TEACHER'S EDITION

GRADE 6

PEARSON

COMMON CORE

Literature

PEARSON

UPPER SADDLE RIVER, NEW JERSEY • BOSTON, MASSACHUSETTS
CHANDLER, ARIZONA • GLENVIEW, ILLINOIS

PEARSON

ISBN-13: 978-0-13-326826-3
ISBN-10: 0-13-326826-8
4 5 6 7 8 9 10 V092 17 16 15 14 13

Teacher's Edition Table of Contents

■ **Contributing Authors** .... CC 4

■ **Author Articles**
    Elfrieda Hiebert: Text Complexity .... CC 6
    Kelly Gallagher: Close Reading Strategies for Common Core .... CC 8
    Diane Fettrow: The Importance of Evidence for Common Core .... CC 9
    William G. Brozo: Building Knowledge Through Nonfiction .... CC 10
    Karen Wixson: The Importance of Assessment .... CC 11
    Ernest Morrell: Digital Instruction in Today's Classrooms .... CC 12
    Donald J. Leu: The Importance of Online Research .... CC 13

■ **Instructional Model** .... CC 14

■ **Table of Contents with Standards and Skills at a Glance**
    Introductory Unit .... CC 20
    Unit 1 .... CC 22
    Unit 2 .... CC 26
    Unit 3 .... CC 30
    Unit 4 .... CC 34
    Unit 5 .... CC 38

■ **Range of Reading** .... CC 42

■ **Features and Workshops** .... CC 46

■ **Skills Navigator**
    Overview .... CC 48
    Unit 1 .... CC 50
    Unit 2 .... CC 52
    Unit 3 .... CC 54
    Unit 4 .... CC 56
    Unit 5 .... CC 58

■ **Common Core State Standards: Key Features and Correlation** .... CC 60

■ **How to Use This Program** .... CC 68

■ **Introductory Unit**
    Building Academic Vocabulary .... CC 82
    Writing an Objective Summary .... CC 92
    Comprehending Complex Texts .... CC 94
    Analyzing Arguments .... CC 100
    Conducting Research .... CC 106

Contributing Authors

The contributing authors guided the direction and philosophy of Pearson Common Core Literature. They helped to build the pedagogical integrity of the program by contributing content expertise, knowledge of the Common Core State Standards, and support for the shifts in instruction the Common Core will bring. Their knowledge, combined with classroom and professional experience, ensures Pearson Common Core Literature is relevant for both teachers and students.

 **William G. Brozo, Ph.D.,** is a Professor of Literacy in the Graduate School of Education at George Mason University in Fairfax, Virginia. He earned his bachelor's degree from the University of North Carolina and his master's and doctorate from the University of South Carolina. He has taught reading and language arts in the Carolinas and is the author of numerous articles on literacy development for children and young adults. His books include *To Be a Boy, To Be a Reader: Engaging Teen and Preteen Boys in Active Literacy; Readers, Teachers, Learners: Expanding Literacy Across the Content Areas; Content Literacy for Today's Adolescents: Honoring Diversity and Building Competence; Supporting Content Area Literacy with Technology* (Pearson); and *Setting the Pace: A Speed, Comprehension, and Study Skills Program.* His newest book is *RTI and the Adolescent Reader: Responsive Literacy Instruction in Secondary Schools.* As an international consultant, Dr. Brozo has provided technical support to teachers from the Balkans to the Middle East, and he is currently a member of a European Union research grant team developing curriculum and providing adolescent literacy professional development for teachers across Europe.

 **Diane Fettrow** spent the majority of her teaching career in Broward County, Florida, teaching high school English courses and serving as department chair. She also worked as an adjunct instructor at Broward College, Nova Southeastern University, and Florida Atlantic University. After she left the classroom, she served as Secondary Language Arts Curriculum Supervisor for several years, working with more than 50 of the district's high schools, centers, and charter schools. During her time as curriculum supervisor, she served on numerous local and state committees; she also served as Florida's K–12 ELA content representative to the PARCC Model Content Frameworks Rapid Response Feedback Group and the PARCC K–12 and Upper Education Engagement Group. Currently she presents workshops on the Common Core State Standards and is working with Pearson on aligning materials to the CCSS.

 **Kelly Gallagher** is a full-time English teacher at Magnolia High School in Anaheim, California, where he has taught for twenty-seven years. He is the former co-director of the South Basin Writing Project at California State University, Long Beach, and the author of *Reading Reasons: Motivational Mini-Lessons for Middle and High School; Deeper Reading: Comprehending Challenging Texts, 4–12; Teaching Adolescent Writers;* and *Readicide: How Schools Are Killing Reading and What You Can Do About It.* He is also a principal author of *Prentice Hall Writing Coach* (Pearson, 2012). Kelly's latest book is *Write Like This* (Stenhouse). Follow Kelly on Twitter @KellyGToGo, and visit him at www.kellygallagher.org.

 **Elfrieda "Freddy' Hiebert, Ph.D.,** is President and CEO of TextProject, a nonprofit that provides resources to support higher reading levels. She is also a research associate at the University of California, Santa Cruz. Dr. Hiebert received her Ph.D. in Educational Psychology from the University of Wisconsin-Madison. She has worked in the field of early reading acquisition for 45 years, first as a teacher's aide and teacher of primary-level students in California and, subsequently, as a teacher educator and researcher at the universities of Kentucky, Colorado-Boulder, Michigan, and California-Berkeley. Her research addresses how fluency, vocabulary,

iv Contributing Authors

and knowledge can be fostered through appropriate texts. Professor Hiebert's research has been published in numerous scholarly journals, and she has authored or edited nine books. Professor Hiebert's model of accessible texts for beginning and struggling readers—TExT—has been used to develop numerous reading programs that are widely used in schools. Dr. Hiebert is the 2008 recipient of the William S. Gray Citation of Merit, awarded by the International Reading Association; is a member of the Reading Hall of Fame; and has chaired a group of experts on early childhood literacy who served in an advisory capacity to the CCSS writers.

 **Donald J. Leu, Ph.D.,** is the John and Maria Neag Endowed Chair in Literacy and Technology and holds a joint appointment in Curriculum and Instruction and Educational Psychology in the Neag School of Education at the University of Connecticut. Don is an international authority on literacy education, especially the new skills and strategies required to read, write, and learn with Internet technologies and the best instructional practices that prepare students for these new literacies. He is a member of the Reading Hall of Fame, a Past President of the National Reading Conference, and a former member of the Board of Directors of the International Reading Association. Don is a Principal Investigator on a number of federal research grants, and his work has been funded by the U.S. Department of Education, the National Science Foundation, and the Bill and Melinda Gates Foundation, among others. He recently edited the *Handbook of Research on New Literacies* (Erlbaum, 2008).

 **Ernest Morrell, Ph.D.,** is a professor of English Education at Teachers College, Columbia University, and the president-elect of the National Council of Teachers of English (NCTE). He is also the Director of Teachers College's Harlem-based Institute for Urban and Minority Education (IUME). Dr. Morrell was an award-winning high school English teacher in California, and he now works with teachers and schools across the country to infuse multicultural literature, youth popular culture, and media production into standards-based literacy curricula and after-school programs. He is the author of nearly 100 articles and book chapters and five books, including *Critical Media Pedagogy: Achievement, Production, and Justice in City Schools* and *Linking Literacy and Popular Culture.* In his spare time he coaches youth sports and writes poems and plays.

 **Karen Wixson, Ph.D.,** is Dean of the School of Education at the University of North Carolina, Greensboro. She has published widely in the areas of literacy curriculum, instruction, and assessment. Dr. Wixson has been an advisor to the National Research Council and helped develop the National Assessment of Educational Progress (NAEP) reading tests. She is a former member of the IRA Board of Directors and co-chair of the IRA Commission on RTI. Recently, Dr. Wixson served on the English Language Arts Work Team that was part of the Common Core State Standards Initiative.

 **Grant Wiggins, Ed.D.,** is the President of Authentic Education in Hopewell, New Jersey. He earned his Ed.D. from Harvard University and his B.A. from St. John's College in Annapolis. Grant consults with schools, districts, and state education departments on a variety of reform matters; organizes conferences and workshops; and develops print materials and Web resources on curricular change. He is perhaps best known for being the co-author, with Jay McTighe, of *Understanding by Design* and *The Understanding by Design Handbook,* the award-winning and highly successful materials on curriculum published by ASCD.

ELFRIEDA HIEBERT, PH.D.

*There will be **exceptions to using quantitative measures** to identify the grade band; sometimes qualitative considerations will trump quantitative measures in identifying the grade band of a text, particularly with narrative fiction in later grades.*

Text Complexity

Students need to read increasingly complex texts in order to be prepared for reading beyond the elementary and high school classroom. Ultimately, greater focus on text complexity will help close the gap that exists between secondary and post-secondary education and prepare students for the increasing demands of required reading in college and in the workplace.

The Common Core State Standards (CCSS) identify a three-part model for measuring a text's complexity:

Quantitative Dimensions are aspects of text complexity that can be measured with traditional readability formulas, such as the Lexile measure. These formulas measure such aspects of a text as word length and frequency, total number of words, average sentence length, and text cohesion.

Qualitative Dimensions consist of "those aspects of text complexity best measured or only measurable by an attentive human reader" and include considerations such as a student's familiarity with a text's structure, levels of meaning, language clarity and conventionality, and knowledge demands, or what the reader needs to know to access the text.

Reader and Task Considerations include an evaluation of student variables, such as the reader's motivation, background knowledge, experience, and cognitive abilities. Evaluating text complexity is best done by the classroom teacher, who brings to bear professional judgments concerning subject matter and individual students.

While this model includes quantitative and qualitative measures as well as variables of individual readers, it is important to note additional key considerations in implementing text complexity since quantitative and qualitative tools are limited and not completely accurate. The CCSS outline in Appendix A that "certain measures are less valid or inappropriate for certain kinds of texts" and "many current quantitative measures underestimate the challenge posed by complex narrative fiction." To further help identify the text complexity levels at which students should be reading, the CCSS provide exemplars to illustrate the kinds of texts students need to read; however, these exemplars are suggestive of the breadth of texts that students should encounter and serve only as guideposts. They "do not represent a complete or partial reading list."

Text Complexity Rubric

Pearson Common Core Literature provides a range of diverse, high-quality, complex texts, including exemplars that adhere to the CCSS model for measuring text complexity—quantitative and qualitative dimensions as well as reader and tasks considerations. The Text Complexity Rubric is provided at point-of-use to guide educators as they implement text complexity in their classrooms.

The Text Complexity Rubric in *Pearson Common Core Literature* The following is a sample from the Teacher's Edition for Grade 9, Unit 1. The leveling of this selection relies on many factors, as depicted in the measures outlined below.

© TEXT COMPLEXITY **RUBRIC** ⑤

The Most Dangerous Game		**Reader and Task Suggestions**	
Qualitative Measures		**Preparing to Read the Text**	**Leveled Tasks**
❶ Context/Knowledge Demands	Small jungle island in Caribbean 1 ② 3 4 5	• Discuss the two kinds of conflict in this story. • Guide students to use Multidraft Reading strategies (TE p. 24).	**Levels of Meaning** Have students first read to identify the main events of the plot. Then, have them reread, taking notes on the motivations of the characters. **Synthesizing** If students will not have difficulty with meaning, have them note the similarities and differences between Rainsford and General Zaroff, and how these similarities and differences affect events.
❷ Structure/Language Conventionality and Clarity	Challenging vocabulary; vocabulary is footnoted 1 2 ③ 4 5		
❸ Levels of Meaning/Purpose/Concept Level	Accessible concept (hunter finds himself the prey in a hunt) 1 2 ③ 4 5		
❹ **Quantitative Measures**			
Lexile	740L	**Text Length**	Word Count: 7,942

❶ **Context/ Knowledge Demands:** The accessibility of texts is dependent in part on the range of students' experiences and their background knowledge.

❷ **Structure/Language Conventionality and Clarity:** Conventional and unconventional structures as well as domain-specific language and vocabulary all affect the ability of students to access text.

❸ **Levels of Meaning/Purpose/Concept Level:** An author's use of either single or multiple levels of meaning impacts the accessibility of a text's concepts.

❹ **Specifics of Text Difficulty:** Pearson has provided two quantitative measures of text complexity—Lexile score and text length.

❺ **Reader and Task Suggestions:** Specific suggestions are given in "Preparing to Read the Text." These are followed by "Leveled Tasks" that will help teachers guide students' comprehension as they analyze, synthesize, or evaluate the concept development of selections. Teachers may adapt the leveled tasks, as appropriate, to suit the needs of their students.

KELLY GALLAGHER

*Students must have opportunities for close-reading texts so they can learn how to gather evidence and **build knowledge** while reading.*

Close Reading Strategies for Common Core

The Common Core State Standards present a vision of what it means to be a literate person in the 21st century, and meeting the standards requires students to master independent, close, attentive reading that is at the heart of understanding complex texts. Students must be able to perform critical reading in order to build knowledge.

The principal strategy that good readers employ when confronted by difficult text is to reread it. If the text is particularly difficult, students should first read the text with the sole purpose of monitoring where they are confused.

Students must have opportunities for close-reading texts so they can learn how to gather evidence and build knowledge. Students should be asking questions while they read: How does what I read compare to what I have learned or thought before? How does the text expand or challenge what I have known before?

As students apply knowledge through reading to build a better understanding of a subject, productive connections and comparisons across texts and ideas should bring students back to careful reading of specific texts. Comprehension questions following selections should require evidence from the text to be answered, so if students have closely read a text, they should be able to find the evidence easily.

Pearson Common Core Literature provides students with strategies for rereading, multi-lens reading, and close reading. An in-depth lesson on Comprehending Complex Texts can be found in the Introductory Unit, and Close Reading Workshops in each unit provide a model selection that demonstrates behaviors and strategies students should use while reading, discussing, researching, and writing. These Close Reading Activities follow each selection throughout the program, and the questions and prompts send students back to the text so they can look for details and evidence that help them build knowledge and respond to the Close Reading Activities.

The Importance of Evidence for Common Core

DIANE FETTROW

Evidence-based learning plays an important role in the Common Core State Standards. In fact, the Common Core State Standards require students to provide evidence in reading, writing, speaking, and listening. In order to use evidence, students must pay close attention to the clues in a text; sometimes the evidence is explicit and other times students must make a logical inference. Every day in the classroom, the teacher and students should get used to hearing as well as saying comments such as "Prove it" or "What's your evidence?"

One reason why evidence is important in the Common Core is the focus on writing for argument. Students are required not only to use evidence in their written arguments, but also to be able to establish the relationships among the claims, counterclaims, reasons, and evidence. Students must supply evidence that points out the strengths as well as the weaknesses of claims and counterclaims fairly.

To demonstrate the importance of evidence as called for in the Common Core State Standards, *Pearson Common Core Literature* embeds evidence-based learning in reading, writing, speaking, and listening throughout the program with lessons on writing to sources, workshops on conducting research, and Close Reading Activities that require students to go back to the texts as they read, discuss, research, and write.

Being able to write about research is also an important aspect of "evidence" in the CCSS. Three of the ten Writing Standards deal with research. Anchor Standard for Writing 9 has students draw "evidence from literary or informational texts to support analysis, reflection, and research." When students conduct research, they must assess whether the reasoning is valid and whether the evidence is relevant and sufficient by identifying false statements and fallacious reasoning.

Students are expected to routinely perform both short-term and long-term research, so *Pearson Common Core Literature* includes a Conducting Research Workshop in the Introductory Unit to teach students strategies for success. In addition, each Writing Process Workshop has an embedded Research strand, and in Part 3, students perform routine research with each selection, taking notes and then using what they have learned to inform their written responses.

> *Every day in the classroom, the teacher and students should get used to hearing as well as saying comments such as 'Prove it' or 'What's your evidence?'*

WILLIAM G. BROZO, PH.D.

*Prevailing **literacy
curriculum** needs to
shift from a focus on
developing reading skills
and building fluency with
simple narratives toward
reading and **writing**
to gain **knowledge**
and express new
understandings with
complex text.*

Building Knowledge Through Nonfiction

The Common Core State Standards Initiative has refocused attention on the goal of ensuring all adolescents are prepared for the reading and learning demands of higher education and the new global economy.

To achieve this goal, there must be an emphasis in secondary English Language Arts on developing independent skills and strategies so students can build knowledge through reading of increasingly complex text. This new focus on literacy in the service of learning is defended on the grounds that building a foundation of knowledge will give students the background to be better readers in all content areas.

Research shows that successful reading involves the orchestration of skills and knowledge. Building a foundation of knowledge through the reading of a variety of genres gives students the background to be better readers. At the same time, teaching students the necessary skills to make meaning from these texts will help them become independent readers.

Pearson Common Core Literature ensures students have engaging and meaningful experiences with texts from a range of genres, including informational texts, biographies, letters, speeches, and essays. The program balances students' skill development with exposure to texts of increasing complexity and variety. Skillful teachers who offer the right texts in the right ways will ensure each student gains knowledge, expresses new understandings, and progresses as a reader and learner.

The Importance of Assessment

KAREN WIXSON, PH.D.

The Common Core State Standards call for development of a common set of K–12 assessments in English and math, anchored in what it takes for students to be ready for college and careers. These new K–12 assessments will build a pathway to college and career readiness by the end of high school, mark students' progress toward this goal from third grade on, and provide teachers with timely information to inform instruction and provide student support.

Students will be required to read passages, perform research, engage with interactive simulations, write an argument, and more—all online. *Pearson Common Core Literature* is prepared to help teachers meet the challenges of the new assessments with a thorough plan that exposes students to the types of items that will appear on the upcoming assessments.

- All program assessments are online so that students can experience the digital aspect of taking tests.

- Questions will require evidence-based responses, so students will need to rely on the passage or text to respond.

- The Close Reading Activities—Read, Discuss, Research, Write—that appear with each selection will prepare students for the rigorous activities they will experience on the new assessments.

- Assessment items that simulate the tasks students will experience are available for additional practice.

In addition to preparing students for the national assessments, *Pearson Common Core Literature* provides formative and summative assessments that can be used to drive instruction. Teachers are able to utilize data to inform instructional emphasis throughout the year and throughout each unit and make decisions related to differentiating instruction for individual students.

> *Assessments must be developed that **inform curriculum and instruction**, as well as measure student progress.*

ERNEST MORRELL, PH.D.

*Adults at work today rarely use pen and paper. We communicate using **mobile media, tablets, laptops,** and other new technologies.*

Digital Instruction in Today's Classrooms

We have to acknowledge that the world is changing, and, as it changes, the world of literacy changes, too. This will have a significant effect on what it means to teach English.

Children entering kindergarten today will retire sometime near 2075. They will be mid-career in 2050. Yet their formal education will end in the next decade and a half. What kind of education do we need to provide for these children to help them be successful in the world of tomorrow?

Two key components of 21st century learning that we need to focus on are the informed use of technology and learning as social interaction. As the world becomes more interconnected, students will need to learn to converse with one another across multiple modes of communication.

Pearson Common Core Literature is designed to motivate today's digital natives while immersing them in a learning environment that prepares them for college and the workplace.

The Online Writer's Notebook and Close Reading Tool present texts in a format that allows for interaction as students respond to the text. Collaborative speaking and listening projects and media-rich content extend core instruction for a connected, dynamic learning experience. Students are encouraged to have conversations while developing their capabilities to become better speakers, stronger writers, and more attuned listeners.

The Importance of Online Research

DONALD J. LEU, PH.D.

Online reading comprehension, it appears, typically takes place within a research and problem-solving task. Unlike reading comprehension when simply reading for a general purpose, online reading comprehension is specifically focused to solve a particular problem or answer a particular question. In short, online reading comprehension is online research.

Online reading also differs from traditional reading because it becomes tightly integrated with writing, as we communicate with others to learn more about the questions we explore and as we communicate our own interpretations. E-mail, text messages, blogs, wikis, and many other new tools become important elements of online research and comprehension. Keyword entry in a search engine becomes an important new literacy skill because search engines are an important new technology for locating information.

Pearson Common Core Literature will help students develop these essential skills for success in their formal education and in the workplace. The Research Workshop in the Introductory Unit will provide students with strategies for these skills. An Online Research Center provides links to Web sites with useful tips and tricks. Close Reading Activities following every selection include a Research activity, and research is embedded within the Writing Workshops.

*To be ready for college, in a technological society, students need the ability to **gather, comprehend, evaluate, synthesize,** and **report on information** and ideas; to conduct original research in order to answer questions or solve problems; and to analyze and create a high volume and extensive range of print and nonprint texts in **media forms old and new.** (Common Core State Standards for English Language Arts, 2010, p. 4)*

Literature for the Common Core

Pearson Common Core Literature is designed to address the instructional shifts in literacy required by the Common Core State Standards.

With this program, students will:

- build content knowledge by reading a range of complex texts—literary and informational—through Text Sets;
- provide written and oral responses to prompts that require students to cite evidence from the text;
- encounter complex texts and analyze and internalize the texts' academic language and vocabulary.

Pearson Common Core Literature delivers an Instructional Model that will help teachers prepare students for the rigors of college and the workplace.

This Instructional Model:

- allows for instructional flexibility depending on the learner levels in the classroom and academic growth needed;
- puts emphasis on the close reading of complex texts and requires students to participate in academic discussions, perform research, and write to sources;
- provides rigorous instruction and guidance in analysis of multiple texts within a genre;
- supports deepening knowledge of a topic through analysis of multiple-genre texts and media in a Text Set;
- provides practice in reading extended texts independently.

Unit-Level Instructional Model

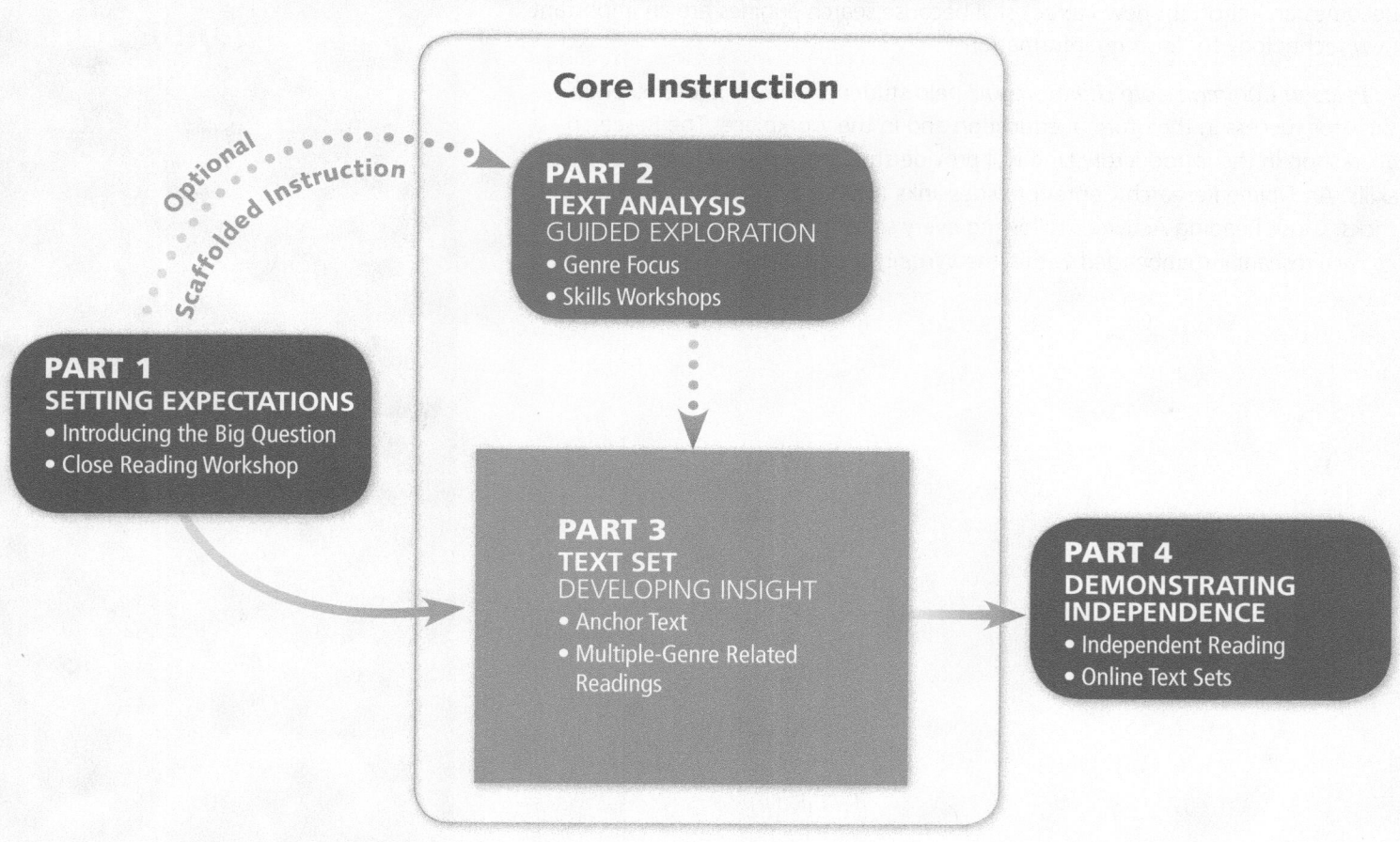

Instructional Model: The Parts

The Instructional Model reflects the learning process: Part 1 models expectations and strategies; Part 2 provides scaffolded supports for reading, writing, speaking and listening, and grammar acquisition; Part 3 enables students to demonstrate learning without scaffolds; Part 4 presents wholly independent reading opportunities.

PART 1: SETTING EXPECTATIONS

Part 1 will set clear expectations for students as they analyze texts, participate in academic discussions, perform research, and present written responses to text. Also introduced are the unit's Big Question and academic vocabulary that students will utilize and revisit in the course of the unit.

PART 2: TEXT ANALYSIS

In Part 2, students will study multiple texts within a genre and master concepts and standards associated with that genre. Learning to closely read and analyze one specific genre will provide students with strategies that guide them toward performing this same analysis across multiple genres.

Direct instruction and scaffolds are provided to ensure that students of all levels are able to comprehend and analyze the complex texts presented in this part. In addition, students are given the opportunity to compare two or more texts and practice writing on demand. Process workshops are also provided for Language Study, Speaking and Listening, and Writing.

PART 3: TEXT SET

In Part 3, the instructional focus shifts from genre study and skill building to the acquisition of content knowledge through multiple-genre Text Sets. Each Text Set is anchored by a text that matches the genre studied in Part 2. The scaffolds fall away, and students are given the opportunity to encounter texts in an authentic reading environment that will mirror what they will experience in college textbooks and in workplace documents.

Throughout the Text Set, students read critically, participate in academic discussions, conduct research, and develop insights on a topic. These are the types of activities students will be required to perform on the national assessments as well as in college and in the workplace.

PART 4: DEMONSTRATING INDEPENDENCE

In Part 4, students are encouraged to read extended texts independently, building stamina and confidence. Online text sets are available, enabling students to practice independent reading of texts within a digital environment.

Flexible Pathways

The Instructional Model in *Pearson Common Core Literature* has been carefully constructed so that it provides you with the ultimate flexibility in meeting the needs of your students. Your pathway through each unit can vary, depending on student performance on the Beginning-of-Year Test and on observation of student performance on Close Reading Activities.

Flexible Pacing

Pearson Common Core Literature is designed to be flexible. Pacing for each Part and each Unit can vary depending on the needs of your students. Pacing recommendations are provided in the Skills Navigator. You will notice that we provide a range of days for some features in the pacing plan; use the number of days that makes the most sense for the ability level of your class.

   The scenarios below are suggestions for how to use the Instructional Model, and the chart that follows provides a visual for these pathways.

On-Level Students

Results from the Beginning-of-Year Test indicate that your students are somewhat familiar with grade-level concepts delineated in the standards for the upcoming unit. Therefore, you begin the unit instruction by reviewing the Part 1 models for reading, discussion, research, and writing, and you assign the Independent Practice selection's Close Reading Activities to confirm that students have the requisite tools for success.

   If students struggle with any aspects of the Close Reading Activities, such as participating in academic discussion, research, or writing, you may opt to assign targeted features in Part 2 in order to provide instruction and practice in those areas.

   If students are successful with the Close Reading Activities following the Independent Practice selection, you might want to move directly to Part 3 where you may assign all or parts of the Text Set, utilizing scaffolds in the Teacher's Edition when necessary. Assign a Part 4 text for students to read independently.

Above-Level Students

Results from the Beginning-of-Year Test indicate that your students are familiar with grade-level concepts for the upcoming unit. Therefore, you may choose to move directly to Part 3 and work with students to build knowledge through independent readings of a range of texts and media. Following Part 3, assign a Part 4 text for students to read independently. Then, instruct students to self-select an extended reading from Part 4 and prepare an oral or written presentation of their learning.

Below-Level Students or English Learners

Results from the Beginning-of-Year Test indicate that your students need intensive instruction in most or all of the upcoming unit skills and concepts. Therefore, you devote class time to modeling expectations in Part 1. You might want to spend more time in Part 2 and assign most or all of the selections and features, to ensure that students develop the requisite reading, writing, and speaking and listening skills needed for success.

Then, assign a portion of the Part 3 Text Set to enable students to develop content knowledge related to the Big Question. Part 4 independent readings may be considered optional.

Unit-Level Pathways

Below is a chart with recommended instructional pathways for the different learner levels in your classroom. These are only recommendations; you know the unique needs of your students and can follow these recommended pathways, follow the units in their entirety, or create your own path through the units. No matter which path you choose, *Pearson Common Core Literature* will help you prepare your students for success in college and in the workplace.

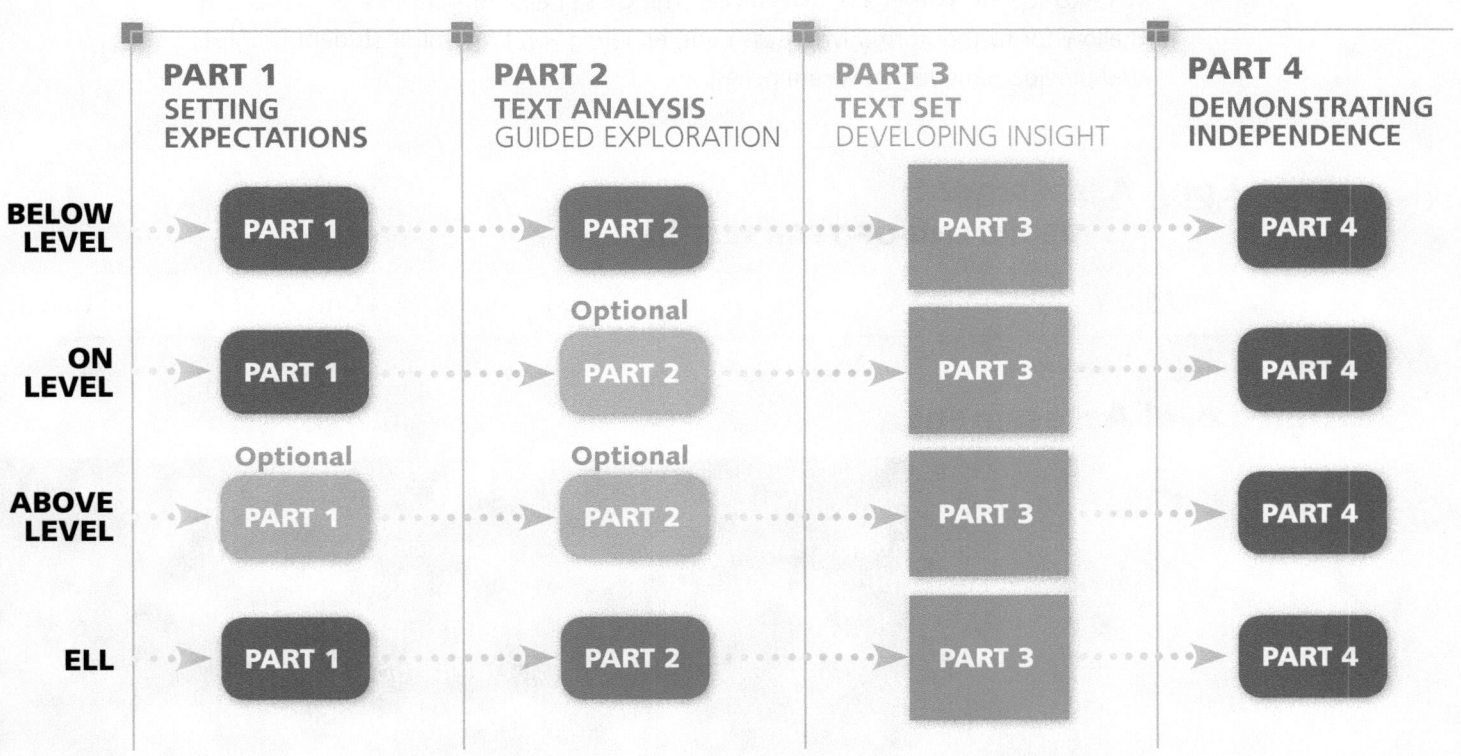

Assessment Overview

Pearson Common Core Literature delivers rigorous instruction through an Instructional Model that provides students with strategies, practice, and skills to independently read and respond thoughtfully and critically to multiple types of complex texts.

Instruction in the program is powered by diagnostic assessment to drive instructional decisions, and various types of assessments are carefully integrated with the Instructional Model of the program.

Types of Assessment

A **Beginning-of-Year Test** assesses students' familiarity with grade-level skills and standards. The results of this assessment enable teachers to choose a pathway through the program. A **Mid-Year** and **End-of-Year Test** revisit these skills to monitor progress.

Close Reading Activities following the Independent Practice selection can be used as a formative assessment to determine students' readiness for Part 2.

These Close Reading Activities assess students' abilities to read closely and analytically, participate in an academic discussion, perform short-term research, and write to sources within a specific mode. The Close Reading Activities in Parts 2 and 3 allow for further formative assessment, enabling you to monitor student progress and provide remediation where necessary.

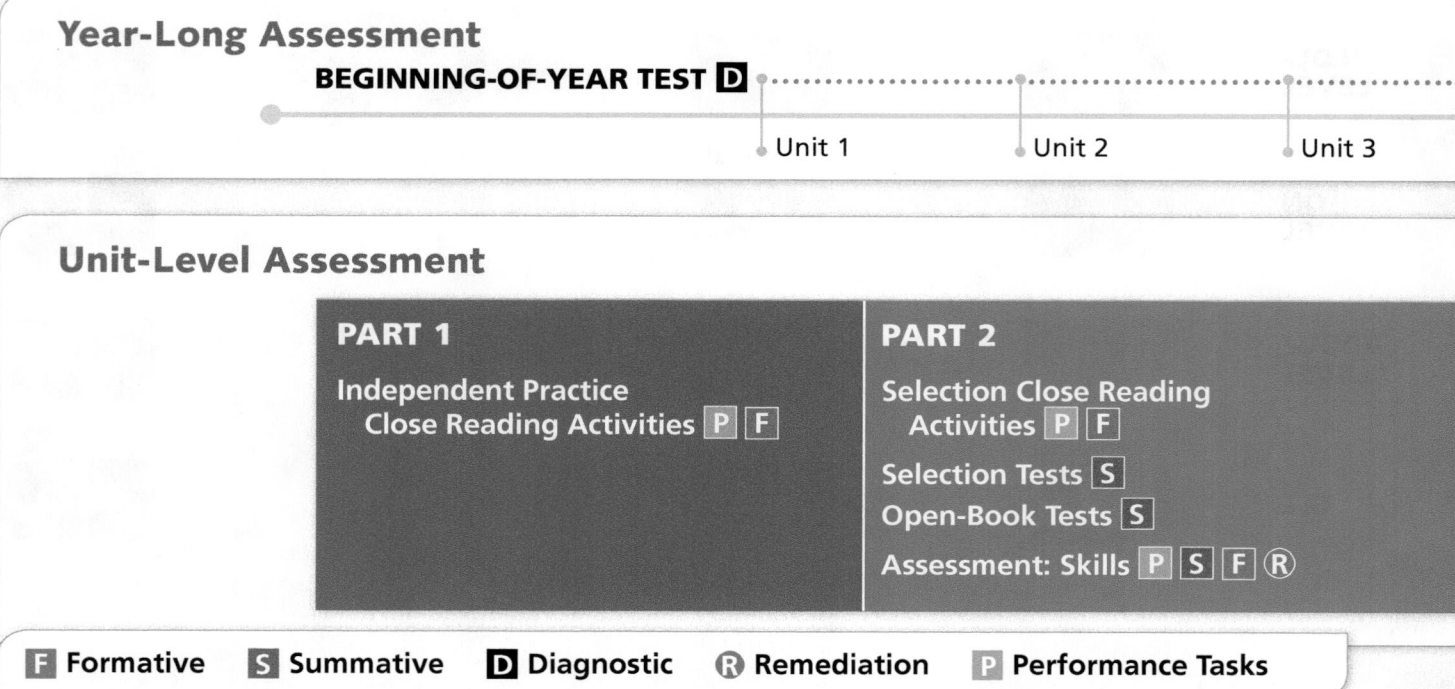

Year-Long Assessment

BEGINNING-OF-YEAR TEST D ··

Unit 1   Unit 2   Unit 3

Unit-Level Assessment

PART 1	PART 2

Independent Practice
    Close Reading Activities P F
	Selection Close Reading
	    Activities P F
	Selection Tests S
	Open-Book Tests S
	Assessment: Skills P S F ®

F Formative   S Summative   D Diagnostic   ® Remediation   P Performance Tasks

A **Selection Test** and **Open-Book Test** monitor mastery of the skills taught with the selections. Selection Tests are in selected-response format, whereas Open-Book Tests are more challenging and require students to provide textual evidence in their responses.

In Part 2, Assessment: Skills is reading-based and tests students' abilities to independently read informational and literary texts and to respond to an array of selected-response items and performance tasks.

The writing portion offers a timed writing activity as well as an opportunity for students to analyze and correct a writing passage.

The items on this assessment are aligned with unit standards and target specific skills to enable teachers to analyze test data and perform remediation as needed.

In Part 3, Assessment: Synthesis is administered at the conclusion of the Text Set. Students will draw upon their learning over the course of the unit, and their progress will be evident in their oral and written responses. Students will complete performance tasks focused on speaking and listening, research, and writing.

A **Benchmark Test** assesses all skills taught within the unit, including reading, writing, vocabulary, and grammar. Questions require students to provide textual evidence in their responses. Remediation recommendations can be found online in the Interpretation Guide.

··▶ **MID-YEAR TEST** S ···▶ **END-OF-YEAR TEST** S

|
Unit 4

|
Unit 5

PART 3

Selection Close Reading
   Activities P F
Selection Tests S
Open-Book Tests S
Assessment: Synthesis P S F

PART 4

Benchmark Test S Ⓡ

INTRODUCTORY UNIT Contents

COMMON CORE FOUNDATIONS

■ Building Academic Vocabulary xlvi
  General Academic Vocabulary xlvi
  Domain-Specific Academic Vocabulary li

■ Writing an Objective Summary lvi
  MODEL: **Summary of "King Midas and the Golden Touch"** lvii

■ Comprehending Complex Texts lviii
  STRATEGY 1: Multidraft Reading lviii
  INDEPENDENT READING: **"Storm"**
  H.D. (Hilda Doolittle) lix

  STRATEGY 2: Close Read the Text lx
  MODEL: *from* **"How to Tell a Story"**
  Mark Twain lxi

  STRATEGY 3: Ask Questions lxii
  MODEL: *from* **"Rendezvous with Despair"**
  Thomas E. Dewey lxiii

  INDEPENDENT PRACTICE: *from* **"The Bill of Rights"**
  Herbert Hoover lxiii

■ Analyzing Arguments lxiv
  MODEL: **"Nelson Mandela's Address Upon His Release From Prison"**
  Nelson Mandela lxv

  **The Art of Argument: Rhetorical Devices
  and Persuasive Techniques** lxvi
  MODEL: *from* **"Speech Celebrating George Washington's Birthday"**
  Jane Addams lxvii

  Composing an Argument lxviii
  Practice lxix

■ Research Workshop lxx
  Conducting Short-term and Long-term Research lxx
  Research Process Workshop lxxii
  STUDENT MODEL: **Research Paper** lxxvii
  Citing Sources and Preparing Manuscript lxxx

COMMON CORE STATE STANDARDS

The following standards are introduced in this unit and revisited throughout the program.

Additional standards addressed in these workshops: **Writing** 1.a, 1.b, 1.e, 2.a, 2.b, 2.d, 2.f; **Language** 6

Reading Literature

2. Determine a theme or central idea of a text and how it is conveyed through particular details; provide a summary of the text distinct from personal opinions or judgments.

10. By the end of the year, read and comprehend literature, including stories, dramas, and poems, at the high end of the grades 6–8 text complexity band proficiently, with scaffolding as needed at the high end of the range.

Reading Informational Text

2. Determine a central idea of a text and how it is conveyed through particular details; provide a summary of the text distinct from personal opinions or judgments.

8. Trace and evaluate the argument and specific claims in a text, distinguishing claims that are supported by reasons and evidence from claims that are not.

Writing

1. Write arguments to support claims with clear reasons and relevant experience.

2. Write informative/explanatory texts to examine and convey complex ideas, concepts, and information clearly and accurately through the effective selection, organization, and analysis of content.

5. With some guidance and support from peers and adults, develop and strengthen writing as needed by planning, revising, editing, rewriting, or trying a new approach.

7. Conduct short research projects to answer a question, drawing on several sources and refocusing the inquiry when appropriate.

8. Gather relevant information from multiple print and digital sources; assess the credibility of each source; and quote or paraphrase the data and conclusions on others while avoiding plagiarism and providing basic bibliographic information for sources.

9. Draw evidence from literary or informational texts to support analysis, reflection, and research.

PART 1
SETTING EXPECTATIONS

Introducing the Big Question
Is conflict always bad?...................... 2

Close Reading Workshop
Read • Discuss • Research • Write............ 4
SHORT STORY
"The Old Grandfather and His Little Grandson"
Leo Tolstoy...................... 5
SHORT STORY
The Wounded Wolf
Jean Craighead George................ 8

PART 2
TEXT ANALYSIS GUIDED EXPLORATION

CHARACTERS AND CONFLICT

Elements of a Short Story 14
Analyzing Structure, Conflict and Characterization 16

SHORT STORY READINGS
Stray
Cynthia Rylant 20

The Tail
Joyce Hansen 30

Zlateh the Goat
Isaac Bashevis Singer 46

The Circuit
Francisco Jiménez 60

COMPARING TEXTS LITERARY ANALYSIS 72
SHORT STORY
Lob's Girl
Joan Aiken 74

SHORT STORY
Jeremiah's Song
Walter Dean Myers 88

LANGUAGE STUDY Using a Dictionary and Thesaurus 98

SPEAKING AND LISTENING Following Oral Directions 100

WRITING PROCESS Narration: Short Story 102

ASSESSMENT SKILLS 110

Selected Response 110

Constructed Response 114

PART 3
TEXT SETS DEVELOPING INSIGHT

THE GOLD RUSH

SHORT STORY | ANCHOR TEXT
The King of Mazy May
Jack London... 118

SONG
To Klondyke We've Paid Our Fare
H.J. Dunham... 132

ANNOTATED MAP
Gold Rush: The Journey by Land
from *The Sacramento Bee*.................................. 136

LETTER
A Woman's View of the Gold Rush
Mary B. Ballou.. 138

WEB ARTICLE
Chinese and African Americans in the Gold Rush
Johns Hopkins University................................... 144

NEWS ARTICLE
Birds Struggle to Recover From Egg Thefts of 1800s
Edie Lau... 148

ASSESSMENT: SYNTHESIS 154

Speaking and Listening: Group Discussion.................. 154

Writing: Historical Fiction................................. 155

Writing to Sources: Argumentative Essay................... 156

PART 4
DEMONSTRATING INDEPENDENCE

Independent Reading

Recommended Titles
for Extended Reading........................... 158

ONLINE TEXT SET

SHORT STORY
Eleven EXEMPLAR TEXT ©
Sandra Cisneros

BIOGRAPHY
A Backwoods Boy
Russell Freedman

LETTER
Letter to Scottie
F. Scott Fitzgerald

■ **READ**

Text Analysis
Plot
Characterization
Conflict and Resolution
Theme
Comparing Foreshadowing and Flashback
Setting
Alliteration
Tone
Author's Purpose
Imagery

Comprehension
Make Predictions
Make Inferences
Draw Conclusions

Language Study
Latin suffix -*ation*
Latin prefix *dis-*
Latin prefix *ex-*
Latin prefix *com-*

Language Study Workshop
Using a Dictionary and Thesaurus

■ **DISCUSS**

Comprehension and Collaboration
Interview

Responding to Text
Group Discussion
Class Discussion

Speaking and Listening Workshop
Following Oral Directions

■ **RESEARCH**

Research and Technology
Brochure
Compare-and-Contrast Chart

Investigate the Topic: The Gold Rush
Gold Rush Struggles
Striking It Rich
Gold Rush Housing
Labor During the Gold Rush
The Gold Rush and Food

■ **WRITE**

Writing to Sources
List of Reasons
Letter of Recommendation
Persuasive Speech
Description
Essay
Cause-and-Effect Essay
Short Story
Journal Entry
Informational Text
Editorial
Argument

Writing Process Workshop
Narration: Short Story

UNIT VOCABULARY

Academic Vocabulary appears in *blue*.

Stray   *timidly, trudged, grudgingly, ignore, exhausted, starvation*
The Tail   *vow, anxious, routine, gnawing, mauled, spasm*
Zlateh the Goat   *bound, astray, exuded, splendor, trace, flickering*
The Circuit   *accompanied, drone, instinctively, savoring, enroll*
Lob's Girl; Jeremiah's Song   *decisively, resolutions, melancholy, diagnosis, anticipate, conclude, refer, reveal*
The King of Mazy May   *endured, liable, summit, passage, contribute, alter*
To Klondyke We've Paid Our Fare   *defiance, privation, invincible, reveal, purpose, challenge*
Gold Rush: The Journey by Land   *similarities, process, indicated*
A Woman's View of the Gold Rush   *associate, scouring, tongues, specific*
Chinese and African Americans in the Gold Rush   *exodus, testify, ambassador, determine, acquired*
Birds Struggle to Recover from Egg Thefts of 1800s   *conservatively, entrepreneurs, faltered, establish, opinion, support*

COMMON CORE STATE STANDARDS

For the full wording of the standards, see the standards chart following the Contents pages.

Reading Literature
RL.6.1, RL.6.2, RL.6.3, RL.6.4, RL.6.5

Reading Informational Text
RI.6.1, RI.6.2, RI.6.3, RI.6.4, RI.6.5, RI.6.6, RI.6.7

Writing
W.6.1, W.6.1.a-d, W.6.2, W.6.2.a-b, W.6.2.e, W.6.3, W.6.3.a-e, W.6.4, W.6.5, W.6.7, W.6.8, W.6.9, W.6.9.a-b, W.6.10

Speaking and Listening
SL.6.1, SL.6.1.a-d, SL.6.2, SL.6.3, SL.6.4, SL.6.5

Language
L.6.1, L.6.1.a-d, L.6.2, L.6.2.b, L.6.3, L.6.4, L.6.4.a-d, L.6.5, L.6.5.c, L.6.6

UNIT 2   What is important to know?

PART 1
SETTING EXPECTATIONS

Introducing the Big Question
What is important to know? 162

Close Reading Workshop
Read • Discuss • Research • Write........ 164

BIOGRAPHY   EXEMPLAR TEXT ©
***from* This Land Was Made**
for You and Me
Elizabeth Partridge 165

NARRATIVE NONFICTION
***from* Zlata's Diary**
Zlata Filipović 168

PART 2
TEXT ANALYSIS GUIDED EXPLORATION

LIFE STORIES

Elements of Nonfiction............................. 180
Determining Author's Purpose, Point of View,
and Development of ideas........................ 182

NONFICTION READINGS
The Drive-In Movies
Gary Soto 186

Names/Nombres
Julia Alvarez 196

Langston Terrace
Eloise Greenfield 208

***from* The Pigman & Me**
Paul Zindel 218

COMPARING TEXTS LITERARY ANALYSIS 230

ONLINE ALMANAC
The Seven Wonders of the World
Infoplease™ 231

TEXTBOOK ARTICLE
Art, Architecture, and Learning in Egypt
Prentice Hall Ancient Civilizations 233

LANGUAGE STUDY Word Origins 236

SPEAKING AND LISTENING Evaluating Media
Messages and Advertisements 238

WRITING PROCESS Informative Text:
Comparison-and-Contrast Essay 240

ASSESSMENT SKILLS.................................. 248

Selected Response 248

Constructed Response 252

PART 3
TEXT SETS DEVELOPING INSIGHT

BASEBALL

EXPOSITORY ESSAY | ANCHOR TEXT
Jackie Robinson: Justice at Last
Geoffrey C. Ward and Ken Burns 256

NEWS ARTICLE
Memories of an All-American Girl
Carmen Pauls 264

PERSUASIVE SPEECH
Preserving a Great American Symbol
Richard Durbin 270

SHORT STORY
The Southpaw
Judith Viorst 274

NEWS ARTICLE
Fenway Park Celebrates 100 Years as America's Oldest Working Major League Ballpark
Molly Line 280

WEB ARTICLE
Why We Love Baseball
Mark Newman 286

BASEBALL CARD
Ted Williams Baseball Card 292

ASSESSMENT SYNTHESIS 294

Speaking and Listening: Group Discussion

Writing: Autobiographical Narrative 295

Writing to Sources: Informative Essay 296

PART 4
DEMONSTRATING INDEPENDENCE

Independent Reading

Recommended
Titles for Extended Reading 298

ONLINE TEXT SET

FOLK TALE
Why Monkeys Live in Trees
Julius Lester

EDITORIAL
Jake Wood Baseball Is the Start of Something Special
Reginald T. Dogan

POEM
Wilbur Wright and Orville Wright
Rosemary and Stephen Vincent Benét

READ

Text Analysis
Narrator and Point of View
Tone
Author's Influences
Mood
Author's Viewpoint
Time Shifts
Hyperbole
Characterization
Figurative Language
Word Choice

Comprehension
Make Predictions
Fact and Opinion
Main Idea
Use Text Aids and Features

Language Study
Latin prefix *pre-*
Latin root *-scrib-* or *-scrip-*
Latin suffix *-ent*
Latin root *-tort-*

Language Study Workshop
Word Origins

DISCUSS

Comprehension and Collaboration
Conversation
Monologue
Informal Discussion

Responding to Text
Group Discussion
Partner Discussion
Panel Discussion

Speaking and Listening Workshop
Evaluating Media Messages and Advertisements

RESEARCH

Research and Technology
Informative Presentation

Investigate the Topic: Baseball
Segregation in Sports
Women and Baseball
Baseball Traditions
Teams and Clubs
Popular Stadiums
Baseball in Literature

WRITE

Writing to Sources
Autobiographical Narrative
Personal Anecdote
Journey Entry
Problem-and-Solution Essay
Position Statement
Comparison-and Contrast Essay
Autobiographical Narrative
Persuasive Speech
Persuasive Letter
Argument
Reflective Essay

Writing Process Workshop
Informative Text: Comparison-and-Contrast Essay

Assessment Synthesis
Speaking and Listening: Group Discussion
Writing: Autobiographical Narrative
Writing to Sources: Expository Essay

UNIT VOCABULARY

Academic Vocabulary appears in *blue*.

The Drive-In Movies   *prelude, pulsating, migrated, evident, winced, vigorously*
Names/Nombres   *mistook, pursue, transport, inevitably, chaotic, inscribed*
Langston Terrace   *applications, community, resident, choral, reunion, homey*
***from* The Pigman & Me**   *exact, demented, observant, undulating, distorted, condemnation*
The Seven Wonders of the World; Art, Architecture, and Learning in Egypt   *archaeologists, architect, colossal*
Jackie Robinson: Justice at Last   *integrate, prejudiced, superb, support, opinions, affect*
Memories of an All-American Girl   *exhilarating, immortality, inductions, visual, reflecting*
Preserving a Great American Symbol   *doomed, extinction, amendment, cite, achieve, argue*
The Southpaw   *former, unreasonable, anticipate, conclude*
Fenway Park Celebrates 100 Years as America's Oldest Working Major League Ballpark   *facade, hallowed, cultivate, unique, position*
Why We Love Baseball   *premise, ventured, diversion, sources, facts, research*
Ted Williams Baseball Card   *reveal, contrast*

COMMON CORE STATE STANDARDS

For the full wording of the standards, see the standards chart following the Contents pages.

Reading Literature
RL.6.1, RL.6.2, RL.6.3, RL.6.4, RL.6.5

Reading Informational Text
RI.6.1, RI.6.2, RI.6.3, RI.6.4, RI.6.5, RI.6.6, RI.6.7, RI.6.8

Writing
W.6.1, W.6.1a-c, W.6.2, W.6.2.a-f, W.6.3, W.6.3.a-e, W.6.4, W.6.5, W.6.7, W.6.8, W.6.9, W.6.10

Speaking and Listening
SL.6.1, SL.6.1.a-d, SL.6.2, SL.6.3, SL.6.4, SL.6.6

Language
L.6.1, L.6.1.b, L.6.2, L.6.2.b, L.6.3, L.6.4, L.6.4.b, L.6.5, L.6.6

 **UNIT 3**   **Do we need words to communicate well?**

PART 1
SETTING EXPECTATIONS

Introducing the Big Question
Do we need words to communicate well? 302

Close Reading Workshop
Read • Discuss • Research • Write 304

POEM   EXEMPLAR TEXT ©
Twelfth Song of Thunder
Navajo 305

POEM   EXEMPLAR TEXT ©
Oranges
Gary Soto 308

POEM
Ode to Family Photographs
Gary Soto 310

PART 2
TEXT ANALYSIS GUIDED EXPLORATION

RHYTHM AND RHYME

Elements of Poetry 314
Analyzing Language, Structure, and
Theme in Poetry 316

POETRY COLLECTION 1
A Dream Within a Dream *Edgar Allan Poe* 321
Adventures of Isabel *Ogden Nash* 322
Life Doesn't Frighten Me *Maya Angelou* 324
The Walrus and the Carpenter *Lewis Carroll* 326

POETRY COLLECTION 2
Abuelito Who *Sandra Cisneros* 337
April Rain Song *Langston Hughes* 338
The World Is Not a Pleasant Place to Be
Nikki Giovanni 339
Fame Is a Bee *Emily Dickinson* 340

POETRY COLLECTION 3
Haiku *Matsuo Bashō* 347
The Sidewalk Racer *Lillian Morrison* 348
Concrete Cat *Dorthi Charles* 349
Limerick *Anonymous* 350

POETRY COLLECTION 4
Wind and water and stone *Octavio Paz* 357
No Thank You *Shel Silverstein* 358
The Fairies' Lullaby *William Shakespeare* 360
Cynthia in the Snow *Gwendolyn Brooks* 362

COMPARING TEXTS LITERARY ANALYSIS 366

POEM
who knows if the moon's
E. E. Cummings 368

POEM
Dust of Snow
Robert Frost 370

LANGUAGE STUDY
Words With Multiple Meanings.................... 372

SPEAKING AND LISTENING
Problem-and-Solution Proposal 374

WRITING PROCESS
Argument: Argumentative Essay 376

ASSESSMENT SKILLS.................... 384

Selected Response 384

Constructed Response 388

PART 3
TEXT SETS DEVELOPING INSIGHT

DETERMINATION

POEM | ANCHOR TEXT
Simile: Willow and Ginkgo
Eva Merriam 392

WEB ARTICLE
Angela Duckworth and the Research on "Grit"
Emily Hanford.................... 398

EXPOSITORY ESSAY
Race to the End of the Earth
William G. Scheller 404

SHORT STORY
The Sound of Summer Running
Ray Bradbury 410

LETTER   EXEMPLAR TEXT Ⓒ
from **Letter on Thomas Jefferson**
John Adams.................... 420

AUTOBIOGRAPHY
Water
Helen Keller 424

POSTER
Determination.................... 430

ASSESSMENT SYNTHESIS 432

Speaking and Listening: Group Discussion.................... 432

Writing: Fictional Narrative 433

Writing to Sources: Argumentative Essay.................... 434

PART 4
DEMONSTRATING INDEPENDENCE

Independent Reading
Recommended
Titles for Extended Reading.................... 436

ONLINE TEXT SET

PERSONAL ESSAY
The Lady and the Spider
Robert Fulghum

SHORT STORY
Dragon, Dragon
John Gardner

POEM
Ankylosaurus
Jack Prelutsky

READ

Text Analysis
Rhythm and Rhyme
Figurative Language
Forms of Poetry
Sound Devices and Tone
Comparing Imagery
Simile
Direct Quotation
Foreshadowing
Symbols
Central Idea
Author's Purpose

Comprehension
Context Clues
Paraphrasing

Language Study
Latin root -mal-
Suffix -ant
Greek prefix auto-
Suffix -y

Language Study Workshop
Words with Multiple Meanings

DISCUSS

Presentation of Ideas
Dramatic Poetry Reading

Responding to Text
Group Discussion
Partner Discussion
Short Response and Group Discussion
Small Group Discussion

Speaking and Listening Workshop
Problem-and-Solution Proposal

RESEARCH

Research and Technology
Illustrated Booklet
Presentation of a Poem
Résumé

Investigate the Topic: Determination
Survival Skills
College Challenges
Expedition to the South Pole
Financial Skills
Determination and the Declaration of
Independence
Learning to Communicate
Politics and Determination

WRITE

Writing to Sources
Letter to an Author
Poem
Prose Description
Essay
Expository Essay
Autobiographical Narrative
Diary Entry
Reflective Essay
Comparison-and-Contrast Essay
Argumentative Essay

Writing Process Workshop
Argument: Argumentative Essay

Student Edition Pages

■ **UNIT VOCABULARY**

Academic Vocabulary appears in *blue*.

Poetry Collection 1 *deem, ravenous, cavernous, beseech, dismal, sympathize*
Poetry Collection 2 *sour, lullaby, pleasant, receive*
Poetry Collection 3 *skimming, asphalt, fellow*
Poetry Collection 4 *hallowed, dispersed, sculpted, thorny, offense, whirs*
who knows if the moon's; Dust of Snow *steeples, rued, achieve, communicate, observe, symbolize*
Simile: Willow and Ginkgo *crude, stubby, thrives, reveal, communicate, establish*
Angela Duckworth and the Research on "Grit" *rigorous, persevere, insurmountable, essential, study, research*
Race to the End of the Earth *plateau, expedition, polar, assess, evidence, perspective*
The Sound of Summer Running *seized, suspended, revelation, symbolize, influence*
from **Letter on Thomas Jefferson** *felicity, explicit, procure, clarifies, evaluate, contrast*
Water *imitate, persisted, barriers, purpose, support, sources*
Determination Poster *context, quotation, facts*

■ **COMMON CORE STATE STANDARDS**

For the full wording of the standards, see the standards chart following the Contents pages.

Reading Literature
RL.6.1, RL.6.2, RL.6.3, RL.6.4, RL.6.5, RL.6.6, RL.6.7

Reading Informational Text
RI.6.1, RI.6.2, RI.6.3, RI.6.4, RI.6.5, RI.6.6, RI.6.7

Writing
W.6.1, W.6.1.a-e, W.6.2, W.6.2.a-b, W.6.2.e-f, W.6.3, W.6.3.d, W.6.4, W.6.5, W.6.6, W.6.7, W.6.8, W.6.9, W.6.9.b, W.6.10

Speaking and Listening
SL.6.1, SL.6.3, SL.6.4, SL.6.5, SL.6.6

Language
L.6.1, L.6.1.e, L.6.2.b, L.6.3, L.6.4, L.6.4.a, L.6.4.c-d, L.6.5, L.6.6

 **UNIT 4** How do we decide who we are?

PART 1
SETTING EXPECTATIONS

Introducing the Big Question
How do we decide who we are? .. 440

Close Reading Workshop
Read • Discuss • Research • Write........ 442
DRAMA
***from* Brighton Beach Memoirs**
Neil Simon 443
DRAMA
Gluskabe and Old Man Winter
Joseph Bruchac...................................... 446

PART 2
TEXT ANALYSIS GUIDED EXPLORATION

ADVENTURE AND IMAGINATION

Elements of Drama 454
Analyzing Dramatic Elements................. 456

DRAMA
The Phantom Tollbooth
Susan Nanus
Act I.. 460
Act II... 490

COMPARING TEXTS LITERARY ANALYSIS............... 522
DRAMA
***from* You're a Good Man, Charlie Brown**
Clark Gesner... 524
REVIEW
Happiness is a Charming Charlie Brown at Orlando Rep
Matthew MacDermid.................................. 530

LANGUAGE STUDY Connotation and Denotation. 534

SPEAKING AND LISTENING Delivering a Persuasive Speech 536

WRITING PROCESS
Argument: Problem-and-Solution Essay.................. 538

ASSESSMENT SKILLS.. 546
Selected Response 546
Constructed Response 550

PART 3
TEXT SETS DEVELOPING INSIGHT

MARK TWAIN

PLAY | ANCHOR TEXT
The Prince and the Pauper 554

NOVEL EXCERPT | ANCHOR TEXT
from **The Prince and the Pauper**
Mark Twain 572

SPEECH
Stage Fright
Mark Twain 580

BIOGRAPHY
My Papa, Mark Twain
Susy Clemens 584

INTERVIEW
Mark Twain's First "Vacation"
The New York World 590

QUOTATIONS
According to Mark Twain
Mark Twain 594

SHORT STORY
An Encounter With an Interviewer
Mark Twain 596

ASSESSMENT SYNTHESIS 604

Speaking and Listening: Group Discussion 604

Writing: Fictional Narrative 605

Writing to Sources: Informative Essay 606

PART 4
DEMONSTRATING INDEPENDENCE

Independent Reading

Recommended
Titles for Extended Reading 608

ONLINE TEXT SET

SPEECH
My Heart Is in the Highlands
Jane Yolen

NOVEL EXCERPT   EXEMPLAR TEXT ©
from **Roll of Thunder, Hear My Cry**
Mildred D. Taylor

POEM
Alphabet
Naomi Shihab Nye

UNIT 4 Unit at a Glance

■ READ

Text Analysis
Dialogue in Drama
Stage Directions
Author's Purpose
Theme
Humor
Point of View
Plot
Tone

Comprehension
Summary
Compare and Contrast

Language Study
Greek root *-eth*
Prefix *trans-*

Language Study Workshop
Connotation and Denotation

■ DISCUSS

Comprehension and Collaboration
Group Discussion

Responding to Text
Partner Discussion
Panel Discussion
Write and Discuss
Group Discussion
Small Group Discussion

Speaking and Listening Workshop
Delivering a Persuasive Speech

■ RESEARCH

Research and Technology
Multimedia Presentation

Investigate the Topic: Mark Twain
The Palace of Westminster
Stage Fright
Twain, According to Others
Twain's First Riverboat Journey
Additional Quotations from Twain
Real Twain Interviews

■ WRITE

Writing to Sources
Summary
Review
Essay
Comparison-and-Contrast Essay
How-To Essay
Argument
Narrative

Writing Process Workshop
Argument: Problem-and-Solution Essay

Student Edition Pages

■ **UNIT VOCABULARY**

Academic Vocabulary appears in *blue*.

The Phantom Tollbooth, Act I *ignorance, precautionary, unethical, ferocious, misapprehension, unabridged*

The Phantom Tollbooth, Act II *dissonance, deficiency, admonishing, iridescent, malicious, transfixed*

from **You're a Good Man, Charlie Brown; Happiness is a Charming Charlie Brown at Orlando Rep** *objectionable, tentatively, civic, evoking, embody, abundantly, opinion, reflect, respond, specific*

The Prince and the Pauper; *from* **The Prince and the Pauper** *pauper, affliction, sauntered, respond, technique, similar*

Stage Fright *compulsion, awed, agonizing, opinion, purpose, common*

My Papa, Mark Twain *striking, incessantly, consequently, identify, credible, convincing*

Mark Twain's First "Vacation" *vigor, deliberate, distinctly, conflict, achieve*

According to Mark Twain *modify, quotation, establish*

An Encounter With An Interviewer *astonishing, rapture, notorious, pose, interviews, refer*

■ **COMMON CORE STATE STANDARDS**

For the full wording of the standards, see the standards chart following the Contents pages.

Reading Literature
RL.6.1, RL.6.2, RL.6.3, RL.6.4, RL.6.5, RL.6.6, RL.6.7, RL.6.9

Reading Informational Text
RI.6.1, RI.6.2, RI.6.3, RI.6.4, RI.6.5, RI.6.6, RI.6.9

Writing
W.6.1, W.6.1.a-e, W.6.2, W.6.2.a-d, W.6.2.e-f, W.6.3, W.6.3.a-e, W.6.4, W.6.6, W.6.8

Speaking and Listening
SL.6.1, SL.6.1.a–d, SL.6.2, SL.6.3, SL.6.4, SL.6.5

Language
L.6.1, L.6.2.a-b, L.6.3, L.6.3.a, L.6.4, L.6.4.a, L.6.4.c-d, L.6.5, L.6.5.c, L.6.6

PART 1
SETTING EXPECTATIONS

Introducing the Big Question
How much do our communities shape us? 612

Close Reading Workshop
Read • Discuss • Research • Write 614
RETELLING OF EPIC   EXEMPLAR TEXT ©
from **Black Ships Before Troy**
Rosemary Sutcliff 615
FOLK LITERATURE
Black Cowboy, Wild Horses
Julius Lester 620

PART 2
TEXT ANALYSIS GUIDED EXPLORATION

SHARED LESSONS

Elements of Folk Literature 628
Analyzing Structure and Theme in Folk Literature 630

FOLK LITERATURE READINGS
The Tiger Who Would Be King • The Ant and the Dove
James Thurber • Leo Tolstoy 634, 636
Arachne
Olivia E. Coolidge 642
The Stone
Lloyd Alexander 652
Why the Tortoise's Shell Is Not Smooth
Chinua Achebe 668

COMPARING TEXTS LITERARY ANALYSIS 676
SHORT STORY
Mowgli's Brothers
Rudyard Kipling 678
FICTION
from **James and the Giant Peach**
Roald Dahl 688

LANGUAGE STUDY Idioms 698

SPEAKING AND LISTENING Oral Response to Literature 700

WRITING PROCESS
Explanatory Text: Cause-and-Effect Essay 702

ASSESSMENT SKILLS 710
Selected Response 710
Constructed Response 714

PART 3
TEXT SETS DEVELOPING INSIGHT

PEOPLE AND ANIMALS

MYTH | ANCHOR TEXT
Prologue from The Whale Rider
Witi Ihimaera 718

MAGAZINE ARTICLE
The Case of the Monkeys That Fell From the Trees
Susan E. Quinlan 726

WEB ARTICLE
Rescuers to Carry Oxygen Masks for Pets
Associated Press 734

INFOGRAPHIC
2012 Pet Ownership Statistics
American Pet Products Association 738

SHORT STORY
The Old Woman Who Lived With the Wolves
Chief Luther Standing Bear 740

NEWS RELEASE
Satellites and Sea Lions
NASA 746

NARRATIVE ESSAY
Turkeys
Bailey White 750

ASSESSMENT SYNTHESIS 756

Speaking and Listening: Small Group Discussion 756

Writing: Narrative 757

Writing to Sources: Explanatory Essay 758

PART 4
DEMONSTRATING INDEPENDENCE

Independent Reading

Recommended
Titles for Extended Reading 760

ONLINE TEXT SET

AUTOBIOGRAPHY
The Market Square Dog
James Herriot

SHORT STORY
Aaron's Gift
Myron Levoy

REFLECTIVE ESSAY
Childhood and Poetry
Pablo Neruda

■ READ

Text Analysis
Fables and Folk Tales
Myths
Universal Theme
Personification
Comparing Elements of Fantasy
Expository Text
Text Features
Conflict and Resolution
Expository Writing
Author's Influences

Comprehension
Cause and Effect
Setting a Purpose
Purpose for Reading

Language Study
Suffix *-ment*
Latin root *-mort-*
Latin root *-van-*
Suffix *–ary*

Language Study Workshop
Idioms

■ DISCUSS

Presentation of Ideas
Oral Report

Comprehension and Collaboration
Dramatic Reading

Responding to Text
Partner Discussion
Panel Discussion
Class Discussion
Group Discussion

Speaking and Listening Workshop
Oral Response to Literature

■ RESEARCH

Research and Technology
Annotated Bibliography Entry
Written and Visual Report

Investigate the Topic: People and Animals
The Role of Myths
Scientific Method
Oxygen Masks
Humans and Animals
Oceanographers
Wild Turkeys

■ WRITE

Writing to Sources
Fable
Comparison-and-Contrast Essay
Plot Proposal
Invitation
Essay
Cause and Effect Essay
Explanation
Nonfiction Narrative
Argument
Informative Essay
Persuasive Letter
Persuasive Essay

Writing Process Workshop
Explanatory Text: Cause-and-Effect Essay

UNIT VOCABULARY

Academic Vocabulary appears in *blue*.

The Tiger Who Would Be King; The Ant and the Dove *prowled, inquired, repulse, monarch, startled, repaid*

Arachne *obscure, humble, mortal, indignantly, obstinacy, strive*

The Stone *feeble, vanished, plight, jubilation, rue, sown*

Why the Tortoise's Shell Is Not Smooth *cunning, famine, orator, custom, eloquent, compound*

Mowgli's Brothers; *from* James and the Giant Peach *quarry, fostering, monotonous, dispute, intently, colossal, conflict, convince, encounter, unique*

***Prologue from* The Whale Rider** *yearning, teemed, apex, sensory, observe, reveal*

The Case of the Monkeys That Fell From the Trees *incidents, abruptly, distress, study, observation, investigate*

Rescuers to Carry Oxygen Masks for Pets *resuscitation, unsolicited, inhalation, support, quotation, authorities*

2012 Pet Ownership Statistics *generalize, explain, subject*

The Old Woman Who Lived With the Wolves *coaxed, traversed, mystified, sensory, indicate, resolve*

Satellites and Sea Lions *navigate, marine, meteorologists, collaboratively, interaction, credible*

Turkeys *dilution, demise, vigilance, crucial*

COMMON CORE STATE STANDARDS

For the full wording of the standards, see the standards chart following the Contents pages.

Reading Literature
RL.6.1, RL.6.2, RL.6.3, RL.6.4, RL.6.5

Reading Informational Text
RI.6.1, RI.6.2, RI.6.5, RI.6.6

Writing
W.6.1, W.6.2, W.6.2.a-f, W.6.3, W.6.3.b-c, W.6.3.e, W.6.4, W.6.5, W.6.6, W.6.7, W.6.8, W.6.9, W.6.9.a-b

Speaking and Listening
SL.6.1, SL.6.2, SL.6.1.c-d, SL.6.4, SL.6.5, SL.6.6, SL.6.7

Language
L.6.1, L.6.2, L.6.2.a-b, L.6.3, L.6.3.a, L.6.4, L.6.4.b, L.6.5, L.6.5.a-b, L.6.6

Range of Reading

Literature

STORIES

Adventure and Suspense Stories

The Wounded Wolf
Jean Craighead George 8

Zlateh the Goat
Isaac Bashevis Singer 46

The King of Mazy May
Jack London 118

Mowgli's Brothers
Rudyard Kipling 678

Fables

The Tiger Who Would Be King
James Thurber 634

The Lion and the Bulls
Aesop .... OLL

Folk Tales and Fairy Tales

Why Monkeys Live in Trees
Julius Lester .... OLL

Dragon, Dragon
John Gardner .... OLL

The Ant and the Dove
Leo Tolstoy 636

The Stone
Lloyd Alexander 652

A Crippled Boy
My-Van Tran .... OLL

Why the Tortoise's Shell Is Not Smooth
Chinua Achebe 668

He Lion, Bruh Bear, and Bruh Rabbit
Virginia Hamilton .... OLL

The Three Wishes
Ricardo E. Alegría .... OLL

Historical Fiction

Roll of Thunder, Hear My Cry EXEMPLAR TEXT ©
Mildred D. Taylor .... OLL

Letter From a Concentration Camp
Yoshiko Uchida .... OLL

Black Cowboy, Wild Horses
Julius Lester 620

Humor

from The Prince and the Pauper
Mark Twain 572

An Encounter With an Interviewer
Mark Twain 596

Myths

**from Black Ships Before Troy:
The Story of the Iliad** EXEMPLAR TEXT ©
Rosemary Sutcliff 615

Arachne
Olivia E. Coolidge 642

Prologue from The Whale Rider
Witi Ihimaera 718

Realistic Fiction

Stray
Cynthia Rylant 20

Eleven EXEMPLAR TEXT ©
Sandra Cisneros

The Tail
Joyce Hansen 30

The Circuit
Francisco Jiménez 60

The All-American Slurp
Lensey Namioka .... OLL

Aaron's Gift
Myron Levoy .... OLL

Jeremiah's Song
Walter Dean Myers 88

The Southpaw
Judith Viorst 274

The Sound of Summer Running
Ray Bradbury 410

Science Fiction and Fantasy

Lob's Girl
Joan Aiken 74

from James and the Giant Peach
Roald Dahl 688

Greyling
Jane Yolen .... OLL

The Homecoming
Laurence Yep .... OLL

The Fun They Had
Isaac Asimov .... OLL

Feathered Friend
Arthur C. Clarke .... OLL

World Literature

The Old Grandfather and His Little Grandson
Leo Tolstoy 5

The Old Woman Who Lived With the Wolves
Chief Luther Standing Bear 740

Becky and the Wheels-and-Brake Boys
James Berry .... OLL

DRAMA

Plays

from **Brighton Beach Memoirs**
Neil Simon 443

Gluskabe and Old Man Winter
Joseph Bruchac 446

The Phantom Tollbooth, Act I
Susan Nanus 460

The Phantom Tollbooth, Act II
Susan Nanus 490

from **You're a Good Man, Charlie Brown**
Clark Gesner 524

The Prince and the Pauper
Mark Twain 554

POETRY

Concrete Poems

The Sidewalk Racer
Lillian Morrison 348

Concrete Cat
Dorthi Charles 349

Haiku

Haiku
Matsuo Bashō 347

Haiku
Musō Soseki .... OLL

Limerick

Limerick
Anonymous .... OLL

Limerick
Anonymous 350

Lyrical Poems

Twelfth Song of Thunder
Navajo 305

Ode to Family Photographs
Gary Soto 310

Adventures of Isabel
Ogden Nash 322

Wilbur Wright and Orville Wright
Rosemary and Stephen Vincent Benét .... OLL

The Walrus and the Carpenter
Lewis Carroll 326

Ankylosaurus
Jack Prelutsky .... OLL

A Dream Within a Dream
Edgar Allan Poe 321

Life Doesn't Frighten Me
Maya Angelou 324

Abuelito Who
Sandra Cisneros 337

April Rain Song
Langston Hughes 338

The World Is Not a Pleasant Place to Be
Nikki Giovanni 339

Fame Is a Bee
Emily Dickinson 340

Wind and water and stone
Octavio Paz 357

No Thank You
Shel Silverstein 358

Cynthia in the Snow
Gwendolyn Brooks 362

who knows if the moon's
E.E. Cummings 368

Dust of Snow
Robert Frost 370

Simile: Willow and Ginkgo
Eve Merriam 392

Child On Top of a Greenhouse
Theodore Roethke .... OLL

Parade
Rachel Field .... OLL

Saying Yes
Diana Chang .... OLL

Alphabet
Naomi Shihab Nye .... OLL

Narrative and Dramatic Poems

Oranges EXEMPLAR TEXT Ⓒ
Gary Soto 308

The Fairies' Lullaby
William Shakespeare 360

To Klondyke We've Paid Our Fare
H.J. Dunham 132

ONLINE LITERATURE LIBRARY

Highlighted selections are found in
the **Online Literature Library** (OLL) in
the Online Student Edition.

Range of Reading **xxix**

Informational Text—Literary Nonfiction

ARGUMENTS

Opinion Pieces

Jake Wood Baseball League Is the Start of Something Special
Reginald T. Dogan .... OLL

Metric Metric: It's so nice, we'll say it twice!
Metric Metric .... OLL

Happiness Is a Charming Charlie Brown at Orlando Rep
Matthew MacDermid 530

Speeches

Preserving a Great American Symbol
Richard Durbin 270

EXPOSITION

Biography

This Land Was Made for You and Me: Life & Songs of Woodie Guthrie EXEMPLAR TEXT ©
Elizabeth Partridge 165

My Papa, Mark Twain
Susy Clemens 584

A Backwoods Boy
Russell Freedman .... OLL

Content-Area Essays and Articles

Chinese and African Americans in the Gold Rush
The Johns Hopkins University 144

Birds Struggle to Recover From Egg Thefts of 1800s
Edie Lau 148

The Seven Wonders of the World
Infoplease™ 231

Art, Architecture, and Learning in Egypt
Prentice Hall Ancient Civilizations 233

The Shutout
Patricia C. McKissack and Fredrick McKissack, Jr. ..... OLL

Satellites and Sea Lions
NASA 746

California Sea Lions .... OLL

Journalism

Memories of an All-American Girl
Carmen Pauls 264

Fenway Park Celebrates 100 Years as America's Oldest Working Major League Ballpark
Molly Line 280

Why We Love Baseball
Mark Newman 286

Angela Duckworth and the Research on "Grit"
Emily Hanford 398

Mark Twain's First "Vacation"
from *The New York World* 590

Rescuers to Carry Oxygen Masks for Pets
Associated Press 734

NASA Finally Goes Metric
SPACE Staff .... OLL

Letters

A Woman's View of the Gold Rush
Mary B. Ballou 138

from **Letter on Thomas Jefferson** EXEMPLAR TEXT ©
John Adams 420

Letter to Scottie
F. Scott Fitzgerald .... OLL

Memoirs and Diaries

from **Zlata's Diary**
Zlata Filipović 168

The Drive-In Movies
Gary Soto 186

Langston Terrace
Eloise Greenfield 208

Water
Helen Keller 424

The Market Square Dog
James Herriot .... OLL

Hard as Nails
Russell Baker .... OLL

from **Something to Declare**
Julia Alvarez .... OLL

Narrative Essays

Jackie Robinson: Justice at Last
Geoffrey C. Ward and Ken Burns 256

Race to the End of the Earth
William G. Scheller 404

The Case of the Monkeys That Fell From the Trees
Susan E. Quinlan 726

Turkeys
Bailey White 750

La Leña Buena
John Phillip Santos .... OLL

Personal Essays

My Heart Is in the Highlands
Jane Yolen .... OLL

Names/ Nombres
Julia Alvarez 196

The Lady and the Spider
Robert Fulghum .... OLL

Reflective Essays

from **The Pigman and Me**
Paul Zindel 218

Childhood and Poetry
Pablo Neruda .... OLL

Speeches

Stage Fright
Mark Twain 580

Literature in Context—Reading in Content Areas

Safety Connection:
Pet Precautions 36

Geography Connection:
Agricultural Seasons 64

Music Connection:
What Is the Delta Blues? (illustrated) 90

Social Studies Connection:
Drive-In Movies 188

Biography Connection:
The Man Langston Terrace Honors 209

Culture Connection:
Turnpike Tollbooth 462

Science Connection:
Measuring Time (illustrated) 467

Culture Connection:
Plumb Line 502

Language Connection:
Allusions 635

Culture Connection:
Athene 645

Literature Connection:
Rocks and Roles 660

FUNCTIONAL TEXT

World of Escher Tessellation Contest .... OLL
Library Card Information
Sara Hightower Regional Library System .... OLL

Library Card Application
Sara Hightower Regional Library System .... OLL

MEDIA

Gold Rush: The Journey by Land
from The Sacramento Bee 136

Ted Williams Baseball Card 292

Determination 430

According to Mark Twain
Mark Twain 594

2012 Pet Ownership Statistics
2011–2012 APPA National Pet Owners Survey 738

ONLINE LITERATURE LIBRARY

Highlighted selections are found in the **Online Literature Library** (OLL) in the Online Student Edition.

Features and Workshops

COMPARING TEXTS

Comparing Foreshadowing and Flashback

SHORT STORY
Lob's Girl
Joan Aiken..74

SHORT STORY
Jeremiah's Song
Walter Dean Myers................................88

Comparing Text Aids and Features

ONLINE ALMANAC
The Seven Wonders of the World
Infoplease™..231

TEXTBOOK ARTICLE
Art, Architecture, and Learning in Egypt
Prentice Hall Ancient Civilizations..........233

Comparing Imagery

POEM
who knows if the moon's
E.E. Cummings.......................................368

POEM
Dust of Snow
Robert Frost...370

Comparing Author's Purpose Across Genres

DRAMA
from **You're a Good Man, Charlie Brown**
Clark Gesner..524

REVIEW
Happiness is a Charming Charlie Brown at Orlando Rep
Matthew MacDermid...............................530

Comparing Elements of Fantasy

SHORT STORY
Mowgli's Brothers
Rudyard Kipling.....................................678

FICTION
from **James and the Giant Peach**
Roald Dahl...688

WRITING PROCESS

Narration: Short Story....................................102
Informative Text: Comparison-and-Contrast Essay....240
Argumentative Text: Argumentative Essay.............376
Argumentative Text: Problem-and-Solution Essay....538
Explanatory Text: Cause-and-Effect Essay...............702

LANGUAGE STUDY

Using a Dictionary and Thesaurus.....................98
Word Origins...236
Words With Multiple Meanings.........................372
Connotation and Denotation............................534
Idioms...698

SPEAKING AND LISTENING

Following Oral Directions................................100
Evaluating Media Messages and Advertisements......238
Problem-and-Solution Proposal........................374
Delivering a Persuasive Speech........................536
Oral Response to Literature.............................700

xxxii Features and Workshops

ONLINE TEXT SETS

These selections can be found in the Online Literature Library in the Online Student Edition

Unit 1

SHORT STORY
Eleven
Sandra Cisneros

BIOGRAPHY
A Backwoods Boy
Russell Freedman

LETTER
Letter to Scottie
F. Scott Fitzgerald

Unit 2

FOLK TALE
Why Monkeys Live in Trees
Julius Lester

EDITORIAL
Jake Wood Baseball Is the Start of Something Special
Reginald T. Dogan

POEM
Wilbur Wright and Orville Wright
Rosemary and Stephen Vincent Benét

Unit 3

PERSONAL ESSAY
The Lady and the Spider
Robert Fulghum

SHORT STORY
Dragon, Dragon
John Gardner

POEM
Ankylosaurus
Jack Prelutsky

Unit 4

SPEECH
My Heart Is in the Highlands
Jane Yolen

NOVEL EXCERPT
from **Roll of Thunder, Hear My Cry**
Mildred D. Taylor

POEM
Alphabet
Naomi Shihab Nye

Unit 5

AUTOBIOGRAPHY
The Market Square Dog
James Herriot

SHORT STORY
Aaron's Gift
Myron Levoy

REFLECTIVE ESSAY
Childhood and Poetry
Pablo Neruda

The Skills Navigator provides a detailed look at the specific features, workshops, skills, and standards covered in each unit. Use these pages to guide you through planning your instruction for a day, unit, or entire year.

The instructional model in *Pearson Common Core Literature* is data driven and provides flexibility based on your students' needs. Therefore, the pacing recommendations on the following pages can be adjusted to meet the needs of your classroom. For example, the recommended number of days for Part 1: Setting Expectations is four days. Depending on your students and their ability to closely read a text, you may choose to use Part 1 for only one day or for as many as five days.

Another example of flexible pacing is shown with Part 2: Guided Exploration. This Part provides scaffolded instruction focused on skills. Again, depending on your students' needs, you may choose to teach one selection over a period of four days or teach three selections over a course of twelve days. The Pacing Recommendations are provided as a guide, but you know your students best and should chart the appropriate pathway through the programs based on students' needs.

INTRODUCTORY UNIT

The Introductory Unit can be used at any time through the year to teach essential Common Core skills and standards. The chart below provides an overview of the features of this unit.

Introductory Unit	Features	Standards Addressed
Building Academic Vocabulary	• General Academic Vocabulary • Domain-specific Academic Vocabulary • Increasing Your Word Knowledge • Building Your Speaking Vocabulary	Language 6
Writing an Objective Summary	• Model Objective Summary	Literature 2; Informational Text 2
Comprehending Complex Texts	• Strategy 1: Multidraft Reading • Strategy 2: Close Read the Text • Strategy 3: Ask Questions	Literature 10
Analyzing Arguments	• The Art of Argument • Composing an Argument	Informational Text 8; Writing 1.a, 1.b, 1.e; Language 6
Conducting Research	• Performing Short-Term and Long-Term Research • Research Process Workshop • Research Model • Citing Sources and Preparing Manuscript	Writing 2, 2.a, 2.b, 2.d, 2.f, 6, 7, 8

UNITS AT A GLANCE

The chart below provides an overview of the features and assessments for each unit. A more detailed listing of each unit's skills begins on the next page.

Unit	Close Reading Workshop	Language Study	Speaking and Listening	Writing Process	Independent Reading	Assessment
1	Focus on Short Story Reading, Writing, Speaking, Research Models Independent Practice	Using a Dictionary and Thesaurus	Following Oral Directions	Narrative: Short Story	Titles for Extended Reading Online Text Set **Eleven** *Sandra Cisneros* **A Backwoods Boy** *Russell Freedman* **Letter to Scotty** *F. Scott Fitzgerald*	Assessment: Skills **Selected Response** **Constructed Response** Assessment: Synthesis **Speaking and Listening:** Group Discussion **Writing:** Historical Fiction **Writing to Sources:** Argumentative Essay
2	Focus on Nonfiction Reading, Writing, Speaking, Research Models Independent Practice	Word Origins	Evaluating Media Messages and Advertisements	Informative Text: Comparison-and-Contrast Essay	Titles for Extended Reading Online Text Set **Why Monkeys Live in Trees** *Julius Lester* **Jake Wood Baseball Is the Start of Something Special** *Reginald T. Dogan* **Wilbur Wright and Orville Wright** *Rosemary and Stephen Vincent Benet*	Assessment: Skills **Selected Response** **Constructed Response** Assessment: Synthesis **Speaking and Listening:** Group Discussion **Writing:** Autobiographical Narrative **Writing to Sources:** Expository Essay
3	Focus on Poetry Reading, Writing, Speaking, Research Models Independent Practice	Words with Multiple Meanings	Problem-and-Solution Proposal	Argumentative Essay	Titles for Extended Reading Online Text Set **The Lady and the Spider** *Robert Fulghum* **Dragon, Dragon** *John Gardner* **Ankylosaurus** *Jack Prelutsky*	Assessment: Skills **Selected Response** **Constructed Response** Assessment: Synthesis **Speaking and Listening:** Group Discussion **Writing:** Fictional Narrative **Writing to Sources:** Argumentative Essay
4	Focus on Drama Reading, Writing, Speaking, Research Models Independent Practice	Connotation and Denotation	Delivering a Persuasive Speech	Argument: Problem-and-Solution Essay	Titles for Extended Reading Online Text Set **My Heart is in the Highlands** *Jane Yolen* from **Roll of Thunder, Hear My Cry** *Mildred D. Taylor* **Alphabet** *Naomi Shihab Nye*	Assessment: Skills **Selected Response** **Constructed Response** Assessment: Synthesis **Speaking and Listening:** Group Discussion **Writing:** Fictional Narrative **Writing to Sources:** Informative/Explanatory Essay
5	Focus on Oral Tradition Reading, Writing, Speaking, Research Models Independent Practice	Idioms	Oral Response to Literature	Explanatory Text: Cause-and-Effect Essay	Titles for Extended Reading Online Text Set **The Market Square Dog** *James Herriot* **Aaron's Gift** *Myron Levoy* **Childhood and Poetry** *Pablo Neruda*	Assessment: Skills **Selected Response** **Constructed Response** Assessment: Synthesis **Speaking and Listening:** Small Group Discussion **Writing:** Narrative **Writing to Sources:** Expository Essay

		Selection/Feature	Pacing	Standards Covered	Common Core Companion Workbook*	Close Reading Focus
PART 1	**IBQ/CLOSE READING WORKSHOP**	**The Old Grandfather and His Little Grandson** Leo Tolstoy **The Wounded Wolf** Jean Craighead George	4 days	RL1, RL2, RL3, RL4, RL5, W2, W4, W7, W8, W9, SL1	pp 2, 15, 28, 41, 54, 184, 207, 246, 253, 267, 286	Close Reading: Short Story
PART 2	**CHARACTERS AND CONFLICT**	**Stray** Cynthia Rylant	4–16 days	RL3, W2b, W2e, W4, W7, SL3, L2, L4b	pp 28, 184, 207, 246, 297, 331, 339	Plot Make Predictions
		The Tail Joyce Hansen		RL1, RL3, W4, SL2, L1, L6	pp 2, 28, 207, 293, 321, 353	Characterization Make Inferences
		Zlateh the Goat Isaac Bashevis Singer		RL1, RL3, W1, SL4, SL5, L1b, L4	pp 2, 28, 173, 304, 311, 321, 339	Conflict and Resolution Make Inferences
		The Circuit Francisco Jiménez		RL2, W4, SL1c, L1a, L4b	pp 15, 207, 286, 321, 339	Theme Draw Conclusions
	COMPARING TEXTS	**Lob's Girl** Joan Aiken **Jeremiah's Song** Walter Dean Myers	2 days	RL5, W2a	pp 54, 184	Plot Techniques
	WORKSHOPS	**Language Study**	1 day	L4c, L4d, L5c	pp 339, 347	
		Speaking and Listening	1 day	SL1c, SL1d	p 286	
		Writing Process	3 days	W3, W3a, W3b, W3c, W3d, W3e, L1c, L1d, L2b	pp 196, 321, 331	
PART 3	**TEXT SET: THE GOLD RUSH**	**Anchor: The King of Mazy May** Jack London	5 days	RL1, RL2, RL3, RL4, RL5, W2, W4, W5, W7, W8, W9, W9a, W10, SL1, SL4, L1, L2, L3, L4, L4a, L5, L6	pp 2, 15, 28, 41, 54, 184, 207, 214, 246, 253, 267, 275, 286, 304, 321, 331, 335, 339, 347, 353	Setting
		To Klondyke We've Paid Our Fare H.J. Dunham	2–3 days	RL1, RL2, RL4, RL5, W3, W4, W7, W8, W9, W9a, W10, SL1, SL4, L1	pp 2, 15, 41, 54, 196, 207, 246, 253, 267, 275, 286, 304, 321	Alliteration
		Gold Rush: The Journey By Land from The Sacramento Bee	1 day	RI1, RI7, W3, W4, SL1, L1, L2, L3, L4, L6	pp 90, 144, 196, 207, 286, 321, 331, 335, 339, 353	
		A Woman's View of the Gold Rush Mary B. Ballou	2–3 days	RL1, RL2, RL4, RL5, W2, W4, W7, W8, W9, W9a, W10, SL1, SL4, L1, L3, L4, L6	pp 2, 15, 41, 54, 184, 207, 246, 253, 267, 275, 286, 304, 321, 335, 339, 353	Tone
		Chinese and African Americans in the Gold Rush Johns Hopkins University	2–3 days	RI1, RI2, RI4, RI5, RI6, W1, W2, W4, W7, W8, W9, W9b, W10, SL1, SL4, L1, L2, L3, L4, L6	pp 90, 103, 123, 130, 137, 173, 184, 207, 246, 253, 267, 275, 286, 304, 321, 331, 335, 339, 353	Author's Purpose
		Birds Struggle to Recover From Egg Thefts of 1800s Edie Lau	2–3 days	RI1, RI2, RI3, RI4, RI5, RI6, RI7, W1, W4, W7, W8, W9, W9b, W10, SL1, SL4, L1, L2, L3, L4, L6	pp 90, 103, 116, 123, 130, 137, 144, 173, 207, 246, 253, 267, 275, 286, 304, 321, 331, 335, 339, 353	Imagery

* represents the first page of multiple-page lessons

Conventions	Language Study**	Speaking and Listening	Research	Writing
		Small-Group Discussion	Explanation: Wolf Behavior	Writing Model: Argument Writing: Explanatory Essay
Common, Proper, and Possessive Nouns	Academic Vocabulary Selection Vocabulary		Brochure	List of Reasons
Personal and Possessive Pronouns	Academic Vocabulary Selection Vocabulary		Compare-and-Contrast Chart	Letter of Recommendation
Pronouns	Academic Vocabulary Selection Vocabulary		Compare-and-Contrast Chart	Persuasive Speech
Pronoun Case	Academic Vocabulary Selection Vocabulary	Interview		Description
				Timed Writing: Explanatory Essay
	Using a Dictionary and Thesaurus			
		Following Oral Directions		
Pronoun-Antecedent Agreement Pronoun Types and Case	Voice		Focus on Research: Narrative	Narrative: Short Story
Nouns Verb Tense	Diction and Style Academic Vocabulary Selection Vocabulary	Group Discussion	Investigate the Topic: Gold Rush Struggles	Informative Text: Cause-and-Effect Essay
	Academic Vocabulary Selection Vocabulary	Group Discussion	Investigate the Topic: Striking It Rich	Fictional Narrative: Short Story
	Academic Vocabulary Selection Vocabulary	Class Discussion		Narrative: Journal Entry
	Academic Vocabulary Selection Vocabulary	Partner Discussion	Investigate the Topic: Gold Rush Housing	Informational Text
	Academic Vocabulary Selection Vocabulary	Group Discussion	Investigate the Topic: Labor During the Gold Rush	Editorial
	Academic Vocabulary Selection Vocabulary	Group Discussion	Investigate the Topic: The Gold Rush and Food	Argumentative Essay

** For a listing of selection and academic vocabulary, see the Table of Contents.

		Selection/Feature	Pacing	Standards Covered	Common Core Companion Workbook*	Close Reading Focus
PART 1	**IBQ/CLOSE READING WORKSHOP**	*from* **This Land Was Made for You and Me** Elizabeth Partridge *from* **Zlata's Diary** Zlata Filipović	4 days	RI1, RI2, RI3, RI4, RI5, RI6, W2, W4, W6, W7, W9b, SL1	pp 90, 103, 116, 123, 130, 137, 184, 207, 227, 246, 267, 286	Close Reading: Nonfiction
PART 2	**LIFE STORIES**	**The Drive-In Movies** Gary Soto	4–16 days	RI6, W3, SL6, L1, L6	pp 137, 196, 313, 321, 353	Narrator and Point of View Make Predictions
		Names/Nombres Julia Alvarez		RL4, RI8, W3d, SL6, L1, L6	pp 41, 151, 196, 313, 321, 353	Tone Fact and Opinion
		Langston Terrace Eloise Greenfield		RI1, RI2, W3, W3b, W8, SL4, L1, L6	pp 90, 103, 196, 253, 304, 321, 353	Author's Influences Main Idea
		from **The Pigman & Me** Paul Zindel		RI2, W2a, W2b, SL1a, SL1b, SL1d, L1, L4b, L6	pp 103, 184, 286, 321, 339, 353	Mood Main Idea
	COMPARING TEXTS	**The Seven Wonders of the Word** Infoplease™ **Art, Architecture, and Learning in Egypt** Prentice Hall Ancient Civilizations	2 days	RI5, RI7, W1, L6	pp 130, 144, 173, 353	Use Text Aids and Features
	WORKSHOPS	**Language Study**	1 day	L4b, L4c	p 339	
		Speaking and Listening	1 day	SL2, SL3	pp 293, 297	
		Writing Process	3 days	W2, W2a, W2b, W2c, L1	pp 184, 321	
PART 3	**TEXT SET: BASEBALL**	**Anchor: Jackie Robinson: Justice at Last** Geoffrey C. Ward and Ken Burns	5 days	RI1, RI2, RI3, RI4, RI5, RI6, W1a, W1b, W1c, W2a, W2b, W2c, W4, W5, W7, SL1, SL4	pp 90, 103, 116, 123, 130, 137, 173, 184, 207, 214, 246, 286, 304	Author's Viewpoint
		Memories of an All-American Girl Carmen Pauls	2–3 days	RI1, RI2, RI3, RI4, RI5, W3, W4, SL1, SL4, L1, L2, L3, L4	pp 90, 103, 116, 123, 130, 196, 207, 286, 304, 321, 331, 335, 339	Time Shifts
		Preserving a Great American Symbol Richard Durbin	2–3 days	RI1, RI2, RI3, RI4, RI5, W2, W4, W7, SL1	pp 90, 103, 116, 123, 130, 184, 207, 246, 286	Hyperbole
		The Southpaw Judith Viorst	2–3 days	RL1, RL2, RL3, RL4, RL5, W2, W4, SL1, SL4	pp 2, 15, 28, 41, 54, 184, 207, 286, 304	Characterization
		Fenway Park Celebrates 100 Years as America's Oldest Working Major League Ballpark Molly Line	2–3 days	RI1, RI2, RI3, RI4, RI5, W1, W4, SL1, SL4, L1, L2, L3, L4, L5	pp 90, 103, 116, 123, 130, 173, 207, 286, 304, 321, 331, 335, 339, 347	Figurative Language
		Why We Love Baseball Mark Newman	2–3 days	RI1, RI2, RI4, W2, W4, W7, W10, SL1, L1, L2, L3, L4, L5	pp 90, 103, 123, 184, 207, 246, 275, 286, 321, 331, 335, 339, 347	Word Choice
		Ted Williams Baseball Card	1 day	RI1, RI6, RI7, W3, W4, SL4	pp 90, 137, 144, 196, 207, 304	

* represents the first page of multiple-page lessons

Conventions	Language Study**	Speaking and Listening	Research	Writing
		Small-Group Discussion	Explanation: Historical Events	Writing Model: Informative Text Writing: Explanatory Essay
Principal Parts of Verbs	Academic Vocabulary Selection Vocabulary	Conversation		Autobiographical Narrative
Action and Linking Verbs	Academic Vocabulary Selection Vocabulary	Monologue		Personal Anecdote
Simple Verb Tenses	Academic Vocabulary Selection Vocabulary		Informative Presentation	Journal Entry
Perfect Tenses of Verbs	Academic Vocabulary Selection Vocabulary	Informal Discussion		Problem-and-Solution Essay
				Timed Writing: Position Statement
	Word Origins			
		Evaluating Media Messages and Advertisements		
Correcting Errors with Verbs Principal Parts of Verbs Verb Tenses	Organizing a Comparison-and-Contrast Essay		Focus on Research: Informative Text	Informative Text: Comparison-and-Contrast Essay
Verb Tenses Past Tense Verbs Past Perfect Tense Verbs	Diction and Style Academic Vocabulary Selection Vocabulary	Group Discussion	Investigate the Topic: Segregation in Sports	Informative Text: Comparison-and-Contrast Essay
	Academic Vocabulary Selection Vocabulary	Partner Discussion	Investigate the Topic: Women and Baseball	Autobiographical Narrative
	Academic Vocabulary Selection Vocabulary	Panel Discussion	Investigate the Topic: Baseball Traditions	Argument: Persuasive Speech
	Academic Vocabulary Selection Vocabulary	Group Discussion	Investigate the Topic: Teams and Clubs	Persuasive Letter
	Academic Vocabulary Selection Vocabulary	Group Discussion	Investigate the Topic: Popular Stadiums	Argumentative Essay
	Academic Vocabulary Selection Vocabulary	Group Discussion	Investigate the Topic: Baseball in Literature	Reflective Essay
	Academic Vocabulary Selection Vocabulary			Narrative: Journal Entry

** For a listing of selection and academic vocabulary, see the Table of Contents.

		Selection/Feature	Pacing	Standards Covered	Common Core Companion Workbook*	Close Reading Focus	
PART 1	**IBQ/CLOSE READING WORKSHOP**	**Twelfth Song of Thunder** Navajo **Oranges** Gary Soto **Ode to Family Photographs** Gary Soto	4 days	RL1, RL2, RL4, RL5, RL6, W2, W7, W9a, SL1	pp 2, 15, 41, 54, 61, 184, 246, 267, 286	Close Reading: Poetry	
PART 2	**RHYTHM AND RHYME**	**Poetry Collection 1** Poe • Nash • Angelou • Caroll	4–16 days	RL4, W2, W2b, W2e, W2f, W9, L1, L4a, L6	pp 41, 184, 267, 321, 339, 353	Rhythm and Rhyme Context Clues	
		Poetry Collection 2 Cisneros • Hughes • Giovanni • Dickinson		RL4, RL7, W3d, SL6, L1, L4a, L4c	pp 41, 68, 196, 313, 321, 339, 353	Figurative Language Context Clues	
		Poetry Collection 3 Bashō • Morrison • Charles • Anonymous		RL5, W4, W6, L1, L3, L6	pp 54, 207, 227, 321, 335, 353	Forms of Poetry Paraphrasing	
		Poetry Collection 4 Paz • Silverstein • Shakespeare • Brooks		RL4, W4, W6, L1, L3, L4c	pp 41, 207, 227, 321, 335, 339	Sound Devices and Tone Paraphrasing	
	COMPARING TEXTS	**who knows if the moon's** e.e. cummings **Dust of Snow** Robert Frost	2 days	RL4, W2a, W2b	pp 41, 184	Imagery	
	WORKSHOPS	**Language Study**	1 day	L4, L4a, L4c, L4d	p 339		
		Speaking and Listening	1 day	SL4, SL5, L1e	pp 304, 311, 321		
		Writing Process	3 days	W1, W1a, W1b, W1c, W1d, W1e, W5, L1, L1e, L2b, L3	pp 173, 214, 321, 331, 335		
PART 3	**TEXT SET: DETERMINA-TION**	**Anchor: Simile: Willow and Ginkgo** Eva Merriam	5 days	RL1, RL2, RL4, RL5, RL6, W2, W4, W6, W7, W8, W9, W9b, W10, SL1, SL4, L3, L4, L5	pp 2, 15, 41, 54, 61, 184, 207, 227, 246, 253, 267, 275, 286, 304, 335, 339, 347	Simile	
		Angela Duckworth and Research on "Grit" Emily Hanford	2–3 days	RI1, RI2, RI3, RI5, W3, W4, W5, W7, W8, SL1, SL4, SL6	pp 90, 103, 116, 130, 196, 207, 214, 246, 253, 286, 304, 313	Direct Quotation	
		Race to the End of the Earth William G. Scheller	2–3 days	RI1, RI2, RI3, RI5, RI6, W3, W4, W7, W8, SL1, SL4, L1	pp 90, 103, 116, 130, 137, 196, 207, 246, 253, 286, 304, 321	Foreshadowing	
		The Sound of Summer Running Ray Bradbury	2–3 days	RL1, RL2, RL3, RL4, RL5, W3, W4, W5, W7, W8, SL1, SL4, L1	pp 2, 15, 28, 41, 54, 196, 207, 214, 246, 253, 286, 304, 321	Symbols	
		from **Letter on Thomas Jefferson** John Adams	2–3 days	RI1, RI2, RI3, RI5, RI6, W1, W2, W4, W5, W7, W8, W9, SL1, SL4	pp 90, 103, 116, 130, 137, 173, 184, 207, 214, 246, 253, 267, 286, 304	Central Idea	
		Water Helen Keller	2–3 days	RI1, RI2, RI3, RI4, RI5, RI6, W1, W4, W5, W7, W8, SL1, SL4	pp 90, 103, 116, 123, 130, 137, 173, 207, 214, 246, 253, 286, 304	Author's Purpose	
		Determination	1 day	RI1, RI2, RI3, RI5, RI6, RI7, W2, W3, W4, W7, W8	pp 90, 103, 116, 130, 137, 144, 184, 196, 207, 246, 253		

* represents the first page of multiple-page lessons

Conventions	Language Study**	Speaking and Listening	Research	Writing
		Small-Group Discussion	Explanation: Importance of Setting	Writing Model: Argument Writing: Explanatory Essay
Adjectives and Adverbs	Academic Vocabulary Selection Vocabulary		Illustrated Booklet	Letter to an Author
Comparisons with Adjectives and Adverbs	Academic Vocabulary Selection Vocabulary	Dramatic Poetry Reading		Poem
Conjunctions and Interjections	Academic Vocabulary Selection Vocabulary		Presentation of a Poem	Poem
Sentence Parts and Types	Academic Vocabulary Selection Vocabulary		Résumé	Prose Description
				Timed Writing: Explanatory Essay
	Words with Multiple Meanings			
		Problem-and-Solution Proposal		
Using Coordinating Conjunctions Adjectives and Adverbs Comparisons with Adjectives	Word Choice		Focus on Research: Argument	Argumentative Essay
Adjectives Present Tense Verbs Past Tense Verbs	Diction and Style Academic Vocabulary Selection Vocabulary	Group Discussion	Investigate the Topic: Survival Skills	Informative Text: Expository Essay
	Academic Vocabulary Selection Vocabulary	Partner Discussion	Investigate the Topic: College Challenges	Autobiographical Narrative
	Academic Vocabulary Selection Vocabulary	Group Discussion	Investigate the Topic: Expedition to the South Pole	Diary Entry
	Academic Vocabulary Selection Vocabulary	Group Discussion	Investigate the Topic: Financial Skills	Reflective Essay
	Academic Vocabulary Selection Vocabulary	Group Discussion	Investigate the Topic: Determination and the Declaration of Independence	Argument: Comparison-and-Contrast Essay
	Academic Vocabulary Selection Vocabulary	Small Group Discussion	Investigate the Topic: Learn to Communicate	Argumentative Essay
	Academic Vocabulary Selection Vocabulary		Investigate the Topic: Politics and Determination	

** For a listing of selection and academic vocabulary, see the Table of Contents.

Skills Navigator: Unit 4

		Selection/Feature	Pacing	Standards Covered	Common Core Companion Workbook*	Close Reading Focus
PART 1	IBQ/CLOSE READING WORKSHOP	*from* **Brighton Beach Memoirs** Neil Simon **Gluskabe and Old Man Winter** Joseph Bruchac	4 days	RL1, RL2, RL3, RL5, W2, W4, W7, W9a, SL1	pp 2, 15, 28, 54, 184, 207, 246, 267, 286	Close Reading: Drama
PART 2	ADVENTURE AND IMAGINATION	**The Phantom Tollbooth Act I** Susan Nanus	4 days	RL2, RL3, RL5, RL6, W4, W6, W8, SL5, L1, L2a	pp 15, 28, 54, 61, 207, 227, 253, 311, 321, 331	Dialogue in Drama Summary
		The Phantom Tollbooth Act II Susan Nanus	4 days	RL5, RL7, W1, W1a, SL1c, SL3, L1, L3, L6	pp 54, 68, 173, 286, 297, 321, 335, 353	Stage Directions Compare and Contrast
	COMPARING TEXTS	*from* **You're a Good Man, Charlie Brown** Clark Gesner **Happiness is a Charming Charlie Brown at Orlando Rep** Matthew MacDermid	2 days	RL9, RI6, RI9	pp 75, 137, 158	Author's Purpose
	WORKSHOPS	**Language Study**	1 day	L4c, L5, L5c	pp 339, 347	
		Speaking and Listening	1 day	SL3, SL4, SL5	pp 297, 304, 311	
		Writing Process	3 days	W1, W1a, W1b, W1c, W1d, W1e, L2b, L3, L3a	pp 173, 331, 335	
PART 3	TEXT SET: MARK TWAIN	**Anchor: The Prince and the Pauper** Mark Twain	5 days	RL1, RL2, RL4, W2a, W2b, SL1a, SL1b, SL1c, SL1d, L4a, L4d, L6	pp 2, 15, 41, 184, 286, 339, 353	Theme
		Stage Fright Mark Twain	2–3 days	RI1, RI2, RI4, RI5, W2, SL1, L4, L5, L6	pp 90, 103, 123, 130, 184, 286, 339, 347, 353	Humor
		My Papa, Mark Twain Susy Clemens	2–3 days	RI1, RI2, RI5, RI6, W1, SL1, L4, L6	pp 90, 103, 130, 137, 173, 286, 339, 353	Point of View
		Mark Twain's First "Vacation" The New York World	2–3 days	RI1, RI2, RI3, RI4, RI5, W3, SL1, SL2, SL5, L4, L6	pp 90, 103, 116, 123, 130, 196, 286, 293, 311, 339, 353	Plot
		According to Mark Twain Mark Twain	1 day	RI1, RI4, W1a	pp 90, 123, 173	
		An Encounter With an Interviewer Mark Twain	2–3 days	RL1, RL2, RL5, RL6, W1, SL1, L4, L6	pp 2, 15, 54, 61, 173, 286, 339, 353	Tone

* represents the first page of multiple-page lessons

Conventions	Language Study**	Speaking and Listening	Research	Writing
		Small-Group Discussion	Explanation: Similarities in Different Texts	Writing Model: Informative Essay Writing: Explanatory Essay
Prepositions and Appositives	Academic Vocabulary Selection Vocabulary		Multimedia Presentation	Summary
Participles and Gerunds	Academic Vocabulary Selection Vocabulary	Group Discussion		Review
				Timed Writing: Explanatory Essay
	Connotation and Denotation			
		Delivering a Persuasive Speech		
Combining Sentences for Variety Prepositions and Appositives Participles and Gerunds	Support Your Ideas		Focus on Research: Argument	Argument: Problem-and-Solution Essay
Appositive Phrases Adverbs	Diction and Style Academic Vocabulary Selection Vocabulary	Partner Discussion	Investigate the Topic: The Palace of Westminster	Informative Text: Comparison-and-Contrast Essay
	Academic Vocabulary Selection Vocabulary	Panel Discussion	Investigate the Topic: Stage Fright	Informational Text: How-To Essay
	Academic Vocabulary Selection Vocabulary	Partner Discussion	Investigate the Topic: Twain According to Others	Argumentative Essay
	Academic Vocabulary Selection Vocabulary	Group Discussion	Investigate the Topic: Twain's First Riverboat Journey	Narrative Text
	Academic Vocabulary Selection Vocabulary		Investigate the Topic: Twain's Quotations	Argumentative Essay
	Academic Vocabulary Selection Vocabulary	Small Group Discussion	Investigate the Topic: Real Twain Interviews	Argumentative Essay

** For a listing of selection and academic vocabulary, see the Table of Contents.

		Selection/Feature	Pacing	Standards Covered	Common Core Companion Workbook*	Close Reading Focus
PART 1	IBQ/CLOSE READING WORKSHOP	*from* **Black Ships Before Troy** Rosemary Sutcliff **Black Cowboy, Wild Horses** Julius Lester	4 days	RL1, RL2, W2b, W7, W9a, SL1	pp 2, 15, 184, 246, 267, 286	Close Reading: Folk Literature
PART 2	SHARED LESSONS	**The Tiger Who Would Be King** James Thurber **The Ant and the Dove** Leo Tolstoy	4–16 days	RL2, W3b, W3e, W6, W7, SL5, L1, L4b	pp 15, 196, 227, 246, 311, 321, 339	Fables and Folktales Cause and Effect
		Arachne Olivia E. Coolidge		RL2, RL5, W2, W2a, W2d, W2e, W8, L3, L4b	pp 2, 54, 184, 253, 335, 339	Myths Cause and Effects
		The Stone Lloyd Alexander		RL2, W4, W6, W8, SL1, L1, L2a, L6	pp 15, 207, 227, 253, 286, 321, 331, 353	Universal Theme Setting a Purpose
		Why the Tortoise's Shell Is Not Smooth Chinua Achebe		RL4, W4, SL6, L1, L3a, L5a, L5b	pp 41, 207, 313, 321, 335, 347	Personification Purpose for Reading
	COMPARING TEXTS	**Mowgli's Brothers** Rudyard Kipling *from* **James and the Giant Peach** Roald Dahl	2 days	RL2, W2a	pp 15, 184	Fantasy
	WORKSHOPS	**Language Study**	1 day	L5	p 347	
		Speaking and Listening	1 day	SL1c, SL1d, SL4	pp 286, 304	
		Writing Process	3 days	W2, W2a, W2b, W2c, W2f, W5, L2, L2a, L2b, L3	pp 184, 214, 331, 335	
PART 3	TEXT SET: PEOPLE AND ANIMALS	**Anchor: Prologue** *from* **The Whale Rider** Witi Ihimaera	5 days	RL1, RL2, RL4, W2a, W2b, W2c, W7, W8, W9a, SL1, SL4, L2, L3, L4, L5, L6	pp 2, 15, 41, 184, 246, 253, 267, 286, 304, 331, 335, 339, 347, 353	Myth
		The Case of the Monkeys That Fell from the Trees Susan E. Quinlan	2–3 days	RI1, RI2, RI6, W2, W7, SL1, SL4, L4b, L6	pp 90, 103, 137, 184, 246, 286, 304, 339, 353	Expository Writing
		Rescuers to Carry Oxygen Masks for Pets Associated Press	2–3 days	RI1, RI2, RI5, W3, W7, SL1, L4, L6	pp 90, 103, 130, 196, 246, 286, 339, 353	Text Features
		2012 Pet Ownership Statistics American Pet Products Association	1 day	RI1, W1, SL1, SL2	pp 90, 173, 286, 293	
		The Old Woman Who Lived With the Wolves Chief Luther Standing Bear	2–3 days	RL1, RL2, RL3, RL4, W1, W7, W8, SL1, SL4, L1, L4	pp 2, 15, 28, 41, 173, 246, 253, 286, 304, 321, 339	Conflict and Resolution
		Satellites and Sea Lions NASA	2–3 days	RI1, RI2, RI5, W1, W6, W7, SL1, L4, L6	pp 90, 103, 130, 173, 227, 246, 286, 339, 353	Expository Writing
		Turkeys Bailey White	2–3 days	RL1, RL2, RL3, W1, W4, SL1, L4, L6	pp 2, 15, 28, 173, 207, 286, 339, 353	Author's Influences

* represents the first page of multiple-page lessons

Conventions	Language Study**	Speaking and Listening	Research	Writing
		Small-Group Discussion	Explanation: Legendary Character	Writing Model: Explanatory Text Writing: Explanatory Essay
Subject Complements	Academic Vocabulary Selection Vocabulary		Oral Report	Fable
Object Complements	Academic Vocabulary Selection Vocabulary		Annotated Bibliography Entry	Compare-and-Contrast Essay
Independent and Dependent Clauses	Academic Vocabulary Selection Vocabulary		Written and Visual Support	Plot Proposal
Sentences	Academic Vocabulary Selection Vocabulary	Dramatic Reading		Invitation
				Timed Writing: Explanatory Essay
	Idioms			
		Oral Response to Literature		
Commas, Parentheses, and Dashes Subject Complements Object Complements	Revising Choppy Sentences		Focus on Research: Explanatory Text	Explanatory Text: Cause-and-Effect Essay
Independent and Dependent Clauses	Diction and Style Academic Vocabulary Selection Vocabulary	Partner Discussion	Investigate the Topic: The Role of Myths	Informative Text: Cause-and-Effect Essay
	Academic Vocabulary Selection Vocabulary	Panel Discussion	Investigate the Topic: The Scientific Method	Informational Text: Explanation
	Academic Vocabulary Selection Vocabulary	Partner Discussion	Investigate the Topic: Oxygen Masks	Nonfiction Narrative
	Academic Vocabulary Selection Vocabulary	Class Discussion		Argumentative Essay
	Academic Vocabulary Selection Vocabulary	Group Discussion	Investigate the Topic: Humans and Animals	Informative Essay
	Academic Vocabulary Selection Vocabulary	Class Discussion	Investigate the Topic: Oceanographers	Argument: Persuasive Letter
	Academic Vocabulary Selection Vocabulary	Class Discussion	Investigate the Topic: Wild Turkeys	Argument: Persuasive Essay

** For a listing of selection and academic vocabulary, see the Table of Contents.

Key Features of the Standards

The following summary of key features is from the Introduction to the Common Core State Standards for English Language Arts © 2010, National Governors Association for Best Practices and Council of Chief State School Officers. All rights reserved.

READING

Text Complexity and the Growth of Comprehension The Reading standards place equal emphasis on the sophistication of what students read and the skill with which they read. Standard 10 defines a grade-by-grade "staircase" of increasing text complexity that rises from beginning reading to the college and career readiness level. Whatever they are reading, students must also show a steadily growing ability to discern more from and make fuller use of text, including making an increasing number of connections among ideas and between texts, considering a wider range of textual evidence, and becoming more sensitive to inconsistencies, ambiguities, and poor reasoning in texts.

WRITING

Text Types, Responding to Reading, and Research The Standards acknowledge the fact that whereas some writing skills, such as the ability to plan, revise, edit, and publish, are applicable to many types of writing, other skills are more properly defined in terms of specific writing types: arguments, informative/explanatory texts, and narratives. Standard 9 stresses the importance of the writing-reading connection by requiring students to draw upon and write about evidence from literary and informational texts. Because of the centrality of writing to most forms of inquiry, research standards are prominently included in this strand, though skills important to research are infused throughout the document.

SPEAKING AND LISTENING

Flexible Communication and Collaboration Including but not limited to skills necessary for formal presentations, the Speaking and Listening standards require students to develop a range of broadly useful oral communication and interpersonal skills. Students must learn to work together, express and listen carefully to ideas, integrate information from oral, visual, quantitative, and media sources, evaluate what they hear, use media and visual displays strategically to help achieve communicative purposes, and adapt speech to context and task.

LANGUAGE

Conventions, Effective Use, and Vocabulary The Language standards include the essential "rules" of standard written and spoken English, but they also approach language as a matter of craft and informed choice among alternatives. The vocabulary standards focus on understanding words and phrases, their relationships, and their nuances and on acquiring new vocabulary, particularly general academic and domain-specific words and phrases.

Correlation to Pearson Literature © 2015

The following correlation shows points at which focused, sustained instruction is provided in the Student Edition. The standards are spiraled and revisited throughout the program, and the Teacher's Edition provides further opportunity to address standards.

Key

SE/TE: Student Edition/Teacher's Edition

© GRADE 6 READING STANDARDS FOR LITERATURE			PEARSON LITERATURE © 2015, GRADE 6
Key Ideas and Details	RL.1	Cite textual evidence to support analysis of what the text says explicitly as well as inferences drawn from the text.	**SE/TE:** 4, 11, 28–29, 41, 44–45, 55, 128–129, 134, 142, 278, 284, 304–305, 311, 394, 395, 418, 442–443, 576, 614, 722, 723, 744, 754
	RL.2	Determine a theme or central idea of a text and how it is conveyed through particular details; provide a summary of the text distinct from personal opinions or judgments.	**SE/TE:** lvi–lvii, 4, 58–59, 69, 128–129, 134, 142, 278, 284, 304–305, 311, 317, 394, 395, 418, 442–443, 458, 550, 576, 614, 630, 632, 637, 640, 647, 650, 663, 677, 714, 715, 722, 744, 754
	RL.3	Describe how a particular story's or drama's plot unfolds in a series of episodes as well as how the characters respond or change as the plot moves toward a resolution.	**SE/TE:** 4, 14–17, 18–19, 25, 28–29, 41, 44–45, 55, 128–129, 278, 284, 418, 442–443, 486–487, 458, 551, 714, 744, 754
Craft and Structure	RL.4	Determine the meaning of words and phrases as they are used in a text, including figurative and connotative meanings; analyze the impact of a specific word choice on meaning and tone.	**SE/TE:** 4, 24, 128, 134, 142, 194, 278, 284, 304–305, 311, 314–315, 316, 318–319, 330, 331, 334–335, 341, 351, 354–355, 363, 367, 371, 388, 389, 394, 395, 418, 550, 576, 666, 715, 722, 723, 744
	RL.5	Analyze how a particular sentence, chapter, scene, or stanza fits into the overall structure of a text and contributes to the development of the theme, setting, or plot.	**SE/TE:** 4, 14–17, 72–73, 128–129, 134, 142, 278, 284, 304–305, 314–315, 317, 344–345, 388, 418, 442–443, 454–457, 458, 488, 550, 576, 640, 714
	RL.6	Explain how an author develops the point of view of the narrator or speaker in a text.	**SE/TE:** 304, 311, 314–315, 394, 395, 458, 551
Integration of Knowledge and Ideas	RL.7	Compare and contrast the experience of reading a story, drama, or poem to listening to or viewing an audio, video, or live version of the text, including contrasting what they "see" and "hear" when reading the text to what they perceive when they listen or watch.	**SE/TE:** 343, 389, 521
	RL.8	(Not applicable to literature)	
	RL.9	Compare and contrast texts in different forms or genres (e.g., stories and poems; historical novels and fantasy stories) in terms of their approaches to similar themes and topics.	**SE/TE:** 523, 533
Range of Reading and Text Complexity	RL.10	By the end of the year, read and comprehend literature, including stories, dramas, and poems, in the grades 6–8 text complexity band proficiently, with scaffolding as needed at the high end of the range.	**SE/TE:** lviii–lxiii, 158–159, 298–299, 436–437, 608–609, 760–761

Common Core State Standards Correlation

GRADE 6 READING STANDARDS FOR INFORMATIONAL TEXT			PEARSON LITERATURE © 2015, GRADE 6
Key Ideas and Details	RI.1	Cite textual evidence to support analysis of what the text says explicitly as well as inferences drawn from the text.	**SE/TE:** 137, 146, 164–165, 177, 206–207, 213, 249, 250, 260, 261, 269, 272, 290, 293, 402, 409, 422, 428, 431, 582, 588, 592, 595, 736, 739, 748
	RI.2	Determine a central idea of a text and how it is conveyed through particular details; provide a summary of the text distinct from personal opinions or judgments.	**SE/TE:** lvi–lvii, 146, 164–165, 177, 206–207, 213, 216–217, 227, 252, 253, 249, 250, 260, 261, 269, 272, 290, 402, 409, 422, 428, 431, 582, 588, 592, 736, 748
	RI.3	Analyze in detail how a key individual, event, or idea is introduced, illustrated, and elaborated in a text (e.g., through examples or anecdotes).	**SE/TE:** 164–165, 180–181, 249, 260, 261, 269, 272, 402, 409, 422, 428, 431, 592
Craft and Structure	RI.4	Determine the meaning of words and phrases as they are used in a text, including figurative, connotative, and technical meanings.	**SE/TE:** 146, 164, 182, 183, 202, 230, 249, 260, 269, 272, 290, 428, 582, 592, 595
	RI.5	Analyze how a particular sentence, paragraph, chapter, or section fits into the overall structure of a text and contributes to the development of the ideas.	**SE/TE:** 146, 164–165, 183, 230, 235, 269, 272, 402, 409, 422, 428, 431, 582, 588, 592, 736, 748
	RI.6	Determine an author's point of view or purpose in a text and explain how it is conveyed in the text.	**SE/TE:** 146, 164, 182–183, 184–185, 191, 252, 249, 250, 261, 293, 409, 422, 428, 431, 523, 588
Integration of Knowledge and Ideas	RI.7	Integrate information presented in different media or formats (e.g., visually, quantitatively) as well as in words to develop a coherent understanding of a topic or issue.	**SE/TE:** 137, 230, 230, 233, 293, 431
	RI.8	Trace and evaluate the argument and specific claims in a text, distinguishing claims that are supported by reasons and evidence from claims that are not.	**SE/TE:** lxiv–lxvii, 194–195, 203, 253
	RI.9	Compare and contrast one author's presentation of events with that of another (e.g., a memoir written by and a biography on the same person).	**SE/TE:** 253, 523, 533
Range of Reading and Text Complexity	RI.10	By the end of the year, read and comprehend literary nonfiction in the grades 6–8 text complexity band proficiently, with scaffolding as needed at the high end of the range.	**SE/TE:** lviii–lxiii, 158–159, 298–299, 436–437, 608–609, 760–761

PEARSON LITERATURE © 2015, GRADE 6

Text Types and Purposes	**W.1**	Write arguments to support claims with clear reasons and relevant evidence.	**SE/TE:** lxviii–lxix, 57, 147, 153, 156–157, 235, 273, 279, 285, 376–383, 423, 462, 434–435, 521, 538–545, 589, 739, 745, 749, 755
	W.1.a	Introduce claim(s) and organize the reasons and evidence clearly.	**SE/TE:** lxviii–lxix, 153, 156–157, 285, 377, 378, 521, 539, 595
	W.1.b	Support claim(s) with clear reasons and relevant evidence, using credible sources and demonstrating an understanding of the topic or text.	**SE/TE:** lxviii–lxix, 147, 153, 156–157, 377, 378, 380, 434, 539, 541
	W.1.c	Use words, phrases, and clauses to clarify the relationships among claim(s) and reasons.	**SE/TE:** 147, 157, 379, 380, 540, 541, 542
	W.1.d	Establish and maintain a formal style.	**SE/TE:** 157, 378, 380, 540, 542
	W.1.e	Provide a concluding statement or section that follows from the argument presented.	**SE/TE:** lxviii–lxix, 157, 273, 279, 285, 380, 540, 542
	W.2	Write informative/explanatory texts to examine a topic and convey ideas, concepts, and information through the selection, organization, and analysis of relevant content.	**SE/TE:** lxx–lxxi, lxxii–lxiii, lxx–lxxi, lxxii–lxviii, 11, 130, 143, 147, 177, 229, 240–247, 249, 262, 291, 296–297, 311, 333, 396, 419, 423, 431, 451, 550, 583, 697, 702–709, 758–759
	W.2.a	Introduce a topic; organize ideas, concepts, and information, using strategies such as definition, classification, comparison/contrast, and cause/effect; include formatting (e.g., headings), graphics (e.g., charts, tables), and multimedia when useful to aiding comprehension.	**SE/TE:** lxxii–lxiii, lxxii–lxviii, lxxiv, lxxxvi, 97, 229, 241, 242, 244, 262, 296, 297, 371, 578, 606–607, 649, 704, 706, 724, 758–759
	W.2.b	Develop the topic with relevant facts, definitions, concrete details, quotations, or other information and examples.	**SE/TE:** lxx–lxxi, lxx–lxxi, lxviii, lxxiv, 27, 229, 242–243, 244, 262, 296, 297, 333, 371, 550, 578, 606–607, 625, 649, 704, 724, 758–759
	W.2.c	Use appropriate transitions to clarify the relationships among ideas and concepts.	**SE/TE:** 242, 262, 297, 550, 578, 606–607, 724
	W.2.d	Use precise language and domain-specific vocabulary to inform about or explain the topic.	**SE/TE:** lxxv, 297, 578, 606–607, 649
	W.2.e	Establish and maintain a formal style.	**SE/TE:** lxxii–lxiii, 27, 333, 388, 606–607, 649
	W.2.f	Provide a concluding statement or section that follows from the information or explanation presented.	**SE/TE:** 143, 291, 297, 333, 578, 706
	W.3	Write narratives to develop real or imagined experiences or events using effective technique, relevant descriptive details, and well-structured event sequences.	**SE/TE:** 102–109, 135, 137, 155, 193, 205, 215, 269, 293, 295, 403, 409, 433, 593, 605, 737, 757
	W.3.a	Engage and orient the reader by establishing a context and introducing a narrator and/or characters; organize an event sequence that unfolds naturally and logically.	**SE/TE:** 103, 104, 155, 295, 605
	W.3.b	Use narrative techniques, such as dialogue, pacing, and description, to develop experiences, events, and/or characters.	**SE/TE:** 104, 105, 106, 155, 215, 295, 605, 639
	W.3.c	Use a variety of transition words, phrases, and clauses to convey sequence and signal shifts from one time frame or setting to another.	**SE/TE:** 106, 155, 269, 295, 605, 639
	W.3.d	Use precise words and phrases, relevant descriptive details, and sensory language to convey experiences and events.	**SE/TE:** 155, 205, 295, 343, 605
	W.3.e	Provide a conclusion that follows from the narrated experiences or events.	**SE/TE:** 104, 135, 269, 293, 295, 403, 605, 639

Common Core State Standards Correlation

GRADE 6 WRITING STANDARDS			PEARSON LITERATURE © 2015, GRADE 6
Production and Distribution of Writing	**W.4**	Produce clear and coherent writing in which the development, organization, and style are appropriate to task, purpose, and audience.	**SE/TE:** 11, 27, 43, 71, 130, 135, 137, 143, 147, 153, 155, 177, 262, 269, 273, 279, 285, 291, 293, 295, 353, 365, 396, 403, 409, 419, 423, 462, 431, 433, 434–435, 451, 487, 665, 755
	W.5	With some guidance and support from peers and adults, develop and strengthen writing as needed by planning, revising, editing, rewriting, or trying a new approach.	**SE/TE:** 130, 240–247, 262, 376–383, 434–435, 700–701, 758–759
	W.6	Use technology, including the Internet, to produce and publish writing as well as to interact and collaborate with others; demonstrate sufficient command of keyboarding skills to type a minimum of three pages in a single sitting.	**SE/TE:** lxxvi, 247, 353, 365, 423, 487, 639, 665
Research to Build and Present Knowledge	**W.7**	Conduct short research projects to answer a question, drawing on several sources and refocusing the inquiry when appropriate.	**SE/TE:** lxx–lxxi, lxxii–lxiii, lxx–lxxi, lxxii–lxviii, 6, 11, 131, 135, 147, 153, 166, 177, 253, 265, 273, 279, 291, 311, 389, 397, 403, 409, 419, 423, 462, 431, 444, 551, 579, 625, 639, 715, 725, 737, 745, 749
	W.8	Gather relevant information from multiple print and digital sources; assess the credibility of each source; and quote or paraphrase the data and conclusions of others while avoiding plagiarism and providing basic bibliographic information for sources.	**SE/TE:** lxx–lxxi, lxxii–lxiii, lxx–lxxi, lxxii–lxviii, lxxvi, lxxix, lxxx–lxxxi, 6, 11, 131, 135, 143, 147, 153, 177, 215, 253, 265, 389, 397, 403, 409, 419, 423, 462, 431, 487, 551, 579, 649, 665, 715, 725, 745, 749
	W.9	Draw evidence from literary or informational texts to support analysis, reflection, and research.	**SE/TE:** 130, 135, 143, 147, 153, 333, 396, 423, 434–435, 758–759
	W.9.a	Apply grade 6 Reading standards to literature (e.g., "Compare and contrast texts in different forms or genres [e.g., stories and poems; historical novels and fantasy stories] in terms of their approaches to similar themes and topics").	**SE/TE:** 130, 135, 143, 388, 451, 625, 714, 724, 758–759
	W.9.b	Apply grade 6 Reading standards to literary nonfiction (e.g., "Trace and evaluate the argument and specific claims in a text, distinguishing claims that are supported by reasons and evidence from claims that are not").	**SE/TE:** 147, 153, 397, 758–759
Range of Writing	**W.10**	Write routinely over extended time frames (time for research, reflection, and revision) and shorter time frames (a single sitting or a day or two) for a range of discipline-specific tasks, purposes, and audiences.	**SE/TE:** 130, 143, 147, 153, 235, 291, 295, 333, 396, 697, 758–759

GRADE 6 SPEAKING AND LISTENING STANDARDS		PEARSON LITERATURE © 2015, GRADE 6
Comprehension and Collaboration	**SL.1** Engage effectively in a range of collaborative discussions (one-on-one, in groups, and teacher-led) with diverse partners on grade 6 topics, texts, and issues, building on others' ideas and expressing their own clearly.	**SE/TE:** 2, 6, 11, 130, 135, 137, 143, 153, 154, 162, 166, 177, 229, 262, 269, 273, 279, 285, 291, 294, 302, 311, 389, 396, 403, 409, 419, 423, 462, 432, 441, 444, 451, 583, 589, 612, 625, 648, 665, 714, 715, 724, 737, 739, 745, 755, 756
	SL.1.a Come to discussions prepared, having read or studied required material; explicitly draw on that preparation by referring to evidence on the topic, text, or issue to probe and reflect on ideas under discussion.	**SE/TE:** 154, 229, 294, 578, 604
	SL.1.b Follow rules for collegial discussions, set specific goals and deadlines, and define individual roles as needed.	**SE/TE:** 154, 229, 294, 432, 578, 604, 665
	SL.1.c Pose and respond to specific questions with elaboration and detail by making comments that contribute to the topic, text, or issue under discussion.	**SE/TE:** 71, 100–101, 154, 294, 521, 578, 604, 700–701
	SL.1.d Review the key ideas expressed and demonstrate understanding of multiple perspectives through reflection and paraphrasing.	**SE/TE:** 100–101, 154, 229, 294, 578, 604, 700–701
	SL.2 Interpret information presented in diverse media and formats (e.g., visually, quantitatively, orally) and explain how it contributes to a topic, text, or issue under study.	**SE/TE:** 43, 238–239, 593, 604, 739
	SL.3 Delineate a speaker's argument and specific claims, distinguishing claims that are supported by reasons and evidence from claims that are not.	**SE/TE:** 27, 238–239, 521, 536–537
Presentation of Knowledge and Ideas	**SL.4** Present claims and findings, sequencing ideas logically and using pertinent descriptions, facts, and details to accentuate main ideas or themes; use appropriate eye contact, adequate volume, and clear pronunciation.	**SE/TE:** 57, 131, 135, 143, 147, 153, 205, 215, 253, 265, 269, 273, 279, 285, 294, 374–375, 389, 396, 403, 409, 419, 423, 462, 536–537, 551, 700–701, 715, 724, 745, 756
	SL.5 Include multimedia components (e.g., graphics, images, music, sound) and visual displays in presentations to clarify information.	**SE/TE:** 57, 374–375, 389, 536–537, 593, 639, 715
	SL.6 Adapt speech to a variety of contexts and tasks, demonstrating command of formal English when indicated or appropriate.	**SE/TE:** 193, 205, 253, 343, 403, 536–537, 675, 756

		GRADE 6 LANGUAGE STANDARDS	PEARSON LITERATURE © 2015, GRADE 6
Conventions of Standard English	L.1	Demonstrate command of the conventions of standard English grammar and usage when writing or speaking.	**SE/TE:** 42, 128, 192, 204, 214, 228, 24, 245, 247, 251, 297, 332, 342, 352, 364, 381, 423, 394, 487, 521, 576, 638, 664, 674
	L.1.a	Ensure that pronouns are in the proper case (subjective, objective, possessive).	**SE/TE:** 42, 43, 70, 71, 113, R21
	L.1.b	Use intensive pronouns (e.g., *myself, ourselves*).	**SE/TE:** 56, 57
	L.1.c	Recognize and correct inappropriate shifts in pronoun number and person.	**SE/TE:** 107
	L.1.d	Recognize and correct vague pronouns (i.e., ones with unclear or ambiguous antecedents).	**SE/TE:** 107
	L.1.e	Recognize variations from standard English in their own and others' writing and speaking, and identify and use strategies to improve expression in conventional language.	**SE/TE:** 374, 380, 381
	L.2	Demonstrate command of the conventions of standard English capitalization, punctuation, and spelling when writing.	**SE/TE:** 26, 27, 128, 297, 487, 705, 724, 759
	L.2.a	Use punctuation (commas, parentheses, dashes) to set off nonrestrictive/parenthetical elements.	**SE/TE:** 664, 665, 705
	L.2.b	Spell correctly.	**SE/TE:** 109, 246, 383, 545, 709
Knowledge of Language	L.3	Use knowledge of language and its conventions when writing, speaking, reading, or listening.	**SE/TE:** 128, 146, 147, 152, 262, 285, 290, 291, 297, 352, 353, 364, 365, 380, 381, 423, 394, 395, 521, 543, 705, 707, 724, 759
	L.3.a	Vary sentence patterns for meaning, reader/listener interest, and style.	**SE/TE:** 521, 543, 674, 707, 724
	L.3.b	Maintain consistency in style and tone.	**SE/TE:** 388
Vocabulary Acquisition and Use	L.4	Determine or clarify the meaning of unknown and multiple-meaning words and phrases based on grade 6 reading and content, choosing flexibly from a range of strategies.	**SE/TE:** 45, 128, 137, 147, 152, 262, 284, 290, 372–373, 394, 582, 588, 592, 722, 737, 748
	L.4.a	Use context (e.g., the overall meaning of a sentence or paragraph; a word's position or function in a sentence) as a clue to the meaning of a word or phrase.	**SE/TE:** 128, 318–319, 331, 334–335, 341, 372, 588, 592, 737
	L.4.b	Use common, grade-appropriate Greek or Latin affixes and roots as clues to the meaning of a word (e.g., *audience, auditory, audible*).	**SE/TE:** 24, 68, 226, 236–237, 518, 545
	L.4.c	Consult reference materials (e.g., dictionaries, glossaries, thesauruses), both print and digital, to find the pronunciation of a word or determine or clarify its precise meaning or its part of speech.	**SE/TE:** 97–98, 237, 343, 354, 372, 373, 534–535

		GRADE 6 LANGUAGE STANDARDS	PEARSON LITERATURE © 2015, GRADE 6
Vocabulary Acquisition and Use	L.4.d	Verify the preliminary determination of the meaning of a word or phrase (e.g., by checking the inferred meaning in context or in a dictionary).	**SE/TE:** 97–98, 163, 372, 373
	L.5	Demonstrate understanding of figurative language, word relationships, and nuances in word meanings.	**SE/TE:** 129, 284, 290, 316, 334–345, 341, 388, 394, 395, 534–535, 582, 722
	L.5.a	Interpret figures of speech (e.g., personification) in context.	**SE/TE:** 316, 334–345, 341, 388, 666, 673, 698–699, 723
	L.5.b	Use the relationship between particular words (e.g., cause/effect, part/whole, item/category) to better understand each of the words.	**SE/TE:** 666, 667, 673
	L.5.c	Distinguish among the connotations (associations) of words with similar denotations (definitions) (e.g., *stingy, scrimping, economical, unwasteful, thrifty*).	**SE/TE:** 97–98, 316, 534–535, 550
	L.6	Acquire and use accurately grade-appropriate general academic and domain-specific words and phrases; gather vocabulary knowledge when considering a word or phrase important to comprehension or expression.	**SE/TE:** xlvi–lv, lxiv–lxvii, 3, 28, 128, 137, 147, 152, 163, 184, 194, 202, 204, 206, 212, 216, 226, 230, 290, 303, 318–319, 344–345, 351, 441, 486, 518, 551, 582, 613, 650, 722, 737, 748

How to Use This Program

Lesson Pacing and Planning

Start your planning with the Time and Resource Manager.

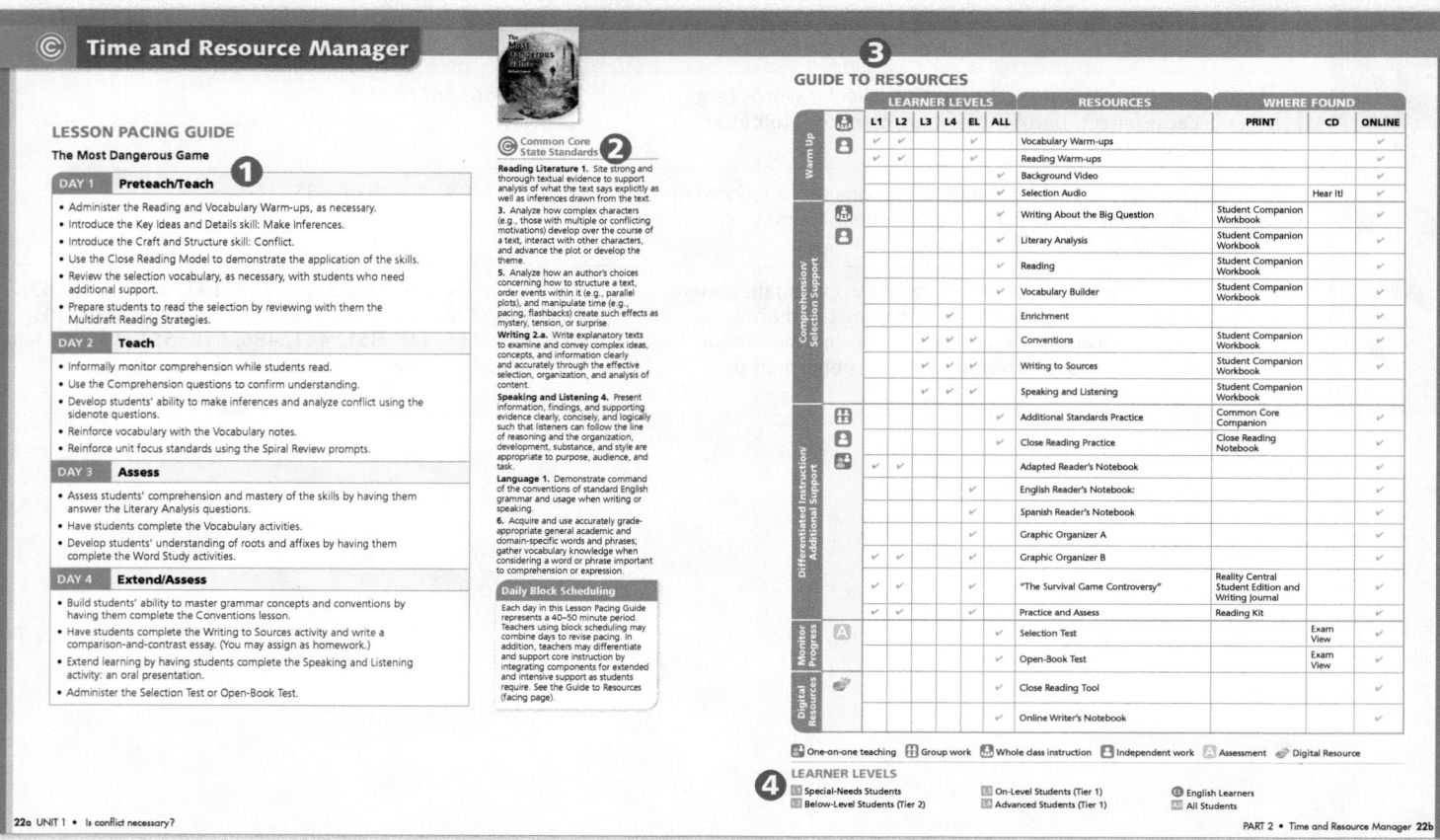

1 Recommended pacing and activities are provided for each day.

2 Standards covered in the lesson are identified.

3 A Guide to Resources includes all resources available for the lesson, where the resources can be found, appropriate learner levels, and recommended class settings.

4 Differentiate instruction with resources for Special-Needs Students, Below-Level Students, On-Level Students, Advanced Students, and English Learners.

Teacher's Edition

The Teacher's Edition provides a variety of support, including point-of-use notes and strategies for Differentiated Instruction, Fluency, and Vocabulary Development.

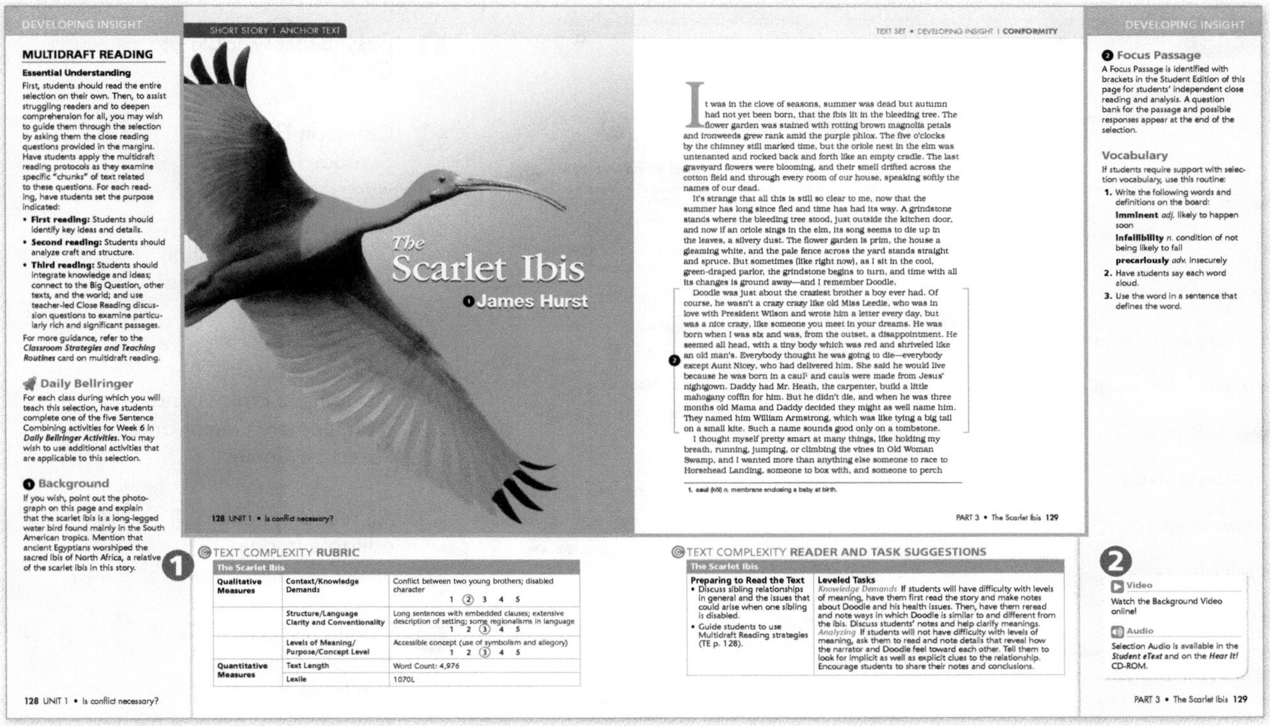

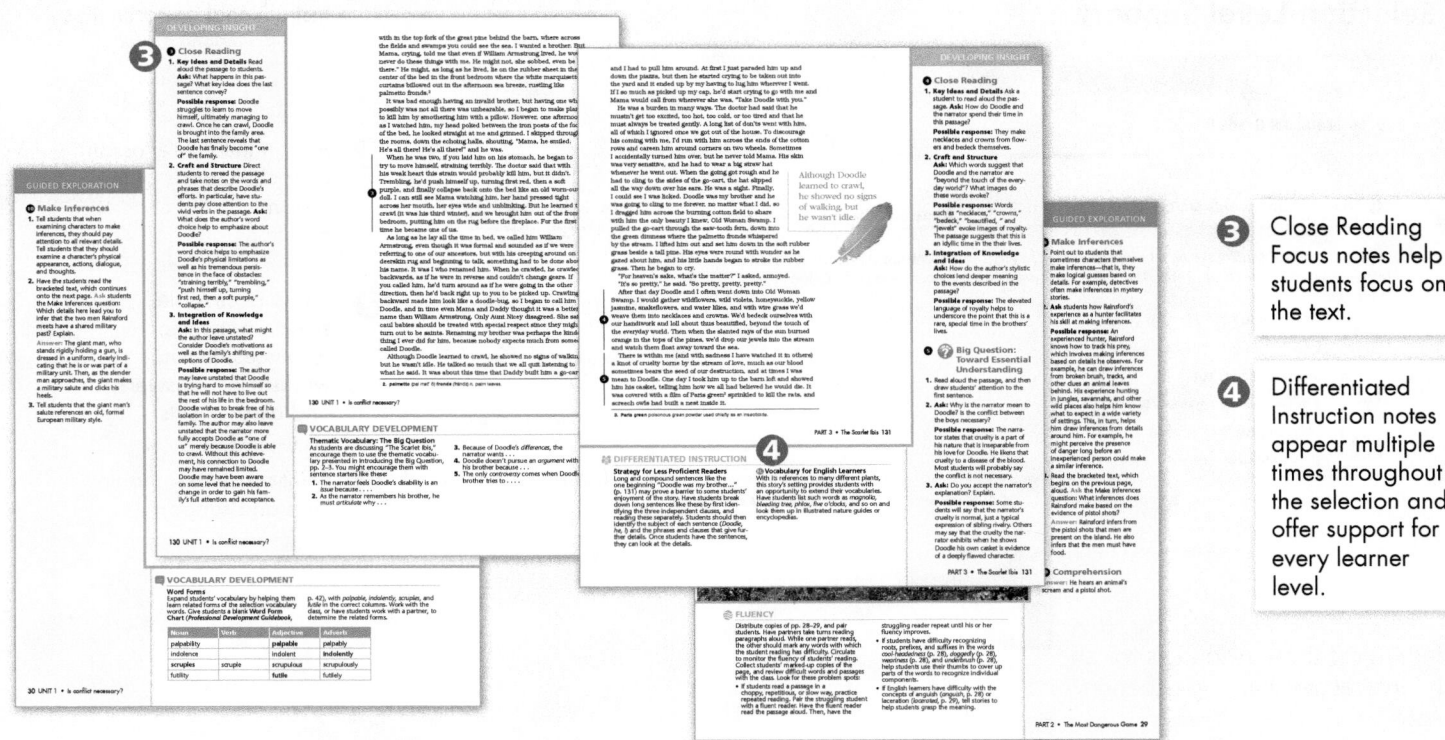

1 Text Complexity Rubrics provide Quantitative, Qualitative, and Reader and Task Suggestions.

2 Digital resources are identified at point-of-use.

3 Close Reading Focus notes help students focus on the text.

4 Differentiated Instruction notes appear multiple times throughout the selection and offer support for every learner level.

Digital Resources

Pearson Common Core Literature offers digital resources at your fingertips.

Find all Digital Resources at **pearsonrealize.com**

Program-Level Table of Contents

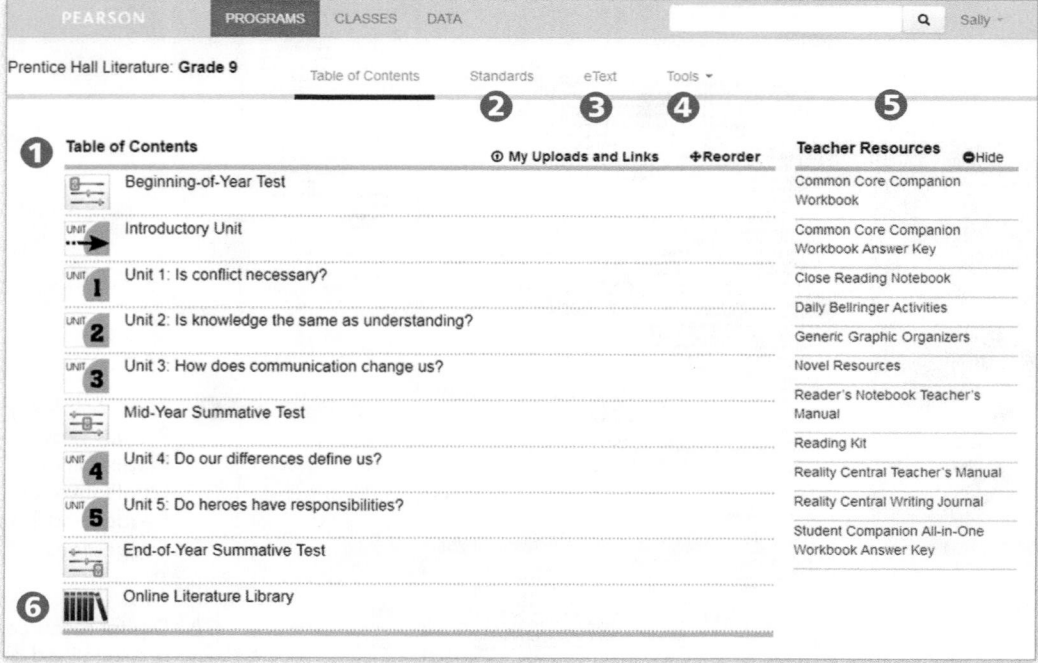

1. Easy-to-follow Table of Contents

2. Common Core State Standards support

3. Quick access to the Online Student Edition, Teacher's Edition, and Reality Central

4. Teacher support, including a Professional Development Center and Research Center

5. All resources are editable in one easy-to-find location

6. Additional selections of multiple genres are available to customize your curriculum or provide extra instructional opportunities

Selection-Level Support

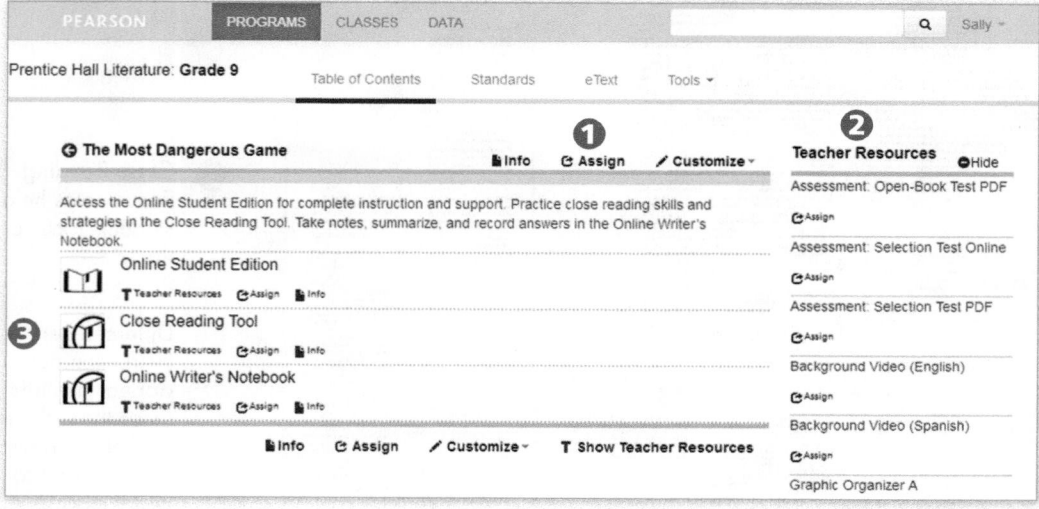

1. Assign the entire lesson or specific parts of the lesson with the click of a button

2. Easily accessible, selection-specific resources, including worksheets, answers, and assessments

3. Point-of-use assignable links and support

Project these resources for an interactive learning experience!

CLOSE READING TOOL ▶

The Close Reading Tool allows students to practice strategies in a digital environment. Prompts and tools for marking the text help students immediately apply what they have learned.

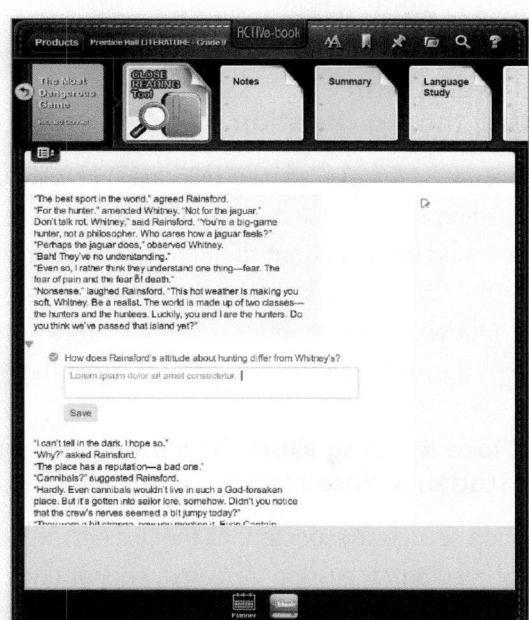

◀ ONLINE WRITER'S NOTEBOOK

Direct students to use the Online Writer's Notebook as a resource for the Close Reading Activities for each selection. You will be able to monitor student progress at all times.

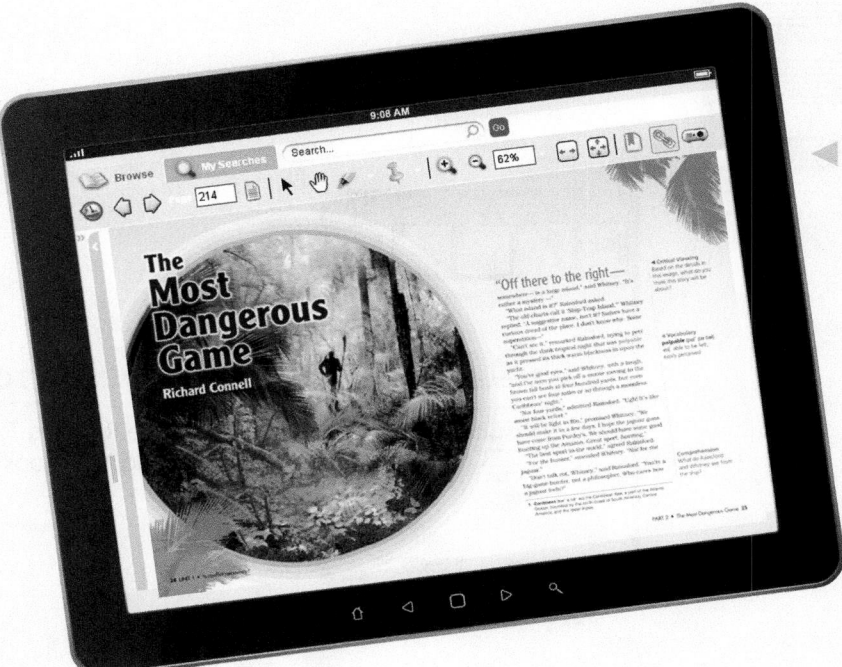

◀ ONLINE STUDENT EDITION

The Online Student Edition provides selection audio and video at point-of-use.

Find all Digital Resources at **pearsonrealize.com**

PART 1: SETTING EXPECTATIONS

Begin each unit with Introducing the Big Question.

The Big Question is the overarching big idea that will guide students' reading throughout the unit. Opportunities for discussing and writing about the Big Question occur throughout the unit, giving students the chance to revisit their ideas. Students are prompted to use the unit's academic vocabulary as they respond to the readings within the unit.

Use the Close Reading Workshop model selection to teach students close reading strategies.

This workshop sets clear expectations for students through modeling of reading, discussion, research, and writing. Learning these strategies will help students as they encounter college texts, workplace documents, and real-life reading.

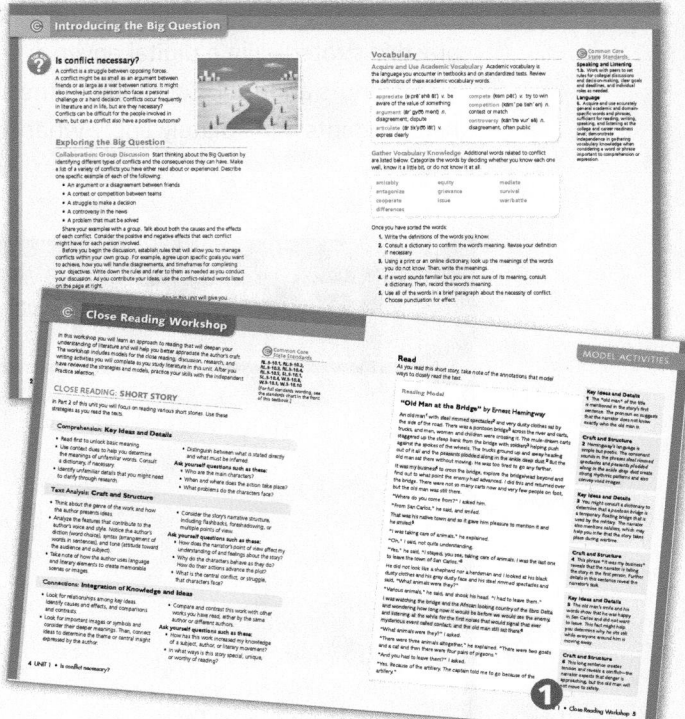

1 Strategies are color-coded and organized according to the sub-domains of the Common Core Reading standards.

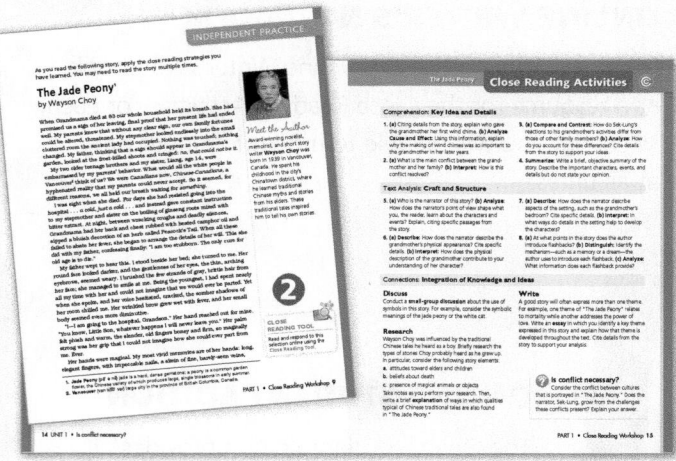

2 The Independent Practice activity provides students with an opportunity to practice and apply close reading strategies.

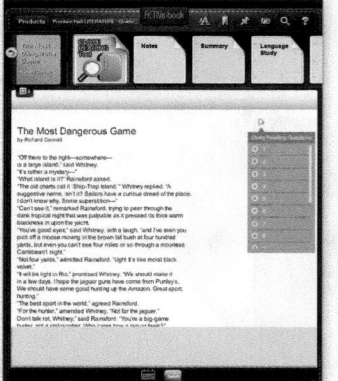

CLOSE READING TOOL

Use the Close Reading Tool or Close Reading Notebook for individual practice.

PART 2: TEXT ANALYSIS GUIDED EXPLORATION

Guide students in an in-depth exploration of the genre by introducing important characteristics, key concepts, and literary terms.

Use Building Knowledge to introduce the Close Reading Focus and selection vocabulary. An excerpt from the selection is provided as a model.

Close Reading Activities following the selection allow students to apply Read, Discuss, Research, and Write strategies. Students can use the Close Reading Tool to mark the text and complete the Close Reading Activities interactively.

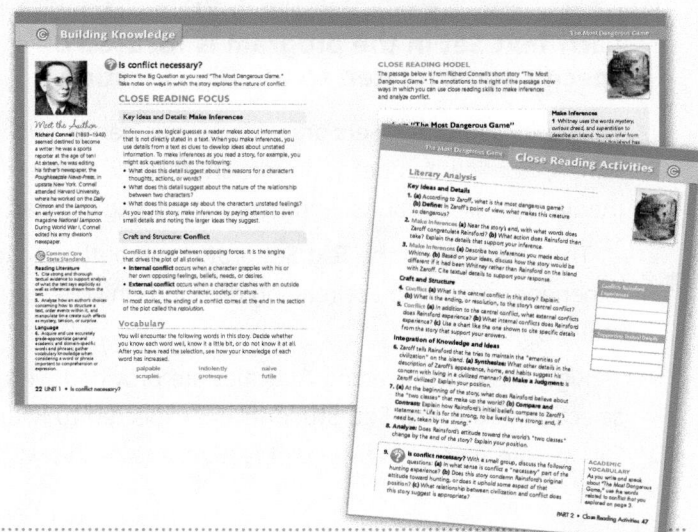

Strengthen process and presentation skills through a series of workshops.

Comparing Texts focuses on texts within one genre or across multiple genres, allowing students to become adept at synthesizing texts and evaluating them critically.

Language Study provides critical vocabulary skills instruction and practice.

Speaking and Listening provides students opportunities to deliver and/or evaluate a speech, collaborate with peers on presentations, and build important communication and collaboration skills.

Writing Process provides step-by-step instruction in the key modes of writing. The rubrics and evaluation criteria for each mode are built on the annotated writing samples contained within the Common Core framework. A research strand is embedded within each writing lesson, ensuring that students become adept at supporting their ideas through evidence. Students may refer to the Online Research Center for additional support.

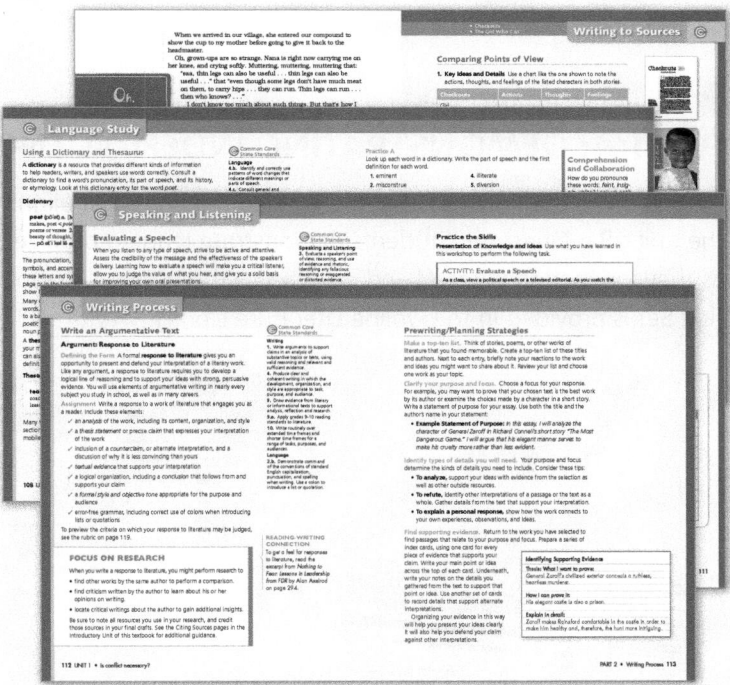

Students can practice writing with EssayScorer, an interactive online writing program that offers immediate feedback and scoring.

How to Use This Program

PART 3: TEXT SET DEVELOPING INSIGHT

Each Text Set in the program is focused on a specific topic related to the Big Question.

The multi-genre Text Sets draw on various genres such as fiction, nonfiction, poetry, drama, short story, Web articles, media clips, illustrations, and newspaper/magazine articles.

The selections in the Text Set provide an authentic reading experience similar to the reading demands in college texts and real-life situations.

Rigorous Close Reading Activities are provided with each selection in the Text Set. Students are expected to Read, Discuss, Research, and Write in response to each text.

PART 4: DEMONSTRATING INDEPENDENCE

Here you will find recommended extended readings that align with the unit's Big Question. Students demonstrate reading proficiency as they independently read and respond to these texts. An Online Text Set is provided in the Online Literature Library.

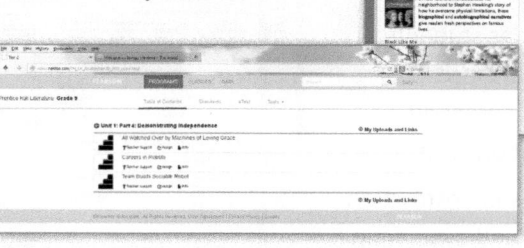

If you teach with novels, you may also want to use the Additional Novel Resources online. Here you will find hundreds of lesson plans, reading guides, rubrics, and tests for popular titles.

You can customize the text set by reordering selections, adding your own resources, or adding selections found in the Online Literature Library!

Assessment

Frequent opportunities for formative and summative assessment are available in the program.

Students can take tests online or in print, or you can use *ExamView® Assessment Suite* to create customized tests.

Selection-Level Support

① PDFs can be printed and tests administered via paper and pencil, or students can complete the tests online and upload for grading.

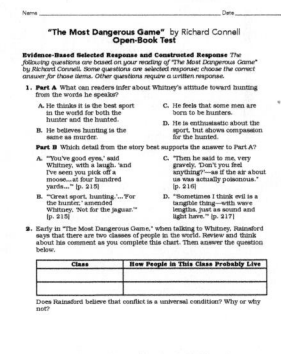

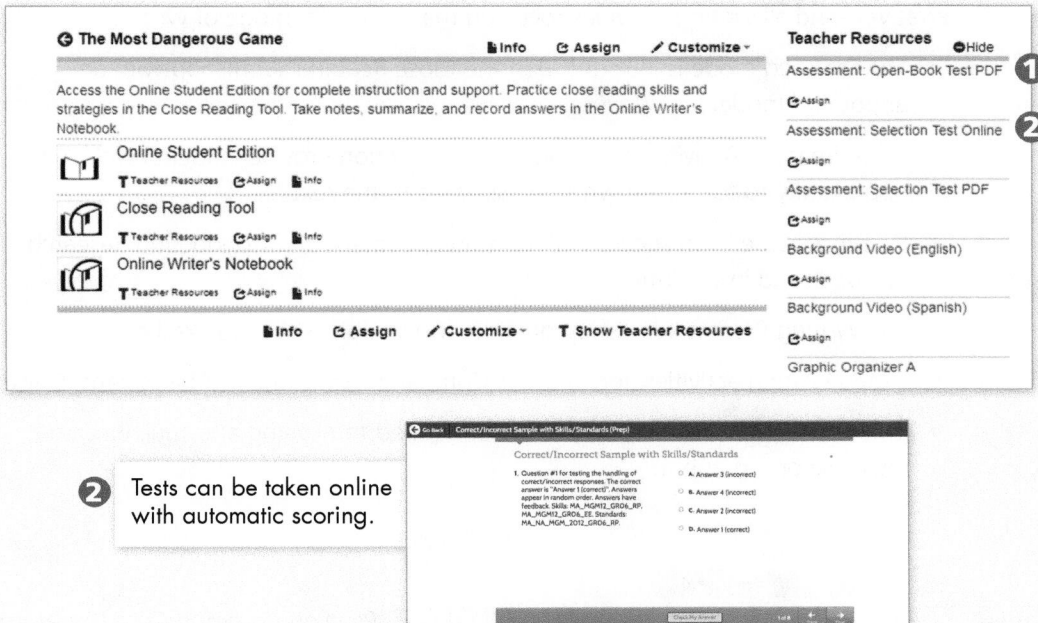

② Tests can be taken online with automatic scoring.

All tests are aligned to Common Core State Standards!

ExamView® Assessment Suite makes it possible to create, administer, and manage assessments to make it easier to assess student performance frequently.

You can personalize the program's existing assessments by customizing questions, creating different versions of tests, and even creating your own! You can also collect results and generate comprehensive reports in minutes so that you are able to analyze student results and identify areas of concern.

How Does the Program Address Writing and Research?

WRITING is an integral part of *Pearson Common Core Literature*. The program adheres to the percentages of writing outcomes as indicated in the Common Core State Standards framework, and most writing outcomes involve writing to sources and writing grounded in evidence.

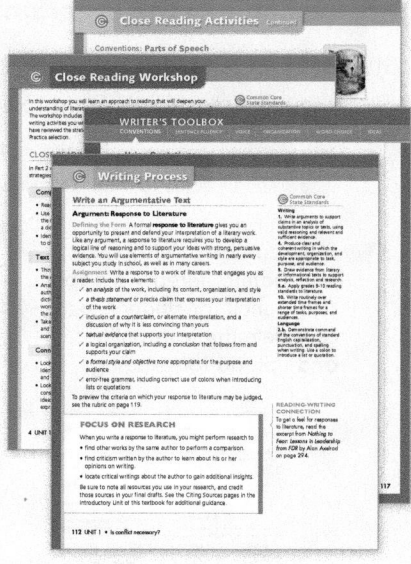

Each unit features a writing mode—argumentative, informative/explanatory, or narrative—and all writing activities focus on that particular mode of writing.

- The featured mode is introduced in the Close Reading Workshop with an annotated model.

- Close Reading Activities that follow each selection provide students with the opportunity to formulate written responses to the text.

- Common Core Workshops on Analyzing Argument and Conducting Research can be found in the Introductory Unit.

- The Writing Process Workshop provides instruction in the featured mode.

- Timed Writing activities appear after Comparing Texts and in Assessment: Skills.

- In Assessment: Synthesis, students are required to develop a formal, written response or argument.

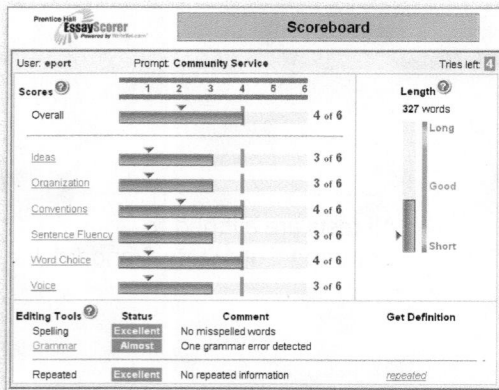

DIGITAL *Pearson Common Core Literature* also offers digital tools to support student writing. *EssayScorer* offers instant feedback and scoring and provides students with instruction and immediate feedback to improve their writing skills.

SummaryScorer is an automated summary writing tool that offers students a motivating, interactive environment for practicing and improving their skills while giving them immediate, easy-to-understand feedback.

ROUTINE RESEARCH Students are expected to perform both short-term and long-term research throughout the program. Each Writing Process Workshop has an embedded Research strand.

In addition, students perform routine research with each text in the Text Set, taking notes and then using what they have learned to inform their written responses to texts.

ONLINE RESEARCH CENTER

Students will find support in the Online Research Center!

How Do I Differentiate Instruction?

***Pearson Common Core Literature* offers support to help you differentiate instruction to ensure all students' needs are met.**

From leveled resources to strategies in the Teacher's Edition, this program will make literature accessible for all learners.

The Instructional Model in the program offers flexibility with each of the parts. Use each part as needed depending on your classroom needs.

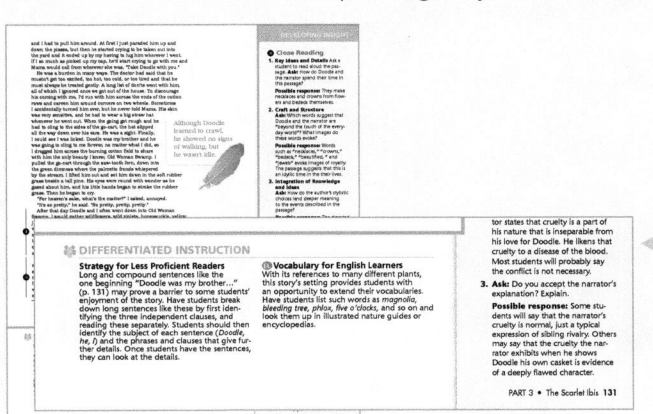

Differentiated Instruction notes in the Teacher's Edition provide strategies at point-of-use.

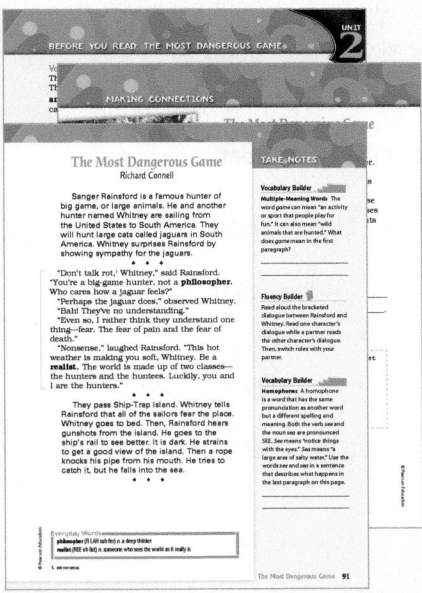

Reader's Notebooks offer support for Below-Level, English Learner, and Spanish-speaking students. Support includes selections in an adapted format with instruction tailored to each learner level.

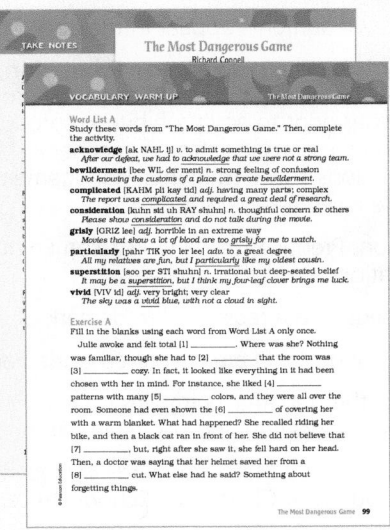

Support for selection vocabulary, building background, and leveled graphic organizers can be found online and assigned as needed.

Reader and Task Suggestions in the Text Complexity Rubrics offer ways to differentiate students' approach to texts.

TEXT COMPLEXITY RUBRIC

The Most Dangerous Game		Reader and Task Suggestions	
Qualitative Measures		**Preparing to Read the Text**	**Leveled Tasks**
Context/Knowledge Demands	Small jungle island in Caribbean 1 ② 3 4 5	• Discuss the two kinds of conflict in this story. • Guide students to use Multidraft Reading strategies (TE p. 24).	**Levels of Meaning** Have students first read to identify the main events of the plot. Then, have them reread, taking notes on the motivations of the characters. **Synthesizing** If students will not have difficulty with meaning, have them note the similarities and differences between Rainsford and General Zaroff, and how these similarities and differences affect events.
Structure/Language Conventionality and Clarity	Challenging vocabulary; vocabulary is footnoted 1 2 ③ 4 5		
Levels of Meaning/Purpose/Concept Level	Accessible concept (hunter finds himself the prey in a hunt) 1 2 ③ 4 5		
Quantitative Measures			
Lexile	740L	Text Length	Word Count: 7,942

COVER: Andrey Bayda/Shutterstock.com

Acknowledgments appear in the back of this book, and constitute an extension of this copyright page.

PEARSON

ISBN-13:   978-0-13-326817-1
ISBN-10:   0-13-326817-9
1 2 3 4 5 6 7 8 9 10 V0RY 17 16 15 14 13

Student Edition Pages

PEARSON

COMMON CORE

Literature

GRADE 6

PEARSON

UPPER SADDLE RIVER, NEW JERSEY • BOSTON, MASSACHUSETTS
CHANDLER, ARIZONA • GLENVIEW, ILLINOIS

xliv

COMMON CORE WORKSHOPS

- BUILDING ACADEMIC VOCABULARY

- WRITING AN OBJECTIVE SUMMARY

- COMPREHENDING COMPLEX TEXTS

- ANALYZING ARGUMENTS

- CONDUCTING RESEARCH

 **Common Core State Standards**

Reading Literature 2, 10
Reading Informational Text 2, 8
Writing 1a, 1b, 1e, 2, 2.a, 2.b, 2.d, 2.f, 6, 7, 8
Language 6

BUILDING ACADEMIC VOCABULARY

Academic vocabulary is the language you encounter in textbooks and on standardized tests and other assessments. Understanding these words and using them in your classroom discussions and writing will help you communicate your ideas clearly and effectively.

There are two basic types of academic vocabulary: general and domain-specific. **General academic vocabulary** includes words that are not specific to any single course of study. For example, the general academic vocabulary word *analyze* is used in language arts, math, social studies, art, and so on.

Domain-specific academic vocabulary includes words that are usually encountered in the study of a specific discipline. For example, the words *factor* and *remainder* are most often used in mathematics classrooms and texts.

General Academic Vocabulary

Word	Definition	Related Words	Word in Context
abandon (uh BAN duhn) *v.*	leave behind; give something up	abandoned abandoning	Maria decided to abandon the book after reading the first chapter.
accompany (uh KUHM puh nee) *v.*	go along; travel with	accompanied accompanying	I will accompany Jake to school to get his backpack.
accurate (AK yer it) *adj.*	free from error	accurately	Her research proved that her facts were accurate.
achieve (uh CHEEV) *v.*	bring to a successful end; gain	achieved achievement	Through hard work, I will achieve my goal of raising my English grade.
anticipate (an TIS uh peyt) *v.*	expect; foresee	anticipated anticipation	Greta can anticipate winning the spelling bee.
approach (uh PROHCH) *v.*	come near or nearer to	approached approaching	The school bus will approach the parking lot in 300 yards.
argue (AHR gyoo) *v.*	fight using words; debate	argument argumentative	During a debate, you must argue your point clearly.
assess (uh SES) *v.*	estimate the value of; evaluate	assessed assessment	The English test will assess our understanding of the poem.
authority (uh THAWR i tee) *n.*	a person with power or expertise; the power to control	authorities authorize	The teacher has authority over her class.
challenge (CHAL uhnj) *n.*	a dare; a calling into question	challenging challenged	The character set a challenge for his opponent.
common (KOM uhn) *adj.*	ordinary or expected	commonplace uncommon	It is common to have a conflict within a story's plot.

Common Core State Standards

Language
6. Acquire and use accurately grade-appropriate general academic and domain-specific words and phrases; gather vocabulary knowledge when considering a word or phrase important to comprehension or expression.

Word	Definition	Related Words	Word in Context
communicate (kuh MYOO nuh kayt) v.	share thoughts or feelings, usually in words	communication communicative	Poets can communicate complex thoughts with very few words.
compile (kuhm PAHYL) v.	put together into one book or work	compiled compilation	The students will compile all their poems into one book.
concept (KON sehpt) n.	general idea or notion	conception	I was able to grasp the broad concept of the news article by skimming.
conclude (kuhn KLOOD) v.	bring to a close; end	conclusion concluded	The story will conclude when the main character has won the race.
confirm (kuhn FURM) v.	support or show to be correct	confirmation confirming	I need to confirm the facts for my research report.
conflict (KON flict) n.	a fight, battle, or struggle	conflicts conflicted	The conflict in the novel was resolved in the end.
consist (kuhn SIST) v.	be made up of or composed of	consisted consistency	The test will consist of multiple-choice and short-answer questions.
context (KON text) n.	the set of circumstances or surrounding words that give a word or phrase its meaning	contexts contextual	We defined the word in its context in the sentence.
contrast (KON trast) v.	show differences between or among	contrasted contrasting	When you contrast two characters, you find the differences between them.
convince (kuhn VIHNS) v.	persuade	convincing convinced	You don't need to convince me that Shakespeare was a brilliant writer!
coordinate (koh AWR dn eyt) v.	show the proper order or relation of things	coordinates coordinating	I had to coordinate my schedule to make time for homework.
correspond (KAWR uh SPOND) v.	agree with or be similar to	correspondence corresponding	My thoughts on the poem did not correspond to my partner's.
crucial (KROO shuhl) adj.	critical; extremely important	crucially	It is crucial that you do well on this test.
defend (dih FEHND) v.	guard from attack; protect	defense defending	The main character was able to defend himself against the bitter cold.
determine (dih TUR muhn) v.	settle; reach a conclusion	imitation imitator	The author's background can help you determine the author's purpose for writing.
display (dih SPLEY) v.	show or exhibit	displayed displaying	The characters display their traits through their words and actions.
distinguish (dihs TIHNG gwihsh) v.	mark as different; set apart	distinguished distinguishing	It is important to notice traits that distinguish characters.
diverse (duh VURS) adj.	many and different; from different backgrounds	diversity	There were diverse cultures represented in the article.
draft (drahft) n.	a rough or preliminary form of any writing	drafts drafting	We had to hand in the first draft of our report.

Word	Definition	Related Words	Word in Context
encounter (en KOUN ter) *v.*	come upon or meet with, usually unexpectedly	encountered encountering	The main character will encounter many difficult situations.
establish (ih STAB lish) *v.*	bring into being; show to be true	established establishment	The author had to establish the reason the character in the book had lied.
evidence (EHV uh duhns) *n.*	proof in support of a claim or statement	evident	The evidence she used in her essay supports her main idea.
examine (ehg ZAM uhn) *v.*	study in depth; look at closely	examination examined	To examine a character, look at what he says and also what is said about him.
fact (fakt) *n.*	idea or thought that is real or true	factual	Be sure something is a fact before you use it to support your argument.
indicate (IN di keyt) *v.*	be a sign of; show	indicates indication	You must indicate where you found your information.
influence (IHN flu uhns) *v.*	sway or affect in some other way	influential influenced	One author can often influence the work of another.
interpret (in TUR prit) *v.*	give or provide the meaning of; explain	interpreting interpretation	We were asked to interpret the poem.
investigate (ihn VEHS tuh gayt) *v.*	examine thoroughly, as an idea	investigation investigating	The characters went to investigate a mysterious disappearance.
involve (ihn VOLV) *v.*	include	involving involved	I want the plot of my short story to involve a space expedition.
isolate (I suh layt) *v.*	set apart	isolated isolation	It is good to isolate each point when using point-by-point organization.
issue (ISH oo) *n.*	a point about which there is disagreement	issues	We discussed the issue of revenge in class.
judge (juhj) *v.*	form an opinion of or pass judgment on	judgment judicial	In the story, the main character had to judge who was a true friend.
measure (MEHZH uhr) *v.*	place a value on	measurement measured	A writer tries to measure many different factors in his or her writing.
modify (MOD uh fahy) *v.*	change the form or quality of	modified modification	We will modify our answers after we finish the book.
motive (MOH tiv) *n.*	something that causes a person to act a certain way	motives, motivation	Her motive for taking my book was that she had lost hers.
observe (uhb ZURV) *v.*	notice or see	observation observed	Observe the shape formed by the lines in this poem.
opinion (uh PIHN yuhn) *n.*	personal view or belief	opinionated	My opinion of the story is very different from that of my friend.
participation (pahr TIHS uh PAY shuhn) *n.*	the act of taking part in an event or activity	participate participant	The teacher appreciated the boy's participation in the group discussion of the novel.

xlviii Introductory Unit

Word	Definition	Related Words	Word in Context
perspective (puhr SPEHK tihv) *n.*	point of view	introspective	I chose to tell my story from the perspective of my family's dog.
pose (pohz) *v.*	display a specific attitude or stance	posture	He might pose as my friend to get my answers to the homework.
process (PROS es) *n.*	a systematic series of actions or changes	processor	Finishing the report was a process of writing and revising.
prove (proov) *v.*	establish the truth of, as in a claim or statement	disprove	I will prove my theory within my report.
purpose (PUR puhs) *n.*	what something is used for	purposeful	The author's purpose for writing became more clear as she read.
quote (kwoht) *v.*	refer to the words of a source	quotation quoted	Quote from a reputable author to add interest to an essay.
refer (rih FUR) *v.*	point back to, as an authority or expert	reference referral	When I write my final draft, I refer to my notes and my outline.
reflect (rih FLEHKT) *v.*	think about or consider	reflection reflecting	The character needed to reflect on what had happened before the conflict could be resolved.
research (REE serch) *n.*	investigation into a subject to find facts	researches researching	The research supported her ideas.
resolve (rih ZOLV) *v.*	settle or bring to an end	resolution resolved	The characters decided to resolve their dispute and became friends.
respond (rih SPOND) *v.*	reply or answer	response responded	To respond to the essay question, I used evidence, examples, and my own thoughts.
reveal (rih VEEL) *v.*	show or uncover	revealing revealed	The detective would reveal the truth in the mystery story.
similar (SIHM uh luhr) *adj.*	alike	similarity similarly	The styles of the two poems are quite similar but the images are very different.
source (sawrs) *n.*	person or book that provides information	resource outsource	Check the source of that quotation to be sure it is trustworthy.

Ordinary Language: She told the story from an interesting angle.

Academic Language: She told the story from an interesting perspective.

Ordinary Language: The conflict in the story was brought to an end.

Academic Language: The conflict in the story was resolved.

Word	Definition	Related Words	Word in Context
specific (spi SIF ik) *adj.*	particular	specify specification	Give specific examples to support your ideas.
structure (STRUHK cher) *n.*	the way in which parts are arranged to make a whole	structures structured	We studied the structure of the poem.
study (STUHD ee) *n.*	research or investigation into a claim	studious	I cited a scientific study in my research report that supported my thesis.
study (STUHD ee) *v.*	look into deeply	studied studying	The two friends in the story liked to study together for English class.
support (suh PAWRT) *v.*	stand behind or back up	supportive supporting	Details in your essay support your main idea.
suspend (suh SPEND) *v.*	hang from something above; keep from falling; to bring to a stop	suspenders suspense	In science lab, we have to suspend an object from a rope.
symbolize (SIHM buh lyz) *v.*	stand for	symbol	What might the flag symbolize in this story?
test (tehst) *n.*	method or process for proving or disproving a claim	testing tested	After the test, I knew my theory was correct.
unique (yoo NEEK) *adj.*	one of a kind	uniqueness	My favorite author has a truly unique writing style.
visual (VIHZH u uhl) *adj.*	able to be seen or understood with the eyes	vision visually	The descriptive passage of the story gives a strong visual image of the scene.

I Introductory Unit

Practice

Examples of various kinds of domain-specific academic vocabulary appear in the charts below. Some chart rows are not filled in. Look up the definitions of the remaining words, provide one or two related words, and use each word in context on a separate piece of paper.

Social Studies: Domain-Specific Academic Vocabulary

Word	Definition	Related Words	Word in Context
epic (EP ik) *adj.*	huge in size, duration, or importance; heroic	epical	*The Odyssey* tells of an epic journey made by Odysseus.
feudalism (FYOOD l iz uhm) *n.*	social system in the Middle Ages based on land ownership by a privileged class	feudal	Feudalism gave power to lords, or men who owned land.
globalization (GLOH buh lih ZAY shun) *n.*	the inclusion of all parts of the globe	globe, global	Computers have made globalization possible.
interdependence (in ter di PEN dunhnts) *n.*	dependence on one another	interdependent	Interdependence between the two countries keeps the peace.
mobility (moh BIL i tee) *n.*	ability of people to change location or position easily	mobile	Mobility increased with the invention of cars.
archaeologist (ahr kee OL uh jist) *n.*			
civilization (siv uh luh ZAY shuhn) *n.*			
irrigation (ir i GAY shuhn) *n.*			
monarchy (MON er kee) *n.*			
nomadic (noh MAD ik) *adj.*			

Mathematics: Domain-Specific Academic Vocabulary

Word	Definition	Related Words	Word in Context
base (bays) *n.*	a number that is raised to a power by an exponent	bases, basic	In the math problem, the base number was 3 and the exponent was 2.
circumference (ser KUHM fer uhns) *n.*	the length of the boundary of a circle	circumvent	We learned how to find the circumference of a circle.
degree (dih GREE) *n.*	unit of measure for temperature and angles	degrees	The teacher drew a 45-degree angle.
equilateral (ee kwuh LAT er uhl) *adj.*	having sides of the same, or equal, length	equal	On the test, we were asked to draw an equilateral triangle.
prime factorization (prym FAK tuh ri ZAY shun) *n.*	the process of breaking down a number into its prime factors	prime, factor	We used prime factorization to find the factors of 39.
percent (per SENT) *n.*			
power (POU er) *n.*			
sample (SAM puhl) *n.*			
similarity (sim uh LAR i tee) *n.*			
simulation (sim yuh LAY shuhn) *n.*			

Science: Domain-Specific Academic Vocabulary

Word	Definition	Related Words	Word in Context
atmosphere (AT muhs feer) *n.*	the air or gaseous area around the earth or a planet	atmospheric	Earth's atmosphere is different from that of Mars.
atom (AT uhm) *n.*	the smallest part of an element with all the element's properties	atomic	An atom is too small to see with the human eye.
cell (sel) *n.*	the basic unit of living organisms	cellular	A plant cell has a cell membrane.
decomposer (dee kuhm POH zer) *n.*	an organism that feeds on and breaks down dead plant or animal matter	decompose	Decomposers are an important part of the food web.
prey (pray) *n.*	an animal hunted for food	preying	The deer was the hungry lion's prey.

Science: Domain-Specific Academic Vocabulary *(continued)*

Word	Definition	Related Words	Word in Context
climate (KLY mit) *n.*			
crystal (KRIS tl) *n.*			
fungus (FUHNG guhs) *n.*			
gene (jeen) *n.*			
molecule (MOL uh kyool) *n.*			

Art: Domain-Specific Academic Vocabulary

Word	Definition	Related Words	Word in Context
diagonal (dy AG uh nl) *adj.*	on a slant	diagonally	The student used diagonal lines to draw a slanted roof.
horizontal (hawr uh ZON tl) *adj.*	side to side	horizontally	Use horizontal lines to draw the floor and ceiling of a room.
hue (hyoo) *n.*	color; form of a color	hues	She used a purple hue in her painting.
tint (tint) *n.*	refers to a hue plus white	tinted, tinting	The art teacher mixed white with red to create a pink tint.
vertical (VUR ti kuhl) *adj.*	straight up and down	vertically	The painter used vertical lines to paint the walls of a building.
color (KUHL er) *n.*			
curved (kurvd) *adj.*			
edge (ej) *n.*			
line (lyn) *n.*			
shade (shayd) *n.*			

Technology: Domain-Specific Academic Vocabulary

Word	Definition	Related Words	Word in Context
desktop (DESK top) *adj.*	a type of computer that fits on a desk but is not portable	laptop	The classroom had many **desktop** computers on long tables.
file (fyl) *n.*	an organized collection of data in a single location	files	I saved my report in a **file** on my computer.
hardware (HAHRD wair) *n.*	electronic devices that make up a computer	software	A computer monitor is an example of **hardware**.
icon (AHY kon) *n.*	a small picture that stands for a command or file	iconic, icons	Click on the folder **icon** to open a new file.
monitor (MON i ter) *n.*	the device that displays images and text	monitored, monitoring	A large **monitor** is handy for showing graphics and photos.
backspace (key) (BAK spays) *n.*			
delete (key) (dih LEET) *n.*			
enter (key) (EN ter) *n.*			
escape (key) (ih SKAYP) *n.*			
online (ON LYN) *adj.*			

Increasing Your Word Knowledge

Increase your word knowledge and chances of success by taking an active role in developing your vocabulary. Here are some tips for you.

To own a word, follow these steps:

Steps to Follow	Model
1. Learn to identify the word and its basic meaning.	The word *examine* means "to look at closely."
2. Take note of the word's spelling.	*Examine* begins and ends with an *e*.
3. Practice pronouncing the word so that you can use it in conversation.	The *e* on the end of the word *examine* is silent. Its second syllable gets the most stress.
4. Visualize the word and illustrate its key meaning.	When I think of the word *examine*, I visualize a doctor checking a patient's health.
5. Learn the various forms of the word and its related words.	*Examination* and *exam* are forms of the word *examine*.
6. Compare the word with similar words.	*Examine*, *peruse*, and *study* are synonyms.
7. Contrast the word with similar words.	*Examine* suggests a more detailed study than *read* or *look at*.
8. Use the word in various contexts.	"I'd like to *examine* the footprints more closely." "I will *examine* the use of imagery in this poem."

Building Your Speaking Vocabulary

Language gives us the ability to express ourselves. The more words you know, the better able you will be to get your points across. There are two main aspects of language: reading and speaking. Using the steps above will help you acquire a rich vocabulary. Follow these steps to help you learn to use this rich vocabulary in discussions, speeches, and conversations.

Steps to Follow	Tip
1. Practice pronouncing the word.	Become familiar with pronunciation guides to allow you to sound out unfamiliar words. Listening to audio books as you read the text will help you learn pronunciations of words.
2. Learn word forms.	Dictionaries often list forms of words following the main word entry. Practice saying word families aloud: "generate," "generated," "generation," "regenerate," "generator."
3. Translate your thoughts.	Restate your own thoughts and ideas in a variety of ways, to inject formality or to change your tone, for example.
4. Hold discussions.	With a classmate, practice using academic vocabulary words in discussions about the text. Choose one term to practice at a time, and see how many statements you can create using that term.
5. Tape-record yourself.	Analyze your word choices by listening to yourself objectively. Note places your word choice could be strengthened or changed.

Building Academic Vocabulary **lv**

WRITING AN OBJECTIVE SUMMARY

The ability to write objective summaries is key to success in college and in many careers. Writing an effective objective summary involves recording the key ideas of a text as well as demonstrating your understanding.

What Is an Objective Summary?

An effective objective summary is a short, accurate, and objective overview of a text. Following are key elements of an objective summary:

- A good summary focuses on a text's main points. It includes specific, relevant details that support the main point, but it leaves out unnecessary details.

- A summary should be a restatement of the text's main points, in the order in which they appear in the original text.

- A summary should accurately capture the essence of the longer text it is describing.

What to Avoid in an Objective Summary

- An objective summary is not a collection of sentences or paragraphs copied from the original source.

- It does not include every event, detail, or point in the original text.

- Finally, a good summary does not include evaluative comments, such as the reader's overall opinion of or reaction to the selection.

- An objective summary is not the reader's interpretation or critical analysis of the text.

Common Core State Standards

Reading Literature
2. Determine a theme or central idea of a text and how it is conveyed through particular details; provide a summary of the text distinct from personal opinions or judgements.

Reading Informational Text
2. Determine a central idea of a text and how it is conveyed through particular details; provide a summary of the text distinct from personal opinions or judgments.

Model Objective Summary

Review the elements of an effective objective summary called out in the sidenotes. Then, write an objective summary of a text you have read. Review your summary. Delete any unnecessary details or opinions.

Summary of "King Midas and the Golden Touch"

"King Midas and the Golden Touch" is a myth that tells the tale of a king who is granted a magical wish.

King Midas, the main character in this ~~popular~~ myth, loved gold. He would go into his dungeon to admire his shiny treasure. However, he did love one thing more than his gold—his daughter Aurelia.

Aurelia loved her father, and every day she would pick a bouquet of colorful, fragrant roses from his garden and bring them to him.

One day the king's guards found an old man asleep in the king's rose garden. Instead of punishing the man, the king invited him to dinner.

After the old man departed, King Midas went to the dungeon to admire his gold. All of a sudden, the glowing figure of a young man appeared. The apparition spoke to the shocked king and explained that he was the old man. To reward Midas for his kindness, the young stranger offered him one wish. King Midas wished that everything he touched would turn to gold.

The next day the king woke up and found that his wish had come true. His bedcovers were spun gold as were his clothes. ~~When he put his glasses on, they, too, turned to gold. That meant he couldn't see through them.~~ Midas rushed out to the garden and excitedly turned his roses into gold.

At breakfast, Aurelia was crying because her roses were made of gold. Midas convinced her to have breakfast with him. Midas lifted a spoonful of porridge to his mouth, but as soon as the porridge touched his lips it turned into a hard golden lump. When Aurelia noticed her father's concern, she went over to comfort him. To the king's horror, Aurelia became a lifeless golden statue at his touch.

As Midas cried, the mysterious stranger suddenly appeared. The stranger told him how to change things back to their original form.

King Midas brought Aurelia and the roses back to life. He did, however, keep one golden rose to remind himself of his experience with the golden touch. ~~Midas learned a good lesson.~~

A one-sentence synopsis highlighting the theme or central idea of the story can be an effective start to a summary.

An adjective describing the story indicates an opinion and should not be included in an objective summary.

Relating the development of the text in chronological order makes a summary easy to follow.

Unnecessary details should be eliminated.

This sentence should be paraphrased rather than copied exactly from the story.

The writer's opinions should not appear in an objective summary.

COMPREHENDING COMPLEX TEXTS

During the coming years in school, you will be required to read increasingly complex texts to prepare you for college and the workplace. A complex text is a text that contains challenging vocabulary; long, complex sentences; figurative language; multiple levels of meaning; or unfamiliar settings and situations. The selections in this textbook include a range of readings, from short stories to autobiographies, poetry, drama, myths, and even science and social studies texts. Some of these texts will fall within your comfort zone; others may be more challenging.

Strategy 1: **Multidraft Reading**

Good readers develop the habit of rereading texts in order to comprehend them completely. Just as an actor practices his lines over and over again in order to learn them, good readers return to texts to more fully enjoy and comprehend them. To fully understand a text, try this multidraft reading strategy:

1st Reading
The first time you read a text, read to gain its basic meaning. If you are reading a narrative text, look for story basics: who the story is about and what happens. If the text is nonfiction, look for main ideas. If you are reading poetry, read first to get an overall impression of the poem.

2nd Reading
During your second reading of a text, focus on ways in which the writer uses language and text structures. Think about why the author chose those words or organizational patterns. Then, examine the author's creative uses of language and the effects of that language. For example, has the author used rhyme, exaggeration, or words with multiple meanings?

3rd Reading
After your third reading, compare and contrast the text with others of its kind you have read. For example, if you have read another myth before, think of ways the myths are alike or different. Evaluate the text's overall effectiveness and its central idea or theme.

Common Core State Standards

Reading Literature
10. By the end of the year, read and comprehend literature, including stories, dramas, and poems, in the grades 6–8 text complexity band proficiently, with scaffolding as needed at the high end of the range.

Independent Practice

As you read this short poem, practice the multidraft reading strategy by completing a chart like the one below.

"Storm" by H. D. (Hilda Doolittle)

You crash over the trees,

you crack the live branch—

the branch is white,

the green crushed,

each leaf is rent like split wood.

You burden the trees

with black drops,

you swirl and crash—

you have broken off a weighted leaf

in the wind,

it is hurled out,

whirls up and sinks,

a green stone.

Multidraft Reading Chart

	My Understanding
1st Reading Look for key ideas and details that unlock basic meaning.	
2nd Reading Read for deeper meanings. Look for ways in which the author used text structures and language to create effects.	
3rd Reading Read to integrate your knowledge and ideas. Connect the text to other texts and to your own experience.	

Strategy 2: Close Read the Text

Complex texts require close reading, a careful analysis of the words, phrases, and sentences. When you close read, use the following tips to comprehend the text:

Tips for Close Reading

1. Break down long sentences into parts. Look for the subject of the sentence and its verb. Then identify which parts of the sentence modify, or give more information about, its subject.

2. Reread passages. When reading complex texts, be sure to reread passages to confirm that you understand their meaning.

3. Look for context clues, such as the types listed below.

   a. Restatement of an idea. For example, in this sentence, "have everlasting life" restates the adjective *immortal*.

     Gilgamesh wanted to be **immortal**, or have everlasting life

   b. Definition of sophisticated words. In this sentence, the underlined information defines the word *empire*.

     An **empire** is a <u>large territory made up of many different places all under the control of a single ruler.</u>

   c. Examples of concepts and topics.

     Flowers <u>such as nasturtiums, daisies, and marigolds</u> grew along the side of the walk.

   d. Contrasts of ideas and topics. In the following sentence, the phrase "on the other hand" indicates a contrast. You can guess that *loquacious* means the opposite of "not talkative."

     President Coolidge was not talkative; President Clinton, <u>on the other hand,</u> was **loquacious.**

4. Identify pronoun antecedents. If long sentences contain pronouns, reread the text to make sure you know to what the pronouns refer. The pronoun *its* in the following sentence refers to Yellowstone National Park, not the U.S. government.

     Yellowstone National Park was set aside by the U.S. government for people to enjoy for **its** natural beauty.

5. Look for conjunctions, such as *and*, *or*, and *yet*, to understand relationships between ideas.

6. Paraphrase, or restate in your own words, passages of difficult text in order to check your understanding. Remember that a paraphrase is a word-for-word rephrasing of an original text; it is not a summary.

Close Reading Model

As you read this complex document, take note of the sidenotes that model ways to unlock meaning in the text.

from "How to Tell a Story" by Mark Twain

. . . The humorous story is American, the comic story is English, the witty story is French. The humorous story depends for its effect upon the manner of the telling; the comic story and the witty story upon the matter. . . .

> The word *but* signals a contrast in ideas.

The humorous story is strictly a work of art—high and delicate art—and only an artist can tell it; but no art is necessary in telling the comic and the witty story; anybody can do it. The art of telling a humorous story—understand, I mean by word of mouth, not print—was created in America, and has remained at home.

> The dashes indicate an interruption of thought. The main part of this sentence appears in yellow highlight. Less important information appears in green.

The humorous story is told gravely; the teller does his best to conceal the fact that he even dimly suspects that there is anything funny about it; but the teller of the comic story tells you beforehand that it is one of the funniest things he has ever heard, then tells it with eager delight, and is the first person to laugh when he gets through. And sometimes, if he has had good success, he is so glad and happy that he will repeat the "nub" of it and glance around from face to face, collecting applause, and then repeat it again. It is a pathetic thing to see.

> Context clues that appear in purple highlighting help you understand the meaning of the word *gravely*.

Very often, of course, the rambling and disjointed humorous story finishes with a nub, point, snapper, or whatever you like to call it. Then the listener must be alert, for in many cases the teller will divert attention from that nub by dropping it in a carefully casual and indifferent way, with the pretence that he does not know it is a nub.

> Additional examples and commentary help you get an idea of the meaning of *nub*.

Strategy 3: **Ask Questions**

Be an attentive reader by asking questions as you read. Throughout this textbook, we have provided questions for you following each selection. These questions are sorted into three basic categories that build in sophistication and lead you to a deeper understanding of the texts you read. Here is an example from this text:

Gluskabe and Old Man Winter **Close Reading Activities**

Some questions are about **Key Ideas and Details** in the text. To answer these questions, you will need to locate and cite explicit information in the text or draw inferences from what you have read.

Some questions are about **Craft and Structure** in the text. To answer these questions, you will need to analyze how the author developed and structured the text. You will also look for ways in which the author artfully used language and how those word choices impacted the meaning and tone of the work.

Comprehension: **Key Ideas and Details**

1. Interpret: In Scene I, what signs do you see that Gluskabe will successfully help the people?

2. (a) Find details in the stage directions that establish the seasons at various points in the play. **(b) Connect:** How are these details connected to the main conflict?

3. (a) Distinguish: How does the playwright characterize Old Man Winter? **(b) Infer:** What does this characterization suggest about the winter season?

4. Summarize: Write a brief objective summary of the drama. Cite story details in your writing.

Text Analysis: **Craft and Structure**

5. (a) What happens in each of the play's four scenes? **(b) Analyze:** Explain how the scenes form a plot with a conflict, rising action, climax, and resolution.

6. (a) Infer: Gluskabe speaks with Grandmother Woodchuck after Old Man Winter defeats him the first time. What

new information about Gluskabe do you learn from this conversation? **(b)** How does the dialogue move the story forward? Explain.

7. (a) What does the last stage direction describe? **(b) Analyze:** How is this stage direction essential to the play's plot?

Connections: **Integration of Knowledge and Ideas**

Discuss
Conduct a **small-group discussion** about the personification of winter and summer in the drama. Discuss why the Abenaki people might give human characteristics to these elements of nature.

Research
Briefly research several stories of the

Write
Many traditional tales helped people make sense of the world. Write an essay in which you describe how *Gluskabe and Old Man Winter* explains an aspect of nature. Cite details from the play to support your analysis.

Some questions are about the **Integration of Knowledge and Ideas** in the text. These questions ask you to evaluate a text in many different ways, such as comparing texts, analyzing arguments in the text, and using many other methods of thinking critically about a text's ideas.

Preparing to Read Complex Texts

Attentive Reading As you read on your own, ask yourself questions like these to enrich your reading experience.

When reading drama, ask yourself...

Comprehension: **Key Ideas and Details**

• Who is the main character? What struggles does this character face?

• What other characters are important? How do these characters relate to the main character?

• Where and when does the play take place? Do the time and place of the setting affect the characters? If so, how?

• Do the characters, settings, and events seem real? Why or why not?

• How does the play end? How does the ending make me feel?

Text Analysis: **Craft and Structure**

• Does the playwright include background information? If so, how does this help me understand what I am reading?

• How many acts are in this play? What happens in each act?

• Does the dialogue sound like real speech? Are there passages that seem especially real? Are there any that seem false?

• What do the stage directions tell me about the ways

Ⓒ Common Core State Standards

Reading Literature/ Informational Text
10. By the end of the year, read and comprehend literature, including stories, dramas, and poems, and literary nonfiction in the grades 6–8 text complexity band proficiently, with scaffolding as needed at the high end of the range.

As you read independently, ask similar types of questions to ensure that you fully enjoy and comprehend texts you read for school and for pleasure. We have provided sets of questions for you on the Independent Reading pages at the end of each unit.

lxii Introductory Unit

Model

Following is an example of a complex text. The sidenotes show sample questions that an attentive reader might ask while reading.

from "Rendezvous with Despair" by Thomas E. Dewey

The President has said we have a rendezvous with destiny. We seem to be on our way toward a rendezvous with despair.

Fellow Republicans, as a party, let us turn away from that rendezvous and let us start going in the other direction and start now.

The one ultimate unforgivable crime is to despair of the republic. The one essential to the survival of the republic is to know it will survive and will survive into a future that is always larger, always better. In every era for a century and a half it has been doomed to death by gloomy young theorists and by tired and hopeless elders. And history laughs at them as each time the dynamic forces of a free republic led by free men have given the lie to the defeatists while the system of free economic enterprise has marched onward, sweeping the nation's increased population to full employment and ever higher living standards.

Sample questions:

Key Ideas and Details Who is the we in these sentences? Who is the us in the next sentence?

Craft and Structure In what ways does Dewey use language creatively in this text?

Integration of Knowledge and Ideas Do you agree with Dewey's point of view? Why or why not?

INFORMATIONAL TEXT

Independent Practice

Write three to five questions you might ask yourself as you read this passage from a speech delivered by Herbert Hoover in 1935.

from "The Bill of Rights" by Herbert Hoover

Our Constitution is not alone the working plan of a great Federation of States under representative government. There is embedded in it also the vital principles of the American system of liberty . . . which not even the government may infringe and which we call the Bill of Rights. It does not require a lawyer to interpret those provisions. . . . Among others the freedom of worship, freedom of speech and of the press, the right of peaceable assembly, equality before the law, just trial for crime, freedom from unreasonable search, and security from being deprived of life, liberty, or property without due process of law, are the principles which distinguish our civilization. . . . Herein is the expression of the spirit of men who would be forever free.

ANALYZING ARGUMENTS

The ability to evaluate an argument, as well as to make one, is an important skill for success in college and in the workplace.

What Is an Argument?

When you think of the word *argument,* you might think of a disagreement between two people. This type of argument involves trading opinions and evidence in a conversation. A formal argument, however, presents one side of a controversial or debatable issue. A good argument is supported by reasoning and evidence.

Purposes of Argument

There are three main purposes for writing a formal argument:

- to change the reader's mind
- to convince the reader to accept what is written
- to motivate the reader to take action, based on what is written

Elements of Argument

Claim (assertion)—what the writer is trying to prove

Example: *Local governments should give vouchers (an allowance to be used for schooling) to parents who send their children to private schools.*

Grounds (evidence)—the support used to convince the reader

Example: *The parents pay taxes to support local schools. Children are required by law to attend school.*

Justification—the link between the grounds and the claim; why the grounds are credible

Example: *If the children don't attend a public school, they are not getting the benefit of the tax dollars their parents have paid. Local governments should support parents' choices of schools for their children by giving them vouchers.*

Evaluating Claims

When reading or listening to a formal argument, critically assess the claims that are made. Which claims are based on fact or can be proved true? Also evaluate evidence that supports the claims. If there is little or no reasoning or evidence provided to support the claims, the argument may not be sound or valid.

Student Edition Pages

Model Argument

Nelson Mandela's Address Upon His Release From Prison

...Today the majority of South Africans, black and white, recognize that apartheid has no future. It has to be ended by our own decisive mass action in order to build peace and security. The mass campaign of defiance and other actions of our organization and people can only culminate in the establishment of democracy. The destruction caused by apartheid on our sub-continent is incalculable. The fabric of family life of millions of my people has been shattered. . . . Our economy lies in ruins and our people are embroiled in political strife. . . .

Claim: All South Africans must work together to end apartheid.

Justification: Apartheid has caused problems for the people as well as the country.

The need to unite the people of our country is as important a task now as it always has been. No individual leader is able to take on this enormous task on his own. . . .

Grounds: No one can do the job alone.

Our struggle has reached a decisive moment. We call on our people to seize this moment so that the process towards democracy is rapid and uninterrupted. We have waited too long for our freedom. We can no longer wait. Now is the time to intensify the struggle on all fronts. To relax our efforts now would be a mistake which generations to come will not be able to forgive. The sight of freedom looming on the horizon should encourage us to redouble our efforts.

Grounds: Black South Africans have waited too long for their freedom.

...We call on the international community to continue the campaign to isolate the apartheid regime. To lift sanctions now would be to run the risk of aborting the process towards the complete eradication of apartheid.

An opposing argument would be to support apartheid. Mandela points out what would happen if the international community lifted sanctions.

Our march to freedom is irreversible. . . . Universal suffrage on a common voters' role in a united democratic and non-racial South Africa is the only way to peace and racial harmony.

Grounds: Universal suffrage is key to peace and racial harmony.

In conclusion I wish to quote my own words during my trial in 1964. They are true today as they were then:

'I have fought against white domination and I have fought against black domination. I have cherished the ideal of a democratic and free society in which all persons live together in harmony and with equal opportunities. It is an ideal which I hope to live for and to achieve. But if needs be, it is an ideal for which I am prepared to die.'

A strong conclusion does more than simply restate the claim.

THE ART OF ARGUMENT: RHETORICAL DEVICES AND PERSUASIVE TECHNIQUES

Rhetorical Devices

Rhetoric is the art of using language in order to make a point or to persuade listeners. Rhetorical devices such as the ones listed below are accepted elements of argument. Their use is regarded as a key part of an effective argument.

Rhetorical Devices	Examples
Repetition The repeated use of certain words, phrases, or sentences	**Vote** for me. **Vote** for honesty. **Vote** for progress.
Parallelism The repeated use of similar grammatical structures	To teach is to inspire. To learn is to explore.
Rhetorical Question Calling attention to the issue by implying an obvious answer	Aren't all people equal under the law?
Sound Devices The use of alliteration, assonance, rhyme, or rhythm	Waste not, want not.
Simile and Metaphor Comparing two like things or asserting that one thing is another	The trees surrounded the house like guards on patrol.

Persuasive Techniques

The persuasive techniques below are often found in informal persuasion.

Persuasive Techniques	Examples
Bandwagon Approach/Anti-Bandwagon Approach Appeals to a person's desire to belong/Encourages or celebrates individuality	You have to see that movie; everyone in our class has seen it. Use your best judgment; don't follow the crowd.
Emotional Appeal Capitalizes on people's fear, anger, or desire	Without a sprinkler system, this school building is a fire trap.
Endorsement/Testimony Employs a well-known person to promote a product or an idea	Meditation and positive thinking have helped me become president of this company.
Loaded Language Uses words charged with emotion	This medal recognizes the integrity of the brave people who defend our beloved country.
"Plain Folks" Appeal Shows a connection to everyday, ordinary people	I worry about rising gas prices just like you do.
Hyperbole Exaggerates to make a point	If I've heard that complaint once, I've heard it a thousand times.

Model Speech

The excerpted speech below includes examples of rhetorical devices and persuasive techniques.

from "Speech Celebrating George Washington's Birthday" by Jane Addams

… What is a great man who has made his mark upon history? Every time, if we think far enough, he is a man who has looked through the confusion of the moment and has seen the moral issue involved; he is a man who has refused to have his sense of justice distorted; he has listened to his conscience until conscience becomes a trumpet call to like-minded men, so that they gather about him and together, with mutual purpose and mutual aid, they make a new period in history. . . .

If we go back to George Washington, and ask what he would be doing were he bearing our burdens now, and facing our problems at this moment, we would, of course, have to study his life bit by bit; his life as a soldier, as a statesman, and as a simple Virginia planter.

First, as a soldier. What is it that we admire about the soldier? It certainly is not that he goes into battle; what we admire about the soldier is that he has the power of losing his own life for the life or a larger cause; that he holds his personal suffering of no account; that he flings down in the gage of battle his all, and says, "I will stand or fall with this cause." That, it seems to me, is the glorious thing we most admire, and if we are going to preserve that same spirit of the soldier, we will have to found a similar spirit in the civil life of the people, the same pride in civil warfare, the spirit of courage, and the spirit of self-surrender which lies back of this. . . .

This rhetorical question gives the reader a purpose for reading.

Repeated grammatical structures give the speech rhythm.

The metaphor comparing conscience to a trumpet call emphasizes the importance of the statement.

Sound devices, such as alliteration, emphasize a phrase.

The parallel grammatical structure provides a rhythm, and introduces the organization of the remainder of the speech.

Addams uses parallelism and repetition to emphasize her main points.

The Art of Argument: Rhetorical Devices and Persuasive Techniques **lxvii**

COMPOSING AN ARGUMENT

Choosing a Topic

You should choose a topic that matters to people—and to you. Once you have chosen a topic, you should check to make sure you can make an arguable claim. Ask yourself:

Once you have chosen a topic, you should check to make sure you can make an arguable claim. Ask yourself:

1. What am I trying to prove? What ideas should I express?
2. Are there people who would disagree with my claim? What opinions might they have?
3. Do I have enough relevant evidence to support my claim?

If you are able to put into words what you want to prove and answered "yes" to questions 2 and 3, you have an arguable claim.

Introducing the Claim and Establishing Its Significance

Before you begin writing, think about your audience and how much you think they already know about your chosen topic. Then, provide only as much background information as necessary. Remember that you are not writing a summary of the issue—you are developing an argument. Once you have provided context for your argument, you should clearly state your claim, or thesis. A written argument's claim often, but not always, appears in the first paragraph.

Developing Your Claim with Reasoning and Evidence

Now that you have made your claim, you must support it with evidence, or grounds. A good argument should have at least three solid pieces of evidence to support the claim. Evidence can range from personal experience to researched data or expert opinion. Knowing your audience's knowledge level, concerns, values, and possible biases can help inform your decision on what kind of evidence will have the strongest impact. Make sure your evidence is up to date and comes from a credible source. Don't forget to credit your sources. You should also address the opposing counterclaim within the body of your argument. Consider points you have made or evidence you have provided that a person might challenge. Decide how best to respond to these counterclaims.

Writing a Concluding Statement or Section

Restate your claim in the conclusion of your argument, and synthesize, or pull together, the evidence you have provided. Make your conclusion strong enough to be memorable to the reader; leave him or her with something to think about.

Common Core State Standards

Writing

1.a. Introduce claim(s) and organize the reasons and evidence clearly.

1.b. Support claim(s) with clear reasons and relevant evidence, using credible sources and demonstrating an understanding of the topic or text.

1.e. Provide a concluding statement or section that follows from the argument presented.

Practice

Complete an outline like the one below to help you plan your own argument.

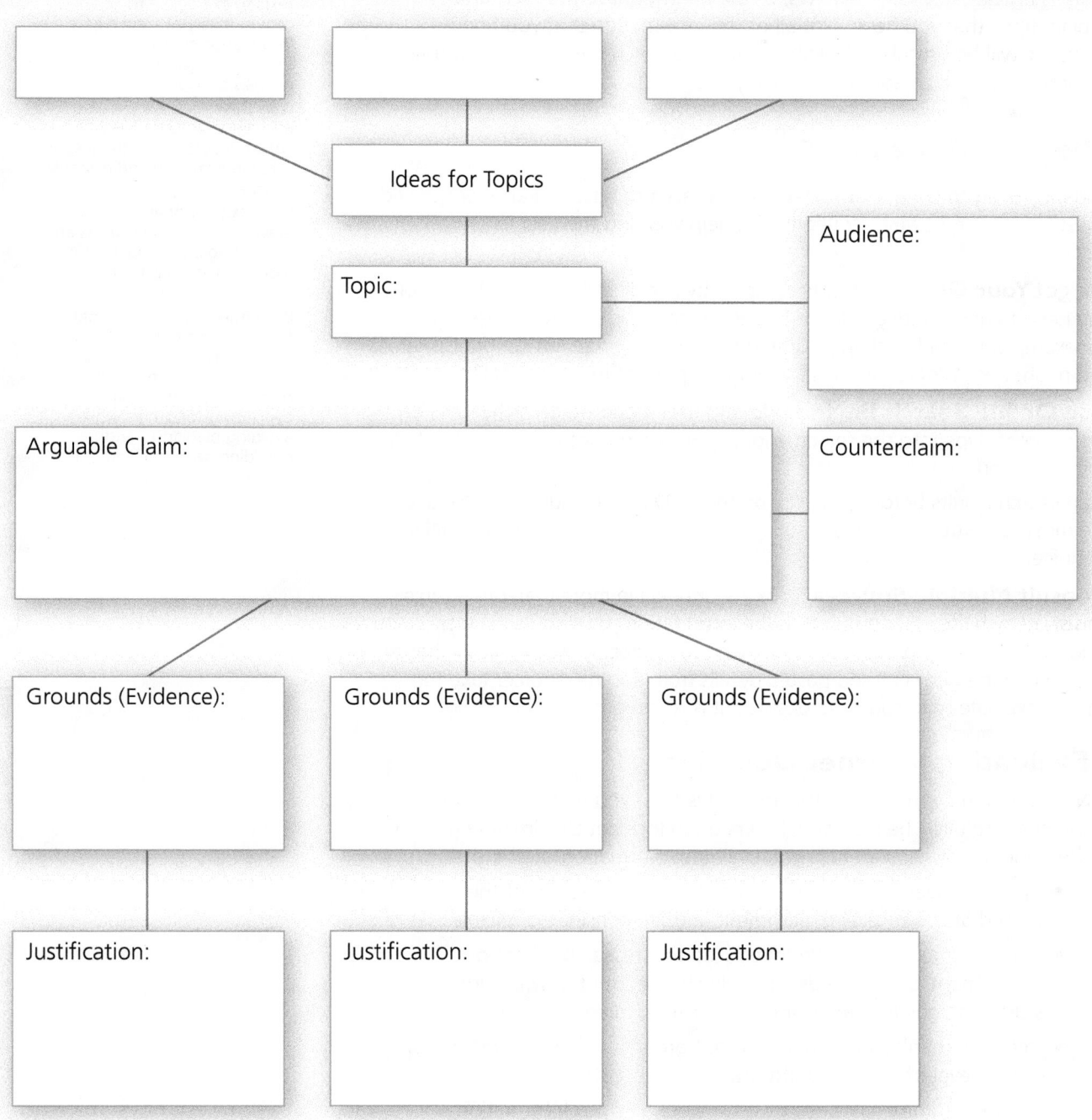

CONDUCTING RESEARCH

To gain more knowledge about a topic, you can conduct research. Sources such as articles, books, interviews, or the Internet have the facts and explanations that you need. Not all of the information that you find, however, will be useful—or reliable. Strong research skills will help you find accurate information about your topic.

Short-term Research

You may need to conduct **short-term research** to help you answer specific questions. The following strategies can help you find the best information quickly.

Target Your Goal Begin your research by deciding the exact information you need to find. Writing a specific question can help you avoid wasting time. For example, instead of simply hunting for information about Sandra Cisneros, you might ask "Why is Cisneros's heritage important to her writing?"

Use Online Search Engines To find useful and trustworthy facts on the Internet, type into the search engine phrases in quotation marks to help you focus your search.

Scan search results before you click on them. The first result is not always the most relevant. Read the text and think about the source before making a choice.

Consult Multiple Sources Look for answers in more than one source. This strategy helps you be sure that the information you find is accurate. If you read the exact same phrases in more than one source, there is a good chance that someone simply cut-and-pasted details from another source. Take the time to evaluate each source to decide if it is trustworthy.

Evaluating Internet Domains

Not everything you read on the Internet is true; you have to evaluate sources carefully. The last three letters of an Internet URL identify the site's domain, which can help you evaluate information on the site.

- .gov — Government sites are sponsored by a branch of the United States federal government and are considered reliable.
- .edu — Information from an educational research center or department is likely to be carefully checked, but may include student pages that are not edited or monitored.
- .org — Organizations are non-profit groups and usually maintain a high level of credibility but may still reflect strong biases.
- .com — Commercial sites exist to make a profit. Information might be biased to show a product or service in a good light.

lxx Introductory Unit

Common Core State Standards

Writing
2. Write informative/explanatory texts to examine a topic and convey ideas, concepts, and information through the selection, organization, and analysis of relevant content.

2.b. Develop the topic with relevant facts, definitions, concrete details, quotations, or other information and examples.

7. Conduct short research projects to answer a question, drawing on several sources and generating additional related, focused questions for further research and investigation.

8. Gather relevant information from multiple print and digital sources; assess the credibility of each source; and quote or paraphrase the data and conclusions of others while avoiding plagiarism and providing basic bibliographic information for sources.

Long-term Research

When you want to really explore a topic, long-term research allows you to carry out a detailed, comprehensive investigation. An organized research plan will help you gather and synthesize information from multiple sources.

As this flow chart shows, long-term research is a flexible process. Throughout your research, you might decide to return to an earlier time to refocus your topic, gather more information, or reflect on what you have learned.

The Research Process

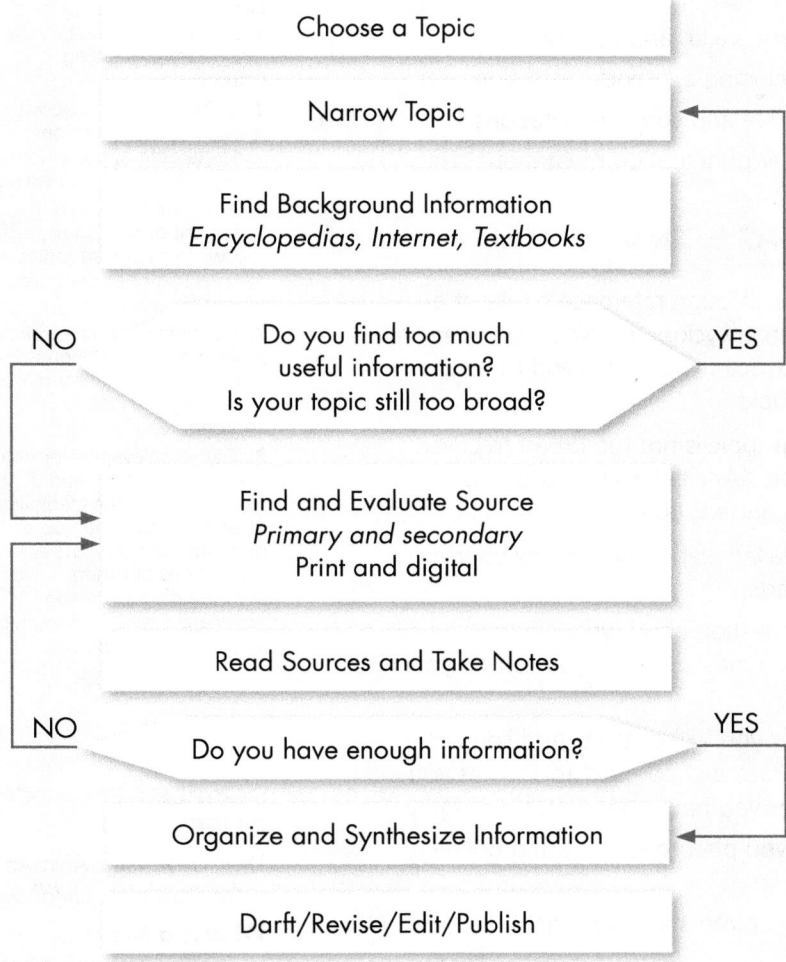

Refer to the Research Process Workshop (pp. lxxii–lxxvi) for more details about the steps in this flowchart.

RESEARCH PROCESS WORKSHOP

Research Writing: Research Paper

A **research paper** presents facts and information gathered from credible sources and includes a Works Cited list that credits each source. You might use elements of this form in reports, articles, or speeches.

Elements of a Research Paper

- a topic for inquiry that is narrow enough to cover thoroughly
- a strong introduction that clearly defines the topic
- facts, details, examples, and explanations from a variety of credible, authoritative sources to support the main ideas
- information that is accurate, relevant, valid, and current
- a clear method of organization, including a strong conclusion
- a Works Cited list containing accurate and complete citations
- error-free grammar, including proper punctuation of citations

PREWRITING/PLANNING STRATEGIES

Browse to choose a topic. Browse through reference books at a library, such as an atlas or a volume of an encyclopedia. Note each person, place, object, or event that interests you. Scan your notes and circle any words or phrases that suggest a good topic.

Narrow your topic. Make sure your topic is not too broad to cover effectively. For example, the general topic "Ancient Rome" could be narrowed down to a specific building in ancient Rome.

Create a research plan. Use a detailed plan to help guide your research. Your plan can include these parts:

- **Research Question** Compose a question about your topic that will help you stay on track. This question may also lead you to find your topic sentence.
- **Source List** Create a list of sources you will consult. Add sources to your list as you discover them. Place a check next to sources you have located, and underline sources you have consulted thoroughly.
- **Search Terms** Write down terms you plan to locate using online search engines.
- **Deadlines** Break a long-term project into short-term goals to prevent last-minute stress.

 **Common Core State Standards**

Writing

2. Write informative/explanatory texts to examine a topic and convey ideas, concepts, and information through the selection, organization, and analysis of relevant content.

2.a. Introduce a topic; organize ideas, concepts, and information, using strategies such as definition, classification, comparison/contrast, and cause/effect; include formatting (e.g., headings), graphics (e.g., charts and tables), and multimedia when useful to aiding comprehension.

2.b. Develop the topic with relevant facts, definitions, concrete details, quotations, or other information and examples.

2.f. Provide a concluding statement or section that follows from and supports the information or explanation presented.

7. Conduct short research projects to answer a question, drawing on several sources and refocusing the inquiry when appropriate.

8. Gather relevant information from multiple print and digital sources; assess the credibility of each source; and quote or paraphrase the data and conclusions of others while avoiding plagiarism and providing basic bibliographic information for sources.

SAMPLE RESEARCH QUESTIONS

Why does Julia Alvarez write about her childhood?

What is a humorous theme in Shel Silverstein's poetry?

GATHERING DETAILS THROUGH RESEARCH

Use multiple sources. An effective research project combines information from multiple sources. It is important not to rely too heavily on a single source. The creativity and originality of your research depends on how you combine ideas from many places. Plan to include a variety of these resources:

- **Primary and Secondary Resources** Use both primary sources (firsthand or original accounts, such as interview transcripts and newspaper articles) and secondary sources (accounts that are not original, such as encyclopedia entries or an online library catalog) in your research.

- **Print and Digital Resources** The Internet allows fast access to data, but print resources are often edited more carefully. Plan to include both print and digital resources in order to guarantee that your work is accurate.

- **Media Resources** You can find valuable information in media resources such as documentaries, television programs, podcasts, and museum exhibitions. Public lectures by experts also offer an opportunity to hear an expert's thoughts on a topic.

- **Original Research** Depending on your topic, you may wish to conduct original research to include among your sources. For example, you might interview experts or eyewitnesses or conduct a survey to find out about beliefs in your community.

Take clear notes from a variety of sources. Use different strategies to take notes:

- Use index cards to create **note cards** and **source cards.** On each source card, record information about each source that you use—title, author, publication date and place, and page numbers. On each note card, record information to use in your report. Use quotation marks when you copy exact words, and indicate the page number on which the quotation appears.

- Photocopy articles and copyright pages; then, highlight relevant information. Remember to include the Web addresses of printouts from online sources.

- Print articles from the Internet or copy them directly into a "notes" folder.

You will use these notes to help you write original text.

Note Card

> ### Education
> Papp, p.5
>
> Only the upper classes could read.
>
> Most of the common people in Shakespeare's time could not read.

Source Card

> Papp, Joseph
> and Kirkland, Elizabeth
>
> **Shakespeare Alive!**
>
> New York: Bantam Books, 1988

DRAFTING STRATEGIES

Use an outline to organize information. Group your notes by categories that break your topic into subtopics. For example, if you are writing about the Colosseum, you might use these topics in your outline:

- architecture
- construction
- events held
- spectators

Use Roman numerals (I, II, III) to number the subtopics and letters (A, B, C) to show details and facts related to each subtopic, as in the outline shown on this page.

Match your draft to your outline. A solid, detailed outline will serve as a map, guiding you through the writing of your draft. The headings with Roman numerals indicate main sections of your report. You may need to write several paragraphs to cover each Roman numeral topic fully. Organize your paragraphs around the topics with capital letters.

Support main ideas with facts. Using your outline, write sentences to express each of your main ideas. Then, refer to your note cards and provide support for your main ideas with facts, details, examples, and explanations that you gathered through your research.

Cite sources. To avoid plagiarism—presenting another's work as your own without giving credit—you must include documentation every time you use another writer's ideas.

It is important to use ethical practices when conducting research.

Plan Your Citations Whether you are paraphrasing, summarizing, or using a direct quotation, you must give credit. As you draft, remember to use quotation marks around any words that you pick-up directly from a source. You should also give credit for ideas or facts that are unique to one source.

Citing Sources Tips:

- For *paraphrased information* or facts that are not common knowledge, insert parentheses for the author's last name and the page number(s) from which the information came:

  The Colosseum holds 50,000 spectators (Smith 87–88).

- For a *direct quotation,* use quotation marks. After the end quotation mark, insert in parentheses the author's last name and the page number(s) from which the quotation came: *"It is the Romans' greatest work of architecture." (Smith 87).*

 **Common Core State Standards**

Writing

2.a. Introduce a topic; organize ideas, concepts, and information, using strategies such as definition, classification, comparison/contrast, and cause/effect; include formatting, graphics, and multimedia when useful to aiding comprehension.

2.b. Develop the topic with relevant facts, definitions, concrete details, quotations, or other information and examples.

2.d. Use precise language and domain-specific vocabulary to inform about or explain the topic.

8. Gather relevant information from multiple print and digital sources; assess the credibility of each source; and quote or paraphrase the data and conclusions of others while avoiding plagiarism and providing basic bibliographic information for sources.

I. Introduction
II. Architecture of Colosseum
   A. measurements
   B. building material
III. Construction of Colosseum
   A. beginning date
   B. workers
IV. Conclusion

REVISING STRATEGIES

Check for effective paragraph structure. In a research report, most body paragraphs should be built according to this plan:

- a **topic sentence (T)** stating the paragraph's main idea
- a **restatement (R)** or elaboration of the topic sentence
- strong **illustrations (I),** including facts, examples, or details about the main idea

Review your draft. Label each of your sentences **T, R,** or **I.** If a paragraph contains a group of I's, make sure that you have a strong **T** that they support. If you find a **T** by itself, add I's to support it.

Revise for unity. In writing that has **unity,** everything comes together to form a complete, self-contained whole. Use the following checklist to assess your report's unity.

Unity Checklist

✓ Every paragraph develops my thesis statement.

✓ All of my paragraphs contain topic sentences that support the thesis.

✓ I have eliminated any sentences that do not support my main idea.

Define technical terms and difficult words. While researching, you may have learned new words—either technical terms related to your topic or difficult words that were unfamiliar to you. Help your readers to understand and enjoy your report by adding context clues or definitions to make these words easier to understand.

Difficult: A popular show at the Roman Colosseum featured **gladiators.**

Defined: A popular show at the Roman Colosseum featured **gladiators,** trained fighters who often faced other men or even wild animals.

Create a works-cited list. A "Works Cited" page provides readers with full bibliographic information on each source you cite. The author and page number within your report will lead your reader to the specific source in your Works Cited page. Readers can use that information to read more about your topic. Review pp. lxxx–lxxxi to see the appropriate format for citing sources.

EDITING AND PROOFREADING

 **Common Core State Standards**

During editing you will focus on giving credit to the sources you used. You should also review your draft to correct errors in grammar, spelling, and punctuation. Demonstrate your keyboarding skills by typing your entire paper carefully and avoiding the introduction of errors.

Proofread for accuracy. Check the names of the authors you quote and the names of the books, articles, or other sources you used. Be sure that you have used quotation marks correctly, and that each open quotation mark has a corresponding closing quotation mark. Carefully reread your draft to find and correct errors in spelling, grammar, and punctuation.

Focus on citations. Cite the sources for quotations, factual information, and ideas that are not your own. Some word-processing programs have features that allow you to create footnotes and endnotes.

Create a reference list. Following the format your teacher prefers, create a Works Cited list of the information you used to write your research report. (For more information, see Citing Sources, pp. lxxx–lxxxi.)

Focus on format. Follow the report requirements by including an appropriate title page, pagination, spacing and margins, and citations. Make sure you have used the preferred system for crediting sources in your paper and for bibliographical sources at the end.

Publishing and Presenting

Consider one of these options for sharing your findings.

Give an oral report. Use your research report as the basis for an oral presentation on your topic. Keep your audience in mind and revise accordingly as you prepare your presentation.

Create a multimedia presentation. Computer software makes it easy to combine interesting videos, sound effects, music, and images in your presentation.

Writing

2.a. Introduce a topic; organize ideas, concepts, and information, using strategies such as definition, classification, comparison/contrast, and cause/effect; include formatting (e.g., headings), graphics (e.g., charts and tables), and multimedia when useful to aiding comprehension.

6. Demonstrate sufficient command of keyboarding skills to type a minimum of three pages in a single sitting.

8. Gather relevant information from multiple print and digital sources; assess the credibility of each source; and quote or paraphrase the data and conclusions of others while avoiding plagiarism and providing basic bibliographic information for sources.

Identifying Missing Citations

These strategies can help you find facts and details that should be cited in your report.

- Look for facts that are not general knowledge. If a fact was unique to one source, it needs a citation.
- Read your report aloud. Listen for words or phrases that do not sound like your writing style. You might have picked them up from a source. If so, use your notes to find the source, place the words in quotation marks, and give credit.
- Review your notes. Look for ideas that you used in your report, but did not cite.

STUDENT MODEL: RESEARCH PAPER

This student includes information to support the topic of her research paper. Notice how she integrates facts and details into her argument. She also uses parentheses to give credit for ideas taken from resources. The Works Cited list at the end of the report gives more details about the reference sources she used during the research process.

Student Model: Elizabeth Cleary, Maplewood, NJ

Ice Ages

Ice ages occur every two hundred million years or so. An ice age is defined as a long period of cold where large amounts of water are trapped under ice. Although ice ages happened long ago, studying their causes and effects helps contemporary scientists understand geological conditions of the world today.

When an ice age does occur, ice covers much of the Earth. This ice forms when the climate changes. The polar regions become very cold and the temperatures drop every-where else. The ice is trapped in enormous mountains of ice called glaciers. Glaciers can be as large as a continent in size. When the Earth's temperature warms up, the glaciers start to melt, forming rivers and lakes. Glaciers' tremendous weight and size can actually wear away mountains and valleys as the

Effects of Ice Age on Eastern Coastline of United States

glaciers melt and move. The melting ice also raises ocean levels.

There are many different theories to explain why ice ages occur, but no one knows for sure. Many scientists agree that it is probably due to a combination of causes, including changes in the sun's intensity, the distance of the Earth from the sun, changes in ocean currents, the continental plates rubbing up against each other, and the varying amounts of carbon dioxide in the atmosphere (*PBS Nova* Web site "The Big Chill").

The author defines her topic clearly in the highlighted sentence.

This map illustrates the writer's point that ice ages caused current conditions.

Here the author presents factual information related to the possible causes of ice ages.

During the last ice age, or the Wisconsin Ice Age, people lived on the Earth. These people saw ice and snow all the time. It was never warm enough for it to melt, so it piled up. In summertime, women fished in chilly streams. The men hunted year-round.

The skeleton of one person who lived and hunted during this time was found by some hikers in 1901 in the European Alps. He had been buried in the ice for nearly 5,000 years. Nicknamed the "Iceman," scientists believe that perhaps he was suddenly caught by a blizzard or that he possibly ran out of food, became weak, and died.

Scientists were able to learn a lot about this ancient period from the leather clothes and animal skins he was wearing and the tools he was carrying (Roberts, p. 38).

> Elizabeth clearly and accurately cites her sources to show where she obtained a set of specific details.

Ice ages also affect life today. The ice sheets that formed weighed a huge amount. When the ice retreated, it left behind large rocks and other debris which otherwise would not be there. Also, without ice ages, large bodies of water like the Great Lakes simply wouldn't exist. We depend on these bodies of water every day for fresh drinking water, recreation, and shipping large quantities of materials.

Scientists discovered ice ages because of Louis Agassiz, a nineteenth-century scientist who is sometimes called the "Father of Glaciology." In Switzerland, he saw boulders of granite far from where any granite should be. He also noticed scrapes and grooves, or striae. He theorized that glaciers had caused all of these geologic features (University of California Museum of Paleontology Web page).

> In each section, Elizabeth explores a different aspect of the ice ages. Here she is explaining scientific discovery.

Many animals that are extinct now lived during the Ice Age. The saber-toothed tiger and the mastodon, an elephant-like animal, formerly lived in North America. They became extinct because of climate change and hunting. Other animals became extinct as well because they could not adapt to the way the Earth was changing.

Baron Gerard de Geer, a Swedish geologist, did pioneering work which estimated the end of the last ice age. In a similar way to the way we count tree rings to estimate a tree's age, De Geer used layers of sediment left by glacier's summer

melts to calculate the history of the Ice Age. He did much of his work in Sweden, but he also visited areas that had been affected by glaciers in New England.

Thanks to scientists like De Geer and Agassiz, we know a great deal about that remote age when glaciers roamed the Earth. We can now estimate the history of ice ages and determine what features—valleys, inland seas, mountains, lakes, rocks—were caused, as you can see by the map displayed here of the Eastern United States. There is still a lot more to be discovered about the causes of ice ages, but one thing is clear: Glaciers had a powerful effect on the world as we know it today.

The author restates the main idea that she presented in the introduction and supported in the body of the paper.

Works Cited

Department of Geosciences, University of Arizona. 10 Nov. 2000. <http://www.geoarizona.edu/Antevs/degeer.html>.

History of the Universe. 11 Nov. 2000. <http://www.historyoftheuniverse.com/iceage.html>.

Ice Age. Compton's Interactive Encyclopedia © The Learning Company, Inc. [CD-ROM] (1998).

Roberts, David. "The Iceman." *National Geographic Magazine,* June 1993: 37–49.

University of California Museum of Paleontology. 11 Nov. 2000. <http://www.ucmp.berkeley.edu/history/agassiz.html>.

PBS Nova "The Big Chill." 10 Nov. 2000. <http://www.pbs.org/wgbh/nova/ice/chill.html>.

In her Works Cited list, Elizabeth cites all the sources used to research her paper.

CITING SOURCES AND PREPARING MANUSCRIPT

Proofreading and Preparing Manuscript

Before preparing a final copy, proofread your manuscript. The chart shows the standard symbols for marking corrections to be made.

Proofreading Symbols	
Insert	∧
delete	ℯ
close space	⌒
new paragraph	¶
add comma	⌄
add period	⊙
transpose (switch)	∼
change to cap	a̲
change to lowercase	A̸

- Choose a standard, easy-to-read font.
- Type or print on one side of unlined 8 1/2" x 11" paper.
- Set the margins for the side, top, and bottom of your paper at approximately one inch. Most word-processing programs have a default setting that is appropriate.
- Double-space the document.
- Indent the first line of each paragraph.
- Number the pages in the upper right corner.

Follow your teacher's directions for formatting formal research papers. Most papers will have the following features:

- Title page
- Table of Contents or Outline
- Works-Cited List

Avoiding Plagiarism

Whether you are presenting a formal research paper or an opinion paper on a current event, you must be careful to give credit for any ideas or opinions that are not your own. Presenting someone else's ideas, research, or opinion as your own—even if you have phrased it in different words—is *plagiarism*, the equivalent of academic stealing, or fraud.

Do not use the ideas or research of others in place of your own. Read from several sources to draw your own conclusions and form your own opinions. Incorporate the ideas and research of others to support your points. Credit the source of the following types of support:

- Statistics
- Direct quotations
- Indirectly quoted statements of opinions
- Conclusions presented by an expert
- Facts available in only one or two sources

Crediting Sources

When you credit a source, you acknowledge where you found your information and you give your readers the details necessary for locating the source themselves. Within the body of the paper, you provide a short citation, a footnote number linked to a footnote, or an endnote number linked to an endnote reference. These brief references show the page numbers on which you found the information. Prepare a reference list at the end of the paper to provide full bibliographic information on your sources. These are two common types of reference lists:

- A bibliography provides a listing of all the resources you consulted during your research.
- A works-cited list indicates the works you have referenced in your paper.

The chart on the next page shows the Modern Language Association format for crediting sources. This is the most common format for papers written in the content areas in middle school and high school. Unless instructed otherwise by your teacher, use this format for crediting sources.

MLA Style for Listing Sources

Book with one author	Pyles, Thomas. *The Origins and Development of the English Language.* 2nd ed. New York: Harcourt, 1971. Print.
Book with two or three authors	McCrum, Robert, William Cran, and Robert MacNeil. *The Story of English.* New York: Penguin, 1987. Print.
Book with an editor	Truth, Sojourner. *Narrative of Sojourner Truth.* Ed. Margaret Washington. New York: Vintage, 1993. Print.
Book with more than three authors or editors	Donald, Robert B., et al. *Writing Clear Essays.* Upper Saddle River: Prentice, 1996. Print.
Single work in an anthology	Hawthorne, Nathaniel. "Young Goodman Brown." *Literature: An Introduction to Reading and Writing.* Ed. Edgar V. Roberts and H. E. Jacobs. Upper Saddle River: Prentice, 1998. 376–385. Print. [Indicate pages for the entire selection.]
Introduction to a work in a published edition	Washington, Margaret. Introduction. *Narrative of Sojourner Truth.* By Sojourner Truth. Ed. Washington. New York: Vintage, 1993. v–xi. Print.
Signed article from an encyclopedia	Askeland, Donald R. "Welding." *World Book Encyclopedia.* 1991 ed. Print.
Signed article in a weekly magazine	Wallace, Charles. "A Vodacious Deal." *Time* 14 Feb. 2000: 63. Print.
Signed article in a monthly magazine	Gustaitis, Joseph. "The Sticky History of Chewing Gum." *American History* Oct. 1998: 30–38. Print.
Newspaper	Thurow, Roger. "South Africans Who Fought for Sanctions Now Scrap for Investors." *Wall Street Journal* 11 Feb. 2000: A1+. Print. [For a multipage article that does not appear on consecutive pages, write only the first page number on which it appears, followed by the plus sign.]
Unsigned editorial or story	"Selective Silence." Editorial. *Wall Street Journal* 11 Feb. 2000: A14. Print. [If the editorial or story is signed, begin with the author's name.]
Signed pamphlet or brochure	[Treat the pamphlet as though it were a book.]
Work from a library subscription service	Ertman, Earl L. "Nefertiti's Eyes." *Archaeology* Mar.–Apr. 2008: 28–32. *Kids Search.* EBSCO. New York Public Library. Web. 18 June 2008 [Indicate the date you accessed the information.]
Filmstrips, slide programs, videocassettes, DVDs, and other audiovisual media	*The Diary of Anne Frank.* Dir. George Stevens. Perf. Millie Perkins, Shelley Winters, Joseph Schildkraut, Lou Jacobi, and Richard Beymer. 1959. Twentieth Century Fox, 2004. DVD.
CD-ROM (with multiple publishers)	Simms, James, ed. *Romeo and Juliet.* By William Shakespeare. Oxford: Attica Cybernetics; London: BBC Education; London: Harper, 1995. CD-ROM.
Radio or television program transcript	"Washington's Crossing of the Delaware." *Weekend Edition Sunday.* Natl. Public Radio. WNYC, New York. 23 Dec. 2003. Television transcript.
Internet Web page	"Fun Facts About Gum." NACGM site. 1999. National Association of Chewing Gum Manufacturers. Web. 19 Dec. 1999 [Indicate the date you accessed the information.]
Personal interview	Smith, Jane. Personal interview. 10 Feb. 2000.

All examples follow the style given in the *MLA Handbook for Writers of Research Papers,* seventh edition, by Joseph Gibaldi.

Is conflict always bad?

THE BIG ?

UNIT PATHWAY

PART 1
SETTING EXPECTATIONS

- INTRODUCING THE BIG QUESTION
- CLOSE READING WORKSHOP

PART 2
TEXT ANALYSIS
GUIDED EXPLORATION

CHARACTERS AND CONFLICT

PART 3
TEXT SET
DEVELOPING INSIGHT

THE GOLD RUSH

PART 4
DEMONSTRATING INDEPENDENCE

- INDEPENDENT READING
- ONLINE TEXT SET

CLOSE READING TOOL

Use this tool to practice the close reading strategies you learn.

STUDENT eTEXT

Bring learning to life with audio, video, and interactive tools.

WRITER'S NOTEBOOK

Easily capture notes and complete assignments online.

 **Is conflict always bad?**

1. Ask a volunteer to read aloud the opening paragraph. Elicit examples of conflicts students have read about, seen on TV or in the movies, and so on.

2. Ask students the Big Question, "Is conflict always bad?"

Possible responses: Yes, one or both sides end up losing. No, sometimes conflicts are worked out, and we learn lessons about how to get along with others.

3. Tell students that the readings in this unit are short stories. As students read, they should think about whether events that occur support or change their first answers to the Big Question.

❷ Exploring the Big Question

Collaboration: One-on-One Discussion

1. Introduce the activity, using the instruction on the student page.

2. Have students work individually to complete their lists. Remind them to include examples for each situation.

3. Review the Big Question vocabulary on the next page, following the teaching suggestions. Have students use the vocabulary as they complete the activity on this page.

Connecting to the Literature

Explain the Big Question strand in the unit, referring to the text at the bottom of this page.

© Introducing the Big Question

Is conflict always bad?

A conflict is a struggle between opposing forces. There are many different types of conflict. One kind of conflict is an argument between people, such as who should get the last cookie. Another type is a battle between nations over freedom and liberty. When you compete against others in a sport or game, that is another kind of conflict. When you struggle over a decision, you are in conflict with yourself. There are many ways to resolve, or work out, conflicts of any kind. There are also many lessons to learn from these situations.

❷ Exploring the Big Question

Collaboration: One-on-One Discussion Start thinking about the Big Question by identifying different types of conflict. Describe one specific example of each of the following types of conflict:

- a disagreement between friends over an issue
- a misunderstanding between two people
- a competition in sports or in a contest
- an individual's struggle to make a decision
- a battle against forces of nature
- a person's fight to overcome or accept a challenge

Share your examples with a partner. Discuss the cause of each conflict and how it was resolved. Listen attentively.

Connecting to the Literature Each reading in this unit will give you additional insight into the Big Question. After you read each text, pause to consider ways in which the characters handled conflict.

2 UNIT 1 • Is conflict always bad?

❓ DEVELOPING ESSENTIAL UNDERSTANDING

Is conflict always bad?

Explain to students that they will continue to consider the Big Question as they work through Unit 1.

- As students read each selection, they will look for details related to the Big Question and take notes.
- At the end of each selection, students will answer a Literary Analysis question that is related to the Big Question.
- Throughout the unit, students will deepen their knowledge of the selections and their understanding of the Big Question through

reading, speaking, listening, researching, and writing. By the end of the unit, students should understand how each selection relates to the Big Question individually and how the selections connect to one another through the Big Question.

- Tell students that their goal will be to gain a deeper understanding of literature and to develop a more sophisticated way of discussing the Big Question. Ultimately, students should use the Big Question as a springboard for their own questions that relate to their interests and concerns.

❸ Vocabulary

Acquire and Use Academic Vocabulary Academic vocabulary is the language you encounter in textbooks and on standardized tests. Review the definitions of these academic vocabulary words.

> **argue** (är´gyōō) v. fight using words; debate
>
> **challenge** (chal´ənj) v. dare; a calling into question
>
> **conclude** (kən klōōd´) v. arrive at a judgment; end
>
> **convince** (kən vins´) v. persuade
>
> **defend** (dē fend´) v. guard from attack; protect
>
> **resolve** (ri zälv´) v. settle; bring to an end

Gather Vocabulary Knowledge Additional vocabulary words are listed below. Categorize the words by deciding whether you know each one well, know it a little bit, or do not know it at all.

> | battle | issue | resist |
> |---|---|---|
> | compete | lose | survival |
> | game | negotiate | win |

Then, do the following:

1. Write the definitions of the words you know.

2. If you think you know a word's meaning, write it down. Consult a dictionary and revise your definition if necessary.

3. Using a print or an online dictionary, look up the meanings of words you do not know. Write down the meanings and study the pronunciations.

4. Use all of the words in two brief paragraphs. In the first paragraph, write about a conflict that had positive results. In the second, discuss a conflict that had negative results.

Common Core State Standards

Speaking and Listening
1. Engage effectively in a range of collaborative discussions with diverse partners on grade 6 topics, texts, and issues, building on others' ideas and expressing their own clearly.

Language
6. Acquire and use accurately grade-appropriate general academic and domain-specific words and phrases; gather vocabulary knowledge when considering a word or phrase important to comprehension or expression.

---

❸ Vocabulary

Acquire and Use Academic Vocabulary

1. Introduce the academic vocabulary words in the first word bank on the student page. Have students preview the words.

2. For each word, have students say the word aloud. Then, use the word in a sentence that defines the word.

Gather Vocabulary Knowledge

1. With the class, review the steps in the activity on the student page. Have students complete the activity independently, with partners, or in small groups.

2. Before students complete the last step, review the words and their meanings as a class. (Definitions appear at the bottom of this page.) Then, have students complete their paragraphs.

🗨 GATHER VOCABULARY KNOWLEDGE

battle (bat´'l) n. fight or major dispute

compete (kəm pēt´) v. contend; take part in a sport, game, or contest

game (gām) n. contest; type of play in which there is usually one winner

issue (ish´ōō) n. problem or point on which you disagree with someone

lose (lōōz) v. fail in a game or dispute

negotiate (ni go´shē āt´) v. settle or come to an agreement

resist (ri zist´) v. oppose actively; refuse to give in

survival (sər vi´vəl) n. the act of lasting or continuing to live

win (win) v. gain a victory or come out ahead

 Video

Watch the Background Video online!

1 Close Reading: Short Story

In the Close Reading Workshop, students will practice using close reading strategies within the context of a particular genre. They will use the features of this genre to help them access the text. All of the close reading strategies align with the Common Core State Standards reading domains:

- **Comprehension:** Key Ideas and Details focuses on what the text says.
- **Text Analysis:** Craft and Structure focuses on how the author conveys the text.
- **Connections:** Integration of Knowledge and Ideas focuses on what the text means and how it changes the reader's view of the world.

MULTIDRAFT READING

Essential Understanding

Explain to students that close reading works best when they read a text multiple times, focusing on different aspects of the text each time.

- **First reading:** Students should read independently to unlock the basic meaning of the text.
- **Second reading:** Students should focus on analyzing key ideas and details and the craft and the structure of the text.
- **Third reading:** Students should focus on integrating knowledge and ideas by connecting the text to the Big Question. The essential understanding students gain from making this connection will help them connect the text to other texts and to the world.

 # Close Reading Workshop

In this workshop you will learn an approach to reading that will deepen your understanding of literature and will help you better appreciate the author's craft. The workshop includes models for close reading, discussion, research, and writing activities. After you have reviewed the strategies and models, practice your skills with the Independent Practice selection.

 **Common Core State Standards**

RL.6.1, RL.6.2, RL.6.3, RL.6.4, RL.6.5; W.6.2, W.6.4, W.6.7, W.6.8, W.6.9; SL.6.1
[For full standards wording, see the standards chart in the front of this book.]

1 CLOSE READING: SHORT STORY

In the beginning of this unit, you will focus on reading various short stories. Use these strategies as you read the texts.

Comprehension: Key Ideas and Details

- Read first to unlock basic meaning.
- Use context clues to define unfamiliar words. Consult a dictionary, if necessary.
- Identify unfamiliar details that you might need to clarify through research.
- Distinguish between what is stated directly and what must be inferred.

Ask yourself questions such as these:
- Who are the main characters?
- What is the setting?
- What is the main conflict?

Text Analysis: Craft and Structure

- Think about the genre of the work and how the author presents ideas.
- Take note of how the author uses dialogue to develop character.
- Determine how the narrator's point of view contributes to the story.

Ask yourself questions such as these:
- Why do the characters behave as they do? How do their actions advance the plot?
- How does the author's word choice affect the story's tone?

Connections: Integration of Knowledge and Ideas

- Look for relationships among key ideas. Identify causes and effects, and comparisons and contrasts.
- Look for important images and symbols and analyze their deeper meaning. Then, connect ideas to determine the theme.
- Compare and contrast this work with other works you have read.

Ask yourself questions such as these:
- How has this work increased my knowledge of a subject or author?
- What is surprising about the story's outcome?

4 UNIT 1 • Is conflict always bad?

@ ACTIVE READING FOR COMMON CORE

Read • Discuss • Research • Write
In this workshop, students will learn how to access text through reading, discussing, researching, and writing. In the first half of the workshop, these activities are modeled for students. In the second half, students have the opportunity to partake in these activities independently.

Read: Students will read and comprehend the Reading Model selection. Annotations call out key points that students should focus on. These annotations model the types of things students should notice when they read the Independent Practice selection later.

Discuss: Students will deepen their understanding of the text through collaborative discussion.

Research: Students will clarify and expand their understanding of the text by conducting research.

Write: Students will synthesize their thoughts and research and will write a response to the text, supporting their ideas with evidence.

2 Read

As you read this short story, take note of the annotations that model ways to closely read the text.

Reading Model

"The Old Grandfather and His Little Grandson" by Leo Tolstoy

The grandfather had become very old. His legs would not carry him, his eyes could not see, his ears could not hear, and he was toothless. When he ate, bits of food sometimes dropped out of his mouth. [1] His son and his son's wife no longer allowed him to eat with them at the table. He had to eat his meals in a corner near the stove. [2]

One day they gave him his food in a bowl. He tried to move the bowl closer; it fell to the floor and broke. [3] His daughter-in-law scolded him. She told him that he spoiled everything in the house and broke their dishes, and she said that from now on he would get his food in a wooden dish. The old man sighed and said nothing. [4]

A few days later, the old man's son and his wife were sitting in their hut, resting and watching their little boy playing on the floor. They saw him putting together something out of small pieces of wood. His father asked him, "What are you making, Misha?"

The little grandson said, "I'm making a wooden bucket. When you and Mamma get old, I'll feed you out of this wooden dish." [5]

[3] The young peasant and his wife looked at each other, and tears filled their eyes. They were ashamed because they had treated the old grandfather so meanly, and from that day they again let the old man eat with them at the table and took better care of him. [6]

Craft and Structure
1 Short, simple words paint a clear picture of the frail and ailing grandfather.

Key Ideas and Details
2 The words "had to" suggest that the grandfather was given no choice; he was forced to eat in a corner.

Integration of Knowledge and Ideas
3 The broken bowl may be a symbol of the grandfather's broken body.

Key Ideas and Details
4 The grandfather's sigh indicates that he is used to being yelled at. His acceptance shows that he is meek and gentle.

Craft and Structure
5 Misha's innocent remark reveals the "lesson" he has learned from his parents. This passage marks the climax of the story.

Integration of Knowledge and Ideas
6 This change in the characters' behavior points to a theme: Treat others the way you wish to be treated.

2 Read

Before students begin reading the model, explain to them that the annotations call out important points in the story related to Key Ideas and Details, Craft and Structure, and Integration of Knowledge and Ideas. Tell students that their understanding and interpretation of the text should not be limited by the existing annotations. Encourage students to use the annotations as a starting point to help them analyze the story further.

3 Integration of Knowledge and Ideas

To move students toward essential understanding, draw their attention to bracketed annotation 3 in the Teacher Edition. **Ask:** What is the outcome of the conflict between the characters? Was the tension between them positive or negative in the end? Explain how the result affects the theme of the story.

Possible response: The outcome is that the parents treat the grandfather with more respect. Before the last sentence, the grandfather's silent suffering indicates that strong people survive through adversity. The theme is not positive or negative but a mixture of both. In the last sentence, the theme shifts to a positive one when the grandfather's suffering results in the parents inviting him back to the table to eat after they learn from their mistakes.

? DEVELOPING ESSENTIAL UNDERSTANDING

Is conflict always bad?
After students have finished reading the model, ask them the following questions to help them deepen their understanding of how the story relates to the Big Question:

- How did the conflict in this story begin? What is the conflict?
- In what ways does this conflict move the plot of the story forward?
- How do the characters react to the conflict?

Remind students that as they read the rest of the selections in this unit, they should ask themselves similar questions to help them connect the texts with the Big Question.

 Audio

Selection Audio is available in the *Student eText* and on the *Hear It!* CD-ROM.

❹ Discuss

Throughout the unit, students will be engaging in discussions about the selections they read. As students discuss, remind them of the following points:

- Come to discussions prepared.
- Support ideas with text evidence.
- Pose and respond to questions that connect the selection to broader themes and ideas.
- Respond thoughtfully to diverse perspectives.

❺ Research

As students conduct research, remind them of the following tips:

- Think carefully about your topic and search terms, and use specific words or phrases whenever possible. For instance, if you want information on the myth of the golden apple, use "golden apple myth" in your search rather than a general term, such as "golden apple."

- Consider the reliability of the sites you visit. Remember that sites with .edu, .gov, and .org are generally more reliable than sites that end with .com.

- Remember to take careful notes as you research. When you include a direct quotation, be sure to use quotation marks in your notes. Later, this strategy will help you remember which pieces of information you quoted directly and which pieces you paraphrased from the source.

❹ Discuss

Sharing your own ideas and listening to the ideas of others can deepen your understanding of a text and help you look at a topic in a whole new way. As you participate in collaborative discussions, work to have a genuine exchange in which classmates build upon one another's ideas. Support your points with evidence and ask meaningful questions.

Discussion Model

Student 1: Tolstoy's description of the grandfather as nearly blind and deaf makes me feel sorry for him. But when I read the sentence, "When he ate, bits of food sometimes dropped out of his mouth," I thought that was a little gross.

Student 2: I agree. I still felt bad for the grandfather, but I also understood where the parents were coming from. Later in the story, when Misha made his parents feel ashamed, I felt kind of ashamed, too.

Student 3: Tolstoy found a good theme for the story. At times, everyone can be hurtful, but we also have the ability to change. This theme seems a lot like the Golden Rule, which says, "Treat others as you want to be treated." I wonder if Tolstoy wrote about the Golden Rule in his other stories and novels.

❺ Research

Targeted research can clarify unfamiliar details and shed light on various aspects of a text. Consider questions that arise in your mind as you read, and use those questions as the basis for research.

Research Model

Question: *What did Tolstoy believe about how we should treat others?*

Key Words for Internet Search: Tolstoy and "Golden Rule"

Result: Journal abstract: <u>Philosophy *Now*</u>, Issue 54

What I Learned: According to scholars, Tolstoy favored "nonresistance to evil." This basically means that he vowed not to harm any human being, even if a person invaded his home and tried to rob him. Tolstoy's theory influenced nonviolent protestors of the twentieth century, including Mohandas Gandhi.

❻ Write

Writing about a text will deepen your understanding of it and will also allow you to share your ideas more formally with others. The following model essay explores the moral tone and characterization of Tolstoy's story and cites evidence to support the main ideas.

Writing Model: Argument

Tolstoy and the Golden Rule

In "The Old Grandfather and His Little Grandson," Tolstoy uses characterizations of the grandfather, his son and daughter-in-law, and his grandson to argue that people should treat others the way they would like to be treated.

> Many effective essays begin with a thesis statement, or summary of the author's argument.

Tolstoy sketches his characters in just a few words. He tells the reader that the grandfather is "very old" and that "his legs would not carry him, his eyes could not see, his ears could not hear, and he was toothless." This description breaks the grandfather down into broken body parts, but it also creates sympathy for him.

> The writer supports claims with specific details from the story.

After the grandfather breaks a bowl, his daughter-in-law scolds him and tells him that he spoils "everything in the house," and he will have to eat from a wooden bowl from now on. The way the son and daughter-in-law treat the grandfather shows that they both lack sympathy. However, the reader can understand the couple's refusal to eat with someone who "drops bits of food" from his mouth.

> The writer cites a specific example to show how Tolstoy creates realistic situations that are complex.

The couple's son, Misha, reflects the idea that children learn the attitudes they observe in adults. Because Misha heard his parents telling his grandfather to eat out of a wooden dish, he assumes that is how to treat elderly people. The little boy's kindness shows when he thinks ahead, making a "wooden dish" for his parents to eat from when they are old. Misha's innocence and kindness make his parents feel ashamed of the way they have treated the grandfather. The couple—and the reader—realize they would not want to be treated that way when they are old and weak.

Tolstoy held several moral beliefs that he often wrote about. He tried to avoid anger, show love for others through the "Golden Rule," and display nonviolent resistance to evil. The grandfather's response to the scolding from his daughter-in-law matches these beliefs: "The old man sighed and said nothing." The grandfather was being attacked, but he did not show anger. Instead, he nonviolently resisted his son's and daughter-in-law's cruel treatment.

> By incorporating information from research, the writer makes a connection between Tolstoy's moral beliefs and the theme of the story.

---

❻ Write

Review the writing model with the class, using the annotations to analyze how the writer uses evidence to support his or her ideas.

Genre Requirements

Remind students that when they write responses to literature, they should do the following:

- Introduce the topic at the beginning of the essay.
- Organize ideas and information in order to make important connections.
- Support claims with specific details from the literary work.
- Provide a conclusion that supports the information presented.

Teaching from the Writing Model

1. Point out to students that the first paragraph states the writer's thesis, or the focus of the essay.
2. Point out that the writer uses specific examples from the text to support his or her argument.
3. The last paragraph reinforces the writer's argument with information from research and restates the thesis.

CLOSE READING TOOL

Students may close read and mark the text using the **Close Reading Tool,** which is available online. Scaffolds are provided for students who need help. Students who do not have online access may use the *Close Reading Notebook* to mark the text with their close reading responses.

7 **Independent Practice**

The Independent Practice is an optional assignment. You may wish to administer it at this point and use it as formative assessment, or you may wish to administer it at the end of Part 1 as summative assessment.

If you wish to administer the Independent Practice but feel your students will struggle with it, you can use the questions in the side margins of this Teacher's Edition to help guide them.

8 **Key Ideas and Details**

Ask: What challenges might a wounded wolf face in a setting like this?

Possible response: A wounded wolf could be further injured by slipping on a rock or ice. It would be difficult for him to stay warm and to keep up with his pack.

9 **Craft and Structure**

Ask: What does this action tell you about Roko?

Possible response: It shows that Roko is brave, protective, and loyal.

10 **Key Ideas and Details**

Ask: What conflict does Roko face?

Possible response: Roko is injured and other animals, including a raven, await his death. The loud winds make it impossible for Roko to get help by letting his pack know he is hurt.

🔊 **Audio**

Selection Audio is available in the *Student eText* and on the *Hear It!* CD-ROM.

---

7 As you read the story, apply the close reading strategies you have learned. You may need to read the story multiple times.

The Wounded Wolf
by Jean Craighead George

Meet the Author **8**

Award-winning novelist, nonfiction writer, short-story writer, and memoirist **Jean Craighead George** (1919–2012) was born in Washington, D.C. A naturalist as much as an author, George wrote more than 100 books about the natural world, most of them for children. Her best-known works are *Julie of the Wolves* (1972) and *My Side of the Mountain* (1959).

CLOSE READING TOOL

Read and respond to this selection online using the **Close Reading Tool.**

A wounded wolf climbs Toklat Ridge,[1] a massive spine of rock and ice. As he limps, dawn strikes the ridge and lights it up with sparks and stars. Roko, the wounded wolf, blinks in the ice fire, then stops to rest and watch his pack run the thawing Arctic valley.

They plunge and turn. They fight the mighty caribou that struck young Roko with his hoof and wounded him. He jumped between the beast and Kiglo, leader of the Toklat pack. Young Roko spun and fell. Hooves, paws, and teeth roared over him. And then his pack and the beast were gone.

Gravely injured, Roko pulls himself toward the shelter rock. Weakness overcomes him. He stops. He and his pack are thin and hungry. This is the season of starvation. The winter's harvest has been taken. The produce of spring has not begun.

Young Roko glances down the valley. He droops his head and stiffens his tail to signal to his pack that he is badly hurt. Winds wail. A frigid blast picks up long shawls of snow and drapes them between young Roko and his pack. And so his message is not read.

A raven scouting Toklat Ridge sees Roko's signal. "Kong, kong, kong," he bells—death is coming to the ridge; there will be flesh and bone for all. His voice rolls out across the valley. It penetrates the rocky cracks where the Toklat ravens rest. One by one they hear and spread their wings. They beat their way to Toklat Ridge. They alight upon the snow and walk behind the wounded wolf.

"Kong," they toll[2] with keen excitement, for the raven clan is hungry, too. "Kong, kong"—there will be flesh and bone for all. Roko snarls and hurries toward the shelter rock. A cloud of snow envelops him. He limps in blinding whiteness now. A ghostly presence flits around. "Hahahahahahaha," the white fox states—death is coming to the Ridge. Roko smells the fox tagging at his heels.

The cloud whirls off. Two golden eyes look up at Roko. The snowy owl has heard the ravens and joined the deathwatch.

---

1. **Toklat Ridge** the top of a mountain located in Alaska's Denali National Park and Preserve.
2. **toll** (tōl) *v.* announce.

Ⓒ **ACTIVE READING FOR COMMON CORE**

Read • Discuss • Research • Write

In the Independent Practice section of the Close Reading Workshop, students will practice the reading, discussing, researching, and writing strategies they learned in the modeling section. They will also deepen their essential understanding of the Big Question.

Read: Students will read and comprehend the selection. They should note significant points in the text that relate to Key Ideas and Details, Craft and Structure, and Integration of Knowledge and Ideas. They should use the annotations in the Reading Model that they read earlier as a guide. After students have

finished reading the story, they will answer Literary Analysis questions.

Discuss: Students will deepen their understanding of the text through collaborative discussion.

Research: Students will clarify and expand their understanding of the text by conducting research.

Write: Students will synthesize their thoughts and research by writing a response to the text, supporting their ideas with evidence.

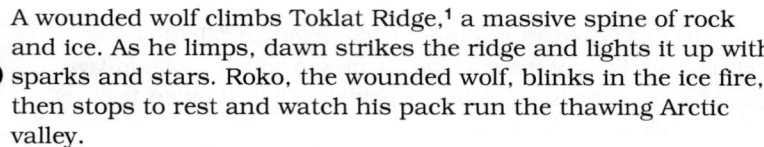

Roko limps along. The ravens walk. The white fox leaps. The snowy owl flies and hops along the rim of Toklat Ridge. Roko stops. Below the ledge out on the flats the musk-ox herd is circling. They form a ring and all face out, a fort of heads and horns and fur that sweeps down to their hooves. Their circle means to Roko that an enemy is present. He squints and smells the wind. It carries scents of thawing ice, broken grass—and earth. The grizzly bear is up! He has awakened from his winter's sleep. A craving need for flesh will drive him.

Roko sees the shelter rock. He strains to reach it. He stumbles. The ravens move in closer. The white fox boldly walks beside him. "Hahaha," he yaps. The snowy owl flies ahead, alights, and waits.

The grizzly hears the eager fox and rises on his flat hind feet. He twists his powerful neck and head. His great paws dangle at his chest. He sees the animal procession and hears the ravens' knell[3] of death. Dropping to all fours, he joins the march up Toklat Ridge.

Roko stops; his breath comes hard. A raven alights upon his back and picks the open wound. Roko snaps. The raven flies and circles back. The white fox nips at Roko's toes. The snowy owl inches closer. The grizzly bear, still dulled by sleep, stumbles onto Toklat Ridge.

Only yards from the shelter rock, Roko falls.

Instantly the ravens mob him. They scream and peck and stab at his eyes. The white fox leaps upon his wound. The snowy owl sits and waits.

Young Roko struggles to his feet. He bites the ravens. Snaps the fox. And lunges at the stoic[4] owl. He turns and warns the grizzly bear. Then he bursts into a run and falls against the shelter rock. The wounded wolf wedges down between the rock and barren ground. Now protected on three sides, he turns and faces all his foes.

The ravens step a few feet closer. The fox slides toward him on his belly. The snowy owl blinks and waits, and on the ridge rim roars the hungry grizzly bear.

Roko growls.

The sun comes up. Far across the Toklat Valley, Roko hears his pack's "hunt's end" song. The music wails and sobs, wilder than the bleating wind. The hunt song ends. Next comes the roll call. Each member of the Toklat pack barks to say that he is home and well.

---

3. **knell** (nel) *n.* mournful sound, like a slowly ringing bell—usually indicating a death.
4. **stoic** (stō ik) *adj.* calm and unaffected by hardship.

11 Key Ideas and Details

Ask: How do Roko's actions in this scene influence the behavior of the other animals on Toklat Ridge?

Possible response: Roko's limping tells the other animals he is injured and might die, which spurs them to follow him.

12 Craft and Structure

Ask: What type of characterization does the author use here? Describe Roko, based on this passage.

Possible response: The author uses indirect characterization because she describes Roko's actions and leaves it up to the reader to determine what those actions say about Roko. Roko is brave and strong because he fights back even though he is hurt. He is clever because he runs to a place where he is protected from the other animals.

13 Key Ideas and Details

Ask: Why is the raven's action important to the plot of the story?

Possible response: The raven's action lets the pack know that Roko is dying.

14 Integration of Knowledge and Ideas

Ask: How does this paragraph affect the central conflict in the story?

Possible response: This paragraph is the height of the tension in the story and also signals the beginning of the resolution of the conflict. After the "deathwatch moves in close" upon Roko, Kiglo comes to help him.

"Kiglo here," Roko hears his leader bark. There is a pause. It is young Roko's turn. He cannot lift his head to answer: the pack is silent. The leader starts the count once more. "Kiglo here."—a pause. Roko cannot answer.

The wounded wolf whimpers softly. A mindful raven hears. "Kong, kong, kong," he tolls—this is the end. His booming sounds across the valley. The wolf pack hears the raven's message that something is dying. They know it is Roko, who has not answered roll call.

The hours pass. The wind slams snow on Toklat Ridge. Massive clouds blot out the sun. In their gloom Roko sees the deathwatch move in closer. Suddenly he hears the musk-oxen thundering into their circle. The ice cracks as the grizzly leaves. The ravens burst into the air. The white fox runs. The snowy owl flaps to the top of the shelter rock. And Kiglo rounds the knoll.

In his mouth he carries meat. He drops it close to Roko's head and wags his tail excitedly. Roko licks Kiglo's chin to honor him. Then Kiglo puts his mouth around Roko's nose. This gesture says "I am your leader." And by mouthing Roko, he binds him and all the wolves together.

The wounded wolf wags his tail. Kiglo trots away.

Already Roko's wound feels better. He gulps the food and feels his strength return. He shatters bone, flesh, and gristle and shakes the scraps out on the snow. The hungry ravens swoop upon them. The white fox snatches up a bone. The snowy owl gulps down flesh and fur. And Roko wags his tail and watches.

For days Kiglo brings young Roko food. He gnashes, gorges, and shatters bits upon the snow.

A purple sandpiper winging north sees ravens, owl, and fox. And he drops in upon the feast. The long-tailed jaeger gull flies down and joins the crowd on Toklat Ridge. Roko wags his tail.

One dawn he moves his wounded leg. He stretches it and pulls himself into the sunlight. He walks—he romps. He runs in circles. He leaps and plays with chunks of ice. Suddenly he stops. The "hunt's end" song rings out. Next comes the roll call.

"Kiglo here."

"Roko here," he barks out strongly.

The pack is silent.

"Kiglo here," the leader repeats.

"Roko here."

Across the distance comes the sound of whoops and yips and barks and howls. They fill the dawn with celebration. And Roko prances down the Ridge.

Vocabulary ►
gnashes (nash′ iz) *v.*
bites with grinding teeth

If you are using the Independent Practice as formative assessment, use the rubric below to evaluate students' performances.

Independent Practice Rubric	Rating Scale				
Close Reading: How well does the student use close reading strategies to answer the questions?	*not very* 1	2	3	4	*very* 5
Support/Elaboration: How well does the student support points with textual or other evidence?	1	2	3	4	5
Insight: How original, sophisticated, or compelling are the insights the student achieves?	1	2	3	4	5
Expression of Ideas: How well does the student use language, including word choice and conventions, in the expression of ideas?	1	2	3	4	5

Close Reading Activities

Comprehension: **Key Ideas and Details**

1. **(a)** How was Roko injured? **(b) Analyze:** What actions does Roko take to save himself?

2. **(a)** How does Kiglo learn that Roko is hurt? **(b) Infer:** What does this evidence show about how wolves take care of pack members?

3. **Summarize:** Write a brief, objective summary of the story. Cite story details in your writing.

Text Analysis: **Craft and Structure**

4. **(a)** What are some specific words the author uses to describe Roko and his actions? **(b) Infer:** What information do these words convey about Roko?

5. **(a) Explain:** What is the main conflict in the story? **(b) Interpret:** How is this conflict resolved?

6. **(a) Describe:** How does the author describe the setting? Cite specific details from the text. **(b) Apply:** How does the story's setting contribute to the conflict?

7. **(a)** List two examples that show how the wolves help each other in this story. **(b) Synthesize:** What insight can you gain from the wolves' behavior?

Connections: **Integration of Knowledge and Ideas**

Discuss
In a **small-group discussion,** share your ideas about where in the story the climax occurs. Use evidence from the text to support your main points.

Research
Jean Craighead George once spent a summer in Alaska, observing wolf packs and learning how they communicate. Briefly research the structure of wolf society, including: **(a)** pecking order; **(b)** the care and education of pups; **(c)** communication.

Take notes as you perform your research. Then, write an **explanation** of how George's depiction of wolf behavior in "The Wounded Wolf" compares with scientists' findings on this topic.

Write
Reread the story to identify ways in which Roko and the other animals behave like humans. Then, write a **comparison-and-contrast essay** in which you describe ways in which the animals are similar to humans and ways in which they are different. Cite details from the story to support your analysis.

> **Is conflict always bad?**
> Consider the conflicts between Roko and the forces of nature that oppose him. Would the story have had a happy ending if George had written it from another animal's point of view? Explain.

Discuss
Students may argue for several different possibilities. Most students, however, will see the climax as the section in which Kiglo "rounds the knoll," bringing meat to Roko. After this point, the conflict is resolved as Roko heals and rejoins his pack.

Research
Students should use the identified aspects of wolf society to compare George's depiction of wolf behavior in "The Wounded Wolf" with scientists' findings.

Write
Student essays should identify details from the story to compare human behavior with animal behavior.

> **Is conflict always bad?**
> Reponses should address other possible points of view and whether those versions of the story would have endings that would be considered "happy."

❶ About the Quotation

At the age of 20, Frederick Douglass (1818–1895) escaped from slavery to become a well-known abolitionist, writer, and defender of the rights of African Americans and women.

Discussion Ask students whether they agree with Douglass's quote. Ask them to define the word *struggle* and give examples of the types of struggles people endure. Have them explain and support their positions with sound reasoning and evidence.

❷ Critical Viewing

Pose the critical viewing question to the class. Then, guide the class in a discussion about the question. Encourage students to build upon each other's ideas as they share responses. Remind students to support their responses with reasons and evidence.

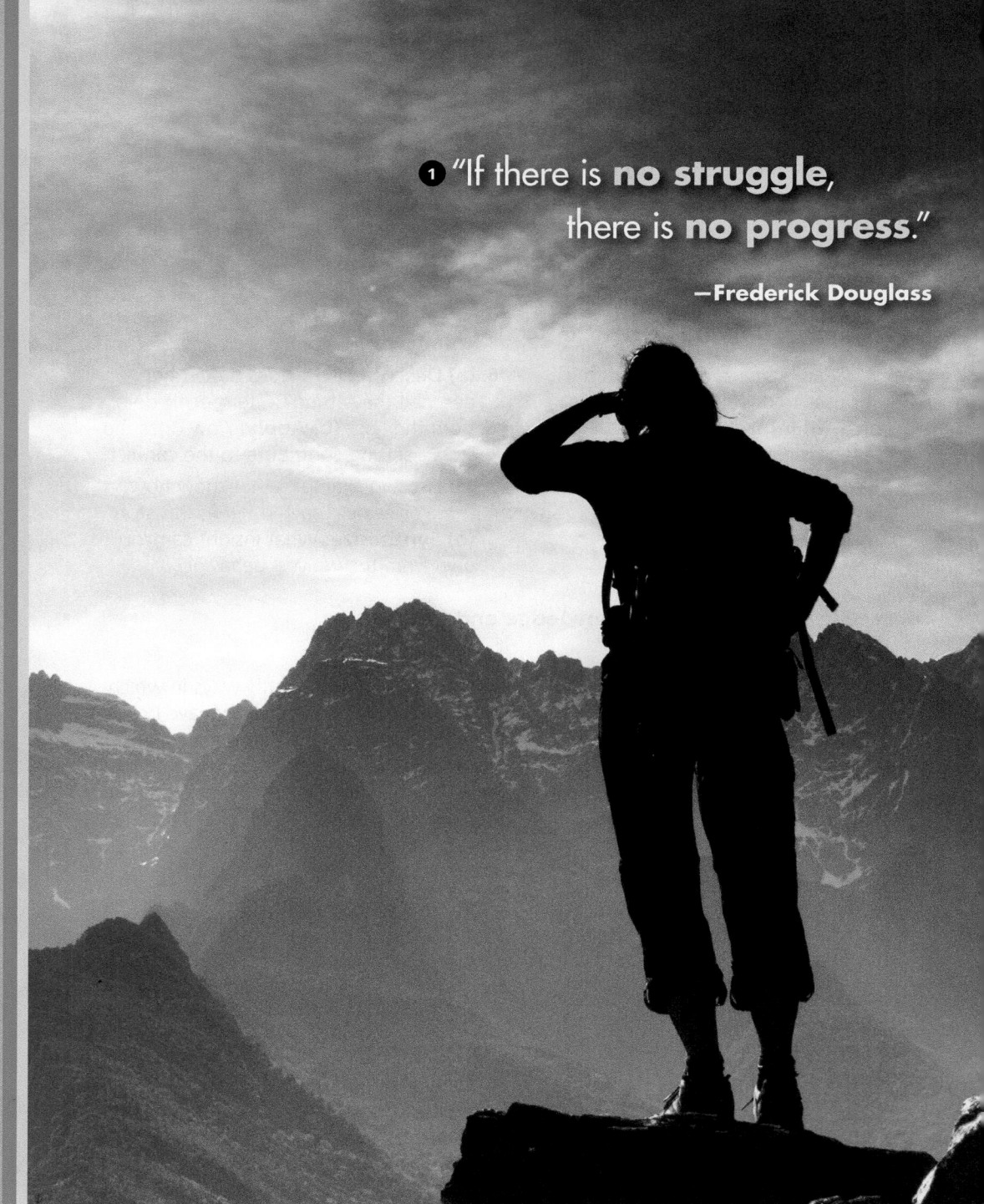

❶ "If there is **no struggle**, there is **no progress**."

—Frederick Douglass

❓ DEVELOPING ESSENTIAL UNDERSTANDING

Is conflict always bad?
Explain to students that they will continue to consider the Big Question as they work through the selections in Part 2 of the unit.

• As students read each selection, they will look for details related to the Big Question and take notes.

• At the end of each selection, students will answer a Literary Analysis question that is related to the Big Question.

• Students will deepen their knowledge of the selections and their understanding of the Big Question through reading, speaking, listening, researching, and writing.

PART 2
TEXT ANALYSIS GUIDED EXPLORATION

CHARACTERS AND CONFLICT

As you read the stories in this section, explore ways in which the authors bring to life various characters who struggle to overcome conflicts. The quotation on the opposite page will help start your thinking about ways in which people triumph even in difficult situations.

2 ◄ **CRITICAL VIEWING** What struggle might the person in this photograph be facing? Can dealing with struggles enhance a person's life? Explain.

3 **READINGS IN PART 2**

SHORT STORY
Stray
Cynthia Rylant (p. 20)

SHORT STORY
The Tail
Joyce Hansen (p. 30)

SHORT STORY
Zlateh the Goat
Isaac Bashevis Singer (p. 46)

SHORT STORY
The Circuit
Francisco Jiménez (p. 60)

CLOSE READING TOOL
Use the Close Reading Tool to practice the strategies you learned in this unit.

PART 2 • Characters and Conflict **13**

CUSTOMIZING THE TEXT SET

Close Reading Tool
Use the Close Reading Tool to project the selections on a whiteboard and work through them as a whole-class activity. Students also have the opportunity to read those selections independently, with scaffolds available as needed.

Curriculum Builder
Customize this program by rearranging existing selections, adding selection titles of your choosing, and uploading your own resources—all online!

3 **Readings in Part 2**
About the Texts
(For quantitative and qualitative measures of text complexity, see the rubrics on the opening pages of each selection.)

SHORT STORY: Stray

Summary Doris rescues an abandoned puppy after a snowstorm despite the fact that her parents have told her they cannot afford a pet. Her parents agree to let her keep the puppy until they can take it to the pound. Doris forms a bond with the puppy and is heartbroken when she must give it up, but her father surprises her with a last-minute decision to keep the dog.

SHORT STORY: The Tail

Summary Tasha's summer plans come to a halt when her parents decide that she is old enough to babysit her younger brother. When she bends the rules and neglects to keep an eye on Junior, he strays. After Tasha finds him, she realizes that one rarely appreciates something until it's almost lost.

SHORT STORY: Zlateh the Goat

Summary Young Aaron is told to sell Zlateh, the family goat, to the butcher so that his family will have money to buy what they need for the Hanukkah celebration. As Aaron sadly leads Zlateh to town, the weather changes and they become lost in a snowstorm and must take shelter in a haystack for several days. When the weather clears, Aaron takes Zlateh home.

SHORT STORY: The Circuit

Summary The son of migrant workers, Panchito goes to school in Fresno, California, while his father and brother pick grapes. A teacher befriends Panchito and offers to teach him to play the trumpet. When Panchito rushes home to share his news, he discovers that his family's belongings are packed and ready for another move.

 **Audio**
Summary Audio is available in the *Student eText* and on the *Hear It!* CD-ROM.

PART 2 • Characters and Conflict **13**

❶ Elements of a Short Story

1. Introduce the elements of a short story, using the instruction on the student page.

Have students provide a specific example of each element, if possible, from a short story they've read.

Sample responses: *Plot*—A mongoose and a snake fight a battle; *Characters*—a mongoose, two evil snakes, a family with a little boy; *Setting*—a jungle; *Conflict*—An external conflict between the mongoose and the two snakes; *Theme*—Courage, hard work, and craftiness pay off in the end

2. Discuss the graphic organizer on the student page. Then, have students tell the story "The Lion and the Mouse" in their own words.

Sample response: A lion and a mouse live in the jungle. One day, the lion catches the mouse, but he kindly agrees to let the mouse go. Later, the lion gets caught in a hunter's trap. The mouse frees his new friend by chewing through the rope, proving that sometimes the weak can help the strong.

 Focus on Craft and Structure

❶ Elements of a Short Story

A short story is a brief work of fiction that contains **plot, characters, setting,** and **theme.**

A **short story** is a brief fictional narrative that can usually be read in one sitting. Although it is short, it is a complete work featuring the same basic elements as longer works of fiction.

Plot is the sequence of events in a story. It consists of a series of scenes or episodes that are linked to each other. Early scenes advance the plot by bringing about later ones.

Conflict is a problem or struggle between opposing forces.

- An **internal conflict** takes place in the mind of a character. The character struggles to make a decision, take an action, or overcome an obstacle.

- An **external conflict** is a conflict in which a character struggles against an outside force, such as nature or another character.

Characters are the people or animals who take part in the action of a story. An author brings a character to life through **characterization**—the art of creating and developing a character.

- A **character's traits,** or qualities, help readers understand the character and his or her actions.

- A **character's motives** are the reasons for his or her actions.

Setting is the time and place of the story's action. Setting can create a specific atmosphere or **mood** in a story. It may even relate directly to the story's conflict.

Theme is the central insight expressed in a short story. It might be stated directly or hinted at through the words and actions of the characters.

Short stories are made up of several key elements.

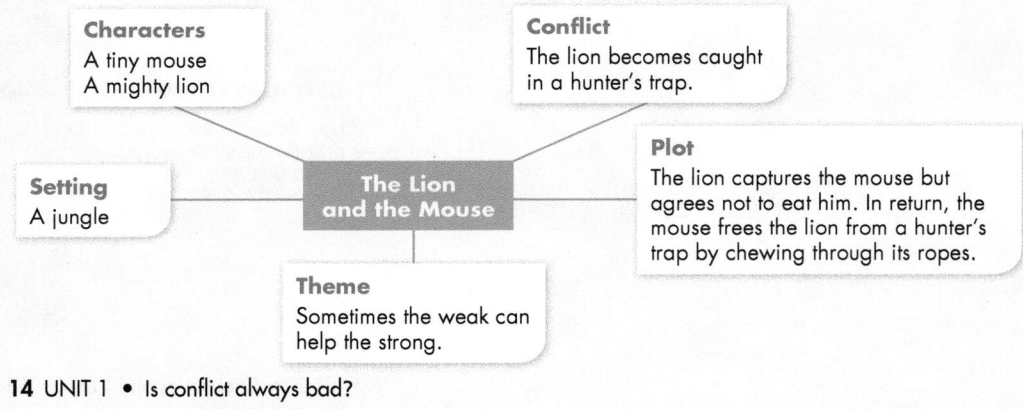

Characters
A tiny mouse
A mighty lion

Conflict
The lion becomes caught in a hunter's trap.

Setting
A jungle

The Lion and the Mouse

Plot
The lion captures the mouse but agrees not to eat him. In return, the mouse frees the lion from a hunter's trap by chewing through its ropes.

Theme
Sometimes the weak can help the strong.

14 UNIT 1 • Is conflict always bad?

❷ Structure in Short Stories

A short story must grab a reader's attention right away. Because the work is brief, every part of the story must move the action forward. The **structure** of a short story is the way it is put together. A story's plot is structured in a way that helps the story progress. These elements make up the basic structure of a plot:

- **Exposition** is the story's setup. This part of the plot introduces the characters, setting, and basic situation. The story's conflict is usually introduced in the exposition.

- **Conflict** is the story's central problem. It might involve a struggle between characters, a struggle between a character and an outside force, or a struggle within the mind of a character.

- **Rising action** is made up of events and complications that increase the tension in the story. This tension builds to a climax.

- **Climax** is the high point of the story—its most intense, exciting, or important part. It is the point at which the story's outcome becomes clear.

- **Falling action** sets up the story's ending. It is the part of the story in which events are settled.

- **Resolution** is the final outcome of the story. Usually, a story's conflict is settled in the resolution. In some stories, however, the conflict is left unsettled.

In the best short stories, readers want to find out what will happen next and how the characters will respond or change.

As you read a short story, notice how particular words, sentences, and events fit into the structure and help you understand the setting, plot, and theme.

Common Core State Standards

Reading Literature

3. Describe how a particular story's or drama's plot unfolds in a series of episodes as well as how the characters respond or change as the plot moves toward a resolution.

5. Analyze how a particular sentence, chapter, scene, or stanza fits into the overall structure of a text and contributes to the development of the theme, setting, or plot.

Plot Structure

PART 2 • Focus on Craft and Structure **15**

❷ Structure in Short Stories

1. Introduce the elements of short stories, using the instruction on the student page.

2. Explain that the plot of each short story will include all the elements listed on the page.

3. **Ask:** If you are reading the part of the story that builds tension, what element are you reading?

   Answer: the rising action

4. **Ask:** What is the most exciting or intense part of the story called?

   Answer: the climax

5. **Ask:** In what part of the story does the author introduce the characters and the background information?

   Answer: the exposition

6. Discuss students' experiences reading short stories. Encourage students to describe specific stories they have read, identifying the conflict and climax in each one.

❖ DIFFERENTIATED INSTRUCTION

Support for Less Proficient Readers
Have students read the **Learning About Short Stories** pages for "The Wounded Wolf" in the *Reader's Notebook: Adapted Version*. This version provides a basic-level introduction to short stories.

EL Support for English Learners
Have students read the **Learning About Short Stories** pages for "The Wounded Wolf" in the *Reader's Notebook: English Learner's Version*. This version provides a basic-level introduction to short stories.

❶ Analyzing Structure, Conflict, and Characterization

1. Introduce the concepts of structure and conflict, using the instruction on the student page.

2. Use the example to show how the elements of a story can have multiple purposes. Explain that in addition to developing the setting, the scene helps set a mysterious, uncertain mood and also gives the reader information about the character and the plot: the character is trying to find his or her way and is shivering and unsteady.

3. Explain that conflict is a key element of plot. Have students suggest examples of internal and external conflicts from stories or their own lives.

   Sample responses: Students may describe internal conflicts, such as struggling to make important decisions or external conflicts, such as arguments with friends.

❶ Analyzing Structure, Conflict, and Characterization

Characters respond and change as a short story's plot unfolds.

The best short stories are **structured,** or put together, in ways that build readers' interest and move the action forward. In a good short story, each scene or episode has a purpose and contributes to the overall impact of the story. For example, the details in a specific scene can develop a key element, such as **setting.**

Example: Scene Developing Setting

The long, narrow hallway was completely deserted. I squinted in the dim light, struggling to see the door at the far end. The musty dampness sent a shiver through my body as I put one unsteady foot in front of the other.

In the example above, the words and sentences work together to develop the setting: a damp, dark, empty hallway. This scene also introduces another key story element. Notice that the narrator is *unsteady.* This detail indicates a possible **conflict,** or problem. Further details in the story will establish what specific conflict the narrator faces. Conflict moves a story forward because a reader must keep reading to find out what the problem is and how it affects the characters.

Types of Conflict As a short story progresses, scenes or events in the plot contribute to the conflict and its **resolution**—the way in which the conflict is settled. Conflicts may be *internal* or *external.* There are different types of external conflict, such as conflict with nature and conflict with society. Review the examples in the chart below. As you read a variety of short stories, you will find that some stories have several conflicts, which are usually related to each other.

Types of Conflict

Internal Conflict: a problem that takes place in a character's mind
  Examples:
  • a fight to overcome a feeling, like insecurity
  • a struggle to do the right thing
  • a struggle to choose between two courses of action

External Conflict: a struggle against an outside force
  Examples:
  • a fight or argument between two people
  • a struggle against a natural force, such as an earthquake
  • a struggle against a social institution, such as a law or a tradition

THINK ALOUD

Conflict

To model the skill of identifying and describing the conflict in a story, use the following think aloud. Say to students:

> To identify the conflict in a story, I can ask myself, "What is the main character trying to do?" The conflict is the problem or struggle that is preventing him or her from taking this action. Perhaps the problem is another character who is standing in the way. Perhaps it is nature or society that causes the struggle. In these cases, the conflict is external. I might also look for details that suggest an internal conflict: perhaps the main character can't make up his or her mind, or perhaps he or she feels too insecure to take action. Once I have identified the conflict, I can read on to find out how the conflict will be resolved.

Characterization A key part of the experience of reading a short story is getting to know the characters and finding out how they respond to the conflicts they face. Characterization is the method an author uses to develop characters and reveal their **traits,** or qualities.

There are two types of characterization. With **direct characterization,** the author makes statements that directly describe what the character is like.

> **Example: Direct Characterization**
>
> Mariah is the bravest girl in the sixth grade. She may be pale and tiny, but nothing scares her—not spiders, not huge barking dogs, not even mean old Mr. Jonas down the block.

With **indirect characterization,** the author reveals a character through that character's words and actions or through the words and actions of other characters.

> **Example: Indirect Characterization**
>
> I don't care what those young fools say; I will not leave this place. I have lived on this mountain since that roaring highway was a dirt road. My body may be bent, but I will stand firm.

Characters and Conflict As characters react to the conflicts in a story, their responses help advance the plot as well as fuel their own growth and development as characters. The example that follows describes a story about a young boy.

Notice how each of the boy's actions brings about a new development in the plot. In turn, each new development causes a change in the boy's actions or attitude.

> **Scene:** A boy stays up late playing video games.

↓

> **Scene:** The next morning, he remembers he has a math test. He fears he will do poorly because he did not study.

↓

> **Scene:** The boy tells his mother he is sick so that she will let him stay home from school.

↓

> **Scene:** The boy's mother says she is sorry he is sick, because the family will have to cancel a surprise trip to a theme park the next day.

↓

> **Scene:** The boy tells his mother he feels better and wants to go to school after all.

Characters and Theme Often, the changes a character undergoes are clues to the story's theme, or the insight the story conveys. For instance, in the example above, the story's theme might be stated like this: *It is always best to tell the truth.* As you read, pay close attention to clues in dialogue or description that might provide a window into a story's theme.

4. Introduce the concept of characterization, using the instruction on the student page.

5. Explain that authors use two types of characterization: direct and indirect. Read and discuss the examples with students.

   Ask: What words and phrases in the first example directly describe Mariah?

   Sample response: "bravest," "pale," "tiny," "nothing scares her"

   Ask: What words in the second example indirectly describe the speaker? What do they tell you about the person?

   Sample responses: "those young fools"; "I will not leave this place"; "since that roaring highway was a dirt road"; "My body may be bent." These words show that the person is old and determined.

6. Review the example plot outline. Emphasize that each decision the character makes furthers the plot.

   Ask: What causes the boy to lie to his mother?

   Sample response: He does not want to go to school because he has not studied for his test.

7. Review the definition of a theme: the central insight expressed in a short story.

   Ask: How can you tell what the theme of this story might be?

   Sample response: The boy tells the truth, so he will probably get to go to the theme park with his family. This tells me that telling the truth is best, which is the theme of the story.

LESSON PACING GUIDE

Stray

DAY 1 — Preteach/Teach

- Administer the Reading and Vocabulary Warm-ups, as necessary.
- Introduce the Key Ideas and Details skill: Make Predictions.
- Introduce the Craft and Structure skill: Plot.
- Use the Close Reading Model to demonstrate the application of the skills.
- Review the selection vocabulary, as necessary, with students who need additional support.
- Prepare students to read the selection by reviewing with them the Multidraft Reading Strategies.

DAY 2 — Teach

- Informally monitor comprehension while students read.
- Use the Comprehension questions to confirm understanding.
- Develop students' ability to make predictions and analyze plot using the sidenote questions.
- Reinforce vocabulary with the Vocabulary notes.
- Reinforce unit focus standards using the Spiral Review prompts.

DAY 3 — Assess

- Assess students' comprehension and mastery of the skills by having them answer the Literary Analysis questions.
- Have students complete the Vocabulary activities.
- Develop students' understanding of roots and affixes by having them complete the Word Study activities.

DAY 4 — Extend/Assess

- Build students' ability to master grammar concepts and conventions by having them complete the Conventions lesson.
- Have students complete the Writing to Sources activity and write an explanatory text. (You may assign as homework.)
- Extend learning by having students complete the Research and Technology activity: a brochure.
- Administer the Selection Test or Open-Book Test.

Common Core State Standards

Reading Literature 3. Describe how a particular story's plot unfolds in a series of episodes as well as how the characters respond or change as the plot moves toward a resolution.

Writing 2.b. Develop the topic with relevant facts, definitions, concrete details, quotations, or other information and examples.

2.e. Establish and maintain a formal style.

4. Produce clear and coherent writing in which the development, organization, and style are appropriate to the task, purpose, and audience.

7. Conduct short research projects to answer a question, drawing on several sources and refocusing the inquiry when appropriate.

Speaking and Listening 3. Delineate a speaker's argument and specific claims, distinguishing claims that are supported by reasons and evidence from claims that are not.

Language 2. Demonstrate command of the conventions of standard English capitalization, punctuation, and spelling when writing.

4.b. Use common, grade-appropriate Greek or Latin affixes and roots as clues to the meaning of a word.

Daily Block Scheduling

Each day in this Lesson Pacing Guide represents a 40–50 minute period. Teachers using block scheduling may combine days to revise pacing. In addition, teachers may differentiate and support core instruction by integrating components for extended and intensive support as students require. See the Guide to Resources (facing page).

GUIDE TO RESOURCES

Section		Learner Levels L1	L2	L3	L4	EL	ALL	Resources	Where Found PRINT	CD	ONLINE
Warm Up		✓	✓			✓		Vocabulary Warm-ups			✓
		✓	✓			✓		Reading Warm-ups			✓
							✓	Background Video			✓
							✓	Selection Audio		Hear It!	✓
Comprehension/ Selection Support							✓	Writing About the Big Question	Student Companion Workbook		✓
							✓	Literary Analysis	Student Companion Workbook		✓
							✓	Reading	Student Companion Workbook		✓
							✓	Vocabulary Builder	Student Companion Workbook		✓
					✓			Enrichment			✓
			✓	✓	✓			Conventions	Student Companion Workbook		✓
			✓	✓	✓			Writing to Sources	Student Companion Workbook		✓
			✓	✓	✓			Research and Technology	Student Companion Workbook		
Differentiated Instruction/ Additional Support							✓	Additional Standards Practice	Common Core Companion		✓
							✓	Close Reading Practice	Close Reading Notebook		✓
		✓	✓					Adapted Reader's Notebook			✓
						✓		English Reader's Notebook:			✓
						✓		Spanish Reader's Notebook			✓
						✓		Graphic Organizer A			✓
		✓	✓			✓		Graphic Organizer B			✓
		✓	✓			✓		"A Place Where Strays Can Stay"	Reality Central Student Edition and Writing Journal		✓
		✓	✓			✓		Practice and Assess	Reading Kit		✓
Monitor Progress							✓	Selection Test		Exam View	✓
							✓	Open-Book Test		Exam View	✓
Digital Resources							✓	Close Reading Tool			✓
							✓	Online Writer's Notebook			✓

One-on-one teaching   Group work   Whole class instruction   Independent work   A Assessment   Digital Resource

LEARNER LEVELS

L1 Special-Needs Students
L2 Below-Level Students (Tier 2)
L3 On-Level Students (Tier 1)
L4 Advanced Students (Tier 1)
EL English Learners
All All Students

① **Is conflict always bad?**

Read • Discuss • Research • Write As students read, they will explore the Big Question through text analysis of the selection. Encourage students to take notes as they read and raise additional questions, using text evidence to support their thoughts. Students should refer to their notes to help them deepen their understanding of the selection through discussion, research, and writing.

② **Close Reading Focus**

1. Encourage students to record their predictions in a three-column chart. Students should note story details in the first column, their own background knowledge or personal experiences in the second column, and their prediction in the third column. Students' predictions should be based on the information in the first two columns.

2. To help students remember plot elements, encourage them to think of a simple story, such as "The Three Little Pigs." The first sentence, "Once upon a time there were three little pigs," is the exposition. The events in the middle, when the pigs each build their house and the wolf destroys it, form the rising action. The climax, or turning point, comes when the wolf falls down the chimney. The rest of the events are the falling action, before the resolution when the pigs win.

Meet the Author

As a child, **Cynthia Rylant** (b. 1954) never imagined that she would become a writer. "I always felt my life was too limited," she says. At age twenty-four, however, she found that her life did in fact contain the seeds of many stories. Her first book, *When I Was Young in the Mountains,* describes her childhood in the hills of West Virginia. Rylant lived with her grandparents for four years in a tiny house without plumbing. The hardships she experienced are reflected in some of her stories. Since her first book, Rylant has written more than sixty children's books. Unlike many writers, she writes by hand, not on a computer.

© **Common Core State Standards**

Reading Literature
3. Describe how a particular story's plot unfolds in a series of episodes as well as how the characters respond or change as the plot moves toward a resolution.

Language
4.b. Use common, grade-appropriate Greek or Latin affixes and roots as clues to the meaning of a word.

© **Building Knowledge**

① **Is conflict always bad?**

Explore the Big Question as you read "Stray." Take notes on ways in which the story explores conflict in its plot.

② **CLOSE READING FOCUS**

Key Ideas and Details: Make Predictions

A **prediction** is a developing idea about what will happen next in a story. You can use your prior knowledge to help you make predictions. To do this, make connections between information you already know and details in the story. For example, if you have ever moved to a new neighborhood, you know that making new friends can be challenging. If the story tells you that a character is shy and has moved to a new neighborhood, you can combine what you know with the information in the story to predict that the character may not make friends easily.

Craft and Structure: Plot

One key element of short stories is **plot**—the arrangement of events in a story. Plot includes the following elements:

- **Exposition:** introduction of setting, characters, and situation
- **Conflict:** the story's central problem
- **Rising Action:** events that increase tension
- **Climax:** high point of the story, when the story's outcome becomes clear and changes in the characters become apparent
- **Falling Action:** events that follow the climax
- **Resolution:** the final outcome

Vocabulary

Copy the following words from "Stray" in your notebook. Which of the words are adverbs? What suffix do they share?

timidly	grudgingly	exhausted
trudged	ignore	starvation

18 UNIT 1 • Is conflict always bad?

© TEXT COMPLEXITY **RUBRIC**

Stray		Reader and Task Suggestions	
Qualitative Measures		**Preparing to Read the Text**	**Leveled Tasks**
Context/Knowledge Demands	Contemporary U.S.; animal shelters ① 2 3 4 5	• Locate the vocabulary words by scanning the selection text and then discuss how each word relates to its sentence. • Guide students to use Multidraft Reading strategies (TE p. 20).	*Structure/Language* If students will have difficulty with selection vocabulary, ask volunteers to relate the vocabulary words to their lives by responding to questions such as, "Have you ever felt timid?" *Analyzing* If students will not have difficulty with vocabulary, have them write a brief paragraph using two or more of the vocabulary words. Have them share and discuss their paragraphs with the class.
Structure/Language Conventionality and Clarity	Simple sentence structure; some challenging vocabulary 1 2 ③ 4 5		
Levels of Meaning/Purpose/Concept Level	Accessible concept (responsibility and pet care) 1 ② 3 4 5		
Quantitative Measures			
Lexile	780L	**Text Length**	Word Count: 1,034

CLOSE READING MODEL

The passage below is from Cynthia Rylant's short story "Stray." The annotations to the right of the passage show ways in which you can use close reading skills to make predictions and analyze plot.

from "Stray"

In January, a puppy wandered onto the property [1] of Mr. Amos Lacey and his wife, Mamie, and their daughter, Doris. Icicles hung three feet or more from the eaves of the houses, snowdrifts swallowed up automobiles [1] and the birds were so fluffed up they looked comic.

The puppy had been abandoned, [1] and it made its way down the road toward the Laceys' small house, its ears tucked, its tail between its legs, shivering.

Doris, whose school had been called off because of the snow, was out shoveling the cinderblock front steps when she spotted the pup on the road. [2] She set down the shovel.

"Hey! Come on!" she called.

The puppy stopped in the road, wagging its tail timidly, trembling with shyness and cold.

Doris trudged through the yard, went up the shoveled drive and met the dog.

"Come on, Pooch."

"Where did *that* come from?" Mrs. Lacey asked as soon as Doris put the dog down in the kitchen. [3]

Mr. Lacey was at the table, cleaning his fingernails with his pocketknife. The snow was keeping him home from his job at the warehouse.

"I don't know where it came from," he said mildly, "but I know for sure where it's going." [4]

Plot

1 The opening paragraphs describe a family home during a heavy snowfall. They also describe an abandoned puppy. This exposition introduces the situation that will set the plot in motion.

Make Predictions

2 Doris spots the abandoned puppy "shivering" in the cold. Based on your prior knowledge, you may predict that she will want to take the puppy home.

Make Predictions

3 Mrs. Lacey's first reaction to the dog is cautious. Based on her words—referring to the puppy as "that"—you might predict that she will not allow the puppy in her home.

Plot

4 At this point, three characters—a daughter and her parents—have been introduced. Each reacts differently to the dog. Their reactions hint at conflicts that will appear as the plot develops.

PART 2 • Building Knowledge: Stray **19**

Daily Bellringer

For each class during which you will teach this selection, have students complete one of the five Quick Write activities for Week 1 in *Daily Bellringer Activities*. You may wish to use additional activities that are applicable to this selection.

Vocabulary

If students require support with selection vocabulary, use this routine:

1. Write the following words and definitions on the board:

   timidly *adv.* in a way that shows fear or shyness

   grudgingly *adv.* in an unwilling or resentful way

   exhausted *adj.* very tired

   trudged *v.* walked as if tired or with effort

   ignore *v.* pay no attention to

   starvation *n.* state of extreme hunger

2. Have students say each word aloud.

3. Use the word in a sentence that defines the word.

DIFFERENTIATED INSTRUCTION

Extended Support—English Learners

Have students complete the **Reading and Vocabulary Warm-ups** for this selection in the *Student Companion All-in-One Workbook* before they read. Assign the prereading pages and the adapted selection in the *Reader's Notebook: English Learner's Version*. Then, have students listen to portions of the selection in the *Student eText* or on the *Hear It!* CD-ROM.

Extended Support—Struggling Readers

Have students complete the **Reading and Vocabulary Warm-ups** for this selection in the *Student Companion All-in-One Workbook* before they read. Assign the prereading pages and the adapted selection in the *Reader's Notebook: Adapted Version*. Then, have students listen to portions of the selection in the *Student eText* or on the *Hear It!* CD-ROM (adapted text).

Extended Support—Reluctant Readers

To build motivation and engagement before assigning the selection, have students read "A Place Where Strays Can Stay," a thematically related selection in *Reality Central*. Then, use the questions at the conclusion of the related selection to guide discussion.

MULTIDRAFT READING

This icon ● marks natural pauses in the selection. To assist struggling readers and to deepen comprehension for all, assign the text in "chunks," separated by the icons, and apply multidraft reading protocols. For each reading, have students set the purpose indicated:

- **First reading:** Students should read the selection independently and think about its basic meaning.
- **Second reading:** Students should analyze the text's key ideas and details and its craft and structure, and respond to the side-column prompts.
- **Third reading:** Students should integrate knowledge and ideas, connect the text to other texts and to the world, and answer the end-of-selection questions.

For more guidance, refer to the *Classroom Strategies and Teaching Routines* card on multidraft reading.

❶ Activating Prior Knowledge

Ask students to imagine watching a puppy in an animal shelter. Then, have partners role-play a scene in which a child tries to convince an adult to adopt the puppy. Ask the partner playing the adult to raise objections to pet ownership.

❶ Stray

Cynthia Rylant

In January, a puppy wandered onto the property of Mr. Amos Lacey and his wife, Mamie, and their daughter, Doris. Icicles hung three feet or more from the eaves of houses, snowdrifts swallowed up automobiles and the birds were so fluffed up they looked comic.

💬 VOCABULARY DEVELOPMENT

Thematic Vocabulary: The Big Question
As students are discussing "Stray," encourage them to use the thematic vocabulary presented in Introducing the Big Question, pp. 2–3. You might encourage them with sentence starters like these:

1. Doris *defends* the puppy by . . .
2. Doris tries to *convince* her parents to let her keep the puppy by . . .
3. Mr. Lacey's decision helps ensure the dog's *survival* because . . .

The puppy had been abandoned, and it made its way down the road toward the Laceys' small house, its ears tucked, its tail between its legs, shivering.

Doris, whose school had been called off because of the snow, was out shoveling the cinderblock front steps when she spotted the pup on the road. She set down the shovel.

"Hey! Come on!" she called.

The puppy stopped in the road, wagging its tail *timidly*, trembling with shyness and cold.

Doris *trudged* through the yard, went up the shoveled drive and met the dog.

"Come on, Pooch."

"Where did *that* come from?" Mrs. Lacey asked as soon as Doris put the dog down in the kitchen.

Mr. Lacey was at the table, cleaning his fingernails with his pocketknife. The snow was keeping him home from his job at the warehouse.

"I don't know where it came from," he said mildly, "but I know for sure where it's going."

Doris hugged the puppy hard against her. She said nothing.

Because the roads would be too bad for travel for many days, Mr. Lacey couldn't get out to take the puppy to the pound[1] in the city right away. He agreed to let it sleep in the basement while Mrs. Lacey *grudgingly* let Doris feed it table scraps. The woman was sensitive about throwing out food.

By the looks of it, Doris figured the puppy was about six months old, and on its way to being a big dog. She thought it might have some shepherd in it.

Four days passed and the puppy did not complain. It never cried in the night or howled at the wind. It didn't tear up everything in the basement. It wouldn't even follow Doris up the basement steps unless it was invited.

It was a good dog.

Several times Doris had opened the door in the kitchen that led to the basement and the puppy had been there, all stretched out, on the top step. Doris knew it had wanted some company and that it had lain against the door,

---

1. pound (pound) *n.* animal shelter.

◄ **Vocabulary**
timidly (tim´ id lē) *adv.* in a way that shows fear or shyness

trudged (trudjd) *v.* walked as if tired or with effort

grudgingly (gruj´ iŋ lē) *adv.* in an unwilling or resentful way

Make Predictions
Based on what you know about big dogs, do you predict that Mr. Lacey will change his mind?

Plot
What action up until this point in the story suggests a conflict? Explain.

Comprehension
How do Doris's parents feel about the puppy?

PART 2 • Stray **21**

---

❷ Make Predictions

1. Remind students that making predictions requires using details from the story and their own knowledge.

2. To help students predict how Mr. Lacey will act, **ask** how the Laceys react to the puppy.

   Answer: Mr. Lacey wants to take the puppy to the pound. Mrs. Lacey unwillingly feeds the dog.

3. **Ask** students what they know about big dogs.

   Possible response: Big dogs eat more food than small dogs.

4. **Ask** the Make Predictions question.

   Answer: Mrs. Lacey objects to feeding a puppy and would be more opposed to feeding a large dog. It is unlikely Mr. Lacey will change his mind.

❸ Plot

1. Remind students that a conflict is the central problem of the story. One type of conflict is when characters disagree with each other.

2. Have students list the events that have happened so far in the story.

3. Have students think about how the characters reacted to events, and **ask** the Plot question.

   Answer: Doris likes the puppy. She hugs it and feeds it. She wants to keep it. Her mother, by contrast, begrudges any food the dog eats, and her father plans to take the dog to the pound when the roads are passable. Her parents will not let Doris keep the animal. The conflict is between Doris and her parents.

❹ Comprehension

Answer: They do not wish to keep the dog because of the expense.

Video

Watch the Background Video online!

Audio

Selection audio is available in the *Student eText* and on the *Hear It!* CD-ROM.

❺ Critical Viewing

Possible response: The puppy's eyes look sad and kind—a characteristic that may cause a sympathetic girl like Doris to become attached to it.

❻ Connecting to the Big Question

1. Point out to students that it is possible to "agree to disagree." In other words, it is possible to respect another's view of what is true, even if we disagree.

2. Direct students' attention to the bracketed passage. **Ask:** What details show that Doris understands her parents' point of view?

   Possible response: She knew that they wouldn't let her keep the dog because they couldn't afford to keep a pet.

3. **Ask:** What details show Doris's feelings about her parents' decision?

   Possible response: She kept telling her parents about the dog's good qualities, even after they had made their decision clear. She didn't name the dog because she wanted to avoid the sadness that would follow giving the dog away. She couldn't keep from crying when her father got ready to go to the pound.

4. Tell students to look for additional details about Doris's feelings and her parents' feelings. **Ask:** Does Doris "agree to disagree" with her parents?

   Possible response: No, she tries to change her parents' minds, and then gives up trying.

Spiral Review

Character

1. Remind students that they studied the concept of character in the Unit 1 Focus on Craft and Structure (pp. 14–17).

2. **Ask** the Spiral Review question.

   Possible response: This shows that Doris is very compassionate, and she cares a great deal for the puppy.

❺ Critical Viewing ▲
Why might a girl like Doris become attached to a dog like this one?

Vocabulary ▶
ignore (ig nôr′) v.
pay no attention to

Spiral Review
CHARACTER
What do Doris's failed efforts to avoid crying tell you about her character?

listening to the talk in the kitchen, smelling the food, being a part of things. It always wagged its tail, eyes all sleepy, when she found it there.

Even after a week had gone by, Doris didn't name the dog. She knew her parents wouldn't let her keep it, that her father made so little money any pets were out of the question, and that the pup would definitely go to the pound when the weather cleared.

Still, she tried talking to them about the dog at dinner one night.

"She's a good dog, isn't she?" Doris said, hoping one of them would agree with her.

Her parents glanced at each other and went on eating.

"She's not much trouble," Doris added. "I like her." She smiled at them, but they continued to ignore her.

"I figure she's real smart," Doris said to her mother. "I could teach her things."

Mrs. Lacey just shook her head and stuffed a forkful of sweet potato in her mouth. Doris fell silent, praying the weather would never clear.

But on Saturday, nine days after the dog had arrived, the sun was shining and the roads were plowed. Mr. Lacey opened up the trunk of his car and came into the house.

Doris was sitting alone in the living room, hugging a pillow and rocking back and forth on the edge of a chair. She was trying not to cry but she was not strong enough. Her face was wet and red, her eyes full of distress.

Mrs. Lacey looked into the room from the doorway.

"Mama," Doris said in a small voice. "Please."

Mrs. Lacey shook her head.

"You know we can't afford a dog, Doris. You try to act more grown-up about this."

Doris pressed her face into the pillow.

Outside, she heard the trunk of the car slam shut, one of the doors open and close, the old engine cough and choke and finally start up.

"Daddy," she whispered. "Please."

She heard the car travel down the road, and, though it was early afternoon, she could do nothing but go to her bed. She cried herself to sleep, and her dreams were full of searching and searching for things lost. •

It was nearly night when she finally woke up. Lying there, like stone, still exhausted, she wondered if she would ever in her life have anything. She stared at the wall for a while.

But she started feeling hungry, and she knew she'd have to make herself get out of bed and eat some dinner. She wanted not to go into the kitchen, past the basement door. She wanted not to face her parents.

But she rose up heavily.

Her parents were sitting at the table, dinner over, drinking coffee. They looked at her when she came in, but she kept her head down. No one spoke.

Doris made herself a glass of powdered milk and drank it all down. Then she picked up a cold biscuit and started out of the room.

"You'd better feed that mutt before it dies of starvation," Mr. Lacey said.

Doris turned around.

"What?"

"I said, you'd better feed your dog. I figure it's looking for you."

Doris put her hand to her mouth.

"You didn't take her?" she asked.

"Oh, I took her all right," her father

"Mama," Doris said in a small voice. "Please."

◀ **Vocabulary**
exhausted (eg zôst′ əd) *adj.* very tired

starvation (stär vā′ shən) *n.* state of extreme hunger

❽ **Comprehension**
Why does Doris not want to get out of bed to eat?

❼ **Draw Conclusions**

1. Have a volunteer read the bracketed passage aloud.

2. **Ask:** When Doris whispers "Daddy, . . . please," to whom is she talking?

   Possible response: She is addressing her father, but he is outside in the car.

3. **Ask:** Why do you think the author included this detail in the story?

   Possible response: It shows that Doris is miserable when she hopelessly whispers her plea. She has given up all hope.

4. **Ask:** What other details in the text tell what Doris is feeling?

   Possible response: She is very sad—she cries herself to sleep, she dreams of searching for things lost, and she wants to avoid her parents.

❽ **Comprehension**

Answer: She does not want to face her parents.

PART 2 • Stray **23**

❾ Plot

1. Remind students that the resolution occurs when the problems are solved.

2. Have students review the events in the story.

3. Tell students to remember what they had predicted would happen in the story. Then, **ask** the Plot question.

Answer: Earlier on, Mr. Lacey does not act as if he will change his mind. The change shows he has a soft side.

▶ **Monitor Progress:** If students have trouble expressing why the resolution is surprising, **ask** them to describe the conflict. **Answer:** It is between Doris, who wants the dog, and her parents, who want to bring it to the pound.

▶ **Reteach:** Review the parts of the plot and help students identify the events that reveal the conflict.

☑ ASSESS

Language Study
Vocabulary

1. The boys _ignore_ the _No Swimming_ sign.

2. Kay _grudgingly_ congratulates the winner.

3. Juan _timidly_ greets the new teacher.

4. Lucy was _exhausted_ after playing soccer for two hours.

5. Betty _trudged_ to school.

Word Study
Part A
Sample answers:

The suffix _-ation_ means "the condition or process of." _Alteration_ means the condition of being altered. _Realization_ means the process of realizing something.

Part B
Sample answers:

1. You might ask for a friend's _recommendation_ of a good book to read, a movie to see, a game to play, or a way to solve a problem.

2. _Experimentation_ is important in science because it is the process by which scientists support their hypotheses.

Plot
What is surprising about the resolution of the conflict?

answered. "Worst looking place I've ever seen. Ten dogs to a cage. Smell was enough to knock you down. And they give an animal six days to live. Then they kill it with some kind of a shot."

Doris stared at her father.

"I wouldn't leave an ant in that place," he said. "So I brought the dog back."

Mrs. Lacey was smiling at him and shaking her head as if she would never, ever, understand him.

Mr. Lacey sipped his coffee.

"Well," he said, "are you going to feed it or not?"

Language Study

Vocabulary The words below appear in "Stray." Rewrite each sentence using one of the words. Your sentence should express a meaning similar to that of the original sentence.

    timidly   trudged   grudgingly   ignore   exhausted

1. The boys pay no attention to the _No Swimming_ sign.

2. Kay forces herself to congratulate the winner.

3. Juan blushes as he greets the new teacher.

4. Lucy was very tired after playing soccer for two hours.

5. Betty walked to school with slow, heavy steps.

WORD STUDY

The **Latin suffix _-ation_** changes a verb to a noun. It means "the condition or process of." In this story, Doris's dad says Doris should feed the dog or it will die of **starvation**, the condition of being starved.

Word Study

Part A Explain how the **Latin suffix _-ation_** contributes to the meaning of _alteration and realization_. Consult a dictionary if necessary.

Part B Use the context of the sentence and your knowledge of the suffix _-ation_ to help you answer each question.

1. When might you ask for a friend's _recommendation_?

2. Why is _experimentation_ important in science?

Literary Analysis

Possible responses appear below. Check to be sure students support their responses with evidence from the text.

1. (a) Doris says nothing and hugs the puppy. **(b)** She wants to keep the puppy but understands her parents' reasoning.

2. (a) Prior Knowledge: Dogs can be expensive to keep. Details From Story: Mrs. Lacey does not want to feed the dog. Mr. Lacey wants to take it to the pound. Prediction: They will not keep the dog. **(b)** Prior Knowledge: People without pets are unlikely to want strays. Details From Story: Mr. Lacey ignores Doris's pleas. Prediction: He will take the dog to the pound.

3. Doris notices that the dog does not cry or tear things up. It waits to be invited, seems smart, and is not a bother. Because the dog is such a good dog, the reader might predict that the family will keep the dog and that the story's resolution will not be tragic.

Literary Analysis

Key Ideas and Details

1. (a) What does Doris do when her father first tells her that she cannot keep the dog? **(b) Analyze:** Why does Doris react in this way?

2. Make Predictions The example in the chart on the right shows how you can use prior knowledge and details from the story to make a prediction. Use a similar chart to show how you make the following predictions. **(a)** What will Doris's parents say about the puppy? **(b)** What will her father do when the weather clears?

3. Make Predictions What characteristics, or personality traits, does Doris notice in the dog? How does the description of these traits help you predict the story's resolution?

Craft and Structure

4. Plot (a) What is the main conflict in this story? **(b)** At what point in the story is the conflict evident? Cite details to support your response.

5. Plot What is the climax, or high point, in the story? Explain your answer.

6. Plot In what way is the snowstorm important to the plot and the resolution of the story?

Integration of Knowledge and Ideas

7. (a) Paraphrase: In the text, find Mr. Lacey's description of the pound and then restate it in your own words. **(b) Analyze:** Why does Mr. Lacey change his mind about keeping the dog?

8. (a) Make a Judgment: Do you think that Doris should have made a stronger case for keeping the dog? Why or why not? **(b) Speculate:** What could Doris do in the future to show her father that he was right about keeping the dog?

---

9. **Is conflict always bad?** Did any of the characters grow or change in a positive way as a result of the conflict in this story? Support your answer with specific details from the text.

Prior Knowledge
Puppies are cute.
(a)
(b)

Details From Story
The puppy is abandoned.
(a)
(b)

Prediction
Doris will want to keep it.
(a)
(b)

ACADEMIC VOCABULARY

As you write and speak about "Stray," use the words related to conflict that you explored on page 3 of this text.

9. **Is conflict always bad?** Mr. Lacey changes as a result of the conflict. He realizes that saving the dog is more important than saving money. His values are not defined by money. In the beginning he is quick to tell Doris that the family can't afford a dog, but it is clear he has changed his mind when he describes the conditions of the pound and says he "wouldn't leave an ant in that place."

---

4. (a) The main conflict is that Doris wants to keep the dog, but her parents do not. **(b)** The conflict becomes apparent when Mrs. Lacey says, "I don't know where it came from, but I know for sure where it's going," indicating that the dog will go to the pound.

5. The climax occurs when Mr. Lacey tells Doris to feed the dog, signaling that he did not leave the dog at the pound.

6. The snowstorm is important because being abandoned in the snow is especially dangerous for the dog and makes Doris more eager to

keep it; the snowstorm also prevents Mr. Lacey from taking the dog to the pound until he has had some time to become fond of it.

7. (a) The pound is a smelly, crowded place, where dogs are put to death after six days. **(b)** He does not want to leave the puppy in such terrible conditions.

8. (a) Doris should have made a stronger case because she truly wanted to keep the dog. **(b)** Doris can take responsibility for the dog by caring for it and training it.

 Online Writer's Notebook

Students can use the Online Writer's Notebook to record all responses.

Conventions

1. Introduce the skill, using the instruction on the student page.

2. Discuss the definitions and the rules for capitalization.

Think Aloud: Model the Skill

Model the skill of using common, proper, and possessive nouns. Say to students:

> To name something, I can use common or proper nouns. For instance, to refer to Ms. Clark, I can say "the lady," using a common noun, or "Ms. Clark," using a proper noun. I will use *Ms. Clark* when I want to be specific. If I am talking about something that Ms. Clark owns, I would use a possessive noun, such as, "That is Ms. Clark's computer."

Practice A

1. *puppy's*: possessive; *face*: common

2. *Mr. Lacey*: proper; *puppy*: common; *pound*: common

3. *Doris*: proper; *Mama's*: possessive (also proper); *words*: common

4. *pound*: common; *place*: common

Reading Application

Sample answers:

Common nouns: *property, daughter, icicles.* Proper nouns: *Amos Lacey, Doris, Mamie.* Possessive noun: *Laceys'*

Practice B

1. *Doris's* house was small.

2. The *Laceys'* love for each other was clear to see.

3. The puppy was *Doris's.*

4. *Mr. Lacey's* opinion changed.

Writing Application

Sample answers:

1. *Doris* hugged the puppy hard against her.

   The *girl* hugged the puppy hard against her.

2. "You'd better feed that mutt before it dies of starvation," *Mr. Lacey* said.

   "You'd better feed that mutt before it dies of starvation," her *father* said.

3. *Mrs. Lacey* just shook her head and stuffed a forkful of sweet potato in her mouth.

   The *woman* just shook her head and stuffed a forkful of sweet potato in her mouth.

Conventions: Common, Proper, and Possessive Nouns

A **common noun** names any one of a group of people, places, or things. A **proper noun** names a particular person, place, or thing. A **possessive noun** shows belonging and is signaled by an apostrophe.

Common nouns are not capitalized unless they are at the beginning of a sentence or in a title. **Proper nouns** are always capitalized. **Possessive nouns** that are *singular* end in an apostrophe followed by the letter s ('s). **Possessive nouns** that are *plural* end in the letter s followed by an apostrophe (s').

Common Nouns	Proper Nouns	Possessive Nouns
Commuters drive **cars** to the **city** and park them on the **street**.	**Ms. Ryan** drove the **Cadillac** to **Miami** and parked it on **Market Street**.	The Cadillac is not **Ms. Ryan's**; it is her **parents'** car.

Practice A

Identify the noun(s) in each sentence and indicate whether they are *common, proper,* or *possessive.*

1. The stray puppy's sad face was pitiful to see.

2. Mr. Lacey said he would take the puppy to the pound.

3. Doris was upset by Mama's words.

4. The pound was a dismal place.

Reading Application In "Stray," find three common nouns, three proper nouns, and one possessive noun.

Practice B

Identify the proper noun in each sentence. Then, rewrite the sentence using the possessive form of that noun, without changing the sentence's meaning.

1. Doris lived in a small house.

2. The love of the Laceys for each other was clear to see.

3. The puppy belonged to Doris.

4. The opinion held by Mr. Lacey changed.

Writing Application In "Stray," find three sentences with proper nouns. Rewrite the sentences using common nouns. Each sentence you choose should have a different proper noun.

▶ EXTEND THE LESSON

Sentence Modeling

Choose the sentence(s) given from the selection:

> "Daddy," she whispered. "Please."

> Four days passed and the puppy did not complain.

Have students identify the common and proper nouns from the sentences. *Daddy* (proper noun); *days* (common noun), *puppy* (common noun)

Then, ask students what they notice about the sentences, eliciting that Rylant has Doris whisper a plea to her father despite the fact that he is outside and cannot hear her, adding poignancy to the scene. In the second sentence the author uses a compound sentence with two common nouns to describe how well-behaved the dog is.

Finally, have students imitate the sentence in a paragraph on a topic of their own choosing, matching the grammatical and stylistic feature discussed. Have volunteers share their sentences.

Writing to Sources

Explanatory Text Write a **list of reasons** Doris could give to her parents explaining why she should be allowed to keep the puppy.

- Reread the story, writing down specific details that show why the puppy would make a good pet.
- State your claim in a brief introduction. Then, list the reasons that support your claim.
- Use formal language to ensure that your ideas will be considered seriously. Write in complete sentences and do not use slang.
- With a small group of classmates, take turns reading your lists aloud. Ask your group to give feedback on whether or not you were successful in supporting your reasons with evidence from the story.

Grammar Application Correctly capitalize and punctuate the proper and possessive nouns in your list.

Research and Technology

Build and Present Knowledge With a group, create a **brochure** about puppy care that Doris could use to help her raise her dog. First, make a list of questions about the topic. Then, search the Internet to find answers.

- Use key words like these to search the Internet: *feeding a new puppy, training a puppy, puppy care, puppy health.*
- Include the following sections in your brochure: "Feeding Your Puppy," "Puppy Training Tips," "Happy, Healthy Puppies." Add other sections if you have ideas and find useful information.
- Assign everyone in your group a specific job, such as writing a section, revising and editing a section, or drawing illustrations.
- Make copies of your brochure to share with your classmates.

 **Common Core State Standards**

Writing
2.b. Develop the topic with relevant facts, definitions, concrete details, quotations, or other information and examples.
2.e. Establish and maintain a formal style.
4. Produce clear and coherent writing in which the development, organization, and style are appropriate to the task, purpose, and audience.
7. Conduct short research projects to answer a question, drawing on several sources and refocusing the inquiry when appropriate.

Speaking and Listening
3. Delineate a speaker's argument and specific claims, distinguishing claims that are supported by reasons and evidence from claims that are not.

Language
2. Demonstrate command of the conventions of standard English capitalization, punctuation, and spelling when writing.

Writing to Sources

1. Review the assignment, using the instruction on the student page.
2. To give students guidance in writing a list, give them the **Support for Writing** page for this selection in the *Student Companion All-in-One Workbook.*
3. To evaluate students' lists, use rubrics for General (Holistic) Writing from *Professional Development Guidebook,* pp. 256–257. You may also evaluate students' writing by checking that they mention all the main points about the selection they have read and that they support each point with at least one detail from the story.

Grammar Application

Have students check their drafts for the correct capitalization and punctuation of proper nouns and possessive nouns.

Six Traits Focus

✓	Ideas		Word Choice
✓	Organization	✓	Sentence Fluency
	Voice		Conventions

Research and Technology

1. Review the assignment, using the instruction on the student page.
2. To support students' work on the assignment, have them complete the **Support for Extend Your Learning** page for this selection in the *Student Companion All-in-One Workbook.*

Time and Resource Manager

The TAIL
Joyce Hansen

LESSON PACING GUIDE

The Tail

DAY 1	Preteach/Teach

- Administer the Reading and Vocabulary Warm-ups, as necessary.
- Introduce the Key Ideas and Details skill: Make Inferences.
- Introduce the Craft and Structure skill: Characterization.
- Use the Close Reading Model to demonstrate the application of the skills.
- Review the selection vocabulary, as necessary, with students who need additional support.
- Prepare students to read the selection by reviewing with them the Multidraft Reading Strategies.

DAY 2	Teach

- Informally monitor comprehension while students read.
- Use the Comprehension questions to confirm understanding.
- Develop students' ability to make inferences and analyze characterization using the sidenote questions.
- Reinforce vocabulary with the Vocabulary notes.
- Reinforce unit focus standards using the Spiral Review prompts.

DAY 3	Assess

- Assess students' comprehension and mastery of the skills by having them answer the Literary Analysis questions.
- Have students complete the Vocabulary activities.
- Develop students' understanding of roots and affixes by having them complete the Word Study activities.

DAY 4	Extend/Assess

- Build students' ability to master grammar concepts and conventions by having them complete the Conventions lesson.
- Have students complete the Writing to Sources activity and write a letter of recommendation. (You may assign as homework.)
- Extend learning by having students complete the Research and Technology activity: a compare-and-contrast chart.
- Administer the Selection Test or Open-Book Test.

Common Core State Standards

Reading Literature 1. Cite textual evidence to support analysis of what the text says explicitly as well as inferences drawn from the text.

3. Describe how the characters respond or change as the plot moves toward a resolution.

Writing 4. Produce clear and coherent writing in which the development, organization, and style are appropriate to task, purpose, and audience.

Speaking and Listening 2. Interpret information presented in diverse media and formats and explain how it contributes to a topic, text, or issue under study.

Language 1. Demonstrate command of the conventions of standard English grammar and usage when writing or speaking.

6. Acquire and use accurately grade-appropriate general academic and domain-specific words and phrases; gather vocabulary knowledge when considering a word or phrase important to comprehension or expression.

Daily Block Scheduling

Each day in this Lesson Pacing Guide represents a 40–50 minute period. Teachers using block scheduling may combine days to revise pacing. In addition, teachers may differentiate and support core instruction by integrating components for extended and intensive support as students require. See the Guide to Resources (facing page).

GUIDE TO RESOURCES

	L1	L2	L3	L4	EL	ALL	RESOURCES	PRINT	CD	ONLINE
Warm Up	✓	✓			✓		Vocabulary Warm-ups			✓
	✓	✓			✓		Reading Warm-ups			✓
						✓	Background Video			✓
						✓	Selection Audio		Hear It!	✓
Comprehension/ Selection Support						✓	Writing About the Big Question	Student Companion Workbook		✓
						✓	Literary Analysis	Student Companion Workbook		✓
						✓	Reading	Student Companion Workbook		✓
						✓	Vocabulary Builder	Student Companion Workbook		✓
				✓			Enrichment			✓
		✓	✓	✓			Conventions	Student Companion Workbook		✓
		✓	✓	✓			Writing to Sources	Student Companion Workbook		✓
		✓	✓	✓			Research and Technology	Student Companion Workbook		
Differentiated Instruction/ Additional Support						✓	Additional Standards Practice	Common Core Companion		✓
						✓	Close Reading Practice	Close Reading Notebook		✓
	✓	✓					Adapted Reader's Notebook			✓
					✓		English Reader's Notebook:			✓
					✓		Spanish Reader's Notebook			✓
					✓		Graphic Organizer A			✓
	✓	✓			✓		Graphic Organizer B			✓
	✓	✓			✓		"Does Birth Order Matter?"	Reality Central Student Edition and Writing Journal		✓
	✓	✓			✓		Practice and Assess	Reading Kit		✓
Monitor Progress						✓	Selection Test		Exam View	✓
						✓	Open-Book Test		Exam View	✓
Digital Resources						✓	Close Reading Tool			✓
						✓	Online Writer's Notebook			✓

👥 One-on-one teaching   👥 Group work   👥 Whole class instruction   👤 Independent work   Ⓐ Assessment   🖳 Digital Resource

LEARNER LEVELS

L1 Special-Needs Students
L2 Below-Level Students (Tier 2)

L3 On-Level Students (Tier 1)
L4 Advanced Students (Tier 1)

EL English Learners
All All Students

Is conflict always bad?

Read • Discuss • Research • Write As students read, they will explore the Big Question through text analysis of the selection. Encourage students to take notes as they read and raise additional questions, using text evidence to support their thoughts. Students should refer to their notes to help them deepen their understanding of the selection through discussion, research, and writing.

② Close Reading Focus

1. Remind students that when they make inferences, they combine details in the text with their own knowledge. In this way, they can understand what the writer does not state directly.

2. Help students understand direct characterization by telling them that your best friend is very kind. Explain that if you describe her acts of kindness (rather than stating that she is kind), this is indirect characterization.

Building Knowledge

Meet the Author

Joyce Hansen (b. 1942) was born and raised in New York City and went to college there. She then spent twenty-two years teaching in the city's public schools. Her first three novels—*The Gift-Giver, Yellow Bird and Me,* and *Home Boy*—are all set in New York and focus on the lives of young people. Hansen, now a full-time writer, believes that writing for young people carries "a special responsibility." Four of her historical novels have earned the Coretta Scott King Honor Book Award.

Common Core State Standards

Reading Literature
1. Cite textual evidence to support analysis of what the text says explicitly as well as inferences drawn from the text.
3. Describe how the characters respond or change as the plot moves toward a resolution.

Language
6. Acquire and use accurately grade-appropriate general academic and domain-specific words and phrases; gather vocabulary knowledge when considering a word or phrase important to comprehension or expression.

① Is conflict always bad?

Explore the Big Question as you read "The Tail." Take notes on ways in which the story explores the nature of conflict.

② CLOSE READING FOCUS

Key Ideas and Details: **Make Inferences**

When you **make inferences**, you make logical assumptions about something that is not stated directly in the text. To make inferences, use details that the writer provides.

Example: Arnie *ran* to the mailbox to see if the package from his aunt had *finally* arrived.

• You can infer from the word *finally* that Arnie has been waiting to get the package.
• You can infer from *ran* that he is eager to get the package.

Craft and Structure: **Characterization**

Characterization is the way writers develop characters and reveal their traits, or qualities.

• With **direct characterization**, a writer makes straightforward statements about a character. For example, "Ron is honest."
• With **indirect characterization**, a writer presents a character's thoughts, words, and actions and reveal what others say and think about the character.

Once you analyze the qualities of a story's main characters, think about ways in which those qualities affect the plot of the story and its outcome. For example, a character's stubbornness may cause him to come into conflict with others in a story.

Vocabulary

You will encounter the following words in "The Tail." In your notebook, list the words in the order of how well you know them, writing the most familiar word first. As you read, record the definitions next to each word.

vow	routine	mauled
anxious	gnawing	spasm

TEXT COMPLEXITY **RUBRIC**

The Tail		Reader and Task Suggestions	
Qualitative Measures		**Preparing to Read the Text**	**Leveled Tasks**
Context/Knowledge Demands	Contemporary; New York City 1　②　3　4　5	• Discuss New York's Central Park and the problem of stray dogs in urban park settings. • Guide students to use Multidraft Reading strategies (TE p. 30)	*Knowledge Demands* If students will have difficulty with knowledge demands, have them first read the passages describing the park, the mother's warning about going into the park, and the discussion about "wild dogs." *Synthesizing* If students will not have difficulty with knowledge demands, have them list the ways in which their summer vacations and activities compare to Tasha's.
Structure/Language Conventionality and Clarity	Informal conversation; relatively short; location-specific vocabulary 1　②　3　4　5		
Levels of Meaning/Purpose/Concept Level	Accessible concept (responsibilities of baby-sitting) 1　2　③　4　5		
Quantitative Measures			
Lexile	570L	**Text Length**	Word Count: 3,012

CLOSE READING MODEL

The passage below is from Joyce Hansen's short story "The Tail." The annotations to the right of the passage show ways in which you can use close reading skills to make inferences and analyze characterization.

from "The Tail"

Junior turned to me and raised his right hand. "This is a vow of obedience." He looked up at the ceiling. "I promise to do whatever Tasha says." [1]

"What do you know about vows?" I asked.

"I saw it on television. A man—"

"Shut up, Junior. I don't feel like hearing about some television show. It's too early in the morning." [2]

I went into the kitchen to start cleaning, when the downstairs bell rang. "Answer the intercom, Junior. If it's Naomi, tell her to wait for me on the stoop," [3] I called out. I knew that it was Naomi, ready to start our big, fun summer. After a few minutes the bell rang again.

"Junior!" I yelled. "Answer the intercom."

The bell rang again and I ran into the living room. Junior was sitting on the couch, looking at cartoons. "What's wrong with you? Why won't you answer the bell?"

He looked at me as if I were crazy. "You told me to shut up. I told you I'd do everything you say." [4]

Make Inferences

1 A vow is a solemn promise. This detail might lead you to infer that Junior is very serious about obeying Tasha.

Characterization

2 The narrator interrupts Junior and speaks rudely to him. These examples of indirect characterization show that Tasha is impatient and not interested in what Junior has to say.

Make Inferences

3 The text mentions *the downstairs bell, the intercom,* and *the stoop.* Based on these details, you might infer that the characters live in an apartment building.

Characterization

4 His words and actions show that Junior is clever and full of mischief. He might not have been serious about obeying Tasha after all.

Daily Bellringer

For each class during which you will teach this selection, have students complete one of the five Sentence Modeling activities for Week 2 in *Daily Bellringer Activities.* You may wish to use additional activities that are applicable to this selection.

Vocabulary

If students require support with selection vocabulary, use this routine:

1. Write the following words and definitions on the board:

    vow *n.* promise or pledge

    routine *n.* usual way in which something is done

    mauled *v.* badly injured by being attacked

    anxious *adj.* eager

    gnawing *v.* biting and cutting with teeth

    spasm *n.* sudden short burst of energy or activity

2. Have students say each word aloud.

3. Use the word in a sentence that defines the word.

:: DIFFERENTIATED INSTRUCTION

EL Extended Support— English Learners
Have students complete the **Reading and Vocabulary Warm-ups** for this selection in the *Student Companion All-in-One Workbook* before they read. Assign the prereading pages and the adapted selection in the *Reader's Notebook: English Learner's Version.* Then, have students listen to portions of the selection in the *Student eText* or on the *Hear It!* CD-ROM.

L1 L2 Extended Support— Struggling Readers
Have students complete the **Reading and Vocabulary Warm-ups** for this selection in the *Student Companion All-in-One Workbook* before they read. Assign the prereading pages and the adapted selection in the *Reader's Notebook: Adapted Version.* Then, have students listen to portions of the selection in the *Student eText* or on the *Hear It!* CD-ROM (adapted text).

Extended Support— Reluctant Readers
To build motivation and engagement before assigning the selection, have students read "Does Birth Order Matter?," a thematically related selection in *Reality Central.* Then, use the questions at the conclusion of the related selection to guide discussion.

MULTIDRAFT READING

This icon ● marks natural pauses in the selection. To assist struggling readers and to deepen comprehension for all, assign the text in "chunks," separated by the icons, and apply multidraft reading protocols. For each reading, have students set the purpose indicated:

- **First reading:** Students should read the selection independently and think about its basic meaning.
- **Second reading:** Students should analyze the text's key ideas and details and its craft and structure, and respond to the side-column prompts.
- **Third reading:** Students should integrate knowledge and ideas, connect the text to other texts and to the world, and answer the end-of-selection questions.

For more guidance, refer to the *Classroom Strategies and Teaching Routines* card on multidraft reading.

❶ Critical Viewing

Possible response: From the fact that they are standing close together, it is possible to infer that they know each other well. From their facial expressions and postures, it is possible to infer that the boy enjoys showing off to the girl. She looks annoyed but appears to be in a good mood.

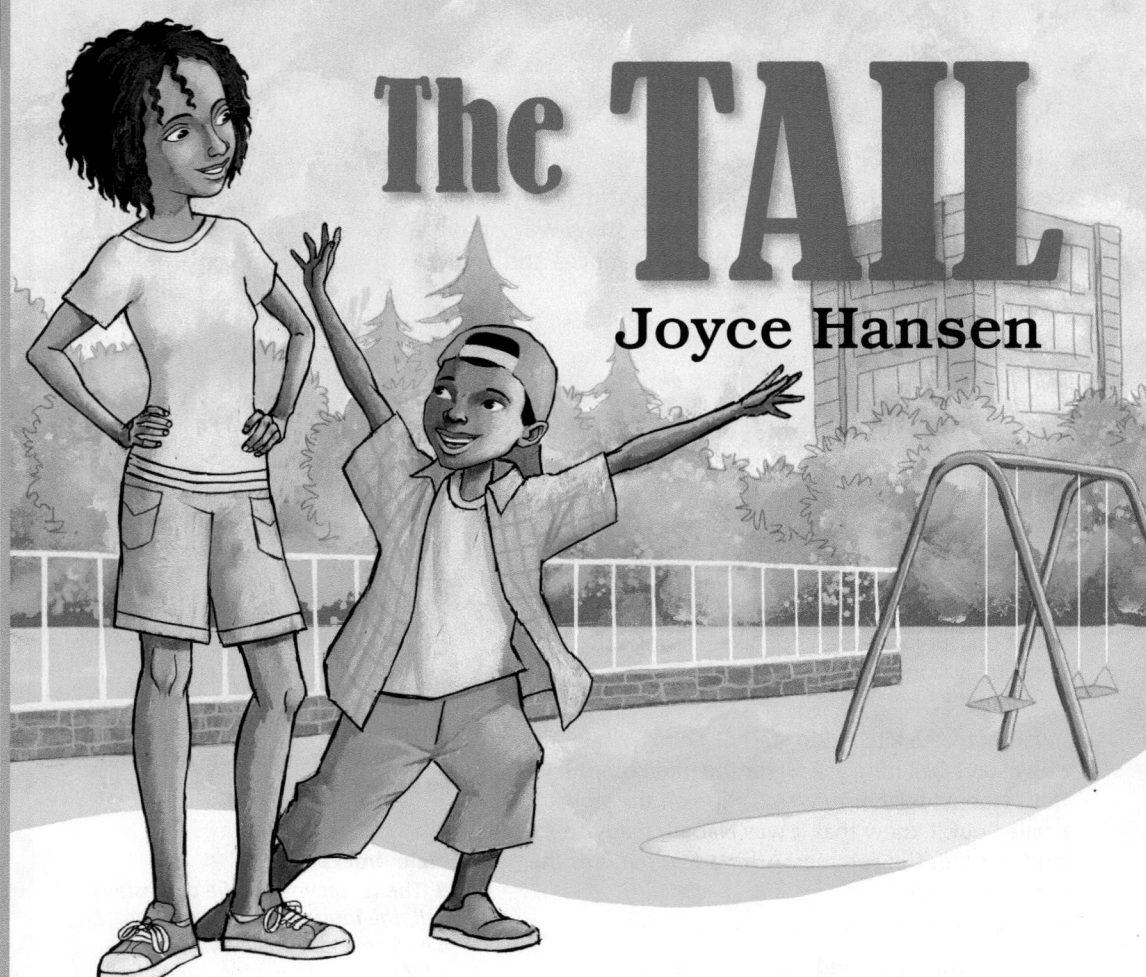

The TAIL
Joyce Hansen

❶ **Critical Viewing ▲**
What can you infer about the relationship between these two characters? Explain.

It began as the worst summer of my life.

The evening before the first day of summer vacation, my mother broke the bad news to me. I was in the kitchen washing dishes and dreaming about the wonderful things my friends and I would be doing for two whole months— practicing for the annual double-dutch[1] contest, which we would definitely win; going to the roller skating rink, the swimming pool, the beach; and sleeping as late in the morning as I wanted to.

---

1. **double-dutch** a jump-rope game in which two ropes are used at the same time.

30 UNIT 1 • Is conflict always bad?

🗨 VOCABULARY DEVELOPMENT

Thematic Vocabulary: The Big Question
As students are discussing "The Tail," encourage them to use the thematic vocabulary presented in Introducing the Big Question, pp. 2–3. You might encourage them with sentence starters like these:

1. Tasha begins to *argue* with her mother when she learns that . . .
2. The children's mother is unwilling to *negotiate* about . . .
3. Tasha tries to *convince* her mother that . . .
4. Boys playing a stickball *game* watched the girls as they . . .
5. Tasha worries that she must *defend* Junior from wild dogs when he . . .

"Tasha," my ma broke into my happy thoughts, "your father and I decided that you're old enough now to take on certain responsibilities."

My heart came to a sudden halt. "Responsibilities?"

"Yes. You do know what that word means, don't you?"

I nodded, watching her dice an onion into small, perfect pieces.

"You're thirteen going on fourteen and your father and I decided that you're old enough to watch Junior this summer, because I'm going to start working again."

"Oh, no!" I broke the dish with a crash. "Not that, Mama." Junior is my seven-year-old brother and has been following me like a tail ever since he learned how to walk. And to make matters worse, there are no kids Junior's age on our block. Everyone is either older or younger than he is.

I'd rather be in school than minding Junior all day. I could've cried.

"Natasha! There won't be a dish left in this house. You're not going to spend all summer ripping and roaring. You'll baby-sit Junior."

"But, Ma," I said, "it'll be miserable. That's not fair. All summer with Junior. I won't be able to play with my friends."

She wiped her hands on her apron. "Life ain't always fair." I knew she'd say that.

"You'll still be able to play with your friends," she continued, "but Junior comes first. He is your responsibility. We're a family and we all have to help out." •

Mama went to work that next morning. Junior and I both stood by the door as she gave her last-minute instructions. Junior held her hand and stared up at her with an innocent look in his bright brown eyes, which everyone thought were so cute. Dimples decorated his round cheeks as he smiled and nodded at me every time Ma gave me an order. I knew he was just waiting for her to leave so he could torment me.

"Tasha, I'm depending on you. Don't leave the block."

"Yes, Ma."

"No company."

"Not even Naomi? She's my best friend."

Make Inferences
Based on her words and actions, how does Tasha feel about baby-sitting her brother?

❸ Comprehension
Why is Tasha unhappy with her mother's request?

---

❷ Make Inferences

1. Remind students that an inference is an assumption a reader makes based on details that the author gives.

2. Tell students to find clues in the bracketed passage about how Tasha is feeling.

   Answer: Clues to Tasha's feelings include her exclamations "'Oh, no!,'" and "'Not that,'" her comment "And to make matters worse," and her dropping the dish.

3. **Ask** the Make Inferences question.

   Possible response: She has negative feelings about baby-sitting her brother.

❸ Comprehension

Possible response: Having to babysit Junior changes her summer plans.

🔧 DIFFERENTIATED INSTRUCTION

Strategy for Less Proficient Readers
Prepare an **Anticipation Guide** (*Professional Development Guidebook*, p. 38) with the following statements:

- Children who are being looked after should obey the babysitter.
- It is acceptable for babysitters to bend the rules and make their own decisions.

   Give students a copy of the Guide and have them respond in the Me column. Have students discuss the statements in groups and respond again in the Group column. Have students complete the After Reading column at the end.

🔵 Strategy for English Learners
Before students read the selection, lead them on a "selection tour." Direct their attention to the title, discuss illustrations, and read aloud the questions in the side margin as well as the Reading Check questions. As you preview the text, help students connect to the text. For example, point out the main characters in the illustrations, and then point out their names in the text.

Video

Watch the Background Video online!

Audio

Selection audio is available in the *Student eText* and on the *Hear It!* CD-ROM.

④ Characterization

1. Ask students to recall the difference between direct and indirect characterization.

Answer: Direct characterization is found in statements about a character. Indirect characterization is found in a character's thoughts, words, and actions, which develop the character.

2. Read the bracketed passage together. **Ask** students the first Characterization question.

Answer: The author uses indirect characterization. We learn about Tasha through her conversation with her mother. The conversation shows that even though she does not want to be stuck with her brother, she is respectful of her mother.

3. Ask students to think about what the author might have written if she were using direct characterization.

Possible response: Tasha was angry and ready to argue with her mother.

⑤ Characterization

1. Give students an auditory clue about the character of Tasha's mother by reading the dialogue aloud. Have a volunteer read Tasha's and Junior's parts of the conversation, as you read the part of Tasha's mother. Say each of her sentences as strong imperative commands.

2. Ask the second Characterization question.

Possible response: Students may say she is strict; she likes rules; she is sure about what she wants.

3. Before discussing the response, you might want to have students use the **Literary Analysis Graphic Organizer** for "The Tail" to create a character map for Tasha. Discuss their choice of words.

Characterization
In this dialogue, does the author use direct or indirect characterization to develop Tasha's personality? Explain.

④

⑤

Characterization
Based on this dialogue, how would you describe Tasha's mother? Explain.

Vocabulary ▶
vow (vou) *n.* promise or pledge

⑥

"No company when your father and I are not home."

"Yes, Ma."

"Don't let Junior hike in the park."

"Yes, Ma."

"Make yourself and Junior a sandwich for lunch."

"Yes, Ma."

"I'll be calling you at twelve, so you'd better be in here fixing lunch. I don't want you all eating junk food all day long."

"Yes, Ma."

"Don't ignore Junior."

"Yes, Ma."

"Clean the breakfast dishes."

"Yes, Ma."

"Don't open the door to strangers."

"Yes, Ma."

Then she turned to Junior. "Now you, young man. You are to listen to your sister."

"Yes, Mommy," he sang out.

"Don't give her a hard time. Show me what a big boy you can be."

"Mommy, I'll do whatever Tasha say."

She kissed us both good-bye and left. I wanted to cry. A whole summer with Junior.

Junior turned to me and raised his right hand. "This is a **vow** of obedience." He looked up at the ceiling. "I promise to do whatever Tasha says."

"What do you know about vows?" I asked.

"I saw it on television. A man—"

"Shut up, Junior. I don't feel like hearing about some television show. It's too early in the morning."

I went into the kitchen to start cleaning, when the downstairs bell rang. "Answer the intercom,[2] Junior. If it's Naomi, tell her to wait for me on the stoop," I called out. I knew that it was Naomi, ready to start our big, fun summer. After a few minutes the bell rang again.

"Junior!" I yelled. "Answer the intercom."

The bell rang again and I ran into the living room. Junior was sitting on the couch, looking at cartoons. "What's wrong with you? Why won't you answer the bell?"

---

2. **intercom** *n.* a communication system used in apartment buildings.

🗫 THINK ALOUD

Vocabulary: Using Context

Direct students' attention to the word *smithereens* in the sentence, "I was so startled that I dropped a plate and it smashed to smithereens" on the next page. Using a think-aloud process, model how to use context to infer the meaning of an unknown word. Say to students:

> I am going to think aloud to show you how to figure out the meaning of *smithereens* from its context.

In this sentence, *smithereens* is the word used to describe the plate after it *smashed* to the floor. I think the word smashed is a clue here. There is a difference between something just falling on the floor and something smashing on the floor. I have dropped plates, and I know that if they smash on the floor, they can break into lots of tiny pieces. So, I think *smithereens* means tiny pieces or fragments.

He looked at me as if I were crazy. "You told me to shut up. I told you I'd do everything you say."

I pulled my hair. "See, you're bugging me already. Do something to help around here."

I pressed the intercom on the wall. "That you, Naomi?"

"Yeah."

"I'll be down in a minute. Wait for me out front."

"Okay."

I quickly washed the dishes. I couldn't believe how messed up my plans were. Suddenly there was a loud blast from the living room. I was so startled that I dropped a plate and it smashed to smithereens. Ma will kill me, I thought as I ran to the living room. It sounded like whole pieces of furniture were being sucked into the vacuum cleaner.

"Junior," I screamed over the racket, "you have it on too high."

He couldn't even hear me. I turned it off myself.

"What's wrong?"

"Ma vacuumed the living room last night. It doesn't need cleaning."

"You told me to do something to help," he whined.

I finished the dishes in a hurry so that I could leave the apartment before Junior bugged out again.

I was so **anxious** to get outside that we ran down the four flights of stairs instead of waiting for the elevator. Junior clutched some comic books and his checkers game. He put his Mets baseball cap on backward as usual. Naomi sat on the stoop and Junior plopped right next to her like they were the best of friends.

"Hi, cutey." She smiled at him, turning his cap to the front of his head the way it was supposed to be.

"What are we going to do today, Naomi?" he asked.

Make Inferences
Why do you think Tasha pulls her hair?

◀ **Vocabulary**
anxious (aŋkˊshəs) *adj.* eager

7 Comprehension
What does Junior do to irritate Tasha?

PART 2 • The Tail **33**

GUIDED EXPLORATION

6 Make Inferences

1. Ask a volunteer to read the bracketed text. Then, ask students to think about whether they have ever been in a situation that made them pull their own hair. If so, ask them to think about why they did so and what emotions they were feeling at the time.

2. **Ask** the Make Inferences question.

   Possible response: By pulling her hair, she shows frustration. She is trying to manage her brother, and he is following her directions in ways that she did not intend.

7 Comprehension

Answer: He follows her orders in ways designed to annoy her: He does not answer the intercom, and he vacuums the living room floor when it does not need to be vacuumed.

DIFFERENTIATED INSTRUCTION

EL Support for English Learners

Expressions that include the multiple-meaning word *bug* or its derivations may be problematic to students learning English. Write the following sentences from this page on the board: "'See, you're bugging me already.'" and "I finished the dishes in a hurry so that I could leave the apartment before Junior bugged out again." Explain that *bug* has more than one meaning. Identify the more familiar meaning of *bug*: "an insect." Then, read the first sentence aloud and underline *bugging*.

Explain that *bug* can also mean "to bother or to annoy," so *bugging* someone means bothering or annoying the person. Ask students to name things that *bug* them.

Then, read aloud the second sentence and underline *bugged out*. Explain that *bugged out* is an expression that can mean "went crazy." Substitute the words in the sentence, "I finished the dishes in a hurry so that I could leave the apartment before Junior went crazy again."

PART 2 • The Tail **33**

8 Analyze

1. After students have read the bracketed passage, **ask** them to compare Naomi's reaction to Junior's presence with Tasha's reaction to Junior's presence.

Answer: Tasha is annoyed that Junior is with them. Naomi thinks he is cute and does not seem to mind that Junior is hanging out with them.

2. Ask students to explain why the girls' reactions are so different.

Possible response: Since Junior is neither her brother nor her responsibility, Naomi thinks he is cute and fun to have around. For Tasha, he is an annoying responsibility.

9 Characterization

1. Ask a volunteer to read the bracketed text. Have students summarize Tasha's thoughts about remaining on the block. Discuss whether she is following her mother's instructions.

2. Ask the Characterization question.

Possible response: She is willing to bend or break the rules in order to do what she wants to do.

3. Ask students to explain why her decision and her reasoning are examples of indirect characterization.

Possible response: The author does not state anything about Tasha. Tasha's words, thoughts, and actions reveal her character.

4. Have students discuss which method of characterization they think is more interesting for the reader.

Characterization
What character trait does Tasha show by deciding to go to the playground?

"Junior, you're not going to be in our faces all day," I snapped at him.

"Mama said you have to watch me. So I have to be in your face."

"You're baby-sitting, Tasha?" Naomi asked.

"Yeah." I told her the whole story.

"Aw, that's not so bad. At least you don't have to stay in the house. Junior will be good. Right, cutey?"

He grinned as she pinched his cheeks.

"See, you think he's cute because you don't have no pesty little brother or sister to watch," I grumbled.

"You ready for double-dutch practice?" she asked. "Yvonne and Keisha are going to meet us in the playground."

"Mama said we have to stay on the block," Junior answered before I could even open my mouth.

"No one's talking to you, Junior." I pulled Naomi up off the stoop. "I promised my mother we'd stay on the block, but the playground is just across the street. I can see the block from there."

"It's still not the block," Junior mumbled as we raced across the street.

We always went over to the playground to jump rope. The playground was just by the entrance to the park. There was a lot of space for us to do our fancy steps. The park was like a big green mountain in the middle of Broadway.

I'd figure out a way to keep Junior from telling that we really didn't stay on the block. "Hey, Tasha, can I go inside the park and look for caves?" People said that if you went deep inside the park, there were caves that had been used centuries ago when Native Americans still lived in northern Manhattan.

"No, Ma said no hiking in the park."

"She said no leaving the block, too, and you left the block."

"Look how close we are to the block. I mean, we can even see it. You could get lost inside the park."

"I'm going to tell Ma you didn't stay on the block."

VOCABULARY DEVELOPMENT

Multiple Meanings
Explain that some words have more than one meaning. Point out the word *stoop* in the sentence, "I pulled Naomi up off the stoop" (this page). Point out that in this sentence, *stoop* is a noun, and it is another word for a small porch or platform with steps at the door of a house. Have students use *stoop* as a noun in sentences. Continue to explain that *stoop* can also be used as a verb, meaning "to bend over." Give students this example sentence: *The man had to stoop to grab the toddler's hand.* Have students use *stoop* as a verb in sentences.

"Okay, me and Naomi will hike with you up to the Cloisters later." That's a museum that sits at the top of the park, overlooking the Hudson River. "Now read your comic books."

"Will you play checkers with me too?"

"You know I hate checkers. Leave me alone." I spotted Keisha and Yvonne walking into the playground. All of us wore shorts and sneakers.

Junior tagged behind me and Naomi as we went to meet them. "Remember you're supposed to be watching me," he said.

"How could I forget."

The playground was crowded. Swings were all taken and the older boys played stickball. Some little kids played in the sandboxes.

Keisha and Yvonne turned and Naomi and I jumped together, practicing a new routine. We were so good that some of the boys in the stickball game watched us. A few elderly people stopped to look at us too. We had an audience, so I really showed off—spinning and doing a lot of fancy footwork.

Suddenly Junior jumped in the ropes with us and people laughed and clapped.

Make Inferences
What are Tasha's feelings as the girls begin to jump?

◀ **Vocabulary**
routine (ro͞o tēn´) *n.* usual way in which something is done

⓫ Comprehension
What does Junior threaten to tell his mother?

⓬ ◀ Critical Viewing
Why might Tasha want to spend her summer in a park like this one?

⓾ Make Inferences

1. Begin by reading the Make Inferences question aloud. Tell students that you are going to read aloud a passage from the story. Ask them to listen closely for details that will help them to make inferences so that they can answer the question.

2. Read the bracketed passage. Then, **ask** the question and have students answer it.

   Possible response: She is proud because their talents have attracted attention. When Junior joins in, she is a bit jealous because he gets attention.

⓫ Comprehension

Answer: He threatens to tell his mother that he and Tasha did not stay on the block.

⓬ Critical Viewing

Possible response: Tasha might enjoy this park because she could jump rope and play with her friends.

DIFFERENTIATED INSTRUCTION

Support for Special-Needs Students
Have students listen to the story up to this point in the *Student eText* or on the *Hear It!* CD-ROM. Tell them to follow along in the book as they hear the text being read. After students listen to the CD, have them reread the pages. As a way of helping them track their reading, tell them to place a self-stick note next to the paragraph that they are reading. Before reading the next paragraph, have them ask themselves one question about what they just read.

Enrichment for Advanced Readers
Point out the reference to the Cloisters on this page. Explain to students that the Cloisters Museum houses the Metropolitan Museum of Art's collection of art from Medieval Europe. Ask students to conduct online research to locate information about the Cloisters Museum art exhibit, tapestries, grounds, and landscaping. Also, have students identify the origin of the word *cloisters*.

13 Literature in Context

Safety Connection The highest rate of injury from dog bites is among children between the ages of 5 and 9. (In the story, Tasha's brother, who befriends a dog, is 7 years old.) It is important for children to know how to act around dogs, and it is just as important for people who are choosing a dog to keep safety in mind when they are choosing. A few recommendations are that you talk with a veterinarian about which breeds of dogs are right for your family; that you spend time with the dog before making a decision; and that you never wrestle or play aggressively with a dog.

Connect to the Literature Have students read the feature, and share the additional background above. Then, **ask** the Connect to the Literature question. Suggest students imagine how Tasha feels when she realizes Junior is missing.

Answer: Tasha is so alarmed by her brother's disappearance that she can think only of finding him, regardless of any harm that might come to her.

---

13 LITERATURE IN CONTEXT

Safety Connection

Pet Precautions Americans love their pets and often think of their dogs and cats as members of their families. However, not all animals are safe to approach. If you confront a stray dog, consider it dangerous until you know better. Follow these safety guidelines:

- Approach the dog slowly and gently and keep your face away from its face.
- If a dog is chasing you, stop running because it encourages the animal to chase you.
- Do not touch a dog that is growling, showing its teeth, or barking excitedly.
- Do not look an aggressive dog in the eye. Instead, back away slowly.

Connect to the Literature

Why might Tasha forget these rules as she searches for Junior?

---

10 "Junior!" I screamed. "Get out of here!"

"Remember, your job is to watch me." He grinned. My foot slipped and all three of us got tangled in the ropes and fell.

"Your feet are too big!" Junior yelled.

Everybody roared. I was too embarrassed. I tried to grab him, but he got away from me. "Get lost," I hollered after him as he ran toward the swings.

I tried to forget how stupid I must've looked and went back to the ropes. I don't know how long we'd been jumping when suddenly a little kid ran by us yelling, "There's a wild dog loose up there!" He pointed to the steps that led deep inside the park.

People had been saying for years that a pack of abandoned dogs who'd turned wild lived in the park, but no one ever really saw them.

We forgot about the kid and kept jumping. Then one of the boys our age who'd been playing stickball came over to us. "We're getting out of here," he said. "A big yellow dog with red eyes just bit a kid."

I took the rope from Yvonne. It was time for me and Naomi to turn. "That's ridiculous. Who ever heard of a yellow dog with red eyes?"

Naomi stopped turning. "Dogs look all kind of ways. Especially wild dogs. I'm leaving."

"Me too," Yvonne said.

Keisha was already gone. No one was in the swings or the sandboxes. I didn't even see the old men who usually sat on the benches. "Guess we'd better get out of here too," I said. Then I realized that I didn't see Junior anywhere.

"Junior!" I shouted.

"Maybe he went home," Naomi said.

We dashed across the street. Our block was empty. Yvonne ran ahead of us and didn't stop until she reached her stoop. When I got to my stoop I expected to see Junior there, but no Junior.

"Maybe he went upstairs," Naomi said.

"I have the key. He can't get in the house."

"Maybe he went to the candy store?"

"He doesn't have any money, I don't think. But let's look."

💬 VOCABULARY DEVELOPMENT

Selection Vocabulary Reinforcement
Students will benefit from practice with the selection vocabulary words. Reinforce their comprehension with "show-you-know" sentences. The first part of the sentence uses the vocabulary word in an appropriate context. The second part of the sentence clarifies the first part. Model the strategy with this example for *vow: Sarah made a vow when she joined the club; she promised to keep the password secret.*

Then, give students these sentence prompts and coach them in creating the clarification portion of each sentence:

1. The soldier made a *vow* when he joined the Army; _____
   Sample answer: he promised to defend his country.
2. The baby was *anxious* when her mother left the room; _____
   Sample answer: she was afraid that she might never come back.
3. Jason changed his workout *routine*; _____
   Sample answer: he found he liked the new order of exercises more.

We ran around the corner to the candy store, but no Junior.

As we walked back to the block, I remembered something.

"Oh, no, Naomi, I told him to get lost. And that's just what he did."

"He's probably hiding from us somewhere. You know how he likes to tease." She looked around as we walked up our block. "He might be hiding and watching us right now looking for him." She peeped behind parked cars, in doorways, and even opened the lid of a trash can.

"Junior," I called. "Junior!"

No answer. Only the sounds of birds and cars, sirens and a distant radio. I looked at the empty stoop where Junior should have been sitting. A part of me was gone and I had to find it. And another part of me would be gone if my mother found out I'd lost Junior.

I ran back toward the playground and Naomi followed me. "He's got to be somewhere right around here," she panted.

I ran past the playground and into the park. "Tasha, you're not going in there, are **14** you? The dog."

I didn't answer her and began climbing the stone steps that wound around and through the park. Naomi's eyes stretched all over her face and she grabbed my arm. "It's dangerous up here!"

I turned around. "If you're scared, don't come. Junior's my only baby brother. Dear God," I said out loud, "please let me find him. I will play any kind of game he wants. I'll never yell at him again. I promise never to be mean to him again in my life!"

Naomi breathed heavily behind me. "I don't think Junior would go this far by himself."

I stopped and caught my breath. The trees were thick and the city street sounds were far away now.

"I know Junior. He's somewhere up here making believe he's the king of this mountain. Hey, Junior," I called, "I was just kidding. Don't get lost." We heard a rustling in the

> "Oh, no, Naomi, I told him to get lost. And that's just what he did."

Spiral Review
THEME What is one theme about brothers and sisters that might apply to the story so far?

Make Inferences
How does Tasha feel about Junior's disappearance? How can you tell?

15 Comprehension
Why is Tasha suddenly worried about Junior?

PART 2 • The Tail **37**

Spiral Review
Theme
1. Remind students that they studied the concept of theme in the Unit 1 Focus on Craft and Structure (pp. 14–17).
2. Then, **ask** students the Spiral Review question.

   Possible response: Brothers and sisters often have differences, but family ties are always important.

14 Make Inferences

1. **Ask** students how they think Tasha feels about her brother up to this point.

   Possible response: Tasha feels that he is a nuisance, and she thinks that he is ruining her vacation.

2. Tell students to listen for clues that the author provides to help readers make inferences about how Tasha feels at this moment.

3. **Ask** the Make Inferences question. Have a volunteer read aloud the bracketed passage.

   Possible response: She is very worried about Junior's safety. She really cares for him or she would not be worried.

▶ **Monitor Progress:** Ask students to identify the specific details they used to infer Tasha's feelings.

▶ **Reteach:** If students have difficulty making this inference, have them reread the explanation of the skill on p. 28. Then reread the bracketed text. Point out that instead of saying "I was very worried about Junior," she shared her thoughts, "A part of me was gone" and her own words such as "Dear God, please let me find him."

15 Comprehension

Answer: She is worried because Junior has disappeared and she knows there are wild dogs in the area.

🌊 FLUENCY

Distribute copies of this page and the previous page and pair students. Have partners take turns reading paragraphs aloud. While one partner reads, the other should mark any words with which the one reading has difficulty. Circulate to monitor the fluency of students' reading. Collect students' marked-up copies of the story, and review difficult words and passages with the class. Look for these problem spots:

• If students struggle with laborious or choppy reading of the text, read a passage fluently and with expression as students track, or

follow along, pointing to each word as you read. Have students echo your reading.

• If students mispronounce *tangled* (previous page), guide them in identifying the letters and sounds in the word. Extend by listing additional words with these letter patterns, such as *angle, bangle, jingle,* and *single.*

• If students are unable to blend syllables in a polysyllabic word such as *ridiculous* (previous page), model the strategy of covering up parts of the word with a thumb and pronouncing each part before blending them together.

16 Make Inferences

1. **Read** the bracketed passage, first telling students to listen for details that reveal how Tasha feels after she discovers Junior's comic book.

2. **Ask** them to identify the details they heard.

   Answer: She started to cry. It occurred to her that the animal might have hurt him.

3. **Ask** the Make Inferences question.

   Possible response: She feels even more panicked and worried than she did before.

Vocabulary ▶
gnawing (nô´ in) v. biting and cutting with the teeth

Vocabulary ▶
mauled (môld) v. badly injured by being attacked

Make Inferences
What can you infer from Tasha's reaction to discovering Junior's comic book?

bushes and grabbed each other. "Probably just a bird," I said, trying to sound brave.

As we climbed some more, I tried not to imagine a huge yellow dog with red eyes gnawing at my heels.

The steps turned a corner and ended. Naomi screamed and pointed up ahead. "What's that?"

I saw a big brown and gray monstrous thing with tentacles reaching toward the sky, jutting out of the curve in the path. I screamed and almost ran.

"What is that, Naomi?"

"I don't know."

"This is a park in the middle of Manhattan. It can't be a bear or anything." I screamed to the top of my lungs, "Junior!" Some birds flew out of a tree, but the thing never moved.

All Naomi could say was, "Dogs, Tasha."

I found a stick. "I'm going up. You wait here. If you hear growling and screaming, run and get some help." I couldn't believe how brave I was. Anyway, that thing, whatever it was, couldn't hurt me any more than my mother would if I didn't find Junior.

"You sure, Tasha?"

"No sense in both of us being mauled," I said.

I tipped lightly up the steps, holding the stick like a club. When I was a few feet away from the thing, I crumpled to the ground and laughed so hard that Naomi ran to me. "Naomi, look at what scared us."

She laughed too. "A dead tree trunk."

We both laughed until we cried. Then I saw one of Junior's comic books near a bush. I picked it up and started to cry. "See, he was here. And that animal probably tore him to pieces." Naomi patted my shaking shoulders.

Suddenly, there was an unbelievable growl. My legs turned to air as I flew down the steps. Naomi was ahead of me. Her two braids stuck out like propellers. My feet didn't even touch the ground. We screamed all the way down the steps. I tripped on the last step and was sprawled out on the ground. Two women passing by bent over me. "Child, are you hurt?" one of them asked.

Then I heard a familiar laugh above me and looked up into Junior's dimpled face. He laughed so hard, he held

17 his stomach with one hand. His checkers game was in the other. A little tan, mangy[3] dog stood next to him, wagging its tail.

I got up slowly. "Junior, I'm going to choke you."

He doubled over with squeals and chuckles. I wiped my filthy shorts with one hand and stretched out the other to snatch Junior's neck. The stupid little dog had the nerve to growl.

"Me and Thunder hid in the bushes. We followed you." He continued laughing. Then he turned to the dog. "Thunder, didn't Tasha look funny holding that stick like she was going to beat up the tree trunk?"

18 I put my hands around Junior's neck. "This is the end of the tail," I said.

Junior grinned. "You promised. 'I'll play any game he wants. I'll never yell at him again. I promise never to be mean to him again in my life.'"

Naomi giggled. "That's what you said, Tasha." The mutt barked at me. Guess he called himself Junior's protector. I took my hands off Junior's neck.

Then Naomi had a laughing spasm. She pointed at the dog. "Is that what everyone was running from?"

"This is my trusted guard. People say he's wild. He just wants a friend."

"Thunder looks like he's already got a lot of friends living inside his fur," I said. We walked back to the block with the dog trotting right by Junior's side.

I checked my watch when we got to my building. "It's ten to twelve. I have to make lunch for Junior," I told Naomi. "But I'll be back out later."

The dog whined after Junior as we entered the building. "I'll be back soon, Thunder," he said, "after I beat my sister in five games of checkers."

Now he was going to blackmail me.

I heard Naomi giggling as Junior and I walked into the building. The phone rang just as we entered the apartment. I knew it was Ma.

_____

3. mangy (mān´ jē) *adj.* shabby and dirty.

> "Me and Thunder hid in the bushes. We followed you."

◄ **Vocabulary**
spasm (spaz´ əm) *n.* sudden short burst of energy or activity

19 **Comprehension**
Where were Junior and the dog?

PART 2 • The Tail **39**

17 **Interpret**

1. Have students read the bracketed passage. Point out that Tasha was very worried about Junior's safety, but then, when she discovers that he is safe, she says, "'Junior, I'm going to choke you.'"

2. **Ask** students to explain this sudden change in attitude.

   Possible response: After Tasha realizes that Junior is safe, she is relieved. Then, she gets upset with him because he has caused her to worry and panic for no reason.

18 **Connecting to the Big Question**

1. Point out that relationships between family members can be strengthened by facing and resolving conflicts together.

2. Have students read the bracketed passage. **Ask:** What does Tasha mean when she says, "'This is the end of the tail'"?

   Possible response: She means two things—Junior is always following her, and that she is going to do away with him, once and for all.

3. **Ask:** Is her threat serious?

   Possible response: No, she is joking. He does bug her, but she is very happy to have found him.

4. **Ask:** How have Tasha's feelings towards Junior probably changed as a result of their conflict?

   Possible response: When she thought that he was lost, she realized how much she loved him. She is glad he has been found, even though she jokes that her feelings are otherwise.

19 **Comprehension**

Answer: They were hiding in the bushes.

 **ASSESS**

Language Study

Vocabulary

Sample answers:

1. No. A back spasm would be a sudden burst of pain.

2. Yes. A dog would enjoy gnawing on a bone, because chewing things, especially bone, is one of its instincts.

3. Yes. Lion tamers are always in danger of being mauled, or attacked, by the animals they work with.

4. Yes. I am anxious about going to the dentist, even though I know that being nervous doesn't improve the situation.

5. Yes. By following a routine each day, I know the order of events.

Word Study

Part A
Sample answers:

The Latin prefix *dis-* can change a word's meaning to its opposite. To *disinfect* is to prevent infection by killing the microorganisms that carry disease. A *dissatisfied* person is not satisfied with the way things are.

Part B
Sample answers:

1. No, I don't enjoy the company of people I dislike and would not invite them to a party.

2. Pain or numbness can be felt when you dislocate your shoulder, as the upper arm bone is pulled out of its normal position in the socket.

Literary Analysis

Possible responses appear below. Check to be sure students support their responses with evidence from the text.

1. Detail: "I couldn't believe how brave I was."

   Inference: Tasha is forming a new picture of herself as a brave person.

   Detail: "I picked it [Junior's comic book] up and started to cry."

   Inference: Tasha has been trying to act brave and holding back her tears.

"Everything okay, Tasha? Nothing happened?"

"No, Ma, everything is fine. Nothing happened at all." ●

Well, the summer didn't turn out to be so terrible after all. My parents got Thunder cleaned up and let Junior keep him for a pet. Me and my friends practiced for the double-dutch contest right in front of my building, so I didn't have to leave the block. After lunch when it was too hot to jump rope, I'd play a game of checkers with Junior or read him a story. He wasn't as pesty as he used to be, because now he had Thunder. We won the double-dutch contest. And Junior never told my parents that I'd lost him. I found out that you never miss a tail until you almost lose it.

Language Study

Vocabulary The words below appear in "The Tail." The questions that follow use the words in context. Answer each question. Then explain your anwer.

anxious   routine   gnawing   mauled   spasm

1. Would having a back *spasm* be pleasant?

2. Would a dog enjoy *gnawing* on a bone?

3. Should lion tamers be afraid of getting *mauled*?

4. Are you *anxious* about your next dentist appointment?

5. Do you know what to expect when you follow a daily *routine*?

Word Study

Part A Explain how the **Latin prefix *dis-*** contributes to the meanings of the words *disinfect* and *dissatisfied.* Consult a dictionary if necessary.

Part B Use your knowledge of the Latin prefix *dis-* to answer each question.

1. Do you usually invite people you *dislike* to a party?

2. How would it feel to *dislocate* your shoulder?

WORD STUDY

The **Latin prefix *dis-*** often changes a word's meaning to its opposite. For example, *vow* and *avow* mean "to declare" or "admit something openly." In this short story, Tasha wants to *disavow*, or deny, responsibility for her brother.

2. **(a)** They hear about a wild dog that bites. **(b)** Just after they hear about the terrible wild dog, they realize that Junior has disappeared and they worry that he might have encountered the dangerous dog.

3. **(a)** Tasha was referring to the possible loss of her brother, "the tail." She means that people do not value what they have until they no longer have it. **(b)** It shows that she has a new appreciation for Junior. The explanation that "he wasn't as pesty as he used to be" shows how she has changed her attitude.

4. Junior says that the dog "just wants a friend." The dog is friendly and not wild. The narrator says Junior "wasn't as pesty as he used to be."

5. **(a)** She drops a plate. This shows that she is surprised and upset. She prays that she will find Junior. This shows that she is worried and ashamed that she was not more responsible. **(b)** By the end of the story, Tasha has a new appreciation for Junior. Instead of being annoyed by him, she treats him nicely. She voluntarily spends time with him. She calls him "my only baby brother."

Close Reading Activities

Literary Analysis

Key Ideas and Details

1. Make Inferences Using a chart like the one on the right, list the details from the story that helped you to make an inference about Tasha. One example is provided. Give at least two more examples.

2. (a) What information are Tasha and her friends given about a danger in the park? **(b) Draw Conclusions:** Why does this information suddenly cause Tasha great worry?

3. (a) Interpret: What does Tasha mean when she says, "I found out that you never miss a tail until you almost lose it"? **(b) Analyze:** How does Tasha's statement show a change in her attitude? Cite textual details to support your response.

Craft and Structure

4. Characterization List two examples of direct characterization from the story. Cite the author's exact words from the text.

5. Characterization (a) In the text, find two descriptions of Tasha's actions or thoughts. What character traits, or qualities, are revealed in these examples of indirect characterization? **(b)** How has Tasha changed by the story's resolution? What details in the text support your answer?

Integration of Knowledge and Ideas

6. Evaluate: Tasha learns some important lessons from her experience. What lesson do you think is most important? Support your ideas with details from the text.

7. At the end of the story, readers learn that Junior never told his parents that Tasha lost him. **Hypothesize:** Why do you think he kept this information to himself? Support your answer with details from the story.

---

8. **Is conflict always bad?** Junior makes a vow to always listen to Tasha. **(a)** How does his vow lead to conflict? **(b)** What positive things can Tasha learn from the conflict? **(c)** What does this story suggest about how conflict is often caused by misunderstandings and miscommunication?

> **Details**
>
> Tasha tells Naomi, "If you're scared, don't come. Junior's my only baby brother."

↓

> **Inferences**
>
> Tasha is worried and is determined to find Junior, with or without Naomi's help.

ACADEMIC VOCABULARY

As you write and speak about "The Tail," use the words related to conflict that you explored on page 3 of this text.

---

6. Some students may cite the lesson about the importance of taking responsibilities seriously. Others may refer to the lesson about valuing family members.

7. After the incident, Tasha played checkers with Junior or read him a story, and he didn't seem as "pesty" as he used to be. Junior wanted to keep this good relationship with Tasha.

8. **Is conflict always bad?**
(a) A conflict develops when Tasha doesn't like the way Junior interprets her instructions and directions, even though he does exactly what she asks. For example, when she tells him to "get lost," he gets lost in the park. **(b)** Tasha will avoid future misunderstandings when she learns to say exactly what she means. This is a positive outcome of the conflict. **(c)** The story suggests that once Tasha and Junior learned how to communicate with each other, they were able to resolve their conflict.

 Online Writer's Notebook

Students can use the Online Writer's Notebook to record all responses.

Conventions

1. Introduce the skill, using the instruction on the student page.
2. Discuss the definitions and the examples in the chart.

Think Aloud: Model the Skill

Model the skill of using pronouns, using the following "think aloud." Say to students:

I can use pronouns to avoid repetition and add variety to my writing. For example, I wouldn't write, "When Janet went to the store, Janet bought what Janet needed for Janet's lunch." Instead, I would replace the proper noun *Janet* with the personal pronoun *she* and the possessive pronoun *her*. "When Janet went to the store, she bought what she needed for her lunch." Using pronouns adds variety to my writing.

Practice A

1. her	**4.** its; it
2. her	**5.** they
3. his	

Reading Application
Sample answers:

Personal: she, you
Possessive: your, his

Practice B

1. her; possessive pronoun
2. his; possessive pronoun
3. she; personal pronoun
4. you; personal pronoun
5. them; personal pronoun

Writing Application:
Sample answers:

We are going to drop our books at the library.

Will you lend me your jacket?

Conventions: Personal and Possessive Pronouns

> A **pronoun** is a word that takes the place of a noun or another pronoun.

A **personal pronoun** refers to a specific noun that is named elsewhere in the text. A **possessive pronoun** shows ownership.

Personal Pronouns	Possessive Pronouns
I, me, you, he, him, she, her, it, we, us, they, them	My, mine, your, yours, his, her, hers, its, our, ours, their, theirs

Practice A

Copy these sentences, choosing the correct pronoun for each.

1. Tasha did not want to watch (she/ her) brother.
2. She wanted to jump rope with (her/ hers) friend Naomi.
3. Junior liked to tease (him/ his) sister.
4. The stray dog wagged (it/ its) tail when (it/its) saw Junior.
5. The girls were relieved when (they/ them) found Junior.

Reading Application Scan "The Tail" to find two personal pronouns and two possessive pronouns.

Practice B

Copy each sentence, adding the missing pronoun. Then, tell whether it is a personal or a possessive pronoun.

1. Tasha promised _____ mother to watch Junior carefully.
2. Junior vowed always to listen to _____ sister.
3. Naomi was afraid of the dog, but _____ kept searching for Junior.
4. "At least _____ don't have to stay in the house," Naomi said to Tasha.
5. Ma turned to Tasha and Junior, kissed _____ both goodbye, and left.

Writing Application Write two sentences that include both personal and possessive pronouns. (Example: *He was nervous about speaking in front of his classmates.*)

▶ EXTEND THE LESSON

Sentence Modeling

Write the following sentence from the selection on the board:

> *He wasn't as pesty as he used to be, because now he had Thunder.*

Have students identify the pronouns in the sentence (*he, he, he*). Ask students how the sentence would be different if each pronoun were replaced with the character's name. (*The sentence would have a lot of repetition.*) Finally, have students imitate the sentence in a paragraph on a topic of their choosing, matching the grammatical and stylistic features discussed. Have volunteers share their sentences.

Writing to Sources

Explanatory Text Tasha's experiences with Junior could help her find a job as a baby sitter. Suppose that Tasha were to apply for a steady baby-sitting job. Write a **letter of recommendation** for her in which you list her qualifications for the job. Address your audience and purpose by following these steps:

- Take notes on the qualities and skills that baby-sitters should have.
- Draft your letter, describing ways in which Tasha is suitable for the job.
- Provide examples of Tasha's previous experiences in baby-sitting her brother.
- Check the organization of your letter to be sure it is clear.
- Revise your word choice, where necessary, to ensure its tone is formal and objective.

Grammar Application Review your letter to be sure you have used personal and possessive pronouns correctly.

Research and Technology

Presentation of Ideas In "The Tail," children play games in a city park. Make a **compare-and-contrast** chart about games that children can play outdoors. Conduct research to learn about Tasha's favorite activity, jumping rope. In addition, research one or two other outdoor games. In your chart, categorize the games based on level of difficulty, age-appropriateness, and number of players.

Follow these steps to complete the assignment:

- Take logical and complete notes on your research findings.
- Keep track of all similarities and differences.
- Be sure to note all of your source materials, or the resources you have consulted.
- Use headings to make your chart as clear as possible.
- Present your findings to your classmates in a brief oral report.

 **Common Core State Standards**

Writing
4. Produce clear and coherent writing in which the development, organization, and style are appropriate to task, purpose, and audience.

Speaking and Listening
2. Interpret information presented in diverse media and formats and explain how it contributes to a topic, text, or issue under study.

Language
1. Demonstrate command of the conventions of standard English grammar and usage when writing or speaking.

Writing to Sources

1. Review the assignment, using the instruction on the student page.
2. To give students guidance in writing the explanatory text, give them the **Support for Writing** page for this selection in the *Student Companion All-in-One Workbook.*
3. To evaluate the writing activity, use one of the Business Letter rubrics from *Professional Development Guidebook,* pp. 265–266. Evaluate how well students identify the job responsibilities and personal qualities needed for applicants.

Grammar Application

Have students check their drafts for the correct use of personal and possessive pronouns.

Six Traits Focus

✓	Ideas	Word Choice
✓	Organization	Sentence Fluency
	Voice	Conventions

Research and Technology

1. Review the assignment, using the instruction on the student page.
2. To support students' work on the assignment, have them complete the **Support for Extend Your Learning** page for this selection in the *Student Companion All-in-One Workbook.*

Zlateh the Goat
Isaac Bashevis Singer

LESSON PACING GUIDE

Zlateh the Goat

DAY 1 Preteach/Teach

- Administer the Reading and Vocabulary Warm-ups, as necessary.
- Introduce the Key Ideas and Details skill: Make Inferences.
- Introduce the Craft and Structure skill: Conflict and Resolution.
- Use the Close Reading Model to demonstrate the application of the skills.
- Review the selection vocabulary, as necessary, with students who need additional support.
- Prepare students to read the selection by reviewing with them the Multidraft Reading Strategies.

DAY 2 Teach

- Informally monitor comprehension while students read.
- Use the Comprehension questions to confirm understanding.
- Develop students' ability to make inferences and analyze conflict and resolution using the sidenote questions.
- Reinforce vocabulary with the Vocabulary notes.
- Reinforce unit focus standards using the Spiral Review prompts.

DAY 3 Assess

- Assess students' comprehension and mastery of the skills by having them answer the Literary Analysis questions.
- Have students complete the Vocabulary activities.
- Develop students' understanding of roots and affixes by having them complete the Word Study activities.

DAY 4 Extend/Assess

- Build students' ability to master grammar concepts and conventions by having them complete the Conventions lesson.
- Have students complete the Writing to Sources activity and write a persuasive speech. (You may assign as homework.)
- Extend learning by having students complete the Research and Technology activity: a compare-and-contrast chart.
- Administer the Selection Test or Open-Book Test.

Common Core State Standards

Reading Literature 1. Cite textual evidence to support analysis of what the text says explicitly as well as inferences drawn from the text.

3. Describe how a particular story's plot unfolds in a series of episodes as well as how the characters respond or change as the plot moves toward a resolution.

Writing 1. Write arguments to support claims with clear reasons and relevant evidence.

Speaking and Listening 4. Present claims and findings, sequencing ideas logically and using pertinent descriptions, facts, and details to accentuate main ideas or themes; use appropriate eye contact, adequate volume, and clear pronunciation.

5. Include multimedia components (e.g., graphics) and visual displays in presentations to clarify information.

Language 1.b Use intensive pronouns (e.g., myself, ourselves).

4. Determine or clarify the meaning of unknown and multiple meaning words and phrases.

Daily Block Scheduling

Each day in this Lesson Pacing Guide represents a 40–50 minute period. Teachers using block scheduling may combine days to revise pacing. In addition, teachers may differentiate and support core instruction by integrating components for extended and intensive support as students require. See the Guide to Resources (facing page).

GUIDE TO RESOURCES

		L1	L2	L3	L4	EL	ALL	RESOURCES	PRINT	CD	ONLINE
Warm Up		✓	✓			✓		Vocabulary Warm-ups			✓
		✓	✓			✓		Reading Warm-ups			✓
							✓	Background Video			✓
							✓	Selection Audio		Hear It!	✓
Comprehension/ Selection Support							✓	Writing About the Big Question	Student Companion Workbook		✓
							✓	Literary Analysis	Student Companion Workbook		✓
							✓	Reading	Student Companion Workbook		✓
							✓	Vocabulary Builder	Student Companion Workbook		✓
					✓			Enrichment			✓
			✓	✓	✓			Conventions	Student Companion Workbook		✓
			✓	✓	✓			Writing to Sources	Student Companion Workbook		✓
			✓	✓	✓			Research and Technology	Student Companion Workbook		
Differentiated Instruction/ Additional Support							✓	Additional Standards Practice	Common Core Companion		✓
							✓	Close Reading Practice	Close Reading Notebook		✓
		✓	✓					Adapted Reader's Notebook			✓
						✓		English Reader's Notebook:			✓
						✓		Spanish Reader's Notebook			✓
						✓		Graphic Organizer A			✓
		✓	✓			✓		Graphic Organizer B			✓
		✓	✓			✓		"Animal Heroes"	Reality Central Student Edition and Writing Journal		✓
		✓	✓			✓		Practice and Assess	Reading Kit		✓
Monitor Progress							✓	Selection Test		Exam View	✓
							✓	Open-Book Test		Exam View	✓
Digital Resources							✓	Close Reading Tool			✓
							✓	Online Writer's Notebook			✓

👥 One-on-one teaching 👥 Group work 👥 Whole class instruction 👤 Independent work Ⓐ Assessment 💻 Digital Resource

LEARNER LEVELS

L1 Special-Needs Students
L2 Below-Level Students (Tier 2)

L3 On-Level Students (Tier 1)
L4 Advanced Students (Tier 1)

EL English Learners
All All Students

❶ Is conflict always bad?

Read • Discuss • Research • Write As students read, they will explore the Big Question through text analysis of the selection. Encourage students to take notes as they read and raise additional questions, using text evidence to support their thoughts. Students should refer to their notes to help them deepen their understanding of the selection through discussion, research, and writing.

❷ Close Reading Focus

1. Remind students that when they make inferences, they combine details in the text with their own knowledge. In this way, they can understand what the writer does not state directly.

2. Help students understand the difference between internal and external conflict by giving them examples. Explain that when a farmer is losing crops because of a drought, the conflict is external: the farmer is struggling against nature. If a girl can't decide which puppy she likes best, the conflict is internal because it's a struggle within in her own mind.

Building Knowledge

Meet the Author

Isaac Bashevis Singer (1904–1991) lived in the United States for half his life, but he never forgot the Polish villages of his youth. Prejudice against Jews led Singer to leave Poland for New York in 1935. After World War II devastated the Jewish villages of Eastern Europe, Singer kept writing about the world he remembered. He wrote in his native Yiddish, translating many stories into English. He said, "I always knew that a writer has to write in his own language or not at all." In 1978 Singer won the Nobel Prize in Literature.

Common Core State Standards

Reading Literature
1. Cite textual evidence to support analysis of what the text says explicitly as well as inferences drawn from the text.
3. Describe how a particular story's plot unfolds in a series of episodes as well as how the characters respond or change as the plot moves toward a resolution.

Language
4. Determine or clarify the meaning of unknown and multiple-meaning words and phrases.

❶ Is conflict always bad?

Explore the Big Question as you read "Zlateh the Goat." Take notes on the different conflicts the main character faces.

❷ CLOSE READING FOCUS

Key Ideas and Details: **Make Inferences**

An **inference** is a logical assumption you develop about information that is not directly stated. To make an inference, combine text clues with your prior knowledge, or what you already know. For example, from the sentence, "Tina smiled when she saw the snow," you might infer that Tina is happy. This inference is based on your prior knowledge that people smile when they are happy. Because Tina is smiling at the snow, you can infer that the snow is the reason she is happy.

Craft and Structure: **Conflict and Resolution**

A **conflict** is a struggle between opposing forces. In a short story, the conflict drives the action. Events in the story contribute to the conflict and to the **resolution**—the way the conflict is settled. A conflict can be *external* or *internal*.

- **External conflict:** a character struggles against an outside force, such as another person or an element of nature.
- **Internal conflict:** a character struggles to make a choice, take an action, or overcome a feeling.

A story may have several conflicts, which may be related. As you read, think about the types of conflict that characters face and how the characters change through their experiences.

Vocabulary

You will encounter the following words in "Zlateh the Goat." Which two words have multiple meanings? List each word and its different definitions.

bound	astray	exuded
splendor	trace	flickering

© TEXT COMPLEXITY **RUBRIC**

Zlateh the Goat		Reader and Task Suggestions	
Qualitative Measures		**Preparing to Read the Text**	**Leveled Tasks**
Context/Knowledge Demands	Rural village in Poland 1 2 ③ 4 5	• Discuss with students the bond people can have with animals.	*Levels of Meaning* If students will have difficulty with the concept, have them read to identify details about how Aaron deals
Structure/Language Conventionality and Clarity	Familiar language; culturally specific vocabulary 1 ② 3 4 5	• Guide students to use Multidraft	with the storm. Discuss how the illustrations help capture the dangers Aaron faces.
Levels of Meaning/Purpose/Concept Level	Accessible concept (survival tale of a boy and his goat who find shelter in a haystack) 1 2 3 ④ 5	Reading strategies (TE p. 46).	*Evaluating* If students will not have difficulty with the concept, have them reread and discuss how Zlateh becomes a
Quantitative Measures			source of strength and courage for Aaron.
Lexile	830L **Text Length** Word Count: 2,115		

CLOSE READING MODEL

The passage below is from Isaac Bashevis Singer's short story "Zlateh the Goat." The annotations to the right of the passage show ways in which you can use close reading skills to make inferences and analyze conflict and resolution.

from "Zlateh the Goat"

The snow grew thicker, falling to the ground in large, whirling flakes. Beneath it Aaron's boots touched the softness of a plowed field. He realized that he was no longer on the road. He had gone astray. He could no longer figure out which was east or west, which way was the village, the town. [1] The wind whistled, howled, whirled the snow about in eddies. It looked as if white imps were playing tag on the fields. A white dust rose above the ground. [2] Zlateh stopped. She could walk no longer. Stubbornly she anchored her cleft hooves in the earth and bleated as if pleading to be taken home. Icicles hung from her white beard, and her horns were glazed with frost.

Aaron did not want to admit the danger, but he knew just the same that if they did not find shelter they would freeze to death. [3] This was no ordinary storm. It was a mighty blizzard. The snow had reached his knees. His hands were numb, and he could no longer feel his toes. He choked when he breathed. His nose felt like wood, and he rubbed it with snow. Zlateh's bleating began to sound like crying.

Conflict and Resolution

1 These sentences introduce an external conflict: Aaron is lost during a terrible snowstorm.

Make Inferences

2 Singer's vivid description of the setting—the whistling and howling wind and the whirling snow—can help you infer that Aaron and Zlateh are in grave danger.

Conflict and Resolution

3 In addition to his external conflict with the storm, Aaron also experiences an internal conflict. He does not want to admit his fear, but he knows he must find shelter. His internal struggle suggests that he must overcome his fear to survive the storm.

For each class during which you will teach this selection, have students complete one of the five Vocabulary activities for Week 3 in *Daily Bellringer Activities*. You may wish to use additional activities that are applicable to this selection.

Vocabulary

If students require support with selection vocabulary, use this routine:

1. Write the following words and definitions on the board:

   bound *v.* tied

   astray *adv.* away from the correct path

   exuded *v.* gave off; oozed

   splendor *n.* gorgeous appearance; magnificence

   trace *n.* mark left behind by something

   flickering *v.* burning unsteadily

2. Have students say each word aloud.

3. Use the word in a sentence that defines the word.

🎯 DIFFERENTIATED INSTRUCTION

🔵 Extended Support—English Learners
Have students complete the **Reading and Vocabulary Warm-ups** for this selection in the *Student Companion All-in-One Workbook* before they read. Assign the prereading pages and the adapted selection in the *Reader's Notebook: English Learner's Version*. Then, have students listen to portions of the selection in the *Student eText* or on the *Hear It!* CD-ROM.

🔲 🔲 Extended Support—Struggling Readers
Have students complete the **Reading and Vocabulary Warm-ups** for this selection in the *Student Companion All-in-One Workbook* before they read. Assign the prereading pages and the adapted selection in the *Reader's Notebook: Adapted Version*. Then, have students listen to portions of the selection in the *Student eText* or on the *Hear It!* CD-ROM (adapted text).

Extended Support—Reluctant Readers
To build motivation and engagement before assigning the selection, have students read "Animal Heroes" a thematically related selection in *Reality Central*. Then, use the questions at the conclusion of the related selection to guide discussion.

MULTIDRAFT READING

This icon ● marks natural pauses in the selection. To assist struggling readers and to deepen comprehension for all, assign the text in "chunks," separated by the icons, and apply multidraft reading protocols. For each reading, have students set the purpose indicated:

- **First reading:** Students should read the selection independently and think about its basic meaning.
- **Second reading:** Students should analyze the text's key ideas and details and its craft and structure, and respond to the side-column prompts.
- **Third reading:** Students should integrate knowledge and ideas, connect the text to other texts and to the world, and answer the end-of-selection questions.

For more guidance, refer to the *Classroom Strategies and Teaching Routines* card on multidraft reading.

❶ Activating Prior Knowledge

Use the **Vocab-o-Gram** strategy (*Professional Development Guidebook,* pp. 39–40) to help students make predictions about the selection. Write the following words on the board or overhead:

village	numb
goat	haystack
blizzard	stillness
shelter	sleigh bells

Then, give students the **Vocab-o-Gram** chart (*Professional Development Guidebook,* p. 40) and have them work with a partner to group words in appropriate categories and make predictions about the story. Have students discuss or explain their word placements, their reasons, and their predictions. Students will return to the **Vocab-o-Gram** after completing the story.

❷ Conflict and Resolution

Ask the Conflict and Resolution question. **Answer:** His decision resolves the conflict between keeping the goat and having money to buy holiday necessities.

❶ # Zlateh the Goat

Isaac Bashevis Singer

Conflict and Resolution
What conflict is resolved by Reuven's decision to sell Zlateh?

At Hanukkah[1] time the road from the village to the town is usually covered with snow, but this year the winter had been a mild one. Hanukkah had almost come, yet little snow had fallen. The sun shone most of the time. The peasants complained that because of the dry weather there would be a poor harvest of winter grain. New grass sprouted, and the peasants sent their cattle out to pasture.

For Reuven the furrier it was a bad year, and after long hesitation he decided to sell Zlateh the goat. She was old and gave little milk. Feivel the town butcher had offered ❷ eight gulden[2] for her. Such a sum would buy Hanukkah candles, potatoes and oil for pancakes, gifts for the children, and other holiday necessaries for the house. Reuven told his oldest boy Aaron to take the goat to town.

1. **Hanukkah** (khä´ noo kä) Jewish festival celebrated for eight days in early winter. Hanukkah is also called the "festival of lights" because a candle is lit on each of the eight days.
2. **gulden** (gool´ den) *n.* unit of money.

💬 VOCABULARY DEVELOPMENT

Thematic Vocabulary: The Big Question
As students are discussing "Zlateh the Goat," encourage them to use the thematic vocabulary presented in Introducing the Big Question, pp. 2–3. You might encourage them with sentence starters like these:

1. Because it was a bad year for Reuven the furrier, he *concluded* that he must . . .
2. Zlateh did not *resist* when Aaron first . . .
3. The sudden change in the weather was a *challenge* to Aaron and Zlateh because . . .
4. Aaron could not *negotiate* with Zlateh when she stubbornly . . .
5. Aaron knew that their *survival* depended on . . .

3

Illustrations copyright © 1966 by Maurice Sendak, copyright renewed 1994 by Maurice Sendak. Printed with permission from HarperCollins Publishers.

Aaron understood what taking the goat to Feivel meant, but had to obey his father. Leah, his mother, wiped the tears from her eyes when she heard the news. Aaron's younger sisters, Anna and Miriam, cried loudly. Aaron put on his quilted jacket and a cap with earmuffs, bound a rope around Zlateh's neck, and took along two slices of bread with cheese to eat on the road. Aaron was supposed

4 ◀ **Critical Viewing**
What do you think life is like in a village like the one in this picture?

◀ **Vocabulary**
bound (bound)
v. tied

5 **Comprehension**
Why is Aaron taking the goat to Feivel?

PART 2 • Zlateh the Goat **47**

🏵 DIFFERENTIATED INSTRUCTION

Support for Less Proficient Readers
Have students listen to the story in the *Student eText* or on the *Hear It!* CD-ROM. Tell them to first listen to the story for pleasure. Then have students read the story with a partner. Tell students to stop several times on each page and ask one another a question about the passage they just read. If they do not agree on the answer, have them reread the section to locate the answer.

Enrichment for Advanced Readers
Suggest that students find and read additional works by Isaac Bashevis Singer. You may wish to recommend the following selections:
• "Shrewd Todie & Lyzer the Miser"
• "Utzel & His Daughter, Poverty"
• "The Parakeet Named Dreidel"
  After students have read these works, have them form discussion groups in which they compare and contrast the selections they have read. Suggest criteria for comparison, such as setting and conflict.

---

3 **Humanities**

Illustration for "Zlateh the Goat," by Maurice Sendak
Writer and illustrator Maurice Sendak was born in 1928 in Brooklyn, New York. He loved books from an early age. He began working as a book illustrator in high school and published his first book at age nineteen. He is best known for his Caldecott Medal–winning book *Where the Wild Things Are.*

Both Sendak and writer Isaac Bashevis Singer had many relatives in Poland who were killed in the Holocaust during World War II. The Holocaust essentially wiped out the Jewish population in the villages. Use these questions for discussion.

1. How does the fact that the way of life described in "Zlateh the Goat" no longer exists affect the importance of the writer's and artist's collaboration?
   Possible response: It makes their effort even more meaningful because it documents a way of life that has been lost.

2. **Ask:** How does your life today compare to Aaron's, as pictured on pages 47, 49, and 51?
   Possible response: Children had more freedom and responsibility in the village. They were allowed to travel great distances on their own.

4 **Critical Viewing**

Possible response: Life in this village is probably quiet and peaceful. Because it is small, everyone probably knows everyone else.

5 **Comprehension**

Answer: Feivel will pay money for the goat. The butcher will turn it into meat to sell to customers.

 **Video**

Watch the Background Video online!

 **Audio**

Selection audio is available in the *Student eText* and on the *Hear It!* CD-ROM.

Spiral Review

Character

1. Remind students that they studied the concept of character in the Unit 1 Focus on Craft and Structure (pp. 14–17).

2. **Ask** students the Spiral Review question.

   Possible response: The fact that Zlateh is so good-natured and trusting makes it especially difficult to say goodbye, as the family knows she will be killed. If the goat were ornery instead, there would probably not be any conflict or sadness about sending her to the butcher.

❻ Conflict and Resolution

1. Remind students that an external conflict occurs when a character struggles against an outside force, such as the wind and snow described in this passage.

2. **Ask** students the Conflict and Resolution question.

   Answer: The snow covers the road and prevents Aaron from seeing anything around him. The wind causes him to become very cold. He can no longer find the road to town.

3. **Ask** students to explain why the weather's action might also cause an *internal* conflict for Aaron.

   Possible response: He might wish to return home at the same time that he wants to complete the task his father has given him.

Spiral Review
CHARACTER How do Zlateh's natural personality traits intensify the conflict at the beginning of the story?

Conflict and Resolution
In what two ways are the snow and wind in conflict with Aaron? ❻

---

to deliver the goat by evening, spend the night at the butcher's, and return the next day with the money.

While the family said goodbye to the goat, and Aaron placed the rope around her neck, Zlateh stood as patiently and good-naturedly as ever. She licked Reuven's hand. She shook her small white beard. Zlateh trusted human beings. She knew that they always fed her and never did her any harm.

When Aaron brought her out on the road to town, she seemed somewhat astonished. She'd never been led in that direction before. She looked back at him questioningly, as if to say, "Where are you taking me?" But after a while she seemed to come to the conclusion that a goat shouldn't ask questions. Still, the road was different. They passed new fields, pastures, and huts with thatched roofs. Here and there a dog barked and came running after them, but Aaron chased it away with his stick.

The sun was shining when Aaron left the village. Suddenly the weather changed. A large black cloud with a bluish center appeared in the east and spread itself rapidly over the sky. A cold wind blew in with it. The crows flew low, croaking. At first it looked as if it would rain, but instead it began to hail as in summer. It was early in the day, but it became dark as dusk. After a while the hail turned to snow.

In his twelve years Aaron had seen all kinds of weather, but he had never experienced a snow like this one. It was so dense it shut out the light of the day. In a short time their path was completely covered. The wind became as cold as ice. The road to town was narrow and winding. Aaron no longer knew where he was. He could not see through the snow. The cold soon penetrated his quilted jacket.

At first Zlateh didn't seem to mind the change in weather. She, too, was twelve years old and knew what winter meant. But when her legs sank deeper and deeper into the snow, she began to turn her head and look at Aaron in wonderment. Her mild eyes seemed to ask, "Why are we out in such a storm?" Aaron hoped that a peasant

---

🍄 THINK ALOUD

Vocabulary: Context

Direct students' attention to the word *anchored* in the first paragraph on the next page. Say to students:

I am going to think aloud to show you how to figure out the meaning of *anchored* from its context.

When I read the sentence in which the word appears, I see that *anchored* is something Zlateh does with or to her hooves: "she anchored her cleft hooves in the earth." I re-read the sentences that come right before this sentence: "Zlateh stopped.

She could walk no longer." These sentences show me that Zlateh is not moving. I realize that the word *anchored* means something like the opposite of moved.

Next, I notice that *anchored* is something Zlateh does "stubbornly." Picturing the scene, I imagine Zlateh stopped, refusing to be led any further. I infer that *anchored* means "stuck or dug firmly in place." Zlateh has stuck her hooves in the ground and will not move. To check my definition, I will look up the word in a dictionary.

would come along with his cart, but no one passed by.

The snow grew thicker, falling to the ground in large, whirling flakes. Beneath it Aaron's boots touched the softness of a plowed field. He realized that he was no longer on the road. He had gone *astray*. He could no longer figure out which was east or west, which way was the village, the town. The wind whistled, howled, whirled the snow about in eddies.[3] It looked as if white imps were playing tag on the fields. A white dust rose above the ground. Zlateh stopped. She could walk no longer. Stubbornly she anchored her cleft hooves in the earth and bleated as if pleading to be taken home. Icicles hung from her white beard, and her horns were glazed with frost.

Aaron did not want to admit the danger, but he knew just the same that if they did not find shelter they would freeze to death. This was no ordinary storm. It was a mighty blizzard. The snow had reached his knees. His hands were numb, and he could no longer feel his toes. He choked when he breathed. His nose felt like wood, and he rubbed it with snow. Zlateh's bleating began to sound like crying. Those humans in whom

Illustrations copyright © 1966 by Maurice Sendak, copyright renewed 1994 by Maurice Sendak. Printed with permission from HarperCollins Publishers.

---

3. eddies (ed´ ēz) *n.* currents of air moving in circular motions like little whirlwinds.

◀ **Vocabulary**
astray (ə strā´)
adv. away from the correct path

❽ Comprehension
What surprises Zlateh when she and Aaron reach the road?

❼ Compare and Contrast

1. Have students read the bracketed passage on the student page.

2. Encourage students to notice details in the passage that describe the setting. Point out the fact that the setting is an important factor in the conflict that is building.

3. **Ask:** What details in the passage show the increasingly dangerous situation that Aaron and Zlateh are both facing?

   Possible response: The snow is falling rapidly and has completely covered the road. They have gone astray and lost their sense of direction. They might freeze to death.

4. **Ask:** How are Aaron's and Zlateh's responses to the storm the same? How are they different?

   Possible response: They are both cold, tired, and frightened. Zlateh wants to stay in one place and go no farther. Aaron knows that they must find shelter.

❽ Comprehension

Answer: She is surprised by the direction they take. She has never been led along the road in that direction before.

≋ FLUENCY

Distribute copies of this page and pair students. Have partners take turns reading sets of five sentences aloud. Listeners should mark any words or sentences with which readers have difficulty. Circulate to monitor students' fluency. Collect students' marked-up copies of the story and review difficult words and passages with the class. Look for these problem spots:

- If students have difficulty pronouncing words such as *whistled* and *anchored*, point out that both words include letters which are not pronounced. Guide students to identify the silent *t* in *whistled*, and the silent *h* in *anchored*.

- If students fail to blend the consonants in *howled*, point out the similarity to the word *owl*. Then, read the passage fluently and with expression while students track, or follow along as you read.

- If students fail to recognize words such as *imps, cleft,* and *blizzard*, encourage them to ask themselves if the words are critical to their understanding. If not, suggest that they skip the words temporarily and read ahead. If the meaning is still unclear, point out that they may need to reread the passage to look for context clues that appeared before the words.

⑨ Conflict and Resolution

1. Ask students to recall the two ways that the snow and wind are in conflict with Aaron.

Answer: They cause him to become lost, and they cause him to become very cold.

2. Ask students what Aaron does when he reaches the haystack.

Answer: He digs through the snow and hollows out a space in the hay for Zlateh and himself.

3. Ask the Conflict and Resolution question.

Possible response: The haystack provides shelter and warmth, so the problem of freezing to death is temporarily solved.

▶ **Monitor Progress:** Ask students to explain why the blizzard is a source of conflict for Aaron.

▶ **Reteach:** If students have difficulty explaining why the blizzard causes conflict, point out that because of the blizzard, Aaron's life is in danger and so is Zlateh's. Have students complete the following cause-and-effect sentences to help understand the struggle that occurs: *The blizzard is a problem for Aaron because _____.* (**Answer:** he cannot take the goat to the butcher.) *Because of the storm, Aaron has to _____.* (**Answer:** find shelter.)

⑩ Connecting to the Big Question

1. Point out that feelings may change while surviving a conflict as people (and animals) work to help themselves and each other.

2. Have students reread the bracketed passage on this page. Remind them that Zlateh had stubbornly refused to go on. **Ask:** In what way do Zlateh's feelings towards Aaron change?

Possible response: She is very grateful that he has brought them to a shelter that is warm and made of hay. She has regained her confidence in people.

3. Ask: Why is Zlateh eager to reward Aaron?

Possible response: She wants to thank him for saving her life.

Conflict and Resolution
How has the discovery of the haystack temporarily resolved Aaron's problem?

Vocabulary ▶
exuded (eg zy $\overline{oo}$ d′ əd)
v. gave off; oozed

she had so much confidence had dragged her into a trap. Aaron began to pray to God for himself and for the innocent animal.

Suddenly he made out the shape of a hill. He wondered what it could be. Who had piled snow into such a huge heap? He moved toward it, dragging Zlateh after him. When he came near it, he realized that it was a large haystack which the snow had blanketed.

Aaron realized immediately that they were saved. With great effort he dug his way through the snow. He was a village boy and knew what to do. When he reached the hay, he hollowed out a nest for himself and the goat. No matter how cold it may be outside, in the hay it is always warm. And hay was food for Zlateh. The moment she smelled it she became contented and began to eat. Outside, the snow continued to fall. It quickly covered the passageway Aaron had dug. But a boy and an animal need to breathe, and there was hardly any air in their hideout. Aaron bored a kind of a window through the hay and snow and carefully kept the passage clear.

Zlateh, having eaten her fill, sat down on her hind legs and seemed to have regained her confidence in man. Aaron ate his two slices of bread and cheese, but after the difficult journey he was still hungry. He looked at Zlateh and noticed her udders were full. He lay down next to her, placing himself so that when he milked her he could squirt the milk into his mouth. It was rich and sweet. Zlateh was not accustomed to being milked that way, but she did not resist. On the contrary, she seemed eager to reward Aaron for bringing her to a shelter whose very walls, floor, and ceiling were made of food. •

Through the window Aaron could catch a glimpse of the chaos outside. The wind carried before it whole drifts of snow. It was completely dark, and he did not know whether night had already come or whether it was the darkness of the storm. Thank God that in the hay it was not cold. The dried hay, grass, and field flowers exuded the warmth of the summer sun. Zlateh ate frequently; she

---

💬 VOCABULARY DEVELOPMENT

Vocabulary Reinforcement

To reinforce and assess students' comprehension of selection Vocabulary words, give them sentences in which the word may or may not be used correctly. Students must tell whether the use is correct and explain their answer.

Use these sentences:

1. She sniffed the blossoms and *exuded* the sweet fragrance of roses.
Answer: No, *exuded* is not used correctly. People do not give off the odor of flowers as they smell them.

2. Emma collected wood and bound it in a pile to make a campfire.
Answer: No, *bound* is not used correctly. It does not make sense to tie wood together when building a fire.

3. Ben thought he had *bound* the canoe to the dock, but it had drifted away.
Answer: Yes, *bound* is used correctly. It would make sense to tie a canoe to a dock.

nibbled from above, below, from the left and right. Her body gave forth an animal warmth, and Aaron cuddled up to her. He had always loved Zlateh, but now she was like a sister. He was alone, cut off from his family, and wanted to talk. He began to talk to Zlateh. "Zlateh, what do you think about what has happened to us?" he asked.

"Maaaa," Zlateh answered.

"If we hadn't found this stack of hay, we would both be frozen stiff by now," Aaron said.

"Maaaa," was the goat's reply.

"If the snow keeps on falling like this, we may have to stay here for days," Aaron explained.

"Maaaa," Zlateh bleated.

"What does 'Maaaa' mean?" Aaron asked. "You'd better speak up clearly."

"Maaaa, Maaaa," Zlateh tried.

"Well, let it be 'Maaaa' then," Aaron said patiently. "You can't speak, but I know you understand. I need you and you need me. Isn't that right?"

"Maaaa."

Aaron became sleepy. He made a pillow out of some hay, leaned his head on it, and dozed off. Zlateh, too, fell asleep.

When Aaron opened his eyes, he didn't know whether it was morning or night. The snow had blocked up his window. He tried

Illustrations copyright © 1966 by Maurice Sendak, copyright renewed 1994 by Maurice Sendak. Printed with permission from HarperCollins Publishers.

⑫ ▲ Critical Viewing
Why does Aaron look sad here?

⑬ Comprehension
What shelter do Aaron and Zlateh find?

⑪ Compare and Contrast

1. Have students read the bracketed passage and point out the contrast between the natural landscape and Zlateh. **Ask** students to name some of the words the author uses to create this contrast.

   Possible responses: Words describing the landscape include *chaos, drifts of snow,* and *darkness.* Words describing Zlateh include *nibbled, warmth, cuddled, sister.*

2. **Ask** students how they think this contrast helps emphasize the conflict in the story.

   Answer: The outside environment is snowy, dark and lifeless, whereas Zlateh provides warmth, comfort, and companionship. It is easy to see how Aaron becomes more attached to Zlateh in light of the natural conditions.

⑫ Critical Viewing

Possible response: He is sad because he is alone, lost, and cold. He is concerned that he and Zlateh will be stuck inside the haystack until the storm passes.

⑬ Comprehension

Answer: They find a haystack to use as shelter.

⚙ DIFFERENTIATED INSTRUCTION

Support for Special-Needs Students
Struggling readers may have trouble understanding the story's examples of external conflict. The concept of a blizzard as an opposing force is less tangible than another person as an opposing force. To help them understand this force, have them reread the story and make a list of everything the blizzard "does." For each of the storm's actions, have students note Aaron's response or reaction.

EL Vocabulary for English Learners
English learners may have trouble understanding some of the idiomatic language in the story. For example, at the top of the previous page, explain that when Aaron "made out" the shape of a hill, it means he *saw* it. In the next paragraph, Aaron "hollowed out" a nest. Explain that this means he dug a hole and used it as a nest, near the top of this page, Explain what it means for Aaron to be "cut off," or distanced from his family. And toward the bottom of this page, Aaron "dozed off," or fell asleep.

⑭ Conflict and Resolution

1. Have students read the bracketed passage that begins on the previous page. Then, **ask** a volunteer to summarize the passage in his or her own words.

Possible response: When Aaron wakes up, it's so dark he doesn't know if it is night or day. The window is blocked with snow. He uses his stick to break through the snow to let air into the haystack. The storm is still going on outside and the wind is wailing. Zlateh wakes up and comforts Aaron with her bleating.

2. Ask students why they think Aaron and Zlateh don't leave the haystack.

Possible response: It is dark outside and still snowing.

3. Ask students the Conflict and Resolution question.

Possible responses: If they leave the haystack they will freeze. The falling snow could suffocate Aaron and Zlateh by covering up the window and cutting off their air supply. The snow could become so deep that Aaron will not be able to dig out an air hole.

⑮ Make Inferences

1. Before reading the bracketed passage aloud, instruct students to listen for details that provide clues about how Aaron is feeling.

2. After reading the passage, explain that the details describe Aaron's point of view about time and place at this point in the story. **Ask** students to summarize that point of view.

Possible response: Aaron feels that he and Zlateh have been inside the haystack forever, that everything else he'd ever experienced never really happened.

3. Ask the Make Inferences question.

Possible response: Aaron is disoriented by the situation. With nothing to do and nothing changing, he loses track of time.

4. Have students add information about Aaron's feelings to the **Reading Skill Graphic Organizer B** for "Zlateh the Goat."

Conflict and Resolution
In what way are Aaron and Zlateh still in danger from the storm?

⑭

Make Inferences
Using your own experience, what inference can you make about how Aaron feels, based on the details in this passage?

⑮

Vocabulary ▶
splendor (splen´dər) *n.* gorgeous appearance; magnificence

---

to clear it, but when he had bored through to the length of his arm, he still hadn't reached the outside. Luckily he had his stick with him and was able to break through to the open air. It was still dark outside. The snow continued to fall and the wind wailed, first with one voice and then with many. Sometimes it had the sound of devilish laughter. Zlateh, too, awoke, and when Aaron greeted her, she answered, "Maaaa." Yes, Zlateh's language consisted of only one word, but it meant many things. Now she was saying, "We must accept all that God gives us—heat, cold, hunger, satisfaction, light, and darkness."

Aaron had awakened hungry. He had eaten up his food, but Zlateh had plenty of milk.

For three days Aaron and Zlateh stayed in the haystack. Aaron had always loved Zlateh, but in these three days he loved her more and more. She fed him with her milk and helped him keep warm. She comforted him with her patience. He told her many stories, and she always cocked her ears and listened. When he patted her, she licked his hand and his face. Then she said, "Maaaa," and he knew it meant, I love you, too.

The snow fell for three days, though after the first day it was not as thick and the wind quieted down. Sometimes Aaron felt that there could never have been a summer, that the snow had always fallen, ever since he could remember. He, Aaron, never had a father or mother or sisters. He was a snow child, born of the snow, and so was Zlateh. It was so quiet in the hay that his ears rang in the stillness. Aaron and Zlateh slept all night and a good part of the day. As for Aaron's dreams, they were all about warm weather. He dreamed of green fields, trees covered with blossoms, clear brooks, and singing birds. By the third night the snow had stopped, but Aaron did not dare to find his way home in the darkness. The sky became clear and the moon shone, casting silvery nets on the snow. Aaron dug his way out and looked at the world. It was all white, quiet, dreaming dreams of heavenly splendor. The stars were large and close. The moon swam in the sky as in a sea.

💬 VOCABULARY DEVELOPMENT

Vocab-o-Gram

Have students return to their **Vocab-o-Grams** to re-evaluate the predictions they made about the story. If they are uncertain about the meaning of any words they recorded on the chart, have them return to the selection to use context clues or look up the words in a dictionary.

On the morning of the fourth day Aaron heard the ringing of sleigh bells. The haystack was not far from the road. The peasant who drove the sleigh pointed out the way to him—not to the town and Feivel the butcher, but home to the village. Aaron had decided in the haystack that he would never part with Zlateh.

Aaron's family and their neighbors had searched for the boy and the goat but had found no trace of them during the storm. They feared they were lost. Aaron's mother and sisters cried for him; his father remained silent and gloomy. Suddenly one of the neighbors came running to their house with the news that Aaron and Zlateh were coming up the road.

There was great joy in the family. Aaron told them how he had found the stack of hay and how Zlateh had fed him with her milk. Aaron's sisters kissed and hugged Zlateh and gave her a special treat of chopped carrots and potato peels, which Zlateh gobbled up hungrily.

Nobody ever again thought of selling Zlateh, and now that the cold weather had finally set in, the villagers needed the services of Reuven the furrier once more. When Hanukkah came, Aaron's mother was able to fry pancakes every evening, and Zlateh got her portion, too. Even though Zlateh had her own pen, she often came to the kitchen, knocking on the door with her horns to indicate that she was ready to visit, and she was always admitted. In the evening Aaron, Miriam, and Anna played dreidel.[4] Zlateh sat near the stove watching the children and the flickering of the Hanukkah candles.

Once in a while Aaron would ask her, "Zlateh, do you remember the three days we spent together?"

And Zlateh would scratch her neck with a horn, shake her white bearded head, and come out with the single sound which expressed all her thoughts, and all her love.

◀ **Vocabulary**
trace (trās) *n.* mark left behind by something

◀ **Vocabulary**
flickering (flik´ər iŋ) *v.* burning unsteadily

Conflict and Resolution
How is the family's conflict over selling Zlateh resolved?

---

4. **dreidel** (drā´ dəl) *n.* small top with Hebrew letters on each of four sides, spun in a game played by children.

PART 2 • Zlateh the Goat **53**

GUIDED EXPLORATION

16 Conflict and Resolution

1. Have students recall the father's conflict that involved Zlateh at the beginning of the story.

   Answer: He had to make a choice between keeping the goat or having money to buy holiday necessities.

2. **Ask** students to identify the details that describe how family members treat Zlateh after she and Aaron return.

   Answer: They kiss and hug her, give her treats, and let her in the house.

3. **Ask** students the Conflict and Resolution question.

   Possible response: The family is so happy that Zlateh kept Aaron alive that they decide to keep her.

 **ASSESS**

Language Study
Vocabulary
Sample answers:

1. Footprints leave a *trace* in the snow.
2. I *bound* the stack of newspapers with twine.
3. I went *astray* in the woods and couldn't find the trail.
4. I gazed up at the *flickering* light from a star.
5. The tourists enjoyed the *splendor* of the royal gardens.

Word Study
Part A
Sample answers:

When you *exceed* the speed limit, you go *beyond* the legal limit. When something *expands,* it grows *outward.*

Part B
Sample answers:

1. When you *exhale* a lot of air, you breathe out a lot of air from your lungs.
2. Most students would vote to *extend,* or stretch out, a school holiday beyond its current limits.

Illustrations copyright © 1966 by Maurice Sendak, copyright renewed 1994 by Maurice Sendak. Printed with permission from HarperCollins Publishers.

Language Study

Vocabulary The words below appear in "Zlateh the Goat." Answer each question that follows, using a word from the list.

bound   astray   splendor   trace   flickering

1. Which word could describe footprints left in the snow?
2. How else could you say that you tied two things together?
3. How can you describe losing your way?
4. How might you describe the light from a star?
5. Which word can apply to a place of great beauty?

WORD STUDY

The **Latin prefix ex-** means "out," "from," or "beyond."

In this story, dried hay, grass, and flowers exuded the sun's warmth, or sent out the warmth of the sun.

Word Study

Part A Explain how the **Latin prefix ex-** contributes to the meanings of the words *exceed* and *expand.* Consult a dictionary if necessary.

Part B Use context and what you know about the Latin prefix *ex-* to explain your answer to each question.

1. What happens when you *exhale* a lot of air?
2. Would you vote to *extend* a school holiday?

Literary Analysis

Key Ideas and Details

1. **Make Inferences** Aaron's mother and sisters cry over selling Zlateh. What inference can you make about their feelings for the goat?

2. **(a)** What happens to Aaron and Zlateh on the way to town? **(b) Deduce:** Why is their situation dangerous? Cite details from the text to support your responses.

3. **Make Inferences** What evidence in the story supports the inference that Aaron is quick-thinking and brave?

Craft and Structure

4. **Conflict and Resolution** In a chart like the one on the right, record each of the following **conflicts**, tell whether it is internal or external, and explain how it was resolved.

   (a) Reuven needs the money he could get for Zlateh, but he loves Zlateh.

   (b) Aaron and Zlateh need food and shelter but are caught in a blizzard.

5. **Conflict and Resolution** Explain how the resolution of the first conflict is connected to the second conflict. Support your response with textual evidence.

Integration of Knowledge and Ideas

6. **(a) Draw Conclusions:** Why does Reuven never again think of selling Zlateh after Aaron and the goat return home? **(b) Apply:** What is the story's message about friendship and trust?

7. **(a) Generalize:** What message does the story convey about animals and their relationships with people? **(b) Support:** What evidence from the story supports this message?

8. **Is conflict always bad? (a)** What does Aaron learn about himself during his struggle to survive the snowstorm? **(b)** What does he learn about Zlateh during this time? **(c)** What lessons does this story suggest about overcoming challenges and dangerous situations?

Conflict

What Kind?

Resolution

ACADEMIC VOCABULARY

As you write and speak about "Zlateh the Goat," use the words related to conflict that you explored on page 3 of this text.

Literary Analysis

Possible responses appear below. Check to be sure students support their responses with evidence from the text.

1. You can infer that they love the goat and that having to sell her breaks their hearts.

2. **(a)** They get caught in a blizzard. **(b)** They lose their way, and Aaron realizes "that if they did not find shelter, they would freeze to death."

3. When he sees the shape covered with snow, he realizes it is a haystack. He decides to take shelter in the haystack, bores a hole in the hay and snow to let in air, and does not panic.

4. Internal conflict; Resolution: He decides he must sell Zlateh to get the money he needs.

   External conflict; Resolution: Aaron finds a haystack that provides shelter and food.

5. When Reuven decides to sell Zlateh, he tells Aaron to take the goat to the butcher, which is why Aaron and Zlateh get caught in a blizzard.

6. **(a)** The family, including Reuven, is grateful that Zlateh saved Aaron by providing him with milk during the storm. **(b)** Friendship and trust are more important than money.

7. **(a)** The story shows that animals and people have a close emotional bond and that animals have feelings and even thoughts, even though they can't express them in words. **(b)** The descriptions of how Zlateh saves Aaron with her milk and how the two huddle together for warmth show their close emotional bond. Singer's imaginative descriptions of Zlateh's thoughts show that animals have feelings.

8. **Is conflict always bad? (a)** Aaron learns that he can think fast in an emergency and can figure out a clever way to survive. **(b)** He learns that Zlateh can supply food, warmth, and companionship in an emergency. **(c)** The story suggests that people can overcome challenges by remaining calm and working together.

 Online Writer's Notebook

Students can use the Online Writer's Notebook to record all responses.

Conventions

1. Introduce the skill, using the instruction on the student page.

2. Discuss the definitions and the examples in the chart.

Think Aloud: Model the Skill

Model the skill of using pronouns. Say to students:

> To tell which words are interrogative pronouns, I look for words that ask questions that are answered by nouns or pronouns. For example, *Which of the dogs has fleas?* includes the interrogative pronoun *which*. It can be answered by a noun, such as *collie*. To tell which words are indefinite pronouns, I look for words that refer to people, places, and things that don't tell exactly which ones. For example, *Some of the books are overdue* doesn't tell exactly which books are overdue. I realize that *some* is an indefinite pronoun.

Practice A

1. *What*: interrogative

2. *whom*: interrogative

3. *Everyone*: indefinite

4. *Who*: interrogative

5. *All*: indefinite

Reading Application

Sample answers:

interrogative:

1. "*Who* had piled snow into a huge heap?

2. "*What* does 'Maaaa' mean?" Aaron asked.

indefinite:

1. Suddenly *one* of the neighbors came running to their house with the news that Aaron and Zlateh were coming up the road.

2. Aaron hoped that a peasant would come along with his cat, but *no one* passed by.

Practice B

1. *himself*: intensive

2. *herself*: reflexive

3. *themselves*: intensive

4. *herself*: intensive

Writing Application

Sample answers:

Aaron and Zlateh helped save *themselves*.

Reuven *himself* decided not to sell the goat.

 ## Close Reading Activities Continued

Conventions: Interrogative, Indefinite, Reflexive, and Intensive Pronouns

> A **pronoun** is a word that takes the place of a noun or another pronoun.

Interrogative pronouns are used in questions.

Indefinite pronouns refer to one or more unspecified objects or people.

Reflexive pronouns are formed by adding *-self* or *-selves* to a pronoun, as in *herself* and *ourselves*. They point to the person or thing receiving the action when that person or thing is the same as the one performing the action.

Intensive pronouns add emphasis to another noun or pronoun in the sentence. Like reflexive pronouns, they are formed by adding *-self* or *-selves* to a pronoun. However, they are not essential to the meaning of the sentence. They are usually found very close to the noun or pronoun they emphasize.

Interrogative Pronouns	Indefinite Pronouns	Reflexive Pronouns	Intensive Pronouns
Who would like an apple?	*Some* of my friends live in Cleveland.	Jeremy gave *himself* a haircut.	Ana *herself* raised the flag.
Which of these hats is yours?	Please serve *all* of the cookies.	I don't want to make *myself* feel bad.	In a democracy, the people *themselves* rule.

Practice A

Identify the pronoun in each sentence as *interrogative* or *indefinite*.

1. What is the name of Aaron's father?

2. To whom does he want to sell his goat?

3. Everyone feels sad about selling Zlateh.

4. Who shows Aaron the way home?

5. All of the family express their joy.

Reading Application In "Zlateh the Goat," find two interrogative pronouns and two indefinite pronouns.

Practice B

Identify the pronoun in each sentence as *reflexive* or *intensive*.

1. Aaron himself had a decision to make.

2. Zlateh helped herself to more hay.

3. The neighbors themselves searched for Aaron and Zlateh.

4. Aaron's mother cooked the Hanukkah meal herself.

Writing Application Write two sentences about the story that include reflexive pronouns and intensive pronouns.

▶ EXTEND THE LESSON

Sentence Modeling

Write the following sentence from the selection on the board:

> *Nobody ever again thought of selling Zlateh, and now that the cold weather had finally set in, the villagers needed the services of Reuven the furrier once more.*

Ask students what they notice about the sentence. Elicit from them that the sentence uses an indefinite pronoun (*nobody*). Then ask what else they notice about the sentence (it includes independent clauses that combine several pieces of information).

Have students imitate the sentence in a sentence on a topic of their own choosing, matching each grammatical and stylistic feature discussed. Collect the sentences, and share them with the class.

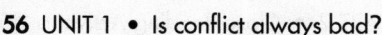

Writing to Sources

Argument Write and present a short **persuasive speech** that Aaron might give to urge his father to keep Zlateh. Address your audience and purpose by following these steps:

- State your position clearly and present at least two reasons that support it.
- Consider Aaron's father's concerns and the counterarguments he might make.
- Conclude your speech by summarizing your position. Avoid using the same words that you used to state your position.
- Rehearse your speech. Consider practicing in front of a mirror or another person. If possible, record your practice.
- Revise your speech to remove less-persuasive details. Then, practice your revised speech once again before presenting it.

Grammar Application Read over your speech and be sure you have used all intensive pronouns correctly.

Research and Technology

Presentation of Ideas Make and present a **compare-and-contrast chart.** Compare and contrast your hometown to a *shtetl*, a Jewish village in Eastern Europe before World War II, like the one in which Aaron and his family live. Follow these steps to complete the assignment:

- Use key words to search online databases for information.
- Organize the information according to categories such as population, resources, way of life, and so on.
- Fill in the chart with information for each category. Include visuals to clarify the information you find.
- Analyze the information and write a summary of your findings.
- Present your findings to the class. Invite comments and feedback when you finish.

 **Common Core State Standards**

Writing
1. Write arguments to support claims with clear reasons and relevant evidence.

Speaking and Listening
4. Present claims and findings, sequencing ideas logically and using pertinent descriptions, facts, and details to accentuate main ideas or themes; use appropriate eye contact, adequate volume, and clear pronunciation.
5. Include multimedia components (e.g., graphics) and visual displays in presentations to clarify information.

Language
1.b Use intensive pronouns (e.g., *myself, ourselves*).

Writing to Sources

1. Review the assignment, using the instruction on the student page.
2. To give students guidance in writing an argument, give them the **Support for Writing** page for this selection in the *Student Companion All-in-One Workbook.*
3. To evaluate the writing activity, use the rubric for Persuasion: Persuasive Composition from *Professional Development Guidebook,* pp. 230–231. Evaluate speeches for how persuasive they are and how well the main points are supported.

Grammar Application

Have students check their drafts for the proper use of pronouns.

Six Traits Focus

✓	Ideas	✓	Word Choice
✓	Organization		Sentence Fluency
	Voice		Conventions

Research and Technology

1. Review the assignment, using the instruction on the student page.
2. To support students' work on the assignment, have them complete the **Support for Extend Your Learning** page for this selection in the *Student Companion All-in-One Workbook.*

LESSON PACING GUIDE

The Circuit

DAY 1	Preteach/Teach

- Administer the Reading and Vocabulary Warm-ups, as necessary.
- Introduce the Key Ideas and Details skill: Draw Conclusions.
- Introduce the Craft and Structure skill: Theme.
- Use the Close Reading Model to demonstrate the application of the skills.
- Review the selection vocabulary, as necessary, with students who need additional support.
- Prepare students to read the selection by reviewing with them the Multidraft Reading Strategies.

DAY 2	Teach

- Informally monitor comprehension while students read.
- Use the Comprehension questions to confirm understanding.
- Develop students' ability to draw conclusions and analyze theme using the sidenote questions.
- Reinforce vocabulary with the Vocabulary notes.
- Reinforce unit focus standards using the Spiral Review prompts.

DAY 3	Assess

- Assess students' comprehension and mastery of the skills by having them answer the Literary Analysis questions.
- Have students complete the Vocabulary activities.
- Develop students' understanding of roots and affixes by having them complete the Word Study activities.

DAY 4	Extend/Assess

- Build students' ability to master grammar concepts and conventions by having them complete the Conventions lesson.
- Have students complete the Writing to Sources activity and write a description of a character. (You may assign as homework.)
- Extend learning by having students complete the Speaking and Listening activity: prepare and role-play an interview.
- Administer the Selection Test or Open-Book Test.

 **Common Core State Standards**

Reading Literature 2. Determine a theme or central idea of a text and how it is conveyed through particular details.

Writing 4. Produce clear and coherent writing in which the development, organization, and style are appropriate to task, purpose, and audience.

Speaking and Listening 1.c. Pose and respond to specific questions with elaboration and detail by making comments that contribute to the topic, text, or issue under discussion.

Language 1.a. Ensure that pronouns are in the proper case.

4.b. Use common, grade appropriate Greek or Latin affixes and roots as clues to the meaning of a word.

Daily Block Scheduling

Each day in this Lesson Pacing Guide represents a 40–50 minute period. Teachers using block scheduling may combine days to revise pacing. In addition, teachers may differentiate and support core instruction by integrating components for extended and intensive support as students require. See the Guide to Resources (facing page).

GUIDE TO RESOURCES

		L1	L2	L3	L4	EL	ALL	RESOURCES	PRINT	CD	ONLINE
Warm Up		✓	✓			✓		Vocabulary Warm-ups			✓
		✓	✓			✓		Reading Warm-ups			✓
							✓	Background Video			✓
							✓	Selection Audio		Hear It!	✓
Comprehension/ Selection Support							✓	Writing About the Big Question	Student Companion Workbook		✓
							✓	Literary Analysis	Student Companion Workbook		✓
							✓	Reading	Student Companion Workbook		✓
							✓	Vocabulary Builder	Student Companion Workbook		✓
					✓			Enrichment			✓
				✓	✓	✓		Conventions	Student Companion Workbook		✓
				✓	✓	✓		Writing to Sources	Student Companion Workbook		✓
				✓	✓	✓		Speaking and Listening	Student Companion Workbook		✓
Differentiated Instruction/ Additional Support							✓	Additional Standards Practice	Common Core Companion		✓
		✓	✓					Adapted Reader's Notebook			✓
						✓		English Reader's Notebook:			✓
						✓		Spanish Reader's Notebook			✓
						✓		Graphic Organizer A			✓
		✓	✓			✓		Graphic Organizer B			✓
		✓	✓			✓		"A Winner On and Off the Field"	Reality Central Student Edition and Writing Journal		✓
		✓	✓			✓		Practice and Assess	Reading Kit		✓
Monitor Progress							✓	Selection Test		Exam View	✓
							✓	Open-Book Test		Exam View	✓
Digital Resources							✓	Close Reading Tool			✓
							✓	Online Writer's Notebook			✓

👥 One-on-one teaching   👫 Group work   👨‍👩 Whole class instruction   👤 Independent work   Ⓐ Assessment   💻 Digital Resource

LEARNER LEVELS

L1 Special-Needs Students   **L3** On-Level Students (Tier 1)   **EL** English Learners
L2 Below-Level Students (Tier 2)   **L4** Advanced Students (Tier 1)   **All** All Students

Is conflict always bad?

Read • Discuss • Research • Write As students read, they will explore the Big Question through text analysis of the selection. Encourage students to take notes as they read and raise additional questions, using text evidence to support their thoughts. Students should refer to their notes to help them deepen their understanding of the selection through discussion, research, and writing.

❷ Close Reading Focus

1. Remind students that when they draw conclusions, they use details in the text to come to a larger understanding about something. For example, if a character repeatedly embarks on extreme adventures, one could conclude that the character is a risk taker.

2. To help students identify the theme of a story, have them think about what happens to the characters. Provide an example of a story about two sisters. One is selfish, and the other is friendly. When the selfish sister has a fight with her best friend, and the friendly one does not, I realize that the writer is showing the consequences of selfishness—it leads to unhappiness.

© Building Knowledge

Meet the Author

Francisco Jiménez (hē mä′ nəz) (b. 1943) was born in Mexico and came to the United States with his family when he was four years old. The family settled in California and became migrant workers. Jiménez could not go to school before the harvest ended, but he studied in the fields and read whenever he had the chance. He once said, "I came to realize that learning and knowledge were the only stable things in my life." In high school, his excellent grades won him three college scholarships. He went on to become an outstanding teacher and award-winning writer.

© **Common Core State Standards**

Reading Literature
2. Determine a theme or central idea of a text and how it is conveyed through particular details.

Language
4.b. Use common, grade-appropriate Greek or Latin affixes and roots as clues to the meaning of a word.

---

❶ ? Is conflict always bad?

Explore the Big Question as you read "The Circuit." Take notes on ways in which the story explores ideas about conflict.

❷ CLOSE READING FOCUS

Key Ideas and Details: **Draw Conclusions**

A **conclusion** is a decision or an opinion you reach based on details in a literary work. To draw conclusions, ask questions as you read, such as *Why is this character alone so often?* Then, look for story details that help you answer the question. For example, the character may like to show off in front of others. You might then draw the conclusion that the character is unpopular because people dislike those who constantly point out their superiority.

Craft and Structure: **Theme**

The **theme**, or central idea of a story, is a thought or an insight about life that the story conveys. Although the theme of a work is sometimes directly stated, more often it is hinted at or suggested. To figure out a theme that is *indirectly* conveyed, consider the following:

• the outcome of the conflict and the effect on characters
• knowledge or insights that characters gain in the course of the story
• the story's title

Together, these details can help you understand the story's theme.

Vocabulary

The following words are critical to understanding "The Circuit." Copy these words into your notebook. Challenge yourself to identify one related word for each listed word. For example, you might write *accompany* next to *accompanied*.

accompanied	drone	instinctively
savoring	enroll	

© TEXT COMPLEXITY **RUBRIC**

The Circuit		Reader and Task Suggestions	
Qualitative Measures		**Preparing to Read the Text**	**Leveled Tasks**
Context/Knowledge Demands	Contemporary; California migrant workers 1 2 ③ 4 5	• Discuss how moving from place to place can affect children's education.	*Levels of Meaning* If students will have difficulty with the meaning, have them read to identify the narrator's conflict. Then have them discuss the difficulties of not belonging.
Structure/Language Conventionality and Clarity	Some Spanish words and phrases; on-level vocabulary 1 2 ③ 4 5	• Guide students to use Multidraft Reading strategies (TE p. 60)	*Synthesizing* If students will not have difficulty with the concept, use the Literature in Context feature (TE p. 64) to discuss migrant work. Discuss how different the lives of migrant children are from their own lives.
Levels of Meaning/Purpose/ Concept Level	Challenging concept (plight of migrant families) 1 2 3 ④ 5		
Quantitative Measures			
Lexile	730L	**Text Length**	Word Count: 2,345

CLOSE READING MODEL

The passage below is from Francisco Jiménez's short story "The Circuit." The annotations to the right of the passage show ways in which you can use close reading skills to draw conclusions and analyze theme.

from "The Circuit"

At sunset we drove into a labor camp near Fresno. Since Papá did not speak English Mamá asked the camp foreman if he needed any more workers. "We don't need no more," said the foreman, scratching his head. "Check with Sullivan down the road.[1] Can't miss him. He lives in a big white house with a fence around it."

When we got there, Mamá walked up to the house. She went through a white gate, past a row of rose bushes, up the stairs to the front door. She rang the doorbell. The porch light went on and a tall husky man came out. They exchanged a few words. After the man went in, Mamá clasped her hands and hurried back to the car. "We have work! Mr. Sullivan said we can stay there the whole season,"[2] she said, gasping and pointing to an old garage near the stables.

The garage was worn out by the years. It had no windows. The walls, eaten by termites, strained to support the roof full of holes. The dirt floor, populated by earthworms, looked like a gray road map.[3]

That night, by the light of a kerosene lamp, we unpacked and cleaned our new home.[4]

Theme

1 These sentences show challenges that the narrator and his migrant family face when they travel to find work in labor camps. These details suggest that the story will deal with themes of hardship and survival.

Theme

2 Mamá's actions show her determination. Her excitement over the job offer conveys her sense of relief—her family is employed and housed for a whole season. Details such as these emphasize the ongoing cycle of working and moving.

Draw Conclusions

3 The family will live in a garage that is filled with termites and earthworms. You may conclude that migrant workers' comfort and health was not a big concern for their employers.

Draw Conclusions

4 The family works to settle their "new home." You might conclude that they want to create a sense of permanence and belonging, even though they move often.

PART 2 • Building Knowledge: The Circuit **59**

🔔 Daily Bellringer

For each class during which you will teach this selection, have students complete one of the five Revision activities for Week 4 in *Daily Bellringer Activities*. You may wish to use additional activities that are applicable to this selection.

Vocabulary

If students require support with selection vocabulary, use this routine:

1. Write the following words and definitions on the board:

   accompanied *v.* went along with; joined

   drone *n.* continuous humming sound

   instinctively *adv.* done automatically, without thinking

   savoring *v.* enjoying; tasting with delight

   enroll *v.* place oneself on a register or list

2. Have students say each word aloud.

3. Use the word in a sentence that defines the word.

👥 DIFFERENTIATED INSTRUCTION

EL Extended Support— English Learners
Have students complete the **Reading and Vocabulary Warm-ups** for this selection in the *Student Companion All-in-One Workbook* before they read. Assign the prereading pages and the adapted selection in the *Reader's Notebook: English Learner's Version*. Then, have students listen to portions of the selection in the *Student eText* or on the *Hear It!* CD-ROM.

L1 L2 Extended Support— Struggling Readers
Have students complete the **Reading and Vocabulary Warm-ups** for this selection in the *Student Companion All-in-One Workbook* before they read. Assign the prereading pages and the adapted selection in the *Reader's Notebook: Adapted Version*. Then, have students listen to portions of the selection in the *Student eText* or on the *Hear It!* CD-ROM (adapted text).

Extended Support— Reluctant Readers
To build motivation and engagement before assigning the selection, have students read "A Winner On and Off the Field" a thematically related selection in *Reality Central*. Then, use the questions at the conclusion of the related selection to guide discussion.

MULTIDRAFT READING

This icon ● marks natural pauses in the selection. To assist struggling readers and to deepen comprehension for all, assign the text in "chunks," separated by the icons, and apply multidraft reading protocols. For each reading, have students set the purpose indicated:

- **First reading:** Students should read the selection independently and think about its basic meaning.
- **Second reading:** Students should analyze the text's key ideas and details and its craft and structure, and respond to the side-column prompts.
- **Third reading:** Students should integrate knowledge and ideas, connect the text to other texts and to the world, and answer the end-of-selection questions.

For more guidance, refer to the *Classroom Strategies and Teaching Routines* card on multidraft reading.

❶ Activating Prior Knowledge

Use the **Vocab-o-Gram** strategy (*Professional Development Guidebook,* pp. 39–40) to introduce students to selection terminology and to make predictions about selection elements. Put the following words or phrases on the board:

sharecropper	broken Spanish
lunch break	cardboard boxes
lump in my throat	jalopy
	termites
soaked in sweat	nervous
play trumpet	

Then, give students the **Vocab-o-Gram Chart** (*Professional Development Guidebook,* p. 40), and have them work with a partner or group to place the words in appropriate categories and make predictions about the story. Have students explain their predictions. Students will re-examine their ideas after reading the story.

💬 VOCABULARY DEVELOPMENT

Thematic Vocabulary: The Big Question
As students are discussing "The Circuit," encourage them to use the thematic vocabulary presented in Introducing the Big Question, pp. 2–3. You might encourage them with sentence starters like these:

1. Children in migrant families face emotional *challenges* when they . . .
2. As migrant families travel in search of paying work, they must *compete* with . . .
3. When children move frequently, they *lose* . . .
4. The migrant worker's *survival* depends on . . .

The
CIRCUIT
Francisco Jiménez

It was that time of year again. Ito, the strawberry sharecropper,[1] did not smile. It was natural. The peak of the strawberry season was almost over and the last few days the workers, most of them braceros,[2] were not picking as many boxes as they had during the months of June and July.

---

1. **sharecropper** (shər′ kräp′ ər) *n.* one who works for a share of a crop; tenant farmer.
2. **braceros** (brä ser′ os) *n.* migrant Mexican farm laborers who harvest crops.

◄ Critical Viewing
Do you think the type of work this man is doing is easy or difficult? Why?

❷ Critical Viewing
Possible response: The work is difficult. There is no shade in the field, so the worker is probably very hot. His back probably aches from bending over and working with the short-handled hoe.

❸ Humanities
"Planting cantaloupe", by Dorothea Lange

Dorothea Lange was an American photographer. Lange began her career as a portrait photographer and later traveled around the United States photographing social issues. She is best known for her documentary photography during the Great Depression, which reveals the hardships that many Americans faced. Use these questions for discussion.

1. Why do you think the photographer didn't show the workers' faces?

   Possible response: The photograph highlights the fact that to many people, migrant workers are invisible—the hardships they endure are not well known to people who buy and enjoy the crops they harvest.

2. Why do you think Lange chose to photograph migrant workers?

   Possible response: Lange may have wanted more people to become aware of migrant workers' hardships in the hope that her images would help bring about social changes.

🐾 DIFFERENTIATED INSTRUCTION

Strategy for Less Proficient Readers
Before students begin reading the selection, explain the meaning of the title to them. Tell them that a *circuit* refers to a circular line or path that goes around an object or an area. In the context of the story, the *circuit* refers to the different harvests that provide work for Panchito's family. Each year, the family must travel the same route, or *circuit,* to harvest the crops as they become ripe. Guide students to make predictions about the selection based on the title.

EL Pronunciation for English Learners
Point out the words *picking* and *during* on this page. Pronounce each in turn, and have students echo you. Then, present these word pairs: *thin/thing, sin/sing,* and *din/ding.* Pronounce each word. Then, call out the words at random, and have students write each in the order in which you call them. Have students compare lists and discuss differences. Finally, lead the class in pronouncing *picking* and *during* again.

 Video

Watch the Background Video online!

 **Audio**

Selection audio is available in the *Student eText* and on the *Hear It!* CD-ROM.

❹ Theme

1. Remind students that a theme is usually not stated directly by the author. Students can use details about the characters and events to draw conclusions about the theme. Encourage them to add details to **Literary Analysis Graphic Organizer A** for "The Circuit" as they read and discuss the story.

2. **Ask** students what the narrator sees when he opens the door.

   Answer: He sees packed cardboard boxes.

3. **Ask** what the packed boxes represent to the narrator.

   Answer: They represent the move to Fresno, which the narrator dreads.

4. Have a volunteer read the bracketed passage. **Ask** the Theme question.

   Possible response: The packed boxes and mention of moving to Fresno, along with the narrator's heavy feeling and tears in his eyes, show that the theme is probably about a child's unhappiness with continual moving and change.

5. Have students add these observations about Panchito to their graphic organizers.

Theme
What clues do this event and the narrator's actions give you about ❹ the story's theme?

Vocabulary ▶
accompanied (ə kum´ pə nēd) v. went along with; joined

As the last days of August disappeared, so did the number of *braceros*. Sunday, only one—the best picker—came to work. I liked him. Sometimes we talked during our half-hour lunch break. That is how I found out he was from Jalisco, the same state in Mexico my family was from. That Sunday was the last time I saw him.

When the sun had tired and sunk behind the mountains, Ito signaled us that it was time to go home. "*Ya esora*,"[3] he yelled in his broken Spanish. Those were the words I waited for twelve hours a day, every day, seven days a week, week after week. And the thought of not hearing them again saddened me.

As we drove home Papá did not say a word. With both hands on the wheel, he stared at the dirt road. My older brother, Roberto, was also silent. He leaned his head back and closed his eyes. Once in a while he cleared from his throat the dust that blew in from outside.

Yes, it was that time of year. When I opened the front door to the shack, I stopped. Everything we owned was neatly packed in cardboard boxes. Suddenly I felt even more the weight of hours, days, weeks, and months of work. I sat down on a box. The thought of having to move to Fresno[4] and knowing what was in store for me there brought tears to my eyes.

That night I could not sleep. I lay in bed thinking about how much I hated this move.

A little before five o'clock in the morning, Papá woke everyone up. A few minutes later, the yelling and screaming of my little brothers and sisters, for whom the move was a great adventure, broke the silence of dawn. Shortly, the barking of the dogs accompanied them.

While we packed the breakfast dishes, Papá went outside to start the "Carcanchita."[5] That was the name Papá gave his old '38 black Plymouth. He bought it in a used-car lot in Santa Rosa in the winter of 1949. Papá was very proud of his little jalopy. He had a right to be

---

3. *Ya esora* (yä es ô rä) Spanish for "It's time" (*Ya es hora*).
4. **Fresno** (frez´ nō) n. city in central California.
5. **Carcanchita** (kär kän chē´ tä) affectionate name for the car.

💬 THINK ALOUD

Making Inferences

Draw students' attention to the second paragraph on this page. Use the following "think aloud" to model the skill of making an inference (introduced on p. 28):

> When I read that Ito yells "*Ya esora*" in broken Spanish, I am curious about the meaning of the phrase. The footnote at the bottom of the page tells me that *Ya esora* is related to the Spanish *Ya es hora*, meaning, "It's time." The narrator says that he waits for these words every day. I read that these words signal the end of the workday and that the boy looks forward to this every day of the week. On this day, he says that "the thought of not hearing them again saddened" him. I realize that he must be moving to another job. I infer that the boy will miss the people and places he is accustomed to. I will read on to see whether my inference is confirmed.

proud of it. He spent a lot of time looking at other cars before buying this one. When he finally chose the "Carcanchita," he checked it thoroughly before driving it out of the car lot. He examined every inch of the car. He listened to the motor, tilting his head from side to side like a parrot, trying to detect any noises that spelled car trouble. After being satisfied with the looks and sounds of the car, Papá then insisted on knowing who the original owner was. He never did find out from the car salesman, but he bought the car anyway. Papá figured the original owner must have been an important man because behind the rear seat of the car he found a blue necktie.

Papá parked the car out in front and left the motor running. "*Listo*,"[6] he yelled. Without saying a word, Roberto and I began to carry the boxes out to the car. Roberto carried the two big boxes and I carried the two smaller ones. Papá then threw the mattress on top of the car roof and tied it with ropes to the front and rear bumpers.

Everything was packed except Mamá's pot. It was an old large galvanized[7] pot she had picked up at an army surplus store in Santa María the year I was born. The pot had many dents and nicks, and the more dents and nicks it acquired the more Mamá liked it. "*Mi olla*,"[8] she used to say proudly.

I held the front door open as Mamá carefully carried out her pot by both handles, making sure not to spill

The grinder (La molendera), 1926, Diego Rivera, Museo Nacional de Arte Moderno, Instituto Nacional de Bellas Artes, Mexico City, D.F., Mexico. ©Banco de Mexico Diego Rivera & Frida Kahlo Museums Trust. Av. Cinco de Mayo No. 2, Col. Centro, Del. Cuauhtemoc 06059, Mexico, D.F. Reproduction authorized by the Instituto Nacional de Bellas Artes y Literatura.

6 ▲ Critical Viewing
What are three words that describe the woman in this painting?

Draw Conclusions
What do the details so far tell you about the family's attitude toward moving again?

8 Comprehension
Why is Papá proud of "Carcanchita"?

---

6. *Listo* (lēs′ tō) Spanish for "Ready."
7. **galvanized** (gal′ və nīzd) *adj.* coated with zinc to prevent rusting.
8. *Mi olla* (mē ō′ yä) Spanish for "My pot."

5 Humanities

The Grinder, by Diego Rivera

Diego Rivera (1886–1957) is considered by many to one the most important Mexican artists of the 20th century. He was inspired by his study of Italian Renaissance frescoes—paintings on plaster. When these paintings dried, they became part of the wall on which they were painted. Rivera painted murals as well as smaller works, many of which featured historical and political themes and celebrated workers. Use this question for discussion: What do details in the painting show about the woman?

Possible response: She is kneeling on the ground, making tortillas in the traditional manner. Her posture shows that she is pressing hard—she appears to be very strong. The setting is very simple. She is surrounded by very few objects, and may be poor.

6 Critical Viewing

Possible response: Words include *strong, quiet,* and *focused.*

7 Draw Conclusions

1. Review what the different family members do in anticipation of the move.

   Answer: The children yell and scream as they get ready for the new adventure; the other family members quietly pack up the belongings and carry them out to the car.

2. **Ask** students the Draw Conclusions question.

   Possible response: The younger children are excited; the older boys and their parents are accepting, but not happy, about the move.

8 Comprehension

Answer: Papá chooses the car after checking every part of it to make sure it works properly. He is proud of making a good choice for his family.

≋ FLUENCY

Distribute copies of this page and pair students. Have partners take turns reading the last two paragraphs aloud, starting with the sentence "Papá parked the car . . . and left the motor running." Listeners should mark any words or sentences with which readers have difficulty. Circulate to monitor students' fluency. Collect students' marked up copies of the story, and review difficult words and passages with the class. Look for these problem spots:

• If students have difficulty with pronouncing the Spanish names, direct their attention to

the accent marks in the names Papá, Mamá, and Santa María and explain that these are an indication of emphasis. Model how to pronounce these names and the Spanish phrases, asking students to echo.

• If students mispronounce *galvanized,* guide them in identifying the letters and sounds in the word. Extend by listing additional words with this letter pattern, such as *elves, evolved,* and *valve.* Once students can pronounce the word, help them use context to be sure they understand its meaning.

9 Literature in Context
Geography Connection

For over fifty years, California has been the largest producer of food and agricultural products in the United States. More than 200 different commodities and crops are grown in California. A few of these crops—almonds, figs, olives, raisins, and walnuts—are grown almost solely in California.

In the United States today, there are more than two million migrant farm workers. About 100,000 of this group are children. Just 14 percent of the farm workers have full-time work, while the others work seasonally.

Connect to the Literature Have students read the Literature in Context feature. Then, provide the additional background above. Finally, ask the Connect to the Literature question.

Answer: When the strawberry season is over, the family has to move to find new work. Because the grape harvest begins in summer, they must work in the hot sun.

---

9 LITERATURE IN CONTEXT
Geography Connection

Agricultural Seasons
With sunny weather and a favorable climate, California produces more crops than any other state. At every point in the year, there is a different crop ready to be harvested in some part of the state. Migrant workers, such as Panchito's family, migrate from place to place to harvest the available crop. Grapes are picked in the summer and fall in the lush valleys of central and northern California. Peak strawberry season hits the southern coastal regions in the spring. Cotton is harvested in the dry valleys of central and southern California during the winter.

Connect to the Literature

Identify two ways the agricultural seasons affect the characters in this story.

---

the cooked beans. When she got to the car, Papá reached out to help her with it. Roberto opened the rear car door and Papá gently placed it on the floor behind the front seat. All of us then climbed in. Papá sighed, wiped the sweat off his forehead with his sleeve, and said wearily: "*Es todo.*"[9]

As we drove away, I felt a lump in my throat. I turned around and looked at our little shack for the last time. •

At sunset we drove into a labor camp near Fresno. Since Papá did not speak English, Mamá asked the camp foreman if he needed any more workers. "We don't need no more," said the foreman, scratching his head. "Check with Sullivan down the road. Can't miss him. He lives in a big white house with a fence around it."

When we got there, Mamá walked up to the house. She went through a white gate, past a row of rose bushes, up the stairs to the front door. She rang the doorbell. The porch light went on and a tall husky man came out. They exchanged a few words. After the man went in, Mamá clasped her hands and hurried back to the car. "We have work! Mr. Sullivan said we can stay there the whole season," she said, gasping and pointing to an old garage near the stables.

The garage was worn out by the years. It had no windows. The walls, eaten by termites, strained to support the roof full of holes. The dirt floor, populated by earthworms, looked like a gray road map.

That night, by the light of a kerosene lamp, we unpacked and cleaned our new home. Roberto swept away the loose dirt, leaving the hard ground. Papá plugged the holes in the walls with old newspapers and tin can tops.

---

9. *Es todo* (es tō′ thō) Spanish for "That's everything."

💬 VOCABULARY DEVELOPMENT

Vocabulary Reinforcement
To reinforce and assess students' comprehension of selection vocabulary words, give them sentences using the words in which the word may or may not be used correctly. Students must tell whether the use is correct and explain their answers. Use these sentences:

1. The *drone* of the bus's horn startled me.
   Answer: No, *drone* is not used correctly. It means "continuous humming sound."
2. The *drone* of the fan put me to sleep.
   Answer: Yes, *drone* is used correctly. A fan makes a continuous humming sound.
3. *Instinctively,* I answered all the questions on the social studies test.
   Answer: No, the word is not used correctly. *Instinctively* means "done without thinking."
4. The driver *instinctively* stopped when he saw a dog in the road.
   Answer: Yes, a driver stops without thinking about it when he or she sees an animal in the road.

Mamá fed my little brothers and sisters. Papá and Roberto then brought in the mattress and placed it on the far corner of the garage. "Mamá, you and the little ones sleep on the mattress. Roberto, Panchito, and I will sleep outside under the trees," Papá said.

Early next morning Mr. Sullivan showed us where his crop was, and after breakfast, Papá, Roberto, and I headed for the vineyard to pick.

Around nine o'clock the temperature had risen to almost one hundred degrees. I was completely soaked in sweat and my mouth felt as if I had been chewing on a handkerchief. I walked over to the end of the row, picked up the jug of water we had brought, and began drinking. "Don't drink too much; you'll get sick," Roberto shouted. No sooner had he said that than I felt sick to my stomach. I dropped to my knees and let the jug roll off my hands. I remained motionless with my eyes glued on the hot sandy ground. All I could hear was the drone of insects. Slowly I began to recover. I poured water over my face and neck and watched the dirty water run down my arms to the ground.

I still felt a little dizzy when we took a break to eat lunch. It was past two o'clock and we sat underneath a large walnut tree that was on the side of the road. While we ate, Papá jotted down the number of boxes we had picked. Roberto drew designs on the ground with a stick. Suddenly I noticed Papá's face turn pale as he looked down the road. "Here comes the school bus," he whispered loudly in alarm. Instinctively, Roberto and I ran and hid in the vineyards. We did not want to get in trouble for not going to school. The neatly dressed boys about my age got off. They carried books under their arms. After they crossed the street, the bus drove away. Roberto and I came out from hiding and joined Papá. "*Tienen que tener cuidado,*"[10] he warned us.

After lunch we went back to work. The sun kept beating down. The buzzing insects, the wet sweat, and the hot dry dust made the afternoon seem to last forever. Finally the mountains around the valley reached out and swallowed the sun. Within an hour it was too dark to continue

"That night, by the light of a kerosene lamp, we unpacked and cleaned our new home."

◀ **Vocabulary**
drone (drōn) *n.* continuous humming sound

instinctively
(in stiŋk′ tiv lē) *adv.* done automatically, without thinking

Comprehension
What makes work in the vineyard hard for Panchito?

---

10. *Tienen que tener cuidado* (tē en′ en kā ten er′ kwē thä′ thō) Spanish for "You have to be careful."

10 **Connecting to the Big Question**

1. Point out to students that while it is not possible to be in two places at the same time, people can still want to be in both places—causing a conflict in themselves. Explain that if the boys are working, they cannot go to school—and if they are in school, they cannot work all day.

2. Have students read the bracketed passage. Then, **ask** why the boys hide when the school bus approaches.

   Possible response: They don't want to get in trouble for not going to school. They can't go to school and work in the fields at the same time. If they get caught, they won't be able to work and help support their family.

3. Tell students to look as they read for details about the conflicts the family faces—wanting to be in two places at once, and wanting to stay longer in one place.

11 **Comprehension**

Answer: It is extremely hot, dry, and dusty in the vineyards. Panchito works all day in these conditions.

DIFFERENTIATED INSTRUCTION

Culturally Responsive Instruction
The characters in this story feel divided from the society they live in. Point out how the school bus incident on this page emphasizes Panchito's isolation from other children his age. Lead students in a discussion to include the causes of this isolation, including his inability to attend school, the difficulties in forming relationships in a community, and his insecurities in speaking English. Encourage students to propose ways they might make Panchito feel welcomed and accepted.

⑫ Theme

1. Remind students that the seasons, and the crops grown during each season, affect the lives of migrant workers. Have students read the paragraph beginning "It was Monday." **Ask** why Roberto is not going to school with Panchito. **Answer:** Roberto has to work until the cotton season is over.

2. Ask: What would happen to the family if the boys went to school and didn't work?

Possible response: The family wouldn't have enough money to buy food for everyone.

3. Ask the Theme question on the student page.

Answer: The sentence shows that Roberto can go to school only when he is not needed to pick crops, because his family's work follows the cycles of nature and crop harvests. The theme it suggests is that the family is caught in a different cycle—because the children must work, they cannot get a good education and so cannot improve their lot.

▶ **Monitor Progress:** Review students' graphic organizers to see whether they are able to identify the events and thoughts that help in understanding the theme.

▶ **Reteach:** If students have difficulty grasping the concept of theme, discuss what the narrator loses by having to work and having to follow the harvest. You may want to provide **Literary Analysis Graphic Organizer A** for "The Circuit" to help students understand the theme as they continue reading.

Vocabulary ▶
savoring (sā´ vər iŋ)
v. enjoying; tasting with delight

Theme
How does the sentence that begins "He would not go" suggest that the family's life follows a cycle? How might this cycle relate to the story's theme?

picking. The vines blanketed the grapes, making it difficult to see the bunches. "*Vámonos*,"[11] said Papá, signaling to us that it was time to quit work. Papá then took out a pencil and began to figure out how much we had earned our first day. He wrote down numbers, crossed some out, wrote down some more. "*Quince*,"[12] he murmured.

When we arrived home, we took a cold shower underneath a waterhose. We then sat down to eat dinner around some wooden crates that served as a table. Mamá had cooked a special meal for us. We had rice and tortillas with "*carne con chile*,"[13] my favorite dish.

The next morning I could hardly move. My body ached all over. I felt little control over my arms and legs. This feeling went on every morning for days until my muscles finally got used to the work. ●

It was Monday, the first week of November. The grape season was over and I could now go to school. I woke up early that morning and lay in bed, looking at the stars and *savoring* the thought of not going to work and of starting sixth grade for the first time that year. Since I could not sleep, I decided to get up and join Papá and Roberto at breakfast. I sat at the table across from Roberto, but I kept my head down. I did not want to look up and face him. I knew he was sad. He was not going to school today. He was not going tomorrow, or next week, or next month. He would not go until the cotton season was over, and that was sometime in February. I rubbed my hands together and watched the dry, acid stained skin fall to the floor in little rolls.

When Papá and Roberto left for work, I felt relief. I walked to the top of a small grade next to the shack and watched the "Carcanchita" disappear in the distance in a cloud of dust.

Two hours later, around eight o'clock, I stood by the side of the road waiting for school bus number twenty. When it arrived I climbed in. Everyone was busy either talking or yelling. I sat in an empty seat in the back.

When the bus stopped in front of the school, I felt very nervous. I looked out the bus window and saw boys

11. ***Vámonos*** (vä´ mō nōs) Spanish for "Let's go."
12. ***Quince*** (kēn´ sā) Spanish for "Fifteen."
13. **"*carne con chile*"** (kär´ nā kən chil´ ā) dish of ground meat, hot peppers, beans, and tomatoes.

💬 VOCABULARY DEVELOPMENT

Vocab-o-Gram
Have students return to their Vocab-o-Grams working on their own or in their original groups. Have students check their predictions and modify them based on their knowledge of the story. Review the vocabulary with the group and clarify words by returning to the selection or other reference sources.

and girls carrying books under their arms. I put my hands in my pant pockets and walked to the principal's office. When I entered I heard a woman's voice say: "May I help you?" I was startled. I had not heard English for months. For a few seconds I remained speechless. I looked at the lady who waited for my answer. My first instinct was to answer her in Spanish, but I held back. Finally, after struggling for English words, I managed to tell her that I wanted to enroll in the sixth grade. After answering many questions, I was led to the classroom.

Mr. Lema, the sixth-grade teacher, greeted me and assigned me a desk. He then introduced me to the class. I was so nervous and scared at that moment when everyone's eyes were on me that I wished I were with Papá and Roberto picking cotton. After taking roll, Mr. Lema gave the class the assignment for the first hour. "The first thing we have to do this morning is finish reading the story we began yesterday," he said enthusiastically. He walked up to me, handed me an English book, and asked me to read. "We are on page 125," he said politely. When I heard this, I felt my blood rush to my head; I felt dizzy. "Would you like to read?" he asked hesitantly. I opened the book to page 125. My mouth was dry. My eyes began to water. I could not begin. "You can read later," Mr. Lema said understandingly.

For the rest of the reading period I kept getting angrier and angrier at myself. I should have read, I thought to myself.

During recess I went into the restroom and opened my English book to page 125. I began to read in a low voice, pretending I was in class. There were many words I did not know. I closed the book and headed back to the classroom.

Mr. Lema was sitting at his desk correcting papers. When I entered he looked up at me and smiled. I felt better. I walked up to him and asked if he could help me with the new words. "Gladly," he said.

◀ **Vocabulary**
enroll (en rōl') *v.*
place oneself on a register or list

Draw Conclusions
What do the details in this paragraph lead you to conclude about Mr. Lema's character?

14 Comprehension
Why is Roberto unable to go back to school?

13 Draw Conclusions

1. After students read through the bracketed paragraph, **ask** if they would like to have Mr. Lema as a teacher. Have them support their answers with details about Mr. Lema.

   Possible response: Students are likely to say that they would like to have Mr. Lema as a teacher, because he is enthusiastic in welcoming a new student, but he doesn't pressure Panchito when he is reluctant to read.

2. **Ask** the Draw Conclusions question.

   Answer: Mr. Lema is kind, sympathetic, and helpful.

14 Comprehension
Answer: Roberto must work through the cotton season.

Spiral Review
Resolution

1. Remind students that they studied the concept of resolution in the Unit 1 Focus on Craft and Structure (pp. 14–17).

2. **Ask** the first Spiral Review question.

   Answer: The cardboard boxes signify that the family is moving.

3. **Ask** the second Spiral Review question.

   Answer: They signal that this chapter in the narrator's life—a happy time—is ending.

 ASSESS

Language Study
Vocabulary

1. savoring   3. drone
2. instinctively   4. enroll

Word Study
Part A

The prefix *com-* means "with," "together," or "next to." A *commission* is a group of people working *together* on a task. *Compression* is the process of pushing the parts of something *together*.

Part B

1. No, if you are alone, there is no one *with* you.
2. No, you would not eat ice cream and vinegar *together*.

Literary Analysis

Possible responses appear below. Check to be sure students support their responses with evidence from the text.

1. *Text Details That Answer Question:*
   - He has to help his family earn money.
   - He has not heard or read English in months.
   - The family has to go look for work again.

   Conclusion:
   - In a migrant family, children may have to work, too.
   - Not being in school for a long time affects a student's confidence.

- The cycle of the crops determines where a migrant family lives and what they do.

2. **(a)** He studies English with Mr. Lema. **(b)** Panchito calls his teacher his best friend because Mr. Lema spends a lot of time with him, helps him study, and offers to teach him to play the trumpet. **(c)** Students may say Panchito is shy, hardworking, thoughtful, and ambitious.

3. **(a)** Mr Lema offers to teach Panchito how to play the trumpet. **(b)** Panchito sees that his family is moving again.

4. **(a)** One theme is that a cycle of poverty is hard to escape. **(b)** Panchito's family moves often to get enough work and make enough money to survive; Panchito and Roberto usually cannot go to school because they have to work with their father.

5. **(a)** A circuit is a closed loop that goes around endlessly. **(b)** Panchito's family depends on a circuit of jobs; they are caught in a circuit of poverty.

The rest of the month I spent my lunch hours working on English with Mr. Lema, my best friend at school.

One Friday during lunch hour Mr. Lema asked me to take a walk with him to the music room. "Do you like music?" he asked me as we entered the building.

"Yes, I like *corridos*,"[14] I answered. He then picked up a trumpet, blew on it and handed it to me. The sound gave me goose bumps. I knew that sound. I had heard it in many corridos. "How would you like to learn how to play it?" he asked. He must have read my face because before I could answer, he added: "I'll teach you how to play it during our lunch hours."

That day I could hardly wait to get home to tell Papá and Mamá the great news. As I got off the bus, my little brothers and sisters ran up to meet me. They were yelling and screaming. I thought they were happy to see me, but when I opened the door to our shack, I saw that everything we owned was neatly packed in cardboard boxes.

Spiral Review
RESOLUTION What do the cardboard boxes signify to the narrator? How do they signal the story's resolution?

---

14. *corridos* (kō rē´ thōs) *n.* ballads.

Language Study

Vocabulary The words below appear in "The Circuit." Match each numbered description with a word from the list.

drone   instinctively   savoring   enroll

1. eating a delicious meal
2. how mother animals protect their young
3. the sound of bees buzzing
4. sign up for guitar lessons

WORD STUDY

The **Latin prefix** *com-* means "with," "together," or "next to." In this story, the narrator says that the barking of dogs accompanied, or mixed together with, his brothers' and sisters' yelling.

Word Study

Part A Explain how the **Latin prefix *com-*** contributes to the meanings of *commission* and *compression*. Use a dictionary if necessary.

Part B Use what you know about the Latin prefix *com-* to answer each question. Then, explain your responses.

1. If you are alone, do you have *company*?
2. Would you eat a *combination* of ice cream and vinegar?

Close Reading Activities

Literary Analysis

Key Ideas and Details

1. **Draw Conclusions** Complete a chart like the one on the right to draw conclusions about the story.

2. **(a)** What does Panchito do on his school lunch hours? **(b) Infer:** Why does Panchito call Mr. Lema his "best friend at school"? **(c) Interpret:** Based on the information in the story, how would you describe Panchito's personality?

3. **(a)** What is the best thing that happens to Panchito on the last day of school? **(b) Infer:** What is the worst thing?

Craft and Structure

4. **Theme (a)** What theme, or insight about life, does the story illustrate? **(b)** What details or events support the theme?

5. **Theme (a)** What is the meaning of "circuit," as used in the story's title? **(b)** How does the title relate to the story's theme?

6. **(a)** How well does the author develop Panchito's character? **(b) Analyze:** What specific details help readers understand Panchito?

Integration of Knowledge and Ideas

7. **(a) Draw Conclusions:** In what ways does Mr. Lema show understanding toward Panchito's situation? **(b)** Does Panchito grow or change as a result of Mr. Lema's help? Support your conclusion with evidence from the text.

8. **(a) Summarize:** Summarize the challenges Panchito's family face as they move from place to place. **(b) Assess:** How have Panchito and Roberto's lives been affected by being part of a migrant family? Cite textual details to support your answer.

9. **? Is conflict always bad?** With a small group, discuss the following questions: **(a)** What might be done to ease the conflicts of families like Panchito's? **(b)** Examine the theme. Will Panchito grow stronger as a result of the conflicts he faces? Explain. **(c)** What ongoing conflicts does this story suggest about child migrant workers?

Question	Text Details that Answer Question	Conclusion
Why does Panchito work so much?		
Why does Panchito not read aloud on the first day of school?		
Why are the family's belongings packed in boxes?		

ACADEMIC VOCABULARY

As you write and speak about "The Circuit," use the words related to conflict that you explored on page 3 of this text.

9. **? Is conflict always bad?** **(a)** Students may suggest the establishment of seasonal schools and the strengthening of tutoring and home-schooling programs. **(b)** Some students may say that Panchito will grow stronger because he is learning to endure conflict. Others may say that the conflict will just make him sad and discouraged. **(c)** Some students may say that the story makes them think about how certain individuals, such as migrant farmworkers and illegal immigrants, face daily conflicts with society that have far-reaching effects on their quality of life and their ability to improve their situations.

6. **(a)** Students might say that the author did a good job of developing Panchito's character because the story shows how he reacts to the different changes in his life. **(b)** Details that help us understand Panchito's character include his feelings about working in the fields, about moving from job to job, and about attending school.

7. **(a)** Mr. Lema does not make Panchito read aloud on the first day of school and helps him study new English words. **(b)** Yes, at first Panchito was scared to read, but he then becomes determined to learn and feels better after getting help from Mr. Lema.

8. **(a)** The family must focus on survival. They have no chance to put down roots anywhere, to have a real home, or to make plans for the future. Students should cite details about the family's living conditions, their constant need to move to find work, and the children's limited chances to attend school. **(b)** Panchito and Roberto's lives have been impacted because they have not been able to go to school regularly. Roberto no longer goes at all. Without an education, they do not have much chance of escaping the cycle of poverty.

 Online Writer's Notebook

Students can use the Online Writer's Notebook to record all responses.

Conventions

1. Introduce the skill, using the instruction on the student page.
2. Discuss the definitions and the examples in the chart.

Think Aloud: Model the Skill

Model the skill of using the correct pronoun case.

I know that pronouns take the place of a noun or another pronoun. But I know that it is not correct to say "I saw she at the store yesterday." Both *she* and *her* are pronouns. However, *she* is a nominative case, which replaces a subject. *Her* is an objective case, which replaces the object of a sentence or clause. In the sentence the woman is a direct object, so *her* should be used. "I saw her at the store yesterday."

Practice A

1. *our*: possessive
2. *him*: objective
3. *You*: nominative
4. *his*: possessive

Reading Application
Sample answers:

nominative: *I* had not heard English for months; objective: Mr. Lema, the sixth-grade teacher, greeted *me* and assigned *me* a desk; possessive: *My* mouth was dry. *My* eyes began to water.

Practice B

1. *She*: nominative
2. *it*: objective
3. *them*: objective
4. *her*: possessive

Writing Application
Sample answers:

1. Panchito is nervous and excited when *he* gets a chance to attend school.
2. Mr. Lema helps *him* succeed at school.
3. Soon, though, *his* family has to move again.

 Close Reading Activities Continued

Conventions: Pronoun Case

> The **pronoun case** is the form a pronoun takes to show whether a pronoun is being used as a subject, an object, or a possessive.

There are three pronoun cases:

- The **nominative case** is used to name the subject of a sentence or clause (the "giver" of an action).
- The **objective case** is used to name the object of a sentence or clause (the "receiver" of an action).
- The **possessive case** is used to show ownership.

Pronoun Cases	Examples
Nominative Case I, you, he, she, it, we, you, they	Subject of a verb: **They** wanted to stay in school.
	Predicate pronoun: The foreman is **he**.
Objective Case me, you, him, her, it, us, you, them	Direct object: Roberto took the pot and gave **it** to them.
	Indirect object: Please give **me** the book.
	Object of a preposition: The man gave the papers to **her**.
Possessive Case my, your, his, her, its, our, their, mine, yours, hers, ours, theirs	I reminded Papá to drive **his** car.

Practice A

Find the pronoun in each sentence and identify its case.

1. "Look at our boxes," Mamá said.
2. Panchito waited for Mr. Lema to walk with him.
3. You are a fine trumpet player.
4. Panchito made his way to the back of the bus.

Reading Application In "The Circuit," find one nominative pronoun, one objective pronoun, and one possessive pronoun.

Practice B

Replace each boldface noun with the appropriate pronoun. Identify the pronoun's case.

1. **Mamá** had cooked a special meal for us.
2. I let the **jug** roll off my hands.
3. Mr. Lema introduced me to the **students**.
4. Everything was packed except for **Mamá's** pot.

Writing Application Write three sentences about "The Circuit." Use one of the three pronoun cases in each sentence.

Writing to Sources

Explanatory Text Write a **description** of a character from "The Circuit."

- Identify details from the story that describe the character's appearance, actions, and personality.
- List details about the character's thoughts and words, and about other characters' reactions to the character you are describing.
- Make a cluster map of words, such as *smart, brave, mean,* or *fun-loving,* that capture the character's personality.
- Using words from your cluster map, write a description that identifies the controlling impression you want to convey.
- Include vivid details to help readers "see" the character.

Grammar Application Identify the pronouns in your description, and make sure they are written in the correct case.

Speaking and Listening

Comprehension and Collaboration With a partner, prepare and role-play an **interview** between a reporter and a migrant worker. The migrant worker may be Panchito or another character in "The Circuit."

Follow these steps to complete the assignment:

- Decide who will play each part.
- Reread the story to gather information.
- Prepare a list of relevant questions for the reporter to ask in the interview.
- Categorize the questions under headings such as Experience, Advice, and Lessons Learned.
- Develop the migrant worker's responses, with elaboration based on details from the story. Write down ideas you develop that you want to use in your interview.
- Rehearse with your partner, and then conduct your interview in front of the class.

 **Common Core State Standards**

Writing
4. Produce clear and coherent writing in which the development, organization, and style are appropriate to task, purpose, and audience.

Speaking and Listening
1.c. Pose and respond to specific questions with elaboration and detail by making comments that contribute to the topic, text, or issue under discussion.

Language
1.a. Ensure that pronouns are in the proper case.

Writing to Sources

1. Review the assignment, using the instruction on the student page.
2. To give students guidance in writing the description, give them the **Support for Writing** page for this selection in the *Student Companion All-in-One Workbook.*
3. To evaluate students' explanatory texts, use the **Writing Rubrics for Descriptive Essay** from *Professional Development Guidebook,* pp. 220–221. In addition, you might evaluate for how well students describe their chosen character and how well they support their descriptions with details from the selection.

Grammar Application

Have students check their drafts for the correct use of nominative, objective, and possessive pronouns.

Six Traits Focus

✓	Ideas	✓	Word Choice
	Organization		Sentence Fluency
	Voice		Conventions

Speaking and Listening

1. Review the assignment, using the instruction on the student page.
2. To support students' work on the assignment, have them complete the **Support for Extend Your Learning** page for this selection in the *Student Companion All-in-One Workbook.*

Comparing Texts

 Daily Bellringer

For each class during which you will teach this selection, have students complete one of the five Research activities for Week 5 in the *Daily Bellringer Activities*. You may wish to use additional activities that are applicable to these selections.

1 **Is conflict always bad?**

1. Review the assignment with the class.

2. Remind students that conflict is a problem or struggle between opposing forces. An internal conflict takes place in the mind of a character. An external conflict is one in which a character struggles against an outside force.

3. Remind students that when they compare and contrast the two works, they should focus on how each story describes the impact of conflict.

MULTIDRAFT READING

To assist struggling readers and to deepen comprehension for all, apply multidraft reading protocols. For each reading, have students set the purpose indicated:

- **First reading:** Students should read the selection independently and think about its basic meaning.

- **Second reading:** Students should analyze the text's key ideas and details and its craft and structure, and respond to the side-column prompts.

- **Third reading:** Students should integrate knowledge and ideas, connect the text to other texts and to the world, and answer the end-of-selection questions.

For more guidance, refer to the *Classroom Strategies and Teaching Routines* card on multidraft reading.

 Is conflict always bad?

1 Explore the Big Question as you read these stories. Take notes on the conflicts in each story. Then compare and contrast what the two stories suggest about the impact of conflict.

READING TO COMPARE FORESHADOWING AND FLASHBACK

Authors Joan Aiken and Walter Dean Myers use foreshadowing and flashback to add interest to their plots. As you read, notice how the authors hint about events that will happen in the future. Also consider how each story moves between past and present. When you finish reading, compare how the two authors use the techniques of foreshadowing and flashback.

SHORT STORY

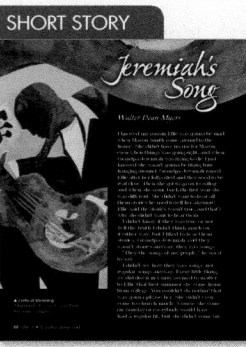

SHORT STORY

"Lob's Girl"

Joan Aiken (1924–2004)
By the time she was a teenager, British author Joan Aiken was a published writer. Aiken's father was poet Conrad Aiken, and two of her sisters are professional writers. Fans of all ages enjoy Aiken's unusual tales. Aiken once said, "Stories are like butterflies, which come fluttering out of nowhere, touch down for a brief instant, may be captured, may not, and then vanish into nowhere again."

"Jeremiah's Song"

Walter Dean Myers (b. 1937)
By age five, Walter Dean Myers was reading a newspaper every day. Despite this impressive start with words, Myers did not think writing would be his career. However, in his twenties, he won a writing contest and had been writing ever since—mostly about his heritage and growing up in Harlem, a part of New York City.

72 UNIT 1 • Is conflict always bad?

💬 VOCABULARY DEVELOPMENT

Vocabulary Knowledge Rating
Create a **Vocabulary Knowledge Rating Chart** (*Professional Development Guidebook,* p. 33) for this selection. Include the selection vocabulary and, if you wish, academic vocabulary from the Introduction to the Big Question (pp. 2–3).

Give students a copy of the chart. Read the words aloud, and have students mark their rating in the Before Reading column. Urge them to be alert to these words as they read and discuss the selection.

Tally how many students think they know a word to gauge how much instruction to provide. As students read and discuss the selection, point out the words and their context.

❷ Comparing Foreshadowing and Flashback

To develop exciting stories, writers use a range of **plot techniques** and literary devices to tell the events in a story.

- **Foreshadowing** is the author's use of clues to hint at what might happen later in a story. For example, the description of a dark cloud in a story might foreshadow something bad that is about to happen. Foreshadowing helps build suspense, the quality that keeps you wondering what will happen next.

- A **flashback** is a scene that interrupts a story to describe an earlier event. Writers use flashback to show something about a character's past. For example, a flashback about a happy childhood journey might explain why an adult character loves to travel.

Plot Devices and Plot Structure Some plots move from the beginning to the end with no interruption. A diagram of such a plot would look like an orderly timeline. Devices such as flashback change a plot's structure by changing the sequence of events.

Flashback takes readers on a short trip to the past. Foreshadowing does not move the plot to the future, but it moves the reader's attention to possible future events. Foreshadowing also adds to a sense of completeness in a plot. First readers recognize a hint, then they read about the event itself. Both devices can make the structure of a plot more interesting and more complex.

Compare the use of foreshadowing and flashback in "Lob's Girl" and "Jeremiah's Song" by using a chart such as the one shown.

	"Lob's Girl"	"Jeremiah's Song"
Foreshadowing		
Flashback		

 **Common Core State Standards**

Reading Literature
5. Analyze how a particular sentence, chapter, scene, or stanza fits into the overall structure of a text and contributes to the development of the theme, setting, or plot.

Writing
2.a. Introduce a topic; organize ideas, concepts, and information, using strategies such as definition, classification, comparison/contrast, and cause/effect; include formatting, graphics, and multimedia when useful to aiding comprehension.

PART 2 • Lob's Girl • Jeremiah's Song **73**

❷ Comparing Foreshadowing and Flashback

Plot Techniques

1. Introduce the skill, using the instruction on the student page.

2. Give students a copy of **Comparing Foreshadowing and Flashback Graphic Organizer B** for these selections. Tell them they will fill it in with details as they read.

Think Aloud: Model the Skill

Model a way to identify foreshadowing. Say to students:

> In the story "Little Red Riding Hood," the mother tells the girl to behave herself and stay on the path to her grandmother's house. When Red takes a shortcut, we know something bad is going to happen.

Plot Devices and Plot Structure

1. Introduce the skill, using the instruction on the student page.

2. Point out that authors write flashbacks into a plot to tell the reader about events that happened in the past or about qualities of the characters that help the reader understand the characters' present situation. Foreshadowing in a plot is a hint about what might happen in the future. Foreshadowing also helps create suspense, as the reader waits for the foreshadowed event to happen.

3. Explain that flashbacks and foreshadowing help enrich a plot. Encourage students to note how flashbacks help them understand what is going on in the story. Have students look for foreshadowing and note when the foreshadowed event occurs.

📋 TEACHING RESOURCES

	Print	Digital
All Common Core Companion, pp. 54–60, 184–195	✓	✓
All Graphic Organizers A and B, *Lob's Girl, Jeremiah's Song*		✓
All Online Student Edition eText with audio and video		✓
All Online Teacher Edition		✓
L1 Professional Development Guidebook, p. 33, 36–38, 42		✓
All Student Companion All-in-One Workbook, *Lob's Girl, Jeremiah's Song*	✓	✓

Lob's Girl

Joan Aiken

GUIDED EXPLORATION

❶ Background

An Incredible Journey Liverpool, Lob's original home, is a bustling port city in west-central England. Cornwall, a region, lies in England's southwestern corner. The story mostly takes place in one of Cornwall's seaside fishing villages. Remarkably, the dog Lob twice travels the more than 400 miles from Liverpool to that village to be reunited with the girl he has chosen as his new owner.

❷ About the Selection

After Lob, a young German shepherd dog, travels more than 400 miles on two different occasions to return to a girl named Sandy, his owner gives him to Sandy and her family. Sandy and Lob become best friends.

Years later, while walking with Lob, Sandy is gravely injured by a speeding truck. Sandy's grandmother sees Lob outside the hospital where Sandy lies in a coma. After some negotiation, the dog is allowed to go to Sandy's room. His whine awakens her.

In a surprise ending, the reader learns that Lob was killed by the truck that hit Sandy. The reader is left to decide what really happened.

© TEXT COMPLEXITY **RUBRIC**

Lob's Girl		
Qualitative Measures	**Context/Knowledge Demands**	20th century England 1 2 ③ 4 5
	Structure/Language Conventionality and Clarity	Formal; challenging vocabulary 1 2 3 ④ 5
	Levels of Meaning/ Purpose/Concept Level	Accessible concept (the bond between people and their pets) 1 2 ③ 4 5
Quantitative Measures	**Text Length**	Word Count: 4,328
	Lexile	970L

74 UNIT 1 • Is conflict always bad?

S ome people choose their dogs, and some dogs choose their people. The Pengelly family had no say in the choosing of Lob; he came to them in the second way, and very decisively.

It began on the beach, the summer when Sandy was five, Don, her older brother, twelve, and the twins were three. Sandy was really Alexandra, because her grandmother had a beautiful picture of a queen in a diamond tiara and high collar of pearls. It hung by Granny Pearce's kitchen sink and was as familiar as the doormat. When Sandy was born everyone agreed that she was the living spit of the picture, and so she was called Alexandra and Sandy for short.

On this summer day she was lying peacefully reading a comic and not keeping an eye on the twins, who didn't need it because they were occupied in seeing which of them could wrap the most seaweed around the other one's legs. Father—Bert Pengelly—and Don were up on the Hard painting the bottom boards of the boat in which Father went fishing for pilchards. And Mother—Jean Pengelly— was getting ahead with making the Christmas puddings because she never felt easy in her mind if they weren't made and safely put away by the end of August. As usual, each member of the family was happily getting on with his or her own affairs. Little did they guess how soon this state of things would be changed by the large new member who was going to erupt into their midst.

Sandy rolled onto her back to make sure that the twins were not climbing on slippery rocks or getting cut off by the tide. At the same moment a large body struck her forcibly in the midriff and she was covered by flying sand. Instinctively she shut her eyes and felt the sand being wiped off her face by something that seemed like a warm, rough, damp flannel. She opened her eyes and looked. It was a tongue. Its owner was a large and bouncy young Alsatian, or German shepherd, with topaz eyes, black-tipped prick ears, a thick, soft coat, and a bushy black-tipped tail.

"*Lob!*" shouted a man farther up the beach. "Lob, come here!"

But Lob, as if trying to atone[1] for the surprise he had given her, went on licking the sand off Sandy's face,

◄ **Vocabulary**
decisively (dē sī´siv lē´)
adv. with determination

Foreshadowing and Flashback
Based on this hint that begins "Little did they guess," what do you think is going to happen in the story?

❹ **Comprehension**
How does Sandy meet Lob?

---

1. atone (ə tōn´) *v.* make up for a wrong.

❸ **Foreshadowing and Flashback**

1. Point out to students the obvious verbal clue in this example of foreshadowing: "Little did they guess . . . " Explain that the clue lets readers know that something unexpected is going to happen.

2. Then **ask** students the Foreshadowing and Flashback question: Based on this hint that begins "Little did they guess," what do you think is going to happen in the story?

   Answer: The Pengelly family would soon have an unexpected, new member who would change their lives.

3. You may wish to suggest that students make a list of phrases that indicate foreshadowing as they read. This can help them fill in the Foreshadowing column in the table on **Comparing Foreshadowing and Flashback Graphic Organizer B** for "Lob's Girl."

❹ **Comprehension**

Answer: Sandy meets Lob when he runs into her at the beach.

ⓒ TEXT COMPLEXITY **READER AND TASK SUGGESTIONS**

Lob's Girl

Preparing to Read the Text
- Using the Background information on TE p. 74, discuss the setting of the story and the distance the dog traveled.
- Point out that the vocabulary in the story includes words that are related to England and English life.
- Guide students to use Multidraft Reading strategies (TE p. 72).

Leveled Tasks
Structure/Language If students will have difficulty with the language in this story, use the Vocabulary Development note on TE p. 76 to guide them through the unfamiliar words.

Evaluating If students will not have difficulty with language, discuss strategies the author uses to make the story effective at pulling the reader in, such as showing the bond between Sandy and Lob. Challenge students to alter some aspect of the story to see what effect it would have. Discuss how changing the story changes its effectiveness.

⑤ Foreshadowing and Flashback

1. Remind students that foreshadowing takes readers into the future, sparking their curiosity about what will happen, without giving the plot away. Then have a volunteer read the bracketed text aloud.

2. Ask students how the author describes the road.

Answer: The author describes the road as narrow, steep, and twisting.

3. Then **ask** the Foreshadowing and Flashback question: What might this description of the road foreshadow?

Possible response: The description might foreshadow an accident on the road.

4. Encourage students to keep the Foreshadowing and Flashback question in mind as they read the story.

⑥ Critical Viewing

Answer: This is a hilly coastal town with little houses and a narrow, twisting road.

Foreshadowing and Flashback
What might this description of the road foreshadow?

⑤

⑥ **Critical Viewing ▶**
What details in this image are like the village described in the story?

wagging his tail so hard while he kept on knocking up more clouds of sand. His owner, a gray-haired man with a limp, walked over as quickly as he could and seized him by the collar.

"I hope he didn't give you a fright?" the man said to Sandy. "He meant it in play—he's only young."

"Oh, no, I think he's *beautiful.*" said Sandy truly. She picked up a bit of driftwood and threw it. Lob, whisking easily out of his master's grip, was after it like a sand-colored bullet. He came back with the stick, beaming, and gave it to Sandy. At the same time he gave himself, though no one else was aware of this at the time. But with Sandy, too, it was love at first sight, and when, after a lot more stick-throwing, she and the twins joined Father and Don to go home for tea, they cast many a backward glance at Lob being led firmly away by his master.

"I wish we could play with him every day." Tess sighed.

"Why can't we?" said Tim.

Sandy explained. "Because Mr. Dodsworth, who owns him, is from Liverpool, and he is only staying at the Fisherman's Arms till Saturday."

"Is Liverpool a long way off?"

"Right at the other end of England from Cornwall, I'm afraid."

It was a Cornish fishing village where the Pengelly family lived, with rocks and cliffs and a strip of beach and a little round harbor, and palm trees growing in the gardens of the little whitewashed stone houses. The village was approached by a narrow, steep, twisting hill-road, and guarded by a notice that said LOW GEAR FOR 1 ½ MILES, DANGEROUS TO CYCLISTS.

The Pengelly children went home to scones with Cornish cream and jam, thinking they had seen the last of Lob. But they were much mistaken. The whole family was

💬 VOCABULARY DEVELOPMENT

Topical Vocabulary

The story employs a number of references to English foods, games, and geography. Give students a partial list of these unfamiliar words and the pages on which they appear: *pilchards* (p. 75), *Christmas puddings* (p. 75), *tea* (p. 76), *scones* (p. 76), *senna* (p. 78), *snakes and ladders* (p. 78), and *thistledown* (p. 82).

Explain to students that if a word is unfamiliar to them, they should try to figure out its meaning based on context clues. For example, the word *dose* is a context clue that suggests *senna* is a kind of medicine. The word *playing* is a context clue that suggests *snakes and ladders* is a game. Work together as a class to figure out the meanings of the remaining words. (*pilchards:* a type of fish; *Christmas puddings:* puddings traditionally served on Christmas; *tea:* refreshments served in the late afternoon; *scones:* pastries eaten as a snack; *thistledown:* tuft of a thistle)

playing cards by the fire in the front room after supper when there was a loud thump and a crash of china in the kitchen.

"My Christmas puddings!" exclaimed Jean, and ran out.

"Did you put TNT in them, then?" her husband said.

But it was Lob, who, finding the front door shut, had gone around to the back and bounced in through the open kitchen window, where the puddings were cooling on the sill. Luckily only the smallest was knocked down and broken.

Lob stood on his hind legs and plastered Sandy's face with licks. Then he did the same for the twins, who shrieked with joy.

"Where does this friend of yours come from?" inquired Mr. Pengelly.

"He's staying at the Fisherman's Arms—I mean his owner is."

"Then he must go back there. Find a bit of string, Sandy, to tie to his collar."

"I wonder how he found his way here," Mrs. Pengelly said, when the reluctant Lob had been led whining away and Sandy had explained about their afternoon's game on the beach. "Fisherman's Arms is right around the other side of the harbor."

Lob's owner scolded him and thanked Mr. Pengelly for bringing him back. Jean Pengelly warned the children that they had better not encourage Lob any more if they met him on the beach, or it would only lead to more trouble. So they dutifully took no notice of him the next day until he spoiled their good resolutions by dashing up to them with joyful barks, wagging his tail so hard that he winded Tess and knocked Tim's legs from under him.

They had a happy day, playing on the sand.

The next day was Saturday. Sandy had found out that Mr. Dodsworth was to catch the half-past-nine train. She went out secretly, down to the station, nodded to Mr. Hoskins, the stationmaster, who wouldn't dream of charging any local for a platform ticket, and climbed up on the footbridge that led over the tracks. She didn't want to be seen, but she did want to see. She saw Mr. Dodsworth get on the train, accompanied by an unhappy-looking Lob with

"*I wish we could play with him every day.*"

◄ **Vocabulary**
resolutions
(rez′ ə lōō′ shənz) *n.*
intentions; things
decided

❼ Comprehension
What causes the
crash in the Pengellys'
kitchen?

❼ Comprehension

Answer: Unable to enter the Pengelly's house by the front door, Lob jumps through the open kitchen window. In doing this, Lob knocks to the floor one of the Christmas puddings that Mrs. Pengelly had cooked earlier that day.

PART 2 • Lob's Girl **77**

✦ DIFFERENTIATED INSTRUCTION

Strategy for Less Proficient Readers
Prepare an **Anticipation Guide** (see *Professional Development Guidebook,* pp. 36–38) with the following statements:

• Animals are forgetful.
• Nothing lasts forever.
• The dog is "man's" best friend.
• Some things cannot be explained.

Give students a copy of the prepared **Anticipation Guide** and have them mark their responses in the Me column. Have students discuss the statements in pairs or groups and mark the Guides again in the Group column. Have students complete their **Guides** after they finish reading the story.

8 ❓ **Connecting to the Big Question**

1. Have students reread the bracketed passage. **Ask** them how Sandy felt.

Answer: She was sad about losing Lob.

2. Ask students what conflict Sandy is experiencing.

Answer: She wishes she hadn't come to the station.

3. Ask them if this conflict is internal or external.

Possible responses: Internal

4. Ask students if this conflict is bad.

Possible response: Students may say that the conflict is only bad if Sandy doesn't find Lob.

9 Critical Viewing

Answer: Sandy and Lob are devoted to one another.

Vocabulary ▶
melancholy
(mel´ ən käl´ ē) *adj.* sad; gloomy

8

9 Critical Viewing ▼
What can you infer about Sandy's relationship with Lob from this picture?

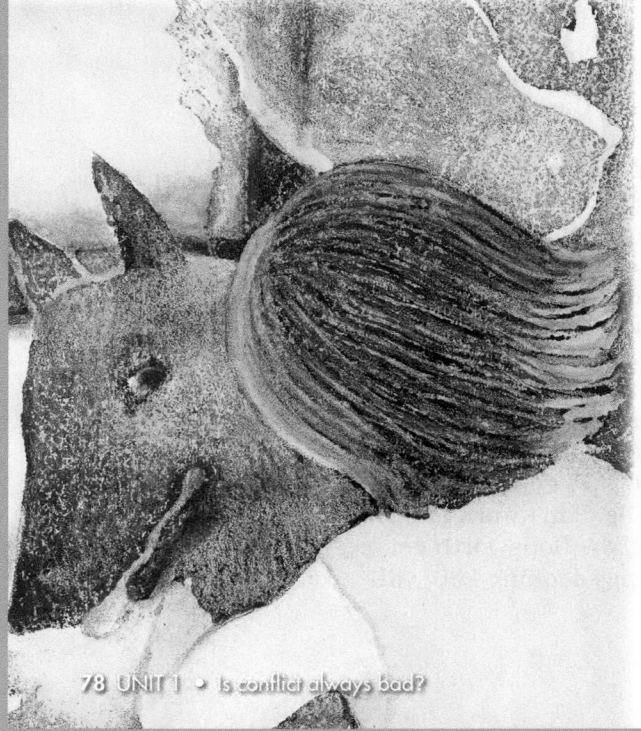

drooping ears and tail. Then she saw the train slide away out of sight around the next headland, with a melancholy wail that sounded like Lob's last good-bye.

Sandy wished she hadn't had the idea of coming to the station. She walked home miserably, with her shoulders hunched and her hands in her pockets. For the rest of the day she was so cross and unlike herself that Tess and Tim were quite surprised, and her mother gave her a dose of senna.

A week passed. Then, one evening, Mrs. Pengelly and the younger children were in the front room playing snakes and ladders. Mr. Pengelly and Don had gone fishing on the evening tide. If your father is a fisherman, he will never be home at the same time from one week to the next.

Suddenly, history repeating itself, there was a crash from the kitchen. Jean Pengelly leaped up, crying, "My blackberry jelly!" She and the children had spent the morning picking and the afternoon boiling fruit.

But Sandy was ahead of her mother. With flushed cheeks and eyes like stars she had darted into the kitchen, where she and Lob were hugging one another in a frenzy of joy.

About a yard of his tongue was out, and he was licking every part of her that he could reach.

"Good heavens!" exclaimed Jean. "How in the world did *he* get here?"

"He must have walked," said Sandy. "Look at his feet."

They were worn, dusty, and tarry. One had a cut on the pad.

"They ought to be bathed," said Jean Pengelly. "Sandy, run a bowl of warm water while I get disinfectant."

"What'll we do about him, Mother?" said Sandy anxiously.

Mrs. Pengelly looked at her daughter's pleading eyes and sighed.

"He must go back to his owner, of course," she said, making her voice firm. "Your dad can get the address

from the Fisherman's tomorrow, and phone him or send a telegram. In the meantime he'd better have a long drink and a good meal."

Lob was very grateful for the drink and the meal, and made no objection to having his feet washed. Then he flopped down on the hearthrug and slept in front of the fire they had lit because it was a cold, wet evening, with his head on Sandy's feet. He was a very tired dog. He had walked all the way from Liverpool to Cornwall, which is more than four hundred miles.

The next day Mr. Pengelly phoned Lob's owner, and the following morning Mr. Dodsworth arrived off the night train, decidedly put out, to take his pet home. That parting was worse than the first. Lob whined, Don walked out of the house, the twins burst out crying, and Sandy crept up to her bedroom afterward and lay with her face pressed into the quilt, feeling as if she were bruised all over.

Jean Pengelly took them all into Plymouth to see the circus on the next day and the twins cheered up a little, but even the hour's ride in the train each way and the Liberty horses and performing seals could not cure Sandy's sore heart.

10 She need not have bothered, though. In ten days' time Lob was back—limping this time, with a torn ear and a patch missing out of his furry coat, as if he had met and tangled with an enemy or two in the course of his four-hundred-mile walk.

Bert Pengelly rang up Liverpool again. Mr. Dodsworth, when he answered, sounded weary. He said, "That dog has already cost me two days that I can't spare away from my work—plus endless time in police stations and drafting newspaper advertisements. I'm too old for these ups and downs. I think we'd better face the fact, Mr. Pengelly, that it's your family he wants to stay with—that is, if you want to have him."

Bert Pengelly gulped. He was not a rich man; and Lob was a pedigreed dog. He said cautiously, "How much would you be asking for him?"

12 "Good heavens, man, I'm not suggesting I'd sell him to you. You must have him as a gift. Think of the train fares I'll be saving. You'll be doing me a good turn."

11 Comprehension
Why does Mr. Dodsworth give Lob to the Pengelly family?

PART 2 • Lob's Girl **79**

GUIDED EXPLORATION

10 Compare and Contrast

1. Tell students that comparing characters is a way of seeing if they have anything in common. Point out that readers can compare and contrast almost any two characters, even those who seem to have little connection in the story.

2. Then **ask** students to compare and contrast Sandy and Mr. Dodsworth, on the basis of their feelings about Lob.

Answer: Both Sandy and Mr. Dodsworth want Lob to have a good home and to be safe. Sandy clearly adores the dog. Mr. Dodsworth likes him but is very frustrated with him.

11 Comprehension

Answer: Mr. Dodsworth gives Lob to the Pengelly family because retrieving Lob from the Pengellys' house is taking up too much of Mr. Dodsworth's time and money.

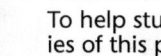

FLUENCY

To help students build fluency, distribute copies of this page to pairs of students. Have the students in each pair take turns reading the paragraph that begins "Lob was very grateful." As each student reads, the other should mark the words the reader had difficulty with. Collect students' marked up copies and review difficult words and passages with them. Look for these potential trouble spots:

• If students have difficulty with *hearthrug*, write the two words that form the compound on the board so they can see and say them independently. Explain that *hearth* means "the area in front of a fireplace" and suggest they picture in their minds what a *hearthrug* is.

• If they have difficulty with *Liverpool* or *Cornwall*, encourage them to look earlier in the story to references to these places.

PART 2 • Lob's Girl **79**

12 Deduce

1. Ask students to picture the scene in their minds as you read the bracketed text that begins on the previous page aloud.

2. Then, **ask** students why the children get so excited when they hear their father ask if Lob is a big eater.

Answer: The father's question suggests that he is considering taking the dog, if the dog is not too costly to feed.

3. Finally, **ask** students how they figured out what was going on.

Possible response: Mr. Pengelly would only ask a question like that if he were thinking about keeping Lob.

"Is he a big eater?" Bert asked doubtfully.

12 By this time the children, breathless in the background listening to one side of this conversation, had realized what was in the wind and were dancing up and down with their hands clasped beseechingly.

"Oh, not for his size," Lob's owner assured Bert. "Two or three pounds of meat a day and some vegetables and gravy and biscuits—he does very well on that."

Alexandra's father looked over the telephone at his daughter's swimming eyes and trembling lips. He reached a decision. "Well, then, Mr. Dodsworth," he said briskly, "we'll accept your offer and thank you very much. The children will be overjoyed and you can be sure Lob has come to a good home. They'll look after him and see he gets enough exercise. But I can tell you," he ended firmly, "if he wants to settle in with us he'll have to learn to eat a lot of fish."

So that was how Lob came to live with the Pengelly family. Everybody loved him and he loved them all. But there was never any question who came first with him. He was Sandy's dog. He slept by her bed and followed her everywhere he was allowed.

Nine years went by, and each summer Mr. Dodsworth came back to stay at the Fisherman's Arms and call on his erstwhile dog. Lob always met him with recognition and dignified pleasure, accompanied him for a walk or two—but showed no signs of wishing to return to Liverpool. His place, he intimated,[2] was definitely with the Pengellys.

In the course of nine years Lob changed less than Sandy. As she went into her teens he became a little slower, a little stiffer, there was a touch of gray on his nose, but he was still a handsome dog. He and Sandy still loved one another devotedly.

One evening in October all the summer visitors had left, and the little fishing town looked empty and secretive. It was a wet, windy dusk. When the children came home from school—even the twins were at high school now, and Don **13** was a full-fledged fisherman—Jean Pengelly said, "Sandy, your Aunt Rebecca says she's lonesome because Uncle Will Hoskins has gone out trawling, and she wants one of you to go and spend the evening with her. You go, dear; you can take your homework with you."

---

2. **intimated** (in´ tə māt´ əd) v. hinted; made known indirectly.

📱 VOCABULARY DEVELOPMENT

Word Forms

Expand students' vocabulary by helping them learn related forms of the selection vocabulary words. All three of the vocabulary words for "Lob's Girl" have related word forms. Give students a blank **Word Form Chart** (*Professional Development Guidebook*, p. 42), with *melancholy, decisively,* and *resolutions* in the correct columns. Work with the class, or have students work with a partner, to determine the related forms. The final chart should look like the one shown.

Hold students accountable for integrating the related forms of the words into their speaking and writing.

Noun	Verb	Adjective	Adverb
melancholy		melancholy	
decisiveness		decisive	**decisively**
resolutions	resolve	resolute	resolutely

Sandy looked far from enthusiastic.

"Can I take Lob with me?"

"You know Aunt Becky doesn't really like dogs—Oh, very well." Mrs. Pengelly sighed. "I suppose she'll have to put up with him as well as you."

Reluctantly Sandy tidied herself, took her schoolbag, put on the damp raincoat she had just taken off, fastened Lob's lead to his collar, and set off to walk through the dusk to Aunt Becky's cottage, which was five minutes' climb up the steep hill.

The wind was howling through the shrouds of boats drawn up on the Hard.

"Put some cheerful music on, do," said Jean Pengelly to the nearest twin. "Anything to drown that wretched sound while I make your dad's supper." So Don, who had just come in, put on some rock music, loud. Which was why the Pengellys did not hear the truck hurtle down the hill and crash against the post office wall a few minutes later.

Dr. Travers was driving through Cornwall with his wife, taking a late holiday before patients began coming down with winter colds and flu. He saw the sign that said STEEP HILL. LOW GEAR FOR 1 ½ MILES. Dutifully he changed into second gear.

"We must be nearly there," said his wife, looking out of her window. "I noticed a sign on the coast road that said the Fisherman's Arms was two miles. What a narrow, dangerous hill! But the cottages are very pretty—Oh, Frank, stop, *stop*! There's a child, I'm sure it's a child—by the wall over there!"

Dr. Travers jammed on his brakes and brought the car to a stop. A little stream ran down by the road in a shallow stone culvert, and half in the water lay something that

Foreshadowing and Flashback
What do you think the descriptions in these paragraphs foreshadow?

🔵14 **Critical Viewing** ▲
What elements of danger do you see in this picture?

🔵15 **Comprehension**
Where are Sandy and Lob going?

PART 2 • Lob's Girl **81**

🔵13 Foreshadowing and Flashback

1. Point out to students that the mood of these paragraphs differs from the mood of those in the paragraphs that immediately precede them. **Ask** students to identify the two moods.

   Answer: The mood of the previous paragraphs is happy as they describe Lob's entry into the family. The mood of the bracketed passage is more ominous and pensive.

2. Remind students that writers can foreshadow a coming event by a change in mood. Then challenge them to think of other stories they have read in which the mood changes as it does here. **Ask** what the mood change foreshadows.

   Possible response: Students may say that in other stories a description such as this often suggests that something unpleasant is about to happen.

   Ask students the Foreshadowing and Flashback question: What do you think the descriptions in these paragraphs foreshadow?

   Possible response: The descriptions might foreshadow an accident on the road.

🔵14 Critical Viewing

Possible response: Students may mention the darkness, and the rain, which makes the driving conditions poor.

🔵15 Comprehension

Answer: They were going to Aunt Rebecca's cottage so Sandy could keep her company.

👥 DIFFERENTIATED INSTRUCTION

Strategies for Special-Needs Students

In the part of the story that begins with Sandy's and Lob's departure and ends with Dr. and Mrs. Travers spotting Sandy's body, special-needs students might benefit by using a chart to keep track of the characters. Offer students the **Three-Column Chart** *Graphic Organizer*. Suggest that they write the name of each member of the Pengelly family in the first column and then use the other two columns to identify who each one is and what he or she is doing. As additional characters appear, they can add information about them to their charts.

16 Foreshadowing and Flashback

1. Have students read the Foreshadowing and Flashback question. Then read the bracketed paragraph aloud as students follow along. Tell students to raise their hands whenever they hear a hint about possible events to come.

Answer: Students should raise their hands when they hear, "Its attendants lifted the child onto a stretcher"; "the ambulance sped off to Plymouth"; and "—for the local cottage hospital did not take serious accident cases."

2. Ask students which plot technique involves providing hints about future story events without giving the plot away.

Answer: The technique is called foreshadowing.

Ask the Foreshadowing and Flashback question: What hints does this paragraph contain about possible events to come?

Possible response: The paragraph hints that Sandy's condition is very serious, and that a possible tragedy is about to happen.

---

looked, in the dusk, like a pile of clothes—or was it the body of the child? Mrs. Travers was out of the car in a flash, but her husband was quicker.

"Don't touch her, Emily!" he said sharply. "She's been hit. Can't be more than a few minutes. Remember that truck that overtook us half a mile back, speeding like the devil? Here, quick, go into that cottage and phone for an ambulance. The girl's in a bad way. I'll stay here and do what I can to stop the bleeding. Don't waste a minute."

Doctors are expert at stopping dangerous bleeding, for they know the right places to press. This Dr. Travers was able to do, but he didn't dare do more; the girl was lying in a queerly crumpled heap, and he guessed she had a number of bones broken and that it would be highly dangerous to move her. He watched her with great concentration, wondering where the truck had got to and what other damage it had done.

Mrs. Travers was very quick. She had seen plenty of accident cases and knew the importance of speed. The first cottage she tried had a phone; in four minutes she was back, and in six an ambulance was wailing down the hill.

16 Its attendants lifted the child onto a stretcher as carefully as if she were made of fine thistledown. The ambulance sped off to Plymouth—for the local cottage hospital did not take serious accident cases—and Dr. Travers went down to the police station to report what he had done.

He found that the police already knew about the speeding truck—which had suffered from loss of brakes and ended up with its radiator halfway through the post-office wall. The driver was concussed and shocked, but the police thought he was the only person injured—until Dr. Travers told his tale.

At half-past nine that night Aunt Rebecca Hoskins was sitting by her fire thinking aggrieved[3] thoughts about the inconsiderateness of nieces who were asked to supper and never turned up, when she was startled by a neighbor, who burst in, exclaiming, "Have you heard about Sandy Pengelly, then, Mrs. Hoskins? Terrible thing, poor little soul, and they don't know if she's likely to live. Police have got the truck driver that hit her—ah, it didn't ought to be allowed,

Foreshadowing and Flashback
What hints does this paragraph contain about possible events to come?

---

3. **aggrieved** (ə grēvd′) *adj.* offended; wronged.

💬 VOCABULARY DEVELOPMENT

Selection Vocabulary Reinforcement

Students will benefit from additional examples and practice with the selection vocabulary words. Reinforce their comprehension with "show-you-know" sentences. The first part of the sentence uses the vocabulary word in an appropriate context. The second part of the sentence—the "show-you-know" part—clarifies the first. Model the strategy with this example for *decisively:*

Mrs. Travers acted *decisively;* she quickly went to phone for an ambulance.

Then give students these sentence prompts and coach them in creating the clarification part:

1. Don's *resolutions* might be very hard to keep; _____.
Sample answer: he may need to go without food or water until he finds Lob.

2. I feel *melancholy* as I read this part of the story; _____.
Sample answer: both Sandy and Lob might die.

speeding through the place like that at umpty miles an hour, they ought to jail him for life—not that that'd be any comfort for poor Bert and Jean."

Horrified, Aunt Rebecca put on a coat and went down to her brother's house. She found the family with white shocked faces; Bert and Jean were about to drive off to the hospital where Sandy had been taken, and the twins were crying bitterly. Lob was nowhere to be seen. But Aunt Rebecca was not interested in dogs; she did not inquire about him.

"Thank the Lord you've come, Beck," said her brother. "Will you stay the night with Don and the twins? Don's out looking for Lob and heaven knows when we'll be back; we may get a bed with Jean's mother in Plymouth."

"Oh, if only I'd never invited the poor child," wailed Mrs. Hoskins. But Bert and Jean hardly heard her.

That night seemed to last forever. The twins cried themselves to sleep. Don came home very late and grim-faced. Bert and Jean sat in a waiting room of the Western Counties Hospital, but Sandy was unconscious, they were told, and she remained so. All that could be done for her was done. She was given transfusions to replace all the blood she had lost. The broken bones were set and put in slings and cradles.

"Is she a healthy girl? Has she a good constitution?" the emergency doctor asked.

"Aye, doctor, she is that," Bert said hoarsely. The lump in Jean's throat prevented her from answering; she merely nodded.

"Then she ought to have a chance. But I won't conceal from you that her condition is very serious, unless she shows signs of coming out from this coma."

But as hour succeeded hour, Sandy showed no signs of recovering consciousness. Her parents sat in the waiting room with haggard faces; sometimes one of them would go to telephone the family at home, or to try to get a little sleep at the home of Granny Pearce, not far away.

At noon next day Dr. and Mrs. Travers went to the Pengelly cottage to inquire how Sandy was doing, but the report was gloomy: "Still in a very serious condition."

Foreshadowing and Flashback
What clues in these paragraphs suggest that Lob may not be safe?

"She's been hit. Can't be more than a few minutes"

⑱ Comprehension
How does Sandy's family react to her condition?

PART 2 • Lob's Girl **83**

---

⑰ Foreshadowing and Flashback

1. Have a volunteer read the bracketed text aloud.
2. **Ask** students what the paragraphs tell about Lob.
   Answer: Lob is missing, and Don has gone to look for him.
3. **Ask** students the Foreshadowing and Flashback question: What clues in these paragraphs suggest that Lob might not be safe?
   Answer: Lob is nowhere to be seen. Don, after searching for him, returns home "grim-faced."

⑱ Comprehension

Possible response: The entire family—Mr. and Mrs. Pengelly, Don, the twins—is feeling miserable and afraid. They do not know what is going to happen to Sandy.

👥 DIFFERENTIATED INSTRUCTION

Strategy for Less Proficient Readers
To enhance their understanding of two characters, have students compare and contrast Mrs. Travers and Mrs. Hoskins. Begin by drawing a Venn diagram on the board. One circle will represent Mrs. Travers and the other, Mrs. Hoskins.

Have students identify one unique action for each character and one similar action for both characters. (Students may say that both women show concern for Sandy but that Mrs. Travers acts quickly and decisively, whereas Mrs. Hoskins carries on.)

Enrichment for Advanced Readers
Challenge students to compare and contrast "Lob's Girl" with another story, book, or movie that has animals as central characters. Have students use a **Venn Diagram** *Graphic Organizer* to show similarities and differences between the two stories. Students may focus on elements other than the characters, such as plot and style.

⓳ Foreshadowing and Flashback

1. Read aloud the bracketed paragraph that begins on the previous page as students follow along.

2. Read aloud the Foreshadowing and Flashback question. Remind students that a flashback interrupts a story to describe an earlier event.

3. **Ask** students to locate the flashback in the paragraph.

   Answer: The third sentence in the paragraph is the flashback.

4. Finally, **ask** the first Foreshadowing and Flashback question: What do you learn about Sandy from the flashback in this paragraph?

   Answer: The flashback tells readers that Sandy has been kind, generous, and helpful with the twins.

⓴ Foreshadowing and Flashback

1. Point out to students that this is the first time Lob has been seen since the accident. **Ask** students if they are surprised that Lob is at the hospital and to explain why they feel this way.

   Possible response: Students may not be surprised, because Lob has walked many miles to be near Sandy in the past.

2. Have students discuss where they think Lob has been since the accident. Then, **ask** the second Foreshadowing and Flashback question: What do you think is foreshadowed when Granny Pearce recognizes the dog?

   Possible responses: Some students might say that the dog's appearance foreshadows that Sandy will survive the accident. Others may see the dog's appearance as foreshadowing that Sandy will not live much longer, and the dog has come to say goodbye.

Foreshadowing and Flashback
What do you learn about Sandy from the flashback in this paragraph?

Foreshadowing and Flashback
What do you think is foreshadowed when Granny Pearce recognizes the dog?

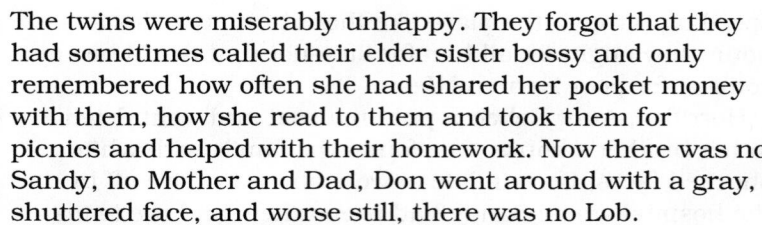

⓳ The twins were miserably unhappy. They forgot that they had sometimes called their elder sister bossy and only remembered how often she had shared her pocket money with them, how she read to them and took them for picnics and helped with their homework. Now there was no Sandy, no Mother and Dad, Don went around with a gray, shuttered face, and worse still, there was no Lob.

The Western Counties Hospital is a large one, with dozens of different departments and five or six connected buildings, each with three or four entrances. By that afternoon it became noticeable that a dog seemed to have taken up position outside the hospital, with the fixed intention of getting in. Patiently he would try first one entrance and then another, all the way around, and then begin again. Sometimes he would get a little way inside, following a visitor, but animals were, of course, forbidden, and he was always kindly but firmly turned out again. Sometimes the guard at the main entrance gave him a pat or offered him a bit of sandwich—he looked so wet and beseeching and desperate. But he never ate the sandwich. No one seemed to own him or to know where he came from; Plymouth is a large city and he might have belonged to anybody.

At tea time Granny Pearce came through the pouring rain to bring a flask of hot tea with brandy in it to her daughter and son-in-law. Just as she reached the main entrance the guard was gently but forcibly shoving out a large, agitated, soaking-wet Alsatian dog.

⓴ "No, old fellow, you can *not* come in. Hospitals are for people, not for dogs."

"Why, bless me," exclaimed old Mrs. Pearce. "That's Lob! Here, Lob, Lobby boy!"

Lob ran to her, whining. Mrs. Pearce walked up to the desk.

"I'm sorry, madam, you can't bring that dog in here," the guard said.

Mrs. Pearce was a very determined old lady. She looked the porter in the eye.

"Now, see here, young man. That dog has walked twenty miles from St. Killan to get to my granddaughter. Heaven knows how he knew she was here, but it's plain he knows. And he ought to have his rights! He ought to get to see her!

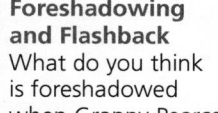 **THINK ALOUD**

Vocabulary: Using Context
Direct students' attention to the word *riveted* on the next page. Model how to use context to infer the meaning of an unknown word with the following "think aloud." Say to students:

> I'm going to think aloud to show you how I would figure out the meaning of *riveted* from its context.

In this sentence, the writer uses *riveted* to describe where Lob's attention lies. Sandy does not know that Lob is in the room. The previous sentence says, "her head was turned away." I think *riveted* refers to Lob's determination to make Sandy aware of his presence. In this sentence, I think *riveted* means "focused completely."

Do you know," she went on, bristling, "that dog has walked the length of England—*twice*—to be with that girl? And you think you can keep him out with your fiddling rules and regulations?"

"I'll have to ask the medical officer," the guard said weakly.

"You do that, young man." Granny Pearce sat down in a determined manner, shutting her umbrella, and Lob sat patiently dripping at her feet. Every now and then he shook his head, as if to dislodge something heavy that was tied around his neck.

Presently a tired, thin, intelligent-looking man in a white coat came downstairs, with an impressive, silver-haired man in a dark suit, and there was a low-voiced discussion. Granny Pearce eyed them, biding her time.

"Frankly. . . not much to lose," said the older man. The man in the white coat approached Granny Pearce.

"It's strictly against every rule, but as it's such a serious case we are making an exception," he said to her quietly. "But only *outside* her bedroom door—and only for a moment or two."

Without a word, Granny Pearce rose and stumped upstairs. Lob followed close to her skirts, as if he knew his hope lay with her.

They waited in the green-floored corridor outside Sandy's room. The door was half shut. Bert and Jean were inside. Everything was terribly quiet. A nurse came out. The white-coated man asked her something and she shook her head. She had left the door ajar and through it could now be seen a high, narrow bed with a lot of gadgets around it. Sandy lay there, very flat under the covers, very still. Her head was turned away. All Lob's attention was riveted on the bed. He strained toward it, but Granny Pearce clasped his collar firmly.

"I've done a lot for you, my boy, now you behave yourself," she whispered grimly. Lob let out a faint whine, anxious and pleading.

㉑ Comprehension
How does Lob get into the hospital to see Sandy?

㉑ Comprehension

Answer: Lob had been trying to enter the hospital all afternoon, but was turned away because animals were forbidden. When Granny Pearce arrives at tea time, she sees Lob and brings him into the lobby. Then she persuades the authorities to let Lob into the hospital to see Sandy.

⚙ DIFFERENTIATED INSTRUCTION

Enrichment for Gifted/Talented Students
Discuss with students what makes the story "Lob's Girl" so effective at pulling the reader in. Students may mention the way the writer carefully shows the depth of the bond between Sandy and her dog, or her use of foreshadowing to create suspense and to move the story along. Challenge students to alter some aspect of the story to see what effect it would have. For example, they could rewrite the story so that it is clear that Lob has been killed by the truck or by making the pet a cat instead of a dog.

Allow students time to write these alternative versions and to share them with the class. Ask the class to comment on how changing details of the story affects it.

22 Determine Cause and Effect

1. Direct students to re-read the bracketed passage. Explain that the white-coated man was probably a doctor. Point out that when doctors revisit patients, they typically check on whether there have been any changes in the patient's condition. **Ask** them how the nurse responds to the doctor, and what they think that means.

Possible response: The nurse shakes her head, which suggests that there is no change in Sandy's condition from earlier.

2. Then, **ask** them how Sandy reacts when she hears Lob.

Answer: She moves, apparently for the first time. After Lob whines again, she moves more and speaks.

3. Ask them how the doctor immediately reacted to Sandy, and what that suggests about his thinking.

Possible response: He gave a sharp intake of his breath, suggesting that he was very surprised by Sandy's movement and speech.

4. Ask them what the doctor did next, and why they think he did it.

Possible response: The doctor allows Granny to bring Lob closer to the bed. He thinks that it is worth trying to find out if Lob's presence can revive Sandy.

23 Critical Viewing

Answer: Sandy is smiling as she pets him. Lob is wagging his tail and looking devotedly at Sandy.

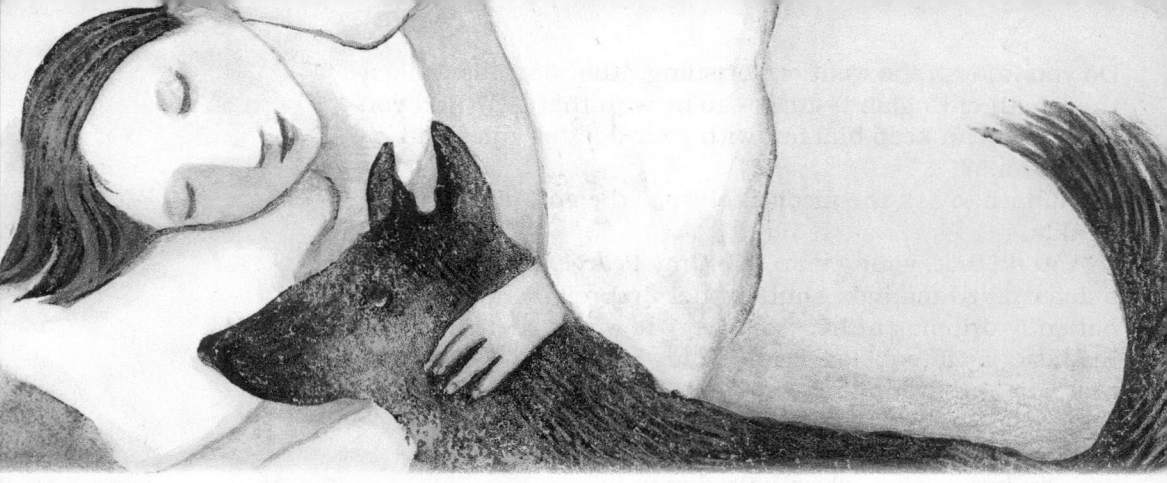

23 Critical Viewing ▲
What details of this final image reinforce the relationship between Sandy and Lob?

At the sound of that whine Sandy stirred just a little. She sighed and moved her head the least fraction. Lob whined again. And then Sandy turned her head right over. Her eyes opened, looking at the door.

"Lob?" she murmured—no more than a breath of sound. "Lobby, boy?"

The doctor by Granny Pearce drew a quick, sharp breath. Sandy moved her left arm—the one that was not broken—from below the covers and let her hand dangle down, feeling, as she always did in the mornings, for Lob's furry head. The doctor nodded slowly.

"All right," he whispered. "Let him go to the bedside. But keep a hold of him."

Granny Pearce and Lob moved to the bedside. Now she could see Bert and Jean, white-faced and shocked, on the far side of the bed. But she didn't look at them. She looked at the smile on her granddaughter's face as the groping fingers found Lob's wet ears and gently pulled them. "Good boy," whispered Sandy, and fell asleep again.

Granny Pearce led Lob out into the passage again. There she let go of him and he ran off swiftly down the stairs. She would have followed him, but Bert and Jean had come out into the passage, and she spoke to Bert fiercely.

"I don't know why you were so foolish as not to bring the dog before! Leaving him to find the way here himself—"

"But, Mother!" said Jean Pengelly. "That can't have been Lob. What a chance to take! Suppose Sandy hadn't—" She stopped, with her handkerchief pressed to her mouth.

🗨 THINK ALOUD

Make Inferences
Model the way to make inferences (introduced on p. 28) with this "think aloud." Say to students:

I'm going to show you how I make inferences. When Granny enters the hospital room with Lob, the narrator says that she sees Sandy's parents, Bert and Jean, "white-faced and shocked." I'm surprised when I read that. I know Sandy is in serious

condition, and it seems that she hasn't moved or spoken since the accident. Now that Lob has appeared, though, she has done both. Sandy's parents should be thrilled and excited, not shocked. Based on their reaction, I think that they know something that Granny doesn't know. Based on their reactions, I think that there's a surprise left in this story.

"Not Lob? I've known that dog nine years! I suppose I ought to know my own granddaughter's dog?"

"Listen, Mother," said Bert. "Lob was killed by the same truck that hit Sandy. Don found him—when he went to look for Sandy's schoolbag. He was—he was dead. Ribs all smashed. No question of that. Don told me on the phone—he and Will Hoskins rowed a half mile out to sea and sank the dog with a lump of concrete tied to his collar. Poor old boy. Still—he was getting on. Couldn't have lasted forever."

"*Sank him at sea?* Then what—?"

Slowly old Mrs. Pearce, and then the other two, turned to look at the trail of dripping-wet footprints that led down the hospital stairs.

In the Pengellys' garden they have a stone, under the palm tree. It says: "Lob. Sandy's dog. Buried at sea."

Foreshadowing and Flashback
Why does the author include this flashback to an earlier event?

Spiral Review
THEME Does this story convey the theme *love conquers all*? Explain.

Critical Thinking

1. **Key Ideas and Details (a)** How do Sandy and her family first meet Lob? **(b) Infer:** Why does Lob travel more than 400 miles to the Pengellys' house? **(c) Analyze:** How does Sandy feel about Lob? Support your answer.

2. **Key Ideas and Details** How do you think Mr. Dodsworth feels about giving the dog away? Support your answer with details from the story.

3. **Key Ideas and Details (a)** What happens when Sandy goes to visit her aunt? **(b)** How does Lob help Sandy at the hospital? **(c) Infer:** What does Lob's mysterious return suggest about his bond with Sandy?

4. **Craft and Structure (a) Analyze:** Why do you think the author chose to end the story in such an unusual way? **(b) Take a Position:** How important is the relationship between people and animals? Explain.

5. **Integration of Knowledge and Ideas (a) Speculate:** What conflicting feelings might the Pengellys experience because of what happened to Sandy and to Lob? **(b) Interpret:** What does the stone in the garden suggest about how they handle those feelings? *[Connect to the Big Question: Is conflict always bad?]*

PART 2 • Lob's Girl **87**

5. **(a)** The Pengellys may have been sad about Lob not surviving the crash, but they were also thankful that Sandy was able to recover from the crash. **(b)** Although they were saddened by Lob's death, they were grateful that his loyalty persisted beyond death and wanted to recognize how valuable he was to them. So they placed the stone in honor of him.

---

24 ## Foreshadowing and Flashback

1. Tell students that writers can use flashback to satisfy readers' curiosity. Then read aloud the bracketed text as students follow along.

2. **Ask** students the Foreshadowing and Flashback question. Why does the author include this flashback to an earlier event?

   Possible responses: This flashback shows why Bert and Jean are shocked to see the dog, and it sets readers up for a surprise ending.

Spiral Review
Theme

1. Remind students that they studied the concept of theme in the Unit 1 Focus on Craft and Structure (pp. 14–17).

2. **Ask** students the Spiral Review question.

   Possible response: Yes. Lob's love for Sandy brought her out of her coma and back to life.

✓ ASSESS

Critical Thinking

Possible responses appear below. Check to be sure students support their responses with evidence from the text.

1. **(a)** They meet Lob at the beach, where Lob runs into Sandy. **(b)** Lob loves Sandy. **(c)** Sandy loves Lob. She is upset each time Lob returns to Liverpool. Over time, she and Lob remain devoted to each other. She awakens from the coma after she hears Lob.

2. Mr. Dodsworth says that, "I think we'd better face the fact, Mr. Pengelly, that it's your family he wants to stay with." He is probably sad but, at the same time, glad that Lob has found a good family.

3. **(a)** Sandy is hit by a speeding truck. **(b)** Lob's whine awakens Sandy from a coma. **(c)** Lob and Sandy will always be close.

4. **(a)** The author may have been commenting on the mysterious and powerful bonds between people and their pets. **(b)** This relationship is very important. A dog like Lob can teach people about unconditional love.

Background

The Blues Blues, the type of music played in "Jeremiah's Song," originated as folk music of African Americans. This musical form had spread across the southern United States by the end of the 1800s. Several types of music have arisen from the blues, including country blues, city blues, jazz, boogie-woogie, and soul music.

26 **About the Selection**

When the narrator's cousin Ellie returns to her small town from college, she no longer wants to hear Grandpa Jeremiah's stories. However, Macon, a young neighbor, shows keen interest in Grandpa. Macon comes over to help the narrator, a younger boy, with household tasks after Grandpa has a stroke. Macon spends hours playing the guitar for Grandpa and listening to Grandpa's stories, or "songs," as he calls them. The narrator is drawn to Macon. Macon's guitar music and Grandpa's "songs" come to represent Grandpa Jeremiah's legacy to the narrator.

27 **Critical Viewing**

Possible response: Students might say that the man is playing the blues because the instrument is a guitar.

Jeremiah's Song

Walter Dean Myers

I knowed my cousin Ellie was gonna be mad when Macon Smith come around to the house. She didn't have no use for Macon even when things was going right, and when Grandpa Jeremiah was fixing to die I just knowed she wasn't gonna be liking him hanging around. Grandpa Jeremiah raised Ellie after her folks died and they used to be real close. Then she got to go on to college and when she come back the first year she was different. She didn't want to hear all them stories he used to tell her anymore. Ellie said the stories wasn't true, and that's why she didn't want to hear them.

I didn't know if they was true or not. Tell the truth I didn't think much on it either way, but I liked to hear them stories. Grandpa Jeremiah said they wasn't stories anyway, they was songs.

"They the songs of my people," he used to say.

I didn't see how they was songs, not regular songs anyway. Every little thing we did down in Curry seemed to matter to Ellie that first summer she come home from college. You couldn't do nothin' that was gonna please her. She didn't even come to church much. 'Course she come on Sunday or everybody would have had a regular fit, but she didn't come on

27 ▲ **Critical Viewing**
What kind of song do you think this man is playing?

88 UNIT 1 • Is conflict always bad?

Jeremiah's Song		
Qualitative Measures	Context/Knowledge Demands	American South, recent past 1 2 ③ 4 5
	Structure/Language Conventionality and Clarity	Conversational; colloquial language; challenging vocabulary 1 2 ③ 4 5
	Levels of Meaning/Purpose/Concept Level	Accessible concept (simple plot line) 1 ② 3 4 5
Quantitative Measures	Text Length	Word Count: 2,097
	Lexile	970L

Thursday nights and she didn't come on Saturday even though she used to sing in the gospel choir.

"I guess they teachin' her somethin' worthwhile up there at Greensboro," Grandpa Jeremiah said to Sister Todd. "I sure don't see what it is, though."

"You ain't never had no book learning, Jeremiah," Sister Todd shot back. She wiped at where a trickle of sweat made a little path through the white dusting powder she put on her chest to keep cool. "Them old ways you got ain't got nothing for these young folks."

"I guess you right," Grandpa Jeremiah said.

He said it but I could see he didn't like it none. He was a big man with a big head and had most all his hair even if it was white. All that summer, instead of sitting on the porch telling stories like he used to when I was real little, he would sit out there by himself while Ellie stayed in the house and watched the television or read a book. Sometimes I would think about asking him to tell me one of them stories he used to tell but they was too scary now that I didn't have nobody to sleep with but myself. I asked Ellie to sleep with me but she wouldn't.

"You're nine years old," she said, sounding real proper. "You're old enough to sleep alone."

I knew that. I just wanted her to sleep with me because I liked sleeping with her. Before she went off to college she used to put cocoa butter on her arms and face and it would smell real nice. When she come back from college she put something else on, but that smelled nice too.

It was right after Ellie went back to school that Grandpa Jeremiah had him a stroke and Macon started coming around. I think his mama probably made him come at first, but you could see he liked it. Macon had always been around, sitting over near the stuck window at church or going on the blueberry truck when we went picking down at Mister Gregory's place. For a long time he was just another kid, even though he was older'n me, but then, all of a sudden, he growed something fierce. I used to be up to his shoulder one time and then, before I could turn around good, I was only up to his shirt pocket. He changed too. When he used to just hang around with the other boys and play ball or shoot at birds he would laugh a lot. He didn't laugh so much anymore and I figured he was just about

Foreshadowing and Flashback

What do you learn about Ellie from this flashback?

29 Comprehension

Why does Grandpa Jeremiah raise Ellie?

28 Foreshadowing and Flashback

1. Remind students that flashback is a scene that interrupts a story. Explain that writers often use flashback to give information about a character.

2. Read the bracketed text aloud. Then, **ask** what period in Ellie's life the flashback is describing.

   Answer: The flashback is describing the summer after Ellie's first year away at college.

3. **Ask** students the Foreshadowing and Flashback question: What do you learn about Ellie from this flashback?

   Possible response: You learn that Ellie's attitudes have changed since she left her small town and went away to college.

29 Comprehension

Answer: Grandpa Jeremiah raises Ellie because Ellie's parents have died.

© **TEXT COMPLEXITY READER AND TASK SUGGESTIONS**

Jeremiah's Song

Preparing to Read the Text
- Using the Background information on TE p. 88, discuss the origins of musical forms developed by African Americans.
- Discuss the importance of passing on songs and stories from one generation to another.
- Guide students to use Multidraft Reading strategies (TE p. 72).

Leveled Tasks
Knowledge Demands If students have difficulty with the setting, have them read to note setting details. Then, have them reread to note how the setting is integral to the story.

Synthesizing If students will not have difficulty with the knowledge demands, point out that people use stories to tell their histories. Invite students to share stories told by an older adult in their family. Discuss what these stories can tell us about our backgrounds.

㉚ Foreshadowing and Flashback

1. Have two volunteers each read half of the bracketed passage aloud. Then **ask** the class what two kinds of things Macon does in Grandpa Jeremiah's household.

   Answer: Macon helps with household chores, and he visits with Grandpa.

2. Have students consider their responses. Then, **ask** the Foreshadowing and Flashback question: What clues here hint at a relationship developing between Macon and Grandpa Jeremiah?

   Answer: Students may say that Macon's helping with household chores and showing interest in Grandpa's stories might hint at the relationship that develops.

㉛ Literature in Context

Music Connection The blues has its roots in the Mississippi Delta. The poorest and most disadvantaged African Americans in the South lived in the Delta. Their suffering found expression in the blues.

Connect to the Literature Delta blues exists in several versions. Two songs that Macon plays, "Just a Closer Walk With Thee" and "Precious Lord," are appropriate for church-going friends. The lyrics to "Precious Lord" were written by Thomas A. Dorsey to go with a tune that was familiar to him and composed by a black gospel musician in 1932.

Ask students the Connect to the Literature question.

Possible response: Grandpa Jeremiah's stories tell about the hardships of people's lives, just as the Delta blues do.

㉚ Foreshadowing and Flashback
What clues here hint at a relationship developing between Macon and Grandpa Jeremiah?

㉚ grown. When Grandpa got sick he used to come around and help out with things around the house that was too hard for me to do. I mean, I could have done all the chores, but it would just take me longer.

When the work for the day was finished and the sows fed, Grandpa would kind of ease into one of his stories and Macon, he would sit and listen to them and be real interested. I didn't mind listening to the stories when Grandpa told them to Macon because he would be telling them in the middle of the afternoon and they would be past my mind by the time I had to go to bed.

Macon had an old guitar he used to mess with, too. He wasn't too bad on it, and sometimes Grandpa would tell him to play us a tune. He could play something he called "the Delta Blues" real good, but when Sister Todd or somebody from the church come around he'd play "Precious Lord" or "Just a Closer Walk With Thee."

Grandpa Jeremiah had been feeling poorly from that stroke, and one of his legs got a little drag to it. Just about the time Ellie come from school the next summer he was

㉛

LITERATURE IN CONTEXT
Music Connection
What Is the Delta Blues?
The hardships of plantation slaves were often told in powerful songs. These were performed by wandering musicians who accompanied themselves on guitar or harmonica.

Tennessee

Arkansas

Memphis

◄ The heart of this music was the Mississippi Delta, home to what is now known as the Delta blues.

Charley Patton is known as the father of the Delta blues. ▼

Mississippi   Alabama

ROBERT JOHNSON

Louisiana

SON HOUSE

◄ The great bluesman Muddy Waters was influenced by Son House and Robert Johnson. In the 1940s, Waters took the Delta blues north to Chicago.

Connect to the Literature In what ways do you think Grandpa Jeremiah's stories resemble the songs of the Delta blues?

💭 THINK ALOUD

Vocabulary: Using Context
Model the way to use context to understand an unfamiliar phrase with this think aloud. Say to students:

I'm going to show you how I come to understand the meaning of an unfamiliar word by using context. The narrator says that after the doctor said Grandpa Jeremiah had little time left to live, "everybody started tiptoeing around the house." I don't think he means that literally, because it doesn't make any sense for people to move on tiptoes. To understand what he does mean, I look at the rest of the paragraph. I see that people began to take extra care to make sure that Grandpa Jeremiah was comfortable. I know that when people walk on tiptoes, they move quietly. Putting these clues together, I think that the narrator means that they were all moving quietly so as not to disturb Grandpa Jeremiah.

real sick. He was breathing loud so you could hear it even in the next room and he would stay in bed a lot even when there was something that needed doing or fixing.

"I don't think he's going to make it much longer," Dr. Crawford said. "The only thing I can do is to give him something for the pain."

"Are you sure of your diagnosis?" Ellie asked. She was sitting around the table with Sister Todd, Deacon Turner, and his little skinny yellow wife.

Dr. Crawford looked at Ellie like he was surprised to hear her talking. "Yes, I'm sure," he said. "He had tests a few weeks ago and his condition was bad then."

"How much time he got?" Sister Todd asked.

"Maybe a week or two at best," Dr. Crawford said.

When he said that, Deacon Turner's wife started crying and goin' on and I give her a hard look but she just went on. I was the one who loved Grandpa Jeremiah the most and she didn't hardly even know him so I didn't see why she was crying.

Everybody started tiptoeing around the house after that. They would go in and ask Grandpa Jeremiah if he was comfortable and stuff like that or take him some food or a cold glass of lemonade. Sister Todd come over and stayed with us. Mostly what she did is make supper and do a lot of praying, which was good because I figured that maybe God would do something to make Grandpa Jeremiah well. When she wasn't doing that she was piecing on a fancy quilt she was making for some white people in Wilmington.

Ellie, she went around asking everybody how they felt about Dr. Crawford and then she went into town and asked about the tests and things. Sister Jenkins asked her if she thought she knowed more than Dr. Crawford, and Ellie rolled her eyes at her, but Sister Jenkins was reading out her Bible and didn't make no notice of it.

Then Macon come over.

He had been away on what he called "a little piece of a job" and hadn't heard how bad off Grandpa Jeremiah was. When he come over he talked to Ellie and she told him what was going on and then he got him a soft drink from the refrigerator and sat out on the porch and before you know it he was crying.

You could look at his face and tell the difference between him sweating and the tears. The sweat was close against his skin and shiny and the tears come down fatter and more sparkly.

◄ **Vocabulary**
diagnosis (dī əg nō′ sis) *n.* identification of a medical condition

Spiral Review
THEME How does the doctor's diagnosis affect the family?

33 **Comprehension**
How does Macon help Grandpa Jeremiah?

PART 2 • Jeremiah's Song **91**

Spiral Review
Theme

1. Remind students that they studied the concept of theme in the Unit 1 Focus on Craft and Structure (pp. 14–17).

2. **Ask** students the Spiral Review question.

   Possible response: Everyone, except for Ellie, is resigned to his death.

32 **Draw Conclusions/ Generalize**

1. **Ask** students what they have learned from the narrator so far about Sister Todd.

   Possible responses: Sister Todd is so religious that Macon has to be careful what music he plays in her presence. She is a trusted friend of Grandpa Jeremiah.

2. Read the bracketed text with students. **Ask** what more it tells about Sister Todd.

   Answer: Sister Todd moves into Grandpa Jeremiah's house toward the end. She cooks supper, prays for Grandpa, and works on a quilt that she is making for some white people.

3. **Ask** students to draw a conclusion about Sister Todd, based on the narrator's presentation of her.

   Possible response: Sister Todd is a true friend and an intelligent woman, with practical skills, such as cooking and quilting, and the know-how to use them to make money.

33 **Comprehension**

Answer: Macon helps Grandpa Jeremiah in two ways—by pitching in with household chores and keeping him company.

DIFFERENTIATED INSTRUCTION

Strategy for Less Proficient Readers
Prepare an **Anticipation Guide** (see *Professional Development Guidebook,* pp. 36–38), with the following statements:

• New ways are better than old ways.
• Adults are tough; their feelings can't be hurt.
• Some friends are like family.

Give students a copy of the prepared **Anticipation Guide** and have them mark their responses in the Me column. Have students discuss the statements in pairs or groups and mark the Guides in the Group column. Have students complete the **Guides** after they've finished reading the story.

EL Vocabulary for English Learners
Direct students' attention to the phrase "rolled her eyes" on this page. Explain that this is an idiom, a phrase that has a meaning that does not match the literal meaning of the words. This phrase means Ellie was showing disapproval. Give students other examples:

• *catch someone's eye* means "to get someone's attention"
• *see eye to eye* means "to agree"

Challenge students to write original sentences using these phrases.

34 Critical Viewing

Possible response: Students may say that the scene is similar to the story's setting because the house seems to be set in the country.

35 Foreshadowing and Flashback

1. Begin by reminding students that authors can use description to hint that something good or bad might happen.

2. Next, have a volunteer read the bracketed paragraph aloud. **Ask** students to summarize the description of Grandpa Jeremiah that it gives.

   Possible response: Grandpa Jeremiah looks untidy, terribly skinny, and very weak. His room smells like disinfectant and medicine.

3. Finally, **ask** students the Foreshadowing and Flashback question: What does this description of Grandpa Jeremiah suggest about events to come?

   Answer: The description suggests that Grandpa might die soon.

34 Critical Viewing ▲
Does this scene seem similar to the story's setting? Explain.

Foreshadowing and Flashback
What does the description of Grandpa Jeremiah suggest about events to come?

Macon sat on the porch, without saying a word, until the sun went down and the crickets started chirping and carrying on. Then he went in to where Grandpa Jeremiah was and stayed in there for a long time.

Sister Todd was saying that Grandpa Jeremiah needed his rest and Ellie went in to see what Macon was doing. Then she come out real mad.

"He got Grandpa telling those old stories again," Ellie said. "I told him Grandpa needed his rest and for him not to be staying all night."

He did leave soon, but bright and early the next morning Macon was back again. This time he brought his guitar with him and he went on in to Grandpa Jeremiah's room. I went in, too.

Grandpa Jeremiah's room smelled terrible. It was all closed up so no drafts could get on him and the whole room was smelled down with disinfect[1] and medicine. Grandpa Jeremiah lay propped up on the bed and he was so gray he looked scary. His hair wasn't combed down and his head on the pillow with his white hair sticking out was enough to send me flying if Macon hadn't been there. He was skinny, too. He looked like his skin got loose on his bones, and when he lifted his arms, it hung down like he was just wearing it instead of it being a part of him.

Macon sat slant-shouldered with his guitar across his lap. He was messin' with the guitar, not making any music, but just going over the strings as Grandpa talked.

"Old Carrie went around out back to where they kept the pigs penned up and she felt a cold wind across her face. . . ." Grandpa Jeremiah was telling the story about how a old woman out-tricked the Devil and got her son back. I had heard the story before, and I knew it was pretty

---

1. **disinfect** (dis' in fect') *n.* dialect, or regional language, for disinfectant, a substance that kills germs.

💬 VOCABULARY DEVELOPMENT

Word Analysis
Call students' attention to the word *disinfect* and its definition, "a substance that kills germs." Tell students that the Latin prefix *dis-* changes the meaning of many root words to their opposites. Therefore, *disinfect* means the opposite of *infect*.

Have students suggest root words that can be used with *dis-* to make new words. Possibilities include: *able, trust, use, similar, repair,* and *qualify*. Suggest that students check the definitions of the new words in a dictionary.

scary. "When she felt the cold breeze she didn't blink nary an eye, but looked straight ahead. . . ."

All the time Grandpa Jeremiah was talking I could see Macon fingering his guitar. I tried to imagine what it would be like if he was actually plucking the strings. I tried to fix my mind on that because I didn't like the way the story went with the old woman wrestling with the Devil.

We sat there for nearly all the afternoon until Ellie and Sister Todd come in and said that supper was ready. Me and Macon went out and ate some collard greens, ham hocks, and rice. Then Macon he went back in and listened to some more of Grandpa's stories until it was time for him to go home. I wasn't about to go in there and listen to no stories at night.

Dr. Crawford come around a few days later and said that Grandpa Jeremiah was doing a little better.

"You think the Good Lord gonna pull him through?" Sister Todd asked.

"I don't tell the Good Lord what He should or should not be doing," Dr. Crawford said, looking over at Sister Todd and at Ellie. "I just said that my patient seems to be doing okay for his condition."

"He been telling Macon all his stories," I said.

"Macon doesn't seem to understand that Grandpa Jeremiah needs his strength," Ellie said. "Now that he's improving, we don't want him to have a setback."

"No use in stopping him from telling his stories," Dr. Crawford said. "If it makes him feel good it's as good as any medicine I can give him."

I saw that this didn't set with Ellie, and when Dr. Crawford had left I asked her why.

"Dr. Crawford means well," she said, "but we have to get away from the kind of life that keeps us in the past."

She didn't say why we should be trying to get away from the stories and I really didn't care too much. All I knew was that when Macon was sitting in the room with Grandpa Jeremiah I wasn't nearly as scared as I used to be when it was just me and Ellie listening. I told that to Macon.

"You getting to be a big man, that's all," he said.

That was true. Me and Macon was getting to be good friends, too. I didn't even mind so much when he started being friends with Ellie later. It seemed kind of natural, almost like Macon was supposed to be there with us instead of just visiting.

Foreshadowing and Flashback
What does Macon's behavior suggest about what he might do later?

37 Comprehension
How does Macon react to Grandpa Jeremiah's illness?

36 Foreshadowing and Flashback

1. Remind students that an author can use foreshadowing to hint at events that happen later in a story. Explain that an author may also use foreshadowing to indicate what will happen in a character's life even after the story ends.

2. Have a volunteer read the bracketed text aloud. Then **ask** the Foreshadowing and Flashback question: What does Macon's behavior suggest about what he might do later?

   Possible response: Macon's behavior suggests that he might set Grandpa Jeremiah's stories to music someday.

37 Comprehension

Answer: Macon continues to visit him and listen to his stories.

DIFFERENTIATED INSTRUCTION

Culturally Responsive Instruction

Point out to students that members of older generations, as in the selection, often hold a wealth of knowledge and stories. Oftentimes, these stories tell a lot about a person's culture or community. Invite students to share experiences that they have had or that their friends have had when they took the time to listen to the stories of a grandparent, for example. Ask students what they learned about their culture from these stories. Ask: why is it important to learn about a culture from a different perspective? Have students discuss the answers to these questions as a class.

③⑧ Foreshadowing and Flashback

1. Have students read the bracketed paragraphs, which begin on the previous page. **Ask** them what kinds of details the paragraph contains. Tell students to use the phrase personal connections in their response.

   Answer: The paragraph contains details about the personal connections between Ellie and Macon and between Macon and the narrator.

2. **Ask** the first Foreshadowing and Flashback question: What details in this passage hint that something pleasant might lie ahead?

   Possible response: Students may say that the details about the growing friendships between Macon and the narrator and Macon and Ellie hint that Macon will become like family.

③⑨ Foreshadowing and Flashback

1. Read the bracketed paragraphs aloud as students follow along. **Ask** students to restate, in their own words, Grandpa's understanding of his stories.

   Possible response: Stories about people who survived hard times in the past can help people in the present get through hard times in their own lives.

2. **Ask** the second Foreshadowing and Flashback question: In what way are Grandpa Jeremiah's stories like flashbacks?

   Possible response: Like flashbacks, Grandpa's stories reveal important information about the past that affects people's present and future selves.

Foreshadowing and Flashback
What details in this passage hint that something pleasant may lie ahead?

③⑧ Grandpa wasn't getting no better, but he wasn't getting no worse, either.

"You liking Macon now?" I asked Ellie when we got to the middle of July. She was dishing out a plate of smothered chops for him and I hadn't even heard him ask for anything to eat.

"Macon's funny," Ellie said, not answering my question. "He's in there listening to all of those old stories like he's really interested in them. It's almost as if he and Grandpa Jeremiah are talking about something more than the stories, a secret language."

I didn't think I was supposed to say anything about that to Macon, but once, when Ellie, Sister Todd, and Macon were out on the porch shelling butter beans after Grandpa got tired and was resting, I went into his room and told him what Ellie had said.

"She said that?" Grandpa Jeremiah's face was skinny and old looking but his eyes looked like a baby's, they was so bright.

"Right there in the kitchen is where she said it," I said. "And I don't know what it mean but I was wondering about it."

"I didn't think she had any feeling for them stories," Grandpa Jeremiah said. "If she think we talking secrets, maybe she don't."

"I think she getting a feeling for Macon," I said,

"That's okay, too," Grandpa Jeremiah said. "They both young."

"Yeah, but them stories you be telling, Grandpa, they about old people who lived a long time ago," I said.

"What you got Grandpa?"

Foreshadowing and Flashback
In what way are Grandpa Jeremiah's stories like flashbacks?

③⑨ "You got you a bridge," Grandpa said. "And a meaning. Then when things get so hard you about to break, you can sneak across that bridge and see some folks who went before you and see how they didn't break. Some got bent and some got twisted and a few fell along the way, but they didn't break."

"Am I going to break, Grandpa?"

"You? As strong as you is?" Grandpa Jeremiah pushed himself up on his elbow and give me a look. "No way you going to break, boy. You gonna be strong as they come. One day you gonna tell all them stories I told you to your young'uns and they'll be as strong as you."

"Suppose I ain't got no stories, can I make some up?"

🗨 THINK ALOUD

Vocabulary: Using Context
Direct students' attention to the word *yellow-jacks* near the bottom of the next page. Model how to use context to infer the meaning of an unfamiliar word with the following think aloud. Say to students:

   I'm going to think aloud to show you how I would figure out the meaning of *yellow-jacks* from its context.

In this sentence, the writer says that *yellow-jacks* 'flew in and buzzed'—first around Sister Todd's niece and then around Deacon Turner's wife. The words *flew* and *buzz* are context clues that tell me *yellowjacks* are a kind of wasp or bee. I think the word is short for the stinging wasps called *yellow jackets*.

"Sure you can, boy. You make 'em up and twist 'em around. Don't make no mind. Long as you got 'em."

"Is that what Macon is doing?" I asked. "Making up stories to play on his guitar?"

"He'll do with 'em what he see fit, I suppose," Grandpa Jeremiah said. "Can't ask more than that from a man."

It rained the first three days of August. It wasn't a hard rain but it rained anyway. The mailman said it was good for the crops over East but I didn't care about that so I didn't pay him no mind. What I did mind was when it rain like that the field mice come in and get in things like the flour bin and I always got the blame for leaving it open.

When the rain stopped I was pretty glad. Macon come over and sat with Grandpa and had something to eat with us. Sister Todd come over, too.

"How Grandpa doing?" Sister Todd asked. "They been asking about him in the church."

"He's doing all right," Ellie said.

"He's kind of quiet today," Macon said. "He was just talking about how the hogs needed breeding."

"He must have run out of stories to tell," Sister Todd said. "He'll be repeating on himself like my father used to do. That's the way I hear old folks get."

Everybody laughed at that because Sister Todd was pretty old, too. Maybe we was all happy because the sun was out after so much rain. When Sister Todd went in to take Grandpa Jeremiah a plate of potato salad with no mayonnaise like he liked it, she told him about how people was asking for him and he told her to tell them he was doing okay and to remember him in their prayers.

Sister Todd came over the next afternoon, too, with some rhubarb pie with cheese on it, which is my favorite pie. When she took a piece into Grandpa Jeremiah's room she come right out again and told Ellie to go fetch the Bible.

It was a hot day when they had the funeral. Mostly everybody was there. The church was hot as anything, even though they had the window open. Some yellowjacks flew in and buzzed around Sister Todd's niece and then around Deacon Turner's wife and settled right on her hat and stayed there until we all stood and sang "Soon-a Will Be Done."

Foreshadowing and Flashback
What event may be foreshadowed in Macon's description? Explain.

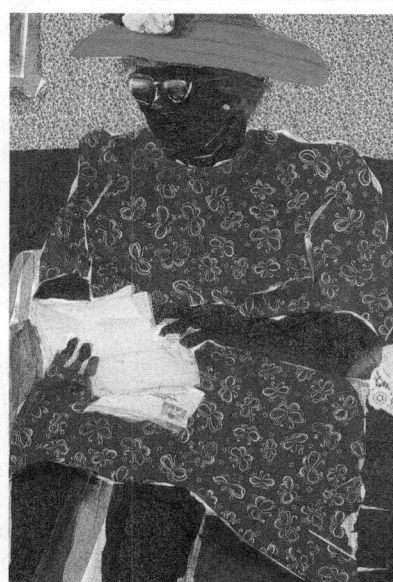

41 Comprehension
How do Ellie's feelings for Macon change?

PART 2 • Jeremiah's Song **95**

40 Foreshadowing and Flashback

1. Read Macon's description aloud. **Ask** students to name the two things Macon mentions about Grandpa in his description.

   Answer: Grandpa seems quiet and says that the hogs need breeding.

2. Remind students that authors can use description, for example, of loudness or quietness, to hint at what might happen next. Then **ask** the Foreshadowing and Flashback question: What event might be foreshadowed in Macon's description? Explain.

   Answer: Macon's describing Grandpa as "kind of quiet today" might foreshadow Grandpa's dying.

41 Comprehension
Answer: Ellie stops resenting Macon and becomes friends with him.

DIFFERENTIATED INSTRUCTION

Enrichment for Gifted/Talented Students
Invite students to illustrate scenes from the story. Allow students to select the setting and characters they wish to portray. Have students use drawing materials to make a poster or use a cardboard box to make a model of part of the narrator's home, such as the porch or Grandpa's room. Where details are not included in the text, have students research typical furnishings of a Southern farm. Have students display their work in the classroom.

Enrichment for Advanced Readers
Have students take notes about the effects of first-person narration, such as the way in which Myers reveals the narrator's impressions of other characters. After they read, have students compare and contrast first-person narration with the previous selection, "Lob's Girl," which has third-person narration.

42 Foreshadowing and Flashback

1. Ask students to describe what is happening in the paragraph.

Answer: The narrator is listening and watching closely as Macon plays the guitar.

2. Then **ask** the Foreshadowing and Flashback question: What event might this last sentence foreshadow?

Possible response: The last sentence might foreshadow the narrator's telling stories with the guitar in the future.

✅ ASSESS

Critical Thinking

Possible responses appear below. Check to be sure students support their responses with evidence from the text.

1. (a) Ellie and the narrator are cousins. **(b)** The narrator likes Ellie but is sad that she has changed while at college.

2. (a) Ellie thinks that Macon is tiring Grandpa. **(b)** The narrator likes Macon. He enjoys Macon's company and is interested in his music.

3. (a) Grandpa's songs are the stories he tells about his life and his people. **(b)** Students may say that songs and stories like Grandpa's are very important because they help people connect with and preserve their heritage.

4.  **(a)** Ellie and Macon both care about Grandpa, but Macon is interested in hearing Grandpa's stories and Ellie no longer wants to hear them. **(b)** Macon thinks that having Grandpa tell stories will help improve his condition. However, Ellie thinks that Grandpa should rest and not tell stories.

At the graveyard Macon played "Precious Lord" and I cried hard even though I told myself that I wasn't going to cry the way Ellie and Sister Todd was, but it was such a sad thing when we left and Grandpa Jeremiah was still out to the grave that I couldn't help it.

During the funeral and all, Macon kind of told everybody where to go and where to sit and which of the three cars to ride in. After it was over he come by the house and sat on the front porch and played on his guitar. Ellie was standing leaning against the rail and she was crying but it wasn't a hard crying. It was a soft crying, the kind that last inside of you for a long time.

Macon was playing a tune I hadn't heard before. I thought it might have been what he was working at when Grandpa Jeremiah was telling him those stories and I watched his fingers but I couldn't tell if it was or not. It wasn't nothing special, that tune Macon was playing, maybe halfway between them Delta blues he would do when Sister Todd wasn't around and something you would play at church. It was something different and something the same at the same time. I watched his fingers go over that guitar and figured I could learn that tune one day if I had a mind to.

42 Foreshadowing and Flashback
What event might this last sentence foreshadow?

Critical Thinking

1. Key Ideas and Details (a) What is Ellie's relationship to the narrator? **(b) Interpret:** Describe the narrator's feelings toward Ellie. Support your response with textual evidence.

2. Key Ideas and Details (a) Why does Ellie not want Macon around Grandpa Jeremiah's house at first? **(b) Draw Conclusions:** How does the narrator feel toward Macon? Cite details to support your response.

3. Key Ideas and Details (a) Interpret: What are Grandpa Jeremiah's "songs"? **(b) Take a Position:** Do you think songs and stories such as those Grandpa tells are important to future generations? Explain.

4. Integration of Knowledge and Ideas (a) How do Ellie and Macon feel about Grandpa? **(b) Draw Conclusions:** Why do they have a conflict over how best to care for him? *[Connect to the Big Question: Is conflict always bad?]*

💬 VOCABULARY DEVELOPMENT

Vocabulary Knowledge Rating
When students have completed reading and discussing "Lob's Girl" and "Jeremiah's Song," have them take out their **Vocabulary Knowledge Rating Chart.** Read the words aloud once more and have students rate their knowledge of the words again in the After Reading column. Clarify any words that are still problematic. Have students write their own definitions and examples or sentences in the appropriate column. Encourage students to use the words in further discussion and written work about these stories. Remind them that they will be accountable for these words on the **Selection Test.**

Writing to Sources

Comparing Foreshadowing and Flashback

1. Key Ideas and Details Create a chart for each story. **(a)** In the left two columns, list clues in the story and the events they foreshadow. **(b)** In the right two columns, list flashbacks and tell what you learn from each one.

Foreshadowing		Flashback	
Clues ──────────► Event		Detail ──────────► Reveals	

2. Craft and Structure Based on your charts, which writer makes more use of these plot devices? Explain.

⏱ Timed Writing

Explanatory Text: Essay
Compare and contrast the authors' use of foreshadowing and flashback in "Lob's Girl" and "Jeremiah's Song." In an essay, discuss the effects of these plot devices. **(30 minutes)**

5-Minute Planner

1. Read the prompt carefully and completely.

2. Review your charts for examples of foreshadowing and flashback in the stories.

3. Organize your thoughts by asking the following questions:

   • Which story has more suspense, based on the use of foreshadowing?

   • Which story's structure includes more flashbacks?

   • What is the effect of the combination of foreshadowing and flashback on each story?

4. Select an organizational strategy that will suit your essay, such as block format or point-by-point organization.

5. Reread the prompt, and then draft your essay.

USE ACADEMIC VOCABULARY

As you write, use academic language, including the following words or their related forms:

anticipate

conclude

refer

reveal

For more information about academic vocabulary, see pages xlvi–l.

Comparing Foreshadowing and Flashback

1. Students' responses will likely be drawn from the clues and events discussed in the Foreshadowing and Flashback questions for the two selections.

   For other sample answers, see **Comparing Foreshadowing and Flashback Graphic Organizer A** for these selections, and the **Additional Answers** section.

2. **Possible response:** My chart shows that Aiken made more use of foreshadowing and flashback, perhaps because her plot was more complex and her ending less predictable.

⏱ Timed Writing

1. Review the prompt with students.

2. Have students use the 5-Minute Planner to structure their time. Guide them in completing the bulleted instructions. Remind them that, generally, flashbacks give information about characters and foreshadowing is about events.

3. Allow students 30 minutes to complete the assignment.

Six Traits Focus

✓	Ideas		Word Choice
✓	Organization		Sentence Fluency
	Voice		Conventions

📋 ASSESSMENT RESOURCES

The following resources can be used to assess students' knowledge and skills.

L1 L2 EL Selection Test
L3 L4 Open-Book Test

✍ Online Writer's Notebook

Students can use the Online Writer's Notebook to record all responses.

Using a Dictionary and Thesaurus

1. Introduce the skill, using the instruction on the student page.

2. Review the explanations of dictionaries and thesauruses and the sample entries.

3. To reinforce the idea that most words that are synonyms do not mean exactly the same thing, write the words *champion* and *winner* on the board. Read this sentence: "The tennis player became a *champion* by defeating her opponent in the tournament's opening round." Ask students what is wrong. (To become *champion*, the player must win the whole tournament, not just the first round.) Then, read the sentence with the word *winner* in place of *champion*. Note that this sentence makes sense. *Winner* and *champion* are not exact synonyms.

4. Review the steps for using the thesaurus and dictionary effectively.

Think Aloud: Model the Skill

Model the skill of using a dictionary and thesaurus to decode words. Say:

Let's say I'm using the word *athlete* while writing about a distance runner. I've used the word several times, and I'd like to add variety by using a synonym. The thesaurus gives me the synonyms but I can't use all of them. I can't replace *athlete* with *acrobat* or *gymnast*, because I'm writing about a runner. The word *player* doesn't make sense. That's for someone who plays a game but not for a racer. I'm not sure if I can use *contestant* because I'm not sure what the word means, so I look the word up in the dictionary. I see that a *contestant* is "someone who takes part in a contest." A race is a kind of contest, so if I am writing about the runner once she has entered the race I can use that synonym.

G Grammar Tutorials

Grammar Tutorials in the *Student eText* provide additional support!

 # Language Study

Using a Dictionary and Thesaurus

A **dictionary** provides the meaning, pronunciation, and part of speech of words in the English language. It also gives a word's **etymology,** or origins. A word's etymology explains how words change, how they are borrowed from other languages, and how new words are invented, or "coined." Notice what this dictionary entry reveals about the word *athlete*.

> **athlete** (ath′ lēt′) *n.* [L *athleta* < Gr athlētēs, contestant in the games] a person trained in exercises, games, or contests requiring such qualities as physical strength, skills, and speed.

A **thesaurus** provides synonyms, or words with similar meanings, for many words in the English language. A thesaurus can help you find a word that means exactly what you want to say. The thesaurus entry shown gives several synonyms for *athlete*. Notice how each word has a slightly different meaning.

> **athlete** *n.* acrobat, gymnast, player, contestant, champion, sportsman, contender, challenger.

Follow these steps to use a thesaurus effectively:

- Identify a word in your writing that could be more precise.
- Read through the words that your thesaurus lists as synonyms.
- Choose the word that best expresses your intended meaning.
- Use a dictionary to make sure you are using the word correctly.

 Common Core State Standards

Language
4.c. Consult reference materials, both print and digital, to find the pronunciation of a word or determine or clarify its precise meaning or its part of speech.

4.d. Verify the preliminary determination of the meaning of a word or phrase (e.g., by checking the inferred meaning in context or in a dictionary).

5.c. Distinguish among the connotations (associations) of words with similar denotations (definitions).

📑 TEACHING RESOURCES

	Print	Digital
All Language Study Worksheet, Using a Dictionary and Thesaurus		✓

Where to Find a Dictionary and Thesaurus You can find these resources in book form at your school or library. You can also find them in electronic form on the Internet. Ask your teacher to recommend the best online word-study resources.

Practice A Find these words in a dictionary. Show how each one breaks into syllables and which syllable is stressed. Then, write each word's definition. Finally, use each word in a sentence that shows its meaning.

1. estimate   2. intuition   3. temporary   4. distinguish

Practice B Find each word in a thesaurus. Select two synonyms for the word. Explain how the meaning of each synonym is different from the meaning of the original word. Then, use each synonym in a sentence that shows its exact meaning. Remember to use a dictionary to check the meanings of your synonyms.

1. laugh (verb)   2. large (adjective)   3. story (noun)

Activity Create a quick-reference thesaurus of some commonly used words. Make notecards like the one shown for the words *strong, happy,* and *smart.* Share your words with classmates, collecting more synonyms. Then, with a partner, discuss the shades of meaning that each word conveys. You can use quick-reference cards like these to help you find precise words when you write.

Word:
Part of Speech:
Definition:
Synonym 1:
Synonym 1 Definition:
Synonym 2:
Synonym 2 Definition:

Comprehension and Collaboration

With a small group, take turns suggesting synonyms for the following words. Use a dictionary and a thesaurus to check your answers and to find additional synonyms.

- **look** (verb)
- **speak** (verb)
- **nervous** (adjective)

PART 2 • Language Study **99**

Practice A
Sample answers:

1. *estimate (v.):* (es'-ti-mate); to judge, approximately, the value of something; They <u>estimate</u> the size of the crowd at 50,000 people, but there could be more. Or (es'-ti-mate) *(n.):* an approximate value; The official <u>estimate</u> of the crowd size was about 50,000 people.

2. *intuition* (in-tu-i'-tion): a quick insight into something; On first entering the new school, the sixth grader's <u>intuition</u> told him he would be happy there.

3. *temporary* (tem'-po-rary): lasting only a limited time; The <u>tempo-rary</u> parking regulations were only for the holiday weekend.

4. *distinguish* (dis-tin'-guish): to see a difference in; The judge at the cooking contest could <u>distinguish</u> between pies made using fresh fruit and those made using frozen fruit.

Practice B
Sample answers:

1. A <u>chuckle</u> is a small laugh; a <u>roar</u> is a loud laugh. The mother <u>chuckled</u> at her daughter's little joke; The audience <u>roared</u> at the comedian's antics on the stage.

2. <u>Big</u> means "great in size"; <u>huge</u> means "extremely great in size." The <u>big</u> bowl held twice as much as the small one; The <u>huge</u> mountain rose high above them.

3. An <u>account</u> is a story of one's own experience; a <u>tale</u> is an impressive or powerful story. Her <u>account</u> of her travels was matter-of-fact; The <u>tale</u> of Abraham Lincoln's early life has inspired many people.

Activity

Pair students, and provide each pair with two sets of index cards to make their quick-reference cards. Invite pairs to take turns offering synonyms for each of the words. Discuss as a class the differences in meaning.

Comprehension and Collaboration

Divide the class into groups to carry out the activity. In their responses, students should be sure to choose synonyms that are the correct part of speech.

DIFFERENTIATED INSTRUCTION

EL Strategy for English Learners
Activate students' prior knowledge in teaching about synonyms. Write the word *move* on the board. Ask students to act out different ways that people *move.* Then, have them use a thesaurus and a dictionary to determine the best word for each style of movement. (Examples are *walk, run, trot, swagger,* and *sprint.*) Invite students to act out each of the new words for the class.

Enrichment for Gifted/Talented Students
Explain that some dictionaries provide notes on the synonyms of certain words. Those notes reveal the differences in meaning that distinguish the various words. Have students choose one such word, such as *copy, estimate, follow,* or *heavy.* Challenge them to write a sentence for each synonym of the word. They should leave a blank in place of the synonym. Then, have them exchange papers with a partner. Each should fill in the correct synonym, working from context.

PART 2 • Language Study **99**

Learn the Skills

1. Introduce the workshop, including the activity on the next page.

2. Mention that a good way to focus your attention is to take notes. Suggest that students number the steps of the directions in their notes.

3. Help students list typical action words they hear in directions, such as *stop, go,* and *make.* Make sure that students understand that *chronology* refers to time. Discuss examples of words that show chronology, such as *first, second, next,* and *finally.*

4. Encourage students to make a note of their questions as they listen to the directions. Then, they can ask the speaker for clarification at the end of the presentation.

5. Tell students to use precise action words in their directions. To illustrate, explain the difference between the sentences "Get the water hot until it has bubbles," and "Heat the water until it boils."

6. Remind students that the paraphrased directions have to be given in the same order as the original directions.

Ⓒ Speaking and Listening

Following Oral Directions

To understand and carry out **multistep oral directions,** or spoken directions with several steps, listen carefully to the speaker. Then, write down or restate the directions in the correct sequence. The following strategies will help you demonstrate effective listening skills.

Learn the Skills

Follow these guidelines to understand and apply oral directions.

Focus your attention. As you listen to directions, pay close attention to the speaker. Try to avoid or ignore distractions and focus on what is being said.

Notice action words and time-order words. Listen for the key action word in each step. These words tell you what to do. In the following directions for a fire drill, the action words are underlined:

- **Example:** First, <u>close</u> the doors and windows. Then, <u>walk</u> to the nearest exit. When you are outside, <u>stand</u> with your class while the teacher counts the people in the group.

Most directions are stated in chronological order, or the sequence in which they are meant to occur. For this reason, they usually include time-order words, such as *first, then, next,* and *last.*

Ask questions. Do not assume that the speaker will give you all the information you need. Instead, identify any information you think is missing or unclear and ask questions. You may need the speaker to be more precise in his or her description or to give you details that will clarify your understanding.

Paraphrase the directions. Clarify your understanding by paraphrasing the directions, or restating them in your own words. Ask the person giving the directions to clear up any misunderstandings.

Use action and time-order words. In your paraphrase, use action words to restate the action in each step. Use time-order words at the beginning of each step to restate multistep directions.

Ⓒ Common Core State Standards

Speaking and Listening
1.c. Pose and respond to specific questions with elaboration and detail by making comments that contribute to the topic, text, or issue under discussion.
1.d. Review the key ideas expressed and demonstrate understanding of multiple perspectives through reflection and paraphrasing.

Checklist

Listen Carefully
- ☑ Focus on the speaker. Listen for main ideas.
- ☑ Notice the action word in each step.
- ☑ Notice time-order words.
- ☑ Ask questions.

Restate Carefully
- ☑ Repeat the directions in your own words.
- ☑ Use action and time-order words.

✔ STRATEGIES **FOR FOLLOWING ORAL DIRECTIONS**

Give students these additional strategies for following directions:

- Remind students that some people learn well from oral directions and remember them easily. Others may need to take notes.

- Have students practice taking notes while you read simple directions aloud. Use gestures as needed. Tell students they may write words or draw symbols or pictures as you speak.

- Have students compare notes with a partner and discuss the different ways of taking notes.

- Ask students to paraphrase your directions using their notes. Then, compare the original directions with the paraphrased versions.

Practice the Skills

Presentation of Knowledge and Ideas Use what you have learned in the workshop to perform the following activity.

> ### ACTIVITY: Giving and Following Oral Directions
> Work with a partner to take turns giving and following oral directions.
> - Choose a multistep task that you can complete in your classroom, such as addressing an envelope, formatting a document, or taking and editing a photograph.
> - Break the task into time-ordered steps, including transition words that show sequence.
> - Deliver the directions clearly, without rushing.
> - Clarify your directions by answering any questions your partner may have.
> - When it is your turn to follow directions, listen carefully. Then, restate the directions, using each step in the checklist on the left page.
> - Ask your partner any questions you have about the directions.
> - Finally, carry out your partner's instructions and complete the task.

Use a guide for following directions like the one shown to take notes on your partner's presentation.

Guide for Following Oral Directions

Steps
Record each step in chronological order. Write the action verb first.

Step 1: _____
Step 2: _____
Step 3: _____
Step 4: _____
Step 5: _____
Step 6: _____

Areas of Confusion
Which steps are confusing?
Do any terms need to be defined?

Summarize
My restatement, or paraphrase, of the directions:
Does my restatement of the directions match those intended by my partner?
Can I successfully carry out these directions?

Comprehension and Collaboration With your classmates, discuss which steps made following oral directions easy and which steps made following oral directions difficult.

Practice the Skills

1. Review the assignment with students. Tell students to choose tasks that can be completed in or near the classroom, such as tying a shoe or doing a pushup. Clarify that partners should not give directions for the same task.

2. Explain to students that they should use a copy of the Guide for Following Oral Directions to evaluate their own presentation and the presentations made by classmates.

3. Before students give their oral directions to the class, remind listeners to ask questions if any points are unclear. To maintain order, encourage them to raise their hands and wait to be acknowledged by the presenter before stating their questions. Suggest that students making presentations scan the classroom from time to time so they will notice any students who have questions.

Evaluate the Activity

1. Evaluate students' presentations on the basis of the clarity, precision, and accuracy of their directions. For example, students should make their steps clear using time-order words. Overall, their directions should be accurate, providing the right information to perform the task.

2. When the class discusses the presentations that were easiest to follow, encourage students to make note of the features of those presentations that made them effective and to incorporate those techniques in their future presentations.

⚙ DIFFERENTIATED INSTRUCTION

ⓔ Strategy for English Learners
Have students demonstrate listening comprehension of the general meaning, main points, and important details of spoken language by following oral directions for performing a familiar classroom procedure:

- Ask students to monitor their comprehension and seek clarification as they follow the directions. Ask students to raise their hands when they have questions.
- Preteach the words *first* and *then*. Then, use the words as you give directions.

- Ask a fluent volunteer to model following your directions. Then, discuss the general meaning, main points, and important details of the directions.
- Give the same directions and have students follow them as a class.
- Have students work with a partner to practice giving and receiving directions for other simple tasks.

Introducing the Writing Assignment

Review the assignment and the criteria, using the instruction on the student page.

Focus on Research

Remind students to keep the following tips in mind as they conduct research.

- Gather information from multiple authoritative print and digital sources.
- Assess the usefulness of each source in answering the research question.
- Integrate information into the text selectively.
- Synthesize information from multiple sources.
- Avoid plagiarism.
- Use a standard format for citations.

 # Writing Process

Write a Narrative

Short Story

Defining the Form **Short stories** are brief works of fiction meant to entertain, to explore ideas, or to tell truths about life. They often feature a conflict, or a problem, faced by one or more characters. You might use elements of a short story in letters, scripts, and screenplays.

Assignment Write a short story about a person who faces a difficult challenge. Your short story should feature these elements:

✓ one or more *well-developed characters*

✓ an *interesting conflict* or problem

✓ a *plot* that moves toward a resolution of the conflict

✓ a clear and accurate *point of view,* or perspective

✓ concrete and *sensory details* that establish the *setting*

✓ *dialogue,* or conversations between characters

✓ error-free grammar, including the use of *correct pronoun-antecedent agreement*

To preview the criteria on which your short story may be judged, see the rubric on page 109.

FOCUS ON RESEARCH

As you prepare to write a short story, you might conduct research to

- find accurate details about the place your story is set.
- locate facts about life during another time period if your story takes place in the past.
- learn about an activity your characters perform or a sport they play.

Be sure to use reliable sources of information for your research. Double-check the accuracy of dates, statistics, and other data by confirming the information in two or more sources.

Common Core State Standards

Writing

3. Write narratives to develop real or imagined experiences or events using effective technique, relevant descriptive details, and well-structured event sequences.

3.a. Engage and orient the reader by establishing a context and introducing a narrator and/or characters; organize an event sequence that unfolds naturally and logically.

READING-WRITING CONNECTION

To get a feel for short stories, read "Stray" by Cynthia Rylant on page 20.

TEACHING RESOURCES

	Print	Digital
All Common Core Companion, pp. 196–206; 321–330; 331–334	✓	✓
All EssayScorer powered by WriteToLearn		✓
All Online Student Edition eText with audio and video		✓
All Online Teacher Edition		✓
L1 Professional Development Guidebook, Rubrics for Narration: Short Story, pp. 226–227		✓
All Student Companion All-in-One Workbook, Unit 1 Writing Process	✓	✓

EssayScorer

Students can use EssayScorer with automatic feedback and scoring to practice summarizing!

Prewriting/Planning Strategies

Freewrite. Set a timer and freewrite for five minutes. Start with an image—a person in a boat in the middle of the ocean—or a feeling: curiosity, fear, or loneliness. During freewriting, focus more on the flow of ideas than on spelling or grammar. After five minutes, review your freewriting. Circle ideas to use in your story.

Review art and photos. Look at several pieces of fine art or photography in your textbooks or other sources. For each, imagine a story based on what the image suggests. Choose one of these ideas as the basis of your story.

Identify the conflict. Once you have a general idea of the story you will tell, get a better idea of its conflict—the struggle between two opposing forces. To develop the conflict, ask yourself these questions:

- What does my main character want?
- Who or what is getting in the way?
- What will the character do to overcome this obstacle?

Create your main character. Fill in a web like the one shown to help you get to know your main character.

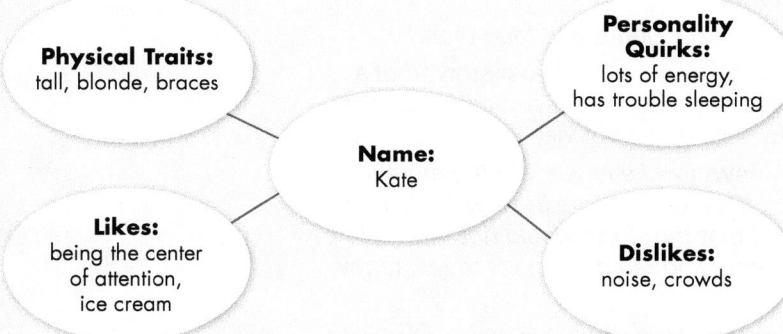

Give your story a title. With a clear idea of your topic and your main character, list possible titles for your story. Scan your list and choose the title that best captures the essence of what your story will convey.

✅ STRATEGIES **FOR CLARIFYING EXPECTED OUTCOMES**

Using Rubrics
- Before students begin work on this assignment, have them preview the Rubric for Self-Assessment (p. 109) to learn what qualities their stories must have. A copy of this rubric appears in the *Graphic Organizer* for this workshop.
- Review the criteria in the Rubric with the class. Before students use the Rubric to assess their own writing, work with them to rate the Student Model (p. 108) using the Rubric.

- If you wish to assess students' short stories with either a 4-point or a 6-point scoring rubric, see *Professional Development Guidebook*, pp. 226–227.

Prewriting/Planning Strategies

1. Introduce the prewriting strategies, using the instruction on the student page.
2. Have students apply the strategies to choose a topic.

Teaching the Strategies

1. In order to help students generate ideas, identify and discuss the topics of their favorite stories from this unit.
2. One way to help students focus is to have them write the image they plan to work from at the top of their papers. Tell students that if they do not have a topic at the end of the freewriting session, they can repeat the technique.
3. As students are narrowing their topics, point out that a topic is not enough to carry a story. Plot is also important. Often a story is about overcoming some type of conflict. Make sure students identify their main characters and the conflicts those characters will face.
4. Review with students the graphic organizer showing details about character. Suggest that students review the ideas from the freewriting activity to see if there are details that pertain to their main characters.
5. Lead students in studying the graphic organizers. Suggest that students review the ideas from the freewriting activity to see if there are details that pertain to their main characters.

Six Traits Focus

✓	Ideas	Word Choice
✓	Organization	Sentence Fluency
	Voice	Conventions

Drafting Strategies

1. Introduce the drafting strategies.
2. Have students apply the strategies as they draft.

Teaching the Strategies

1. Before students begin drafting their stories, use the plot diagram to help them visualize a plot. Explain that they should reveal information gradually so readers will want to keep reading to find out what happens.

2. Point out that suspense is essential to keep readers interested in the rising action of a plot.

3. Remind students to use their five senses when describing the setting and characters. Read each of the following sentences and then the revision in parentheses:

   Harry was afraid. (Revision: An icy shiver ran down Harry's spine; goose bumps broke out on his arms. He gasped.)

   Leroy noticed it was a beautiful spring day. (Revision: Leroy could smell the sweetness of lilacs, as the warm breeze caressed his skin.)

4. Discuss point of view with students. Remind them that in third-person point of view narrative, all characters are referred to in the third person. Point out that first-person point of view is useful for understanding the story from the narrator's perspective.

Six Traits Focus

✓	Ideas	✓	Word Choice
✓	Organization		Sentence Fluency
	Voice		Conventions

Drafting Strategies

Develop your plot. Use a plot diagram like the one shown to organize the sequence of events in your short story. Make sure the events follow a sequence that unfolds naturally and logically. Plot often follows this pattern:

- **Exposition** introduces the characters and situation, including the conflict.
- The **conflict** develops during the **rising action,** which leads to the climax of the story.
- The **climax** is the point of greatest tension in the story.
- In the **falling action,** events and emotions wind down.
- In the **resolution,** the conflict is resolved and loose ends are tied up. The conclusion of your story should logically follow the events in the plot.

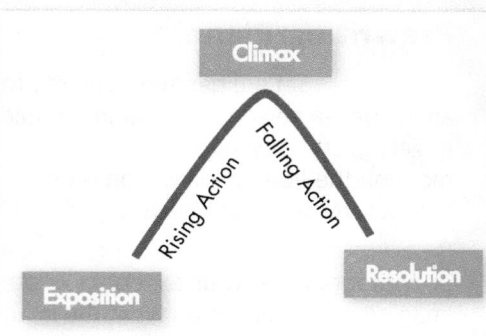

Use sensory details. As you draft your story, make your characters and setting come to life by including **sensory details**—language that describes how things look, sound, feel, taste, and smell. Having descriptive details will help you to develop a setting that the reader can visualize.

Dull: The sky *looked stormy*.

Vivid: The sky *boiled with black clouds and loud thunder*.

Write from a specific point of view. Tell your story from a single point of view, either as a participant (first-person point of view) or an observer (third-person point of view).

First-person point of view: *I woke up early in the morning to the sound of thunder. I couldn't believe it! How could it rain on my big day? I worried that the storm would not stop before noon. I pulled on my clothes and ran downstairs to talk to my mom.*

Third-person point of view: *Harry woke up early in the morning to the sound of thunder. He couldn't believe it! How could it rain on his big day? Harry's face revealed signs of worry and frustration. After dressing, he ran downstairs to talk to his mom.*

Common Core State Standards

Writing
3.a. Engage and orient the reader by establishing a context and introducing a narrator and/or characters; organize an event sequence that unfolds naturally and logically.
3.d. Use precise words and phrases, relevant descriptive details, and sensory language to convey experiences and events.
3.e. Provide a conclusion that follows from the narrated experiences or events.

🔅 DIFFERENTIATED INSTRUCTION

Strategy for Less Proficient Writers
As students consider how to develop their topics, suggest that they write about something with which they are familiar. They might model the events on places, people, or events that they know about. Have students write a list of familiar events that could be developed into a plot.

EL Strategy for English Learners
Encourage students to write five words that describe an event. Suggest that they add words that relate to the five senses to extend their descriptions. Then, have students perform the same exercise for their main character. This strategy will help them by creating a word list from which they can build a plot.

Voice

Voice is the personality behind a piece of writing. When voice comes through in an essay or a story, readers can almost hear someone speaking. Voice reveals the speaker's personality and attitude toward the world.

Finding a Fictional Voice When you write an essay, the voice you use should be a reflection of you. It should allow your personality and your ideas to shine through. When you write a short story, however, the narrator is not necessarily you.

If you write your story from a first-person point of view, the narrator is a character in the story. This character's way of speaking and attitude toward the other characters must reflect his or her personality.

If you write your story from a third-person point of view, the narrator is outside the story. You must imagine the character of that narrator.

Consider the following points as you develop your narrator's voice:

Characteristics	What the narrator is like will shape the way he or she tells the story.	**Consider these questions:** • How old is the narrator? • Is the narrator male or female?
Attitude	The narrator's attitude toward the different characters and their conflict will affect how he or she tells the story.	**Consider this question:** • Is the narrator sympathetic toward the main character? Why or why not?
Tone	Tone is the author's attitude toward his or her audience and subject. If your story is funny, you might want your narrator to convey a humorous tone.	**Consider this question:** • What word describes the tone of your story? • How can your narrator convey that tone?
Word Choice	The narrator's words can reflect his or her traits. For example, a teen is likely to speak differently than an adult.	**Consider this question:** • What words or phrases would someone with the characteristics of the narrator use?

Evaluating Your Narrative Voice After you have drafted your story, read it aloud. Does the narrator sound right to you? Does his or her voice come across the way you want it to? If not, revise your word choice and sentence structures to better reflect your narrator's voice.

Voice

1. **Remind** students that a story's narrator has a personality and attitude that affect the way the story is told. The narrator's voice should reflect his or her personality. Creating the words and actions of a character requires using language that reveals who the character is.

2. **Ask** students to answer the following question prior to reviewing the chart on the student page: If your best friend were the narrator of a story, would the story sound the same as it would if it were told by a young child?

   Possible response: No, people of different ages have different experiences and that affects the way they tell a story and their attitude toward the characters in the story.

3. Review the questions on the chart with the class, asking students to write down their responses.

4. Tell students that as they read their drafts, they should picture the person who is narrating the story. Tell students that if they cannot picture this person clearly, they should go back and add words and phrases that reflect the narrator's personality.

Revising Strategies

1. Introduce the revising strategies, using the instruction on the student page.

2. Have students apply the strategies as they revise.

Teaching the Strategies

1. Before students begin their bead charts, explain that in order for their stories to make sense, none of the events of the plot should happen "out of the blue." Their stories will not be believable unless one event leads to another. Remind them to limit their stories to one or two settings and a limited time span.

2. Have volunteers read aloud the Student Model. Remind students that the plot was advanced through dialogue. Elicit that dialogue reveals the personality of the speakers.

3. As students exchange papers to evaluate each other's dialogue, suggest they try to imagine the words they read being spoken aloud by a real person to determine if the character's speech is believable.

Think Aloud: Modeling How to Create Dialogue

Model the strategy of creating dialogue, using the following "think aloud." Say to students:

I can use dialogue to make my short story more lively. For instance, let's say that my story is about two friends, Mary and Jeanette, who enter a cave to hunt for rare stones. I could write, "The two friends entered the cave, hoping to find rocks that no one had ever discovered." However, it would be much more interesting to have them speak to one another. For instance, Mary could say, "I can't wait to see what we'll find in here!" And Jeanette could respond by saying, "Me, too. We might become world-famous archeologists someday!"

Six Traits Focus

Ideas		Word Choice	
Organization		Sentence Fluency	
Voice		Conventions	✓

Revising Strategies

Create logical connections between events. Use a bead chart to make sure that events in your plot are logically connected.

- Underline the major events in your story.

- Summarize each event in a "bead" on a chart like the one shown.

- Show the connections between events by writing a word or phrase in the connector string. Make sure that these ideas have been developed in your story.

- If most of your connectors say *next*, review your story. If you cannot think of a good connection between events, delete or reshape one of the events.

- Transitional words, phrases, and clauses, such as *meanwhile, back in town, while Mike waited,* can help you show a shift in time or setting.

- Consider using literary devices such as suspense, foreshadowing, or flashback to add variety to your "string" of events.

> Troy starts wondering where Leonard is.
>
> he's curious, annoyed
>
> Troy yells to Leonard to stop searching.
>
> next
>
> Troy goes into woods to look for Leonard.
>
> Troy doesn't hear any response from Leonard.
>
> he starts to worry

Evaluate point of view. Check that the point of view in your story remains the same throughout the story. For example, if the story begins with the point of view of a young boy named Daniel, it should not end with the point of view of Daniel's mother.

Use dialogue to give characters a voice. Review your draft for places to bring your story to life with dialogue. Keep in mind that realistic characters may use slang and interrupt each other.

Vary your sentences and word choices. Revise your story to include a variety of words and sentence lengths. Be sure to use a thesaurus to make descriptions more vivid and to choose precise words. Look for a balance of short and long sentences. Providing a variety of sentences will improve your story's flow.

Common Core State Standards

Writing
3.b. Use narrative techniques, such as dialogue, pacing, and description, to develop experiences, events, and/or characters.
3.c. Use a variety of transition words, phrases, and clauses to convey sequence and signal shifts from one time frame or setting to another.

Language
1.c. Recognize and correct inappropriate shifts in pronoun number and person.
1.d. Recognize and correct vague pronouns (i.e., ones with unclear or ambiguous antecedents).

✔ STRATEGIES **FOR USING TECHNOLOGY IN WRITING**

Have students use the "search" or "find" feature in the word-processing program to find overused words in their writing. For example, students may find that they used the word *said* in every instance of using dialogue. Encourage them to use more colorful words, such as *whispered, yelled,* or *replied* to create a better sense of tone and mood when something is said.

Revising for Pronoun-Antecedent Agreement

A **pronoun** takes the place of a noun. The noun that the pronoun refers to is called the **antecedent**.

Agreement in Number A pronoun and its antecedent must agree in number. Use a singular pronoun with a singular antecedent. Use a plural pronoun with a plural antecedent.

Singular Pronoun and Antecedent

<u>California</u> is a popular vacation spot because **_it_** has many beautiful beaches.

Plural Pronoun and Antecedent

My <u>**parents**</u> said that **_they_** would attend my play.

Agreement in Person A pronoun and its antecedent must agree in person. Use a first-person pronoun with a first-person antecedent. Use a third-person pronoun with a third-person antecedent.

First-Person Pronoun and Antecedent

<u>Shandra</u> said, "Could **_I_** borrow that book?"

Third-Person Pronoun and Antecedent

<u>Shandra</u> said **_she_** wanted to borrow a book.

Clear Antecedent Every pronoun must have a clear antecedent. Problems may arise if a pronoun has more than one possible antecedent.

Unclear: <u>Patel</u> told <u>George</u> that **_he_** was late.

Clear: <u>Patel</u> told <u>George,</u> "**_I_** am late."

Clear: <u>Patel</u> told <u>George,</u> "**_You_** are late."

Fixing Errors To find and fix errors related to pronoun use, follow these steps:

1. Identify each pronoun/antecedent pair that you used.
- Decide whether the antecedent is singular or plural.
- Determine whether the antecedent is in the first, second, or third person.
- Make sure pronouns refer to specific antecedents.

2. Follow the rules of agreement to fix any errors.

Grammar in Your Writing

Reread your short story. Look for pronouns and their antecedents. Then, use the rules above to make corrections.

Revising for Pronoun–Antecedent Agreement

1. Introduce the grammar skill, using the instruction on the student page.

2. Discuss the rules and examples, as well as the strategies for fixing incorrect usage.

3. Have students follow the instruction under Grammar in Your Writing to correct errors in their drafts.

Teaching the Grammar Skill

1. Errors in pronoun–antecedent agreement most often occur when the antecedent is an indefinite pronoun. Point out the following examples to reinforce the rule that a singular pronoun is used with a singular antecedent.

   Has anyone in the boys' class misplaced his textbook?

   Ask the girls if somebody left her coat in the living room.

2. Have students identify the sentences with errors in pronoun–antecedent agreement and fix them:

   They took their fishing rods.
   (**Answer:** correct as is)

   Each of the two girls has their passport.
   (**Answer:** Each of the two girls has her passport.)

   All of them liked their dinner.
   (**Answer:** correct as is)

   Nobody in the Boy Scout troop has earned all their merit badges.
   (**Answer:** Nobody in the Boy Scout troop has earned all his merit badges.)

3. Have students identify if the antecedent is singular and plural. Then have them choose the correct pronoun.

   Yesterday Rick said that _____ will go to the lake this weekend. (he, us) (**Answer:** singular, he)

   Each person on the soccer team said _____ will be on time for the game. (they, she) (**Answer:** singular, she)

   My cousins said _____ want to visit us during the summer (she, they) (**Answer:** plural, they)

☑ STRATEGIES **FOR USING DIALOGUE**

Students should be careful to ensure that their dialogue sounds realistic. To make characters sound like real people, writers use contractions, colloquialisms, interrupted speech, and other types of informal language that occur frequently in conversation. Have students practice using these techniques in writing assignments.

Student Model

Review the Student Model with the class, using the annotations to analyze the writer's use of the elements of a short story.

Teaching From the Student Model

1. Explain that the Student Model is a sample and that stories may be longer.

2. **Ask** students to summarize the conflict of "Math Mackerel."

   Answer: The narrator has difficulty understanding math.

3. **Ask** students what the dialogue between the narrator and Math Mackerel suggests about their respective personalities.

   Possible responses: The narrator seems hesitant and skeptical ("Yes, but…" "Are you going to give me all the knowledge I need?"); Math Mackerel seems confident ("I am Math Mackerel," the fish stated proudly. "Good, I'll go first…").

4. Discuss the reasons the writer might have chosen to tell the story from the first-person point of view.

   Possible response: This point of view gives us the best insight into the character's math anxiety.

5. **Ask** students how the writer makes the resolution of the story believable.

   Answer: The character practices for three weeks, and keeps improving her skills.

Connecting to Real-Life Writing

Let students know that there will be many times when they can use short-story writing skills. Magazines and newspapers often have story writing contests and many high schools and colleges have literary magazines that print student work. In addition, the skills used to write stories can be transferred easily to writing for the stage, television, and movies. News reporters use narration to tell stories that are true.

STUDENT MODEL: **Karina McCorkle, Raleigh, NC**

Common Core State Standards
Language
2.b. Spell correctly.

Math Mackerel

I sat staring blankly at the sheet of notebook paper in front of me. My teacher had just finished explaining how to divide fractions. I didn't understand it at all. I hated math, and now in sixth grade, math was much harder.

"I wish someone could help me understand math." I whispered.

Suddenly, a fish appeared out of thin air. I stared at him. He was standing on his tail with a flowing red cape and on his chest he had a yellow emblem with the red letters "MM."

"W-who are you?" I stammered.

"I am Math Mackerel. I thought I heard someone asking for help with math," the fish stated proudly.

"Oh, that was me," I said.

"I'll see you at recess." Math Mackerel said as he disappeared with a swish of his tail and a flick of fins.

My teacher called out, "Time to put your math in your notebooks." I realized I hadn't written down a single problem on my paper.

"Drat!" I thought and put away my paper.

Outside, I sat in a secluded spot behind a bush and waited. Suddenly, Math Mackerel appeared.

"Greetings," said Math Mackerel happily. "I am here to help you with math."

"Are you going to give me all the knowledge I need?" I asked curiously.

"I could do that, but that would be cheating," scoffed Math Mackerel. He whipped out a deck of cards. I raised my eyebrows at him. I couldn't see how a deck of cards could help me with math.

"Do you know how to play Go Fish?" asked Math Mackerel.

"Yes, but how is . . ." I tried to ask.

"Good, I'll go first." And he began to deal the cards with his fins.

Twenty minutes later, we were still playing a hearty game of Go Fish.

"Got any nines?" I asked, peering over my cards.

"Yes, what is one and seven ninths divided by two thirds?" he asked.

"Two and two thirds," I answered.

"Good job!" Math Mackerel said as he slammed his nines on the ground. Suddenly I heard my teacher's whistle. It was time to go inside.

"I will see you tomorrow," Math Mackerel called as he disappeared.

Math Mackerel and I played Go Fish for three weeks, and I got better and better at math. Then one day, my teacher announced a math test to review what we had learned. Suddenly, all my confidence evaporated. Playing with Math Mackerel was something I could handle easily, but a test was a different matter.

At recess, Math Mackerel was already waiting for me.

"Time to continue yesterday's game," Math Mackerel said happily.

"There is going to be a math test on Friday! You have to be there!" I gasped.

"Just remember Go Fish, and you'll be fine." And he disappeared, as his cape swirled around him.

All week, I dreaded Friday. I gulped as the teacher passed out the papers. I worked through the problems and found them easy as I thought about Go Fish. My teacher returned the tests on Monday. I picked mine up and saw an A!

Karina introduces the conflict in the first paragraph of her story.

Karina chooses to write her story from the first-person point of view.

Karina creates dialogue between two central characters.

Here, Karina moves the plot forward to its climax.

Karina includes an exciting climax and ends with the resolution.

✔ STRATEGIES **FOR TIME MANAGEMENT**

When writing a short story or narrative in a timed situation such as a test, it is easy to lose track of time. Remind students that using a plot diagram will save them time in the long run. They should spend some of their drafting time creating and filling in the chart to help organize their thoughts about character and conflict. By doing this planning, they will find that drafting and revising go much faster.

Editing and Proofreading

Revise to correct errors in grammar, spelling, and punctuation.

Focus on spelling. **Homophones** are words that sound the same and have similar spellings but have very different meanings. A spell checker will not find an error if a word is spelled correctly but is the wrong word choice; therefore, proofread carefully. Here are just a few examples of easily confused words: *our/are, than/then, know/now, lose/loose, accept/except, it's/its*

Publishing and Presenting

Consider one of the following ways to share your writing:

Submit your story. Submit your story to your school's literary magazine, a national magazine, or an e-zine, or enter a contest that publishes student writing. Ask your teacher for suggestions.

Give a reading. Get together with a group of classmates and present a literary reading for an audience at your school.

Reflecting on Your Writing

Writer's Journal Jot down your answer to this question:

The next time you write a story, what do you think you might do differently as a result of this writing experience?

Rubric for Self-Assessment

Find evidence in your writing to address each category. Then use the rating scale to grade your work.

Rubric for Self-Assessment

Criteria	Rating Scale
Purpose/Focus Clearly presents a narrative that develops real experiences and events	*not very* .... *very* 1 2 3 4
Organization Organizes events clearly and logically; presents a strong conclusion that follows from and reflects on events in the narrative	1 2 3 4
Development of Ideas/Elaboration Establishes a clear context and point of view; effectively uses narrative techniques, such as dialogue, pacing, and description	1 2 3 4
Language Uses precise words, descriptive details, and sensory language to convey experiences and events	1 2 3 4
Conventions Uses proper grammar, including correct use of pronouns and antecedents	1 2 3 4

Spiral Review Earlier in this unit, you learned about **personal and possessive pronouns** (p. 42) and **pronoun case** (p. 70). As you review your short story, be sure you have used pronouns correctly.

Editing and Proofreading

1. Introduce the editing and proofreading focus, using the instruction on the student page.
2. Have students edit and proofread their narratives, correcting grammar, spelling, punctuation, and word choice. Make sure they check for errors of the type noted in the lesson focus and the Spiral Review.

Teaching the Editing Focus

1. Tell students that homophones are also often described as "easily confused words," because misuse of homophones is common. Have students carefully check for words with similar spellings but different meanings by circling these types of words in their writing.
2. Invite students to share words with spellings they sometimes confuse. **Possible responses:** chose, choose; desert, dessert; capital, capitol; hearty, hardy; miner, minor; root, route.
3. Ask students to spell the following confusing words: **Answers:** lose, loose; accept, except; than, then; our, are; know, now.

Six Traits Focus

Ideas	Word Choice
Organization	Sentence Fluency
Voice	✓ Conventions

ASSESS

Publishing and Presenting

Find out whether the town newspaper or other local publications accept student fiction, and encourage students to submit to these venues. Emphasize the importance of students acquainting themselves with the type of work that is accepted by each publication before they submit their writing. Suggest that students organize a reading for another class at your school. Have students practice their readings beforehand, using appropriate gestures and expression. If possible, tape-record or videotape rehearsals, so students can review their performance.

Reflecting on Your Writing

Emphasize that as students record their thoughts in their journals, they should focus on the process of writing the short story rather than the finished product. Tell students that rather than comparing their stories to those of their favorite author, they should think and write about the challenges and rewards of stretching their imaginations.

 Interactive Whiteboard Activities

Use this tool to project and edit student writing!

Assessment

In this Assessment (pp. 110–115), students apply and reinforce their mastery of the Common Core State Standards and the skills taught in Unit 1. The practice is divided into four sections, including a section of Constructed Response tasks addressing CCS Reading standards.

1. Before assigning each section, review the relevant Common Core State Standards and unit skills with students.

2. Set a time limit for the multiple-choice items in each section, allowing a little over one minute per question. Allow twenty minutes for any Timed Writing questions.

3. Administer each of the first three sections of the Assessment (pp. 110–113).

4. Use the Constructed Response tasks on pages 114–115 to assess the depth of students' mastery of standards taught in the unit. Follow the suggestions on teacher pages 114–115 for assigning tasks and for supporting and evaluating student performance.

Reteaching Plan

For each practice, use the Reteaching Plan chart on the same page as the answers to determine which skills require reteaching, given the items students answered incorrectly.

Question	Instructional Pages to Reteach
1	18
2	28
3	44
4	58
5	44
6	28
7	—
8	28

 Assessment: Skills

SELECTED RESPONSE

I. Reading Literature

Directions: *Read the excerpt from "Becky and the Wheels-and-Brake Boys" by James Berry. Then, answer each question that follows.*

I found myself in the center of town, going through the busy Saturday crowd. I hoped Mum wouldn't be too cross. I went into the fire station. With lots of luck I came face to face with a round-faced man in uniform. He talked to me. "Little miss, can I help you?"

I told him I'd like to talk to the head man. He took me into the office and gave me a chair. I sat down. I opened out my brown paper parcel. I showed him my dad's sun helmet. I told him I thought it would make a good fireman's hat. I wanted to sell the helmet for some money toward a bike, I told him.

The fireman laughed a lot. I began to laugh, too. The fireman put me in a car and drove me back home.

Mum's eyes popped to see me bringing home the fireman. The round-faced fireman laughed at my adventure. Mum laughed, too, which was really good. The fireman gave Mum my dad's hat back. Then—mystery, mystery—Mum sent me outside while they talked.

My mum was only a little cross with me. Then—mystery and more mystery—my mum took me with the fireman in his car to his house.

The fireman brought out what? A bicycle! A beautiful, shining bicycle! His nephew's bike. His nephew had been taken away, all the way to America. The bike had been left with the fireman-uncle for him to sell it. And the good, kind fireman-uncle decided we could have the bike—on small payments. My mum looked uncertain. But in a big, big way, the fireman knew it was all right. And Mum smiled a little. My mum had good sense to know it was all right. My mum took the bike from the fireman Mr. Dean.

And guess what? Seeing my bike much, much newer than his, my cousin Ben's eyes <u>popped</u> with envy. But he took on the big job. He taught me to ride. Then he taught Shirnette.

Common Core State Standards

RL.6.1, RL.6.2, RL.6.3, RL.6.4; W.6.3
[For the full wording of the standards, see the standards chart in the front of your textbook.]

1. **Part A** What is the best summary of the **plot** of this passage?

   A. Becky should save her money and buy a bike.

   B. Becky finds a way, with a stranger's help, to get a bike.

   C. Becky's family does not have enough money to buy a bike.

   D. Becky cannot have a bike.

   Part B Which phrase from the passage best supports the answer to Part A?

   A. "I wanted to sell the helmet"

   B. "The fireman gave Mum my Dad's hat back."

   C. "And the good, kind fireman-uncle decided we could have the bike"

   D. "The round-faced fireman laughed"

2. Based on the writer's **characterization**, which words best describe Mr. Dean?

   A. cross and suspicious

   B. uncertain and confused

   C. quiet and determined

   D. polite and friendly

3. **Part A** What is the **internal conflict** felt by Becky's mother?

   A. She is worried that the family cannot afford a bike for Becky.

   B. She does not like bicycles.

   C. She does not want Becky to talk to strangers.

   D. She does not trust the fireman.

   Part B Which detail from the story best supports the answer to Part A?

   A. "Mum's eyes popped to see me bringing home the fireman."

   B. "My mum was only a little cross with me."

   C. "My mum looked uncertain."

   D. "And Mum smiled a little."

4. Which sentence best sums up the **theme** of the story?

   A. You should not want something too much—you might not be able to get it.

   B. If you cannot get something yourself, it's probably not worth it.

   C. Parents should get you what you want.

   D. If you really want something, you need to work with others to get it.

5. Which phrase from the passage best represents the **resolution** of the internal conflict felt by Becky's mother?

   A. "Mum laughed, too, which was really good."

   B. "My mum had good sense to know it was all right."

   C. "Mum sent me outside while they talked"

   D. "Mum smiled a little"

6. Which of the following best describes Becky?

   A. She has not earned her mother's trust.

   B. She is filled with pride by her new bike.

   C. She is willing to take a chance to get what she wants.

   D. She only wants what she cannot have.

7. Which phrase is closest in meaning to the underlined word *popped*?

   A. filled with tears

   B. looked angry

   C. narrowed suspiciously

   D. opened wide

   ⏱ Timed Writing

8. Write an original narrative that provides an alternative ending to the passage. Include both **direct characterization** and **indirect characterization**.

   GO ON →

☑ **ASSESS**

I. Reading Literature

1. **Part A:** B
   Part B: C

2. D

3. **Part A:** A
   Part B: C

4. D

5. B

6. C

7. D

⏱ **Timed Writing**

8. Student narratives should include both direct characterization and indirect characterization.

 **ASSESS**

II. Reading Informational Text

Part A: A
Part B: C

II. Reading Informational Text

Directions: *Read the passage. Then, answer each question that follows.*

Common Core State Standards

RI.6.1; L.6.1; L.6.1.a, L.6.1.b, L.6.1.c, L.6.1.d, L.6.2
[For the full wording of the standards, see the standards chart in the front of your textbook.]

Paper or Plastic?

After unloading your cart of groceries at the supermarket, you are faced with an important question: paper bags or plastic bags? How will you answer?

Paper comes from trees. The process of turning wood into paper uses great amounts of energy. Recycling paper requires the use of many different chemicals and a lot of energy. Even though paper is recyclable, it still fills half of all landfill space. Paper biodegrades more easily than plastic, but it is still a process that takes years.

Plastics come from the waste products of oil refining. Plastic bags require less energy to produce than do paper bags. They can also be recycled for uses such as relining wastebaskets. In landfills, plastic bags take up less room. However, plastic bags are often carelessly thrown away, harming marine life and causing clogs in sewers.

Conclusion Both paper bags and plastic bags use precious natural resources, but both can be recycled. So, what's the best choice? Neither one, we think. Our bag of choice? A reusable cotton bag.

Quick Facts: Why we should switch to reusable shopping bags
In one year, the average American uses about 350 plastic bags.
In one year, 14 million trees are cut down to make 10 billion paper bags.
Reusable bags are stronger and can be used for most shopping trips.

1. Part A The "Paper" and "Plastic" sections of the article answer these questions: *Where does it come from?* and *How much energy is used in making it?* What third question is answered by both sections?

A. Can it be recycled?
B. Will it harm the environment?
C. Which is stronger?
D. How much landfill space is used?

Part B Which detail from the article best supports the answer to Part A?

A. "Both paper bags and plastic bags use precious natural resources."
B. "Plastic bags require less energy to produce than do paper bags."
C. "They can also be recycled for uses such as relining wastebaskets."
D. "In landfills, plastic bags take up less room."

III. Writing and Language Conventions

Directions: *Read the passage. Then, answer each question that follows.*

(1) Suddenly, Poppa stopped the car. (2) He wanted to show us something. (3) In my minds eye, I tried to picture what it might be. (4) Outside, the air was cool and damp. (5) I breathed in the rich, spicy odor of pine. (6) We hiked along, our feet padding on the soft, moist ground. (7) Poppa told us to follow them closely. (8) Beauty surrounded us completely. (9) Then I heard water splashing onto water. (10) A small sign pointed north to angel falls. (11) What would we see around the next turn? (12) Suddenly, there it was: a long white strip of water rushing over a tall cliff and plunging into a blue pool below.

1. What **personal pronoun** is used in sentence 2?
   - **A.** He
   - **B.** wanted
   - **C.** show
   - **D.** something

2. Which revision to sentence 10 uses correct capitalization of **proper nouns?**
   - **A.** A small sign pointed North to Angel Falls.
   - **B.** A small sign pointed north to Angel falls.
   - **C.** A small sign pointed North to angel falls.
   - **D.** A small sign pointed north to Angel Falls.

3. Which revision to sentence 7 uses correct **pronoun-antecedent agreement?**
   - **A.** Poppa told we to follow them closely.
   - **B.** Poppa told us to follow her closely.
   - **C.** Poppa told us to follow him closely.
   - **D.** Poppa told us to follow their closely.

4. Which sentence contains an example of an **interrogative pronoun?**
   - **A.** sentence 1
   - **B.** sentence 4
   - **C.** sentence 8
   - **D.** sentence 11

5. In sentence 3, what is the correct way to rewrite the **possessive noun** in the phrase "minds eye"?
   - **A.** minds' eye
   - **B.** mind's eye
   - **C.** minds's eye
   - **D.** mindes' eye

☑ ASSESS

III. Writing and Language Conventions

1. A
2. D
3. C
4. D
5. B

Reteaching Plan

Question	Pages to Reteach
1	42
2	26
3	107
4	56
5	26

Constructed Response
Assigning Tasks/Reteaching Skills

Use the chart below to choose appropriate Constructed Response tasks by identifying which tasks assess lessons in the textbook that you have taught. Use the same lessons for reteaching when students' performance indicates a failure to fully master a standard. For additional instruction and practice, assign the *Common Core Companion* pages indicated for each task.

Task	Where Taught/ Pages to Reteach	Common Core Companion Pages
1	14–17, 18	28–40
2	14–17, 28	28–40, 321–330
3	14–17, 58	15–27, 28–40, 321–330
4	14–17, 18	28–40, 304–310
5	14–17, 58	15–27, 286–292
6	14–17, 44	15–27, 246–252, 253–266

Assessment Pacing

In assigning the Writing tasks on this student page, allow a class period for the completion of a task. As an alternative, assign tasks as homework. In assigning the Speaking and Listening and Research tasks on the facing page, consider having students do any required preparation as a homework assignment. Then, allow a class period for the presentations themselves.

Evaluating Constructed Response

Use the rubric at the bottom of this Teacher Edition page to evaluate students' mastery of the standards as demonstrated in their Constructed Responses. Review the rubric with students before they begin work so they know the criteria by which their work will be evaluated.

CONSTRUCTED RESPONSE

Directions: *Follow the instructions to complete the tasks below as required by your teacher.*

As you work on each task, incorporate both general academic vocabulary and literary terms you learned in Parts 1 and 2.

Common Core State Standards

RL.6.2, RL.6.3; W.6.7, W.6.8; SL.6.1, SL.6.4; L.6.1
[For the full wording of the standards, see the standards chart in the front of your textbook.]

Writing

TASK 1 Literature [RL.6.3]
Analyze the Development of Plot

Write an essay in which you describe how a plot unfolds in a story from Part 2.

- Determine which story you will write about and begin your essay by briefly describing the basic plot.
- Explain the conflict or problem that starts the story moving. Tell whether the conflict or problem is internal or external.
- Then, describe how the plot unfolds in a series of scenes. Explain which scenes make up the exposition, the rising action, the climax, and the falling action.
- Tell how each scene adds information that finally leads to the resolution.

TASK 2 Literature [RL.6.3; L.6.1]
Describe Characters

Write an essay in which you describe characters from two stories in Part 2.

- Tell which stories and which characters you will discuss.
- Describe your chosen characters. Include details about the characters' looks, age, thoughts, feelings, and actions.
- Explain how the characters respond to the events of the stories. Describe what those responses tell you about the characters.

- Discuss how the characters change from the beginning to the end of the stories.
- Check to be sure you have used personal and possessive pronouns correctly.

TASK 3 Literature [RL.6.2; RL.6.3; L.6.1]
Determine the Theme

Write an essay in which you explain the theme of a story from Part 2.

Part 1

- Explain which story you will discuss in your essay and write a brief summary of the text.
- Determine the theme of the story. Then, choose three key details from the story that convey the theme. Consider plot events, characters' actions and reactions, and characters' feelings.

Part 2

- Write an essay about what the characters learn about themselves or the world around them. Be sure to consider how the characters change by the end of the story.
- Organize your ideas logically, using transitional words and phrases. Pay close attention to your use of common, proper, and possessive nouns.

CONSTRUCTED RESPONSE RUBRIC: STANDARDS MASTERY

	Rating Scale
Critical Thinking: How clearly and consistently does the student pursue the specific mode of reasoning or discourse required by the standard, as specified in the prompt (e.g., comparing and contrasting, analyzing, explaining)?	*not very* *very* 1 2 3 4 5
Focus: How well does the student understand and apply the focus concepts of the standard, as specified in the prompt (e.g., development of theme or of complex characters, effects of structure, and so on)?	*not very* *very* 1 2 3 4 5
Support/Elaboration: How well does the student support points with textual or other evidence? How relevant, sufficient, and varied is the evidence provided?	*not very* *very* 1 2 3 4 5
Insight: How original, sophisticated, or compelling are the insights the student achieves by applying the standard to the text(s)?	*not very* *very* 1 2 3 4 5
Expression of Ideas: How well does the student organize and support ideas? How well does the student use language, including word choice and conventions, in the expression of ideas?	*not very* *very* 1 2 3 4 5

Speaking and Listening

TASK 4 Literature [RL.6.3; SL.6.4]

Describe a Story's Structure

Prepare a visual presentation of a story's structure by analyzing the main episodes, or scenes, from a story in Part 2.

- Break your chosen story into its major scenes. Identify how each scene fits into the parts of a story—exposition, rising action, climax, falling action, and resolution.
- Choose a graphic, such as a plot diagram, sequence-of-events chart, or storyboard, to visually present the episodes in order.
- As you present information to the class, describe how the story's plot unfolds and how the characters respond as the story moves toward its resolution.
- Practice your presentation in front of a mirror to make sure that you speak clearly and use appropriate eye contact.

TASK 5 Literature [RL.6.2; SL.6.1]

Determine the Theme

Lead a small-group discussion about the theme of a story from Part 2.

- Prepare for the discussion by choosing a story and writing a paragraph about it. State the story's theme and note three details that add to the theme.
- Write down at least three questions you have about the story and its theme.
- Gather with your group and read the paragraph you wrote about the story. Invite the group to respond to your ideas.
- If you find the discussion slowing down, ask one of the questions you wrote down earlier.
- As a group, arrive at an agreement about the story's theme.

Research

TASK 6 Literature [RL.6.2; W.6.7, W.6.8]

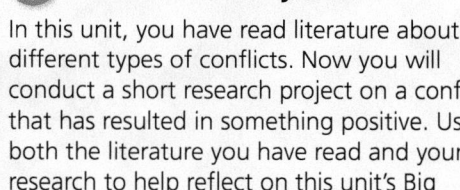 **Is conflict always bad?**

In this unit, you have read literature about different types of conflicts. Now you will conduct a short research project on a conflict that has resulted in something positive. Use both the literature you have read and your research to help reflect on this unit's Big Question. Review the following guidelines before you begin your research:

- Focus your research on one conflict. Try to determine benefits that have resulted from the conflict.

- Gather relevant information from at least two reliable sources. Your sources may be print or digital.
- Take notes as you research the conflict and its benefits.
- Cite your sources.

When you have completed your research, write a response to the Big Question. Discuss how your initial ideas about conflict have changed or been reinforced. Support your response with an example from the literature you read and an example from your research.

Supporting Speaking and Listening

1. Consider having students work with partners or in groups to complete Constructed Response tasks involving speaking and listening. For tasks that you assign for individual work, you may still wish to have students rehearse with partners, who can provide constructive feedback.

2. As students rehearse, have them keep in mind these tips:
   - Present findings and evidence clearly and concisely.
   - Observe conventions of standard English grammar and usage.
   - Be relaxed and friendly but maintain a formal tone.
   - Make eye contact with the audience, pronounce words clearly, and vary your pace.
   - When working with a group, respond thoughtfully to others' positions, modifying your own in response to new evidence.

Linking Constructed Response to Independent Reading

If you wish to cover the standards with students' independent reading, adapt Constructed Response tasks of your choice to the works they have selected. (Independent reading suggestions appear on the next page.)

Is conflict always bad?

1. Remind students that the unit Big Question is "Is conflict always bad?"

2. Have students complete their responses to the prompt on the student page. Point out that they have read selections in this unit about different types of struggles and conflicts and that they should draw on these selections in their responses. Remind them that they can also draw on their own experiences and what they have learned in other subject areas in formulating their answers.

🔧 DIFFERENTIATED INSTRUCTION

Strategy for Less Proficient Readers
Assign a Constructed Response task, and then have students meet in groups to review the standard assessed in that task. Remind students of the selections or independent readings to which they have previously applied the standard. Have groups summarize what they learned in applying the standard and then present their summaries. Discuss, clarifying any points of confusion. After students have completed their tasks, have groups meet again to evaluate members' work. Encourage members to revise their work based on the feedback they receive.

🔵 Strategy for English Learners
For each assigned Constructed Response task, review the instructions with students. Clarify the meaning of any unfamiliar vocabulary, emphasizing routine classroom words such as *diagram, chart,* and *report,* and academic vocabulary such as *organize.*

Next, have students note ideas for their responses. Pair students, and have them review each other's notes, asking questions to clarify meaning and suggesting improvements. Encourage students to ask for your assistance in supplying English words or expressions they may require.

❶ About the Quotation

Ralph Waldo Emerson (1803–1882) was an American writer who was at the forefront of the Transcendentalist movement. He was also a staunch individualist.

Discussion Ask students to discuss the meaning of Emerson's quotation about gold. Then, ask them to decide whether they agree with the quotation. Have them explain and support their positions with sound reasoning and evidence.

❷ Critical Viewing

Pose the critical viewing question to the class. Then, guide the class in a discussion about the question. Encourage students to build upon each other's ideas as they share their responses. Remind students to support their responses with reasons and evidence.

"The **desire of gold** is not for gold. ❶ It is for the means of **freedom and benefit**."

—Ralph Waldo Emerson

❓ DEVELOPING ESSENTIAL UNDERSTANDING

The Gold Rush

After gold was discovered in California in 1848 and later in the Yukon Territory, people swarmed to those regions. The adventurous arrived from every corner of the globe, seeking their fortune. They faced challenges and conflicts in the gold fields while the American Dream glittered in their eyes. The selections in this multi-genre text set will help students develop essential understanding about the Gold Rush by raising questions such as:

- Why would someone undertake a journey to search for gold?
- What qualities might help that person in his or her quest?
- What obstacles in the gold fields could lead to conflict?
- Why is conflict a natural and necessary part of life?

PART 3
TEXT SETS DEVELOPING INSIGHT

THE GOLD RUSH

The selections in this unit all deal with the Big Question: **Is conflict always bad?** Conflict can take place on a range of scales, from individual battles of will to life-and-death situations brought on by hardship and severe climate conditions. The selections that follow explore the challenges faced by those who sought their fortunes in the unsettled American West and Yukon Territory during the gold rushes. As you read the selections, take note of the various conflicts and their consequences—both good and bad.

2 ◄ **CRITICAL VIEWING** Based on this photograph, what might have been some of the challenges faced by miners who panned for gold in the 1850s?

CLOSE READING TOOL
Use the **Close Reading** Tool to practice the strategies you learned in this unit.

3 READINGS IN PART 3

ANCHOR TEXT **SHORT STORY**
The King of Mazy May
Jack London (p. 118)

SONG
To Klondyke We've Paid Our Fare
H. J. Dunham (p. 132)

ANNOTATED MAP
Gold Rush: The Journey by Land
from The Sacramento Bee (p. 136)

LETTER
A Woman's View of the Gold Rush
Mary B. Ballou (p. 138)

WEB ARTICLE
Chinese and African Americans in the Gold Rush
The Johns Hopkins University (p. 144)

NEWS ARTICLE
Birds Struggle to Recover From Egg Thefts of 1800s
Edie Lau (p. 148)

CUSTOMIZING THE TEXT SET

Close Reading Tool
Use the Close Reading Tool to project the anchor text on a whiteboard and work through it as a whole-class activity. Students also have the opportunity to read this selection independently, with scaffolds available as needed.

Curriculum Builder
Customize this program by rearranging existing selections, adding selection titles of your choosing, and uploading your own resources—all online!

---

3 **Readings in Part 3**
About the Texts
(For quantitative and qualitative measures of text complexity, see the rubrics on the opening pages of each selection.)

SHORT STORY: The King of Mazy May

Summary Teenager Walt Masters grows to manhood when he takes a wild dog sled ride to protect his neighbor's gold claim from thieves.

SONG: To Klondyke We've Paid Our Fare

Summary This song about the 1897 Alaska-Klondike Gold Rush focuses on miners of "the last frontier."

ANNOTATED MAP: Gold Rush: The Journey by Land

LETTER: A Woman's View of the Gold Rush

Summary One of the few women in a California gold mining town in 1852 describes a boarding house for "forty-niners."

WEB ARTICLE: Chinese and African Americans in the Gold Rush

Summary Both of these minority groups believed California offered a golden opportunity.

NEWS ARTICLE: Birds Struggle to Recover from Egg Thefts of 1800s

Summary The population of common murres was nearly wiped out when their eggs were harvested during the Gold Rush.

Extended Reading Opportunity

INFORMATIONAL TEXT: Discoveries: Trouble Ahead

You may want to assign this extended reading to accompany the readings in Part 3. Further details about this text and other extended readings appear on the Independent Reading pages at the end of this unit.

 Audio

Summary Audio is available in the *Student eText* and on the *Hear It!* CD-ROM.

LESSON PACING GUIDE

ANCHOR TEXT (5 DAYS)

The King of Mazy May

DAY 1 Preteach/Teach

- Introduce the topic of the text set and its relationship to the Big Question.
- To motivate and engage students, discuss the quotation and the Critical Viewing question.
- Direct students to read the selection independently.

DAYS 2–4 Teach/Extend

- Use the Comprehension questions to confirm student understanding of the text.
- Develop vocabulary by assigning and monitoring the Language Study activities.
- Develop analytic ability by reviewing the Literary Analysis questions and instruction.
- Assign the Group Discussion and monitor responses to discussion questions.
- Assign the Writing to Sources activity, distributing copies of the Take Notes worksheet to help students organize their thoughts and information.

DAY 5 Extend/Assess

- Preview the Research activity, distributing copies of the Take Notes worksheet to help students plan their note-taking strategy. Assign the activity as homework.
- Administer the Selection Test or the Open-Book Test to monitor student progress.

RELATED TEXTS (2 DAYS EACH)

To Klondyke We've Paid Our Fare • Gold Rush: The Journey by Land • A Woman's View of the Gold Rush • Chinese and African Americans in the Gold Rush • Birds Struggle to Recover from Egg Thefts of 1800s

DAY 1 Preteach/Teach

- Review with students the topic of the text set and what they have learned from the previous readings.
- Build knowledge of the topic by directing students to read the text independently.
- Develop vocabulary by reviewing the Language Study activities.
- Build students' ability to think critically using the Literary Analysis questions.

DAY 2 Extend/Assess

- Extend exploration of the text through the Discuss, Research, and Write activities.
- Administer the Selection Test or the Open-Book Test to monitor student progress.

ASSESSMENT: SYNTHESIS (1–2 DAYS)

DAYS 1–2 Assess

- Review with the class the Criteria for Success for the Speaking and Listening activity. Assign the activity, and monitor student progress.
- Review with students the Criteria for Success for the Writing assignment, and assign the activity.
- Review with students the Self-Evaluation Rubric for the Writing to Sources activity. Direct students to complete the assignment.

ⓒ Common Core State Standards

Reading Literature 1, 2, 3, 4, 5
Reading Informational Text 1, 2, 4, 5, 6, 7
Writing 1, 2, 3, 4, 5, 7, 8, 9, 9a, 9b, 10
Speaking and Listening 1, 4
Language 1, 2, 3, 4, 4a, 5, 6

Daily Block Scheduling

Each day in this Lesson Pacing Guide represents a 40–50 minute period. Teachers using block scheduling may combine days to revise pacing. In addition, teachers may differentiate and support core instruction by integrating components for extended and intensive support as students require. See the Guide to Resources (facing page).

GUIDE TO RESOURCES

RESOURCES	WHERE FOUND			ANCHOR TEXT The King of Mazy May	To Klondyke We've Paid Our Fare	Gold Rush: The Journey by Land	A Woman's View of the Gold Rush	Chinese and African Americans in the Gold Rush	Birds Struggle to Recover from Egg Thefts of 1800s
	PRINT	CD	ONLINE						
SELECTION SUPPORT									
Close Reading Practice	CRN		✓	✓					
Academic Vocabulary	SCW		✓	✓	✓	✓	✓	✓	✓
Discussion: Take Notes worksheet	SCW		✓	✓	✓		✓	✓	✓
Writing to Sources	SCW		✓	✓	✓	✓	✓	✓	✓
Research: Take Notes worksheet	SCW		✓	✓	✓		✓	✓	✓
STANDARDS SUPPORT									
Standards Instruction and Practice	CCC		✓	✓	✓	✓	✓	✓	✓
MONITOR PROGRESS									
Selection Test		EV	✓	✓	✓		✓	✓	✓
Open-Book Test		EV	✓	✓	✓		✓	✓	✓
ASSESSMENT: SYNTHESIS GRAPHIC ORGANIZERS AND RUBRICS									
Speaking and Listening: Graphic Organizer			✓						
Writing: Graphic Organizer			✓						
Writing to Sources: Graphic Organizer			✓						
Self-Evaluation Rubric			✓						
DIGITAL RESOURCES									
Close Reading Tool			✓	✓					
Online Writer's Notebook			✓	✓	✓	✓	✓	✓	✓

CRN Close Reading Notebook   **SCW** Student Companion All-in-One Workbook   **EV** ExamView   **CCC** Common Core Companion

Group work   Whole class instruction   Independent work   Assessment   Digital Resource

MULTIDRAFT READING

Essential Understanding

First, students should read the entire selection on their own. Then, to assist struggling readers and to deepen comprehension for all, you may wish to guide them through the selection by asking them the close reading questions provided in the margins. Have students apply the multidraft reading protocols as they examine specific "chunks" of text related to these questions. For each reading, have students set the purpose indicated:

- **First reading:** Students should read the selection independently and think about its basic meaning.
- **Second reading:** Students should analyze the text's key ideas and details and its craft and structure.
- **Third reading:** Students should integrate knowledge and ideas; connect to the Big Question, other texts, and the world; and use teacher-led Close Reading discussion questions to examine particularly rich and significant passages.

For more guidance, refer to the ***Classroom Strategies and Teaching Routines*** card on multidraft reading.

🔔 Daily Bellringer

For each class during which you teach this selection, have students complete one of the Sentence Combining activities for Week 6 in ***Daily Bellringer Activities***. You may wish to use additional activities that are applicable to this selection.

❶ Background

If you wish, explain that during the Klondike Gold Rush, approximately 100,000 prospectors set off to the Klondike region of the Yukon in northwestern Canada after George Carmack discovered gold there in 1896. Only 30,000 completed the trip due to difficult trails and freezing temperatures. For those who persevered, more than 1 billion dollars' worth of gold was discovered.

❶ The King of Mazy May

Jack London

118 UNIT 1 • Is conflict always bad?

ⓒ TEXT COMPLEXITY **RUBRIC**

The King of Mazy May		
Qualitative Measures	Context/Knowledge Demands	Yukon wilderness; Gold Rush 1 2 3 ④ 5
	Structure/Language Conventionality and Clarity	Conversational, folksy style; Long sentences; Historical and geographical vocabulary 1 2 ③ 4 5
	Levels of Meaning/ Purpose/Concept Level	Accessible concept (standing up for oneself) 1 2 ③ 4 5
Quantitative Measures	Text Length	Word Count: 3,240
	Lexile	1250L

Walt Masters is not a very large boy, but there is manliness in his make-up, and he himself, although he does not know a great deal that most boys know, knows much that other boys do not know. He has never seen a train of cars nor an elevator in his life, and for that matter he has never once looked upon a cornfield, a plow, a cow, or even a chicken. He has never had a pair of shoes on his feet, nor gone to a picnic or a party, nor talked to a girl. But he has seen the sun at midnight, watched the ice jams on one of the mightiest of rivers, and played beneath the northern lights,[1] the one white child in thousands of square miles of frozen wilderness.

Walt has walked all the fourteen years of his life in suntanned, moose-hide moccasins, and he can go to the Indian camps and "talk big" with the men, and trade calico and beads with them for their precious furs. He can make bread without baking powder, yeast, or hops, shoot a moose at three hundred yards, and drive the wild wolf dogs fifty miles a day on the packed trail.

Last of all, he has a good heart, and is not afraid of the darkness and loneliness, of man or beast or thing. His father is a good man, strong and brave, and Walt is growing up like him.

Walt was born a thousand miles or so down the Yukon,[2] in a trading post below the Ramparts. After his mother died, his father and he came up on the river, step by step, from camp to camp, till now they are settled down on the Mazy May Creek in the Klondike country. Last year they and several others had spent much toil and time on the Mazy

---

1. **northern lights** glowing bands or streamers of light, sometimes appearing in the night sky of the Northern Hemisphere.
2. **Yukon** (yoo´ kän) river flowing through the Yukon Territory of northwest Canada.

PART 3 • The King of Mazy May **119**

❷ Close Reading

1. **Key Ideas and Details** Read aloud the passage to students. **Ask:** What does the list of the things that Walt has done tell you about Walt's life?

   Possible response: These details show that Walt lives in a wilderness without friends his age, but he has seen amazing sights.

2. **Craft and Structure** **Ask:** How does the author emphasize the contrast between Walt's life and that of most boys his age? What does the author mean in the alliterative phrase "manliness in his makeup"? What image does the author create with the description "the one white child in thousands of square miles of frozen wilderness"?

   Possible response: The author repeats the phrase "he has never" to point out that Walt is different. He uses alliteration to emphasize that Walt is mature. The final sentence emphasizes that Walt is isolated from other boys like him.

3. **Integration of Knowledge and Ideas** **Ask:** From the author's description of the boy's life in the Yukon, what ideas can you develop about the kind of person Walt is?

   Possible response: Walt had to shoulder adult responsibilities in order to survive the dangers of the wilderness.

Vocabulary

1. Write the following words and definitions on the board:

   endured *v.* suffered through

   liable *adj.* likely to do something or to happen

   summit *n.* highest part

2. Have students say each word aloud.

 Video

Watch the Background Video online!

 **Audio**

Selection Audio is available in the *Student eText* and on the *Hear It!* CD-ROM.

© **TEXT COMPLEXITY READER AND TASK SUGGESTIONS**

The King of Mazy May	
Preparing to Read the Text • Have students use the photographs to preview the selection. • Guide students to use Multidraft Reading strategies on the previous page.	**Leveled Tasks** *Knowledge Demands* If students will have difficulty with the context, discuss how the geography of the area affects the action of the story. *Synthesizing* If students will not have difficulty with the context in the selection, have them review the photographs in the selection. Then have them write a caption for each photo.

endured ▶
(en doord´) v. suffered through

liable ▶
(lī´ ə bəl) adj. likely to do something or to happen

May, and endured great hardships; the creek, in turn, was just beginning to show up its richness and to reward them for their heavy labor. But with the news of their discoveries, strange men began to come and go through the short days and long nights, and many unjust things they did to the men who had worked so long upon the creek.

Si Hartman had gone away on a moose hunt, to return and find new stakes driven and his claim jumped.[3] George Lukens and his brother had lost their claims in a like manner, having delayed too long on the way to Dawson to record them. In short, it was the old story, and quite a number of the earnest, industrious prospectors had suffered similar losses.

But Walt Masters's father had recorded his claim at the start, so Walt had nothing to fear now that his father had gone on a short trip up the White River prospecting for quartz. Walt was well able to stay by himself in the cabin, cook his three meals a day, and look after things. Not only did he look after his father's claim, but he had agreed to keep an eye on the adjoining one of Loren Hall, who had started for Dawson to record it.

Loren Hall was an old man, and he had no dogs, so he had to travel very slowly. After he had been gone some time, word came up the river that he had broken through the ice at Rosebud Creek and frozen his feet so badly that he would not be able to travel for a couple of weeks. Then Walt Masters received the news that old Loren was nearly all right again, and about to move on afoot for Dawson as fast as a weakened man could.

Walt was worried, however; the claim was liable to be jumped at any moment because of this delay, and a fresh stampede had started in on the Mazy May. He did not like the looks of the newcomers, and one day, when five of them came by with crack dog teams and the lightest of camping outfits, he could see that they were prepared to make speed, and resolved to keep an eye on them. So he locked up the cabin and followed them, being at the same time careful to remain hidden.

He had not watched them long before he was sure that

---

3. **claim jumped** A claim is a piece of land marked by a miner with stakes to show where the borders are. A claim that is jumped is stolen by someone else.

💬 VOCABULARY DEVELOPMENT

Thematic Vocabulary: The Big Question

As students are discussing "The King of Mazy May," encourage them to use the thematic vocabulary presented in Introducing the Big Question, pp. 2–3. You might encourage them with sentence starters like these:

1. By registering his claim, Walt's father hoped he wouldn't have to *argue* . . .

2. Because old Loren had no sled dogs, Walt *concluded* that . . .

3. Walt decided that he must *defend* old Loren's claim because . . .

4. Walt knew that there was no use trying to *convince* the thieves to change their minds because . . .

they were professional stampeders, bent on jumping all the claims in sight. Walt crept along the snow at the rim of the creek and saw them change many stakes, destroy old ones, and set up new ones.

In the afternoon, with Walt always trailing on their heels, they came back down the creek, unharnessed their dogs, and went into camp within two claims of his cabin. When he saw them make preparations to cook, he hurried home to get something to eat himself, and then hurried back. He crept so close that he could hear them talking quite plainly, and by pushing the underbrush aside he could catch occasional glimpses of them. They had finished eating and were smoking around the fire.

"The creek is all right, boys," a large, black-bearded man, evidently the leader, said, "and I think the best thing we can do is to pull out tonight. The dogs can follow the trail; besides, it's going to be moonlight. What say you?"

"But it's going to be beastly cold," objected one of the party. "It's forty below zero now."

"An' sure, can't ye keep warm by jumpin' off the sleds an' runnin' after the dogs?" cried an Irishman. "An' who wouldn't? The creek's as rich as a United States mint! Faith, it's an ilegant chanst to be gettin' a run fer yer money! An' if ye don't run, it's mebbe you'll not get the money at all, at all."

"That's it," said the leader. "If we can get to Dawson and record, we're rich men; and there's no telling who's been sneaking along in our tracks, watching us, and perhaps now off to give the alarm. The thing for us to do is to rest the dogs a bit, and then hit the trail as hard as we can. What do you say?"

Evidently the men had agreed with their leader, for Walt Masters could hear nothing but the rattle of the tin dishes which were being washed. Peering out cautiously, he could see the leader studying a piece of paper. Walt knew what it was at a glance—a list of all the unrecorded claims on Mazy May. Any man could get these lists by applying to the gold commissioner at Dawson.

"Thirty-two," the leader said, lifting his face to the men. "Thirty-two isn't recorded, and this is thirty-three. Come on; let's take a look at it. I saw somebody had been working on it when we came up this morning."

❸ Close Reading

1. **Key Ideas and Details** Invite a student to read aloud the passage. **Ask:** What does the Irishman suggest to one of the stampeders who has complained about the cold?

   Possible response: The Irishman tells him to keep warm by jumping off the dogsled and running along with the dogs.

2. **Craft and Structure** Reread the passage aloud, and tell students to listen for the sound of the dialect and a simile. **Ask:** How does the dialect help characterize the Irishman? What simile does he use, and what does this figure of speech mean?

   Possible response: The Irishman uses a colorful dialect. He drops the d's in *and* and the g's in words ending in "-ing," and changes other words, such as *you* and *for*. The dialect shows that he is more concerned with actions than words. The Irishman uses the simile "the creek's as rich as a United States mint" to express his belief that the claims on the Mazy May Creek would yield large quantities of gold because the mint is where U.S. coins are made.

3. **Integration of Knowledge and Ideas**
   Ask: What does the Irishman's dialogue suggest about people who journeyed to northwestern Canada in search of Klondike gold?

   Possible response: The dialect suggests that men from other countries came to the region in search of a better life. Some people believed that the river flowed with gold and that they would strike it rich with little effort or hardship.

👥 DIFFERENTIATED INSTRUCTION

Strategy for Less Proficient Readers
Ask students to identify passages in the story that they had trouble visualizing. Then have them listen to the audio version of the passage they have read in the **Student eText** or on the **Hear It!** CD-ROM. Tell students that closing their eyes while listening may help them visualize what is happening. After students listen have them reread the passages. Discuss how the audio helped them visualize the story.

Enrichment for Advanced Readers
Invite students to note how Jack London makes his writing descriptive. Have students record descriptive phrases from the part of the story they have read so far, such as "beastly cold" or "The creek's as rich as a United States mint." Have students analyze the story for personification, such as "the creek … just beginning … to reward them for their heavy labor." Ask students to comment on how the descriptions add to the effect of the story.

④ ❓ Big Question: Toward Essential Understanding

1. Point out to students that conflict can often be avoided—if people do not stand up for what they believe.

2. Ask: When Walt watches the men discover gold, what conflict is set in motion?

Possible response: Walt is responsible for Loren Hall's claim, and he knows that the men will try to steal it in his neighbor's absence. He feels strongly that it is important for him to defend old Loren's claim.

3. Ask: Is Walt's decision sensible? What would you do in his place?

Possible response: Walt realizes that he faces a dangerous conflict with the men; however, after considering what they are trying to do, he resolves to do something to stop the theft. Walt risks danger but has no guarantee of safety if he stops running. He chooses to take a chance. Some students may agree with Walt's decision. Other students may say that it is too dangerous and they would go for help instead.

Three of the men went with him, leaving one to remain in camp. Walt crept carefully after them till they came to Loren Hall's shaft. One of the men went down and built a fire on the bottom to thaw out the frozen gravel, while the others built another fire on the dump and melted water in a couple of gold pans. This they poured into a piece of canvas stretched between two logs, used by Loren Hall in which to wash his gold.

In a short time a couple of buckets of dirt were sent up by the man in the shaft, and Walt could see the others grouped anxiously about their leader as he proceeded to wash it. When this was finished, they stared at the broad streak of black sand and yellow gold grains on the bottom of the pan, and one of them called excitedly for the man who had remained in camp to come. Loren Hall had struck it rich and his claim was not yet recorded. It was plain that they were going to jump it.

Walt lay in the snow, thinking rapidly. He was only a boy, but in the face of the threatened injustice to old lame Loren Hall he felt that he must do something. He waited and watched, with his mind made up, till he saw the men begin to square up new stakes. Then he crawled away till out of hearing, and broke into a run for the camp of the stampeders. Walt's father had taken their own dogs with him prospecting, and the boy knew how impossible it was for him to undertake the seventy miles to Dawson without the aid of dogs.

Gaining the camp, he picked out, with an experienced eye, the easiest running sled and started to harness up the stampeders' dogs. There were three teams of six each, and from these he chose ten of the best. Realizing how necessary it was to have a good head dog, he strove to discover a leader amongst them; but he had little time in which to do it, for he could hear the voices of the returning men. By the time the team was in shape and everything ready, the claim-jumpers came into sight in an open place not more than a hundred yards from the trail, which ran down the bed of the creek. They cried out to Walt, but instead of giving heed to them he grabbed up one of their fur sleeping robes, which lay loosely in the snow, and leaped upon the sled.

"Mush! Hi! Mush on!" he cried to the animals, snapping the keen-lashed whip among them.

💬 VOCABULARY DEVELOPMENT

Word Analysis

Draw students' attention to the word *injustice* in the phrase "in the face of the threatened injustice." Model the skill of word analysis. Say to students: When I see the word *injustice,* I look at its parts to find the meaning. I see the base word *justice,* which means "fairness or reasonableness," as in the way people are treated. I know that the prefix *in-* changes the meaning of the base word, so that it means *not* or *without.* When I put these clues together, I know that an *injustice* is an unfair or unjust treatment of somebody. Encourage students to consider the importance of treating people with fairness as they read the rest of the story.

The dogs sprang against the yoke straps, and the sled jerked under way so suddenly as to almost throw him off. Then it curved into the creek, poising perilously on the runner. He was almost breathless with suspense, when it finally righted with a bound and sprang ahead again. The creek bank was high and he could not see the men, although he could hear their cries and knew they were running to cut him off. He did not dare to think what would happen if they caught him; he just clung to the sled, his heart beating wildly, and watched the snow rim of the bank above him.

Suddenly, over this snow rim came the flying body of the Irishman, who had leaped straight for the sled in a desperate attempt to capture it; but he was an instant too late. Striking on the very rear of it, he was thrown from his feet, backward, into the snow. Yet, with the quickness of a cat, he had clutched the end of the sled with one hand, turned over, and was dragging behind on his breast, swearing at the boy and threatening all kinds of terrible things if he did not stop the dogs; but Walt cracked him sharply across the knuckles with the butt of the dog whip till he let go.

It was eight miles from Walt's claim to the Yukon—eight very crooked miles, for the creek wound back and forth like a snake, "tying knots in itself," as George Lukens said. And because it was so crooked the dogs could not get up their best speed, while the sled ground heavily on its side against the curves, now to the right, now to the left.

Travelers who had come up and down the Mazy May on foot, with packs on their backs, had declined to go round all the bends, and instead had made shortcuts across the narrow necks of creek bottom. Two of his pursuers

PART 3 • The King of Mazy May **123**

Close Reading

1. **Key Ideas and Details** Read aloud the passage to students. **Ask:** What happens when Walt first gets the dogs to run?

   Possible response: Walt is almost thrown off the sled, and the sled almost turns over.

2. **Craft and Structure** Have students focus on the vivid verbs and alliteration. **Ask:** How does the author's verb choice help create tension? What is an example of alliteration that also conveys suspense in this passage?

   Possible response: The author uses strong action verbs to convey suspense, such as *sprang, jerked, clung,* and *beating. Poising perilously* is an example of alliteration and indicates danger and uncertainty.

3. **Integration of Knowledge and Ideas**
   Ask: How do the author's stylistic choices heighten the conflict in the story?

   Possible response: The descriptive language reveals the dangerous situation that Walt is in. Not only does Walt have to battle the harsh conditions of the environment, but he also has to contend with the other stampeders.

Focus Passage

A Focus Passage is identified with brackets in the Student Edition of this page for students' independent close reading and analysis. A question bank for the passage and possible responses appear at the end of the selection.

DIFFERENTIATED INSTRUCTION

Vocabulary for English Learners
Lead students in pronouncing the words *claim-jumpers* (p. 122) and *jerked* on p. 123. Then, present these word pairs: *jeer/year* and *jarred/yard.* Pronounce each word. Station two volunteers at the board. Call out the words at random, and have the volunteers point at the word you have called while the class judges their responses. Finally, lead the class in pronouncing the selection words again.

Enrichment for Gifted/Talented Students
Have students role-play an interview between Walt and a reporter for the *Klondike News.* Tell students that the reporter should ask questions beginning with *who, what, where, why, when,* and *how* to get information about events in the story so far. Walt should supply facts for the reporter.

Tell students that they can present the interview as a dramatic breaking news story. Allow students to make up details that are not mentioned in the story. Invite students to use objects from the classroom as props. Encourage students to present their work to the class.

❼ Close Reading

1. Key Ideas and Details Ask a student to read aloud the passage. **Ask:** What does Walt see when he finally reaches the mighty Yukon?

Possible response: Although it is starting to get dark, he views a great white path so wide that he can't see from one side of the river to the other.

2. Craft and Structure Direct students to carefully reread the paragraph and examine sound devices, sensory details, and imagery. **Ask:** What words tell you what Walt is seeing and hearing at this moment in the story? How do these images affect your ability to feel you are with Walt on the sled?

Possible response: The author uses the words *failing twilight* and *great white sea* to describe what Walt sees, and *frozen stillness, not a sound,* and *breathing of the dogs* to tell what Walt hears. This paints a portrait of the mighty Yukon. This helps readers see and hear as though they were on the sled with Walt.

3. Integration of Knowledge and Ideas

Ask: How does the vivid imagery in this passage help create the setting of a faraway place in a different era?

Possible response: The author uses strong and distinct images to appeal to the senses and help readers imagine how the Yukon looked during the Gold Rush.

had gone back to harness the remaining dogs, but the others took advantage of these shortcuts, running on foot, and before he knew it they had almost overtaken him.

"Halt!" they cried after him. "Stop, or we'll shoot!"

But Walt only yelled the harder at the dogs, and dashed around the bend with a couple of revolver bullets singing after him. At the next bend they had drawn up closer still, and the bullets struck uncomfortably near him but at this point the Mazy May straightened out and ran for half a mile as the crow flies. Here the dogs stretched out in their long wolf swing, and the stampeders, quickly winded, slowed down and waited for their own sled to come up.

Looking over his shoulder, Walt reasoned that they had not given up the chase for good, and that they would soon be after him again. So he wrapped the fur robe about him to shut out the stinging air, and lay flat on the empty sled, encouraging the dogs, as he well knew how.

❼ At last, twisting abruptly between two river islands, he came upon the mighty Yukon sweeping grandly to the north. He could not see from bank to bank, and in the quick-falling twilight it loomed a great white sea of frozen stillness. There was not a sound, save the breathing of the dogs, and the churn of the steel-shod sled.

No snow had fallen for several weeks, and the traffic had packed the main river trail till it was hard and glassy as glare

124 UNIT 1 • Is conflict always bad?

💬 VOCABULARY DEVELOPMENT

Selection Vocabulary Reinforcement
To reinforce and assess students' comprehension of selection vocabulary words, give them sentences in which the word may or may not be used correctly. Students must tell whether the use is correct and explain their answer. Use these sentences:

1. I *endured* the frigid ocean temperatures as I trained for the triathlon.
Answer: Yes, *endured* is used correctly. People training for triathlons usually suffer through the process to improve their physical fitness.

2. As the hiker climbed up the mountain, she gazed down at the *summit.*
Answer: No, *summit* is not used correctly. The hiker would be gazing up at the highest peak.

3. My little brother is *liable* to fidget whenever I drag him along to the ballet.
Answer: Yes, *liable* is used correctly. Younger brothers typically are likely to be restless when watching a performance.

ice. Over this the sled flew along, and the dogs kept the trail fairly well, although Walt quickly discovered that he had made a mistake in choosing the leader. As they were driven in single file, without reins, he had to guide them by his voice, and it was evident the head dog had never learned the meaning of "gee" and "haw." He hugged the inside of the curves too closely, often forcing his comrades behind him into the soft snow, while several times he thus capsized the sled.

There was no wind, but the speed at which he traveled created a bitter blast, and with the thermometer down to forty below, this bit through fur and flesh to the very bones. Aware that if he remained constantly upon the sled he would freeze to death, and knowing the practice of Arctic travelers, Walt shortened up one of the lashing thongs, and whenever he felt chilled, seized hold of it, jumped off, and ran behind till warmth was restored. Then he would climb on and rest till the process had to be repeated.

Looking back he could see the sled of his pursuers, drawn by eight dogs, rising and falling over the ice hummocks like a boat in a seaway. The Irishman and the black-bearded leader were with it, taking turns in running and riding.

Night fell, and in the blackness of the first hour or so Walt toiled desperately with his dogs. On account of the poor lead dog, they were continually floundering off the beaten track into the soft snow, and the sled was as often riding on its side or top as it was in the proper way. This work and strain tried his strength sorely. Had he not been in such haste he could have avoided much of it, but he feared the stampeders would creep up in the darkness and overtake him. However, he could hear them yelling to their dogs, and knew from the sounds they were coming up very slowly.

When the moon rose he was off Sixty Mile, and Dawson was only fifty miles away. He was almost exhausted, and breathed a sigh of relief as he climbed on the sled again. Looking back, he saw his enemies had crawled up within four hundred yards. At this space they remained, a black speck of motion on the white river breast. Strive as they would, they could not shorten this distance, and strive as he would, he could not increase it.

Walt had now discovered the proper lead dog, and he knew he could easily run away from them if he could only change

---

 DIFFERENTIATED INSTRUCTION

Strategy for Special-Needs Students
Students may have trouble visualizing the action sequence. Have them use sticky notes to summarize the main action in each paragraph. Then help students combine their notes into a chart to review the key elements in this passage.

Strategy for Gifted/Talented Students
Ask students to rewrite the paragraph that begins, "When the moon rose he was off Sixty Mile." Ask students to write using the paragraph from Walt's point of view. Their versions should be no longer than one page and should reflect Walt's feelings as he races through the moonlight on the dog sled and his thoughts as his enemies are behind him. Have volunteers act out their versions for the class.

8 Close Reading

1. Key Ideas and Details Ask a student to read aloud the passage. **Ask:** Why is it fortunate for Walt that both his sled and the sled of the black-bearded leader were moving erratically?

Possible response: The leader was unable to make a straight shot and hit Walt.

2. Craft and Structure Direct students to explore how the language shifts slightly as the narrator explains events. Have students highlight the simile in the paragraph *(yawing like a boat before the wind)*. **Ask:** How does the language in the first sentence of the paragraph change compared with the second sentence? How does this help you to understand Walt's dilemma? How does the simile add to your understanding?

Possible response: In this passage, the narrator first uses a lengthy sentence with vivid verbs to explain what happens on a moving sled. This description of jumping and plunging and yawing" reflects the actions on the sled. The author then switches to a direct style that explains Walt was not hit. The simile helps readers visualize how Walt's sled was pitching and rolling like a boat in rough water as he raced up and down the summits of the ice jams with bullets zinging around him.

3. Integration of Knowledge and Ideas

Ask: How does the fictionalized narrator intrude upon this story to offer a commentary to the reader? Why does the narrator interrupt the narration?

Possible response: In this passage, the narrator steps away from Walt's emotions and struggles and gives an idea of what is going on in the whole scene, on both Walt's sled and that of the men chasing him. The narrator wants to place the reader in the scene to realize how dangerous Walt's position is.

summit ▶
(sum´ it) *n.*
highest part

the bad leader for the good one. But this was impossible, for a moment's delay, at the speed they were running, would bring the men behind upon him.

When he was off the mouth of Rosebud Creek, just as he was topping a rise, the report of a gun and the ping of a bullet on the ice beside him told him that they were this time shooting at him with a rifle. And from then on, as he cleared the summit of each ice jam, he stretched flat on the leaping sled till the rifle shot from the rear warned him that he was safe till the next ice jam was reached.

8 Now it is very hard to lie on a moving sled, jumping and plunging and yawing[4] like a boat before the wind, and to shoot through the deceiving moonlight at an object four hundred yards away on another moving sled performing equally wild antics. So it is not to be wondered at that the black-bearded leader did not hit him.

After several hours of this, during which, perhaps, a score of bullets had struck about him, their ammunition began to give out and their fire slackened. They took greater care, and shot at him at the most favorable opportunities. He was also leaving them behind, the distance slowly increasing to six hundred yards.

Lifting clear on the crest of a great jam off Indian River, Walt Masters met with his first accident. A bullet sang past his ears, and struck the bad lead dog.

The poor brute plunged in a heap, with the rest of the team on top of him.

Like a flash Walt was by the leader. Cutting the traces with his hunting knife, he dragged the dying animal to one side and straightened out the team.

He glanced back. The other sled was coming up like an express train. With half the dogs still over their traces, he cried "Mush on!" and leaped upon the sled just as the pursuers dashed abreast[5] of him.

The Irishman was preparing to spring for him—they were so sure they had him that they did not shoot—when Walt turned fiercely upon them with his whip.

9 He struck at their faces, and men must save their faces with their hands. So there was no shooting just then. Before

---

4. **yawing** (yô´ iŋ) *adj.* swinging from side to side.
5. **abreast** (ə brest´) *adv.* alongside.

VOCABULARY DEVELOPMENT

Using Context to Determine Meaning
Model the process of using context clues to determine the meaning of a word. Then, have students practice on their own.

1. Read aloud the sentence on p. 127 that contains the word *capsizing.* **Say:** After Walt grabs the men's wheel dog by his front legs and throws him, he sets in motion a sequence of events. His quick reaction causes the dog team to be *snarled,* which affects the sled and then

tangles up his enemies. I can visualize this chain of events. They help me understand that *capsizing* means "causing to tip over."

2. Have students use a similar process to determine the meaning of the word *silvering* on page 127. Guide them to recognize and use context clues, including "just as daylight."

they could recover from the hot rain of blows, Walt reached out from his sled, catching their wheel dog by the forelegs in midspring, and throwing him heavily. This snarled the team, capsizing the sled and tangling his enemies up beautifully.

Away Walt flew, the runners of his sled fairly screaming as they bounded over the frozen surface. And what had seemed an accident proved to be a blessing in disguise. The proper lead dog was now to the fore, and he stretched low and whined with joy as he jerked his comrades along.

By the time he reached Ainslie's Creek, seventeen miles from Dawson, Walt had left his pursuers, a tiny speck, far behind. At Monte Cristo Island he could no longer see them. And at Swede Creek, just as daylight was silvering the pines, he ran plump into the camp of old Loren Hall.

Almost as quick as it takes to tell it, Loren had his sleeping furs rolled up, and had joined Walt on the sled. They permitted the dogs to travel more slowly, as there was no sign of the chase in the rear, and just as they pulled up at the gold commissioner's office in Dawson, Walt, who had kept his eyes open to the last, fell asleep.

And because of what Walt Masters did on this night, the men of the Yukon have become proud of him, and speak of him now as the King of Mazy May.

ABOUT THE AUTHOR

Jack London (1876–1916)

Jack London lived an adventurous life. Before the age of 20, this Californian had worked in a factory, traveled as a hobo, captained a pirate ship, and searched for gold. Though he dropped out of college, he taught himself by reading at public libraries and giving himself daily writing assignments. London's love of reading and his own adventures inspired him to write.

In 1897, London went to northwestern Canada, where gold had just been discovered. He did not find any gold, but he did have adventures on the way to Dawson, a town in the Yukon Territory. Once, for instance, he made a boat from trees and ran the dangerous White Horse rapids on the Yukon River. London wrote more than fifty books, including *The Call of the Wild* and *White Fang*.

PART 3 • The King of Mazy May **127**

🔹 DIFFERENTIATED INSTRUCTION

Culturally Responsive Instruction

Point out to students that the main character in this story is a teenage boy who has spent most of his life in Klondike country. Explain that in this different culture, teenagers like Walt have different experiences and knowledge than other teens living in the United States. Ask students to reread the beginning of this short story and create a T-chart comparing and contrasting what Walt has seen and done with the experiences of other fourteen-year-olds. Ask students to discuss how Walt's experiences are similar to and different from those of students' own cultures.

---

⑨ Focus Passage

A Focus Passage is identified with brackets in the Student Edition of this page for students' independent close reading and analysis. A question bank for the passage and possible responses appear at the end of the selection.

⑩ Close Reading

1. **Key Ideas and Details** Read aloud the passage to students. **Ask:** What does the author refer to when he says, "And because of what Walt Masters did on this night"?

   Possible response: All by himself, Walt stopped the claim-jumpers from stealing Loren's claim.

2. **Craft and Structure** Draw students' attention to the final paragraph. **Ask:** How is the language reminiscent of folk tales? Give specific examples.

   Possible response: The phrasing "And because of" wraps up the story in a way that is similar to how a folk tale would end. "Men … speak of him now as the King of Mazy May" elevates Walt to a folk hero or the hero of a legend.

3. **Integration of Knowledge and Ideas**
   Ask: Why might the setting, during the Yukon Gold Rush, be used in a North American legend?

   Possible response: The discovery of gold in the Klondike was a legendary time in North American history, when fortunes were made and lost, and there was conflict between hardworking prospectors and those who wanted to steal from them. This exciting time period and setting provides a background for great tales that are retold through the years.

READ

Comprehension

1. He can make bread without yeast, baking powder, or hops; he can trade with Native Americans; he can shoot moose; he can drive a team of sled dogs.

2. Walt lives on Mazy May Creek in the Klondike country.

3. Walt is shot at by the claim-jumpers; he has to rearrange his dogs after one of them dies; he has to keep himself warm in the frigid temperatures.

4. The men call him the King of Mazy May out of respect, because he risked his life to help a fellow prospector.

Research: Clarify Details

Students should use their research to clarify a detail that is unfamiliar.

Summarize

Student summaries should include descriptions of the main characters and events of the story.

Language Study

Selection Vocabulary
Possible responses:
- *endured:* suffered through
- *liable:* likely to happen
- *summit:* the highest point

Students' paragraphs should use all three words in an appropriate context.

Diction and Style

1. **(a)** The adverb describing the verb comes before the subject and the verb. **(b)** The word order emphasizes Walt's movement.

2. **(a)** The runners of the sled are described as "fairly screaming." **(b)** This description personifies the sled and shows how quickly Walt moved along the difficult terrain.

Close Reading Activities

READ

Comprehension

Reread all or part of the text to help you answer the following questions.

1. What special skills does Walt possess?

2. Where does Walt live?

3. What events take place after Walt begins the trip to Dawson?

4. Why do the men of the Yukon call Walt the "King of Mazy May"?

Language Study

Selection Vocabulary The following phrases appear in "The King of Mazy May." Define each boldfaced word, and use all three words in a brief story of your own.

- …they and several others had spent much toil and time on the Mazy May, and **endured** great hardships…
- …the claim was **liable** to be jumped at any moment because of this delay…
- …as he cleared the **summit** of each ice jam, he stretched flat on the leaping sled…

Diction and Style Study the sentence below. Then, answer the questions.

> Away Walt flew, the runners of his sled fairly screaming as they bounded over the frozen surface.

1. **(a)** What do you notice about the word order in the phrase "Away Walt flew"? **(b)** What effect does the word order create?

2. **(a)** How is the sled described? **(b)** What effect is created through this use of description?

Research: Clarify Details This story may include references to life in the Yukon that are unfamiliar to you. Choose at least one detail and briefly research it. Explain how the information clarifies an aspect of the story.

Summarize Write an objective summary of the story. Remember that an objective summary is free from opinion and evaluation.

Conventions Read this passage from the story. Identify the common, proper, and possessive nouns. Then, explain how you identified the possessive noun.

> But Walt Masters's father had recorded his claim at the start, so Walt had nothing to fear now that his father had gone on a short trip up the White River prospecting for quartz…. Not only did he look after his father's claim, but he had agreed to keep an eye on the adjoining one of Loren Hall, who had started for Dawson to record it.

Academic Vocabulary

The following words appear in the instructions and questions on the facing page.

passage   contribute   alter

Categorize the words by deciding whether you know each one well, know it a little bit, or do not know it at all. Then, use a print or online dictionary to look up the definitions of the words you are unsure of or do not know at all.

Conventions

Students should identify common nouns such as *claim, start, father, trip, quartz,* and *eye;* proper nouns such as *Walt, White River, Loren Hall,* and *Dawson;* and possessive nouns such as *Masters's* and *father's.*

Academic Vocabulary

If students struggle with categorizing and defining the academic vocabulary words, use this routine:

Write the words and definitions on the board.

passage: a brief portion of a written work

contribute: to help bring about a result; to supply

alter: to change

Have students say each word aloud. Then have students use each word in a sentence.

Literary Analysis

Reread the identified passages. Then, respond to the questions that follow:

> **Focus Passage 1** *(p. 123)*
> Suddenly, over this snow rim … till he let go.

> **Focus Passage 2** *(pp. 126–127)*
> He struck at their faces … tangling his enemies up beautifully.

Key Ideas and Details

1. Infer Which character seems to be winning the struggle in this **passage**? Cite details to support your answer.

Craft and Structure

2. (a) Interpret: What effect do word choices such as "suddenly," "clutched," and "threatening" create? **(b) Evaluate:** Would the passage be as suspenseful if London had chosen more neutral words? Explain.

3. Analyze: Examine London's sentence length and structures. What effect do these elements create?

Integration of Knowledge and Ideas

4. (a) Analyze: In what way has the author made the Irishman unsympathetic? **(b) Evaluate:** Does the character of the Irishman make you "root" harder for Walt? Explain.

Key Ideas and Details

1. (a) What are the two main events in this passage? **(b)** What does Walt do to keep the men from shooting at him?

Craft and Structure

2. (a) Analyze: What descriptive details express the main events of the passage? **(b) Interpret:** What images do these descriptions bring to mind?

3. Evaluate: How does this paragraph **contribute** to the plot of the story?

4. (a) Analyze: How would you describe the narrator's tone? **(b)** What clues point to the idea that the narrator admires Walt?

Integration of Knowledge and Ideas

5. Draw Conclusions: How does this passage illustrate the relationship between the humans and the dogs?

Setting

The **setting** of a literary work is the time and place of the action. The setting can **alter** the tone or mood of a story. Reread the story, and take notes on ways in which the author uses setting.

1. What story details bring to life its setting?

2. The Gold Rush In what way do the events of the Gold Rush affect the story's action and characters?

 **Common Core State Standards**

RL.6.1, RL.6.2, RL.6.3, RL.6.4, RL.6.5; L.6.1, L.6.2, L.6.3, L.6.4, L.6.4a, L.6.5, L.6.6
[For full standards wording, see the chart in the front of this book.]

PART 3 • Close Reading Activities **129**

Focus Passage 2

1. (a) Walt whips his attackers' faces; he trips one of the dogs and makes the sled turn over. **(b)** Walt uses his whip to attack the men's faces; they have to protect their faces with their hands, so they don't have free hands to shoot at him.

2. (a) London uses figurative language such as "hot rain of blows" and descriptive details such as "snarled" and "capsized." He tangles up his enemies "beautifully." **(b)** "Snarled" brings to mind the image of a tangled knot or a snarling dog; "capsized" creates a picture of a sinking ship.

3. This paragraph is the climax of the story; this is the last encounter between Walt and the claim-jumpers before he gets to Dawson.

4. (a) The tone shows the narrator's admiration for Walt's quick thinking. The tone also reflects the intense and dangerous situation that Walt is in. **(b)** The words *tangling his enemies up beautifully* show the narrator's admiration for how Walt handled the situation.

5. The humans depend on the dogs for transportation, but in this passage, both Walt and the men hurt the animals to achieve their goals.

Setting

1. The descriptions of the setting, such as "a great white sea of frozen stillness," help readers imagine what it would be like to live in the Klondike area.

2. The Klondike Gold Rush was a time when many people traveled to northwestern Canada to mine or pan rivers for gold. The action takes place during the Gold Rush, and the characters are prospectors. The actions of the characters are based on the desire to obtain gold.

Literary Analysis

Focus Passage 1

Possible responses appear below. Check to be sure students support their responses with evidence from the text.

1. Walter is winning the struggle. The details describe how "Walt cracked him sharply across the knuckles." The Irishman was being "dragged behind" and eventually had to "let go."

2. (a) The word choices create a feeling of tension and describe the seriousness of the situation. **(b)** If more neutral words were used, readers would not realize the intense struggle between the characters.

3. The long and complex sentence at the end of the paragraph adds to the suspense by dragging out the conclusion of each event or idea.

4. (a) Although the Irishman is being hurt, the fact that he is trying to attack Walt may make readers feel unsympathetic toward him. **(b)** Oftentimes, readers "root" for the underdog, who in this case is a boy being chased by grown men.

DISCUSS

From Text to Topic: Group Discussion

1. **Possible response:** The narrator explains that while some boys go to school or talk to girls, Walt has other useful knowledge, such as survival skills.

2. **Possible response:** The tone of admiration shows the narrator respects Walt.

3. **Possible response:** Having lived in the wilderness, he is aware of the difficulties of the land and is mature enough to know how to survive in this environment.

WRITE

Writing to Sources: Informative Text

Introduce the assignment using the instruction on the student page.

Prewriting and Planning

1. To guide students' rereading and note taking, remind them that a *cause* is an event that makes something else happen; an *effect* is what happens as a result of the cause. Provide struggling students with guiding questions, such as these: *To determine the cause, ask "Why did this event happen?" To determine the effect, ask "What happened as a result?"*

2. Provide students with copies of a web diagram.

Drafting

1. Review the two organizational patterns with students, and remind them that they can use one pattern or the other but they cannot combine both patterns.

2. Remind students to focus on the main causes. Advise them that they can use pairs of signal words (such as *if/then, before/after*) to show the relationships between cause and effect.

DISCUSS

From Text to Topic **Group Discussion**

Discuss the following passage with a group of classmates. Take notes during the discussion. Contribute your own ideas, and support them with examples from the text.

> Walt Masters is not a very large boy, but there is manliness in his make-up, and he himself, although he does not know a great deal that most boys know, knows much that other boys do not know. He has never seen a train of cars nor an elevator in his life, and for that matter he has never once looked upon a cornfield, a plow, a cow, or even a chicken. He has never had a pair of shoes on his feet, nor gone to a picnic or a party, nor talked to a girl. But he has seen the sun at midnight, watched the ice jams on one of the mightiest of rivers, and played beneath the northern lights, the one white child in thousands of square miles of frozen wilderness.

WRITE

Writing to Sources **Informative Text**

Assignment

Write a **cause-and-effect essay** in which you analyze the main events of the story. Identify the causes and effects of these events or actions.

Prewriting and Planning Reread the story, looking for details, definitions, and examples that describe causes and effects of important events. Record your notes in a web diagram.

Drafting Choose a way to organize your essay. For example, if a number of unrelated events leads to a single result, focus one paragraph on each cause. If one cause leads to several effects, focus one paragraph on each effect. In your draft, cite specific examples and show clear relationships between your points.

Revising Reread your essay, making sure you have clearly explained links between ideas. Add transitional words and phrases where needed.

Editing and Proofreading Make sure your transitions clearly explain the relationships between events. In addition, make sure the verb tenses correctly reflect the order of the causes and effects.

1. How does the author compare Walt's experiences with those of other boys?

2. What do the details in this passage tell you about the narrator's attitude toward Walt?

3. In what way is Walt well suited to the challenges of his environment and circumstance?

CONVENTIONS

A **verb tense** tells whether the time of an action or a condition is in the past, present, or future. Clearly explain the timeline of events and relationships by using verb tenses to show sequence.

Revising

1. Encourage students to review their drafts to ensure they have used transitional words and phrases to effectively link ideas.

2. Remind students that they should focus on outcomes that result from the character's action(s).

Editing and Proofreading

1. Encourage students to check that they have correctly used transitional words and phrases. For example, did they use *due to* or *because of* to show the cause and *as a result* or *consequently* to show the effect?

2. Have students check that they used the correct verb tenses to ensure clarity and show sequence.

RESEARCH

Research **Investigate the Topic**

Gold Rush Struggles "The King of Mazy May" reveals some of the hardships gold prospectors faced in the Yukon, such as frigid temperatures and hard physical labor. Jack London had some personal experience with these hardships when he worked as a gold prospector, and he included details from his own experiences in this story.

> ### Assignment
> Conduct research to learn more about living conditions for gold prospectors in Canada in the 1890s. Consult books such as memoirs to learn about the prospectors' personal experiences. Take clear notes and carefully identify your sources so that you can easily access the information later. Share your findings in an **informal speech or presentation** for the class.

Gather Sources Find reliable print and electronic sources. Primary sources, such as letters, journals, or memoirs, provide firsthand accounts of experiences. These types of sources illustrate events in people's daily lives. You should also consult secondary sources, such as history books or encyclopedias. Look for sources that feature expert authors and up-to-date information.

Take Notes Take notes on each source, either electronically or on note cards. Use an organized note-taking strategy.

- Label each note card with its source information and main idea.
- Include important notes or quotations that support the main idea. Use quotation marks to indicate direct quotes.
- Create a timeline or web diagram to organize your main ideas.

Synthesize Multiple Sources Gather data from your sources and organize them into a presentation. Use information you learned from your research to draw conclusions about struggles during the Gold Rush. Use your notes to write an outline for your presentation. See the Citing Sources pages in the Introductory Unit of this textbook for help in creating a Works Cited list.

Organize and Present Ideas Review your outline and practice delivering your presentation. Be ready to answer questions from your audience.

PREPARATION FOR ESSAY
You may use the knowledge you gain during this research assignment to support your claims in an essay at the end of this section.

 **Common Core State Standards**

W.6.2, W.6.4, W.6.5, W.6.7, W.6.8, W.6.9, W.6.9.a, W.6.10; SL.6.1, SL.6.4
[For full standards wording, see the chart in the front of this book.]

RESEARCH

Investigate the Topic
Introduce the assignment, using the instruction on the student page.

Gather Sources
1. Arrange for students to visit your school's library or computer lab.
2. Remind students that primary sources were written during a specific time period and offer an inside view of a specific event. Secondary sources analyze and interpret the primary sources, and were usually written after the event.

Take Notes
1. Explain to students that direct quotes should match the primary or secondary source word for word. These original quotes need to be placed within quotation marks. Students must give proper credit to the original author(s).
2. Remind students that they can paraphrase, or put passages from sources into their own words. They can also summarize, or write a shortened version that states the main points.

Synthesize Multiple Sources
1. Encourage students to combine different ideas from a variety of sources to draw conclusions.
2. Explain how an outline is composed of a list of the main points of a subject. Tell students that this rough draft will help them focus on what should be included in their presentations. Give students copies of the Outline in *Graphic Organizer Transparencies*, p. 206.

Organize and Present Ideas
Suggest that pairs of students practice delivering their presentations prior to facing their audience. Students can ask each other questions so they can rehearse answers.

MULTIDRAFT READING

Essential Understanding

First, students should read the entire selection on their own. Then, to assist struggling readers and to deepen comprehension for all, you may wish to guide them through the selection by asking them the close reading questions provided in the margins. Have students apply the multidraft reading protocols as they examine specific "chunks" of text related to these questions. For each reading, have students set the purpose indicated:

- **First reading:** Students should read the selection independently and think about its basic meaning.

- **Second reading:** Students should analyze the text's key ideas and details and its craft and structure.

- **Third reading:** Students should integrate knowledge and ideas; connect to the Big Question, other texts, and the world; and use teacher-led Close Reading discussion questions to examine particularly rich and significant passages.

For more guidance, refer to the *Classroom Strategies and Teaching Routines* card on multidraft reading.

 Daily Bellringer

For each class during which you teach this selection, have students complete one of the five Quick Write activities for Week 7 in *Daily Bellringer Activities.* You may wish to use additional activities that are applicable to this selection.

 Big Question: Toward Essential Understanding

1. **Ask:** What conflicts or "stuff" might these adventurers expect?

   Possible response: They might have to battle nature to get the gold from the river, or struggle against thieves who want to steal their claims.

2. **Ask:** What does this line indicate about the gold seekers' attitudes toward potential conflict?

   Possible response: This line shows that the gold seekers are determined to make their fortunes in gold no matter what it takes.

SONG

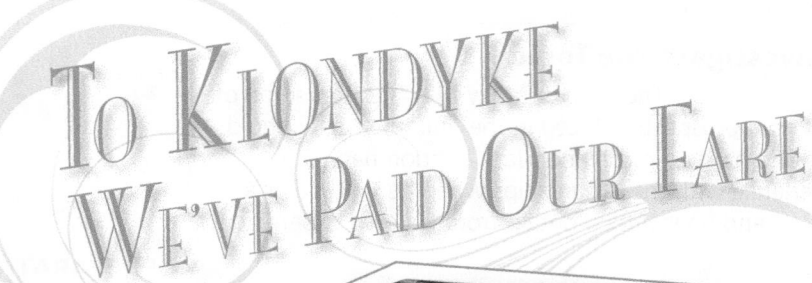

TO KLONDYKE WE'VE PAID OUR FARE

WRITTEN AND COMPOSED BY H.J. DUNHAM

We're a band of Argonauts[1] bold,
With a feverish fancy for gold.
1 We're ready and rough, and "out for the stuff,"
Tho the weather up north is cold.
We've carefully counted the cost,
Defiance we bid to Jack-Frost.
We're fill'd to the brim with courage and vim,
No tales of privation our vision can dim,
our vision of treasure untold.
We'll work the rich earth, for all it is worth,
And each with a fortune will feather his berth.[2]

defiance ▶
(de fi´əns) *n.* open resistance to authority

privation ▶
(prĭ vā´ shən) *n.* lack of necessities

---

1. **Argonauts** (är´gə nôts´) sailors on the *Argo*, the ship in the Greek myth of Jason and the Golden Fleece; adventurers.
2. **feather his berth** stuff his mattress; in this case, a figure of speech: he will be rich enough to stuff his mattress with money.

© TEXT COMPLEXITY **RUBRIC**

To Klondyke We've Paid Our Fare		
Qualitative Measures	Context/Knowledge Demands	The Klondike Gold Rush, 1890s; the increase of gold-seekers in western Canada 1 2 ③ 4 5
	Structure/Language Conventionality and Clarity	Song; misspellings and dialect reflective of the period; some difficult vocabulary and unfamiliar colloquial phrases 1 2 3 ④ 5
	Levels of Meaning/Purpose/Concept Level	Accessible concepts (the spirit of adventure and the promise of a better life) 1 2 ③ 4 5
Quantitative Measures	Text Length	Word Count: 282
	Lexile	NP

Refrain

To Klondyke we've paid our fare, our golden slippers we
soon will wear,
We'll live on pig and polar bear, and gather the nuggets we
know are there.

2
"We're a strictly respectable crowd,
No political pluggers allowed,
We've a preacher or two, to keep it in view,
That sobriety all have vowed.
We've maidens aged and young,
And Chinamen fresh from Hong Kong.
While a jolly street faker, a fat undertaker,
A lively grass widow, a dude and a quaker,[3]
have join'd our invincible throng,
We're not all alike, but we're bound for Klondyke,
And each is determin'd to make a big strike."

◄ **invincible**
(in vin′sə bəl) *adj.*
incapable of being
harmed or defeated

Repeat Refrain

If you're tired of tedious delay,
In the dawn of prosperity's day,
We'll give you a chance, your wealth to enhance,
In a venture that's sure to pay.
Our band-wagon's waiting below,
3 To carry us straight to Juneau[4],
So get into line, and in with us climb,
Put on your best clothes, get a shave and a shine,
Put a lunch in your pocket and go!
And when you return, your friends will all learn,
That you've come from the Klondyke with "money to burn."

Repeat Refrain

---

3. **grass widow** a woman who is separated from her husband; **dude** a city-dweller whose fancy
clothes make him stand out from other adventurers; **quaker** member of a Christian group that
opposes war.
4. **Juneau** (jŭ′nō) capital city of Alaska.

2 Focus Passage

A Focus Passage is identified with
brackets in the Student Edition of this
page for students' independent close
reading and analysis. A question
bank for the passage and possible
responses appear at the end of the
selection.

3 Close Reading

1. **Key Ideas and Details**
   Ask: What actions does this song
   tell people to take?

   Possible response: It tells
   people to get in line, climb into
   the band-wagon, dress up, bring
   some food, and go to Juneau.

2. **Craft and Structure**
   Ask: What is the rhyme scheme
   in the refrain? How does the
   rhythm mirror the attitude of the
   gold seekers?

   Possible response: The rhyme
   scheme is: *aabaccddcee*. The
   rhythm is upbeat and fast-paced,
   like the gold seekers themselves.

3. **Integration of Knowledge
   and Ideas**
   Ask: Why might this song attract
   others to join the adventurers on
   their way to Klondike?

   Possible response: The people
   singing the song seem uncon-
   querable and destined for riches.
   Their "can-do" attitude might
   appeal to others who seek adventure, gold, and a better life.

Vocabulary

1. Write the following words and
   definitions on the board:

   defiance *n.* open resistance to
   authority

   privation *n.* lack of necessities

   invincible *adj.* incapable of
   being harmed or defeated

2. Have students say each word
   aloud.

3. Use the word in a sentence that
   defines the word.

🔊 **Audio**

Selection Audio is available in the
Student eText and on the ***Hear It!***
CD-ROM.

© **TEXT COMPLEXITY READER AND TASK SUGGESTIONS**

To Klondyke We've Paid Our Fare	
Preparing to Read the Text	**Leveled Tasks**
• Discuss how song lyrics can offer comments about society. Examine how these lyrics reflect the spirit of adventure and hope for a better life felt by many gold seekers of that time. Have students give examples of modern song lyrics and how the words might motivate listeners. • Guide students to use Multidraft Reading strategies (TE p. 132).	*Language Conventionality and Clarity* If students will have difficulty with language conventionality, have them read first and take notes about the variety of people mentioned in the second verse. Then, have them reread the verse, consulting their notes. Discuss their notes, offering clarification. *Analyzing* If students will not have difficulty with the language in the selection, have them note possible meanings as they read the optimistic viewpoint of this song. As a class, discuss why the gold seekers might be encouraged to journey to Klondike to begin a new life.

READ

Comprehension

1. The song is about the Klondike Gold Rush.

2. The rhythm, word choice, and punctuation suggest it is a happy song.

3. The song tells you that the Klondike Gold Rush is an exciting and profitable, yet difficult and serious event to participate in.

Research: Clarify Details

Students' paragraphs should identify and describe at least one element in the song with which they are not familiar.

Summarize

Students should describe the events of each stanza and the main idea of the song.

Language Study

Possible responses:

- *defiance*: show of resistance
- *privation*: great lack or need
- *invincible*: incapable of being harmed

Check students' sentences for appropriate use of words in context.

Literary Analysis

Possible responses appear below. Check to be sure students support their responses with evidence from the text.

1. **(a)** The main idea is that many different types of people are heading to Klondike, and everyone is hopeful and ready to work hard to strike gold. **(b)** The words *sobriety, respectable,* and *invincible* show that the people are confident and serious.

2. The new society will be diverse, and people with many different jobs will contribute.

3. The song has repeated sounds, the refrain has a rhyme scheme of *aabaccddcee,* and consistent rhythm.

4. **(a)** The song's purpose might be to convince listeners to join the adventurers. **(b)** The song challenges listeners to "get into line."

 Close Reading Activities

READ

Comprehension

Reread all or part of the text to help you answer the following questions.

1. What is the song about?

2. When set to music, would this song be happy or sad? How do you know?

3. What does the song tell you about the Klondike Gold Rush?

Language Study

Selection Vocabulary The following phrases appear in "To Klondyke We've Paid Our Fare." Define each boldfaced word, and then write a sentence for each word.

Literary Analysis

Reread the identified passage. Then, respond to the questions that follow:

> **Focus Passage** *(p. 133)*
> We're a strictly respectable crowd, ... make a big strike.

Key Ideas and Details

1. **(a) Interpret:** What is the main idea of this verse? **(b) Analyze:** What specific words **reveal** the main idea?

2. **Draw Conclusions:** What does the listing of people indicate about the society the settlers will form?

Alliteration

Alliteration is the repetition of initial consonant sounds, such as the *b* sound in *big blue ball*. Reread the song, and note ways in which the author uses alliteration.

Research: Clarify Details Choose one unfamiliar detail and briefly research it. Then, explain how the information you learned from research sheds light on an aspect of the song.

Summarize Write an objective summary of the song. Do not include opinions.

- **Defiance** we bid to Jack-Frost
- No tales of **privation** our vision can dim
- have join'd our **invincible** throng

Craft and Structure

3. **(a)** Read the verse aloud to notice its rhythm and rhyme. **(b) Evaluate:** Does the song have a regular pattern of sounds when read aloud? Explain.

Integration of Knowledge and Ideas

4. **(a) Interpret:** What might be the **purpose** of a song like this one? **(b)** What does the song **challenge** the listener to do?

1. **(a)** Point out two examples of alliteration in the song. **(b) Analyze:** What effect does the alliteration create?

2. **The Gold Rush (a) Evaluate:** Does this song effectively capture the spirit of the Gold Rush? Why or why not?

Alliteration

1. **(a)** Examples are the *f* sound in "feverish fancy" and the *r* sound in "ready and rough." **(b)** The alliteration makes the hard consonant sounds stand out. The effect is to make the song sound energized and upbeat.

2. The song's positive tone and energetic rhythm effectively capture the spirit and excitement of the adventurers who are about to join in the Gold Rush. The song almost functions as an advertisement for the Gold Rush.

DISCUSS • RESEARCH • WRITE

From Text to Topic **Group Discussion**

Discuss the following passage with classmates. Contribute your own ideas, and support them with examples from the text.

> **Refrain:** To Klondyke we've paid our fare, our golden slippers we soon will wear,
> We'll live on pig and polar bear, and gather the nuggets we know are there.

Research **Investigate the Topic**

Striking It Rich The Klondike Gold Rush of 1898 was one of the last gold rushes, following the major rushes in California and Australia that had occurred fifty years earlier.

Assignment

Conduct research to find out information about the Klondike Gold Rush. Consult online and print sources such as encyclopedias, Klondike National Park's Web site, or news articles from the 1890s. Take clear notes, and carefully identify your sources so that you can easily access the information later. Capture your findings in a detailed **outline.**

Writing to Sources **Fictional Narrative**

"To Klondyke We've Paid Our Fare" captures the spirit of adventure that characterized the Gold Rush. The promise of riches and a new start made many people journey west.

Assignment

Write a **short story** from the point of view of someone who has heard this song and joins the Klondike Gold Rush. Follow these steps as you draft your story:

- Introduce your character and establish the setting.
- Create a smooth progression of events that build on one another.
- Use information from your research, where appropriate.
- Provide a logical, satisfying conclusion to your story.

QUESTIONS FOR DISCUSSION

1. How would you describe the mood of the song's refrain?
2. Why might a song like this have been popular with Gold Rush settlers?

PREPARATION FOR ESSAY

You may use the results of this research project to support your ideas in the essay at the end of this section.

ACADEMIC VOCABULARY

Academic terms appear in blue on these pages. If these words are not familiar to you, use a dictionary to find their definitions. Then, use them as you speak and write about the text.

Ⓒ **Common Core State Standards**

RL.6.1, RL.6.2, RL.6.4, RL.6.5; L.6.1; W.6.3, W.6.4, W.6.7, W.6.8, W.6.9, W.6.9a, W.6.10; SL.6.1, SL.6.4
[For full standards wording, see the chart in the front of this book.]

Writing to Sources: Fictional Narrative

Students' stories should take the point of view of an individual who will decide to participate in the Gold Rush, and should introduce the character, establish the setting, and provide smooth transitions between events.

 **Online Writer's Notebook**

Students can use the Online Writer's Notebook to record all responses.

DISCUSS • RESEARCH • WRITE

From Text to Topic: Group Discussion

1. The mood of the song's refrain is positive and encouraging. It describes the riches that people will have.
2. The Gold Rush settlers had to have been optimistic and believe that they would be successful in their search for gold. This song reinforces those ideas.

Research: Investigate the Topic

Introduce the assignment, using the instruction on the student page.

1. Arrange for students to visit your school's library or computer lab.
2. Remind students to locate authoritative electronic sources when they conduct research on the Internet. Web sites the end in .gov, .edu, and .org are generally reliable. Demonstrate how to access archived newspaper articles from online sources.
3. Encourage students to paraphrase and summarize information by restating it in their own words. If they discover unfamiliar terms, they should search for definitions in a dictionary.
4. Suggest that students act out their story. Prompt them to pay attention to body language and diction.

Academic Vocabulary

If students struggle with categorizing and defining the academic vocabulary words, use this routine:

Write the words and definitions on the board.

reveal: to make known

purpose: reason why something is done

challenge: to call into question

Have students say each word aloud. Then have them use the word in a sentence. Sample sentences should demonstrate that the word can be used across disciplines.

Big Question:
Toward Essential Understanding

1. Have students view the map and review the features listed in the annotations and the Key. **Ask:** What information do the annotations add to the map?

Possible response: The annotations highlight important points along the route and show major obstacles that travelers encountered along different passages.

2. Have students read the annotation for Note A and locate it on the map. **Ask:** How does this note connect to the Big Question: *Is conflict always bad?*

Possible response: According to Note A, the dreaded area of Humboldt Basin could lead to many problems, such as severe heat, deep sand, and no food or water. In these situations, problems could lead to death.

Critical Viewing

Tell students that annotated maps contain brief chunks of text that clarify or give additional information about a region. This annotated map contains different features, such as colors and symbols, that present geographical and historical information. In addition to the various trails that travelers took on their journey westward, the map shows milestones, or significant points along each route. Two of these points—Independence Rock and Chimney Rock—were literally milestones, or rocks that marked the miles traveled in a journey.

Also discuss how cartographers use colors and shading to represent various geographic features. For example, point out how higher elevations, such as the Rocky Mountains, are depicted in shades of brown, while green is used for lower elevations and shades of blue indicate water.

Gold Rush: The Journey by Land
from The Sacramento Bee

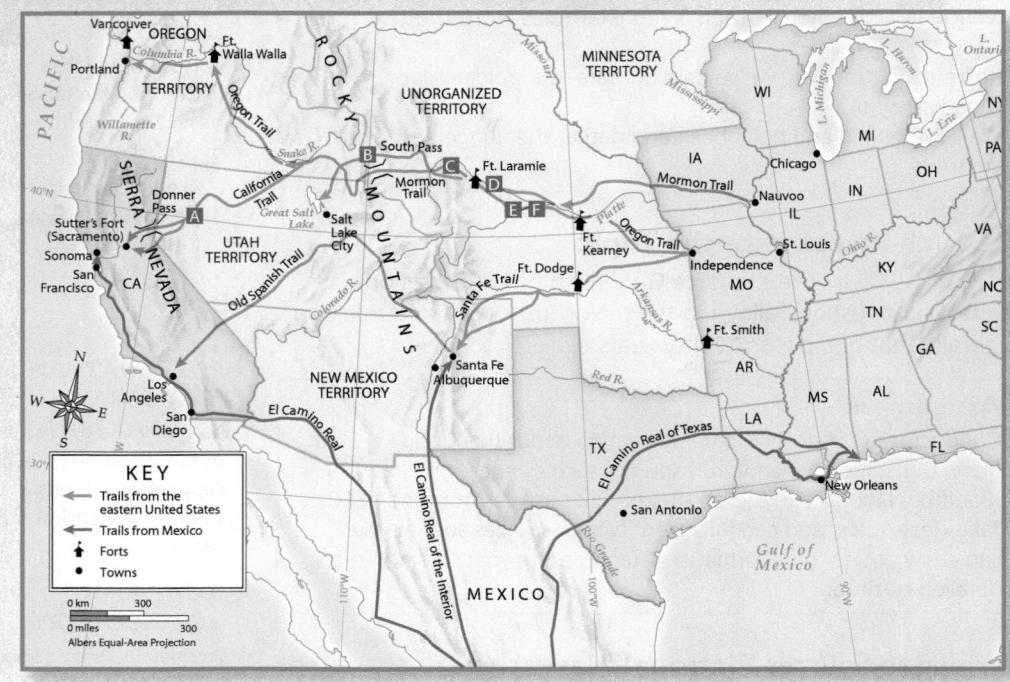

The Routes Taken

A The Humboldt Basin
The dreaded 40-mile stretch of Humboldt Basin promised severe heat, sand deep enough to trap oxen, and no food or water.

B The Continental Divide
Rivers to the east flowed toward the Atlantic. Rivers to the west flowed toward the Pacific.

C Independence Rock
This rock was marked on by hundreds of pioneers who passed it.

D Fort Laramie
More than 39,000 people were recorded passing through Fort Laramie in the first six months of 1849.

E The Platte River
The rains of 1849 made the overland journey difficult.

F Chimney Rock
This 500-foot column marks 550 miles from Independence, Missouri.

VOCABULARY DEVELOPMENT

Academic Vocabulary

If students require support with academic vocabulary, write the following words and definitions on the board:

- **similarity:** a quality of being alike
- **process:** a series of actions that bring about a result
- **indicated:** pointed out

Have students say each word aloud. Then use the word in a sentence that defines it. Point out that academic vocabulary can be used across disciplines. For example, *indicate* is a verb that means "to point out" when it is used this way: *Please indicate which books belong to you.* However, indicate can also mean "represent" when it is used to explain a map: *Blue indicates water and dotted lines indicate county lines.*

Close Reading Activities

READ • DISCUSS • WRITE

Comprehension

Study the map and answer the following questions.

1. What tools help you read and analyze the map?
2. **(a)** What two major trails did people take on the journey? **(b)** Choose a trail and identify two sites that travelers on the trail might pass along the way.

Critical Analysis

Key Ideas and Details

1. **(a) Interpret:** What are the main end points for each of the trails? **(b) Infer:** Why did people want to travel to these places?
2. **Compare and Contrast:** What are some similarities and differences between the routes?

Craft and Structure

3. **Draw Conclusions:** Why did the mapmaker choose to call attention to the sites labeled with letters?

Integration of Knowledge and Ideas

4. **Interpret:** What does this map tell you about the hardships people encountered during the Gold Rush?

From Text to Topic **Class Discussion**

Discuss the map with classmates. Use the following discussion questions to focus your conversation.

1. What might have motivated people to endure hardships to travel such great distances?
2. How does the process of traveling across the country in the 1850s differ from the way we travel today?
3. How might the Gold Rush have changed the population of the western United States?

Writing to Sources **Narrative**

Write a brief **journal entry** from the point of view of a traveler on the Oregon or Mormon Trail. Briefly research one of the sites indicated on the map. Then write about your character's experiences there.

Common Core State Standards

RI.6.1, RI.6.7; L.6.1, L.6.2, L.6.3, L.6.4, L.6.6; W.6.3, W.6.4; SL.6.1
[For full standards wording, see the chart in the front of this book.]

ACADEMIC VOCABULARY

Academic terms appear in blue on these pages. If these words are not familiar to you, use a dictionary to find their definitions. Then, use them as you speak and write about the text.

READ • DISCUSS • WRITE

Comprehension

1. The tools are the key and the annotations.
2. **(a)** The two major trails were the Oregon and Mormon Trails. **(b)** Check that students choose appropriate sites for the chosen trail.

Critical Analysis

Possible responses appear below. Check to be sure students support their responses with evidence from the text.

1. **(a)** Oregon: Portland; Mormon: Salt Lake City; Santa Fe: Santa Fe; Old Spanish: Los Angeles; El Camino Real: Sonoma; El Camino Interior: Santa Fe; El Camino Real of Texas: New Orleans; California: Sutter's Fort **(b)** People traveled in search of gold or new opportunities.
2. Students should point out that some trails pass over the Rocky Mountains while others cross the desert. All of the trails cross one or more rivers.
3. The mapmaker wanted to show some major landmarks and point out some of the hardships faced by pioneers.
4. The map points out places such as the Humboldt Basin and other parts of the terrain that made traveling difficult.

From Text to Topic: Class Discussion

1. Students may suggest that the promise of riches, or even just a new start, might have motivated people to travel.
2. Students should mention that traveling today is much faster and generally less dangerous than it was during the Gold Rush era.
3. Students may mention that some of California towns listed on the map are now very large cities and that the Gold Rush led people to move there.

Writing to Sources: Narrative

Students' journal entries should clearly describe the site they've researched and indicate some reasons why their character decided to travel west.

 Online Writer's Notebook

Students can use the Online Writer's Notebook to record all responses.

MULTIDRAFT READING

Essential Understanding

First, students should read the entire selection on their own. Then, to assist struggling readers and to deepen comprehension for all, you may wish to guide them through the selection by asking them the close reading questions provided in the margins. Have students apply the multidraft reading protocols as they examine specific "chunks" of text related to these questions. For each reading, have students set the purpose indicated:

- **First reading:** Students should read the selection independently and think about its basic meaning.
- **Second reading:** Students should analyze the text's key ideas and details and its craft and structure.
- **Third reading:** Students should integrate knowledge and ideas; connect to the Big Question, other texts, and the world; and use teacher-led Close Reading discussion questions to examine particularly rich and significant passages.

For more guidance, refer to the *Classroom Strategies and Teaching Routines* card on multidraft reading.

❶ Background

If you wish, explain that during the Gold Rush, the majority of people who flooded into California from 1848 to 1855 were prospecting for gold. Others sought their fortunes by providing services to miners, such as running boarding homes that offered a place to sleep and providing home-cooked meals and laundry services for a high price.

Vocabulary

If students require support with selection vocabulary, use this routine:

1. Write the following words and definitions on the board:

   associate *n.* friend or partner

   scouring *v.* cleaning or polishing by vigorous rubbing

   tongues *n.* languages or dialects

2. Have students say each word aloud.

3. Use the word in a sentence that defines the word.

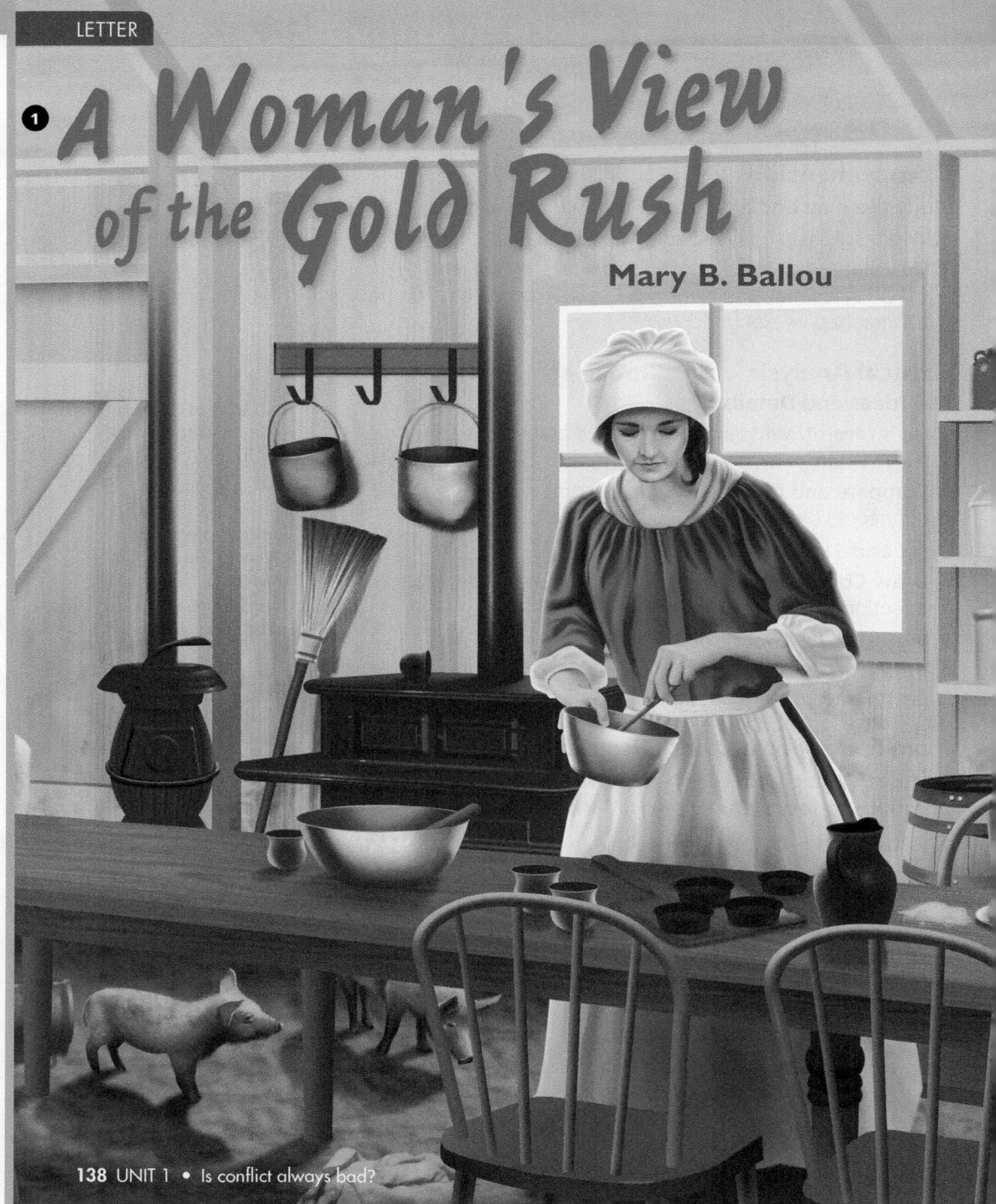

LETTER

A Woman's View of the Gold Rush

Mary B. Ballou

138 UNIT 1 • Is conflict always bad?

Ⓒ TEXT COMPLEXITY **RUBRIC**

A Woman's View of the Gold Rush		
Qualitative Measures	**Context/Knowledge Demands**	The California Gold Rush, 1840s; the hardships of boarding house life 1 2 ③ 4 5
	Structure/Language Conventionality and Clarity	Conversational letter; dialect, misspellings, unconventional punctuation and capitalization; on-level vocabulary 1 2 3 ④ 5
	Levels of Meaning/ Purpose/Concept Level	Accessible concepts (challenging work and poor living conditions) 1 2 ③ 4 5
Quantitative Measures	**Text Length**	Word Count: 1,058
	Lexile	1230L

October 30, 1852

My Dear Selden:

We are about as usual in health. Well I suppose you would like to know what I am doing in this gold region. Well I will try to tell you what my work is here in this muddy Place. All the kitchen that I have is four posts stuck down into the ground and covered over the top with factory cloth no floor but the ground. This is a Boarding House kitchen....

Now I will try to tell you what my work is in this Boarding House. Well somtimes[1] I am washing and Ironing somtimes I am making mince pie and Apple pie and squash pies. Somtimes frying mince turnovers and Donuts. I make Buiscuit and now and then Indian jonny cake[2] and then again I am making minute puding filled with rasons and Indian Bake pudings and then again a nice Plum Puding and then again I am Stuffing a Ham of pork that cost forty cents a pound.... Three times a day I set my Table which is about thirty feet in length and do all the little fixings about it such as filling pepper boxes and vinegar cruits and mustard pots and Butter cups. Somtimes I am feeding my chickens and then again I am scareing the Hogs out of my kitchen and Driving the mules out of my Dining room. You can see by the description of that I have given you of my kitchen that anything can walk into the kitchen that chooses to walk in and there being no door to shut from the kitchen into the Dining room ... Hogs and mules can walk in any time day or night if they choose to do so. Somtimes I am up all times a night scaring the Hogs and mules out of the House. Last night there a large rat came down pounce down onto our bed in the night. Sometimes I take my fan and try to fan myself but I work so hard that my Arms pain me so severely that I kneed some

---

1. Misspellings in this selection reflect Mary Ballou's original letter.
2. jonny cake (jän´ ē kāk´) *n.* a thin, flat corn bread baked on a griddle.

❷ Close Reading

1. **Key Ideas and Details** Read aloud the passage to students. **Ask:** What do these details tell you about Mary Ballou's daily life of running her boarding house?

   Possible response: The details show that Mary works nonstop for long hours every day, cooking, serving meals, washing, ironing, and taking care of the livestock.

2. **Craft and Structure** Have students focus on the author's unconventional spelling, grammar, and punctuation. **Ask:** How does this style add to the overall description of life during the California Gold Rush?

   Possible response: This letter is a primary source written by a real woman living in California in 1852. The misspellings and unconventional grammar and punctuation add to the authenticity of her description of her life in this time period. In her own words, she reveals what life was really like for her, and the capitalization can indicate the things that were an important part of her life. The informal writing shows that ordinary people such as her were willing to work hard to earn a living during the Gold Rush.

3. **Integration of Knowledge and Ideas**
   Ask: Why might Mary be including this information in a letter home to her son?

   Possible response: Mary wants to describe how difficult and overwhelming her daily chores are. She probably doesn't have much free time to write letters home. However, she wants to let her family know the details of her life and what she is doing while she is away from her family.

ⓒ TEXT COMPLEXITY **READER AND TASK SUGGESTIONS**

A Woman's View of the Gold Rush

Preparing to Read the Text	**Leveled Tasks**
• Have students explain how a conversational letter can provide interesting and authentic information about a particular time period. • Guide students to use Multidraft Reading strategies (TE p. 138).	*Language Conventionality and Clarity* If students will have difficulty with the context, have them read first to identify misspellings. Then have them reread and provide them with a list of properly spelled words to which they can refer. *Synthesizing* If students will not have difficulty with the context in the selection, have them note what challenging work conditions the proprietress of a boarding house might face. As a class, discuss difficult work conditions people face in a modern environment.

 **Audio**

Selection Audio is available in the *Student eText* and on the *Hear It!* CD-ROM.

❸ Close Reading

1. Key Ideas and Details Read aloud the passage to students. **Ask:** What does Mary do when she visits Jane and Mrs. Durphy? Why do you think she seeks them out?

Possible response: Mary talks with them. There are probably few women among the male miners. Mary and the other women seek each other out for companionship and to share their struggles.

2. Craft and Structure Have students focus on the sentence, "No one but my maker knows my feelings." **Ask:** How is this line different from the other descriptions in the letter?

Possible response: The previous sections of text describe all of the chores and activities she does. In this part of the letter, Mary is acknowledging that she hides her feelings from other people. How she acts in public while working is different from how she feels inside. Although she keeps her emotions in check unless she is alone, she feels free to express them in her letter.

3. Integration of Knowledge and Ideas

Ask: How does injecting an emotional detail about Mary's sadness into the middle of routine details about cooking and household chores affect the reader?

Possible response: The description of how Mary often has a "hearty cry" and goes to her cellar to be alone allows readers to learn more about the internal conflict Mary has. Her life is more than just what she does each day. She also has strong feelings about being homesick.

---

one to fan me so I do not find much comfort anywhere. I made a Bluberry puding to day for Dinner. Somtimes I am making soups and cramberry tarts and Baking chicken that cost four Dollars a head and cooking Eggs at three Dollars a Dozen. Somtimes boiling cabbage and Turnips and frying fritters and Broiling stake and cooking codfish and potatoes. I often cook nice Salmon trout that weigh from ten to twenty pound apiece. Somtimes I am taking care of Babies and nursing at the rate of Fifty Dollars a week but I would not advise any Lady to come out here and suffer the toil and fatigue that I have suffered for the sake of a little gold neither do I advise any one to come. Clarks Simmon wife says if she was safe in the States she would not care if she had not one cent. She came in here last night and said, "Oh dear I am so homesick that I must die," and then again my other **associate** came in with tears in her eyes and said that she had cried all day. She said if she had as good a home as I had got she would not stay twenty five minutes in California....

◀ **associate**
(ə sō′ shē it) *n.* friend or partner

Now I will tell you a little more about my cooking. Somtimes I am cooking rabbits and Birds that are called quails here and I cook squrrels. Occasionly I run in and have a chat with Jane and Mrs. Durphy and I often have a hearty cry. No one but my maker knows my feelings. And then I run into my little cellar which is about four feet square as I have no other place to run that is cool....

The wind Blows verry hard here to day. I have three lights Burning and the wind blows so hard that it almost puts my lights out while I am trying to write. If you could but step in and see the inconvience that I have for writing you would not wonder that I cannot write any better you would wonder that I could write at all. Notwithstanding all the dificulty in writing I improve every leishure moment. It is quite cool here my fingers are so cold that I can hardly hold my pen. Well it is ten o'clock at night while I am writing....

There I hear the Hogs in my kitchen turning the Pots and kettles upside down so I must drop my pen and

---

💬 VOCABULARY DEVELOPMENT

Selection Vocabulary Reinforcement

Students will benefit from additional examples and practice with the selection vocabulary words. Reinforce their comprehension with "show-you-know" sentences. The first part of the sentence uses the vocabulary word in an appropriate context. The second part of the sentence—the "show-you-know" part—clarifies the first. Model the strategy with this example for *scouring*:

She spent the evening *scouring* the pans; when she finished, the copper bottoms of the pans shined.

Then, give students these sentence prompts, and coach them in creating the clarification part:

1. He spent an hour *scouring* his dirty shirts in the wash basin; _____.
Sample answer: when he was finished, his hands were raw but the stains had vanished.

2. My sister and an associate went _____.
Sample answer: to the business meeting in the afternoon.

run and drive them out. So you [see] this is the way that I have to write—jump up every five minutes for somthing and then again I washed out about a Dollars worth of gold dust the fourth of July in the cradle so you see that I am doing a little mining in this gold region but I think it harder to rock the cradle to wash out gold than it is to rock the cradle for the Babies in the States....

I am making Flags with all the rest of the various kinds of work that I am doing and then again I am scouring candle sticks and washing the floor and making soft soap. The People tell me that it is the first Soft Soap they knew made in California. Somtimes I am making mattresses and sheets. I have no windows in my room. All the light that I have shines through canvas that covers the House and my eyes are so dim that I can hardly see to make a mark so I think you will excuse me for not writing any better. I have three Lights burning now but I am so tired and Blind that I can scearcely see and here I am among the French and Duch and Scoth and Jews and Italions and Sweeds and Chineese and Indians and all manner of tongues and nations but I am treated with due respect by them all....

I must close soon for I am so tired and almost sick. Oh my Dear Selden I am so Home sick.... I worry a great deal about my Dear children. It seems as though my heart would break when I realise how far I am from my Dear Loved ones. This from your affectionate mother,

Mary B. Ballou

◄ **scouring**
(skour´ in) *v.* cleaning or polishing by vigorous rubbing

◄ **tongues**
(tuŋs) *n.* languages or dialects

---

4 ❓ **Big Question: Toward Essential Understanding**

1. Read aloud the passage. **Ask:** What conflicts does the author experience?

   Possible response: The author is constantly struggling in very hard conditions to earn money. She is interrupted in all of her tasks, especially by animals who can enter her roughly built home and disrupt her kitchen whenever they wish. She is making a living by providing services to miners and panning for gold, but she struggles with her feelings of homesickness for her children and family.

2. **Ask:** How might the author's reference to "rock the cradle" illustrate the conflict she is experiencing?

   Possible response: She has tried to do some mining for gold and found it harder to "rock the cradle" for mining than it is to "rock the cradle" when taking care of children. She must choose what work to do.

5 **Focus Passage**

A Focus Passage is identified with brackets in the Student Edition of this page for students' independent close reading and analysis. A question bank for the passage and possible responses appear at the end of the selection.

👥 DIFFERENTIATED INSTRUCTION

Enrichment for Advanced Readers
Tell students that throughout history, ordinary Americans have described their experiences in letters and other texts, along with images. Have students conduct research to discover a text or an image created during the California Gold Rush (1848–1855). Have them explain how the text or image sheds light on the historical significance of this time. What details made history come alive for them?

Enrichment for Gifted/Talented Students
Invite students to use details in the letter to collaborate on a brief play about Mary Ballou's life. Suggest that students focus on a particular scene that is representative of the chaos and hardship she endures on a daily basis. Have students perform their scene for the class.

READ

Comprehension

1. She runs a boarding house. Mary Ballou cooks, drives animals out of her home, does laundry, and sews.

2. (a) Mary writes to her son, Selden. **(b)** She left family behind to go to California.

Research: Clarify Details

Students should clarify a detail from the text and explain its relationship to the letter.

Summarize

Students' summaries should describe Ballou's thoughts and activities.

Language Study

Possible responses:

- *associate*: fellow worker; *v.* to connect or join
- *scouring*: cleaning and polishing; *v.* searching through
- *tongues*: languages; *n.* tongue: an organ used for speaking

Literary Analysis

Possible responses appear below. Check to be sure students support their responses with evidence from the text.

1. (a) It is "dim" and without windows. **(b)** The lack of light and comfort frustrates her. She says that she "can hardly see to make a mark so I think you will excuse me for not writing any better." She wishes there was more light to make it easier to write her letter.

2. The long sentences reflect Ballou's long list of chores; the letter is disorganized, which may reflect her fatigue from hard work.

3. People have come from many different communities, and if others work hard and provide good service, it is important to respect others so that there aren't any conflicts.

Tone

1. The words *muddy Place* and *All the kitchen that I have* indicate that Ballou's environment is poor and she is not happy with it.

 Close Reading Activities

READ

Comprehension

Reread all or part of the text to help you answer the following questions.

1. What is Mary Ballou's job in the gold region? List three of her daily chores.

2. (a) To whom does Ballou write? **(b)** What information does this detail provide?

Language Study

Selection Vocabulary The following phrases appear in the selection. Define each boldfaced word. Then, identify another meaning for the word.

- … my other **associate** came in with tears in her eyes…
- … I am **scouring** candle sticks…
- … all manner of **tongues** and nations…

Literary Analysis

Reread the identified passage. Then, respond to the questions that follow:

> **Focus Passage** *(p. 141)*
> I am making Flags with all the rest… I am treated with due respect by them all.

Key Ideas and Details

1. (a) How does Ballou describe her environment? **(b) Analyze:** How does Ballou's environment affect her mood?

Tone

Tone, the attitude a writer displays toward his or her subject, is created through word choice.

1. The Gold Rush Find at least two details in the first paragraph of the letter that create a disapproving tone about Ballou's home environment.

Research: Clarify Details Choose one unfamiliar detail from the text and briefly research it. Then, explain how your research clarifies an aspect of the letter.

Summarize Write an objective summary of the letter to confirm your comprehension.

Cite details from the text to support your response.

Craft and Structure

2. Infer: What can you infer about Mary Ballou from her writing style? Cite details to support your response.

Integration of Knowledge and Ideas

3. Draw Conclusions: Why do you think the settlers treat one another with "respect"? Support your response with details.

2. Re-read the final paragraph of the letter. What tone is revealed by the writer's word choice? Support your response with details from the text.

2. The tone is sad yet caring. She describes how her "heart would break" because she misses her son and family. However, she still wants to be a caring and "affectionate mother."

DISCUSS • RESEARCH • WRITE

From Text to Topic **Partner Discussion**

Discuss the following passage with a partner. Take notes during the discussion. Contribute your own ideas, and support them with examples from the text.

> Somtimes I am taking care of Babies and nursing at the rate of Fifty Dollars a week but I would not advise any Lady to come out here and suffer the toil and fatigue that I have suffered for the sake of a little gold neither do I advise any one to come. Clarks Simmon wife says if she was safe in the States she would not care if she had not one cent.

Research **Investigate the Topic**

Gold Rush Housing Mary Ballou runs a boarding house in California during the Gold Rush. When miners came to California for gold, they found that housing conditions were usually poor.

Assignment

Conduct research to find information about housing during the Gold Rush. Consult the Internet or other reliable sources. Take clear notes, and carefully identify your sources so that you can easily access the information later. Share your findings in a brief **descriptive essay.**

Writing to Sources **Informational Text**

"A Woman's View of the Gold Rush" is an account of one woman's experience in California. Use information from Mary Ballou's letter to write about daily life for women during the Gold Rush.

Assignment

Write an **informational text** in which you explain living conditions and daily life for women during the Gold Rush. Follow these steps:

- Introduce the topic.
- Explain women's duties and jobs during the Gold Rush.
- Use specific information from the text to make generalizations.
- Write a conclusion in which you summarize your ideas.

QUESTIONS FOR DISCUSSION

1. Has Mary Ballou been successful in California? Cite specific details to support your answer.

2. California was a state in 1852. Explain the meaning of the comment by Simmon's wife about being "safe in the States."

PREPARATION FOR ESSAY

You may use the results of your research to support your ideas in the essay at the end of this section.

ACADEMIC VOCABULARY

Academic terms appear in blue on these pages. If these words are not familiar to you, use a dictionary to find their definitions. Then, use them as you speak and write about the text.

Common Core State Standards

RL.6.1, RL.6.2, RL.6.4, RL.6.5; L.6.1, L.6.3, L.6.4, L.6.6; W.6.2, W.6.4, W.6.7, W.6.8, W.6.9, W.6.9.a, W.6.10; SL.6.1, SL.6.4
[For full standards wording, see the chart in the front of this book.]

DISCUSS • RESEARCH • WRITE

From Text to Topic: Partner Discussion

1. **Possible response:** Ballou may be seen as being successful. She is busy and people have said her soft soap is the first "they knew made in California."

2. **Possible response:** Although California was a state, it seemed as uncomfortable and unfamiliar as a foreign country.

Research: Investigate the Topic

Introduce the assignment, using the instruction on the student page.

1. Arrange for students to visit your school's library or computer lab. Review strategies for identifying reliable sources on the Internet, stressing that students should focus on Web sites that end in .gov, .edu., and .org.

2. As students take notes on main ideas found in their source materials, tell them to write down exact quotes using quotation marks or summarize their findings using their own words.

3. Encourage students to make connections between multiple sources. Suggest that they create a Works Cited list that accurately identifies each source they reference. Advise them to print out any photographs of Gold Rush housing in California that they discover.

4. Suggest that students practice until they are comfortable reading without constantly consulting their presentation outlines. Remind them to be prepared to answer any questions.

Academic Vocabulary

If students struggle with defining the academic vocabulary word, use this routine:

Write the following word and definition on the board.

specific: precise or particular

Have students say the word aloud. Then have them use the word in a sentence. Sample sentences should demonstrate that the word can be used across disciplines.

Writing to Sources: Informational Text

Students' informational essays should use evidence from the text to form generalizations.

 Online Writer's Notebook

Students can use the Online Writer's Notebook to record all responses.

MULTIDRAFT READING

Essential Understanding

First, students should read the entire selection on their own. Then, to assist struggling readers and to deepen comprehension for all, you may wish to guide them through the selection by asking them the close reading questions provided in the margins. Have students apply the multidraft reading protocols as they examine specific "chunks" of text related to these questions. For each reading, have students set the purpose indicated:

- **First reading:** Students should read the selection independently and think about its basic meaning.
- **Second reading:** Students should analyze the text's key ideas and details and its craft and structure.
- **Third reading:** Students should integrate knowledge and ideas; connect to the Big Question, other texts, and the world; and use teacher-led Close Reading discussion questions to examine particularly rich and significant passages.

For more guidance, refer to the *Classroom Strategies and Teaching Routines* card on multidraft reading.

Vocabulary

If students require support with selection vocabulary, use this routine:

1. Write the following words and definitions on the board:

   exodus *n.* departure of a large group of people

   testing *v.* bear witness in court

   ambassador *n.* special representative, often one nation's official representative in another nation

2. Have students say each word aloud.

3. Use the word in a sentence that defines the word.

❶ Focus Passage

A Focus Passage is identified with brackets in the Student Edition of this page for students' independent close reading and analysis. A question bank for the passage and possible responses appear at the end of the selection.

Gold Miners in Auburn, California

Chinese and African Americans in the Gold Rush
The Johns Hopkins University

exodus ▶
(eks´ ə dəs) *n.*
departure of
a large group
of people

People from around the globe rushed to California in 1848. They came from China, Mexico, South America, Sweden, Ireland, Germany, and other lands. What caused this mad dash? Gold—and the promise of a better life. Free African Americans also joined the exodus west, hoping to find not only gold but greater freedom.

When news of the gold rush reached China, in 1848, thousands of Chinese headed to California. They wanted to escape the civil war, floods, droughts, and typhoons they faced back home. They thought they would get rich in "Gold Mountain," as California was known. Before the gold rush, only a few Chinese people lived in California, but by 1852, over twenty thousand Chinese immigrants had settled there.

© TEXT COMPLEXITY **RUBRIC**

Chinese and African Americans in the Gold Rush		
Qualitative Measures	Context/Knowledge Demands	The California Gold Rush, 1840s–1850s; immigration, minorities 1 ② 3 4 5
	Structure/Language Conventionality and Clarity	Some unfamiliar words; on-level vocabulary; straightforward narrative 1 2 ③ 4 5
	Levels of Meaning/ Purpose/Concept Level	Challenging concepts (obstacles of immigrants and minorities, racial inequality) 1 2 ③ 4 5
Quantitative Measures	Text Length	Word Count: 484
	Lexile	890L

The Chinese immigrants hoped for jobs and riches, but they faced many problems. They worked long hours for low pay. Some white miners thought the Chinese should be sent back to China. The Chinese miners (along with Mexican American miners) had to pay a special tax. Some places wouldn't hire Chinese workers or threw them out. They were not allowed to testify in court. But the Chinese stayed, and started organizations and unions. They also started newspapers and public schools.

Many African Americans came to California as well. They hoped to find freedom and good jobs. Most were free men and women from eastern cities. Some free African Americans had fled the east to escape the Fugitive Slave Law. This law punished anyone who helped runaway slaves. Even free men and women were afraid that a slave catcher would claim they were runaways and sell them south. Some free blacks came to California after reading success stories in Frederick Douglass'[1] newspaper, *North Star*. Others came as slaves and bought their freedom with gold they panned[2] from streams or dug out of mines. In the first three years of the gold rush, over a thousand African Americans came to California. About half of the three hundred and fifty African Americans in Sacramento, California, were free. Some miners formed all-black settlements such as Negro Bar and Negro Slide. Like other minorities in California, African Americans could not vote, testify in court, or attend public schools. In spite of this, they worked hard. They used their gold to free their families, start churches, schools, libraries and newspapers, and work for greater legal rights.

Mifflin Gibbs came to California in 1850 to work as a carpenter. After white carpenters refused to work with him because of his race, he started a business shining shoes and boots. A few years later, he and Peter Lester, another African American, opened a store. They worked hard and became rich. They later moved to Canada because California law did not protect their rights. Gibbs returned to the United States, became a lawyer, and was appointed an ambassador. Both men worked in the antislavery movement and to protect the rights of African Americans.

◀ **testify**
(tes´ tə fī) *v.* bear witness in court

◀ **ambassador**
(am bas´ ə dər) *n.* special representative, often one nation's official representative in another nation

1. **Frederick Douglass** escaped slave and noted scholar and speaker who lived during the nineteenth century. Douglass was a leader in the antislavery movement.
2. **gold they panned** Gold prospectors filled pans with river mud and then systematically shook and rinsed the mud several times. Since gold is heavier than dirt and water, gold particles sunk to the bottom of the pan as the dirt washed away.

PART 3 • Chinese and African Americans in the Gold Rush **145**

❷ Close Reading

1. Key Ideas and Details
Ask: What lured free African Americans to California from eastern cities?

Possible response: Along with the promise of good jobs, African Americans hoped to remain free.

2. Craft and Structure
Ask: How is the language in this passage fair and impartial rather than biased?

Possible response: The language makes no judgment about the Fugitive Slave Law or the actions of slave catchers.

3. Integration of Knowledge and Ideas
Ask: What effect did the Fugitive Slave Law have on the California Gold Rush?

Possible response: The threat of being captured and sold as slaves motivated many to head to California in a search of freedom.

❸  Big Question: Toward Essential Understanding

1. Ask: How did the two African Americans profiled in this passage overcome the hardships they faced?

Possible answer: Through hard work, the men were able to accomplish their goals of becoming rich.

2. Ask: How did the conflict between Gibbs and white carpenters lead to a gain for African Americans?

Possible answer: Gibbs ultimately became successful and worked in the antislavery movement.

© **TEXT COMPLEXITY READER AND TASK SUGGESTIONS**

Chinese and African Americans in the Gold Rush

Preparing to Read the Text	**Leveled Tasks**
• Discuss how other immigrants and minorities have overcome racial inequality. • Guide students to use Multidraft Reading strategies (TE p. 144).	*Levels of Meaning* If students will have difficulty with the concepts of racial inequality and challenges for immigrants, have them read first to identify details about immigration and minorities during the California Gold Rush. Then, have them reread to identify similarities and differences between Chinese and African American experiences during the Gold Rush. *Analyzing* If students will not have difficulty with the concepts of racial inequality, have them note how Frederick Douglass inspired African Americans to head to California. As a class, discuss how success stories printed in newspapers inspire others to take action.

 **Audio**

Selection Audio is available in the *Student eText* and on the *Hear It!* CD-ROM.

READ

Comprehension

1. (a) Chinese immigrants came to California to escape civil war, droughts, floods, and typhoons and to find jobs and riches. **(b)** African Americans hoped to find good jobs and freedom from slavery. They hoped to earn enough money to free family members who were still enslaved.

2. These minorities were not allowed to vote, attend school, or testify in court.

3. African Americans started schools, churches, libraries, and newspapers. Chinese Americans started organizations and unions to protect their rights, in addition to schools and newspapers.

Research: Clarify Details

Students' paragraphs should explain an aspect of the text and how research helped them understand the text better.

Summarize

Students' summaries should include which minorities joined the Gold Rush, why they came, and how they overcame the hardships they faced.

Language Study

- *exodus*: leaving in a large group
- *testify*: to bear witness
- *ambassador*: special representative to another country

Students' sentences should correctly use the vocabulary words in context.

Literary Analysis

Possible responses appear below. Check to be sure students support their responses with evidence from the text.

1. (a) Chinese immigrants faced many obstacles when they arrived in California, but they managed to establish a place for themselves despite the difficulties. **(b)** The details that the Chinese had to work long hours for low pay, had to pay a special tax, and could not testify in court show the difficulties they faced. The details that they started unions, newspapers and schools show that they overcame the difficulties.

 Close Reading Activities

READ

Comprehension

Answer the following questions.

1. (a) Why did Chinese immigrants come to California? **(b)** What benefits did African Americans hope to find there?

2. What obstacles did minorities face during the Gold Rush?

3. What did African Americans and Chinese immigrants do in response to these obstacles?

Language Study

Selection Vocabulary Define each boldfaced word, and use the word in a sentence of your own.

- Free African Americans also joined the **exodus** west, …

Literary Analysis

Reread the identified passage. Then, respond to the questions that follow.

> **Focus Passage** *(p. 145)*
> The Chinese immigrants … public schools.

Key Ideas and Details

1. (a) Explain: What is the main idea of the passage? **(b)** What details support your response?

Author's Purpose

An **author's purpose** is his or her reason for writing about a subject. A reader can **determine** an author's purpose by analyzing word choice and tone.

Research: Clarify Details This informative text may include references that are unfamiliar to you. Choose at least one unfamiliar detail, and briefly research it. Then, explain how the information you learned from research sheds light on an aspect of the text.

Summarize Write an objective summary of the text. Remember that an objective summary is free from opinion and evaluation.

- They were not allowed to **testify** in court.
- Gibbs … became a lawyer, and was appointed an **ambassador**.

Craft and Structure

2. Analyze: How and when does the mood, or overall feeling, of the passage change? Support your response with textual evidence.

Integration of Knowledge and Ideas

3. Infer: Why do you think some white miners wanted the Chinese immigrants to be sent home?

1. Re-read the first paragraph. **(a)** What type of details does the author provide? **(b)** What purpose do these details serve?

2. The Gold Rush (a) What information is provided in the final paragraph? **(b)** Why might the author have chosen to end the text with this information?

---

2. In the first sentence, the author states that the Chinese hoped for good lives but faced obstacles. The many obstacles are then detailed. The mood changes in the seventh sentence when the author says that despite obstacles, they stayed and built a community.

3. They may have been afraid that Chinese workers would take their jobs or find lots of gold. Also, some white miners may have been prejudiced against people of different races and ethnicities.

Author's Purpose

1. (a) The author provides details about the different people who rushed to California in search of gold and freedom. **(b)** These details provide reasons why so many different people went to California.

2. (a) In the last paragraph, the author explains that some African Americans experienced prejudice but were able to still become successful and even helped fight for the rights of others. **(b)** The author may have wanted to show how people overcame prejudice and helped others.

DISCUSS • RESEARCH • WRITE

From Text to Topic **Group Discussion**

Discuss the following passage with a group of classmates. Take notes during the discussion. Contribute your own ideas, and support them with examples from the text.

> Many African Americans came to California as well. They hoped to find freedom and good jobs. Most were free men and women from eastern cities. Some free African Americans had fled the east to escape the Fugitive Slave Law.

Research **Investigate the Topic**

Labor During the Gold Rush Mining and panning were the two main ways that people acquired gold during the Gold Rush. This labor was time-consuming and often difficult and dangerous.

Assignment

Conduct research to learn more about the process of mining or panning for gold. Consult print and online sources such as encyclopedias. Also search for primary sources such as letters, journals, and memoirs. Present your findings in an **annotated poster**.

Writing to Sources **Editorial**

"Chinese and African Americans in the Gold Rush" describes obstacles faced by two groups of workers during the Gold Rush. While some people mistreated these workers, many others believed that mistreatment of the workers was unfair and should be changed.

Assignment

Write an **editorial** from the point of view of a resident of Sacramento, California, in 1849. Present the argument that Chinese and African American workers are being treated badly. Follow these steps:

• Clearly state your position on the issue.

• Use facts and details from the text or from outside research to support your position and claims.

• Clarify the relationships among ideas with transitional words and phrases.

QUESTIONS FOR DISCUSSION

1. How did slavery affect the Gold Rush?

2. What issues motivated African American workers to travel west?

PREPARATION FOR ESSAY

You may use the results of this research project to support your ideas in the essay at the end of this section.

ACADEMIC VOCABULARY

Academic terms appear in blue on these pages. If these words are not familiar to you, use a dictionary to find their definitions. Then, use them as you speak and write about the text.

 **Common Core State Standards**

RI.6.1, RI.6.2, RI.6.4, RI.6.5, RI.6.6; L.6.1, L.6.2, L.6.3, L.6.4, L.6.6; W.6.1, W.6.2, W.6.4, W.6.7, W.6.8, W.6.9, W.6.9.b, W.6.10; SL.6.1, SL.6.4
[For full standards wording, see the chart in the front of this book.]

PART 3 • Close Reading Activities **147**

Writing to Sources: Editorial

Students' editorials should clearly express the Sacramento resident's position on the issue of the maltreatment of minorities during the Gold Rush using evidence from the text and from outside research.

 Online Writer's Notebook

Students can use the Online Writer's Notebook to record all responses.

DISCUSS • RESEARCH • WRITE

From Text to Topic: Group Discussion

1. African Americans who were eager to escape slavery joined the Gold Rush in search of freedom and better opportunities.

2. African American workers were looking to escape the possibility of being sold into slavery and hoped to have better lives and to gain wealth.

Research: Investigate the Topic

Introduce the assignment, using the instruction on the student page.

1. Arrange for students to visit your school's library or computer lab. Review strategies for identifying reliable sources on the Internet, stressing that students should focus on Web sites that end in .gov, .edu., and .org.

2. As students take notes on main ideas found in their source materials, tell them to write down exact quotes using quotation marks or summarize their findings using their own words.

3. Encourage students to make connections between multiple sources. Suggest that they create a Works Cited list that accurately identifies each source they reference.

4. Suggest that students create an outline or diagram of the mining process.

Academic Vocabulary

If students struggle with defining the academic vocabulary words, use this routine:

Write the words and definitions on the board.

determine: to find out or make a decision

acquired: got

Have students say the word aloud. Then have them use the word in a sentence. Sample sentences should demonstrate that the word can be used across disciplines.

MULTIDRAFT READING

Essential Understanding

First, students should read the entire selection on their own. Then, to assist struggling readers and to deepen comprehension for all, you may wish to guide them through the selection by asking them the close reading questions provided in the margins. Have students apply the multidraft reading protocols as they examine specific "chunks" of text related to these questions. For each reading, have students set the purpose indicated:

- **First reading:** Students should read the selection independently and think about its basic meaning.
- **Second reading:** Students should analyze the text's key ideas and details and its craft and structure.
- **Third reading:** Students should integrate knowledge and ideas; connect to the Big Question, other texts, and the world; and use teacher-led Close Reading discussion questions to examine particularly rich and significant passages.

For more guidance, refer to the *Classroom Strategies and Teaching Routines* card on multidraft reading.

❶ Background

If you wish, explain that the Gold Rush era spurred a demand for eggs as prospectors flocked to California. With no poultry industry, people raided the nests of sea birds on the Farallon Islands. These "eggers" nearly wiped out the common murre population, which is still struggling to recover.

Vocabulary

If students require support with selection vocabulary, use this routine:

1. Write the following words and definitions on the board:

   conservatively *adv.* moderately or cautiously; safely

   entrepreneurs *n.* people who organize or manage a business

   faltered *v.* lost strength; weakened

2. Have students say each word aloud.

3. Use the word in a sentence that defines the word.

---

❶ Birds Struggle to Recover from Egg Thefts of 1800s

By Edie Lau
Bee Staff Writer

This time of year, sea birds that look somewhat like penguins are busy breeding on the Farallon Islands. Within a month after mating, these birds—called common murres—will lay speckled eggs, one per couple. The eggs are a gorgeous mixture of hues, and big.

The eggs also are said to taste good.

People who poured into Northern California for the Gold Rush ate millions of murre eggs that were collected from the Farallons, pointy rocks that jut from the ocean 27 miles west of San Francisco. The newcomers' hunger nearly wiped out the islands' most populous bird.

One-and-a-half centuries later, the Farallons' common murre colony is still trying to recover.

"It's growing, but it's not growing as fast as it could be," said William Sydeman, director of marine studies at the Point Reyes Bird Observatory. "If we get an oil spill at the wrong place at the wrong time, we could lose easily 50 percent. There's no cushion."

Murres (pronounced merz) once again are the most plentiful bird on the islands, breeding adults numbering about 80,000. But that's not many

---

Ⓒ TEXT COMPLEXITY **RUBRIC**

Birds Struggle to Recover from Egg Thefts of 1800s		
Qualitative Measures	Context/Knowledge Demands	The California Gold Rush, 1840s; ornithology 1 2 ③ 4 5
	Structure/Language Conventionality and Clarity	Informative article; some content-area vocabulary; straightforward exposition 1 2 ③ 4 5
	Levels of Meaning/ Purpose/Concept Level	Challenging concept (a decreasing bird population) 1 2 ③ 4 5
Quantitative Measures	Text Length	Word Count: 917
	Lexile	1150L

compared with their numbers before the Gold Rush. Biologists **conservatively** estimate that 500,000 adult murres—and possibly many more—raised chicks on the islands.

The Farallon Islands and surrounding ocean make a rich marine environment. The islands are known as the largest sea bird rookery[1] in the continental United States. The Farallons are alive and noisy with seagulls, puffins, auklets and cormorants, to name a few; the air is thick with the pungent scent of their guano. Sea lions and seals lounge on ledges or cavort in coves.

The Farallons' abundant wildlife impressed Yankee seamen and Russian explorers in the early nineteenth century. They hunted the seals for their pelts, meat and blubber. The Russians also enthusiastically collected sea bird eggs—for which they and Scandinavian peoples had developed a taste long before—according to Peter White of Martinez, an amateur naturalist and author of "The Farallon Islands: Sentinels of the Golden Gate."

Mining the National Archives in Washington, D.C., the California State Library in Sacramento and the public library in San Francisco, White found many colorful accounts of the commercial egging spurred by the Gold Rush.

One of the first to profit from the Farallon egg trade reportedly was a pharmacist from Maine known as "Doc" Robinson. Shortly after he arrived in San Francisco in 1849, Robinson

People who poured into Northern Califoria for the Gold Rush ate millions of murre eggs. . .

and a companion sailed to the islands. By selling the eggs he gathered there, Robinson earned enough money to open a drug store.

Two years later, another group of **entrepreneurs** established a business known as the Pacific Egg Co. or the Farallone Egg Co. The company constructed buildings, roads and landing facilities on the island. During the months of May, June and July, as many as 30 laborers gathered eggs.

◄ **conservatively**
(kən sər′ və tiv lē)
adv. moderately or cautiously; safely

◄ **entrepreneurs**
(än′ trə prə nərz′)
n. people who organize and manage a business

---

1. **rookery** (rook′ ər ē) *n.* a breeding place or colony of birds or animals, such as penguins or seals.

PART 3 • Birds Struggle to Recover from Egg Thefts of 1800s **149**

② Close Reading

1. **Key Ideas and Details** Read aloud the passage to students. **Ask:** What are the Farallon Islands known for according to this passage?

   Possible response: The Farallon Islands are known as the largest sea bird breeding place in the continental United States. They are an important habitat for many species of sea birds, along with sea lions and seals.

2. **Craft and Structure** Have students focus on the vivid verbs and adjectives that help set the scene in this passage. **Ask:** What verbs and adjectives does the author use to help you see, hear, and even smell the scene?

   Possible response: The author uses adjectives, such as *alive, noisy,* and *pungent,* to make you feel like you are on the island. You can imagine the sea lions and seals as they "lounge" or "cavort." You hear the noise of the different kinds of seabirds. You smell the "pungent" scents from the animals.

3. **Integration of Knowledge and Ideas**
   Ask: Why is it important for readers to know these descriptive details? How do these descriptive details relate to the plight of the birds?

   Possible response: The descriptive language helps readers visual the setting and realize that the birds and other animals need space to live. If their environment is threatened, then they have nowhere to live.

© **TEXT COMPLEXITY READER AND TASK SUGGESTIONS**

Birds Struggle to Recover from Egg Thefts of 1800s	
Preparing to Read the Text	**Leveled Tasks**
• Use the Background information on TE p. 148 to discuss how the human population explosion created by the Gold Rush led to a shortage of food and a demand for sea bird eggs. • Have students consider how bird populations can be adversely affected by human activities. • Guide students to use Multidraft Reading strategies (TE p. 148).	*Concept Level* If students will have difficulty with the concept that human activity may threaten birds with extinction, have them read first to identify threats to common murres and other birds on the Farallons. Then, have them reread and list the dangers that humans present to birds. *Synthesizing* If students will not have difficulty understanding how humans may threaten wildlife, have them note other challenges that sea birds face on an island rookery. As a class, discuss why banning egging and gill nets was necessary for population recovery.

 **Audio**

Selection Audio is available in the *Student eText* and on the *Hear It!* CD-ROM.

❸ Focus Passage

A Focus Passage is identified with brackets in the Student Edition of this page for students' independent close reading and analysis. A question bank for the passage and possible responses appear at the end of the selection.

In search of fresh eggs—not those with a visibly developing chick embryo—the gatherers, when they arrived for the season, would smash eggs that had already been laid, Sydeman said. That forced the birds to lay a second egg. Normally, murre ❸ couples produce a single chick in a year.

Eggers were rough men in a rough environment, according to witnesses' descriptions. Earnest Peixotto, a San Francisco artist who sketched the egg gatherers at work, wrote, "It made one shudder to see (the men)…scramble down the slippery cliffs, with boiling surf straight below, steadying themselves with one hand while with the other, they reached for the eggs."

While there were many bird eggs to choose from, murre eggs apparently were particularly desirable for their taste and ease of harvest, said Harry R. Carter, a sea bird biologist at the U.S. Geological Survey's Western Ecological Research Center in Dixon.

"They nested on the surface, so you could just walk along

The Farallon Islands

🗨 THINK ALOUD

Vocabulary: Using Context

Direct students' attention to the word *desirable* on this page. Using a think-aloud process, model how to use context to infer the meaning of an unknown word. Say to students:

I'm going to think aloud to show you how I would figure out the meaning of *desirable* from its context. In this sentence, *desirable* is being used to describe why murre eggs were preferred above other types of bird eggs. We learned that these eggs are laid on the surface rather than in holes, making them easy to harvest, and taste delicious. The word *particularly* is used as an adverb to modify the noun *desirable,* so I think that *desirable* refers to something that is sought after, like the murre eggs.

and pick them up," Carter said. "Other birds nested in holes on the ground."

In its infancy, California had no poultry industry, which further boosted the value of murre eggs. Carter cited one account of eggs sold away from market for as much as $6 to $9 a dozen. In San Francisco, prices began at $1.50 a dozen; by 1896, they had dropped to 12 cents a dozen.

The eggs were used predominantly by restaurants and bakeries in San Francisco, but Carter surmises that miners carried the nuggets of protein inland. "I imagine that these eggs were…transported wherever they could get to before they got bad," Carter said. "I imagine they went up to Sacramento, at least."

The egging company was ousted from the islands in 1881 by the federal government, which operated a lighthouse on the Farallons and challenged the company's presence from the start. Lighthouse keepers continued the practice of egg gathering until late 1896, when ornithologists[2] at the California Academy of Sciences successfully pressured the federal government to ban egging once and for all.

In the years since, the Farallons' breeding murre colony has swelled and shrunk. Chronic coastal oil pollution depressed the population's

> In the years since, the Farallon's breeding murre colony has swelled and shrunk.

growth for much of this century, Sydeman said.

By the early 1980s, murre numbers rose to about 100,000. But the population faltered less than a decade later, this time because the birds were drowning in gill nets[3]. Now those fishing nets, for the most part, are not allowed where murres dive for food.

Around the world, common murres are, in fact, common, Sydeman said, with a global population of about 20 million. But Sydeman thinks the Farallon murres will never regain their pre-Gold Rush abundance. The environment has probably changed too much.

copyright © The Sacramento Bee

◄ **faltered**
(fol´ tərd) *v.* lost strength; weakened

---

2. **ornithologists** (or´ nə thäl´ ə jists) people who study the branch of zoology dealing with birds.
3. **gill nets** *n.* nets set upright in the water to catch fish by entangling their gills.

④ **?** **Big Question: Toward Essential Understanding**

1. Read aloud the passage.
   Ask: What conflict did the Gold Rush create for the birds?

   Possible answer: The Gold Rush created a conflict between the needs of people for food and the needs of the birds to survive by laying and hatching their eggs. The population of California surged during the Gold Rush, creating a huge need for foods such as eggs. To supply this need, people collected huge numbers of eggs from the common murres and nearly wiped out this bird population.

2. **Ask:** Was this conflict ever really resolved?

   Possible answer: The government finally banned egg gathering on the islands in 1896. Although common murres are widespread in other locations, it is doubtful that they will ever recover their plentiful population on the Farallon Islands prior to the Gold Rush.

≈ **FLUENCY**

Distribute copies of pages 150–151, and pair students. Have partners take turns reading paragraphs aloud. While one partner reads, the other should mark any words with which the one reading has difficulty. Circulate to monitor the fluency of students' reading. Collect students' marked up copies of the story, and review difficult words and passages with the class. Look for these problem spots:

• If students have difficulty with the word *embryo* (p. 150), remind them to use context clues. Point out that if they read the rest of the sentence containing the word, clues such as *chick* and *eggs* will help them recognize the word.

• If students have difficulty with the word *predominantly* (p. 151), point out that the word features a common prefix, *pre-*, and a common suffix, *-ly*. Have students cover up parts of the word with their thumb to sound out each syllable in turn. Then, explain that *predominantly* means "in the greatest number or amount."

• If students have difficulty with the word *ousted* (p. 151), practice cloze reading with the sentence. First, read the sentence with the word *ousted* omitted. Then, reread the sentence, asking students to "fill in the blank" with a word that makes the most sense.

READ

Comprehension

1. They were good to eat and easy to sell.

2. Eggers stole murre eggs; oil pollution killed the birds; the birds got caught in gill nets.

Research: Clarify Details

Students' paragraphs should clarify an aspect of the text that was unfamiliar, and explain how the research relates the topic.

Summarize

Students' research should include the relationship between the Gold Rush and egging, and its effects on the murres.

Language Study

• *conservatively*: with caution
• *entrepreneurs*: people who start and manage businesses
• *faltered*: weakened

Students should use vocabulary words in the appropriate context.

Literary Analysis

Possible responses appear below. Check to be sure students support their responses with evidence from the text.

1. (a) They smashed murre eggs that had been laid. **(b)** The birds were forced to lay more eggs.

2. The environment was dangerous; they worked on slippery cliffs above the sea.

3. (a) The verbs are *smash, scramble,* and *steadying.* **(b)** The eggers are skilled and brave, but destructive.

4. The writer thinks they are destructive. The eggers are "rough" and they "forced" the birds to lay more eggs.

Imagery

1. (a) Examples include "boiling surf straight below" and "birds that look somewhat like penguins." **(b)** Both of the images appeal to one's sense of sight.

2. (a) "Pointy rocks that jut out" **(b)** The mood is dangerous and harsh.

 Close Reading Activities

READ

Comprehension

Reread all or part of the text to help you answer the following questions.

1. Why were Californians interested in common murre eggs?

2. Name three reasons the common murre population in the Farallon Islands has decreased.

Research: Clarify Details Choose at least one unfamiliar detail from the text, and briefly research it. Then, explain how the information you learned from research sheds light on an aspect of the article.

Summarize Write an objective summary of the text to clarify your understanding.

Language Study

Selection Vocabulary Define each boldfaced word, and use the word in a sentence of your own.

• Biologists **conservatively** estimate that 500,000 adult murres…

• Two years later, another group of **entrepreneurs** established a business…

• But the population **faltered** less than a decade later, …

Literary Analysis

Reread the identified passage. Then, respond to the questions that follow:

> **Focus Passage** *(p. 150)*
> In search of fresh eggs … reached for the eggs."

Key Ideas and Details

1. (a) What did the gatherer do when they arrived for the season? **(b) Analyze Causes and Effects:** How did their actions change the birds' behavior?

2. Analyze: In what kind of environment did the eggers work?

Craft and Structure

3. (a) List the verbs the writer uses to describe the eggers' actions. **(b) Interpret:** How do these verbs **establish** the eggers' characters?

Integration of Knowledge and Ideas

4. What is the writer's attitude toward the eggers? Use details from the text to support your response.

Imagery

Imagery is descriptive language that appeals to the five senses. Reread the article, and note the author's use of imagery.

1. (a) Find two examples of imagery in the text. **(b) Interpret:** To what senses do those images appeal?

2. (a) Find imagery that describes the Farallon Islands. **(b) Interpret:** What mood does the imagery develop?

DISCUSS • RESEARCH • WRITE

From Text to Topic **Group Discussion**

Discuss the following passage with a group of classmates. Take notes during the discussion. Contribute your own ideas, and support them with examples from the text.

> The Farallon Islands and surrounding ocean make a rich marine environment. The islands are known as the largest sea bird rookery in the continental United States. The Farallons are alive and noisy with seagulls, puffins, auklets and cormorants, to name a few; the air is thick with the pungent scent of their guano. Sea lions and seals lounge on ledges or cavort in caves.
>
> The Farallons' abundant wildlife impressed Yankee seamen and Russian explorers in the early nineteenth century. They hunted the seals for their pelts, meat and blubber.

Research **Investigate the Topic**

The Gold Rush and Food When people rushed to California, they had to adjust to unfamiliar plants and foods.

Assignment

Conduct research to find the types of food miners and their families ate during the Gold Rush. Consult the Internet and other sources. Take clear notes, and carefully identify your sources so that you can easily access the information later. Share your findings by creating a **menu** that lists popular food items.

Writing to Sources **Argument**

In the late 1800s, the federal government banned egging in California. While some people pushed for the ban, others disagreed with the decision.

Assignment

Write an **argument** in which you agree or disagree with the egging ban in California. Follow these steps:

- Introduce a problem or issue, and explain both sides.
- Clearly state your **opinion**.
- Cite evidence from the article to **support** your position.

QUESTIONS FOR DISCUSSION

1. How do the words the writer uses to describe the Farallon Islands suggest her attitude toward the subject?

2. Contrast the ways the islands' wildlife impresses the writer and the explorers.

PREPARATION FOR ESSAY

You may use the results of this research project to support your ideas in the essay at the end of this section.

ACADEMIC VOCABULARY

Academic terms appear in blue on these pages. If these words are not familiar to you, use a dictionary to find their definitions. Then, use them as you speak and write about the text.

 Common Core State Standards

RI.6.1, RI. 6.2, RI.6.3, RI.6.4, RI.6.5, RI6.6, RI.6.7; L.6.1, L.6.2, L.6.3, L.6.4, L.6.6; W.6.1, W.6.4, W.6.7, W.6.8, W.6.9, W.6.9.b, W.6.10; SL6.1, SL.6.4
[For full standards wording, see the chart in the front of this book.]

DISCUSS • RESEARCH • WRITE

From Text to Topic: Group Discussion

1. Imagery and poetic language, such as "lounge on ledges or cavort in caves," show admiration for nature.

2. To the explorers, wildlife is a way to make money and find food. To the writer, wildlife is impressive for its beauty.

Research: Investigate the Topic

Introduce the assignment, using the instruction on the student page.

1. Arrange for students to visit your school's library or computer lab.

2. Encourage students to look for primary source documents, such as journal or diaries, which may include details about the types of food people ate.

3. Urge students to draw conclusions and make connections between multiple sources.

4. Remind students of the importance of an outline, which can help them to organize the information that they find. Have students use outlines to identify and organize the types of plants and foods.

Academic Vocabulary

If students struggle with defining the academic vocabulary words, use this routine:

Write the words and definitions on the board.

establish: to show to be true

opinion: personal belief

support: to provide evidence for

Have students say the word aloud. Then have them use the word in a sentence. Sample sentences should demonstrate that the word can be used across disciplines.

Writing to Sources: Argument

Students' arguments should follow the steps in order to clearly present their argument using evidence from the text.

📝 **Online Writer's Notebook**

Students can use the Online Writer's Notebook to record all responses.

Speaking and Listening: Group Discussion

Introduce the assignment using the instruction on the student page.

1. **Conduct discussions.** Help students recall and apply their knowledge of the selections in this section to answer the discussion questions. For example, **ask:**

   • Why did the Klondike Gold Rush cause a conflict between Yukon residents like Walt and newcomers who journeyed to northwestern Canada in search of gold?

   • Which aspects of the California Gold Rush does Mary view as positive in her letter? Which aspects does she view as negative?

   • How did the Gold Rush affect California's population and its environment?

   • What consequences did the Gold Rush have for Chinese immigrants and African Americans?

2. **Summarize and present your ideas.** Remind students that when they summarize their findings, they should strive to represent a range of ideas that emerged from their group's discussion.

Criteria for Success

Circulate around the room and observe group discussions. Support groups in their efforts to conduct organized, focused, balanced, and respectful discussions. Ask guiding questions if the conversation stagnates, and encourage students to make connections between ideas and experiences from different sources and to explore contrasts in the texts' portrayals or points of view. Emphasize that students should support all points with specific text evidence.

Use New Vocabulary

Assist students in using new vocabulary during group discussion. For example, **ask:**

• What hardships were *endured* by women during the California Gold Rush?

• How did *entrepreneurs* from various backgrounds use innovation to make profits?

 Assessment: Synthesis

Speaking and Listening: **Group Discussion**

The Gold Rush and Conflict The texts in this section vary in genre, length, style, and perspective. However, all of the texts focus on an aspect or outcome of the Gold Rush. The effects of the Gold Rush on the environment, population, civil rights, and popular culture are fundamentally related to the Big Question addressed in this unit: **Is conflict always bad?**

> **Assignment**
>
> **Conduct discussions.** With a small group of classmates, conduct a discussion about issues of the Gold Rush and conflict. Refer to the texts in this section, other texts you have read, and your personal experience and knowledge to support your ideas. Begin your discussion by addressing the following questions:
>
> • Why do significant international events, such as the Gold Rush, sometimes cause conflict?
>
> • Was the outcome of the Gold Rush positive or negative? Why?
>
> • How did the Gold Rush affect the following: U.S. population, the environment, and the treatment of minorities?
>
> **Summarize and present your ideas.** After you have fully explored the topic, summarize your discussion and present your ideas to the class as a whole.

Criteria for Success

✓ **Organizes the group effectively**
Appoint a group leader and a timekeeper. The group leader should present the discussion questions. The timekeeper should make sure the discussion takes no longer than 20 minutes.

✓ **Maintains focus of discussion**
As a group, stay on topic and avoid straying into other subject areas.

✓ **Involves all participants equally and fully**
No one person should monopolize the conversation. Rather, everyone should take turns speaking and contributing ideas.

✓ **Follows the rules for collegial discussion**
As each group member speaks, others should listen carefully. Build on one another's ideas and support viewpoints and opinions with sound reasoning and evidence. Express disagreement respectfully.

Common Core State Standards

SL.6.1.a-d
[For full standards wording, see the chart in the front of this book.]

USE NEW VOCABULARY

As you speak and share ideas, strive to use the vocabulary words you have learned in this unit. The more you use new words, the more you will "own" them.

Writing: Historical Fiction

The Gold Rush and Conflict Conflict characterizes the stories we read and many of the historical events we study. Just as we face conflict in our daily lives, those who participated in the Gold Rush also dealt with conflict.

> **Assignment**
>
> Write a **short story** in which you include real events, places, or people in a made-up narrative about the Gold Rush. This form of writing is known as historical fiction. Your story should develop conflicts between characters or highlight conflicts that result from historical events or situations.

Criteria for Success

Purpose/Focus
✓ **Connects specific incidents with larger ideas**
Make clear connections between your characters and plot, and the texts you have read in this section.

✓ **Clearly conveys the significance of the story**
Provide a conclusion in which the conflict is resolved in a satisfying and logical manner.

Organization
✓ **Sequences events logically**
Structure your narrative so that individual events build on one another to create a coherent whole.

Development of Ideas/Elaboration
✓ **Supports insights**
Draw on your knowledge of the historical time period as you develop your setting, conflict, and characters.

✓ **Uses narrative techniques effectively**
Consider using dialogue to help readers "hear" characters speak.

Language
✓ **Uses description effectively**
Use sensory details that bring to life settings and characters.

Conventions
✓ **Does not have errors**
Correct errors in grammar, spelling, and punctuation.

Common Core State Standards

W.6.3.a-d, W.6.4
[For full standards wording, see the chart in the front of this book.]

INCORPORATE RESEARCH

As you plan your story, refer to the notes you took as you researched the Gold Rush. Use what you have learned about that historic time period as you develop your story's characters and settings.

Writing: Historical Fiction

Introduce the assignment, using the instruction on the student page.

Criteria for Success

1. **Purpose/Focus** Encourage students to identify meaningful connections between their experiences and those of characters introduced in the texts. For example, **ask:** What might you have done if you were faced with a dangerous conflict with people who were attempting to steal a neighbor's gold claim?

2. **Organization** Encourage students to sequence the events in their short stories in a logical way. A clear and smooth sequence of events will add up to a coherent whole.

3. **Development of Ideas/Elaboration** Encourage students to focus on realistic dialogue to help their audience envision different characters. Point out colorful models in the texts, such as the Irishman's simile, "the creek's as rich as a United States mint."

4. **Language** Instruct students to use descriptive details that appeal to the five senses.

5. **Conventions** In addition to self-review, students should swap their narratives with partners to check for errors.

Incorporate Research

Remind students to consider how they might use their prior research about the Gold Rush to explain what conditions the characters faced and what living in the 1800s was like.

Writing to Sources: Argumentative Essay

Introduce the assignment using the instruction on the student page.

Prewriting and Planning

1. **Choose texts.** Explain that in order to identify and develop their own claims about the effects of the Gold Rush on individuals, groups, or the environment, students will need to review and analyze the conflicts presented in two or more of the texts that they explored.

2. **Gather details and craft a working thesis, or claim.**
   - Remind students that a thesis is a declarative statement that a writer is attempting to prove to readers.
   - Instruct students to go back into the two or more texts they have selected and review passages that are connected to the effects of the Gold Rush.
   - Encourage students to use a chart like the one shown to record the texts they have selected, appropriate passages, and notes pertaining to the effects of the Gold Rush.
   - Students may also wish to raise counterclaims that the passage might help answer, such as

   What positive outcomes could conflict have on individuals during the Gold Rush? How might a negative conflict result in a beneficial outcome for the environment?

3. **Prepare counterarguments.**
   - Remind students that they should plan ahead by predicting potential counterarguments. By responding to readers' objections, students ultimately will make their own arguments more powerful and credible.
   - Explain how to recognize and refute a counterargument for the sample claim, "Even though there were conflicts during the Gold Rush, the conflicts had many positive outcomes, such as making people stronger as individuals and more unified as groups."

Writing to Sources: Argumentative Essay

 **Common Core State Standards**

W.6.1.a-d, W.6.4, W.6.5, W.6.9
[For full standards wording, see the chart in the front of this book.]

The Gold Rush and Conflict The related readings in this section present a range of ideas about the Gold Rush and conflict. They raise questions, such as the following:

- How did individuals deal with the Gold Rush?
- What were the effects of the Gold Rush on minorities?
- How did people resolve conflicts during the Gold Rush?

Focus on the question that interests you the most, and then complete the following assignment.

> **Assignment**
>
> Write an **essay** in which you state and defend a claim about the effects of the Gold Rush on individuals, groups, or on the environment. Build evidence for your claim by analyzing the conflicts presented in two or more texts from this section. Clearly present, develop, and support your ideas with examples and details from the texts.

Prewriting and Planning

Choose texts. Review the texts in the section, and choose at least two to cite in your essay. Select at least two that will provide strong material to support your argument.

Gather details and craft a working thesis, or claim. Use a chart like the one shown to develop your claim.

Focus Question: Was conflict during the Gold Rush always negative?

Text	Passage	Notes
"The King of Mazy May"	"He did not like the looks of the newcomers, and one day, when five of them came by with crack dog teams and the lightest of camping outfits, he could see that they were prepared to make speed, and resolved to keep an eye on them."	narrator indicates that the Gold Rush has created conflict—in this case, suspicion—between the main characters
"Chinese and African Americans in the Gold Rush"	"They used their gold to free their families, start churches, schools, libraries and newspapers, and work for greater legal rights."	positive outcomes of hardship during the Gold Rush

Example Claim: Even though there were conflicts during the Gold Rush, the conflicts had many positive outcomes, such as making people stronger as individuals and more unified as groups.

Prepare counterarguments. Note a possible objection to each point that supports your claim. Plan to include the strongest of these counterclaims in your essay: Be sure to introduce and supply evidence to disprove it.

- Offer the following counterargument to this claim: "Conflicts during the Gold Rush were caused by greed and always resulted in negative outcomes."
- Then demonstrate how students might refute this counterargument. For example, point out that Walt wasn't motivated by greed but rather the innate desire to do the right thing and help defend his neighbor Loren's claim.

INCORPORATE RESEARCH

Refer to the notes you took as you researched various aspects of the Gold Rush. Cite relevant details from your research in your argument.

Incorporate Research

Remind students to consider how they might use their prior research—about living conditions for gold prospectors in Canada in the 1890s—to support their claim in this essay.

Drafting

Structure your ideas and evidence. Create an informal outline or list of ideas you want to present. Decide where you will include evidence and which evidence you will use to support each point.

Address counterclaims. Strong argumentation takes differing ideas into account and addresses them directly. As you order your ideas, explain opposing opinions or differing interpretations. Then, write a reasoned, well-supported response to those counterclaims.

Frame and connect ideas. Write an introduction that will grab the reader's attention. Consider beginning with a compelling quotation or a detail. Then, write a strong conclusion that ends your essay with a clear statement. Use words, phrases, and clauses to link the major sections of your essay and clarify the relationships between your claims and reasons, evidence, and counterclaims.

Revising and Editing

Review content. Make sure that your claim is clearly stated and that you have supported it with convincing evidence from the texts. Underline main ideas in your paper and confirm that each one is supported. Add more proof as needed.

Review style. Revise to cut wordy language. Adapt your language, as needed, to achieve a formal, objective tone. Then, proofread to eliminate errors in spelling and grammar.

CITE RESEARCH CORRECTLY

Review your argument, and note the details that came from an outside source. Cite your source material for each detail. Refer to the Research Workshop in the front of this book for citation guidelines.

Self-Evaluation Rubric

Use the following criteria to evaluate the effectiveness of your essay.

Criteria	Rating Scale			
Purpose/Focus Introduces a precise claim and supports the argument with clear reasons and evidence	*not very .... very*			
	1	2	3	4
Organization Establishes a logical organization; uses words, phrases, and clauses to clarify the relationships among ideas	1	2	3	4
Development of Ideas/Elaboration Develops the claim and counterclaims fairly, supplying evidence for each; provides a concluding statement that follows from the argument presented	1	2	3	4
Language Establishes and maintains a formal style and an objective tone	1	2	3	4
Conventions Uses correct conventions of grammar, spelling, and punctuation	1	2	3	4

Drafting

1. **Structure your ideas and evidence.**
   - Encourage students to create lists or informal outlines to present the main ideas in their argumentative essays.
   - Remind students to use evidence to support main points.
2. **Address counterclaims.**
   - Have students review their prewriting and planning notes about preparing counterclaims.
   - Remind students to explain opposing opinions and then support these counterclaims with evidence.
3. **Frame and connect ideas.**
   - Point out that one of the best ways to grab a reader's attention is to begin an essay with a compelling quote.
   - The body of students' essays should provide evidence that supports their claims. Major sections of their essays should be clearly linked together.
   - The conclusion should end with a clear, strong statement that sums up the claim for readers and makes them reflect on its validity.

Revising and Editing

1. **Review content.** After students are certain that their claim is as strong and clear as possible, suggest that they exchange their essays with partners. Have students ask:
   - Is my claim clearly stated?
   - Have I presented a convincing argument?
   - What areas of my argument need to be strengthened?
   - Are there other counterarguments I should include?

   Remind students to clarify the relationships between their claims and reasons, evidence, and counterarguments.

2. **Review style.** Instruct students to communicate their ideas clearly and simply. Tell them to delete wordy language. Remind them to use a print or online thesaurus to find precise and descriptive words.

Self-Evaluation Rubric

Encourage students to rate their own essays objectively and to use the results to guide their revision process.

Cite Research Correctly

Review with students the correct format for citing different sources, such as books and print or online news articles. Provide examples of proper citations. Then have students create a Works Cited list that correctly lists each source they refer to in their essays.

Independent Reading

Titles featured on the Independent Reading pages at the end of each unit represent a range of reading, including stories, dramas, and poetry, as well as literary nonfiction and other types of informational text. Throughout, labels indicate the works that are CCSS Exemplar Texts. Choosing from among these featured titles will help students read works at increasing levels of text complexity in the grades 6–8 text complexity band.

Online Text Set

The selections that are a part of the Online Text Set are located in the *Student eText.*

Using Literature Circles

A literature circle is a temporary group in which students independently discuss a book.

Use the guidance in the *Professional Development Guidebook*, pp. 47–49, as well as the teaching notes on the facing page, for additional suggestions for literature circles.

Meeting Unit 1 Common Core State Standards

Students can use books listed on this page to apply and to reinforce their mastery of the Common Core State Standards covered in this unit.

Introducing Featured Titles

Have students choose a book or books for independent reading. Assist them by previewing the titles, noting their subject matter and level of difficulty. **Note:** Before recommending a work to students, preview it, taking into account the values of your community as well as the maturity of your students.

Independent Reading

Titles for Extended Reading

In this unit, you have read texts in a variety of genres. Continue to read on your own. Select works that you enjoy, but challenge yourself to explore new authors and works of increasing depth and complexity. These titles will help you get started.

INFORMATIONAL TEXT

All Creatures Great and Small
by James Herriot

 James Herriot describes his first years as a veterinarian in this collection of **narrative nonfiction.** His tales of helping animals in the English countryside have delighted readers for over twenty-five years.

Discoveries: Trouble Ahead

 The **essays** in this collection cover topics that range from ancient Greece to baseball. Each essay features a conflict that the participants turn into an advantage.

Cathedral: The Story of Its Construction
by David Macaulay   EXEMPLAR TEXT ⓒ

In this illustrated **informational text**, David Macaulay uses detailed pen-and-ink drawings to show how a magnificent cathedral would have been built in the year 1252.

LITERATURE

The Sherlock Holmes Mysteries
by Sir Arthur Conan Doyle
Signet, 1985

 Sherlock Holmes is considered one of the greatest fictional detectives of all time. In this **short story** collection, the brilliant Holmes solves baffling crimes with the help of his partner, Dr. Watson.

An Island Like You: Stories of the Barrio
by Judith Ortiz Cofer
Orchard Books, 1995

 In this collection of **short stories**, teenagers deal with conflicts between their American culture and their parents' Puerto Rican heritage.

My Side of the Mountain
by Jean Craighead George
Scholastic Book Services, 1988

 In this gripping adventure **novel**, Sam Gribley leaves his comfortable home in New York City, bound for the Catskill Mountains. Read how he bravely endures a harsh year in the wilderness.

The Book of Questions
by Pablo Neruda   EXEMPLAR TEXT ⓒ

 Pablo Neruda wrote this collection of **poems** near the end of his life. Each poem is a thought-provoking question, or series of questions, about nature, life, or death.

ONLINE TEXT SET

SHORT STORY
Eleven Sandra Cisneros

BIOGRAPHY
A Backwoods Boy Russell Freedman

LETTER
Letter to Scottie F. Scott Fitzgerald

ⓒ TEXT COMPLEXITY **ALIGNING TEXTS WITH READERS AND TASKS**

Texts	Readers and Tasks
• *The Sherlock Holmes Mysteries*	**Below-Level Readers** Allow students to focus on reading for content, and challenge them to interpret multiple perspectives.
• *My Side of the Mountain* (Lexile: 810L) • *An Island Like You: Stories of the Barrio* (Lexile: 910L) • *Discoveries: Trouble Ahead* • *All Creatures Great and Small* (Lexile: 990L)	**Below-Level Readers** Challenge students as they read for content. **On-Level Readers** Allow students to focus on reading for content, and challenge them to interpret multiple perspectives. **Advanced Readers** Allow students to focus on interpreting multiple perspectives.
• *Cathedral: The Story of Its Construction* (Lexile: 1120L) • *The Book of Questions*	**On-Level Readers** Challenge students as they read for content. **Advanced Readers** Allow students to focus on reading for content, and challenge them to interpret multiple perspectives.

Preparing to Read Complex Texts

Attentive Reading As you read on your own, ask yourself questions like these to enrich your reading experience.

When reading short stories, ask yourself...

Comprehension: **Key Ideas and Details**

- Can I clearly picture the time and place of the action? Which details help me do so?
- Can I picture the characters clearly? Why or why not?
- Do the characters behave like real people? Why or why not?
- Which characters do I like and which do I dislike? Why?
- Do I understand why the characters act as they do? Why or why not?
- What does the story mean to me? Does it express a meaning or an insight I find important and true?

Text Analysis: **Craft and Structure**

- Does the story grab my attention immediately? Why or why not?
- Do I want to keep reading? Why or why not?
- Can I follow the sequence of events in the story? Am I confused at any point? If so, what information would make the sequence clearer?
- Do the characters change as the story progresses? If so, do the changes seem believable?
- Are there any passages that I find especially moving, interesting, or well written? If so, why?

Connections: **Integration of Knowledge and Ideas**

- How is this story similar to and different from other stories I have read?
- How do my feelings toward the characters affect my experience of reading the story?
- Did the story teach me something new or cause me to look at something in a new way? If so, what did I learn?
- Would I recommend this story to others? Why or why not?
- Would I like to read other works by this author? Why or why not?

Common Core State Standards

Reading Literature/ Informational Text
10. By the end of the year, read and comprehend literature, including stories, dramas, and poems, and literary nonfiction in the grades 6–8 text complexity band proficiently, with scaffolding as needed at the high end of the range.

Preparing to Read Complex Texts

1. Tell students they can be attentive readers by bringing their experience and imagination to the texts they read and by actively questioning those texts. Explain that the questions they see on the student page are examples of types of questions to ask about short stories.

2. Point out that, like writing, reading is a "multidraft" process, involving several readings of complete works or passages, revising and refining one's understanding each time.

Key Ideas and Details

3. As an example, review and amplify the second bulleted item. **Ask:** What key ideas and details would you use to evaluate if you can picture characters clearly?

   Possible response: You might point to the author's effective use of descriptive language or devices like figurative language that compare the character to someone (or something) else.

Craft and Structure

4. **Ask:** What details of craft and structure would you use to evaluate whether or not a character's behavior seems believable?

   Possible response: You might point to the author's effective description of the character's motivations or use of devices like foreshadowing.

Integration of Knowledge and Ideas

5. **Ask:** How would you decide if you want to read other works by the same author?

   Possible response: You might consider whether or not you enjoyed the author's writing style or if you agreed with the story's message.

6. Finally, explain to students that they should cite key ideas and details, examples of craft and structure, or instances of the integration of knowledge and ideas as evidence to support their points during a book discussion. After hearing the evidence, the group might reach a consensus or might agree to disagree.

TEXT COMPLEXITY **READER AND TASK SUPPORT SUGGESTIONS**

Independent Reading

Increased Support Suggest that students choose a book that they feel comfortable reading and one that is a bit more challenging. Pair a more proficient reader with a less proficient reader and have them work together on the more challenging text. Partners can prepare to read the book by reviewing questions on this student page. They can also read difficult passages together, sharing questions and insights. They can use the questions on the student page to guide after-reading discussion.

Increased Challenge Encourage students to integrate knowledge and ideas by combining the Big Question and the Unit Focus concepts in their approach to two or more featured titles.

For example, students might consider who are the "winners" and "losers" of the conflicts described in *My Side of the Mountain* and *All Creatures Great and Small.* In addition, students can focus on similarities and differences in the motives that drive characters in works of fiction and nonfiction.

UNIT 2

101010
101001101010
0011

 **THE BIG ?**

What is important to know?

UNIT PATHWAY

PART 1
SETTING EXPECTATIONS

- INTRODUCING THE BIG QUESTION
- CLOSE READING WORKSHOP

PART 2
TEXT ANALYSIS
GUIDED EXPLORATION

LIFE STORIES

PART 3
TEXT SET
DEVELOPING INSIGHT

BASEBALL

PART 4
DEMONSTRATING INDEPENDENCE

- INDEPENDENT READING
- ONLINE TEXT SET

CLOSE READING TOOL

Use this tool to practice the close
reading strategies you learn.

STUDENT eTEXT

Bring learning to life
with audio, video, and
interactive tools.

WRITER'S NOTEBOOK

Easily capture notes and
complete assignments online.

1 What is important to know?

1. Have students read the introductory text. Then, have them imagine they are voting for a student government president. **Ask:** What would you need to know to make an informed decision? **Possible responses:** what the person believes in; what other positions, if any, she or he has held

2. Note that it is always important to determine how much information you need to know about a situation.

3. **Ask** students the Big Question. **Possible responses:** just enough to succeed with regards to a task; as much as you can so you can be prepared

4. Note that the selections in this unit provide factual information. Remind students to keep the Big Question in mind as they read.

2 Exploring the Big Question

Collaboration: One-on-One Discussion

1. Introduce the activity, using the instruction on the student page.

2. Have students work individually to list examples. If students have difficulty with the last item, prompt ideas about different kinds of challenges:

   - What kinds of physical challenges do people have? **Sample response:** They could be disabled or have a chronic illness.

   - What kinds of change can cause challenges? **Sample response:** moving from one city or state to another or changing your diet

3. Review the Big Question vocabulary on the next page. Have students use the vocabulary as they complete the activity on this page.

Connecting to the Literature

Explain the Big Question strand in the unit, referring to the text at the bottom of this page.

© Introducing the Big Question

1 What is important to know?

Knowledge does not come only from books and the Internet. It also comes from participating in life. You gain knowledge from your daily experience—when you observe what happens around you and when you examine the ideas and events that spark your curiosity. On the one hand, there is no limit to what you can know. Yet, on the other hand, you cannot know everything.

With all the information that is available to you, it is helpful to decide what you think is most important to know.

2 Exploring the Big Question

Collaboration: One-on-One Discussion Start thinking about the Big Question by exploring what you already know and what you would like to learn. Begin by making a list. Give at least two examples of things that you think are important to know in each of these situations:

- Getting along with family members
- Doing well in school
- Making new friends
- Learning about the world around you
- Facing challenges

Share your examples with a partner. Discuss why you believe the examples on your list are important. Work together to decide which information seems important. Use the vocabulary words in your discussion.

Connecting to the Literature Each reading in this unit will give you additional insight into the Big Question. After you read each text, pause to consider the ways that we gain and use knowledge about ourselves and the world.

❓ DEVELOPING ESSENTIAL UNDERSTANDING

What is important to know?

Explain to students that they will continue to consider the Big Question as they work through Unit 2.

- As students read each selection, they will look for details related to the Big Question and take notes.

- At the end of each selection, students will answer a Literary Analysis question that is related to the Big Question.

- Throughout the unit, students will deepen their knowledge of the selections and their understanding of the Big Question through reading, speaking, listening, researching, and writing. By the end of the unit, students should understand how each selection relates to the Big Question individually and how the selections connect to one another through the Big Question.

- Tell students that their goal will be to gain a deeper understanding of literature and to develop a more sophisticated way of discussing the Big Question. Ultimately, students should use the Big Question as a springboard for their own questions that relate to their interests and concerns.

❸ Vocabulary

Acquire and Use Academic Vocabulary Academic vocabulary is the language you encounter in textbooks and on standardized tests. Review the definitions of these academic vocabulary words.

> **concept** (kän´ sept´) *n.* general idea or notion
>
> **distinguish** (di stiŋ´ gwish) *v.* mark as different; set apart
>
> **examine** (eg zam´ ən) *v.* study or look at closely
>
> **judge** (juj) *v.* form an opinion about; decide on
>
> **measure** (mezh´ ər) *v.* find the value of
>
> **observe** (əb zʉrv´) *v.* see or notice
>
> **purpose** (pʉr´ pəs) *n.* use; function
>
> **question** (kwes´ chən) *v.* doubt; wonder about
>
> **refer** (ri fʉr´) *v.* turn to for information such as to a book or an expert
>
> **source** (sôrs) *n.* something that gives information, such as a book, Web site, or person
>
> **study** (stud´ ē) *v.* look into deeply; examine

Gather Vocabulary Knowledge Additional vocabulary words are listed below. Categorize the words by deciding whether you know each one well, know it a little bit, or do not know it at all.

> guess   limit
> knowledge   narrow

Then, do the following:

1. Write the definitions of the words you know.
2. Consult a dictionary to confirm the meanings of the words you know. Revise your definitions if necessary.
3. Next, use a print or an online dictionary to look up the meanings of the words you do not know. Then, write the meanings.
4. Use all of the words in a brief paragraph about knowledge.

Common Core State Standards

Speaking and Listening

1. Engage effectively in a range of collaborative discussions with diverse partners on grade 6 topics, texts, and issues, building on others' ideas and expressing their own clearly.

Language

4.d. Verify the preliminary determination of the meaning of a word or phrase.

6. Acquire and use accurately grade-appropriate general academic and domain-specific words and phrases; gather vocabulary knowledge when considering a word or phrase important to comprehension or expression.

---

❸ Vocabulary

Acquire and Use Academic Vocabulary

1. Introduce the academic vocabulary words in the first word bank on the student page. Have students preview the words.
2. For each word, have students say the word aloud. Then, use the word in a sentence that defines the word.

Gather Vocabulary Knowledge

1. With the class, review the steps in the activity on the student page. Have students complete the activity independently, with partners, or in small groups.
2. Before students complete the last step, review the words and their meanings as a class. (Definitions appear at the bottom of this page.) Then, have students complete their paragraphs.

💬 GATHER VOCABULARY KNOWLEDGE

guess (ges) *n.* estimate; hunch

knowledge (näl´ij) *n.* learning; awareness

limit (lim´it) *n.* farthest point

narrow (nar´ō) *adj.* limited; not wide

▶ **Video**

Watch the Background Video online!

Close Reading Workshop

1 Close Reading: Nonfiction

In the Close Reading Workshop, students will practice using close reading strategies within the context of a particular genre. They will use the features of this genre to help them access the text. All of the close reading strategies align with the Common Core State Standards reading domains:

- **Comprehension:** Key Ideas and Details focuses on what the text says.

- **Text Analysis:** Craft and Structure focuses on how the author conveys the text.

- **Connections:** Integration of Knowledge and Ideas focuses on what the text means and how it changes the reader's view of the world.

MULTIDRAFT READING

Essential Understanding
Explain to students that close reading works best when they read a text multiple times, focusing on different aspects of the text each time.

- **First reading:** Students should read independently to unlock the basic meaning of the text.

- **Second reading:** Students should focus on analyzing key ideas and details and the craft and the structure of the text.

- **Third reading:** Students should focus on integrating knowledge and ideas by connecting the text to the Big Question. The essential understanding students gain from making this connection will help them connect the text to other texts and to the world.

In this workshop you will learn an approach to reading that will deepen your understanding of literature and will help you better appreciate author's craft. The workshop includes models for the close reading, discussion, research, and writing activities. After you have reviewed the strategies and models, practice your skills with the Independent Practice selection.

Common Core State Standards

RI.6.1, RI.6.2, RI.6.3, RI.6.4, RI.6.5, RI.6.6; W.6.2, W.6.4, W.6.7, W.6.9.b; SL.6.1
[For full standards wording, see the standards chart in the front of this book.]

1 CLOSE READING: NONFICTION

In the beginning of this unit you will focus on reading various types of nonfiction. Use these strategies as you read the texts.

Comprehension: **Key Ideas and Details**

- Read first to unlock basic meaning.
- Use context clues to help you determine the meanings of unfamiliar words. Consult a dictionary, if necessary.
- Identify unfamiliar details that you can clarify through research.
- Distinguish between what is stated directly and what must be inferred.

Ask yourself questions such as these:
- Who or what is the subject?
- When and where do the events take place?
- What are the main ideas in the text?

Text Analysis: **Craft and Structure**

- Think about the genre of the work and how the author presents facts and details.
- Analyze the author's word choice, writing style, and tone.
- Determine the author's point of view. Notice how this perspective affects what the author says.

Ask yourself questions such as these:
- What do I learn from the quotations and *anecdotes*—stories that make a point—that the author includes?
- How does the author's word choice help convey his or her point of view?
- What is the author's attitude toward his or her subject?

Connections: **Integration of Knowledge and Ideas**

- Look for relationships among key ideas. Identify causes and effects, and comparisons and contrasts.
- Look for clues that help you identify the purpose of the text.

Ask yourself questions such as these:
- How has this work increased my knowledge of a subject or author?
- Why is it worthwhile to learn about this subject?

164 UNIT 2 • What is important to know?

ACTIVE READING FOR COMMON CORE

Read • Discuss • Research • Write
In this workshop, students will learn how to access text through reading, discussing, researching, and writing. In the first half of the workshop, these activities are modeled for students. In the second half, students have the opportunity to partake in these activities independently.

Read: Students will read and comprehend the Reading Model selection. Annotations call out key points that students should focus on. These annotations model the types of things students should notice when they read the Independent Practice selection later.

Discuss: Students will deepen their understanding of the text through collaborative discussion.

Research: Students will clarify and expand their understanding of the text by conducting research.

Write: Students will synthesize their thoughts and research and will write a response to the text, supporting their ideas with evidence.

❷ Read

As you read this selection from a biography, take note of the annotations that model ways to closely read the text.

Reading Model

from **"Rambling 'Round"** [1] by Elizabeth Partridge

"I hate a song that makes you think that you're not any good. I hate a song that makes you think you are just born to lose. I am out to fight those kind of songs to my very last breath of air and my last drop of blood." [2]

Woody Guthrie could never cure himself of wandering off. One minute he'd be there, the next he'd be gone, vanishing without a word to anyone, abandoning those he loved best. He'd throw on a few extra shirts, one on top of the other, sling his guitar over his shoulder, and hit the road. He'd stick out his thumb and hitchhike, swing onto moving freight trains, and hunker down with other traveling men [3] in flophouses, hobo jungles, and Hoovervilles across Depression America. [4]

He moved restlessly from state to state, soaking up songs: work songs, mountain and cowboy songs, sea chanteys, songs from the southern chain gangs. He added them to the dozens he already knew from his childhood until he was bursting with American folk songs. Playing the guitar and singing, he started making up new ones: hardbitten, rough-edged songs that told it like it was, full of anger and hardship and hope and love.

Woody said the best songs came to him when he was walking down a road. He always had fifteen or twenty songs running around in his mind, [5] just waiting to be put together. Sometimes he knew the words, but not the melody. Usually he'd borrow a tune that was already well known—the simpler the better. As he walked along, he tried to catch a good, easy song [5] that people could sing the first time they heard it, remember, and sing again later.

Key Ideas and Details
1 The title suggests that this work will be about a person on the move. The repeated *r* sounds give the title a musical quality.

Craft and Structure
2 The author introduces her subject with the words of Woody Guthrie himself. Well-chosen quotations are an important feature of biographies.

Craft and Structure
3 The author uses long sentences that contain many clauses. Her sentences seem to "ramble" around just like Guthrie.

Key Ideas and Details
4 Through research you can learn that that *flophouses* and *Hoovervilles* were temporary houses for poor people during the Great Depression of the 1930s.

Integration of Knowledge and Ideas
5 These details reinforce the main idea that Guthrie was a "rambler." The author's word choice and tone throughout the passage suggest that she wants readers to learn about and like Guthrie.

---

❷ Read

Before students begin reading the model, explain to them that the annotations call out important points in the story related to Key Ideas and Details, Craft and Structure, and Integration of Knowledge and Ideas. Tell students that their understanding and interpretation of the text should not be limited by the existing annotations. Encourage students to use the annotations as a starting point to help them analyze the story further.

❸ Integration of Knowledge and Ideas

To move students toward essential understanding, draw their attention to the bracketed annotation 3 in the Teacher Edition. **Ask:** Why might Woody Guthrie have chosen to spend time in "flophouses, hobo jungles, and Hoovervilles"? Explain.

Possible response: Students may infer that Guthrie believed it was important to understand what life was like for poor people during the 1930s. Students may conclude that these experiences influenced the songs Guthrie wrote.

---

❷ DEVELOPING ESSENTIAL UNDERSTANDING

What is important to know?

After students have finished reading the model, ask them the following questions to help them deepen their understanding of how the story relates to the Big Question:

- What information does the author think is important to know about Woodie Guthrie?
- Do the facts presented about Guthrie influence your understanding of his life and work? Explain.

- From the passage, infer what information Guthrie thought people should know about. How did he communicate that information?

Remind students that as they read the rest of the selections in this unit, they should ask themselves similar questions to help them connect the texts with the Big Question.

 **Audio**

Selection Audio is available in the *Student eText* and on the *Hear It!* CD-ROM.

❹ Discuss

Throughout the unit, students will be engaging in discussions about the selections they read. As students discuss, remind them of the following points:

- Come to discussions prepared.
- Support ideas with text evidence.
- Pose and respond to questions that connect the selection to broader themes and ideas.
- Respond thoughtfully to diverse perspectives.

❺ Research

As students conduct research, remind them of the following tips:

- Narrow your search terms by using precise details if the results of your first searches are too general.
- Try using more than one search engine to gather a broad range of information.
- Remember to use reputable Web sites, such as those that end in .gov, .edu, and .org.

❹ Discuss

Sharing your own ideas and listening to the ideas of others can deepen your understanding of a text and help you look at a topic in a whole new way. As you participate in collaborative discussions, work to have a genuine exchange in which classmates build upon one another's ideas. Support your points with evidence and ask meaningful questions.

Discussion Model

Student 1: I think the quote from Woody Guthrie is really interesting. Usually, I think of songs as entertainment, but for him, they meant a lot more. It seems like he learned as many songs as he could during his travels.

Student 2: And Guthrie spent a lot of time with people who had lost everything in hard times. Maybe he understood how important music was to the people he met. There wasn't much to be happy about during the Great Depression.

Student 3: That's a good point. He wanted his songs to make people feel good about themselves and their lives. I wonder what his songs say and what they sound like.

❺ Research

Targeted research can clarify unfamiliar details and shed light on various aspects of a text. Consider questions that arise in your mind as you read, and use those questions as the basis for research.

Research Model

Questions: *What songs did Woody Guthrie write? How did his songs influence other musicians?*

Key Words for Internet Search: "Woody Guthrie" and music

Result: WoodyGuthrie.org, The Guardian (U.K.)

What I Learned: Woody Guthrie was an important writer of folk and children's songs, including "This Land Is Your Land" and "So Long (It's Been Good to Know You)." His music inspired many modern songwriters, including Bob Dylan and Bruce Springsteen.

❻ Write

Writing about a text will deepen your understanding of it and will also allow you to share your ideas more formally with others. The following model essay evaluates the author's biographical essay about Woody Guthrie and cites evidence to support the main ideas.

Writing Model: Informative Text

An Introduction to Woody Guthrie

In "Rambling 'Round," Elizabeth Partridge introduces readers to Woody Guthrie, a free-spirited man who traveled across America writing songs inspired by the people he met. The author's engaging portrait of Guthrie makes readers want to learn more about the man and his music.

> In the first paragraph, the writer clearly states the purpose of the essay.

Partridge begins the biography with a quotation from Guthrie, allowing readers to hear his "voice." "I hate a song that makes you think you are just born to lose," he says. "I am out to fight those kind of songs to my very last breath of air and my last drop of blood." In other words, songs were more to Guthrie than just words and a melody. Instead, Guthrie saw his music as a way to give people hope.

> The writer includes direct quotations from the text and analyzes what they mean.

Guthrie lived and wrote during a period of great hardship. In the 1930s, the Great Depression caused many banks to fail and factories to close, leaving people without jobs or money. The "flophouses, hobo jungles, and Hoovervilles" in which Guthrie spent time were temporary shelters for people who were looking for ways to make a living.

However, even though Guthrie lived during hard times, Partridge portrays him as easygoing. She uses short clauses, strung together into long, descriptive sentences that paint a clear picture of the songwriter: "He'd stick out his thumb and hitchhike, swing onto moving freight trains, and hunker down with other traveling men." Partridge also gives readers a clear sense of Guthrie's "ramblin'." She uses phrases such as "hit the road," "hunker down," "restlessly," and "running around" to describe his actions. Partridge rounds out her portrayal of Guthrie by showing that even though he acted carefree, he told the truth in his music: Even if it is sometimes "rough-edged" and "hard-bitten," life is still full of "hope and love."

> Examples from the text support the writer's claims about the author's style.

"Rambling 'Round" should encourage readers to find recordings of Guthrie's music and listen to songs like "This Land Is Your Land" and "So Long (Been Good to Know You)." Guthrie died in 1967, but his influence upon songwriters lives on. Today, musicians such as Bob Dylan and Bruce Springsteen keep Guthrie's legacy alive in their own music.

> Details and facts obtained through research support the writer's evaluation of the text and provide a useful reference for the reader.

---

❻ Write

Review the writing model with the class, using the annotations to analyze how the writer uses evidence to support his or her ideas.

Genre Requirements

Remind students that when they write responses to literature, they should do the following:

- Introduce the topic at the beginning of the essay.
- Organize ideas and information in order to make important connections.
- Support claims with specific details from the literary work.
- Provide a conclusion that supports the information presented.

Teaching from the Writing Model

1. Point out that the thesis, or subject of the essay, is clearly stated in the first paragraph.

2. Note that the writer cites examples from the text and from outside research to support the claims.

3. Point out that the last paragraph restates the thesis and calls readers to action.

CLOSE READING TOOL

Students may close read and mark the text using the **Close Reading Tool**, which is available online. Scaffolds are provided for students who need help. Students who do not have online access may use the *Close Reading Notebook* to mark the text with their close reading responses.

(7) Independent Practice

The Independent Practice is an optional assignment. You may wish to administer it at this point and use it as formative assessment, or you may wish to administer it at the end of Part 1 as summative assessment.

If you wish to administer the Independent Practice but feel your students will struggle with it, you can use the questions in the side margins of this Teacher Edition to help guide them.

(8) Craft and Structure

Ask: What does the title tell you about this text and the author's purpose?

Possible response: It is a diary. It was probably written to record the author's feelings and experiences.

(9) Key Ideas and Details

Ask: How would you describe the author and her point of view about the world?

Possible response: Her point of view is that of an 11-year-old girl. She is a normal child who goes to school, takes tests, goes on field trips, and listens to her mother.

◄)) Audio

Selection Audio is available in the *Student eText* and on the *Hear It!* CD-ROM.

As you read the following selection, apply the close reading strategies you have learned. You may need to read the selection multiple times.

(8) from Zlata's Diary

by Zlata Filipović

Monday, March 30, 1992

Hey, Diary! You know what I think? Since Anne Frank[1] called her diary Kitty, maybe I could give you a name too. What about:
   ASFALTINA PIDZAMETA
   SEFIKA HIKMETA
   SEVALA MIMMY
or something else???
   I'm thinking, thinking . . .
   I've decided! I'm going to call you
   MIMMY
   All right, then, let's start.

Dear Mimmy,
It's almost half-term. We're all studying for our tests. Tomorrow we're supposed to go to a classical music concert at the Skenderija Hall. Our teacher says we shouldn't go because there will be 10,000 people, pardon me, children, there, and somebody might take us as hostages or plant a bomb in the concert hall. Mommy says I shouldn't go. So I won't.

Hey! You know who won the Yugovision Song Contest?! EXTRA NENA!!!???

I'm afraid to say this next thing. Melica says she heard at the hairdresser's that on Saturday, April 4, 1992, there's going to be BOOM—BOOM, BANG—BANG, CRASH Sarajevo. Translation: they're going to bomb Sarajevo.

Love,
Zlata

Meet the Author

When she was a girl, **Zlata Filipović** (b. 1980) kept a diary in which she wrote about life in the war-torn city of Sarajevo, which was under attack between 1992 and 1996. Her diary has been translated into over 30 languages and is read around the world.

CLOSE READING TOOL

Read and respond to this selection online using the Close Reading Tool.

---

1. **Anne Frank** In 1942, 13-year-old Anne Frank began a diary that she kept for the two years she and her family and some others hid from the Nazis in an attic in Amsterdam. Anne died in a concentration camp in 1945. Her father published parts of the diary in 1947, and it has since become a classic.

© ACTIVE READING FOR COMMON CORE

Read • Discuss • Research • Write
In the Independent Practice section of the Close Reading Workshop, students will practice the reading, discussing, researching, and writing strategies they learned in the modeling section. They will also deepen their essential understanding of the Big Question.

Read: Students will read and comprehend the selection. They should note significant points in the text that relate to Key Ideas and Details, Craft and Structure, and Integration of Knowledge and Ideas. They should use the annotations in the Reading Model that they read earlier as a guide. After students have

finished reading the story, they will answer Literary Analysis questions.

Discuss: Students will deepen their understanding of the text through collaborative discussion.

Research: Students will clarify and expand their understanding of the text by conducting research.

Write: Students will synthesize their thoughts and research by writing a response to the text, supporting their ideas with evidence.

Sunday, April 12, 1992

Dear Mimmy,

The new sections of town—Dobrinja, Mojmilo, Vojnicko polje—are being badly shelled. Everything is being destroyed, burned, the people are in shelters. Here in the middle of town, where we live, it's different. It's quiet.

People go out. It was a nice warm spring day today. We went out too. Vaso Miskin Street was full of people, children. It looked like a peace march. People came out to be together, they don't want war. They want to live and enjoy themselves the way they used to. That's only natural, isn't it? Who likes or wants war, when it's the worst thing in the world?

I keep thinking about the march I joined today. It's bigger and stronger than war. That's why it will win. The people must be the ones to win, not the war, because war has nothing to do with humanity. War is something inhuman.

                                                      Zlata

Tuesday, April 14, 1992

Dear Mimmy,

People are leaving Sarajevo. The airport, train and bus stations are packed. I saw sad pictures on TV of people parting. Families, friends separating. Some are leaving, others staying. It's so sad. Why? These people and children aren't guilty of anything. Keka and Braco[2] came early this morning. They're in the kitchen with Mommy and Daddy, whispering. Keka and Mommy are crying. I don't think they know what to do—whether to stay or to go. Neither way is good.

                                                      Zlata

---

2. **Keka and Braco** nicknames of a husband and wife who are friends of Zlata's parents.

10 Craft and Structure

Ask: To what does Zlata compare the crowd of people? Why does she say it will "win"?

Possible response: She compares it to a peace march. She says it will "win" because people are stronger than war, which "has nothing to do with humanity."

11 Integration of Knowledge and Ideas

Ask: What fact does Zlata offer at the beginning of this entry? What earlier idea about war does this fact support?

Possible response: Many people are leaving the city. People are leaving because "War is something inhuman."

12 Craft and Structure

Ask: Compare this entry to the first one. How has Zlata's purpose for writing changed?

Possible response: Earlier, she wanted to record the happy events in the life of an 11-year-old girl. Now, she is recording and processing the terrible events she is experiencing.

13 Craft and Structure

Ask: Which word in this sentence has strong negative connotations? What does this word make you see or feel?

Possible response: The word *devoured* has strong negative connotations. It causes the reader to imagine a wild animal doing something violent; it creates feelings of fear and dread.

14 Craft and Structure

Ask: How would you describe the tone of these sentences?

Possible response: The tone might be described as sad, mournful, hopeless, or pained.

Dear Mimmy,

Today was truly, absolutely the worst day ever in Sarajevo. The shooting started around noon. Mommy and I moved into the hall. Daddy was in his office, under our apartment, at the time. We **12** told him on the intercom to run quickly to the downstairs lobby where we'd meet him. We brought Cicko[3] with us. The gunfire was getting worse, and we couldn't get over the wall to the Bobars',[4] so we ran down to our own cellar.

The cellar is ugly, dark, smelly. Mommy, who's terrified of mice, had two fears to cope with. The three of us were in the same corner as the other day. We listened to the pounding shells, the shooting, the thundering noise overhead. We even heard planes. At one moment I realized that this awful cellar was the only place that could save our lives. Suddenly, it started to look almost warm and nice. It was the only way we could defend ourselves against all this terrible shooting. We heard glass shattering in our street. Horrible. I put my fingers in my ears to block out the terrible sounds. I was worried about Cicko. We had left him behind in the lobby. Would he catch cold there? Would something hit him? I was terribly hungry and thirsty. We had left our half-cooked lunch in the kitchen.

When the shooting died down a bit, Daddy ran over to our apartment and brought us back some sandwiches. He said he could smell something burning and that the phones weren't working. He brought our TV set down to the cellar. That's when we learned that the main post office (near us) was on fire and that they had kidnapped our President. At around 8:00 we went back up to our apartment. Almost every window in our street was broken. Ours were all right, thank God. I saw the post office in flames. A terrible sight. The fire-fighters battled with **13** the raging fire. Daddy took a few photos of the post office being devoured by the flames. He said they wouldn't come out because I had been fiddling with something on the camera. I was sorry. The whole apartment smelled of the burning fire. God, and I used to pass by there every day. It had just been done up. It was **14** huge and beautiful, and now it was being swallowed up by the flames. It was disappearing. That's what this neighborhood of mine looks like, my Mimmy.

---

3. **Cicko** (chēk´ ō) Zlata's canary.
4. **Bobars'** (Bō´ bërs) next-door neighbors.

I wonder what it's like in other parts of town? I heard on the radio that it was awful around the Eternal Flame.[5] The place is knee-deep in glass. We're worried about Grandma and Granddad. They live there. Tomorrow, if we can go out, we'll see how they are. A terrible day. This has been the worst, most awful day in my eleven-year-old life. I hope it will be the only one. Mommy and Daddy are very edgy. I have to go to bed.

Ciao![6]
Zlata

Tuesday, May 5, 1992

Dear Mimmy,
The shooting seems to be dying down. I guess they've caused enough misery, although I don't know why. It has something to do with politics. I just hope the "kids" come to some agreement. Oh, if only they would, so we could live and breathe as human beings again. The things that have happened here these past few days are terrible. I want it to stop forever. PEACE! PEACE!

I didn't tell you, Mimmy, that we've rearranged things in the apartment. My room and Mommy and Daddy's are too dangerous to be in. They face the hills, which is where they're shooting from. If only you knew how scared I am to go near the windows and into those rooms. So, we turned a safe corner of the sitting room into a "bedroom." We sleep on mattresses on the floor. It's strange and awful. But, it's safer that way. We've turned everything around for safety. We put Cicko in the kitchen. He's safe there, although once the shooting starts there's nowhere safe except the cellar. I suppose all this will stop and we'll all go back to our usual places.

Ciao!
Zlata

---

5. **Eternal Flame** Sarajevo landmark that honors those who died resisting the Nazi occupation during World War II.
6. **Ciao!** (chou) *interj.* hello or goodbye.

15 Key Ideas and Details
Ask: What idea has Zlata begun to repeat? State it in your own words.

Possible response: War is terrible.

16 Key Ideas and Details
Ask: Do you think Zlata is being realistic about the situation she and her family are in? Explain.

Possible response: No, there is no indication that the violence will end and things will return to normal.

17 Integration of Knowledge and Ideas

Ask: How does this anecdote help Zlata express what she is experiencing? Why might Zlata have thought it was important to record this information in her diary?

Possible response: It starts with a hopeful idea but then presents a violent event. The anecdote shows how Zlata's emotions fluctuate between hope and fear. Zlata may have wanted to record Nina's death in her diary because it affected her personally. This is the first time in the diary when someone Zlata knows personally has suffered death because of the war.

18 Craft and Structure

Ask: What feeling does Zlata convey by capitalizing these words?

Possible response: The capital letters convey extreme anger and frustration.

Thursday, May 7, 1992

Dear Mimmy,

I was almost positive the war would stop, but today . . . Today a shell fell on the park in front of my house, the park where I used to play and sit with my girlfriends. A lot of people were hurt. From what I hear Jaca, Jaca's mother, Selma, Nina, our neighbor Dado and who knows how many other people who happened to be there were wounded. Dado, Jaca and her mother have come home from the hospital, Selma lost a kidney but I don't know how she is, because she's still in the hospital. AND NINA IS DEAD. A piece of shrapnel lodged in her brain and she died. She was such a sweet, nice little girl. We went to kindergarten together, and we used to play together in the park. Is it possible I'll never see Nina again? Nina, an innocent eleven-year-old little girl—the victim of a stupid war. I feel sad. I cry and wonder why? She didn't do anything. A disgusting war has destroyed a young child's life. Nina. I'll always remember you as a wonderful little girl.

Love, Mimmy,
Zlata

Monday, June 29, 1992

Dear Mimmy,

BOREDOM!!! SHOOTING!!! SHELLING!!! PEOPLE BEING KILLED!!! DESPAIR!!! HUNGER!!! MISERY!!! FEAR!!!

That's my life! The life of an innocent eleven-year-old schoolgirl!! A schoolgirl without a school, without the fun and excitement of school. A child without games, without friends, without the sun, without birds, without nature, without fruit, without chocolate or sweets, with just a little powdered milk. In short, a child without a childhood. A wartime child. I now realize that I am really living through a war, I am witnessing an ugly, disgusting war. I and thousands of other children in this town that is being destroyed, that is crying, weeping, seeking help, but getting none. God, will this ever stop, will I ever be a schoolgirl again, will I ever enjoy my childhood again? I once heard that childhood is the most wonderful time of your life. And it is. I loved it, and now an ugly war is taking it all away from me. Why? I feel sad. I feel like crying. I am crying.

Your Zlata

Thursday, October 29, 1992

Dear Mimmy,

Mommy and Auntie Ivanka (from her office) have received grants to specialize in Holland. They have letters of guarantee,[7] and there's even one for me. But Mommy can't decide. If she accepts, she leaves behind Daddy, her parents, her brother. I think it's a hard decision to make. One minute I think—no, I'm against it. But then I remember the war, winter, hunger, my stolen childhood and I feel like going. Then I think of Daddy, Grandma and Granddad, and I don't want to go. It's hard to know what to do. I'm really on edge, Mimmy, I can't write anymore.

Your Zlata

Monday, November 2, 1992

Dear Mimmy,

Mommy thought it over, talked to Daddy, Grandma and Granddad, and to me, and she's decided to go. The reason for her decision is—ME. What's happening in Sarajevo is already too much for me, and the coming winter will make it even harder. All right. But . . . well, I suppose it's better for me to go. I really can't stand it here anymore. I talked to Auntie Ivanka today and she told me that this war is hardest on the children, and that the children should be got out of the city. Daddy will manage, maybe he'll even get to come with us.

Ciao!
Zlata

---

7. **letters of guarantee** letters from people or companies promising to help individuals who wanted to leave the country during the war.

19 Craft and Structure

Ask: These two entries tell a story. What elements make the story suspenseful? What key idea does the story support?

Possible response: Several elements make the story suspenseful: the break between the two entries, the "on the one hand … on the other hand" structure of the ideas, and the author's own mixed feelings. The story supports the idea that war makes life unbearable.

20 Key Ideas and Details

Ask: What kind of supporting details does Zlata provide here?

Possible response: Zlata describes the birthday gifts she received and the food she ate at her party. These details support the idea that her family made a great effort to provide the presents and food that Zlata enjoys for her birthday.

21 Integration of Knowledge and Ideas

Ask: How do all the examples given above strengthen Zlata's key idea?

Possible response: They highlight the fact that peace is far more valuable than any collection of things.

Thursday, December 3, 1992

Dear Mimmy,

Today is my birthday. My first wartime birthday. Twelve years old. Congratulations. Happy birthday to me!

The day started off with kisses and congratulations. First Mommy and Daddy, then everyone else. Mommy and Daddy gave me three Chinese vanity cases—with flowers on them!

As usual there was no electricity. Auntie Melica came with her family (Kenan, Naida, Nihad) and gave me a book. And Braco Lajtner came, of course. The whole neighborhood got together in the evening. I got chocolate, vitamins, a heart-shaped soap (small, orange), a key chain with a picture of Maja and Bojana, a pendant made of a stone from Cyprus, a ring (silver) and **20** earrings (bingo!).

The table was nicely laid, with little rolls, fish and rice salad, cream cheese (with Feta), canned corned beef, a pie, and, of course—a birthday cake. Not how it used to be, but there's a war on. Luckily there was no shooting, so we could celebrate.

21 It was nice, but something was missing. It's called peace!

Your Zlata

Tuesday, July 27, 1993

Dear Mimmy,

Journalists, reporters, TV and radio crews from all over the world (even Japan). They're interested in you, Mimmy, and ask me about you, but also about me. It's exciting. Nice. Unusual for a wartime child.

My days have changed a little. They're more interesting now. It takes my mind off things. When I go to bed at night I think about the day behind me. Nice, as though it weren't wartime, and with such thoughts I happily fall asleep.

But in the morning, when the wheels of the water carts wake me up, I realize that there's a war on, that mine is a wartime life. SHOOTING, NO ELECTRICITY, NO WATER, NO GAS, NO FOOD. Almost no life.

Zlata

Thursday, October 7, 1993

Dear Mimmy,

Things are the way they used to be, lately. There's no shooting (thank God), I go to school, read, play the piano . . .

Winter is approaching, but we have nothing to heat with.

I look at the calendar and it seems as though this year of 1993 will again be marked by war. God, we've lost two years listening to gunfire, battling with electricity, water, food, and waiting for peace.

I look at Mommy and Daddy. In two years they've aged ten. And me? I haven't aged, but I've grown, although I honestly don't know how. I don't eat fruit or vegetables, I don't drink juices, I don't eat meat . . . I am a child of rice, peas and spaghetti. There I am talking about food again. I often catch myself dreaming about chicken, a good cutlet, pizza, lasagna . . . Oh, enough of that.

Zlata

22 **Key Ideas and Details**
Ask: Why does Zlata find the journalists' attention "unusual"?

Possible response: She is used to hiding to stay safe and making do with too little.

23 **Craft and Structure**
Ask: Zlata says her family battled with the electricity. What attitude toward life does this word suggest?

Possible response: It suggests that life is a constant struggle.

SETTING EXPECTATIONS

24 Craft and Structure

Ask: What is Zlata's tone in this entry? Why?

Possible response: Zlata's tone is happy and upbeat because she has made a new friend.

25 Integration of Knowledge and Ideas

Ask: How does the key idea of this entry differ from earlier ones?

Possible response: Earlier, Zlata repeated the idea that war is horrible. Here, she expresses the idea that the terrible times are behind her and better times lie ahead.

26 Key Ideas and Details

Ask: What does Zlata want her readers—and herself—to believe is true?

Possible response: She wants to convince herself and her readers that her nightmare of living in a war-torn nation has ended.

Tuesday, October 12, 1993

Dear Mimmy,
I don't remember whether I told you that last summer I sent a letter through school to a pen-pal in America. It was a letter for an American girl or boy.

Today I got an answer. A boy wrote to me. His name is Brandon, he's twelve like me, and lives in Harrisburg, Pennsylvania. It really made me happy.

24 I don't know who invented the mail and letters, but thank you whoever you are. I now have a friend in America, and Brandon has a friend in Sarajevo. This is my first letter from across the Atlantic. And in it is a reply envelope, and a lovely pencil.

A Canadian TV crew and journalist from *The Sunday Times* (Janine) came to our gym class today. They brought me two chocolate bars. What a treat. It's been a long time since I've had sweets.

Love,
Zlata

December 1993

Dear Mimmy,
PARIS. There's electricity, there's water, there's gas. There's, there's . . . life, Mimmy. Yes, life; bright lights, traffic, people, food . . . Don't think I've gone nuts, Mimmy. Hey, listen to me, Paris!? No, I'm not crazy, I'm not kidding, it really is Paris and (can you believe it?) me in it. Me, my Mommy and my Daddy. At last. You're 100% sure I'm crazy, but I'm serious, I'm telling you, dear Mimmy, that I have arrived in Paris. I've come to be with you. You're mine again now and together we're moving into the light. The darkness has played out its part. The darkness **25** is behind us; now we're bathed in light lit by good people. Remember that—good people. Bulb by bulb, not candles, but bulb by bulb, and me bathing in the lights of Paris. Yes, Paris. Incredible. You don't understand. You know, I don't think I **26** understand either. I feel as though I must be crazy, dreaming, as though it's a fairy tale, but it's all TRUE.

If you are using the Independent Practice as formative assessment, use the rubric below to evaluate students' performances.

Independent Practice Rubric	Rating Scale				
Close Reading: How well does the student use close reading strategies to answer the questions?	*not very* 1	2	3	4	*very* 5
Support/Elaboration: How well does the student support points with textual or other evidence?	1	2	3	4	5
Insight: How original, sophisticated, or compelling are the insights the student achieves?	1	2	3	4	5
Expression of Ideas: How well does the student use language, including word choice and conventions, in the expression of ideas?	1	2	3	4	5

Close Reading Activities

Comprehension: **Key Ideas and Details**

1. Infer: Why does Zlata decide to give her diary a name?

2. (a) What hardships do Zlata and her family endure during the war? **(b) Analyze:** Why did Zlata still have mixed feelings about leaving Sarajevo?

3. (a) Describe Zlata's birthday party. **(b) Connect:** Based on earlier diary entries, what gift does she most want?

4. Summarize: Write a brief, objective summary of the diary. Cite story details.

Text Analysis: **Craft and Structure**

5. Zlata describes the horrors of war from a specific point of view. How might her perspective differ from that of her parents?

6. (a) Analyze: Why is the fact that this is a diary important to consider? **(b) Explain:** How would your understanding of the text change if *Zlata's Diary* was a fictional story?

7. (a) What is Zlata's purpose for starting a diary? **(b) Analyze:** How does this purpose change over time?

8. (a) Describe the *tone*—the writer's attitude—of the last entry. **(b) Analyze:** What words and phrases create this tone?

Connections: **Integration of Knowledge and Ideas**

Discuss
Conduct a **small-group discussion** about the themes that develop over the course of *Zlata's Diary.* Why do you think she does not talk about the causes of the war or about the politics of either side?

Research
The events in *Zlata's Diary* happen in a particular time and place. Briefly research the following:

a. Sarajevo

b. The civil war in the former Yugoslavia

c. Similar texts, such as the *Diary of Anne Frank*

Take notes as you perform your research. Then, write a brief **explanation** of why

information about historical events and setting helps you understand Zlata's experiences.

Write
Zlata describes a peace march as being "bigger and stronger than war." Write an **essay** in which you analyze her statement. What does Zlata mean? How is the theme of peace emphasized throughout the diary? Cite details to support your analysis.

> **What is important to know?**
> *Zlata's Diary* is read all over the world. What does Zlata write about in her diary that is important to know? Explain your answer.

Discuss
Responses should include discussions of innocence and the way ordinary people cope with and survive hardships.

Research
Students should use the research topics to understand the setting of Zlata's story.

Write
Student essays should identify the meaning of the statement and cite passages from the story that illustrate the theme of peace.

> **What is important to know?**
> Responses should build on the research topic and address the universal themes in *Zlata's Diary.* Students should state the aspects of the story they think are important to know and tell why.

☑ **ASSESS**

Possible responses appear below. Check to be sure students support their responses with evidence from the text.

1. She is following the style of Anne Frank, who also lived during conflict and named her diary. It also makes the diary more personable, as if it were a friend.

2. (a) They hid in a cellar; they lost friends; they were hungry and afraid. **(b)** She did not want to leave her family, but she was eager to get away from the war.

3. (a) She celebrates with a special meal and a birthday cake. **(b)** peace and an end to the war

4. Summaries should include key points in the diary's time line, such as the bombings, Nina's death, and the escape to Paris.

5. She is a child who misses the carefree life she had before the war. Her parents may have written more about the causes of the war.

6. (a) The events are true (nonfiction) and come from the point of view of one person with whom the reader identifies (autobiography). **(b)** The story might be more difficult to believe if the events happened to a made-up character rather than to a real person.

7. (a) to have a "friend" to confide in **(b)** The diary became a historical record of living through a war.

8. (a) relieved, disbelieving **(b)** She talks about moving out the "darkness" into the "light." That shows relief—because dark is frightening—and disbelieving because light is dazzling if you have been in the dark for a long time.

❶ About the Quotation

John Barth (b. 1930) is an American novelist and short-story writer.

Discussion Ask students to discuss the meaning of Barth's quotation about life stories. Then ask them to decide whether they agree with the quotation. Have them explain and support their positions with sound reasoning and evidence.

❷ Critical Viewing

Pose the critical viewing question to the class. Then, guide the class in a discussion about the question. Encourage students to build upon each other's ideas as they share their responses. Remind students to support their responses with reasons and evidence.

❶ "**Everyone** is necessarily the **hero** of his own life story."

—John Barth

❓ DEVELOPING ESSENTIAL UNDERSTANDING

What is important to know?
Explain to students that they will continue to consider the Big Question as they work through the selections in Part 2 of the unit.

• As students read each selection, they will look for details related to the Big Question and take notes.

• At the end of each selection, students will answer a Literary Analysis question that is related to the Big Question.

• Students will deepen their knowledge of the selections and their understanding of the Big Question through reading, speaking, listening, researching, and writing.

PART 2
TEXT ANALYSIS GUIDED EXPLORATION

LIFE STORIES

In this section, authors share their own memories of personal struggles and unique achievements. Consider the quotation on the opposite page, and think about the ways a person can triumph from both mistakes and accomplishments, no matter how big or small.

2 ◄ CRITICAL VIEWING How does this photograph represent the idea of looking both forward and back over one's life and experiences?

3 READINGS IN PART 2

AUTOBIOGRAPHY
The Drive-In Movies
Gary Soto
(p. 186)

PERSONAL NARRATIVE
Names/Nombres
Julia Alvarez
(p. 196)

MEMOIR
Langston Terrace
Eloise Greenfield
(p. 208)

REFLECTIVE ESSAY
from **The Pigman & Me**
Paul Zindel
(p. 218)

CLOSE READING TOOL

Use the Close Reading Tool to practice the strategies you learned in this unit.

PART 2 • Life Stories **179**

CUSTOMIZING THE TEXT SET

Close Reading Tool
Use the Close Reading Tool to project the selections on a whiteboard and work through them as a whole-class activity. Students also have the opportunity to read these selections independently, with scaffolds available as needed.

Curriculum Builder
Customize this program by rearranging existing selections, adding selection titles of your choosing, and uploading your own resources—all online!

---

3 Readings in Part 2
About the Texts
(For quantitative and qualitative measures of text complexity, see the rubrics on the opening pages of each selection.)

AUTOBIOGRAPHY: The Drive-In Movies

Summary A young Gary Soto works extra hard doing chores so that he can go to a drive-in movie. Unfortunately, he is so tired when he gets there that he falls asleep.

PERSONAL NARRATIVE: Names/Nombres

Summary Julia Alvarez recalls her family's early years as Dominican immigrants in America. Eager to fit in at school, Alvarez allows herself to be called American names and nicknames.

MEMOIR: Langston Terrace

Summary On Eloise Greenfield's ninth birthday, she and her family moved to a newly built low-rent housing project in Washington, D.C. She describes this "growing-up place," where she and her friends experienced a real sense of community.

REFLECTIVE ESSAY: *from* The Pigman & Me

Summary In this memoir excerpt, Paul is at a new school where he accidentally hits John with a paddle. When John vows revenge after school, Paul is terrified to fight. He gets advice from Nonno Frankie. Paul survives the fight, using this advice, his own wits, and the help of an unexpected savior.

 **Audio**

Summary Audio is available in the *Student eText* and on the *Hear It!* CD-ROM.

❶ Elements of Nonfiction

1. Introduce the elements of nonfiction, using the instruction on the student page.

Have students name as many forms of nonfiction as they can. Write students' responses on the board. Then, ask students to identify the purpose of each form listed and to tell whether it is informative, narrative, or literary.

Sample responses: encyclopedia (to inform; informative); newspaper article (to inform, persuade, and/or entertain; informative); history book (to provide information and to tell a story; informative and narrative); biography (to inform and to entertain; informative, narrative, literary).

Guide students to understand that nonfiction works can have several purposes and can therefore be difficult to categorize.

2. Referring to the chart on the student page, introduce the elements of nonfiction texts. Explain that these elements are not unique to nonfiction: works of fiction employ them, too. However, nonfiction writers use these elements to communicate ideas or experiences related to real life.

3. Write *letter to the editor* on the board. Guide students to generate a possible purpose and point of view for an editorial letter about a topic such as women in sports, as well as words and images that might appear in the letter.

Sample response: *Purpose—* urging more coverage of women's sports; *Point of view—*women's sports fan; *Words—unpredictable, fast-paced; Imagery—*players have the "hearts of warriors" and deserve "the spotlight."

 # Focus on Craft and Structure

❶ Elements of Nonfiction

Nonfiction writing tells about **real people, places, objects,** or **events.**

Nonfiction writing is about real life. Some forms of nonfiction, such as histories, have been around since ancient times. Others, such as blogs and Web pages, came into being more recently. Nonfiction writing changes with people and technology. It is a large, ever-developing category of literature. Still, all forms of nonfiction have certain basic elements.

- They are written for one or more **purposes,** or reasons.
- They express the writer's unique **point of view,** or perspective, about a subject.
- They use words and phrases that project a certain **tone,** or attitude.
- They **develop or explain ideas** in a logical, organized way.

Informative Texts Many nonfiction texts—like this textbook—are informative. Their main purpose is to inform, or give information to the reader. Newspaper reports, encyclopedia articles, and science books are examples of informative texts.

Narrative Nonfiction Narrative nonfiction tells the story of real people, places, things, and events. These texts usually aim to entertain *and* inform the reader. They might tell the story of a single person's life or the story of an entire group of people. They might describe a dramatic, real-life event.

Literary Nonfiction Authors of literary nonfiction use elements of literature, such as language, in creative ways. They choose words that stir up feelings in the reader. These writers may also use the kinds of comparisons you might find in a poem, or they may include vivid details to make their writing rich and interesting.

The best nonfiction writing opens new windows on the world for the reader. It says, "This is what I see, from the place where I happen to be."

Nonfiction texts . . .	This element of nonfiction is called . . .
Are written from the unique perspective of the author.	Point of View
Are written for one or more reasons.	Author's Purpose
Use specific words to convey specific meanings.	Word Choice
Use vivid details that appeal to the five senses: sight, sound, touch, taste, and smell.	Imagery
Organize ideas in ways that are easy for readers to follow.	Organization

② Forms of Nonfiction

There are many forms of nonfiction.

An **autobiography** is a story about the writer's own life, told by the writer. Autobiographies take many different forms.

- A **memoir** describes one or more meaningful events, and may express strong feelings.
- A **diary** is a personal record of events and experiences. Most diaries are updated regularly.
- An **autobiographical sketch** is a brief description of the high points of a person's life.

An **essay** is a short work about a single subject. Essays are written for many purposes.

- A **persuasive essay, or argument,** is meant to convince readers to adopt a particular point of view or take a certain action.
- A **narrative essay** tells the story of an event that

happened in real life, often one that the writer witnessed, or saw.

- An **expository essay** presents facts, ideas, and explanations.
- A **reflective essay** presents the writer's thoughts and beliefs about a subject or an event.

A **speech** is an oral, or spoken, presentation of a speaker's ideas and beliefs.

- **Persuasive speeches** urge listeners to adopt certain beliefs or take certain actions.
- An **address** is a formal speech to a specific group of people. It may offer deep thoughts on an important occasion.
- A **talk** is an informal presentation in which the speaker shares his or her knowledge on a subject.

**Common Core
State Standards**

Reading Informational Text

3. Analyze in detail how a key individual, event, or idea is introduced, illustrated, and elaborated in a text.

4. Determine the meaning of words and phrases as they are used in a text, including the figurative, connotative, and technical meanings.

5. Analyze how a particular sentence, paragraph, chapter, or section fits into the overall structure of a text and contributes to the development of the ideas.

6. Determine an author's point of view or purpose in a text and explain how it is conveyed in the text.

③ Other Forms of Nonfiction

Advertisement	Letter	Editorial	Functional Text
• Written for a target audience who might be interested in a product or service • Often includes visuals • Aims to persuade	• Addressed to a specific individual or group • May be personal or formal • Aims to share thoughts, describe events, or request action or information	• States the writer's position on an issue • Featured in newspapers or magazines • Aims to persuade	• Presents facts in an easy-to-read form • Examples include schedules, menus, charts • Aims to inform

② Forms of Nonfiction

1. Introduce the forms of nonfiction, using the instruction on the student page.
2. Discuss students' experiences in reading the various forms described on this page. Ask whether students are more interested in some forms than in others, and why. If students have attended speeches, addresses, or talks, have them describe the occasion and qualities that made each presentation effective or ineffective, in their view.

③ Other Forms of Nonfiction

1. Introduce the additional forms of nonfiction, using the chart.
2. **Ask:** What type of nonfiction text is a thank-you note to your aunt?
   Answer: a letter
3. **Ask:** What type of nonfiction text is an instruction manual for a toaster?
   Answer: a functional text
4. **Ask:** What type of nonfiction text is a poster for a bake sale?
   Answer: an advertisement

❶ Determining Author's Purpose, Point of View, and Development of Ideas

1. Introduce the concepts of author's purpose and point of view, using the instruction on the student page.

2. On the board, write the following: *a biography of a pop star; a diary written during a move to a new city; an essay about the impacts of an oil spill; a political campaign speech.* Then, have students identify likely purposes for each text. Remind students that many nonfiction texts have more than one purpose.

   Sample responses:
   Biography—to inform, to entertain; *Diary*—to describe, to express feelings; *Essay*—to describe, to inform, to persuade; *Speech*—to persuade, to inform, to entertain

3. Discuss point of view, using the example provided. Explain that every text contains clues that hint at the author's values and beliefs. **Ask:** What words in the speech tell you that the author values the students and believes life is a learning process?

   Answer: *celebrate, lessons*

4. Discuss connotations, using the examples in the chart. **Ask:** Which words in the graduation speech stir up positive feelings?

   Answer: *celebrate, accomplishments, learn*

5. After discussing tone, read the graduation speech excerpt aloud in a formal but upbeat voice. Then, **ask:** How would you describe the tone of this speech?

   Possible responses: formal, respectful, reverent

---

❶ Determining Author's Purpose, Point of View, and Development of Ideas

A nonfiction text is written for specific **purposes**. Its **key ideas** convey the author's unique **point of view**.

Author's Purpose An author's purpose is his or her main reason for writing. Nonfiction texts are often written to **inform, persuade, entertain, describe,** or **express feelings.** In many cases, an author has more than one reason for writing. For example, an author might write an essay about the impacts of an oil spill to describe and to persuade.

Point of View Every writer views his or her subject through a certain lens, or **point of view,** that is shaped by the writer's values and beliefs.

> **Example: Graduation Speech**
> Today we celebrate your goals and accomplishments. We also celebrate your past and future failures—and the lessons that you have learned and will learn from them.

> **Point of View**
> The author respects the students, values the marking of occasions, and views life as a learning process.

Word Choice Looking closely at an author's word choice can help you understand his or her point of view. Authors choose specific words and phrases to stir up positive or negative feelings, or **connotations.**

Idea: "Love your neighbor"	Author's Point of View
Positive Connotation: We all know the **timeless truth** "Love your neighbor."	The author values the saying.
Negative Connotation: We have all heard the **tired cliché** "Love your neighbor."	The author finds the saying meaningless.

Tone Tone is the feeling or attitude that you can "hear" in the lines of a work. Tone can usually be summed up in a single word. The tone of the first sentence in the chart shown above might be described as approving. The tone of the second sentence might be described as critical.

 THINK ALOUD

Theme
To model the skill of determining an author's point of view, use the following think aloud. Say to students:

> To determine an author's point of view, I do two things: I look at the text, and I think about the author of the text. When I look at the text, I look at the specific words, phrases, and sentences the author uses. In the graduation speech example, the author uses the words *celebrate* and *accomplishments*. These tell me that the author has a positive point of view. However, she also refers to "past and future failures" and "lessons you will learn." Why would she mention failures if she has a positive point of view?
>
> To figure this out, I think about the person writing the text. I think about the author's larger worldview. She says that she celebrates the students' failures because they will learn from them. In her worldview, failures are valuable; they are positive, not negative, experiences. This verifies that the author's point of view is positive. She respects the students and values life as a learning process.

Key Idea All nonfiction texts center on one or more **key ideas.** A key idea is the central idea a writer wishes to convey. Key ideas are usually linked to an author's purpose and the type of text he or she is writing.

- In a persuasive speech meant to convince listeners to vote, the key idea might be: Voting is an important right and responsibility for Americans.
- In an essay meant to reflect on sports in society, the key idea might be: Athletes should be role models.

Key ideas are sometimes stated directly; other times, they are *implied,* or suggested. To understand implied ideas, examine all the parts and details of the text to see what they have in common. Look for the key idea of each paragraph and see how it relates to the overall key idea of the text.

Developing and Supporting the Key Idea Whether stated or unstated, a key idea must be developed and supported. Writers use different types of details to elaborate a key idea. The following chart provides examples of various kinds of support that may be used to devlop a key idea.

Type of Support	Example
Anecdotes: brief stories used to make a point	"When I was a boy," Uncle Ramos began . . .
Facts: pieces of data that can be proven	4,000 tons of cans have been recycled.
Figurative language: colorful comparisons	Rivers are the bloodstreams of the world.
Examples: specific cases that illustrate ideas	Boots are "in." Cowboy boots are the most popular.
Quotations: the exact words of a key person	"I have a dream," said Dr. Martin Luther King, Jr.

Writers arrange supporting details in logical, artful ways.

- Writers may introduce the key idea with an anecdote or example at the beginning of a work.
- Writers develop the key idea with blocks of supporting ideas. They group related **sentences** into **paragraphs** and may divide long works into **chapters** or **sections.**
- Writers give their piece an **overall structure.** If the work tells a story, for example, a writer may arrange the events in time order.

6. Introduce the concept of key ideas, using the instruction on the student page.

7. Discuss the bulleted items, emphasizing the link between author's purpose, type of text, and key idea. Then, **ask:** In a biography meant to tell the story of Helen Keller, what might the key idea be?

   Sample response: Keller overcame enormous odds.

8. Explain that individual paragraphs within a text may have their own key ideas and that these ideas point to, or support, the key idea of the entire text. Then, write the following sentences on the board: *This backpack is roomy. This backpack is durable. This backpack is stylish.* Explain that these are the key ideas of three body paragraphs of a persuasive essay. **Ask:** What might the key idea of the entire essay be?

   Sample response: You should buy this backpack.

9. Explore with students the types of support shown in the chart. Ask students for additional examples of each type. Then, review with students the ways writers give their ideas a structure using sentences, paragraphs, chapters, and sections.

Time and Resource Manager

LESSON PACING GUIDE

The Drive-In Movies

DAY 1	Preteach/Teach

- Administer the Reading and Vocabulary Warm-ups, as necessary.
- Introduce the Key Ideas and Details skill: Make Predictions.
- Introduce the Craft and Structure skill: Narrator and Point of View.
- Use the Close Reading Model to demonstrate the application of the skills.
- Review the selection vocabulary, as necessary, with students who need additional support.
- Prepare students to read the selection by reviewing with them the Multidraft Reading Strategies.

DAY 2	Teach

- Informally monitor comprehension while students read.
- Use the Comprehension questions to confirm understanding.
- Develop students' ability to make predictions and analyze narrator and point of view using the sidenote questions.
- Reinforce vocabulary with the Vocabulary notes.
- Reinforce unit focus standards using the Spiral Review prompts.

DAY 3	Assess

- Assess students' comprehension and mastery of the skills by having them answer the Literary Analysis questions.
- Have students complete the Vocabulary activities.
- Develop students' understanding of roots and affixes by having them complete the Word Study activities.

DAY 4	Extend/Assess

- Build students' ability to master grammar concepts and conventions by having them complete the Conventions lesson.
- Have students complete the Writing to Sources activity and write an autobiographical narrative. (You may assign as homework.)
- Extend learning by having students complete the Speaking and Listening activity: write a conversation.
- Administer the Selection Test or Open-Book Test.

Common Core State Standards

Reading Informational Text 6. Determine an author's point of view or purpose in a text and explain how it is conveyed in the text.

Writing 3. Write narratives to develop real or imagined experiences or events using effective technique, relevant descriptive details, and well-structured event sequences.

Speaking and Listening 6. Adapt speech to a variety of contexts and tasks.

Language 1. Demonstrate command of the conventions of standard English grammar and usage when writing or speaking.

6. Acquire and use accurately grade-appropriate general academic and domain-specific words and phrases.

Daily Block Scheduling

Each day in this Lesson Pacing Guide represents a 40–50 minute period. Teachers using block scheduling may combine days to revise pacing. In addition, teachers may differentiate and support core instruction by integrating components for extended and intensive support as students require. See the Guide to Resources (facing page).

GUIDE TO RESOURCES

		L1	L2	L3	L4	EL	ALL	RESOURCES	PRINT	CD	ONLINE
Warm Up		✓	✓			✓		Vocabulary Warm-ups			✓
		✓	✓			✓		Reading Warm-ups			✓
							✓	Background Video			✓
							✓	Selection Audio		Hear It!	✓
Comprehension/ Selection Support							✓	Writing About the Big Question	Student Companion Workbook		✓
							✓	Literary Analysis	Student Companion Workbook		✓
							✓	Reading	Student Companion Workbook		✓
							✓	Vocabulary Builder	Student Companion Workbook		✓
					✓			Enrichment			✓
			✓	✓	✓			Conventions	Student Companion Workbook		✓
			✓	✓	✓			Writing to Sources	Student Companion Workbook		✓
			✓	✓	✓			Speaking and Listening	Student Companion Workbook		✓
Differentiated Instruction/ Additional Support							✓	Additional Standards Practice	Common Core Companion		✓
							✓	Close Reading Practice	Close Reading Notebook		✓
		✓	✓					Adapted Reader's Notebook			✓
						✓		English Reader's Notebook:			✓
						✓		Spanish Reader's Notebook			✓
						✓		Graphic Organizer A			✓
		✓	✓			✓		Graphic Organizer B			✓
		✓	✓			✓		"Smart Money"	Reality Central Student Edition and Writing Journal		✓
		✓	✓			✓		Practice and Assess	Reading Kit		✓
Monitor Progress							✓	Selection Test		Exam View	✓
							✓	Open-Book Test		Exam View	✓
Digital Resources							✓	Close Reading Tool			✓
							✓	Online Writer's Notebook			✓

One-on-one teaching   Group work   Whole class instruction   Independent work   A Assessment   Digital Resource

LEARNER LEVELS

L1 Special-Needs Students
L2 Below-Level Students (Tier 2)
L3 On-Level Students (Tier 1)
L4 Advanced Students (Tier 1)
EL English Learners
All All Students

❶ ❓ What is important to know?

Read • Discuss • Research • Write As students read, they will explore the Big Question through text analysis of the selection. Encourage students to note comments and additional questions as they read, using text evidence to support their thoughts. Students may wish to log their comments, questions, and evidence in a three-column chart. Students should refer to their notes to help them deepen their understanding of the selection through discussion, research, and writing.

❷ Close Reading Focus

1. Encourage students to record their predictions in a three-column chart. Students should note story details in the first column, their own background knowledge or personal experiences in the second column, and their prediction in the third column. Students' predictions should be based on the information in the first two columns.

2. Tell students that when they read the word *I* in a story, it is a clue that the narrator is a person in the story. Therefore, the story is told in the first-person point of view. When the narrator is outside the story, the story is told from the third-person point of view.

Ⓒ Building Knowledge

❶ ❓ What is important to know?

Explore the Big Question as you read "The Drive-In Movies." Take notes on what the narrator learns through his experiences.

❷ CLOSE READING FOCUS

Key Ideas and Details: **Make Predictions**

When you **make predictions,** you develop ideas about what is most likely to happen next. Base your predictions on details in the text and on your own experience. Keep track of your predictions by writing them down. Then, read ahead to check each prediction. When you find details that show your original prediction may be wrong, revise your prediction. Use these new details to correct and change your ideas.

Craft and Structure: **Narrator and Point of View**

The **narrator** is the voice that tells a true or imagined story. **Point of view** is the perspective from which the story is told. The narrator's point of view affects the kinds of details that are revealed to the reader.

- **First-person point of view:** The narrator takes part in the action of the story and refers to himself or herself as "I." Readers know only what the narrator sees, thinks, and feels.
- **Third-person point of view:** The narrator does not take part in the action. As an outside observer, a third-person narrator can share information that the characters do not know.

Most true stories about a writer's life are told from the first person point of view.

Vocabulary

Write these words from "The Drive-In Movies" in your notebook. Which words are past-tense verbs? How do you know?

prelude	pulsating	migrated
evident	winced	vigorously

Meet the Author

As a child, Gary Soto (b. 1952) loved the bustle and energy of his Fresno, California, neighborhood. When Soto was six years old, however, a government program changed his neighborhood by replacing many run-down buildings with new ones. "It didn't work in our area," Soto says. "The houses were bulldozed, and in their place grew weeds." As he grew older, Soto continued to feel a sense of loss over his old neighborhood. Writing helped him get his feelings down on paper, where he could see and think about them.

Ⓒ **Common Core State Standards**

Reading Informational Text
6. Determine an author's point of view or purpose in a text and explain how it is conveyed in the text.

Language
6. Acquire and use accurately grade-appropriate general academic and domain-specific words and phrases.

Ⓒ TEXT COMPLEXITY **RUBRIC**

The Drive-In Movies		Reader and Task Suggestions	
Qualitative Measures		**Preparing to Read the Text**	**Leveled Tasks**
Context/Knowledge Demands	1950s U.S. suburbs; drive-in movies 1　2　③　4　5	• Using the background information on TE p. 185, discuss the impact of drive-in movies. • Guide students to use Multidraft Reading strategies (TE p. 186).	*Knowledge Demands* If students will have difficulty with knowledge demands, have them examine the image on SE pages 186–187. Discuss the size of the drive-in theater screen and the privacy of the car. *Synthesizing* If students will not have difficulty with knowledge demands, have them note as they read the importance of the drive-in to people during that time.
Structure/Language Conventionality and Clarity	Informal; some figures of speech; on-level vocabulary 1　②　3　4　5		
Levels of Meaning/Purpose/Concept Level	Accessible concept (hard work brings rewards) 1　②　3　4　5		
Quantitative Measures			
Lexile	920L	Text Length	Word Count: 1,003

CLOSE READING MODEL

The passage below is from Gary Soto's autobiographical narrative "The Drive-In Movies." The annotations to the right of the passage show ways in which you can use close reading skills to make predictions and analyze narrator and point of view.

from "The Drive-In Movies"

For our family, moviegoing was rare. But if our mom, tired from a week of candling eggs, woke up happy on a Saturday morning, there was a chance we might later scramble to our blue Chevy and beat nightfall to the Starlight Drive-In. [1] My brother and sister knew this. I knew this. So on Saturday we tried to be good. [2] We sat in the cool shadows of the TV with the volume low and watched cartoons, a prelude of what was to come.

One Saturday I decided to be extra good. [3] When she came out of the bedroom tying her robe, she yawned a hat-sized yawn and blinked red eyes at the weak brew of coffee I had fixed for her. I made her toast with strawberry jam spread to all the corners and set the three boxes of cereal in front of her. If she didn't care to eat cereal, she could always look at the back of the boxes as she drank her coffee.

I went outside. The lawn was tall but too wet with dew to mow. I picked up a trowel and began to weed the flower bed. [4]

Make Predictions
1 Based on the title and these sentences, you might predict that this selection will describe a family's "rare" trip to the drive-in movies.

Narrator and Point of View
2 The first-person pronouns *I* and *we* indicate that this narrative is told from the first-person point of view.

Narrator and Point of View
3 Soto shares his decision to be extra good. As a first-person narrator, he can share his own thoughts and feelings, but not the thoughts of his mother or any other character.

Make Predictions
4 Soto has been working hard to be "extra good." At this point you might make a prediction about whether or not his efforts will earn him a trip to the movies.

❸ Background
Drive-In Theaters

Drive-in movies reached their high point in the U.S. in the 1950s and remained popular until the 1980s when cable TV and VCRs became available. People could then watch movies in their own homes.

🔔 Daily Bellringer

For each class during which you will teach this selection, have students complete one of the five Sentence Modeling activities for Week 8 in *Daily Bellringer Activities*. You may wish to use additional activities that are applicable to this selection.

Vocabulary

If students require support with selection vocabulary, use this routine:

1. Write the following words and definitions on the board:

   prelude *n.* introduction to a main event

   pulsating *adj.* beating or throbbing in a steady rhythm

   migrated *v.* moved from one place to another

   evident *adj.* easy to see; very clear

   winced *v.* pulled back slightly as if in pain

   vigorously *adv.* forcefully or energetically

2. Have students say each word aloud.

3. Use the word in a sentence that defines the word.

PART 2 • Building Knowledge: The Drive-In Movies **185**

🔧 DIFFERENTIATED INSTRUCTION

🔵 Extended Support— English Learners
Have students complete the **Reading and Vocabulary Warm-ups** for this selection in the *Student Companion All-in-One Workbook* before they read. Assign the prereading pages and the adapted selection in the *Reader's Notebook: English Learner's Version*. Then, have students listen to portions of the selection in the *Student eText* or on the *Hear It!* CD-ROM.

🔲 🔲 Extended Support— Struggling Readers
Have students complete the **Reading and Vocabulary Warm-ups** for this selection in the *Student Companion All-in-One Workbook* before they read. Assign the prereading pages and the adapted selection in the *Reader's Notebook: Adapted Version*. Then, have students listen to portions of the selection in the *Student eText* or on the *Hear It!* CD-ROM (adapted text).

Extended Support— Reluctant Readers
To build motivation and engagement before assigning the selection, have students read "Smart Money," a thematically related selection in *Reality Central*. Then, use the questions at the conclusion of the related selection to guide discussion.

MULTIDRAFT READING

This icon ● marks natural pauses in the selection. To assist struggling readers and to deepen comprehension for all, assign the text in "chunks," separated by the icons, and apply multidraft reading protocols. For each reading, have students set the purpose indicated:

- **First reading:** Students should read the selection independently and think about its basic meaning.

- **Second reading:** Students should analyze the text's key ideas and details and its craft and structure, and respond to the side-column prompts.

- **Third reading:** Students should integrate knowledge and ideas, connect the text to other texts and to the world, and answer the end-of-selection questions.

For more guidance, refer to the *Classroom Strategies and Teaching Routines* card on multidraft reading.

❶ Narrator and Point of View

1. Remind students that the *point of view* is the perspective from which the story is told.

2. On the chalkboard list these pronouns: **First Person:** *I, we, me, us, my, mine, our, ours;* **Third Person:** *he, she, it, they, his, her, hers, its, their, theirs.*

3. Tell students that the pronouns indicate a story's point of view. **Ask** students the Narrator and Point of View question. **Answer:** Soto uses first-person pronouns *our, we, my, I.*

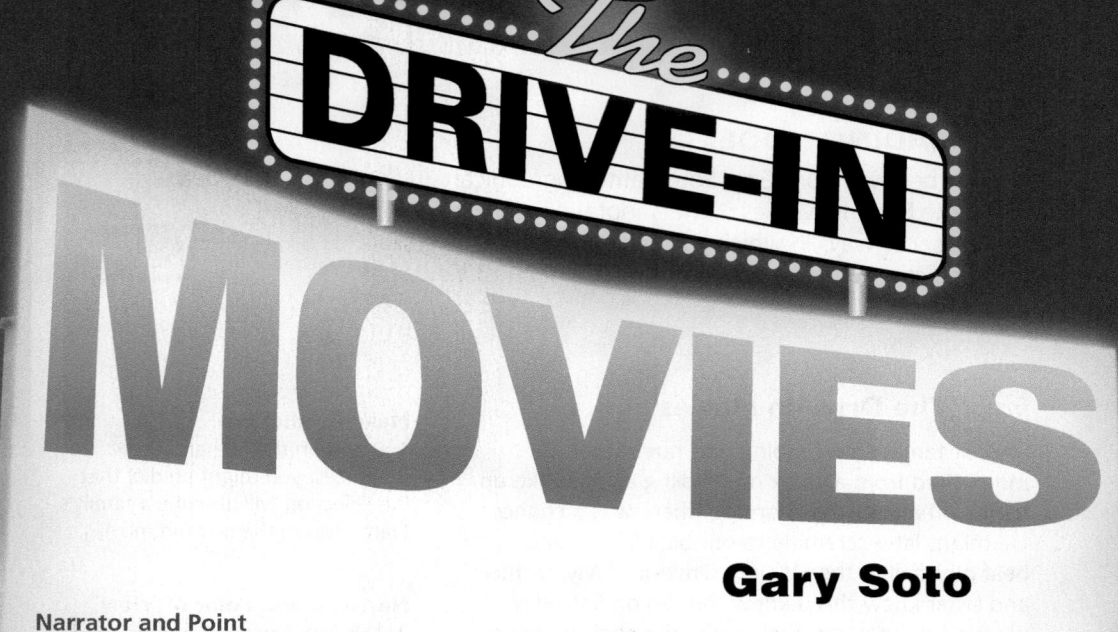

The DRIVE-IN MOVIES

Gary Soto

Narrator and Point of View
What clues here indicate the narrator is telling the story from the first-person point of view?

Vocabulary ▶
prelude (prā′ lōōd′) *n.* introduction to a main event

❶

F or our family, moviegoing was rare. But if our mom, tired from a week of candling eggs,[1] woke up happy on a Saturday morning, there was a chance we might later scramble to our blue Chevy and beat nightfall to the Starlight Drive-In. My brother and sister knew this. I knew this. So on Saturday we tried to be good. We sat in the cool shadows of the TV with the volume low and watched cartoons, a prelude of what was to come.

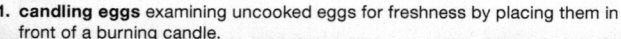

1. **candling eggs** examining uncooked eggs for freshness by placing them in front of a burning candle.

186 UNIT 2 • What is important to know?

💬 VOCABULARY DEVELOPMENT

Thematic Vocabulary: The Big Question
As students are discussing "The Drive-In Movies," encourage them to use the thematic vocabulary presented in Introducing the Big Question, pp. 162–163. You might provide them with sentence starters like these:

1. The *purpose* of the children's hard work is to . . .
2. Their mother *observed* that they . . .
3. In the end, they were surprised when she *judged* their work as being . . .

One Saturday I decided to be extra good. When she came out of the bedroom tying her robe, she yawned a hat-sized yawn and blinked red eyes at the weak brew of coffee I had fixed for her. I made her toast with strawberry jam spread to all the corners and set the three boxes of cereal in front of her. If she didn't care to eat cereal, she could always look at the back of the boxes as she drank her coffee.

I went outside. The lawn was tall but too wet with dew to mow. I picked up a trowel² and began to weed the flower bed. The weeds were really bermuda grass, long stringers that ran finger-deep in the ground. I got to work quickly and in no time crescents of earth began rising under my fingernails. I was sweaty hot. My knees hurt from kneeling, and my brain was dull from making the trowel go up and down, dribbling crumbs of earth. I dug for half an hour, then stopped to play with the neighbor's dog and pop ticks from his poor snout.

2. **trowel** (trou´ əl) *n.* a small hand tool used by gardeners to weed or dig.

▼ Critical Viewing
How might seeing a movie at a drive-in like this one differ from seeing it in a regular theater?

Comprehension
Why is the narrator being extra good?

PART 2 • The Drive-In Movies **187**

DIFFERENTIATED INSTRUCTION

Strategy for Less-Proficient Readers
Prepare an *Anticipation Guide (Professional Development Guidebook,* pp. 36–38) with the following statements:

• Children should be paid for doing chores around the house.

• Household chores can be fun if family members cooperate.

After allowing students time to respond to the statements, read each statement aloud and ask for a hand count of responses. Call on students to discuss their responses. After students are done reading, have them respond to statements again in the After Reading column. For further guidance, use the *Classroom Strategies and Teaching Routines* card for **Anticipation Guides.**

 Video

Watch the Background Video online!

 Audio

Selection Audio is available in the *Student eText* and on the *Hear It!* CD-ROM.

❺ Literature in Context

Social Studies Connection

Some drive-in complexes provided such features as playgrounds equipped with swings and merry-go-rounds; restaurants and cafeterias; and swimming pools. At some drive-ins it was possible to rent car heaters during cold weather.

Connect to the Literature

1. Direct students back to the opening paragraph of the narrative. Ask a volunteer to read the passage.

2. Have students list the various chores Soto did around the house.

3. Then, **ask** the Connect to the Literature question.
   Possible response: In the opening paragraph the narrator says that going to the movies was rare in his family. Therefore, it would be considered a treat that was reserved for special occasions, such as when the narrator and his siblings have been well-behaved.

Spiral Review

Central Idea

1. Remind students that they studied the concept of central idea in the Unit 2 Focus on Craft and Structure (pp. 180–183).

2. Have students reread this page. Then, **ask** students the Spiral Review question.

   Answer: They show the extent to which the narrator is willing to go in order to get what he wants. These details show that he is doing everything he can to be "extra good."

---

❺ LITERATURE IN CONTEXT

Social Studies Connection

Drive-In Movies
The first drive-in theater had three speakers near the screen to project sound. If you parked near the screen, you could hear every word perfectly. If you lived nearby, you heard every word, too. A later system of individual speakers, placed on the car door when the window was rolled down, satisfied angry neighbors.

Connect to the Literature

Why might a trip to the drive-in movies be a reward for the narrator?

Vocabulary ▶
pulsating (pul´ sāt´ iŋ)
adj. beating or throbbing in a steady rhythm

migrated (mī´ grāt əd)
v. moved from one place to another

Spiral Review
CENTRAL IDEA How do these vivid details contribute to the author's central idea?

❻

I then mowed the lawn, which was still beaded with dew and noisy with bees hovering over clover. This job was less dull because as I pushed the mower over the shaggy lawn, I could see it looked tidier. My brother and sister watched from the window. Their faces were fat with cereal, a third helping. I made a face at them when they asked how come I was working. Rick pointed to part of the lawn. "You missed some over there." I ignored him and kept my attention on the windmill of grassy blades. ●

While I was emptying the catcher, a bee stung the bottom of my foot. I danced on one leg and was ready to cry when Mother showed her face at the window. I sat down on the grass and examined my foot: the stinger was **pulsating**. I pulled it out quickly, ran water over the sting and packed it with mud, Grandmother's remedy.

Hobbling, I returned to the flower bed where I pulled more stringers and again played with the dog. More ticks had **migrated** to his snout. I swept the front steps, took out the garbage, cleaned the lint filter to the dryer (easy), plucked hair from the industrial wash basin in the garage (also easy), hosed off the patio, smashed three snails sucking paint from the house (disgusting but fun), tied a bundle of newspapers, put away toys, and, finally, seeing that almost everything was done and the sun was not too high, started waxing the car.

My brother joined me with an old gym sock, and our sister watched us while sucking on a cherry Kool-Aid ice cube. The liquid wax drooled onto the sock, and we began to swirl the white slop on the chrome. My arms ached from

buffing, which though less boring than weeding, was harder. But the beauty was evident. The shine, hurting our eyes and glinting like an armful of dimes, brought Mother out. She looked around the yard and said, "Pretty good." She winced at the grille and returned inside the house.

We began to wax the paint. My brother applied the liquid and I followed him rubbing hard in wide circles as we moved around the car. I began to hurry because my arms were hurting and my stung foot looked like a water balloon. We were working around the trunk when Rick pounded on the bottle of wax. He squeezed the bottle and it sneezed a few more white drops.

We looked at each other. "There's some on the sock," I said. "Let's keep going."

We polished and buffed, sweat weeping on our brows. We got scared when we noticed that the gym sock was now blue. The paint was coming off. Our sister fit ice cubes into our mouths and we worked harder, more intently, more dedicated to the car and our mother. We ran the sock over the chrome, trying to pick up extra wax. But there wasn't enough to cover the entire car. Only half got waxed, but we thought it was better than nothing and went inside for lunch. After lunch, we returned outside with tasty sandwiches.

Rick and I nearly jumped. The waxed side of the car was foggy white. We took a rag and began to polish vigorously and nearly in tears, but the fog wouldn't come off. I blamed Rick and he blamed me. Debra stood at the window, not wanting to get involved. Now, not only would we not go to the movies, but Mom would surely snap a branch from the plum tree and chase us around the yard.

◀ **Vocabulary**
evident (ev´ ə dənt)
adj. easy to see;
very clear

winced (winst)
v. pulled back
slightly, as if in pain

Make Predictions
How do you predict the narrator will feel at the drive-in, after his long day of hard work? Read on to check whether you are correct.

◀ **Vocabulary**
vigorously (vig´ ər
əs lē) *adv.* forcefully
or energetically

6 Make Predictions

1. Remind students that a prediction is a reasonable guess about what will happen next.

2. To help students predict how the narrator will feel at the movies, **ask** students to find details in the bracketed passage that show how he feels physically.

Possible responses: He talks of being "sweaty hot"; his knees hurt from kneeling; the bee sting makes him hobble in pain; his arms ache from buffing the car; he and his brother have "sweat weeping" on their brows.

3. Ask students the Make Predictions question.
Possible response: He will probably be weary and may not be able to enjoy the movie.

▶ **Monitor Progress:** As students read the passage, have them fill in *Reading Skill Graphic Organizer B* for "The Drive-In Movies" with their predictions. Ask students to name one prediction they have made based on the clues in the story and what they already know.

▶ **Reteach:** If students have trouble making predictions, have them list events on this page and the previous page. The narrator gets stung by a bee and performs a long list of chores. These are clues that he may be tired and in pain. Based on the knowledge that when one doesn't feel well, one is not likely to enjoy going out, students can predict that Soto may not be able to go to the movies, or that he may not enjoy the movie if he does go.

❼ Make Predictions

1. Instruct students to evaluate their predictions and to indicate if their expectations were fulfilled.

2. Have students explore the possibility of other endings. What else might have happened? Then, challenge them to defend their outcomes based on their own experience and the events in the narrative.

3. **Ask** students the Make Predictions question.

   Possible response: The outcome is logical. After so much hard work, the narrator would feel fatigued and would fall asleep.

☑ ASSESS

Language Study
Vocabulary

1. evident
2. winced
3. pulsating
4. vigorously
5. migrated

Word Study
Part A
Sample answers:

A *precaution* is an action taken <u>before</u> something goes wrong. To *predict* means to say what is going to happen <u>before</u> it does. When you *preheat* the oven, you turn it on so that it can reach the correct temperature <u>before</u> you put something in to bake.

Part B
Sample answers:

1. A *preview* will feature highlights from the movie <u>before</u> it is shown to give viewers a chance to predict whether they will like the movie.

2. A *preface* is an introduction, so it comes at the beginning, <u>before</u> the main story or text.

Literary Analysis

Possible responses appear below. Check to be sure students support their responses with evidence from the text.

1. **(a)** Students may have predicted that she would take the family to

---

Mom came out and looked at us with hands on her aproned hips. Finally, she said, "You boys worked so hard." She turned on the garden hose and washed the car. That night we did go to the drive-in. The first feature was about nothing, and the second feature, starring Jerry Lewis, was *Cinderfella.* I tried to stay awake. I kept a wad of homemade popcorn in my cheek and laughed when Jerry Lewis fit golf tees in his nose. I rubbed my watery eyes. I laughed and looked at my mom. I promised myself I would remember that scene with the golf tees and promised myself not to work so hard the coming Saturday. Twenty minutes into the movie, I fell asleep with one hand in the popcorn.

❼

Make Predictions
How does this outcome fit with your prediction about how the narrator would feel after his day of work?

Language Study

Vocabulary The following words appear in "The Drive-In Movies." For each item, choose a synonym, or word with a similar meaning, from the vocabulary list.

| pulsating | migrated | evident | winced | vigorously |

1. clear, obvious, ?
2. shrank back, cringed, ?
3. throbbing, beating, ?
4. actively, energetically, ?
5. traveled, roamed, ?

WORD STUDY

The **Latin prefix *pre-*** means "before" or "in advance."

In this story, the narrator and his siblings begin Saturday mornings by watching television. This activity is a **prelude** to all the activities that they will do later on. It happens *before* the other activities.

Word Study

Part A Explain how the **Latin prefix *pre-*** contributes to the meaning of *precaution, predict,* and *preheat.* Consult a dictionary if necessary.

Part B Use sentence context and what you know about the Latin prefix *pre-* to explain your responses to the following questions.

1. How might a movie's *preview* help people decide whether or not to see that movie?

2. Does the *preface* appear at the end of a book?

---

the movies. **(b)** Students should support predictions with details such as the mother's comment that the yard looked "Pretty good" and her compliment to the boys.

2. Students may say that they predicted that the boys would be punished for waxing the car badly, but revised their predictions when they read the mother's reaction to the mess.

3. *Events:*
   The narrator weeds the flowerbed.
   The narrator waxes the car.
   The waxed half of the car turns "foggy white."

Details Provided by Narrator:
He sweats and his knees hurt.
His arm aches from buffing. The shine is like "an armful of dimes."
The boys blame each other for the way the car looks.

4. She would reveal her own thoughts and feelings about the mess the boys made with the car wax.

5. **(a)** He works very hard doing various chores around the house. **(b)** She understands that they didn't intend to make a mess, and she appreciates that they worked hard.

Close Reading Activities

Literary Analysis

Key Ideas and Details

1. (a) Make Predictions Did you predict that Soto's mother would take the family to the drive-in movies? **(b)** On what details did you base your prediction?

2. Make Predictions As you read, did you change any of your predictions? Explain.

Craft and Structure

3. Narrator and Point of View Make a chart like the one on the right to note how the author develops point of view in the narrative. Include at least three examples.

4. Narrator and Point of View What details about the events described in the narrative would you expect to find if the narrator were Soto's mother?

Integration of Knowledge and Ideas

5. (a) How does Soto persuade his mother to take the family to the drive-in movies? **(b) Draw Conclusions:** Why do you think Soto's mother does not get angry with the children for making a mess with the car wax?

6. (a) What two things does Soto promise himself to remember? **(b) Assess:** Do you think he still has fond memories of that day and night? Explain.

7. Make a Judgment: Do you think children should have to do chores before their parents allow them to do something enjoyable? Why or why not? With a partner, discuss and support your responses.

8. **What is important to know?** With a small group, discuss the following questions. **(a)** As a child, what did Soto know and consider important about his family's Saturday activities? **(b)** As an adult, what does Soto know and consider important about his childhood Saturdays?

Event
The narrator is stung by a bee.

Details Provided by Narrator
The narrator wants to cry but takes the stinger out and packs the wound with mud.

ACADEMIC VOCABULARY

As you write and speak about "The Drive-In Movies," use the words related to gaining knowledge that you explored on page 163 of this text.

PART 2 • Close Reading Activities **191**

---

6. (a) He promises to remember the funny scene from the movie and not to work so hard the following Saturday. **(b)** He probably remembers how much fun they had as a family. He now can see the humor in what happened to the car.

7. Some students may say that working for a reward makes it more valuable.

8. **What is important to know?** **(a)** As a child, Soto thought it was important whether or not his mother took him and his siblings to the movies. He knew that if he and his siblings helped make their mother happy, the chances of going to the movies were better. **(b)** As an adult, Soto understands that whether he was allowed to go to the movies or not, and whether he stayed awake at the movies or not, are less important than the fact that he was part of a close, loving family.

 Online Writer's Notebook

Students can use the Online Writer's Notebook to record all responses.

Conventions

1. Introduce the skill, using the instruction on the student page.

2. Discuss the definitions and the examples.

Think Aloud: Model the Skill

Model the skill of using the principal parts of verbs. Say to students:

I *brush* my teeth every day. When I say that I *brushed* my teeth yesterday, I'm talking about something that started and ended in the past. When I say that I *have brushed* my teeth thousands of times, I'm using the past participle to form a tense that shows I have brushed my teeth many times before now. When I say that I *am brushing* regularly, you know that I started brushing in the past, and will continue into the future. By using the principal parts to form tenses, I tell when an activity started, when it ended, and whether or not it is still continuing.

Practice A

1. *worked*: past tense

2. *falls*: present tense

3. *(is) trying*: present participle

4. *(has) taken*: past participle

Speaking Application

Students' discussions of the autobiography should include the use of at least three of the four principal parts of verbs.

Practice B

1. One Saturday, Gary *made* breakfast for his mom.

2. Gary *is kneeling* as he weeds the lawn.

3. The boys *have waxed* the car.

4. On Saturday night, they *go* to the drive-in.

Writing Application

Sample answers: (Past tense) I rubbed my watery eyes. (Past participle) I *have rubbed* my watery eyes. (Past tense) Twenty minutes into the movie, I fell asleep with one hand in the popcorn. (Past participle) Twenty minutes into the movie, I *had fallen* asleep with one hand in the popcorn.

Close Reading Activities Continued

Conventions: Principal Parts of Verbs

Every verb has four main forms, or principal parts. These parts are used to form verb tenses that show time.

Regular verbs form their past tense and past participles by adding *-ed* or *–d*.

Irregular verbs, such as *be*, form their past tense and past participles in different ways.

	Present	Present Participle	Past	Past Participle
Regular	talk(s)	(am, is, are) talking	talked	(has, have) talked
	serve(s)	(am, is, are) serving	served	(has, have) served
Irregular	be (am, is, are)	(am, is, are) being	was, were	(has, have) been
	has, have	(am, is, are) having	had	(has, have) had
	rise(s)	(am, is, are) rising	rose	(has, have) risen

Practice A

Identify the verb or verbs in each sentence. For each verb, indicate which of the four principal parts is used.

1. Soto's mother worked hard.

2. Soto falls asleep in the middle of the movie.

3. Soto is trying to be extra good.

4. His mother has taken them to the movies before.

Speaking Application Describe "The Drive-In Movies" to a partner. In your discussion, use at least three of the four principal parts of verbs.

Practice B

Rewrite each sentence, replacing the italicized verb with the principal part indicated in parentheses.

1. One Saturday, Gary *makes* breakfast for his mom. (past tense)

2. Gary *kneels* as he weeds the lawn. (present participle)

3. The boys *waxed* the car. (past participle)

4. On Saturday night, they *went* to the drive-in. (present tense)

Writing Application Find two sentences in "The Drive-In Movies" that use verbs in the past tense. Rewrite the sentences to use the past participle forms.

Writing to Sources

Narrative Text "The Drive-In Movies" is filled with details about events in author Gary Soto's early life. Write an **autobiographical narrative** about an interesting experience in your life. In your narrative, compare and contrast your experience to the one Soto describes.

- Think of important or humorous events in your life and jot them down.
- Narrow your topic and choose one experience.
- List the details of where, when, and with whom the experience took place. Number the events in the order in which they happened.
- Note ways in which your experience is similar to and different from Soto's experience. You might compare characters, settings, final outcomes, or lessons learned. Review "The Drive-In Movies" to find details to use in your comparisons.
- Use your notes and numbered list to write your narrative.

Grammar Application Use appropriate principal parts or the verbs you write in your narrative. Look for ways in which you can vary your use of principal parts.

Speaking and Listening

Comprehension and Collaboration With a partner, write a **conversation** that Gary Soto and his mother might have had the morning after their trip to the drive-in. Then, act out the conversation for the class or a small group.

Follow these steps to complete the assignment:

- Review the selection, jotting down details about each character that will help you invent interesting dialogue.
- Ask your partner questions and make observations, keeping each character's traits, goals, and feelings in mind.
- Practice using eye contact when listening and speaking.
- Finally, when you act out your conversation, use expressive tones of voice and gestures to engage your audience.

 **Common Core State Standards**

Writing
3. Write narratives to develop real or imagined experiences or events using effective technique, relevant descriptive details, and well-structured event sequences.

Speaking and Listening
6. Adapt speech to a variety of contexts and tasks.

Language
1. Demonstrate command of the conventions of standard English grammar and usage when writing or speaking.

Writing to Sources

1. Review the assignment, using the instruction on the student page.
2. To give students guidance in writing a narrative text, give them the **Support for Writing** page for this selection in the *Student Companion All-in-One Workbook.*
3. To evaluate the writing activity, use the rubrics for Autobiographical Narrative, pp. 222–223 in *Professional Development Guidebook.*

Grammar Application

Have students check their drafts for the correct principal parts of verbs.

Six Traits Focus

✓	Ideas	✓	Word Choice
✓	Organization	✓	Sentence Fluency
✓	Voice		Conventions

Speaking and Listening

1. Review the assignment, using the instruction on the student page.
2. To support students' work on the assignment, have them complete the **Support for Extend Your Learning** page for this selection in the *Student Companion All-in-One Workbook.*

Time and Resource Manager

LESSON PACING GUIDE

Names/Nombres

| DAY 1 | **Preteach/Teach** |

- Administer the Reading and Vocabulary Warm-ups, as necessary.
- Introduce the Key Ideas and Details skill: Fact and Opinion.
- Introduce the Craft and Structure skill: Tone.
- Use the Close Reading Model to demonstrate the application of the skills.
- Review the selection vocabulary, as necessary, with students who need additional support.
- Prepare students to read the selection by reviewing with them the Multidraft Reading Strategies.

| DAY 2 | **Teach** |

- Informally monitor comprehension while students read.
- Use the Comprehension questions to confirm understanding.
- Develop students' ability to differentiate fact and opinion and analyze tone using the sidenote questions.
- Reinforce vocabulary with the Vocabulary notes.
- Reinforce unit focus standards using the Spiral Review prompts.

| DAY 3 | **Assess** |

- Assess students' comprehension and mastery of the skills by having them answer the Literary Analysis questions.
- Have students complete the Vocabulary activities.
- Develop students' understanding of roots and affixes by having them complete the Word Study activities.

| DAY 4 | **Extend/Assess** |

- Build students' ability to master grammar concepts and conventions by having them complete the Conventions lesson.
- Have students complete the Writing to Sources activity and write a personal anecdote. (You may assign as homework.)
- Extend learning by having students complete the Speaking and Listening activity: write and deliver a monologue.
- Administer the Selection Test or Open-Book Test.

 **Common Core State Standards**

Reading Literature 4. Determine the meanings of words and phrases as they are used in a text, including figurative and connotative meanings; analyze the impact of specific word choice on meaning and tone.

Reading Informational Text 8. Trace and evaluate the argument and specific claims in a text, distinguishing claims that are supported by reasons and evidence from claims that are not.

Writing 3.d. Use precise words and phrases, relevant descriptive details, and sensory language to convey experiences and events.

Speaking and Listening 6. Adapt speech to a variety of contexts and tasks.

Language 1. Demonstrate command of the conventions of standard English grammar and usage when writing or speaking.

6. Acquire and use accurately grade-appropriate general academic and domain-specific words and phrases; gather vocabulary knowledge when considering a word or phrase important to comprehension or expression.

Daily Block Scheduling

Each day in this Lesson Pacing Guide represents a 40–50 minute period. Teachers using block scheduling may combine days to revise pacing. In addition, teachers may differentiate and support core instruction by integrating components for extended and intensive support as students require. See the Guide to Resources (facing page).

GUIDE TO RESOURCES

		L1	L2	L3	L4	EL	ALL	RESOURCES	PRINT	CD	ONLINE
Warm Up		✔	✔			✔		Vocabulary Warm-ups			✔
		✔	✔			✔		Reading Warm-ups			✔
							✔	Background Video			✔
							✔	Selection Audio		Hear It!	✔
Comprehension/ Selection Support							✔	Writing About the Big Question	Student Companion Workbook		✔
							✔	Literary Analysis	Student Companion Workbook		✔
							✔	Reading	Student Companion Workbook		✔
							✔	Vocabulary Builder	Student Companion Workbook		✔
					✔			Enrichment			✔
				✔	✔	✔		Conventions	Student Companion Workbook		✔
				✔	✔	✔		Writing to Sources	Student Companion Workbook		✔
				✔	✔	✔		Speaking and Listening	Student Companion Workbook		
Differentiated Instruction/ Additional Support							✔	Additional Standards Practice	Common Core Companion		✔
		✔	✔					Adapted Reader's Notebook			✔
						✔		English Reader's Notebook:			✔
						✔		Spanish Reader's Notebook			✔
						✔		Graphic Organizer A			✔
		✔	✔			✔		Graphic Organizer B			✔
		✔	✔			✔		"Facebook or Face-to-Face?"	Reality Central Student Edition and Writing Journal		✔
		✔	✔			✔		Practice and Assess	Reading Kit		✔
Monitor Progress							✔	Selection Test		Exam View	✔
							✔	Open-Book Test		Exam View	✔
Digital Resources							✔	Close Reading Tool			✔
							✔	Online Writer's Notebook			✔

One-on-one teaching   Group work   Whole class instruction   Independent work   A Assessment   Digital Resource

LEARNER LEVELS

L1 Special-Needs Students   L3 On-Level Students (Tier 1)   EL English Learners
L2 Below-Level Students (Tier 2)   L4 Advanced Students (Tier 1)   All All Students

1 **What is important to know?**

Read • Discuss • Research • Write As students read, they will explore the Big Question through text analysis of the selection. Encourage students to note comments and additional questions as they read, using text evidence to support their thoughts. Students may wish to log their comments, questions, and evidence in a three-column chart. Students should refer to their notes to help them deepen their understanding of the selection through discussion, research, and writing.

2 **Close Reading Focus**

1. To help students understand the difference between fact and opinion, read the following statements: *Cardinals are birds. Cardinals are the best birds.* Explain that the first statement is a fact because it can be proven. The second statement is an opinion because it's impossible to prove that cardinals are the best bird.

2. Tell students that in writing, an author's word choice and punctuation are clues to an author's tone. For example, in the sentence *Good grief! The mayor's plan will never work,* the writer's tone is casual and concerned. The tone affects how the reader interprets a piece of writing.

© Building Knowledge

Meet the Author

Although **Julia Alvarez** (b. 1950) was born in New York City, her family soon returned to their original home, the Dominican Republic. After Julia's father worked to overthrow the dictator there, he and his family fled the country. Julia was ten years old when they arrived in the United States again. From the moment she landed in New York City, she felt she had to "translate her experience into English." Today, she says, "I write to find out what I'm thinking."

© Common Core State Standards

Reading Literature
4. Determine the meanings of words and phrases as they are used in a text, including figurative and connotative meanings; analyze the impact of specific word choice on meaning and tone.

Reading Informational Text
8. Trace and evaluate the argument and specific claims in a text, distinguishing claims that are supported by reasons and evidence from claims that are not.

Language
6. Acquire and use accurately grade-appropriate general academic and domain-specific words and phrases.

194 UNIT 2 • What is important to know?

1 **What is important to know?**

Explore the Big Question as you read "Names/Nombres." Take notes on ways in which the story explores the importance of personal identity.

2 **CLOSE READING FOCUS**

Key Ideas and Details: Fact and Opinion

To evaluate the author's claims or ideas in a work of nonfiction, you must understand the difference between **fact** and **opinion.** A fact, unlike an opinion, can be proved. An opinion expresses a judgment that can be supported but not proved. You can check facts by using resources such as the following:

- dictionaries
- encyclopedias
- reliable Web sites

Craft and Structure: Tone

The **tone** of a literary work is the writer's attitude toward his or her audience and subject. The tone can often be described in one word, such as *playful, serious,* or *humorous.* Factors that contribute to tone include word choice, sentence structure, and sentence length. Notice how word choice creates a friendly tone in this example:

If you plan ahead, I promise you, you'll have the best party ever!

As you read, look for details that convey a certain tone.

Vocabulary

You will encounter the following words in "Names/Nombres." Write the words in your notebook, and rate them from the one you know most best (6) to the one you know least (1). As you read, look for the words and their definitions.

mistook	transport	chaotic
pursue	inevitably	inscribed

© TEXT COMPLEXITY RUBRIC

Names/Nombres		Reader and Task Suggestions	
Qualitative Measures		**Preparing to Read the Text**	**Leveled Tasks**
Context/Knowledge Demands	Contemporary U.S.; immigrant experience 1 ②(2) 3 4 5	• Discuss ways in which foreign languages can lead to misunderstandings.	*Structure/Language* If students will have difficulty with Spanish words, have them work in pairs to find context clues around the words. Have them use these clues to determine the meaning of each word.
Structure/Language Conventionality and Clarity	Includes Spanish words and words spelled to show accents 1 2 ③(3) 4 5	• Guide students to use Multidraft Reading Strategies (TE p. 196).	*Evaluating* If students will not have difficulty with the Spanish words, have them find examples of the author's sense of humor with pronunciations of names.
Levels of Meaning/ Purpose/Concept Level	Accessible concept (a young adult's experience fitting in) 1 ②(2) 3 4 5		
Quantitative Measures			
Lexile	1060L	Text Length	Word Count: 1,367

CLOSE READING MODEL

The passage below is from Julia Alvarez's autobiographical essay "Names/Nombres." The annotations to the right of the passage show ways in which you can use close reading skills to distinguish fact and opinion and to analyze tone.

from **"Names/Nombres"**

My little sister, Ana, had the easiest time of all. [1] She was plain *Anne*—that is, only her name was plain, for she turned out to be the pale, blond "American beauty" in the family. . . . [2]

Later, during her college years in the late '60s, there was a push to pronounce Third World names correctly. I remember calling her long distance at her group house and a roommate answering.

"Can I speak to Ana?" I asked, pronouncing her name the American way.

"Ana?" The man's voice hesitated. "Oh! You must mean *Ah-nah*!" [3]

Our first few years in the States, though, ethnicity was not yet "in." Those were the blond, blue-eyed, bobby sock years of junior high and high school before the '60s ushered in peasant blouses, hoop earrings, serapes. [4] My initial desire to be known by my correct Dominican name faded. I just wanted to be Judy and merge with the Sallys and Janes in my class.

Fact and Opinion

1 Alvarez states a personal feeling about her sister. It is an opinion because it cannot be proved. Ana might have a different opinion from Alvarez's.

Tone

2 In the phrases "plain Anne" and "that is, only her name was plain," Alvarez's word choice creates a humorous and friendly tone.

Tone

3 Alvarez uses a casual, humorous tone to share a funny story about mispronouncing her sister's name.

Fact and Opinion

4 You could consult print or online resources to confirm these facts about U.S. clothing fads of the 1950s and '60s.

Daily Bellringer

For each class during which you will teach this selection, have students complete one of the five Vocabulary activities for Week 9 in *Daily Bellringer Activities*. You may wish to use additional activities that are applicable to this selection.

Vocabulary

If students require support with selection vocabulary, use this routine:

1. Write the following words and definitions on the board:

   mistook *v.* identified incorrectly; misunderstood

   transport *v.* carry from one place to another

   chaotic *adj.* completely confused

   pursue *v.* be involved in; follow

   inevitably *adv.* unavoidably

   inscribed *v.* written on

2. Have students say each word aloud.

3. Use the word in a sentence that defines the word.

DIFFERENTIATED INSTRUCTION

Extended Support— English Learners

Have students complete the **Reading and Vocabulary Warm-ups** for this selection in the *Student Companion All-in-One Workbook* before they read. Assign the prereading pages and the adapted selection in the *Reader's Notebook: English Learner's Version*. Then, have students listen to portions of the selection in the *Student eText* or on the *Hear It!* CD-ROM.

L1 L2 Extended Support— Struggling Readers

Have students complete the **Reading and Vocabulary Warm-ups** for this selection in the *Student Companion All-in-One Workbook* before they read. Assign the prereading pages and the adapted selection in the *Reader's Notebook: Adapted Version*. Then, have students listen to portions of the selection in the *Student eText* or on the *Hear It!* CD-ROM (adapted text).

Extended Support— Reluctant Readers

To build motivation and engagement before assigning the selection, have students read "Facebook or Face-to-Face?," a thematically related selection in *Reality Central*. Then, use the questions at the conclusion of the related selection to guide discussion.

MULTIDRAFT READING

This icon ● marks natural pauses in the selection. To assist struggling readers and to deepen comprehension for all, assign the text in "chunks," separated by the icons, and apply multidraft reading protocols. For each reading, have students set the purpose indicated:

- **First reading:** Students should read the selection independently and think about its basic meaning.
- **Second reading:** Students should analyze the text's key ideas and details and its craft and structure, and respond to the side-column prompts.
- **Third reading:** Students should integrate knowledge and ideas, connect the text to other texts and to the world, and answer the end-of-selection questions.

For more guidance, refer to the *Classroom Strategies and Teaching Routines* card on multidraft reading.

❶ Fact and Opinion

Ask the Fact and Opinion question.

Answer: She states that the immigration officer asked her father if he had anything to declare.

Give students a blank copy of the partially filled-in **Reading Skill Graphic Organizer A** for this selection. Have students record facts and resources as they read.

Names/Nombres

Julia Alvarez

Fact and Opinion
What fact does the narrator state in the first paragraph?

When we arrived in New York City, our names changed almost immediately. At Immigration,[1] the officer asked my father, *Mister Elbures,* if he had anything to declare. My father shook his head, "No," and we were waved through. I ❶ was too afraid we wouldn't be let in if I corrected the man's pronunciation, but I said our name to myself, opening my mouth wide for the organ blast of the *a,* trilling my tongue for the drum-roll of the *r, All-vah-rrr-es!* How could anyone get *Elbures* out of that orchestra of sound?

At the hotel my mother was *Missus Alburest,* and I was little girl, as in, "Hey, *little girl,* stop riding the elevator up and down. It's *not* a toy."

---

1. **Immigration** government agency that processes people who have recently moved to the United States.

When we moved into our new apartment building, the super[2] called my father *Mister Alberase*, and the neighbors who became mother's friends pronounced her name *Jew-lee-ah* instead of *Hoo-lee-ah*. I, her namesake, was known as *Hoo-lee-tah* at home. But at school, I was *Judy* or *Judith*, and once an English teacher **mistook** me for *Juliet*.

2 It took awhile to get used to my new names. I wondered if I shouldn't correct my teachers and new friends. But my mother argued that it didn't matter. "You know what your friend Shakespeare said, *'A rose by any other name would smell as sweet.'*" My father had gotten into the habit of calling any famous author "my friend" because I had begun to write poems and stories in English class.

By the time I was in high school, I was a popular kid, and it showed in my name. Friends called me *Jules* or *Hey Jude*, and once a group of troublemaking friends my mother forbade me to hang out with called me *Alcatraz*. I was *Hoo-lee-tah* only to Mami and Papi and uncles and aunts who came over to eat *sancocho* on Sunday afternoons—old world folk whom I would just as soon go back to where they came from and leave me to **pursue** whatever mischief I wanted to in America. JUDY ALCATRAZ: the name on the Wanted Poster would read. Who would ever trace her to me?

3 My older sister had the hardest time getting an American name for herself because *Mauricia* did not translate into English. Ironically, although she had the most foreign-sounding name, she and I were the Americans in the family. We had been born in New York City when our parents had first tried immigration and then gone back "home," too homesick to

2. **super** *n.* superintendent; person who manages an apartment building.

◄ **Vocabulary**
mistook (mis to͝ok′) *v.* identified incorrectly; misunderstood

pursue (pər so͞o′) *v.* be involved in; follow

Tone
What attitude does the author have toward her different names?

Fact and Opinion
What opinion does the narrator give in this paragraph?

4
Comprehension
What does Julia experience when she arrives in New York City?

GUIDED EXPLORATION

2 Tone

1. **Ask** students what attitude they think Alvarez expresses so far in this essay.
   Possible response: She has a humorous attitude.
2. Point out that in the first bracketed passage, Alvarez focuses on her names.
3. **Ask** students the Tone question.
   Possible response: She seems to accept the names and wants to embrace life in America and be accepted. However, the American names are not entirely connected to who she really is.
4. Have a volunteer read the first bracketed passage aloud.
   Ask: How does the name Judy Alcatraz express Alvarez's attitude toward her dual identity?
   Possible response: Alvarez is ready to leave her heritage behind. She wants to be Judy Alcatraz so she can be mischievous in America without hearing criticism from her relatives, who wouldn't know that name.

3 Fact and Opinion

1. As review, **ask** students how they can identify an opinion in a literary work.
   Answer: They can identify opinions by finding words that express personal judgment.
2. **Ask** students the Fact and Opinion question.
   Answer: Her sister had the hardest time finding an American name.
3. **Ask** students what clue led them to the answer.
   Answer: The word *hardest* is an expression of personal judgment.

4 Comprehension

Answer: People mispronounce her family's name.

Video
Watch the Background Video online!

Audio
Selection Audio is available in the ***Student eText*** and on the ***Hear It!*** CD-ROM.

DIFFERENTIATED INSTRUCTION

EL Pronunciation for English Learners
Point out the words *stop* and *not* on page 196. Pronounce each in turn, and have students echo you. Then, present the following word pairs: *not/gnat, cot/cat,* and *pot/pat*. Pronounce each in turn. Then, arrange a game of telephone in which each student passes one of the words on to the next. When the last student repeats the word aloud, have the first student judge whether the word was relayed correctly. Have all pronounce the original word, then the word that arrived at the end of the chain.

Strategy for Less-Proficient Readers
Prepare an **Anticipation Guide** ***(Professional Development Guidebook,*** pp. 36–38) with the following statements:

- You should correct people who mispronounce your name.
- You should change to fit in.

Give students a copy of the prepared **Guide** and have them mark their responses in the Me column. Have students discuss the statements in pairs and mark their responses in the Group column. After they're done reading the selection, have students fill in the After Reading column.

❺ Infer

1. Have students reread the episode describing the narrator's older sister's name.

2. Help students find the words that various people use to describe names, such as *pretty, ugliest, beautiful,* or *awful.*

3. Ask: What is the narrator's tone as she describes people's reactions to her sister's name?

Possible responses: Her tone is sympathetic to both her mother's embarrassment and her sister's plight; at the same time, she is amused—and slightly dismayed—that people don't pronounce the name properly even as they say how beautiful it is.

4. Ask students to point out details in the text that support their answers to the previous question.

Answer: Alvarez says her mother was embarrassed, apologetic, and blushing. She says she pities her sister. She also makes the group of women seem silly as they are cooing, and saying *"Moor-ee-sha."* She is dismayed that "American tongues found even that mispronunciation tough to say."

❻ Critical Viewing

Possible response: The mother has mixed feelings about the name Mauricia, but this photo shows a woman adoring a baby. In the story the mother feels a little embarrassed to say her baby's name among the American names. Still, she finds it beautiful as she created the name and it is related to her own name.

❻ ▶ Critical Viewing
Does this picture accurately reflect Mami's feelings about baby Mauricia's name? Why or why not?

❸ stay. My mother often told the story of how she had almost changed my sister's name in the hospital.

After the delivery, Mami and some other new mothers were cooing over their new baby sons and daughters and exchanging names and weights and delivery stories. My mother was embarrassed among the Sallys and Janes and Georges and Johns to reveal the rich, noisy name of *Mauricia,* so when her turn came to brag, she gave her baby's name as *Maureen.*

"Why'd ya give her an Irish name with so many pretty Spanish names to choose from?" one of the women asked.

My mother blushed and admitted her baby's real name to the group. Her mother-in-law had recently died, she apologized, and her husband had insisted that the first daughter be named after his mother, *Mauran.* My mother thought it the ugliest name she had ever heard, and she talked my father into what she believed was an improvement, a combination of *Mauran* and her own mother's name, *Felicia.*

❺ "Her name is *Mao-ree-shee-ah,*" my mother said to the group of women.

"Why that's a beautiful name," the new mothers cried. "*Moor-ee-sha, Moor-ee-sha,*" they cooed into the pink blanket. *Moor-ee-sha* it was when we returned to the States eleven years later. Sometimes, American tongues found even that mispronunciation tough to say and called her *Maria* or *Marsha* or *Maudy* from her nickname *Maury.* I pitied her. What an awful name to have to transport across borders!

Vocabulary ▶
transport (trans pôrt′) *v.* carry from one place to another

💭 THINK ALOUD

Making Predictions

Draw students' attention to the paragraph in the middle of the next page that begins, "Our first few years in the States . . ." Use this think aloud to model the skill of predicting (introduced on p. 184):

> When I read the sentence, "Our first few years in the States, though, ethnicity was not yet 'in,'" I realize that it holds clues about what will happen to the author as she grows up. "Our first few years in the States" tells me that she is talking about America when she was young, in the 1950s.

> "Ethnicity was not yet 'in'" uses a slang term, *in,* to mean "in fashion." *Ethnicity* puzzles me, so I check a dictionary and find that *ethnicity* refers to a group of people who share a racial or national heritage. I realize the author is saying that in America in the 1950s, it was not fashionable to have an unusual national or cultural heritage. However, the author uses the word *yet,* so I infer that this will change and her ethnicity will one day be "in." I'll read on to see if my prediction is confirmed.

My little sister, Ana, had the easiest time of all. She was plain *Anne*—that is, only her name was plain, for she turned out to be the pale, blond "American beauty" in the family. The only Hispanic thing about her was the affectionate nicknames her boyfriends sometimes gave her. *Anita*, or as one goofy guy used to sing to her to the tune of the banana advertisement, *Anita Banana*.[3]

Later, during her college years in the late '60s, there was a push to pronounce Third World names correctly. I remember calling her long distance at her group house and a roommate answering.

"Can I speak to Ana?" I asked, pronouncing her name the American way.

"Ana?" The man's voice hesitated. "Oh! you must mean *Ah-nah*!"

Our first few years in the States, though, ethnicity was not yet "in." Those were the blond, blue-eyed, bobby sock years of junior high and high school before the '60s ushered in peasant blouses, hoop earrings, serapes.[4] My initial desire to be known by my correct Dominican name faded. I just wanted to be Judy and merge with the Sallys and Janes in my class. But inevitably, my accent and coloring gave me away. "So where are you from, Judy?"

"New York," I told my classmates. After all, I had been born blocks away at Columbia Presbyterian Hospital.

"I mean, *originally*."

"From the Caribbean," I answered vaguely, for if I specified, no one was quite sure on what continent our island was located.

"Really? I've been to Bermuda. We went last April for spring vacation. I got the worst sunburn! So, are you from Portoriko?"

"No," I sighed. "From the Dominican Republic."

"Where's that?"

"South of Bermuda."

---

3. **Anita Banana** play on the name *Chiquita Banana*, a character in a company's ad.
4. **serapes** (sə rä′ pēz) *n.* colorful shawls worn in Latin America.

"Her name is Mao-ree-shee-ah," my mother said to the group of women.

◄ **Vocabulary**
inevitably
(in ev′ i tə blē) *adv.*
unavoidably

Fact and Opinion
How could you check the fact that the narrator was born in Columbia Presbyterian Hospital?

8 Comprehension
What other names was Julia known by when she came to the United States?

7 Fact and Opinion

1. **Ask** the Fact and Opinion question.

   Answer: That fact could be checked in public records at a courthouse. It could also be checked with the hospital itself, if those records are still available.

2. Ask students to fill in their answers in **Reading Skill Graphic Organizer A.**

3. Point out to students that the author is using this fact to support her claim that she is from New York.

4. Explain that she realizes that even though she is from New York, her heritage is Dominican.

5. **Ask:** Do you think she wants to deny her heritage?

   Possible response: She wants to fit in with the kids at her school, but she also wants to tell the truth about her place of birth.

► **Monitor Progress:** Make sure that students understand there is a variety of reliable sources in which to check facts. Review their completed graphic organizers to evaluate their understanding.

► **Reteach:** If students have difficulty identifying the appropriate resources to use for fact-checking, review the different options available and help students match kinds of information with specific resources.

8 Comprehension

Answer: She is known as Julia, Jules, Hey Jude, Alcatraz, and Judy.

 FLUENCY

Distribute copies of this page, and pair students. Direct students' attention to the paragraph in the middle of the page that begins, "Our first few years in the States . . ." Have partners take turns reading sentences aloud until they have completed the paragraph and the rest of the page. While one partner reads, the other should mark any words with which the reader has difficulty.

Circulate to monitor fluency. Collect students' marked up copies of the page, and review difficult words and passages. Look for these problem spots:

• If students have difficulty with the word *initial*, help them sound out each syllable in turn. Then, explain that *initial* means "first." Encourage students to pair *initial* with the following word, *desire*, to result in "what she wanted at first."

• If students have difficulty with the word *Portoriko*, explain that the spelling is incorrect although the sound is similar to that of the correct spelling, *Puerto Rico*. Point out that the author is making a point about variations in pronunciation by speakers of different backgrounds.

9 **?** **Connecting to the Big Question**

1. Point out to students that a person can feel more than one feeling at a time based on what they know.

2. **Ask:** What details of the author's feelings about her family are revealed in this passage?

   Possible response: She is self-conscious about how many family members attend her graduation and how they stick out.

3. **Ask:** Do you think the author has any other feelings for her family members?

   Possible response: Yes, she probably feels love and affection for her family, even though she is self-conscious about them.

4. Tell students to look for additional situations in which Julia Alvarez seems to feel more than one feeling based on her knowledge.

Spiral Review

Central Idea

1. Remind students that they studied the concept of central idea in the Unit 2 Focus on Craft and Structure (pp. 180–183)

2. Have students reread this page. Then, **ask** students the Spiral Review question.

   Answer: Her Spanish name carries with it her proud Dominican heritage, the history of her family for several generations, and the close bonds she has with her family today. She wants to fit in with her peers, but she feels ashamed of being singled out as a "foreigner."

Vocabulary ►
chaotic (kā ät´ ik) *adj.* completely confused

Spiral Review
CENTRAL IDEA Explain why Alvarez's Spanish name is an important detail in this essay.

9

They were just being curious, I knew, but I burned with shame whenever they singled me out as a "foreigner," a rare, exotic friend.

"Say your name in Spanish, oh please say it!" I had made mouths drop one day by rattling off my full name, which according to Dominican custom, included my middle names, Mother's and Father's surnames for four generations back.

"Julia Altagracia María Teresa Álvarez Tavares Perello Espaillat Julia Pérez Rochet González," I pronounced it slowly, a name as chaotic with sounds as a Middle Eastern bazaar[5] or market day in a South American village. •

My Dominican heritage was never more apparent than when my extended family attended school occasions. For my graduation, they all came, the whole lot of aunts and uncles and the many little cousins who snuck in without tickets. They sat in the first row in order to better understand the Americans' fast-spoken English. But how

---

5. **bazaar** (bə zär´) *n.* marketplace, frequently outdoors.

could they listen when they were constantly speaking among themselves in florid-sounding phrases, rococo[6] consonants, rich, rhyming vowels?

Introducing them to my friends was a further trial to me. These relatives had such complicated names and there were so many of them, and their relationships to myself were so convoluted. There was my Tía Josefina, who was not really an aunt but a much older cousin. And her daughter, Aida Margarita, who was adopted, *una hija de crianza.* My uncle of affection, Tío José, brought my *madrina* Tía Amelia and her *comadre* Tía Pilar. My friends rarely had more than a "Mom and Dad" to introduce.

After the commencement ceremony my family waited outside in the parking lot while my friends and I signed yearbooks with nicknames which recalled our high school good times: "Beans" and "Pepperoni" and "Alcatraz." We hugged and cried and promised to keep in touch.

---

6. **rococo** (rə kō′ kō) *adj.* fancy style of art of the early eighteenth century.

"Say your name in Spanish, oh please say it!"

10 Compare

1. With students, compare Alvarez's attitude toward her status as an immigrant at the beginning of the essay to the attitude she reflects at the end of the essay. First, have students reread the text on p. 196 through the first full paragraph on p. 197.

2. Invite students to describe Alvarez's view of being an immigrant at that time in her life.

   Possible responses: She feels different, like an outsider. She is bothered by the way Americans mispronounce her family's names. She defends her language. She feels torn between her Hispanic culture and the new culture in which she lives.

3. Have a volunteer read the bracketed paragraph on this page. **Ask:** Has Alvarez found acceptance among her friends? How can you tell?

   Possible response: The author has found acceptance. She mentions signing yearbooks and recalls her nicknames as part of "good times."

4. Point out that, although the author's attitude toward her status as an immigrant seems to have changed during the essay, her friendly and humorous tone has remained the same throughout.

ASSESS

Language Study
Vocabulary

1. False. A *chaotic* place is completed confused, not calm.

2. False. *Inevitably* describes something that is going to happen no matter what. It is more likely you will fail a test, not pass, if you do not study.

3. False. To *transport*, or carry, water from one place to another you would need to use something that could hold the water, unlike a net with holes in it.

4. True. When students *pursue,* or follow, a career path in medicine, they often study in hospitals as part of their training.

5. False. If someone identified another person incorrectly, he or she *mistook,* that person. Identical twins look alike and are often identified incorrectly, so it would not be surprising.

Word Study
Part A
Sample answers:

A *prescription* is a <u>written</u> order from a doctor. A *scribe* is someone who <u>writes</u>. A *manuscript* is a text <u>written</u> by a person.

Part B
Sample answers:

1. The root "-scrip-" means "to write." A *script* consists of written lines and directions telling an actor what to say and do.

2. The root "-scrib-" means "to write." *Scribbling* may be fun to do, but to write a mark in a book makes it difficult for the next person to read and enjoy it.

Literary Analysis

Possible responses appear below. Check to be sure students support their responses with evidence from the text.

1. **(a)** Her family pronounces her name "Hoo-*lee*-ah." **(b)** In English, the *J* in *Julia* makes the /j/ sound, but in Spanish it makes the /h/ sound. Also, it sounds similar in its English pronunciation to common names like *Julie, Judy,* and even *Juliet.*

Our goodbyes went on too long. I heard my father's voice calling out across the parking lot, "*Hoo-lee-tah! Vamonos!*"

Back home, my *tíos* and *tías* and *primas*, Mami and Papi, and *mis hermanas* had a party for me with *sancocho* and a storebought *pudín*, inscribed with *Happy Graduation, Julie.* There were many gifts—that was a plus to a large family! I got several wallets and a suitcase with my initials and a graduation charm from my godmother and money from my uncles. The biggest gift was a portable typewriter from my parents for writing my stories and poems.

Someday, the family predicted, my name would be well-known throughout the United States. I laughed to myself, wondering which one I would go by.

Vocabulary ▶
inscribed (in skrībd´)
v. written on

Language Study

Vocabulary Each statement below includes one of the following words from "Names/Nombres." Explain why you think each statement is true or false.

> mistook   pursue   transport   inevitably   chaotic

1. A *chaotic* place is calm and relaxing.
2. If you do not study for a test, you will *inevitably* pass.
3. A net is a useful tool if you want to *transport* water.
4. A hospital is a good place to *pursue* a medical career.
5. If someone *mistook* you for your identical twin, you would be surprised.

WORD STUDY

The **Latin root -scrib-** or **-scrip-** means "to write."

In this story, the narrator's family buys a special cake for her graduation party. The cake is **inscribed** with writing that says "Happy Graduation."

Word Study

Part A Explain how the **Latin root -scrib-** or **-scrip-** contributes to the meanings of *prescription, scribe,* and *manuscript.* Consult a dictionary if necessary.

Part B Use context and what you know about the Latin root *-scrib-* or *-scrip-* to explain your answers.

1. How is the *script* of a play helpful to an actor?
2. Why might you get in trouble for *scribbling* in a book?

---

2. You might check public records or hospital records.

3. Her mother is stating an opinion that is expressed through the word *ugliest,* which is a judgment.

4. Later, during her college years in the late 1960s, it was more appropriate to pronounce Third World names correctly. During the first years that we lived in the United States, though, ethnicity was not yet popular.

5. **(a)** This sentence has a serious tone as it says, "I burned with shame," which is a serious emotion. **(b)** This sentence has a humorous tone as it mentions getting many gifts, which is a pleasant experience, and the idea that getting many gifts is a plus of having a large family is amusing.

6. **(a)** Julia says she is from New York. **(b)** She doesn't want to appear foreign. **(c)** Some students may say no because they are proud of their heritage. Others may say yes because they want to fit in.

Literary Analysis

Key Ideas and Details: Fact and Opinion

1. **(a)** How does Julia's family say her name? **(b) Analyze Cause and Effect** Explain why some English speakers mispronounce her name.

2. **Fact and Opinion** How might you check the fact that Julia Alvarez was born in New York City?

3. **Fact and Opinion** Alvarez relates the story of her sister's name by saying, "My mother thought it the ugliest name she had ever heard." Is her mother stating a fact or an opinion? Explain.

Craft and Structure: Tone

4. **Tone** "Names/Nombres" is written in an informal, or friendly, tone. In a chart like the one on the right, rewrite the two sentences in a more serious, or formal, tone.

5. **Tone** Tell which of the following sentences from "Names/Nombres" has a humorous tone, and which has a serious tone. Explain your answers. **(a)** *They were just being curious, I knew, but I burned with shame whenever they singled me out as a "foreigner," a rare exotic friend.* **(b)** *There were many gifts—that was a plus to a large family!*

Integration of Knowledge and Ideas

6. **(a)** How does Julia respond when her classmates ask her where she comes from? **(b) Draw Conclusions:** Why does she respond as she does? **(c) Evaluate:** Would you make the same decision in the same situation? Why or why not?

7. **(a)** Explain how the title captures the focus, or main topic, of Alvarez's narrative. **(b) Analyze:** How do Alvarez's feelings about the topic change over time? **(c) Synthesize:** What do names represent for Alvarez and others?

8. **What is important to know?** With a small group, discuss the following questions: **(a)** What do you think Alvarez learned about language differences from her experience as a young bilingual speaker? **(b)** Would it have been valuable for her to correct people who mispronounced her name? Explain your answer.

| **Informal Tone** |
| "Later, during her college years in the late '60s, there was a push to pronounce Third World names correctly."

"Our first few years in the States, though, ethnicity was not yet 'in'." |

↓

| **Formal Tone** |
| |

ACADEMIC VOCABULARY

As you write and speak about "Names/Nombres," use the words related to conflict that you explored on page 163 of this text.

---

7. **(a)** The title contains the English and Spanish words for *names,* and it reflects the author's dual identity as an immigrant. **(b)** She starts by feeling proud of her heritage, and then, as a teenager, she tries to deny it. Finally, she seems to accept it and take pride in it again. **(c)** Names reflect Alvarez's desire to fit in and allow her the choice of sharing different aspects of her identity. For Alvarez and others, nicknames can reflect affection or admiration.

8. **What is important to know?**
   (a) Student responses may reflect an understanding that language can identify people and their culture. Sometimes this can set people apart and make them feel different. But it can also be the thing that holds families and friends together and helps them celebrate their culture. **(b)** Some students may feel that it would have been valuable to correct mispronunciations of Alvarez's name as it would educate people and celebrate diversity. Others may think it would be better to not correct people and draw less attention to the foreign sound of the name.

Online Writer's Notebook

Students can use the Online Writer's Notebook to record all responses.

Close Reading Activities Continued

Conventions

1. Introduce the skill, using the instruction on the student page.

2. Discuss the definitions and the examples.

Think Aloud: Model the Skill

To model the skill of distinguishing between action and linking verbs, use the following think aloud. Say to students:

> Sometimes I have trouble deciding if a verb is an action verb or a linking verb. If the words after the verb are a description of the subject, I know that the verb is probably a linking verb. Suppose a friend tells me, "The baby leopard grew tired." Because *tired* is a description of the leopard, I know *grew* is a linking verb in this sentence. On the other hand, let's say that someone else tells me, "The baby leopard grew quickly." I know that *quickly* is not a description of the baby leopard, so in this sentence *grew* must be an action verb.

Practice A

1. *was*: linking verb

2. *celebrated*: action

3. *moved*: action

4. *made*: action

5. *wished*: action

Reading Application

But at school I *was* Judy or Judith, and once an English teacher *mistook* me for Juliet.

Practice B
Sample answers:

1. The family *lived* in an apartment building where they *were* very comfortable.

2. Of the three sisters, Ana *acted* most like an American, and she *felt* more at home here.

3. Mauricia *said* her name was hard to pronounce, but that did not *seem* to bother her.

4. Julia's relatives *celebrated* her graduation, and they *were* very proud of her.

Conventions: Action and Linking Verbs

A **verb** expresses an action or a state of being. Every complete sentence includes at least one verb.

An **action verb** such as *jump* or *dance* expresses an action of a person or thing. Some verbs, such as *guess, believe,* and *wish,* express mental actions rather than physical actions.

A **linking verb** such as *am, is,* and *were,* connects a noun or pronoun to a word that identifies, renames, or describes it. Other common linking verbs include *seem, feel, look,* and *become.*

Action Verbs	Linking Verbs
Jacob *jumped* over the rocks. (The action is *jumping*.)	Katie *is* an artist. (*Is* links *Katie* to *artist*. *Artist* renames *Katie*.)
Tamara *guessed* the answer. (The action is *guessing*.)	The blanket *feels* soft. (*Feels* links *blanket* to *soft*. *Soft* describes the *blanket*.)

Practice A
Identify the verb(s) in each sentence and indicate whether they are action verbs or linking verbs.

1. Julia's mother was embarrassed.

2. The whole family celebrated Julia's graduation.

3. The family moved from the Dominican Republic.

4. Julia made many friends at school.

5. Julia's friends wished to hear her name.

Reading Application In "Names/Nombres," find one sentence that includes both an action verb and a linking verb.

Practice B
Rewrite each sentence so that it contains both an action verb and a linking verb.

1. Julia's family lived in an apartment building.

2. Of the three sisters, Ana fit in most easily.

3. Mauricia thought that her name was hard to pronounce.

4. Julia's relatives celebrated her graduation.

Writing Application Write a short paragraph about "Names/Nombres." Use at least three action verbs and two linking verbs.

Writing Application
Sample answer:

When the Alvarez family <u>arrived</u> in New York City, it <u>seemed</u> that everyone <u>said</u> their names differently. Even the teachers at Julia Alvarez's school <u>called</u> her by different names like Judy or Judith. By the time Julia got to high school she <u>was</u> very popular and it <u>showed</u> in the nicknames her friends <u>gave</u> her, such as Jules or Hey Jude.

Writing to Sources

Narrative Text "Names/Nombres" relates a **personal anecdote**, a brief true story about a personal experience. Write a personal anecdote about a happy experience you had growing up.

- Brainstorm a list of interesting experiences you have had.
- Choose the experience you will most enjoy writing about.
- Review "Names/ Nombres" to see how a writer uses vivid details to convey an experience. Then, use descriptive and sensory language that captures what you saw, heard, and felt.
- Include brief descriptions of the setting in which the experience took place, and of other people who took part in the experience.
- Write down your reactions to the experience.
- Use your notes to write your personal narrative.

Grammar Application Use both action verbs and linking verbs in your anecdote.

Speaking and Listening

Comprehension and Collaboration A **monologue** is a speech in which someone expresses his or her thoughts. Write and deliver a monologue that presents the thoughts of young Julia Alvarez as she hears someone mispronounce her name for the first time. Deliver your monologue to a partner.

Follow these steps to complete the assignment:

- Jot down words and phrases that express the feelings you think Alvarez experienced.
- Describe why you, in the character of Alvarez, would feel that way.
- Use vocabulary that reflects Alvarez's personality. Review the selection to find words and phrases that Alvarez typically uses.
- Be sure to consistently use first-person pronouns such as *I, my, me, we,* and *us.*

Common Core State Standards

Writing
3.d. Use precise words and phrases, relevant descriptive details, and sensory language to convey experiences and events.

Speaking and Listening
6. Adapt speech to a variety of contexts and tasks.

Language
1. Demonstrate command of the conventions of standard English grammar and usage when writing or speaking.
6. Acquire and use accurately grade-appropriate general academic and domain-specific words and phrases; gather vocabulary knowledge when considering a word or phrase important to comprehension or expression.

Writing to Sources

1. Review the assignment, using the instruction on the student page.
2. In order to help students brainstorm for ideas for their personal anecdotes, have them make a list of funny stories about their families. Help them add details by asking them to describe what is funny about the story. To give students guidance for writing this personal anecdote, provide them with the **Support for Writing** page for this selection in the *Student Companion All-in-One Workbook.*
3. To evaluate students' personal anecdotes, use the General (Holistic) Writing Rubrics pp. 256–257 in *Professional Development Guidebook.* In addition, you might evaluate the organization, the word choice, and the tone.

Grammar Application
Have students check their drafts for action and linking verbs.

Six Traits Focus

✓	Ideas	✓	Word Choice
	Organization		Sentence Fluency
✓	Voice		Conventions

Speaking and Listening

1. Review the assignment, using the instruction on the student page.
2. To support students' work on the assignment, have them complete the **Support for Extend Your Learning** page for this selection in the *Student Companion All-in-One Workbook.*

Time and Resource Manager

LESSON PACING GUIDE

Langston Terrace

| DAY 1 | **Preteach/Teach** |

- Administer the Reading and Vocabulary Warm-ups, as necessary.
- Introduce the Key Ideas and Details skill: Main Idea.
- Introduce the Craft and Structure skill: Author's Influences.
- Use the Close Reading Model to demonstrate the application of the skills.
- Review the selection vocabulary, as necessary, with students who need additional support.
- Prepare students to read the selection by reviewing with them the Multidraft Reading Strategies.

| DAY 2 | **Teach** |

- Informally monitor comprehension while students read.
- Use the Comprehension questions to confirm understanding.
- Develop students' ability to know the main idea and analyze the author's influences using the sidenote questions.
- Reinforce vocabulary with the Vocabulary notes.
- Reinforce unit focus standards using the Spiral Review prompts.

| DAY 3 | **Assess** |

- Assess students' comprehension and mastery of the skills by having them answer the Literary Analysis questions.
- Have students complete the Vocabulary activities.
- Develop students' understanding of roots and affixes by having them complete the Word Study activities.

| DAY 4 | **Extend/Assess** |

- Build students' ability to master grammar concepts and conventions by having them complete the Conventions lesson.
- Have students complete the Writing to Sources activity and write a journal entry. (You may assign as homework.)
- Extend learning by having students complete the Research and Technology activity: an informative presentation.
- Administer the Selection Test or Open-Book Test.

Common Core State Standards

Reading Informational Texts 1. Cite textual evidence to support analysis of what the text says explicitly as well as inferences drawn from the text.

2. Determine a central idea of a text and how it is conveyed through particular details; provide a summary of the text distinct from personal opinions or judgments.

Writing 3. Write narratives to develop real or imagined experiences or events using effective technique, relevant descriptive details, and well-structured event sequences.

3.b. Use narrative techniques, such as dialogue, pacing, and description, to develop experiences, events, and/or characters.

8. Gather relevant information from multiple print and digital sources; assess the credibility of each source.

Speaking and Listening 4. Present claims and findings, sequencing ideas logically and using pertinent descriptions, facts, and details to accentuate main ideas or themes; use appropriate eye contact, adequate volume, and clear pronunciation.

Language 1. Demonstrate command of standard English grammar and usage when writing or speaking.

6. Acquire and use accurately grade-appropriate general academic and domain-specific words and phrases; gather vocabulary knowledge when considering a word or phrase important to comprehension or expression.

Daily Block Scheduling

Each day in this Lesson Pacing Guide represents a 40–50 minute period. Teachers using block scheduling may combine days to revise pacing. In addition, teachers may differentiate and support core instruction by integrating components for extended and intensive support as students require. See the Guide to Resources (facing page).

Section		L1	L2	L3	L4	EL	ALL	RESOURCES	PRINT	CD	ONLINE
Warm Up		✔	✔			✔		Vocabulary Warm-ups			✔
		✔	✔			✔		Reading Warm-ups			✔
							✔	Background Video			✔
							✔	Selection Audio		Hear It!	✔
Comprehension/ Selection Support							✔	Writing About the Big Question	Student Companion Workbook		✔
							✔	Literary Analysis	Student Companion Workbook		✔
							✔	Reading	Student Companion Workbook		✔
							✔	Vocabulary Builder	Student Companion Workbook		✔
					✔			Enrichment			✔
				✔	✔	✔		Conventions	Student Companion Workbook		✔
				✔	✔	✔		Writing to Sources	Student Companion Workbook		✔
				✔	✔	✔		Research and Technology	Student Companion Workbook		
Differentiated Instruction/ Additional Support							✔	Additional Standards Practice	Common Core Companion		✔
							✔	Close Reading Practice	Close Reading Notebook		✔
		✔	✔					Adapted Reader's Notebook			✔
						✔		English Reader's Notebook:			✔
						✔		Spanish Reader's Notebook			✔
						✔		Graphic Organizer A			✔
		✔	✔			✔		Graphic Organizer B			✔
		✔	✔			✔		"Response to a Tragedy"	Reality Central Student Edition and Writing Journal		✔
		✔	✔			✔		Practice and Assess	Reading Kit		✔
Monitor Progress							✔	Selection Test		Exam View	✔
							✔	Open-Book Test		Exam View	✔
Digital Resources							✔	Close Reading Tool			✔
							✔	Online Writer's Notebook			✔

One-on-one teaching Group work Whole class instruction Independent work A Assessment Digital Resource

LEARNER LEVELS

L1 Special-Needs Students
L2 Below-Level Students (Tier 2)
L3 On-Level Students (Tier 1)
L4 Advanced Students (Tier 1)
EL English Learners
All All Students

❶ What is important to know?

Read • Discuss • Research • Write As students read, they will explore the Big Question through text analysis of the selection. Encourage students to note comments and additional questions as they read, using text evidence to support their thoughts. Students may wish to log their comments, questions, and evidence in a three-column chart. Students should refer to their notes to help them deepen their understanding of the selection through discussion, research, and writing.

❷ Close Reading Focus

1. Explain to students that the main idea of an essay is often presented near the beginning. Students may be able to understand the main idea more clearly after they have finished reading the essay and they can consider all the information the author has presented.

2. Explain to students that examining an author's influences can help them to better understand and enjoy a selection. For example, if you are reading a journal entry by a man who immigrated to the U.S. in the early 1900s, you might realize that his view of the trip is influenced by the time in which he lived.

ⓒ Building Knowledge

Meet the Author

Young **Eloise Greenfield** (b. 1929) loved reading, but she did not enjoy writing. One day, though, she sat down and began to write. Since then, she has published more than thirty books. She once said, "I love words . . . sometimes they make me laugh. Other times, I feel a kind of pain in struggling to find the right ones. But I keep struggling because I want to do my best, and because I want children to have the best."

ⓒ **Common Core State Standards**

Reading Informational Texts
1. Cite textual evidence to support analysis of what the text says explicitly as well as inferences drawn from the text.
2. Determine a central idea of a text and how it is conveyed through particular details; provide a summary of the text distinct from personal opinions or judgments.

Language
6. Acquire and use accurately grade-appropriate general academic and domain-specific words and phrases; gather vocabulary knowledge when considering a word or phrase important to comprehension or expression.

❶ What is important to know?

Explore the Big Question as you read "Langston Terrace." Take notes on ways in which the story explores the importance of knowing about place, culture, and history.

❷ CLOSE READING FOCUS

Key Ideas and Details: **Main Idea**

The **main idea** is the most important point in a literary work. Sometimes the main idea is stated directly. At other times, you must infer, or figure out, the main idea by identifying key details in the text.
- Key details often reveal what a work is about.
- They are sometimes repeated throughout a work.
- They are related to other details in a work.
- Together, the key details support the main idea.

Craft and Structure: **Author's Influences**

An **author's influences** are the factors that affect his or her writing. These influences may include historical factors, such as world events that happened during the author's lifetime. For example, the gold rush of 1849 might have influenced the ideas of an author who grew up in California in the 1850s. Authors are also influenced by cultural factors such as the way they live and the issues they think are important. As you read, look for details that indicate the author's influences.

❸ Vocabulary

You will encounter the following words in "Langston Terrace." Identify the ones that relate to the idea of people living together. Jot down the words in your notebook and find their definitions as you read.

applications	resident	reunion
community	choral	homey

ⓒ TEXT COMPLEXITY **RUBRIC**

Langston Terrace	
Qualitative Measures	
Context/Knowledge Demands	Urban Washington, D.C., housing project, 1930s 1 2 ③ 4 5
Structure/Language Conventionality and Clarity	Longer sentences; on-level vocabulary 1 2 ③ 4 5
Levels of Meaning/ Purpose/Concept Level	Challenging concept (reflective thoughts about life in a housing project) 1 2 3 ④ 5
Quantitative Measures	

Lexile	1000L	**Text Length**	Word Count: 1,125

Reader and Task Suggestions	
Preparing to Read the Text	**Leveled Tasks**
• Have students list the effects of experiencing a sense of community.	*Levels of Meaning* If students will have difficulty with author's point of view, ask students to describe how the author felt about her home and give specific details from the text.
• Guide students to use Multidraft Reading strategies (TE p. 208).	*Analyzing* If students will not have difficulty with point of view, discuss what elements the author describes as making a good "growing-up place."

CLOSE READING MODEL

The passage below is from Eloise Greenfield's memoir "Langston Terrace." The annotations to the right of the passage show ways in which you can use close reading skills to find the main idea and analyze the author's influences.

from "Langston Terrace"

I fell in love with Langston Terrace the very first time I saw it. **1** Our family had been living in two rooms of a three-story house when Mama and Daddy saw the newspaper article telling of the plans to build it. **2** It was going to be a low-rent housing project in northeast Washington, and it would be named in honor of John Mercer Langston, the famous black lawyer, educator, and congressman. **3**

So many people needed housing and wanted to live there, many more than there would be room for. They were all filling out applications, hoping to be one of the 274 families chosen. My parents filled one out, too.

I didn't want to move. I knew our house was crowded—there were eleven of us, six adults and five children—but I didn't want to leave my friends, and I didn't want to go to a strange place and be the new person in a neighborhood and a school where most of the other children already knew each other. I was eight years old, and I had been to three schools. We had moved five times since we'd been in Washington, each time trying to get more space and a better place to live. But rent was high so we'd always lived in a house with relatives and friends, and shared the rent. **4**

Main Idea
1 Greenfield states a main idea in this topic sentence: she "fell in love with Langston Terrace" the first time she saw it.

Author's Influences
2 Here Greenfield describes her family's living situation. An author's early life and experiences can strongly influence his or her writing.

Author's Influences
3 Greenfield explains that the housing project was named after a famous African American. You may infer that this detail influenced her feelings about Langston Terrace.

Main Idea
4 Greenfield states key details about her family, friends, and school to support the main idea that she did not want to move.

🔔 Daily Bellringer

For each class during which you will teach this selection, have students complete one of the five Revision activities for Week 10 in *Daily Bellringer Activities*. You may wish to use additional activities that are applicable to this selection.

Vocabulary

If students require support with selection vocabulary, use this routine:

1. Write the following words and definitions on the board:

   applications *n.* forms filled out to make a request

   resident *adj.* living in a particular place

   reunion *n.* a gathering of people who have been separated

   community *n.* group of people living in the same area

   choral *adj.* related to a singing group or choir

   homey *adj.* comfortable; having a feeling of home

2. Have students say each word aloud.

3. Use the word in a sentence that defines the word.

🧑‍🤝‍🧑 DIFFERENTIATED INSTRUCTION

🟢 Extended Support— English Learners
Have students complete the **Reading and Vocabulary Warm-ups** for this selection in the *Student Companion All-in-One Workbook* before they read. Assign the prereading pages and the adapted selection in the *Reader's Notebook: English Learner's Version*. Then, have students listen to portions of the selection in the *Student eText* or on the *Hear It!* CD-ROM.

🔲 🔲 Extended Support— Struggling Readers
Have students complete the **Reading and Vocabulary Warm-ups** for this selection in the *Student Companion All-in-One Workbook* before they read. Assign the prereading pages and the adapted selection in the *Reader's Notebook: Adapted Version*. Then, have students listen to portions of the selection in the *Student eText* or on the *Hear It!* CD-ROM (adapted text).

Extended Support— Reluctant Readers
To build motivation and engagement before assigning the selection, have students read "Response to a Tragedy," a thematically related selection in *Reality Central*. Then, use the questions at the conclusion of the related selection to guide discussion.

MULTIDRAFT READING

This icon ● marks natural pauses in the selection. To assist struggling readers and to deepen comprehension for all, assign the text in "chunks," separated by the icons, and apply multidraft reading protocols. For each reading, have students set the purpose indicated:

- **First reading:** Students should read the selection independently and think about its basic meaning.
- **Second reading:** Students should analyze the text's key ideas and details and its craft and structure, and respond to the side-column prompts.
- **Third reading:** Students should integrate knowledge and ideas, connect the text to other texts and to the world, and answer the end-of-selection questions.

For more guidance, refer to the *Classroom Strategies and Teaching Routines* card on multidraft reading.

❶ Critical Viewing

Possible response: The men may be building a large building or several buildings. The size of the crew, the extensive collection of tools, and the tall ladder show it is a big project.

Langston Terrace
—Eloise Greenfield—

Builders in the City, 1993, Jacob Lawrence, The Jacob and Gwendolyn Lawrence Foundation/© Artists Rights Society (ARS), New York

❶ ▲ **Critical Viewing**
What do you think these men are building? Why do you think so?

Vocabulary ▶
applications (ap´ li kā´ shənz) *n.* forms filled out to make a request

I fell in love with Langston Terrace the very first time I saw it. Our family had been living in two rooms of a three-story house when Mama and Daddy saw the newspaper article telling of the plans to build it. It was going to be a low-rent housing project in northeast Washington, and it would be named in honor of John Mercer Langston, the famous black lawyer, educator, and congressman.

So many people needed housing and wanted to live there, many more than there would be room for. They were all filling out applications, hoping to be one of the 274 families chosen. My parents filled out one, too.

I didn't want to move. I knew our house was crowded—there were eleven of us, six adults and five children—but I didn't want to leave my friends, and I didn't want to go

💬 VOCABULARY DEVELOPMENT

Thematic Vocabulary: The Big Question
As students are discussing "Langston Terrace," encourage them to use the words for discussing the Big Question presented on pp. 162–163. You might encourage them with sentence starters like these:

1. The *concept* behind naming Langston Terrace in honor of John Mercer Langston was . . .

2. The *purpose* of the application for residency at Langston Terrace was . . .
3. It was the author's *guess* that most parents thought of Langston Terrace as . . .
4. A resident council was formed to *study* . . .
5. Langston Terrace was the *source* of many happy memories for the author, including . . .

to a strange place and be the new person in a neighborhood and a school where most of the other children already knew each other. I was eight years old, and I had been to three schools. We had moved five times since we'd been in Washington, each time trying to get more space and a better place to live. But rent was high so we'd always lived in a house with relatives and friends, and shared the rent.

One of the people in our big household was Lillie, Daddy's cousin and Mama's best friend. She and her husband also applied for a place in the new project, and during the months that it was being built, Lillie and Mama would sometimes walk fifteen blocks just to stand and watch the workmen digging holes and laying bricks. They'd just stand there watching and wishing. And at home, that was all they could talk about. "When we get our new place . . ." "If we get our new place . . ."

Lillie got her good news first. I can still see her and Mama standing at the bottom of the hall steps, hugging and laughing and crying, happy for Lillie, then sitting on the steps, worrying and wishing again for Mama.

Finally, one evening, a woman came to the house with our good news, and Mama and Daddy went over and picked out the house they wanted. We moved on my ninth birthday. Wilbur, Gerald, and I went to school that morning from one house, and when Daddy came to pick us up, he took us home to another one. All the furniture had been moved while we were in school.

Langston Terrace was a lovely birthday present. It was built on a hill, a group of tan brick houses and apartments with a playground as its center. The red mud surrounding the concrete walks had not yet been covered with black soil and grass seed, and the holes that would soon be homes for young trees were filled with rainwater. But it still looked beautiful to me.

We had a whole house all to ourselves. Upstairs and downstairs. Two bedrooms, and the living room would be my bedroom at night. Best of all, I wasn't the only new

LITERATURE IN CONTEXT

Biography Connection

The Man Langston Terrace Honors

John Mercer Langston (1829–1897) became Ohio's first African American lawyer in 1854. Langston helped runaway slaves escape along the Ohio part of the Underground Railroad. In 1868, he started the law department at Howard University in Washington, D.C., becoming the department's dean and later the university's acting president. Langston became the first African American congressman from Virginia when he was elected to the U.S. House of Representatives in 1888.

Connect to the Literature

Does this information support Eloise Greenfield's description of Langston? Why or why not?

Comprehension
Why is the move to Langston Terrace exciting for the whole family?

PART 2 • Langston Terrace **209**

:::: DIFFERENTIATED INSTRUCTION

Support for Less Proficient Readers
Prepare an **Anticipation Guide** (*Professional Development Guidebook,* p. 38) with the following statements:

• People are not influenced by the places they live as children.

• In a large community, an individual's behavior does not affect others.

Give students a copy of the prepared **Guide** and have them mark their responses in the Me column. Have pairs discuss the statements and mark the Group column. After students have read the selection, have them fill in the After Reading column.

Support for English Learners
Before students read, preteach vocabulary that will help them comprehend the selection. Write the following words and phrases on the board and discuss their meanings: *housing project* (public housing for lower-income families), *neighborhood* (area near and including where you live), *move* (relocate), *relatives* (people related to you by blood; family members), *good news* (information that is agreeable or pleasant). As students learn each, have them write sentences to show their understanding.

---

❷ Literature in Context
Biography Connection

1. Have students read the Literature in Context feature.

2. Then, have students reread the first paragraph of the selection. **Ask** them what information is provided by Eloise about John Langston.

   Answer: He was a famous African American lawyer, an educator, and a congressman.

Connect to the Literature

Ask students the question on the student page.

Answer: Yes, the information confirms that he was an African American lawyer who taught and who is probably famous for his "firsts"—his achievements as a lawyer and congressman.

❸ Summarize

1. Remind students that as they read, they should pause occasionally to think about events that have happened so far.

2. To summarize, students should organize the most important events and ideas in order. Then they identify their connections.

3. **Ask** students to read and summarize the bracketed text.

   Possible response: Mama and Lillie want to live in the new housing project. They are so interested in it that they walk a long way to watch it being built.

❹ Comprehension

Answer: The family has always shared a house with others in order to afford the rent. For the first time, the family has a whole house to themselves.

 **Video**

Watch the Background Video online!

 **Audio**

Selection Audio is available in the *Student eText* and on the *Hear It!* CD-ROM.

PART 2 • Langston Terrace **209**

❺ Main Idea

1. Remind students that key details often reveal the main idea of the selection. Point out that if the main idea is not directly stated, it can be found by weaving together key details that are repeated in the selection.

2. **Ask** the Main Idea question. Have students use one of the **Reading Skill Graphic Organizers** for this selection to arrive at an answer to the question.

Possible responses: There was a resident council. There were music and poetry programs. There was a playground. People cared for one another.

❻ Humanities

Builders in the City (p. 208)
Students with Books (p. 210)
Street Scene (Boy with Kite) (p. 211)
by Jacob Lawrence

The celebrated African American artist Jacob Lawrence (1917–2000) painted many colorful images of his experience of the vibrant urban black community of Harlem, New York, and the history of African Americans in general. He celebrated workers and families and wasn't afraid to portray images of poverty, violence, and social injustice. He not only painted what he saw with his own eyes but also stories that were passed down to him. Some of these stories were presented as narratives—series of small paintings with texts. His work is included in the collections of nearly 200 museums.

Vocabulary ▶
community (kə my$\overline{oo}'$ nə tē) *n.* group of people living in the same area

Main Idea
What key details so far support the main idea that Langston Terrace is a good place to live?

Vocabulary ▶
resident (rez' i dənt) *adj.* living in a particular place

choral (kôr' əl) *adj.* relating to a singing group or choir

person. Everybody was new to this new little community, and by the time school opened in the fall, we had gotten used to each other and had made friends with other children in the neighborhood, too. •

I guess most of the parents thought of the new place as an in-between place. They were glad to be there, but their dream was to save enough money to pay for a house that would be their own. Saving was hard, though, and slow, because each time somebody in a family got a raise on the job, it had to be reported to the manager of the project so that the rent could be raised, too. Most people stayed years longer than they had planned to, but they didn't let that stop them from enjoying life.

They formed a resident council to look into any neighborhood problems that might come up. They started a choral group and presented music and poetry programs on Sunday evenings in the social room or on the playground. On weekends, they played horseshoes and softball and other games. They had a reading club that met once a week at the Langston branch of the public library, after it opened in the basement of one of the apartment buildings.

Students with Books, 1966, Jacob Lawrence, The Jacob and Gwendolyn Lawrence Foundation/© Artists Rights Society (ARS), New York

210 UNIT 2 • What is important to know?

Street Scene (Boy with Kite), 1962, Jacob Lawrence, The Jacob and Gwendolyn Lawrence Foundation/© Artists Rights Society (ARS), New York.

The library was very close to my house. I could leave by my back door and be there in two minutes. The playground was right in front of my house, and after my sister Vedie was born and we moved a few doors down to a three-bedroom house, I could just look out of my bedroom window to see if any of my friends were out playing.

There were so many games to play and things to do. We played hide-and-seek at the lamppost, paddle tennis and shuffleboard, dodge ball and jacks. We danced in fireplug showers, jumped rope to rhymes, played "Bouncy, Bouncy,
8 Bally," swinging one leg over a bouncing ball, played baseball on a nearby field, had parties in the social room and bus trips to the beach. In the playroom, we played Ping-Pong and pool, learned to sew and embroider and crochet.

For us, Langston Terrace wasn't an in-between place. It was a growing-up place, a good growing-up place. Neighbors who cared, family and friends, and a lot of fun. Life was good. Not perfect, but good. We knew about problems, heard about them, saw them, lived through some hard ones ourselves, but our community wrapped itself around us, put itself between us and the hard knocks, to cushion the blows.

It's been many years since I moved away, but every once in a long while I go back, just to look at things and

7 ◄ Critical Viewing What details in this painting would appeal to children? Why?

Spiral Review
DEVELOPMENT OF IDEAS How important are memories to the author?

Author's Influences
How do the author's childhood experiences influence her attitude about the importance of family and friends?

PART 2 • Langston Terrace **211**

GUIDED EXPLORATION

7 Critical Viewing

Possible response: The bright and contrasting colors create a vivid portrait of an urban neighborhood. The boy with the kite and the girl walking the dog play on the lively city street, in the middle of everything.

8 Connecting to the Big Question

1. Point out to students that the setting, people, and events are all important features of life at Langston Terrace.

   Ask: What details described in the bracketed passage show why the author felt at home there?

   Possible response: The library and the playground were very close to her house. There were many opportunities to have fun—at the lamppost, in a nearby field, in the social room, and at the beach.

Spiral Review
Development of Ideas

1. Remind students that they studied the concept of development of ideas in the Unit 2 Focus on Craft and Structure (pp. 180–183).
2. **Ask** students the Spiral Review question.

   Possible response: The memories are very important; the details add up to a happy childhood.

9 Author's Influences

1. Remind students that cultural and historical factors include the routines, habits, and resources of a community.
2. **Ask** students how Eloise Greenfield feels about the importance of family and friends.

   Possible response: She believes they are very important and are to be treasured.
3. **Ask** the Author's Influences question.

   Possible response: She was very close to her family members and had lots of friends at Langston Terrace. She believes the love, caring, and support of family and friends are very important.

☑ ASSESS

Language Study

Vocabulary

1. Yes. An *application* is a form that is filled out to make a request. A job application is a form that is filled out by a person who is requesting a job.

2. Yes. As a group of people living in the same area, a *community* can join together to help someone in need.

3. Yes. A *reunion* is a gathering of people who have been apart.

4. No. A *choral* group is made up of people who enjoy singing.

5. Yes. A school that is comfortable and has some of the feelings of home can be *homey*.

Word Study

Part A

Sample answers:

The suffix *–ent* can mean "has," "shows," or "does." Someone who is *persistent* <u>does</u> persist, or continue steadily. One thing that <u>does</u> differ from another is *different,* or not the same. If something is *evident,* it is easily <u>shown,</u> seen, or understood.

Part B

Sample answers:

1. No, I am not *patient* when I cannot wait for something. I do not have patience, and I want it now.

2. Yes. By being *insistent,* I do insist that I really want something and I don't stop until I get it.

Literary Analysis

Possible responses appear below. Check to be sure students support their responses with evidence from the text.

1. **(a)** They keep moving to get more space and a better place to live. **(b)** Both homes are houses, not apartments. The family lives in the new house alone and uses the upstairs and the downstairs.

2. **(a)** They move on Eloise's ninth birthday. **(b)** She probably feels both excited and sad. She could be excited about moving to a larger, brand new house. She could feel a little sad about leaving her friends.

---

remember. The large stone animals that decorated the playground are still there. A walrus, a hippo, a frog, and two horses. They've started to crack now, but I remember when they first came to live with us. They were friends, to climb on or to lean against, or to gather around in the evening. You could sit on the frog's head and look way out over the city at the tall trees and rooftops.

Nowadays, whenever I run into old friends, mostly at a funeral, or maybe a wedding, after we've talked about how we've been and what we've been doing, and how old our children are, we always end up talking about our childtime in our old neighborhood. And somebody will say, "One of these days we ought to have a Langston reunion." That's what we always called it, just "Langston," without the "Terrace." I guess because it sounded more homey. And that's what Langston was. It was home.

Vocabulary ▶
reunion (rē yoo̅n′ yən) *n.* a gathering of people who have been separated

homey (hōm′ ē) *adj.* comfortable; having a feeling of home

Language Study

Vocabulary The following words appear in "Langston Terrace." Answer each question with either *yes* or *no.* Then explain your answer.

   applications   community   choral   reunion   homey

1. If someone wants a job, should he or she fill out an *application*?
2. Can a *community* help someone in need?
3. To see an old friend, should you go to a *reunion*?
4. If you hate to sing, should you join a *choral* group?
5. Does your school feel *homey*?

WORD STUDY

The **Latin suffix -ent** can form an adjective or a noun. As a word part, it means "has," "shows," or "does."

In this story, the narrator is a **resident** of Langston Terrace, which means she has a residence, or home, there.

Word Study

Part A Explain how the **Latin suffix -ent** contributes to the meanings of the words *persistent, different,* and *evident.* Consult a dictionary if necessary.

Part B Use the context of the sentence and what you know about the suffix -ent to explain your answers to these questions.

1. Are you *patient* when you cannot wait for something?
2. If you really want something, should you be *insistent*?

---

3. (1) There were many games to play and things to do. (2) The community "wrapped itself around us, put itself between us and the hard knocks, to cushion the blows." (3) "It was…a good growing-up place." (4) "It was home."

4. Langston Terrace was a wonderful place to grow up.

5. *Time and Place:* She lived in Washington, D.C., in the 1930s. *Cultural Background:* She came from a working-class African American family. *World Events:* She grew up in a time before civil rights laws were passed to stop discrimination against African Americans.

6. The place where Eloise grew up influenced her the most. Growing up in Washington, D.C., she had experienced crowded living conditions. Langston Terrace seemed to be like a paradise to her after all the other places she had lived.

7. **(a)** They expect to be there only long enough to save money to buy a house of their own. **(b)** She might not have developed such strong friendships and feelings about the community.

Close Reading Activities

Literary Analysis

Key Ideas and Details

1. **(a)** Why does Greenfield's family move many times before moving to Langston Terrace? **(b) Compare and Contrast:** How is the family's new home similar to the old home? How is it different?

2. **(a)** What is significant about the day Greenfield's family moves to Langston Terrace? **(b) Draw Conclusions:** How does Greenfield feel on that day?

3. **Main Idea** Greenfield's thoughts and feelings about Langston Terrace make up the main body of this essay. List four key details in the essay that show Greenfield's thoughts and feelings.

4. **Main Idea** In your own words, state the main idea of this essay.

Craft and Structure

5. **Author's Influences** In a chart like the one on the right, list cultural and historical factors that may have influenced Greenfield's writing of "Langston Terrace."

6. **Author's Influences** Which factors on your completed chart do you think influenced the author's writing the most? Explain.

Time and Place	Cultural Background	World Events

Integration of Knowledge and Ideas

7. **(a)** Why do some of the parents think of Langston Terrace as an "in-between place"? **(b) Speculate:** How might Greenfield's essay have been different if Langston Terrace had been an "in-between" place for her?

8. **(a)** As an adult, how does Greenfield feel about Langston Terrace? **(b) Speculate:** Why might former residents of Langston Terrace want to have a reunion? Explain.

9. **What is important to know? (a)** What made Langston Terrace feel like home to Greenfield and her family? **(b)** Why is it important for a community to make newcomers feel comfortable?

ACADEMIC VOCABULARY

As you write and speak about "Langston Terrace," use the words related to gaining knowledge that you explored on page 163 of this text.

---

8. **(a)** She feels that it was a wonderful place to grow up. **(b)** They might want to find out what happened to their old friends and talk about childhood memories.

9. **What is important to know?**
(a) It was a safe community of friends and had many public spaces for work, study, and play. **(b)** A community grows strong when all members contribute their talents and skills. Newcomers who are welcomed into a new community are more likely to join with others in activities that benefit everyone.

 Online Writer's Notebook

Students can use the Online Writer's Notebook to record all responses.

Conventions

1. Introduce the skill, using the instruction on the student page.

2. Discuss the definition and the examples in the chart.

Think Aloud: Model the Skill

Model the skill of using simple verb tenses. Say to students:

I am teaching the students today. When I say *I am teaching* it indicates that the action is occurring now, in the present. If I want to describe this action as something that happened in the past, I would have to use the past tense and say *I taught the students yesterday.* When I say *I will teach the students tomorrow,* it indicates that the action will be taking place in the future. The verb tense—present, past, and future—shows the time of the action or the condition being expressed.

Practice A

1. *loved*: past
2. *want*: present
3. *will become*: future
4. *walked*: past
5. *remembers*: present

Reading Application

fell (past), saw (past), needed (past), filled (past)

Practice B

1. had   **3.** will fill out
2. think   **4.** need

Writing Application

Present tense: *Students with Books* shows people in a library. Some of them are sitting and reading. Others are standing and looking for books on the shelves. *Street Scene* shows a street crowded with people. Most of them are walking. One boy is flying a kite.

Future Tense: If you look at *Students with Books,* you will see people in a library. Some of them will be sitting and reading. Others will be standing and looking for books on the shelves. If you look at *Street Scene,* you will see a street crowded with people. Most of them will be walking. One boy will be flying a kite.

Conventions: Simple Verb Tenses

> A **verb** expresses an action or a state of being. A verb tense shows the time of the action or the state of being expressed by the verb.

There are three simple tenses.

Present tense indicates an action or a condition in the present. It may also indicate an action or a condition that occurs regularly.

Past tense tells that an action took place in the past.

Future tense tells that an action will take place in the future.

Tenses	Regular Verb: *cheer*	Irregular Verb: *have*
Present	I cheer; I am cheering	She has
Past	I cheered	She had
Future	I will cheer	She will have

Practice A

Identify the verb in each sentence and indicate its tense.

1. Eloise loved her new home.

2. Many people want to live at Langston Terrace.

3. Eloise will become a famous writer some day.

4. Eloise's mother walked to the building.

5. Eloise remembers Langston Terrace.

Reading Application Reread the first two paragraphs of "Langston Terrace." Select four verbs and identify the tense of each.

Practice B

Change the tense of each of the following sentences to the tense listed in parentheses.

1. Eloise will have vivid memories of her home. (past)

2. Some people thought of Langston Terrace as an in-between place. (present)

3. Eloise's parents filled out an application. (future)

4. Many people needed low-cost housing. (present)

Writing Application Choose two pictures in "Langston Terrace." Write a few sentences to describe each picture in the present tense. Then, convert the sentences to the future tense.

▶ EXTEND THE LESSON

Sentence Modeling

Use this sentence from the selection students have read:

It was going to be a low-rent housing project in northeast Washington, and it would be named in honor of John Mercer Langston, the famous black lawyer, educator, and congressman. ("Langston Terrace")

Ask students what they notice about the sentence.

Elicit from them that the sentence is in the future tense. Then, ask what else they notice. (Commas indicate the various professions of John Mercer Langston.)

Have students imitate the sentence in a sentence on a topic of their own choosing, matching each grammatical and stylistic feature discussed. Collect the sentences, and share them with the class.

Writing to Sources

Narrative Text Write a **journal entry** as Eloise Greenfield.

- Review the essay to choose an event that especially interests you.
- Jot down notes about Greenfield's reaction to the event.
- Write an entry from Greenfield's point of view. Use descriptions to make the entry vivid.
- Adjust the pacing throughout your entry. Pacing is like rhythm. You can speed up the action or slow it down, depending on the effect you want. Pacing can help you build anticipation or draw attention to an important event or detail.
- Remember to include the thoughts, feelings, and reactions you think Greenfield might feel.
- Consider using dialogue to show what you or others said during the event.

Grammar Application Check your writing to make sure that you have used verb tenses correctly.

Research and Technology

Build and Present Knowledge In a small group, use Internet or library resources to prepare an **informative presentation** on the importance of community.

Follow these steps to complete the assignment:

- Narrow your focus to two or three ways in which community is important.
- Research your topic using a variety of resource materials, including reputable online sources.
- Use details in "Langston Terrace" as a resource for information.
- Prepare a poster that highlights the most important facts about your topic. Use art or photographs to engage viewers.
- Present your findings to the class. Have each group member discuss a different aspect of your topic.

 **Common Core State Standards**

Writing
3. Write narratives to develop real or imagined experiences or events using effective technique, relevant descriptive details, and well-structured event sequences.
3.b. Use narrative techniques, such as dialogue, pacing, and description, to develop experiences, events, and/or characters.
8. Gather relevant information from multiple print and digital sources; assess the credibility of each source.

Speaking and Listening
4. Present claims and findings, sequencing ideas logically and using pertinent descriptions, facts, and details to accentuate main ideas or themes; use appropriate eye contact, adequate volume, and clear pronunciation.

Language
1. Demonstrate command of standard English grammar and usage when writing or speaking.

Writing to Sources

1. Review the assignment, using the instruction on the student page.
2. Suggest to students that they choose one event from the essay and then imagine themselves in that scene. What do they see? What do they feel? Students can use this imagined information to help them draft their journal entries.
3. To give students guidance in writing the journal entry, give them the **Support for Writing** page for this selection in the *Student Companion All-in-One Workbook.*
4. To evaluate the writing activity, use the rubrics for Generic (Holistic) Writing, *Professional Development Guidebook,* pp. 256–257. Evaluate for how well students describe the event and their feelings about it.

Grammar Application

Have students check their drafts for the correct use of simple verb tenses.

Six Traits Focus

✓	Ideas		Word Choice
✓	Organization		Sentence Fluency
✓	Voice		Conventions

Research and Technology

1. Review the assignment, using the instruction on the student page.
2. To support students' work on the assignment, have them complete the **Support for Extend Your Learning** page for this selection in the *Student Companion All-in-One Workbook.*

Time and Resource Manager

LESSON PACING GUIDE

from The Pigman & Me

| DAY 1 | **Preteach/Teach** |

- Administer the Reading and Vocabulary Warm-ups, as necessary.
- Introduce the Key Ideas and Details skill: Main Idea.
- Introduce the Craft and Structure skill: Mood.
- Use the Close Reading Model to demonstrate the application of the skills.
- Review the selection vocabulary, as necessary, with students who need additional support.
- Prepare students to read the selection by reviewing with them the Multidraft Reading Strategies.

| DAY 2 | **Teach** |

- Informally monitor comprehension while students read.
- Use the Comprehension questions to confirm understanding.
- Develop students' ability to know the main idea and analyze mood using the sidenote questions.
- Reinforce vocabulary with the Vocabulary notes.
- Reinforce unit focus standards using the Spiral Review prompts.

| DAY 3 | **Assess** |

- Assess students' comprehension and mastery of the skills by having them answer the Literary Analysis questions.
- Have students complete the Vocabulary activities.
- Develop students' understanding of roots and affixes by having them complete the Word Study activities.

| DAY 4 | **Extend/Assess** |

- Build students' ability to master grammar concepts and conventions by having them complete the Conventions lesson.
- Have students complete the Writing to Sources activity and write a problem-and-solution essay. (You may assign as homework.)
- Extend learning by having students complete the Speaking and Listening activity: an informal discussion.
- Administer the Selection Test or Open-Book Test.

Common Core State Standards

Reading Informational Texts 2. Determine a central idea of a text and how it is conveyed through particular details; provide a summary of the text distinct from personal opinion or judgments.

Writing 2.a. Introduce a topic; organize ideas, concepts, and information, using strategies such as definition, classification, comparison/contrast, and cause/ effect.

2.b. Develop the topic with relevant facts, definitions, concrete examples, quotations, or other information and examples.

Speaking and Listening 1.a. Come to discussions prepared, having read or studied required material; explicitly draw on that preparation by referring to evidence on the topic, text, or issue to probe and reflect on ideas under discussion.

1.b. Follow rules for collegial discussion.

1.d. Review the key ideas expressed and demonstrate understanding of multiple perspectives through reflection and paraphrasing.

Language 1. Demonstrate command of the conventions of standard English grammar and usage when writing or speaking.

4.b. Use common grade-appropriate Greek or Latin affixes and roots as clues to the meaning of a word.

6. Acquire and use accurately grade-appropriate general academic and domain-specific words and phrases; gather vocabulary knowledge when considering a word or phrase important to comprehension or expression.

Daily Block Scheduling

Each day in this Lesson Pacing Guide represents a 40–50 minute period. Teachers using block scheduling may combine days to revise pacing. In addition, teachers may differentiate and support core instruction by integrating components for extended and intensive support as students require. See the Guide to Resources (facing page).

GUIDE TO RESOURCES

Section	L1	L2	L3	L4	EL	ALL	RESOURCES	PRINT	CD	ONLINE
Warm Up	✓	✓			✓		Vocabulary Warm-ups			✓
Warm Up	✓	✓			✓		Reading Warm-ups			✓
Warm Up						✓	Background Video			✓
Warm Up						✓	Selection Audio		Hear It!	✓
Comprehension/Selection Support						✓	Writing About the Big Question	Student Companion Workbook		✓
Comprehension/Selection Support						✓	Literary Analysis	Student Companion Workbook		✓
Comprehension/Selection Support						✓	Reading	Student Companion Workbook		✓
Comprehension/Selection Support						✓	Vocabulary Builder	Student Companion Workbook		✓
Comprehension/Selection Support				✓			Enrichment			✓
Comprehension/Selection Support			✓	✓	✓		Conventions	Student Companion Workbook		✓
Comprehension/Selection Support			✓	✓	✓		Writing to Sources	Student Companion Workbook		✓
Comprehension/Selection Support			✓	✓	✓		Speaking and Listening	Student Companion Workbook		✓
Differentiated Instruction/Additional Support						✓	Additional Standards Practice	Common Core Companion		✓
Differentiated Instruction/Additional Support	✓	✓					Adapted Reader's Notebook			✓
Differentiated Instruction/Additional Support					✓		English Reader's Notebook:			✓
Differentiated Instruction/Additional Support					✓		Spanish Reader's Notebook			✓
Differentiated Instruction/Additional Support					✓		Graphic Organizer A			✓
Differentiated Instruction/Additional Support	✓	✓			✓		Graphic Organizer B			✓
Differentiated Instruction/Additional Support	✓	✓			✓		"Fighting Sports Stereotypes"	Reality Central Student Edition and Writing Journal	·	✓
Differentiated Instruction/Additional Support	✓	✓			✓		Practice and Assess	Reading Kit		✓
Monitor Progress						✓	Selection Test		Exam View	✓
Monitor Progress						✓	Open-Book Test		Exam View	✓
Digital Resources						✓	Close Reading Tool			✓
Digital Resources						✓	Online Writer's Notebook			✓

One-on-one teaching   Group work   Whole class instruction   Independent work   A Assessment   Digital Resource

LEARNER LEVELS

L1 Special-Needs Students
L2 Below-Level Students (Tier 2)
L3 On-Level Students (Tier 1)
L4 Advanced Students (Tier 1)
EL English Learners
All All Students

❶ What is important to know?

Read • Discuss • Research • Write As students read, they will explore the Big Question through text analysis of the selection. Encourage students to note comments and additional questions as they read, using text evidence to support their thoughts. Students may wish to log their comments, questions, and evidence in a three-column chart. Students should refer to their notes to help them deepen their understanding of the selection through discussion, research, and writing.

❷ Close Reading Focus

1. Explain to students that the main idea of an essay is often presented near the beginning. Students may be able to understand the main idea more clearly after they have finished reading the essay and they can consider all the information the author has presented.

2. Explain to students that they can identify the mood of a selection by examining the author's word choice. For example, the words *thunder, heavy rain, wet hair,* and *soggy* shoes create a picture of someone soaked by rain, creating a mood of discomfort. If the words *slippery* and *hilarious laughter* are added, however, the mood becomes more playful.

© Building Knowledge

Meet the Author

As a teenager, **Paul Zindel** (1936–2003) lived for a while on Staten Island, New York, with his mother and sister. Before he wrote his famous novel *The Pigman*, Zindel taught high school science while writing in his spare time. After the success of *The Pigman*, he started writing full time. "I felt I could do more for teenagers by writing for them," he once said. Zindel discovered that most young adult books did not relate to the teenagers he knew. He made a list of pointers and then wrote another novel, following his own advice.

© **Common Core State Standards**

Reading Informational Texts
2. Determine a central idea of a text and how it is conveyed through particular details; provide a summary of the text distinct from personal opinion or judgments.

Language
6. Acquire and use accurately grade-appropriate general academic and domain-specific words and phrases; gather vocabulary knowledge when considering a word or phrase important to comprehension or expression.

❶ What is important to know?

Explore the Big Question as you read the excerpt from *The Pigman & Me*. Take notes on ways in which the selection explores the importance of knowing the rules.

❷ CLOSE READING FOCUS

Key Ideas and Details: **Main Idea**

The **main idea** is the most important point in a literary work. Individual paragraphs or sections may also have a central idea that supports the main idea of the work. To determine the main idea, distinguish between important and unimportant details. Important, or key, details support or tell more about the main idea.

- Ask yourself questions such as these about details in a literary work: *Why did the author include this detail? Does this detail help readers understand the main idea of the work?*
- Keep in mind that not all details support the main idea.

Craft and Structure: **Mood**

Mood is the overall feeling a literary work produces in a reader. For example, the mood of a work may be happy, scary, or hopeful. To create a particular mood, writers carefully choose words and create word pictures that appeal to the reader's senses.

Some literary works convey a single mood. In other works, the mood changes within the selection.

Vocabulary

You will encounter the following words in the excerpt from *The Pigman & Me*. Write the words in your notebook. Choose one and write its related forms in other parts of speech. For example, if you choose an adjective, write a related word in noun and verb form.

exact	observant	distorted
demented	undulating	condemnation

© TEXT COMPLEXITY **RUBRIC**

from The Pigman & Me		Reader and Task Suggestions	
Qualitative Measures		**Preparing to Read the Text**	**Leveled Tasks**
Context/Knowledge Demands	New York City; playground behavior 1 2 ③ 4 5	• Encourage students to note what the narrator says about the character of John Quinn. • Guide students to use Multidraft Reading strategies (TE p. 218).	*Levels of Meaning* If students will have difficulty with the concepts, as they read have them note qualities of the narrator and John Quinn. Discuss how these affect the plot. *Analyzing* If students will not have difficulty with concepts, have them review the text for unwritten rules. Have students list other unwritten rules they know.
Structure/Language Conventionality and Clarity	Longer selection; conversational language 1 2 ③ 4 5		
Levels of Meaning/Purpose/Concept Level	Challenging concept (boy is forced into fighting another boy in school) 1 2 3 ④ 5		
Quantitative Measures			
Lexile	840L	Text Length	Word Count: 2,780

CLOSE READING MODEL

The passage below is from Paul Zindel's reflective essay *The Pigman & Me*. The annotations to the right of the passage show ways in which you can use close reading skills to find the main idea and analyze mood.

from *The Pigman & Me*

There, across the street in a field behind Ronkewitz's Candy Store, was a crowd of about 300 kids standing around like a big, undulating horseshoe, with John Quinn standing at the center bend glaring at me. **1**

"You could run," Jennifer suggested, tossing her hair all to the left side of her face. She looked much more than pretty now. She looked loyal to the bone.

"No," I said. I just walked forward toward my fate, with the blood in my temples pounding so hard I thought I was going to pass out. **2** Moose and Leon and Mike and Conehead and Little Frankfurter were sprinkled out in front of me, goading me forward. I didn't even hear what they said. I saw only their faces distorted in ecstasy and expectation. They looked like the mob I had seen in a sixteenth-century etching where folks in London had bought tickets to watch bulldogs attacking water buffalo. **3**

John stood with his black eye, and his fists up.

I stopped a few feet from him and put my fists up. A lot of kids in the crowd started to shout, "Kill him, Johnny!" but I may have imagined that part. **4**

Main Idea

1 Based on the details "about 300 kids" and "glaring at me," you can determine the main idea of this passage: the narrator, young Paul Zindel, feels alone and threatened.

Mood

2 Zindel's blood is pounding and he almost passes out. He describes himself as walking toward his "fate." These details create a mood of fearful acceptance.

Main Idea

3 Zindel compares the other boys to a "mob," and imagines himself as a buffalo being attacked by bulldogs. These details support the idea that he feels alone, different, and picked on.

Mood

4 Paul hears—or thinks he hears—the crowd shouting, "Kill him, Johnny!" His confusion between what is real and imagined intensifies the fearful mood.

Daily Bellringer

For each class during which you will teach this selection, have students complete one of the five Research activities for Week 11 in *Daily Bellringer Activities.* You may wish to use additional activities that are applicable to this selection.

Vocabulary

If students require support with selection vocabulary, use this routine:

1. Write the following words and definitions on the board:

   exact *v.* demand with force or authority

   observant *adj.* quick to notice; alert

   distorted *adj.* twisted out of normal shape

   demented *adj.* insane; mad

   undulating *adj.* moving in waves, like a snake

   condemnation *n.* expression of strong disapproval

2. Have students say each word aloud.

3. Use the word in a sentence that defines the word.

DIFFERENTIATED INSTRUCTION

EL Extended Support—English Learners
Have students complete the **Reading and Vocabulary Warm-ups** for this selection in the *Student Companion All-in-One Workbook* before they read. Assign the prereading pages and the adapted selection in the *Reader's Notebook: English Learner's Version.* Then, have students listen to portions of the selection in the *Student eText* or on the *Hear It!* CD-ROM.

L1 L2 Extended Support—Struggling Readers
Have students complete the **Reading and Vocabulary Warm-ups** for this selection in the *Student Companion All-in-One Workbook* before they read. Assign the prereading pages and the adapted selection in the *Reader's Notebook: Adapted Version.* Then, have students listen to portions of the selection in the *Student eText* or on the *Hear It!* CD-ROM (adapted text).

Extended Support—Reluctant Readers
To build motivation and engagement before assigning the selection, have students read "Fighting Sports Stereotypes," a thematically related selection in *Reality Central.* Then, use the questions at the conclusion of the related selection to guide discussion.

MULTIDRAFT READING

This icon ● marks natural pauses in the selection. To assist struggling readers and to deepen comprehension for all, assign the text in "chunks," separated by the icons, and apply multidraft reading protocols. For each reading, have students set the purpose indicated:

- **First reading:** Students should read the selection independently and think about its basic meaning.
- **Second reading:** Students should analyze the text's key ideas and details and its craft and structure, and respond to the side-column prompts.
- **Third reading:** Students should integrate knowledge and ideas, connect the text to other texts and to the world, and answer the end-of-selection questions.

For more guidance, refer to the *Classroom Strategies and Teaching Routines* card on multidraft reading.

❶ Critical Viewing

Possible responses: Students might argue about the rules of their playground games, about each other's behavior, and about the use of sports equipment.

from
The Pigman & Me
Paul Zindel

❶ ▲ **Critical Viewing**
What are some conflicts among students that might occur in a scene like this one?

When trouble came to me, it didn't involve anybody I thought it would. It involved the nice, normal, smart boy by the name of John Quinn. Life does that to us a lot. Just when we think something awful's going to happen one way, it throws you a curve and the something awful happens another way. This happened on the first Friday, during gym period, when we were allowed to play games in the school yard. A boy by the name of Richard Cahill, who lived near an old linoleum factory, asked me if I'd like to play paddle ball with him, and I said, "Yes." Some of the kids played

218 UNIT 2 • What is important to know?

💬 VOCABULARY DEVELOPMENT

Thematic Vocabulary: The Big Question
As students are discussing the excerpt from *The Pigman & Me*, encourage them to use the words for discussing the Big Question presented on pp. 162–163. You might encourage them with sentence starters like these:

1. The rule stated that the time *limit* for signing out paddles and other equipment was . . .

2. The *purpose* of the rule was . . .
3. Paul had no *knowledge* of the rule when he . . .
4. When trouble came to Paul, its *source* was . . .
5. To prepare for the fight, Nonno Frankie encouraged Paul to *study* . . .

softball, some played warball, and there were a few other games where you could sign out equipment and do what you wanted. What I didn't know was that you were allowed to sign out the paddles for only fifteen minutes per period so more kids could get a chance to use them. I just didn't happen to know that little rule, and Richard Cahill didn't think to tell me about it. Richard was getting a drink from the water fountain when John Quinn came up to me and told me I had to give him my paddle.

"No," I said, being a little paranoid about being the new kid and thinking everyone was going to try to take advantage of me.

"Look, you *have* to give it to me," John Quinn insisted.

That was when I did something berserk. I was so wound up and frightened that I didn't think, and I struck out at him with my right fist. I had forgotten I was holding the paddle, and it smacked into his face, giving him an instant black eye. John was shocked. I was shocked. Richard Cahill came running back and he was shocked.

"What's going on here?" Mr. Trellis, the gym teacher, growled.

"He hit me with the paddle," John moaned, holding his eye. He was red as a beet, as Little Frankfurter, Conehead, Moose, and lots of the others gathered around.

"He tried to take the paddle away from me!" I complained.

"His time was up," John said.

Mr. Trellis set me wise to the rules as he took John over to a supply locker and pulled out a first-aid kit.

"I'm sorry," I said, over and over again.

Then the bell rang, and all John Quinn whispered to me was that he was going to get even. He didn't say it like a nasty rotten kid, just more like an all-American boy who knew he'd have to regain his dignity about having to walk around school with a black eye. Before the end of school, Jennifer came running up to me in the halls and told me John Quinn had announced to everyone he was going to exact revenge on me after school on Monday. That was the note of disaster my first week at school ended on, and I was terrified because I didn't know how to fight. I had never even been in a fight. What had happened was all an accident. It really was.

◄ Main Idea
What details support the main idea that Paul did not expect or intend to injure John?

◄ Vocabulary
exact (eg zakt´) *v.*
demand with force or authority

❹ Comprehension
What misunderstanding takes place in the school yard?

PART 2 • *from* The Pigman & Me **219**

---

❷ Main Idea

1. Remind students of these questions that readers can ask themselves about details in a selection: *Why did the author include this detail? Does this detail help me to understand the main idea?*

2. Have students ask themselves these questions as they independently read the first bracketed passage. **Ask** the Main Idea question. **Answer:** The narrator admits that he went berserk and he didn't think. He had forgotten that he was holding the paddle. He says he was shocked.

❸ ? Connecting to the Big Question

1. Have students read the second bracketed passage on the page. **Ask:** What did John Quinn assume when the fight started, and why did Mr. Trellis need to inform Paul about the rules? **Answer:** John Quinn assumed that Paul knew about the time limit and was disregarding it. Paul didn't know the rules, so Mr. Trellis explained them.

2. **Ask** students how knowing these rules would have helped Paul avoid the conflict with John Quinn. **Possible response:** Paul would have known to return the paddle on time. He wouldn't have felt that he was being singled out as the new kid and taken advantage of.

3. Tell students to look for additional rules that Paul learns.

❹ Comprehension

Answer: John Quinn thought that Paul was being greedy in keeping the paddle longer than fifteen minutes. Paul didn't know about the time limit and thought that John Quinn was picking on him.

Video
Watch the Background Video online!

Audio
Selection Audio is available in the *Student eText* and on the *Hear It!* CD-ROM.

⁑ DIFFERENTIATED INSTRUCTION

Support for Less Proficient Readers
To help students distinguish between important and unimportant details, show them the **Reading Skill Graphic Organizer A** for this selection. Guide them through the sample answers, and explain that the transparency will help them identify the kinds of details that support a main idea. Encourage students to refer to the graphic organizer as a model for identifying their own details as they read.

Strategy for Less-Proficient Readers
Prepare an **Anticipation Guide** (*Professional Development Guidebook*, pp. 36–38) with the following statements:

• People should not be expected to follow unwritten rules.

• In some situations, it's okay to bend the rules among friends and family.

Give students a copy of the prepared **Guide** and have students mark their responses in the Me column. Have students discuss the statements in groups and fill in the Group column. After students are done reading the selection, have them complete the After Reading column.

⑤ Main Idea

1. Have students read the first bracketed passage on this page, beginning with, "I was expecting him to notice. . ." **Ask** them to identify the main idea of that passage.

   Answer: The kids had harmed the tree by carving their names in it.

2. **Ask** the Main Idea question.

   Possible response: Students may say it is not an important detail. The fact that the twins added their names to Paul's and Jennifer's is important, but the fact that the twins are copycats is not important to the main idea.

⑥ Mood

1. Read aloud the Mood question, but do not ask students to answer it at this point.

2. Tell students to listen carefully for words that create a threatening mood as you read aloud the second bracketed passage.

3. **Ask** the Mood question.

   Possible response: Students may say that the words *heart and blood, slitting its throat,* and *kill* create a threatening mood. They may say that the words create a picture that makes them think of murder.

Main Idea
Is the detail about "the twins, being such copycats" important to the main idea of the paragraph? Explain.

⑤

Mood
What words create a threatening mood in this paragraph?

⑥

When Nonno Frankie arrived on Saturday morning, he found me sitting in the apple tree alone. Mom had told him it was O.K. to walk around the whole yard now, as long as he didn't do any diggings or mutilations other than weed-pulling on her side. I was expecting him to notice right off the bat that I was white with fear, but instead he stood looking at the carvings Jennifer and I had made in the trunk of the tree. I thought he was just intensely curious about what "ESCAPE! PAUL & JENNIFER!" meant. Of course, the twins, being such copycats, had already added their names so the full carving away of the bark now read, "ESCAPE! PAUL & JENNIFER! & NICKY & JOEY!" And the letters circled halfway around the tree.

"You're killing it," Nonno Frankie said sadly.

"What?" I jumped down to his side.

"The tree will die if you cut any more."

I thought he was kidding, because all we had done was carve off the outer pieces of bark. We hadn't carved deep into the tree, not into the *heart* of the tree. The tree was too important to us. It was the most crucial place to me and Jennifer, and the last thing we'd want to do was hurt it.

"The heart of a tree isn't deep inside of it. Its heart and blood are on the *outside*, just under the bark," Nonno Frankie explained. "That's the living part of a tree. If you carve in a circle all around the trunk, it's like slitting its throat. The water and juices and life of the tree can't move up from the roots!" I knew about the living layer of a tree, but I didn't know exposing it would kill the whole tree. I just never thought about it, or I figured trees patched themselves up.

"Now it can feed itself from only half its trunk," Nonno Frankie explained. "You must not cut any more."

"I won't," I promised. Then I felt worse than ever. Not only was I scheduled to get beat up by John Quinn after school on Monday, I was also a near tree-killer. Nonno Frankie finally looked closely at me.

"Your first week at school wasn't all juicy meatballs?" he asked.

That was all he had to say, and I spilled out each and every horrifying detail. Nonno Frankie let me babble on and on. He

🧠 THINK ALOUD

Vocabulary: Dictionary Use

Direct students' attention to the word *retreat* on the next page. Using a think-aloud process, model how to choose the correct definition of the word, using the actual definitions in your own dictionary. Say to students:

> I'm going to think-aloud to show you how to choose the definition of *retreat,* as it is used here. Let's find *retreat* in the dictionary. I see that there are two entries for *retreat*—a verb and a noun.

I can tell from the sentence that I am looking for the definition of it as a verb. The first definition is "to withdraw from what is difficult, dangerous, or disagreeable." The second is "to slope backward." When I replace the word *retreat* with each definition, I find that the first definition makes sense: *you can also yell it if you have to withdraw from what is difficult, dangerous, or disagreeable.*

looked as if he understood exactly how I felt and wasn't going to call me stupid or demented or a big yellow coward. When I didn't have another word left in me, I just shut up and stared down at the ground.

"Stab nail at ill Italian bats!" Nonno Frankie finally said. "What?"

He repeated the weird sentence and asked me what was special about it. I guessed, "It reads the same wbackward as forward?"

"Right! Ho! Ho! Ho! See, you learn! You remember things I teach you. So today I will teach you how to fight, and you will smack this John Quinn around like floured pizza dough."

"But I can't fight."

"I'll show you Sicilian combat tactics."

"Like what?"

"Everything about Italian fighting. It has to do with your mind and body. Things you have to know so you don't have to be afraid of bullies. Street smarts my father taught me. Like 'Never miss a good chance to shut up!'"

VAROOOOOOOOOOOM!

A plane took off over our heads. We walked out beyond the yard to the great field overlooking the airport.

Nonno Frankie suddenly let out a yell. "Aaeeeeeyaaaayeeeeeh!" It was so blood-curdlingly weird, I decided to wait until he felt like explaining it.

"Aaeeeeeyaaaayeeeeeh!" he bellowed again. "It's good to be able to yell like Tarzan!" he said. "This confuses your enemy, and you can also yell it if you have to retreat. You run away roaring and everyone thinks you at least have guts! It confuses everybody!"

"Is that all I need to know?" I asked, now more afraid than ever of facing John Quinn in front of all the kids.

"No. Tonight I will cut your hair."

"Cut it?"

"Yes. It's too long!"

"It is?"

"Ah," Nonno Frankie said, "you'd be surprised how many kids lose fights because of their hair. Alexander the Great always ordered his entire army to shave their heads. Long hair makes it easy for an enemy to grab it and cut off your head."

◄ **Vocabulary**
demented (dē ment´ əd) *adj.* insane; mad

"Aaeeeeeyaaaayeeeeeh!" he bellowed again. "It's good to be able to yell like Tarzan!"

8 Comprehension
What advice does Paul get from Nonno Frankie?

7 Infer

1. Read aloud with expression the bracketed passage. Then, **ask** students why Nonno Frankie compares John Quinn to pizza dough.

   Possible answer: The comparison vividly illustrates the physical technique of smacking that he is describing. It is also humorous, which is the style of much of Nonno Frankie's advice.

2. **Ask** students to infer what Sicilian combat tactics are.

   Possible answer: Sicilian combat tactics are techniques of street fighting that Nonno Frankie learned from his father in Sicily. These include physical and mental tactics.

8 Comprehension

Possible response: Nonno Frankie gives Paul advice about fighting techniques and using his mind and body so that he won't have to be afraid of bullies.

PART 2 • *from* The Pigman & Me **221**

DIFFERENTIATED INSTRUCTION

Culturally Responsive Instruction

In this selection, Nonno Frankie is a colorful character who is full of advice for his nephew—some of it based on his childhood experiences in Sicily. Invite students to share what they know about the culture of extended families. Explain to students that giving advice and passing on suggestions is part of the tradition of any culture. Encourage students to describe the advice they have received from older family members or elders in their communities. Then, have them consider ways in which family and cultural traditions are preserved by passing down advice.

9 Main Idea

1. Ask students to recall the details they have learned about Nonno Frankie up to this point, before the bracketed text.

2. Have a student read the bracketed text.

3. **Ask** students the Main Idea question.

   Possible responses: He tells Paul surprising and funny stories to cheer him up. He yells and carries on to get Paul's mind off his worries.

10 Mood

1. Read aloud the bracketed passage. **Ask** students to identify the mood this conversation creates.

   Possible response: It creates a funny, or humorous, mood.

2. **Ask** students the Mood question.

   Possible response: He creates a humorous mood by helping readers form a mental picture of people attacking one another with giant yo-yos. He also talks about a ridiculous law about camels and a silly detail about a cartoon character.

Main Idea
What details support the main idea that Nonno Frankie is an unusual character? **9**

Mood
How does the author create a humorous mood?

**Vocabulary ▶
observant** (əb zʉrv´ ənt) *adj.* quick to notice; alert

"John Quinn just wants to beat me up!"

"You can never be too sure. This boy might have the spirit of Genghis Khan!"

"Who was Genghis Khan?"

"Who? He once killed two million enemies in one hour. Some of them he killed with yo-yos."

"Yo-yos?"

"See, these are the things you need to know. The yo-yo was first invented as a weapon. Of course, they were as heavy as steel pipes and had long rope cords, but they were still yo-yos!"

"I didn't know that," I admitted.

"That's why I'm telling you. You should always ask about the rules when you go to a new place."

"I didn't think there'd be a time limit on handball paddles."

"That's why you must ask."

"I can't ask everything," I complained.

10 "Then you *read*. You need to know all the rules wherever you go. Did you know it's illegal to hunt camels in Arizona?"

"No."

"See? These are little facts you pick up from books and teachers and parents as you grow older. Some facts and rules come in handy, some don't. You've got to be observant. Did you know that Mickey Mouse has only *four* fingers on each hand?"

"No."

"All you have to do is look. And rules change! You've got to remember that. In ancient Rome, my ancestors worshipped a god who ruled over mildew. Nobody does anymore, but it's an interesting thing to know. You have to be connected to the past and present and future. At NBC, when they put in a new cookie-cutting machine, I had to have an open mind. I had to prepare and draw upon everything I knew so that I didn't get hurt."

Nonno Frankie must have seen my mouth was open so wide a baseball could have flown into my throat and choked me to death. He stopped at the highest point in the rise of land above the airport. "I can see you want some meat and potatoes. You want to know exactly how to beat this vicious John Quinn."

"He's not vicious."

💬 **VOCABULARY DEVELOPMENT**

Selection Vocabulary Reinforcement
Students will benefit from additional examples and practice with the selection vocabulary words. Reinforce their comprehension with "show-you-know" sentences. The first part of the sentence uses the vocabulary word in an appropriate context. The second part of the sentence—the "show-you-know" part—clarifies the first. Model the strategy with this example: *The lawyer tried to* exact *a statement from his client; however, the man refused to talk.* Then, give students these sentence starters and coach them in creating the clarification part:

1. The customer tried to *exact* a refund from the store; _____.
   Sample answer: he claimed that the lawnmower didn't work.
2. When the dog was stung by a wasp, he appeared to be *demented;* ____.
   Sample answer: he ran in circles, howling loudly as if he were crazy.
3. The *observant* bus driver grabbed some paper towels; _____.
   Sample answer: he was the first to notice that juice had spilled on the front seat.

"Make believe he is. It'll give you more energy for the fight. When he comes at you, don't underestimate the power of negative thinking! You must have only positive thoughts in your heart that you're going to cripple this monster. Stick a piece of garlic in your pocket for good luck. A woman my mother knew in Palermo did this, and she was able to fight off a dozen three-foot-tall muscular Greeks who landed and tried to eat her. You think this is not true, but half her town saw it. The Greeks all had rough skin and wore backpacks and one-piece clothes. You have to go with what you feel in your heart. One of my teachers in Sicily believed the Portuguese man-of-war jellyfish originally came from England. He felt that in his heart, and he eventually proved it. He later went on to be awarded a government grant to study tourist swooning sickness in Florence."

"But how do I hold my hands to fight? How do I hold my fists?" I wanted to know.

"Like this!" Nonno Frankie demonstrated, taking a boxing stance with his left foot and fist forward.

"And then I just swing my right fist forward as hard as I can?"

"No. First you curse him."

"Curse him?"

"Yes, you curse this John Quinn. You tell him, 'May your left ear wither and fall into your right pocket!' And you tell him he looks like a fugitive from a brain gang! And tell him he has a face like a mattress! And that an espresso coffee cup would fit on his head like a sombrero. And then you just give him the big Sicilian surprise!"

"What?"

"You kick him in the shins!" •

By the time Monday morning came, I was a nervous wreck. Nonno Frankie had gone back to New York the night before, but had left me a special bowl of pasta and steamed octopus that he said I should eat for breakfast so I'd have "gusto" for combat. I had asked him not to discuss my upcoming bout with my mother or sister, and Betty didn't say anything so I assumed she hadn't heard about it.

Jennifer had offered to get one of her older brothers to protect me, and, if I wanted, she was willing to tell Miss

Main Idea
What is the main idea of this paragraph?

Spiral Review
FIGURATIVE LANGUAGE Identify the similes in this paragraph. How do they contribute to the intended effect?

⑫ **Comprehension**
Why does Nonno Frankie insist that Paul always know the rules?

✿ DIFFERENTIATED INSTRUCTION

🔵 Vocabulary for English Learners
Preteach some additional vocabulary that will enable students to better comprehend and enjoy the selection. Briefly explain *mildew* (a growth produced by fungus). Help students see the humor of "ruling over mildew." Explain that *espresso* is a coffee drink served in tiny cups and a *sombrero* is a large hat with a wide brim. Help students visualize the picture suggested by "an espresso coffee cup would fit on his head like a sombrero."

Enrichment for Advanced Readers
Challenge students to check up on some of Nonno Frankie's lessons. Assign some students to find out if Alexander the Great really ordered his army to shave or if Genghis Khan really killed two million enemies. Assign others to research the yo-yo. Encourage students to organize their research around a main idea and present the information orally to the class.

---

⑪ **Main Idea**

1. Help students consider the details in the bracketed paragraph as they figure out the main idea. Discuss details such as having only positive thoughts, putting garlic in your pocket, and going with what you feel in your heart.

2. **Ask** the Main Idea question.
   Possible response: The main idea is that if you believe you can do something, you will be able to do it.

3. Invite volunteers to point out important details in the paragraph that led them to this main idea.
   Possible responses: Believing that he can "cripple" John Quinn and believing that his luck will be good will help him.

▶ **Reteach:** If students are struggling to distinguish between important and unimportant details, give them a photocopy of the bracketed paragraph and a highlighter. State the main idea (*Think positively and you will accomplish what you might think is impossible.*) and have them write it above the paragraph. Tell them to reread the paragraph and highlight only the important details, that is, the sentences that support that main idea (*make believe the opponent is vicious, keep only positive thoughts, have a good luck charm, go with what you feel in your heart*). Discuss the choices they make.

Spiral Review

Figurative Language

Ask students the Spiral Review question.

Possible response: The similes are "face like a mattress," "he looks like a fugitive from a brain gang," and "a coffee cup . . . like a sombrero." They are humorous and light, suggesting that Paul will easily defeat John Quinn.

⑫ **Comprehension**

Answer: He believes that if people make a point of knowing the rules, they will never accidentally do something wrong.

⑬ Mood

1. Have a student reread the paragraph on the previous page, beginning with "Yes, you curse this John Quinn."

2. Point out that the mood of that paragraph is humorous. **Ask** students to explain how the author creates that mood.

   Answer: He uses funny words to describe the opponent, such as "a fugitive from a brain gang," "a face like a mattress," and "an espresso coffee cup would fit on his head like a sombrero."

3. Direct students' attention to the bracketed text. Remind them that it's now Monday morning in the story, and Paul is returning to school. Have a student read the two paragraphs.

4. **Ask** the Mood question.

   Possible response: He uses words and phrases such as "nervous wreck," "combat," "revenge," and "my mind was numb with fear" to show that Paul was very anxious.

Mood
How does the author create a different mood in this passage?
⑬

Vocabulary ▶
undulating (un´ jə lā tin) *adj.* moving in waves, like a snake

distorted (di stôrt´ əd) *adj.* twisted out of normal shape

Haines so she could stop anything from happening. I told her, "No." I thought there was a chance John Quinn would have even forgotten the whole incident and wouldn't make good on his revenge threat. Nevertheless, my mind was numb with fear all day at school. In every class I went to, it seemed there were a dozen different kids coming over to me and telling me they heard John Quinn was going to beat me up after school.

At 3 p.m. sharp, the bell rang.

All the kids started to leave school.

I dawdled.

I cleaned my desk and took time packing up my books. Jennifer was at my side as we left the main exit of the building. There, across the street in a field behind Ronkewitz's Candy Store, was a crowd of about 300 kids standing around like a big, undulating horseshoe, with John Quinn standing at the center bend glaring at me.

"You could run," Jennifer suggested, tossing her hair all to the left side of her face. She looked much more than pretty now. She looked loyal to the bone.

"No," I said. I just walked forward toward my fate, with the blood in my temples pounding so hard I thought I was going to pass out. Moose and Leon and Mike and Conehead and Little Frankfurter were sprinkled out in front of me, goading me forward. I didn't even hear what they said. I saw only their faces distorted in ecstasy and expectation. They looked like the mob I had seen in a sixteenth-century etching where folks in London had bought tickets to watch bulldogs attacking water buffalo.

John stood with his black eye, and his fists up.

I stopped a few feet from him and put my fists up. A lot of kids in the crowd started to shout, "Kill him, Johnny!" but I may have imagined that part.

John came closer. He started to dance on his feet like all father-trained fighters do. I danced, too, as best I could. The crowd began to scream for blood. Jennifer kept shouting, "Hey, there's no need to fight! You don't have to fight, guys!"

But John came in for the kill. He was close enough now so any punch he threw could hit me. All I thought of was Nonno Frankie, but I couldn't remember half of what he told me and I didn't think any of it would work anyway.

14 Critical Viewing

Possible response: They seem to be about the same age. They seem to be having a similar schoolyard fight.

15 Comprehension

Answer: He has been feeling very nervous and wishes he didn't have to go through with it.

"Aaeeeeeyaaaayeeeeeh!" I suddenly screamed at John. He stopped in his tracks and the crowd froze in amazed silence. Instantly, I brought back my right foot, and shot it forward to kick John in his left shin. The crowd was shocked, and booed me with mass condemnation for my Sicilian fighting technique. I missed John's shin, and kicked vainly again. He threw a punch at me. It barely touched me, but I was so busy kicking, I tripped myself and fell down. The crowd cheered. I realized everyone including John thought his punch had floored me. I decided to go along with it. I groveled in the dirt for a few moments, and then stood up slowly holding my head as though I'd received a death blow. John put his fists down. He was satisfied justice had been done and his black eye had been avenged. He turned to leave, but Moose wasn't happy.

"Hey, ya didn't punch him enough," Moose complained to John.

"It's over," John said, like the decent kid he was.

"No, it's not," Moose yelled, and the crowd began to call for more blood. Now it was Moose coming toward me, and I figured I was dead meat. He came closer and closer. Jennifer shouted for him to stop and threatened to pull his eyeballs out, but he kept coming. And that was when something amazing happened. I was aware of a figure taller than me, running, charging. The figure had long blond hair, and it struck Moose from behind. I could see it was a girl and she had her hands right around Moose's neck,

14 ▲ Critical Viewing
How are these boys similar to John and Paul?

◄ Vocabulary
condemnation
(kän´ dem nā´ shən)
n. expression of strong disapproval

15 Comprehension
How has Paul been feeling about this fight?

Mood

Ask the Mood question.

Possible responses: The scream, the description of how Paul tripped himself, and the amazing fighting abilities of his sister are funny.

17 Main Idea

Ask the Main Idea question.

Possible response: Students may say the main idea is that the support of one's friends and family helps in difficult times.

☑️ **ASSESS**

Language Study

Vocabulary

Sample answers:

1. The bill collector was sent to *exact payment* from the customer.

2. The women's *necklace* was *undulating* slightly as she ran to her car.

3. Celebrating New Year's Day by swimming in a freezing lake or ocean may seem like a *demented idea,* but some people enjoy doing so.

4. The *observant spy* quickly noticed that someone was following him.

5. People generally disapprove of *thieves,* except in the case of Robin Hood, who escapes this *condemnation.*

Word Study

Part A

Sample Answers:

The Latin root *-tort-* means "twist out of shape." A *retort* is a witty reply that may take another person's remark and twist it out of shape. To *contort* something is to twist it out of shape. *Torturous* means having many twists and turns.

Part B

Sample Answers:

1. A *contortionist* is a person who can twist his or her body and perform amazing gymnastic acts.

2. It is difficult to watch television when *distortion* causes the image to be twisted out of shape.

Mood
A fight scene would normally be scary. What details make the mood of this scene humorous?

16 choking him. When she let him go, she threw him about ten feet, accidentally tearing off a religious medal from around his neck. Everyone stopped dead in their tracks, and I could see my savior was my sister.

"If any of you tries to hurt my brother again, I'll rip your guts out," she announced.

Moose was not happy. Conehead and Little Frankfurter were not happy. But the crowd broke up fast and everyone headed home. I guess that was the first day everybody **17** learned that if nothing else, the Zindel kids stick together. As for Nonno Frankie's Sicilian fighting technique, I came to realize he was ahead of his time. In fact, these days it's called karate.

Main Idea
What is the main idea of this final paragraph?

Language Study

Vocabulary The following words appear in *The Pigman & Me.* Write sentences that correctly use each word pair below.

exact   demented   observant   undulating   condemnation

1. exact (as a verb); payment

2. undulating; necklace

3. demented; idea

4. observant; spy

5. condemnation; thieves

Word Study

WORD STUDY
The **Latin root *-tort-*** means "twist out of shape." In this story, the author describes his classmates' faces as distorted, or twisted out of normal shape.

Part A Explain how the **Latin root *-tort-*** contributes to the meanings of *retort, contort* and *torturous*. Consult a dictionary if necessary.

Part B Use the context of each sentence and what you know about the root *-tort-* to explain your answers to the following questions.

1. What can a *contortionist* do?

2. Can you watch television if the screen has a *distortion*?

Literary Analysis

Possible responses appear below. Check to be sure students support their responses with evidence from the text.

1. **(a)** Life is full of written and unwritten rules. **(b)** Paul got into a fight because he did not know a school rule. Nonno Frankie, Jennifer, and Betty follow the unwritten rule that friends and family should support one another.

2. About 300 kids came to watch the fight. The exact number of kids who came to watch the fight did not affect what happened.

3. **(a)** The overall mood is humorous. **(b)** Nonno Frankie is a funny character and what happens at the fight is comical.

4. **(a)** *Words*: revenge, disaster; *Images*: Paul is white with fear.; *Mood*: tense, suspenseful **(b)** The reader may think the humorous story is turning serious.

For other sample answers, see the **Literary Analysis Graphic Organizer A** for "The Pigman & Me."

5. **(a)** Nonno Frankie tells Paul to yell like Tarzan; he tells him to pretend his opponent is vicious. **(b)** Yes, for example, he tells Paul to keep positive thoughts in his heart.

Literary Analysis

Key Ideas and Details

1. **Main Idea (a)** What is the main idea of this selection? **(b)** What are two important details in the selection that support this main idea?

2. **Main Idea** What is one unimportant detail that does not support the main idea? Explain your choice.

Craft and Structure

3. **Mood (a)** What is one **mood**, or overall feeling, that the author creates in this selection? **(b)** What details create that mood?

4. **Mood (a)** Complete a chart like the one on the right to analyze a passage that has a different mood. **(b)** What effect does the change in mood have on readers?

Integration of Knowledge and Ideas

5. **(a)** Identify two pieces of advice that Nonno Frankie gives Paul. **(b) Analyze:** Does Frankie's advice apply to more than the fight itself? Explain.

6. **(a)** What does Paul do after he falls down during the fight? **(b) Infer:** Why does he do this? **(c) Criticize:** Is his strategy a good one? Explain your answer and support it with details from the selection.

7. **(a) Compare and Contrast:** Explain the difference between John's attitude and the attitude of the other students after Paul falls down. **(b) Analyze:** What problems does the attitude of the other students create for John and Paul?

8. **What is important to know? (a)** How does a lack of knowledge cause trouble for Paul? **(b) Draw Conclusions:** Was Nonno Frankie's advice helpful to Paul in his fight with John Quinn? Use specific details to support your answer. **(c) Speculate:** Will any of Nonno Frankie's advice be helpful to Paul in the future? Explain.

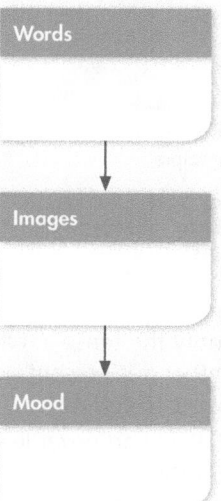

Words

Images

Mood

ACADEMIC VOCABULARY

As you write and speak about the excerpt from *The Pigman & Me,* use the words related to gaining knowledge that you explored on page 163 of this text.

6. **(a)** Paul acts as if he is hurt. **(b)** He wants the fight to be over. **(c)** It is a good strategy because it saves Paul from getting hurt.

7. **(a)** John wants the fight to end; the other students want it to continue. **(b)** Both John and Paul want the fight to end, but the cheers of the other kids make it difficult for them to stop fighting.

8. **What is important to know?** **(a)** Because Paul did not know the rule about the use of paddles, he kept one past the time limit, provoking a fight. **(b)** Yes, it was helpful. Paul didn't apply all of Nonno Frankie's specific advice, but followed the spirit of the advice when he pretended to be hurt and distracted John Quinn. **(c)** Nonno Frankie's advice may be helpful to Paul in the future if Paul ever finds himself in a similar situation where conflict is involved.

 Online Writer's Notebook

Students can use the Online Writer's Notebook to record all responses.

Conventions

1. Introduce the skill, using the instruction on the student page.

2. Discuss the definitions and the examples in the chart.

Think Aloud: Model the Skill

Say to students:

To decide which perfect tense of a verb to choose when I write, I ask, "When did the action start?" and "When did the action stop?" If I'm writing about my vacation in Hawaii, I might say, "I *had applied* sunscreen before swimming" to tell about something I did in the past that is now finished. "I *have applied* sunscreen many times" indicates that I am still doing something that I started in the past.

Practice A

1. past perfect   **3.** present perfect

2. future perfect   **4.** present perfect

Reading Application

Sample answers:
Before the end of school, Jennifer came running up to me in the halls and told me John Quinn *had announced* to everyone he was going to exact revenge on me after school on Monday. (*… has announced … he is going to*)

I *had* never even *been* in a fight. (*have….been*)

I thought he was kidding, because all we *had done* was carve off the outer pieces of bark. (*…will have done is…*)

Practice B

1. Paul *has listened* carefully to Nonno Frankie.

2. Soon, Paul *will have recovered* from his fear.

3. Before long, Paul and John *had become* friends.

4. A huge crowd of students *has appeared*.

5. Paul *had learned* an important lesson.

Writing Application

Sample answers:
Paul had gone to school eager to see his new friends.

John has forgiven Paul for the black eye.

Paul and Jennifer will have spent more time together.

 Close Reading Activities Continued

Conventions: Perfect Tenses of Verbs

The **perfect tense** of a verb combines a form of *have* with the past participle of the verb.

- The **present perfect** tense shows an action that began in the past and continues in the present.
- The **past perfect** tense shows a past action or condition that ended before another past action began.
- The **future perfect** tense shows a future action or condition that will have ended before another begins.

Present Perfect	Past Perfect	Future Perfect
have, has + past participle	*had* + past participle	*will have* + past participle
They *have voted* in this city for seventeen years.	They *had voted* by the time we arrived.	The council *will have* voted by summer.

Practice A

Identify the tense in each sentence. Indicate whether it is present perfect, past perfect, or future perfect.

1. Paul had never learned to fight before facing John.

2. Nanno Frankie will have returned home by then.

3. Paul has never been so afraid.

4. The other kids have decided to be mean to Paul.

Reading Application Find three sentences in the past perfect tense in the selection. Rewrite each sentence in either the present perfect or the future perfect tense. You may have to change other verbs in the sentence or add words to the sentence.

Practice B

Rewrite each sentence using the tense indicated in parentheses.

1. Paul had listened carefully to Nanno Frankie. (present perfect)

2. Paul has recovered from his fear. (future perfect)

3. Before long, Paul and John will have become friends. (past perfect)

4. A huge crowd of students had appeared. (present perfect)

5. Paul will have learned an important lesson. (past perfect)

Writing Application Write three sentences describing a future day in Paul's life. In each sentence, use one of the perfect tenses.

Writing to Sources

Explanatory Text Write a **problem-and-solution essay** based on the excerpt from *The Pigman & Me*. Your essay should help a newcomer adjust to a new school.

- State a problem that newcomers might face. Review *The Pigman and Me* for possible ideas.
- Provide a step-by-step solution to the problem. Clearly explain the rules a newcomer should know.
- Explain why your solution will help solve the problem.
- Support each step of your suggested solution with concrete details, examples, and anecdotes, including ones from *The Pigman & Me*.

Grammar Application Check your writing to be sure that you have used perfect tenses correctly.

Speaking and Listening

Comprehension and Collaboration In a small group, hold an **informal discussion** based on the excerpt from *The Pigman & Me*. Discuss how students should act in order to make friends at a new school. Identify the social rules that students should know and follow. Include details from the selection and from your prior knowledge to make suggestions. You may also include things that student should *not* do.

Follow these steps to complete the assignment:

- Allow each person in the group an opportunity to offer opinions about the topic.
- Support opinions with facts and examples.
- Use good listening skills when others are talking.
- Jot down notes to remember important ideas and details. Your notes do not have to be a complete record of the discussion.
- At the end of the discussion, reflect on the group's responses and paraphrase the group's ideas.
- Share your paraphrase with the rest of the class.

 **Common Core State Standards**

Writing
2.a. Introduce a topic; organize ideas, concepts, and information, using strategies such as definition, classification, comparison/contrast, and cause/effect. **2.b.** Develop the topic with relevant facts, definitions, concrete examples, quotations, or other information and examples.

Speaking and Listening
1.a. Come to discussions prepared, having read or studied required material; explicitly draw on that preparation by referring to evidence on the topic, text, or issue to probe and reflect on ideas under discussion. **1.b.** Follow rules for collegial discussion. **1.d.** Review the key ideas expressed and demonstrate understanding of multiple perspectives through reflection and paraphrasing.

Language
1. Demonstrate command of the conventions of standard English grammar and usage when writing or speaking. **4.b.** Use common grade-appropriate Greek or Latin affixes and roots as clues to the meaning of a word.

Writing to Sources

1. Review the assignment, using the instruction on the student page.
2. Help students to brainstorm for problems that new students might face at your school, such as not understanding unwritten rules or dress codes.
3. To give students guidance in writing their essay, give them the **Support for Writing** page for this selection in the *Student Companion All-in-One Workbook.*
4. To evaluate the writing activity, use the rubrics for **Problem-Solution Essay**, in *Professional Development Guidebook,* pp. 244–245. Evaluate how students select and discuss the issues.

Grammar Application

Have students check their drafts for the correct use of perfect tenses of verbs.

Six Traits Focus

✓	Ideas	✓	Word Choice
✓	Organization		Sentence Fluency
	Voice	✓	Conventions

Speaking and Listening

1. Review the assignment, using the instruction on the student page.
2. To support students' work on the assignment, have them complete the **Support for Extend Your Learning** page for this selection in the *Student Companion All-in-One Workbook.*

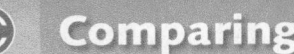 **Comparing Texts**

ANALYZING EXPOSITORY TEXTS

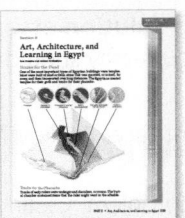

Reading Skill: Use Text Aids and Features

Many writers of expository texts use **text aids and features** to organize details and highlight important information, including central ideas. Identifying text features as you read can help you locate specific information and understand key ideas. Text aids and features can also help you see the relationships among ideas in a text. As you read expository texts, identify the items listed in the chart below, and use them to guide your reading.

Text Aids	
Title	Identifies the subject of a chapter or complete work
Main heading	Identifies the general topic of a section
Subheading	Identifies a specific topic within the section's main topic
Highlighted vocabulary	Introduces and defines key terms
Text Features	
Maps, graphs, and charts	Provide visual and statistical information that supports the topic
Photographs, drawings, and diagrams with captions	Illustrate information in the text and provide additional details

Content-Area Vocabulary

These words appear in the selections that follow. You may also encounter them in other content-area texts.

- **archaeologists** (är′kē äl′ə jists) *n.* people who study human history by analyzing ancient objects and remains
- **architect** (är′ kə tekt) *n.* person who designs buildings
- **colossal** (kə läs′əl) *adj.* extremely large

Reading Skill

1. Introduce the skill, using the instruction on the student page.

2. Provide students with an example of how to use text aids and features. If they are researching lions online and come across an article with the boldfaced subheadings, "Size," "Feeding," and "Social Structure," they will easily find the information they need.

MULTIDRAFT READING

To assist struggling readers and to deepen comprehension for all, apply multidraft reading protocols. For each reading, have students set the purpose indicated:

- **First reading:** Students should read the selection independently and think about its basic meaning.
- **Second reading:** Students should analyze the text's key ideas and details and its craft and structure, and respond to the side-column prompts.
- **Third reading:** Students should integrate knowledge and ideas, connect the text to other texts and to the world, and answer the end-of-selection questions.

For more guidance, refer to the *Classroom Strategies and Teaching Routines* card on multidraft reading.

What is important to know?

Have students look for statements of fact and think about what kinds of sources they might use to double-check these claims.

Content-Area Vocabulary

If students require support with selection vocabulary, use this routine:

1. Write the following words and definitions on the board:

   archaeologists *n.* people who study human history by finding and analyzing ancient objects and other remains

   architect *n.* person who designs buildings

   colossal *adj.* extremely large

2. Have students say each word aloud.

3. Use the word in a sentence that defines the word.

Common Core State Standards

Reading Informational Text

5. Analyze how a particular sentence, paragraph, chapter, or section fits into the overall structure of a text and contributes to the development of the ideas.

7. Integrate information presented in different media or formats as well as in words to develop a coherent understanding of a topic or issue.

Writing

1. Write arguments to support claims with clear reasons and relevant evidence.

Language

6. Acquire and use accurately grade-appropriate general academic and domain-specific words and phrases; gather vocabulary knowledge when considering a word or phrase important to comprehension or expression.

TEACHING RESOURCES

	Print	Digital
All Common Core Companion, pp. 130–136, 144–150, 173–183, 353–354	✓	✓
All Graphic Organizers A and B, The Seven Wonders of the World; Art, Architecture, and Learning in Egypt		✓
All Online Student Edition eText with audio and video		✓
All Online Teacher Edition		✓
L1 Professional Development Guidebook, p. 33		✓
All Student Companion All-in-One Workbook, The Seven Wonders of the World; Art, Architecture, and Learning in Egypt	✓	✓

The Seven Wonders of the World

from Infoplease®

Since ancient times, numerous "seven wonders" lists have been created. The content of these lists tends to vary and none is definitive. The seven wonders that are most widely agreed upon as being in the original list are the Seven Wonders of the Ancient World, which was compiled by ancient Greek historians and is thus confined to the most magnificent structures known to the ancient Greek world. Of all the Ancient Wonders, the pyramids alone survive.

The Pyramids of Egypt are three pyramids at Giza, outside modern Cairo. The largest pyramid, built by Khufu (Cheops), a king of the fourth dynasty, had an original estimated height of 482 feet (now approximately 450 feet). The base has sides 755 feet long. It contains 2,300,000 blocks; the average weight of each is 2.5 tons. The estimated date of completion is 2680 B.C.

The Hanging Gardens of Babylon were supposedly built by Nebuchadnezzar around 600 B.C. to please his queen, Amuhia. They are also associated with the mythical Assyrian queen Semiramis. Archaeologists surmise that the gardens were laid out atop a vaulted building, with provisions for raising water. The terraces were said to rise from 75 to 300 feet.

The Statue of Zeus (Jupiter) at Olympia was made of gold and ivory by the Greek sculptor Phidias (5th century B.C.). Reputed to be 40 feet high, the statue has been lost without a trace, except for reproductions on coins.

PART 2 • The Seven Wonders of the World **231**

Use Text Aids and Features

1. Remind students that as they look at this online source, they should pay attention to text aids. The main heading and subheadings help them in organizing and comprehending the content. Links help them quickly find additional information, and illustrations help them visualize what is being described.

2. Direct students' attention to the online almanac entry on the student page. **Ask:** What features of the page help organize the information?

   Answer: The main heading identifies the topic, the Seven Wonders of the World. The subheadings divide the overall topic into smaller subtopics—each of the wonders. The slight bit of extra space around each subtopic also separates them from one another.

3. **Ask** them why this particular source does not have captions for the illustrations.

   Possible response: Students may say that because the illustrations simply depict the structures detailed in the text passages, there is no need to have captions.

DIFFERENTIATED INSTRUCTION

Strategies for Less Proficient Readers

Students might have difficulty with some of the words in the entries. Help them by giving them definitions of the following:

- *compiled:* put together
- *confined:* limited
- *surmise:* conclude
- *vaulted:* raised in an arch
- *provisions:* steps taken
- *reputed:* believed to be

Enrichment for Advanced Readers

Remind students that this list of ancient wonders is limited to the structures that Greek historians knew. Have groups research the major achievements of the peoples of ancient East Asia, South Asia, Southeast Asia, Europe, Africa, and the Americas. Challenge them to develop their own list of the "Seven Wonders of All Ancient Worlds." Have them create and present their own almanac, with brief text descriptions and pictures. Remind them that their choices should all date from before A.D. 1.

Use Text Aids and Features

1. Tell students to look at the sub-headings and the paragraphs about each wonder.

2. Ask them what information the subheadings convey.

Answer: Each subheading identifies the name of the structure and its location.

3. Ask what information is common to the entries.

Answer: Each entry gives more information about what the structure was and when it was built. Several entries state the size of the structures and when they were destroyed.

4. Explain that reference sources often give similar information about related subjects to make it easier for people who consult the sources to compare one subject to another.

5. Ask students to identify text features that the online almanac could have used to present this information in a way that would make the parallels, or similarities, stand out more.

Possible responses: Students may suggest the information could be further organized in a list with headings such as *Date of Construction; Size;* and so on. Others might say that the source could have organized the information into a chart.

The Temple of Artemis (Diana) at Ephesus was begun about 350 B.C., in honor of a non-Hellenic goddess who later became identified with the Greek goddess of the same name. The temple, with Ionic columns 60 feet high, was destroyed by invading Goths in A.D. 262.

The Mausoleum at Halicarnassus was erected by Queen Artemisia in memory of her husband, King Mausolus of Caria in Asia Minor, who died in 353 B.C. Some remains of the structure are in the British Museum. This shrine is the source of the modern word mausoleum.

The Colossus at Rhodes was a bronze statue of Helios (Apollo), about 105 feet high. The work of the sculptor Chares, who reputedly labored for 12 years before completing it in 280 B.C., it was destroyed during an earthquake in 224 B.C.

The Pharos (Lighthouse) of Alexandria was built by Sostratus of Cnidus during the 3rd century B.C. on the island of Pharos off the coast of Egypt. It was destroyed by an earthquake in the 13th century.

(Some lists include the Walls of Babylon in place of the second or seventh wonder.)

See also The Seven Wonders of the Modern World.

232 UNIT 2 • What is important to know?

💬 **VOCABULARY DEVELOPMENT**

Content-Area Vocabulary: History
The entries on the Seven Wonders of the World use several words common to history writing. Challenge pairs of students to develop definitions of these terms. They might consult a history textbook, where they can find definitions in the glossary. They could also use a dictionary.

Call on the students not only to define the terms but to collaborate on writing a paragraph that employs them. Terms to include, found on this page and the previous page, include *ancient, pyramids, dynasty,* B.C., *mythical, archeological, Hellenic, Ionic,* A.D., and *Goths.*

Section 5

Art, Architecture, and Learning in Egypt

from *Prentice Hall Ancient Civilizations*

Homes for the Dead

One of the most important types of Egyptian buildings were temples. Most were built of mud or from stone that was quarried, or mined, far away, and then transported over long distances. The Egyptians created temples for their gods and tombs for their pharaohs.

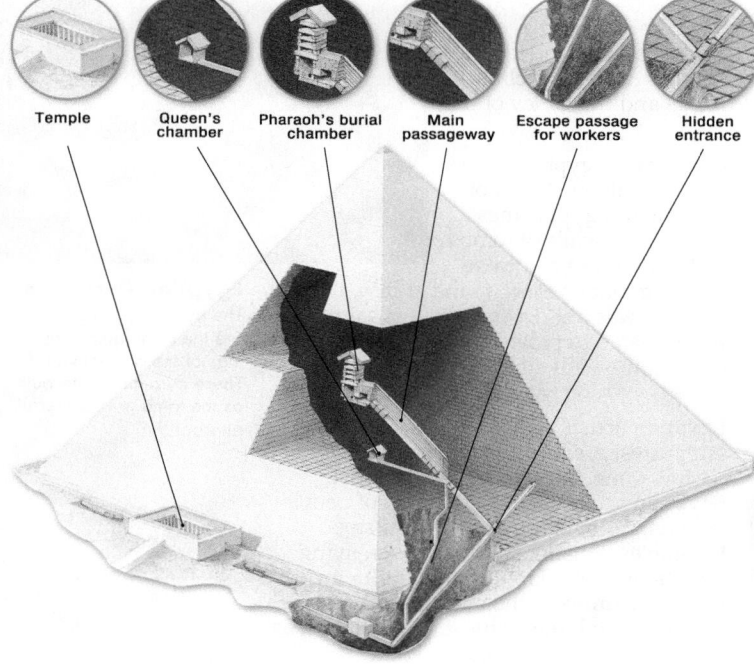

Temple   Queen's chamber   Pharaoh's burial chamber   Main passageway   Escape passage for workers   Hidden entrance

Tombs for the Pharaohs

Tombs of early rulers were underground chambers, or rooms. The burial chamber contained items that the ruler might want in the afterlife.

Use Text Aids and Features

1. Tell students that this selection is from a history textbook. **Ask** them to study the page and identify the text aids and features on it.

   Answer: Features include the section number, title, subheadings, illustrations, and captions.

2. **Ask** students to identify the purpose of each text aid and feature.

   Answer: The section number shows the division of topics into smaller parts. The title states the subject of the section. Subheadings divide the topic further and provide an outline of the subject. The illustrations show objects that are more easily understood if seen than if described in words. The captions explain details about the illustrations.

3. Direct students' attention to the main illustration. **Ask** them to explain why a section of the walls seems to be eliminated.

   Answer: The walls are cut away so the illustration can reveal what is inside the structure.

⚙ DIFFERENTIATED INSTRUCTION

Strategy for Special-Needs Students

To help students understand what is meant by "text aids" and "text features," lead them on a "tour" of the selection. Explain that text aids help organize information. Point out the main heading and the subheadings on this page and the next page. Discuss how these headings help structure the text and guide students as they read about the topic. Direct students to the photograph and caption on the next page. Have them identify how the caption aids in their understanding of the text.

ⒺⓁ Strategies for English Learners

Direct students' attention to the two uses of *or* to signal the definition of a term. One appears in the first paragraph ("was quarried, or mined"); the second is in the second paragraph ("chambers, or rooms"). Explain that when a word or phrase is preceded by *or* and set off by commas in this way, the word or phrase is often a definition or an explanation of the word that came before it. Invite students to create original sentences using *or* to link the words *temple* and *religious building* or the words *tombs* and *burial places*.

Use Text Aids and Features

1. Point out to students that to identify text aids and text features, they need to take an overall look at the page rather than focusing on particular words. The idea is to identify features on the page that stand out from the rest of the text.

2. **Ask** students to identify the features that stand out on this page.

   Possible responses: The features that stand out are the boldfaced words *Imhotep, King Khufu, sculpture,* and *mummies;* the subheading "Painting and Sculpture"; and the caption to the photograph.

3. Explain that students can use the subheadings to organize notes they take as they read a textbook. Point out that it is a good idea to record boldfaced names and terms, like *King Khufu* and *mummies,* when they take notes because such words are likely to be important terms.

An **architect** named **Imhotep** designed a new kind of tomb for his pharaoh, with six stone mounds, one on top of the other. The result is known as the Step Pyramid. Later architects made the sides smoother to create a true pyramid.

Three enormous pyramids were built at Giza by **King Khufu**, his son Khafre, and his grandson Menkaure. The tallest of these is the Great Pyramid of Khufu. For more than 4,000 years, this pyramid was the world's tallest building. Nearby stands the famous statue known as the Sphinx. The Sphinx guarded the road to Khafre's pyramid.

The great age of pyramid building ended about 2200 B.C. Pharaohs who ruled after that time carved tombs from the cliffs in the Valley of the Kings and the Valley of the Queens.

Painting and Sculpture Egyptians were skilled artists as well as builders. Much of what we know about life in Egypt comes from paintings found on the walls of tombs. Although these paintings show Egyptians at work and at play, their purpose was not decoration. The paintings were created to provide the person buried in the tomb with all of the objects and pleasures shown on the walls.

Egyptian artists also created wonderful sculptures. A **sculpture** is a statue made of clay, stone, or other materials. Most Egyptian sculptures were statues of people or gods. **Colossal** statues of gods stood in temples. Smaller statues of once-living Egyptians were placed in tombs along with their **mummies**. If the person's mummy was destroyed, the statue could replace it as a home for the dead person's spirit.

Egyptian Pyramids
The pyramids of Egypt are the most famous buildings of the ancient world. These pyramids were built as the tomb of a powerful pharaoh.

🔊 THINK ALOUD

Vocabulary: Using Context
Model the way to use context clues to clarify the meaning of unfamiliar words with this think aloud. Say to students:

I'm going to show you how I determine the meaning of the word *pharaoh* by using context clues. In the paragraph that begins "An architect named **Imhotep**," I see the word *pharaoh*. I notice the word is not defined on page 233, but I also see that the first sentence under the "Tombs for the Pharaohs" subheading includes the phrase "Tombs of early rulers." From this phrase,

I think that *pharaoh* might be another name for *ruler*. On page 234, I learn that three large pyramids were built by King Khufu and his son and grandson. My definition makes sense, because I know that a king is a kind of ruler. In the next paragraph, I read that later pharaohs were buried in places called the "Valley of the Kings" and the "Valley of the Queens." I conclude that *pharaoh* is another word for the kings or queens of ancient Egypt.

Writing to Sources

Comparing Expository Texts

1. Craft and Structure (a) Identify a text aid or structural feature that you would find in both an online almanac and a textbook. **(b)** Identify a text aid or structural feature that you would find in an online almanac, but not in a textbook. **(c)** In which text—the almanac or the textbook—is it easier to find specific information? Explain.

Content-Area Vocabulary

2. Use *archaeologists, architect,* and *colossal* in a brief paragraph that shows you understand the meaning of each word.

⏱ Timed Writing

Argument: Position Statement

Throughout history, there have been different lists of the Seven Wonders of the World. Take a position on whether or not the Egyptian pyramids should be classified as one of the Seven Wonders of the World. Support your position by integrating details from the texts you have read. **(25 minutes)**

5-Minute Planner

Complete these steps before you begin to write:

1. Read the prompt carefully and completely. Note that the prompt asks you to take a position based on what you have read.

2. Review the two texts. Use text aids and features to locate information about your topic. **TIP:** Relying on text aids and text features alone may lead you to incorrect conclusions. Be sure to review the text completely.

3. Compare the information that is presented in the two texts to connect and clarify main ideas.

4. Write a statement of your opinion, and make notes about the facts you will use to support your position.

5. Use your notes to prepare a quick outline. Then, use your outline to help you organize your response.

☑ ASSESS

Comparing Expository Texts

Possible responses appear below. Check to be sure students support their responses with evidence from the text.

1. (a) Students may identify subheadings or illustrations. **(b)** Students may say that links to more in-depth information or to other references would appear in an online almanac but not a textbook. **(c)** An online almanac makes it easier to look up information quickly on a related topic. Rather than flip through pages or look in another book, all a reader must do is click on a link.

2. Sample response: Archaeologists in Mexico have been learning about the ancient Mayan culture by exploring sites where these people once lived. Recently, they discovered a colossal temple that had been hidden over the centuries by the spreading jungle. The architects of this enormous building had designed a tomb inside for a Mayan king. Who knows what else the archaeologists will find

⏱ Timed Writing

1. Guide students in identifying and analyzing key words and phrases in the prompt.

2. Work with students to draw up guidelines for their essays:
   - **Thesis** The writer states whether the pyramids should be a wonder of the world.
   - **Organization** The writer explains what makes a structure qualify as a wonder of the world.
   - **Support** The writer offers facts to explain why the pyramids qualify as a wonder.
   - **Rhetoric** The writer should use persuasive techniques to make the argument convincing.

3. Have students use the 5-Minute Planner to structure their time.

4. Allow students 25 minutes to complete the assignment. Evaluate their work using the guidelines they have developed.

✎ Online Writer's Notebook

Students can use the Online Writer's Notebook to record all responses.

ASSESSMENT **RESOURCES**

The following resources can be used to assess students' knowledge and skills.

 Selection Test
 Open-Book Test

Word Origins

1. Introduce the skill, using the instruction on the student page.

2. Review the examples in the chart.

3. Invite students to give examples of familiar words that have come into English from other languages. If they have difficulty, prompt them with examples of foods from other countries, such as *pizza, taco,* and *sushi.*

Think Aloud: Model the Skill

Model the skill of using word origins to decode word meanings. Say to students:

> Learning the origins of a word helps me remember the meaning of the word. For instance, I know that *herculean* comes from the name of the Greek hero Hercules, who was famous for his strength. Knowing this fact makes it easy to remember that the word means "requiring great strength."

Practice A

1. *Solo* means "alone." Its origin is the Latin word *solus,* which has the same meaning.

2. *Martial* means "warlike." It comes from Mars, the Roman god of war.

3. *Skill* means "the ability to use knowledge effectively." Its origin is an Old Norse word meaning "distinction."

4. A *marathon* is a race that covers 26 miles and 385 yards. Its origin is the plain of Marathon, where Greek armies defeated Persian armies, prompting one man to run from that location to Athens to deliver news of the victory.

5. *Edict* means "a proclamation that has the force of law." The origin is from the Latin *dicere,* which means "to say."

6. *Mentor* means "a trusted counselor or guide." It comes from the name of a person to whom the Greek hero Odysseus entrusted his son.

 **Grammar Tutorials**

Grammar Tutorials in the *Student eText* provide additional support!

 Language Study

Word Origins

The English language continues to grow and change. New words enter the language from many sources. The **etymology** of a word describes its **origin** and development. A word's etymology identifies the language in which the word first appeared. It also tells how the word's spelling and meaning have changed over time.

Many English words come from ancient Latin or Greek words or word roots. Some modern words are **allusions,** references to well-known characters, places, or events in history, art, or literature. This chart shows some examples.

Word	Origin	Definition	Example Sentence
prove	Latin word *probare,* which means "test"	to show that something is true	This experiment will prove that light travels faster than sound.
biography	Greek words *bios* ("life") and *graphein* ("to write")	the story of a person's life	The biography of George Washington includes many facts about the American Revolution.
herculean	allusion to Hercules, a hero in ancient Greek myths, known for his great strength	requiring great strength	Moving the heavy box was a herculean task.

Practice A

Find each of the following words in a dictionary. Define each word and explain its origin.

1. solo
2. martial
3. skill
4. marathon
5. edict
6. mentor

Common Core State Standards

Language

4.b. Use common, grade-appropriate Greek or Latin affixes and roots as clues to the meaning of a word (e.g., *audience, auditory, audible*).

4.c. Consult reference materials, both print and digital, to find the pronunciation of a word or determine or clarify its precise meaning or its part of speech.

TEACHING RESOURCES

	Print	Digital
All Language Study Worksheet, Word Origins		✓

Practice B

Each question contains a word that has come into the English language from the Greek or Latin language or from mythology. Use a dictionary to find each italicized word's origin and meaning. Then, use that information to answer each question.

1. What special ability does an *ambidextrous* person have?

2. How did *cereal* get its name?

3. Where will you go if you *circumnavigate* our planet?

4. What does a *dermatologist* treat?

5. Why is the word "goat" a *tetragram*?

6. Why is the word *colossal* used to describe something that is very big?

7. Why is a kangaroo considered a *marsupial*?

8. How would you describe the personality of someone who is *jovial*?

Comprehension and Collaboration

With a partner, research the following characters from Greek mythology. Then, use a dictionary to find an English word that is based on each character's name. Finally, write a few sentences that explain how the word's meaning relates to the character.

- **Helios**
- **Pan**
- **Arachne**

Activity Identify the source of each of the following English words. Then, use a graphic organizer like the one shown to explain how the English word and the source word are related. The first item has been completed as an example.

1. stampede   2. mercurial   3. kindergarten   4. phobia

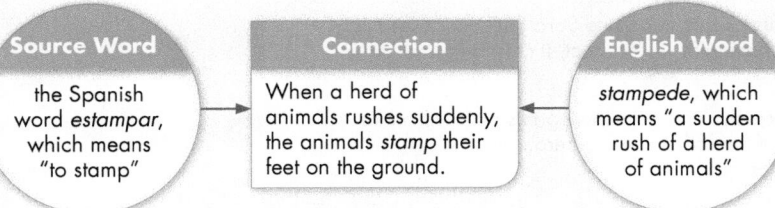

Source Word	Connection	English Word
the Spanish word *estampar*, which means "to stamp"	When a herd of animals rushes suddenly, the animals *stamp* their feet on the ground.	*stampede*, which means "a sudden rush of a herd of animals"

🎯 DIFFERENTIATED INSTRUCTION

Support for Special-Needs Students

Guide special-needs students in carrying out the activity by walking them through the origin of the word *stampede*, shown in the chart. Help them see how to demonstrate the connection between the origin word and the English word. Then, give them a chance to prepare their graphic organizer for the first word. Review their work to make sure that they are on the right track before they proceed to the remaining words.

🔵 Enrichment for English Learners

Invite English learners to name words from their native language—or related languages—that have been adopted in English. Give them time to use Internet sources or the library to find examples. They might prepare a bulletin board or slide show to present their examples to the class.

Practice B

1. *Ambidextrous* is an adjective used to describe someone who can use both hands effectively. It comes from the Latin *ambi-*, meaning "both," and *dexter*, or "right hand," suggesting that "both hands are as effective as the right hand."

2. *Cereal*, which refers to grain products, comes from the Roman goddess Ceres, who was the goddess of agriculture.

3. If you *circumnavigate* Earth, you travel around it. The word comes from the Latin words *circum*, meaning "around," and *navigare*, "to navigate."

4. A *dermatologist* treats problems of the skin. The word comes from the Greek roots *derma-*, meaning "skin," and *-ologu*, which means "the study of."

5. *Goat* is a *tetragram* because it has four letters. In Greek, *tetra* means "four," and *gramma* means "letter."

6. *Colossal* describes something very large because it is based on an ancient statue, the Colossus of Rhodes, which stood more than 100 feet high.

7. A kangaroo is a *marsupial* because it carries its young in a pouch. The word comes from the Greek word *marsypion*, which means "pouch" or "pocket."

8. A *jovial* person is jolly or happy. Its origin is the Roman god Jove.

Activity

Provide dictionaries for students so they can carry out the activity. Also provide students with copies of the Three-column Chart Graphic Organizer to record their ideas.

In their responses, students should show the connections between the English word and its source word.

Comprehension and Collaboration

Divide the class into groups. Provide dictionaries for students so they can carry out the activity.

Students should explain how the word's meaning in English relates to the character's story.

Learn the Skills

1. Introduce the workshop, including the activity on the next page.

2. Explain that companies may "slant" the information in an advertisement by providing only those facts that reflect positively on their product.

3. Review with students the difference between a fact and an opinion. Read this example to students: "People need more time outdoors, so purchase your camping supplies from Joe's Sporting Goods." Explain that the statement is not a fact because it can't be proved.

4. Review with students each of the persuasive techniques listed. Explain that bandwagon appeals, testimonials, and emotional appeals can lead people to adopt beliefs they would not hold if they reasoned from the facts alone.

5. Point out that commercials are paid advertisements on television and radio. Paid advertisements that appear in print media, such as newspapers, are called advertisements or ads.

© Speaking and Listening

Evaluating Media Messages and Advertisements

A persuasive message encourages the audience to think or act in a certain way. This is especially true of media messages such as advertisements.

Learn the Skills

Identify the source of the message. When you encounter media messages and advertisements, think about who is delivering the "information" and why. Facts supplied by the person or group may be slanted to favor a point of view.

Evaluate the content of the message. A fact is something that can be proved or demonstrated. An *opinion* can be supported but not proved. Notice whether or not the claims in a media message are supported by facts and evidence.

Recognize propaganda. When the information is completely one-sided, it is called *propaganda*. Propaganda is the spreading of misleading ideas. The chart below shows three types of propaganda. These are media techniques that are used in place of factual information.

Technique	Example
Bandwagon appeals rely on the idea that people make choices to be part of a crowd.	Every sixth-grader thinks this, and you should too.
Testimonials portray famous people giving their opinions or behaving in a certain way.	Since Sara Superstar uses this product, it must be good.
Emotional appeals influence an audience through the use of loaded language that appeals to feelings rather than logic.	Following this plan will make you a hero.

Evaluate the delivery of the message. Persuasive messages can be delivered through a variety of media—writing, radio, television, film, or billboards. Ask yourself if the words, sounds, and pictures in a message or ad are meant to make you feel a certain way or *think* a certain way.

238 UNIT 2 • What is important to know?

© Common Core State Standards

Speaking and Listening

2. Interpret information presented in diverse media and formats and explain how it contributes to a topic, text, or issue under study.

3. Delineate a speaker's argument and specific claims, distinguishing claims that are supported by reasons and evidence from claims that are not.

✔ STRATEGIES FOR EVALUATING MEDIA MESSAGES AND ADVERTISEMENTS

Model the skill of evaluating persuasive messages by describing your thought process as you watch a commercial.

• First, describe the commercial. Say to students: *I have seen a commercial that shows a famous actor and her dog. The dog has a shiny coat and is playing with the actor. She says, "Come on, Cruiser! It's time for dinner!" The dog eagerly eats his bowl of Brand X dog food, wagging his tail. The actor says, "This food sure does keep you healthy and happy, doesn't it, Cruiser?"*

• Explain how you would evaluate the commercial. Say: *I ask myself, "What is being said about the dog food?" The commercial is telling me that the dog food is good. Dogs love to eat it. The actor says it makes her dog healthy and happy. These statements cannot be proved, so they are not facts. Because the person is a famous actor, I think the commercial is suggesting that I buy this dog food because the actor thinks it is good. This persuasive technique is called a testimonial.*

Practice the Skills

Presentation of Knowledge and Ideas Use what you have learned in this workshop to perform the following task.

ACTIVITY: **Evaluate a Persuasive Message**

Evaluate a television commercial by following these steps:
- Identify and explain the commercial's message.
- Analyze the propaganda used in the message.
- Decide whether or not the claims in the commercial are supported by evidence.
- Explain how propaganda in the commercial influences your emotions.

Use the Evaluation Checklist to help you evaluate the commercial.

Evaluation Checklist

Message
What is the source and content of the message?
Explain the message and its purpose.

Propaganda and Persuasive Techniques
What persuasive techniques are used to influence the viewer? Briefly explain each one used.
❑ Bandwagon appeal ❑ Testimonial ❑ Emotional appeal

Influence on Emotion
How does each technique make you feel? Briefly explain your reasons.
The message made me want to
❑ buy the product. ❑ not buy the product. ❑ Other (explain).

Conclusion
What claims in the commercial are supported by evidence?
What claims are supported by propaganda?
Is the commercial effective? Why or why not?

Technique(s) Used:

Effect of the Message:

Comprehension and Collaboration For three days, view several types of advertisements. Take notes on the propaganda used in each one. Also note whether or not the claims in the ads are supported by facts. Compare your findings with those of a partner.

Practice the Skills

1. Review the assignment with students. Make sure they understand that their evaluations should explain the content of the commercial's message. Tell them to discuss specific persuasive techniques such as bandwagon appeal, testimonial, and emotional appeal.

2. Explain to students that they should use a copy of the Evaluation Checklist to evaluate their own presentation and the presentations made by classmates.

3. Before students give their presentations to the class, remind listeners to ask questions if any points are unclear. To maintain order, encourage them to raise their hands and wait to be acknowledged by the presenter before stating their questions. Suggest that students making presentations scan the classroom from time to time so they will notice any students who have questions.

Evaluate the Activity

1. Evaluate students' analysis of commercials on the basis of their understanding of persuasive techniques. They should identify the persuasive techniques used in the message by presenting specific details.

2. When the class discusses the evaluations that were most effective, encourage students to make note of the features of those presentations that made them effective and to incorporate those techniques in their future presentations.

Comprehension and Collaboration

After students make charts showing propaganda and whether it is supported, pair students so they can compare their results.

DIFFERENTIATED INSTRUCTION

Strategy for Special-Needs Students
Have students name a few products with which they are familiar. Then, single out the products with which all of the students are familiar, and have them discuss the words and slogans used to market each product. As students discuss the words and slogans, write them on the board so students can experience their impact. Then, challenge students to question the slogans and words and the impact they make.

Strategy for Less Proficient Readers
Have students write a short advertisement for a product they use or with which they are familiar. Tell students to write a couple of paragraphs describing the product in an ordinary and honest manner. Then, have students compare their own descriptions with the actual advertisement. Challenge students to notice persuasive language in the advertisement and whether or not the content is factual.

Introducing the Writing Assignment

Review the assignment and the criteria.

Focus on Research

Remind students to keep the following tips in mind as they conduct research.

- Gather information from multiple authoritative print and digital sources.
- Assess the usefulness of each source in answering the research question.
- Integrate information into the text selectively.
- Synthesize information from multiple sources.
- Avoid plagiarism.
- Use a standard format for citations.

 Writing Process

Write an Informative Text

Comparison-and-Contrast Essay

Defining the Form In a **comparison-and-contrast essay,** an author uses factual details to analyze similarities and differences between two or more subjects. You may use elements of a comparison and contrast essay in literary reviews, movie reviews, and comparisons.

Assignment Write a comparison-and-contrast essay in which you examine the similarities and differences between two subjects. Include these elements:

✓ *two subjects that are similar and different*

✓ a *thesis,* or purpose, stated in a *strong opening paragraph*

✓ an *organizational pattern* that clearly shows similarities and differences

✓ facts, descriptions, and examples that *support your assertions* of how the subjects are alike and how they are different

✓ a *well-supported conclusion* that wraps up your essay

✓ error-free writing, including correct usage of *verbs*

To preview the criteria on which your comparison-and-contrast essay may be judged, see the rubric on page 247.

FOCUS ON RESEARCH

When you write a comparison-and-contrast essay, you might have to conduct research in order to:

- find statistics or other data on the two subjects you are comparing.
- obtain background information on the two subjects.
- locate statements that experts have made about the two subjects.

Be sure to note all the sources you use and to cite them in your essay. Refer to the Research Workshop in the Introductory Unit for information on how to cite sources properly.

Common Core State Standards

Writing

2. Write informative/explanatory texts to examine a topic and convey ideas, concepts, and information through the selection, organization, and analysis of relevant content.

2.a. Introduce a topic; organize ideas, concepts, and information, using strategies such as definition, classification, comparison/contrast, and cause/effect; include formatting, graphics, and multimedia when useful to aiding comprehension.

READING-WRITING CONNECTION

To get a feel for comparison-and-contrast essays, read "Race to the End of the Earth" by William G. Scheller on page 404.

TEACHING RESOURCES

		Print	Digital
All	Common Core Companion, pp. 184–195, 321–334	✓	✓
All	EssayScorer powered by WriteToLearn		✓
All	Online Student Edition eText with audio and video		✓
All	Online Teacher Edition		✓
L1	Professional Development Guidebook, Rubrics for Self-Assessment: Comparison-Contrast Essay, pp. 234–235		✓
All	Student Companion All-in-One Workbook, Unit 2 Writing Process	✓	✓

EssayScorer

Students can use EssayScorer with automatic feedback and scoring to practice summarizing!

Prewriting/Planning Strategies

Choose subjects that are similar and different in important ways. Use one of these strategies to find a topic:

Use a quicklist to choose your topic. Make a three-column chart. In the first column, jot down people, places, and things that are interesting to you. In the second column, list an adjective to describe each one. Then, in the third column, provide a detail about each. Review your list, looking for ideas that it suggests, such as two brands of frozen pizza or two sports you enjoy. Choose one of those ideas as your topic.

Narrow your topic. You could probably write an entire book comparing and contrasting Mexico and Spain. To make your broad topic more manageable, divide it into smaller subtopics. Then, choose one subtopic, such as Mexican and Spanish food, as the focus of your essay.

Gather details. Conduct research to find relevant details about the subjects you are comparing and contrasting. Be sure to note the source of each detail you plan to use in your essay.

Organize your details. You can see similarities and differences clearly by organizing your details into a Venn diagram like the one shown. In the two outer sections, record details about how each subject is different. In the overlapping area, record similarities. Refer to your diagram as you draft your essay.

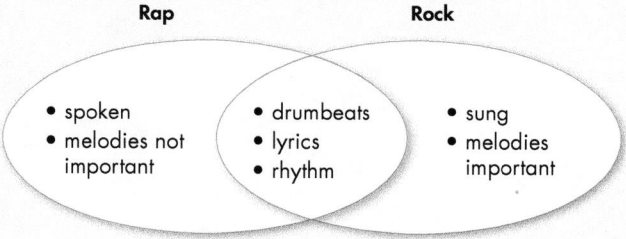

Rap — Rock

- spoken
- melodies not important

- drumbeats
- lyrics
- rhythm

- sung
- melodies important

✓ STRATEGIES **FOR CLARIFYING EXPECTED OUTCOMES**

Using Rubrics

- Before students begin work on this assignment, have them preview the Rubric for Self-Assessment (p. 247) to know what qualities their essays must have. A copy of this rubric appears in the *Graphic Organizers* for this workshop.
- Review the criteria in the rubric with the class. Before students use the rubric to assess

their own writing, work with them to rate the Student Model (p. 246) using the rubric.

- If you wish to assess students' Comparison-Contrast Essays with either a 4-point or a 6-point scoring rubric, see the *Professional Development Guidebook*, pp. 234–235.

Prewriting/Planning Strategies

1. Introduce the prewriting strategies.
2. Have students apply the strategies to choose a topic.

Teaching the Strategies

1. Provide examples of people, places, and things students might want to use to develop their quiklists, such as historical figures, athletes, actors, vacation spots, or types of music.
2. Model a quicklist with the following chart.

Choice	*Description*	*Detail*
Skiing	Exhilarating	Gliding in snow

3. Make sure students understand the importance of choosing a narrow topic. Tell them, for example, that comparing two entire countries would involve comparing too many areas of information.
4. Remind students to gather relevant details and to note their sources.
5. Whatever strategy students use, have them use a Venn diagram to organize their details and begin to plan their essays.

Think Aloud: Model Making Comparisons

Say to students:

To write a comparison-contrast essay, I can start with a Venn diagram to record similarities and differences between two subjects. If I want to compare Mexican food and Chinese food, I try to put three things they have in common in the overlapping portion of the Venn diagram. By listing the things the two kinds of food have in common, I have done the comparison part. Next, I will list differences in the outer parts of the diagram.

Six Traits Focus

✓	Ideas		Word Choice
✓	Organization		Sentence Fluency
	Voice		Conventions

Drafting Strategies

1. Introduce the drafting strategies.
2. Have students apply the strategies as they draft.

Teaching the Strategies

1. Remind students that their thesis statement and introduction should state the main point of their essay and introduce the significance of the facts, ideas, and details they will be comparing and contrasting.
2. Guide students in the importance of using specific details and how to use transitions.

Think Aloud: Model Using Specific Details

Say to students:

When drafting a comparison-and-contrast essay, it is important to use specific details. For example, simply making a reference to a "holiday meal" doesn't really tell the reader anything, and there are basically no details to compare or contrast. If I describe a "holiday breakfast" and list the specific foods served at the breakfast, I have specific details to compare and contrast with the details of another meal.

Think Aloud: Model Using Transitions

Say to students:

Suppose I have written: *Baseball is a team sport. Basketball is a team sport.* I can better show that I am making a comparison by adding a transition: *Baseball is a team sport. Similarly, basketball is a team sport.* To illustrate a contrast, let's say I have written: *Professional baseball is usually played outside. Professional basketball is played indoors.* I show that I am making a contrast by writing: *Professional baseball is usually played outside. However, professional basketball is played indoors.*

Six Traits Focus

✓	Ideas	✓	Word Choice
✓	Organization		Sentence Fluency
	Voice		Conventions

Drafting Strategies

Develop a thesis statement. Your thesis should explain your overall point about the two subjects. It should identify the significance of your comparisons and contrasts. For example, a thesis statement for a comparison-and-contrast essay on baseball and basketball might be: *Teamwork is more essential in basketball than in baseball.*

Draft your introduction. Begin your essay with a strong introductory paragraph that does the following:

- introduces the subjects you are comparing and contrasting
- identifies the features or aspects you will discuss
- states a main idea about your subjects

Use specific details. Develop your topic by citing details. The more you can pinpoint similarities and differences, the more interesting and vibrant your essay will be. Compare the following examples:

General: holiday meal

Concrete: holiday breakfast of omelets, berries, and cinnamon rolls

Use transitions. Use transitional words and phrases to signal that you are discussing either a similarity or a difference. Transitions that show similarity include *similarly, also, both,* and *like.* Transitions that show difference include *in contrast, unlike, on the other hand, but,* and *however.*

Common Core State Standards

Writing

2.a. Introduce a topic; organize ideas, concepts, and information, using strategies such as definition, classification, comparison/contrast, and cause/effect; include formatting, graphics, and multimedia when useful to aiding comprehension.

2.b. Develop the topic with relevant facts, definitions, concrete details, quotations, or other information and examples.

2.c. Use appropriate transitions to clarify the relationships among ideas and concepts.

STRATEGIES **FOR USING TRANSITIONS**

Transitions make the connection between ideas "visible." If students have difficulty finding a transition to join two sentences, their ideas may not be well connected.

Have students consider rearranging such sentences so that they can connect them to others with transitions.

Organizing a Comparison-and-Contrast Essay

The organization of a comparison-and-contrast essay is extremely important. To clearly show the relationships between the items you are comparing, choose one of these organizational patterns:

- **Block Method:** Present all the details about one subject first. Then, present all the details about the other subject. This method works well when you are writing about more than two things or are covering many different types of details. In following this organization, it is a good idea to refer back to the first subject when you discuss the second. Doing so will help your essay hold together. This technique can also be used to support your thesis.

> **Block Method**
>
> 1. Introduction
> 2. Tyrannosaurus: diet, size, and mobility
> 3. Velociraptor: diet, size, and mobility
> 4. Conclusion

Example: Relating Back to First Subject

Velociraptors were carnivores. In this respect, they are similar to tyrannosaurus.

- **Point-by-Point Method:** Discuss each aspect of your subjects in turn. For example, if you are comparing two types of dinosaurs, you could first discuss the diet of each one, then the size and mobility, and so on.

When using the point-by-point organization, think about your thesis when you arrange the details. Suppose you want to emphasize the differences between the two subjects. In that case, discuss the similarities first and then focus on the differences, as this example shows.

> **Point-by-Point Method**
>
> 1. Introduction
> 2. Diet of tyrannosaurus vs. velociraptor
> 3. Size and mobility of tyrannosaurus vs. velociraptor
> 4. Conclusion

Example: From Similarities to Differences

1. Both velociraptor and tyrannosaurus were meat-eaters.
2. Both were able hunters.
3. Tyrannosaurus was much larger then velociraptor.
4. Velociraptor was faster than tyrannosaurus.
5. Differences in size and mobility made them hunt differently.

Organizing a Comparison-and-Contrast Essay

1. Students who had more than three points of comparison on their Venn diagrams should use the block method of organization; students with fewer points should use the point-by-point method.

2. Direct students who are using the block method to outline their draft with a separate list of details under each of the two items being compared. Outlines for the point-by-point method should list features. Details should be grouped with the appropriate feature.

3. Encourage students to review their introductions after they have completed the body of their essays. They will then have a firmer grasp of their main idea.

4. Discuss how concrete details engage readers' senses. Challenge students to provide more examples for the following chart. General: good movie; More specific: exciting action picture; Concrete: fast-paced action picture

:: DIFFERENTIATED INSTRUCTION

Strategies for Less Proficient Writers
Suggest that students limit their topics to objects or ideas from their own experiences. This choice will allow them to focus on their writing rather than on researching facts and details. Remind students that they should identify at least three similarities and differences between their topics.

EL Strategies for English Learners
Challenge students to compare and contrast one object or idea from their native culture with one from American culture. Students may focus on something simple, such as food or music, or they may try to explain larger cultural differences.

Strategies for Advanced Writers
Suggest that students compare and contrast two ideas or issues rather than two people, places, or things. This choice would require them to go beyond a straightforward description and to seek information from outside sources such as newspapers and books.

Revising Strategies

1. Introduce the revising strategies, using the instruction on the student page.

2. Have students apply the strategies as they revise.

Teaching the Strategies

1. Provide highlighters to allow students to apply the revision strategy.

Think Aloud: Model Revising for Balance

Model the strategy of revising for balance, using the following think aloud. Say to students:

In my comparison-contrast essay, I can revise to be sure that I make the same number of points about both subjects. If I find that I have written ten facts about baseball and only six facts about basketball, I can go back and delete some of the baseball facts—or add some basketball facts—to make my writing more balanced and better organized.

2. Have students check the following sentences for subject-verb agreement, correcting the verbs as needed.

Like Brahms, Beethoven <u>was</u> a great German composer.
Answer: correct

Neither a German shepherd nor a poodle <u>are</u> as smart as a border collie. **Answer:** is

Softball, like baseball, <u>require</u> bats. **Answer:** requires

Both Monet and Manet <u>were</u> French Impressionist painters.
Answer: correct

Six Traits Focus

✓	Ideas	✓	Word Choice
✓	Organization		Sentence Fluency
	Voice	✓	Conventions

Revising Strategies

Check organization and balance. Your essay should give equal space to each subject and should be organized consistently. To check the balance of your essay, take a moment to reread it.

- Use a red marker to underline or highlight all the features and details related to one subject. Use a yellow marker for the other subject.
- If one color dominates, add additional features and details related to the other subject.
- If one color appears in large chunks, followed by other places where the colors seem to alternate, revise your organizational plan. For example, you may have made the mistake of starting with block organization and then switching to point-by-point organization.

Use a chart like the one below to help you figure out what features or details are missing from your essay.

	Subject #1	Subject #2
Point 1		
Point 2		
Point 3		
Point 4		

Check subject-verb agreement. Check your draft for correct subject-verb agreement. Make sure that sentences with singular subjects have singular verbs and that sentences with plural subjects have plural verbs.

Example: Unlike football, hockey **is** played on ice. (singular subject, singular verb)
Both football and hockey **are** fast-paced games. (plural subject, plural verb)

Peer Review

Have a classmate read your draft. Ask your reader to give you feedback about the organization and balance, and to show you places where more information would improve your essay.

Common Core State Standards

Writing
2.a. Introduce a topic; organize ideas, concepts, and information, using strategies such as definition, classification, comparison/contrast, and cause/effect; include formatting, graphics, and multimedia when useful to aiding comprehension.
2.b. Develop the topic with relevant facts, definitions, concrete details, quotations, or other information and examples.

Language
1. Demonstrate command of the conventions of standard English grammar and usage when writing or speaking.

✅ STRATEGIES **FOR USING TECHNOLOGY**

Remind students that they should assign a color to each object or idea being compared and highlight information about each in a different color. If students are using a word-processing program, they can use a different font or highlighting color. This will help them to see if their comparisons are balanced and well-organized.

Correcting Errors With Verbs

Irregular verbs are those in which the past tense and past participle are not formed by adding -*ed* or -*d* to the present tense. **Troublesome verbs** are verb pairs that are easily confused.

Identifying Incorrect Forms of Irregular Verbs Memorize these verb forms that occur frequently in reading and writing.

Examples of Irregular Verbs			
Present	**Present Participle**	**Past**	**Past Participle**
drink	(am) drinking	drank	(have) drunk
do	(am) doing	did	(have) done
bring	(am) bringing	brought	(have) brought

Identifying Incorrect Forms of Troublesome Verbs The two verbs in each of these pairs are often confused:

Lay/Lie *Lay* means "to put or place something." It takes a direct object. Example: *Shelly will lay the guitar on the table*.

Lie means "to rest in a reclining position" or "to be situated." Example: *I like to lie in the hammock*.

Raise/Rise *Raise* means "to lift up" or "to cause to rise." It takes a direct object. Example: *Please raise the curtain*.

Rise means "to get up" or "to go up." It does not take a direct object. Example: *My neighbors rise early in the morning*.

Fixing Errors To fix incorrect irregular verbs, identify which principal part of the verb is needed.

- **Refer to a chart of principal parts of verbs.**
- **Use a dictionary to find the correct form of the verb.**

To fix an incorrectly used troublesome verb:

- **Look up the verb in a glossary or resource of troublesome words.**
- **Use a dictionary to determine which verb to use.**

Grammar in Your Writing

Circle the verbs used in your comparison-and-contrast essay. If any verbs are used incorrectly, fix them using the methods above.

Correcting Errors With Verbs

1. Introduce the grammar skill, using the instruction on the student page.
2. Have students follow the instruction under Grammar in Your Writing to correct errors in their drafts.

Teaching the Grammar Skill

1. Students often make errors in forming the past and past participle of irregular verbs. Remind students that when they are unsure of the past tense of an irregular verb, they can check a dictionary, where they will find this form listed after the present tense of the verb.

2. Have students rewrite the following sentences using the verb tense in parentheses to replace the underlined verb.

   The boy *drinks* the *milk*. (past) (**Answer:** drank)

   I *bring* this to your attention. (past participle) (**Answer:** have brought)

   She *put* the hat on the bed. (present participle) (**Answer:** is putting)

3. Students may also confuse troublesome verbs, such as *lie/lay* and *rise/raise*. Have them choose the correct verb from the pair in parentheses to complete the following sentences.

   The hat was _____ right there on the table all this time. (laying/lying) (**Answer:** lying)

   The dog _____ his head at the sound of the can opener. (rose/raised) (**Answer:** raised)

   The fragile vase _____ on a high shelf (sat/set) (**Answer:** sat)

   Barbara _____ asleep for hours. (laid/lay) (**Answer:** lay)

   Terry _____ his books down on the kitchen counter. (sat/set) (**Answer:** set)

Student Model

Review the Student Model with the class, using the annotations to analyze the writer's use of the elements of a comparison-contrast essay.

Teaching From the Student Model

1. Explain that the Student Model is a sample and that essays can be longer.

2. Have students identify two points of comparison Jessica uses.

   Possible response: uses of numbers and letters, precision

3. Have students name two similarities between numbers and letters.

   Possible response: Both are used in everyday speech. Both must be used precisely.

4. Have students identify two differences between numbers and letters.

   Possible response: There is an infinite number of numbers but a limited number of letters. You can represent numbers with letters but you cannot easily replace letters with numbers.

Connecting to Real-Life Writing

Managers, business owners, and others in the workforce need to know the pros and cons of an idea to make an informed decision. Decision makers may ask for a report that compares and contrasts two ideas or items, such as prices of office supplies or productivity of two departments. These reports, like the students' papers, must provide accurate facts and details in an organized manner.

STUDENT MODEL: Jessica Kursan, Franklin Lakes, NJ

Common Core State Standards

Language
2.b. Spell correctly.

Letters . . . Or Numbers?

Have you ever heard the saying, "You can't compare apples and oranges"? Well, I've done it, so I know it's possible. But I'm not here to compare apples and oranges. I'm here to compare something else: numbers and letters. Numbers and letters have so many unusual properties about them. They are probably two of the most difficult things to compare, but I'll tackle them anyway.

> Jessica's introduction grabs the reader's attention and identifies her topics for comparison.

We'll start off with their differences. Numbers and letters have a lot of differences, obviously, but I'm only going to name a few. For one thing, letters are used to spell words, and numbers are used to, well, write numbers! Also, numbers go on forever, while letters stop at z, the twenty-sixth letter. No matter how many letters you have in your alphabet, whether it's Hebrew, Spanish, Greek, or anything else, it will always end somewhere. But numbers just keep right on going.

Also, letters can represent numbers, but not the other way around, unless you're a computer programmer. For example, you could have a list of instructions, and the steps could be labeled A, B, C, instead of 1, 2, 3. But you can't say that 586 spells *car*.

> Jessica uses a point-by-point organization, first addressing differences and then addressing similarities.

Numbers and letters have about as many similarities as they do differences, and they are just as simple. For one thing, words and numbers are both used in everyday speech. For example, you could say, "Mr. Johnson, may I walk your dog?" "But I have two dogs." Just the words themselves that you speak are made up of letters and numbers.

In addition, letters and numbers must be precise. This is tough to explain. Letters cannot just be arranged into any order. They have to spell out a real word. For example, you can't just grab a bunch of letters and stick them together because they look pretty. If you had a word like *sdlkhjiower*, what would it mean? Where would you use it? How would you pronounce it? None of these questions has a real answer because *sdlkhjiower* is not a real word. It's the same with numbers. You need to make sure your answer is precise. Also, you can't just say, "Well, I like 14, so I'm going to make 93 and 27 equal 14." That's not how it works. As with letters, you can't put numbers together just because they look good.

> Jessica uses examples to explain each point she presents.

As you see, numbers and letters have many differences, but also many similarities. If you take the time, I'm sure you can find even more on your own.

> In her conclusion, Jessica sums up her ideas and invites readers to consider the topic further.

Editing and Proofreading

Revise to correct errors in grammar, spelling, and punctuation.

Focus on double comparisons. Comparison-and-contrast essays often contain comparative adjectives. Avoid using double comparisons. Never use *-er* or *-est* and *more* or *most* to form the comparative and superlative degrees in the same sentence.

Incorrect: The Great Dane was the *most biggest* dog in the show.

Correct: The Great Dane was the *biggest* dog in the show.

Publishing and Presenting

Consider one of the following ways to share your writing:

Create an illustrated essay. Find photographs to illustrate the similarities and differences you have discussed. Then, share your illustrated essay with classmates.

Make a recording. Practice reading your essay aloud a few times. Read slowly and clearly, emphasizing the strongest points. Then, record and share your essay with a group of classmates.

Reflecting on Your Writing

Writer's Journal Jot down your answer to this question:

How has your writing changed your view on your topic?

Spiral Review Earlier in this unit, you learned about **principal parts of verbs** (p. 192) and **verb tenses** (p. 214). Check your essay to be sure you have used verbs correctly.

Rubric for Self-Assessment

Find evidence in your writing to address each category. Then, use the rating scale to grade your work.

Criteria	Rating Scale
Purpose/Focus Examines and conveys complex ideas about the similarities and differences between two subjects	*not very* .... *very* 1 2 3 4
Organization Organizes information effectively using the block or point-by-point method	1 2 3 4
Development of Ideas/Elaboration Develops the topic and supports the thesis with relevant facts, definitions, concrete details, quotations, and other examples; establishes and maintains a formal style	1 2 3 4
Language Uses transition words to signal similarities or differences; effectively combines sentences with related ideas	1 2 3 4
Conventions Uses proper grammar, including correct use of verbs	1 2 3 4

☑ STRATEGIES **FOR TEST TAKING**

When taking a test that includes a comparison-contrast writing prompt, students should reread the prompt to see whether it specifies the items to be compared. If not required to write on a given topic, students should select two items that have clear points of comparison and contrast. If possible, students should consider items that have physical characteristics, which are easier to describe than ideas. Students should set aside time for prewriting and use a Venn diagram to plan their essays.

Editing and Proofreading

1. Introduce the editing and proofreading focus, using the instruction on the student page.

2. Have students edit and proofread their essays, correcting grammar, spelling, punctuation, and word choice. Make sure they look for errors of the type noted in the lesson focus and the Spiral Review.

Teaching the Editing Focus

Students may make errors using comparative adjectives. Have them correct the following sentences.

She did more better on the test than I did. (**Answer:** She did better on the test than I did.)

It was the most best movie I ever saw. (**Answer:** It was the best movie I ever saw.)

He is the more quicker runner. (**Answer:** He is the quicker runner.)

Six Traits Focus

Ideas		Word Choice
Organization		Sentence Fluency
Voice	✓	Conventions

☑ ASSESS

Publishing and Presenting

1. Students who illustrate their essays may also want to add tables or charts.

2. Have students who want to record their essays make a practice recording and play it back for themselves so they can evaluate and improve their performance before making the final presentation.

Reflecting on Your Writing

Suggest that students compare their Venn diagram from the prewriting stage to their final essays to identify any new insights they had during the writing process.

 **Interactive Whiteboard Activities**

Use this tool to project and edit student writing!

Assessment

In this assessment (pp. 248–253), students apply and reinforce their mastery of the Common Core State Standards and the skills taught in Unit 2. The assessment is divided into four sections, including a section of Constructed Response tasks addressing CCS Reading standards.

1. Before assigning each section, review the relevant Common Core State Standards and unit skills with students.

2. Set a time limit for the multiple choice items in each section, allowing a little over one minute per question. Allow twenty minutes for any Timed Writing questions.

3. Administer each of the first three sections of the Assessment (pp. 248–251).

4. Use the Constructed Response tasks on pages 252–253 to assess the depth of students' mastery of standards taught in the unit. Follow the suggestions on teacher pages 252–253 for assigning tasks and for supporting and evaluating student performance.

Reteaching Plan

For each practice, use the Reteaching Plan on the same page as the answers to determine which skills require reteaching, given the items students answered incorrectly.

Question	Instructional Pages to Reteach
1	184
2	206
3	194
4	216
5	206, 216
6	—
7	180–183

Assessment: Skills

SELECTED RESPONSE

I. Reading Literature/Informational Text

Common Core State Standards
RI.6.1, RI.6.2, RI.6.3, RI.6.4, RI.6.6; W.6.2
[For the full wording of the standards, see the standards chart in the front of your textbook.]

Directions: *Read the excerpt from* Something to Declare *by Julia Alvarez. Then, answer each question that follows.*

The first time I received a letter from one of my readers, I was surprised. I had just published my first book of poems, *Homecoming*, which concludes with a sonnet sequence titled "33." My reader wanted to know why I had included forty-one sonnets when the title of the sequence was "33."

I considered not answering. Often, it is the little <u>perplexities</u> and curiosities and quandaries that remain after I have finished reading a book that send me to buy another book by that author. If I want to know more, the best way to find out is to read all the books that the author has written….

Many of the essays in this book began in just that way—as answers to such queries. Jessica Peet, a high-school student, read my first novel, *How the García Girls Lost Their Accents,* in her Vermont Authors class and wanted to know if I considered myself a Vermonter. The Lane Series, our local arts and entertainment series, wanted to know what I might have to say about opera. Share Our Strength was putting together a fund-raising anthology. Did I have anything at all to declare about food?

I could not really say to any of them, "Read my novels or my poems or my stories." These folks wanted what my boarding-school housemother used to call a straight answer. Which is where essays start. Not that they obey housemothers. Not that they list everything you are supposed to list on that Customs Declaration form. (How could the wild, multitudinous, daily things in anyone's head be inventoried in a form?) But that is the pretext of essays: *we have something to declare.*

And so this essay book is dedicated to you, my readers, who have asked me so many good questions and who want to know more than I have told you in my novels and poems. About my experience of immigration, about switching languages, about the writing life, the teaching life, the family life, about all of those combined.

Your many questions boil down finally to this one question: Do you have anything more to declare?

Yes, I do.

✓ STRATEGIES **FOR TEST TAKING**

Remind students to use their time wisely, especially on long tests like this unit review test. Explain that if they find that they cannot answer a question after spending a reasonable amount of time on it, they should skip that question and move on. They can always return to it after they have completed the test if time still remains. If they do use this strategy, caution them to leave blank the answer space for the skipped question to be sure that all later answers appear in the appropriate spaces.

1. **Part A** Who is the **narrator** of the passage, and what is the narrator's **point of view**?
   A. Jessica Peet is the narrator; first person
   B. Jessica Peet is the narrator; third person
   C. Julia Alvarez is the narrator; first person
   D. Julia Alvarez is the narrator; third person

   Part B Which phrase from the passage best supports the answer to Part A?
   A. "Jessica Peet, a high-school student, read my first novel"
   B. "Not that they obey housemothers."
   C. "Save Our Strength was putting together a fund-raising anthology"
   D. "Do you have anything more to declare? Yes, I do."

2. Which **influence** has the greatest effect on the author of this passage?
   A. her desire to contribute to the Lane Series
   B. her desire to list things on a Customs Declaration form
   C. her desire to be considered a Vermonter
   D. her desire to provide straight answers to questions from readers

3. **Part A** What is the author's **tone** in this passage?
   A. angry   **C.** humorous
   B. respectful   **D.** alarmed

   Part B Which detail from the essay best supports the answer to Part A?
   A. "And so this essay book is dedicated to you, my readers"
   B. "Did I have anything at all to declare about food?"
   C. "Not that they obey housemothers."
   D. "How could the wild, multitudinous, daily things in anyone's head be inventoried in a form?"

4. Why does the author consider not answering the reader's question about the sonnets in *Homecoming*?
   A. She does not have time to answer every question sent to her by readers.
   B. She would rather answer questions about the writing life.
   C. She would rather write sonnets and essays than answers to questions.
   D. She wants readers to read her books to find answers to their questions.

5. What is the **main idea** of this passage?
   A. The author will share her insights about life in a series of essays.
   B. Writing creatively is more important to the author than writing nonfiction.
   C. Readers expect to learn personal details about the author.
   D. Writing to readers takes the mystery out of creative writing.

6. Which phrase is closest in meaning to the underlined word *perplexities*?
   A. confusing or puzzling details
   B. angry or fearful details
   C. creative or imaginative details
   D. scientific or numeric details

 Timed Writing

7. In an essay, explain whether the **author's style** in this passage is formal or informal. Support your ideas with details from the text.

GO ON

☑ ASSESS

I. Reading Literature/ Informational Text

1. Part A: C
   Part B: D

2. D

3. Part A: B
   Part B: A

4. D

5. A

6. A

🕐 Timed Writing

7. Students' essays should include an explanation of how formal the passage is.

 **ASSESS**

II. Reading Informational Text

1. Part A: C
Part B: D
2. C
3. A

Reteaching Plan

Question	Pages to Reteach
1	206, 216
2	194
3	194

II. Reading Informational Text

Directions: *Read this speech. Then, answer each question that follows.*

© Common Core State Standards

RI.6.1, RI.6.2, RI.6.6, RI.6.9; L.6.1
[For the full wording of the standards, see the standards chart in the front of your textbook.]

> Do you ever wonder why students are lethargic after lunch, or why they cannot seem to pay attention in afternoon classes? This is most likely due to the foods students eat during lunch.
>
> I believe that our school cafeteria needs healthier foods. If you look at the monthly menu, you will see that fried foods, pizza, and pasta dominate the daily specials. Although the daily specials are not our only options, the alternatives are soggy, wilting salads, bagels, or the fried chips, candy, and soda in the vending machines.
>
> In the news, and in our health classes, we are lectured about eating well. Studies show that eating healthful foods provides teens with the energy to succeed in school, along with a positive self-image. Statistics reveal that there is a growing obesity problem among children in America. This is quite evident here at Milton Middle School. So, why are we being tempted by battered onion rings and fatty nachos. Why can't we be tempted by fresh salad bars, grilled chicken sandwiches, and healthy soups? These healthier options teach us good habits and could save us from developing serious illnesses later in life.
>
> If nutritious foods are served, every student in school will buy them, and you will see an increase in student achievement.

1. Part A Which statement best summarizes the author's main idea?
   A. Students are lazy and tired.
   B. Eating lunch causes a lack of focus.
   C. Students eat foods that make them tired and unfocused.
   D. Teachers are annoyed after lunch.

   Part B Which phrase from the speech best supports the answer to Part A?
   A. "we are lectured about eating well"
   B. "the alternatives are soggy, wilting salads"
   C. "This is quite evident here at Milton Middle School"
   D. "This is most likely due to the foods students eat during lunch"

2. What is the tone of the speech?
   A. threatening
   B. funny
   C. disapproving
   D. lighthearted

3. Which of the following claims in the speech is an opinion rather than a fact?
   A. "If nutritious foods are served, every student in school will buy them"
   B. "Statistics reveal that there is a growing obesity problem among children"
   C. "eating healthy food provides teens with the energy to succeed in school"
   D. "These healthier options teach us good habits and could save us from developing serious illnesses"

250 UNIT 2 • What is important to know?

III. Writing and Language Conventions

Directions: *Read the passage. Then, answer each question.*

> (1) I have read my favorite book, *Charlotte's Web*, four times. (2) Each time I find a new treasure. (3) This time, it was the sadness and beauty of growing up. (4) Fern, a young girl, rescues Wilbur the pig. (5) She is devoted to Wilbur, even when he leaves her farm. (6) Charlotte the spider soon becomes Wilbur's friend. (7) Later, though, Fern's interests change. (8) She is more interested in her friends than in the farm animals. (9) Through these changes, Fern shows what lays ahead for all of us. (10) When leaving childhood, we gain much, but we lose much, too.

1. Which **verb tense** does the writer use in sentence 1?

A. present
B. present perfect
C. past
D. past perfect

2. How could the writer revise sentence 2 to **maintain the verb tense** of sentence 1?

A. Each time I have found a new treasure.
B. Each time I am finding a new treasure.
C. Each time I was finding a new treasure.
D. Each time I had found a new treasure.

3. Which **linking verb** would *best* replace the word *is* in sentence 8?

A. was
B. looks
C. felt
D. becomes

4. What is the correct way to rewrite sentence 9 to fix the **troublesome verb?**

A. Through these changes, Fern shows what lay ahead for all of us.
B. Through these changes, Fern shows what laid ahead for all of us.
C. Through these changes, Fern shows what will lay ahead for all of us.
D. Through these changes, Fern shows what lies ahead for all of us.

5. Which word in sentence 10 is a verb in the **present tense?**

A. leaving
B. childhood
C. gain
D. too

 ASSESS

III. Writing and Language Conventions

1. B
2. A
3. D
4. D
5. A

Reteaching Plan

Question	Pages to Reteach
1	214
2	214
3	204
4	245
5	214

Constructed Response

Assigning Tasks/Reteaching Skills

Use the chart below to choose appropriate Constructed Response tasks by identifying which tasks assess lessons in the textbook that you have taught. Use the same lessons for reteaching when students' performance indicates a failure to fully master a standard. For additional instruction and practice, assign the *Common Core Companion* pages indicated for each task.

Task	Where Taught/ Pages to Reteach	Common Core Companion Pages
1	180–183, 184	137–143
2	180–183, 194	103–115
3	180–183, 184	137–143
4	180–183	151–157, 313–319
5	180–183	158–164, 304–310
6	180–183	103–115, 246–252, 253–266

Assessment Pacing

In assigning the Writing tasks on this student page, allow a class period for the completion of a task. As an alternative, assign tasks as homework. In assigning the Speaking and Listening and Research tasks on the facing page, consider having students do any required preparation as a homework assignment. Then, allow a class period for the presentations themselves.

Evaluating Constructed Response

Use the rubric at the bottom of this Teacher Edition page to evaluate students' mastery of the standards as demonstrated in their Constructed Response tasks. Review the rubric with students before they begin work so they know the criteria by which their work will be evaluated.

CONSTRUCTED RESPONSE

Directions: *Follow the instructions to complete the tasks below as required by your teacher.*

As you work on each task, incorporate both general academic vocabulary and literary terms you learned in Parts 1 and 2.

 **Common Core State Standards**

RI.6.2, RI.6.4, RI.6.5, RI.6.6, RI.6.8, RI.6.9; W.6.7, W.6.8; SL.6.4, SL.6.6

[For the full wording of the standards, see the standards chart in the front of your textbook.]

Writing

TASK 1 Informational Text [RI.6.6]

Determine the Author's Point of View

Write an essay in which you determine the author's point of view in a nonfiction text from Part 2.

- Tell which work you chose and identify the topic it discusses.
- Explain the author's purpose and main idea by answering the question: What does this author want me to know or to do?
- Explain the point of view you think the author expresses in the text. Support your ideas by identifying any direct statements the author makes about his or her point of view.
- Further support your ideas by citing other details that show the author's point of view.
- In your conclusion, restate your explanation of the author's point of view.

TASK 2 Informational Text [RI.6.2]

Analyze Tone

Write an essay in which you determine the tone of a nonfiction work from Part 2.

- Choose one selection from the unit, and review the author's tone throughout the selection.
- Write an essay in which you analyze the overall tone of the text. Then, explain whether or not the author's tone changes from the beginning to the end of the selection.
- Cite particular details that contribute to the development of the author's tone.

TASK 3 Informational Text [RI.6.6]

Determine the Author's Point of View

Write an essay in which you determine the author's point of view in a nonfiction text from Part 2.

Part 1

- Choose a selection in which the author presents a clear point of view on a topic.
- Take notes on how the author develops a main idea by emphasizing certain evidence or by presenting an interpretation of facts.

Part 2

- Write an essay in which you explain the author's point of view and how the author used facts and evidence to support his or her perspective.
- Further support your ideas by citing other details that show the author's point of view.
- In your conclusion, restate your key findings.

CONSTRUCTED RESPONSE RUBRIC: **STANDARDS MASTERY**

	Rating Scale
Critical Thinking: How clearly and consistently does the student pursue the specific mode of reasoning or discourse required by the standard, as specified in the prompt (e.g., comparing and contrasting, analyzing, explaining)?	*not very* 1 2 3 4 *very* 5
Focus: How well does the student understand and apply the focus concepts of the standard, as specified in the prompt (e.g., development of theme or of complex characters, effects of structure, and so on)?	*not very* 1 2 3 4 *very* 5
Support/Elaboration: How well does the student support points with textual or other evidence? How relevant, sufficient, and varied is the evidence provided?	*not very* 1 2 3 4 *very* 5
Insight: How original, sophisticated, or compelling are the insights the student achieves by applying the standard to the text(s)?	*not very* 1 2 3 4 *very* 5
Expression of Ideas: How well does the student organize and support ideas? How well does the student use language, including word choice and conventions, in the expression of ideas?	*not very* 1 2 3 4 *very* 5

Speaking and Listening

TASK 4 Informational Text [RI.6.8; SL.6.6]

Trace and Evaluate an Argument

Write and present an essay in which you trace and evaluate the argument in a nonfiction work from Part 2.

- Write an essay in which you explain the argument an author presents in one of this unit's selections.

- Trace the argument, showing how the author introduces, develops, and concludes it.

- Note specific claims, or separate ideas, that contribute to the overall argument.

- Include your evaluation of the argument, explaining whether it is logical and supported with strong evidence.

- Take turns orally presenting essays in a small group.

- Listen for slang or informal language in both your own and others' presentations. Discuss how to improve the use of formal language.

- Apply the feedback to revise your essay.

Research

TASK 6 Informational Text [RI.6.2; W.6.7, W.6.8]

 What is important to know?

In Part 2, you have read nonfiction and informational texts about many different ideas and events. Now you will conduct a short research project about something from this unit that you would like to learn more about. Use both the Part 2 texts and your research to reflect on this unit's Big Question. Review the following guidelines before you begin your research:

- Focus your research on ideas and events from one of the texts in Part 2.

TASK 5 Informational Text [RI.6.9; SL.6.4]

Compare Presentations of Events

Give an oral presentation of an essay in which you compare and contrast one author's presentation of events with that of another.

- Choose two nonfiction works from this unit written about similar subjects.

- Compare and contrast one author's presentation of events with that of another. Use examples from the texts to support your analysis.

- Present your ideas in logical order, using specific details to support main ideas.

- As you speak, use appropriate eye contact. Speak clearly and loudly enough to be understood in a classroom setting.

- Gather relevant information from at least two reliable sources. Your sources may be print or digital.

- Take notes as you research the ideas and events.

- Cite your sources.

When you have completed your research, write a response to the Big Question. Discuss how your initial thoughts may have been either changed or reinforced. Support your response with examples from the text you chose and from your research.

PART 2 • Assessment: Skills **253**

Supporting Speaking and Listening

1. Consider having students work with partners or in groups to complete Constructed Response tasks involving listening and speaking. For tasks that you assign for individual work, you may still wish to have students rehearse with partners, who can provide constructive feedback.

2. As students rehearse, have them keep in mind these tips:

   - Present findings and evidence clearly and concisely.

   - Observe conventions of standard English grammar and usage.

   - Be relaxed and friendly but maintain a formal tone.

   - Make eye contact with the audience, pronounce words clearly, and vary your pace.

   - When working with a group, respond thoughtfully to others' positions, modifying your own in response to new evidence.

Linking Constructed Response to Independent Reading

If you wish to cover the standards with students' independent reading, adapt Constructed Response tasks of your choice to the works they have selected. (Independent reading suggestions appear on the next page.)

What is important to know?

1. Remind students that the unit Big Question is "What is important to know?"

2. Have students complete their responses to the prompt on the student page. Point out that they have read selections in this unit about different approaches to or views of knowledge and that they should draw on these selections in their responses.

DIFFERENTIATED INSTRUCTION

Strategy for Less Proficient Readers

Assign a Constructed Response task, and then have students meet in groups to review the standard assessed in that task. Remind students of the selections or independent readings to which they have previously applied the standard. Have groups summarize what they learned in applying the standard and then present their summaries. Discuss, clarifying any points of confusion. After students have completed their tasks, have groups meet again to evaluate members' work. Encourage members to revise their work based on the feedback they receive.

Strategy for English Learners

For each assigned Constructed Response task, review the instructions with students. Clarify the meaning of any unfamiliar vocabulary, emphasizing routine classroom words such as *summary, feedback,* and *graphic,* and academic vocabulary such as *analyze.*

Next, have students note ideas for their responses. Pair students, and have them review each other's notes, asking questions to clarify meaning and suggesting improvements. Encourage students to ask for your assistance in supplying English words or expressions they may require.

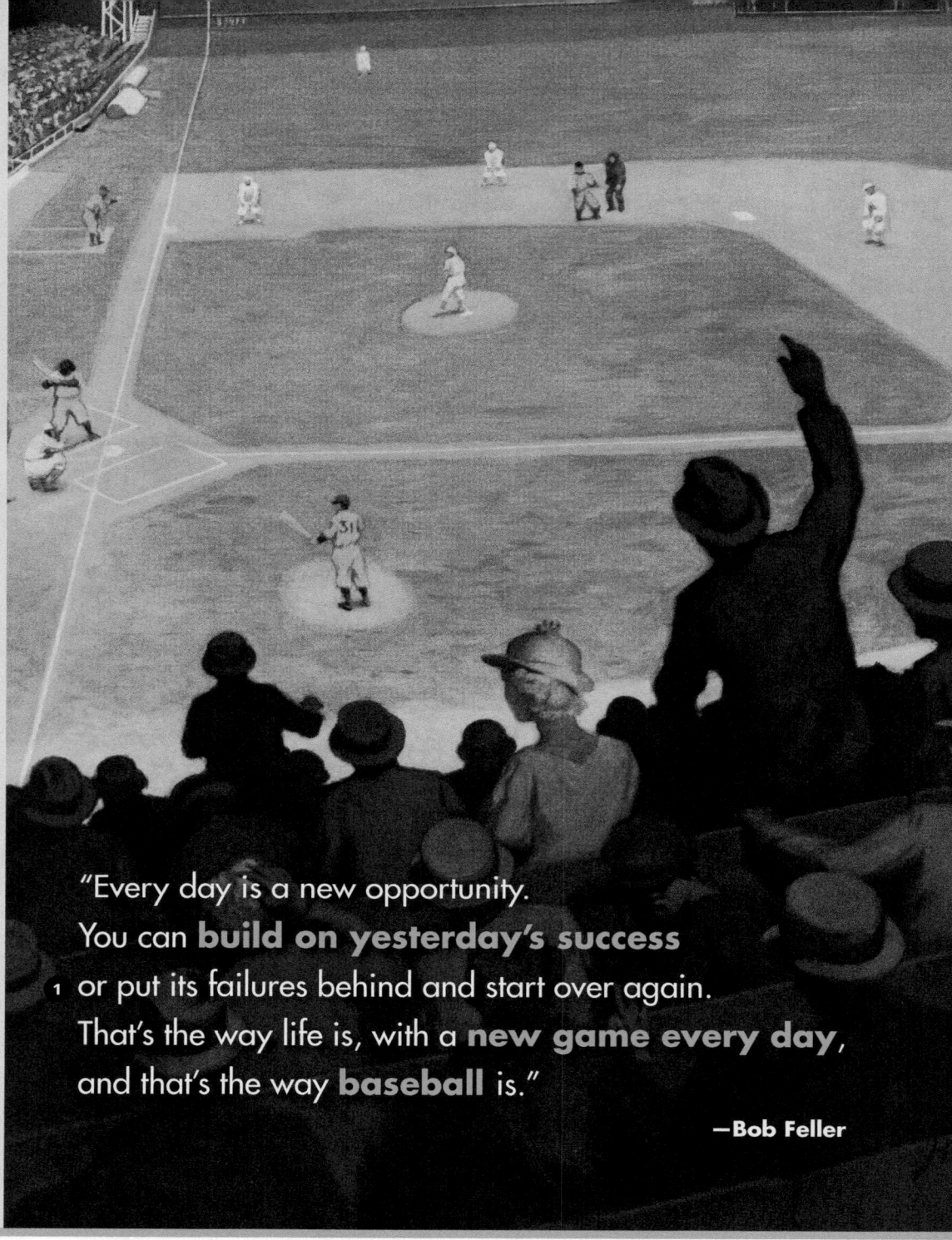

1 About the Quotation

Bob Feller (1918–2010) was a famous pitcher for the Cleveland Indians for 18 years. He began pitching in the major leagues when he was just 17 years old.

Discussion Ask students to discuss the meaning of Feller's quotation about baseball. Then, ask them to decide whether they agree with the quotation. Have them explain and support their positions with sound reasoning and evidence.

2 Critical Viewing

Pose the critical viewing question to the class. Then, guide the class in a discussion about the question. Encourage students to build upon each other's ideas as they share their responses. Remind students to support their responses with reasons and evidence.

"Every day is a new opportunity.
You can **build on yesterday's success**
or put its failures behind and start over again.
That's the way life is, with a **new game every day**,
and that's the way **baseball** is."

—**Bob Feller**

? DEVELOPING ESSENTIAL UNDERSTANDING

Baseball

Students should relate easily to the subject of baseball; yet the selections about prejudice in baseball, the symbols of baseball, and a century-old ballpark will give them new perspectives on the traditions surrounding this sport. The nonfiction selections, the short story, and the media selection in this text set will help students develop essential understanding about baseball by raising questions such as:

- Why do so many people of all ages and from different walks of life relate to the game of baseball?
- What was the significance of integrating the major leagues?
- Should girls and boys play on the same team?
- How does the history of baseball reflect changes in our society?

PART 3
TEXT SETS DEVELOPING INSIGHT

BASEBALL

The selections in this unit all deal with the Big Question: **What is important to know?** You gain knowledge every day: by studying, talking with others, meeting new people, or learning a new skill. As you read the texts that follow, you will explore the ways that baseball players and fans gain knowledge about themselves and the world around them by participating in this "great American pastime."

② ◀ CRITICAL VIEWING Can baseball be as rewarding for spectators, such as those in this picture, as it is for players? Explain.

CLOSE READING TOOL
Use the Close Reading Tool to practice the strategies you learned in this unit.

③ READINGS IN PART 3

ANCHOR TEXT
EXPOSITORY ESSAY
Jackie Robinson: Justice at Last
Geoffrey C. Ward and Ken Burns (p. 256)

NEWS ARTICLE
Memories of an All-American Girl
Carmen Pauls (p. 264)

PERSUASIVE SPEECH
Preserving a Great American Symbol
Richard Durbin (p. 270)

SHORT STORY
The Southpaw
Judith Viorst (p. 274)

NEWS ARTICLE
Fenway Park Celebrates 100 Years . . .
Molly Line (p. 280)

WEB ARTICLE
Why We Love Baseball
Mark Newman (p. 286)

BASEBALL CARD
Ted Williams Baseball Card
(p. 292)

CUSTOMIZING THE TEXT SET

Close Reading Tool
Use the Close Reading Tool to project the anchor text on a whiteboard and work through it as a whole-class activity. Students also have the opportunity to read this selection independently, with scaffolds available as needed.

Curriculum Builder
Customize this program by rearranging existing selections, adding selection titles of your choosing, and uploading your own resources—all online!

③ Readings in Part 3
About the Texts
(For quantitative and qualitative measures of text complexity, see the rubrics on the opening pages of each selection.)

EXPOSITORY ESSAY: Jackie Robinson: Justice at Last
Summary Branch Rickey wanted to integrate the major league baseball teams. He chose Jackie Robinson.

NEWS ARTICLE: Memories of an All-American Girl
Summary Daisy Junor describes playing in the All-American Girls Professional Baseball League in the 1940s.

PERSUASIVE SPEECH: Preserving a Great American Symbol
Summary Senator Durbin argues that wooden bats should be kept.

SHORT STORY: The Southpaw
Summary Friends Richard and Janet finally resolve the issue of her playing on the boys' baseball team.

NEWS ARTICLE: Fenway Park Celebrates 100 Years ...
Summary The Boston Red Sox celebrate the players and events at their historic ballpark.

WEB ARTICLE: Why We Love Baseball
Summary People tell why they love baseball.

BASEBALL CARD: Ted Williams Baseball Card

Extended Reading Opportunity

INFORMATIONAL TEXT: Boy: Tales of Childhood
You may want to assign this extended reading to accompany the readings in Part 3. Further details about this text and other extended readings appear on the Independent Reading pages at the end of this unit.

 Audio
Summary Audio is available in the *Student eText* and on the *Hear It!* CD-ROM.

Time and Resource Manager

LESSON PACING GUIDE

ANCHOR TEXT (5 DAYS)

Jackie Robinson: Justice at Last

DAY 1 Preteach/Teach

- Introduce the topic of the text set and its relationship to the Big Question.
- To motivate and engage students, discuss the quotation and the Critical Viewing question.
- Direct students to read the selection independently.

DAYS 2–4 Teach/Extend

- Use the Comprehension questions to confirm student understanding of the text.
- Develop vocabulary by assigning and monitoring the Language Study activities.
- Develop analytic ability by reviewing the Literary Analysis questions and instruction.
- Assign the Group Discussion and monitor responses to discussion questions.
- Assign the Writing to Sources activity, distributing copies of the Take Notes worksheet to help students organize their thoughts and information.

DAY 5 Extend/Assess

- Preview the Research activity, distributing copies of the Take Notes worksheet to help students plan their note-taking strategy. Assign the activity as homework.
- Administer the Selection Test or the Open-Book Test to monitor student progress.

RELATED TEXTS (2 DAYS EACH)

Memories of an All-American Girl • Preserving a Great American Symbol • The Southpaw • Fenway Park Celebrates 100 Years as America's Oldest Working Major League Ballpark • Why We Love Baseball • Ted Williams Baseball Card

DAY 1 Preteach/Teach

- Review with students the topic of the text set and what they have learned from the previous readings.
- Build knowledge of the topic by directing students to read the text independently.
- Develop vocabulary by reviewing the Language Study activities.
- Build students' ability to think critically using the Literary Analysis questions.

DAY 2 Extend/Assess

- Extend exploration of the text through the Discuss, Research, and Write activities.
- Administer the Selection Test or the Open-Book Test to monitor student progress.

ASSESSMENT: SYNTHESIS (1–2 DAYS)

DAYS 1–2 Assess

- Review with the class the Criteria for Success for the Speaking and Listening activity. Assign the activity, and monitor student progress.
- Review with students the Criteria for Success for the Writing assignment, and assign the activity.
- Review with students the Self-Evaluation Rubric for the Writing to Sources activity. Direct students to complete the assignment.

**Common Core
State Standards**

Reading Literature 1, 2, 3, 4, 5
Reading Informational Texts 1, 2, 3, 4, 5, 6
Writing 1, 1.a-c, 2, 2.a-c, 3, 4, 5, 6, 7, 10
Speaking and Listening 1, 4
Language 1, 2, 3, 4, 5

Daily Block Scheduling

Each day in this Lesson Pacing Guide represents a 40–50 minute period. Teachers using block scheduling may combine days to revise pacing. In addition, teachers may differentiate and support core instruction by integrating components for extended and intensive support as students require. See the Guide to Resources (facing page).

GUIDE TO RESOURCES

RESOURCES	PRINT	CD	ONLINE	ANCHOR TEXT Jackie Robinson	All-American Girl	Preserving a Great American Symbol	The Southpaw	Fenway Park Celebrates 100 Years	Why We Love Baseball	Ted Williams Baseball Card
SELECTION SUPPORT 👤 👥 👨‍👩‍👧										
Close Reading Practice	CRN		✔	✔						
Academic Vocabulary	SCW		✔	✔	✔	✔	✔	✔	✔	✔
Discussion: Take Notes worksheet	SCW		✔	✔	✔	✔	✔	✔	✔	
Writing to Sources	SCW		✔	✔	✔	✔	✔	✔	✔	✔
Research: Take Notes worksheet	SCW		✔	✔	✔	✔	✔	✔	✔	
STANDARDS SUPPORT 👨‍👩‍👧										
Standards Instruction and Practice	CCC		✔	✔	✔	✔	✔	✔	✔	✔
MONITOR PROGRESS Ⓐ										
Selection Test		EV	✔	✔	✔	✔	✔	✔	✔	
Open-Book Test		EV	✔	✔	✔	✔	✔	✔	✔	
ASSESSMENT: SYNTHESIS GRAPHIC ORGANIZERS AND RUBRICS 👤										
Speaking and Listening: Graphic Organizer			✔							
Writing: Graphic Organizer			✔							
Writing to Sources: Graphic Organizer			✔							
Self-Evaluation Rubric			✔							
DIGITAL RESOURCES 🖱️										
Close Reading Tool			✔	✔						
Online Writer's Notebook			✔	✔	✔	✔	✔	✔	✔	✔

CRN Close Reading Notebook **SCW** Student Companion All-in-One Workbook **EV** ExamView **CCC** Common Core Companion

👥 Group work 👨‍👩‍👧 Whole class instruction 👤 Independent work Ⓐ Assessment 🖱️ Digital Resource

Essential Understanding

First, students should read the entire selection on their own. Then, to assist struggling readers and to deepen comprehension for all, you may wish to guide them through the selection by asking them the close reading questions provided in the margins. Have students apply the multidraft reading protocols as they examine specific "chunks" of text related to these questions. For each reading, have students set the purpose indicated:

- **First reading:** Students should read the selection independently and think about its basic meaning.
- **Second reading:** Students should analyze the text's key ideas and details and its craft and structure.
- **Third reading:** Students should integrate knowledge and ideas; connect to the Big Question, other texts, and the world; and use teacher-led Close Reading discussion questions to examine particularly rich and significant passages.

For more guidance, refer to the **Classroom Strategies and Teaching Routines** card on multidraft reading.

Daily Bellringer

For each class during which you teach this selection, have students complete one of the five Sentence Combining activities for Week 12 in **Daily Bellringer Activities**. You may wish to use additional activities that are applicable to this selection.

❶ Background

The Kansas City Monarchs, a celebrated team in the Negro National League, played from 1920 to the 1950s. The Monarchs won two World Series and ten pennants. They introduced night baseball in 1930, five years before the major leagues held night games. More than 20 African American baseball players from the Monarchs were sent to the major leagues. Jackie Robinson was one of them.

¹ JACKIE ROBINSON
Justice at Last

© TEXT COMPLEXITY **RUBRIC**

Jackie Robinson: Justice at Last		
Qualitative Measures	Context/Knowledge Demands	1940s: American baseball; integration 1 2 ③ 4 5
	Structure/Language Conventionality	Conversational; on-level vocabulary 1 ② 3 4 5
	Levels of Meaning/ Purpose/Concepts	Accessible concept (fighting against prejudice) 1 2 ③ 4 5
Quantitative Measures	Text Length	Word Count: 682
	Lexile	710L

Geoffrey C. Ward
and Ken Burns

It was 1945, and World War II had ended. Americans of all races had died for their country. Yet black men were still not allowed in the major leagues. The national pastime was loved by all America, but the major leagues were for white men only.

Branch Rickey of the Brooklyn Dodgers thought that was wrong. He was the only team owner who believed blacks and whites should play together. Baseball, he felt, would become even more thrilling, and fans of all colors would swarm to his ballpark.

PART 3 • Jackie Robinson: Justice at Last **257**

Vocabulary

If students require support with selection vocabulary, use this routine:

1. Write the following words and definitions on the board:

   integrate *v.* remove all barriers and allow free association; bring together as a whole

   prejudiced *adj.* having unfair feelings of dislike for a specific group

   superb *adj.* extremely fine; excellent

2. Have students say each word aloud.

3. Use the word in a sentence that defines the word.

ⒸTEXT COMPLEXITY **READER AND TASK SUGGESTIONS**

Jackie Robinson: Justice at Last

Preparing to Read the Text
- Using the Background information on the previous page, discuss the impact and contributions of the Kansas City Monarchs to the sport of baseball.
- Discuss Jackie Robinson and what the word *justice* in the title might mean.
- Guide students to use Multidraft Reading strategies (TE p. 256).

Leveled Tasks
Knowledge Demands If students will have difficulty with the context of this essay, discuss what they know about Jackie Robinson and segregation in baseball before the 1950s.

Evaluating If students will not have difficulty with the context of the essay, encourage them to discuss what professional sports owe to Jackie Robinson and Branch Rickey.

 Video

Watch the Background Video online!

 Audio

Selection Audio is available in the *Student eText* and on the *Hear It!* CD-ROM.

2 Close Reading

1. Key Ideas and Details Read aloud the passage to students.
Ask: What is the key idea in this passage?

Possible response: Rickey wants the first black major league player to be someone who will not fight back when insulted or booed. He realizes that many people are prejudiced and a fight would give them a reason to oppose integration.

2. Craft and Structure Direct students to reread the passage and take notes on words and phrases that reflect people's prejudices. In particular, have students pay close attention to the action verbs and repeated phrases in the passage.
Ask: What do the authors' word choices help to reveal about people's reactions to integration in baseball?

Possible response: The authors' choice of the action verbs *throw, spike, cursed,* and *booed* helps to show the intensity of feelings against integration. The repeated phrases "no matter what" and "he must never" emphasize Rickey's belief in the importance of not reacting in anger.

3. Integration of Knowledge and Ideas
Ask: In this passage, what might the authors leave unstated? Consider whether fighting back or enduring insults for a greater purpose takes more courage.

Possible response: Students should understand that it often takes more courage to endure insults than to lash out in anger. African American players would have faced repeated threats, but fighting back would have caused additional problems.

3 Focus Passage

A Focus Passage is identified with brackets in the Student Edition of this page for students' independent close reading and analysis. A question bank for the passage and possible responses appear at the end of the selection.

---

integrate ▶
(in´ tə grāt) *v.* remove all barriers and allow free association; bring together as a whole

prejudiced ▶
(prej´ ə dist) *adj.* having unfair feelings of dislike for a specific group

superb ▶
(sə purb´) *adj.* extremely fine; excellent

Rickey decided his team would be the first to integrate. There were plenty of brilliant Negro league players, but he knew the first black major leaguer would need much more than athletic ability.

Many fans and players were prejudiced—they didn't want the races to play together. Rickey knew the first black player would be cursed and booed. Pitchers would throw at him; runners would spike him. Even his own teammates might try to pick a fight.

But somehow this man had to rise above that. No matter what happened, he must never lose his temper. No matter what was said to him, he must never answer back. If he had even one fight, people might say integration wouldn't work.

When Rickey met Jackie Robinson, he thought he'd found the right man. Robinson was 28 years old, and a superb athlete. In his first season in the Negro leagues, he hit .387. But just as importantly, he had great intelligence and sensitivity. Robinson was college-educated, and knew what joining the majors would mean for blacks. The grandson of a slave, he was proud of his race and wanted others to feel the same.

In the past, Robinson had always stood up for his rights. But now Rickey told him he would have to stop. The Dodgers needed "a man that will take abuse."

At first Robinson thought Rickey wanted someone who was afraid to defend himself. But as they talked, he realized that in this case a truly brave man would have to avoid fighting. He thought for a while, then promised Rickey he would not fight back.

Robinson signed with the Dodgers and went to play in the minors in 1946. Rickey was right—fans insulted him, and so did players. But he performed brilliantly and avoided fights. Then, in 1947, he came to the majors.

Many Dodgers were angry. Some signed a petition demanding to be traded. But Robinson and Rickey were determined to make their experiment work.

On April 15—Opening Day—26,623 fans came out to Ebbets Field. More than half of them were black—Robinson was already their hero. Now he was making history just by being on the field.

The afternoon was cold and wet, but no one left the ballpark. The Dodgers beat the Boston Braves, 5–3.

💬 VOCABULARY DEVELOPMENT

Thematic Vocabulary: The Big Question
As students are discussing "Jackie Robinson: Justice at Last," encourage them to use the thematic vocabulary presented in Introducing the Big Question, pp. 162–163. You might encourage them with sentence starters like these:

1. Rickey's *purpose* in hiring Jacking Robinson was that . . .

2. *Knowledge* about Robinson led Rickey to choose him because . . .
3. Allowing only white men to play the game places a *limit* on . . .
4. Prejudiced fans show a *narrow* view because . . .

Robinson went hitless, but the hometown fans didn't seem to care—they cheered his every move.

Robinson's first season was difficult. Fans threatened to kill him; players tried to hurt him. The St. Louis Cardinals said they would strike if he took the field. And because of laws separating the races in certain states, he often couldn't eat or sleep in the same places as his teammates.

Yet through it all, he kept his promise to Rickey. No matter who insulted him, he never retaliated.

Robinson's dignity paid off. Thousands of fans jammed stadiums to see him play. The Dodgers set attendance records in a number of cities.

Slowly his teammates accepted him, realizing that he was the spark that made them a winning team. No one was more daring on the base paths or better with the glove. At the plate, he had great bat control—he could hit the ball anywhere. That season, he was named baseball's first Rookie of the Year.

Jackie Robinson went on to a glorious career. But he did more than play the game well—his bravery taught Americans a lesson. Branch Rickey opened a door, and Jackie Robinson stepped through it, making sure it could never be closed again. Something wonderful happened to baseball—and America—the day Jackie Robinson joined the Dodgers.

ABOUT THE AUTHORS

Geoffrey C. Ward (b. 1940)
The author of many award-winning books, Geoffrey C. Ward is also a screenwriter and a former editor of *American Heritage* magazine. For more than twenty years, Ward has worked with Ken Burns, writing award-winning television documentaries including *Baseball*, *The Civil War*, and *The West*.

Ken Burns (b. 1953)
Ken Burns has co-written, produced, and directed several television documentaries and mini-series and has directed movies that have been nominated for Academy Awards. "Jackie Robinson: Justice at Last" is from a book based on Ward's and Burns's 1994 television documentary *Baseball*. The documentary won numerous awards, including an Emmy.

④ ？ Big Question: Toward Essential Understanding

1. Have a student read aloud the passage.

2. **Ask:** How was Robinson treated during his first season? Why is this important to know?

   Possible response: Fans threatened to kill him. Other players tried to hurt him, and one team threatened to strike if he played. While on the road, he could not always stay in the same places as his teammates because of the laws in some states. It is important for people to understand the struggles that people in the past faced.

3. **Ask:** What do you learn about Robinson by knowing that his first season was very difficult? Would Robinson have acted as he did if Rickey were not the owner? Explain.

   Possible response: The difficulties Robinson faced show his courage in refusing to fight back. Some students will say that even without Rickey's leadership, Robinson would have ignored the insults because he understood the consequences. Others may say that Rickey's insistence on not fighting back made all the difference.

⑤ Focus Passage

A Focus Passage is identified with brackets in the Student Edition of this page for students' independent close reading and analysis. A question bank for the passage and possible responses appear at the end of the selection.

⚙ DIFFERENTIATED INSTRUCTION

Strategy for Less Proficient Readers
The use of dashes in long sentences like the one beginning "At the plate, he" on this page may prove a barrier to some students' understanding. Point out that a dash is often used to show emphasis. It takes the place of another punctuation mark, such as a comma or a semicolon. Have students read the sentence as two independent clauses, pausing after the word *control*. With the last sentence in the selection, have students pause for each dash and explain that in this sentence the punctuation emphasizes the words *and America*.

EL Strategy for English Learners
For students unfamiliar with this favorite American sport, check understanding of baseball terms. Provide definitions if they cannot explain the following terms in the selection: *hitless*—in baseball, a player gets a hit by batting a pitched ball and running to first base before being tagged out, so to be *hitless* is to fail to get a hit; *base paths*—the area between any two of the four bases that runners must touch in order to score; *plate*—the base at home, or home plate; *glove*—a large leather glove used for catching; *Rookie of the Year*—an award given each year to one player in each major league.

Close Reading Activities

READ

Comprehension

1. He thought African Americans and whites should play baseball together. Robinson was an outstanding player who was intelligent and sensitive.
2. Jackie Robinson was supposed to avoid fights and not respond to those who threatened him.
3. Fans cheered everything Robinson did.

Research: Clarify Details

Students should use their research to explain the significance of a particular detail in the story.

Summarize

Student summaries should include details about segregation in major league baseball in 1945, Branch Rickey's goals in hiring Jackie Robinson, the abuse Robinson suffered, Robinson's performance, and the effects of Robinson's joining the Dodgers.

Language Study

Selection Vocabulary
Possible responses:
- *integrate:* synonym—*mix*
- *prejudiced:* synonym—*biased*
- *superb:* synonym—*excellent*

Students' sentences should demonstrate an understanding of each word's meaning.

Diction and Style
Possible responses:
1. **(a)** When people *insulted* Robinson, they treated him as if he were not worthy of any respect. **(b)** Fans might boo someone they normally like if they think the person performs badly, but booing doesn't necessarily mean disrespect. Insults are usually given to people whom you do not like.
2. **(a)** *Brilliantly* suggests that Robinson's play shone in comparison to the play of others. **(b)** The images suggested include a diamond, stars shining on a clear dark night, and the sun on a summer day. **(c)** *Brilliantly* is more sensory than *well.*

READ

Comprehension
Reread all or part of the text to help you answer the following questions.
1. Why did Branch Rickey want Jackie Robinson on his team?
2. How did Branch Rickey want Jackie Robinson to act?
3. How did the hometown fans react when Robinson played in his first game with the Dodgers?

Language Study
Selection Vocabulary The following sentences appear in the essay. Write a synonym for each boldfaced word, and then use each word in a sentence of your own.
- Rickey decided his team would be the first to **integrate**.
- Many fans and players were **prejudiced**— they didn't want the races to play together.
- Robinson was 28 years old, and a **superb** athlete.

Diction and Style Study these sentences from the essay, then answer the questions.

> Rickey was right—fans insulted him, and so did players. But he performed brilliantly and avoided fights.

1. **(a)** What does *insulted* mean? **(b)** How is being *insulted* different from being *booed*?
2. **(a)** What does *brilliantly* mean as it is used here? **(b)** What images does the word call to mind? **(c)** Why is *brilliantly* a more

effective word choice than *well* would be in this sentence?

Conventions Read this passage from the essay. Identify the tense of each verb. Then, explain how that tense indicates when the events took place.

> It was 1945, and World War II had ended. Americans of all races had died for their country. Yet black men were still not allowed in the major leagues. The national pastime was loved by all America, but the major leagues were for white men only.

Academic Vocabulary
These words appear in blue in the instructions and questions on the facing page.

support   opinions   affect

Categorize the words by deciding whether you know each one well, know it a little bit, or do not know it at all. Then, use a dictionary to look up the definitions of the words you do not know.

Research: Clarify Details This essay may include references that are unfamiliar to you. Choose an unfamiliar detail and briefly research it. Then, explain how your research sheds light on an aspect of the article.

Summarize Write an objective summary of the article. Remember that an objective summary is free from opinion and evaluation.

Conventions
Students should identify and label the tenses of the following verbs: *was* (past), *had ended* (past perfect), *had died* (past perfect), *were . . . allowed* (past), *were* (past). The use of past perfect tense means those events and situations occurred before those described using past tense.

Academic Vocabulary
If students struggle with categorizing and defining the academic vocabulary words, use this routine:
Write the words and definitions on the board.

support: stand behind or back up

opinions: personal views or beliefs

affect: to influence

Have students say the word aloud. Then have them use the word in a sentence. Sample sentences should demonstrate that the words can be used across disciplines.

Literary Analysis

Reread the identified passages. Then, respond to the questions that follow:

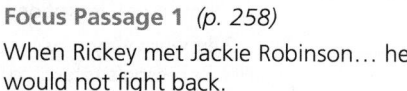

Focus Passage 1 *(p. 258)*
When Rickey met Jackie Robinson… he would not fight back.

Focus Passage 2 *(p. 259)*
"Robinson's dignity paid off… the day Jackie Robinson joined the Dodgers."

Key Ideas and Details

1. (a) According to the authors, what kind of athlete was Jackie Robinson?
(b) Support: What detail do the authors provide to **support** this claim?

Craft and Structure

2. Draw Conclusions: Why do the authors emphasize the idea that intelligence and sensitivity were as important for Robinson as his physical ability?

3. (a) Analyze: Why do the authors share the thoughts and insights of both Robinson and Rickey in this passage?
(b) Connect: How does this technique help clarify the authors' purpose?

Integration of Knowledge and Ideas

4. Given the historical context, why would "a truly brave man … have to avoid fighting"?

Author's Viewpoint

An author's **viewpoint** is the author's attitude and feelings about a subject. Authors use words with strong connotations, or associations, to express positive or negative viewpoints. Reread the essay and take notes on how the authors express their viewpoint.

1. Baseball (a) What is the authors' attitude toward Branch Rickey and his effect

Key Ideas and Details

1. (a) Interpret: How did Robinson's teammates change their **opinions** about him? **(b) Analyze:** What caused them to change?

Craft and Structure

2. How does the authors' choice of the word *jammed* instead of *attended* **affect** the meaning of the second sentence?

3. (a) Interpret: Why do the authors compare Robinson to a spark in the fourth sentence?
(b) Evaluate: Is the metaphor, or comparison, effective? Explain.

Integration of Knowledge and Ideas

4. Interpret: Reread the sentence that begins "Branch Rickey opened a door." In your own words, explain what the authors mean and tell how this sentence expresses a main idea of the essay.

on major league baseball? **(b)** Support your answer with details from the text.

2. What does the title of the selection reveal about the authors' viewpoint?

Common Core State Standards

RI.6.1, RI.6.2, RI.6.3, RI.6.4, RI.6.5, RI.6.6
[For full standards wording, see the chart in the front of this book.]

Focus Passage 2

1. (a) At first they rejected him, but then they began accepting him as a team member. **(b)** He helped them win more games.

2. Connotations of *jammed* suggest that stadiums were filled beyond their normal capacity and some fans probably had to be turned away. A word such as *attended* would not suggest that more fans than usual came.

3. (a) A spark can start a fire. In this case, Robinson started the Dodgers' winning. **(b)** It is effective because it conveys that the Dodgers without Robinson were dull, but with Robinson they were on fire.

4. By breaking the segregation rule in baseball, Rickey and Robinson gave other African Americans the opportunity to play in the major leagues. The metaphor effectively compares this opportunity to a door (which Rickey opened and Robinson stepped through) that could never close.

Author's Viewpoint

1. (a) They believe Rickey was a courageous and fair man who changed the nature of baseball in America. **(b)** The text shows that Rickey opposed other owners and many fans to integrate the major leagues. The last paragraph indicates that Rickey and Robinson changed baseball forever.

2. The phrase "Justice at Last" shows that the authors felt segregation in baseball was unfair. Robinson's entry into the major leagues helped correct that injustice.

Literary Analysis

Possible responses appear below. Check to be sure students support their responses with evidence from the text.

Focus Passage 1

1. (a) Robinson was an excellent ("superb") athlete. **(b)** His batting average in his first year in the Negro leagues was .387, which is extremely high.

2. They foreshadow that Robinson will need these abilities to survive the difficulties he will face both on and off the field, and they establish

the fact that the first African American major league baseball player must meet a higher standard than other players.

3. (a) Including both men's thoughts and insights shows how the white owner and black player worked toward one goal. **(b)** It clarifies the authors' purpose by showing how Rickey and Robinson together overcame obstacles to integrate major league baseball.

4. Fighting the abuse would be a normal reaction, but it wouldn't help the cause of integrating the major leagues. Not fighting would be much harder but would help achieve the bigger goal.

 Online Writers Notebook

Students can use the Online Writer's Notebook to record all responses.

DISCUSS

From Text to Topic: Group Discussion

1. **Possible response:** People who opposed integration would say that any fight was evidence that black and white players could not get along together.

2. **Possible response:** By not fighting back, Robinson proved that African Americans had the discipline and dignity to play major league baseball without resorting to violence.

WRITE

Writng to Sources: Informative Text

Introduce the assignment using the instruction on the student page.

Prewriting and Planning

1. The events took place more than 60 years ago, so students may not have background information about the time period. In addition, some risks and obstacles are only implied. To guide students' rereading and note-taking, provide questions, such as these: *Could Rickey count on support from other team owners and fans? What might happen if fans stopped coming to games? What if Robinson were injured, either intentionally or accidentally during a game? What if all of the teams threatened to strike as the Cardinals did? What if Robinson did not perform well under the stress?*

2. Remind students to use a two-column chart to organize their notes. Point out that they should head one column "Rickey" and another "Robinson." Then they should list the risks and obstacles each faced.

3. Students can use sticky notes to mark passages they may wish to cite.

Drafting

1. Review the block method of organizing. Remind students to present all of the details about Robinson together, and all of the details about Rickey together.

DISCUSS

From Text to Topic **Group Discussion**

Discuss this passage with a group of classmates. Take notes during the discussion. Contribute your own ideas, and support them with examples from the text.

> But somehow this man had to rise above that. No matter what happened, he must never lose his temper. No matter what was said to him, he must never answer back. If he had even one fight, people might say integration wouldn't work.

WRITE

Writing to Sources **Informative Text**

> **Assignment**
> Branch Rickey and Jackie Robinson shared a common goal—to integrate baseball—but they faced different challenges on the way to achieving that goal. Write a **comparison-and-contrast essay** in which you compare the risks and obstacles Branch Rickey faced and overcame with those that Jackie Robinson faced and overcame. Use details from the essay to support your ideas.

Prewriting and Planning Reread the essay to find details about the risks and obstacles Robinson and Rickey each faced. Some risks and obstacles may be suggested but not directly stated. Record your notes in a two-column chart.

Drafting Use the **block method** to organize your essay. Present all the details about one of the men, and then all the details about the other man. Cite specific examples from the essay to support your points.

Revising Reread your essay, making sure you have explained which risks and obstacles were the same for both Robinson and Rickey and which were different. Use transitional words and phrases like these to connect your ideas:

in the same way   similarly   in contrast   on the other hand

Editing and Proofreading Make sure the transitions you use clearly show your comparisons and contrasts. In addition, review your essay to ensure you have correctly used past tense and past perfect tense verbs to express time relationships.

QUESTIONS FOR DISCUSSION

1. Why could a single fight damage the cause of integration?

2. In what way was Robinson's refusal to fight back a way of fighting *for* something?

CONVENTIONS

Use past tense verbs to describe the main events that occurred during the timeframe of the article. Use verbs in the past perfect tense to describe background events or situations that occurred before the main events.

2. Suggest that students use the notes in their two-column charts as they cite examples.

Revising

1. Encourage students to review their drafts to make sure that they have used past tense and past perfect tense verbs correctly.

2. Remind students to make sure that they have used specific examples of risks and challenges.

Editing and Proofreading

1. Encourage students to check that they have used appropriate transitional words and phrases. For example, did they use *similarly* to show comparison and *in contrast to* for contrast?

2. Have students check that their verbs show time relationships.

RESEARCH

Research **Investigate the Topic**

Segregation in Sports The courage and wisdom of Jackie Robinson and Branch Rickey helped break down the barrier of racial prejudice in major league baseball. However, another type of segregation in sports exists. Many team sports are segregated by gender: Few sports teams include both men and women.

> ### Assignment
>
> Conduct research to find out how gender segregation is still practiced in amateur and professional baseball and how some people have fought against this bias. Look for articles about gender discrimination in baseball and firsthand accounts of people who have fought the gender barrier. Take clear notes. Share your findings in a short **presentation** to the class.

Gather Sources Locate authoritative print and electronic sources. Primary sources, such as interviews and letters written by people who have tried to break the gender barrier, provide authentic firsthand information. You may also use secondary sources, such as articles and news accounts by expert authors.

Take Notes Take notes on each source, either electronically or on note cards. Use an organized note-taking strategy.

- Make separate notes for each source. Label each note with the incident(s) it describes.
- Record source information for each note. For Internet sources, record the web address and the date you accessed the site.

Synthesize Multiple Sources Organize information from your sources into a well-structured presentation. Use what you learned to draw conclusions about gender discrimination in baseball. Use your notes to outline your presentation. Create a Works Cited list as described in the Research Workshop in the front of this book.

Organize and Present Ideas Review your outline and draft your presentation. Practice delivering your presentation before you present it to a group of classmates. Be prepared to answer questions from your audience.

PREPARATION FOR ESSAY

You may use the knowledge you gain during this research assignment to support your claims in an essay at the end of this section.

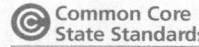 **Common Core State Standards**

W.6.1a-c, W.6.2a-c, W.6.4, W.6.5, W.6.7; SL.6.1; SL.6.4
[For full standards wording, see the chart in the front of this book.]

RESEARCH

Introduce the assignment, using the instruction on the student page.

Gather Sources

1. Arrange for students to visit your school library or have access to computers.

2. Remind students that some Internet sites are unreliable. Tell them that Web addresses ending in .gov, .edu, and .org are generally more reliable than .com sites. Searches for "baseball and gender" or "gender barriers in baseball" may be helpful.

Take Notes

1. Remind students about using quotation marks for direct quotes from primary sources, such as interviews and personal essays. For other sources, they can summarize in their own words.

2. Stress the importance of writing the complete information for each source, whether it is a direct quote or a summary.

Synthesize Multiple Sources

1. Encourage students to draw conclusions by connecting ideas from multiple sources.

2. Have students create an outline for their presentation. Point out that creating an outline will help them identify and organize the main points that will give focus to the presentation. Model the format of an outline for students.

3. Review the MLA style requirements for citing different kinds of print and online sources, and provide examples. Have students create a Works Cited list that accurately identifies each source they reference.

Organize and Present Ideas

Point out that reviewing their outlines and drafts will help students become familiar with their information. They will then be well prepared to deliver their presentations without reading directly from their outlines and also to answer questions.

MULTIDRAFT READING

Essential Understanding

First, students should read the entire selection on their own. Then, to assist struggling readers and to deepen comprehension for all, you may wish to guide them through the selection by asking them the close reading questions provided in the margins. Have students apply the multidraft reading protocols as they examine specific "chunks" of text related to these questions. For each reading, have students set the purpose indicated:

- **First reading:** Students should read the selection independently and think about its basic meaning.
- **Second reading:** Students should analyze the text's key ideas and details and its craft and structure.
- **Third reading:** Students should integrate knowledge and ideas; connect to the Big Question, other texts, and the world; and use teacher-led Close Reading discussion questions to examine particularly rich and significant passages.

For more guidance, refer to the *Classroom Strategies and Teaching Routines* card on multidraft reading.

Daily Bellringer

For each class during which you teach this selection, have students complete one of the five Quick Write activities for Week 13 in *Daily Bellringer Activities*. You may wish to use additional activities that are applicable to this selection.

Vocabulary

If students require support with selection vocabulary, use this routine:

1. Write the following words and definitions on the board:

   exhilarating *adj.* exciting; stimulating

   immortality *n.* the ability to live forever

   inductions *n.* introductions; acts of being brought into something

2. Have students say each word aloud.

3. Use the word in a sentence that defines the word.

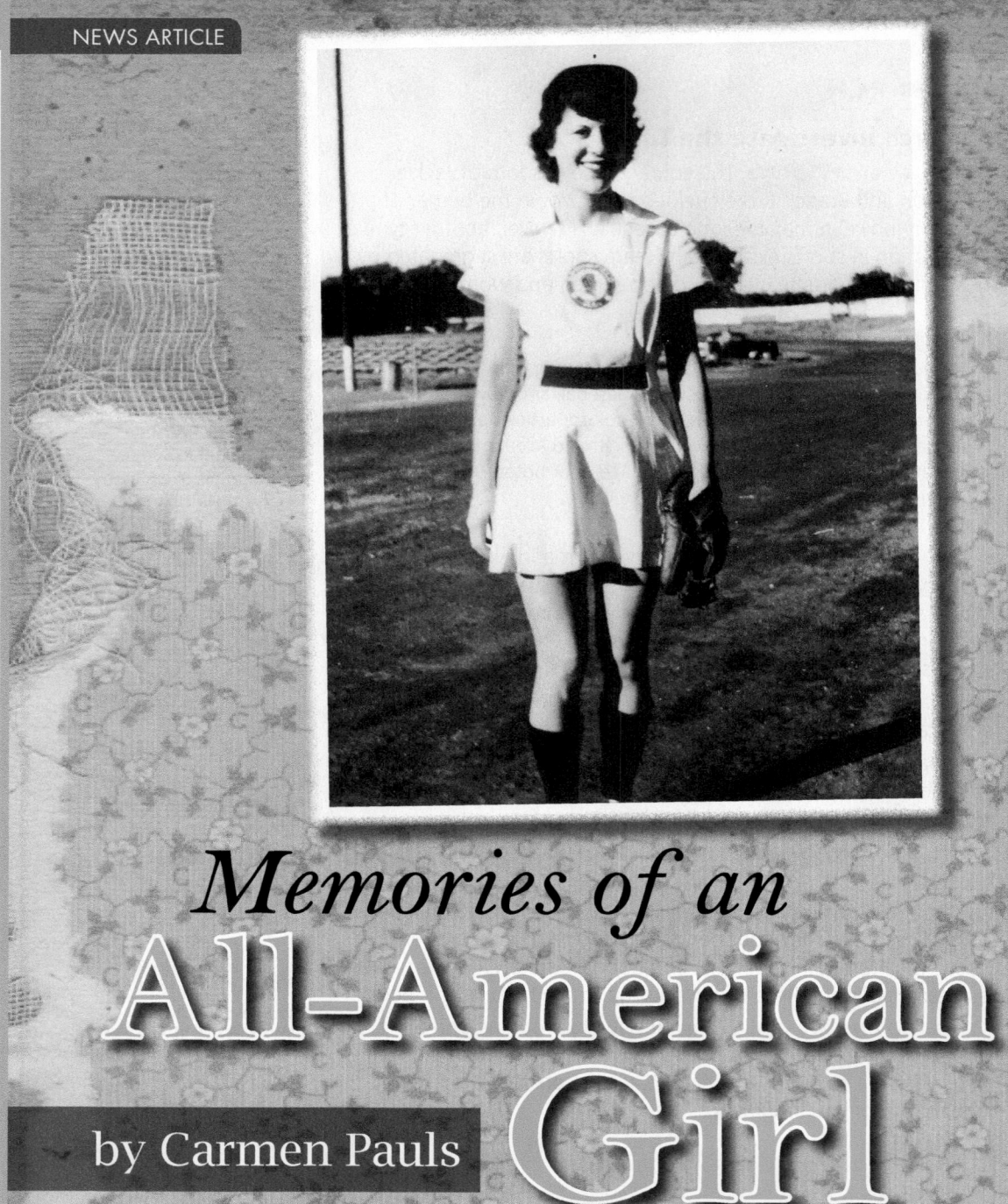

Memories of an All-American Girl

by Carmen Pauls

264 UNIT 2 • What is important to know?

TEXT COMPLEXITY **RUBRIC**

Memories of an All-American Girl		
Qualitative Measures	**Context/Knowledge Demands**	The All-American Girls Professional Baseball League, 1940s; professional baseball players 1　2　③　4　5
	Structure/Language Conventionality and Clarity	Conversational tone; direct quotations; flashbacks; simple sentences 1　2　③　4　5
	Levels of Meaning/ Purpose/Concept Level	Challenging concept (gender differences in professional baseball league) 1　2　3　④　5
Quantitative Measures	**Text Length**	Word Count: 722
	Lexile	990L

Daisy Junor is waiting for me outside her south Regina apartment, a smile on her young-looking, 76-year-old face. She shakes my hand, then holds it in hers. Looking at me, she says, "You've got soft hands. You don't play ball, do you?" Then she gently leads me into her apartment, still holding my hand.

She's right. I don't play baseball. But Daisy does—or did, in the glory days of women's baseball, the 1946–49 seasons of the All-American Girls Professional Baseball League.

The baseball league began in 1943, the brainchild of chewing gum magnate Philip Wrigley. Wrigley, who owned the Chicago Cubs, feared American baseball was going down the tubes. With major-league players going off to fight in World War II, Wrigley was afraid the ball parks might soon be empty.

Wrigley decided to satisfy the craving for America's game with a professional women's baseball league. He sent scouts all over North America, including southern Saskatchewan.

Daisy's team, with players from Regina, Moose Jaw and Estevan, had just won the Western Canada Softball League tournament, and Wrigley's scout came to see them play. Pleased with what he saw, he invited players to come down to Chicago for spring training.

Twenty-two-year-old Daisy had just gotten married, so she turned down the offer. But her sister Ruby went, and was picked to play for the Racine Belles. Over the next couple of years, as her sister and other girls came back to Saskatchewan with glowing reports, Daisy became more and more eager to go.

In the spring of 1946, Daisy heard that the training season would be in Pascagoula, Mississippi, on the Gulf of Mexico. Dave Junor, Daisy's husband, told her he'd never be able to

---

❶ Close Reading

1. **Key Ideas and Details** Read aloud the passage to students. **Ask:** Who are the people in the news article? What are they doing?

   Possible response: A news reporter is meeting Daisy Junor. They are meeting because Daisy played women's baseball in the 1940s.

2. **Craft and Structure** Direct students to reread the passage. In particular, have them pay close attention to the author's descriptions and contrasts. **Ask:** What contrasts does the author describe? What can you infer from Daisy's description of "soft hands"?

   Possible response: The author shows contrast when saying that the reporter doesn't play baseball but Daisy did. From the description of "soft hands" readers can infer that Daisy did not have soft hands because she identifies the reporter as not playing baseball through this observation.

3. **Integration of Knowledge and Ideas** Explain that writers begin news articles with a "hook" that will capture readers' interest. **Ask:** Why is beginning the article in the present and then showing a contrast by going back to an earlier time in the next paragraph an effective way to interest readers?

   Possible response: Daisy is first shown to be a kind and gentle older woman. Then readers learn she was a pioneer in women's baseball in the 1940s. They will want to know more about this interesting woman.

Ⓒ TEXT COMPLEXITY **READER AND TASK SUGGESTIONS**

Memories of an All-American Girl

Preparing to Read the Text	Leveled Tasks
• Discuss baseball. Encourage students to talk about professional teams and players. • Ask them how young players participate in the sport. They may mention Little League and T-ball teams of boys and girls. • Guide students to use Multidraft Reading strategies (TE p. 264).	*Knowledge Demands* If students will have difficulty with the challenging concept of gender differences in professional baseball, have them read the selection and make notes about Daisy and what she recalls of playing the game. Then, have them reread the selection and note the similarities and differences between men and women's professional baseball in the 1940s. Discuss students' notes and help clarify their understanding. *Analyzing* If students will not have difficulty with the concept of gender differences in professional baseball, then have them read and note details that Daisy mentions as she recalls playing in the 1940s. Have them analyze how the participation of women in sports has changed since the 1940s.

 **Audio**

Selection Audio is available in the *Student eText* and on the *Hear It!* CD-ROM.

❷ Focus Passage

A Focus Passage is identified with brackets in the Student Edition of this page for students' independent close reading and analysis. A question bank for the passage and possible responses appear at the end of the selection.

❸ Close Reading

1. **Key Ideas and Details** Have a student read aloud the passage. **Ask:** What is the author's main idea in this paragraph?

   Possible response: The girls were expected to be glamorous and at the same time play as tough a game of baseball as the men.

2. **Craft and Structure** Direct students to reread the passage and consider the author's use of comparison and contrast. **Ask:** How does the author compare and contrast men's and women's baseball?

   Possible response: The author compares the two by saying that the girls were "expected to play ball like men." To show a contrast, she explains that the game was tougher for the women because they were expected to wear short skirts, resulting in less protective wear and more injuries.

3. **Integration of Knowledge and Ideas**

   Ask: How does the author's use of comparison and contrast reveal the cultural expectations for women in the 1940s?

   Possible response: The comparison and contrast reveals that women were expected to be glamorous, as shown by their nickname "American Glamor League," yet fans also wanted them to play hard. Students may infer what the author has not stated: Women were beginning to fight for equality and recognition of their abilities, yet the culture of the times was changing slowly.

afford to take her there, so she might as well go. She did, and was signed with the South Bend (Indiana) Blue Sox, as a left-fielder.

❷ "It was a very serious game," Daisy remembers. The girls would play every night, with double-headers on weekends, and only got a day or two off all summer. At home in South Bend, the girls trained every morning and played at night under the hot stadium lights, so there was little time for socializing. In the movie *A League of Their Own*, the girls lived together in a rooming house, but the real players boarded with South Bend baseball fans.

The travel schedule was grueling.

The girls headed out to away games every week or two. "We were always coming and going. We were living out of a suitcase most of the time," Daisy recalls. "I always said, 'Gee, it'd be good to have some home-made mashed potatoes.'"

…[T]he girls, from what was sometimes called the "American Glamor League," had a tougher time than their male counterparts. ❸ The girls were expected to play ball like men, even though they were wearing short skirts, which caused serious leg burns and bruises during slides.

The girls received lessons on how to charm a date, wear makeup ❹ and skirts, and sip tea like a lady.

💬 VOCABULARY DEVELOPMENT

Related Word Forms

Expand students' vocabulary by helping them learn related forms of the selection vocabulary words. The selection vocabulary words for "Memories of an All-American Girl" have related forms. Give students a blank **Word Form Chart** (*Professional Development* *Guidebook*, p. 42) with *exhilarating, immortality,* and *inductions* in the correct columns. Work with the class, or have students work with a partner, to determine the related forms. The final chart:

Noun	Verb	Adjective	Adverb
exhilaration	exhilarate	**exhilarating**	exhilaratingly
immortality	immortalize	immortal	immortally
inductions	induct	inductive	inductively

The All-American Girls were to be every boy's ideal woman as well as the girl next door. "Frankly, I'll tell you, it didn't work with some of them," Daisy says. "Almost all these girls were tomboys, and they all looked so funny in skirts."

But whether it was the posture lessons or their skills on the field, fans loved the All-Americans. Fans would grab a player's glove as a souvenir, or stake out players' homes to catch a glimpse of them. "It was very **exhilarating**," Daisy says. "After the ball game, we could hardly get to the dressing room (because of the requests) for autographs."

Fifty years later, the fans are still coming for autographs. In Arizona, four of Daisy's friends from the league regularly go to local shopping malls to sign and sell autographed baseball cards. "It's almost a living for them," Daisy says. "They say the people just love (them) there."

Daisy herself rarely signs autographs these days. But she's already achieved a sort of **immortality**, with **inductions** into the Saskatchewan Sports Hall of Fame in Regina, the Saskatchewan Baseball Hall of Fame in North Battleford, and the grand-daddy of them all, the Baseball Hall of Fame in Cooperstown, N.Y.

And if you let her get her ball and glove, she'll come play catch with you any time.

◄ **immortality**
(im´ôr tal´i tē) *n.*
ability to live
forever

◄ **inductions**
(in duk´shənz) *n.*
introductions; acts
of being brought
into something

◄ **exhilarating**
(eg zil´ə rāt´ iŋ) *adj.*
exciting; stimulating

ABOUT THE AUTHOR

Carmen Pauls
At the age of eight, Carmen Pauls wrote an essay about the wonders of reading that was published in her local newspaper. Since that time, she has been an award-winning news reporter, screenwriter, and photographer. She currently lives and works in Saskatchewan, Canada.

PART 3 • Memories of an All-American Girl **267**

❹ 🔵 **Big Question:
Toward Essential
Understanding**

1. Read aloud the passage. **Ask:** Was it important for women to have lessons on being a lady?

   Possible response: The lessons were not important because they had nothing to do with playing the tough game of baseball.

2. **Ask:** What was the contradiction between expectations in the 1940s for the players in the professional league and the characteristics of most of the women who were attracted to the game of baseball?

   Possible response: The girls were expected to be glamorous as well as good players. In contrast, most of the girls who wanted to play in the league were tomboys, according to Daisy.

🔧 DIFFERENTIATED INSTRUCTION

Strategy for Special-Needs Students
Have students create a two-column chart to identify the positive and negative aspects of being in the baseball league. Then, have them add specific details from the news article that show what Daisy liked about being in the league and what she didn't like. Ask them to determine whether the benefits outweighed the negative aspects.

Enrichment for Advanced Readers
Tell students that many women played in the professional league at the time Daisy did. For example, Doris Sams pitched a perfect game in 1947 and was the inspiration for the film *A League of Their Own,* and Ann Harnett was the first woman to sign a contract with the league. Have students do preliminary research, choose a woman for more in-depth research, and write an essay comparing Daisy Junor's viewpoint with how other women baseball players viewed the league.

Close Reading Activities

READ

Comprehension

1. It was formed to fill the gap left when many male baseball players went to war.

2. The women wore short skirts that didn't protect their legs during slides, and they had to take classes on proper behavior.

3. She was a left fielder for a team from South Bend. She was eventually inducted into the Baseball Hall of Fame.

Research: Clarify Details

Students should describe the results of their research and explain how their research helped them understand the article.

Summarize

Students' summaries should briefly describe why the women's league was formed, Daisy's involvement, the life of the players, and the league's effects.

Language Study

Possible responses:

• *exhilarating: Exhilarate* is a verb meaning to excite or to stimulate. Adding *-ing* makes it an adjective.

• *immortality: Immortal* is an adjective meaning never dying. Adding *-ity* changes it to a noun.

• *inductions: Induct* is a verb meaning to introduce or bring into. Adding *-ions* makes it a plural noun.

Literary Analysis

Possible responses appear below. Check to be sure students support their responses with evidence from the text.

1. (a) The girls worked hard and had a demanding travel schedule. **(b)** They trained in the morning, played at night and on the weekends, and went out of town every week or two.

2. (a) The direct quotations make the experience more real. **(b)** No, the article would not be as effective without the quotations because they express the feelings of a woman who was directly involved.

READ

Comprehension

Reread all or part of the text to help you answer the following questions.

1. Why was the All-American Girls Professional Baseball League formed?

2. Why did women have a "tougher time" than the men playing professional baseball?

3. What was Daisy Junor's role in the women's baseball league?

Language Study

Selection Vocabulary Explain how the suffix changes each base word in each boldfaced word from the article. If necessary, use a dictionary to help you answer.

Literary Analysis

Reread the identified passage. Then, respond to the questions that follow.

> **Focus Passage** *(p. 266)*
> "It was a very serious game… home-made mashed potatoes.'"

Key Ideas and Details

1. (a) Infer: What is the main idea of this passage? **(b) Support:** What details in the passage support the main idea?

Craft and Structure

2. (a) Analyze: In these paragraphs, the author uses direct quotations from Daisy.

Time Shifts

Narrative **time shifts** are scenes that jump from the present to the past or even the future.

1. (a) Identify the section of the article that takes place in the past. **(b)** What

Research: Clarify Details Choose at least one unfamiliar detail from the article and research it. Then, explain how your research helped you understand the article.

Summarize Write an objective summary of the article. Include main ideas and details, but do not include opinions.

• "It was very **exhilarating**," Daisy says.

• But she's already achieved a sort of **immortality**, with **inductions** into the Saskatchewan Sports Hall of Fame . . .

What is the effect of the quotations? **(b) Make a Judgment:** Would the article be as effective if it did not contain quotations? Why or why not?

Integration of Knowledge and Ideas

3. (a) Evaluate: The author mentions the movie *A League of Their Own*. Do you think the experiences of Daisy and her teammates would make an interesting subject for a movie? Use details from the passage to support your answer.

words does the author use to signal shifts in time?

2. What effect does the author achieve by using time shifts in this article?

3. Students may say it would be interesting to see a movie about the positive and negative aspects of the women's league, or that it would not be interesting because the article does not have enough action for a movie.

Time Shifts

1. (a) The middle of the article is set in the past, from the third paragraph to the twelfth paragraph. **(b)** In the second paragraph the author notes that "Daisy does—or did" play baseball. This shows the shift that will occur. The third

paragraph uses past tense verbs, such as *began* and *feared*.

2. The time shifts allow readers to step back into time and understand the experiences that Daisy Junor had when she was playing baseball.

DISCUSS • RESEARCH • WRITE

From Text to Topic **Partner Discussion**

Discuss this passage with a partner. Take notes during the discussion. Contribute your own ideas, and support them with examples from the text.

> … [T]he girls, from what was sometimes called the "American Glamor League,"… they all looked so funny in skirts." (p. 266)

Research **Investigate the Topic**

Women and Baseball Although the All-American Girls Professional Baseball League was the first women's sports league to gain national fame, women continue to play baseball at the collegiate and semi-pro level.

Assignment

Conduct research to find out about another woman's contribution to baseball history. Take clear notes and carefully identify your sources. Share your findings in an **informal discussion** with the class.

Writing to Sources **Autobiographical Narrative**

"Memories of an All-American Girl" focuses on one woman's experiences during an extraordinary time in her life.

Assignment

Write an **autobiographical narrative** that describes an opportunity or event that had a positive effect on your life. Follow these steps:

- Introduce the significant opportunity or event.
- Include **visual** descriptions to create vivid images for your audience.
- Use transitions to smoothly connect events.
- Conclude by **reflecting** on the impact of the event, and by making a connection between your experience and Daisy Junor's.

QUESTIONS FOR DISCUSSION

1. How were women treated differently from male players?
2. Do you think the women were treated unfairly? Why or why not?

PREPARATION FOR ESSAY

You may use the results of this research project to support your ideas in the essay at the end of this section.

ACADEMIC VOCABULARY

Academic terms appear in blue on these pages. If these words are not familiar to you, use a dictionary to find their definitions. Then, use them as you speak and write about the text.

Common Core State Standards

RI.6.1, RI6.2, RI6.3, RI6.4, RI6.5; L.6.1, L.6.2, L.6.3, L.6.4; SL.6.1, SL.6.4; W.6.3, W.6.4
[For full standards wording, see the chart in the front of this book.]

PART 3 • Close Reading Activities **269**

Writing to Sources: Autobiographical Narrative

Students' autobiographical narratives should follow the steps listed. Encourage students to use word choices that appeal to the reader's senses to make the event come alive. Remind students to draw a connection between the opportunity or event they faced and Daisy Junor's experience.

DISCUSS • RESEARCH • WRITE

From Text to Topic: Partner Discussion

1. **Possible response:** For the sake of appearance, women couldn't wear the proper safety equipment.
2. **Possible response:** Some probably felt they should be treated like the male players. Others may have felt that the opportunity to earn money and travel was worth the different treatment.

Research: Investigate the Topic

Introduce the assignment, using the instruction on the student page.

1. Arrange for students to visit your school library or computer lab. Review strategies for identifying reliable electronic sources.
2. Remind students to take notes and write complete details about the source. They can quote directly or paraphrase.
3. Encourage students to draw conclusions and make connections between multiple sources. Suggest using an outline for their discussion. They should also prepare a Works Cited list that includes each source they reference.
4. Suggest that students review their notes before the discussion. They should be prepared to answer questions about what they found.

Academic Vocabulary

If students struggle with defining the academic vocabulary words, use this routine:

Write the words and definitions on the board.

visual: used in seeing

reflecting: showing

Have students say the word aloud. Then have them use the word in a sentence. Sample sentences should demonstrate that the words can be used across disciplines.

 Online Writer's Notebook

Students can use the Online Writer's Notebook to record all responses.

PART 3 • Close Reading Activities **269**

MULTIDRAFT READING

Essential Understanding

First, students should read the entire selection on their own. Then, to assist struggling readers and to deepen comprehension for all, you may wish to guide them through the selection by asking them the close reading questions provided in the margins. Have students apply the multidraft reading protocols as they examine specific "chunks" of text related to these questions. For each reading, have students set the purpose indicated:

- **First reading:** Students should read the selection independently and think about its basic meaning.
- **Second reading:** Students should analyze the text's key ideas and details and its craft and structure.
- **Third reading:** Students should integrate knowledge and ideas; connect to the Big Question, other texts, and the world; and use teacher-led Close Reading discussion questions to examine particularly rich and significant passages.

For more guidance, refer to the *Classroom Strategies and Teaching Routines* card on multidraft reading.

❶ Focus Passage

A Focus Passage is identified with brackets on the following page of the Student Edition for students' independent close reading and analysis. A question bank for the passage and possible responses appear at the end of the selection.

Vocabulary

If students require support with selection vocabulary, use this routine:

1. Write the following words and definitions on the board:

   doomed *v.* condemned to destruction or death

   extinction *n.* act of bring to an end; destruction

   amendment *n.* change made to a law or bill by adding, deleting, or altering its language

2. Have students say each word aloud.

3. Use the word in a sentence that defines the word.

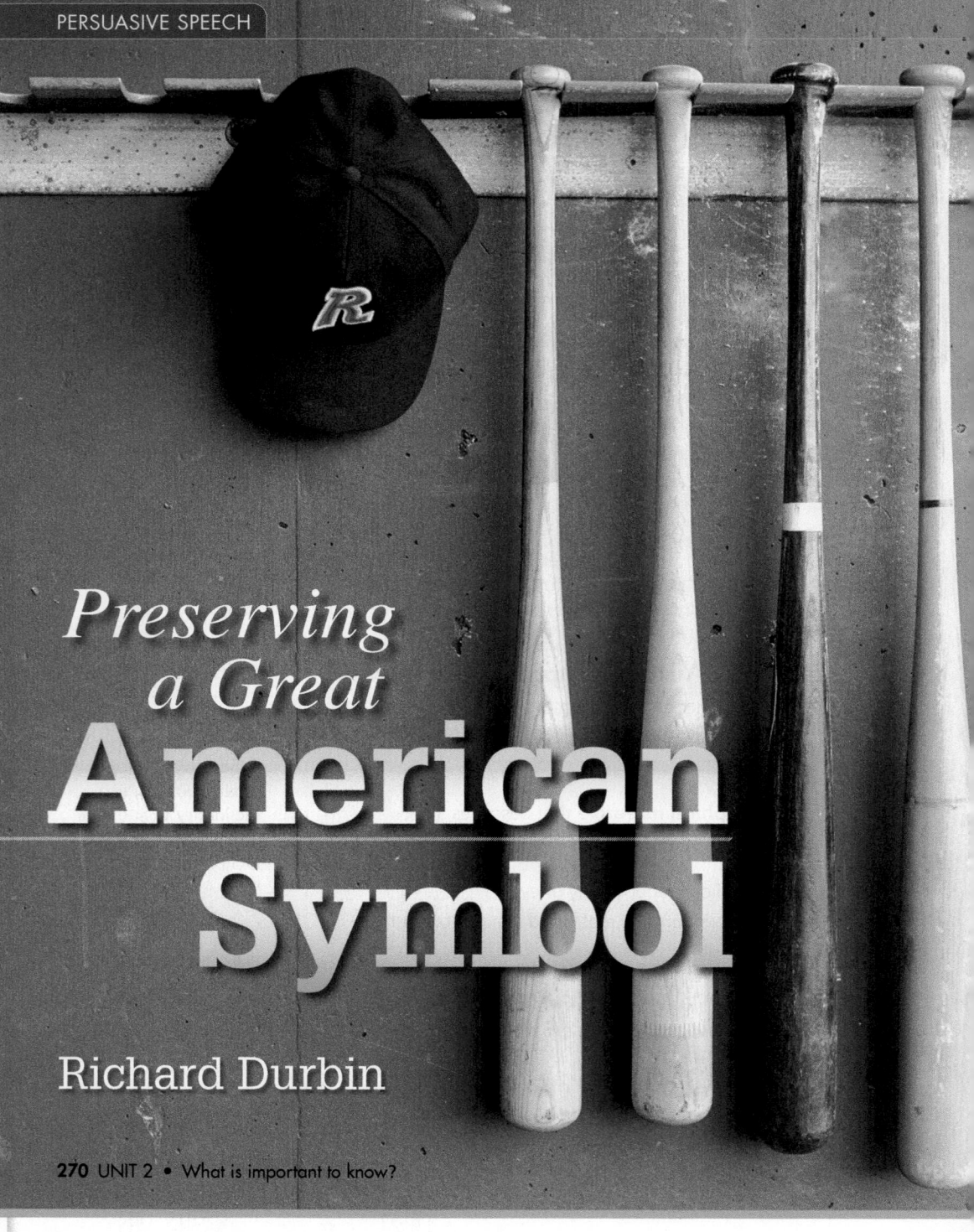

PERSUASIVE SPEECH

Preserving a Great
American Symbol

Richard Durbin

270 UNIT 2 • What is important to know?

Ⓒ TEXT COMPLEXITY **RUBRIC**

Preserving a Great American Symbol		
Qualitative Measures	**Context/Knowledge Demands**	Baseball traditions in U.S.; speeches in Congress 1 2 ③ 4 5
	Structure/Language Conventionality and Clarity	Humorous tone; some specialized vocabulary; figurative language 1 2 ③ 4 5
	Levels of Meaning/ Purpose/Concept Level	Accessible concept (use of wooden versus aluminum bats) 1 ② 3 4 5
Quantitative Measures	**Text Length**	Word Count: 302
	Lexile	1130L

Mr. Speaker, I rise to condemn the desecration of a great American symbol. No, I am not referring to flagburning; I am referring to the baseball bat.

Several experts tell us that the wooden baseball bat is doomed to extinction, that major league baseball players will soon be standing at home plate with aluminum bats in their hands.

Baseball fans have been forced to endure countless indignities by those who just cannot leave well enough alone: designated hitters,[1] plastic grass, uniforms that look like pajamas, chicken clowns dancing on the base lines, and, of course, the most heinous sacrilege, lights in Wrigley Field.[2]

Are we willing to hear the crack of a bat replaced by the dinky ping? Are we ready to see the Louisville Slugger replaced by the aluminum ping dinger? Is nothing sacred?

Please do not tell me that wooden bats are too expensive, when players who cannot hit their weight are being paid more money than the President of the United States.

Please do not try to sell me on the notion that these metal clubs will make better hitters.

What will be next? Teflon baseballs? Radar-enhanced gloves? I ask you.

I do not want to hear about saving trees. Any tree in America would gladly give its life for the glory of a day at home plate.

I do not know if it will take a constitutional amendment to keep our baseball traditions alive, but if we forsake the great Americana of broken-bat singles and pine tar,[3] we will have certainly lost our way as a nation.

◄ **doomed**
(d⁻o⁻omd) *v.*
condemned
to destruction
or death

◄ **extinction**
(ek stiŋk′shən) *n.*
act of bringing
to an end;
destruction

◄ **amendment**
(ə mend′mənt) *n.*
change made to
a law or bill by
adding, deleting,
or altering its
language

---

1. **designated hitter** player who bats in place of the pitcher and does not play any other position. The position was created in 1973 in the American League. Some fans argue that it has changed the game for the worse.
2. **Wrigley Field** historic baseball field in Chicago. It did not have lights for night games until 1988. Some fans regretted the change.
3. **broken-bat singles . . . pine tar** when a batter breaks a wooden bat while hitting the ball and makes it to first base, it is a notable event in a baseball game; pine tar is a substance used to improve the batter's grip on a wooden bat.

ABOUT THE AUTHOR

Richard Durbin (b. 1944)

Richard (Dick) Durbin has been a United States senator from Illinois since 1997. Before being elected to the Senate, Durbin served six terms as a congressman from Illinois in the United States House of Representatives. He gave this humorous speech in the House of Representatives on July 26, 1989.

---

❷ Close Reading

1. **Key Ideas and Details**
   Ask: Why does Durbin bring up the point about saving trees?

   Possible response: Durbin offers a counterargument against preserving trees.

2. **Craft and Structure**
   Ask: How does Durbin use exaggeration and personification?

   Possible response: Suggesting that baseballs might be made of Teflon is hyberbole. Saying that a tree could sacrifice its life is personification.

3. **Integration of Knowledge and Ideas**
   Ask: How does his use of exaggeration and personification show the level of seriousness and humor in this speech?

   Possible response: These rhetorical devices add humor to the speech. Durbin's language is serious and shows his strong desire to keep wooden bats, yet in relation to other political matters, this issue is not a serious issue.

❸ ❓ Big Question: Toward Essential Understanding

1. **Ask:** Are baseball traditions an important issue for the nation?

   Possible response: Students will probably say no.

2. **Ask:** Do you think that giving up traditions means America has lost its identity as a nation?

   Possible response: Some students may say that certain traditions are important to America's identity, but others may say some traditions need to change to reflect the times.

ⓒ TEXT COMPLEXITY **READER AND TASK SUGGESTIONS**

Preserving a Great American Symbol

Preparing to Read the Text	Leveled Tasks
• Discuss the bats used in baseball and ask whether students have ever seen a player break a bat while hitting. • Point out that for some people, wooden bats have come to represent, or symbolize, the game. • Guide students to use Multidraft Reading strategies on the previous page.	*Knowledge Demands* If students will have difficulty with the humorous tone in this speech before Congress, discuss what they know about exaggeration and how it often leads to humor. *Evaluating* If students will not have difficulty with the humorous tone of the speech, encourage them to discuss baseball traditions with which they are familiar and whether they think it's okay to change traditions.

 **Audio**

Summary Audio is available in the *Student eText* and on the *Hear It!* CD-ROM.

Close Reading Activities

READ

Comprehension

1. He is arguing to keep wooden bats in major league baseball.

2. They have "endured" plastic grass, silly-looking uniforms, clowns on the field, and lights in Wrigley Field.

3. Aluminum is cheaper; trees will be saved; players will become better hitters with aluminum bats.

Research: Clarify Details

Students' explanations should describe the results of their research and explain how their research helped them understand the selection.

Summarize

Students' summaries should describe Durbin's position on the issue of wooden versus aluminum bats, and briefly and objectively list Durbin's main arguments.

Language Study

Possible responses:

- *doomed*: condemned; *extinction*: elimination; The Ice Age *doomed* dinosaurs to *extinction*.

- *amendment*: change made to a law or bill by adding, deleting, or altering its language; An *amendment* to the U.S. Constitution gave women the right to vote.

Check students' new sentences.

Literary Analysis

Possible responses appear below. Check to be sure students support their responses with evidence from the text.

1. **(a)** He thinks they are ruining the sport. **(b)** He provides examples of the changes and describes them in a humorous, exaggerated manner to make them sound silly.

2. **(a)** The word *crack* has rough or tough connotations while *dinky ping* sounds weak and silly. This creates contrasting images of a rough, tough sport versus a weak, silly game. **(b)** Comparing a Slugger to a ping dinger heightens the contrast between the tough-sounding proper noun Louisville Slugger and the silly-sounding, made-up *ping dinger*.

READ

Comprehension

Reread all or part of the text to help you answer the following questions.

1. What is the purpose of Durbin's speech?
2. What "indignities" have baseball fans already endured?
3. What advantages of aluminum bats does Durbin dismiss?

Language Study

Selection Vocabulary The following phrases come from the selection. Define the boldfaced words. Then, use each word in a sentence of your own.

Literary Analysis

Reread the identified passage. Then, respond to the questions that follow:

> **Focus Passage** *(p. 271)*
> Baseball fans have been forced … Is nothing sacred?

Key Ideas and Details

1. **(a) Interpret:** What is Durbin's position on the changes in major league baseball? **(b) Analyze:** How does he support his position?

Hyperbole

Hyperbole is a form of figurative language in which an author uses exaggeration to **achieve** an effect. Reread the speech, noting examples of hyperbole.

Research: Clarify Details Choose an unfamiliar reference from the speech and briefly research it. Then, explain how your research helped clarify the speech.

Summarize Write an objective summary of the speech. Objective summaries are free of opinions and evaluation.

- Several experts tell us that the wooden baseball bat is **doomed** to **extinction** . . .
- I do not know if it will take a constitutional **amendment** . . .

Craft and Structure

2. **(a) Analyze:** What effect does Durbin achieve by comparing the "crack" of a wooden bat to the "dinky ping" of an aluminum bat? **(b)** Use details from the speech to explain how the next sentence strengthens this effect.

Integration of Knowledge and Ideas

3. To what type of audience would this speech most appeal? **Cite** details from the text to support your answer.

1. **Analyze:** Identify two examples of hyperbole in the speech, and explain their effects.

2. **Evaluate:** Does Durbin's use of hyperbole strengthen his overall message? Explain.

3. This speech would most likely appeal to audiences who are in support of tradition and the baseball fans that Durbin refers to.

Hyperbole

1. In saying that lights in Wrigley Field were a "heinous sacrilege," he implies that Wrigley Field is a sacred site, and putting lights in was like vandalizing a sacred site. It is humorous, but it also emphasizes the value of tradition in baseball. References to a constitutional amendment and saying we have "lost our

way" as a nation exaggerate the seriousness of the issue. The exaggeration emphasizes that Americans should protect national traditions.

2. Some students may say that the use of hyperbole strengthens the argument because it shows people that tradition is important. Others may say that the hyperboles are not realistic and cause readers to question whether the topic is a serious matter.

DISCUSS • RESEARCH • WRITE

From Text to Topic **Panel Discussion**

Discuss the following passage with a group of classmates. Take notes during the discussion. Contribute your own ideas, and support them with examples from the text.

> Please do not try to sell me on the notion that these metal clubs will make better hitters.
> What will be next? Teflon baseballs? Radar-enhanced gloves? I ask you.

Research **Investigate the Topic**

Baseball Traditions For close to a century, baseball has been America's "National Pastime." Many valued traditions have developed around the game and the players, teams, and stadiums associated with it.

Assignment

Conduct research to learn about some of baseball's most well-known traditions and how these traditions affect players and fans today. Consult electronic and print sources. Take clear notes and carefully identify your sources so that you can easily access the information later. Share your findings in an **informal presentation** for the class.

Writing to Sources **Argument**

Some people, like Durbin, argue for preserving traditions such as the wooden bat in baseball. Others argue for the use of new technology such as advanced camera systems for instant replays.

Assignment

Write a **persuasive speech** in which you **argue** for or against the use of new technology in baseball. Follow these steps:

- Identify the issue and clearly state your claim.
- Use statistics, quotations, and other details to support your claim. You may also draw upon information presented in Durbin's speech.
- Conclude your speech by summarizing the impact that new technology will have upon established baseball traditions.

QUESTIONS FOR DISCUSSION

1. What might be the effects of "radar-enhanced gloves"?
2. What does Durbin imply about the effects of technology? In sports, how much technology is too much?

PREPARATION FOR ESSAY

You may use the results of this research project to support your ideas in the essay at the end of this section.

ACADEMIC VOCABULARY

Academic terms appear in blue on these pages. If these words are not familiar to you, use a dictionary to find their definitions. Then, use them as you speak and write about the text.

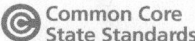 **Common Core State Standards**

RI.6.1, RI6.2, RI6.3, RI6.4, RI6.5; W.6.2, W.6.4, W.6.7; SL.6.1
[For full standards wording, see the chart in the front of this book.]

DISCUSS • RESEARCH • WRITE

From Text to Topic: Panel Discussion

1. Fielders would have an easier time making plays.
2. **Possible response:** Technological advances could change the basic nature of the game, making it too easy; if technology changes the game, it may also change our enjoyment of it. He thinks there is already too much technology.

Research: Investigate the Topic

Introduce the assignment, using the instruction on the student page.

1. Arrange for students to visit a library or your school's computer lab. Review strategies for identifying reliable sources.
2. Have students take notes on what they learn about baseball traditions. Whether they choose to use note cards or type the notes on a laptop or tablet, they should include source information. They will need complete information for their Works Cited list when they prepare their presentation. Suggest that their notes include both direct quotations and paraphrases or summaries of the information.
3. Students should include multiple sources to draw conclusions and make connections. Suggest that they prepare an outline for their presentation. They may want to consider using visuals, such as graphic organizers or sketches.
4. Point out that being well prepared will give them confidence when it's time for the presentation.

Academic Vocabulary

If students struggle with defining the academic vocabulary words, use this routine:

Write the words and definitions on the board.

cite: quote, refer to

achieve: accomplish

argue: give reasons for or against something

Have students say the word aloud. Then have them use the word in a sentence. Sample sentences should demonstrate that the words can be used across disciplines.

Writing to Sources: Argument

Students' persuasive speeches should follow the steps listed in order. They should identify the issue and state a claim; use statistics, quotations, and other details to support the claim; and provide a summary that appeals directly to the audience.

 Online Writer's Notebook

Students can use the Online Writer's Notebook to record all responses.

MULTIDRAFT READING

Essential Understanding

First, students should read the entire selection on their own. Then, to assist struggling readers and to deepen comprehension for all, you may wish to guide them through the selection by asking them the close reading questions provided in the margins. Have students apply the multidraft reading protocols as they examine specific "chunks" of text related to these questions. For each reading, have students set the purpose indicated:

- **First reading:** Students should read the selection independently and think about its basic meaning.
- **Second reading:** Students should analyze the text's key ideas and details and its craft and structure.
- **Third reading:** Students should integrate knowledge and ideas; connect to the Big Question, other texts, and the world; and use teacher-led Close Reading discussion questions to examine particularly rich and significant passages.

For more guidance, refer to the *Classroom Strategies and Teaching Routines* card on multidraft reading.

Vocabulary

If students require support with selection vocabulary, use this routine:

1. Write the following words and definitions on the board:

former *adj.* existing in an earlier time; past

unreasonable *adj.* not fair; not sensible

2. Have students say each word aloud.

3. Use the word in a sentence that defines the word.

SHORT STORY

The Southpaw
Judith Viorst

former ▶
(fôr´ mər) *adj.*
existing in an
earlier time; past

❶ *Dear Richard,*
Don't invite me to your birthday party because I'm not coming. And give back the Disneyland sweatshirt I said you could wear. If I'm not good enough to play on your team, I'm not good enough to be friends with.
Your former friend,
Janet

P.S. I hope when you go to the dentist he finds 20 cavities.

Dear Janet,
Here is your stupid Disneyland sweatshirt, if that's how you're going to be. I want my comic books now—finished or not. No girl had ever played on the Mapes Street baseball team, and as long as I'm captain, no girl ever will.
Your former friend,
Richard

P.S. I hope when you go for your checkup you need a tetanus shot.

Dear Richard,
I'm changing my goldfish's name from Richard to Stanley. Don't count on my vote for class president next year. Just because I'm a member of the ballet club doesn't mean I'm not a terrific ballplayer.
Your former friend,
Janet

P.S. I see you lost your first game 28-0.

274 UNIT 2 • What is important to know?

© TEXT COMPLEXITY **RUBRIC**

The Southpaw		
Qualitative Measures	Context/Knowledge Demands	1970s America; baseball 1 ②(2) 3 4 5
	Structure/Language Conventionality and Clarity	Letter format; conversational; on-level vocabulary 1 2 ③(3) 4 5
	Levels of Meaning/ Purpose/Concept Level	Accessible concept (girl wants to be on all-boys baseball team) 1 ②(2) 3 4 5
Quantitative Measures	Text Length	Word Count: 538
	Lexile	650L

Dear Janet,

I'm not saving any more seats for you on the bus. For all I care you can stand the whole way to school. Why don't you just forget about baseball and learn something nice like knitting?
Your former friend,
    Richard

P.S. Wait until Wednesday.

Dear Richard,

My father said I could call someone to go with us for a ride and hot-fudge sundaes. In case you didn't notice, I didn't call you.
Your former friend,
    Janet

P.S. I see you lost your second game, 34-0.

Dear Janet,

Remember when I took the laces out of my blue-and-white sneakers and gave them to you? I want them back.
Your former friend,
    Richard

P.S. Wait until Friday.

Dear Richard,

Congratulations on your un-broken record. Eight straight loses, wow! I understand you're the laughingstock of New Jersey.
Your former friend,
    Janet

P.S. Why don't you and your team forget about baseball and learn something nice like knitting maybe?

PART 3 • The Southpaw **275**

ⓒ TEXT COMPLEXITY **READER AND TASK SUGGESTIONS**

The Southpaw

Preparing to Read the Text
- Have students identify the meaning of *southpaw* in the title. (a left-handed person; a left-handed pitcher)
- Discuss how disagreements can develop and be resolved between two friends. Ask them how sending notes might help or hinder the resolution of conflicts.
- Guide students to use Multidraft Reading strategies on the previous page.

Leveled Tasks
Knowledge Demands If students will have difficulty with the letter format of this story, have volunteers take the role of each character and read the notes. Encourage them to express the angry feelings of each character. Then discuss with students how the story develops through the notes.

Synthesizing If students will not have difficulty with the format, have them discuss the progression of the disagreement as it is revealed in the notes and discuss what information in the letters gives the reader clues about how the argument will be resolved.

❶ Close Reading

1. **Key Ideas and Details**
   Ask: From whose point of view do readers learn about the problem?

   Possible response: The point of view is that of the writer of the letter, Janet.

2. **Craft and Structure**
   Ask: How does the word choice express Janet's feelings? What does the repeated phrase show?

   Possible response: The author uses the negative phrases "don't invite me" and "not coming," to show she is angry. The phrase "I'm not good enough" shows she is upset that Richard questions her skills.

3. **Integration of Knowledge and Ideas**
   Ask: Why would the author choose to use a letter format to show the character's perspective?

   Possible response: The format allows the author to show two viewpoints about the situation.

❷ Close Reading

1. **Key Ideas and Details**
   Ask: What event does Janet recount to Richard here?

   Possible response: Janet tells Richard that her father could take her and "someone" for hot-fudge sundaes and points out that she didn't go with Richard.

2. **Craft and Structure**
   Ask: What is the significance of the repetition of *didn't*?

   Possible response: Janet didn't call Richard, and she wants him to notice.

3. **Integration of Knowledge and Ideas**
   Ask: How do Janet's descriptions of what she could and didn't do help you understand her relationship with Richard?

   Possible response: The descriptions say that she is no longer friends with him. However, she still writes him.

 **Audio**

Summary Audio is available in the *Student eText* and on the *Hear It!* CD-ROM.

❸ Focus Passage

A Focus Passage is identified with brackets in the Student Edition of the previous page and this page for students' independent close reading and analysis. A question bank for the passage and possible responses appear at the end of the selection.

❹ Close Reading

1. Key Ideas and Details Read aloud the passage to students. **Ask:** What does Janet say in her letter, and what is Richard's response?

Possible response: Janet's note declares that she pitches. Richard offers her first base.

2. Craft and Structure Ask students to compare the difference in length of each person's letter.

Ask: What does Janet's one-sentence note show about her determination, and why does Richard write a longer note?

Possible response: Janet's simple "I pitch" shows her insistence on being the pitcher, and her unwillingness to compromise. Richard's longer note explains why various players cannot play. Richard is still not willing to let Janet pitch, and makes a counteroffer.

3. Integration of Knowledge and Ideas
Ask: In this passage, whose position is becoming stronger, Janet's or Richard's? How does the sentence length reflect that?

Possible response: Janet is not willing to change her demand, while Richard lists a variety of reasons why his team is losing a number of players. Janet's position is clearly getting stronger.

Dear Janet,
    Here's the silver horseback riding trophy that you gave me. I don't think I want to keep it anymore.
Your former friend,
    Richard

P.S. I didn't think you'd be the kind who'd kick a man when he's down.

❸ *Dear Richard,*
    I wasn't kicking exactly. I was kicking back.
Your former friend,
    Janet

P.S. In case you were wondering, my batting average is .345.

Dear Janet,
    Alfie is having his tonsils out tomorrow. We might be able to let you catch next week.
    Richard

Dear Richard,
    I pitch.
Janet

Dear Janet,
    Joel is moving to Kansas and Danny sprained his wrist. How about a permanent place in the outfield?
    Richard

Dear Richard,
    I pitch.
Janet

❹ *Dear Janet,*
    Ronnie caught the chicken pox and Leo broke his toe and Elwood has these stupid violin lessons. I'll give you first base, and that's my final offer.
    Richard

276 UNIT 2 • What is important to know?

🗨 VOCABULARY DEVELOPMENT

Selection Vocabulary Reinforcement
Students will benefit from additional examples and practice with the selection vocabulary words. Reinforce their comprehension with a "show-you-know" sentence. The first part of the sentence uses the vocabulary word in an appropriate context. The second part of the sentence—the "show-you-know" part—clarifies the first. Model the strategy with this example for *former*:

The conductor is my *former* teacher; she taught me to play the violin.

Then give students this sentence prompt, and coach them in creating the clarification part:

Her demand for a bigger allowance is *unreasonable*; _____.
Sample answer: Her parents will never agree to her unfair request.

Dear Richard

Susan Reilly plays first base, Marilyn Jackson catches, Ethel Kahn plays center field, I pitch. It's a package deal.
    Janet

P.S. Sorry about your 12-game losing streak.

⑤ *Dear Janet,*

Please! Not Marilyn Jackson.
Richard

Dear Richard

Nobody ever said that I was unreasonable. How about Lizzie Martindale instead?
    Janet

⑥ *Dear Janet,*

At least could you call your goldfish Richard again?
Your friend,
    Richard

◄ **unreasonable**
(un rē´ zən ə bəl)
adj. not fair;
not sensible

ABOUT THE AUTHOR

Judith Viorst (b. 1931)

Born in Newark, New Jersey, Judith Viorst knew as a child that she wanted to be a writer. She kept writing, and eventually found success with her stories and poetry. Many of Viorst's characters are based on people she knows. When she saw the musical version of her book *Alexander and the Terrible, Horrible, No Good, Very Bad Day*, Viorst said the experience of seeing her family and friends come to life through seven actors was a "truly weird and thrilling thing."

PART 3 • The Southpaw **277**

---

⑤ Close Reading

1. Key Ideas and Details
Ask: What does Janet want in this passage? What key idea does Janet's second response in this passage convey?

Possible response: Janet wants girls to play the positions Richard has offered her. When Richard objects to one of them, for the first time Janet offers to compromise by suggesting another girl.

2. Craft and Structure
Ask: How does Richard's "Please! Not Marilyn Jackson" point to a change in the situation?

Possible response: Richard does not object to Susan or Ethel or, more significantly, to Janet being the pitcher. This suggests he has changed his position and wants the girls to play.

3. Integration of Knowledge and Ideas
Ask: How is the team taking shape at the end of the passage? How important are the changes?

Possible response: Janet is now willing to make a compromise, by replacing Marilyn with Lizzie. The team that once had only boys will now have four girls—Janet, Susan, Ethel, and Lizzie. This new roster of players is a significant change for Richard's team.

⑥ Big Question: Toward Essential Understanding

1. Ask: How does the letter format affect the information that readers are given?

Possible response: In this format, the reader can only know what the letter writers, Janet and Richard, are thinking and saying. However, what the writers say reveals a lot about their characters and the situation.

2. Ask: Why is the way that Richard signs the last letter important to understanding what happens in the end?

Possible response: He signs this letter "Your friend." The sequence of letters began with "Your former friend." Signing "Your friend" in the last letter is important because it suggests that Richard and Janet are friends again.

PART 3 • The Southpaw **277**

👥 DIFFERENTIATED INSTRUCTION

Strategy for Special-Needs Students
Students may need help in understanding the letter format. Provide each student with sticky notes in two colors, and have them mark letters from Janet with one color and letters from Richard with another color.

🟢 Strategy for English Learners
Some informal phrases in the story may need explanation. For example, Richard accuses Janet of being "the kind who'd kick a man when he's down." This phrase means she is being deliberately cruel in her comments because she knows he already has a lot of problems with the team. Janet offers Richard a "package deal." This response means he must agree to take all four girls.

Close Reading Activities

READ

Comprehension

1. They had been close friends.

2. Richard won't let her play on his baseball team.

3. The team keeps losing games and players.

4. Richard agrees to let Janet pitch and to let Janet's friends play on the team.

Research: Clarify Details

Students' paragraphs should explain how their research helped them understand the selection.

Summarize

Students' summaries should describe the conflict and the general nature of the dialogue, identify events that change Richard's negotiating position, and describe the conflict resolution.

Language Study

Possible responses:

• *former*: synonym—*previous*; Melanie visited her *former* school when she came home from college.

• *unreasonable*: not rational; His boss made *unreasonable* demands so he quit and found another job.

Students' sentences should show an understanding of the meaning of each word.

Literary Analysis

Possible responses appear below. Check to be sure students support their responses with evidence from the text.

1. (a) Janet explains that Richard's team has lost eight games in a row. **(b)** Richard's team has an "un-broken record" of losing, so people may make fun of him being on a losing team.

2. Janet wants to show that she is a good player.

3. (a) Janet is expressing that she didn't start the fight. She is only responding to being hurt first. **(b)** Students may suggest that the passage would have been less effective because it would have been less interesting for readers if Janet simply stated what she felt.

READ

Comprehension

Reread the text to help you answer these questions.

1. What was Janet's and Richard's relationship before their argument?

2. Why is Janet angry?

3. What happens to Richard's baseball team?

4. What does Richard finally agree to do?

Language Study

Selection Vocabulary Write a synonym for each boldfaced word. Then, use the boldfaced words in sentences.

Literary Analysis

Reread the identified passage. Then, respond to the questions:

> **Focus Passage** *(pp. 275–276)*
> Congratulations on your un-broken record... We might be able to let you catch next week.

Key Ideas and Details

1. (a) Infer: Why is Richard a "laughingstock"? **(b)** What story details support your inference?

2. Infer: Why does Janet tell Richard her batting average?

Characterization

Authors use characterization to develop characters and reveal their unique traits, or qualities.

1. What traits are revealed in the notes the two characters write to each other?

Research: Clarify Details Choose one unfamiliar reference in the story and research it. Then, write a brief paragraph explaining how your research helped you understand the story.

Summarize Write an objective summary of the story. Objective summaries are free from opinions.

• Your **former** friend, Janet."

• Nobody ever said that I was **unreasonable**.

Craft and Structure

3. (a) Interpret: What feeling does Janet express when she says, "I wasn't kicking exactly. I was kicking back"? **(b) Evaluate:** Would this passage have been as effective if the author had directly stated Janet's feelings? Explain.

Integration of Knowledge and Ideas

4. (a) Describe the format of this story. **(b) Analyze:** Why do you think the author chose this structure?

2. What character traits help Janet resolve her conflict with Richard?

4. (a) The story is presented in a series of letters. **(b)** The format allows the author to create an interesting dialogue that reveals the events.

Characterization

1. Both characters are angry at each other and determined to have the baseball team only include the people they want.

2. When both characters are willing to compromise and respect each other's skills and viewpoints, they are able to resolve the conflict.

DISCUSS • RESEARCH • WRITE

From Text to Topic **Group Discussion**

Discuss the first exchange between Janet and Richard with a group of classmates. Take notes during the discussion. Contribute your own ideas, and support them with examples from the text.

> "Dear Richard, Don't invite me to your birthday party… when you go for your checkup you need a tetanus shot." (p. 274)

Research **Investigate the Topic**

Teams and Clubs Youth baseball teams are popular around the world.

Assignment

Conduct research to learn about the worldwide popularity of baseball. Take clear notes that identify your sources so that you can easily access the information later. Share your findings in an **annotated list.**

Writing to Sources **Persuasive Letter**

"The Southpaw" focuses on a girl's efforts to join a baseball team. People often have to persuade others about the value of their skills and talents.

Assignment

From Janet's perspective, write a formal **persuasive letter** to Richard's team, presenting your qualifications and arguing that you are a good candidate for membership. You can make up additional skills and experience. Follow these steps:

- Present facts and evidence to support your claim that you are qualified to be a member of the team.
- **Anticipate** and respond to any arguments the group might have against your becoming a member.
- **Conclude** by restating your position and summarizing how your membership will benefit the team.

QUESTIONS FOR DISCUSSION

1. In this quarrel, which statements are fair? Which are not?
2. Is this disagreement worthy of breaking up a friendship? Why or why not?

PREPARATION FOR ESSAY

You may use the results of this research project to support your ideas in the essay at the end of this section.

ACADEMIC VOCABULARY

Academic terms appear in blue on these pages. If these words are not familiar to you, use a dictionary to find their definitions. Then, use them as you speak and write.

Common Core State Standards

RL.6.1, RL.6.2, RL.6.3, RL.6.4, RL.6.5; W.6.2, W.6.4; SL.6.1, SL.6.4
[For full standards wording, see the chart in the front of this book.]

Writing to Sources: Persuasive Letter

Students' persuasive letters should follow the steps listed in order. The letter should be from Janet's perspective and use and expand on information from the text. Remind students to end their letter with strong restatement of how they can help the team become more successful.

 Online Writer's Notebook

Students can use the Online Writer's Notebook to record all responses.

DISCUSS • RESEARCH • WRITE

From Text to Topic: Group Discussion

1. **Possible response:** It's fair for Janet to talk about the baseball team, and for Richard to respond. It's not fair to bring up unrelated things like comic books or wish bad luck on one another.
2. **Possible response:** No, because they can find an easy solution to the disagreement.

Research: Investigate the Topic

Introduce the assignment, using the instruction on the student page.

1. Arrange for students to visit your school's library or computer lab. Review strategies for identifying reliable sources. Students are likely to need Internet sources for research on the worldwide popularity of baseball. Review that sites ending in .edu or .gov. are usually more reliable than sites ending in .com.
2. Have students take notes, either by directly quoting or by summarizing in their own words. Their notes should include information about each source.
3. Encourage students to draw conclusions from multiple sources.
4. Remind students to practice so that they do not need to read directly from their list when presenting. In addition, preparation will help them be prepared to answer questions.

Academic Vocabulary

If students struggle with defining the academic vocabulary words, use this routine:

Write the words and definitions on the board.

anticipate: expect

conclude: to determine by reason

Have students say the word aloud. Then have them use the word in a sentence. Sample sentences should demonstrate that the words can be used across disciplines.

MULTIDRAFT READING

Essential Understanding

First, students should read the entire selection on their own. Then, to assist struggling readers and to deepen comprehension for all, you may wish to guide them through the selection by asking them the close reading questions provided in the margins. Have students apply the multidraft reading protocols as they examine specific "chunks" of text related to these questions. For each reading, have students set the purpose indicated:

- **First reading:** Students should read the selection independently and think about its basic meaning.
- **Second reading:** Students should analyze the text's key ideas and details and its craft and structure.
- **Third reading:** Students should integrate knowledge and ideas; connect to the Big Question, other texts, and the world; and use teacher-led Close Reading discussion questions to examine particularly rich and significant passages.

For more guidance, refer to the *Classroom Strategies and Teaching Routines* card on multidraft reading.

❶ Focus Passage

A Focus Passage is identified with brackets in the Student Edition of this page for students' independent close reading and analysis. A question bank for the passage and possible responses appear at the end of the selection.

Vocabulary

If students require support with selection vocabulary, use this routine:

1. Write the following words and definitions on the board:

   hallowed *adj.* sacred; highly honored; holy

   cultivate *v.* to grow or nurture

   facade *n.* front or face of a building

2. Have students say each word aloud.

3. Use the word in a sentence that defines the word.

Published April 20, 2012 / FoxNews.com

Fenway Park Celebrates 100 Years as America's Oldest Working Major League Ballpark

By Molly Line

America's oldest working Major League ballpark, Boston's Fenway Park, is 100 years old Friday, and the park is celebrating.

What better way to kick off the next century of competition between two teams that make up one of the greatest rivalries in sports than with a rematch?

The Red Sox played the New York Yankees, the same team they played on April 20, 1912, when the opponent was called the New York Highlanders.

Both teams wore throwback uniforms, and fans manned the stands as they've done for generations—staring out across the hallowed ground where the greats of the game, like Babe Ruth and Ted Williams, once rounded the bases.

And while the hometown team ended up losing 6–2 on Friday to the Bronx Bombers,[1] the season is young and Fenway remains.

"This is what I like about Fenway...the family feel of it. Generations upon generations upon generations have brought their kids here for a long time," said Cory Sprague, a father who brought his family, including three sons, to enjoy Thursday's Open House held at Fenway Park. The Red Sox invited the public to wander the historic grounds and soak up the history.

"You want to drape the atmosphere in sentiment, emotion, and nostalgia, and try to stimulate memories," said Charles Steinberg, a senior advisor to team president Larry Lucchino. Steinberg was the executive vice president of public affairs for the Red Sox from 2002 through 2007.

hallowed ▶
(hal´ōd) *adj.* sacred; highly honored; holy

1. **Bronx Bombers** popular nickname for the New York Yankees baseball team.

Ⓒ TEXT COMPLEXITY **RUBRIC**

Fenway Park Celebrates 100 Years as America's Oldest Working Major League Ballpark		
Qualitative Measures	Context/Knowledge Demands	Contemporary U.S.; baseball 1 ② 3 4 5
	Structure/Language Conventionality and Clarity	Conversational; direct quotations; some difficult vocabulary; longer sentences 1 2 ③ 4 5
	Levels of Meaning/ Purpose/Concept Level	Accessible concept (appreciating a beloved national landmark) 1 2 ③ 4 5
Quantitative Measures	Text Length	Word Count: 788
	Lexile	1200L

Memories are easy to **cultivate** on the historic grounds. Fans still pack the park's narrow wooden seats, built for a slimmer population, surrounded by hallowed ground.

"If you come up on the **facade** on Yawkey Way it still looks very much the same as it did in 1912," said Saul Wisnia, the author of "Fenway Park, The Centennial: 100 Years of Red Sox Baseball." That volume is packed with historic photos and a DVD hosted by retired Red Sox catcher Carlton Fisk.

◄ **cultivate**
(kul′tə vāt′) *v.* to grow or nurture

◄ **facade**
(fə säd′) *n.* front or face of a building

1. **Key Ideas and Details** Read aloud the passage to students. **Ask:** Why does Cory Sprague visit Fenway Park?

   Possible response: The ballpark had an Open House and invited people to visit the historic grounds.

2. **Craft and Structure**
   Ask: What does the author's repetition of *generations* mean?

   Possible response: The author repeats this phrase three times to emphasize how families have been coming to the ballpark for many years.

   Integration of Knowledge and Ideas
   Ask: How does the repetition of *generations* reflect the importance of Fenway Park?

   Possible response: The ballpark is important to many families because it is a continued tradition in which they go to the games with friends and family.

PART 3 • Fenway Park Celebrates 100 Years **281**

© **TEXT COMPLEXITY READER AND TASK SUGGESTIONS**

Fenway Park Celebrates 100 Years as America's Oldest Working Major League Ballpark

Preparing to Read the Text
• Discuss baseball stadiums and their typical design. Where do the players sit when they are not on the field? Where do the fans sit?
• Talk about specific experiences students have had at ballparks, either major league or neighborhood parks.
• Guide students to use Multidraft Reading strategies on the previous page.

Leveled Tasks
Knowledge Demands If students will have difficulty with the use of direct quotations, have them read the article, make notes about several quotes, and identify the person who is quoted in each. Then have students take turns rereading aloud a quote they chose and discuss with the class the meaning and significance of the words as they relate to the 100th celebration of Fenway Park.

Evaluating If students will not have difficulty with the use of direct quotations, then have them read and note details about memorable occasions in the ballpark and why Fenway Park is unique among ballparks.

 **Audio**

Selection Audio is available in the **Student eText** and on the **Hear It!** CD-ROM.

❸ Close Reading

1. Key Ideas and Details Have a student read the passage aloud. **Ask:** What important change happened in the 1960s, and what was its effect on Fenway Park?

Possible response: The 1967 team started winning. The effect was that people started coming back to the ballpark to watch games.

2. Craft and Structure
Ask: What words and phrases does the author choose to describe the ballpark before and after the team started winning? What figure of speech does the author use?

Possible response: The author describes the ballpark in 1967 as "broken down," and then says it became a "magical spot" when the "Impossible Dream Team" began winning. Describing the change as "a stay of execution" gives the inanimate park a human quality, which is called *personification*.

3. Integration of Knowledge and Ideas
Ask: How is it possible for the park to go from "broken down" to "magical" without changes to the furnishings or physical structure? What really changed?

Possible response: The ballpark changed in the fans' perception when they had a chance to cheer for a winning team.

"I really think what makes Fenway so unique—and maybe Wrigley Field is the only (other) park that can say this is—it really goes back to the early days of baseball," Wisnia said. "These new ballparks kind of have that feel, but Fenway, you can actually say Babe Ruth played here. Ted Williams played here."

Throughout the decades, onlookers from every walk of life cheered in the stands. In 1944, President Franklin D. Roosevelt gave his final campaign speech from Fenway. In the '60s, Catholic nuns had their own day, filling the stands in their black and white habits.

Fenway has lasted a century but its future has not always been secure.

"There's actually been two times when Fenway was on the endangered species list," said Wisnia. "First in the 1960s when the Red Sox were drawing terribly after Ted Williams retired. They actually had a couple games where there were under 500 people here, if you can believe that, and Tom Yawkey, the owner, was really thinking of trying to get a new stadium, a dome stadium perhaps or moving it out to the suburbs."

The headlines didn't look good for Fenway but then something incredible happened. The 1967 team started winning.

"That was the Impossible Dream Team. The ballpark started getting filled up and all of a sudden Fenway went from kind of this broken down old park to kind of a magical spot and that kind of gave it a stay of execution," said Wisnia.

Fenway was on the chopping block again in the 90s. The owners thought a new park was needed to stay competitive with other big-city teams that were laying the groundwork for new mega-stadiums with shopping plazas and vast parking lots.

A grassroots movement to save Fenway was organized. Soon new ownership took over and under the leadership of John Henry, Tom Werner and Larry Lucchino, Fenway got a $285 million dollar facelift, including added seats above the famous Green Monster[2] and other spots, new restaurants, widened concourses,[3] HD monitors and more.

---

2. **Green Monster** popular name for a 37-foot-high green wall in left field at Fenway Park.
3. **concourse** (kän′kôrs′) *n.* large open area inside or outside of a building.

 THINK ALOUD

Compare and Contrast
Direct students' attention to the paragraph beginning "I really think what makes Fenway so unique." Use the following think aloud process to model identifying and analyzing comparisons and contrasts.

> I see that this paragraph is a quote from another writer. In the first sentence, I read that the writer claims Fenway Park is "unique." In the rest of the sentence, the writer compares Fenway to Wrigley Field because both have long histories as baseball parks. In the next sentence, I read the writer's contrast of Fenway to new parks. He believes Fenway is different because some of the greats in baseball, like Babe Ruth, played in Fenway. Through comparison and contrast, the author shows that Fenway's long history makes it special.

Ted Williams bats against the New York Yankees, 1960

"It is so wonderful to be here. This is home for anybody in Red Sox Nation to come in here, with what's going on in the world, it is a very happy place," said Jeannette Gallagher. The 70-year-old says she's been a fan since she was a little girl.

"As we have been planning the 100th anniversary, one of the things you wonder is what did they think 100 years ago?"

mused Steinberg. "Did they have the vision to imagine that the ballpark would live 100 years and then, what is our vision? Will it be here for its 200th—can you imagine the Fenway Park bicentennial?"

Many in Red Sox Nation, sitting in the stands where their grandparents cheered, hope their own grandchildren will see the day.

Big Question: Toward Essential Understanding

❹

1. Read aloud the passage. **Ask:** Why did the owners think it was necessary to change or replace Fenway in the 90s?

   Possible response: The owners thought it was important to have a ballpark that was up-to-date in order to compete with the planned mega-stadiums of other teams.

2. **Ask:** What happened to save the park?

   Possible response: People organized a grassroots effort, meaning that the movement started at the lowest level with the fans. Then new ownership decided on a costly renovation instead of a new park.

3. Have students compare and contrast the enthusiasm of 1967 and the 1990s.

   Ask: What was the difference between what saved Fenway Park each time? What actions by the fans played a role in each situation?

   Possible response: The winning "Impossible Dream Team" brought fans to the games in 1967. In the 1990s, a big investment in the ballpark facilities turned the situation around. In the first case, the renewed enthusiasm of fans for a winning team saved the park. In the second case, the fans' grassroots efforts gained the attention of the new owners and helped to save Fenway Park.

✺ DIFFERENTIATED INSTRUCTION

Strategy for Less Proficient Readers
Students may need help with some of the informal expressions and specialized vocabulary in the article. Provide the following words and definitions, read the sentence context in the selection, and then have students use the word in a sentence of their own.

kick off: begin or start (p. 280)

soak up: spend time experiencing and feeling something (p. 280)

on the chopping block: at risk of being gone (p. 282)

mega-stadium: large, important stadium (p. 282)

facelift: a renovation that improves the outward appearance (p. 282)

ⓒ **Close Reading Activities**

READ

Comprehension

1. They are both very old. They go back to the early days of baseball.

2. The team's success saved the ballpark from being torn down.

3. It got a "facelift" with added seats and features, such as restaurants, TV monitors, and enlarged areas.

Research: Clarify Details

Students should identify the detail they researched, describe what they found, and explain how their research helped them understand the article.

Summarize

Students' summaries should identify Fenway Park as major league baseball's oldest park, briefly recap the opinions expressed by the sources quoted, and describe changes that Fenway Park has undergone.

Language Study

Possible responses:

- *hallowed*: sacred; highly honored; holy
- *cultivate*: to grow or nurture
- *facade*: front or face of a building

Student sentences should demonstrate an understanding of the word's meaning.

Literary Analysis

Possible responses appear below. Check to be sure students support their responses with evidence from the text.

1. The Red Sox and the Yankees are rivals. The text describes a rematch between "One of the greatest rivalries in sports."

2. **(a)** She means that there are still more games left to play during the baseball season. **(b)** One game is a small number of games and "young" compared to the many games played over the years at Fenway Park. The article is about the history of Fenway Park, and the word *young* contrasts with its history.

3. *Hallowed ground* suggests the author considers Fenway Park almost sacred. This echoes the article's reverent tone.

READ

Comprehension

Reread all or part of the text to help you answer the following questions.

1. How are Fenway Park and Wrigley Field different from other ballparks?

2. Why was the "Impossible Dream Team" important to Fenway Park?

3. How was Fenway Park changed in the 1990s?

Language Study

Selection Vocabulary Define these words from the article. Then, use each word in a sentence of your own.

- … staring out across the **hallowed** ground …

Literary Analysis

Reread the identified passage. Then, respond to the questions that follow:

> **Focus Passage** *(p. 280)*
> What better way to kick off … the season is young and Fenway remains.

Key Ideas and Details

1. What is the relationship between the Red Sox and the Yankees? **Cite** details to support your answer.

Figurative Language

Writers and speakers use figurative language, such as creative comparisons, to create vivid images and emphasize key points. Note specific comparisons in the article.

1. **Baseball (a)** What is the writer comparing in this sentence: "Fenway

Research: Clarify Details Briefly research one unfamiliar detail from the article. Then, explain how your research sheds light on an aspect of the article.

Summarize Write an objective summary of the article. Objective summaries are free from opinion and evaluation.

- Memories are easy to **cultivate** on the historic grounds.
- If you come up on the **facade** …

Craft and Structure

2. **(a) Interpret:** What does the author mean when she says, "the season is young"?
   (b) Analyze: Why might she have used *young*, and not a different word?

Integration of Knowledge and Ideas

3. **Analyze:** How does the author's use of the term "hallowed ground" reflect the overall message of the article?

was on the endangered species list"?
(b) What idea does this comparison express?

2. Identify one other creative comparison in the article and explain its effect.

Figurative Language

1. **(a)** The author compares the park to an animal about to become extinct. **(b)** The comparison evokes sympathy for the park.

2. "Fenway was on the chopping block" compares the park to an object on a piece of wood used to chop food or wood. It suggests that Fenway was to be chopped up, or destroyed.

DISCUSS • RESEARCH • WRITE

From Text to Topic **Group Discussion**

Compose a quick written response to the following passage. Then share and discuss your response with a small group of classmates. Support your ideas with examples from the text and from your own experience.

> "That was the Impossible Dream Team. The ballpark started getting filled up and all of sudden Fenway went from kind of this broken down old park to kind of a magical spot and that kind of gave it a stay of execution," said Wisnia.

Research **Investigate the Topic**

Popular Stadiums Fenway Park may be the oldest major league ballpark still in use, but many sports stadiums are well-loved and **unique** in their own ways.

Assignment

Conduct research to identify and learn about a ballpark or sports stadium that interests you. Consult electronic and print resources. Take clear notes and carefully identify your sources so that you can easily access the information later. Share your findings in an **informal presentation** to a group of students.

Writing to Sources **Argument**

Fenway has lasted for more than 100 years, but some fans think the park should be replaced with a newer facility.

Assignment

Write an **argument** in which you take a position on whether or not Fenway Park should be replaced with a new, modern stadium. Follow these steps:

- Introduce Fenway Park and its history.
- Explain the issue and clearly state your **position**.
- Support your claim with evidence from the text.
- Conclude by reflecting on the issue and restating your claim.

QUESTIONS FOR DISCUSSION

1. How did people's opinion of Fenway Park change?
2. What caused the change of opinon?

PREPARATION FOR ESSAY

You may use the results of this research project to support your ideas in the essay at the end of this section.

ACADEMIC VOCABULARY

Academic terms appear in blue on these pages. If these words are not familiar to you, use a dictionary to find their definitions. Then, use them as you speak and write about the text.

 **Common Core State Standards**

RI.6.1, RI6.2, RI6.3, RI6.4, RI6.5; L.6.1, L.6.2, L.6.3, L.6.4, L.6.5; W.6.1, W.6.4; SL.6.1, SL.6.4
[For full standards wording, see the chart in the front of this book.]

DISCUSS • RESEARCH • WRITE

From Text to Topic: Group Discussion

1. **Possible response:** People liked the park again because it was associated with a winning team.
2. **Possible response:** People might come to associate the park with memories or with the emotions of winning seasons.

Research: Investigate the Topic

Introduce the assignment, using the instruction on the student page.

- Arrange for students to use your school's library or to have access to computers. Review the strategies for identifying reliable sources.
- Remind students to take notes, either by quoting directly or summarizing in their own words. They can use note cards or take notes on an electronic device such as a tablet.
- Encourage students to draw conclusions and make connections between multiple sources. Suggest that they prepare an outline for their presentation and create a Works Cited list that accurately identifies each source they reference.
- Suggest that students practice so that they do not need to read directly from their presentation outlines and are prepared to answer any questions.

Academic Vocabulary

If students struggle with defining the academic vocabulary words, use this routine:

Write the words and definitions on the board.

cite: to quote or mention in support

unique: different, unusual

position: a stand taken on a question

Have students say the word aloud. Then have them use the word in a sentence. Sample sentences should demonstrate that the words can be used across disciplines.

Writing to Sources: Argument

Students' arguments should clearly take a position for or against replacing Fenway Park and support it with evidence from the text.

 Online Writer's Notebook

Students can use the Online Writer's Notebook to record all responses.

MULTIDRAFT READING

Essential Understanding

First, students should read the entire selection on their own. Then, to assist struggling readers and to deepen comprehension for all, you may wish to guide them through the selection by asking them the close reading questions provided in the margins. Have students apply the multidraft reading protocols as they examine specific "chunks" of text related to these questions. For each reading, have students set the purpose indicated:

- **First reading:** Students should read the selection independently and think about its basic meaning.
- **Second reading:** Students should analyze the text's key ideas and details and its craft and structure.
- **Third reading:** Students should integrate knowledge and ideas; connect to the Big Question, other texts, and the world; and use teacher-led Close Reading discussion questions to examine particularly rich and significant passages.

For more guidance, refer to the *Classroom Strategies and Teaching Routines* card on multidraft reading.

❶ Close Reading

1. Key Ideas and Details

Ask: Why does Derek Jeter say he loves the game of baseball?

Possible response: Everyone can identify with the game's ups and downs.

2. Craft and Structure

Ask: What metaphors and similes does Jeter use?

Possible response: Jeter compares baseball's ups and downs to life and a soap opera.

3. Integration of Knowledge and Ideas

Ask: What effect do the metaphors and similes have on readers?

Possible response: The metaphors and similes help readers see the connection between baseball and life.

Why We Love Baseball

Players, management and fans chime in on Valentine's Day By Mark Newman / MLB.com

A record 76 million fans attended Major League Baseball games in 2006, and all signs point toward yet another single-season mark in 2007. On this Valentine's Day, MLB.com decided to investigate this torrid love affair more closely by asking people around the game this simple question: "Why do you love baseball?"

Yankees shortstop Derek Jeter: "I think because everybody can relate. You don't have to be seven feet tall; you don't have to be a certain size to play. Baseball is up and down. I think life's like that sometimes, you know. Back and forth, up and down, you're going through this grind. I think people like watching it. Baseball's like a soap opera every day."

Ernie Banks, Cubs legend and Hall of Famer: "It's just life. When I think about baseball, it's just life. It's really the way life is. It requires a lot of mental capacity to be involved in it. It creates a lot of joy for people and memories for people who follow it. It's a family. You like it because it's a family. You started with it and know all these people—it's family, it's friends, it's

286 UNIT 2 • What is important to know?

ⓒ TEXT COMPLEXITY **RUBRIC**

Why We Love Baseball		
Qualitative Measures	**Context/Knowledge Demands**	Contemporary U.S.; franchise management and player terms 1 2 ③ 4 5
	Structure/Language Conventionality and Clarity	Conversational tone; direct quotations; some difficult vocabulary; longer sentences 1 2 3 ④ 5
	Levels of Meaning/ Purpose/Concept Level	Accessible concept (enjoyment of a sport) 1 ② 3 4 5
Quantitative Measures	**Text Length**	Word Count: 1,175
	Lexile	840L

fun, it's a beautiful game. All in all, baseball is amazing. I wish everybody could play it for at least two years. I wish everybody—men and women."

Indians manager Eric Wedge: "The game gets inside you. It becomes a part of who you are, and you don't know anything different. It's just something you feel passionate about. If you really feel that strong about something and you feel something that special, it's really hard to put it into words. For me, the love of the game is a given. It's been the one constant that I've known, for as far back as I can remember."

A's general manager Billy Beane: "What I love is that when it is Valentine's Day you're getting real close going to Arizona, and to me there is something real pure about Spring Training. Most of us are getting out of a long winter, and it's nice to get outside and be in the sunshine in February. To me, Spring Training is my favorite time of year for baseball. It's the most relaxing time as an executive."

Phillies first baseman Ryan Howard: "I think it's just the overall atmosphere: to be able to come out in the summer, nice weather—you can bring

your kids and make it a family event. People just can come out and have fun."

Joel Kweskin, 56, White Sox fan based in Charlotte, N.C.: "It's unique unto itself. Football, basketball and hockey are variations of the same concept—back and forth in a linear progression to score a goal. Baseball, however, is mapped out on the field unlike any other sport. A running back or return specialist can run 100 yards, tops; a baserunner legging out an inside-the-park homer runs 20 yards farther. Baseball is the most democratic of sports— any size can play, and because the ball is not controlled by the offense but rather the defense, every player at any given time is involved in a play. Along with the anecdotally accepted premise that hitting a pitched baseball is the single most difficult thing to do in sports, so might be fielding a 175-mph line drive or grounder down the line. I love baseball because it is the greatest game ever invented."

Devil Rays manager Joe Maddon: "Makes you feel like a kid again every day, you do it every day. And that's what makes it so attractive."

Giants bench coach Ron Wotus: "Baseball has always

◄ **premise**
(prē′məs) *n.*
something assumed
or taken for granted

2 ❓ **Big Question: Toward Essential Understanding**

1. Read aloud the passage.

   Ask: Why does Ernie Banks love baseball?

   Possible response: He thinks it has all the elements of life.

2. Have students reread the passage and consider how Banks describes baseball.

   Ask: What does Banks value most in life and in baseball?

   Possible response: His answers focus on people, good memories, and a joy in living.

3. **Ask:** How is baseball important to people?

   Possible response: It mirrors what is enjoyable in life and it helps people create memories.

3 **Focus Passage**

A Focus Passage is identified with brackets in the Student Edition of this page for students' independent close reading and analysis. A question bank for the passage and possible responses appear at the end of the selection.

Vocabulary

If students require support with selection vocabulary, use this routine:

1. Write the following words and definitions on the board:

   premise *n.* something assumed or taken for granted

   ventured *v.* dared to do something risky

   diversion *n.* recreation; distraction from everyday tasks

2. Have students say each word aloud.

3. Use the word in a sentence that defines the word.

 **Audio**

Selection Audio is available in the **Student eText** and on the **Hear It!** CD-ROM.

ⓒ TEXT COMPLEXITY **READER AND TASK SUGGESTIONS**

Why We Love Baseball

Preparing to Read the Text
• Discuss major league baseball teams and players familiar to students.
• Talk about the positions in baseball, including players, coaches, and managers.
• Guide students to use Multidraft Reading strategies on the previous page.

Leveled Tasks
Knowledge Demands If students will have difficulty with the longer sentences in the quotations, remind them to use punctuation to read in meaningful units. For example, a period indicates the end of a thought, while a comma indicates a brief pause. A semicolon is used to separate two closely related ideas.

Synthesizing If students will not have difficulty with the longer sentences, then have them read and note details about the reasons people give for why they love baseball. Have them note reasons that are repeated by several people.

➍ Close Reading

1. Key Ideas and Details Have a student read the passage aloud. **Ask:** According to Willie Wilson, what makes baseball so well-loved?

Possible response: He says a player's size is not important in baseball, so anyone can play. Since many people have played softball or baseball of some kind, they can relate to the sport.

2. Craft and Structure Have students reread the passage and make notes on how Wilson compares and contrasts baseball and other sports.

Ask: How does Willie compare and contrast baseball to other sports?

Possible response: In basketball, players have to be tall and able to jump. Football players are usually big, meaning that not everyone is able to play the game. In contrast, most people have played some kind of softball or baseball, and the skills needed are common ones—catching a ball, swinging a bat, and hitting the ball.

3. Integration of Knowledge and Ideas
Ask: How do the comparisons and contrasts reveal the importance of baseball in America?

Possible response: Americans embrace, or cherish, baseball because they feel it is part of their own experience. No one is excluded because they lack size or special skills; many people grow up playing on teams or with a group of friends.

ventured ▶
(ven´chərd) *v.* dared to do something risky

been in my blood, and there's nothing like being on grass outdoors, playing the game. It's a great feeling just to hit the ball and have some success. The pace is slower and it's a thinking man's game, and there are so many different facets of it. And because so many people have played it, from Little League on up, they can still give their opinion on what's happening on the field, what kind of pitch should be thrown next."

Former Royals star Willie Wilson: "The first thing is, I don't think there's any criteria for size, so anybody can play. I think people can relate. A lot of people never played football; basketball, you've gotta be tall and be able to jump. But baseball is a game where you pick up a bat and a ball, and you catch it, you swing the bat and you hit the ball. Most people have played softball or some kind of baseball, so they can relate to the sport. For me, that's why I think America just embraces baseball, man."

A's outfielder Milton Bradley: "I just love getting together

diversion ▶
(də vʉr´zhən) *n.* recreation; distraction from everyday tasks

with a group of 25 guys and everybody is working together on a common goal. I like competition whatever the sport. Baseball for me is the hardest thing to do. That's why I **ventured** into baseball. It's more difficult than any other sport and I just liked the difficulty of it. I like a challenge."

Cyn Donnelly, 38-year-old Boston author of Red Sox Chick, the most popular fan-written MLBlog: "I love baseball because my parents love baseball and even as a kid I knew it could be something that connected us no matter what else was going on in our lives. I love watching young players come up, I love watching mediocre players do well, even if only for a game. I love watching a struggling player come out of a slump. I love seeing the unexpected, which happens an awful lot in baseball. Unlike any of the other major sports, baseball gives a team many chances to do well. In a three-game series with the opposing team, you can lose one game and still come out of the series up. It makes every minute of the game 'important'. Baseball is a wonderful **diversion** from my real life. Especially when my real life isn't going quite the way I planned."

🗨 VOCABULARY DEVELOPMENT

Selection Vocabulary Reinforcement
To reinforce and assess students' comprehension of selection vocabulary words, give them sentences using the words in which the word may or may not be used correctly. Students must tell whether the use is correct and explain their answer. Use these sentences.

1. Jamie explained her *premise* for wanting to take guitar lessons.
Answer: Yes, a *premise* can give an assumption or explanation.

2. Joe left the rest of us in the city and *ventured* off to see the countryside.
Answer: Yes, *ventured* is used correctly. Joe dared to go in spite of possible risks.

3. Mom takes work home every night as a *diversion* from her job.
Answer: No, a *diversion* is done for fun.

Royals outfielder David DeJesus: "It's such a team game. You can't rely on one guy to win the game. You build relationships, you make good friends out here, and you're having fun with 25 guys from different places all over the country. I grew up loving it because my Dad always loved it. We practiced together, we watched baseball games together, so it's one of those things I've always been around."

Royals outfielder Joey Gathright: "I can't really put it into words. It's not something I really grew up around in Mississippi. All they do is play football. But, when I was a kid, I was in awe of Rickey Henderson and Ken Griffey Jr., so I just fell in love with those guys and later I fell in love with baseball."

The Lealie family of Spring Valley, Calif.: During the recent FriarFest event, Jazmine, 4, tugged at father Marc all the way into PETCO Park, with 2-year-old brother Quincy bouncing in stride, eyes bright and alive. "Man, she loves this place," said Marc, formerly of Chicago. "I mean, Jazmine really loves PETCO Park, everything about it. These two are Junior Padres now. They come to games every Sunday. Her favorite player is Mike Cameron."

Lorenzo Bundy, manager of Mexico at the Caribbean Series and manager of the Dodgers' Triple-A Las Vegas affiliate: "I love the camaraderie and being around the guys. There is nothing like coming to the park and smelling the grass every day. It's the greatest game in the world … and on any given day anybody can win. That's how the ball bounces and that's fun. They are probably going to have to bury me in this uniform."

ABOUT THE AUTHOR

Mark Newman

Mark Newman has been a vice president of Nascar.com and *Sporting News* and the founder of two Internet firms. As Enterprise Editor at MLB.com, he has interviewed dozens of baseball professionals and fans. Newman is also a lifetime honorary member of the Baseball Writers Association of America.

---

⑤ Close Reading

1. **Key Ideas and Details** Read aloud the passage to students.
   Ask: What key idea does the first sentence of the quote from Cyn Donnelly convey?

   Possible response: Donnelly learned to love baseball while growing up. It was an interest that connected the family.

2. **Craft and Structure** Direct students to reread the passage and take notes on the ways that baseball appeals to Donnelly.

   Ask: What does the author's repetition of *I love* convey?

   Possible response: The repetition shows the emotion and family connection to baseball. It emphasizes that Donnelly is passionate about baseball. The listings of why baseball appeals to Donnelly explain his passionate love of the game.

3. **Integration of Knowledge and Ideas**
   Ask: How do the reasons Donnelly gives for loving baseball relate to the widespread appeal of baseball?

   Possible response: Most people like to watch a young person succeed, as well as cheer for someone who has been struggling and then achieves success. A game in which the unexpected is likely to happen draws and holds fans with the anticipation of being surprised. Each person may have many and unique reasons for loving the game.

DIFFERENTIATED INSTRUCTION

Strategy for Special-Needs Students
Before students read, lead a quick "selection tour." Focus their attention on the title and identify the selection as a Web article. Read with students the first paragraph that explains the article shows people's responses to the question, "Why do you love baseball?" Point to the boldface headings, and explain that these tell the name of the person and the person's connection to baseball.

Enrichment for Gifted/Talented Students
Ask students to work together to plan and then give a reader theater's performance of this article. Depending on the size of the group, they can do the entire selection or choose a number of responses. Suggest that students practice their roles and begin each comment by introducing the person who said the words. Remind students to express the person's enthusiasm for baseball.

Close Reading Activities

READ

Comprehension

1. The article was written for Valentine's Day, and it describes why people love baseball.

2. There are no size requirements. Anyone can play.

3. **Possible response:** Baseball creates a family, anyone can play, and the game requires thought.

Research: Clarify Details

Students should describe the results of their research and explain how it helped them understand the article.

Summarize

Students' summaries should explain that the article consists of comments in response to the question "Why do you love baseball?" and include brief statements of several key reasons mentioned by the responders.

Language Study

Possible responses:

• *premise*: something assumed or taken for granted

• *ventured*: dared to do something risky

• *diversion*: distraction from everyday tasks

Jenny *ventured* forth to try the martial arts class. She told her parents that her *premise* for taking the classes was to develop self-discipline. She assured them that this was not just a *diversion* for her.

Literary Analysis

Possible responses appear below. Check to be sure students support their responses with evidence from the text.

1. Teams move back and forth to score a goal.

2. **(a)** Main idea: Baseball is unique. **(b)** Three supporting details: (1) Baseball's playing field and scoring method are different from other sports; (2) Baseball is the most "democratic" sport; (3) Hitting a baseball is the most difficult task in sports. **(c)** Kweskin claims that baseball "is the greatest game ever invented" and effectively supports

READ

Comprehension

Reread all or part of the text to help you answer the following questions.

1. What is the connection between the timing of this article and its topic?

2. What observation do multiple speakers make about the physical size requirements of baseball?

3. Identify three reasons speakers give for loving baseball.

Language Study

Selection Vocabulary Define these words from the article, and then write a paragraph that includes all three words.

• premise
• ventured
• diversion

Literary Analysis

Reread the identified passage. Then, respond to the questions that follow.

> **Focus Passage** *(p. 287)*
> **Joel Kweskin, 56 ...** the greatest game ever invented.

Key Ideas and Details

1. What characteristics do football, basketball, and hockey have in common?

Word Choice

Word choice can have a powerful affect on the strength and meaning of a writer's or speaker's message. Highly charged words bring to mind strong feelings. Reread this article, noting each speaker's word choice.

290 UNIT 2 • What is important to know?

Research: Clarify Details Choose at least one unfamiliar detail from this article and briefly research it. Then, explain how your research helps you understand the article.

Summarize Write an objective summary of the article. Describe the nature of the article and state key ideas that are mentioned in at least two comments.

Craft and Structure

2. **(a) Infer:** What is the main idea in Joel Kweskin's response? **(b) Connect:** Cite three details Kweskin uses to support his main idea. **(c) Evaluate:** Does Kweskin support his claim effectively? Explain.

Integration of Knowledge and Ideas

3. **Compare and Contrast:** How are Kweskin's remarks similar to and different from the remarks of the sepakers quoted earlier in the article?

1. **Baseball** What do you think Derek Jeter means when he says, "Baseball's like a soap opera … ? Support your answer.

2. Ron Wotus says, "it's a thinking man's game"? What impression about baseball do these words create?

this claim with facts and examples about baseball and other sports before he concludes with the statement.

3. Kweskin's comments are similar to others because he compares and contrasts baseball with other sports. His descriptions are different because he discusses the difficult skills involved in playing baseball.

Word Choice

1. Jeter believes that baseball is like a soap opera because it is always changing. There are also frequent games, so people can watch them daily during baseball season.

2. Wotus's description of baseball as "a thinking man's game" shows people that a lot of thought goes into the game. Usually people think of games, such as chess, when they imagine "a thinking man's game." This reference shows that baseball requires more than just physical strength.

DISCUSS • RESEARCH • WRITE

From Text to Topic **Group Discussion**

Discuss the comment from Eric Wedge with a small group of classmates. Take notes during the discussion. Contribute your own ideas, and support them with examples from the text.

> The game gets inside you.... as far back as I can remember." (p. 287)

Research **Investigate the Topic**

Baseball in Literature The love of baseball has inspired many works of literature.

Assignment

Conduct research to find poems, novels, short stories, and essays about baseball. Consult print or Internet sources. Take clear notes and carefully identify your sources so that you can easily access the information later. Record your findings in an **annotated bibliography.**

Writing to Sources **Reflective Essay**

"Why We Love Baseball" presents the reasons why fans and players love baseball. The article makes clear the fact that different people enjoy things for different reasons.

Assignment

Write a **reflective essay** in which you describe your thoughts and feelings about a favorite interest or activity and explain why you like it. Follow these steps:

- Introduce the activity, briefly stating why it is interesting or fun.
- Present the reasons you like the activity, supporting each reason with personal examples, logic, **facts**, or details.
- Use transitional words and phrases to help you move smoothly from point to point.
- Conclude by reflecting upon the impact the activity has had on you. Make a connection between your feelings and the feelings expressed by the people quoted in the Web article.

QUESTIONS FOR DISCUSSION

1. What does Wedge mean by "The game gets inside you"?
2. Does Wedge's argument appeal to emotion or to reason? Which do you think makes a stronger argument? Why?

PREPARATION FOR ESSAY

You may use the results of this **research** project to support your ideas in the essay at the end of this section.

ACADEMIC VOCABULARY

Academic terms appear in blue on these pages. If these words are not familiar to you, use a dictionary to find their definitions. Then, use them as you speak and write about the text.

 Common Core State Standards

RI.6.1, RI.6.2, RI.6.4; L.6.1, L.6.2, L.6.3, L.6.4, L.6.5; W.6.2, W.6.4, W.6.7, W.6.10; SL.6.1
[For full standards wording, see the chart in the front of this book.]

Academic Vocabulary

If students struggle with defining the academic vocabulary words, use this routine:

Write the words and definitions on the board.

sources: books, people, or other publications that supply information

research: a collection of information about a subject

facts: truths from experience or observation

Have students say the word aloud. Then have them use the word in a sentence. Sample sentences should demonstrate that the words can be used across disciplines.

DISCUSS • RESEARCH • WRITE

From Text to Topic: Group Discussion

1. **Possible response:** The game becomes something that is always on your mind. You are thinking about it even when you are not actively involved in it.

2. Emotion; students may say emotion makes a stronger argument because it comes from a passionate belief, or they may say that reason makes a stronger argument because it is based on logic; students should support their responses.

Research: Investigate the Topic

Introduce the assignment, using the instruction on the student page.

1. Arrange for students to visit your school's library or computer lab. Review strategies for making sure sources are reliable.

2. Remind students to take notes. If they quote a print or Internet source, they should be sure the words are enclosed in quotation marks. They can also paraphrase or summarize in their own words.

3. Encourage students to draw conclusions and make connections between multiple sources.

4. Students should create a Works Cited list that includes each source they reference. Remind students to use proper formatting for the annotated bibliography.

Writing to Sources: Reflective Essay

Students' reflective essays should include all the elements mentioned and should connect students' feelings about their chosen interest back to the reasons that people give for loving baseball in "Why We Love Baseball."

 Online Writer's Notebook

Students can use the Online Writer's Notebook to record all responses.

Big Question: Toward Essential Understanding

1. Have students view the pictures on the front of the card and read the words that appear. **Ask:** What information do the pictures give? How is this information clarified by the words? How does this card connect to the topic of baseball?

Possible response: The pictures show a baseball hitter from two angles and a fanciful red sock with a bat. The information is clarified by the text because the player is identified as Ted Williams, who played in the outfield for the Boston Red Sox. The red sock with a bat is a kind of logo that represents the Boston Red Sox.

2. Direct students' attention to the back of the card. **Ask:** How does the factual information relate to the Big Question: *What is important to know?*

Possible response: The facts are important to know because they show that Williams was an outstanding hitter and a Most Valuable Player. Thus, they explain why he is remembered and honored today as a player.

Critical Viewing

Tell students that the card has different kinds of images: photographs, an imaginative cartoon character of a Red Sox player, and comic-strip style drawings of Williams at different times in his life. Explain that the photographs of Williams show him in two batting positions, which reflect his strengths. Point out that the fanciful red sock "batter" immediately lets viewers know that Ted Williams played for the Boston Red Sox and that the comic strip illustrations help to convey information about Williams' life in a brief, easy-to-follow format. Discuss how the two illustrations differ from each other and from the photographs.

292 UNIT 2 • What is important to know?

💬 VOCABULARY DEVELOPMENT

Academic Vocabulary

If students require support with academic vocabulary, write the following words and definitions on the board:

- **reveal:** make known or shown
- **contrast:** show differences between things

Have students say each word aloud. Then, use the word in a sentence that defines it.

Point out that academic vocabulary words can be used across print and visual disciplines. For example, both visual art forms and written text can *reveal* ideas and information. A text can *contrast* ideas and visual images can show a *contrast* of colors.

READ • WRITE

Comprehension

Review the baseball card to answer these questions.

1. Identify Ted Williams's team and position.
2. Was Williams still playing baseball when this card was issued? Cite evidence to support your answer.

Critical Analysis

Key Ideas and Details

1. Interpret: Does the information on the card emphasize Williams's career as a hitter or as a fielder? Explain.

2. Draw Conclusions: Did Williams get on base in the majority of games he played? Support your answer.

Craft and Structure

3. (a) Interpret: Describe the tone, or attitude, of the paragraph and captions on the back of the card. **(b) Analyze:** What specific details reveal the tone?

Integration of Knowledge and Ideas

4. Draw Conclusions: Do you think this baseball card holds a high value for collectors? Explain why or why not.

Writing to Sources **Narrative**

Write a brief **journal entry** from the point of view of a fan who recently watched Ted Williams hit a home run during a Red Sox game. Compare and **contrast** Williams' performance with that of other players. Describe the mood of the crowd and your character's feelings when Williams hit the home run. Use data and details from the baseball card, the other texts in this section, and your own experiences. Follow these steps:

• Describe the setting, characters, and events.
• Include sensory and concrete details to enrich your descriptions.
• Conclude by explaining your character's thoughts about the game and Ted Williams' performance.

ACADEMIC VOCABULARY

Academic terms appear in blue on these pages. If these words are not familiar to you, use a dictionary to find their definitions. Then, use them as you speak and write about the text.

 **Common Core State Standards**

RI.6.1, RI.6.6, RI.6.7; W.6.3, W.6.4; SL.6.4
[For full standards wording, see the chart in the front of this book.]

READ • WRITE

Comprehension

1. Williams played for the Boston Red Sox. He played in the outfield.

2. Williams was still playing when the baseball card was published. You can tell because the card refers to him as an "active player"—one who is still playing the game.

Critical Analysis

Possible responses appear below. Check to be sure students support their responses with evidence from the text.

1. The card emphasizes his career as a hitter. It describes Ted as one of the "greatest hitters of all time" and that he had "the highest Lifetime B.A (batting average) of any active player."

2. Yes, in his lifetime he played 1,464 games. He had 1,292 runs, which shows that he was on base the majority of times.

3. (a) The writer's tone is one of enthusiasm and admiration for Williams as a baseball player. **(b)** The writer's attitude is revealed in the first sentence of the paragraph on the back of the card: "Ted is one of the greatest hitters of all time!" Later details presented in the paragraph also reflect this tone.

4. It would probably be very valuable because Williams was a great baseball player with high averages; the card was issued while Williams was still playing—over 50 years ago—and pieces of baseball history, like this card, are highly valued by baseball fans.

Writing to Sources: Narrative

Students' journal entries should follow the steps listed and relate information from the baseball card, descriptive details from their own experiences, and additional facts and ideas from other texts in the section.

 Online Writer's Notebook

Students can use the Online Writer's Notebook to record all responses.

Speaking and Listening: Group Discussion

Introduce the assignment using the instruction on the student page.

1. Conduct discussions. Help students recall and apply their knowledge of the selections in this section to answer the discussion questions. For example, **ask:**

- Why is it important to Janet that she is allowed to play on Richard's team, and why does he at first refuse to let her join the team?

- Why are old baseball stadiums important to baseball fans?

- What do we learn about ourselves by reading about the courage of the first black player to integrate the major leagues, a speech in Congress to preserve the tradition of wooden bats, and an article on why people love baseball?

2. Summarize and present your ideas. Remind students that when they summarize their findings, they should try to represent a range of ideas that came out of their group's discussion.

Criteria for Success

Circulate around the room and observe group discussions. Support groups in their efforts to conduct organized, focused, balanced, and respectful discussions. Ask guiding questions if the conversation lags, and encourage students to make connections between ideas and experiences from different sources and to explore contrasts in the texts' portrayals or points of view. Emphasize that students should support all points with specific text evidence.

Use New Vocabulary

Assist students in using new vocabulary during group discussion. For example, **ask:**

- What characteristics about baseball makes it *exhilarating* for so many people of both genders and all ages?

- What *former* players and baseball traditions are important to fans today?

 Assessment: Synthesis

Speaking and Listening: **Group Discussion**

Baseball and Knowledge The texts in this section vary in genre, length, style, and perspective. However, all of the texts relate in some way to America's love of baseball, as a game and as an institution. The subject of American baseball and the traditions that surround it is fundamentally related to the Big Question this unit addresses: **What is important to know?**

> **Assignment**
>
> **Conduct discussions.** With a small group of classmates, conduct a discussion about people's love and knowledge of baseball. Refer to the texts in this section, other texts you have read, and your personal experience and knowledge to support your ideas. Begin your discussion by addressing the following questions:
>
> - Why is baseball in all its forms—from T-ball to the major leagues—important to Americans of all ages?
> - What traditions have grown around baseball, and how do they affect the people who play and love the game?
> - How can knowing about the game of baseball, its history, and its traditions help us understand ourselves?
>
> **Summarize and present your ideas.** After you have fully explored the topic, summarize your discussion for the class.

Criteria for Success

✓ **Organizes the group effectively**
Appoint a group leader and a timekeeper. The group leader should present the discussion questions. The timekeeper should make sure the discussion takes no longer than 20 minutes.

✓ **Maintains focus of discussion**
As a group, stay on topic and avoid straying into other subject areas.

✓ **Involves all participants equally and fully**
No one person should monopolize the conversation. Rather, everyone should take turns speaking and contributing ideas.

✓ **Follows the rules for collegial discussion**
As each group member speaks, others should listen carefully. Build on one another's ideas, and support viewpoints and opinions with sound reasoning and evidence. Express disagreement respectfully.

294 UNIT 2 • What is important to know?

Common Core State Standards

SL.6.1.a-d, SL.6.4
[For full standards wording, see the chart in the front of this book.]

USE NEW VOCABULARY

As you speak and share ideas, work to use the vocabulary words you have learned in this unit. The more you use new words, the more you will "own" them.

Writing: Autobiographical Narrative

Baseball and Knowledge All writing is rooted in the author's knowledge and experience. Sports, such as baseball, play a large role in the lives of many Americans.

Common Core State Standards

W.6.3.a-e, W.6.4, W.6.10
[For full standards wording, see the chart in the front of this book.]

> **Assignment**
>
> In an **autobiographical narrative**, describe a situation in which your level of knowledge about a sport affected you either positively or negatively. Focus on a time when you either participated in or observed the sport. Present a sequence of significant events and thoughts that, taken together, create a picture of an experience that had a lasting effect upon you.

Criteria for Success

Purpose/Focus

✓ **Connects specific incidents with larger ideas**
Make meaningful connections between your experiences and the texts you have read in this section.

✓ **Clearly conveys the significance of the story**
Provide a conclusion in which you reflect on what you experienced.

Organization

✓ **Sequences events logically**
Structure your narrative so that individual events build on one another to create a coherent whole.

Development of Ideas/Elaboration

✓ **Supports insights**
Include both personal examples and details from the texts you have read in this section.

✓ **Uses narrative techniques effectively**
Even though an autobiographical narrative is nonfiction, it may include storytelling elements like those found in fiction. Consider using dialogue to help readers "hear" how characters sound.

Language

✓ **Uses description effectively**
Use sensory language and vivid descriptive details.

Conventions

✓ **Does not have errors**
Correct any errors in grammar, spelling, and punctuation.

WRITE TO EXPLORE

Writing is a way to clarify what you feel and think. This means that you may change your mind or get new ideas as you work. Allowing for this will improve your final draft.

Writing: Autobiographical Narrative

Introduce the assignment using the instruction on the student page.

Criteria for Success

1. **Purpose/Focus** Encourage students to identify meaningful connections or contrasts between their experiences, their research, and ideas explored in the texts. For example, **ask:**

   Have you, like Janet and Richard, ever argued or disagreed with someone about a sport? How did you resolve the issue or question?

2. **Organization** Encourage your students to structure their narratives in a logical way. Chronological order may be the most practical structure for most students.

3. **Development of Ideas/ Elaboration** Encourage students to vividly convey real people and events through the use of detail and dialogue. Point out effective models in the texts, such as Janet's statement in her letter to Richard, "Just because I'm a member of the ballet club doesn't mean I'm not a terrific ballplayer."

4. **Language** Instruct students to use strong verbs and descriptive images to portray the people and events.

5. **Conventions** In addition to a self-review, students should have someone else read their narratives to check for errors.

Write to Explore

Point out that students' thoughts and feelings about what they experienced might deepen or change as they write and reflect. As they conclude their narratives, encourage them to carefully consider what they have learned over the course of the writing experience in order to identify important observations they have made, insights they have gained, or conclusions they have drawn.

Writing to Sources: Expository Essay

Introduce the assignment using the instruction on the student page.

Prewriting and Planning

1. Choose texts. Explain that in order to identify and develop their own claims about the history and traditions of baseball, students will need to analyze in depth the people and ideas in two or more of the texts that they explored.

2. Gather details and identify key ideas.

- Remind students that details and key ideas should support the points of comparison and contrast.

- Instruct students to go back into the texts they have selected and review passages that are connected to the topic of baseball and how each passage reflects the author's attitude toward the sport.

- Encourage them to use a chart like the one shown to record each significant passage and identify what ideas it suggests about the concepts.

- Students may also wish to raise questions that the passage may help answer, such as *To what extent do injustices in baseball reflect society? To what extent do they reflect issues within organized baseball?*

- Students can then use these ideas to identify and develop an overall thesis about how understanding the place of baseball in American history and culture can help them learn more about themselves and a changing society.

Incorporate Research

Remind students to consider how they might use their prior research—about how gender discrimination in baseball is still practiced and how people have fought against the bias—to support their key idea in this essay.

Writing to Sources: Expository Essay

Baseball and Knowledge The related readings in this section represent a wide range of knowledge and insight about the game of baseball, its traditions, and its players. The selections raise questions, such as the following:

- What can we learn about our society from baseball?
- What draws people to a sport such as baseball? Is it the competition, the game itself, a specific team, traditions surrounding the sport, or a combination of these factors?
- How can we benefit from participating in sports such as baseball?

Focus on the question that intrigues you the most, and then complete the following assignment.

> **Assignment**
>
> Write an essay in which you compare and contrast the ways that two or more authors in this section portray baseball history and tradition. As you analyze each selection, pay particular attention to the details each author includes to support his or her claims. Clearly present, develop, and support your ideas with examples and details from the texts.

Prewriting and Planning

Choose texts. Review the texts in this section to determine which ones you will cite in your essay. Select at least two selections that will provide strong material to support comparisons and contrasts.

Gather details and identify key ideas. Use a chart like the one shown to develop your key ideas.

Focus Question: What can we learn about our society from baseball?

Text	Passage	Notes
"Jackie Robinson: Justice at Last"	The national pastime was loved by all America, but the major leagues were for white men only.	Authors imply criticism of major league baseball
"Memories of an All-American Girl"	The girls received lessons on how to charm a date, wear makeup and skirts, and sip tea like a lady.	Author reports on an unjust situation objectively, without judging it
Example key idea: While some authors view injustices in baseball as a reflection of society at large, others blame organized baseball for injustices in the sport.		

Common Core
State Standards

L.6.1, L.6.2, L.6.3; W.6.2.a-f,
W.6.4, W.6.5, W.6.9, W.6.10
[For full standards wording, see the chart in the front of this book.]

INCORPORATE RESEARCH

In your essay, use information you gathered as you completed the brief research assignments related to the selections in this section.

Drafting

Plan your ideas and support. Create an informal outline or list of ideas you want to present. Decide where you will include facts, quotations, and examples to support each point.

Organize to show comparisons and contrasts. Choose an organizational structure that will clearly show similarities and differences. You might use the block method, in which you present all of the details about one of the selections, then all the details about the other selection. Alternatively, you might use the point-by-point method, in which you discuss one feature of both selections, then another feature of both selections, and so on.

Frame and connect ideas. Consider beginning your essay with a compelling story or quotation to capture your readers' interest. Use transitional words and phrases to link the major sections of your essay and to clarify the relationships among your main ideas and supporting details. Write a strong conclusion that sums up your key points.

Revising and Editing

Focus on comparative and superlative adjectives. Review your essay to be sure you have used adjectives correctly. Use comparative adjectives—such as *older* and *more popular*—to compare two things. Use superlative adjectives—such as *oldest* and *most popular*—to compare three or more things.

© Common Core State Standards

L.6.1, L.6.2, L.6.3; W.6.2.a-d, f; W.6.4
[For full standards wording, see the chart in the front of this book.]

CITE RESEARCH CORRECTLY

When you quote from a source directly, use quotation marks to indicate that the words are not your own.

Self-Evaluation Rubric

Use the following criteria to evaluate the effectiveness of your essay.

Criteria	Rating Scale
Purpose/Focus Introduces a specific topic; provides a concluding section that follows from and supports the information or explanation presented	*not very .... very* 1 2 3 4
Organization Organizes complex ideas, concepts, and information to make important connections and distinctions; clearly shows comparisons and contrasts, uses appropriate and varied transitions to link the major sections, create cohesion, and clarify relationships among ideas	1 2 3 4
Development of Ideas/Elaboration Develops the topic with well-chosen, relevant, and sufficient facts, extended definitions, concrete details, quotations, or other information and examples appropriate to the audience's knowledge of the topic	1 2 3 4
Language Uses precise language and domain-specific vocabulary to manage the complexity of the topic; establishes and maintains a formal style and objective tone	1 2 3 4
Conventions Uses correct conventions of grammar, spelling, and punctuation	1 2 3 4

Self-Evaluation Rubric

Encourage students to rate their own essays objectively and to use the results to guide their revision process.

Cite Research Correctly

Review with students the correct format for citing different sources, such as books and print or online news articles. Provide examples of proper citations. Then, have students create a Works Cited list that correctly lists each source they reference in their essays.

Drafting

1. **Plan your ideas and support.**
   - Encourage students to create informal outlines to organize the main ideas in their essays.
   - Remind students that each of their points should be supported by evidence.

2. **Organize to show comparisons and contrasts.**
   - Have students refer to their prewriting and planning notes on preparing examples and details.
   - Remind students to choose one structure to use in presenting their comparisons and contrasts.

3. **Frame and connect ideas.**
   - Remind students that the introduction of their essay should make the reader want to know more.
   - The body of the essay should provide examples that support the thesis. They should include specific details that show comparisons and contrasts in the ways the author views and presents baseball history and traditions.
   - The conclusion should restate the thesis and leave readers with a lasting impression of its validity and insight.

Revising and Editing

Focus on comparative and superlative adjectives. Suggest that students share a draft of their comparison and contrast essay with a classmate or family member. Students should ask the reviewer the following questions:

- What comparative and superlative adjectives are used?
- Are comparative adjectives used when discussing two things?
- Are superlative adjectives used when discussing three or more things?
- What additional comparisons and contrasts might be included?

Explain that if students are only comparing and contrasting the information from two authors, they would use comparative adjectives.

Independent Reading

Titles featured on the Independent Reading pages at the end of each unit represent a range of reading, including stories, dramas, and poetry, as well as literary nonfiction and other types of informational text. Throughout, labels indicate the works that are CCSS Exemplar Texts. Choosing from among these featured titles will help students read works at increasing levels of text complexity in the grades 6–8 text complexity band.

Online Text Set

The selections that are a part of the Online Text Set are located in the **Student eText.**

Using Literature Circles

A literature circle is a temporary group in which students independently discuss a book.

Use the guidance in the *Professional Development Guidebook,* pp. 47–49, as well as the teaching notes on the facing page, for additional suggestions for literature circles.

ⓒ **Meeting Unit 2 Common Core State Standards**

Students can use books listed on this page to apply and to reinforce their mastery of the Common Core State Standards covered in this unit.

Introducing Featured Titles

Have students choose a book or books for independent reading. Assist them by previewing the titles, noting their subject matter and level of difficulty. **Note:** Before recommending a work to students, preview it, taking into account the values of your community as well as the maturity of your students.

ⓒ Independent Reading

Titles for Extended Reading

In this unit, you have read texts in a variety of genres, including literary nonfiction. Continue to read on your own. Select works that you enjoy, but challenge yourself to explore new topics, new authors, and works of increasing depth and complexity. The titles suggested below will help you get started.

INFORMATIONAL TEXT

Boy: Tales of Childhood
by Roald Dahl

Read this collection of funny—and true—stories to learn what Roald Dahl found important and fascinating in his own childhood. This **autobiography** shows that life can be just as comical and exciting as fiction.

Zlata's Diary: A Child's Life in Wartime Sarajevo
by Zlata Filipović

During the war in Bosnia and Herzegovina in the early 1990s, Zlata kept a **diary** recording the desperate situations her family faced in Sarajevo. Her diary provides an honest, unique view of what it is like to live during a war.

Adams on Adams
by John Adams   EXEMPLAR TEXT ⓒ

Editor Paul M. Zall explores John Adams's own writings to present this founding father's life and worldview. This **autobiographical** collection includes Adams's "Letter on Thomas Jefferson."

Discoveries: Digging for Answers

Build your knowledge in many subject areas as you read these **essays,** including "Searching for Pompeii," "Identifying Birds," "The Story of American Sign Language," and "The Measure of a Good Cook."

LITERATURE

A Wrinkle in Time
by Madeleine L'Engle
Square Fish, 2007   EXEMPLAR TEXT ⓒ

In this **fantasy novel,** two children, along with a friend, set out on a quest through time and space to find their missing father. In their travels, they become part of a galactic battle between good and evil.

The Number Devil: A Mathematical Adventure
by Hans Magnus Enzensberger
Granta Books, 2000   EXEMPLAR TEXT ⓒ

In this book, which is part math instruction and part good-humored **fantasy,** a boy who dislikes math dreams of meeting a number devil who teaches basic mathematical concepts in an entertaining way.

ONLINE TEXT SET

FOLK TALE
Why Monkeys Live in Trees Julius Lester

EDITORIAL
Jake Wood Baseball Is the Start of Something Special Reginald T. Dogan

POEM
Wilbur Wright and Orville Wright Rosemary and Stephen Vincent Benet

---

ⓒ TEXT COMPLEXITY **ALIGNING TEXTS WITH READERS AND TASKS**

Texts	Readers and Tasks
• *The Number Devil: A Mathematical Adventure* (Lexile: 580L) • *Zlata's Diary: A Child's Life in Wartime Sarajevo* (640L)	**Below-Level Readers** Allow students to focus on reading for content, and challenge them to interpret multiple perspectives.
• *A Wrinkle in Time* (Lexile: 740L) • *Discoveries: Digging for Answers* (Lexile: 785L)	**Below-Level Readers** Challenge students as they read for content. **On-Level Readers** Allow students to focus on reading for content, and challenge them to interpret multiple perspectives. **Advanced Readers** Allow students to focus on interpreting multiple perspectives.
• *Adams on Adams* • *Boy: Tales of Childhood* (Lexile: 1090L)	**On-Level Readers** Challenge students as they read for content. **Advanced Readers** Allow students to focus on reading for content, and challenge them to interpret multiple perspectives.

Preparing to Read Complex Texts

Attentive Reading As you read on your own, ask yourself questions like these to enrich your reading experience.

Common Core State Standards

Reading Literature/ Informational Text
10. By the end of the year, read and comprehend literature, including stories, dramas, and poems, and literary nonfiction in the grades 6–8 text complexity band proficiently, with scaffolding as needed at the high end of the range.

When reading literary nonfiction, ask yourself...

Comprehension: Key Ideas and Details

- Is the author writing about a personal experience or a topic he or she has studied? In either case, what are my expectations about the work?
- Are the ideas the author expresses important? Why or why not?
- Did the author live at a different time and place than the present? If so, how does that affect his or her choice of topic and attitude?
- Does the author express beliefs that are very different from mine? If so, how does that affect what I understand and feel about the text?

Text Analysis: Craft and Structure

- Does the author organize ideas so that I can understand them? If not, what is unclear?
- Does the author give me a new way of looking at a topic? If so, how? If not, why?
- Is the author an expert on the topic? How do I know?
- Does the author use a variety of evidence that makes sense? If not, what is weak?
- Does the author use words in ways that are both interesting and clear?

Connections: Integration of Knowledge and Ideas

- Does the work seem believable? Why or why not?
- Do I agree or disagree with the author's arguments or ideas? Why or why not?
- Does this work remind me of others I have read? If so, how?
- Does this work make me want to read more about this topic or explore a related topic? Why or why not?

Preparing to Read Complex Texts

1. Tell students they can be attentive readers by bringing their experience and imagination to the texts they read and by actively questioning those texts. Explain that the questions they see on the student page are examples of types of questions to ask about works of literary nonfiction.

2. Point out that, like writing, reading is a "multidraft" process, involving several readings of complete works or passages, revising and refining one's understanding each time.

Key Ideas and Details

3. As an example, review and amplify the first bulleted item. **Ask:** What key ideas and details could you cite as evidence that the author is writing about a personal experience?

   Possible response: You might cite evidence that the author uses the first-person pronoun "I" to narrate the story or that the author shares anecdotes from his or her own life to support the main idea.

Craft and Structure

4. **Ask:** What details of craft and structure would you use to evaluate whether or not a work captures your interest?

   Possible response: You might point to the author's effective use of descriptive language to pull you into the story or to something interesting that happens in the first paragraph.

Integration of Knowledge and Ideas

5. **Ask:** How would you determine whether or not a work seems believable?

   Possible response: You might point to the author's use of realistic details or a familiar setting.

6. Finally, explain to students that they should cite key ideas and details, examples of craft and structure, or instances of the integration of knowledge and ideas as evidence to support their points during a book discussion. After hearing the evidence, the group might reach a consensus or might agree to disagree.

TEXT COMPLEXITY **READER AND TASK SUPPORT SUGGESTIONS**

Independent Reading

Increased Support Suggest that students choose a book that they feel comfortable reading and one that is a bit more challenging. Pair a more proficient reader with a less proficient reader and have them work together on the more challenging text. Partners can prepare to read the book by reviewing questions on this student page. They can also read difficult passages together, sharing questions and insights. They can use the questions on the student page to guide after-reading discussion.

Increased Challenge Encourage students to integrate knowledge and ideas by combining the Big Question and the Unit Focus concepts in their approach to two or more featured titles.

For example, students might consider how characters in *The Number Devil: A Mathematical Adventure* and *A Wrinkle in Time* search for knowledge. In addition, students can focus on looking for details that indicate the author's purpose in literary nonfiction.

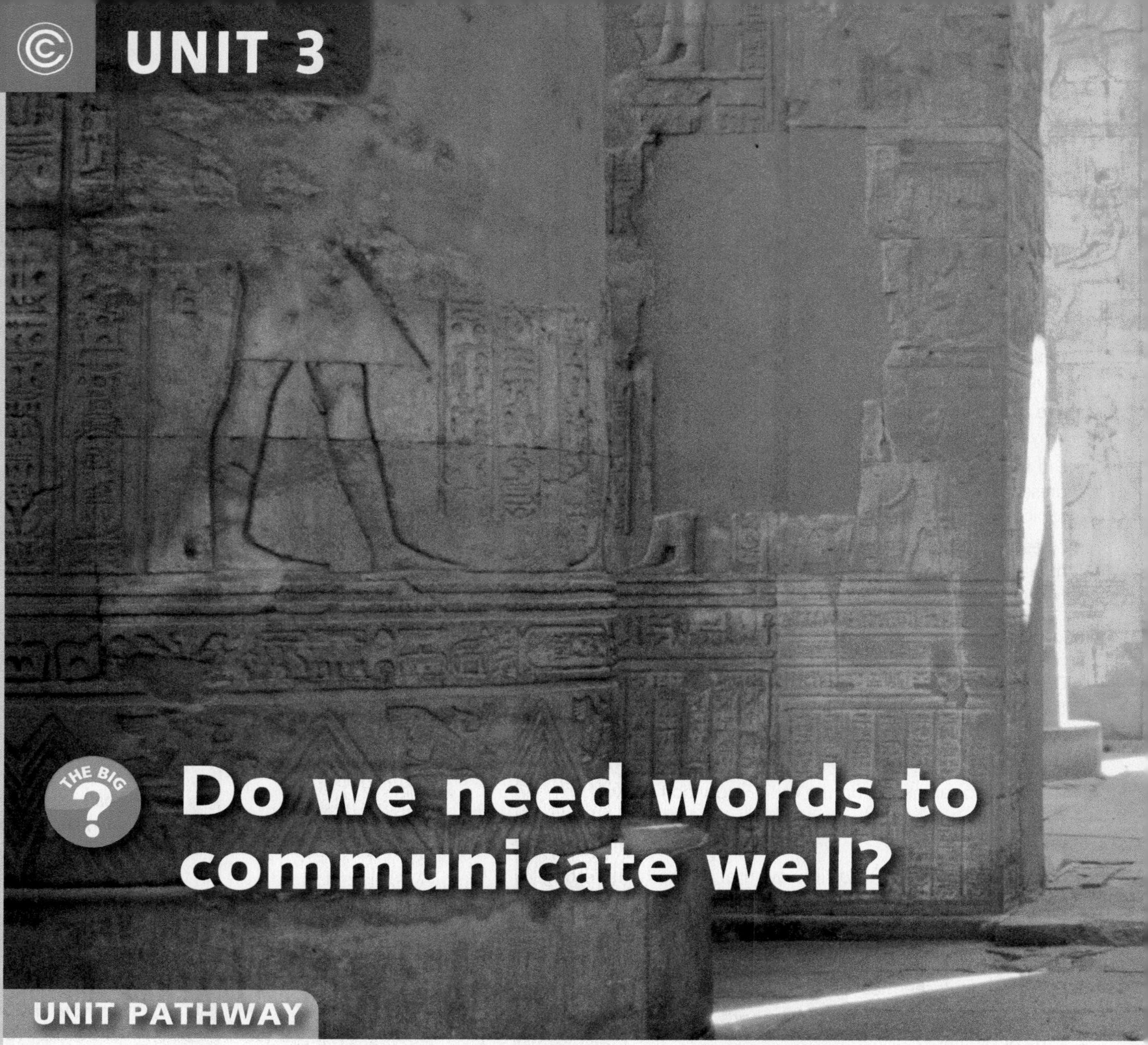

THE BIG ? Do we need words to communicate well?

UNIT PATHWAY

PART 1	PART 2	PART 3	PART 4
SETTING EXPECTATIONS	**TEXT ANALYSIS** GUIDED EXPLORATION	**TEXT SET** DEVELOPING INSIGHT	**DEMONSTRATING INDEPENDENCE**

- INTRODUCING THE BIG QUESTION
- CLOSE READING WORKSHOP

RHYTHM AND RHYME

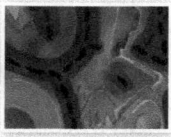

DETERMINATION

- INDEPENDENT READING
- ONLINE TEXT SET

CLOSE READING TOOL

Use this tool to practice the close reading strategies you learn.

STUDENT eTEXT

Bring learning to life with audio, video, and interactive tools.

WRITER'S NOTEBOOK

Easily capture notes and complete assignments online.

1 **Do we need words to communicate well?**

1. Shake your head side to side, and then **ask** students what that means. ("*No.*") **Ask** students to show and explain other gestures.

    Possible responses: waving, shrugging shoulders, shaking head up and down

2. **Ask** students the Big Question, Do we need words to communicate well?

    Possible response: No, we can use gestures and expressions.

3. Explain that the selections in this unit are poems, which express meaning with both words and the sound of words.

2 Exploring the Big Question

Collaboration: One-on-One Discussion

1. Introduce the activity, using the instruction on the student page.

2. Have students work individually to list examples. As they complete their lists, remind them to include some examples of nonverbal communication.

3. Review the Big Question vocabulary on the next page, following the teaching suggestions. Have students use the vocabulary as they complete the activity on this page.

Connecting to the Literature

Explain the Big Question strand in the unit, referring to the text at the bottom of this page.

 Introducing the Big Question

1  **Do we need words to communicate well?**

To communicate means to interact with others to promote understanding. Often, we use words to communicate our thoughts and feelings. However, we also use nonverbal communication methods that do not depend on words. An expression such as a smile or a frown can reveal your feelings. A gesture such as a wave or a nod can send a clear message, too.

2 Exploring the Big Question

Collaboration: One-on-One Discussion Start thinking about the Big Question by identifying various ways that we communicate with one another. List ways that people share thoughts and feelings. Describe examples of communicating information in the following situations:

- thanking someone for a gift
- asking for something you need or want
- persuading someone to change his or her mind
- sharing an important wish or dream
- listening to a friend share a difficult problem

Share ideas with a partner. Highlight examples that use nonverbal communication. Which of these examples are *at least* as effective as using words?

Connecting to the Literature Each reading in this unit will give you additional insight into the Big Question. As you read, consider the different methods authors use to communicate their ideas.

? DEVELOPING ESSENTIAL UNDERSTANDING

Do we need words to communicate well?
Explain to students that they will continue to consider the Big Question as they work through Unit 3.

- As students read each selection, they will look for details related to the Big Question and take notes.

- At the end of each selection, students will answer a Literary Analysis question that is related to the Big Question.

- Throughout the unit, students will deepen their knowledge of the selections and their understanding of the Big Question through

reading, speaking, listening, researching, and writing. By the end of the unit, students should understand how each selection relates to the Big Question individually and how the selections connect to one another through the Big Question.

- Tell students that their goal will be to gain a deeper understanding of literature and to develop a more sophisticated way of discussing the Big Question. Ultimately, students should use the Big Question as a springboard for their own questions that relate to their interests and concerns.

❸ Vocabulary

Acquire and Use Academic Vocabulary Academic vocabulary is the language you encounter in textbooks and on standardized tests. Review the definitions of these academic vocabulary words.

communicate (kə myōō´ ni kāt´) *v.* share thoughts or feelings, usually in words

correspond (kôr´ ə spänd´) *v.* communicate with by letter; agree with

quote (kwōt) *v.* use a speaker's or writer's words

reveal (ri vēl´) *v.* show; uncover

symbolize (sim´ bə līz´) *v.* stand for

visual (vizh´ ōō əl) *adj.* able to be seen with the eyes

Gather Vocabulary Knowledge Additional vocabulary words are listed below. Categorize the words by deciding whether you know each one well, know it a little bit, or do not know it at all.

connection	gesture	nonverbal
dialogue	language	share
expression	message	verbal

Then, do the following:

1. Write the definitions of the words you know.
2. If a word sounds familiar but you are not sure of its meaning, write down what you think the word means.
3. Then, using a print or an online dictionary, look up the meanings of the words you do not know or are not certain of. Write down their meanings.
4. Use all of the words in a brief paragraph about the various ways you communicate with others in your daily life.

Common Core State Standards

Speaking and Listening
1. Engage effectively in a range of collaborative discussions with diverse partners on grade 6 topics, texts, and issues, building on others' ideas and expressing their own clearly.

Language
6. Acquire and use accurately grade-appropriate general academic and domain-specific words and phrases; gather vocabulary knowledge when considering a word or phrase important to comprehension or expression.

❸ Vocabulary

Acquire and Use Academic Vocabulary

1. Introduce the academic vocabulary words in the first word bank on the student page. Have students preview the words.
2. For each word, have students say the word aloud. Then, use the word in a sentence that defines the word.

Gather Vocabulary Knowledge

1. With the class, review the steps in the activity on the student page. Have students complete the activity independently, with partners, or in small groups.
2. Before students complete the last step, review the words and their meanings as a class. (Definitions appear at the bottom of this page.) Then, have students complete their paragraphs.

PART 1 • Introducing the Big Question **303**

💬 GATHER VOCABULARY KNOWLEDGE

connection (kə nek´ shən) *n.* link or tie
dialogue (dī´ ə lôg´) *n.* conversation; words between two people
expression (ek spresh´ ən) *n.* a look that shows feeling
gesture (jes´ chər) *n.* motion of the hand or body
language (laŋ´ gwij) *n.* form of communication, often speech

message (mes´ ij) *n.* a written or spoken communication
nonverbal (nän vʉr´ bəl) *adj.* not using words
share (sher) *v.* tell, such as an idea or an experience
verbal (vʉr´ bəl) *adj.* using words or speech

Video

Watch the Background Video online!

Close Reading Workshop

❶ Close Reading: Poetry

In the Close Reading Workshop, students will practice using close reading strategies within the context of a particular genre. They will use the features of this genre to help them access the text. All of the close reading strategies align with the Common Core State Standards reading domains:

- **Comprehension:** Key Ideas and Details focuses on what the text says.
- **Text Analysis:** Craft and Structure focuses on how the author conveys the text.
- **Connections:** Integration of Knowledge and Ideas focuses on what the text means and how it changes the reader's view of the world.

MULTIDRAFT READING

Essential Understanding

Explain to students that close reading works best when they read a text multiple times, focusing on different aspects of the text each time.

- **First reading:** Students should read independently to unlock the basic meaning of the text.
- **Second reading:** Students should focus on analyzing key ideas and details and the craft and the structure of the text.
- **Third reading:** Students should focus on integrating knowledge and ideas by connecting the text to the Big Question. The essential understanding students gain from making this connection will help them connect the text to other texts and to the world.

In this workshop you will learn an approach to reading that will deepen your understanding of literature and will help you better appreciate author's craft. The workshop includes models for close reading, discussion, research, and writing. After you have reviewed the strategies and models, practice your skills with the Independent Practice selection.

 Common Core State Standards

RL.6.1, RL.6.2, RL.6.4, RL.6.5, RL.6.6; W.6.2, W.6.7, W.6.9.a; SL.6.1
[For full standards wording, see the standards chart in the front of this book.]

❶ CLOSE READING: POETRY

Use these strategies as you read the poems in this unit.

Comprehension: **Key Ideas and Details**

- Read first to unlock basic meaning.
- Use context clues to help you determine the meanings of unfamiliar words. Consult a dictionary, if necessary.
- Identify unfamiliar details that you might need to clarify through research.
- Distinguish between what is stated directly and what must be inferred.

Ask yourself questions such as these:
- Who is the speaker in this poem?
- What is the speaker describing?
- What is the tone of the poem?

Text Analysis: **Craft and Structure**

- Analyze how sound devices, rhythm, and rhyme add meaning to the poem.
- Identify how the poet uses figurative language to express familiar ideas in new ways.
- Consider how the poem's structure relates to its meaning.

Ask yourself questions such as these:
- How do the poet's descriptive words appeal to my senses and help me determine the poem's theme?
- How does the poet's word choice create an atmosphere, or mood?

Connections: **Integration of Knowledge and Ideas**

- Look for relationships among key ideas. Identify causes and effects, and comparisons and contrasts.
- Connect ideas to determine the poem's theme.
- Compare and contrast this work with other poems you have read.

Ask yourself questions such as these:
- How has this work increased my knowledge of a subject, author, or theme?
- What images are most important to the poem's meaning?

304 UNIT 3 • Do we need words to communicate well?

❡ ACTIVE READING FOR COMMON CORE

Read • Discuss • Research • Write
In this workshop, students will learn how to access text through reading, discussing, researching, and writing. In the first half of the workshop, these activities are modeled for students. In the second half, students have the opportunity to partake in these activities independently.

Read: Students will read and comprehend the Reading Model selection. Annotations call out key points that students should focus on. These annotations model the types of things students should notice when they read the Independent Practice selection later.

Discuss: Students will deepen their understanding of the text through collaborative discussion.

Research: Students will clarify and expand their understanding of the text by conducting research.

Write: Students will synthesize their thoughts and research and will write a response to the text, supporting their ideas with evidence.

➋ Read

As you read this poem, take note of the annotations that model ways to closely read the text.

Reading Model

"Twelfth Song of Thunder" from the Navajo Mountain Chant[1]

The voice that beautifies the land!

The voice above,

➌ The voice of thunder

Within the dark cloud[2]

5 Again and again it sounds,

The voice that beautifies the land.

The voice that beautifies the land!

The voice below,

The voice of the grasshopper

10 Among the plants[3]

Again and again it sounds,

The voice that beautifies the land. [4]

Key Ideas and Details

1 The title suggests that the Navajo perform a number of chants about nature. This information may lead you to conclude that nature is important to Navajo culture.

Craft and Structure

2 Throughout the poem, the poet uses personification to give the human quality of a voice to elements of nature that are not human.

Integration of Knowledge and Ideas

3 Each stanza focuses on details of the natural world, such as "thunder," "dark cloud," "grasshopper," and "plants." The stanzas work together to convey the poem's larger theme: Nature's beauty is far-reaching.

Craft and Structure

4 The repetition of these lines at the end of each stanza, and the repetition of *voice* throughout the poem creates a musical quality and rhythm that celebrate the sounds of nature.

❓ DEVELOPING ESSENTIAL UNDERSTANDING

Do we need words to communicate well?

After students have finished reading the model, ask them the following questions to help them deepen their understanding of how the poem relates to the Big Question:

- What kind of "voice" is communicating in this poem?
- Does the "voice" of the poem communicate with words? Does the "voice" communicate well?

- Does the structure of poetry communicate ideas better than other kinds of writing? Why or why not?

  Remind students that as they read the rest of the selections in this unit, they should ask themselves similar questions to help them connect the texts with the Big Question.

➋ Read

Before students begin reading the model, explain to them that the annotations call out important points in the poem related to Key Ideas and Details, Craft and Structure, and Integration of Knowledge and Ideas. Tell students that their understanding and interpretation of the text should not be limited by the existing annotations. Encourage students to use the annotations as a starting point to help them analyze the poem further.

➌ Integration of Knowledge and Ideas

To move students toward essential understanding, draw their attention to bracketed annotation 3 in the Teacher Edition. **Ask:** In what way is personification an effective way to communicate a poem's theme?

Possible response: Giving human traits to things that are not human can help readers see familiar ideas and objects in a new way.

 **Audio**

Selection Audio is available in the *Student eText* and on the *Hear It!* CD-ROM.

❹ Discuss

Throughout the unit, students will be engaging in discussions about the selections they read. As students discuss, remind them of the following points:

- Come to discussions prepared.
- Support ideas with text evidence.
- Pose and respond to questions that connect the selection to broader themes and ideas.
- Respond thoughtfully to diverse perspectives.

❺ Research

As students conduct research, remind them of the following tips:

- Focus your research question so that it is neither too broad nor too complex.
- Think carefully about your topic and search terms, and use specific words or phrases whenever possible. You might also try using more than one search engine.
- Consider the reliability of the sites you visit. Remember that sites with .edu, .gov, and .org are generally more reliable than sites that end in .com.

❹ Discuss

Sharing your own ideas and listening to the ideas of others can deepen your understanding of a text and help you look at a topic in a whole new way. As you participate in collaborative discussions, work to have a genuine exchange in which classmates build upon one another's ideas. Support your points with evidence and ask meaningful questions.

Discussion Model

Student 1: The word *chant* in the title made me think about how the poem is supposed to be read. A chant seems different from a typical poem. When I think of a chant, I think of something with a rhythm that a group of people might speak together.

Student 2: I think you're right. The poem seems like it's meant to be read out loud. The way some words are repeated, like "voice" and "again" give the chant rhythm, and it seems almost like a song.

Student 3: I also notice the word *twelfth* in the title. That might mean this chant is part of a large ceremony, or maybe one of many chants about thunder or nature. I wonder what that ceremony is about.

❺ Research

Targeted research can clarify unfamiliar details and shed light on various aspects of a text. Consider questions that arise in your mind as you read, and use those questions as the basis for research.

Research Model

Questions: *What is the purpose and history of the Navajo Mountain Chant?*

Key Words for Internet Search: Navajo AND Mountain AND Chant

Results: Encyclopedia2, Navajo Mountain Chant; Internet Sacred Text Archive

What I Learned: The Navajo Mountain Chant is a nine-day ceremony that is performed in the late winter, sometime after the season of thunderstorms but before the arrival of spring. The chant marks the change from one season to another. It also is a healing ceremony to cure diseases and mend troubled human relationships.

⑥ Write

Writing about a text will deepen your understanding of it and will also allow you to share your ideas more formally with others. The following model essay analyzes the use of various poetic elements in "Twelfth Song of Thunder" and cites evidence to support the main ideas.

Writing Model: Argument

Poetic Elements in "Twelfth Song of Thunder"

"Twelfth Song of Thunder" expresses the theme that the beauty of nature is all around us. The poet develops this theme through the use of poetic elements. Repetition, descriptive language, personification, and rhythm all highlight nature's beauty.

The poet repeats key words, phrases, and lines. The word "voice" appears eight times. The phrase "again and again" is used twice. The line "The voice that beautifies the land" is used four times in the twelve-line poem. This constant repetition focuses the reader's attention on the idea of nature's beauty, and adds a meaningful rhythm that celebrates the sounds of nature.

The poet also uses imagery to appeal to the senses and highlight nature's beauty. The description of the "dark cloud" in line 4 appeals to the reader's sense of sight and helps set the scene. In addition, the mention of the "voice of the grasshopper" in line 9 appeals to the reader's sense of hearing. These examples of imagery suggest that nature's beauty can be appreciated by different senses.

Perhaps the strongest poetic element is the use of personification, or the way in which nonhuman subjects are given human qualities. Thunder clearly makes a sound, and so does a grasshopper, but we do not usually call these sounds "voices." However, the poet does give voices to the thunder and the grasshopper. Giving human characteristics to elements of nature makes a connection that helps us relate to nature.

As with many other chants, this one is meant to be spoken or sung out loud. A Navajo medicine man performs this meaningful chant at sunset on the last day of the nine-day Mountain Chant ceremony to celebrate the seasons and to cure illnesses. The pattern of beats and repetition of words and lines give the chant a powerful musical quality that rejoices in the sounds of nature. The descriptive language and use of personification show the all-reaching beauty of nature.

> The writer begins by stating a claim about the theme of the poem. This is an effective way to structure a short response.

> Specific details from the poem support the writer's claim.

> The writer provides an important example to reinforce a key idea.

> In the conclusion, the writer includes evidence from research to make a connection between the purpose and theme of the poem.

---

⑥ Write

Review the writing model with the class, using the annotations to analyze how the writer uses evidence to support his or her ideas.

Genre Requirements

Remind students that when they write responses to literature, they should do the following:

- Introduce the topic at the beginning of the essay.
- Organize ideas and information in order to make important connections.
- Support claims with specific details from the literary work.
- Provide a conclusion that supports the information presented.

Teaching from the Writing Model

1. Point out to students that the first sentence states the writer's claim, or the focus of the essay.
2. Point out that each body paragraph explains poetic elements by using details in the text.
3. The conclusion uses research to tie back to the claim about the theme of the poem.

CLOSE READING TOOL

Students may close read and mark the text using the **Close Reading Tool**, which is available online. Scaffolds are provided for students who need help. Students who do not have online access may use the *Close Reading Notebook* to mark the text with their close reading responses.

7 Independent Practice

The Independent Practice is an optional assignment. You may wish to administer it at this point and use it as formative assessment, or you may wish to administer it at the end of Part 1 as summative assessment.

If you wish to administer the Independent Practice but feel your students will struggle with it, you can use the questions in the side margins of this Teacher Edition to help guide them.

8 Craft and Structure

Ask: To which senses do these lines appeal? What idea do they convey?

Possible response: The lines appeal to the senses of sight, touch, and hearing. They convey the idea of a cold day.

9 Key Ideas and Details

Ask: How does the speaker feel about the girl? How can you tell?

Possible response: The boy likes the girl. He describes her face as "bright" and he smiles at her.

10 Craft and Structure

Ask: Which type of figurative language does the poet use in these lines? What two things are being compared?

Possible response: The poet uses a simile to compare the shelves of candy to rows of bleachers.

 **Audio**

Selection Audio is available in the *Student eText* and on the *Hear It!* CD-ROM.

7 As you read the following poems, apply the close reading strategies you have learned. You may need to read the poems multiple times.

"Oranges"
by Gary Soto

The first time I walked
With a girl, I was twelve,
Cold, and weighted down
With two oranges in my jacket.
5 December. Frost cracking
Beneath my steps, my breath
Before me, then gone,
As I walked toward
Her house, the one whose
10 Porch light burned yellow
Night and day, in any weather.
A dog barked at me, until
She came out pulling
At her gloves, face bright
15 With rouge[1]. I smiled,
Touched her shoulder, and led
Her down the street, across
A used car lot and a line
Of newly planted trees,
20 Until we were breathing
Before a drugstore. We
Entered, the tiny bell
Bringing a saleslady
Down a narrow aisle of goods.
25 I turned to the candies
Tiered[2] like bleachers,
And asked what she wanted—

---

1. **rouge** (roo zh) *n.* a reddish cosmetic used to color the cheeks.
2. **tiered** (tē r´d) *adj.* arranged in levels, one above another.

308 UNIT 3 • Do we need words to communicate well?

Meet the Author

A native of Fresno, California, **Gary Soto** (b. 1952) is an award-winning poet and author of children's books. Much of his work focuses on life in Mexican-American communities and is based on his own childhood and experiences as a young adult.

CLOSE READING TOOL

Read and respond to this selection online using the **Close Reading Tool**.

C ACTIVE READING FOR COMMON CORE

Read • Discuss • Research • Write
In the **Independent Practice** section of the Close Reading Workshop, students will practice the reading, discussing, researching, and writing strategies they learned in the modeling section. They will also deepen their essential understanding of the Big Question.

Read: Students will read and comprehend the selection. They should note significant points in the text that relate to Key Ideas and Details, Craft and Structure, and Integration of Knowledge and Ideas. They should use the annotations in the Reading Model that they read earlier as a guide. After students have

finished reading the poem, they will answer Literary Analysis questions.

Discuss: Students will deepen their understanding of the text through collaborative discussion.

Research: Students will clarify and expand their understanding of the text by conducting research.

Write: Students will synthesize their thoughts and research by writing a response to the text, supporting their ideas with evidence.

Light in her eyes, a smile
Starting at the corners
30 Of her mouth. I fingered
A nickel in my pocket,
And when she lifted a chocolate
That cost a dime,
I didn't say anything.
35 I took the nickel from
My pocket, then an orange,
And set them quietly on
The counter. When I looked up,
The lady's eyes met mine,
40 And held them, knowing
Very well what it was all
About.
        Outside,
A few cars hissing past,
45 Fog hanging like old
Coats between the trees.
I took my girl's hand
In mine for two blocks,
Then released it to let
50 Her unwrap the chocolate.
I peeled my orange
That was so bright against
The gray of December
That, from some distance,
55 Someone might have thought
I was making a fire in my hands.

11 **Craft and Structure**
Ask: What tone does the speaker convey in these lines? Explain.

Possible response: The speaker conveys a tone of shy determination. He does not have enough money for the candy, but he attempts to pay with what he does have.

12 **Craft and Structure**
Ask: The word *outside* indicates the beginning of a new stanza. What shift has occurred between the first and second stanzas?

Possible response: The speaker and the girl are back outdoors. It implies that the speaker has successfully overcome a potentially awkward situation.

13 **Craft and Structure**
Ask: Which sound device does the poet use in this line?
Answer: onomatopoeia

14 **Integration of Knowledge and Ideas**
Ask: How does the image presented in these lines sum up the poem and help convey a possible theme?

Possible response: The orange is "so bright against" the cold winter sky, conveying the theme that there is hope and love in a world otherwise bleak and cold.

15 Craft and Structure

Ask: How would you describe the tone of these lines?

Possible response: Students may describe the tone of these lines as amused, fond, nostalgic, or affectionate.

16 Craft and Structure

Ask: What is the effect of the repeated phrase *This is*?

Possible response: The repeated phrase *This is* moves the reader's eyes from one image or object to another. It creates the sense that the speaker and the reader are looking through a photo album together.

17 Key Ideas and Details

Ask: What can you tell about the speaker's family based on the photographs described in this stanza?

Possible response: The family went on adventures together and enjoyed one another's company.

18 Integration of Knowledge and Ideas

Ask: These lines are an example of which type of figurative language? What theme does this description suggest?

Possible response: This line contains a simile comparing the "dizzy" angles of the photographs to a ride on a merry-go-round. The description supports the idea that the speaker's family life was unpredictable and fun.

"Ode to Family Photographs"
by Gary Soto

15
This is the pond, and these are my feet.
This is the rooster, and this is more of my feet.

Mamá was never good at pictures.

This is a statue of a famous general who lost an
    arm
5 And this is me with my head cut off.

16
This is a trash can chained to a gate,
This is my father with his eyes half-closed.

This is a photograph of my sister
And a giraffe looking over her
    shoulder.

10 This is our car's front bumper.
17
This is a bird with a pretzel in its
    beak.
This is my brother Pedro standing
    on one leg on a rock,
With a smear of chocolate on his
    face.

Mamá sneezed when she looked
15 *Behind the camera: the snapshots*
    are blurry,
18
The angles dizzy as a spin on a
    merry-go-round.

But we had fun when Mamá picked
    up the camera.
How can I tell?
Each of us laughing hard.
20 Can you see? I have candy in my
    mouth.

310 UNIT 3 • Do we need words to communicate well?

If you are using the Independent Practice as formative assessment, use the rubric below to evaluate students' performances.

Independent Practice Rubric	Rating Scale				
Close Reading: How well does the student use close reading strategies to answer the questions?	*not very* 1	2	3	4	*very* 5
Support/Elaboration: How well does the student support points with textual or other evidence?	1	2	3	4	5
Insight: How original, sophisticated, or compelling are the insights the student achieves?	1	2	3	4	5
Expression of Ideas: How well does the student use language, including word choice and conventions, in the expression of ideas?	1	2	3	4	5

Close Reading Activities

Comprehension: **Key Ideas and Details**

1. **(a) Deduce:** In "Oranges," why does the speaker put the nickel and the orange on the counter? **(b) Interpret:** What does the saleslady's response suggest about her attitude toward the speaker?

2. **(a)** Identify details the speaker uses to describe the girl in "Oranges." **(b) Interpret:** What do these details tell you about his attitude toward the girl?

3. **(a) Identify:** In "Ode to Family Photographs," why does the poet repeat the phrase "This is"? **(b) Interpret:** What is the meaning of the images in lines 5 and 7?

4. **(a)** Describe the speaker's mother's ability as a photographer. **(b) Interpret:** How does the speaker feel about the photographs? How do you know?

Text Analysis: **Craft and Structure**

5. **(a)** In "Ode to Family Photographs," what is the difference between the sentences in italics and the other lines? **(b) Analyze:** How is the last stanza different from the rest of the poem?

6. **Compare and Contrast:** How are "Oranges" and "Ode to Family

Photographs" similar and different? Consider each poem's speaker, descriptive language, and structure.

7. **(a) Analyze:** Find a comparison that is made in one of the poems. **(b) Interpret:** Explain what this comparison means and how it relates to the poem's theme.

Connections: **Integration of Knowledge and Ideas**

Discuss
In a **small-group discussion**, explore the ways in which descriptive and sensory language develop a mood in each poem.

Research
Briefly research Gary Soto's life and speculate about the influence of his upbringing on the two poems you read. Focus on the following aspects:
a. Soto's Mexican-American heritage
b. his childhood in Central California
Take notes as you research. Then, write a brief **explanation** of why setting is important to Soto's writing.

Write
Common advice for writers is "Write what you know." Write an **essay** in which you evaluate this advice based on an analysis of Soto's poems. Cite details from the poems and from your research to support your analysis.

 Do we need words to communicate well?
What feelings and ideas do the characters in these poems express without words?

Discuss
Students should cite specific examples of descriptive and sensory language from each poem and discuss how language conveys a particular mood.

Research
Students should use reliable resources to conduct research on Soto's life. They should incorporate details from their research to explain Soto's heritage and childhood.

Write
Student essays should evaluate the advice "Write what you know," based on an analysis of Soto's poems. Students should cite details from the poems and research to support their analysis.

 Do we need words to communicate well?
Students should consider examples such as the interaction between the speaker and the saleslady in "Oranges," noting that characters are able to communicate their needs and feelings without using words.

☑ **ASSESS**

Possible responses appear below. Check to be sure students support their responses with evidence from the text.

1. **(a)** He hopes the saleslady will accept the orange and the nickel as payment for the chocolate. **(b)** She is sympathetic; she understands he cannot afford the candy, and is willing to accept the payment.

2. **(a)** "face bright/With rouge"; "Light in her eyes" **(b)** The descriptive words suggest the boy likes and admires the girl.

3. **(a)** The speaker is pointing out photographs. **(b)** The photographer missed the boy's head in the frame; the father's eyes aren't open for the picture.

4. **(a)** Mamá does not carefully compose her shots; she is distracted, maybe by having too much fun. **(b)** The speaker loves the photographs because they reflect his mother's carefree personality and the fun he had with his family.

5. **(a)** The sentences in italics describe the speaker's mother and her way of taking photographs. The other lines describe the photographs themselves. **(b)** The first several stanzas are objective—they contain descriptions of people and events. The last stanza is subjective—it describes the speaker's affection for his family and for the good times they have shared.

6. Similarities—Both have first-person speakers; both use language that appeals to the senses ("frost cracking"; "a smear of chocolate on his face," "blurry," "dizzy"). Differences—"Oranges" tells a story, while "Ode to Family Photographs" describes family activities in the form of snapshots.

7. **(a)** "Ode to Family Photographs": the line "The angles dizzy as a spin on a merry-go-round" **(b)** The photographs are out of focus. Although the photographs are blurry, they are important to the speaker because they bring back family memories.

❶ About the Quotation

Rita Dove (b. 1952) is an award-winning poet who served as Poet Laureate of the United States from 1993 to 1995. Dove was the 1987 Pulitzer Prize winner in poetry and the 1996 Heinz Award in the Arts and Humanities.

Discussion: Ask students to discuss the meaning of Dove's quotation about poetry. Then ask them to decide whether they agree with the quotation. Have them explain and support their positions with sound reasoning and evidence.

❷ Critical Viewing

Pose the critical viewing question to the class. Then, guide the class in a discussion about the question. Encourage students to build upon each other's ideas as they share their responses. Remind students to support their responses with reasons and evidence.

❶ "Poetry is **language** at its most distilled and most **powerful**."

—Rita Dove

❓ DEVELOPING ESSENTIAL UNDERSTANDING

Do we need words to communicate well?
Explain to students that they will continue to consider the Big Question as they work through the selections in Part 2 of the unit.

- As students read each selection, they will look for details related to the Big Question and take notes.

- At the end of each selection, students will answer a Literary Analysis question that is related to the Big Question.

- Students will deepen their knowledge of the selections and their understanding of the Big Question through reading, speaking, listening, researching, and writing.

PART 2
TEXT ANALYSIS GUIDED EXPLORATION

RHYTHM AND RHYME

As you read the poetry collections in this section, consider ways in which rhyme, rhythm, and other sound devices create meaning. The quotation on the opposite page will help you start thinking about ways in which poets use language and sound to express significant ideas and important themes.

2 ◀ **CRITICAL VIEWING** How do the images in this painting represent the language of poetry?

CLOSE READING TOOL

Use the **Close Reading** Tool to practice the strategies you learned in this unit.

3 READINGS IN PART 2

POETRY COLLECTION I
• **A Dream Within a Dream** • **Adventures of Isabel** • **Life Doesn't Frighten Me** • **The Walrus and the Carpenter**
(p. 321)

POETRY COLLECTION 2
• **Abuelito Who** • **April Rain Song** • **The World Is Not a Pleasant Place to Be** • **Fame Is a Bee**
(p. 337)

POETRY COLLECTION 3
• **Haiku** • **The Sidewalk Racer** • **Concrete Cat** • **Limerick**
(p. 347)

POETRY COLLECTION 4
• **Wind and water and stone** • **No Thank You** • **The Fairies' Lullaby** • **Cynthia in the Snow**
(p. 357)

PART 2 • Rhythm And Rhyme **313**

 CUSTOMIZING THE TEXT SET

Close Reading Tool
Use the Close Reading Tool to project the selections on a whiteboard and work through them as a whole-class activity. Students also have the opportunity to read the selection(s) independently, with scaffolds available as needed.

Curriculum Builder
Customize this program by rearranging existing selections, adding selection titles of your choosing, and uploading your own resources—all online!

---

3 **Readings in Part 2**
About the Texts
(For quantitative and qualitative measures of text complexity, see the rubrics on the opening pages of each selection.)

POETRY COLLECTION 1: A Dream Within a Dream • Adventures of Isabel • Life Doesn't Frighten Me • The Walrus and the Carpenter

Summary "A Dream Within a Dream" describes having lost a love. "Adventures of Isabel" tells of a girl who encounters different characters. "Life Doesn't Frighten Me" deals with frightening aspects of life. "The Walrus and the Carpenter" tells of a walrus who tricks oysters.

POETRY COLLECTION 2: Abuelito Who • April Rain Song • The World Is Not a Pleasant Place to Be • Fame Is a Bee

Summaries "Abuelito Who" weaves impressions of a grandfather. "April Rain Song" describes gentle rain. "The World Is Not a Pleasant Place to Be" expresses that the world is pleasant only when shared with friends. "Fame Is a Bee," compares fame and a bee.

POETRY COLLECTION 3: Haiku • The Sidewalk Racer • Concrete Cat • Limerick

Summaries Bashō's haiku presents a glimpse into nature. "The Sidewalk Racer" describes skateboarding. The author of "Concrete Cat" arranges the nouns into the shape of a cat. In the limerick the poet tells of a misadventure.

POETRY COLLECTION 4: Wind and water and stone • No Thank You • The Fairies' Lullaby • Cynthia in the Snow

Summaries "Wind and water and stone" describes the three elements. "No Thank You" describes getting a kitten. "The Fairies' Lullaby," warns unpleasant creatures to stay away. "Cynthia in the Snow" creates imagery of snow.

 Audio

Summary Audio is available in the **Student eText** and on the **Hear It!** CD-ROM.

PART 2 • Rhythm And Rhyme **313**

Focus on Craft and Structure

❶ Elements of Poetry

1. Introduce the elements of poetry, using the instruction on the student page.

   Have students list some of their favorite poems or poets and tell what kinds of poems they like best.

2. Help students distinguish between rhythm and rhyme. Emphasize that these elements give poems their musical quality. Explain that some poems have set rhythms and rhyme schemes, while other poems do not.

3. **Ask** students to describe the structure of "Snowflake," the example poem.

   Sample response: It has three lines—one long, one medium, and one short. The last line is indented.

   Explain that, often, all the stanzas of a poem have the same structure. For example, if "Snowflake" had a second stanza, that stanza might follow the same structural pattern as the stanza shown.

4. Emphasize that the speaker of a poem may resemble the poet himself or herself but is often a distinct character.

5. Read aloud "The Cat" and discuss with students the poem's structure. **Ask:** How does the final line of each stanza help communicate the poem's meaning?

   Sample response: It is short and quick, like the swipe of a cat's paw.

❶ Elements of Poetry

Poetry uses musical elements of **language** to help express thoughts and feelings.

Poetry is a type of literature in which the rhythms and sounds of words are as important as their definitions. When you read most poems, you can hear a **rhythm,** or beat. Other sound devices, such as **rhyme,** add to a poem's musical effect. Rhythm and sound help support a poem's meaning and shape its structure.

Structure Poems are arranged in **lines**, or groups of words, that help create rhythm and emphasis.

> **Example: Snowflake**
>
> A cold little star, spun from the sky,
> landed on the ground,
>   then vanished.

Poetry looks different from prose because the lengths of individual lines in a poem may vary. In the example above, each of the snowflake's actions is presented on its own line.

The lines of a poem are arranged in units called stanzas. A **stanza** is a group of lines that work together to express a central idea. Like the paragraphs in an essay, the stanzas in a poem divide the text into logical parts.

Speaker When you read a poem, you can "hear" a voice speaking to you. The voice that narrates a poem is called the **speaker.** Like the narrator in a story, the speaker in a poem is an imaginary voice created by the poet. The speaker may present a unique point of view that is not necessarily the point of view of the poet.

Read the poem below, taking special note of its speaker and its structure. Notice the effects of these elements on the poem's meaning.

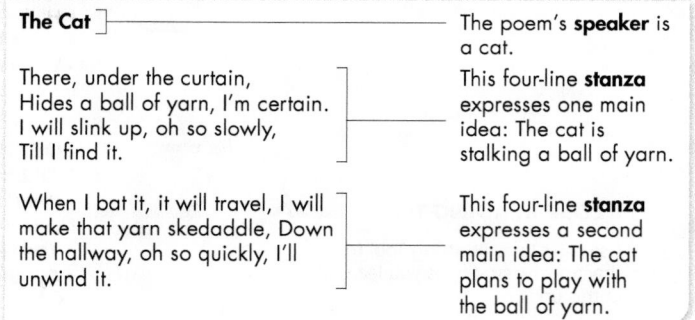

The Cat — The poem's **speaker** is a cat.

There, under the curtain,
Hides a ball of yarn, I'm certain.
I will slink up, oh so slowly,
Till I find it.

This four-line **stanza** expresses one main idea: The cat is stalking a ball of yarn.

When I bat it, it will travel, I will make that yarn skedaddle, Down the hallway, oh so quickly, I'll unwind it.

This four-line **stanza** expresses a second main idea: The cat plans to play with the ball of yarn.

Sound devices add a musical quality to poetry. Poets use the following devices to enhance a poem's mood and meaning.

Rhythm The rhythm of a poem is the beat created by its pattern of stressed and unstressed syllables. A stressed syllable is emphasized when it is spoken. An unstressed syllable is not emphasized. Rhythm can support meaning and make a poem memorable.

Read the following example aloud to hear its rhythm. Stressed syllables are printed in dark type.

> **Example:**
>
> The **anxious fans** shot **to** their **feet**,
> Their **faces filled** with **fear.**
> But **when** the **ball** swished **through** the **net**,
> They **cheered** a **migh**ty **cheer!**

In this poem, the regular rhythm is like the bouncing of a basketball. Not all poems have such a predictable rhythmic pattern, however. Poets may vary rhythms to emphasize certain words or to enhance meaning.

Rhyme is the repetition of sounds at the ends of words, as in *pool, rule,* and *fool.* As you read the following example, notice how rhyme connects ideas in the poem.

> **Example:**
>
> I was angry with my fri<u>end</u>:
> I told my wrath, my wrath did <u>end</u>.
> I was angry with my f<u>oe</u>:
> I told it not, my wrath did <u>grow</u>.
> — from "The Poison Tree" by William Blake

The rhyming words *friend* and *end* create a connection between the first two lines of the poem. Together these lines state a sentence with a central idea. Likewise, rhyming words connect the next two lines, which state a second sentence and a new, but related, idea.

Repetition is the use of any element of language—a sound, word, phrase, or sentence—more than once.

Alliteration is the repetition of similar consonant sounds at the beginnings of words.

Onomatopoeia is the use of words to imitate sounds. In the poem below, examples of alliteration are highlighted in color and examples of onomatopoeia are underlined.

> **Example:**
>
> Outside, clouds curl before the storm.
> I snuggle inside, safe from the <u>whooshing</u> wind.
> I watch as the sky darkens,
> And put my hand to the cold window.

Common Core State Standards

Reading Literature

4. Determine the meaning of words and phrases as they are used in a text, including figurative and connotative meanings; analyze the impact of a specific word choice on meaning and tone.

5. Analyze how a particular sentence, chapter, scene, or stanza fits into the overall structure of a text and contributes to the development of the theme, setting, or plot.

6. Explain how an author develops the point of view of the narrator or speaker in a text.

6. Ask a volunteer to clap his or her hands to demonstrate a rhythm that includes lighter and heavier beats, for example, *light, light, heavy . . . light, light, heavy.* Then, invite the rest of the class to join in. Explain that because the rhythm was regular, it was easy to learn and predict, and that poets use rhythm in a similar way to carry readers forward through a poem. Point out that in language, "lighter" syllables are referred to as *unstressed,* and "heavier" syllables are referred to as *stressed.* Reinforce this concept by reading the example poem in the first column aloud.

7. Review with students the sound device of rhyme. Emphasize that in poetry, rhyme creates a musical sound, but it also builds meaning by connecting related ideas. Use the example poem by William Blake to ensure that students understand this concept.

8. After discussing repetition, alliteration, and onomatopoeia, have students work in pairs to generate original examples of each of these sound devices. Invite pairs to share their examples with the class.

❶ Analyzing Language, Structure, and Theme in Poetry

1. Introduce poetic language, using the instruction on the student page.

2. Define *connotation* and *denotation,* using the information and examples on the student page. Then, write the following words on the board: *curious, bold, fragrant, lively.* Explain that these words have positive connotations. Challenge students to generate synonyms with negative connotations for each word.

   Sample responses: *curious—snoopy, nosey; bold—aggressive, pushy; fragrant—smelly, stinky; lively—hyper, overwhelming*

3. Lead students in a discussion of tone, using the two lines of poetry at the bottom of the first column. Point out that negative and positive connotations help to create tone. **Ask** students to come up with a third example that expresses the same meaning but creates a playful tone.

   Sample response: They tumbled over the waves until they splashed ashore.

4. Emphasize that poets use figurative language to surprise their readers or to help them see a subject from a new angle. After reviewing the types of figurative language in the chart, have partners work together to generate an additional example of each type. As students share their ideas with the class, ask other students to explain why an example fits (or doesn't fit) the definition given.

❶ Analyzing Language, Structure, and Theme in Poetry

Poets choose and arrange words carefully to convey a **theme** about life.

Connotation and Denotation
A word can convey different kinds of meanings. One kind is the word's **denotation,** or dictionary definition. Another kind is the word's **connotation,** or the feelings and associations it evokes in people.

A word with positive connotations is associated with positive feelings and ideas. A word with negative connotations is associated with negative feelings and ideas. Think about the difference between the words *fragrance* and *odor.* Both words literally mean "smell." However, their connotative meanings are very different.

Meaning and Tone Tone is a writer's attitude toward his or her subject. A poem's **tone** can usually be described in one word, such as *joyful* or *lonely.* The connotations of the words in a poem can help convey its tone. Compare the following lines of poetry:

- They rolled over the swells until they slid ashore.
- They slammed over the waves until they hit land.

Both examples convey roughly the same information. However, in the first example, the words *rolled, swells,* and *slid* create a peaceful tone. In the second example, the words *slammed, waves,* and *hit* create an anxious tone.

Figurative Language Poets use **figurative language** to help readers see familiar ideas in fresh new ways. Figurative language is writing or speech that is not meant to be taken literally. Common types of figurative language are described below.

Types of Figurative Language
Simile compares two unlike things using the words *like* or *as.* **Example:** The man was as gruff as a grizzly bear.
Metaphor compares two unlike things without using *like* or *as.* **Example:** My aching feet were two bricks at the ends of my legs.
Personification gives human qualities to something that is not human. **Example:** The flames of the campfire licked the night air.
Hyperbole is an extreme exaggeration. **Example:** You've broken my heart into a million pieces!

Imagery Poets use **imagery,** also known as *sensory language,* to create vivid word pictures for readers. Imagery is language that appeals to the five senses of sight, hearing, smell, taste, and touch. The following lines of poetry appeal to the senses of sight and smell:

The bright crimson roses
Filled the air with their perfume.

Structure and Theme The **theme** of a poem is the message or insight about life that it conveys. Often, the structure of a poem contributes to its meaning. For example, each stanza may develop a central idea. Combining the central ideas of all the stanzas can lead you to the poem's theme.

As you read the following example, look for the theme of the poem.

> **Example: Waiting**
>
> The hands of the clock
> creep
> over
> the
> numbers
> until . . .
>
> The bell rings and sets me free.

Notice the different lengths of the poem's two stanzas. The first stanza has six lines, and the second stanza has only one. However, both stanzas contribute to the overall theme of the poem. In the first stanza, beginning with the second line, the poet puts one word on each line. This structure imitates the slow-ticking hands of a clock. The second stanza flows as one sentence. This suggests the speaker's relief upon hearing the bell. Together,

the stanzas develop the theme of the poem: Time seems to move slowly when you are waiting for something you want.

Forms of Poetry Poetry comes in many different forms. Following are some of the common forms of poetry, which you will explore in this unit.

A **narrative** poem tells a story in verse. Narrative poetry has elements similar to those in short stories, such as plot and characters.

A **lyric** poem expresses the thoughts and feelings of a single speaker, often in highly musical verse.

A **concrete** poem is shaped to look like its subject. The poet arranges the lines to create a picture on the page.

A **haiku** is a Japanese form of poetry about nature, made up of three lines. The first and third lines have five syllables each. The second line has seven syllables.

A **limerick** is a humorous, rhyming five-line poem with a specific rhythm and pattern of rhyme.

A **free verse** poem does not have a strict structure, regular rhythm, or pattern of rhyme.

5. Introduce the concepts of structure and theme, using the instruction on the student page.

6. Explain that in some ways, a poem's stanzas are like the paragraphs in a work of prose: each one provides additional details or support for the central idea. Then, **ask:** How are the stanzas of a poem *different* from the paragraphs of an article or essay?

   Sample responses: Stanzas in a poem are not necessarily made up of sentences. They can be very long, or they can be as short as one word or phrase. The lines in a stanza can break in different places.

   Ask: Imagine you are writing a poem called "Freedom"—a sequel to the "Waiting" poem. What kinds of stanzas and lines would you use to reinforce your theme?

   Sample response: Students might use longer, unbroken lines and stanzas to reflect the feeling of being free.

7. Explore students' familiarity with the different forms of poetry. Challenge partners to find an example of one of the forms in this unit's poetry selections.

DIFFERENTIATED INSTRUCTION

Support for Less-Proficient Readers
Have students read the **Learning About Poetry** pages for these selections in the *Reader's Notebook: Adapted Version*. This version provides a basic-level introduction to poetry.

EL Support for English Learners
Have students read the **Learning About Poetry** pages for these selections in the *Reader's Notebook: English Learner's Version*. This version provides a basic-level introduction to poetry.

Time and Resource Manager

LESSON PACING GUIDE

Poetry Collection 1: A Dream Within a Dream • Adventures of Isabel • Life Doesn't Frighten Me • The Walrus and the Carpenter

 **Common Core State Standards**

DAY 1	**Preteach/Teach**

- Administer the Reading and Vocabulary Warm-ups, as necessary.
- Introduce the Key Ideas and Details skill: Context Clues.
- Introduce the Craft and Structure skill: Rhythm and Rhyme.
- Use the Close Reading Model to demonstrate the application of the skills.
- Review the selection vocabulary, as necessary, with students who need additional support.
- Prepare students to read the selection by reviewing with them the Multidraft Reading Strategies.

DAY 2	**Teach**

- Informally monitor comprehension while students read.
- Use the Comprehension questions to confirm understanding.
- Develop students' ability to identify context clues and analyze rhythm and rhyme using the sidenote questions.
- Reinforce vocabulary with the Vocabulary notes.
- Reinforce unit focus standards using the Spiral Review prompts.

DAY 3	**Assess**

- Assess students' comprehension and mastery of the skills by having them answer the Literary Analysis questions.
- Have students complete the Vocabulary activities.
- Develop students' understanding of roots and affixes by having them complete the Word Study activities.

DAY 4	**Extend/Assess**

- Build students' ability to master grammar concepts and conventions by having them complete the Conventions lesson.
- Have students complete the Writing to Sources activity and write a letter to an author. (You may assign as homework.)
- Extend learning by having students complete the Research and Technology activity: an illustrated booklet.
- Administer the Selection Test or Open-Book Test.

Reading Literature 4. Determine the meaning of words and phrases as they are used in the text, including figurative and connotative meanings; analyze the impact of a specific word choice on meaning and tone.

Writing 2. Write informative/ explanatory texts to examine a topic and convey ideas, concepts, and information through the selection, organization, and analysis of relevant content.

2.b. Develop the content with relevant facts, definitions, concrete details, quotations, or other information and examples.

2.e. Establish and maintain a formal style.

2.f. Provide a concluding statement or section that follows from the information or explanation presented.

9. Draw evidence from literary or informational texts to support analysis, refection, and research.

Language 1. Demonstrate command of the conventions of standard English grammar and usage when writing or speaking.

4.a. Use context as a clue to the meaning of a word or phrase.

6. Acquire and use accurately grade-appropriate general academic and domain-specific words and phrases; gather vocabulary knowledge when considering a word or phrase important to comprehension or expression.

Daily Block Scheduling

Each day in this Lesson Pacing Guide represents a 40–50 minute period. Teachers using block scheduling may combine days to revise pacing. In addition, teachers may differentiate and support core instruction by integrating components for extended and intensive support as students require. See the Guide to Resources (facing page).

GUIDE TO RESOURCES

		L1	L2	L3	L4	EL	ALL	RESOURCES	PRINT	CD	ONLINE
Warm Up		✔	✔			✔		Vocabulary Warm-ups			✔
		✔	✔			✔		Reading Warm-ups			✔
							✔	Background Video			✔
							✔	Selection Audio		Hear It!	✔
Comprehension/ Selection Support							✔	Writing About the Big Question	Student Companion Workbook		✔
							✔	Literary Analysis	Student Companion Workbook		✔
							✔	Reading	Student Companion Workbook		✔
							✔	Vocabulary Builder	Student Companion Workbook		✔
					✔			Enrichment			✔
			✔	✔	✔			Conventions	Student Companion Workbook		✔
			✔	✔	✔			Writing to Sources	Student Companion Workbook		✔
			✔	✔	✔			Research and Technology	Student Companion Workbook		
Differentiated Instruction/ Additional Support							✔	Additional Standards Practice	Common Core Companion		✔
							✔	Close Reading Practice	Close Reading Notebook		✔
		✔	✔					Adapted Reader's Notebook			✔
						✔		English Reader's Notebook:			✔
						✔		Spanish Reader's Notebook			✔
						✔		Graphic Organizer A			✔
		✔	✔			✔		Graphic Organizer B			✔
		✔	✔			✔		"Dancing in the Streets"	Reality Central Student Edition and Writing Journal		✔
		✔	✔			✔		Practice and Assess	Reading Kit		✔
Monitor Progress							✔	Selection Test		Exam View	✔
							✔	Open-Book Test		Exam View	✔
Digital Resources							✔	Close Reading Tool			✔
							✔	Online Writer's Notebook			✔

👥 One-on-one teaching   👥 Group work   👥 Whole class instruction   👤 Independent work   Ⓐ Assessment   🖥 Digital Resource

LEARNER LEVELS

L1 Special-Needs Students   L3 On-Level Students (Tier 1)   EL English Learners

L2 Below-Level Students (Tier 2)   L4 Advanced Students (Tier 1)   All All Students

❶ Do we need words to communicate well?

Read • Discuss • Research • Write As students read, they will explore the Big Question through text analysis of the selection. Encourage students to note comments and additional questions as they read, using text evidence to support their thoughts. Students should refer to their notes to help them deepen their understanding of the selection through discussion, research, and writing.

❷ Close Reading Focus

1. Explain to students that context clues can also be synonyms or antonyms of the unknown word. For example, in the sentence, *The desert was so arid, the opposite of the humid jungle,* "humid" is an antonym for "arid."

2. Explain to students that recognizing rhythm and rhyme in poetry can help them enjoy and understand it more. Not every poem has a regular rhyme scheme or rhythm. It often helps to read a poem aloud to feel the beat.

 Building Knowledge

Poetry Collection 1

 Common Core State Standards

Reading Literature
4. Determine the meaning of words and phrases as they are used in the text, including figurative and connotative meanings; analyze the impact of a specific word choice on meaning and tone.

Language
4.a. Use context as a clue to the meaning of a word or phrase.
6. Acquire and use accurately grade-appropriate general academic and domain-specific words and phrases; gather vocabulary knowledge when considering a word or phrase important to comprehension or expression.

❶ Do we need words to communicate well?

Explore the Big Question as you read the poems in Collection 1. Take notes on ways in which the poems explore relationships between action and communication.

❷ CLOSE READING FOCUS

Key Ideas and Details: **Context Clues**

Context clues are found in the text surrounding an unfamiliar word. These clues help you determine the meaning of a word you may not know. Context clues may be explanations or words with the same meaning. To use context clues, ask questions like these:
- *Which words restate, explain, or contrast with the word?*
- *What word can I use in place of the unfamiliar word?*
- *Does the new sentence I created make sense?*

Craft and Structure: **Rhythm and Rhyme**

Rhythm and rhyme add a musical quality to poems.
- **Rhythm** is the beat, or sound pattern, created by stressed and unstressed syllables.

Jack and **Jill** went **up** the **hill**

(4 stressed / 3 unstressed)

- **Rhyme** is the repetition of sounds at the ends of words, such as *delight* and *excite.* Once a rhyme pattern, or *scheme,* is established, you come to expect rhymes.

As you read, listen for ways in which these sound patterns add layers of meaning and convey each poem's *tone,* or speaker's attitude.

Vocabulary

You will encounter the following words in this collection. Write the words in your notebook. Next to the verb *sympathize,* write its noun and adjective forms.

ravenous	cavernous	deem
beseech	dismal	sympathize

318 UNIT 3 • Do we need words to communicate well?

© TEXT COMPLEXITY **RUBRIC**

Poetry Collection 1				Reader and Task Suggestions	
Qualitative Measures				**Preparing to Read the Text**	**Leveled Tasks**
Context/Knowledge Demands	Personal reflections; fearless adventure; humor 1 2 ③ 4 5			• Use the summary information on p. 313 to help students understand the poems.	*Levels of Meaning* If students will have difficulty with levels of meaning, have them read to understand the literal meaning of each poem. Have them reread to determine the theme of each poem.
Structure/Language Conventionality and Clarity	Challenging vocabulary and diction; humorous language 1 2 3 ④ 5				
Levels of Meaning/Purpose/Concept Level	Challenging concepts (lost love; amazing feats; facing fears; funny and sad at one time) 1 2 3 ④ 5			• Guide students to use Multidraft Reading strategies (TE p. 320)	*Evaluating* If students will not have difficulty with the levels of meaning, have them read to note vivid images in each poem. Discuss how these devices help determine the meaning.
Quantitative Measures					
Lexile	NP	**Text Length**	Word Count: 140; 271; 199; 610		

CLOSE READING MODEL

The passages below are from Edgar Allan Poe's "A Dream Within a Dream" and Ogden Nash's "Adventures of Isabel." The annotations to the right of each passage show ways in which you can use close reading skills to understand context clues and analyze rhythm and rhyme.

from "A Dream within a Dream"

Take this kiss upon the brow!
And, in parting from you now,
Thus much let me avow— [1]
You are not wrong, who deem
That my days have been a dream;

Rhythm and Rhyme

1 The words *brow* and *now* share the end sound "ow," which also occurs at the end of line 3. Lines 1 and 2 have the same rhythm. The rhythm changes slightly in line 3. In some poems, a change in rhythm indicates an important new thought or idea.

from "Adventures of Isabel"

Once in a night as black as pitch [2]
Isabel met a wicked old witch.
The witch's face was cross and wrinkled,
The witch's gums with teeth were sprinkled. [3]

Context Clues

2 The context clues *night* and *black* can help you infer that *pitch* is something that is black. To get more information, you might use a dictionary to learn that pitch is a form of tar.

Rhythm and Rhyme

3 When you read these lines aloud, you can hear the pattern of stressed and unstressed syllables. This rhythm creates a humorous tone.

Daily Bellringer

For each class during which you will teach this selection, have students complete one of the five Sentence Modeling activities for Week 14 in *Daily Bellringer Activities*. You may wish to use additional activities that are applicable to this selection.

Vocabulary

If students require support with selection vocabulary, use this routine:

1. Write the following words and definitions on the board:

   ravenous *adj.* greedily hungry

   cavernous *adj.* huge and hollow; like a cavern

   deem *v.* hold as an opinion; judge

   beseech *v.* beg

   dismal *adj.* causing gloom or misery

   sympathize *v.* share in a feeling; feel compassion

2. Have students say each word aloud.

3. Use the word in a sentence that defines the word.

DIFFERENTIATED INSTRUCTION

EL Extended Support— English Learners
Have students complete the **Reading and Vocabulary Warm-ups** for this collection in the *Student Companion All-in-One Workbook* before they read. Assign the prereading pages and the selections in the *Reader's Notebook: English Learner's Version*. Then, have students listen to portions of the collection in the *Student eText* or on the *Hear It!* CD-ROM.

L1 L2 Extended Support— Struggling Readers
Have students complete the **Reading and Vocabulary Warm-ups** for this collection in the *Student Companion All-in-One Workbook* before they read. Assign the prereading pages and the selections in the *Reader's Notebook: Adapted Version*. Then, have students listen to portions of the collection in the *Student eText* or on the *Hear It!* CD-ROM.

Extended Support— Reluctant Readers
To build motivation and engagement before assigning the collection, have students read "Dancing in the Streets," a thematically related selection in *Reality Central*. Then, use the questions at the conclusion of the related selection to guide discussion.

MULTIDRAFT READING

To assist struggling readers and to deepen comprehension for all, assign the text in "chunks" and apply multidraft reading protocols. For each reading, have students set the purpose indicated:

- **First reading:** Students should read the selection independently and think about its basic meaning.
- **Second reading:** Students should analyze the text's key ideas and details and its craft and structure, and respond to the side-column prompts.
- **Third reading:** Students should integrate knowledge and ideas, connect the text to other texts and to the world, and answer the end-of-selection questions.

For more guidance, refer to the *Classroom Strategies and Teaching Routines* card on multidraft reading.

Meet the Poets

 **Edgar Allan Poe** (1809–1849) led a troubled life. His father deserted him, his mother died before he was three, and his wife died young. Despite his problems, Poe produced some of the world's best-known short stories, essays, and poems.

 **Ogden Nash** (1902–1971), one of America's best-loved poets and humorists, threw away his first poetry attempt. Luckily, he pulled it out of the trash and sent it to the *New Yorker* magazine—which published it immediately. During his forty-year career, Nash wrote more than thirty poetry books.

 **Maya Angelou** (b. 1928) changed her childhood name from Marguerite Johnson, and she has never stopped exploring who she is. In addition to being a poet and best-selling author, she has been an educator, historian, actress, playwright, civil-rights activist, producer, and director.

 **Lewis Carroll** (1832–1898) is the pen name of Charles Lutwidge Dodgson, an English math professor who taught at Oxford University. He wrote two children's classics, *Alice's Adventures in Wonderland* (1865) and *Through the Looking Glass,* (1872), which contains "The Walrus and the Carpenter."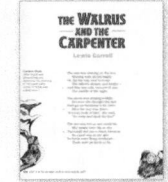

320 UNIT 3 • Do we need words to communicate well?

💬 VOCABULARY DEVELOPMENT

Thematic Vocabulary: The Big Question
As students are discussing Poetry Collection 1, encourage them to use the words for discussing the Big Question presented on pp. 302–303. You might encourage them with sentence starters like these:

1. Poets *communicate* thoughts and feelings by . . .
2. The *connection* between the title of Edgar Allan Poe's poem and the poem itself can be described as . . .

3. In Maya Angelou's poem, calling Mother Goose "mean" may be an *expression* of the poet's feeling that . . .
4. The main *message* of "Life Doesn't Frighten Me" is . . .
5. The walrus and the carpenter *share* . . .

A Dream Within a Dream

Edgar Allan Poe

Take this kiss upon the brow!
And, in parting from you now,
Thus much let me avow—
You are not wrong, who deem
5   That my days have been a dream;
Yet if hope has flown away
In a night, or in a day,
In a vision, or in none,
Is it therefore the less *gone*?
10 *All* that we see or seem
Is but a dream within a dream.
I stand amid the roar
Of a surf-tormented shore,
And I hold within my hand
15 Grains of the golden sand—
How few! yet how they creep
Through my fingers to the deep,
While I weep—while I weep!
O God! can I not grasp
20 Them with a tighter clasp?
O God! can I not save
One from the pitiless wave?
Is *all* that we see or seem
But a dream within a dream?

◄ **Vocabulary**
deem (dēm) *v.* hold an opinion; judge

Spiral Review
IMAGERY How does the image of the "surf-tormented shore" reflect the speaker's state of mind?

Rhythm and Rhyme
When read aloud, how many stressed syllables are there in most lines of this poem?

Spiral Review
Imagery

1. Remind students that they learned about imagery in the Unit 3 Focus on Craft and Structure (pp. 314–317).

2. Have students reread the poem. Then, **ask** students the Spiral Review question.

   Possible response: He, too, is tormented; perhaps he remembers an awful event.

❶ **Rhythm and Rhyme**

Ask the Rhythm and Rhyme question.

Answer: Most lines of this poem have three stressed syllables, but many have four.

❷ **Interpret**

1. Remind students that a metaphor describes something as if it were something else.

2. **Ask** students what is meant by the metaphor in Poe's question in lines 23–24.

   Possible response: Students may say Poe is asking how someone can distinguish between what is real and what is not, especially when life seems to slip away like the sand.

3. **Ask** students what they think may have prompted Poe to write this poem.

   Possible responses: Some students may say they think he lost a loved one, or he is realizing how time has passed and his life and the things in it seem to be slipping away.

👥 DIFFERENTIATED INSTRUCTION

EL Pronunciation for English Learners
Refer students to the word *deem* on this page. Write the word on the board, pronounce it distinctly, and have students repeat it. Next, write the word *dim* on the board. Model its pronunciation, and have students repeat it. Then, call a volunteer to the board. Say one or the other word, and have the volunteer point to the word you have said. Repeat with additional volunteers.

Strategy for Less Proficient Readers
Prepare an **Anticipation Guide** (*Professional Development Guidebook,* p. 38) with the following statements:

- A confident person is not afraid of anything.
- Dreams have no connection to real life.
- You can't always trust a friendly face.

   Give students a copy of the prepared **Guide** and have them mark their responses in the Me column. Have students discuss the statements in groups and then mark their responses in the Group column. After students are done reading the poems, have them complete the After Reading column.

Video

Watch the Background Video online!

Audio

Selection Audio is available in the *Student eText* and on the *Hear It!* CD-ROM.

Adventures of
Isabel

Ogden Nash

Isabel met an enormous bear,
Isabel, Isabel, didn't care;
The bear was hungry, the bear was ravenous,
The bear's big mouth was cruel and cavernous.
5 The bear said, Isabel, glad to meet you,
How do, Isabel, now I'll eat you!
Isabel, Isabel, didn't worry,
Isabel didn't scream or scurry.
She washed her hands and
    she straightened her hair up,
10 Then Isabel quietly ate the bear up.

Vocabulary ▶
ravenous
(rav´ ə nəs) *adj.*
greedily hungry

cavernous (kav´
ər nəs) *adj.* huge
and hollow;
like a cavern

Once in a night as black as pitch
Isabel met a wicked old witch.
The witch's face was cross and wrinkled,
The witch's gums with teeth were sprinkled.
15 Ho ho, Isabel! the old witch crowed,
I'll turn you into an ugly toad!
Isabel, Isabel, didn't worry,
Isabel didn't scream or scurry,
She showed no rage and she showed no rancor,
20 But she turned the witch into milk and drank her.

Isabel met a hideous giant,
Isabel continued self-reliant.
The giant was hairy, the giant was horrid,
He had one eye in the middle of his forehead.
25 Good morning Isabel, the giant said,
I'll grind your bones to make my bread.
Isabel, Isabel, didn't worry,
Isabel didn't scream or scurry.
She nibbled the zwieback that she always fed off,
30 And when it was gone, she cut the giant's head off.

Isabel met a troublesome doctor,
He punched and he poked till he really shocked her.
The doctor's talk was of coughs and chills
And the doctor's satchel bulged with pills.
35 The doctor said unto Isabel,
Swallow this, it will make you well.
Isabel, Isabel, didn't worry,
Isabel didn't scream or scurry.
She took those pills from the pill concocter,
40 And Isabel calmly cured the doctor.

Spiral Review
IMAGERY What do the poem's images suggest about Isabel's personality?

Rhythm and Rhyme
What two-word rhymes are used in lines 29 and 30?

Context Clues
What clues help you understand that a satchel (line 34) is something that holds things?

PART 2 • Poetry Collection 1 **323**

Spiral Review
Imagery
1. Remind students that they studied imagery in the Unit 3 Focus on Craft and Structure (pp. 314–317).
2. **Ask** students the Spiral Review question.

    Possible response: Like the first stanza, this one tells of an instance when Isabel did not "scream or scurry." This repeating image of Isabel facing a scary bear and witch reinforces the idea that Isabel is calm and decisive in tense situations.

❸ Rhythm and Rhyme
1. Review that rhyme is the repetition of sounds at the ends of words. Explain that rhyming can involve more than a single word, and the words do not always rhyme perfectly.
2. **Ask** the Rhythm and Rhyme question.

    Answer: The two-word rhymes are "fed off" and "head off."

❹ Context Clues
1. Remind students that context clues are words surrounding a given word that give clues to the word's meaning. Have students read lines 33 and 34. **Ask:** Is a *satchel* a person, place, or thing? How do you know?

    Answer: It's a thing; it is stuffed with pills.
2. **Ask** what word students could use in place of *satchel*.

    Answer: Bag.
3. Have students reread the sentence, replacing *satchel* with *bag*. **Ask** if the new sentence makes sense.

    Answer: Yes.
4. **Ask** the Context Clues question.

    Answer: bulged, pills.

≈ FLUENCY

Distribute copies of this page. Have pairs of students take turns reading the first stanza on the page aloud as a partner marks areas of difficulty, paying particular attention to mispronounced words or letters. Collect the copies and review problem areas, focusing on mispronounced words, such as *wrinkled* and *sprinkled*.

Guide students in identifying the letters and sounds in each word. Next, list other words with these letter patterns, such as *crackled*, *tackled*, and *chuckled*. Once students can pronounce each word, help them use context to understand its meaning.

Point out that they might find clues about the correct pronunciation of unfamiliar words in poetry by noting regular rhyme schemes. For example, have students look at the last two words of the first stanza (*drank her*) as a clue to the pronunciation of the vocabulary word *rancor*.

⑤ Rhythm and Rhyme

1. Explain to students that a list has its own rhythm because it is a grouping of similar items. Have students reread the first stanza of the poem and note the things that don't frighten the speaker.

2. Ask the Rhythm and Rhyme question.

Answer: The poet lists shadows, noises, bad dogs, and ghosts.

⑥ Context Clues

1. Ask a volunteer to pantomime the actions in the third stanza while you read it aloud. **Ask** how the speaker reacts to the scary things mentioned in Stanzas 1 and 2.

Possible response: She doesn't cry, she just smiles and scares them away.

2. Ask the Context Clues question.

Answer: The words *boo, make fun, run* and *fly* are context clues for the word *shoo. Shoo* means to drive or frighten away.

Life Doesn't Frighten Me

MAYA ANGELOU

Rhythm and Rhyme
The poet uses lists of things to build rhythm and rhyme. What things does she list in the first stanza?

Shadows on the wall
Noises down the hall
Life doesn't frighten me at all
Bad dogs barking loud
5 Big ghosts in a cloud
Life doesn't frighten me at all.

Mean old Mother Goose
Lions on the loose
They don't frighten me at all
10 Dragons breathing flame
On my counterpane[1]
That doesn't frighten me at all.

Context Clues
What words help you understand the meaning of *shoo* in line 14? What does *shoo* mean?

I go boo
Make them shoo
15 I make fun
Way they run
I won't cry
So they fly
I just smile
20 They go wild
Life doesn't frighten me at all.
Tough guys in a fight
All alone at night
Life doesn't frighten me at all.

---

1. **counterpane** *n.* bedspread.

💬 VOCABULARY DEVELOPMENT

Expressive Vocabulary
To develop students' expressive vocabulary, present the following words: *interpret, perceive, respond, distinguish,* and *react.* Have them use each of the words in sentences about the poems. Use these sentence starters:

1. You can *interpret* Angelou's phrase "I make fun" as . . .

2. The speaker in "Life Doesn't Frighten Me" doesn't *perceive* . . .

3. She might *respond* to a challenge by . . .

4. In "The Walrus and the Carpenter," the walrus failed to *distinguish* . . .

5. The Carpenter was slow to *react* . . .

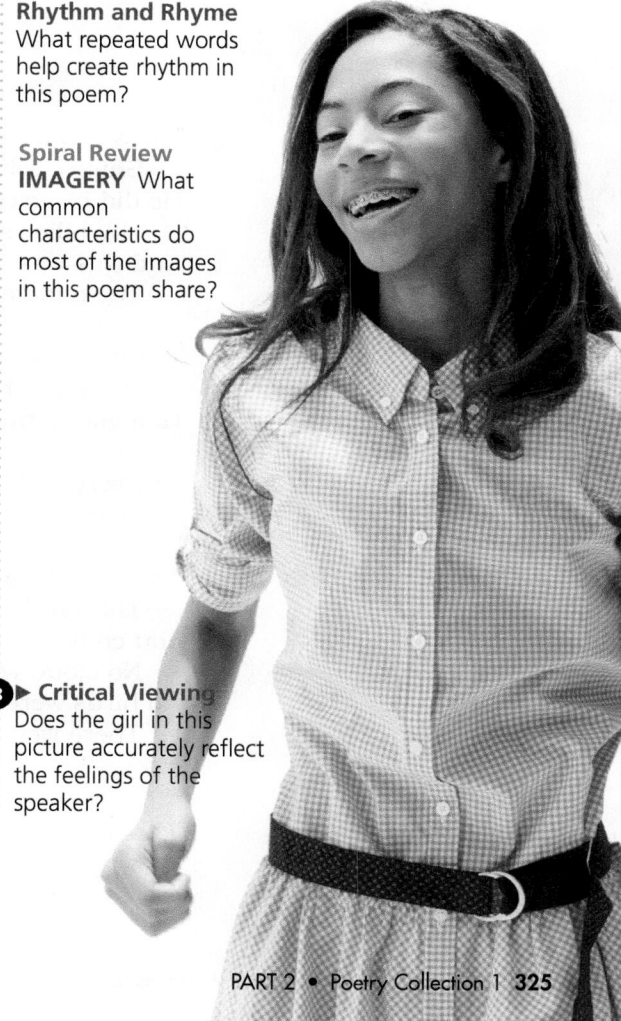

25　Panthers in the park
　　Strangers in the dark
　　No, they don't frighten me at all.

　　That new classroom where
　　Boys all pull my hair
30　(Kissy little girls
　　With their hair in curls)
　　They don't frighten me at all.

　　Don't show me frogs and snakes
　　And listen for my scream,
35　If I'm afraid at all
　　It's only in my dreams.

　　I've got a magic charm
　　That I keep up my sleeve,
　　I can walk the ocean floor
40　And never have to breathe.

　　Life doesn't frighten me at all
　　Not at all
　　Not at all.
　　Life doesn't frighten me at all.

Rhythm and Rhyme
What repeated words help create rhythm in this poem?

Spiral Review
IMAGERY What common characteristics do most of the images in this poem share?

8 ▶ Critical Viewing
Does the girl in this picture accurately reflect the feelings of the speaker?

PART 2 • Poetry Collection 1　**325**

---

❼ Rhythm and Rhyme

1. Remind students that repetition can give a poem a musical quality. Have students scan the poem to find the repeated words in each stanza.

2. Ask the Rhythm and Rhyme question.

　　Answer: "Life doesn't frighten me at all," along with "They don't frighten me at all."

Spiral Review
Imagery

1. Remind students that they studied imagery in the Unit 3 Focus on Craft and Structure (pp. 314–317).

2. Ask students the Spiral Review question.

　　Possible response: The images are all of situations that would be particularly frightening to a child.

❽ Critical Viewing

Possible response: The girl's facial expression shows she is happy and her posture indicates that she is not afraid. The girl pictured reflects the speaker's feelings of not being frightened.

⁂ DIFFERENTIATED INSTRUCTION

🔵L Strategy for English Learners
Students may benefit from reading the poem in small sections. Ask students to take out several sheets of paper and copy the poem, writing one stanza on each side of a page. Read aloud one section of the poem at a time. Then, allow students time to write questions and notes about words they do not know. Guide students to interpret the images. After students complete the poem, ask them to write a summary of it.

Enrichment for Advanced Learners
Point out to students that Maya Angelou uses lists of potentially scary things and repeats the phrase "life doesn't frighten me at all" to reveal the personality of the speaker of her poem. Challenge students to create short poems of their own that describe themselves or someone they know well. Have them include repetition and lists of ideas or characteristics in their poems.

❾ Context Clues

1. Read the second stanza aloud with students. **Ask** students why the sun has no business being out.

Answer: It isn't daytime; it is the middle of the night.

2. Ask students to identify the word that describes how the moon reacts to this situation.

Answer: The word is *sulkily*.

3. Ask the Context Clues question.

Possible response: *Had got no business, very rude,* and *spoil the fun* provide context clues for the word's meaning. *Sulkily* means "grumpily," "sullenly," or "resentfully."

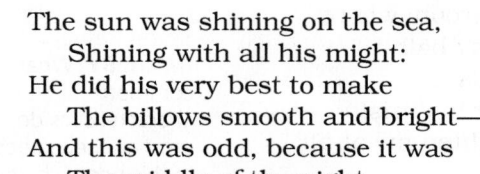

THE WALRUS AND THE CARPENTER

Lewis Carroll

Context Clues
What words and phrases help you determine the meaning of the word *sulkily* in line 7? What does *sulkily* mean?

❾

The sun was shining on the sea,
   Shining with all his might:
He did his very best to make
   The billows smooth and bright—
5 And this was odd, because it was
   The middle of the night.

The moon was shining sulkily,
   Because she thought the sun
Had got no business to be there
10   After the day was done—
"It's very rude of him," she said,
   "To come and spoil the fun!"

The sea was wet as wet could be,
   The sands were dry as dry.
15 You could not see a cloud, because
   No cloud was in the sky:
No birds were flying overhead—
   There were no birds to fly.

326 UNIT 3 • Do we need words to communicate well?

💭 THINK ALOUD

Making Inferences

Model the skill of making inferences, introduced on p. 28. Say to students:

When I read the first line of "The Walrus and the Carpenter," I learn that the sun is shining on the sea. However, when I read lines 5 and 6, I am confused: "And this was odd, because it was / The middle of the night." I realize that the poem is not entirely realistic—it calls the sun "he" and talks about the great effort the sun is making: "He did his very best to make / The billows smooth and bright." Knowing that the poem is not intended to describe reality truly, I make an inference: The writer intends the surprise in the last two lines of this stanza to be humorous. As I read further, I'll look for more funny details that will confirm, or prove, my inference.

The Walrus and the Carpenter
20 Were walking close at hand:
They wept like anything to see
Such quantities of sand:
"If this were only cleared away,"
  They said, "it would be grand!"

25 "If seven maids with seven mops
  Swept it for half a year,
Do you suppose," the Walrus said,
  "That they could get it clear?"
"I doubt it," said the Carpenter,
30 And shed a bitter tear.

"O Oysters, come and walk with us!"
  The Walrus did beseech.
"A pleasant walk, a pleasant talk,
  Along the briny beach:
35 We cannot do with more than four,
  To give a hand to each."

The eldest Oyster looked at him,
  But never a word he said:
The eldest Oyster winked his eye,
40 And shook his heavy head—
Meaning to say he did not choose
  To leave the oyster-bed.

◀ **Vocabulary**
beseech (bē sēch´)
v. beg

PART 2 • Poetry Collection 1 327

10 **Connecting to the Big Question**

1. Point out that verbal and non-verbal communication work together to create successful communication.

2. Have students read the last two verses on this page. **Ask:** What invitation does the Walrus extend to the oysters?

   Possible response: He begs them to come for a pleasant walk with him and the Carpenter.

3. **Ask:** Why does the eldest Oyster shake his head?

   Possible response: He doesn't believe that the Walrus is saying what he means. He is suspicious of the Walrus and the Carpenter, based on his previous knowledge of walruses and human beings.

4. **Ask:** What other methods of communication could the Walrus have used to better communicate?

   Possible response: None, since the oyster is already suspicious of the Walrus.

🌐 DIFFERENTIATED INSTRUCTION

Support for Special-Needs Students
Remind students that sometimes the speaker in a poem is inside the action, and other times the speaker is watching and describing the action. Encourage students to discuss whether the speaker in the first two stanzas of "The Walrus and the Carpenter" is inside or outside the action and to say what clues they used to determine the speaker's position.

Enrichment for Gifted/Talented Students
Invite students to rewrite the "The Walrus and the Carpenter" from the point of view of one of the characters: the Walrus, the Carpenter, the Oysters, or even, the moon. Before they write, encourage students to generate a list of qualities for their character. Students should cover the same events and include the same dialogue, but change the perspective to that of the character speaking. Have students read their poems to the class. Invite listeners to respond to the changes.

❶❶ Critical Viewing

Possible response: The Walrus in formal wear, the flying pig, and the baby oysters with arms and legs are colorful and fanciful illustrations reflecting the nonsensical nature of the humor of the poem. The picnic scene emphasizes the innocence of the Walrus' invitation, while the ship sailing off in a stormy sea hints at the dark message behind it.

❶❷ Context Clues

1. Read lines 49–54 with students. **Ask** students who joins the Walrus and the Carpenter in their walk.

Answer: many young oysters

2. Have students reread lines 53–54 silently. **Ask** what image the writer creates in these lines.

Possible response: The image is of many oysters bobbing over the waves as they try to get to shore.

3. Ask the Context Clues question.

Answer: *Frothy* describes the waves. The actions *hopping* and *scrambling* provide clues to the word's meaning.

❶❸ Rhythm and Rhyme

1. Read lines 55–60 aloud as a group. Ask students to identify the number of beats in lines 55, 57, and 59, and in lines 56, 58, and 60.

Answer: Lines 55, 57, and 59 have four beats. Lines 56, 58, and 60 have three beats.

2. Ask the Rhythm and Rhyme question.

Answer: You should pronounce the word as if it had five syllables rather than four to keep the rhythmic pattern.

❶❶ ▼ Critical Viewing
In what way do the illustrations on pp. 326–330 reflect the feeling of the poem?

Context Clues ❶❷
What word does *frothy* describe in line 53? What actions help you know it means "churning or foamy"?

Rhythm and Rhyme ❶❸
How many syllables should you pronounce in *conveniently* to keep the poem's rhythmic pattern?

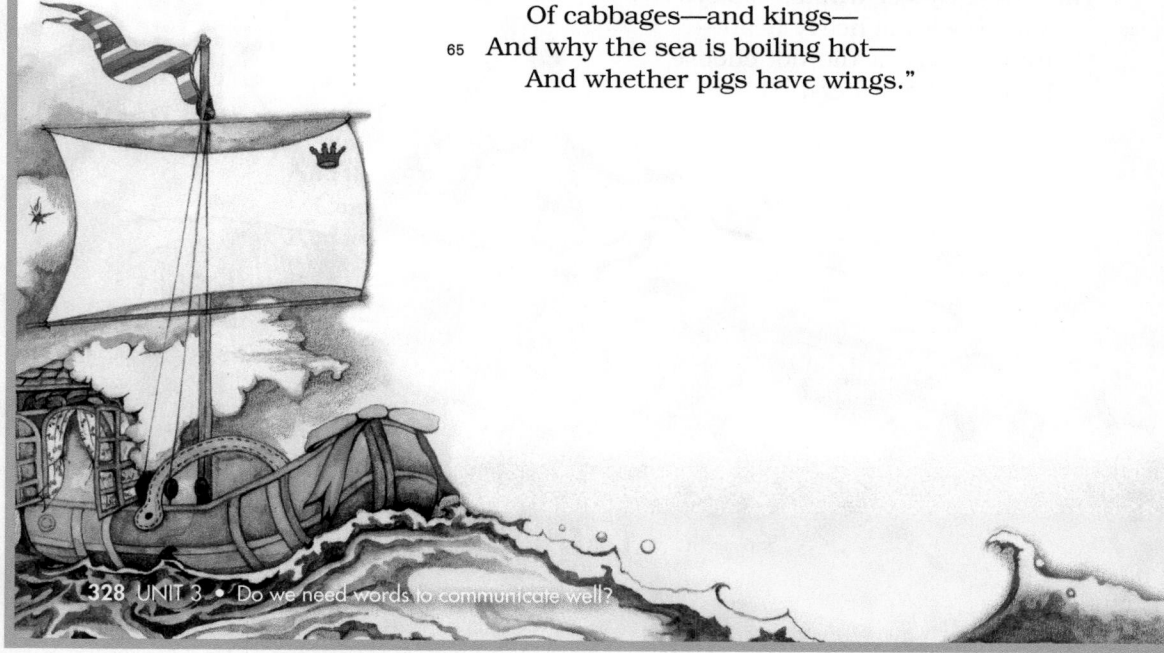

But four young Oysters hurried up,
    All eager for this treat:
45 Their coats were brushed, their faces washed,

    Their shoes were clean and neat—
And this was odd, because, you know,
    They hadn't any feet.
Four other Oysters followed them,
50   And yet another four;
And thick and fast they came at last,
    And more, and more, and more—
All hopping through the frothy waves,
    And scrambling to the shore.

55 The Walrus and the Carpenter
        Walked on a mile or so,
And then they rested on a rock
    Conveniently low:
And all the little Oysters stood
60   And waited in a row.

"The time has come," the Walrus said,
    "To talk of many things:
Of shoes—and ships—and sealing wax—
    Of cabbages—and kings—
65 And why the sea is boiling hot—
    And whether pigs have wings."

328 UNIT 3 • Do we need words to communicate well?

"But wait a bit," the Oysters cried,
    "Before we have our chat;
For some of us are out of breath,
    And all of us are fat!"
70 "No hurry!" said the Carpenter.
    They thanked him much for that.

"A loaf of bread," the Walrus said,
    "Is what we chiefly need:
75 Pepper and vinegar besides
    Are very good indeed—
Now, if you're ready, Oysters dear,
    We can begin to feed."

"But not on us!" the Oysters cried,
80 Turning a little blue.
"After such kindness, that would be
    A dismal thing to do!"
"The night is fine," the Walrus said.
    "Do you admire the view?"

85 "It was so kind of you to come!
    And you are very nice!"
The Carpenter said nothing but
    "Cut us another slice.
I wish you were not quite so deaf—
90 I've had to ask you twice!"

Rhythm and Rhyme
In each six-line stanza of
this poem, which lines
rhyme?

◀ **Vocabulary**
dismal (diz´ məl) *adj.*
causing gloom
or misery

⑭ Rhythm and Rhyme

1. Remind students that rhythm is
   the sound pattern created by
   stressed and unstressed syllables.
   Rhyme is the repetition of sounds
   at the ends of words. **Ask** students to reread the last stanza on
   the previous page and identify
   the rhyming words.

   Answer: *things, kings, wings*

2. Have students review other stanzas and note which words rhyme.
   Then **ask** the Rhythm and Rhyme
   question.

   Answer: In each stanza, lines 2,
   4, and 6 rhyme.

 **ASSESS**

Language Study
Vocabulary

1. Claire *beseeched* her parents to buy her the black pony for her birthday.

2. Our veterinarian never fails to *sympathize* with her clients when a pet dies.

3. Entering the small, dark space, we discovered a wide, *cavernous* opening.

4. The judge announced, "I *deem* that Bailey Jones' painting "Tree in Winter" deserves the first-place prize in this art show."

5. Jenny was *ravenous* after missing breakfast and lunch.

Word Study
Part A
Sample answers:

The Latin root *–mal-* means "bad" or "evil". A person who is *malnourished* suffers from the effects of a <u>bad</u> diet. Something that is *malodorous* smells <u>bad</u>. A *malicious* act is motivated by an <u>evil</u> desire to cause harm or pain.

Part B
Sample answers:

1. A plant that is *maladapted* to an environment will find <u>bad</u> conditions for survival and will not grow well.

2. Yes, a bully's expression of *malice* would indicate his or her intent to do <u>harm</u>.

Literary Analysis
Possible responses appear below. Check to be sure students support their responses with evidence from the text.

1. (a) The words *roar* and *shore* are clues that indicate *surf-tormented* describes the effect of noisy ocean waves on a beach. **(b)** The phrases *showed no rage* and *showed no ___* are clues that *rancor* is hatred. **(c)** The words *weep* and *deeply* are clues that to *sympathize* is to feel pity.

2. (a) A charm is an object that a person believes will protect himself or herself from danger or evil. **(b)** The speaker says that the charm is "magic" and that she can keep it "up my sleeve" so she

---

"It seems a shame," the Walrus said,
"To play them such a trick.
After we've brought them out so far,
And made them trot so quick!"
95 The Carpenter said nothing but
"The butter's spread too thick!"

"I weep for you," the Walrus said:
"I deeply sympathize."
With sobs and tears he sorted out
100 Those of the largest size,
Holding his pocket-handkerchief
Before his streaming eyes.

"O Oysters," said the Carpenter,
"You've had a pleasant run!
105 Shall we be trotting home again?"
But answer came there none—
And this was scarcely odd, because
They'd eaten every one.

Vocabulary ▶
sympathize (sim′ pə thīz) *v.* share in a feeling; feel compassion

---

Language Study

Vocabulary For each numbered item below, write a sentence that includes one of the blue vocabulary words.

ravenous   cavernous   deem   beseech   sympathize

1. a child who asks her parents for a pony

2. someone who feels sorry for another person's loss

3. a large cave you discover on a hike

4. a decision to award a prize

5. a person who has not eaten all day

WORD STUDY

The **Latin root -mal-** means "bad" or "evil." In "The Walrus and the Carpenter," the two title characters do something dismal, or something that causes bad feelings.

Word Study

Part A Explain how the **Latin root -mal-** contributes to the meanings of *malnourished, malodorous,* and *malicious.* Consult a dictionary if necessary.

Part B Explain your answers to these questions.

1. If a plant is *maladapted* to its environment, will it grow?

2. If a bully's face showed *malice,* would you be frightened?

330 UNIT 3 • Do we need words to communicate well?

---

can "walk the ocean floor/And never have to breathe"

3. "Adventures of Isabel": bear/care; ravenous/cavernous

"A Dream Within a Dream": brow/now/avow; seem/dream; roar/shore

"Life Doesn't Frighten Me": goose/loose; flight/night

"The Walrus and the Carpenter": might/bright/night; year/clear/tear; beseech/beach/each

4. The rhyming patterns in "Adventures of Isabel" and "The Walrus and the Carpenter" create a humorous, playful, fantastic tone and mood.

The rhyming pattern in "Life Doesn't Frighten Me" helps establish a humorous, but confident tone and mood. The rhyming pattern in "A Dream Within a Dream" contributes to a serious, solemn tone and mood.

5. There are seven stressed syllables.

6. (a) Isabel is calmly confident. She faces foes without fussing or straining. **(b)** Yes. She's not afraid to stand up for herself and would not tolerate bullying.

7. (a) Shadows on the wall, bad dogs barking loud, and lions on the loose. **(b)** Smiling shows courage and bravery when confronting scary things.

Literary Analysis

Poetry Collection 1

Key Ideas and Details

1. Context Clues Explain how the italicized context clues help you find the meanings of the underlined words.

(a) I stand amid the *roar* / of a <u>surf-tormented</u> *shore*
(b) "She *showed no rage* and she *showed no* <u>rancor</u>."
(c) "I *weep* for you," the Walrus said: / I *deeply* <u>sympathize</u>."

2. Context Clues Read this stanza from "Life Doesn't Frighten Me": "I've got a magic *charm* / That I keep up my sleeve, / I can walk the ocean floor / And never have to breathe."

(a) What is a *charm*? **(b)** What context clues help you understand the meaning of the word in this context?

Craft and Structure

3. Rhythm and Rhyme Complete a chart like the one on the right to give examples of rhyming words each poet uses.

4. Rhythm and Rhyme How does each pair of the words listed in the chart affect the tone and meaning of the poem?

5. Rhythm and Rhyme How many stressed syllables are in this line of poetry?
"If seven maids with seven mops/Swept it for half a year"

Integration of Knowledge and Ideas

6. (a) Support: Describe Isabel's personality, using details from "Adventures of Isabel" to support your answer. **(b) Assess:** Is Isabel someone you would want as a friend? Explain.

7. (a) Name three things that do not frighten the speaker of "Life Doesn't Frighten Me." **(b) Infer:** Why does she smile at frightening things?

8. 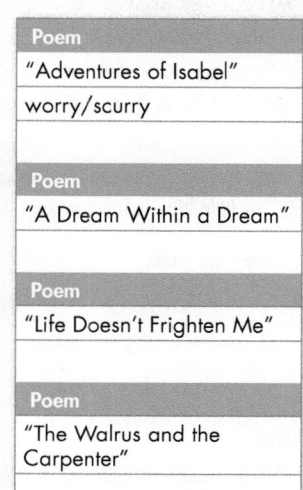 **Do we need words to communicate well? (a) Infer:**
In "The Walrus and the Carpenter," how does the old oyster know to be wary of the Walrus and the Carpenter?
(b) Generalize: In real life, how might someone know that a situation is dangerous if no one has described the danger in words?

Poem
"Adventures of Isabel"
worry/scurry

Poem
"A Dream Within a Dream"

Poem
"Life Doesn't Frighten Me"

Poem
"The Walrus and the Carpenter"

ACADEMIC VOCABULARY

As you write and speak about the poems in Collection 1, use the words related to communication that you explored on page 303 of this text.

---

8. **Do we need words to communicate well?**
(a) The old oyster had previous encounters with human beings who harvested oysters from the bed. **(b)** Someone might sense danger from prior knowledge and from clues such as sounds, smells, and people's faces or gestures.

Online Writer's Notebook

Students can use the Online Writer's Notebook to record all responses.

Conventions

Introduce the skill using the instruction on the student page.

Think Aloud: Model the Skill

Say to students:

If I say, "She ran away from the dog," you might wonder if she ran quickly or slowly. To give you this information, I would have to add an adverb that tells you how she ran. I would say, "She quickly ran away from the dog." The word *quickly* modifies the verb and clearly tells you how fast she ran. Similarly, I might say, "I gave her a book." This doesn't give any information about the book. However, if I say, "I gave her an *interesting* book," it tells you more about it. The word *interesting* is an adjectives that modifies, or tells more about the word *book*.

Practice A

1. adjective: *largest*—modifies *bag*
2. adverb: *quietly*—modifies *thinks*
3. adverb: *briskly*—modifies *walked*
4. adjective: *thrilling*—modifies *idea*

Reading Application
Sample answer:

Adjectives: *frothy*—modifies *waves*; *odd*—modifies *this*

Adverbs: *sulkily*—shining; *conveniently*—modifies *low*

Practice B

1. *quickly*: adverb Answers the question *How?*
2. *four*: adjective Answers the question *How many?*
3. *Slowly*: adverb; Answers the question *How?*
4. *yesterday*: adverb; Answers the question *When?*

Writing Application
Sample answer:

new/quickly; tall/slowly; little/sneakily; neighbor/quietly

Conventions: Adjectives and Adverbs

Adjectives and adverbs are called **modifiers** because they modify, or make clearer, the meaning of another word in the sentence.

An **adjective** describes a person, place, thing, or idea. It modifies a noun or pronoun.

An **adverb** modifies a verb, an adjective, or another adverb.

Poetry Collection 1

Adjectives answer the questions, *What kind? Which one? How many? How much?*

Many adverbs end in *-ly*. Adverbs answer the questions, *Where? When? How? To what extent?*

Sentence	Adjective or Adverb	Word It Modifies
The *little* kittens love milk.	*little*: adjective	*kittens* (noun)
They are *cute*.	*cute*: adjective	*They* (pronoun)
He ran *slowly*.	*slowly*: adverb	*ran* (verb)
Maples are *very* tall trees.	*very*: adverb	*tall* (adjective)
He went *extremely* slowly.	*extremely*: adverb	*slowly* (adverb)

Practice A

Write each sentence. Underline each adjective, circle each adverb, and draw an arrow to the word that each modifies.

1. Isabel's doctor gave her the largest bag.
2. The speaker thinks quietly to himself.
3. The girl walked briskly past the dog.
4. The Walrus and the Carpenter have a thrilling idea.

Reading Application Identify two adjectives and two adverbs in "The Walrus and the Carpenter," and state the word each modifies.

Practice B

Identify the modifier in each sentence. Tell whether it is an adjective or an adverb. Then, say what question the modifier answers.

1. The frogs jumped quickly over the snakes.
2. Four oysters crawled across the sand.
3. Slowly, the creature turned to Isabel.
4. The speaker had a nightmare yesterday.

Writing Application Rewrite this sentence four times, using a different adjective and adverb each time: *I saw the (adjective) girl run (adverb).*

332 UNIT 3 • Do we need words to communicate well?

▶ EXTEND THE LESSON

Sentence Modeling

Write the following sentence from "The Walrus and the Carpenter" on the board:

And thick and fast they came at last, and more and more, and more—all hopping through the frothy waves, and scrambling to the shore.

Ask students what they notice about the sentence. Elicit from them that the sentence

uses adjectives and adverbs (adjective: *frothy*; adverb: *fast*). Have students imitate the sentence in a sentence on a topic of their own choosing, matching the grammatical and stylistic features. Collect the sentences and share them with the class.

Writing to Sources

Explanatory Text One way to respond to literature is to write a **letter to an author**—even if you never send it. Write a letter to the author of one of the poems in Collection 1. In your letter, evaluate the poem's message, tone, rhythm, and rhyme.

- Begin by telling the poet which poem you read and explaining why you are writing about that poem.
- Quote lines, stanzas, or particular words to support your analysis of the poem's message, tone and sound devices.
- Write at least two well-organized paragraphs. Establish and maintain a formal style.
- End with a brief conclusion that summarizes your ideas.
- Use correct business letter format. Review a sample business letter in the Resources section in the back of your textbook.

Grammar Application Use at least three adjectives and two adverbs in your letter.

Research and Technology

Build and Present Knowledge Use library resources to find poems to include in an **illustrated booklet** about facing fears. Follow these steps to complete the assignment:

- Plan to include "Life Doesn't Frighten Me" and other poems you enjoy reading.
- Copy the poems into your booklet, leaving space for illustrations and annotations. Double-check your work to make sure you have copied the poems accurately. Pay particular attention to line breaks and punctuation.
- Illustrate your booklet to capture the spirit of the poems.
- Prepare annotations to summarize selections and point out details for readers. Use these questions as a guide:

  What message(s) do these poems express about facing fears?

  How do the poets use language and literary devices, such as rhyme and rhythm to convey their ideas?

 **Common Core State Standards**

Writing

2. Write informative/explanatory texts to examine a topic and convey ideas, concepts, and information through the selection, organization, and analysis of relevant content. **2.b.** Develop the content with relevant facts, definitions, concrete details, quotations, or other information and examples. **2.e.** Establish and maintain a formal style. **2.f.** Provide a concluding statement or section that follows from the information or explanation presented.

9. Draw evidence from literary or informational texts to support analysis, refection, and research.

Language

1. Demonstrate command of the conventions of standard English grammar and usage when writing or speaking.

Writing to Sources

1. Review the assignment, using the instruction on the student page.
2. To give students guidance in writing their letters, provide them with the **Support for Writing** page for this selection in the *Student Companion All-in-One Workbook.*
3. To evaluate students' explanatory texts, use one of the rubrics for **Letters**, pp. 236–237 in *Professional Development Guidebook.* In addition, you might evaluate how well students express their reactions and opinions and organize their thoughts.

Grammar Application

Have students check their drafts for the correct use of adjectives and adverbs.

Six Traits Focus

✓	Ideas		Word Choice
✓	Organization		Sentence Fluency
✓	Voice		Conventions

Research and Technology

1. Review the assignment, using the instruction on the student page.
2. To support students' work on the assignment, have them complete the **Support for Extend Your Learning** page for this selection in the *Student Companion All-in-One Workbook.*

LESSON PACING GUIDE

Poetry Collection 2: Abuelito Who • April Rain Song • The World Is Not a Pleasant Place to Be • Fame Is a Bee

DAY 1 — Preteach/Teach

- Administer the Reading and Vocabulary Warm-ups, as necessary.
- Introduce the Key Ideas and Details skill: Context Clues.
- Introduce the Craft and Structure skill: Figurative Language.
- Use the Close Reading Model to demonstrate the application of the skills.
- Review the selection vocabulary, as necessary, with students who need additional support.
- Prepare students to read the selection by reviewing with them the Multidraft Reading Strategies.

DAY 2 — Teach

- Informally monitor comprehension while students read.
- Use the Comprehension questions to confirm understanding.
- Develop students' ability to identify context clues and analyze figurative language using the sidenote questions.
- Reinforce vocabulary with the Vocabulary notes.
- Reinforce unit focus standards using the Spiral Review prompts.

DAY 3 — Assess

- Assess students' comprehension and mastery of the skills by having them answer the Literary Analysis questions.
- Have students complete the Vocabulary activities.
- Develop students' understanding of roots and affixes by having them complete the Word Study activities.

DAY 4 — Extend/Assess

- Build students' ability to master grammar concepts and conventions by having them complete the Conventions lesson.
- Have students complete the Writing to Sources activity and write a poem. (You may assign as homework.)
- Extend learning by having students complete the Speaking and Listening activity: a dramatic poetry reading.
- Administer the Selection Test or Open-Book Test.

Common Core State Standards

Reading Literature 4. Determine the meaning of words and phrases as they are used in a text, including figurative and connotative meanings; analyze the impact of a specific word choice on meaning and tone.

7. Compare and contrast the experience of reading a story, drama, or poem to listening to or viewing an audio, video, or live version of the text, including contrasting what they "see" and "hear" when reading the text to what they perceive when they listen or watch.

Writing 3.d. Use precise words and phrases, relevant descriptive details, and sensory language to convey experiences and events.

Speaking and Listening 6. Adapt speech to a variety of contexts and tasks, demonstrating command of formal English when indicated or appropriate.

Language 1. Demonstrate command of the conventions of standard English grammar and usage when writing or speaking.

4.a. Use context as a clue to the meaning of a word or phrase.

4.c. Consult reference materials, both print and digital, to find the pronunciation of a word or determine or clarify its precise meaning or its part of speech.

Daily Block Scheduling

Each day in this Lesson Pacing Guide represents a 40–50 minute period. Teachers using block scheduling may combine days to revise pacing. In addition, teachers may differentiate and support core instruction by integrating components for extended and intensive support as students require. See the Guide to Resources (facing page).

GUIDE TO RESOURCES

	LEARNER LEVELS						RESOURCES	WHERE FOUND		
	L1	L2	L3	L4	EL	ALL		PRINT	CD	ONLINE
Warm Up	✓	✓			✓		Vocabulary Warm-ups			✓
	✓	✓			✓		Reading Warm-ups			✓
						✓	Background Video			✓
						✓	Selection Audio		Hear It!	✓
Comprehension/ Selection Support						✓	Writing About the Big Question	Student Companion Workbook		✓
						✓	Literary Analysis	Student Companion Workbook		✓
						✓	Reading	Student Companion Workbook		✓
						✓	Vocabulary Builder	Student Companion Workbook		✓
				✓			Enrichment			✓
			✓	✓	✓		Conventions	Student Companion Workbook		✓
			✓	✓	✓		Writing to Sources	Student Companion Workbook		✓
			✓	✓	✓		Speaking and Listening	Student Companion Workbook		✓
Differentiated Instruction/ Additional Support						✓	Additional Standards Practice	Common Core Companion		✓
						✓	Close Reading Practice	Close Reading Notebook		✓
	✓	✓					Adapted Reader's Notebook			✓
					✓		English Reader's Notebook:			✓
					✓		Spanish Reader's Notebook			✓
					✓		Graphic Organizer A			✓
	✓	✓			✓		Graphic Organizer B			✓
	✓	✓			✓		"Acts of Kindness"	Reality Central Student Edition and Writing Journal		✓
	✓	✓			✓		Practice and Assess	Reading Kit		✓
Monitor Progress						✓	Selection Test		Exam View	✓
						✓	Open-Book Test		Exam View	✓
Digital Resources						✓	Close Reading Tool			✓
						✓	Online Writer's Notebook			✓

One-on-one teaching   Group work   Whole class instruction   Independent work   Assessment   Digital Resource

LEARNER LEVELS

L1 Special-Needs Students
L2 Below-Level Students (Tier 2)
L3 On-Level Students (Tier 1)
L4 Advanced Students (Tier 1)
EL English Learners
All All Students

Building Knowledge

❶ Do we need words to communicate well?

Read • Discuss • Research • Write As students read, they will explore the Big Question through text analysis of the selection. Encourage students to note comments and additional questions as they read, using text evidence to support their thoughts. Students should refer to their notes to help them deepen their understanding of the selection through discussion, research, and writing.

❷ Close Reading Focus

1. Remind students that context clues can also be synonyms or antonyms of the unknown word. For example, in the sentence, *The class felt sorrow and sadness for the girl who broke her leg,* "sadness" is a synonym for "sorrow."

2. Explain to students that we use figurative language in conversation all the time. For example, if we say, "She took off like a rocket," we're using a simile to compare a girl's speed to a rocket. Figurative language can be very effective for making a point.

Poetry Collection 2

❶ Do we need words to communicate well?

Explore the Big Question as you read the poems in Collection 2. Note ways in which the poets communicate feelings.

❷ CLOSE READING FOCUS

Key Ideas and Details: **Context Clues**

Context clues are details in a text that give you clues about a word's meaning. When you encounter an unfamiliar word, or a word with multiple meanings, reread and read ahead to look for context clues. This example shows how context clarifies the meaning of the multiple-meaning word *beat*:

Let the <u>rain</u> beat your <u>head with silver liquid drops</u>.

From the underlined context clues, you can figure out that *beat* is a verb that describes a gentle tap.

Craft and Structure: **Figurative Language**

Figurative language is language that is not meant to be taken literally. Authors and poets use figurative language to state ideas in fresh ways. They may use one or more of the following types of figurative language:

- **Similes** compare two unlike things using *like* or *as*.
- **Metaphors** compare two unlike things by stating that one thing *is* another.
- **Personification** compares an object or animal to a human by giving the object or animal human characteristics.

Vocabulary

You will encounter the following words in the poems in Collection 2. Decide whether you know each word well, know it a little bit, or do not know it at all. After you read, see how your knowledge of each word has increased.

  lullaby   sour   pleasant   receive

© **Common Core State Standards**

Reading Literature
4. Determine the meaning of words and phrases as they are used in a text, including figurative and connotative meanings; analyze the impact of a specific word choice on meaning and tone.

Language
4.a. Use context as a clue to the meaning of a word or phrase.

334 UNIT 3 • Do we need words to communicate well?

© TEXT COMPLEXITY **RUBRIC**

Poetry Collection 2		Reader and Task Suggestions	
Qualitative Measures		**Preparing to Read the Text**	**Leveled Tasks**
Context/Knowledge Demands	Reflections on nature and those around us 1 2 ③ 4 5	• Review various types of figurative language and other poetic devices prior to reading the poems.	*Levels of Meaning* If students will have difficulty with levels of meaning, have them take notes on the sensory language the poets use.
Structure/Language Conventionality and Clarity	Challenging vocabulary and diction; short poems and stanzas 1 2 ③ 4 5	• Guide students to use Multidraft Reading strategies (TE p. 336)	*Analyzing* If students will not have difficulty with levels of meaning, have them read to determine poetic devices the poets use to communicate.
Levels of Meaning/Purpose/Concept Level	Challenging concepts (feelings about others; need to belong) and accessible concepts (nature, fame) 1 2 ③ 4 5		
Quantitative Measures			
Lexile	NP **Text Length** Word Count: 151; 23; 56; 19		

CLOSE READING MODEL

The passages below are from Sandra Cisneros's "Abuelito Who" and Langston Hughes's "April Rain Song." The annotations to the right of each passage show ways in which you can use close reading skills to understand context clues and analyze figurative language.

from "Abuelito Who"

Abuelito who throws coins like rain [1]
And asks who loves him
Who is dough and feathers
Who is a watch and glass of water [2]

Figurative Language

1 The simile "throws coins like rain" may make you think of many sparkling coins falling with a tinkling sound. The image suggests that Abuelito's generosity pleases the speaker.

Figurative Language

2 The poet uses metaphors to describe Abuelito. He is "dough," "feathers," "a watch," and "a glass of water." These everyday items convey images of familiarity and a feeling of home.

from "April Rain Song"

The rain makes still pools on the sidewalk.
The rain makes running pools in the gutter. [3]

Context Clues

3 You can determine the meaning of the multiple-meaning word *still* by reading ahead. The speaker contrasts the "still pools" with "running pools." This contrast can help you figure out that here *still* means "unmoving."

Daily Bellringer

For each class during which you will teach this selection, have students complete one of the five Vocabulary activities for Week 15 in *Daily Bellringer Activities*. You may wish to use additional activities that are applicable to this selection.

Vocabulary

If students require support with selection vocabulary, use this routine:

1. Write the following words and definitions on the board:

lullaby *n.* a song to help a baby fall asleep

sour *adj.* having the sharp acid taste of lemon or vinegar

pleasant *adj.* agreeable; delightful

receive *v.* to get something

2. Have students say each word aloud.

3. Use the word in a sentence that defines the word.

DIFFERENTIATED INSTRUCTION

EL Extended Support— English Learners
Have students complete the **Reading and Vocabulary Warm-ups** for this collection in the *Student Companion All-in-One Workbook* before they read. Assign the prereading pages and the selections in the *Reader's Notebook: English Learner's Version*. Then, have students listen to portions of the collection in the *Student eText* or on the *Hear It!* CD-ROM.

L1 L2 Extended Support— Struggling Readers
Have students complete the **Reading and Vocabulary Warm-ups** for this collection in the *Student Companion All-in-One Workbook* before they read. Assign the prereading pages and the selections in the *Reader's Notebook: Adapted Version*. Then, have students listen to portions of the collection in the *Student eText* or on the *Hear It!* CD-ROM.

Extended Support— Reluctant Readers
To build motivation and engagement before assigning the collection, have students read "Acts of Kindness," a thematically related selection in *Reality Central*. Then, use the questions at the conclusion of the related selection to guide discussion.

MULTIDRAFT READING

To assist struggling readers and to deepen comprehension for all, assign the text in "chunks" and apply multidraft reading protocols. For each reading, have students set the purpose indicated:

- **First reading:** Students should read the selection independently and think about its basic meaning.
- **Second reading:** Students should analyze the text's key ideas and details and its craft and structure, and respond to the side-column prompts.
- **Third reading:** Students should integrate knowledge and ideas, connect the text to other texts and to the world, and answer the end-of-selection questions.

For more guidance, refer to the *Classroom Strategies and Teaching Routines* card on multidraft reading.

Meet the Poets

 **Sandra Cisneros** (b. 1954) was born in Chicago, but her family often traveled to Mexico to live with her grandfather, the *abuelito* in her poem "Abuelito Who." The frequent moves left Cisneros with few friends, and she remembers that she "retreated inside" herself, reading books and writing. Cisneros has won several awards for her poetry and short stories.

 **Langston Hughes** (1902–1967), an award-winning poet, dramatist, and novelist, traveled to Africa and Europe as a young man before settling in Harlem in New York City. In the 1920s, he was one of the leaders of the Harlem Renaissance, a period in which African American writers, artists, and musicians produced brilliant works.

 **Nikki Giovanni** (b. 1943), born in Knoxville, Tennessee, has become one of America's most popular poets. Her awards include the National Association for the Advancement of Colored People (NAACP) Image Award for Distinguished Contributions to Arts and Letters. She is a college professor.

 **Emily Dickinson** (1830–1886) spent one year in college, but then became homesick and returned to her parents' house in Amherst, Massachusetts. For her remaining years, she seldom traveled or received guests. Dickinson read many books and wrote more than 1,700 poems, which form a kind of lifelong diary of her deepest thoughts. She is considered one of the leading voices of American poetry.

336 UNIT 3 • Do we need words to communicate well?

💬 VOCABULARY DEVELOPMENT

Thematic Vocabulary: The Big Question
As students are discussing Poetry Collection 2, encourage them to use the thematic vocabulary presented in Introducing the Big Question, pp. 302–303. You might encourage them with sentence starters like these:

1. The speaker in "Abuelito Who" *reveals* feelings about . . .

2. Langston Hughes creates a *visual* image of . . .

3. In the poem "The World is NOT a Pleasant Place to Be" the author *shares* feelings about . . .

4. Dickinson makes a *connection* between. . .

ABUELITO WHO

SANDRA CISNEROS

Abuelito[1] who throws coins like rain
and asks who loves him
who is dough and feathers
who is a watch and glass of water
5   whose hair is made of fur
is too sad to come downstairs today
who tells me in Spanish you are my diamond
who tells me in English you are my sky
whose little eyes are string
10   can't come out to play
sleeps in his little room all night and day
who used to laugh like the letter k
is sick
is a doorknob tied to a sour stick
15   is tired shut the door
doesn't live here anymore
is hiding underneath the bed
who talks to me inside my head
is blankets and spoons and big brown shoes
20   who snores up and down up and down up and down again
is the rain on the roof that falls like coins
asking who loves him
who loves him who?

---

1. **Abuelito** (ä bwä lē′ tō) *n.* in Spanish, an affectionate term for a grandfather.

Context Clues
What meaning of the word *watch* does the poet use in line 4?

Spiral Review
WORD CHOICE What attitude is suggested by the words the author uses to describe her grandfather?

◄ **Vocabulary**
sour (sour) *adj.* having the sharp acid taste of lemon or vinegar

Figurative Language
What type of figurative language does the poet use to describe Abuelito in lines 14–19?

❶ Context Clues

1. **Ask:** Why does the poet compare Abuelito to a watch and a glass of water in line 4?

   Possible response: To show that Abuelito was always available to provide for simple needs.

2. **Ask** the Context Clues question on the student page.

   Answer: The word watch refers to a timepiece in line 4.

Spiral Review
Word Choice

1. Remind students that they studied the concept of word choice in the Unit 2 Focus on Craft and Structure (pp. 180–183).

2. **Ask** students the Spiral Review question.

   Possible response: The word choices indicate that the author has an attitude of love and concern for Abuelito ("tells me . . . you are my sky,"), but there is also sadness about Abuelito being sick ("is too sad," "can't come out to play").

❷ Figurative Language

1. Review the types of figurative language you have discussed with the class.

2. **Ask** the Figurative Language question.

   Answer: The poet is using metaphor.

 Video

Watch the Background Video online!

 **Audio**

Selection Audio is available in the *Student eText* and on the *Hear It!* CD-ROM.

❸ Context Clues

1. Remind students that context clues are words or phrases that can help them figure out a word with multiple possible meanings. Have students reread lines 4 and 5. **Ask** which meaning of *still* the poet uses in line 4.

   Answer: In this case, *still* means "not moving."

2. Then **ask** the Context Clues question.

   Answer: The word *running* means "flowing" or "streaming" in line 5 of the poem. The poet contrasts the "running pools" with the "still pools" from line 4.

❹ Connecting to the Big Question

1. Point out that uncommon connections can be made between common words to create a strong impression. Tell students that poets often choose words as much for their sound as for their meaning.

2. Have students read the poem on this page. **Ask:** How does the rhythm of *silver liquid drops* emphasize the poet's description of the rain?

   Possible response: The words *silver* and *liquid* imply the regular rhythmic sound of falling raindrops.

3. **Ask** students: How do the words *still* and *pools* connect and create an image of the rain?

   Possible response: Both words have an -*l* sound. The sound of the words together creates a peaceful feeling.

4. **Ask** students to explain if and how the poet could communicate his love for the rain any better.

   Possible responses: Some students may say a drawing could show the poet enjoying the rain. Others may say his poem works the best because of the images he creates.

April Rain Song

LANGSTON HUGHES

Vocabulary ▶
lullaby (lul′ə bī) *n.* quiet, gentle song sung to send a child to sleep

❸ Context Clues
Which meaning of the word *running* does the poet use in line 5? How can you tell?

❹ Let the rain kiss you.
Let the rain beat upon your head with silver liquid drops.
Let the rain sing you a lullaby.

The rain makes still pools on the sidewalk.
5 The rain makes running pools in the gutter.
The rain plays a little sleep-song on our roof
   at night—

And I love the rain.

338 UNIT 3 • Do we need words to communicate well?

The World is **NOT** a Pleasant Place to Be

Nikki Giovanni

6

the world is not a pleasant place
to be without
someone to hold and be held by

a river would stop
5 its flow if only
a stream were there
to receive it

an ocean would never laugh
if clouds weren't there
10 to kiss her tears

the world is not
a pleasant place to be without
someone

◄ **Vocabulary**
pleasant (plez´ ənt) *adj.*
agreeable; delightful

◄ **Vocabulary**
receive (ri sēv´) *v.* be given

Figurative Language
What type of figurative
language is used in
lines 8–10? What do
you think the poet
means?

5 Figurative Language

1. Have students reread lines 8 through 10. **Ask** what qualities the poet gives the ocean and the clouds in this passage.

   Answer: The ocean laughs, the clouds kiss away her tears.

2. **Ask** the Figurative Language question.

   Answer: The poet uses personification in lines 8 through 10. The poet means that even one part of nature, the ocean, seems to be able to be happy only because another part of nature, the clouds, is there to comfort her when she is sad.

6 Connecting to the Big Question

1. Point out that poets often use personification: They compare an object or animal to a human by giving it human characteristics.

2. Direct students to read the poem. **Ask:** How does the poet describe a river and an ocean?

   Possible response: Both are described as having human emotions, such as wanting to be welcomed and appreciated, sadness, and sympathy.

3. Direct students to read the poem again. **Ask:** Does the last verse seem unfinished? What do you think about when you read the final word "someone"?

   Possible response: The last line doesn't follow the form of the earlier verses and feels incomplete. The reader is left with an empty, lonely feeling.

4. **Ask** students if the images created in the first three stanzas or the omission of words in the last stanza communicates the overall mood of the poem better.

   Possible responses: Students may say the last stanza because the lack of an image reinforces the feeling of loneliness.

❼ Figurative Language

1. **Ask** the Figurative Language question.

   Answer: The poet uses metaphor to compare fame to a bee.

2. **Ask** students to explain why the poet compared fame to a bee.

   Possible responses: Fame can be good and bad, like a bee. It also come and goes quickly, like a bee.

☑ ASSESS

Language Study

Vocabulary

1. A parent would be most likely to sing a *lullaby* at night, because a lullaby is a bedtime song.

2. No, I am not *pleasant* after a sleepless night, because going without sleep makes me grouchy, the opposite of pleasant.

3. No, I do not want to drink *sour* milk, as this means it has been standing too long and has gone bad. It could make me sick.

4. I like to *receive* gifts because when someone gives me something, I feel loved.

Word Study

Part A

Sample answers:

The suffix *–ant* means "state" or "condition of being." *Vigilant* is the <u>state</u> of being watchful and alert. *Important* is the <u>state</u> of being valuable or having much value.

Part B

Sample answers:

1. The suffix *–ant* means "state" or "condition of being." Yes, *expectant* is the <u>state</u> of expecting, so the person is expecting or waiting for something.

2. The suffix *–ant* means "state" or "condition of being." No, a water-*resistant* jacket has the <u>condition of being</u> resistant to water, so it does not soak up much rain.

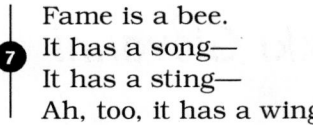

Fame Is a Bee

Emily Dickinson

Figurative Language
What type of figurative language is used to compare fame to a bee?

❼ Fame is a bee.
It has a song—
It has a sting—
Ah, too, it has a wing.

Language Study

Vocabulary The words listed below appear in the poems in Collection 2. Answer each question, explaining your responses.

lullaby   sour   pleasant   receive

1. When would a parent be most likely to sing a *lullaby*?
2. Are you *pleasant* after a sleepless night?
3. Would you want to drink *sour* milk?
4. Why do you like to *receive* gifts?

WORD STUDY

The **suffix -ant** means "state" or "condition of being." In "The World Is Not a Pleasant Place to Be," the speaker tells of ways in which the world is not **pleasant** or in a pleasing state.

Word Study

Part A Explain how the **suffix -ant** contributes to the meanings of *vigilant* and *important*. Consult a dictionary if necessary.

Part B Use the context of the sentence and what you know about the suffix -ant to explain your answers to each question.

1. Is an *expectant* person waiting for something?
2. Does a water-*resistant* jacket get soaking wet in the rain?

340 UNIT 3 • Do we need words to communicate well?

Literary Analysis

Possible responses appear below. Check to be sure students support their responses with evidence from the text.

1. *Pools* means "puddles of standing water." The phrases "on the sidewalk" and "in the gutter" provide clues to the word's meaning.

2. *Flow* means "route" or "path." The words *river* and *stops its* provide clues to the word's meaning in the poem.

3. **(a)** Abuelito is aging and becoming more ill.
   (b) *can't come out to play, sleeps in his little room all night and day*

4. Students answers should include figures of speech similar to the following:

   "April Rain Song"; personification: *let the rain kiss you*

   "The World Is Not a Pleasant Place to Be"; personification: *an ocean would never laugh*

   "Abuelito Who"; personification: *who is dough and feathers*; simile: *throws coins like rain*

   "Fame Is a Bee"; metaphor: *fame is a bee*

Literary Analysis

Key Ideas and Details

1. **Context Clues** In "April Rain Song," what is the meaning of *pools* (line 4)? What context clues in the poem help you determine the meaning?

2. **Context Clues** In "The World Is Not a Pleasant Place to Be," what is the meaning of *flow* (line 5)? What context clues in the poem help you decide?

3. **(a) Make Inferences:** In "Abuelito Who," what is happening with Abuelito? **(b) Interpret:** What words in the poem convey Abuelito's situation?

Craft and Structure

4. **Figurative Language** For each poem, fill in a graphic organizer like the one on the right with examples of the different types of figurative language.

5. **Figurative Language** How does the use of figurative language contribute to the tone of each poem? Cite specific examples from the texts to support your responses.

Integration of Knowledge and Ideas

6. **(a)** In "April Rain Song," what kind of song does the rain sing? **(b) Infer:** What does the song tell you about the speaker's feelings about rain? **(c) Speculate:** How would the poem be different if it were about the rain that comes with a hurricane?

7. **(a) Interpret:** Fill out a three-column chart in response to the ideas in "Fame Is a Bee." In the first column, list the good things about fame. In the second, list the bad things about fame. **(b) Compare and Contrast:** Trade charts with a partner and discuss how your responses are similar and different. **(c) Assess:** In the third column of your chart, evaluate how your response has or has not changed based on your discussion.

8. **Do we need words to communicate well?**
   (a) In "Abuelito Who" and "April Rain Song," find examples of common things that are described in uncommon ways. **(b)** Does this technique help the poets communicate their ideas effectively? Explain.

Poetry Collection 2

Title of Poem
Metaphor
Personification
Simile

ACADEMIC VOCABULARY

As you write and speak about the poems in Poetry Collection 2, use the words related to communication that you explored on page 303 of this text.

GUIDED EXPLORATION

8. **Do we need words to communicate well?**
   (a) In "April Rain Song," rain is compared to silver. In "Abuelito Who," the writer compares her grandfather to several unusual things such as dough, feathers, a watch, and a glass of water.
   (b) By comparing rain to silver, the rain seems extraordinary, valuable, and beautiful. The unusual comparisons used in "Abuelito Who" convey the idea that the grandfather was once larger than life and charismatic while also clearly depicting the impact of age and illness on his life now.

5. The figurative language in "Abuelito Who" reflects and enhances the speaker's respect, admiration, and love for the grandfather. The language in "The World Is Not a Pleasant Place to Be" contributes to the lonesome tone because the images seem lonesome. In "April Rain Song" and "Fame Is a Bee" the figurative language allows the poets to convey a playful or informal tone because the comparisons are quirky, original, and amusing.

6. **(a)** The rain sings a lullaby. **(b)** The speaker finds rain to be soothing and restful. **(c)** The speaker might talk about rain that is hard and violent.

7. **(a)** Good things about fame: attracts attention and admiration. Bad things about fame: attracts criticism and is fleeting. **(b)** Some students may think that fame is good because famous people make more money; others may note that it is bad because with fame comes a lack of privacy. **(d)** Discussion gives people another perspective or way of looking at things that may influence students' responses.

 Online Writer's Notebook

Students can use the Online Writer's Notebook to record all responses.

Close Reading Activities Continued

Conventions

Introduce the skill using the instruction on the student page.

Teaching the Skill

Give students examples of comparative and superlative adjectives in sentences. *Oranges are <u>sweeter</u> than lemons. Apples are the <u>sweetest</u> of the three fruits.* Have students discuss what each adjective compares. *Sweeter* compares lemons and oranges; *sweetest* compares all three fruits.

Practice A
Sample answers:

1. The speaker of "The World Is Not a Pleasant Place to Be" is *sadder* than the speaker of "April Rain Song."

2. Rain that falls like silver droplets is *quieter* than rain that falls like coins.

3. In my opinion, "April Rain Song" has the *most beautiful* descriptions of any poem in this collection.

4. I can understand the feelings expressed in "Abuelito Who" *more easily* than those expressed in "The World Is Not a Pleasant Place to Be."

5. "April Rain Song" is not the *shortest* poem in this collection.

Reading Application
Sample answers:

Sentence 1: two

Sentence 2: two

Sentence 3: four

Sentence 4: two

Sentence 5: four

Practice B
Sample answers:

1. most softly; Greta sings the most softly of the members in the group.

2. more famous; The President is more famous than the mayor of our town.

3. kindest; The black and white kitten is the kindest kitten from the litter.

4. most frightened; During the storm I was most frightened when the power went out.

Conventions: Comparisons with Adjectives and Adverbs

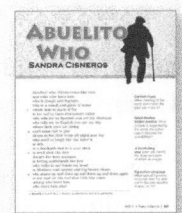

Poetry Collection 2

> An **adjective** describes a person, a place, a thing, or an idea. An **adverb** describes a verb, an adjective, or another adverb. Adjectives and adverbs are **modifiers** that can be used to compare two or more items or actions.

Type of Modifier	Definition	Adjective Example	Adverb Example
positive	not used to compare	new	calmly
comparative	used to compare *two* examples	newer	more calmly
superlative	used to compare *three* or more examples	newest	most calmly

Comparative and **superlative modifiers** are formed from **positive modifiers**.

1. If a positive adjective contains one or two syllables, you can usually add the ending *-er* or *-est*.

2. If a positive adjective contains three or more syllables, you can usually use the words *more* or *most*.

3. For most adverbs, use the words *more* or *most*.

Practice A
Write sentences about any of the poems in Collection 2, using the comparative or superlative modifiers listed below.

1. sadder
2. quieter
3. most beautiful
4. more easily
5. shortest

Reading Application For each sentence you wrote in Practice A, tell how many examples are being compared.

Practice B
Write each modifier in the form indicated. Then, use each word in an original sentence.

1. softly (superlative)
2. famous (comparative)
3. kind (superlative)
4. frightened (superlative)
5. carefully (comparative)

Writing Application Write one sentence about a poem in Collection 2 using a comparative adjective and one sentence using a superlative adjective.

5. more carefully: My teacher said that next time I need to work more carefully.

Writing Application
Sample answers:

comparative: "April Rain Song" is *easier* to read than "Abuelito Who."

superlative: "Fame Is a Bee" is the *shortest* poem in the collection.

Writing to Sources

Poetry Write a **poem** using figurative language.

- Think about something that makes you happy—the beach on a sunny day, the stars twinkling in the dark sky, your favorite flavor of ice cream, or anything that comes to your mind.
- Use questions to think about your topic: *What qualities does this thing have? To what can I compare this thing? What vivid words can I use to describe it?* List ideas.
- Review the poems in this collection to see how the poets use figurative and descriptive language.
- Write your poem using precise descriptions, unique comparisons, and figurative language. Experiment with rhyme and rhythm.

Grammar Application In your poem, include at least one comparative adjective and one comparative adverb.

Speaking and Listening

Presentation of Ideas Prepare a **dramatic poetry reading**. Select a poem you have read that is meaningful to you. It may be a poem in Poetry Collection 2 or a different poem.

- First, be sure you know how to pronounce all the words in the poem. Use a dictionary to learn the pronunciations of unfamiliar words.
- Practice reading the poem aloud, using expression and pauses where appropriate. Speak clearly.
- Pay attention to the end-of-line punctuation.
- Vary your volume and pitch to show emotion and to convey tone.
- Memorize your poem.
- Use gestures and body language to enhance your interpretation.
- Ask your classmates to silently read your poem.
- Now, present your dramatic poetry reading to the class.
- Discuss with classmates how reading the poem silently compared and contrasted with hearing it read aloud.

 Common Core
State Standards

Reading Literature
7. Compare and contrast the experience of reading a story, drama, or poem to listening to or viewing an audio, video, or live version of the text, including contrasting what they "see" and "hear" when reading the text to what they perceive when they listen or watch.

Writing
3.d. Use precise words and phrases, relevant descriptive details, and sensory language to convey experiences and events.

Speaking and Listening
6. Adapt speech to a variety of contexts and tasks, demonstrating command of formal English when indicated or appropriate.

Language
1. Demonstrate command of the conventions of standard English grammar and usage when writing or speaking.
4.c. Consult reference materials, both print and digital, to find the pronunciation of a word or determine or clarify its precise meaning or its part of speech.

Writing to Sources

1. Review the assignment, using the instruction on the student page.
2. To give students guidance in writing a poem with figurative language, give them the **Support for Writing** page for this selection in the *Student Companion All-in-One Workbook.*
3. To evaluate students' poems, adapt one of the rubrics for Poetry, pp. 248–249 in the *Professional Development Guidebook.* In addition, you might evaluate how well students identify the qualities of their subject and create comparisons using figurative language.

Grammar Application

Have students check their drafts for the use of comparisons with adjectives and adverbs.

Six Traits Focus

✓	Ideas	✓	Word Choice
	Organization		Sentence Fluency
	Voice		Conventions

Speaking and Listening

1. Review the assignment, using the instruction on the student page.
2. To support students' work on the assignment, have them complete the **Support for Extend Your Learning** page for this selection in the *Student Companion All-in-One Workbook.*

Time and Resource Manager

LESSON PACING GUIDE

Poetry Collection 3: Haiku • The Sidewalk Racer • Concrete Cat • Limerick

DAY 1 Preteach/Teach

- Administer the Reading and Vocabulary Warm-ups, as necessary.
- Introduce the Key Ideas and Details skill: Paraphrasing.
- Introduce the Craft and Structure skill: Forms of Poetry.
- Use the Close Reading Model to demonstrate the application of the skills.
- Review the selection vocabulary, as necessary, with students who need additional support.
- Prepare students to read the selection by reviewing with them the Multidraft Reading Strategies.

DAY 2 Teach

- Informally monitor comprehension while students read.
- Use the Comprehension questions to confirm understanding.
- Develop students' ability to paraphrase and analyze forms of poetry using the sidenote questions.
- Reinforce vocabulary with the Vocabulary notes.
- Reinforce unit focus standards using the Spiral Review prompts.

DAY 3 Assess

- Assess students' comprehension and mastery of the skills by having them answer the Literary Analysis questions.
- Have students complete the Vocabulary activities.
- Develop students' understanding of roots and affixes by having them complete the Word Study activities.

DAY 4 Extend/Assess

- Build students' ability to master grammar concepts and conventions by having them complete the Conventions lesson.
- Have students complete the Writing to Sources activity and write a haiku, limerick, or concrete poem. (You may assign as homework.)
- Extend learning by having students complete the Research and Technology activity: a presentation of a poem.
- Administer the Selection Test or Open-Book Test.

Poetry Collection 3

Common Core State Standards

Reading Literature 5. Analyze how a particular sentence, chapter, scene, or stanza fits into the overall structure of a text and contributes to the development of the theme, setting, or plot.

Writing 4. Produce clear and coherent writing in which the development, organization, and style are appropriate to task, purpose, and audience.

6. Use technology, including the Internet, to produce and publish writing as well as to interact and collaborate with others; demonstrate sufficient command of keyboarding skills to type a minimum of three pages in a single sitting.

Language 1. Demonstrate command of the conventions of standard English grammar and usage when writing or speaking.

3. Use knowledge of language and its conventions when writing, speaking, reading, or listening.

6. Acquire and use accurately grade-appropriate general academic and domain-specific words and phrases; gather vocabulary knowledge when considering a word or phrase important to comprehension or expression.

Daily Block Scheduling

Each day in this Lesson Pacing Guide represents a 40–50 minute period. Teachers using block scheduling may combine days to revise pacing. In addition, teachers may differentiate and support core instruction by integrating components for extended and intensive support as students require. See the Guide to Resources (facing page).

GUIDE TO RESOURCES

		L1	L2	L3	L4	EL	ALL	RESOURCES	PRINT	CD	ONLINE
Warm Up		✔	✔			✔		Vocabulary Warm-ups			✔
		✔	✔			✔		Reading Warm-ups			✔
							✔	Background Video			✔
							✔	Selection Audio		Hear It!	✔
Comprehension/ Selection Support							✔	Writing About the Big Question	Student Companion Workbook		✔
							✔	Literary Analysis	Student Companion Workbook		✔
							✔	Reading	Student Companion Workbook		✔
							✔	Vocabulary Builder	Student Companion Workbook		✔
					✔			Enrichment			✔
				✔	✔	✔		Conventions	Student Companion Workbook		✔
				✔	✔	✔		Writing to Sources	Student Companion Workbook		✔
				✔	✔	✔		Research and Technology	Student Companion Workbook		✔
Differentiated Instruction/ Additional Support							✔	Additional Standards Practice	Common Core Companion		✔
							✔	Close Reading Practice	Close Reading Notebook		✔
		✔	✔					Adapted Reader's Notebook			✔
						✔		English Reader's Notebook:			✔
						✔		Spanish Reader's Notebook			✔
						✔		Graphic Organizer A			✔
		✔	✔			✔		Graphic Organizer B			✔
		✔	✔			✔		"Decks and Trucks"	Reality Central Student Edition and Writing Journal		✔
		✔	✔			✔		Practice and Assess	Reading Kit		✔
Monitor Progress							✔	Selection Test		Exam View	✔
							✔	Open-Book Test		Exam View	✔
Digital Resources							✔	Close Reading Tool			✔
							✔	Online Writer's Notebook			✔

👥 One-on-one teaching ▦ Group work 👥 Whole class instruction 👤 Independent work Ⓐ Assessment 🖥 Digital Resource

LEARNER LEVELS

L1 Special-Needs Students
L2 Below-Level Students (Tier 2)
L3 On-Level Students (Tier 1)
L4 Advanced Students (Tier 1)
EL English Learners
All All Students

1 **Do we need words to communicate well?**

Read • Discuss • Research • Write As students read, they will explore the Big Question through text analysis of the selection. Encourage students to note comments and additional questions as they read, using text evidence to support their thoughts. Students should refer to their notes to help them deepen their understanding of the selection through discussion, research, and writing.

2 **Close Reading Focus**

1. Explain to students that, in general, a paraphrase is much shorter than the original text. Since poems are already fairly short, however, it's possible that paraphrases of lines may be around the same length as the original.

2. Explain to students that the form a poet chooses may depend on what the poet hopes to convey. For example, if you want to write a poem about the flight of a seagull, you might choose to write a concrete poem with the words arranged in the shape of a gull.

Building Knowledge

Poetry Collection 3

1 **Do we need words to communicate well?**

Explore the Big Question as you read the poems in Collection 3. Take notes on the different ways in which the poets communicate experiences.

2 **CLOSE READING FOCUS**

Key Ideas and Details: **Paraphrasing**

When you **paraphrase** a literary work, you restate the author's words in your own words. Paraphrasing difficult or confusing passages in a poem helps you identify the main idea and monitor your understanding. Use the following steps to help you paraphrase challenging text:

- Stop and reread any difficult lines or passages.
- Identify unfamiliar words, find their meanings, and replace them with words that mean nearly the same thing.
- Restate the lines in your own words.
- Reread to see whether your paraphrase makes sense.

Craft and Structure: **Forms of Poetry**

Poets use **forms of poetry** suited to the meaning, images, and feelings they want to express. Here are three poetic forms:

- In a **concrete poem**, words are arranged in a shape that reflects the subject of the poem.
- A **haiku** is a Japanese verse form with three lines. Line 1 has five syllables, line 2 has seven, and line 3 has five.
- A **limerick** is a funny poem of five lines. Lines 1, 2, and 5 rhyme and have three beats, or stressed syllables. Lines 3 and 4 rhyme and have two beats.

Vocabulary

You will encounter these words in the poems in Collection 3. Choose one of the words and write at least two of its *synonyms*. After you read, see how your knowledge of each word has increased.

skimming   asphalt   fellow

Common Core State Standards

Reading Literature
5. Analyze how a particular sentence, chapter, scene, or stanza fits into the overall structure of a text and contributes to the development of the theme, setting, or plot.

Language
6. Acquire and use accurately grade-appropriate general academic and domain-specific words and phrases; gather vocabulary knowledge when considering a word or phrase important to comprehension or expression.

TEXT COMPLEXITY RUBRIC

Poetry Collection 3			Reader and Task Suggestions	
Qualitative Measures			**Preparing to Read the Text**	**Leveled Tasks**
Context/Knowledge Demands	A pond, an asphalt street, animals, amusing situation 1 2 ③ 4 5		• Review various types of figurative language and other poetic devices prior to reading the poems.	*Levels of Meaning* If students will have difficulty with levels of meaning, have them take notes on the sensory language the poets use.
Structure/Language Conventionality and Clarity	Some on-level and some challenging vocabulary 1 2 ③ 4 5			*Analyzing* If students will not have difficulty with levels of meaning, have them read to determine poetic devices the poets use to communicate.
Levels of Meaning/ Purpose/Concept Level	Challenging concepts (concrete poetry; wordplay); accessible concepts (frog jumping into pond; skateboarder) 1 2 ③ 4 5		• Guide students to use Multidraft Reading strategies (TE p. 346)	
Quantitative Measures				
Lexile	NP	**Text Length**	Word Count: 13; 43; 14; 34	

CLOSE READING MODEL

The passages below are from a limerick by an anonymous poet. The annotations to the right of the passage show ways in which you can use close reading skills to paraphrase lines and analyze forms of poetry.

from Limerick

There was a young fellow named Hall, [1]
Who fell in the spring in the fall [2]
   'Twould have been a sad thing
   If he'd died in the spring,
But he didn't—he died in the fall.

Forms of Poetry

1 You can often identify a limerick from its opening lines. Limericks have an instantly recognizable, bouncy rhythm, and many begin with the words "There was a...."

Paraphrase

2 This line may be confusing, since both *spring* and *fall* have multiple meanings. When you reread, you can understand that *spring* refers to a spring of water, and *fall* refers to a season of the year. You could paraphrase the line this way: "Who fell into water in autumn."

🔔 Daily Bellringer

For each class during which you will teach this selection, have students complete one of the five Revision activities for Week 16 in *Daily Bellringer Activities*. You may wish to use additional activities that are applicable to this selection.

Vocabulary

If students require support with selection vocabulary, use this routine:

1. Write the following words and definitions on the board:

   skimming *v.* gliding; moving swiftly and lightly

   asphalt *n.* brown or black mixture of substances used to pave roads

   fellow *n.* man or boy

2. Have students say each word aloud.

3. Use the word in a sentence that defines the word.

👥 DIFFERENTIATED INSTRUCTION

🅴🅻 Extended Support— English Learners
Have students complete the **Reading and Vocabulary Warm-ups** for this collection in the *Student Companion All-in-One Workbook* before they read. Assign the prereading pages and the selections in the *Reader's Notebook: English Learner's Version*. Then, have students listen to portions of the collection in the *Student eText* or on the *Hear It!* CD-ROM.

🅻🅸 🅻🅸 Extended Support— Struggling Readers
Have students complete the **Reading and Vocabulary Warm-ups** for this collection in the *Student Companion All-in-One Workbook* before they read. Assign the prereading pages and the selections in the *Reader's Notebook: Adapted Version*. Then, have students listen to portions of the collection in the *Student eText* or on the *Hear It!* CD-ROM.

Extended Support— Reluctant Readers
To build motivation and engagement before assigning the collection, have students read "Decks and Trucks," a thematically related selection in *Reality Central*. Then, use the questions at the conclusion of the related selection to guide discussion.

MULTIDRAFT READING

To assist struggling readers and to deepen comprehension for all, assign the text in "chunks" and apply multidraft reading protocols. For each reading, have students set the purpose indicated:

- **First reading:** Students should read the selection independently and think about its basic meaning.
- **Second reading:** Students should analyze the text's key ideas and details and its craft and structure, and respond to the side-column prompts.
- **Third reading:** Students should integrate knowledge and ideas, connect the text to other texts and to the world, and answer the end-of-selection questions.

For more guidance, refer to the *Classroom Strategies and Teaching Routines* card on multidraft reading.

❸ Activating Prior Knowledge

Cut out paper silhouettes of several animals or objects that are familiar to students. Display the silhouettes and ask students to identify each one. Elicit from students that they are able to recognize each silhouette's form. Then tell students that each poem in this collection has a specific form with special characteristics that define it. Concrete poems are most like the silhouettes because their form is a physical shape; however, the other poems—the haiku and the limerick—also have form. After reading the poetry collection, have students return to the silhouettes and have them explain how they relate to each of the three forms of poetry—concrete, haiku, and limerick.

Meet the Poets

Matsuo Bashō (1644–1694) was born into a family of Japanese landowners. When Bashō was five, his father died. Bashō then entered the service of a local lord and began to write poetry. He was an important developer of the haíku form and one of its greatest masters. The Japanese have built a monument near the place where Bashō is believed to have written the haiku in Poetry Collection 3.

Lillian Morrison (b. 1917) played street games and sports as a child in Jersey City, New Jersey. The rhymes and chants she heard on the playground inspired her love of poetry. As an adult, Morrison spent nearly forty years working in the New York Public Library. She has written several books of poetry, including *The Sidewalk Racer and Other Poems of Sports and Motion.* Morrison has said, "I love rhythms, the body movement implicit in poetry, explicit in sports." Many of her poems, such as "The Sidewalk Racer," celebrate the human body in motion.

Dorthi Charles (b. 1960) was a student when she wrote "Concrete Cat." Readers especially enjoy the creative way that Charles presents her subject. This poem is featured in the book *Knock at a Star: A Child's Introduction to Poetry.*

Anonymous

💬 VOCABULARY DEVELOPMENT

Thematic Vocabulary: The Big Question
As students are discussing Poetry Collection 3, encourage them to use the thematic vocabulary presented in Introducing the Big Question, pp. 302–303. You might encourage them with sentence starters like these:

1. A few words in "Haiku" *communicate* . . .

2. In "The Sidewalk Raceer or On the Skateboard" the *gestures* of the speaker emphasize . . .
3. The words in "Concrete Cat" *symbolize* . . .
4. The *language* in "Limerick" is . . .

❶ HAIKU

BASHŌ

An old silent pond . . .
A frog jumps into the pond,
splash! Silence again.

PART 2 • Poetry Collection 3 **347**

❶ Forms of Poetry

Before students read the poems, review the definitions of haiku, concrete poem, and limerick.

A haiku has three lines; the first and third lines have five syllables, and the second has seven. A concrete poem is one in which the words are arranged in a shape that reflects the poem's subject. A limerick is a short, funny five-line poem. The first, second, and fifth lines rhyme and have three beats each. The third and fourth lines rhyme and have two beats.

Video

Watch the Background Video online!

Audio

Selection audio is available in the **Student eText** and on the **Hear It!** CD-ROM.

❷ Critical Viewing

Possible responses: The skateboarder in the photograph and the poem both make me think of the words *sailing, soaring, exhilarating,* and *speeding.*

❸ ⑦ Connecting to the Big Question

1. Point out that poets can make word choices and order words to create the impression of the sound or feeling that words describe.

2. Have students read the poem. **Ask:** How do common verbs and uncommon comparisons describe the movement of the sidewalk racer?

   Possible response: The common verbs *swerve, curve, sway,* and *speed* name the various moves. "Speed to whirring sound," and the description of the sidewalk racer as a sailor, a sail, and a human machine are uncommon.

3. **Ask:** How does the rhythm of the words and the shape created by the lines on the page communicate the poet's ideas?

   Possible response: "I swerve, I curve, I sway" implies fast, gliding motion and changes of direction. The rhythm of the words at the end of the poem gives a feeling of flight and power. The lines are arranged to make a shape similar to that of a skateboard.

The Sidewalk Racer

or On the Skateboard

Lillian Morrison

Vocabulary ▶
skimming (skim´ iŋ)
v. gliding; moving swiftly and lightly over a surface

asphalt (as´ fôlt)
n. brown or black mixture of substances used to pave roads

❷ Critical Viewing ▶
What words might describe the spirit of both this skateboarder and the poem?

❸

Skimming
an asphalt sea
I swerve, I curve, I
sway; I speed to whirring
5 sound an inch above the
ground; I'm the sailor
and the sail, I'm the
driver and the wheel
I'm the one and only
10 single engine
human auto
mobile.

Concrete Cat

Dorthi Charles

A   A
e r   e r

        stripestripestripestripe
eYe eYe   stripestripestripe
whisker   whisker stripestripestripestripe   t a i l
whisker m h whisker stripestripestripe
    o t   stripestripestripestripe
     U

    paw paw   paw paw   ǝsnoɯ

dishdish   litterbox
               litterbox

4 Evaluate

1. Prompt a discussion about how the individual words and letters in "Concrete Cat" are arranged to create the visual of a cat and items associated with a cat.

2. **Ask** students why the word *mouse* is printed upside down.

   Possible response: It brings to mind the image of a dead mouse.

3. **Ask** students to offer their opinions about which of the words in the poem are placed most cleverly.

   Possible response: The letters in *ear* are placed most cleverly. They are arranged to look like ears, with a capital *A* forming the tip of each ear.

5 ? Connecting to the Big Question

1. Point out that readers usually start reading at the top of a page of text. Tell students that concrete poems may offer different points of entry.

2. Have students read "Concrete Cat" and examine the design created by the words on the page. **Ask:** Where do you begin reading this poem?

   Possible response: Some students may notice the tail and whiskers before they "see" the cat.

3. **Ask** students: How does the design created by the arrangement of the words reflect the meaning of the poem?

   Possible response: The positions of the whiskers, ears and tail make the cat look alert. The words *stripes* are arranged to create a picture of striped fur, and the letters of the word *mouth* are arranged to show a satisfied expression. The position of the word *mouse* makes the mouse look dead.

6 Forms of Poetry

Ask the Forms of Poetry question.

Answer: The stressed syllables in line 1 are *was, fel-,* and *Hall.* In line 2, the stressed syllables are *fell, spring,* and *fall.* In line 5, the stressed syllables are *did-, died,* and *fall.*

7 Critical Viewing

Answer: It illustrates fall, the season, referred to in line 2.

 **ASSESS**

Language Study

Vocabulary

Sample answers:

1. Suzy grimaced as she ran after the ice cream truck, because the *asphalt* burned her bare feet.

2. The young *fellow* walked to school in the pouring rain.

3. Jane watched as the geese *skimmed* gracefully over the surface of the lake.

Word Study

Part A

Sample answers:

The Greek prefix *auto-* means "self." An *autobiography* is a biography—a life story—that the person has written about <u>himself</u> or <u>herself</u>. An action that is *automatic* seems almost to perform <u>itself</u>.

Part B

Sample answers:

1. The inventors of the *automobile* may have given it that name because it moves under its own power, unlike a horse-drawn cart.

2. If a factory becomes *automated,* fewer people work there because the machines operate themselves.

Literary Analysis

Possible responses appear below. Check to be sure students support their responses with evidence from the text.

1. **(a)** The pond is still and peaceful. A frog hops into the water and makes a splash. Then the water is still again. **(b)** Paraphrasing helps to clarify that the pond moves from silence and stillness

---

Vocabulary ▶
fellow (fel′ ō) *n.*
man or boy

6

Forms of Poetry
What are the stressed syllables in lines 1, 2, and 5?

7 Critical Viewing ▶
What part of the limerick does this image illustrate?

WORD STUDY

The **Greek prefix** *auto-* means "self."

The speaker in "The Sidewalk Racer" compares herself to a "human auto mobile," because she moves by herself under her own power.

Limerick
Anonymous

There was a young fellow named Hall,
Who fell in the spring in the fall;
   'Twould have been a sad thing
    If he'd died in the spring,
5 But he didn't—he died in the fall.

Language Study

Vocabulary The words listed below appear in the poems in Collection 3. Write a sentence that connects the situation in each numbered item below with a vocabulary word.

  skimming   asphalt   fellow

1. children run after an ice cream truck, their bare feet burning
2. a young man walks to school in the rain
3. a girl watches birds glide across a lake

Word Study

Part A Explain how the **Greek prefix** *auto-* contributes to the meanings of *autobiography* and *automatic.* You may consult a dictionary if necessary.

Part B Use context and what you know about the Greek prefix *auto-* to explain your answer to each question.

1. Why might the inventors of the *automobile* have given their machine that name?
2. If a factory becomes *automated,* do more people work there, or fewer people?

---

to a noisy splash, and then returns to silence and stillness. **(c)** Shorter sentences with fewer words convey silence, while longer sentences with more words convey loudness.

2. As well as being a passenger, the rider feels like part of the vehicle.

3. Crouching near its dish and litterbox, a striped cat smiles after killing a mouse.

4. **(a)** Line 1: a calm pond; Line 2: a frog leaping into the water; Line 3: water rippling, then becoming still again **(b)** Line one gives the setting. Line 2 describes the action. Line

3 describes the change and its momentary effect. The frog changes the silent old pond by jumping into it, creating a ripple in the water and making a splashing sound. The pond quickly returns to its former state, however. Through this image, the poem contrasts the eternal nature of the pond with the brief and transient nature of animal life.

5. The poem would be less effective because it would just contain repeated words instead of the cat's image. For example, it would lack the witty use of the *U* for the tongue and the upside-down mouse.

Literary Analysis

Key Ideas and Details

1. **Paraphrase (a)** Paraphrase the haiku in your own words. **(b)** How does paraphrasing the haiku help you clarify your understanding of the poem's main idea? **(c)** How does line length impact the meaning of the haiku?

2. **Paraphrase** Paraphrase lines 6–12 of "The Sidewalk Racer."

3. **Paraphrase** Review "Concrete Cat." Then, write a sentence in which you use your own words to restate the meaning of the poem.

Craft and Structure

4. **Forms of Poetry (a)** What image appears in each line of the haiku? Record answers in a web like the one on the right. **(b)** How does each line develop the scene in the poem and help you understand its message?

5. **Forms of Poetry** Would "Concrete Cat" be more effective or less effective if it were written in a different shape? Explain.

Integration of Knowledge and Ideas

6. **(a) Interpret:** Which words and phrases help show motion in "The Sidewalk Racer?" **(b) Analyze:** How can the speaker be both "the sailor / and the sail"? **(c) Assess:** Which image do you think most successfully conveys the sense of being on a skateboard? Explain.

7. **(a)** What incident does the limerick describe? **(b) Analyze:** How do the double meanings of *spring* and *fall* contribute to the humor in the limerick? **(c) Speculate:** Do you think it would be possible to write a serious limerick? Explain.

8. **Do we need words to communicate well?** With a small group, discuss these questions: **(a)** The poems in this collection use few words to convey meaning. How is the form of a poem as much a part of the meaning as the words of the poem? **(b) Analyze:** Can you separate the form from the meaning in any of these poems? Explain. **(c) Draw Conclusions:** Are poems more effective when they are longer and use more words? Explain, citing evidence from the poems you have read.

Poetry Collection 3

Haiku

Line 1:

Line 2:

Line 3:

ACADEMIC VOCABULARY

As you write and speak about the poems in Poetry Collection 3, use the words related to communication that you explored on page 303 of this text.

PART 2 • Close Reading Activities **351**

---

description would not improve the clear and simple image at the core of each poem. For example, in "The Sidewalk Racer," four short phrases convey the idea of movement just as well as would four full lines or stanzas.

---

6. **(a)** The images that suggest motion are, "I swerve, I curve, I sway; I speed" and "I'm the driver and the wheel." **(b)** The speaker can be a sailor who is guiding the skateboard; the speaker can also be the sail propelling the board. **(c)** The image of a "single engine human auto mobile," conveys the sense of being on a skateboard because it reflects someone being in charge of moving through the air.

7. **(a)** A young man named Hall falls into a spring and dies. **(b)** A spring is a source of water and a season; fall is also a season and the motion of going down. The wordplay allows the last two lines to be interpreted in two different ways. **(c)** No. Part of the definition of a limerick is that it is funny. However, at times, serious points can be made through humor.

8. **Do we need words to communicate well?**
(a) In each of the poems, words and form are tightly interwoven to create meaning. **(b)** To one degree or another, each poem would be different in effect and meaning if its form were changed. **(c)** These poems are effective precisely because of their brevity. Further

 Online Writer's Notebook

Students can use the Online Writer's Notebook to record all responses.

Close Reading Activities Continued

Conventions

Introduce the skill, using the instruction on the student page.

Think Aloud: Model the Skill

Model the skill of identifying conjunctions and interjections. Say:

Conjunctions connect words and show how information is related. When I say, "Go to the store *and* buy me a kiwi," I am telling you to do two things: *go* to the store and *buy* something. Interjections add feeling to a sentence. When I say, "*Golly,* I love kiwis!" you know that I am enthusiastic about kiwis: I have included an interjection (*golly*).

Practice A
Sample answers:

1. but
2. Hey, Oh
3. and
4. Wow; Hey; Whoa, Whew

Reading Application
Sample answer:

In "The Sidewalk Racer," the conjunction *and* in "I'm the sailor/and the sail" combines the two images. In the same poem, the conjunction *and* in "I'm the one and only" intensifies the speaker's claim. In the limerick, the conjunction *But* creates a contrast between "If he'd died in the spring" and "he didn't—he died in the fall."

Practice B
Sample answers:

1. Some poems are only three lines long, but others are very long, with many stanzas.
2. Lily and I like limericks, so we decided to write one together.
3. "Aha! Now I understand that poem," Sam said.

Writing Application

Students' answers should include four circled conjunctions and two underlined interjections.

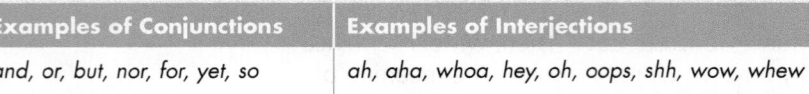

Conventions: **Conjunctions and Interjections**

> **Conjunctions** connect sentence parts and help show the relationships between those parts. **Interjections** express feelings. The use of conjunctions helps to improve the flow of your writing. Interjections add liveliness to dialogue and narration.

Poetry Collection 3

Examples of Conjunctions	Examples of Interjections
and, or, but, nor, for, yet, so	*ah, aha, whoa, hey, oh, oops, shh, wow, whew*

A conjunction that joins two independent clauses is preceded by a comma.

> The corn grew tall that summer**, and** the harvest was plentiful.

> The party was fun**, but** I had to leave early.

In some cases, an interjection is followed by an exclamation point. In other cases, an interjection may be followed by a comma, and an exclamation point may appear at the end of the sentence.

> Hey**,** that new song is really great**!**

> Aha**!** I've found you at last**!**

Practice A
Fill in the blanks with a conjunction or interjection that completes the sentence.

1. The pond was old, _____ the frog was young.
2. _____, did you hear a splash?
3. The poem is about a cat, _____ it is in the shape of a cat.
4. _____! I love to ride my skateboard.

Reading Application Find three conjunctions in the poems in Collection 3. Explain the relationships between the words, phrases, or clauses that are connected by the conjunctions.

Practice B
Improve these sentences by following the directions in parentheses. Be sure to use commas and exclamation points correctly.

1. Some poems are only three lines long. Others are very long, with many stanzas. (combine with a conjunction)
2. Lily and I like limericks. We decided to write one together. (combine with a conjunction)
3. "Now I understand that poem," Sam said. (add an interjection)

Writing Application Write a paragraph about jumping into a pond. Use at least four conjunctions and two interjections. Circle the conjunctions and underline the interjections.

⇨ **EXTEND THE LESSON**

Write the following excerpt from "The Sidewalk Racer" on the board:

> I'm the sailor and the sail, I'm the driver and the wheel

Ask students what they notice about the excerpt. Elicit from them that the excerpt uses the conjunction *and*. Then ask what else they notice (the conjunction creates repetition and rhythm).

Have students imitate the excerpt in a sentence on a topic of their own choosing, matching the grammatical and stylistic features discussed. Collect the sentences and share them with the class.

Writing to Sources

Poetry Write your own haiku, limerick, or concrete **poem.**

- Brainstorm for a list of topics that inspire you. Think about an element of nature, an event from your daily life, an amusing incident, or a visual image that you want to describe.

- Review the poems in this collection as models of the different poetic forms. Decide which of the three forms fits your topic best.

- Write your poem. Choose the correct pattern for the poetic form you have selected. Use a visual layout if you are writing a concrete poem, and use humor, rhythm, and rhyme if you are writing a limerick.

- Make copies of your poem for a small group of classmates. Read the poem aloud as they follow along.

Grammar Application Look for places in your poem where conjunctions can help you connect ideas and improve the rhythm and flow of your writing. Consider using interjections to add liveliness or feeling to your poem.

Research and Technology

Build and Present Knowledge Use a computer word processing program to develop and design a **presentation of a poem**.

- Choose a poem from this collection or another poem that you enjoyed reading.

- Type the poem exactly as the poet wrote it. You may have to set your margins extra wide to accommodate the poem's line breaks, or use tabs to set off indented lines.

- Choose a font or style that is easy to read. Use a larger font size for the title.

- Proofread your poem. Remember to add the poet's name. Use "Anonymous" if the poet is unknown.

- Add pictures or illustrations to enhance the appearance of the poem.

- Post a copy of your poem as part of a class display.

 **Common Core State Standards**

Writing
4. Produce clear and coherent writing in which the development, organization, and style are appropriate to task, purpose, and audience.
6. Use technology, including the Internet, to produce and publish writing as well as to interact and collaborate with others; demonstrate sufficient command of keyboarding skills to type a minimum of three pages in a single sitting.

Language
1. Demonstrate command of the conventions of standard English grammar and usage when writing or speaking.
3. Use knowledge of language and its conventions when writing, speaking, reading, or listening.

Writing to Sources

1. Review the assignment, using the instruction on the student page.

2. Encourage students to try to create a mental image with the words they choose.

3. To give students guidance for writing their own poetry, give them the **Support for Writing** page for this selection in the **Student Companion All-in-One Workbook**.

4. To evaluate the writing activity, use the rubrics from **Professional Development Guidebook** (pp. 248–249). Evaluate for how well students write the form of poetry they choose.

Grammar Application

Have students check their drafts for correct use of conjunctions and interjections.

Six Traits Focus

✓	Ideas		Word Choice
✓	Organization		Sentence Fluency
	Voice		Conventions

Research and Technology

1. Review the assignment, using the instruction on the student page.

2. To support students' work on the assignment, have them complete the **Support for Extend Your Learning** page for this selection in the **Student Companion All-in-One Workbook**.

Poetry Collection 4

LESSON PACING GUIDE

Poetry Collection 4: Wind and water and stone • No Thank You • The Fairies' Lullaby • Cynthia in the Snow

DAY 1   Preteach/Teach

- Administer the Reading and Vocabulary Warm-ups, as necessary.
- Introduce the Key Ideas and Details skill: Paraphrasing.
- Introduce the Craft and Structure skill: Sound Devices and Tone.
- Use the Close Reading Model to demonstrate the application of the skills.
- Review the selection vocabulary, as necessary, with students who need additional support.
- Prepare students to read the selection by reviewing with them the Multidraft Reading Strategies.

DAY 2   Teach

- Informally monitor comprehension while students read.
- Use the Comprehension questions to confirm understanding.
- Develop students' ability to paraphrase and analyze sound devices and tone using the sidenote questions.
- Reinforce vocabulary with the Vocabulary notes.
- Reinforce unit focus standards using the Spiral Review prompts.

DAY 3   Assess

- Assess students' comprehension and mastery of the skills by having them answer the Literary Analysis questions.
- Have students complete the Vocabulary activities.
- Develop students' understanding of roots and affixes by having them complete the Word Study activities.

DAY 4   Extend/Assess

- Build students' ability to master grammar concepts and conventions by having them complete the Conventions lesson.
- Have students complete the Writing to Sources activity and write a prose description. (You may assign as homework.)
- Extend learning by having students complete the Research and Technology activity: a resume.
- Administer the Selection Test or Open-Book Test.

Common Core State Standards

Reading Literature 4. Determine the meaning of words and phrases as they are used in a text, including figurative and connotative meanings; analyze the impact of a specific word choice on meaning and tone.

Writing 4. Produce clear and coherent writing in which the development, organization, and style are appropriate to task, purpose, and audience.

6. Use technology, including the Internet, to make and publish writing as well as to interact and collaborate with others; demonstrate sufficient command of keyboarding skills to type a minimum of three pages in a single sitting.

Language 1. Demonstrate command of the conventions of standard English grammar and usage when writing or speaking.

3. Use knowledge of language and its conventions when writing, speaking, reading, or listening.

4.c. Consult reference materials (e.g., dictionaries, glossaries, thesauruses), both print and digital, to find the pronunciation of a word or determine or clarify its precise meaning or its part of speech.

Daily Block Scheduling

Each day in this Lesson Pacing Guide represents a 40–50 minute period. Teachers using block scheduling may combine days to revise pacing. In addition, teachers may differentiate and support core instruction by integrating components for extended and intensive support as students require. See the Guide to Resources (facing page).

GUIDE TO RESOURCES

		LEARNER LEVELS						RESOURCES	WHERE FOUND		
		L1	L2	L3	L4	EL	ALL		PRINT	CD	ONLINE
Warm Up		✔	✔			✔		Vocabulary Warm-ups			✔
		✔	✔			✔		Reading Warm-ups			✔
							✔	Background Video			✔
							✔	Selection Audio		Hear It!	✔
Comprehension/ Selection Support							✔	Writing About the Big Question	Student Companion Workbook		✔
							✔	Literary Analysis	Student Companion Workbook		✔
							✔	Reading	Student Companion Workbook		✔
							✔	Vocabulary Builder	Student Companion Workbook		✔
					✔			Enrichment			✔
				✔	✔	✔		Conventions	Student Companion Workbook		✔
				✔	✔	✔		Writing to Sources	Student Companion Workbook		✔
				✔	✔	✔		Research and Technology	Student Companion Workbook		
Differentiated Instruction/ Additional Support							✔	Additional Standards Practice	Common Core Companion		✔
							✔	Close Reading Practice	Close Reading Notebook		✔
		✔	✔					Adapted Reader's Notebook			✔
						✔		English Reader's Notebook:			✔
						✔		Spanish Reader's Notebook			✔
						✔		Graphic Organizer A			✔
		✔	✔			✔		Graphic Organizer B			✔
		✔	✔			✔		"Everyday Art"	Reality Central Student Edition and Writing Journal		✔
		✔	✔			✔		Practice and Assess	Reading Kit		✔
Monitor Progress							✔	Selection Test		Exam View	✔
							✔	Open-Book Test		Exam View	✔
Digital Resources							✔	Close Reading Tool			✔
							✔	Online Writer's Notebook			✔

👥 One-on-one teaching   👥 Group work   👥 Whole class instruction   👤 Independent work   Ⓐ Assessment   🖥 Digital Resource

LEARNER LEVELS

L1 Special-Needs Students   L3 On-Level Students (Tier 1)   EL English Learners

L2 Below-Level Students (Tier 2)   L4 Advanced Students (Tier 1)   All All Students

1 **Do we need words to communicate well?**

Read • Discuss • Research • Write As students read, they will explore the Big Question through text analysis of the selection. Encourage students to note comments and additional questions as they read, using text evidence to support their thoughts. Students should refer to their notes to help them deepen their understanding of the selection through discussion, research, and writing.

2 Close Reading Focus

1. Explain to students that as they read a poem, they may want to take notes about the main ideas. Students can use those ideas to help paraphrase the poem using their own words.

2. Tell students that often, the easiest way to identify sound devices in a poem is by reading it aloud. Repetition, alliteration, and onomatopoeia are all more apparent when heard or spoken.

© **Building Knowledge**

Poetry Collection 4

1 **Do we need words to communicate well?**

Explore the Big Question as you read the poems in Collection 4.

2 CLOSE READING FOCUS

Key Ideas and Details: **Paraphrasing**

Before you **paraphrase** a poem, read it aloud according to its punctuation to help you group words for meaning. Do not automatically stop at the ends of lines. Instead, use the punctuation in the poem to decide where to pause.

- Use a slight pause after a comma.
- Use a longer pause after a colon, semicolon, or dash.
- Your longest pause should come after a period, a question mark, or an exclamation point.
- If there is no punctuation, do not pause at all.

Craft and Structure: **Sound Devices and Tone**

A poet uses **sound devices** to create musical effects, reinforce meaning, and develop **tone**, the poet's attitude toward his or her audience and subject. The following sound devices are commonly used in poetry.

- **Repetition** is the repeated use of any element of language—a sound, word, phrase, or sentence—as in *of the people, by the people, for the people.*
- **Alliteration** is the repetition of initial consonant sounds, such as the *b* sound in *big beautiful bird.*
- **Onomatopoeia** is the use of a word that sounds like what it means, such as *roar* or *buzz.*

Vocabulary

You will encounter the following words in the poems in Collection 4. Write each word, noting whether you think it is a noun, an adjective, or a verb. Use a dictionary to check your responses.

hollowed	dispersed	sculpted
thorny	offense	whirs

© **Common Core State Standards**

Reading Literature
4. Determine the meaning of words and phrases as they are used in a text, including figurative and connotative meanings; analyze the impact of a specific word choice on meaning and tone.

Language
4.c. Consult reference materials (e.g., dictionaries, glossaries, thesauruses), both print and digital, to find the pronunciation of a word or determine or clarify its precise meaning or itspart of speech.

© TEXT COMPLEXITY **RUBRIC**

Poetry Collection 4		Reader and Task Suggestions	
Qualitative Measures		**Preparing to Read the Text**	**Leveled Tasks**
Context/Knowledge Demands	Natural elements; being charmed by a kitten; fairies; snowy day 1 2 ③ 4 5	• Use the Vocabulary note on TE p. 355 to preview the vocabulary. • Guide students to use Multidraft Reading strategies (TE p. 356)	*Structure/Language* If students will have difficulty with vocabulary and language in these poems, have them identify difficult language on a first reading. *Analyzing* If students will not have difficulty with language, have them discuss how sound devices help poets develop vivid descriptions.
Structure/Language Conventionality and Clarity	Some challenging vocabulary; alliteration; difficult Shakespearean diction 1 2 3 ④ 5		
Levels of Meaning/Purpose/ Concept Level	Accessible concepts (kittens; changing landscape); challenging concepts (protecting fairy queen) 1 2 ③ 4 5		
Quantitative Measures			
Lexile	NP	Text Length	Word Count: 66; 132; 109; 39

CLOSE READING MODEL

The passage below is from Shel Silverstein's poem "No Thank You." The annotations to the right of the passage show ways in which you can use close reading skills to paraphrase the poem and analyze sound devices and tone.

from "No Thank You"

No I do not want a kitten,
No cute, cuddly kitty-poo,
No more long hair in my cornflakes,
No more midnight meowing mews. [1]

. . .

No I will not take that kitten—
I've had lice and I've had fleas,
I've been scratched and sprayed and bitten,
I've developed allergies. [2]

Sound Devices and Tone

1 The speaker repeats the word, "No" at the beginning of each line. This repetition, along with the alliteration in "cute, cuddly kitty-poo" and "midnight meowing mews" creates a bouncy, humorous tone.

Paraphrasing

2 When reading this stanza aloud, you would take a long pause after the line that ends with a dash. You would pause only briefly after the lines that end with commas, and take the longest pause after the line that ends with a period.

🔔 Daily Bellringer

For each class during which you will teach this selection, have students complete one of the five Research activities for Week 17 in *Daily Bellringer Activities.* You may wish to use additional activities that are applicable to this selection.

Vocabulary

If students require support with selection vocabulary, use this routine:

1. Write the following words and definitions on the board:

hollowed *v.* created a hole or a space within

dispersed *v.* distributed in many directions

sculpted *v.* shaped or molded

thorny *adj.* irritating or annoying

offense *n.* harmful act; violation of a law

whirs *v.* flies or moves quickly with a buzzing sound

2. Have students say each word aloud.

3. Use the word in a sentence that defines the word.

🌐 DIFFERENTIATED INSTRUCTION

EL Extended Support—English Learners
Have students complete the **Reading and Vocabulary Warm-ups** for this collection in the *Student Companion All-in-One Workbook* before they read. Assign the prereading pages and the selections in the *Reader's Notebook: English Learner's Version.* Then, have students listen to portions of the collection in the *Student eText* or on the *Hear It!* CD-ROM.

L1 L2 Extended Support—Struggling Readers
Have students complete the **Reading and Vocabulary Warm-ups** for this collection in the *Student Companion All-in-One Workbook* before they read. Assign the prereading pages and the selections in the *Reader's Notebook: Adapted Version.* Then, have students listen to portions of the collection in the *Student eText* or on the *Hear It!* CD-ROM.

Extended Support—Reluctant Readers
To build motivation and engagement before assigning the collection, have students read "Everyday Art," a thematically related selection in *Reality Central.* Then, use the questions at the conclusion of the related selection to guide discussion.

MULTIDRAFT READING

To assist struggling readers and to deepen comprehension for all, assign the text in "chunks" and apply multidraft reading protocols. For each reading, have students set the purpose indicated:

- **First reading:** Students should read the selection independently and think about its basic meaning.

- **Second reading:** Students should analyze the text's key ideas and details and its craft and structure, and respond to the side-column prompts.

- **Third reading:** Students should integrate knowledge and ideas, connect the text to other texts and to the world, and answer the end-of-selection questions.

For more guidance, refer to the *Classroom Strategies and Teaching Routines* card on multidraft reading.

Meet the Poets

 **Octavio Paz** (1914–1998), a famous Mexican poet, lived in and visited many countries, but always remained deeply committed to his Mexican heritage. In 1990, Paz received the Nobel Prize in Literature.

 **Shel Silverstein** (1932–1999), a Chicago native, was a talented poet, cartoonist, playwright, and songwriter. His popular poetry collections— such as *Where the Sidewalk Ends* and *A Light in the Attic*—show his imaginative sense of humor, which both children and adults enjoy. Silverstein also wrote the classic children's book *The Giving Tree*.

 **William Shakespeare** (1564–1616) is probably the most highly regarded writer in the English language. Born in the English town of Stratford-upon-Avon, Shakespeare went to London as a young man. There he began writing and acting in plays. He wrote at least thirty-seven plays and more than one hundred fifty poems. "The Fairies' Lullaby" comes from the play *A Midsummer Night's Dream*.

 **Gwendolyn Brooks** (1917–2000) wrote many poems about her neighbors in Chicago, the city she lived in for most of her life. She started writing when she was seven years old and published her work in a well-known magazine as a teenager. In 1950, Brooks became the first African American writer to win a Pulitzer Prize.

356 UNIT 3 • Do we need words to communicate well?

🗨 VOCABULARY DEVELOPMENT

Thematic Vocabulary: The Big Question

As students are discussing Poetry Collection 4, encourage them to use the thematic vocabulary presented in Introducing the Big Question, pp. 302–303. You might encourage them with sentence starters like these:

1. Using few words, poetry can clearly focus and *communicate* . . .
2. Poetry is often used for the *expression* of feelings because . . .

3. The *message* of "No Thank You" is . . .
4. The imagery in "Wind and water and stone" may *symbolize* the poet's feelings about . . .

Wind and water and stone

Octavio Paz

The water hollowed the stone,
the wind dispersed the water,
the stone stopped the wind.
Water and wind and stone.

5 The wind sculpted the stone,
the stone is a cup of water,
the water runs off and is wind.
Stone and wind and water.

The wind sings in its turnings,
10 the water murmurs as it goes,
the motionless stone is quiet.
Wind and water and stone.

One is the other, and is neither:
among their empty names
15 they pass and disappear,
water and stone and wind.

◄ **Vocabulary**
hollowed (häl´ ōd)
v. created a hole
or a space within

dispersed (di spʉrst´)
v. distributed in
many directions

sculpted (sculpt´ əd)
v. shaped or molded

Sound Devices
What effect is created
by the repetition of the
words in the fourth line
of each stanza?

GUIDED EXPLORATION

❶ Sound Devices

1. **Ask** the Sound Devices question.

   Possible response: It creates a solemn effect that makes the elements seem ageless and important.

2. **Ask:** In addition to repetition, what other sound device appears in these lines?

   Answer: alliteration (water, wind)

 Video

Watch the Background Video online!

 Audio

Selection Audio is available in the *Student eText* and on the *Hear It!* CD-ROM.

❷ ? Connecting to the Big Question

1. Point out that a poet's feelings about a subject can be communicated by word choice and arrangement.

2. Have students read the first stanza of the poem. **Ask:** How does the first line signal the mood of the poem?

   Possible response: The first line is negative. The speaker immediately announces what he or she does not want.

3. **Ask:** What effect does the repetition of the word *no* create?

   Possible response: It makes the speaker sound very emphatic and sure of his or her position.

No
Thank You

SHEL SILVERSTEIN

No I do not want a kitten,
No cute, cuddly kitty-poo,
No more long hair in my cornflakes,
No more midnight meowing mews.

5 No more scratchin', snarlin', spitters,
No more sofas clawed to shreds,
No more smell of kitty litter,
No more mousies in my bed.

No I will not take that kitten—
10 I've had lice and I've had fleas,
I've been scratched and sprayed and bitten,
I've developed allergies.

If you've got an ape, I'll take him,
If you have a lion, that's fine,
15 If you brought some walking bacon,
Leave him here, I'll treat him kind.

I have room for mice and gerbils,
I have beds for boars and bats,
But please, *please* take away that kitten—
20 Quick—'fore it becomes a cat.
Well . . . it is kind of cute at that.

Sound Devices
What sound device is
used in lines 5 and 6?

Paraphrasing
How do the ellipsis
points (. . .) help you
understand the poet's
meaning?

❸ Sound Devices

1. Invite a volunteer to read aloud the bracketed lines of the poem.

2. **Ask** students if they notice the repetition of a particular beginning consonant sound in these lines.

   Answer: Yes, several words begin with *s* or an *s* blend.

3. **Ask** the Sound Devices question.

   Answer: The sound device is alliteration—the repetition of initial consonant sounds.

4. Point out that the poet may also have chosen the *s* sound because it sounds like the hiss of a cat. **Ask** what literary device the poet would be using.

   Answer: The poet would be using onomatopoeia along with alliteration.

❹ Paraphrasing

1. Read aloud the final line of the poem. As you pause at the ellipses, make an expression as if you are pondering a decision.

2. **Ask** the Paraphrasing question.

   Possible response: It tells the reader to slow down because the narrator is thinking and perhaps changing his mind.

👥 DIFFERENTIATED INSTRUCTION

🔵 Vocabulary for English Learners
Preteach vocabulary that students will encounter in each poem: "No Thank You," *sofa, lice, allergies, boars;* "The Fairies' Lullaby," *thorny, offense;* "Wind and water and stone," *hollowed, dispersed, sculpted.* Explain the meaning of each word. Then write sentences on the board, omitting the targeted word. Read the sentences with students and ask them to supply the missing word. Example: *You can sit on a ___.* (sofa)

Strategy for Less Proficient Readers
Prepare an **Anticipation Guide** (*Professional Development Guidebook,* p. 38) with the following statements:

• Onomatopoeia is the best sound device to use to create a vivid image in a poem.

• Poets should not combine different sound devices within one poem.

   Give students a copy of the prepared **Guide** and have them mark their responses in the Me column. Have students discuss the statements in pairs and have them mark the **Guides** again in the Group column. After students read the poems, have them complete the After Reading column.

⑤ Paraphrasing

1. Read aloud lines 5 and 6. **Ask** the first part of the Paraphrasing question.

Answer: There is no punctuation mark.

2. **Ask** the second part of the Paraphrasing question.

Possible response: Nightingale, use your sweet voice to sing a lullaby with us.

THE FAIRIES' LULLABY

from A MIDSUMMER NIGHT'S DREAM

WILLIAM SHAKESPEARE

Fairies. You spotted snakes with double tongue,
    Thorny hedgehogs, be not seen.
  Newts and blindworms,[1] do no wrong,
    Come not near our fairy Queen.

5 **Chorus.** Philomel,[2] with melody
    Sing in our sweet lullaby;
  Lulla, lulla, lullaby, lulla, lulla, lullaby.
    Never harm,
    Nor spell, nor charm,
10 Come our lovely lady nigh.
  So, good night, with lullaby.

Vocabulary ▶
thorny (thôr´ nē) *adj.*
prickly; full of thorns

Paraphrasing
In reading aloud, why would you keep reading at the end of line 5? How would you paraphrase lines 5 and 6?

---

1. **newts** (nōōts) **and blindworms** *n.* newts are salamanders, which look like lizards but are related to frogs. Blindworms are legless lizards.
2. **Philomel** (fil´ ə mel´) *n.* nightingale.

Fairies. Weaving spiders, come not here.
        Hence, you long-legged spinners, hence!
    Beetles black, approach not near.
15   Worm nor snail do no offense.

Chorus. Philomel, with melody
        Sing in our sweet lullaby;
    Lulla, lulla, lullaby, lulla, lulla, lullaby.
        Never harm,
20   Nor spell, nor charm,
    Come our lovely lady nigh.
    So, good night, with lullaby.

offense (ə fens´)
n. harmful act;
violation of a law

6 Sound Devices

1. Ask the Sound Devices question.

Answer: They are examples of onomatopoeia. The words express a magical, dream-like experience.

2. Point out that *sushes* is a word that the author made up. **Ask** students to suggest why it works so well as onomatopoeia.

Possible response: It is a soft-sounding word that sounds like a combination of quiet words and images, such as *soft*, *snow*, and *hush*.

☑ ASSESS

Language Study

Vocabulary

Sample answers:

1. A crowd might have suddenly *dispersed*, or run away, if an alarm sounded.

2. A small *hollowed* stone could be strung as a bead on a necklace.

3. Snowmen and animals can be *sculpted* out of snow.

4. A child who interrupts an adult who is speaking commits a minor *offense*.

5. A windmill *whirs* as its blades turn, generating power.

Word Study

Part A

Sample answers:

The suffix *-y* forms adjectives that mean "having," full of," or "characterized by." A *wordy* answer is <u>full of</u> words, or <u>characterized by</u> the use of many words. A *grouchy* person is <u>full of</u> grouchiness or bad temper. A *drowsy* child is <u>characterized by</u> sleepiness.

Part B

Sample answers:

1. A *thirsty* person is <u>full of</u> thirst, and should drink water.

2. A child's hands might have a *sticky* coating after eating a jam sandwich.

Cynthia in the Snow
Gwendolyn Brooks

Vocabulary ▶
whirs (wʉrz) *v.* flies or moves quickly with a buzzing sound

6

Sound Devices
What sound device is at work in the words *SUSHES, hushes,* and *flitter-twitters?* What do these words express?

It SUSHES.
It hushes
The loudness in the road.
It flitter-twitters,
5   And laughs away from me.
It laughs a lovely whiteness,
And whitely whirs away,
To be
Some otherwhere,
10   Still white as milk or shirts.
So beautiful it hurts.

Language Study

Vocabulary The words listed below appear in the poems in Collection 4. Answer each numbered question based on the meaning of the italicized vocabulary word.

> hollowed   dispersed   sculpted   offense   whirs

1. Why might a crowd have suddenly *dispersed*?
2. What could you do with a *hollowed* stone?
3. What things can be *sculpted* out of snow?
4. What is an example of a child's minor *offense*?
5. What is an example of something that *whirs*?

Word Study

Part A Explain how the **suffix -y** contributes to the meanings of the words *wordy, grouchy,* and *drowsy*. Consult a dictionary if necessary.

Part B Use context and what you know about the suffix *-y* to explain your answer to each question.

1. If a person is *thirsty*, what should he or she do?
2. When might a child's hands be *sticky*?

WORD STUDY

The **suffix -y** forms adjectives that mean "having," full of," or "characterized by." In "The Fairies' Lullaby," William Shakespeare uses the word **thorny** to describe hedgehogs—small animals that have sharp, thorn-like spines.

Literary Analysis

Possible responses appear below. Check to be sure students support their responses with evidence from the text.

1. (a) Wind and water and stone are similar, yet different; names are meaningless as one becomes the other over time. **(b)** The forces of nature are interconnected, one affecting the other in a never-ending, timeless way. Some may see this as an analogy to life itself and the forces and interactions that shape our lives.

2. (a) The chorus should pause after lines 6, 7 (8, 9 short pause), 10, 11, 17, 18 (19, 20 short pause), 21 and 22. **(b)** Nightingale, sing with us, because your song is sweet and it will put the queen to sleep.

3. (a) The punctuation gives the poem the uneven rhythm of falling snow. **(b)** The punctuation helps the reader know where and how long to pause, which makes it easier to "hear" the poem and understand its meaning.

4. (a) snakes, hedgehogs, newts, blindworms, spiders, beetles, worms, snails **(b)** The creatures are all small animals that people generally do not like. However, most of them are not that threatening.

Close Reading Activities ©

Literary Analysis

Key Ideas and Details

1. **Paraphrase (a)** Paraphrase the final stanza of "Wind and water and stone." **(b)** What ideas become clear after paraphrasing?

2. **Paraphrase (a)** In "The Fairies' Lullaby," after which words should the chorus pause? **(b)** Paraphrase the chorus's lines.

3. **Paraphrase (a)** How does punctuation affect the pace, or timing, of the words in "Cynthia in the Snow"? **(b)** How does reading the poem aloud help you paraphrase the poem?

4. **(a)** Name all the creatures the fairies address in "The Fairies' Lullaby." **(b) Classify:** What do all these creatures have in common?

Craft and Structure

5. **Sound Devices and Tone** Complete a chart like the one on the right by listing examples of repetition, alliteration, and onomatopoeia in each poem.

6. **Sound Devices and Tone** What tone do sound devices create in each poem?

Integration of Knowledge and Ideas

7. **(a)** According to the speaker in "Wind and water and stone," what does each of the three natural elements do? **(b) Connect:** What is the three elements' overall effect on nature?

8. **(a)** In "No Thank You," what are three reasons the speaker gives for not wanting a kitten? **(b) Make a Judgment:** Are the reasons convincing? Explain.

9. **(a)** In "Cynthia in the Snow," what five things does the snow do? **(b) Analyze:** What is the speaker's overall reaction to the snow?

10. ❓ **Do we need words to communicate well? (a)** Choose two images in the poems that make you think of something familiar in a whole new way. **(b) Interpret:** For each image, explain what the poet communicates by making you think this way.

Poetry Collection 4

"Wind and water and stone"

"No Thank You"

"The Fairies' Lullaby"

"Cynthia in the Snow"

ACADEMIC VOCABULARY

As you write and speak about the poems in Collection 4, use the words related to communication that you explored on page 303 of this text.

8. **(a)** Kittens claw the sofa, bring mice to the bed, and shed hair. **(b)** These seem to be convincing reasons until the speaker changes his mind in the last line because the kitten is so cute.

9. **(a)** The snow shushes, hushes, flitter-twitters, laughs, and whirls. **(b)** Her reaction is delight.

10. ❓ **Do we need words to communicate well?**
(a) Cat hair in a bowl of corn-flakes and "walking bacon" are two images that describe familiar objects in new ways. **(b)** The first image details the unpleasant side of living with a kitten—its hair can end up in your mouth. The description of the pig combines the movement of the live animal and the product of its death in a single humorous image.

---

5. "Wind and water and stone": repetition: *wind, water, stone;* alliteration: *sculpted the stone, wind and water;* onomatopoeia: *murmurs*

   "No Thank You": repetition: *no, no more, I've, I, if you, I have;* alliteration: *cute, cuddly kitty-poo; more midnight meowing mews; scratchin', snarlin', spitters . . . sofas; boars and bats;* onomatopoeia: *meowing*

   "The Fairies' Lullaby": repetition: the lines of the chorus; alliteration: *spotted snakes, lulla, lulla, lullaby; lovely lady; long-legged*

   "Cynthia in the Snow": repetition: *it, laughs;* alliteration: *laughs . . . lovely, whitely whirs;* onomatopoeia: *sushes, flitter-twitters, whirs.*

6. "No Thank You"—a playful, humorous tone; "Wind and water and stone"—a tone of time-lessness; "The Fairies' Lullaby"—a magical, lyrical tone; "Cynthia in the Snow"—a quiet, peaceful tone

7. **(a)** The water shapes stone, runs off, and murmurs; the wind scatters water, shapes stone, and sings, the stone stops wind, forms a cup for water, and is quiet. **(b)** The overall effect of the three elements' work is to shape nature into beautiful forms.

 Online Writer's Notebook

Students can use the Online Writer's Notebook to record all responses.

Close Reading Activities Continued

Conventions

1. Introduction the skill, using the instruction on the student page.
2. Discuss the examples in the chart.

Think Aloud: Model the Skill

Model the skill of identifying simple and compound subjects. Say:

> To help me remember the difference between simple and compound subjects, I think "simple equals single." A simple subject contains one singular or one plural noun or pronoun. In the sentence *Wasps and bees sting, wasps and bees* is a compound subject made up of two plural nouns joined by a conjunction (*and*).

Practice A

1. Does the speaker of the poem want to own a kitten?
2. Sing me a lullaby.
3. I love watching snow fall!
4. Water and wind change stone.

Reading Application
Sample answers:

"Cynthia in the Snow:" "It laughs a lovely whiteness." *It*—simple. "The Fairies' Lullaby:" "Worm nor snail do no offense." *worm nor snail*—compound. "No Thank You:" "No I will not take that kitten." *I*—simple.

Practice B
Sample answers:

1. The speaker of "No Thank You" complains about hair in his cereal.
2. The poem "Cynthia in the Snow" includes sound devices.
3. The fairies sing a lullaby.
4. Wind and water change stone.

Writing Application
Sample answers:

(a) Cynthia loves watching snow fall. **(b)** How do wind, water, and stone work together? **(c)** So many nasty little creatures live in the forest!

Conventions: Sentence Parts and Types

Poetry Collection 4

A **sentence** consists of a subject and a predicate, and expresses a complete thought. A sentence always begins with a capital letter.

A **simple subject** is the person, place, or thing about which the sentence is written. A **complete subject** includes the simple subject and any words related to it. A **simple predicate** is the verb that expresses the main action in the sentence. A **complete predicate** includes the verb and any words related to it.

A **compound subject** is made up of two or more nouns that share the same verb and are joined by conjunctions such as *and*.

Sentences can be classified according to their functions.

Type of Sentence	Function	Sample Sentence	End Punctuation
Declarative	states an idea	The sky is blue.	period
Interrogative	asks a question	What time is it?	question mark
Imperative	gives an order or direction	Do not enter this room.	period or exclamation mark
Exclamatory	expresses strong emotion	This is amazing!	exclamation mark

Practice A
Rewrite each sentence, changing it to the type indicated.

1. The speaker of the poem does not want to own a kitten. (*interrogative*)
2. Will you please sing me a lullaby? (*imperative*)
3. I love watching snow fall. (*exclamatory*)
4. How do water and wind change a stone? (*declarative*)

Reading Application Identify three subjects in the poems in this collection. In each case, explain whether the subject is simple or compound.

Practice B
Write a sentence that combines each complete subject below with a complete predicate.

1. the speaker of "No Thank You"
2. the poem "Cynthia in the Snow"
3. the fairies
4. wind and water

Writing Application Write a sentence for each item based on one of the poems you read. **(a)** a declarative sentence with a simple subject, **(b)** an interrogative sentence with a compound subject, **(c)** an exclamatory sentence.

364 UNIT 3 • Do we need words to communicate well?

⇒ EXTEND THE LESSON

Sentence Modeling
Write the following sentence from "The Fairies' Lullaby" on the board:

> *Newts and blindworms, do no wrong, come not near our fairy Queen.*

Ask students what they notice about the sentence. Elicit from them that the subject is compound (*newts and blindworms*) because it contains two nouns. Then ask what else they notice (the sentence structure seems archaic, i.e., "come not near").

Have students imitate the sentence in a sentence on a topic of their choosing, matching each grammatical and stylistic feature discussed. Collect the sentences, and share them with the class.

Writing to Sources

Description Write a **prose description** inspired by one of the poems you read in Poetry Collection 4. Read your description to the class.

- Review Collection 4, and select the poem you will use as your subject.
- Jot down notes that capture the poem's images and feelings, as well as your reactions to the poem.
- Use words that appeal to the senses of sight, sound, smell, taste, and touch.
- Write a paragraph in which you describe and support your impression of the poem.

Grammar Application Make sure each sentence in your description includes a subject and a predicate. To add interest in your writing, use a variety of sentence types.

Research and Technology

Build and Present Knowledge A **résumé** is a specially formatted summary of information about a person's career and education. Prepare a résumé for one of the poets in this collection.

- Conduct research on the poet of your choice. Focus on specific categories such as schools attended, books written, awards won, and related jobs.
- Search online for examples of résumé formats. Look for writers' résumés to use as models.
- Write a résumé that showcases what you have learned about the poet. Organize your information, using the example résumés you found as a guide. Include categories such as *Education, Publishing History,* and *Honors.*
- Type your résumé using a word-processing program. Use tabs and settings in the program to correctly format the résumé.

Common Core State Standards

Writing

4. Produce clear and coherent writing in which the development, organization, and style are appropriate to task, purpose, and audience.

6. Use technology, including the Internet, to make and publish writing as well as to interact and collaborate with others; demonstrate sufficient command of keyboarding skills to type a minimum of three pages in a single sitting.

Language

1. Demonstrate command of the conventions of standard English grammar and usage when writing or speaking.

3. Use knowledge of language and its conventions when writing, speaking, reading, or listening.

Writing to Sources

1. Review the assignment, using the instruction on the student page.
2. To help students with their notes, have them think of synonyms for some of the words in the poem they choose, so that they can describe the details and emotions in their own words.
3. To give students guidance in writing a description, give them **Support for Writing** for this selection in the *Student Companion All-in-One Workbook.*
4. To evaluate the writing activity, use one of the rubrics for a narrative text from *Professional Development Guidebook* (pp. 220–221). Evaluate for how well students describe a scene suggested in the poems they choose.

Grammar Application

Have students check their drafts to make sure they have used complete sentences and a variety of sentence types correctly.

Six Traits Focus

✓	Ideas	✓	Word Choice
✓	Organization	✓	Sentence Fluency
	Voice		Conventions

Research and Technology

1. Review the assignment, using the instruction on the student page.
2. To support students' work on the assignment, have them complete the **Support for Extend Your Learning** page for this selection in the *Student Companion All-in-One Workbook.*

Daily Bellringer

For each class during which you will teach this selection, have students complete one of the five Sentence Combining activities for Week 18 in the *Daily Bellringer Activities*. You may wish to use additional activities that are applicable to these selections.

❶ **Do we need words to communicate well?**

1. Review the assignment with the class.

2. Remind students that to communicate means to interact with others, with the goal of reaching understanding. Communication can be verbal and nonverbal. Encourage students to think about how they communicate by using nonverbal methods, such as facial expressions, gestures, and eye contact.

3. Remind students that when they read the poems, they should focus on how poets use imagery to express moods or emotions.

MULTIDRAFT READING

To assist struggling readers and to deepen comprehension for all, apply multidraft reading protocols. For each reading, have students set the purpose indicated:

- **First reading:** Students should read the selection independently and think about its basic meaning.

- **Second reading:** Students should analyze the text's key ideas and details and its craft and structure, and respond to the side-column prompts.

- **Third reading:** Students should integrate knowledge and ideas, connect the text to other texts and to the world, and answer the end-of-selection questions.

For more guidance, refer to the *Classroom Strategies and Teaching Routines* card on multidraft reading.

  Do we need words to communicate well?

❶ Explore the Big Question as you read these poems. Take notes on how the poets paint pictures with words. Then compare and contrast what the two poems suggest about communication.

READING TO COMPARE IMAGERY

Poets E.E. Cummings and Robert Frost use descriptive language that includes vivid images. As you read the poems that follow, consider the effects of each poet's word choice. When you finish reading, compare and contrast the ways in which the two poets use imagery.

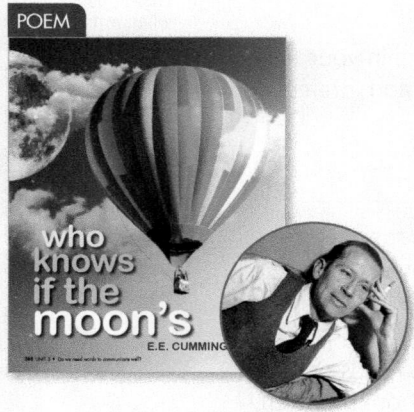

"who know's if the moon's"

E.E. Cummings (1894–1962)
As a poet, E.E. (Edward Estlin) Cummings experimented with punctuation, capitalization, spelling, and the arrangement of words on the page. In many poems, his words seem to be scattered on the page. However, the scattered words create the effects he wanted to achieve, especially when the poems are read aloud. Cummings studied painting, which may explain why he became interested in the visual effect of his poems.

"Dust of Snow"

Robert Frost (1874–1963)
Although he was born in California, Robert Frost is often associated with New England. Frost's family moved to Massachusetts when he was eleven years old, and he spent most of his life in the Northeast. Frost began writing poetry in high school. He kept writing while he worked as a farmer, mill worker, newspaper reporter, and teacher. Frost won the Pulitzer Prize four times—more than any other poet.

366 UNIT 3 • Do we need words to communicate well?

 VOCABULARY DEVELOPMENT

Vocabulary Knowledge Rating
Create a **Vocabulary Knowledge Rating Chart (Professional Development Guidebook**, p. 33) featuring the words glossed in the selections:

steeples (p. 369)   *rued* (p. 370)

Give students a copy of the chart, and read the words aloud. Have students mark their rating of each in the Before You Read column.

To gauge how much instruction to provide, tally the students who think they know each word.

Explain that the words are defined in the margin at the point where they appear in the selection. Urge students to be alert to these words as they read the selections. They will rate their knowledge again when they finish.

❷ Comparing Imagery

An **image** is a word picture that appeals to one or more of the five senses of sight, hearing, smell, taste, and touch. Writers use descriptive language and sensory details to develop **imagery**.

- An image can appeal to more than one sense. For example, "soft carpet of yellow prairie flowers" appeals to both touch and sight.
- An image can create a feeling of movement. For example, "the autumn leaves floated gently to the ground" shows the reader how the leaves fell.
- Imagery helps writers express moods or emotions. Mood is the feeling that a poem creates in the reader. A poem can have many moods, including frightening, fanciful, thoughtful, and lonely.

In the poems "who knows if the moon's" and "Dust of Snow," each poet uses imagery to achieve a different effect. As you read each poem, use a chart such as the one below to record the picture the poem creates in your mind, the sense or senses to which each image appeals, and the overall mood or emotion the poet communicates through imagery.

Poem title	Image	Sight	Hearing	Smell	Taste	Touch	Mood

Common Core State Standards

Reading Literature
4. Determine the meaning of words and phrases as they are used in a text, including figurative and connotative meanings; analyze the impact of a specific word choice on meaning and tone.

Writing
2.a. Introduce a topic; organize ideas, concepts, and information, using strategies such as definition, classification, comparison/contrast, and cause/effect; include formatting, graphics, and multimedia when useful to aiding comprehension.
2.b. Develop the topic with relevant facts, definitions, concrete details, quotations, or other information and examples.

❷ Comparing Imagery

1. Introduce the skill.
2. Discuss the information in the bulleted list.
3. Give students a copy of **Comparing Imagery Graphic Organizer B** for these selections. Tell them they will fill it in with examples of images as they read.

Think Aloud: Model the Skill

Model a way to understand the effects of imagery. Say to students:

When I read poetry that uses imagery, I first try to picture the sights, hear the sounds, or smell the smells that the images describe. Then, I try to think about what emotions those sense experiences call forth. For instance, in the song "America, the Beautiful," the phrase "amber waves of grain" makes me imagine a huge wheat field stretching off as far as I can see. That picture makes me feel grateful that we Americans have land that can produce such crops.

TEACHING RESOURCES

	Print	Digital
All Common Core Companion, pp. 41–53; 184–195	✓	✓
All Graphic Organizers A and B, *who knows if the moon's; Dust of Snow*		✓
All Online Student Edition eText with audio and video		✓
All Online Teacher Edition		✓
L1 Professional Development Guidebook, p. 33		✓
All Student Companion All-in-One Workbook, *who knows if the moon's; Dust of Snow*	✓	✓

❶ Background

Punctuation and Capitalization

E. E. Cummings is known for his deviation from grammatical conventions. In his poems, he uses unconventional capitalization, spacing, and punctuation. His style contributes to the mood of the poems.

❷ Activating Prior Knowledge

Ask students if they have ever looked down on Earth from a plane, and if so, to describe their impressions. Then have them imagine what it would be like to travel away from Earth in a balloon. Ask volunteers to describe their imagined journey.

❸ About the Selection

In E. E. Cummings's "who knows if the moon's," the speaker ponders what it would be like to travel in a balloon to a city where it's always spring.

who knows if the moon's ... ❶ ❷ ❸

E.E. CUMMINGS

368 UNIT 3 • Do we need words to communicate well?

© TEXT COMPLEXITY **RUBRIC**

who knows if the moon's		
Qualitative Measures	Context/Knowledge Demands	Imaginative, fantastic journey 1 ② 3 4 5
	Structure/Language Conventionality	Difficult style; on-level vocabulary 1 2 ③ 4 5
	Levels of Meaning/ Purpose/Concepts	Accessible concept (an imaginary world) 1 ② 3 4 5
Quantitative Measures	Text Length	Word Count: 83
	Lexile	NP

who knows if the moon's
a balloon, coming out of a keen¹ city
in the sky—filled with pretty people?
(and if you and i should

5   get into it, if they
should take me and take you into their balloon,
why then
we'd go up higher with all the pretty people

4

than houses and steeples and clouds:
10   go sailing
away and away sailing into a keen
city which nobody's ever visited, where

always
5   it's
15   Spring) and everyone's
in love and flowers pick themselves

---

1. keen (kēn) *adj.* slang for *good, fine.*

Imagery
What kind of movement does the balloon image suggest to you?

◄ **Vocabulary**
steeples (stē′ pəlz) *n.* towers rising above churches or other structures

Critical Thinking

1. **Key Ideas and Details** Why might a place where everything is perfect be appealing to Cummings and his readers?

2. **Craft and Structure (a)** What words are repeated in the poem? **(b)** What ideas do these words emphasize?

3. **Craft and Structure** Why do you think lines 13–15 are arranged differently from the other lines in the poem?

4. **Integration of Knowledge and Ideas** Identify an image in the poem and think about how you might capture it in a drawing. **(a)** What information do the words of the poem give you? What information is missing? **(b)** How could you fill in the missing information? **(c)** Describe or draw the picture you would make. **(d)** How are the idea and mood you convey similar to and different from the image in the poem? *[Connect to the Big Question: Do we need words to communicate well?]*

PART 2 • who knows if the moon's **369**

ⓒ TEXT COMPLEXITY **READER AND TASK SUGGESTIONS**

who knows if the moon's

Preparing to Read the Text
• Using the Background information on TE p. 368, discuss the poet's style.
• Tell students that there is limited punctuation separating sentences and ideas, but there are still places to pause naturally.
• Guide students to use Multidraft Reading strategies (TE p. 366).

Leveled Tasks
Structure/Language If students will have difficulty with the style, read the poem aloud, emphasizing the natural pauses in the lines. Discuss the inverted syntax in lines 8–10. Then have students read the poem.

Analyzing If students will not have difficulty with the style, ask them to locate the one capitalized word in the poem. Discuss why the poet chose to capitalize the word *spring.*

❹ Imagery

Ask students the Imagery question.

Possible response: Students may say that the balloon image suggests a floating movement. They may also describe an image of the balloon sailing, as clouds do in the air.

❺ 🅱 Connecting to the Big Question

1. Remind students of the Big Question.

2. Direct students' attention to the bracketed passage. **Ask** students what ideas or feelings they associate with *spring.*

   Possible responses: Students might mention warmer weather, blooming flowers, and similar ideas.

3. Discuss how commonly shared these ideas about spring are. Explain that writers rely on these powerful words to help deliver the same message to all readers. Tell students to look for other powerful words and ideas.

☑ ASSESS

Critical Thinking

Possible responses appear below. Check to be sure students support their responses with evidence from the text.

1. A perfect place would be appealing to people because they wouldn't have to deal with disappointment or sadness.

2. **(a)** "Sailing" and "away" are repeated. **(b)** They emphasize the ideas of movement and freedom.

3. The lines mimic the movement of the balloon as it gently lands in the keen city. The lines also look like someone hopping down steps.

4. 🅱 **(a)** If the image were the balloon, the poem says that it would have a container large enough to hold "you," "me," and many other people. The poem, however, does not describe the balloon's shape or color. **(b)** You would need to use your imagination. You might decide that the balloon looks like the moon, white and glowing. **(c)** Students might describe a large hot-air balloon. **(d)** Students should compare the mood created by their imagined balloon to the delighted mood of the poem.

PART 2 • who knows if the moon's **369**

❻ Background

Circumstances may present themselves in ways that we do not expect. How people perceive these circumstances varies. Robert Frost appreciated simple events, which reflects his perception of change and new possibility.

❼ Activating Prior Knowledge

Ask students to recall a recent surprise they've had. Encourage them to think about whether it had an effect on their life. Have volunteers describe the surprise and the effects it had on them.

❽ About the Selection

In "Dust of Snow" Robert Frost describes a small incident in nature and how it makes him feel.

✓ ASSESS

Critical Thinking

Possible responses appear below. Check to be sure students support their responses with evidence from the text.

1. **(a)** A crow shakes snow on the speaker. **(b)** It happens by chance; it is a coincidence that the speaker and the crow are in the same place at the same time.

2. **(a)** The crow's action makes the speaker feel better. **(b)** Perhaps the action reminds the speaker of the beauty of nature and other good things. **(c)** Small pleasures can help ease a bad day.

3. Similar events do happen every day, but people often don't notice them. The impact of such events might be less as people began to take them for granted.

4.  **(a)** Students' sketches should show the scene. **(b)** Students might mention the crow, the tree, and the speaker. **(c)** Students might say that the emotional effect of the incident is better conveyed in words.

❻❼❽ Dust of Snow
Robert Frost

The way a crow
Shook down on me
The dust of snow
From a hemlock[1] tree

5   Has given my heart
A change of mood
And saved some part
Of a day I had rued.

Vocabulary ▶
rued (rōōd) *v.*
regretted

---

1. **hemlock** (hem' läk) *n.* evergreen tree; member of the pine family.

Critical Thinking

1. **Key Ideas and Details (a)** What is the action that changes the speaker's mood? **(b) Classify:** Is this action planned or does it occur by chance? Explain.

2. **Key Ideas and Details (a)** Describe the change that the action brings about in the speaker. **(b) Analyze:** Why does the action have this effect? **(c) Generalize:** What lesson do you think the speaker learns from this experience?

3. **Key Ideas and Details** If such small, unexpected natural events happened every day, would they have the same impact on a person? Explain.

4. **Integration of Knowledge and Ideas (a)** Draw a quick sketch of an image like the one described in the poem. **(b)** What parts of the poem could you convey in your picture? **(c)** What parts of the poem are better conveyed in words? *[Connect to the Big Question: Do we need words to communicate well?]*

370 UNIT 3 • Do we need words to communicate well?

© TEXT COMPLEXITY **RUBRIC**

Dust of Snow		
Qualitative Measures	Context/Knowledge Demands	Event in nature on an average day 1　②　3　4　5
	Structure/Language Clarity and Conventionality	On-level vocabulary; challenging style; complex syntax 1　2　③　4　5
	Levels of Meaning/ Purpose/Concept Level	Accessible concept (simple event can change one's outlook) 1　②　3　4　5
Quantitative Measures	Text Length	Word Count: 34
	Lexile	NP

Comparing Imagery

1. **Craft and Structure** **(a)** Choose an image from each poem. To which senses does each image appeal? **(b)** Complete a graphic organizer like the one shown for each poem to analyze the poem's mood. In the center, write a word that describes the mood. Then, in the outer circles, list images, words, or phrases in the poem that help develop that mood.

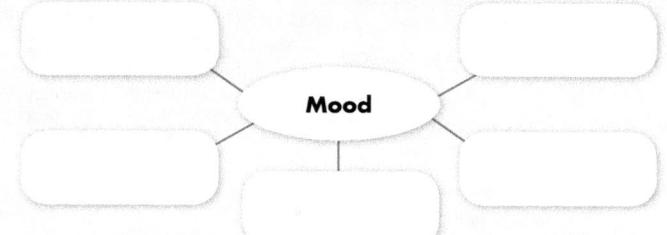

2. **Key Ideas and Details** In "who knows if the moon's," how does the imagery create a feeling of floating or weightlessness? List details that suggest this movement.

 Timed Writing

Explanatory Text: Essay
Write an essay in which you draw conclusions about the role nature plays in each poem. In your essay, note which descriptive words or phrases contribute to the image of nature, and decide whether the image of nature is positive or negative. **(25 minutes)**

5-Minute Planner

1. Read the prompt carefully and completely.
2. Use these questions to help you get started:
   • In each poem, does nature play a central role, or is it a part of the background for the action?
   • What sensory language contributes to the images of nature?
   • Which words help you tell whether the images of nature are negative or positive?
3. Reread the prompt, and then draft your essay. Include quotations from the two poems.

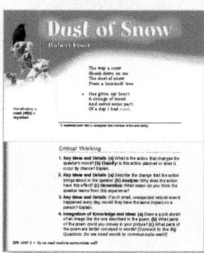

Comparing Imagery

1. **(a) Possible responses:** The image of the moon as a balloon evokes the sight and feeling of a hot-air balloon floating across the sky. The image of the crow shaking snow appeals to the senses of sight, hearing, and touch.

   (b) "who knows if the moon's": joyful mood, supported by spring, love, flowers

   "Dust of Snow": contented mood, supported by the words heart, change, saved

   For other sample answers, see *Graphic Organizer Transparencies,* **Comparing Imagery Graphic Organizer A** for the selections and the Additional Answers section.

2. The imagery refers to the moon, hanging in the sky, and a balloon, floating in the air.

Timed Writing

1. Review the prompt with students.
2. Have students use the 5-Minute Planner to structure their time. Guide them in completing the bulleted instructions. For example, point out that the response to the second and third prompts are related, as sensory language can suggest positive or negative images.
3. Allow students 25 minutes to complete the assignment.

Six Traits Focus

✓	Ideas	✓	Word Choice
✓	Organization		Sentence Fluency
	Voice		Conventions

© TEXT COMPLEXITY **READER AND TASK SUGGESTIONS**

Dust of Snow

Preparing to Read the Text
• Using the Background information on TE p. 370, discuss how a simple event can change our perception of something and help us discover new possibilities.
• Point out that the poem is a single sentence.
• Guide students to use Multidraft Reading strategies (TE p. 366).

Leveled Tasks
Structure/Language If students will have difficulty with syntax, have them read the poem aloud as a single sentence and note the rhyme scheme. Point out that the first stanza makes up the complete subject; the last stanza is the complete predicate.

Analyzing If students will not have difficulty with the syntax, point out that all but two of the words in the poem are single-syllables. Discuss how short words and the simple rhyme evoke a light-hearted mood.

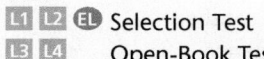 ASSESSMENT **RESOURCES**

The following resources can be used to assess students' knowledge and skills.

L1 L2 EL Selection Test
L3 L4 Open-Book Test

 **Online Writer's Notebook**

Students can use the Online Writer's Notebook to record all responses.

Words with Multiple Meanings

1. Introduce the skill, using the instruction on the student page.

2. Review the examples in the chart.

3. Explain to students that sometimes words that have different meanings have different parts of speech. Direct their attention to the chart and point out the different parts of speech stated for the word *key*.

4. Introduce the concept of multiple meanings by writing the familiar word *save* on the board. Call on volunteers to state a meaning of the word and use it in a sentence. You might prompt students by asking for a meaning related to computers, money, danger, and so on.

Think Aloud: Model the Skill

Model the skill of identifying words with multiple meanings. Say to students:

When I think of words with multiple meanings, words used in sports come to mind. Many words used to describe objects or actions in a game, such as *base, bat, double, run,* and *strike,* have specific meanings in baseball and different meanings in other contexts. Usually, it's pretty clear from the context which meaning is intended. If I hear that a "player swung a bat," I know that he or she was swinging a wooden or an aluminum stick, not a flying animal!

Practice A

Sample answers:

1. a. fine particles of dirt
   b. cover with a fine coating of material

2. a. to look at a performance, an event, or a program
   b. device to keep time

3. a. the topic of or information in a written work
   b. pleased; satisfied

4. a. in attendance
   b. a gift

 **G Grammar Tutorials**

Grammar Tutorials in the *Student eText* provide additional support!

Words with Multiple Meanings

A **multiple-meaning word** is a word that has more than one basic definition. To determine the meaning intended in a sentence, look at the context—the words surrounding the multiple-meaning word. This chart shows three different definitions and usages for the word *key*. Note how context clues suggest the meaning of *key* in each sentence.

Word	Use	Definition	Example Sentence
key	noun	a device used to open a lock	Use this **key** to unlock the door.
key	noun	a reef or low island	We paddled our boat out to the **key**.
key	adjective	important	The **key** point of the article is that tigers are an endangered species.

Practice A

Use context and your prior knowledge to write the meaning of the italicized word in each sentence. Then, use a print or an online dictionary to verify, or confirm, the meanings.

1. a. The old chair was covered with *dust.*
   b. When you take the cookies out of the oven, *dust* them with powdered sugar.

2. a. Let's *watch* the news on television at six o'clock.
   b. Check your *watch* to see if we need to leave for home yet.

3. a. I think the *content* of that poem is beautiful.
   b. The applause made Mary feel *content* with her performance.

4. a. How many people were *present* at the meeting?
   b. I made a birthday *present* for my grandfather.

 **Common Core State Standards**

Language

4. Determine or clarify the meaning of unknown and multiple-meaning words and phrases based on grade 6 reading and content, choosing flexibly from a range of strategies.

4.a. Use context as a clue to the meaning of a word or phrase.

4.c. Consult reference materials, both print and digital, to find the pronunciation of a word or determine or clarify its precise meaning or its part of speech.

4.d. Verify the preliminary determination of the meaning of a word or phrase.

TEACHING RESOURCES

	Print	Digital
All Language Study Worksheet, Words with Multiple Meanings		✓

Practice B

For each word listed, write two sentences that use different meanings of the word. If necessary, look up the meanings in a dictionary.

1. bow
2. set
3. draft
4. cast

5. tip
6. cape
7. current
8. ruler

Activity Look in a dictionary to find five words that have multiple meanings. You may use the five numbered words below, or you may choose words of your own. Write each word on a separate notecard like the one shown. Fill in the left-hand column of the notecard based on one of the word's meanings. Fill in the right-hand column based on another of the word's meanings. Then, trade note cards with a partner. Discuss the different meanings and uses of the words that each of you found.

1. pitcher
2. entry
3. hide
4. line
5. fast

Word: _____	
Part of Speech:	Part of Speech:
Definition:	Definition:
Example Sentence:	Example Sentence:

Comprehension and Collaboration

Work with two or three classmates. Write a sentence for each of the following words, using two different meanings of the word in the same sentence. For example, "My brother can't *bear* to be without his teddy *bear*."

charge
hard
wave

⚙ DIFFERENTIATED INSTRUCTION

ᴱᴸ Strategy for English Learners

Explain that some words have different pronunciations in their different uses. Point to these examples in the exercises:

- *content* (CAHN-tent as a noun, cuhn-TENT as an adjective) (Practice A, item 3)
- *bow* (BAU as a noun or verb, meaning "bend in respect;" or noun, meaning "the front of a ship;" BOH as a noun, meaning "a decoration") (Practice B, item 1)

Review these pronunciations to help students recognize and make the different sounds.

Enrichment for Advanced Readers

Give students practice in decoding meanings from context by telling them to insert the word *well* in the following blank spaces. Then, have them define the word as it is used.

- They lowered the bucket into the _____ to get water. (in-ground storage area for water)
- Tears would _____ up in his eyes when he saw a sad movie. (rise to the surface)
- The recommendation spoke _____ of the applicant's abilities. (favorably)

Practice B
Sample answers:

1. The crew gathered at the <u>bow</u> of the ship. The gift was wrapped and topped with a <u>bow</u>.
2. The network issued a <u>set</u> of DVDs for its popular show. He <u>set</u> the book on the table.
3. The writer began with a rough <u>draft</u>. The <u>draft</u> from the window chilled the room.
4. The artist <u>cast</u> the figure in bronze. The full <u>cast</u> was on hand for the show.
5. The customer left a <u>tip</u> after paying the bill. The teacher gave a useful <u>tip</u> for taking the test.
6. The ship sailed around the <u>cape</u>. The pirate wore a <u>cape</u> and a plumed hat.
7. The switch opened the electric <u>current</u>. The magazine focused on <u>current</u> events.
8. The <u>ruler</u> issued a decree. Nadia used a <u>ruler</u> to draw a straight line.

Activity

Provide dictionaries for students and guide them in their use so they can carry out the activity.

- Have pairs of students create the notecards.
- In their responses, students should be sure to list words that have distinct meanings. Allow students time to discuss their results.

Comprehension and Collaboration

Provide dictionaries for students and guide them in their use so they can carry out the activity.

- Divide the class into small groups to carry out the activity.
- Remind students that in their responses, they should use distinct meanings of each word in the same sentence.

Sample Answers:

1. The babysitter felt in <u>charge</u> after her <u>charge</u> listened to her and went to bed.
2. The frozen, <u>hard</u> ground made drilling <u>hard</u>.
3. The surfer was able to <u>wave</u> to her friends before catching the next big <u>wave</u>.

Learn the Skills

1. Introduce the workshop, including the activity on page 375.

2. Urge students to start with a problem within your school or community that can be improved, if not entirely solved. Suggest that students use a graphic organizer to gather their ideas about the problem and potential solutions.

3. Explain to students they need to establish connections between the problem and a proposed solution and to provide evidence to persuade their audience.

4. Review qualities that make speakers effective, such as clear knowledge of the topic and a confident tone of voice.

5. Remind students that graphs, charts, and other visual aids must be based on accurate facts from reliable sources.

6. Tell students that practicing their presentations at home before giving them in class can help to calm nerves.

Speaking and Listening

Problem-and-Solution Proposal

A **problem-and-solution proposal** is a formal plan that suggests a course of action for solving a problem. The following strategies can help you present a convincing problem-and-solution proposal.

Learn the Skills

Organize your ideas. First, identify the problem and make a list of its causes. Use statistics and examples to demonstrate these causes. Then, describe your proposed solution and list the reasons you think the solution will work. Add details that provide evidence and support for each point of your solution.

Establish connections and provide evidence. Use visual aids to show connections or provide evidence. For example, a bar graph or chart can show the connection between the problem you defined and the solution you are proposing. In the example shown, the bar graph illustrates the increase in accidents each year and provides support for the solution of installing a traffic light. Draw your visual aids or create them on a computer.

Plan your delivery. Practice your proposal and prepare any notes and visuals before your presentation so you do not forget your key points.

Remember your listener. Speak slowly and clearly so that your audience will be able to follow your presentation. Adjust your tone for emphasis when you introduce impotant information, then pause after you make a key point. Refer to your visuals at appropriate points during your presentation.

Use standard English. Your argument will be stronger if you use formal, correct language. As you speak, avoid slang and errors in grammar and usage.

Use eye contact and gestures. Make eye contact with members of the audience to keep them engaged, and use gestures to emphasize your points.

 Common Core State Standards

Speaking and Listening
4. Present claims and findings, sequencing ideas logically and using pertinent descriptions, facts, and details to accentuate main ideas or themes; use appropriate eye contact, adequate volume, and clear pronunciation.
5. Include multimedia components and visual displays in presentations to clarify information.

Language
1.e. Recognize variations from standard English in their own and others' writing and speaking, and identify and use strategies to improve expression in conventional language.

> **Problem:** Car accidents have increased each year.
> **Solution:** Replace stop signs with traffic lights.

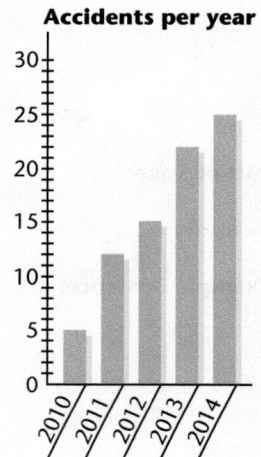

Accidents per year

✔ STRATEGIES **FOR DELIVERING AN ORAL PRESENTATION**

Tell students that oral presentations sound more natural when the speaker has an outline rather than a full script. Students may write a full script if that helps them collect their thoughts, but after reading the script aloud several times, they should condense it to an outline of the major points that they will discuss.

Each point should serve to remind the speaker what he or she wants to say next. After a brief glance at the next point, the speaker should make eye contact with the audience. Tell students to practice presenting their outlines at home and to add brief additional notes if their outlines do not sufficiently remind them of their points.

Practice the Skills

Presentation of Knowledge and Ideas Use what you have learned in this workshop to complete the following activity.

ACTIVITY: Present a Problem-and-Solution Proposal

Find a problem and think of a solution for it. Then, follow the steps below.

- List the causes of the problem.
- Use statistics and examples to demonstrate the causes.
- Organize your ideas around your solution.
- Use visual aids and evidence to support your solution.
- When delivering your proposal, make eye contact with the audience and use gestures. Be sure to use adequate volume and clear pronunciation.

Use the Speaking Guide to organize and plan your problem-and-solution proposal.

Speaking Guide

Problem: _____

Solution: _____

Supporting Points: _____

Visual Aids

Which visual aid will best support your solution? Briefly explain.

- ❏ graph
- ❏ chart
- ❏ table
- ❏ slide show
- ❏ diagram
- ❏ video

Delivery of Presentation

Employ the following techniques when you present your proposal.

- ❏ eye contact
- ❏ speaking rate
- ❏ volume level
- ❏ clear pronunciation
- ❏ natural gestures
- ❏ conventions of language

Comprehension and Collaboration Ask a classmate to evaluate your proposal based on the clarity of your presentation and whether or not your proposed solution seems reasonable. Then, evaluate your partner's proposal. If necessary, offer each other suggestions for improvement.

Practice the Skills

1. Review the assignment with students. Make sure that they understand the solution must be specific. Tell students to carefully plan and explain how the solution will be carried out. For example, if a student suggests beautifying the school by planting a garden, the student should pick a specific date for planting and describe what will be planted.

2. Explain to students that they should use a copy of the Speaking Guide to evaluate their own presentation and the presentations made by classmates.

3. Before students give their presentations to the class, remind listeners to ask questions if any points are unclear. To maintain order, encourage them to raise their hands and wait to be acknowledged by the presenter before stating their questions. Suggest that students making presentations scan the classroom from time to time so they will notice any students who have questions.

Evaluate the Activity

1. Evaluate students' presentations on the basis of the thoughtfulness of their ideas and the connection between their ideas and supporting details.

2. When the class discusses the presentations that were easiest to follow, encourage students to make note of the features of those presentations that made them effective and to incorporate those techniques in their future presentations.

❖ DIFFERENTIATED INSTRUCTION

Strategy for Special-Needs Students

Point out to students that when they give oral presentations, they should use body language to help convey their message. Show students a videotape of someone delivering a speech. Have them watch the nonverbal messages the person sends. Use questions, such as the following, to introduce further clarification:

- What kind of eye contact is the speaker making? Effective speakers make good eye contact with the audience. If the speaker looks interested in the audience, the audience will be interested in what the speaker has to say.

- What kind of speaking voice does the speaker have? An effective speech starts with a clear, strong, confident speaking voice.

- What kind of posture does the speaker have? Standing up straight sends the audience a message of confidence.

Encourage students to incorporate effective body language and a confident voice into their presentations.

Introducing the Writing Assignment

Review the assignment and the criteria, using the instruction on the student page.

Focus on Research

Remind students to keep the following tips in mind as they conduct research.

- Gather information from multiple authoritative print and digital sources.
- Assess the usefulness of each source in answering the research question.
- Integrate information into the text selectively.
- Synthesize information from multiple sources.
- Avoid plagiarism.
- Use a standard format for citations.

Writing Process

Write an Argument

Argumentative Essay

Defining the Form In an **argumentative essay**, the writer states a claim based on factual evidence. The writer then uses logic, reasoning, and strong support to convince readers to agree with the claim.

Assignment Write an argumentative essay in which you state and support a claim. Include these elements:

✓ a *clear thesis statement* that presents a position on an issue that has at least two sides

✓ a *clear organization,* including an introduction, a body, and a conclusion

✓ facts and examples from *credible sources* that *support your position*

✓ *evidence and support* to address the *counterarguments*

✓ a *formal style* that takes the subject and audience seriously

✓ *precise language* that clearly shows the *relationships between claims and evidence*

✓ *correct usage of coordinating conjunctions*

To preview the criteria on which your argumentative essay may be judged, see the rubric on page 383.

FOCUS ON RESEARCH

When you write an argumentative essay, use strong evidence to support your claim. Evidence should be

- *credible,* or from a trustworthy source.
- *accurate,* or recorded correctly from the source.
- *current,* or reflecting up-to-date information.
- *relevant,* or suitable to prove a specific point.

Be sure to cite your sources properly. Refer to the Research Workshop in the Introductory Unit for help on citing sources.

Common Core State Standards

Writing
1. Write arguments to support claims with clear reasons and relevant evidence.
1.a. Introduce claim(s) and organize the reasons and evidence clearly.
1.b. Support claim(s) with clear reasons and relevant evidence, using credible sources and demonstrating an nderstanding of the topic or text.

READING-WRITING CONNECTION

To get the feel for argument, read the persuasive speech "Preserving a Great American Symbol" on page 270.

TEACHING RESOURCES

	Print	Digital
All Common Core Companion, pp. 173–183, 214–226; 321–338	✓	✓
All EssayScorer powered by WriteToLearn		✓
All Online Student Edition eText with audio and video		✓
All Online Teacher Edition		✓
L1 Professional Development Guidebook, Rubrics for Self-Assessment: Argumentative Essay pp. 230–231		✓
All Student Companion All-in-One Workbook, Unit 3 Writing Process	✓	✓

 EssayScorer

Students can use EssayScorer with automatic feedback and scoring to practice summarizing!

Prewriting/Planning Strategies

Choose a two-sided topic. Select a topic that is important to you and that has two clear sides—one that you can support and one that you can oppose. Use these tips to zero in on an interesting topic:

- **Conduct a media review.** Think about the local issues in the news now. Look at print and online news sources, read letters to the editor, and watch and listen to local television and radio news programs to list all the topics that appeal to you. Then, choose one for your essay.
- **Organize a round table.** Gather classmates for a discussion of places and groups that are important to you. Think of issues that affect the locations and groups you have listed. Jot down any ideas that interest you, and choose a topic.

Narrow your topic to a manageable size. Make sure your topic is not too big to cover in an argumentative essay. Use a graphic organizer like the one shown to narrow your topic.

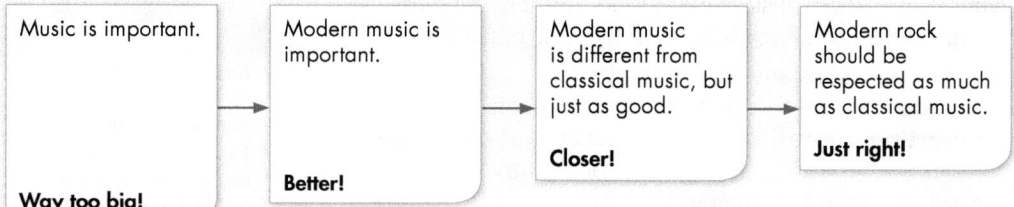

| Music is important.

Way too big! | → | Modern music is important.

Better! | → | Modern music is different from classical music, but just as good.

Closer! | → | Modern rock should be respected as much as classical music.

Just right! |

Build your argument. Plan how you will support your position with facts and strong details. In addition, decide how you will address opposing points of view. Use these tips:

- **Collect evidence.** Identify facts, examples, statistics, quotations, and personal observations that support your position. Take notes on the sources of your information, because you need to credit any ideas or words that are not your own.
- **Anticipate counterarguments.** Look ahead to identify readers' questions and points of view that might differ from your position. Plan to include facts that will successfully address counterarguments and questions.

Prewriting/Planning Strategies

1. Introduce the prewriting and planning strategies.
2. Have students apply the strategies to choose a topic and gather details.

Teaching the Strategies

1. Students should choose an issue that is open to debate. A scandal about neglected animals, for example, would not make a good topic. No one is in favor of neglecting animals. Animal testing, on the other hand, would make a good topic. People either strongly oppose or support it.
2. Remind students that it is usually wise to focus on a specific issue associated with a topic, rather than trying to cover too much.
3. Suggest that students list their arguments and facts and then list possible counterargument. Encourage students to try to come up with facts that can be used against each counterargument.

Think Aloud: Model Gathering Support

Say to students:

I want to write an essay arguing that students should be outside at lunchtime. I have to find evidence that will convince readers. I have read that being in the sun triggers some beneficial chemical reactions in our bodies. I think that will be a convincing idea. I start to think of other ideas that will persuade my readers. I am gathering evidence.

Six Traits Focus

✓	Ideas		Word Choice
✓	Organization		Sentence Fluency
	Voice		Conventions

✅ STRATEGIES **FOR CLARIFYING EXPECTED OUTCOMES**

Using Rubrics

- Before students begin work on this assignment, have them preview the Rubric for Self-Assessment (p. 383) to know what is expected. A copy of this rubric appears in the *Graphic Organizers* for this workshop.
- Review the criteria in the rubric with the class. Before students use the rubric to assess their own writing, work with them to rate the Student Model (p. 382) using the rubric.

- If you wish to assess students' argumentative essays with either a 4-point or a 6-point scoring rubric, see *Professional Development Guidebook*, pp. 230–231.

Drafting Strategies

1. Introduce the drafting strategies.
2. Have students apply the strategies as they draft.

Teaching the Strategies

1. Students should realize that a strong argumentative paper takes readers step by step through each idea and supports each idea with evidence.

2. Explain that words such as *all, best, every, never, none,* and *worst* signal a strong opinion that would be difficult to support: *That is the worst movie ever.* A good thesis statement is one that can be proved: *The movie was dull and copied other, better movies.*

3. Discuss the graphic organizer with students. Point out that the body of the composition develops the thesis statement.

4. Remind students to tailor their vocabulary and sentence structure, as well as their argument, to their audience. If targeting a younger audience, students should keep the vocabulary simple and the sentences short.

Think Aloud: Model Using Evidence

Say to students:

When I write an argumentative essay, I try not to rely only on my personal experience. Let's say I have written this statement: *I get nervous when I see drivers talking on their cell phones.* I look for a statistic, expert opinion, or quotation that gives more weight to my statement. For example, if I write: *The Highway Safety Board has recorded a significant increase in the number of traffic accidents in cases where the driver was using a cell phone,* I know my reader will pay attention to this fact supporting my position. As I write, I strive to include many forms of evidence.

Six Traits Focus

✓	Ideas	✓	Word Choice
✓	Organization		Sentence Fluency
	Voice		Conventions

Drafting Strategies

Write a thesis statement. The evidence you have gathered will help support your position. Prepare a thesis statement—one sentence that names your issue and expresses your position.

Sample Thesis Statements

1. Our school should have recycling bins.
2. Young people should exercise for twenty minutes every day.

Create a clear organization. Review the chart on the right to organize your thoughts. Include your thesis in your introduction. Support your thesis statement in the body of your essay. Organize supporting information into paragraphs. Conclude with a restatement of your thesis.

Support each point. As you develop your evidence, be sure to support it fully.

- Find and use examples.
  Main idea: Vegetables are healthy snacks.
  Supporting example: Carrots are a source of Vitamin A.
- Use facts or statistics.
  Main idea: Rock music is often loud, but it is still music.
  Supporting fact: Rock follows a rhythmic pattern.
- Include quotations and expert opinions.
  Main idea: Our nation depends on volunteers.
  Supporting quotation: "Ask not what your country can do for you; ask what you can do for your country."
  —President John F. Kennedy

Address counterarguments. An effective argumentative essay addresses the opposing point of view. Introduce one or two objections to your position. Use facts or other evidence to show why those objections are not strong enough to overcome your position.

Maintain a formal style. Do not weaken your argument by using slang or informal language. Instead, use a formal, authoritative tone. Maintain that tone by using sophisticated vocabulary and mixing in longer sentences with shorter ones.

Target your audience. As you write, keep in mind your readers' ages and their knowledge about your topic. Use language and details that are appropriate for your audience.

Common Core State Standards

Writing
1.a. Introduce claim(s) and organize the reasons and evidence clearly.
1.b. Support claim(s) with clear reasons and relevant evidence, using credible sources and demonstrating an understanding of the topic or text.
1.d. Establish and maintain a formal style.
Language
1.e. Recognize variations from standard English in their own and others' writing and speaking, and identify and use strategies to improve expression in conventional language.

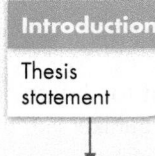

Introduction

Thesis statement

Body

Main point followed by facts, details, statistics, expert opinions. Explanations and evidence to address readers' concerns and counterarguments.

Conclusion

Summary of arguments. Strong restatement of position.

Word Choice

Word choice is the specific language a writer uses to create a strong impression. You can construct an effective argument by using precise language.

Choosing Accurate Words The success of your argument will depend on how credible, or believable, you are. Choose words carefully to make your statements accurate. Avoid using exaggerations. Vivid words create lively writing, but use them only if they are accurate.

Fixing Exaggerations
The number of families vacationing there has ~~skyrocketed~~ doubled in the last five years.

Another way to make your words accurate is to avoid absolute words. Words such as *all, always, never,* and *only* can lead to generalizations that are too broad. Replace them with words you can defend.

Revising Absolute Words
~~All the~~ Some people who object to reality shows have never even seen one.

Using Reasonable Words Strengthen your arguments by appealing to your readers' sense of reason. Highly-charged words can capture readers' interest, but be sure to back up your strongest arguments with words that can be supported by facts.

Appealing to Reason, Not Emotion
Recycling can save ~~the planet.~~ resources.

Another way to keep your argument based on reason is by staying away from name calling. Stick to arguments that are based on evidence.

Fixing Name-Calling
Riding a bicycle without wearing a helmet is ~~stupid.~~ risky.

Word Traps to Avoid

✓ Exaggerated words

✓ Absolute words

✓ Emotional words

✓ Name-calling

Checking Your Language Review your essay, focusing on your word choice. Revise words that fall into the word traps in the chart. Choose words that will support your argument and make it more credible.

Word Choice in Argumentative Essays

1. Direct students to read through their drafts and circle the words that create a strong impression or make a strong statement.

2. Tell students to make a list of these words in a two-column chart and then evaluate each of them. For each word, they may ask questions like *Is this word believable? Is it exaggerated? Does it appeal to reason rather than emotion?*

3. Students should then use this evaluative process to edit their words as necessary, writing the revised word in the second column of their chart.

⚙ DIFFERENTIATED INSTRUCTION

Strategy for Less Proficient Writers
If students have trouble gathering evidence, suggest that they choose a topic, such as recycling, for which ample factual evidence is available. Guide students to evaluate their sources and use only convincing and relevant evidence. Ask students if the evidence would convince *them.*

🔵 Strategy for English Learners
For students using the Internet to conduct their research, help them to narrow their searches by using the most effective keywords and phrases. Ensure that the librarian can assist students in areas such as reference materials if students conduct their research in the library.

Enrichment for Advanced Writers
Challenge students to gather a variety of evidence, such as an interview with a person who has first-hand knowledge or experience of the topic. Encourage students also to use strong sources when examining the counter-arguments for their topics.

Revising Strategies

1. Introduce the revising strategies, using the instruction on the student page.

2. Have students apply the strategies as they revise.

Teaching the Strategies

1. Write the following two sentences on the board to help students understand how using transitions can help show the relationships between ideas.

   People who don't recycle harm the environment.

   People who don't recycle harm the environment because they are contributing waste rather than reusing it.

   Work with students to see how the second sentence clarifies the relationship between the ideas.

2. Supply students with colored pencils, pens, or highlighters to use as they follow the revising instructions on the student page.

Think Aloud: Model Revising for Support

Model the strategy of revising to find adequate support for each argument, using the following think aloud. Say to students:

   I can go back over each idea that I have written and check to see that it is well-supported. Each idea should have at least two supporting points, and each point should be identified in terms of the type of evidence it represents. For instance, if I have written *The price of postage stamps is too high*, I go back and check to make sure that I have evidence, such as the number of increases in cost over the past 10 years (a fact), or the cost of stamps in other countries compared to our costs (a statistical comparison). If not, I can do more research to add this support.

Six Traits Focus

✓	Ideas	✓	Word Choice
✓	Organization		Sentence Fluency
	Voice		Conventions

Revising Strategies

Revise to improve support. Review your draft to find places where you can strengthen the arguments that support your thesis. Follow these steps:

1. Underline your thesis statement.

2. Put a star next to each supporting point. Add more support if you have only one star.

3. If you find a paragraph without support, review your prewriting notes and add evidence. If necessary, conduct additional research to find a fact, statistic, or quotation you can use.

4. Draw attention to a well-supported point by adding powerful language or a colorful comparison that helps readers connect one main point with another.

5. Pay careful attention to how you present counterarguments. Make sure that you fairly state the other point of view. Provide two or more pieces of evidence to explain why you reject that view.

6. Review your conclusion to be sure that it follows logically from the argument you presented in the body of your essay.

Revise sentences to show relationships. Revise your sentences to clarify the relationships between the claims you make and the evidence you provide. Use transition words like the ones on the chart to show the connections among ideas.

because	therefore	as a result
consequently	however	alternatively
on the other hand	in fact	for example

Peer Review

Ask a partner to read your draft and identify places where the support for your argument seems weak. Consider adding details to strengthen your claims. In addition, have your partner review your use of standard English, and suggest any necessary corrections.

Common Core State Standards

Writing

1.b. Support claim(s) with clear reasons and relevant evidence, using credible sources and demonstrating an understanding of the topic or text.

1.c. Use words, phrases, and clauses to clarify the relationships among claim(s) and reasons.

1.d. Establish and maintain a formal style.

1.e. Provide a concluding statement or section that follows from the argument presented.

5. With some guidance and support from peers and adults, develop and strengthen writing as needed by planning, editing, rewriting, or trying a new approach.

Language

1. Demonstrate command of the conventions of standard English grammar and usage when writing or speaking.

1.e. Recognize variations from standard English in their own and others' writing and speaking, and identify and use strategies to improve expression in conventional language.

3. Use knowledge of language and its conventions when writing, speaking, reading, or listening.

☑ STRATEGIES FOR PEER REVIEW

Tell students that it may be encouraging to hear peers say they like their work. However, students should challenge readers to give them specific feedback that will help them revise their writing. Avoid asking readers to answer questions that can be answered with a *yes* or *no* answer, such as, "Is my message clear?" Instead, students should ask their readers more focused questions, such as:

- How could I make my message more clear?
- How could I improve my argument?
- Can you think of other examples I might provide to support my position?
- What would you like to know more about?

Combining Sentences Using Coordinating Conjunctions

Coordinating conjunctions such as *and, but, or,* and *so* are used to connect words, groups of words, or sentences that are similar in form.

Identifying Which Coordinating Conjunction to Use Each coordinating conjunction has a specific purpose. To join a pair of related sentences, first determine the relationship between the ideas in each sentence. Then use the correct coordinating conjunction. Place a comma *after* the first sentence and *before* the coordinating conjunction.

Coordinating Conjunction	Purpose	Use
and	to join similar or related ideas	I live in an apartment, **and** it is on the fourth floor.
but	to highlight differences or contrast	I like soccer, **but** my brother does not.
or	to show choices	You can have your lunch now, **or** you can wait for Molly.
so	to show cause and effect	I enjoy adventure stories, **so** I loved *Treasure Island.*

Fixing Comma Splices You can also use coordinating conjunctions to fix a **comma splice**. In a comma splice, two sentences are incorrectly joined together by only a comma.

Incorrect: He saw the movie, he liked the movie.
Correct: He saw the movie, and he liked it.

Using Coordinating Conjunctions Follow these steps:

1. **Identify the relationship between the sentences you wish to combine.**
2. **Choose a coordinating conjunction based on your purpose.**
3. **Join the two sentences using a comma and the coordinating conjunction.**

Grammar in Your Writing

Reread your argumentative essay, looking for short sentences with related ideas. Use coordinating conjunctions to combine sentences.

Combining Sentences Using Coordinating Conjunctions

1. Introduce the grammar skill, using the instruction on the student page.
2. Discuss the rules and examples.
3. Have students follow the instruction under Grammar in Your Writing to correct repetitive sentence structure in their drafts.

Teaching the Grammar Skill

1. Students may need help using coordinating conjunctions to turn short, repetitive sentences into longer, more complex ones. Challenge students to revise the following paragraph using coordinating conjunctions.

   Sea lions have ear flaps. Furred seals just have ear holes. These two animals are similar. They are also different. The seals' fur is very valuable. The seals are hunted frequently.

   Possible response: Sea lions have ear flaps, but only furred seals just have ear holes. These two animals are similar, **but** they are also different. The seals' fur is very valuable, **so** they are hunted frequently.

2. Call on volunteers to come to the board and write sample sentences with different coordinating conjunctions. Have students circle the conjunctions in their sentences.

Student Model

Review the Student Model with the class, using the annotations to analyze the writer's use of the elements of a successful argumentative essay.

Teaching From the Student Model

1. Explain that the Student Model is a sample and that essays can be longer.

2. Have students identify the topic or issue and its counter argument. **Answer:** The topic is the musical merit of contemporary rock music. The counter argument is that some people who prefer the melodic sound of classical music think that rock music is not musical.

3. Talk with students about how Isaac supports his ideas with evidence. Students should notice that Isaac provides facts ("the lowest string of the guitar is an E") and personal observations ("Chopin is like elegant figure skating"). Challenge students to think of other forms of evidence, such as quotations or statistics, that would help the argument.

4. Have students identify the evidence that the writer gives that disproves the counter argument. **Answer:** The writer explains that rock musicians have developed techniques to help change the pitch and key of songs, so that songs no longer sound the same.

5. Point out how Isaac saves most of his evidence for the fourth paragraph, where he disproves his counter argument. By saving his strongest ideas for the end, Isaac makes a lasting impression.

6. Discuss how Isaac compares music to sports. Point out how these images make the reader see the difference between the two types of music.

Connecting to Real-Life Writing

Argumentative writing has many uses in the real world. Businesses use it in advertisements, hoping to convince people to buy or use their products or services. Politicians use arguments in campaigns to get people to vote for them. Editorial writers in newspapers and magazines use arguments to change people's minds.

STUDENT MODEL: **Isaac Tetenbaum, Reseda, CA**

Common Core State Standards

Language
2.b. Spell correctly.

Modern Rock Is Music, Too

Maybe you think Chopin is really cool—the blissful tones of the piano, played to serenade and mesmerize, the dazzling cadenzas and glistening high notes. For a change, though, why don't you pop in a modern rock CD? Contemporary music gets very little respect, yet most of the people who put it down haven't even listened to it. Modern rock deserves to be regarded and respected as music.

Music can be classified as any group of organized sounds. Yet while the roars of today's lead vocalists don't seem to make sense, even they are organized and related to the message of the song. Is it music? Yes. It follows a precise rhythmic pattern. It repeats. Just because howls from a modern vocalist don't follow any pitches doesn't mean they can't be classified as perfectly good music. You might not like the style, but you cannot deny it is music.

Once you've accepted rock as music, you might say all rock songs are in the same key—E. Just because the lowest string of the guitar is an E doesn't mean modern rock musicians continuously strum that string and open and end a tune with it. Nowadays, as new musicians experiment with different pitches, the common E of rock has almost disappeared.

In a technique called "dropping," guitarists and bassists of modern rock bands have been able to use lower pitches in their songs. In fact, a well-known modern guitarist has successfully created a seven-string guitar. Its seventh string has the default pitch of a B. Although you might have to listen a little harder to hear the evidence, the musicians of contemporary bands know their music. How else could they come up with "dropping" and the seven-string guitar?

I think anyone, even the most classical music lover, can appreciate today's sounds if given a chance. (Notice I didn't say love, just appreciate.) I listen to Chopin and modern rock. I respect both kinds of music because each one has its place. Chopin is like elegant figure skating—rock is like snowboarding. I feel free when I listen to my favorite rock group. Why don't you listen with me?

Isaac clearly establishes the two sides—those who like contemporary music and those who prefer classical. The last sentence in the introduction is the thesis.

Isaac provides evidence that contemporary artists would be considered musical even by classical definitions.

Here, Isaac admits that readers might think that all rock music is written in the same key—an argument he says is no longer true.

Isaac gives details supporting his statement that rock music is no longer written in the key of E. Notice that he has more than one piece of evidence.

A powerful image helps readers understand Isaac's argument.

Editing and Proofreading

Proofread to fix grammar, spelling, and punctuation errors.

Spelling Errors: Irregular Plurals Review these rules and examples, then double-check your work for spelling errors.

- Change the *f* to *v* and add *-es*: *elf, elves; wife, wives*
- Use the same spelling for words that have the same singular and plural forms: *one fish, two fish; one deer, two deer*
- Some words change vowel form to make them plural: *tooth, teeth; mouse, mice; goose, geese; foot, feet*

Publishing and Presenting

Consider one of the following ways to share your writing:

Deliver a speech. Use your argumentative essay as the basis for a speech that you present to your classmates.

Post your essay. Post your argumentative essay on a community bulletin board or online so that others can read it and discuss your position.

Reflecting on Your Writing

Writer's Journal Jot down your answer to this question:

How did your evidence change or deepen your view on the issue?

Rubric for Self-Assessment

Find evidence in your writing to address each category. Then, use the rating scale to grade your work.

Criteria	Rating Scale			
Purpose/Focus In a clear thesis statement, presents a position on an issue that has at least two sides	*not very* .... *very* 1	2	3	4
Organization Introduces the topic and makes a clear claim; organizes reasons and evidence clearly and logically; provides a concluding section that follows from the argument presented	1	2	3	4
Development of Ideas/Elaboration Supports the claim with clear reasons and relevant evidence, using credible sources; addresses counterarguments; establishes and maintains a formal style	1	2	3	4
Language Uses precise language to strengthen the argument; uses words, phrases, and clauses to clarify the relationships among claims and reasons	1	2	3	4
Conventions Uses proper grammar, including correct use of coordinating conjunctions	1	2	3	4

Spiral Review
Earlier in the unit, you learned about **adjectives and adverbs** (p. 332) and **making comparisons with adjectives** (p. 342). Review your essay to be sure that you have used these modifiers correctly.

PART 2 • Writing Process **383**

☑ STRATEGIES **FOR TEST TAKING**

Students should remember to be practical when arguing an issue on a test—even if they do not agree with it. Because students will not be able to do research during a test, their evidence will be limited to examples and personal observations. They should spend most of their limited time thinking about the evidence they already have to support their point. Tell students that outlining their ideas before they begin to write is always a good idea. Students should make sure that their strongest ideas appear at the end of their essay, just before the conclusion.

Editing and Proofreading

1. Introduce the editing and proofreading focus, using the instruction on the student page.
2. Have students edit and proofread their essays, correcting grammar, spelling, punctuation, and word choice. Make sure they look for errors of the type noted in the lesson focus and the Spiral Review.

Teaching the Editing Focus

Encourage students to memorize examples of each rule. Suggest that when unsure of how to form a plural, students should check a dictionary, where the spellings of irregular plurals are usually listed right after the pronunciation. If no plural form is given, students should assume it has a regular plural.

Six Traits Focus

Ideas	Word Choice
Organization	Sentence Fluency
Voice	✓ Conventions

☑ ASSESS

Publishing and Presenting

1. Have students consider how they might revise their essays to create an effective speech. Remind them that, after making a key point, they should repeat it in a single sentence.
2. Hold a response day on which students read and respond to each other's work.

Reflecting on Your Writing

Suggest that students compare their graphic organizers from the drafting stage to their final essays to identify any new insights they had during the writing process.

 Interactive Whiteboard Activities

Use this tool to project and edit student writing!

PART 2 • Writing Process **383**

Assessment: Skills

Assessment

In this assessment (pp. 384–389), students apply and reinforce their mastery of the Common Core Standards and the skills taught in Unit 3. The assessment is divided into four sections including a section of Constructed Response tasks addressing CCSS Reading standards.

1. Before assigning each section, review the relevant Common Core Standards and unit skills with students.

2. Set a time limit for the multiple choice items in each section, allowing a little over one minute per question. Allow twenty minutes for any Timed Writing questions.

3. Administer each of the first three sections of the assessment (pp. 384–387).

4. Use the Constructed Response tasks on pages 388–389 to assess the depth of students' mastery of standards taught in the unit. Follow the suggestions on teacher pages 388–389 for assigning tasks and for supporting and evaluating student performance.

Reteaching Plan

For each practice, use the Reteach chart on the same page as the answers to determine which skills require reteaching, given the items students answered incorrectly.

Question	Instructional Pages to Reteach
1	334
2	318
3	334
4	316
5	354
6	344
7	—
8	354

SELECTED RESPONSE

I. Reading Literature

Directions: *Read the poem "Wilbur Wright and Orville Wright" by Rosemary and Stephen Vincent Benét. Then, answer each question that follows.*

> Said Orville Wright to Wilbur Wright,
> "These birds are very <u>trying</u>.
> I'm sick of hearing them cheep-cheep
> About the fun of flying.
> 5 A bird has feathers, it is true.
> That much I freely grant.
> But must that stop us, W?"
> Said Wilbur Wright, "It shan't."
>
> And so they built a glider, first,
> 10 And then they built another.
> —There never were two brothers more
> Devoted to each other.
> They ran a dusty little shop
> For bicycle repairing.
> 15 And bought each other soda-pop
> And praised each other's daring.
>
> They glided here, they glided there,
> They sometimes skinned their noses.
> —For learning how to rule the air
> 20 Was not a bed of roses—
> But each would murmer, afterward,
> While patching up his bro,
> "Are we discouraged, W?"
> "Of course we are not, O!"
>
> 25 And finally at Kitty Hawk
> In Nineteen-Three (let's cheer it!)
> The first real airplane really flew
> With Orville there to steer it!
> —And kingdoms may forget their kings
> 30 And dogs forget their bites.
> But, not till Man forgets his wings,
> Will men forget the Wrights.

384 UNIT 3 • Do we need words to communicate well?

 **Common Core State Standards**

RL.6.1, RL.6.2, RL.6.3, RL.6.4; W.6.3, W.6.4
[For the full wording of the standards, see the standards chart in the front of your textbook.]

1. Part A What type of **figurative language** is used in the first stanza of the poem?

A. simile   **C.** personification

B. metaphor   **D.** rhyme

Part B Which lines from the first stanza of the poem give you an idea of the brothers' spirit?

A. "Said Orville Wright to Wilbur Wright, "These birds are very trying."

B. "I'm sick of hearing them cheep-cheep About the fun of flying."

C. "A bird has feathers, it is true. That much I freely grant."

D. "But must that stop us, W?" Said Wilbur Wright, "It shan't."

2. Which of the following lines could replace line 16 without interrupting the **rhyme scheme**?

A. And made sure the other came out on top

B. And showed each other caring

C. And made sure the other did not stop

D. And praised the other brother

3. Part A What type of **figurative language** is used in the third stanza of the poem?

A. simile   **C.** personification

B. metaphor   **D.** rhyme

Part B Which lines from the first stanza of the poem contain the **figurative language** you identified in Part A?

A. "They glided here, they glided there, They sometimes skinned their noses."

B. "—For learning how to rule the air Was not a bed of roses—"

C. "But each would murmur, afterward, While patching up his bro"

D. "Are we discouraged, W?" "Of course we are not, O!"

4. Which word best summarizes the tone of this poem?

A. confident   **C.** hysterical

B. defeated   **D.** hesitant

5. How do the authors use **repetition** to enhance the poem's mood and meaning?

A. They repeatedly mention inventions, such as bicycles, gliders, and airplanes.

B. They repeatedly mention failures, such as skinned noses and a dusty little shop.

C. They have Wilbur and Orville question each other several times and answer positively.

D. Over the course of the poem, they make fun of birds and dogs to prove the superiority of humans.

6. What **form of poetry** is used in "Wilbur and Orville Wright"?

A. haiku

B. concrete poem

C. limerick

D. narrative poem

7. Which word is closest in meaning to the underlined word *trying*?

A. attempting   **C.** achieving

B. bothersome   **D.** happening

⏱ Timed Writing

8. Write an essay or a poem about modern-day flight. Use sound devices such as **repetition**, **alliteration**, and **onomatopoeia** to add to your poem's or essay's mood and meaning.

GO ON ➡

☑ ASSESS

I. Reading Literature

1. Part A: C
Part B: B

2. B

3. Part A: B
Part B: B

4. A

5. C

6. D

7. B

⏱ Timed Writing

8. Student essays or poem should include sound devices to add to the mood and meaning.

 **ASSESS**

II. Reading Informational Text

1. B

2. Part A: B
   Part B: D

II. Reading Informational Text

Directions: *Read this application. Then, answer each question that follows.*

Common Core State Standards

RI.6.1; L.6.1, L.6.3
[For the full wording of the standards, see the standards chart in the front of your textbook.]

Application for Adventure Summer Camp

About our camp: Our summer program is for *students entering the 7th or 8th grades.* Applicants must be highly motivated and must see the value in helping others. An adventurous spirit is important because we will be hiking, kayaking, and camping. We will also spend time doing volunteer work in the community.

To apply for our camp: Answer the following questions. Type or print neatly. Provide one brief letter of reference from an adult who is not your parent. A second reference is optional.
No applications will be accepted after March 31.

(1) Name: _____ (2) Age: _____ (3) Entering grade: _____
(4) Address: _____
(5) Phone number: _____
(6) Hobbies: _____
(7) Why do you want to attend Adventure Camp? _____
(8) What skills make you a good candidate for Adventure Camp?
_____

(9) What type(s) of volunteer work would interest you most?
_____

---

1. Why does some information in the application appear in italics?

   A. to make the application easier to read
   B. to show that the information is important
   C. to make the application more interesting to look at
   D. to show that people do not have to read this information

2. Part A What is one thing students must do when applying to Adventure Summer Camp?

   A. do volunteer work
   B. provide a letter of reference
   C. see the value in helping others
   D. go hiking, kayaking and camping

Part B What detail from the application best supports the answer to Part A?

   A. "we will be hiking, kayaking, and camping"
   B. "Applicants must be highly motivated and must see the value in helping others"
   C. "We will also spend time doing volunteer work in the community"
   D. "Provide one brief letter of reference"

III. Writing and Language Conventions

Directions: *Read the passage. Then, answer each question that follows.*

> (1) Unfortunately, six band students recently quit the band because they could not afford to buy or rent needed instruments. (2) Our school band is in desperate need of new instruments. (3) If everyone contributed a mere $5, we could purchase those six instruments. (4) This might be the most important contribution students could make to our school. (5) Most of us spend $5 a week on snacks after school anyway. (6) We should stop buying snacks for just one week. (7) Music enriches the whole school, not just band students. (8) We must all work together to solve this problem.

1. What **adverb** modifies the verb *quit* in sentence 1?
- **A.** Unfortunately
- **B.** band
- **C.** students
- **D.** recently

2. Which sentence contains an example of a **comparative adjective**?
- **A.** sentence 2
- **B.** sentence 3
- **C.** sentence 4
- **D.** sentence 5

3. Which of the following **compound subjects** could best be substituted to clarify the subject in sentence 1?
- **A.** Four saxophone students
- **B.** Four saxophones and two oboes
- **C.** Three artists and three students
- **D.** Four saxophone students and two oboe students

4. How could the writer revise sentence 6 to make it an **imperative sentence?**
- **A.** Is it not possible to stop buying snacks for just one week?
- **B.** We will stop buying snacks for one week.
- **C.** We can stop buying snacks!
- **D.** Stop buying snacks for one week.

5. How could the writer revise sentence 8 to make it an **interrogative sentence?**
- **A.** We must work to solve this problem!
- **B.** Work together to solve this problem.
- **C.** Shouldn't we all work together to solve this problem?
- **D.** Working on this problem together will solve this problem.

6. What **conjunctions** are used in sentence 1?
- **A.** students, recently
- **B.** quit, band
- **C.** because, or
- **D.** buy, rent

✔ ASSESS

III. Writing and Language Conventions

1. D
2. C
3. D
4. D
5. C
6. C

Reteaching Plan

Question	Pages to Reteach
1	332
2	342
3	364
4	364
5	364
6	352

Constructed Response
Assigning Tasks/Reteaching Skills

Use the chart below to choose appropriate Constructed Response tasks by identifying which tasks assess lessons in the textbook that you have taught. Use the same lessons for reteaching when students' performance indicates a failure to fully master a standard. For additional instruction and practice, assign the *Common Core Companion* pages indicated for each task.

Task	Where Taught/ Pages to Reteach	Common Core Companion Pages
1	314–317, 334	41–53, 347–352
2	314–317, 344	54–60, 184–195, 267–274
3	314–317, 354	41–53, 335–338
4	314–317, 354	41–53, 311–312
5	314–317	68–74, 286–292, 304–310
6	314–317	41–53, 246–252, 253–266

Assessment Pacing

In assigning the Writing tasks on this student page, allow a class period for the completion of a task. As an alternative, assign tasks as homework. In assigning the Speaking and Listening and Research tasks on the facing page, consider having students do any required preparation as a homework assignment. Then, allow a class period for the presentations themselves.

Evaluating Constructed Response

Use the rubric at the bottom of this Teacher Edition page to evaluate students' mastery of the standards as demonstrated in their Constructed Responses. Review the rubric with students before they begin work so they know the criteria by which their work will be evaluated.

CONSTRUCTED RESPONSE

Directions: *Follow the instructions to complete the tasks below as required by your teacher.*

As you work on each task, incorporate both general academic vocabulary and literary terms you learned in Parts 1 and 2.

 **Common Core State Standards**

RL.6.4, RL.6.5, RL.6.7; W.6.2.e, W.6.7, W.6.8, W.6.9.a; SL.6.1, SL.6.4, SL.6.5; L.6.3.b, L.6.5.a

[For the full wording of the standards, see the standards chart in the front of your textbook.]

Writing

TASK 1 Literature [RL.6.4; L.6.5.a]
Analyze Figurative Language
Write an essay in which you analyze the figurative language used in two poems from Part 2.

- Choose two poems from Part 2 that include several examples of figurative language, such as simile, metaphor, or personification.
- Determine the meanings of the figurative phrases as they are used in the context of the poems. Analyze their impact on the poems' meaning and tone.
- If possible, use a word-processing program to type your essay and prepare it for publication.

TASK 2 Literature [RL.6.5; W.6.9.a; W.6.2.e]
Use Forms of Poetry
Write two poems using different forms of poetry.

- Determine a theme about which you would like to write two poems.
- Write a poem about that theme using one of the forms of poetry, such as narrative poetry, lyric poetry, concrete poetry, haiku, a limerick, or free verse.
- Write a second poem using the same theme but a different form of poetry.

- Finally, write a short response to this assignment in which you explain which form of poetry you felt was most effective in conveying your chosen theme.

TASK 3 Literature [RL.6.4; L.6.3.b]
Analyze Sound Devices and Tone
Write an essay in which you analyze the effects of sound devices upon tone in poetry from Part 2.

Part 1
- Review the poetry you studied in Part 2. Find examples of sound devices, such as rhythm, rhyme, repetition, alliteration, and onomatopoeia.
- Take notes about how these devices contribute to tone in the poems.

Part 2
- Write an essay in which you analyze the sound devices used in one or more poems from this unit. Describe the effect of the sound devices on the tone of the poem or poems you choose.
- Revise your work to vary sentences and maintain consistency in style and tone.
- Publish your finished essay in the classroom library. Include a copy of the original text of the poem or poems about which you wrote.

388 UNIT 3 • Do we need words to communicate well?

CONSTRUCTED RESPONSE RUBRIC: **STANDARDS MASTERY**

	Rating Scale
Critical Thinking: How clearly and consistently does the student pursue the specific mode of reasoning or discourse required by the standard?	*not very* *very* 1 2 3 4 5
Focus: How well does the student understand and apply the focus concepts of the standard?	*not very* *very* 1 2 3 4 5
Support/Elaboration: How well does the student support points with textual or other evidence? How relevant, sufficient, and varied is the evidence provided?	*not very* *very* 1 2 3 4 5
Insight: How original, sophisticated, or compelling are the insights the student achieves by applying the standard to the text(s)?	*not very* *very* 1 2 3 4 5
Expression of Ideas: How well does the student organize and support ideas? How well does the student use language in the expression of ideas?	*not very* *very* 1 2 3 4 5

Speaking and Listening

TASK 4 ▶ Literature [RL.6.4; SL.6.5]
Analyze Sound Devices

Create a multimedia presentation in which you use visuals and audio to enhance the sound devices used in a poem from Part 2.

- Determine the purpose of the sound devices in your chosen poem, using evidence from the text to support your analysis.
- Prepare a multimedia presentation of the poem. Choose visuals, music, sound effects, or video that supports the author's use of sound devices in the poem and enhance your oral reading of it.
- Follow your oral reading with an explanation of your multimedia choices. Accurately use academic vocabulary in your explanation.

TASK 5 ▶ Literature [RL.6.7; SL.6.1, SL.6.4]
Compare Reading to Listening

Deliver an oral presentation in which you compare the experience of reading a poem from Part 2 with the experience of hearing the poem read aloud.

- With a partner, identify a poem you will discuss.
- Read the poem, and then listen to a recording of it. If no recording of the poem exists, read the poem aloud to each other.
- Take notes about your experiences, contrasting what you imagine and feel when reading with what you imagine and feel when listening.
- Organize and present your observations, sequencing them logically. Pronounce words clearly, both when speaking your own words and when reading the poem.

Research

TASK 6 ▶ Literature [RL.6.4; W.6.7, W.6.8]

Do we need words to communicate well?

In Part 2, you have read poetry in which many speakers use words to communicate. Now you will conduct a short research project on one type of communication that does not use words. Review the following guidelines before you begin your research:

- Focus your research on one type of communication that does not use words.
- Gather relevant information from at least two reliable sources. Your sources may be print or digital.

- Take notes as you research the type of communication.
- Cite your sources.

When you have completed your research, write a response to the Big Question. Use both the literature you have read and your research to reflect on this unit's Big Question. Discuss how your initial ideas have been either changed or reinforced. Support your response with an example from literature and an example from your research.

✦ DIFFERENTIATED INSTRUCTION

Strategy for Less Proficient Readers
Assign a Constructed Response task, and then have students meet in groups to review the standard assessed in that task. Remind students of the selections or independent readings to which they have previously applied the standard. Have groups summarize what they learned in applying the standard and then present their summaries. Discuss, clarifying any points of confusion. After students have completed their tasks, have groups meet again to evaluate members' work. Encourage members to revise their work based on the feedback they receive.

⏃ Strategy for English Learners
For each assigned Constructed Response task, review the instructions with students. Clarify the meaning of any unfamiliar vocabulary, emphasizing routine classroom words, such as *context, impact,* and *stanza,* and academic vocabulary, such as *support.*

Next, have students note ideas for their responses. Pair students, and have them review each other's notes, asking questions to clarify meaning and suggesting improvements. Encourage students to ask for your assistance in supplying English words or expressions they may require.

Supporting Speaking and Listening

1. Consider having students work with partners or in groups to complete Constructed Response tasks involving listening and speaking. For tasks that you assign for individual work, you may still wish to have students rehearse with partners, who can provide constructive feedback.

2. As students rehearse, have them keep in mind these tips:
   - Present findings and evidence clearly and concisely.
   - Observe conventions of standard English grammar and usage.
   - Be relaxed and friendly but maintain a formal tone.
   - Make eye contact with the audience, pronounce words clearly, and vary your pace.
   - When working with a group, respond thoughtfully to others' positions, modifying your own in response to new evidence.

Linking Constructed Response to Independent Reading

If you wish to cover the standards with students' independent reading, adapt Constructed Response tasks of your choice to the works they have selected. (Independent reading suggestions appear on the next page.)

Do we need words to communicate well?

1. Remind students that the unit Big Question is "Do we need words to communicate well?"

2. Have students complete their responses to the prompt on the student page. Point out that they have read selections in this unit about different approaches to or views of communication and that they should draw on these selections in their responses. Remind them that they can also draw on their own experiences and what they have learned in other subject areas in formulating their answers.

❶ About the Quotation

Maya Angelou (b. 1928) is an American author and poet.

Discussion Ask students to discuss the meaning of Angelou's quotation about determination, and then rewrite the quotation using their own words. Then, ask them how this quotation might affect them in their daily lives. Have students explain how they can deal with difficult circumstances without feeling overwhelmed.

❷ Critical Viewing

Pose the critical viewing question to the class. Then, guide the class in a discussion about the question. Encourage students to build upon each other's ideas as they share their responses. Remind students to support their responses with reasons and evidence.

1 "You may not **control** all the events that happen to you, but you can **decide** not to be reduced by them."

—**Maya Angelou**

❓ DEVELOPING ESSENTIAL UNDERSTANDING

Determination

A combination of determination and self-discipline can enable students to reach a goal despite the obstacles they may need to overcome. Many people refuse to let anything or anyone prevent them from doing what they have made up their minds to do; they persevere, inspiring others with their determination. The selections in this multi-genre text set will help students develop essential understanding about the power of determination by raising questions, such as

- How can determination help someone overcome difficulties?
- What other qualities might help a determined person succeed?
- Is determination inborn or can you develop it?
- How can we express our determination through words and nonverbal communication?

PART 3
TEXT SETS DEVELOPING INSIGHT

DETERMINATION

The selections in this unit all deal with the Big Question: **Do we need words to communicate well?** In the texts that follow, you will explore the many ways—both verbal and nonverbal—that people communicate their efforts to achieve their goals. As you read, consider how individuals use determination as they strive for success.

② ◄ CRITICAL VIEWING Does this photograph effectively convey the idea of determination? Why or why not?

CLOSE READING TOOL

Use the Close Reading Tool to practice the strategies you learned in this unit.

③ READINGS IN PART 3

ANCHOR TEXT **POEM**
Simile: Willow and Gingko
Eve Merriam (p. 392)

WEB ARTICLE
Angela Duckworth and the Research on "Grit"
Emily Hanford (p. 398)

EXPOSITORY ESSAY
Race to the End of the Earth
William G. Scheller (p. 404)

SHORT STORY
The Sound of Summer Running
Ray Bradbury (p. 410)

LETTER
from **Letter on Thomas Jefferson**
John Adams (p. 420)

AUTOBIOGRAPHY
Water
Helen Keller (p. 424)

POSTER
Determination (p. 430)

PART 3 • Determination **391**

CUSTOMIZING THE TEXT SET

Close Reading Tool
Use the Close Reading Tool to project the anchor text on a whiteboard and work through it as a whole-class activity. Students also have the opportunity to read this selection independently, with scaffolds available as needed.

Curriculum Builder
Customize this program by rearranging existing selections, adding selection titles of your choosing, and uploading your own resources—all online!

③ Readings in Part 3
About the Texts
(For quantitative and qualitative measures of text complexity, see the rubrics on the opening pages of each selection.)

POEM: Simile: Willow and Gingko
Summary The poet compares the delicate beauty of the willow tree and the sturdy toughness of the ginkgo.

WEB ARTICLE: Angela Duckworth and the Research on "Grit"
Summary Grit is a trait that a psychology professor researches.

EXPOSITORY ESSAY: Race to the End of the Earth
Summary Two teams compete to be the first to reach the South Pole.

SHORT STORY: The Sound of Summer Running
Summary A boy's desire for new sneakers inspires a shoe salesman.

LETTER: *from* Letter on Thomas Jefferson
Summary John Adams wrote a letter about how Thomas Jefferson was chosen to draft the Declaration of Independence.

AUTOBIOGRAPHY: Water
Summary Helen Keller tells how she began to understand words.

POSTER: Determination
Summary Winston Churchill's resolve is explored in a poster.

Extended Reading Opportunity
LITERATURE: Code Talker
You may want to assign this extended reading to accompany the readings in Part 3. Further details about this text and other extended readings appear on the Independent Reading pages at the end of this unit.

 **Audio**

Summary Audio is available in the *Student eText* and on the *Hear It!* CD-ROM.

LESSON PACING GUIDE

ANCHOR TEXT (5 DAYS)

Simile: Willow and Ginkgo

DAY 1 Preteach/Teach

- Introduce the topic of the text set and its relationship to the Big Question.
- To motivate and engage students, discuss the quotation and the Critical Viewing question.
- Direct students to read the selection independently.

DAYS 2–4 Teach/Extend

- Use the Comprehension questions to confirm student understanding of the text.
- Develop vocabulary by assigning and monitoring the Language Study activities.
- Develop analytic ability by reviewing the Literary Analysis questions and instruction.
- Assign the Group Discussion and monitor responses to discussion questions.
- Assign the Writing to Sources activity, distributing copies of the Take Notes worksheet to help students organize their thoughts and information.

DAY 5 Extend/Assess

- Preview the Research activity, distributing copies of the Take Notes worksheet to help students plan their note-taking strategy. Assign the activity as homework.
- Administer the Selection Test or the Open-Book Test to monitor student progress.

 **Common Core State Standards**

Reading Literature 1, 2, 3, 4, 5, 6

Reading Informational Text 1, 2, 3, 4, 5, 6, 7

Writing 1, 2, 3, 4, 5, 7, 8, 9, 9b, 10

Speaking and Listening 1, 4, 6

Language 1, 3, 4, 5

RELATED TEXTS (2 DAYS EACH)

Angela Duckworth and the Research on "Grit" • Race to the End of the Earth • The Sound of Summer Running • *from* **Letter on Thomas Jefferson • Water • Determination**

DAY 1 Preteach/Teach

- Review with students the topic of the text set and what they have learned from the previous readings.
- Build knowledge of the topic by directing students to read the text independently.
- Develop vocabulary by reviewing the Language Study activities.
- Build students' ability to think critically using the Literary Analysis questions.

DAY 2 Extend/Assess

- Extend exploration of the text through the Discuss, Research, and Write activities.
- Administer the Selection Test or the Open-Book Test to monitor student progress.

ASSESSMENT: SYNTHESIS (1–2 DAYS)

DAYS 1–2 Assess

- Review with the class the Criteria for Success for the Speaking and Listening activity. Assign the activity, and monitor student progress.
- Review with students the Criteria for Success for the Writing assignment, and assign the activity.
- Review with students the Self-Evaluation Rubric for the Writing to Sources activity. Direct students to complete the assignment.

Daily Block Scheduling

Each day in this Lesson Pacing Guide represents a 40–50 minute period. Teachers using block scheduling may combine days to revise pacing. In addition, teachers may differentiate and support core instruction by integrating components for extended and intensive support as students require. See the Guide to Resources (facing page).

GUIDE TO RESOURCES

RESOURCES	PRINT	CD	ONLINE	ANCHOR TEXT Simile: Willow and Ginkgo	Angela Duckworth and the Research on "Grit"	Race to the End of the Earth	The Sound of Summer Running	from Letter on Thomas Jefferson	Water	Determination
SELECTION SUPPORT 👤 👥 👨‍🏫										
Close Reading Practice	CRN		✔	✔						
Academic Vocabulary	SCW		✔	✔	✔	✔	✔	✔	✔	✔
Discussion: Take Notes worksheet	SCW		✔	✔	✔	✔	✔	✔	✔	
Writing to Sources	SCW		✔	✔	✔	✔	✔	✔	✔	✔
Research: Take Notes worksheet	SCW		✔	✔	✔	✔	✔	✔	✔	
STANDARDS SUPPORT 👨‍🏫										
Standards Instruction and Practice	CCC		✔	✔	✔	✔	✔	✔	✔	✔
MONITOR PROGRESS A										
Selection Test		EV	✔	✔	✔	✔	✔	✔	✔	
Open-Book Test		EV	✔	✔	✔	✔	✔	✔	✔	
ASSESSMENT: SYNTHESIS GRAPHIC ORGANIZERS AND RUBRICS 👤										
Speaking and Listening: Graphic Organizer			✔	✔						
Writing: Graphic Organizer			✔	✔						
Writing to Sources: Graphic Organizer			✔	✔						
Self-Evaluation Rubric			✔	✔						
DIGITAL RESOURCES 🖥️										
Close Reading Tool			✔	✔						
Online Writer's Notebook			✔	✔	✔	✔	✔	✔	✔	✔

CRN Close Reading Notebook   **SCW** Student Companion All-in-One Workbook   **EV** ExamView   **CCC** Common Core Companion

👥 Group work   👨‍🏫 Whole class instruction   👤 Independent work   A Assessment   🖥️ Digital Resource

MULTIDRAFT READING

Essential Understanding

First, students should read the entire selection on their own. Then, to assist struggling readers and to deepen comprehension for all, you may wish to guide them through the selection by asking them the close reading questions provided in the margins. Have students apply the multidraft reading protocols as they examine specific "chunks" of text related to these questions. For each read-ing, have students set the purpose indicated:

- **First reading:** Students should read the selection independently and think about its basic meaning.
- **Second reading:** Students should analyze the text's key ideas and details and its craft and structure.
- **Third reading:** Students should integrate knowledge and ideas; connect to the Big Question, other texts, and the world; and use teacher-led Close Reading discus-sion questions to examine particu-larly rich and significant passages.

For more guidance, refer to the *Classroom Strategies and Teaching Routines* card on multidraft reading.

Daily Bellringer

For each class during which you teach this selection, have students complete one of the five Quick Write activities for Week 19 in *Daily Bellringer Activities*. You may wish to use additional activities that are applicable to this selection.

Background

If you wish, explain that the willow tree has long flexible branches, narrow leaves, and catkins (flower clusters). The tall ginkgo has fan shaped leaves and edible seeds.

Vocabulary

1. Write the following words and definitions on the board:

   crude *adj.* lacking polish; not carefully made

   stubby *adj.* short and thick; bristly

   thrives *v.* grows well

2. Have students say each word aloud.

SIMILE: WILLOW AND GINKGO

EVE MERRIAM

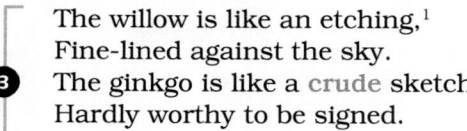
crude ▶
(krood) *adj.*
lacking
polish;
not carefully
made

The willow is like an etching,[1]
Fine-lined against the sky.
The ginkgo is like a crude sketch,
Hardly worthy to be signed.

5 The willow's music is like a soprano,
Delicate and thin.
The ginkgo's tune is like a chorus
With everyone joining in.

---

1. **etching** (ech´ in) *n.* print of a drawing made on metal, glass, or wood.

392 UNIT 3 • Do we need words to communicate well?

© TEXT COMPLEXITY **RUBRIC**

Simile: Willow and Ginkgo		
Qualitative Measures	Context/Knowledge Demands	Reflections on nature 1 ② 3 4 5
	Structure/Language Conventionality and Clarity	Short poems and stanzas; similes; simple sentences and on-level vocabulary 1 2 ③ 4 5
	Levels of Meaning/ Purpose/Concept Level	Accessible concepts (nature) 1 2 ③ 4 5
Quantitative Measures	Text Length	Word Count: 171
	Lexile	NP

The willow is sleek as a velvet-nosed calf;
10 The ginkgo is leathery as an old bull.
The willow's branches are like silken thread;
The ginkgo's like stubby rough wool.

The willow is like a nymph² with streaming hair;
Wherever it grows, there is green and gold and fair.
15 The willow dips to the water,
Protected and precious, like the king's favorite
daughter.

The ginkgo forces its way through gray concrete;
Like a city child, it grows up in the street.
Thrust against the metal sky,
20 Somehow it survives and even thrives.

My eyes feast upon the willow,
But my heart goes to the ginkgo.

◀ **stubby**
(stub´ ē) *adj.*
short and
thick; bristly

◀ **thrives**
(thrīvz) *v.*
grows well

---

2. **nymph** (nimf) *n.* goddess of nature, thought of as a beautiful maiden.

ABOUT THE AUTHOR

Eve Merriam (1916–1992)

As a young child, Eve Merriam fell in love with the music of language. She was also influenced by musical plays that she saw during her childhood. After writing her first poem at age eight, Merriam went on to write award-winning poetry for adults and children. She also wrote and directed theater productions, some of them musicals. Her many books for young readers include *There is No Rhyme for Silver, Out Loud,* and *Rainbow Writing.* "Simile: Willow and Ginkgo" comes from her second collection of poetry, *It Doesn't Always Have to Rhyme.*

 Big Question: Toward Essential Understanding

1. Read aloud the passage. **Ask:** What literary devices does the poet use in this poem? To what does the poet compare the willow and ginkgo?

Possible answer: The poet uses simile and personification to contrast the willow tree and the ginkgo. The poet compares the trees to drawings, singers, animals, fabrics, and humans.

2. Ask: How do the words in this poem paint vivid and contrasting pictures?

Possible answer: The poet uses vivid adjectives and similes to create vibrant images of both trees for the reader to imagine. The willow seems elegant, delicate, and gorgeous; the ginkgo seems rough, sturdy, and brave.

3. Ask: How does this poem demonstrate that words help us to communicate ideas and feelings, as well as images?

Possible answer: The poet uses language to describe common things in uncommon ways. By contrasting the two trees through similes, the poet vividly conveys not only visual details, but also her feelings about each tree.

❸ ❹ Focus Passage

Two Focus Passages are identified with brackets in the Student Edition of the previous page and this page for students' independent close reading and analysis. A question bank for each passage and possible responses appear at the end of the selection.

 Video

Watch the Background Video online!

 Audio

Selection Audio is available in the *Student eText* and on the *Hear It!* CD-ROM.

ⓒ TEXT COMPLEXITY **READER AND TASK SUGGESTIONS**

Simile: Willow and Ginkgo

Preparing to Read the Text
- Using the Background information on the previous page, discuss the differences between these two types of trees.
- Have students use similes to compare nature with a different object using *like* or *as.*
- Guide students to use Multidraft Reading strategies on the previous page.

Leveled Tasks
Structure/Language If students will have difficulty with the stanza structure, have them review the number of lines in each stanza and the number of stanzas in the poem. Then, have them read carefully and note how the number of lines devoted to each tree in each stanza changes in the fourth and fifth stanzas. Then, discuss the purpose of the final short stanza.

Synthesizing If students will not have difficulty with the structure of the selection, have them review the similes the poet has used in each stanza. Then, have them write a stanza using similes to compare two different types of trees, animals, or other living things. Have volunteers read aloud their stanzas and discuss the similes students have used.

Close Reading Activities

READ

Comprehension

1. The speaker of the poem contrasts willow and ginkgo trees.
2. Responses should mention an etching, a soprano, a calf, a thread, a nymph, or the king's favorite daughter.
3. Responses should mention a sketch, a chorus, a bull, wool, or a city child.
4. The speaker thinks the willow is beautiful but prefers the ginkgo.

Research: Clarify Details

Students should use their research to explain the significance of a particular detail in the poem.

Summarize

Summaries should briefly describe ways in which the speaker compares and contrasts the two trees and how the speaker feels about them.

Language Study

Selection Vocabulary

Possible responses:

- *crude*: synonym: *rough*; antonym: *refined*; I drew a *crude* map of the area.
- *stubby*: synonym: *short*; antonym: *long*; My fingers are so *stubby* that I can wear my little brother's gloves.
- *thrives*: synonym: *flourishes*; antonym: *fails*; Mia *thrives* in her new arts-focused school.

Diction and Style

1. **(a)** Here, *feast* means to find great pleasure in, enjoy, or devour. **(b)** *Feast* may also mean to eat a large, fancy dinner, overindulge, or celebrate.

2. **(a)** She means that she gives her love, sympathy, and admiration to the ginkgo. **(b)** Because of its double meaning, *heart* refers to positive emotions and gives the sense that part of the author herself is drawn to the tree.

READ

Comprehension

Reread all or part of the text to help you answer the following questions.

1. What two objects does the speaker in the poem contrast?
2. Name one thing to which the speaker compares the willow.
3. Name one thing to which the speaker compares the ginkgo.
4. What idea does the speaker express at the end of the poem?

Language Study

Selection Vocabulary Identify at least one synonym and one antonym for each boldfaced word from the poem. Then, use each word in a sentence of your own.

- The ginkgo is like a **crude** sketch,
- The gingko's like **stubby** rough wool.
- Somehow it survives and even **thrives**.

Diction and Style Study the following lines from the poem. Then, answer the questions.

> My eyes feast upon the willow,
> But my heart goes to the ginkgo.

1. **(a)** What does the word *feast* mean in these lines? **(b)** What other meanings does *feast* have?
2. **(a)** What does the speaker mean when she says, *"My heart goes to the ginkgo"*? **(b)** Why do you think the poet uses the word *heart* instead of a synonym?

Research: Clarify Details This poem may include references that are unfamiliar to you. Choose an unfamiliar detail and briefly research it. Then, explain how your research helps you understand the poem.

Summarize Write an objective summary of the poem. An objective summary does not include opinions or evaluations.

Conventions Identify the adjectives in this stanza. Then, explain how the poet uses the adjectives to contrast the trees.

> The willow is sleek as a velvet-nosed calf;
> The ginkgo is leathery as an old bull.
> The willow's branches are like silken thread;
> The ginkgo's like stubby rough wool.

Academic Vocabulary

The following words appear in blue in the instructions and questions on the facing page.

reveal   communicate   establish

Categorize the words by deciding whether you know each one well, know it a little bit, or do not know it at all. Then, use a print or online dictionary to look up the definitions of the words you do not know well or do not know at all.

Conventions

Students should identify and label the following adjectives: *sleek, velvet-nosed, leathery, old, silken, stubby,* and *rough*. Students should explain that Merriam's use of adjectives clarifies the sensory, tactile differences between the trees.

Academic Vocabulary

If students struggle with categorizing and defining the academic vocabulary words, use this routine:

Write the words and definitions on the board.

reveal: show, uncover

communicate: share thoughts and feelings, usually in words

establish: bring into existence

Have students say each word aloud and then use the word in a sentence. Sample sentences should demonstrate that the words can be used across disciplines.

Literary Analysis

Reread the identified passages. Then, respond to the questions that follow:

Focus Passage 1 *(p. 392–393)*
The willow is like an etching ... like stubby rough wool.

Focus Passage 2 *(p. 392)*
The willow is like a nymph ... *But my heart goes to the ginkgo.*

Key Ideas and Details

1. Name the categories in which the speaker compares the trees.
2. **Analyze:** What do the comparisons **reveal** about each tree?

Craft and Structure

3. **(a) Summarize:** What sensory information does each stanza **communicate**? **(b) Compare and Contrast:** How are the trees different in terms of strength?
4. **(a) Analyze:** Describe the pattern of rhyming words in these stanzas. **(b)** What is the effect of this rhyme scheme?

Integration of Knowledge and Ideas

5. **(a) Synthesize:** In these stanzas, is the speaker more positive toward the willow or the ginkgo? **(b) Compare:** How does this tone compare with commonly-held ideas about beauty?

Simile

In a **simile**, the writer uses *like* or *as* to make a comparison. Reread the poem, taking notes on the poet's use of similes.

1. **(a)** How do the similes in the poem contrast the trees? **(b)** What do comparisons to "silken thread" and "stubby rough wool" show?

Key Ideas and Details

1. **Analyze:** What gives the willow "streaming hair"?
2. **(a) Analyze:** What does "metal sky" mean? **(b) Interpret:** What does this description say about the ginkgo's environment?

Craft and Structure

3. **(a)** What colors and materials do the fourth and fifth stanzas name? **(b) Analyze:** What do these words suggest about the trees' environments?
4. **(a)** List the verbs in the fourth and fifth stanzas. **(b) Interpret:** What contrasting moods do these verbs **establish**?

Integration of Knowledge and Ideas

5. **(a)** In the last two stanzas, how does the speaker's attitude change? **(b) Analyze:** What does this change suggest about the poem's message?

2. **Determination** Explain how the simile that compares the ginkgo to a "city child" relates to the idea of determination.

 **Common Core State Standards**

RL.6.1, RL.6.2, RL.6.4, RL.6.5, RL.6.6; L.6.3, L.6.4, L.6.5
[For full standards wording, see the chart in the front of this book.]

PART 3 • Close Reading Activities **395**

Focus Passage 2

1. Its branches hang down like hair.
2. **(a)** The phrase may refer to skyscrapers or to a cloudy sky. **(b)** The ginkgo's environment is urban, possibly harsh, and man-made.
3. **(a)** *Green, gold, water; gray, concrete, metal.* **(b)** The willow is growing in a natural, nurturing environment, while the ginkgo is growing in a harsher man-made environment.
4. **(a)** Verbs: *grows, is,* and *dips; forces, grows up, survives,* and *thrives.* **(b)** The fourth stanza has a calm, nurturing mood while the fifth stanza has an aggressive, tough mood.
5. **(a)** The speaker describes the ginkgo in a heroic way. **(b)** This description suggests the speaker admires overcoming difficulties.

Simile

1. **(a)** The willow seems to be made up of fine lines, while the ginkgo is more squat and clumpy-looking. **(b)** The willow's branches are slender and fragile and sway in the wind, while the ginkgo's branches look short and sturdy.
2. The tough gingko has to work harder in its urban environment to "survive and thrive."

Literary Analysis

Possible responses appear below. Check to be sure students support their responses with evidence from the text.

Focus Passage 1

1. The speaker compares the trees to different kinds of artwork, music, cattle, and fibers.
2. The willow is refined, delicate, and beautiful. The ginkgo is unrefined, hardy, rough, and tough.
3. **(a)** The first stanza communicates visual information; the second, sound; the third, texture.

(b) The willow is more delicate (*fine lined, delicate, thin, sleek, silken*), and the ginkgo is tougher (*leathery, stubby, rough*).
4. **(a)** The second and fourth lines have end rhymes (*sky, signed; thin, in; bull, wool*). **(b)** The rhymes emphasize the contrast between the two trees.
5. **(a)** The speaker's tone seems more positive toward the willow. **(b)** The tone seems to agree with the popular idea of favoring the young and beautiful (the willow) over the old and weathered (the ginkgo).

 Online Writer's Notebook

Students can use the Online Writer's Notebook to record all responses.

DISCUSS

From Text to Topic: Group Discussion

Possible responses:

1. The gingko's leaves are larger and would appear more like a group than the willow's leaves, which are more singular and delicate.

2. The ginkgo's tune sounds more positive, because it comes from "everyone," while the willow's music is described as being "thin."

WRITE

Writing to Sources: Informative Text

Introduce the assignment using the instruction on the student page.

Prewriting and Planning

1. To guide students' rereading and note taking remind them that a poet sometimes uses subtle language to express ideas and make connections. The reader must "read between the lines" to discover these ideas.

2. Suggest that students use sticky notes to mark lines of the poem that help them understand how the environment can influence determination.

Drafting

1. Review the organizational pattern with students.

2. Remind students that the introduction should present the thesis of their essay.

3. The body of their essay should offer explanations that support their claim. It should include specific details from both the poem and their own experiences about how conditions in nature may create a need for determination.

4. The conclusion should summarize the main points made in the body of the essay and restate the thesis that the points support.

Revising

1. Encourage students to review their drafts to ensure they have clearly differentiated between

DISCUSS

From Text to Topic **Group Discussion**

Discuss the following stanza with classmates. Take notes during the discussion. Contribute your own ideas, and support them with examples from the text.

> The willow's music is like a soprano, ... everyone joining in. (p. 392)

WRITE

Writing to Sources **Informative Text**

> **Assignment**
> Write an **expository essay** in which you discuss the relationship between environment and determination. Cite evidence from both the poem and your own experience to support your ideas.

Prewriting and Planning Reread the poem to find details that describe how an environment can create the need for determination. The connection might not be stated directly. Instead, it may be implied through the language of the poem. Record your notes.

Drafting Select an organizational structure. Most expository writing includes an introduction, a body, and a conclusion.

- **Introduction** Begin by introducing the poem and stating your thesis.
- **Body** Explain the qualities of a particular environment, and explain how it creates a need for determination.
- **Conclusion** End by drawing a conclusion about the relationship between environment and determination.

Revising Reread your essay. If you have included examples of personal experiences as evidence, make sure it is clear when you are talking about the poem and when you are talking about yourself. Use present-tense verbs to discuss the poem. Use past-tense verbs to discuss your past experiences and present-tense verbs to discuss something that is happening now.

Editing and Proofreading Make sure you have used the correct verb tense in each section. If you are not sure of how to form a tense, look it up in a grammar handbook. Correct any errors you find.

QUESTIONS FOR DISCUSSION

1. Why does the speaker describe the ginkgo's music as a "chorus"?

2. Which is more positive, the description of the willow's music or of the ginkgo's tune? Why?

CONVENTIONS

When you shift from the present to the past, you must use the correct verb tense. Use present-tense verbs (*go, sing, eat*) to discuss the present, and past-tense verbs (*went, sang, ate*) to discuss the past.

references to the poem and to personal experiences.

2. Remind students to reread and make certain that they have used the correct verb tenses to ensure clarity.

Editing and Proofreading

1. Encourage students to double check all verb tenses by identifying the tenses of the verbs they used.

2. Have students check that each sentence in their essays does not continuously change verb tenses.

RESEARCH

Research **Investigate the Topic**

Survival Skills In this poem, the speaker compares the ginkgo to a "city child" who, through determination, "survives and even thrives." Social scientists have identified certain factors that help children develop the determination they need to succeed. For example, strong family support helps children develop self-esteem and seek positive paths in life.

> **Assignment**
>
> Conduct research to find out what social scientists have learned about factors that help children use determination to make positive choices and thrive in their environments. Consult credible sources, such as scientific journals. Take clear notes and carefully identify your sources so that you can easily access the information later. Share your findings in a brief **research report**.

Gather Sources Locate authoritative print and electronic sources. Scientific journals provide the latest social science research. These types of sources are peer-reviewed and usually credible. You may also want to use online sources. Look for sources that feature expert authors and up-to-date information.

Take Notes Take notes on each source, either electronically or on note cards. Use an organized note-taking strategy.

- Use a separate electronic file, sheet of paper, or note card for each source.
- Put quotation marks around each direct quotation from a source. This way, you will not accidentally plagiarize material.
- Record source information for use in your bibliography.

Synthesize Multiple Sources Gather data from your sources and use it to construct an outline. Use your outline to draft a cohesive research report on the factors that help children develop the determination they need to succeed. Create a Works Cited list as described in the Research Workshop in the Introductory Unit of your textbook.

Organize and Present Ideas Review your report and double-check that you have accurately quoted or paraphrased your sources.

PREPARATION FOR ESSAY

You may use the knowledge you gain during this research assignment to support your claims in an essay at the end of this section.

 **Common Core State Standards**

W.6.2, W.6.4, W.6.7, W.6.8, W.6.9, W.6.9.b, W.6.10; SL.6.1, SL.6.4
[For full standards wording, see the chart in the front of this book.]

RESEARCH

Research: Investigate the Topic

Introduce the assignment, using the instruction on the student page.

Gather Sources

1. Arrange for students to visit your school's library or computer lab.
2. Explain to students that scientific journals are print or online periodicals that are published for scientists and contain relevant and credible scientific information. Many of these journals contain the latest research.

Take Notes

1. Reinforce how a structured method of note taking can save time when students start to write their research reports.
2. Emphasize that students should place any original quotes within quotation marks and give proper credit to the sources of the quotes. All source information from scientific journals should be recorded because it will appear in students' bibliographies.

Synthesize Multiple Sources

1. Encourage students to create outlines to organize data for their research reports.
2. Explain how to examine research findings in order to discover similarities and differences between them. After considering the relevant facts, students should be able to draw conclusions about factors that help children develop the determination to succeed.
3. Review the MLA style requirements for citing different kinds of print and online sources, and provide examples. Have students create a Works Cited list that accurately identifies each source they reference.

Organize and Present Ideas

After writing their reports, students should re-examine their work to make certain that quotes are accurate and properly attributed.

WEB ARTICLE

MULTIDRAFT READING

Essential Understanding

First, students should read the entire selection on their own. Then, to assist struggling readers and to deepen comprehension for all, you may wish to guide them through the selection by asking them the close reading questions provided in the margins. Have students apply the multidraft reading protocols as they examine specific "chunks" of text related to these questions. For each reading, have students set the purpose indicated:

- **First reading:** Students should read the selection independently and think about its basic meaning.
- **Second reading:** Students should analyze the text's key ideas and details and its craft and structure.
- **Third reading:** Students should integrate knowledge and ideas; connect to the Big Question, other texts, and the world; and use teacher-led Close Reading discussion questions to examine particularly rich and significant passages.

For more guidance, refer to the ***Classroom Strategies and Teaching Routines*** card on multidraft reading.

🔔 Daily Bellringer

For each class during which you teach this selection, have students complete one of the five Sentence Modeling activities for Week 20 in ***Daily Bellringer Activities***. You may wish to use additional activities that are applicable to this selection.

❶ Background

Explain that psychology professors conduct research and often publish in academic journals. Researchers explain the methods and the results of an experiment.

Vocabulary

1. Write the following words and definitions on the board:

   rigorous *adj.* difficult; demanding

   persevere *v.* continue although faced with difficulties

   insurmountable *adj.* impossible to overcome

2. Have students say each word aloud.

---

❶ # Angela Duckworth and the Research on

"GRIT"

Emily Hanford

Before she was a psychology professor, Angela Duckworth taught in middle school and high school. She spent a lot of time thinking about something that might seem obvious: The students who tried hardest did the best, and the students who didn't try very hard didn't do very well. Duckworth wanted to know: What is the role of effort in a person's success?

❷ Now Duckworth is an assistant professor at the University of Pennsylvania, and her research focuses on a personality trait she calls "grit." She defines grit as "sticking with things over the very long term until you master them." In a paper, she writes that "the gritty individual approaches achievement as a marathon; his or her advantage is stamina."[1]

---

1. **stamina** (stam´ ə nə) *n.* endurance; ability to resist fatigue.

Ⓒ TEXT COMPLEXITY **RUBRIC**

Angela Duckworth and the Research on "Grit"		
Qualitative Measures	Context/Knowledge Demands	Contemporary U.S.; demands for college readiness and career success 1 2 3 ④ 5
	Structure/Language Conventionality and Clarity	Informative article; some difficult vocabulary; longer sentences; straightforward exposition 1 2 3 ④ 5
	Levels of Meaning/Purpose/Concept Level	Challenging concept (determining why grit is essential to success) 1 2 3 ④ 5
Quantitative Measures	Text Length	Word Count: 826
	Lexile	1070L

Duckworth's research suggests that when it comes to high achievement, grit may be as essential as intelligence. That's a significant finding because for a long time, intelligence was considered *the* key to success.

Intelligence "is probably the best-measured trait that there is in all of human psychology," says Duckworth. "We know how to measure intelligence in a matter of minutes."

But intelligence leaves a lot unexplained. There are smart people who aren't high achievers, and there are people who achieve a lot without having the highest test scores. In one study, Duckworth found that smarter students actually had *less* grit than their peers who scored lower on an intelligence test. This finding suggests that, among the study participants—all students at an Ivy League school—people who are not as bright as their peers "compensate by working harder and with more determination." And their effort pays off: The grittiest students—not the smartest ones—had the highest GPAs.

The Grit Test

Duckworth's work is part of a growing area of psychology research focused on what are loosely called "noncognitive skills."[2] The goal is to identify and measure the various skills and traits other than intelligence that contribute to human development and success.

Duckworth has developed a test called the "Grit Scale." You rate yourself on a series of 8 to 12 items. Two examples: "I have overcome setbacks to conquer an important challenge" and "Setbacks don't discourage me." It's entirely self-reported, so you could game[3] the test, and yet what Duckworth has found is that a person's grit score is highly predictive of achievement under challenging circumstances.

At the elite United States Military Academy, West Point, a cadet's grit score was the best predictor of success in the

---

2. **noncognitive skills** processes that involve emotions and decision-making, rather than cognitive skills such as intelligence, memory, perception, judgment, and reasoning.
3. **game** here, game means "bending the rules" or "cheating."

© TEXT COMPLEXITY **READER AND TASK SUGGESTIONS**

Angela Duckworth and the Research on "Grit"

Preparing to Read the Text	Leveled Tasks
• Have students discuss how people can research a person's intelligence, success, and determination. • Guide students to use Multidraft Reading strategies (TE p. 398).	*Concept Level* If students will have difficulty with the concept of the importance of grit to being successful, have them explore ways to develop grit. As a class, have students take the author's "Grit Scale" test, rating themselves on a series of items to discover their grit score. *Synthesizing* If students will not have difficulty with the concept presented in the selection, have them note where the author uses compare and contrast to show an inverse relationship between intelligence and grit. Discuss with students how people with grit might be inspired to work harder when presented with obstacles. Ask students to share some examples of this from their own experiences in school, sports, or other areas of their lives.

❷ Focus Passage

A Focus Passage is identified with brackets in the Student Edition of the previous page and this page for students' independent close reading and analysis. A question bank for the passage and possible responses appear at the end of the selection.

❸ Close Reading

1. **Key Ideas and Details** Read aloud the passage to students.
   Ask: Why does Duckworth believe that "intelligence leaves a lot unexplained"?

   Possible response: She discovered that intelligence doesn't ensure that people are successful. Students with lower scores on intelligence tests but with a lot of grit had the best grades.

2. **Craft and Structure**
   Ask: How does the author organize her concepts and ideas in this paragraph?

   Possible response: The author introduces her theory that the most intelligent people aren't the highest achievers. She illustrates this concept with a real-life example of a study at an Ivy League school where she discovered that the students with grit, rather than those with the highest scores on intelligence tests, had the highest GPAs.

3. **Integration of Knowledge and Ideas**
   Ask: How does the author's inclusion of a real-life study make her thesis more convincing?

   Possible response: The study showed that among students at a top college, those with lower intelligence scores but more grit achieved higher grades. The real-life situations support the author's thesis that grit may be as important as intelligence in attaining success.

🔊 **Audio**

Selection Audio is available in the *Student eText* and on the *Hear It!* CD-ROM.

❹ Close Reading

1. Key Ideas and Details Have a student read aloud the passage. **Ask:** What main idea does the author develop in this passage?

Possible response: Grit can increase and decrease over a period of time or in response to different issues.

2. Craft and Structure Have students focus on the descriptive language in this paragraph. **Ask:** What does the expression wax and wane mean? Why is it effective here?

Possible response: It means to become stronger and then weaker. This expression brings to mind the phases of the moon, presenting a vivid visual image of how a person's grit can change over time.

3. Integration of Knowledge and Ideas Have students relate the phrase wax and wane to the way people might use grit in life experiences. **Ask:** Why is the concept of waxing and waning important in understanding a person's determination?

Possible response: Although a person may be determined in one area, he or she may not have the same type of determination in other areas. A person's determination can also change if his or her interests change.

rigorous ▶
(rig´ ər əs)
adj. difficult; demanding

rigorous summer training program known as "Beast Barracks." Grit mattered more than intelligence, leadership ability or physical fitness.

At the Scripps National Spelling Bee, the grittiest contestants were the most likely to advance to the finals—at least in part because they studied longer, not because they were smarter or were better spellers....

Learning to Be Gritty

It's not clear what makes some people grittier than others, but Angela Duckworth believes grit is something people can probably learn.

She says every human quality that has been studied has proven to be affected at least in part by a person's environment—even intelligence. In addition, people change over time.

"Think about things about your personality like, 'I'm a pretty extroverted[4] person,'" says Duckworth. "Well, how fixed is that?"

It turns out a personality trait like extroversion can change a lot over a person's life. "If you look at large population data, people get more or less extroverted over time," says Duckworth. "There's no reason to think that grit is any different."

❹ She believes grit can wax and wane in response to experiences. In addition, people might be gritty about some things and not others.

"You can see a child be exceptionally self-disciplined about their basketball practicing, and yet when you see them in math class,

The Scripps Spelling Bee

---

4. **extroverted** (eks´ trə vʉrt´ id) *adj.* outgoing; sociable.

💬 VOCABULARY DEVELOPMENT

Selection Vocabulary Reinforcement

Students will benefit from additional practice with the selection vocabulary. Reinforce their comprehension with "show-you-know" sentences. The first part of the sentence uses the vocabulary word in an appropriate context. The show-you-know part clarifies the first part of the sentence. Model the strategy:

The photographer made the *rigorous* journey to the Antarctic; the sub zero temperatures gave her frostbite.

Give students these sentence prompts, and coach them in creating the clarification part:

1. Dana *persevered* in the grueling triathlon, _____.

Sample answer: despite temperatures that soared above 100 degrees and a pulled hamstring.

2. My sister faced *insurmountable* obstacles when she joined the all-male archery team; _____.

Sample answer: however, she impressed the team with a series of bull's eyes.

they give up at the slightest frustration," says Duckworth.

Donald Kamentz, director of college initiatives at YES Prep, says students he's worked with are some of the grittiest people he's ever met. They "deal with things and persevere through situations that most people would find insurmountable," he says.

He's known students who get jobs to pay the bills when their parents are laid off, or figure out how to get the electricity back on until the power company shuts it off.

"And then they go to college and they're struggling with financial aid or their financial aid didn't come through and they don't know what to do," he says. Some of them drop out when confronted with these kinds of challenges. He says they're not gritty enough when it comes to college.

A question for YES Prep and other charter schools in Duckworth's study is not necessarily how to get students to be gritty, but how to get them to be gritty about college completion.

"Which experiences do we give kids to get them in the direction of more grit and not less?" asks Duckworth.

One of the goals of Duckworth's research is to figure this out. Her current project began in the fall of 2011 and is scheduled to wrap up in 2014.

◄ **persevere**
(pur´ sə vir´) *v.*
continue although faced with difficulties

◄ **insurmountable**
(in´ sər mount´ ə bəl) *adj.*
impossible to overcome

ABOUT THE AUTHOR

Emily Hanford

Emily Hanford began working in radio immediately after graduating from Amherst College in Amherst, Massachusetts. She has worked as a news producer, director, and reporter for several public radio stations. As the senior editor/ producer for the series *North Carolina Voices*, Hanford contributed to a reporting project about high school reform that eventually became the documentary *Put to the Test*. In 2008, Hanford began reporting on education for American RadioWorks.

5 **Big Question: Toward Essential Understanding**

1. Read aloud the passage. **Ask:** How can actions communicate information about a person's determination?

   Possible response: Actions can show that someone is determined to succeed despite facing difficulties that often seem impossible to overcome.

2. **Ask:** Are people's actions more or less effective than their words as a form of communication?

   Possible response: People's actions often speak louder than their words because what people actually do is sometimes different from what they say they will do.

FLUENCY

Distribute copies of pp. 398–401, and pair students. Have partners take turns reading paragraphs aloud. While one partner reads, the other should mark any words with which the one reading has difficulty. Circulate to monitor the fluency of students' reading. Collect students' marked-up copies of the story, and review difficult words and passages with the class. Look for these problem spots:

• If students have difficulty with the word *confronted* (p. 401), practice oral cloze with the sentence. First, read the sentence with the word *confronted* omitted. Then, reread the sentence, asking students to fill in the blank with a word that makes the most sense.

• If students have difficulty with the word *setback* (p. 399), point out that this is a compound noun that is made up of two other words. Have students write the word on an index card and then cut the card apart to form the two words *set* and *back*. Tell students that compound nouns often have a meaning that is different from the two separate words. Then, explain that *setback* means "an unexpected reversal in progress; a change from better to worse."

READ

Comprehension

1. It is stamina, or "sticking with things over the very long term until you master them."

2. Grit is as essential as intelligence

3. The "Grit Scale" is a self-reported test that rates people on noncognitive skills, such as how he or she responds to setbacks.

Research: Clarify Details

Students should explain how their findings helped them understand an unfamiliar reference.

Summarize

Students' summaries should define *grit,* explain Angela Duckworth's research, and discuss how people can learn to be gritty.

Language Study

Possible responses:

• *rigorous*: difficult; demanding; The journalism class is *rigorous.*

• *persevere*: continue in spite of difficulties; Although I fell during the marathon, I *persevered* and finished the race.

• *insurmountable*: impossible to overcome; The obstacles in the firefighter's path seemed *insurmountable,* but she managed to rescue the child.

Literary Analysis

Possible responses appear below. Check to be sure students support their responses with evidence from the text.

1. (a) Duckworth's teaching experiences interested her in the idea of grit. (b) Students who have grit generally have higher GPAs.

2. (a) Factors such as grit and motivation can be just as important. (b) Duckworth describes the Ivy League students from one her studies as examples.

3. (a) She uses passive voice. (b) Passive voice implies that everyone assumed or accepted the idea that intelligence was the key for a long time.

READ

Comprehension

Reread all or part of the text to help you answer the following questions.

1. What is "grit"?

2. According to Angela Duckworth's research, grit is as **essential** to achievement as which trait?

3. What is the "Grit Scale"?

Language Study

Selection Vocabulary Define each word from the article and use the word in a sentence of your own.

Literary Analysis

Reread the identified passages. Then, respond to the questions that follow:

> **Focus Passage** *(pp. 398–399)*
> Before she was a psychology professor … in a matter of minutes."

Key Ideas and Details

1. (a) What observation sparked Duckworth's interest in "grit"? (b) **Connect:** How does grit affect students' success?

2. (a) **Speculate:** Why might intelligence fail to predict success? (b) **Support:** What examples from the text support this idea?

Direct Quotation

A **direct quotation** states a person's exact words. Reread the article, taking notes on Hanford's use of direct quotation.

1. (a) Which two people does Hanford quote directly? (b) Why does she quote these people?

402 UNIT 3 • Do we need words to communicate well?

Research: Clarify Details This article may include references that are unfamiliar to you. Choose an unfamiliar detail and briefly research it. Then, explain how your research clarifies the article.

Summarize Write an objective summary of the article, free from opinion and evaluation.

• rigorous
• persevere
• insurmountable

Craft and Structure

3. (a) Does the author use the active or passive voice when she says "for a long time, intelligence was considered *the* key to success"? (b) **Infer:** Why do you think the author phrased the idea this way?

Integration of Knowledge and Ideas

4. **Draw Conclusions:** What do you learn from this passage about the ways in which researchers choose topics for study?

2. **Determination (a)** Which direct quotation expresses Duckworth's current research question? (b) How might this research contribute to the **study** of determination?

4. Researchers choose topics that intrigue them, such as the growing focus on noncognitive skills

Direct Quotation

1. (a) She quotes Angela Duckworth and Donald Kamentz. (b) They are experts on her topic.

2. (a) "Which experiences do we give kids to get them in the direction of more grit and not less?" The article says that answering this question is a goal of Duckworth's research.

(b) Grit is a trait that indicates determination, so the research will help kids develop ways to act on their determination.

DISCUSS • RESEARCH • WRITE

From Text to Topic **Partner Discussion**

Discuss the following passage with a partner. Take notes during the discussion. Contribute your own ideas, and support them with examples from the text.

> Donald Kamentz, director of college initiatives … when it comes to college. (p. 401)

Research **Investigate the Topic**

College Challenges As the article says, problems with financial aid can cause students to drop out of college. Other factors contribute to the drop-out rate as well.

Assignment

Conduct **research** to find out what factors can cause students to drop out of college. Consult government education websites and reputable magazines and journals. Take clear notes and carefully identify your sources so that you can easily access the information later. Share your findings in a **chart**. Create separate categories for factors that are related to determination and factors that are not.

Writing to Sources **Autobiographical Narrative**

People can use "grit" in many different situations.

Assignment

Write an **autobiographical narrative** in which you describe how you used grit to succeed in a situation. Follow these steps:

- Explain the meaning of grit and introduce a situation in which you needed it.
- Describe how you used grit in that situation. Use transitions to create a smooth progression of ideas that build on one another.
- Use literary elements such as description, dialogue, foreshadowing, and suspense to create an engaging narrative.
- Provide a conclusion in which reflect on your "gritty" experience and connect it to the experiences of people described in Hanford's article.

QUESTIONS FOR DISCUSSION

1. What makes some gritty people "not gritty enough when it comes to college"?

2. Why might people be gritty about some things and not others?

PREPARATION FOR ESSAY

You may use the results of this research project to support your ideas in the essay at the end of this section.

ACADEMIC VOCABULARY

Academic terms appear in blue on these pages. If these words are not familiar to you, use a dictionary to find their definitions. Then, use them as you speak and write about the text.

 **Common Core State Standards**

RI.6.1, RI.6.2, RI.6.3, RI.6.5; W.6.3, W.6.4, W.6.5, W.6.7, W.6.8; SL.6.1, SL.6.4, SL.6.6
[For full standards wording, see the chart in the front of this book.]

Writing to Sources: Autobiographical Narrative

Students' autobiographical narratives should follow the steps listed to relate a situation in which they used grit to succeed. Remind them to connect their experience to those of people described in Hanford's article.

DISCUSS • RESEARCH • WRITE

From Text to Topic: Partner Discussion

Possible responses:

1. Some students are unable or unwilling to apply their "grit skills" in a new context, such as college.

2. People might be gritty about things they have knowledge about or things they care about. Unfamiliar situations may make some people more or less determined.

Research: Investigate the Topic

Introduce the assignment, using the instruction on the student page.

1. Arrange for students to visit your school's library or computer lab. Review strategies for identifying reliable sources. Stress that students should focus on government education Web sites that end in either .gov or .edu.

2. Remind students that they should create a Works Cited list for each source they use.

3. Suggest that students exchange their papers with a partner to obtain feedback.

Academic Vocabulary

If students struggle with defining the academic vocabulary words, use this routine:

Write the words and definitions.

essential: necessary

study: report based on research

research: study of a topic

Have students say each word aloud and then use the word in a sentence. Sample sentences should demonstrate that the words can be used across disciplines.

 Online Writer's Notebook

Students can use the Online Writer's Notebook to record all responses.

MULTIDRAFT READING

Essential Understanding

First, students should read the entire selection on their own. Then, to assist struggling readers and to deepen comprehension for all, you may wish to guide them through the selection by asking them the close reading questions provided in the margins. Have students apply the multidraft reading protocols as they examine specific "chunks" of text related to these questions. For each reading, have students set the purpose indicated:

- **First reading:** Students should read the selection independently and think about its basic meaning.

- **Second reading:** Students should analyze the text's key ideas and details and its craft and structure.

- **Third reading:** Students should integrate knowledge and ideas; connect to the Big Question, other texts, and the world; and use teacher-led Close Reading discussion questions to examine particularly rich and significant passages.

For more guidance, refer to the *Classroom Strategies and Teaching Routines* card on multidraft reading.

Vocabulary

If students require support with selection vocabulary, use this routine:

1. Write the following words and definitions on the board:

   plateau *n.* raised area of land with a level surface

   expedition *n.* journey for a particular purpose, such as exploration or scientific study

   polar *adj.* near, of, or relating to the North or South pole

2. Have students say each word aloud.

3. Use the word in a sentence that defines the word.

RACE
TO THE END OF
THE EARTH

William G. Scheller

plateau ▶
(pla tō´) *n.* raised area of land with a level surface

expedition ▶
(eks´pə dish´ən) *n.* journey for a particular purpose, such as exploration or scientific study

polar ▶
(pō´lər) *adj.* near, of, or relating to the North or South Pole

1

Two explorers competed against each other and a brutal environment to reach the South Pole.

The drifts were so deep and the snow was falling so heavily that the team of five Norwegian explorers could hardly see their sled dogs a few feet ahead of them. Behind rose a monstrous mountain barrier. The men had been the first to cross it. But now they and their dogs were stumbling toward a stark and desolate plateau continually blasted by blizzards. The landscape was broken only by the towering peaks of mountains that lay buried beneath a mile of ancient ice. Led by Roald Amundsen, the men were still 300 miles from their goal: the South Pole.

On that same day, a party of 14 British explorers was also struggling across a similarly terrifying landscape toward the same destination. But they were almost twice as far from success. Their commander was Capt. Robert Falcon Scott, a naval officer. Amundsen was Scott's rival.

Preparation Both expedition leaders had long been preparing for their race to the South Pole. Amundsen came from a family of hardy sailors, and he had decided at the age of 15 to become a polar explorer. He conditioned himself by taking long ski trips across the Norwegian countryside

404 UNIT 3 • Do we need words to communicate well?

© TEXT COMPLEXITY **RUBRIC**

Race to the End of the Earth		
Qualitative Measures	**Context/Knowledge Demands**	America in the early 1900s; polar expeditions 1 2 3 ④ 5
	Structure/Language Conventionality and Clarity	Compare and contrast essay; point-by-point organization; geographical vocabulary; longer sentences; sarcasm 1 2 3 ④ 5
	Levels of Meaning/Purpose/Concept Level	Accessible concept (how differences in explorers' expeditions affected the outcomes) 1 2 ③ 4 5
Quantitative Measures	**Text Length**	Word Count 712
	Lexile	1000L

and by sleeping with his windows open in winter.

By the time of his South Pole attempt, Amundsen was an experienced explorer. He had sailed as a naval officer on an expedition in 1897 that charted sections of the Antarctic coast. Between 1903 and 1906 he commanded the ship that made the first voyage through the Northwest Passage, the icy route that threads its way through the Canadian islands separating the Atlantic and Pacific Oceans. During that long journey Amundsen learned how the native people of the Arctic dress and eat to survive in extreme cold. He also learned that the dogsled was the most efficient method of polar transportation. These lessons would serve him well at Earth's frozen southern end.

Robert Scott was an officer in the British Navy. He had decided that leading a daring expedition of discovery would be an immediate route to higher rank. He heard that Great Britain's Royal Geographical Society was organizing such an exploration, and he volunteered in 1899 to be its commander. Now he was in command again.

The two expedition leaders had different styles. Scott followed a British tradition of brave sacrifice. He felt that he and his men should be able to reach the South Pole with as little help as possible from sled dogs and special equipment. He did bring dogs to Antarctica, as well as 19 ponies and three gasoline-powered sledges, or sturdy sleds. But his plan was for his team to "man-haul," or carry, all of their own supplies along the final portion of the route.

Roald Amundsen had spent much time in the far north, and he was a practical man. He'd seen how useful dogs were to Arctic inhabitants. He would be traveling in one of the most dangerous places on Earth, and he knew that sled dogs would be able to get his party all the way to the South Pole and make a safe return.

PART 3 • Race to the End of the Earth **405**

❶ Close Reading

1. Key Ideas and Details Read aloud the passage to students. **Ask:** What makes this landscape so brutal for the Norwegian explorers?

Possible response: The explorers and their sled dogs have to navigate deep drifts of snow, cross an enormous barrier, and plot a route over a plateau while a severe snowstorm causes limited visibility.

2. Craft and Structure Have students focus on the repetition of *so* and the alliteration of *m, s,* and *b* in this passage. **Ask:** Why does the author repeat *so* in the first sentence? What do the alliterations describe? Give examples.

Possible response: The author wants to focus attention on the brutal conditions. Repeating *so* emphasizes the intensity of the storm. Alliterations, such as *monstrous mountain; stumbling* and *stark, blasted by blizzards, broken,* and *buried,* are used to reveal how harsh and severe this environment is.

3. Integration of Knowledge and Ideas **Ask:** How do the author's vivid descriptions of the dangerous environment increase your understanding of the explorers' determination and bravery in attempting this journey?

Possible response: Amundsen and his team had to be incredibly determined, as well as brave, to continue their efforts to reach the South Pole despite the wild and dangerous environment. The trials and tribulations they underwent did not deter Amundsen or his men.

❷ Focus Passage

A Focus Passage is identified with brackets in the Student Edition of this page and the next for students' independent close reading and analysis. A question bank for the passage and possible responses appear at the end of the selection.

 **Audio**

Selection Audio is available in the *Student eText* and on the *Hear It!* CD-ROM.

ⓒ TEXT COMPLEXITY **READER AND TASK SUGGESTIONS**

Race to the End of the Earth

Preparing to Read the Text	Leveled Tasks
• Have students discuss possible motivations for exploring Antarctica. Explain that this essay is about explorers in the past, so motivations may be different throughout history. • Guide students to use Multidraft Reading strategies on the previous page.	*Structure* If students will have difficulty with the point-by-point structure of this compare and contrast selection, have them create a Venn diagram to compare and contrast Roald Amundsen and Robert Falcon Scott. Remind them to write details about how the subjects are different in the outer circles and to write details how they are alike where the circles overlap. *Evaluating* If students will not have difficulty with the structure of the selection, have them discuss how they think the differences in skills, motivation, and leadership contributed to the outcome of the race to the South Pole. Discuss with students various ways that leaders motivate their followers.

❸ Close Reading

1. Key Ideas and Details Have a student read aloud the passage. **Ask:** What is the key idea the author is communicating in this passage?

Possible response: He is describing the many difficulties that Scott and his men encountered on their Antarctic journey. These struggles delayed and weakened Scott's team.

2. Craft and Structure Have students focus on the cause-and-effect text structure. **Ask:** Think about what happened (the effect) and why it happened (the cause). What causes and their effects can you link together in this passage?

Possible response: The sledges had to be discarded because they broke down. The ponies did not survive because, unlike the dogs, they perspired and their sweat froze so they couldn't handle the frigid Antarctic climate. The men had little energy to travel far because food and fuel were extremely limited.

3. Integration of Knowledge and Ideas

Ask: How does the cause-and-effect text structure relate to the determination of Scott's team?

Possible response: Despite all the daunting challenges, Scott and his five followers were determined to keep trying to reach the South Pole ahead of Amundsen and his team. They took the competition seriously and relied on their willpower to keep going.

FOR SCOTT AND HIS MEN, THE JOURNEY WAS LONG AND BRUTAL.

Amundsen also placed great faith in skis, which he and his Norwegian team members had used since childhood. The British explorers had rarely used skis before this expedition and did not understand their great value.

❷ The two leaders even had different ideas about diet. Scott's men would rely on canned meat. But Amundsen's plan made more sense. He and his men would eat plenty of fresh seal meat. Amundsen may not have fully understood the importance of vitamins, but fresh meat is a better source of vitamin C, which prevents scurvy, a painful and sometimes deadly disease.

The Race Is On! After making long sea voyages from Europe, Scott and Amundsen set up base camps in January on opposite edges of the Ross Ice Shelf. Each team spent the dark winter months making preparations to push on to the Pole when spring would arrive in Antarctica.

Amundsen left base camp on October 20, 1911, with a party of four. Scott, accompanied by nine men, set off from his camp 11 days later. Four others had already gone ahead on the motorized sledges.

Scott's Final Diary Entry Things went wrong for Scott from the beginning. The sledges broke down and had to be abandoned. Scott and his men soon met up with the drivers, who were traveling on foot. Blizzards then struck and lasted several weeks into December. Scott's ponies were proving to be a poor choice for Antarctic travel as well. Their hooves sank deep into the snow, and their perspiration froze on their bodies, forming sheets of ice. (Dogs do not perspire; they pant.) On December 9, the men shot the last of the surviving weak and frozen ponies. Two days later Scott sent his remaining dogs back to base camp along with several members of the expedition. Over the next month, most of the men returned to the camp. Scott's plan from here on was for the five men remaining to manhaul supplies the rest of the way to the Pole and back. ❸

For Scott and his men, the journey was long and brutal. To cover only ten miles each day, the team toiled like dogs—like the dogs they no longer had. Food and fuel were in short supply, so the men lacked the energy they needed for such a crushing task.

💬 VOCABULARY DEVELOPMENT

Content-Area Vocabulary: Geography

Point out to students that the article uses many terms related to geography. Some are nouns referring to specific places (*South Pole, Northwest Passage*). Others are adjectives derived from the names of places (*Norwegian, British, polar, Antarctic, Canadian, Arctic*). Direct students to identify the related noun for each adjective. (*Norway, Britain, Antarctica, Canada, the Arctic.*)

Robert F. Scott (center) and his team.

Roald Amundsen's careful planning and Arctic experience were paying off. Even so, there's no such thing as easy travel by land in Antarctica. To the men who had just crossed those terrible mountains, the Polar Plateau might have looked easy. But Amundsen's team still had to cross a long stretch they later named the "Devil's Ballroom." It was a thin crust of ice that concealed crevasses, or deep gaps, that could swallow men, sleds, and dogs. Stumbling into one crevasse, a team of dogs dangled by their harnesses until the men could pull them up to safety.

Reaching the Goal On skis, with the "ballroom" behind them and well-fed dogs pulling their supply sleds, Amundsen and his men swept across the ice. The going was smooth for them, and the weather was fine. The Norwegians' only worry was that they'd find Scott had gotten to the Pole first. On the afternoon of December 14, 1911, it was plain that no one was ahead of them. At three o'clock, Amundsen skied in front of the team's sleds, then stopped to look at his navigation instruments. There was no point further south. He was at the South Pole!

Big Question: Toward Essential Understanding

❹

1. Read aloud the passage. **Ask:** What hazard did the team face as they crossed the "Devil's Ballroom"?

   Possible response: There were great crevasses hidden under the ice that men, dogs, and sleds could fall into.

2. **Ask:** Do you think that words were necessary when Amundsen's team crossed the "Devil's Ballroom"? Why or why not?

   Possible response: Some students may say no because Amundsen's team was too intent on surviving the treacherous crevasses to speak. One wrong step and the men and their dogs could vanish beneath the ice. They were probably too apprehensive to talk during this dangerous situation. Others may say that the team may have given warnings to let other team members know what to watch out for. Note that the naming of the area came after they crossed. At the time of the crossing, they were focused on survival.

DIFFERENTIATED INSTRUCTION

Enrichment for Gifted/Talented Students
After students have read and discussed "Race to the End of the Earth," have them think about lessons in the story, such as being well prepared for an extreme and demanding journey. Then, ask students to consider how this article reminds them of fables they have read. Challenge students to rewrite the story as a fable. Remind students to include fantastic or imaginary details that lead to some type of instruction or moral lesson. Point out that their stories can contain factual details, but they should also contain fantastic elements that make it impossible to confuse the fable with nonfiction. Provide an opportunity for students to share their fables.

READ

Comprehension

1. They were competing to be first to reach the South Pole.

2. **Possible response:** They both faced dangerous conditions, a long and tiring journey, and very cold weather.

3. Amundsen and his team reached the South Pole first.

Research: Clarify Details

Students should explain how their research helped them understand an unfamiliar detail from the text.

Summarize

Students' summaries should describe how Amundsen and Scott prepared for their expeditions, how their expeditions fared, and which team reached the South Pole first.

Language Study

- *plateau*: a piece of flat land that is at a high elevation; a period of little change

- *expedition*: a journey that has a purpose; promptness or speed

- *polar*: near, of, or relating to the North or South Pole; opposite

Literary Analysis

Possible responses appear below. Check to be sure students support their responses with evidence from the text.

1. **(a)** Amundsen brought dogs, skis, and dogsleds. Scott brought dogs, ponies, sledges, and canned meat. **(b)** Amundsen was better prepared because he chose items that were practical and made sense in the environment.

2. **(a)** Amundsen planned to eat fresh seal meat. Scott planned to eat canned meat. **(b)** Scott's team had to carry the cans, and the canned meat was not as nutritious as fresh meat.

3. **(a)** The passage has a point-by-point comparison/contrast structure. **(b)** This approach helps the author compare and contrast the explorers' methods, which explains why Amundsen reached the South Pole first.

READ

Comprehension

Reread all or part of the text to help you answer the following questions.

1. For what were Amundsen and Scott competing?

2. What problems did both men face?

3. What was the outcome of the competition?

Language Study

Selection Vocabulary: Science Give the scientific meaning of each boldfaced word. Then, give another meaning of each word.

- … a stark and desolate **plateau** continually blasted by blizzards.

- Both **expedition** leaders had long been preparing for their race to the South Pole.

- … dogsled was the most efficient method of **polar** transportation.

Literary Analysis

Reread the identified passage. Then, respond to the questions that follow:

> **Focus Passage** *(pp. 405–406)*
> The two expedition leaders had different styles … sometimes deadly disease.

Key Ideas and Details

1. **(a)** What equipment and supplies did Amundsen and Scott each bring on their expeditions? **(b) Assess:** Which man was better prepared? Why?

2. **(a)** What food did Amundsen and Scott plan to eat on their expeditions? **(b) Evaluate:** What were the disadvantages of Scott's plan?

Craft and Structure

3. **(a) Classify:** How is the passage organized? **(b) Analyze:** Why did the author approach the topic this way?

Integration of Knowledge and Ideas

4. **(a) Infer:** Which explorer does the author seem to admire more? **(b) Support:** Cite evidence that supports your choice.

Foreshadowing

Foreshadowing is the use of clues to hint at what might happen later in a narrative.

1. **(a)** Find two examples of foreshadowing in the essay. **(b)** What future event does each example suggest?

2. **Determination** Based on foreshadowing in the essay, would you say that determination always leads to success? Explain.

Research: Clarify Details This essay may include unfamiliar references. Choose one to briefly research. Then, explain how your research helps you understand the essay.

Summarize Write an objective summary of the essay. Include main ideas, but do not include opinions.

4. **(a)** He prefers Amundsen. **(b)** The author says Amundsen is practical, makes use of his knowledge and experience, and has a meal plan that makes more sense than Scott's. The author also says that Scott's team "did not understand" the value of skis.

Foreshadowing

1. **(a)** "The British explorers had rarely used skis before and did not understand their great value" and "Behind rose a monstrous mountain barrier."

(b) The first example foreshadows that Scott is not properly prepared for the expedition. The second example hints that the journey will be difficult.

2. This article shows that determination does not always lead to success. Scott was determined, but he wasn't fully prepared for the dangerous journey.

DISCUSS • RESEARCH • WRITE

From Text to Topic **Group Discussion**

Discuss the following passage with a partner. Take notes during the discussion. Contribute your own ideas, and support them with examples from the text.

> The drifts were so deep and the snow was falling so heavily … their goal: the South Pole. (p. 404)

Research **Investigate the Topic**

Expedition to the South Pole "Race to the End of the Earth" reveals who won the "race," but does not tell what happened to Scott and his team. Specifically, readers do not learn whether Scott and his team ever reached the South Pole.

Assignment

Conduct research to learn more about Scott's background, and to find out whether or not Scott's determination ever carried him and his team to the South Pole. Consult credible historical sources. Take clear notes and carefully identify your sources so that you can easily access the information later. Share your findings in a **short research paper**.

Writing to Sources **Diary Entry**

Scott kept a journal of his adventures and struggles on the expedition.

Assignment

Write a diary entry, from Scott's point of view, describing something that happens in the final days of his journey to the South Pole.

- Use first-person pronouns such as *I, me,* and *mine* to convey Scott's **perspective**.
- Describe your experiences using vivid language that appeals to the five senses.
- Expand on information presented in the essay, adding details to build Scott's character, feelings, and personality.
- Use transitions to build suspense and connect your ideas.

QUESTIONS FOR DISCUSSION

1. How does the author emphasize the danger of South Pole expeditions?
2. How does this passage relate to the idea of determination?

PREPARATION FOR ESSAY

You may use the results of this research project to support your ideas in the essay at the end of this section.

ACADEMIC VOCABULARY

Academic terms appear in blue on these pages. If these words are not familiar to you, use a dictionary to find their definitions. Then, use them as you speak and write about the text.

Ⓒ **Common Core State Standards**

RI.6.1, RI.6.2, RI.6.3, RI.6.5, RI.6.6; W.6.3, W.6.4, W.6.7, W.6.8; SL.6.1, SL.6.4; L.6.1
[For full standards wording, see the chart in the front of this book.]

PART 3 • Close Reading Activities **409**

DISCUSS • RESEARCH • WRITE

From Text to Topic: Group Discussion

Possible responses:

1. Descriptions such as "monstrous mountain barrier" and "stark and desolate plateau continually blasted by blizzards" create mental pictures of the dangers.
2. The passage emphasizes that anyone trying to reach the South Pole would need determination to overcome the harsh conditions.

Research: Investigate the Topic

Introduce the assignment, using the instruction on the student page.

1. Arrange for students to visit your school's library or computer lab. Remind students to locate authoritative electronic sources when they conduct research on the Internet. Web sites that end in .gov, .edu., and .org are generally reliable. Demonstrate how to access articles, photos, and journal entries from credible online historical sources.

2. Remind students to take clear notes and keep track of all sources that they reference. Explain to students that they need to give proper credit whenever they use direct quotes from Web sites, news articles, and other print and online sources. Emphasize that they must place direct quotes within quotation marks. Encourage students to paraphrase and summarize information by restating it in their own words.

3. Suggest that students exchange their research papers with a partner to obtain feedback.

Academic Vocabulary

If students struggle with defining the academic vocabulary words, use this routine:

Write the words and definitions on the board.

assess: evaluate

evidence: proof

perspective: point of view

Have students say each word aloud and then use the word in a sentence. Sample sentences should demonstrate that the words can be used across disciplines.

Writing to Sources: Diary Entry

Students' diary entries should be written from Scott's perspective, use vivid language, expand on the text, and use transitions that build suspense and connect ideas.

 Online Writer's Notebook

Students can use the Online Writer's Notebook to record all responses.

MULTIDRAFT READING

Essential Understanding

First, students should read the entire selection on their own. Then, to assist struggling readers and to deepen comprehension for all, you may wish to guide them through the selection by asking them the close reading questions provided in the margins. Have students apply the multidraft reading protocols as they examine specific "chunks" of text related to these questions. For each reading, have students set the purpose indicated:

- **First reading:** Students should read the selection independently and think about its basic meaning.
- **Second reading:** Students should analyze the text's key ideas and details and its craft and structure.
- **Third reading:** Students should integrate knowledge and ideas; connect to the Big Question, other texts, and the world; and use teacher-led Close Reading discussion questions to examine particularly rich and significant passages.

For more guidance, refer to the *Classroom Strategies and Teaching Routines* card on multidraft reading.

❶ Background

If you wish, explain that objects can be named differently in various regions. For example, in "The Sound of Summer Running," the author refers to *tennis shoes,* which can also be called *sneakers* or *gym shoes* in other regions. Discuss other regional differences in word use that students might be aware of in their specific region.

Vocabulary

If students require support with selection vocabulary, use this routine:

1. Write the following words and definitions on the board:

   seized *v.* grabbed; taken hold of

   suspended *v.* stopped for a time

   revelation *n.* sudden rush of understanding

2. Have students say each word aloud.

3. Use the word in a sentence that defines the word.

❶ # The Sound of Summer Running

from Dandelion Wine

Ray Bradbury

410 UNIT 3 • Do we need words to communicate well?

ⓒ TEXT COMPLEXITY **RUBRIC**

The Sound of Summer Running		
Qualitative Measures	Context/Knowledge Demands	Contemporary America; new shoes 1　2　③　4　5
	Structure/Language Conventionality and Clarity	Conversational tone; challenging vocabulary 1　2　③　4　5
	Levels of Meaning/ Purpose/Concept Level	Accessible concept (tennis shoes as a symbol of the freedom and joy of summer) 1　2　③　4　5
Quantitative Measures	Text Length	Word Count: 2,145
	Lexile	920L

Late that night, going home from the show with his mother and father and his brother Tom, Douglas saw the tennis shoes in the bright store window.

He glanced quickly away, but his ankles were seized, his feet suspended, then rushed. The earth spun; the shop awnings slammed their canvas wings overhead with the thrust of his body running. His mother and father and brother walked quietly on both sides of him. Douglas walked backward, watching the tennis shoes in the midnight window left behind.

"It was a nice movie," said Mother.

Douglas murmured, "It was . . ."

It was June and long past time for buying the special shoes that were quiet as a summer rain falling on the walks. June and the earth full of raw power and everything everywhere in motion. The grass was still pouring in from the country, surrounding the sidewalks, stranding the houses. Any moment the town would capsize, go down and leave not a stir in the clover and weeds. And here Douglas stood, trapped on the dead cement and the red-brick streets, hardly able to move.

"Dad!" He blurted it out. "Back there in that window, those Cream-Sponge Para Litefoot Shoes . . ."

His father didn't even turn. "Suppose you tell me why you need a new pair of sneakers. Can you do that?"

"Well . . ."

It was because they felt the way it feels every summer when you take off your shoes for the first time and run in the grass. They felt like it feels sticking your feet out of the hot covers in wintertime to let the cold wind from the open window blow on them suddenly and you let them stay out a

◄ **seized**
(sēzd) *v.* grabbed; taken hold of

◄ **suspended**
(sə spend´ əd) *v.* stopped for a time

PART 3 • The Sound of Summer Running **411**

❷ Close Reading

1. Key Ideas and Details
Ask: What happens to Douglas?

Possible response: He reacts to a pair of tennis shoes in a store window.

2. Craft and Structure
Ask: What does the author communicate by using alliteration?

Possible response: Verbs such as *seized, suspended, spun,* and *slammed* reveal the powerful impact of the shoes on Douglas.

3. Integration of Knowledge and Ideas
Ask: How do the author's stylistic choices deepen your understanding of Douglas and his family?

Possible response: The words show that Douglas has different feelings about the world and the shoes than his familly.

❸ Close Reading

1. Key Ideas and Details
Ask: How does the narrator describe how new sneakers feel?

Possible response: He compares the feeling to other pleasant sensations.

2. Craft and Structure
Ask: What simile does the narrator use? Why are the descriptions effective?

Possible response: He describes how feet can feel "like packed snow." The paragraph helps readers imagine the sensations of bare feet during different seasons.

3. Integration of Knowledge and Ideas
Ask: Why is Douglas unable to communicate the feelings he has about the sneakers?

Possible response: He may not think that his father will understand, or he may not know how to express his feelings.

 **Audio**

Selection Audio is available in the *Student eText* and on the *Hear It!* CD-ROM.

ⓒTEXT COMPLEXITY **READER AND TASK SUGGESTIONS**

The Sound of Summer Running

Preparing to Read the Text
- Using the Background information on the previous page, discuss how people in specific regions of America speak different dialects and may use different words to name the same thing.
- Tell students that symbols often represent something universal about the human experience. They may represent feelings or experiences that we share in common. Ask students to describe symbols they have seen in literature.
- Guide students to use Multidraft Reading strategies on the previous page.

Leveled Tasks
Levels of Meaning If students will have difficulty with the symbolism in the selection, point out that the nation's flag is a symbol. It is a real object—a piece of cloth—but it stands for the history and values of the whole nation. Discuss the feelings or ideas associated with the flag, and why it causes people to feel patriotic when they see it.

Synthesizing If students will not have difficulty with the symbolism in the selection, have them identify other symbols we commonly use. As a class, discuss the meaning of these symbols. Then, ask volunteers to describe other things that symbolize freedom and summer.

❹ Close Reading

1. Key Ideas and Details Have a student read aloud the passage. **Ask:** What does the old pair of sneakers represent to Douglas? What does the new pair represent?

Possible response: The old pair represents the end of last summer and the knowledge that he couldn't really jump over rivers, trees, and houses. The new pair represents the beginning of another summer and his renewed sense that anything is possible.

2. Craft and Structure Have students focus on the repetition of the words *dead* and *new* in this paragraph. **Ask:** What is being contrasting with the words *dead* and *new*?

Possible response: The old pair of sneakers was dead inside; they no longer offered possibilities to Douglas. The new pair of tennis shoes would start the new summer off by making him feel like he can do anything.

3. Integration of Knowledge and Ideas
Ask: How does the word choice reflect Douglas's determination to get the new shoes?

Possible response: Douglas doesn't feel that he could be successful at anything while wearing last year's pair. The new shoes help him to dream that anything is possible. His strong feelings about not using last year's shoes make him determined to get the new pair.

long time until you pull them back in under the covers again to feel them, like packed snow. The tennis shoes felt like it always feels the first time every year wading in the slow waters of the creek and seeing your feet below, half an inch further downstream, with refraction, than the real part of you above water.

"Dad," said Douglas, "it's hard to explain."

Somehow the people who made tennis shoes knew what boys needed and wanted. They put marshmallows and coiled springs in the soles and they wove the rest out of grasses bleached and fired in the wilderness. Somewhere deep in the soft loam of the shoes the thin hard sinews of the buck deer were hidden. The people that made the shoes must have watched a lot of winds blow the trees and a lot of rivers going down to the lakes. Whatever it was, it was in the shoes, and it was summer.

Douglas tried to get all this in words.

"Yes," said Father, "but what's wrong with last year's sneakers? Why can't you dig *them* out of the closet?"

Well, he felt sorry for boys who lived in California where they wore tennis shoes all year and never knew what it was to get winter off your feet, peel off the iron leather shoes all full of snow and rain and run barefoot for a day and then lace on the first new tennis shoes of the season, which was better than barefoot. The magic was always in the new pair of shoes. The magic might die by the first of September, but now in late June there was still plenty of magic, and shoes like these could jump you over trees and rivers and houses. And if you wanted, they could jump you over fences and sidewalks and dogs.

"Don't you see?" said Douglas. "I just *can't* use last year's pair."

For last year's pair were dead inside. They had been fine when he started them out, last year. But by the end of summer, every year, you always found out, you always knew, you couldn't really jump over rivers and trees and houses in them, and they were dead. But this was a new year, and he felt that this time, with this new pair of shoes, he could do anything, anything at all.

They walked up on the steps to their house. "Save your money," said Dad. "In five or six weeks—"

💬 THINK ALOUD

Vocabulary: Using Context
Direct students' attention to the word *refraction* on this page. Using the following think aloud process, model how to use context to infer the meaning of an unknown word. Say to students:

I'm going to think aloud to show you how I can figure out the meaning of *refraction* from its context.

In this sentence, *refraction* is used to describe how Douglas's feet look in the creek. The narrator describes how his feet below the water appear "half an inch further downstream" compared with "the real part of you above water." Using this description, and my own experience with seeing things under water, I think *refraction* means the bending of light in water that causes a visual distortion.

"Summer'll be over!"

Lights out, with Tom asleep, Douglas lay watching his feet, far away down there at the end of the bed in the moonlight, free of the heavy iron shoes, the big chunks of winter fallen away from them.

"Reason. I've got to think of reasons for the shoes."

Well, as anyone knew, the hills around town were wild with friends putting cows to riot, playing barometer[1] to the atmospheric changes, taking sun, peeling like calendars each day to take more sun. To catch those friends, you must run much faster than foxes or squirrels. As for the town, it steamed with enemies grown irritable with heat, so remembering every winter argument and insult. *Find friends, ditch enemies!* That was the Cream-Sponge Para Litefoot motto. *Does the world run too fast? Want to catch up? Want to be alert, stay alert? Litefoot, then! Litefoot!*

He held his coin bank up and heard the faint small tinkling, the airy weight of money there.

"Reason. I've got to think of reasons for the shoes."

Whatever you want, he thought, you got to make your own way. During the night now, let's find that path through the forest. . . .

Downtown, the store lights went out, one by one. A wind blew in the window. It was like a river going downstream and his feet wanting to go with it.

In his dreams he heard a rabbit running running running in the deep warm grass.

Old Mr. Sanderson moved through his shoe store as the proprietor of a pet shop must move through his shop where are kenneled animals from everywhere in the world, touching each one briefly along the way. Mr. Sanderson brushed his hands over the shoes in the window, and some of them were like cats to him and some were like dogs; he touched each pair with concern, adjusting laces, fixing tongues. Then he stood in the exact center of the carpet and looked around, nodding.

There was a sound of growing thunder.

---

1. **barometer** (bə räm′ ət ər) *n.* device that measures air pressure, to predict weather changes.

❺ Close Reading

1. **Key Ideas and Details** Have a student read aloud the passage. **Ask:** What is Mr. Sanderson doing in this passage?

   Possible response: Mr. Sanderson is checking on the shoes in his shop as if they were alive. He seems to be caring for his shoes with concern and affection as he brushes his hands over them and adjusts the laces and tongues until he is satisfied with how they look.

2. **Craft and Structure** Have students focus on the simile of Mr. Sanderson being the proprietor of a pet shop. **Ask:** What simile about the shoes does the narrator use in this paragraph? Is this comparison successful here?

   Possible response: The narrator compares the shoes to cats and dogs. The comparison is successful because Mr. Sanderson's shoes are like pets to him. He is fond of the shoes, petting and fussing over them.

3. **Integration of Knowledge and Ideas** **Ask:** How are Mr. Sanderson's and Douglas's thoughts about new shoes similar?

   Possible response: Both give new shoes special meanings, elevating them above the status of inanimate objects. They both believe that the shoes can be alive and influence people.

 **FLUENCY**

To help students build fluency, distribute copies of this page to pairs of students. Have partners take turns reading the paragraph that begins "Well, as anyone knew." As each student reads, the other should mark the words with which the reader had difficulty. Collect students' marked-up copies, and review difficult words and passages with them. Look for these potential trouble spots:

- If students have difficulty with *barometer,* prompt them to name a more familiar word with the same ending (*thermometer*).

- If students have difficulty with *atmospheric,* show them how to split the word into its four syllables and then sound out each one.

- If students say *irritate* rather than *irritable,* have them read the sentence twice, placing first one word and then the other in the sentence. Then, ask which word makes more sense. Guide students to see that the adjective form works while the verb form does not.

One moment, the door to Sanderson's Shoe Emporium was empty. The next, Douglas Spaulding stood clumsily there, staring down at his leather shoes as if these heavy things could not be pulled up out of the cement. The thunder had stopped when his shoes stopped. Now, with painful slowness, daring to look only at the money in his cupped hand, Douglas moved out of the bright sunlight of Saturday noon. He made careful stacks of nickels, dimes, and quarters on the counter, like someone playing chess and worried if the next move carried him out into sun or deep into shadow.

"Don't say a word!" said Mr. Sanderson.

Douglas froze.

"First, I know just what you want to buy," said Mr. Sanderson. "Second, I see you every afternoon at my window; you think I don't see? You're wrong. Third, to give it its full name, you want the Royal Crown Cream-Sponge Para Litefoot Tennis Shoes: 'Like Menthol On Your Feet!' Fourth, you want credit."

"No!" cried Douglas, breathing hard, as if he'd run all night in his dreams. "I got something better than credit to offer!" he gasped. "Before I tell, Mr. Sanderson, you got to do me one small favor. Can you remember when was the last time you yourself wore a pair of Litefoot sneakers, sir?"

Mr. Sanderson's face darkened. "Oh, ten, twenty, say, thirty years ago. Why . . . ?"

"Mr. Sanderson, don't you think you owe it to your customers, sir, to at least try the tennis shoes you sell, for just one minute, so you know how they feel? People forget if they don't keep testing things. United Cigar Store man smokes cigars, don't he? Candy-store man samples his own stuff, I should think. So . . ."

"You may have noticed," said the old man, "I'm wearing shoes."

"But not sneakers, sir! How you going to sell sneakers unless you can rave about them and how you going to rave about them unless you know them?"

Mr. Sanderson backed off a little distance from the boy's fever, one hand to his chin. "Well . . ."

VOCABULARY DEVELOPMENT

Word Forms

Expand students' vocabulary by helping them learn related forms of the selection vocabulary words. Focus on the two selection vocabulary words for "The Sound of Summer Running" that have related forms. Give students a blank Word Form Chart (*Professional Development* *Guidebook*, p. 42), with *suspended* and *revelation* in the correct columns. Work with the class, or have students work with a partner, to determine the related forms. The final chart should look like the one shown below.

Noun	Verb	Adjective	Adverb
suspension	suspend	suspended	
revelation	reveal	revealable revealing	revealingly

"Mr. Sanderson," said Douglas, "you sell me something and I'll sell you something just as valuable."

"Is it absolutely necessary to the sale that I put on a pair of the sneakers, boy?" said the old man.

"I sure wish you could, sir!"

The old man sighed. A minute later, seated panting quietly, he laced the tennis shoes to his long narrow feet. They looked detached and alien[2] down there next to the dark cuffs of his business suit. Mr. Sanderson stood up.

"How do they *feel*?" asked the boy.

"How do they feel, he asks; they feel fine." He started to sit down.

"Please!" Douglas held out his hand. "Mr. Sanderson, now could you kind of rock back and forth a little, sponge around, bounce kind of, while I tell you the rest? It's this: I give you my money, you give me the shoes, I owe you a dollar. But, Mr. Sanderson, *but*—soon as I get those shoes on, you know what *happens*?"

"What?"

"Bang! I deliver your packages, pick up packages, bring you coffee, burn your trash, run to the post office, telegraph office, library! You'll see twelve of me in and out, in and out, every minute. Feel those shoes, Mr. Sanderson, *feel* how fast they'd take me? All those springs inside? Feel all the running inside? Feel how they kind of grab hold and can't let you alone and don't like you just *standing* there? Feel how quick I'd be doing the things you'd rather not bother with? You stay in the nice cool store while I'm jumping all around town! But it's not me really, it's the shoes. They're going like mad down alleys, cutting corners, and back! There they go!"

Mr. Sanderson stood amazed with the rush of words. When the words got going the flow carried him; he began to sink deep in the shoes, to flex his toes, limber[3] his arches, test his ankles. He rocked softly, secretly, back and forth in a small breeze from the open door. The tennis shoes silently hushed themselves deep in the carpet, sank as in a jungle grass, in loam and resilient clay. He gave one solemn bounce of his heels in the yeasty dough, in the yielding and welcoming earth. Emotions hurried over his face as if many

---

2. **alien** (āl´ yən) *adj.* foreign; unfamiliar.
3. **limber** (lim´ bər) *v.* loosen up (a muscle or limb); make easy to bend.

⑥ Close Reading

1. **Key Ideas and Details** Read aloud the passage to students. **Ask:** What is Douglas doing in this passage?

   Possible response: He lists the many chores and errands he will be able to do with speed and energy once he is wearing the new sneakers. Mr. Sanderson can remain comfortable in the cool store. He is trying to persuade Mr. Sanderson to let him have the shoes.

2. **Craft and Structure** Have students focus on the author's repetition of exclamation marks at the beginning and end of the passage. Then have students note the repetition of the word *feel* in the middle sentences. **Ask:** What does the author communicate with his repeated use of this punctuation and word choice?

   Possible response: The exclamation marks help the reader understand the excitement in Douglas's words. He begins his appeal with "Bang!" and ends with "There they go!" By repeating the word *feel,* the author shows that Douglas is using an emotional appeal to persuade Mr. Sanderson to give him the shoes.

3. **Integration of Knowledge and Ideas**
   Ask: How is Douglas able to use words? Why is he able to describe his feelings?

   Possible response: Douglas is able to describe the feelings that the shoes will make him and Mr. Sanderson feel, possibly because he knows that Mr. Sanderson will understand how special shoes can be.

⑦ Focus Passage

A Focus Passage is identified with brackets in the Student Edition of this page and the next for students' independent close reading and analysis. A question bank for the passage and possible responses appear at the end of the selection.

🎎 DIFFERENTIATED INSTRUCTION

🇪🇱 Support for English Learners
English learners might have difficulty with the passage that begins "Bang!" because at certain points it breaks grammatical rules and piles on words to convey Douglas's breathless excitement. For instance, "All those springs inside?" is a sentence fragment. Preteach the passage by reading it aloud. Hearing Douglas's words will allow students to understand the rhythm of speech. Invite volunteers to read parts of the passage aloud. This will help students understand the meaning of each thought.

Enrichment for Gifted/Talented Students
Divide gifted and talented readers into groups. Have each group find a way to express, in a medium of their choice, some of the ideas and emotions in the story. Instruct groups to select a particular passage and then identify the ideas they associate with it. For example, what comes to mind when they read how the shoes looked "alien" on Mr. Sanderson? Then, have students interpret the passage by making a collage, sculpture, or drawing or by performing a pantomime.

revelation ▶
(rev´ ə lā´ shən) *n.*
sudden rush of
understanding

colored lights had been switched on and off. His mouth hung slightly open. Slowly he gentled and rocked himself to a halt, and the boy's voice faded and they stood there looking at each other in a tremendous and natural silence.

7 A few people drifted by on the sidewalk outside, in the hot sun.

Still the man and boy stood there, the boy glowing, the man with revelation in his face.

"Boy," said the old man at last, "in five years, how would you like a job selling shoes in this emporium?"

"Gosh, thanks, Mr. Sanderson, but I don't know what I'm going to be yet."

"Anything you want to be, son," said the old man, "you'll be. No one will ever stop you."

The old man walked lightly across the store to the wall of ten thousand boxes, came back with some shoes for the boy, and wrote up a list on some paper while the boy was lacing the shoes on his feet and then standing there, waiting.

The old man held out his list. "A dozen things you got to do for me this afternoon. Finish them, we're even Stephen, and you're fired."

"Thanks, Mr. Sanderson!" Douglas bounded away.

"Stop!" cried the old man.

Douglas pulled up and turned.

Mr. Sanderson leaned forward. "How do they *feel*?"

8 The boy looked down at his feet deep in the rivers, in the fields of wheat, in the wind that already was rushing him out of the town. He looked up at the old man, his eyes burning, his mouth moving, but no sound came out.

"Antelopes?" said the old man, looking from the boy's face to his shoes. "Gazelles?"

The boy thought about it, hesitated, and nodded a quick nod. Almost immediately he vanished. He just spun about

9 with a whisper and went off. The door stood empty. The sound of the tennis shoes faded in the jungle heat.

Mr. Sanderson stood in the sun-blazed door, listening. From a long time ago, when he dreamed as a boy, he remembered the sound. Beautiful creatures leaping under

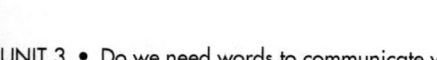

THINK ALOUD

Vocabulary: Using Context
Direct students' attention to the word *vanished* on this page. Using the following think aloud process, model how to use context to infer the meaning of an unknown word. Say to students:

   I'm going to think aloud to show you how I can figure out the meaning of *vanished*

from its context. I know Douglas is standing in the door of the store. The word *vanished* describes something he did.

   If I read further, I see that he "spun about . . . and went off." The next sentence says he wasn't in the door anymore. So, *vanished* must mean he left or disappeared.

the sky, gone through brush, under trees, away, and only the soft echo their running left behind.

"Antelopes," said Mr. Sanderson. "Gazelles."

He bent to pick up the boy's abandoned winter shoes, heavy with forgotten rains and long-melted snows. Moving out of the blazing sun, walking softly, lightly, slowly, he headed back toward civilization. . . .

ABOUT THE AUTHOR

Ray Bradbury (1920–2012)

As a boy, Ray Bradbury nourished his imagination by attending circuses, watching magicians, and reading science fiction. He once stated, "My life filled up with these wonderful events and people and images, and they stirred my imagination so that by the time I was twelve, I decided to become a writer. Just like that."

Bradbury began publishing short stories in magazines in 1940. His best-known works are the short story collections *The Martian Chronicles* (1950), *The Illustrated Man* (1951), and *The Golden Apples of the Sun* (1953) and the novels *Fahrenheit 451* (1953), *Dandelion Wine* (1957), and *Something Wicked This Way Comes* (1962). Bradbury's stories and novels are known for their sharp social criticism and warnings about human reliance on technology.

❾ Close Reading

1. **Key Ideas and Details** Read aloud the passage to students. **Ask:** What happens in this passage?

   Possible response: Mr. Sanderson suggests that Douglas feels like an antelope or gazelle running because of the shoes. Douglas runs off.

2. **Craft and Structure** Have students focus on how words such as *antelopes* and *gazelles* are used as metaphors for how Douglas feels in his new shoes. **Ask:** What does this imagery bring to mind?

   Possible response: This language makes readers envision beautiful, fast, wild creatures running and exploring in the wilderness.

3. **Integration of Knowledge and Ideas**
   Ask: How do the spoken words influence Douglas and Mr. Sanderson?

   Possible response: The suggestions of *antelopes* and *gazelles* allow the characters to imagine themselves in the heat of the jungle. The images remind Mr. Sanderson being young and free during summer days long ago.

🎭 DIFFERENTIATED INSTRUCTION

Strategy for Special-Needs Students
Students may have trouble identifying what is real and what Douglas and Mr. Sanderson dream or imagine. Have students create two-column charts, one column labeled "Reality" and the other labeled "Dream." Ask students to reread the last two pages and fill in the chart with examples of actions that actually happened and events that Douglas and Mr. Sanderson imagine. Then, ask students to write two sentences that summarize what was real and what was imaginary.

EL Strategy for English Learners
English learners may have difficulty with the idiom *even Stephen* on p. 416. Explain that this phrase means that someone has repaid a debt. Ask students to locate any other idioms or phrases that they have difficulty understanding.

Close Reading Activities

READ

Comprehension

1. **Possible response:** Douglas wants new tennis shoes because his old ones are "dead" and new shoes have a special meaning for him.

2. His father thinks Douglas can wear last year's tennis shoes.

3. Douglas convinces Mr. Sanderson to give him the shoes in exchange for some money and an afternoon's worth of running errands.

Research: Clarify Details

Students should explain how research findings helped them understand an unfamiliar detail in the text.

Summarize

Students' summaries should describe Douglas's longing for the new tennis shoes, his father's response, and how Douglas gets the shoes.

Language Study

Possible responses:

• *seized*: verb
I *seized* my brother by the hand and dragged him away from the railroad tracks.

• *suspended*: verb
Time was *suspended* when I saw the train roaring down the tracks toward me.

• *revelation*: noun
After the *revelation* that the main character was lying, I quickly guessed the ending of the book.

Literary Analysis

Possible responses appear below. Check to be sure students support their responses with evidence from the text.

1. The "rush of words" is Douglas trying to persuade Mr. Sanderson to give him the new sneakers.

2. Mr. Sanderson rocks back and forth in the sneakers as he recalls how he felt about new shoes as a youth.

READ

Comprehension

Reread all or part of the text to help you answer the following questions.

1. What does Douglas want, and why?
2. Why does Douglas's father refuse to get him what he wants?
3. How does Douglas acquire what he wants?

Language Study

Selection Vocabulary Write the part of speech of each boldfaced word. Then, use each word in a sentence.

• He glanced quickly away, but his ankles were **seized** …

Literary Analysis

Reread the identified passage. Then, respond to the questions that follow.

> **Focus Passage** *(pp. 415–416)*
> Mr. Sanderson stood amazed … the man with revelation in his face.

Key Ideas and Details

1. What is the "rush of words" Mr. Sanderson hears?
2. What does Mr. Sanderson do as he listens?

Symbols

A **symbol** is an object or idea that represents something other than itself. For example, an owl can be a symbol of wisdom. Reread the passage and take notes on the author's use of symbols.

Research: Clarify Details This story may include details that are unfamiliar to you. Choose one unfamiliar detail, and briefly research it. Then, explain your research clarifies the story.

Summarize Write an objective summary of the story. Do not include your opinions.

• … his feet **suspended**, then rushed.

• Still the man and boy stood there, the boy glowing, the man with **revelation** in his face.

Craft and Structure

3. **(a)** What sensory images does Bradbury use to describe how the shoes feel to Mr. Sanderson? **(b) Connect:** To what senses do these images appeal? **(c) Interpret:** What ideas do the images convey?

Integration of Knowledge and Ideas

4. **Draw Conclusions:** What "revelation" comes to Mr. Sanderson after he tries on the shoes?

1. What do the tennis shoes **symbolize** for Douglas? Use details in the story to support your interpretation.

2. What do the tennis shoes come to symbolize for Mr. Sanderson? Support your response.

---

3. **(a)** The author describes how the shoes feel like they are sinking *in a jungle grass, in loam and resilient clay*. **(b)** These images appeal to the sense of touch. **(c)** The images make it appear that Mr. Sanderson is in a jungle instead of in a store.

4. Mr. Sanderson realizes that new shoes feel like summer and speed to Douglas, and he realizes that he has forgotten how good it feels to run outdoors.

Symbols

1. To Douglas, they represent the feeling of running in the grass in summer or dipping his feet in a stream and other moments when everything is new and fresh.

2. To Mr. Sanderson, they represent youth and energy. They make him feel like he sinks into "jungle grass," like an antelope or a gazelle.

The Sound of Summer Running
from Dandelion Wine
Ray Bradbury

DISCUSS • RESEARCH • WRITE

From Text to Topic **Group Discussion**

Discuss the following passage with a group of classmates. Take notes during the discussion. Contribute your own ideas, and support them with examples from the text.

> He held the coin bank up and heard the faint small tinkling, the airy weight of money there ...
> Whatever you want, he thought, you got to make your own way. During the night now, let's find that path through the forest ... Downtown, the store lights went out, one by one. A wind blew in the window. It was like a river going downstream and his feet wanting to go with it.

Research **Investigate the Topic**

Financial Skills Douglas's father teaches him that if you are determined to have something that costs money, you must earn the money to buy it.

Assignment

Conduct research to find out how young people can learn financial, or money-related, skills. Consult the Web sites of state treasurers' offices, as well as financial magazines and books. Take clear notes and carefully identify your sources so that you can easily access the information later. Share your findings in a **presentation** for the class. Explain how determination can help a person learn and use financial skills.

Writing to Sources **Reflective Essay**

"The Sound of Summer Running" vividly describes how an item of clothing has a symbolic meaning for the main character.

Assignment

Write a **reflective essay** in which you describe an object that has a symbolic meaning for you and explain what makes the object special.
- Begin by introducing an item that has a symbolic meaning for you.
- In the body of your essay, explain how the item developed its meaning. Use vivid imagery to tell your story.
- Provide a conclusion in which you make connections between your symbolic object and Douglas's shoes.

QUESTIONS FOR DISCUSSION

1. Why does Douglas think that "you got to make your own way"?
2. How does the wind **influence** Douglas's determination?

PREPARATION FOR ESSAY

You may use the knowledge you gain during this research assignment to support your claims in an essay at the end of this section.

ACADEMIC VOCABULARY

Academic terms appear in blue on these pages. If these words are not familiar to you, use a dictionary to find their definitions. Then, use them as you speak and write about the text.

 **Common Core State Standards**

RL.6.1, RL.6.2, RL.6.3, RL.6.4, RL.6.5; W.6.3, W.6.4, W.6.5, W.6.7, W.6.8; SL.6.1, SL.6.4; L.6.1
[For full standards wording, see the chart in the front of this book.]

DISCUSS • RESEARCH • WRITE

From Text to Topic: Group Discussion

1. Douglas's father taught him that if he wants something, he has to find a way to make it happen.
2. It strengthens his determination and makes him feel like "his feet [are] wanting to go with it," so he has to find a way to get the shoes.

Research: Investigate the Topic

Introduce the assignment using the instruction on the student page.

1. Arrange for students to visit your school's library or computer lab. Review strategies for identifying reliable sources.
2. Demonstrate to students how to locate Web sites for state treasurer's offices, including the one in their state. Remind students that these Web sites are run by the government, and therefore end in .gov.
3. Encourage students to take clear notes and consult a variety of sources. Suggest that they paraphrase and summarize information by restating it in their own words. When they directly quote from a source, emphasize that they need to give proper credit and place the quote within quotation marks. Recommend that students identify each source they reference in a Works Cited list.
4. Suggest that students practice their presentations prior to sharing them with the class. As they rehearse, ask students to anticipate potential questions from the audience.

Academic Vocabulary

If students struggle with defining the academic vocabulary words, use this routine:

Write the words and definitions on the board.

symbolize: to represent by a symbol

influence: have a power or effect on something

Have students say each word aloud and then use the word in a sentence. Sample sentences should demonstrate that the words can be used across disciplines.

Writing to Sources: Reflective Essay

Students' reflective essays should follow the steps listed to describe something that has a symbolic meaning for them and to vividly explain the symbolic meaning using adjectives and adverbs correctly. Remind students to connect their experience to that of Douglas and his new shoes.

 Online Writer's Notebook

Students can use the Online Writer's Notebook to record all responses.

MULTIDRAFT READING

Essential Understanding

First, students should read the entire selection on their own. Then, to assist struggling readers and to deepen comprehension for all, you may wish to guide them through the selection by asking them the close reading questions provided in the margins. Have students apply the multidraft reading protocols as they examine specific "chunks" of text related to these questions. For each reading, have students set the purpose indicated:

- **First reading:** Students should read the selection independently and think about its basic meaning.
- **Second reading:** Students should analyze the text's key ideas and details and its craft and structure.
- **Third reading:** Students should integrate knowledge and ideas; connect to the Big Question, other texts, and the world; and use teacher-led Close Reading discussion questions to examine particularly rich and significant passages.

For more guidance, refer to the *Classroom Strategies and Teaching Routines* card on multidraft reading.

Vocabulary

If students require support with selection vocabulary, use this routine:

1. Write the following words and definitions on the board:

   felicity *n.* ability to find appropriate expression for one's thoughts

   explicit *adj.* clear; definite

   procure *v.* get or obtain by some effort

2. Have students say each word aloud.

3. Use the word in a sentence that defines the word.

❶ Focus Passage

A Focus Passage is identified with brackets in the Student Edition of the next page for students' independent close reading and analysis. A question bank for the passage and possible responses appear at the end of the selection.

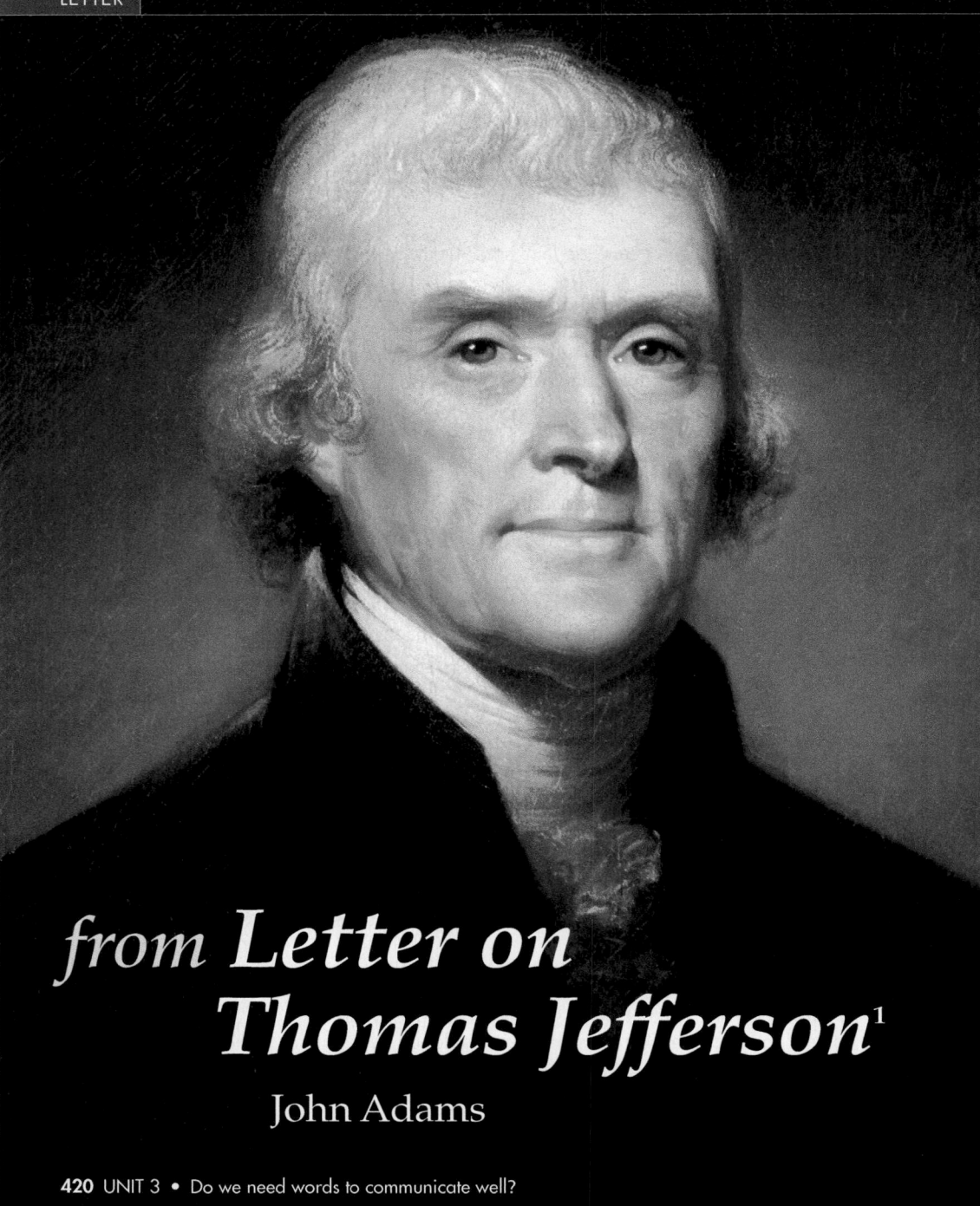

from Letter on Thomas Jefferson[1]

John Adams

420 UNIT 3 • Do we need words to communicate well?

ⓒ TEXT COMPLEXITY **RUBRIC**

from **Letter on Thomas Jefferson**		
Qualitative Measures	**Context/Knowledge Demands**	U.S history; basic knowledge that Thomas Jefferson drafted the Declaration of Independence 1 2 3 4 ⑤
	Structure/Language Conventionality and Clarity	Formal tone; direct quotations; difficult vocabulary 1 2 3 ④ 5
	Levels of Meaning/ Purpose/Concept Level	Challenging concept (writing of the Declaration of Independence) 1 2 3 ④ 5
Quantitative Measures	**Text Length**	Word Count: 261
	Lexile	700L

Mr. Jefferson came into Congress, in June, 1775, and brought with him a reputation for literature, science, and a happy talent of composition. Writings of his were handed about, remarkable for the peculiar felicity of expression. Though a silent member in Congress, he was so prompt, frank, explicit, and decisive upon committees and in conversation, not even Samuel **1** Adams was more so, that he soon seized upon my heart; and upon this occasion I gave him my vote, and did all in my power to procure the votes of others. I think he had one more vote than any other, and that placed him at the head of the committee. I had the next highest number, and that placed me second. The committee met, discussed the subject, and then appointed Mr. Jefferson and me to make the draft, I suppose because we were the two first on the list.

The sub-committee met. Jefferson proposed to me to make the draught. I said, "I will not."

"You should do it."

"Oh! no."

2 "Why will you not? You ought to do it."

"I will not."

"Why?"

"Reasons enough."

"What can be your reasons?"

"Reason first—You are a Virginian, and a Virginian ought to appear at the head of this business. Reason second—I am obnoxious, suspected, and unpopular. You are much otherwise. Reason third—You can write **3** ten times better than I can."

"Well," said Jefferson, "if you are decided, I will do as well as I can."

"Very well. When you have drawn it up, we will have a meeting."

---

1. **Letter on Thomas Jefferson** John Adams wrote this letter in 1822 telling what happened when a committee appointed him and Thomas Jefferson to write a "Declaration of Independence."

◄ **felicity**
(fə lis′i tē) *n.* ability to find appropriate expression for one's thoughts

◄ **explicit**
(eks plis′it) *adj.* clear; definite

◄ **procure**
(prō kyoor′) *v.* get or obtain by some effort

ABOUT THE AUTHOR

John Adams
(1735–1826)

John Adams was born in the Massachusetts Bay Colony and attended Harvard University, where he studied law. He was among the men who supported independence from Great Britain for the United States. Adams was a diplomat in France and Holland during the Revolutionary War. He served as George Washington's vice president for two terms and was then elected the new nation's second president.

2 Close Reading

1. Key Ideas and Details
Ask: What did Jefferson ask Adams to do? How did Adams respond?

Possible response: Jefferson asked Adams to draft the Constitution, and Adams responded, "I will not."

2. Craft and Structure
Ask: What do you notice about the length of the sentences and the style of the argument?

Possible response: The sentences are short, and the argument bounces back and forth as Jefferson repeatedly asks Adams to write the draft and Adams repeatedly answers no.

3. Integration of Knowledge and Ideas
Ask: What do the short sentences and lack of reasons show about the argument?

Possible response: The short sentences and lack of reasons show that each man is determined to have his way and does not want to bother with reasons.

3 Big Question: Toward Essential Understanding

1. **Ask:** In this passage, what was different in Adams's response to Jefferson?

Possible response: This time he offered three logical responses.

2. **Ask:** How are words shown to be important in communicating? What may Adams have left unstated but implied in Jefferson's quick agreement?

Possible response: By using words, Adams was able to provide reasons to persuade Jefferson. Adams may have left unstated that Jefferson wanted to be persuaded to use his writing ability to draft this important document.

◄))) Audio

Selection Audio is available in the *Student eText* and on the *Hear It!* CD-ROM.

© TEXT COMPLEXITY **READER AND TASK SUGGESTIONS**

from **Letter on Thomas Jefferson**

Preparing to Read the Text	Leveled Tasks
• Discuss what students know about the writing of the Declaration of Independence. • Explain that John Adams later became the second President and Thomas Jefferson the third President. • Guide students to use Multidraft Reading strategies on the previous page.	*Knowledge Demands* If students will have difficulty understanding the context in which this letter was written, have them read and take notes about why Jefferson was chosen to head the committee. Have them identify the speakers in each line of dialogue. *Analyzing* If students will not have difficulty understanding the context, then ask them to read and explain why Jefferson was the best choice to write the Declaration of Independence.

READ

Comprehension

1. John Adams explains why Jefferson wrote the first draft of the Declaration of Independence.

2. Adams describes Jefferson as an agreeable, popular, educated man who expresses himself very well.

3. Adams describes himself as "obnoxious, suspected, and unpopular."

Research: Clarify Details

Students should explain how their research helped them understand an unfamiliar detail in the letter.

Summarize

Students' summaries should explain how Adams and Jefferson came to be on the subcommittee and how they decided Jefferson would draft the Declaration of Independence.

Language Study

Possible responses:

- *felicity*: ability to find appropriate expression for one's thoughts; The author had many fans who enjoyed her *felicity* with words in her writing.

- *explicit*: clearly expressed; My teacher was *explicit* about the materials we should use in our projects.

- *procure*: to get or obtain by some effort; I managed to *procure* a rare comic book for her birthday.

Literary Analysis

Possible responses appear below. Check to be sure students support their responses with evidence from the text.

1. **(a)** Jefferson won by one vote. **(b)** Adams voted for Jefferson. **(c)** Adams is showing that he is responsible for Jefferson being appointed head of the committee.

2. **(a)** Adams uses words and phrases that show his admiration, such as "prompt, frank, explicit, and decisive upon committees and in conversation." **(b)** The descriptions convey that Jefferson

Close Reading Activities

READ

Comprehension

Reread all or part of the text to help you answer the following questions.

1. What does John Adams explain in this letter?

2. How does Adams view Jefferson?

3. How does Adams describe himself?

Language Study

Selection Vocabulary Define each boldfaced word, and use the word in a sentence of your own.

- Writings of his were handed about, remarkable for the peculiar **felicity** of expression.

Literary Analysis

Reread the identified passage. Then, respond to the questions that follow.

> **Focus Passage** *(p. 421)*
> Mr. Jefferson came into Congress … the two first on the list.

Key Ideas and Details

1. **(a)** By how many votes was Jefferson elected to head the committee? **(b)** For whom did Adams vote? **(c) Analyze:** Why does Adams reveal this?

Central Idea

The **central idea** is the key point in a work of nonfiction. Reread the letter, and take notes on how Adams expresses a central idea.

Research: Clarify Details This letter may include references that are unfamiliar to you. Choose one unfamiliar detail, briefly research it, and then explain how your research **clarifies** the letter.

Summarize Write an objective summary of the letter. Do not include your opinions.

- Though a silent member in Congress, he was so prompt, frank, **explicit**, and decisive …

- … and upon this occasion I gave him my vote, and did all in my power to **procure** the votes of others.

Craft and Structure

2. **(a)** What words and phrases does Adams use to describe Jefferson? **(b) Analyze:** What information about Jefferson do these descriptions convey? **(c) Evaluate:** What do you learn about Adams, based on his use of descriptive language?

Integration of Knowledge and Ideas

3. **Make a Judgment:** Based on this passage, do you think Adams and Jefferson were good choices to be co-authors of the Declaration of Independence? Support your answer.

1. What is the letter's central idea?

2. **Determination** How does the central idea show Adams's determination?

was hard-working, honest, and determined. **(c)** Adams himself was also at ease with words.

3. Yes, both men were leaders in Congress and skilled in written expression.

Central Idea

1. Adams persuaded Jefferson to write the first draft of the Declaration of Independence.

2. Adams worked to get Jefferson on the committee. When he and Jefferson were chosen,

he asked Jefferson to write the draft and gave reasons why he should. Adams was determined that Jefferson should write the draft and Adams repeatedly refused to write it.

from Letter on Thomas Jefferson

DISCUSS • RESEARCH • WRITE

From Text to Topic **Group Discussion**

Discuss the following passage with a small group of classmates. When it is your turn to speak, respond to the previous speaker and then add your own ideas. Support your ideas with examples from the text.

> I said, "I will not.… You can write ten times better than I can." (p. 421)

Research **Investigate the Topic**

Determination and the Declaration of Independence In some cases, it can take time and determination for a group to reach a consensus, or agreement.

Assignment

Conduct research to learn about the process that the Continental Congress followed in order to write and approve the Declaration of Independence. Consult government sources and first-hand accounts. Share your findings in an **informal speech** to the class. Explain why the Continental Congress needed determination to get the job done.

Writing to Sources **Argument**

In this letter, John Adams compares himself to Thomas Jefferson as he tries to convince Jefferson to draft the Declaration of Independence.

Assignment

Write a **comparison-and-contrast essay** in which you analyze John Adams and Thomas Jefferson. Follow these steps:

- As you reread Adams's letter, record details about each man in a chart or Venn diagram.
- Organize your essay in a way that clearly shows similarities and differences.
- Use transitional words and phrases, such as *similarly* and *on the other hand* to show comparisons and contrasts.
- Correct errors in grammar, spelling, and punctuation.

QUESTIONS FOR DISCUSSION

1. Do you think Adams's version of the conversation matches what was really said? Why or why not?
2. How does Adams' version of the conversation characterize Adams himself?

PREPARATION FOR ESSAY

You may use the knowledge you gain during this research assignment to support your claims in an essay at the end of this section.

ACADEMIC VOCABULARY

Academic terms appear in blue on these pages. If these words are not familiar to you, use a dictionary to find their definitions. Then, use them as you speak and write about the text.

 **Common Core State Standards**

RI.6.1, RI.6.2, RI.6.3, RI.6.5, RI.6.6; W.6.1, W.6.2, W.6.4, W.6.5, W.6.7, W.6.8, W.6.9; SL.6.1, SL.6.4.
[For full standards wording, see the chart in the front of this book.]

DISCUSS • RESEARCH • WRITE

From Text to Topic: Group Discussion

Possible responses:

1. The letter was written more than 40 years after the events it describes. Adams may have forgotten the exact conversation, removed Jefferson's counterarguments, and/or edited the conversation for effect.
2. Adams makes himself appear generous and modest.

Research: Investigate the Topic

Introduce the assignment using the instruction on the student page.

1. Arrange for students to visit your school's library to use reference sources or American history Web sites.
2. Remind students to take notes on main ideas they find in each source. They can quote directly or summarize in their own words.
3. Encourage students to draw conclusions and make connections between multiple sources. Suggest that they prepare an outline for their presentation and create a Works Cited list.
4. Advise students to practice so that they do not need to read directly from their outlines and are prepared to answer any questions.

Academic Vocabulary

If students struggle with defining the academic vocabulary words, use this routine:

Write the words and definitions on the board.

clarifies: to make easier to understand

evaluate: to find the importance or value

contrast: difference

Have students say each word aloud and then use the word in a sentence. Sample sentences should demonstrate that the words can be used across disciplines.

Writing to Sources: Argument

Students' comparison-and-contrast essays should follow the steps listed and use text evidence to explain what similarities and differences they have learned about Adams and Jefferson.

 Online Writer's Notebook

Students can use the Online Writer's Notebook to record all responses.

MULTIDRAFT READING

Essential Understanding

First, students should read the entire selection on their own. Then, to assist struggling readers and to deepen comprehension for all, you may wish to guide them through the selection by asking them the close reading questions provided in the margins. Have students apply the multidraft reading protocols as they examine specific "chunks" of text related to these questions. For each reading, have students set the purpose indicated:

- **First reading:** Students should read the selection independently and think about its basic meaning.
- **Second reading:** Students should analyze the text's key ideas and details and its craft and structure.
- **Third reading:** Students should integrate knowledge and ideas; connect to the Big Question, other texts, and the world; and use teacher-led Close Reading discussion questions to examine particularly rich and significant passages.

For more guidance, refer to the **Classroom Strategies and Teaching Routines** card on multidraft reading.

❶ Background

If you wish, share this information about Helen Keller's life. She was born in Alabama in 1880. For the first year and a half of her life, she could see and hear. Then she became ill and lost both sight and hearing. Her temper outbursts were upsetting to her family until Anne Sullivan came to teach Keller when she was 7 years old. Mis Sullivan taught Keller how to communicate using sign language. Keller later went on to college, lectured and wrote books to share her experiences, and became a leading educator and humanitarian.

Vocabulary

If students require support with selection vocabulary, use this routine:

1. Write the following words and definitions on the board:
   imitate *v.* copy; mimic.
   persisted *v.* refused to give up
   barriers *n.* things that make progress difficult; obstacles
2. Have students say each word aloud.
3. Use the word in a sentence that defines the word.

AUTOBIOGRAPHY

Water
Helen Keller

Helen Keller as a young girl.

424 UNIT 3 • Do we need words to communicate well?

Ⓒ TEXT COMPLEXITY **RUBRIC**

Water		
Qualitative Measures	Context/Knowledge Demands	Late 19th century; life of Helen Keller 1 ② 3 4 5
	Structure/Language Conventionality and Clarity	Informal; lively; some challenging vocabulary 1 ② 3 4 5
	Levels of Meaning/ Purpose/Concept Level	Accessible concept (learning from adversity) 1 2 ③ 4 5
Quantitative Measures	Text Length	Word Count: 731
	Lexile	910L

The morning after my teacher came she led me into her room and gave me a doll. The little blind children at the Perkins Institution had sent it and Laura Bridgman had dressed it; but I did not know this until afterward.

When I had played with it a little while, Miss Sullivan slowly spelled into my hand the word "d-o-l-l." I was at once interested in this finger play and tried to imitate it. When I finally succeeded in making the letters correctly I was flushed with childish pleasure and pride. Running downstairs to my mother I held up my hand and made the letters for doll. I did not know that I was spelling a word or even that words existed; I was simply making my fingers go in monkey-like imitation. In the days that followed I learned to spell in this uncomprehending way a great many words, among them *pin, hat, cup* and a few verbs like *sit, stand* and *walk.* But my teacher had been with me several weeks before I understood that everything has a name.

One day, while I was playing with my new doll, Miss Sullivan put my big rag doll into my lap also, spelled "d-o-l-l" and tried to make me understand that "d-o-l-l" applied to both. Earlier in the day we had had a tussle over the words "m-u-g" and "w-a-t-e-r." Miss Sullivan had tried to impress it upon me that "m-u-g" is *mug* and that "w-a-t-e-r" is *water,* but I persisted in confounding the two. In despair she had dropped the subject for the time, only to renew it at the first opportunity. I became impatient at her repeated attempts and, seizing the new doll, I dashed it upon the floor. I was keenly delighted when I felt the

◄ **imitate**
(im′ i tāt′) *v.*
copy; mimic

But my teacher had been with me several weeks before I understood that everything has a name.

◄ **persisted**
(pər sist′ əd) *v.*
refused to give up

❷ Close Reading

1. **Key Ideas and Details** Read aloud the passage to students. **Ask:** What is Miss Sullivan trying to achieve in this passage?

   Possible response: Miss Sullivan is determined to teach Keller that words are names that stand for objects.

2. **Craft and Structure** Have students reread the passage looking for word repetition, alliteration, and word choice. **Ask:** What does the repetition of *tried to* emphasize? What is the effect of the alliteration of *d* in *despair* and *dropped*?

   Possible response: The repetition of *tried to* emphasizes Miss Sullivan's determination. The alliteration with *d* calls attention to her frustration in not being able to communicate the concept that words stand for objects, such as *mug* and *water.*

3. **Integration of Knowledge and Ideas**
   Ask: How do the author's stylistic choices reveal the determination of Miss Sullivan and the tension between her and Keller?

   Possible response: The author uses words, such as *tussle, persisted,* and *renew* to show the continued tension between the teacher and student. Miss Sullivan keeps trying, and although she may drop an effort temporarily, she renews it as soon as possible. Keller is frustrated and the result is a series of struggles between them.

©TEXT COMPLEXITY **READER AND TASK SUGGESTIONS**

Water

Preparing to Read the Text	Leveled Tasks
• Use the background note on the previous page to discuss Helen Keller's background and life achievements. • Discuss what difficulties a person who is deaf and blind would face. • Guide students to use Multidraft Reading strategies on the previous page.	*Knowledge Demands* If students will have difficulty with the vocabulary and sentence structure in this autobiography, have them reread one page at a time and note sentences that they have trouble understanding. Then, discuss with them the sentences and their meanings. *Analylzing* If students will not have difficulty understanding the vocabulary and sentence structure, then ask them to read and note examples of sentences with vivid descriptions. Have them look up unfamiliar vocabulary in a dictionary and share the meanings with other students.

 **Audio**

Selection Audio is available in the *Student eText* and on the *Hear It!* CD-ROM.

❸ Close Reading

1. Key Ideas and Details Read aloud the passage to students. **Ask:** What does Keller do in this passage?

Possible response: Keller smashes her doll in frustration.

2. Craft and Structure Ask students to reread the passage and note the words that describe Keller actions and those that describe her feelings. **Ask:** What action verbs does Keller use to describe what she did? What are the emotions she feels in this passage?

Possible response: Keller uses the verbs *seized* and *dashed* to describe her destruction of the doll. In the passage, she first feels impatient, then feels keenly delighted, then has a sense of satisfaction, and finally she feels pleasure.

3. Integration of Knowledge and Ideas
Ask: What does Keller's description of her actions and feelings reveal about her way of dealing with the "still, dark world" in which she lives?

Possible response: Keller moves from one emotion to another in response to what she feels physically. She reacts emotionally to the world of sensation. She feels satisfaction when her feet feel the fragments of the doll she has destroyed, and pleasure at the anticipation of being out in the warm sunshine.

❹ Focus Passage

A Focus Passage is identified with brackets in the Student Edition of this page and the next for students' independent close reading and analysis. A question bank for the passage and possible responses appear at the end of the selection.

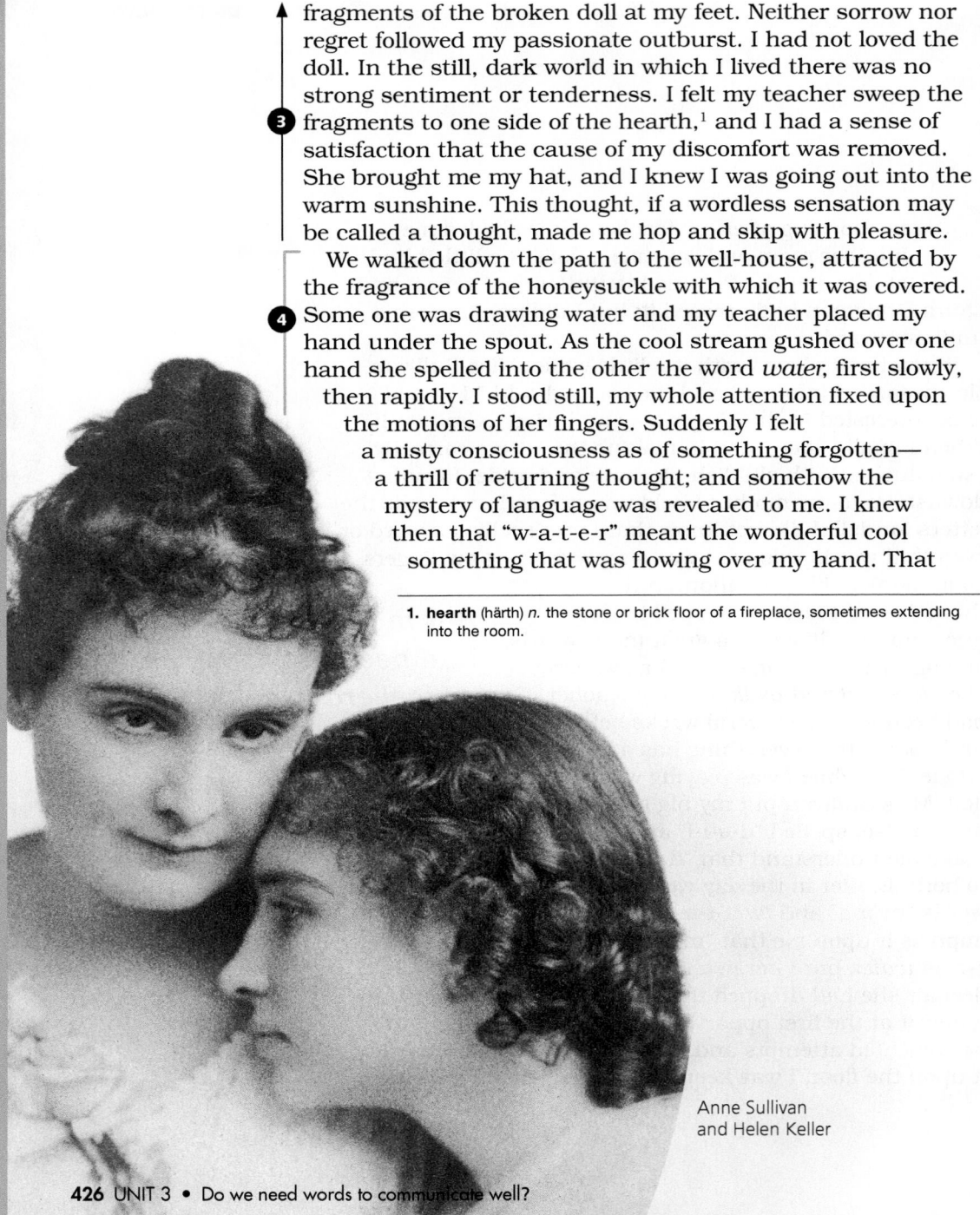

Anne Sullivan and Helen Keller

❸ fragments of the broken doll at my feet. Neither sorrow nor regret followed my passionate outburst. I had not loved the doll. In the still, dark world in which I lived there was no strong sentiment or tenderness. I felt my teacher sweep the fragments to one side of the hearth,[1] and I had a sense of satisfaction that the cause of my discomfort was removed. She brought me my hat, and I knew I was going out into the warm sunshine. This thought, if a wordless sensation may be called a thought, made me hop and skip with pleasure.

❹ We walked down the path to the well-house, attracted by the fragrance of the honeysuckle with which it was covered. Some one was drawing water and my teacher placed my hand under the spout. As the cool stream gushed over one hand she spelled into the other the word *water*, first slowly, then rapidly. I stood still, my whole attention fixed upon the motions of her fingers. Suddenly I felt a misty consciousness as of something forgotten— a thrill of returning thought; and somehow the mystery of language was revealed to me. I knew then that "w-a-t-e-r" meant the wonderful cool something that was flowing over my hand. That

---

1. hearth (härth) *n.* the stone or brick floor of a fireplace, sometimes extending into the room.

426 UNIT 3 • Do we need words to communicate well?

🗨 THINK ALOUD

Vocabulary: Using Context
Direct students' attention to the word *well-house* on this page. Using a think-aloud process, model how to use context to infer the meaning of an unknown word. Say to students:

I'm going to think aloud to show you how I would figure out the meaning of *well-house* from its context.

In this sentence, *well-house* is used to describe a place for getting water. Since I know that a *well* is a hole in the ground from which people can get water and a *house* is a shelter, I can use these clues to figure out that a *well-house* is a shed or small house built around a well.

living word awakened my soul, gave it light, hope, joy, set it free! There were barriers still, it is true, but barriers that could in time be swept away.

I left the well-house eager to learn. Everything had a name, and each name gave birth to a new thought. As we returned to the house every object which I touched seemed to quiver with life. That was because I saw everything with the strange, new sight that had come to me. On entering the door I remembered the doll I had broken. I felt my way to the hearth and picked up the pieces. I tried vainly to put them together. Then my eyes filled with tears; for I realized what I had done, and for the first time I felt repentance and sorrow.

I learned a great many new words that day. I do not remember what they all were; but I do know that *mother, father, sister, teacher* were among them—words that were to make the world blossom for me, "like Aaron's rod, with flowers." It would have been difficult to find a happier child than I was as I lay in my crib at the close of that eventful day and lived over the joys it had brought me, and for the first time longed for a new day to come.

◀ **barriers**
(bar' ē ərz) *n.* things that make progress difficult; obstacles

ABOUT THE AUTHOR

Helen Keller (1880–1968)

A serious illness left Helen Keller blind and deaf before she was two years old. When Keller was nearly seven, her family hired Anne Sullivan, a teacher from the Perkins Institute for the Blind, to help her learn to communicate. In this excerpt from her autobiography, Keller describes her early lessons with Sullivan. Eventually, Keller learned to read by using Braille (raised dots that stand for letters), to type, and to speak. Keller and Sullivan developed a remarkable teacher and student relationship as well as a unique friendship.

PART 3 • Water **427**

---

5 ❓ **Big Question: Toward Essential Understanding**

1. Have a student read aloud the passage. **Ask:** What is Keller's attitude when she returns to the house?

   Possible response: She is eager to learn because every object now has a name and therefore new meaning and life.

2. Have students reread the passage and compare and contrast Keller's life before and after she learned words. **Ask:** Why is it important for Keller to learn language?

   Possible response: Language puts her in touch with others, with the world, and with herself. Without language she did not care about what she did or how she acted.

6 **Close Reading**

1. **Key Ideas and Details** Have students read the passage aloud. **Ask:** What words does Keller remember learning that day? Why do you think these might have special meaning for her?

   Possible response: She learned the meaning of *mother, father, sister,* and *teacher.* These are the people who love and care for her; they are the most important people in her life.

2. **Craft and Structure** Ask students to reread the passage, looking for figurative language. **Ask:** To what does she compare words?

   Possible response: She compares words to flowers opening up in blossom.

3. **Integration of Knowledge and Ideas**
   Ask: How does Keller's view of life change based on her new knowledge of words?

   Possible response: Keller is full of joy as she thinks about the world full of words that are waiting for her to learn. The world is filled with beauty for her now that she can learn and communicate with words.

👥 DIFFERENTIATED INSTRUCTION

Strategy for Less Proficient Readers
Sentences that start with independent clauses, such as the one beginning "As the cool stream gushed" (p. 426), may interfere with students' understanding. Have students analyze such sentences by first finding and reading aloud the independent clause, and then identifying the subject. Finally, have them identify the dependent clause.

EL Strategy for English Learners
Since some words in this selection are not common in contemporary speech, you may want to preteach them by providing definitions and sentence contexts for English learners. For example, **uncomprehending:** not understanding. The student looked at her teacher in an *uncomprehending* way. **confounding:** confusing. These two words keep *confounding* me because they look and sound so similar.

Other words you may want to preteach include *tussle, discomfort, consciousness,* and *repentance.*

Close Reading Activities

READ

Comprehension

1. Miss Sullivan teaches Keller how to spell the word *doll*.

2. Keller becomes frustrated when Mis Sullivan keeps trying to teach her the word *doll*. She was already frustrated because she mixed up *mug* and *water*.

3. Miss Sullivan puts Keller's hand under running water while spelling the word *water* into her other hand.

Research: Clarify Details

Students should explain how their research findings helped them understand an unfamiliar reference in the text.

Summarize

Students' summaries should describe the frustrations that Miss Sullivan and Keller experienced, how Helen finally came to understand the meaning of the word *water*, and what Keller's new understanding of language meant to her.

Language Study
Possible responses:

• *imitate*: copy; mimic
• *persisted*: persevered
• *barriers*: obstacles

Literary Analysis

Possible responses appear below. Check to be sure students support their responses with evidence from the text.

1. **(a)** Feeling the water on one hand and the spelling of the letters in her other hand at the same time. **(b)** Water from the pump streams freely over Keller's hand, but water in a mug would be contained.

2. **(a)** The fragrance of the honeysuckle appeals to the sense of smell. The cool water on Keller's hand and the motions of Miss Sullivan's fingers appeals to the sense of touch. **(b)** She experiences the world around her through her sense of touch and smell.

3. She will have a new enthusiasm for life, and she may learn to

READ

Comprehension

Reread all or part of the text to help you answer the following questions.

1. What does Miss Sullivan do after giving Keller the doll?

2. Why does Keller break the new doll?

3. How does Keller learn what the word *water* means?

Language Study

Selection Vocabulary Name a synonym for each boldfaced word from the selection. Consult a thesaurus if necessary.

• I was at once interested in this finger play and tried to **imitate** it.

Literary Analysis

Reread the identified passage. Then, respond to the questions that follow.

> **Focus Passage** *(pp. 426–427)*
> We walked down the path… barriers that could in time be swept away.

Key Ideas and Details

1. **(a)** What event helps Keller recognize the meaning of *w-a-t-e-r*? **(b) Compare and Contrast:** Explain how water from the pump is the same as and different from water in a mug.

Author's Purpose

The **author's purpose** is his or her reason for writing. Reread the selection and take notes on how Keller expresses her purpose.

1. What are two possible purposes Keller may have had for writing

Research: Clarify Details Choose an unfamiliar detail in the selection and briefly research it. Then, explain how research helps you better understand the autobiography.

Summarize Write an objective summary of the autobiography. An objective summary is free from opinions and evaluations.

• … "w-a-t-e-r" is *water,* but I **persisted** in confounding the two.

• There were **barriers** still, it is true, but barriers that could in time be swept away.

Craft and Structure

2. **(a)** Give three examples of sensory language that Keller uses in this paragraph. **(b) Infer:** What do these examples reveal about the ways in which Keller experiences the world around her?

Integration of Knowledge and Ideas

3. **(a) Speculate:** How might Keller's life change after the "water" incident? Cite details in the autobiography to support your response.

her autobiography? **Support** your answer.

2. **Determination** How does writing an autobiography express Keller's determination?

communicate more effectively. Keller says that "There were barriers still, it is true, but barriers that could in time be swept away." Although she will face difficulties, she has more hope about her life and future.

Author's Purpose

1. One purpose is to inform readers about the important event that helped her recognize words. The title of the text reflects the importance of how water helped Keller understand words. Another is to express emotions about

her language breakthrough: "That living word awakened my soul, gave it light, hope, joy, set it free!"

2. It shows how determination enabled her to master words, to appreciate the joys of life, and to share her story with others.

Water
Helen Keller

DISCUSS • RESEARCH • WRITE

From Text to Topic **Small Group Discussion**

Discuss the following passage with a group of classmates. Take notes during the discussion. Contribute your own ideas, and support them with examples from the text.

> Running downstairs to my mother I held up my hand and made the letters for doll. … I understood that everything has a name. (p. 425)

Research **Investigate the Topic**

Learning to Communicate In "Water," Helen Keller shows tremendous determination in her quest to learn to communicate.

Assignment

Conduct research to find out how people with visual impairments learn to read, or how people with hearing impairments learn to communicate without speaking. Consult credible health **sources**. Take clear notes and carefully identify your sources so that you can easily access the information later. Share your findings in a **presentation with graphics** for the class.

Writing to Sources **Argumentative Writing**

"Water" focuses on the moment Anne Sullivan held Helen Keller's hand under running water. In that moment, Keller's world changed.

Assignment

Write an **argumentative essay** in which you argue that the person Helen Keller was before the "water" incident was profoundly different from the person she became after the incident. Follow these steps:

- Reread the text and take notes about Helen's personality and character both before and after the "water" incident.
- Write an introduction in which you state your claim.
- In the body of your essay, use a point-by-point organizational structure to compare and contrast the "before" Helen with the "after" Helen.
- Provide a conclusion in which you summarize your argument and explain how the incident will affect Helen's future.

QUESTIONS FOR DISCUSSION

1. In this passage, how does Keller show determination?
2. How will her determination aid her in years to come?

PREPARATION FOR ESSAY

You may use the results of this research project to support your ideas in the essay at the end of this section.

ACADEMIC VOCABULARY

Academic terms appear in blue on these pages. If these words are not familiar to you, use a dictionary to find their definitions. Then, use them as you speak and write about the text.

 **Common Core State Standards**

RI.6.1, RI.6.2, RI.6.3, RI.6.4, RI.6.5, RI.6.6; W.6.1, W.6.4, W.6.5, W.6.7, W.6.8; SL.6.1, SL.6.4
[For full standards wording, see the chart in the front of this book.]

DISCUSS • RESEARCH • WRITE

From Text to Topic: Small Group Discussion

1. Keller shows that she is eager to learn and will persist until she has mastered something, even if she doesn't understand it right away.
2. She will need determination to learn to communicate through sign language and writing.

Research: Investigate the Topic

Introduce the assignment using the instruction on the student page.

1. Arrange for students to visit your school's library or have access to computers. Review strategies for identifying reliable health resources. Students might look up "Braille" and "devices to help the deaf communicate."
2. Remind students to take notes on the main ideas in the sources. They may choose to take notes on cards or electronically, and they may quote directly or paraphrase the information.
3. Encourage students to draw conclusions and make connections between multiple sources. Suggest that they prepare an outline for their presentation and create a Works Cited list.
4. Point out that practice will make their presentation go smoothly and get them ready to answer any questions.

Academic Vocabulary

If students struggle with defining the academic vocabulary words, use this routine:

Write the words and definitions on the board.

purpose: the reason something is done

support: to provide evidence for

sources: a person or publication that provides information

Have students say each word aloud and then use the word in a sentence. Sample sentences should demonstrate that the words can be used across disciplines.

Writing to Sources: Argumentative Essay

Students' argumentative essays should follow the steps listed in order to demonstrate the differences between the person Keller was before the "water" incident and the person she was afterward. Remind them to include in the conclusion ideas about how the incident will affect Keller's future.

 Online Writer's Notebook

Students can use the Online Writer's Notebook to record all responses.

Big Question: Toward Essential Understanding

1. Have students read the title, study the poster, and read the quotation. **Ask:** What details in the photograph communicate determination? What clue is given to the identity of the man in the photograph?

   Possible response: The man in the photograph communicates determination in his intense gaze, serious expression, and erect stance. The quote below the picture is from Winston Churchill. He is likely the man shown on the poster.

2. Reread the quotation below the photograph. **Ask:** What is the relationship between the poster title and the quotation? How does this poster connect to the Big Question: *Do we need words to communicate well?*

   Possible response: The quotation says that what matters is "the courage to continue." It takes determination to continue your efforts after either a success or a failure. The title and photo may give a sense of what determination is, but the quotation clarifies and emphasizes the message the poster is intended to communicate.

Critical Viewing

Tell students that this poster demonstrates the ability of the photographer to capture a feeling and attitude in black and white. The focus is clearly the man. The background is simple, forcing the viewers' attention to the subject, Winston Churchill.

Also discuss the photographer's decision to focus on the figure. It allows the viewer to examine evidence of determination in Churchill's face and posture. His brow is furrowed, and his arms are stiff as he grabs the walking stick. His face and posture show that he is intent about where he is going and what he wants to do. Since Churchill is in the foreground, viewers focus on his stance and action.

DETERMINATION

"Success is not final,
failure is not fatal:
it is the courage to continue
that counts."
—Winston Churchill

430 UNIT 3 • Do we need words to communicate well?

 VOCABULARY DEVELOPMENT

Academic Vocabulary

If students require support with academic vocabulary, write the following words and definitions on the board:

- **context:** setting or text that influences a word's meaning
- **quotation:** exact words cited
- **facts:** truths known from experience or observation

Have students say each word aloud. Then, use the word in a sentence that defines it. Point out that academic vocabulary words can be used across disciplines. For example, the *context* is the setting in a visual form, and it is the surrounding words in a text. A *fact* can be from an event that is seen, or it can be something learned while reading.

VIEW • RESEARCH • DISCUSS

Comprehension

Look at the poster to help you answer the following questions.

1. What is the topic of the poster?
2. According to the poster, what is one possible definition of the topic?

Critical Analysis

Key Ideas and Details

1. **(a)** Describe Churchill's facial expression in the photograph. **(b) Analyze:** What idea or feeling does his expression convey?

2. **(a)** What type of clothing is Churchill wearing? **(b) Interpret:** What does his clothing imply about the **context** of the photograph?

Craft and Structure

3. **(a) Analyze:** How does the poster's title draw the viewer's attention? **(b) Speculate:** If *Kindness* were the title, what image might the poster's designer have chosen to show?

4. **(a)** Identify the parallelism in the **quotation**. **(b) Analyze:** What effect does this construction have on meaning? **(c) Interpret:** What message does the quotation express?

Integration of Knowledge and Ideas

5. **Synthesize:** Why do you think the poster's creator accompanied the quotation with this particular photograph?

Research **Investigate the Topic**

Politics and Determination Winston Churchill was the prime minister of Great Britain from 1940–1945, during World War II.

> **Assignment**
>
> Conduct research to learn how Winston Churchill used his determination to lead Great Britain to victory in WWII. Consult credible historical sources, including both primary and secondary sources. Share your findings in a **report**. With a partner, discuss the **facts** you learned about Churchill through your research.

Common Core State Standards

RI.6.1, RI.6.2, RI.6.3, RI.6.5, RI.6.6, RI.6.7, W.6.2, W.6.3, W.6.4, W.6.7, W.6.8
[For full standards wording, see the chart in the front of this book.]

ACADEMIC VOCABULARY

Academic terms appear in blue on these pages. If these words are not familiar to you, use a dictionary to find their definitions. Then, use them as you speak and write about the text.

VIEW • RESEARCH • DISCUSS

Comprehension

1. The topic is determination.

2. **Possible response:** A definition of *determination* is "the persistence to stick with a goal or task."

Critical Analysis

Possible responses appear below. Check to be sure students support their responses with evidence from the text.

1. **(a)** Churchill's expression is serious, and it shows a firmness of purpose. **(b)** His serious expression shows he is certain about what he will do.

2. **(a)** His clothing is formal, with the vest, top hat, and cutaway suit coat. **(b)** The context may be that he is on the way to a ceremonial or political event.

3. **(a)** The large white-on-gray, all-capital letters draw the viewer's attention. **(b)** If *Kindness* were the title, the designer might have chosen the image of a smiling, relaxed person.

4. **(a)** The repeat of *is not* shows the parallel construction. **(b)** The construction shows that neither success nor failure is fatal, or final. **(c)** Since neither success nor failure is permanent, what counts is that people have "courage to continue."

5. The photograph shows Churchill in a formal context, with a serious expression, as if announcing that he is determined and will continue on.

Research: Investigate the Topic

Introduce the assignment, using the instruction on the student page. Students' reports should include facts that show Churchill's determination to lead his country to victory during WWII.

> **Online Writer's Notebook**
>
> Students can use the Online Writer's Notebook to record all responses.

Speaking and Listening: Group Discussion

Introduce the assignment using the instruction on the student page.

1. **Conduct discussions.** Help students recall and apply their knowledge of the selections in this section to answer the discussion questions. For example, **ask:**

   - Both Roald Amundsen and Robert Scott had the determination to reach the South Pole. Why was this not enough to make Scott successful?

   - In what positive ways did Douglas and Helen Keller demonstrate their determination to reach their goals?

   - How did Anne Sullivan's determination to teach Helen result in anger, frustration, and conflict at first?

   - What does Angela Duckworth's research show about people who demonstrate "grit" through actions and not words?

   - Can an inanimate object, such as a ginkgo tree, show determination? Explain.

2. **Summarize and present your ideas.** Remind students that when they summarize their findings, they should try to represent a range of ideas that came out of their group's discussion.

Criteria for Success

Circulate around the room and observe group discussions. Support groups in their efforts to conduct organized, focused, balanced, and respectful discussions. Ask guiding questions if the conversation lags, and encourage students to make connections between ideas and experiences from different sources and to explore contrasts in the texts' portrayals or points of view. Emphasize that students should support all points with specific text evidence.

Use New Vocabulary

Assist students in using new vocabulary during group discussion. For example, **ask:**

- How can determination help people overcome what seem to be *insurmountable* obstacles?

- What characters *persisted* in spite of difficult *barriers* to their success?

 ## Assessment: Synthesis

Speaking and Listening: **Group Discussion**

Determination and Communication The texts in this section explore the idea of determination and show that people often express determination through their communication with others. This idea is fundamentally related to the Big Question addressed in this unit: **Do we need words to communicate well?**

> **Assignment**
>
> **Conduct discussions.** With a small group of classmates, conduct a discussion about issues of determination and communication. Refer to the texts in this section, other texts you have read, and your own prior knowledge to support your ideas. Begin your discussion by addressing the following questions:
>
> - Is determination always a positive trait?
>
> - What are some constructive ways that people can communicate their determination to take an action or reach a goal?
>
> - Do people sometimes communicate their determination in ways that anger, frighten, annoy, or confuse others? How?
>
> - What are nonverbal ways people can show determination?
>
> **Summarize and present your ideas.** After you have fully explored the topic, summarize your discussion for the class.

Criteria for Success

✓ **Organizes the group effectively**
Appoint a group leader and a timekeeper. The group leader should present the discussion questions. The timekeeper should make sure the discussion takes no longer than 20 minutes.

✓ **Maintains focus of discussion**
As a group, stay on topic and avoid straying into other subject areas.

✓ **Involves all participants equally and fully**
No one person should monopolize the conversation. Rather, everyone should take turns speaking and contributing ideas.

✓ **Follows the rules for collegial discussion**
As each group member speaks, others should listen carefully. Build on one another's ideas and support viewpoints and opinions with sound reasoning and evidence. Express disagreement respectfully.

Common Core State Standards

SL.6.1, SL.6.3, SL.6.4, SL.6.6
[For full standards wording, see the chart in the front of this book.]

USE NEW VOCABULARY

As you speak and share ideas, work to use the vocabulary words you have learned in this unit. The more you use new words, the more you will "own" them.

Writing: Fictional Narrative

Determination and Communication In many stories, conflict may result from a character's determination to accomplish a goal. Often, the character's success or failure depends on how he or she communicates with others.

Common Core State Standards

W.6.3, W.6.4, W.6.5
[For full standards wording, see the chart in the front of this book.]

> ### Assignment
> Write a **fictional narrative** that follows from the events described in Ray Bradbury's story "The Sound of Summer Running." Invent a new challenge for Douglas, and describe how he uses determination in his attempts to succeed. Tell how Douglas communicates his determination to others, and how that communication either aids or hinders him.

Criteria for Success

Purpose/Focus
✓ **Connects specific incidents with larger ideas**
Make meaningful connections between Douglas's experiences and other texts you have read in this section.

✓ **Clearly conveys the significance of the story**
Provide a conclusion that makes clear the meaning of Douglas's experiences.

Organization
✓ **Sequences events logically**
Structure your narrative so that individual events build on one another to create a coherent whole.

Development of Ideas/Elaboration
✓ **Supports insights**
Include ideas from other texts you have read and the research you have conducted in this section.

✓ **Uses narrative techniques effectively**
Use dialogue to help readers "hear" how the characters sound. Consider telling your story from the first-person point of view.

Language
✓ **Uses description effectively**
Use sensory language to develop your setting and characters.

Conventions
✓ **Does not have errors**
Eliminate errors in grammar, spelling, and punctuation.

WRITE TO EXPLORE

Writing is a way to clarify what you feel and think. This means that you may change your mind or get new ideas as you work. Allowing for this will improve your final draft.

Writing: Fictional Narrative

Introduce the assignment using the instruction on the student page.

Criteria for Success

1. **Purpose/Focus** Encourage students to draw from the challenges characters faced in other texts in this section when they invent a new challenge for Douglas. For example, **ask:**

   How would you compare and contrast what Douglas and Anne Sullivan wanted? What role did communication play in each of their efforts to succeed?

2. **Organization** Encourage your students to structure their narratives in a logical way.

3. **Development of Ideas/ Elaboration** Encourage students to tell their stories through the use of detail and dialogue. Point out effective models in the texts, such as "The magic was always in the new pair of shoes. The magic might die by the first of September, but now in late June there was still plenty of magic, and shoes like these could jump you over trees and rivers and houses."

4. **Language** Instruct students to use strong verbs and vivid descriptive images to portray the characters and events in their fictional narratives.

5. **Conventions** In addition to a self-review, students should have someone else read their narratives to check for errors.

Write to Explore

Point out that students' thoughts and feelings about their stories might deepen or change as they write and reflect. As they conclude their narratives, encourage them to carefully consider what they have learned over the course of the writing experience in order to identify important observations they have made, insights they have gained, or conclusions they have drawn.

Writing to Sources: **Argumentative Essay**

Introduce the assignment using the instruction on the student page.

Prewriting and Planning

1. Choose texts. Explain that in order to identify and develop their own claims about determination and communication, students will need to analyze in depth the people and ideas in two or more of the texts that they explored.

2. Gather details and craft a working thesis, or claim.

- Remind students that a claim is an assertion that a writer is trying to prove to readers.

- Instruct students to go back into the texts they have selected and review passages that are connected to the topic of determination or communication.

- Encourage them to use a chart like the one shown to record each significant passage and identify the ideas it suggests about the concepts.

- Students may also wish to raise questions that the passage may help answer, such as *What happens when being determined leads to conflict? Can too much determination cause a person to lose sight of the big picture?*

- Students can then use these ideas to identify and develop an overall claim about communication and determination.

Incorporate Research

Remind students to consider how they might use their prior research—about the process that the Continental Congress went through to write and approve the Declaration of Independence—to support their claim in this essay.

Writing to Sources: **Argumentative Essay**

Determination and Communication The related readings in this section present a range of ideas about determination and communication. They raise questions, such as the following, about the value of determination, and a person's ability to communicate his or her determination to others:

- What does it mean to be determined? Is it enough to feel and act determined, or must a person always communicate his or her determination to others?

- What are the different ways that a person can show determination? Are some ways better than others? Why?

- What actions, if any, should people take to turn their determination into success?

- Can there be any drawbacks to having or communicating determination? If so, what are the drawbacks?

Focus on the question that intrigues you the most, and then complete the following assignment.

> **Assignment**
>
> Write an **essay** in which you state and defend a claim about the values of determination and communication. Build evidence for your claim by analyzing the presentation of determination and communication in two or more texts from this section. Clearly present and develop your ideas, and support them with details from the texts.

Prewriting and Planning

Choose texts. Review the texts in the section to determine which ones you will cite in your essay. Select at least two selections that will provide strong material to support your argument.

Gather details and craft a working thesis, or claim. Use a chart like the one shown to develop your claim. As you reread the texts, gather details that relate to your focus question. Use your notes to develop your claim.

Focus Question: Can there be drawbacks to communicating determination?
In "The Sound of Summer Running," when Douglas says he wants new shoes, he comes into conflict with his father.
In "Letter on Thomas Jefferson," Adams and Jefferson disagree about who should write the draft.
Example Claim: Communicating determination to others can lead to conflict.

 **Common Core State Standards**

W.6.1, W.6.4, W.6.5, W.6.9
[For full standards wording, see the chart in the front of this book.]

INCORPORATE RESEARCH

In your essay, use information you gathered as you completed the brief research assignments related to the selections in this section.

Drafting

Organize your ideas and evidence. Create an informal outline or a list of ideas you will to present. Decide where you will include evidence and which evidence you will use to support each point.

Address counterclaims. Strong argumentation takes differing ideas into account and addresses those ideas directly. As you organize your essay, build in sections in which you explain opposing opinions or differing interpretations. Then, write a reasoned, well-supported response to those counterclaims.

Frame and connect ideas. Grab your readers' attention with a strong introduction. Consider beginning with a compelling quotation or a startling fact. In the body of your essay, make sure to show clear connections among your claims, evidence, and counterclaims. Finally, write a strong conclusion in which you sum up your main idea.

Revising and Editing

Strengthen support. Make sure that your claim is clearly stated and that you have supported it with convincing evidence from the texts. Underline main ideas in your essay and confirm that each one is fully supported. Add more evidence as needed.

Review style. Revise to cut wordy passages. Check that you have found the clearest, simplest way to communicate your ideas.

CITE RESEARCH CORRECTLY

Avoid plagiarism by properly crediting the ideas of others. Refer to the Research Workshop in the Introductory Unit of this textbook for information on citing sources.

Self-Evaluation Rubric

Use the following criteria to evaluate the effectiveness of your essay.

Criteria	Rating Scale			
	not very .... very			
Purpose/Focus Introduces a precise claim and distinguishes the claim from alternate or opposing claims; provides a concluding section that follows from and supports the argument presented	1	2	3	4
Organization Organizes reasons and evidence clearly and logically; provides a concluding section that follows from the argument presented	1	2	3	4
Development of Ideas/Elaboration Supports the claim with clear reasons and relevant evidence, using credible sources; addresses counterarguments; establishes and maintains a formal style	1	2	3	4
Language Uses precise language to strengthen the argument; uses words, phrases, and clauses to clarify the relationships among claims and reasons	1	2	3	4
Conventions Uses proper grammar, punctuation, and spelling	1	2	3	4

Drafting

1. **Organize your ideas and evidence.**
   - Encourage students to create informal outlines to organize the main ideas in their essays.
   - Remind students that each of their points should be supported by evidence from the texts.

2. **Address counterclaims.**
   - Demonstrate how to identify and refute a counterclaim for the sample claim, "Instead of conflict, communicating determination can encourage others to join in to help reach a goal."

3. **Frame and connect ideas.**
   - Remind students that the introduction to their essay should grab the reader's attention and present the claim.
   - The body of their essay should identify reasons that support the claim and provide evidence that supports each reason. This evidence should include specific details from the texts.
   - The conclusion should restate the claim and leave readers with a lasting impression of its validity and insight.

Revising and Editing

1. **Strengthen support.** Suggest that students share a draft of their argument with a classmate or family member. Students should ask the reviewer the following questions.
   - Is my argument convincing?
   - What areas of my argument seem weak?
   - What connections among claims and evidence seem faulty?
   - What additional or stronger counterarguments might I offer?
   - What additional reasons or evidence should I include?

   Remind students to confirm that the relationships among their claim, reasons, and evidence are clear. Encourage them to include words, phrases, and clauses to reinforce these links.

2. **Review style.** If students are using a computer to type their papers, remind them to utilize the grammar and spell-check features.

Self-Evaluation Rubric

Encourage students to rate their own essays objectively and to use the results to guide their revision process.

Cite Research Correctly

Review with students the correct format for citing different sources, such as books and print or online news articles. Provide examples of proper citations. Then have students create a Works Cited list that correctly lists each source they reference in their essays.

Independent Reading

Titles featured on the Independent Reading pages at the end of each unit represent a range of reading, including stories, dramas, and poetry, as well as literary nonfiction and other types of informational text. Throughout, labels indicate the works that are CCSS Exemplar Texts. Choosing from among these featured titles will help students read works at increasing levels of text complexity in the grades 6–8 text complexity band.

Online Text Set

The selections that are a part of the Online Text Set are located in the *Student eText*.

Using Literature Circles

A literature circle is a temporary group in which students independently discuss a book.

Use the guidance in the *Professional Development Guidebook*, pp. 47–49, as well as the teaching notes on the facing page, for additional suggestions for literature circles.

ⓒ Meeting Unit 3 Common Core State Standards

Students can use books listed on this page to apply and to reinforce their mastery of the Common Core State Standards covered in this unit.

Introducing Featured Titles

Have students choose a book or books for independent reading. Assist them by previewing the titles, noting their subject matter and level of difficulty. **Note:** Before recommending a work to students, preview it, taking into account the values of your community as well as the maturity of your students.

ⓒ Independent Reading

Titles for Extended Reading

In this unit, you have read texts in a wide variety of genres. Continue to read on your own. Select works that you enjoy, but challenge yourself to explore new authors and works of increasing depth and complexity. The titles suggested below will help you get started.

INFORMATIONAL TEXT

A Short Walk Around the Pyramids and through the World of Art
by Philip Isaacson
Knopf Books for Young Readers   EXEMPLAR TEXT ⓒ

This **nonfiction art book** takes the reader on a journey through the art world. More than 70 pictures of paintings, crafts, sculptures, architecture, and other works of art accompany Isaacson's lively discussion of art.

Restless Spirit: The Life and Work of Dorothea Lange
by Elizabeth Partridge

 Dorothea Lange recorded a **photographic history** of people struggling through some of the most difficult periods in American history.

Free at Last! The Story of Martin Luther King, Jr.
by Angela Bull

 This **biography** provides facts on how the slain civil rights leader raised the American social conscience about equality and nonviolence. Read about King's struggle to deliver a message of peace.

LITERATURE

Acolytes
by Nikki Giovanni
William Morrow, 2007   EXEMPLAR TEXT ⓒ

 In this inspiring collection of **poems**, Nikki Giovanni honors men and women who have sacrificed and struggled for freedom, justice, and civil rights.

The Fields of Praise: New and Selected Poems
by Marilyn Nelson
Louisiana State University Press, 1997

 In this collection of **poems**, Nelson describes the struggles as well as the joys of the African American experience. In powerful language, she writes about faith, love, tragedy, heartbreak, and pride.

Code Talker
by Joseph Bruchac
Speak, 2006

 This **novel** tells the story of Ned Bega, who joins the Marines during World War II. He becomes one of the "code talkers," Navajo soldiers who used their own language as an unbreakable code, and saved many American lives.

ONLINE TEXT SET

PERSONAL ESSAY
The Lady and the Spider Robert Fulghum

SHORT STORY
Dragon, Dragon John Gardner

POEM
Ankylosaurus Jack Prelutsky

436 UNIT 3 • Do we need words to communicate well?

ⓒ TEXT COMPLEXITY **ALIGNING TEXTS WITH READERS AND TASKS**

Texts	Readers and Tasks
• *The Fields of Praise: New and Selected Poems* • *Code Talker*	**Below-Level Readers** Allow students to focus on reading for content, and challenge them to interpret multiple perspectives.
• *Free at Last! The Story of Martin Luther King, Jr.* • *Acolytes* • *Restless Spirit: The Life and Work of Dorothea Lange* (Lexile: 970L)	**Below-Level Readers** Challenge students as they read for content. **On-Level Readers** Allow students to focus on reading for content, and challenge them to interpret multiple perspectives. **Advanced Readers** Allow students to focus on interpreting multiple perspectives.
• *A Short Walk Around the Pyramids and through the World of Art* (Lexile: 1110L)	**On-Level Readers** Challenge students as they read for content. **Advanced Readers** Allow students to focus on reading for content, and challenge them to interpret multiple perspectives.

Preparing to Read Complex Texts

Attentive Reading As you read on your own, ask yourself questions like these to enrich your reading experience.

When reading poetry, ask yourself...

Comprehension: Key Ideas and Details

- Who is the speaker of the poem? What kind of person does the speaker seem to be? How do I know?
- What is the poem about?
- Does any one line or section state the poem's theme, or meaning, directly? If so, what is that line or section?
- If there is no direct statement of a theme, what details help me to see the poem's deeper meaning?

Text Analysis: Craft and Structure

- Does the poem have a formal structure, or is it free verse?
- How many stanzas form this poem? What does each stanza tell me?
- Do I notice repetition, rhyme, meter, or other sound devices? How do these elements affect how I read the poem?
- Do any of the poet's word choices seem especially interesting or unusual? Why?
- What images do I notice? Do they create clear word-pictures in my mind? Why or why not?
- Would I like to read this poem aloud? Why or why not?

Connections: Integration of Knowledge and Ideas

- Has the poem helped me understand its subject in a new way? If so, how?
- Does the poem remind me of others I have read? If so, how?
- In what ways is the poem different from others I have read?
- What information, ideas, or insights have I gained from reading this poem?
- Do I find the poem moving, funny, or mysterious? How does the poem make me feel?
- Would I like to read more poems by this poet? Why or why not? .

Common Core State Standards

Reading Literature/ Informational Text
10. By the end of the year, read and comprehend literature, including stories, dramas, and poems, and literary nonfiction in the grades 6–8 text complexity band proficiently, with scaffolding as needed at the high end of the range.

PART 4 • Independent Reading **437**

Preparing to Read Complex Texts

1. Tell students they can be attentive readers by bringing their experience and imagination to the texts they read and by actively questioning those texts. Explain that the questions they see on the student page are examples of types of questions to ask about poetry.

2. Point out that, like writing, reading is a "multidraft" process, involving several readings of complete works or passages, revising and refining one's understanding each time.

Key Ideas and Details

3. As an example, read and amplify the second bulleted item. **Ask:** What key ideas and details could you cite as evidence to explain what the poem is about?

   Possible response: You might point to the characters or events described in the poem.

Craft and Structure

4. **Ask:** What details of craft and structure would you use to describe how the poem looks on the page?

   Possible response: You might discuss whether or not the lines look like prose sentences (with capital letters and punctuation) or count the number of stanzas in the poem.

Integration of Knowledge and Ideas

5. **Ask:** How would you determine how the poem makes you feel?

   Possible response: You might monitor your emotional reactions as you read the poem or look for words that help create a certain mood.

6. Finally, explain to students that they should cite key ideas and details, examples of craft and structure, or instances of the integration of knowledge and ideas as evidence to support their points during a book discussion. After hearing the evidence, the group might reach a consensus or might agree to disagree.

TEXT COMPLEXITY READER AND TASK SUPPORT SUGGESTIONS

Independent Reading

Increased Support Suggest that students choose a book that they feel comfortable reading and one that is a bit more challenging. Pair a more proficient reader with a less proficient reader and have them work together on the more challenging text. Partners can prepare to read the book by reviewing questions on this student page. They can also read difficult passages together, sharing questions and insights. They can use the questions on the student page to guide after-reading discussion.

Increased Challenge Encourage students to integrate knowledge and ideas by combining the Big Question and the Unit Focus concepts in their approach to two or more featured titles.
   For example, students might consider how characters express themselves in *Code Talker* and *Restless Spirit: The Life and Work of Dorothea Lange*. In addition, students can focus on sound devices such as rhythm, rhyme, repetition, and alliteration in poetry.

UNIT 4

THE BIG ?

How do we decide who we are?

UNIT PATHWAY

PART 1
SETTING EXPECTATIONS

- INTRODUCING THE BIG QUESTION
- CLOSE READING WORKSHOP

PART 2
TEXT ANALYSIS
GUIDED EXPLORATION

ADVENTURE AND IMAGINATION

PART 3
TEXT SET
DEVELOPING INSIGHT

MARK TWAIN

PART 4
DEMONSTRATING INDEPENDENCE

- INDEPENDENT READING
- ONLINE TEXT SET

CLOSE READING TOOL

Use this tool to practice the close
reading strategies you learn.

STUDENT eTEXT

Bring learning to life
with audio, video, and
interactive tools.

WRITER'S NOTEBOOK

Easily capture notes and
complete assignments online.

439

① How do we decide who we are?

1. Discuss how, like snowflakes, no two people are alike.

2. Have students read the introduction on this page. Have them write profiles of themselves like Angela's profile. Then point out that a profile is not a complete portrait of a person. Many more qualities and traits define a person.

3. **Ask** students the Big Question. **Possible response:** We examine our likes, dislikes, values, beliefs, and goals.

4. Have students think about the Big Question as they read the plays and think about how each play helps them understand what makes a person him- or herself.

② Exploring the Big Question

Collaboration: One-on-One Discussion

1. Introduce the activity, using the instruction on the student page.

2. Have students work individually to list examples. As they complete their lists, remind them to include some examples of nonverbal communication.

3. Review the Big Question vocabulary on the next page, following the teaching suggestions. Have students use the vocabulary as they complete the activity on this page.

Connecting to the Literature

Explain the Big Question strand in the unit, referring to the text at the bottom of this page.

© Introducing the Big Question

① How do we decide who we are?

Who are you? You might answer this question by stating your name: *I am Angela Reyna.* Instead, you might give a description: *I am a 12-year-old African American girl.* Perhaps you would answer by naming your skills or interests: *I am a good swimmer. I like music and art.*

Many qualities make up who you are: your personality, your values, your hopes and dreams, and your experiences. Some of us may look alike, or we may have similar beliefs. In the end, however, each of us is unique.

How do we come to know exactly who we are?

② Exploring the Big Question

Collaboration: One-on-One Discussion Start thinking about the Big Question by identifying ways that we learn about ourselves. Make a list of different situations that have revealed something about you or about another person. Make notes about what you can learn about yourself in each of the following situations:

- being in a contest or other type of competition
- making a mistake
- going to an unfamiliar place
- listening to what others say about you
- getting to know someone who is very different from you
- facing a difficult challenge

Share your examples with a partner. Talk about what each situation can teach a person about himself or herself. Use the vocabulary words in your discussion.

Connecting to the Literature Each reading in this unit will give you additional insight into the Big Question. As you read, consider the ways in which the characters learn more about themselves.

❓ DEVELOPING ESSENTIAL UNDERSTANDING

How do we decide who we are?

Explain to students that they will continue to consider the Big Question as they work through Unit 4.

- As students read each selection, they will look for details related to the Big Question and take notes.

- At the end of each selection, students will answer a Literary Analysis question that is related to the Big Question.

- Throughout the unit, students will deepen their knowledge of the selections and their understanding of the Big Question through reading, speaking, listening, researching, and writing. By the end of the unit, students should understand how each selection relates to the Big Question individually and how the selections connect to one another through the Big Question.

- Tell students that their goal will be to gain a deeper understanding of literature and to develop a more sophisticated way of discussing the Big Question. Ultimately, students should use the Big Question as a springboard for their own questions that relate to their interests and concerns.

❸ Vocabulary

Acquire and Use Academic Vocabulary Academic vocabulary is the language you encounter in textbooks and on standardized tests. Review the definitions of these academic vocabulary words.

diverse (də vʉrs´) *adj.* many and different; from different backgrounds

perspective (per spek´ tiv) *n.* point of view

reaction (rē´ ak´ shən) *n.* response to something said or done

reflect (ri flekt´) *v.* think or wonder about

respond (ri spänd´) *v.* answer or reply

similar (sim´ ə lər) *adj.* alike

unique (yoō nēk´) *adj.* one of a kind

Gather Vocabulary Knowledge Additional vocabulary words are listed below. Categorize the words by deciding whether you know each one well, know it a little bit, or do not know it at all.

appearance	expectations	personality
conscious	ideals	trend
custom	individuality	

Then, do the following:

1. Write the definitions of the words you know.
2. Consult a dictionary to confirm the meanings of the words whose definitions you wrote down. Revise your definitions if necessary.
3. Using a print or an online dictionary, look up the meanings of the words you are unsure of or do not know. Then, write the meanings.
4. Use all of the words in a brief paragraph about expressing individuality.

Common Core State Standards

Speaking and Listening

1. Engage effectively in a range of collaborative discussions with diverse partners on grade 6 topics, texts, and issues, building on others' ideas and expressing their own clearly.

Language

6. Acquire and use accurately grade-appropriate general academic and domain-specific words and phrases; gather vocabulary knowledge when considering a word or phrase important to comprehension or expression.

❸ Vocabulary

Acquire and Use Academic Vocabulary

1. Introduce the academic vocabulary words in the first word bank on the student page. Have students preview the words.
2. For each word, have students say the word aloud. Then, use the word in a sentence that defines the word.

Gather Vocabulary Knowledge

1. With the class, review the steps in the activity on the student page. Have students complete the activity independently, with partners, or in small groups.
2. Before students complete the last step, review the words and their meanings as a class. (Definitions appear at the bottom of this page.) Then, have students complete their paragraphs.

💬 GATHER VOCABULARY KNOWLEDGE

appearance (ə pir´əns) *n.* the way a person or thing looks

conscious (kän´shəs) *adj.* awake or aware

custom (kus´təm) *n.* accepted practice

expectations (ek´spek tā´shənz) *n.* feelings that something will happen

ideals (ī dē´əlz) *n.* models of excellence

individuality (in´də vij oō al´ə tē) *n.* the way a person or thing stands apart

personality (pʉr´sə nal´ə tē) *n.* the ways of acting, being, and feeling that define a person

trend (trend) *n.* tendency; pattern of events

▶ **Video**

Watch the Background Video online!

❶ Close Reading: Drama

In the Close Reading Workshop, students will practice using close reading strategies within the context of a particular genre. They will use the features of this genre to help them access the text. All of the close reading strategies align with the Common Core State Standards reading domains:

- **Comprehension:** Key Ideas and Details focuses on what the text says.
- **Text Analysis:** Craft and Structure focuses on how the author conveys the text.
- **Connections:** Integration of Knowledge and Ideas focuses on what the text means and how it changes the reader's view of the world.

MULTIDRAFT READING

Essential Understanding

Explain to students that close reading works best when they read a text multiple times, focusing on different aspects of the text each time.

- **First reading:** Students should read independently to unlock the basic meaning of the text.
- **Second reading:** Students should focus on analyzing key ideas and details and the craft and the structure of the text.
- **Third reading:** Students should focus on integrating knowledge and ideas by connecting the text to the Big Question. The essential understanding students gain from making this connection will help them connect the text to other texts and to the world.

© Close Reading Workshop

In this workshop you will learn an approach to reading that will deepen your understanding of literature and will help you better appreciate the author's craft. The workshop includes models for close reading, discussion, research, and writing activities. After you have reviewed the strategies and models, practice your skills with the Independent Practice selection.

© Common Core State Standards

RL.6.1, RL.6.2, RL.6.3, RL.6.5; W.6.2, W.6.4, W.6.7, W.6.9a; SL.6.1
[For full standards wording, see the standards chart in the front of this book.]

❶ CLOSE READING: DRAMA

Use these strategies as you read the drama in this unit.

Comprehension: **Key Ideas and Details**

- Read first to unlock basic meaning.
- Identify unfamiliar details that you might need to clarify through research.
- Distinguish between what is stated directly and what must be inferred.

Ask yourself questions such as these:
- Who are the main characters?
- What internal and external conflicts do the characters face?
- When and where does the action take place?

Text Analysis: **Craft and Structure**

- Think about the genre of the work and how the author presents ideas.
- Analyze how dialogue and stage directions provide information about character and setting.
- Think about how scenes introduce characters, begin or end action, and change setting or mood.

Ask yourself questions such as these:
- How do details in the stage directions help me picture the action?
- How does each scene move the story forward?
- How does dialogue provide clues to characters' personalities?

Connections: **Integration of Knowledge and Ideas**

- Look for relationships among key ideas.
- Look for characters that represent universal, or common, personality types.
- Compare and contrast this work with other dramas you have read.

Ask yourself questions such as these:
- How has this work increased my knowledge of a subject or a playwright?
- What is the theme of the drama?
- What actors would I choose to play each role in this play?

442 UNIT 4 • How do we decide who we are?

© ACTIVE READING FOR COMMON CORE

Read • Discuss • Research • Write

In this workshop, students will learn how to access text through reading, discussing, researching, and writing. In the first half of the workshop, these activities are modeled for students. In the second half, students have the opportunity to partake in these activities independently.

Read: Students will read and comprehend the Reading Model selection. Annotations call out key points that students should focus on. These annotations model the types of things students should notice when they read the Independent Practice selection later.

Discuss: Students will deepen their understanding of the text through collaborative discussion.

Research: Students will clarify and expand their understanding of the text by conducting research.

Write: Students will synthesize their thoughts and research and will write a response to the text, supporting their ideas with evidence.

❷ Read

As you read this excerpt from a drama, take note of the annotations that model ways to closely read the text.

Reading Model

from *Brighton Beach Memoirs* by Neil Simon

STAN. [*half whisper*] Hey! Eugie!

EUGENE. Hi, Stan! [*to audience*] My brother, Stan. He's okay. You'll like him. **1** [*to* STAN] What are you doing home so early?

STAN. [*looks around, lowers his voice*] **2** Is Pop home yet?

EUGENE. No ... Did you ask about the tickets?

STAN. What tickets?

EUGENE. For the Yankee game. You said your boss knew this guy who could get passes. You didn't ask him?

STAN. Me and my boss had other things to talk about. [*He sits on steps, his head down, almost in tears*] **2** I'm in trouble, Eug. I mean really big trouble.

3 EUGENE. [*to audience*] This really shocked me. Because Stan is the kind of guy who could talk himself out of *any* kind of trouble. [*to* STAN] What kind of trouble?

STAN. ... I got fired today! **3**

EUGENE. [*shocked*] Fired? ... You mean for good?

STAN. You don't get fired temporarily. It's permanent. It's a lifetime firing. **4**

EUGENE. Why? What happened? **5**

Craft and Structure

1 An *aside* is a comment made by a character that the audience can hear but other characters cannot hear. In this aside, Eugene introduces his brother to the audience.

Craft and Structure

2 Stage directions can give important clues about a character's feelings. Stan's body language reveals that he is nervous and upset.

Key Ideas and Details

3 Stan pauses before revealing that he has been fired. His hesitation suggests a conflict: he is worried about how his family will react to his news.

Craft and Structure

4 By stating the obvious, Stan makes the audience laugh. The situation is serious, but the playwright presents it with humor.

Integration of Knowledge and Ideas

5 Eugene asks the same question the audience is thinking. The audience knows only what Eugene knows, which deepens their connection with his character.

❷ Read

Before students begin reading the model, explain to them that the annotations call out important points in the story related to Key Ideas and Details, Craft and Structure, and Integration of Knowledge and Ideas. Tell students that their understanding and interpretation of the text should not be limited by the existing annotations. Encourage students to use the annotations as a starting point to help them analyze the story further.

❸ Integration of Knowledge and Ideas

To move students toward essential understanding, draw their attention to bracketed annotation 3 in the Teacher Edition. **Ask:** How has Stan's problem affected him? How does he react to being fired? Explain.

Possible response: Students should point out that Stan is upset and worried about being fired. It was hard for him to say what happened. He is not acting like his usual self.

❓ DEVELOPING ESSENTIAL UNDERSTANDING

How do we decide who we are?

After students have finished reading the model, ask them the following questions to help them deepen their understanding of how the story relates to the Big Question:

• How does what happened to Eugene affect who he is?

• What role does a person's feelings play in how they define themselves?

• How do the opinion of others influence people?

Remind students that as they read the rest of the selections in this unit, they should ask themselves similar questions to help them connect the texts with the Big Question.

 Audio

Selection Audio is available in the *Student eText* and on the *Hear It!* CD-ROM.

4 Discuss

Throughout the unit, students will be engaging in discussions about the selections they read. As students discuss, remind them of the following points:

- Come to discussions prepared.
- Support ideas with text evidence.
- Pose and respond to questions that connect the selection to broader themes and ideas.
- Respond thoughtfully to diverse perspectives.

5 Research

As students conduct research, remind them of the following tips:

- Focus your research question so that it's not too broad or too complex.
- Try to be as precise as possible when doing a key word search online. Otherwise, you'll have too many results to evaluate. You might also try using more than one search engine.
- Make sure the Web sites you use are reputable ones. Sites that end in .gov, .edu, or .org are generally reliable.

4 Discuss

Sharing your own ideas and listening to the ideas of others can deepen your understanding of a text and help you look at a topic in a whole new way. As you participate in collaborative discussions, work to have a genuine exchange in which classmates build upon one another's ideas. Support your points with evidence and ask meaningful questions.

> **Discussion Model**
>
> **Student 1:** In most plays I've seen, the characters only talk to each other. It's interesting that Eugene talks to the audience, too, almost as though the audience is a character in the play.
>
> **Student 2:** Why do you think the playwright did that? It seems as if Eugene's comments to the audience are just extra information, and the dialogue would make sense without them. For example, Eugene says, "this really shocked me," but we can see that he's shocked through his dialogue with Stan.
>
> **Student 3:** I think Eugene is probably the main character, and that's why he talks to the audience. The audience sees the action and the other characters through his eyes. I wonder what Eugene's role is in the rest of the play, and whether the audience experiences the whole play from his point of view.

5 Research

Targeted research can clarify unfamiliar details and shed light on various aspects of a text. Consider questions that arise in your mind as you read, and use those questions as the basis for research.

> **Research Model**
>
> **Questions:** *What is Eugene's role in* Brighton Beach Memoirs*?*
>
> **Key Words for Internet Search:** "Brighton Beach Memoirs"
>
> **What I Learned:** In earlier scenes in the play, the audience learns that Eugene is writing his memoirs in a journal. He wants to be a baseball player or a writer. He shares his experiences growing up in the Brighton Beach area of New York City with his family during the Great Depression.

⑥ Write

Writing about a text will deepen your understanding of it and will also allow you to share your ideas more formally with others. The following model essay analyzes how the playwright creates meaningful dialogue and cites evidence to support the main ideas.

Writing Model: Informative Essay

Finding Meaning in Dialogue

When Stan gets fired in this scene from *Brighton Beach Memoirs*, playwright Neil Simon gives the audience reasons to laugh. Eugene's comments to the audience reveal his amusing personality while lightening the scene's mood. Most importantly, the dialogue between Eugene and Stan helps the audience understand the brothers' situation and their feelings about each other and their family.

> Stating the main idea at the beginning makes the writer's intentions clear.

Eugene makes comments to the audience that Stan does not hear. For example, he introduces his brother Stan in an aside: "My brother, Stan. He's okay. You'll like him." As the audience, we can form our own opinions about Stan. Eugene's aside, therefore, has another purpose. These lines convey how close Eugene is to his brother.

> Specific details from the play help support the writer's key points.

In his next aside, Eugene shares his amazement when he sees how upset Stan is: "This really shocked me. Because Stan is the kind of guy who can talk himself out of *any* kind of trouble." This amusing comment allows Eugene to lighten the serious mood. Eugene also wants the audience to know more about Stan's personality by sharing a funny detail.

> The writer provides an example to reinforce a main idea.

Similarly, Neil Simon shows Stan's humorous side in his response to Eugene. When Eugene numbly asks, "You mean for good?" Stan wryly responds with, "You don't get fired temporarily." This exchange helps the audience understand that Stan can find humor in the situation, while Eugene still needs to process the bad news.

> This example provides further elaboration and support for the main idea.

Whether Eugene is talking with Stan or commenting to the audience through his asides, his humorous dialogue conveys a sense of realism and give the audience important information. In earlier scenes of the play, the audience learns that the play is about a family who live in the Brighton Beach area of New York City during the Depression. This scene establishes a situation that points to a potential theme: hard times and struggles can bring families together. The dialogue between Eugene and Stan helps the audience understand the conflict that the brothers face.

> In the conclusion, the writer includes evidence from research to support an interpretation of the play's meaning.

⑥ Write

Review the writing model with the class, using the annotations to analyze how the writer uses evidence to support his or her ideas.

Genre Requirements

Remind students that when they write responses to literature, they should do the following:

- Introduce the topic at the beginning of the essay.
- Organize ideas and information in order to make important connections.
- Support claims with specific details from the literary work.
- Provide a conclusion that supports the information presented.

Teaching from the Writing Model

1. Point out to students that the last sentence of the introduction is the writer's main idea.
2. Point out that each body paragraph uses text evidence or facts to support the main idea.
3. The conclusion presents further evidence and restates the main idea.

CLOSE READING TOOL

Students may close read and mark the text using the **Close Reading Tool**, which is available online. Scaffolds are provided for students who need help. Students who do not have online access may use the *Close Reading Notebook* to mark the text with their close reading responses.

7 Independent Practice

The Independent Practice is an optional assignment. You may wish to administer it at this point and use it as formative assessment, or you may wish to administer it at the end of Part 1 as summative assessment.

If you wish to administer the Independent Practice but feel your students will struggle with it, you can use the questions in the side margins of this Teacher Edition to help guide them.

8 Craft and Structure

Ask: What do the stage directions reveal about the setting and characters?

Possible response: The setting is a wigwam where Gluskabe and his grandmother live. The reader can tell that the weather is cold because the characters are covered by blankets.

9 Key Ideas and Details

Ask: What conflict do the characters face?

Possible response: Gluskbe and his grandmother are very cold because there is very deep snow and it has been winter for a long time.

🔊 Audio

Selection Audio is available in the *Student eText* and on the *Hear It!* CD-ROM.

---

7 As you read the following play, apply the close reading strategies you have learned. You may need to read the drama multiple times.

Gluskabe and Old Man Winter

by Joseph Bruchac

CHARACTERS

Speaking Roles:	**Non-speaking Roles:**
NARRATOR	SUN
GLUSKABE	FLOWERS
GRANDMOTHER WOODCHUCK	PLANTS
HUMAN BEING	
OLD MAN WINTER	
FOUR OR MORE SUMMER LAND PEOPLE, including the leader	
FOUR CROWS	

Scene I: Gluskabe and Grandmother Woodchuck's Wigwam

8 GLUSKABE *and* GRANDMOTHER WOODCHUCK *sit inside with their blankets over their shoulders.*

NARRATOR: Long ago Gluskabe (gloo-SKAH-bey) lived with his grandmother, Woodchuck, who was old and very wise. Gluskabe's job was to help the people.

GLUSKABE: It is very cold this winter, Grandmother.

GRANDMOTHER WOODCHUCK: *Ni ya yo* (nee yah yo), Grandson. You are right!

9 **GLUSKABE:** The snow is very deep, Grandmother.

GRANDMOTHER WOODCHUCK: *Ni ya yo*, Grandson.

GLUSKABE: It has been winter for a very long time, Grandmother.

GRANDMOTHER WOODCHUCK: *Ni ya yo*, Grandson. But look, here comes one of those human beings who are our friends.

HUMAN BEING: *Kwai, Kwai, nidobak* (kwy kwy nee-DOH-bahk). Hello, my friends.

Meet the Author

A professional storyteller and writer from New York State, **Joseph Bruchac** (b. 1942) often draws upon the traditions of his Native American ancestors, the Abenaki people. He has written more than seventy books for children and has performed worldwide as a teller of Native American folk tales.

CLOSE READING TOOL

Read and respond to this selection online using the **Close Reading Tool.**

© ACTIVE READING FOR COMMON CORE

Read • Discuss • Research • Write

In the Independent Practice section of the Close Reading Workshop, students will practice the reading, discussing, researching, and writing strategies they learned in the modeling section. They will also deepen their essential understanding of the Big Question.

Read: Students will read and comprehend the selection. They should note significant points in the text that relate to Key Ideas and Details, Craft and Structure, and Integration of Knowledge and Ideas. They should use the annotations in the Reading Model that they read earlier as a guide. After students have

finished reading the story, they will answer Literary Analysis questions.

Discuss: Students will deepen their understanding of the text through collaborative discussion.

Research: Students will clarify and expand their understanding of the text by conducting research.

Write: Students will synthesize their thoughts and research by writing a response to the text, supporting their ideas with evidence.

GLUSKABE and **GRANDMOTHER WOODCHUCK:** *Kwai, Kwai, nidoba* (kwy kwy nee-DOH-bah).

HUMAN BEING: Gluskabe, I have been sent by the other human beings to ask you for help. This winter has been too long. If it does not end soon, we will all die.

GLUSKABE: I will do what I can. I will go to the wigwam of Old Man Winter. He has stayed here too long. I will ask him to go back to his home in the Winter Land to the north.

GRANDMOTHER WOODCHUCK: Be careful, Gluskabe.

GLUSKABE: Don't worry, Grandmother. Winter cannot beat me.

Scene II: The Wigwam of Old Man Winter

OLD MAN WINTER *sits in his wigwam, "warming" his hands over his fire made of ice. The four balls of summer are on one side of the stage.* **GLUSKABE** *enters stage carrying his bag and stands to the side of the wigwam door. He taps on the wigwam.*

OLD MAN WINTER: Who is there!

GLUSKABE: It is Gluskabe.

OLD MAN WINTER: Ah, come inside and sit by my fire.

GLUSKABE *enters the wigwam.*

GLUSKABE: The people are suffering. You must go back to your home in the Winter Land.

OLD MAN WINTER: Oh, I must, eh? But tell me, do you like my fire?

GLUSKABE: I do not like your fire. Your fire is not warm. It is cold.

OLD MAN WINTER: Yes, my fire is made of ice. And so are you!

OLD MAN WINTER *throws his white sheet over* **GLUSKABE.** **GLUSKABE** *falls down.* **OLD MAN WINTER** *stands up.*

OLD MAN WINTER: No one can defeat me!

OLD MAN WINTER *pulls* **GLUSKABE** *out of the lodge. Then he goes back inside and closes the door flap. The Sun comes out and shines on* **GLUSKABE.** **GLUSKABE** *sits up and looks at the Sun.*

GLUSKABE: Ah, that was a good nap! But I am not going into Old Man Winter's lodge again until I talk with my grandmother.

🔟 Craft and Structure

Ask: What does the repetition of "I will" reveal about Gluskabe?

Possible response: Gluskabe feels positive and determined that he can get Old Man Winter to leave.

⓫ Key Ideas and Details

Ask: What conflict is revealed by the exchange between Gluskabe and Old Man Winter?

Possible response: Gluskabe wants Old Man Winter to go home to the Winter Land, but Old Man Winter refuses to leave.

⓬ Integration of Knowledge and Ideas

Ask: How do Gluskabe's feelings about himself and what he can do change based on his experiences?

Possible response: After being frozen by Old Man Winter, Gluskabe no longer feels confident that he can change the situation on his own.

13 **Key Ideas and Details**

Ask: What new complication does Grandmother Woodchuck's speech describe?

Possible response: The Summer Land people refuse to give up summer, and crows guard the pot full of summer.

14 **Craft and Structure**

Ask: What do the descriptions of the Summer Land People reveal about them?

Possible response: The Summer Land people are dancing and singing, so they are enjoying themselves.

GLUSKABE begins walking across the stage toward the four balls. GRANDMOTHER WOODCHUCK enters.

GRANDMOTHER WOODCHUCK: It is still winter, Gluskabe! Did Old Man Winter refuse to speak to you?

GLUSKABE: We spoke, but he did not listen. I will speak to him again; and I will make him listen. But tell me, Grandmother, where does the warm weather come from?

GRANDMOTHER WOODCHUCK: It is kept in the Summer Land.

GLUSKABE: I will go there and bring summer back here.

GRANDMOTHER WOODCHUCK: Grandson, the Summer Land people are strange people. Each of them has one eye. They are also greedy. They do not want to share the warm weather. It will be dangerous.

GLUSKABE: Why will it be dangerous?

13 **GRANDMOTHER WOODCHUCK:** The Summer Land people keep the summer in a big pot. They dance around it. Four giant crows guard the pot full of summer. Whenever a stranger tries to steal summer, those crows fly down and pull off his head!

GLUSKABE: Grandmother, I will go to the summer land. I will cover up one eye and look like the people there. And I will take these four balls of sinew with me.

GLUSKABE picks up the four balls, places them in his bag, and puts the bag over his shoulder.

Scene III: *The Summer Land Village*

14 *The SUMMER LAND PEOPLE are dancing around the pot full of summer. They are singing a snake dance song, following their leader, who shakes a rattle in one hand. FOUR CROWS stand guard around the pot as the people dance.*

SUMMER LAND PEOPLE: *Wee gai wah neh* (wee guy wah ney),

Wee gai wah neh,

Wee gai wah neh, wee gai wah neh,

Wee gai wah neh, wee gai wah neh,

Wee gai wah neh.

Gluskabe enters, wearing an eye patch and carrying his bag with the balls in it.

Gluskabe: *Kwai, kwai, nidobak!* Hello, my friends.

Everyone stops dancing. They gather around Gluskabe.

Leader of The Summer Land People: Who are you?

Gluskabe: I am not a stranger. I am one of you. See, I have one eye.

Second Summer Land Person: I do not remember you.

Gluskabe: I have been gone a long time.

Third Summer Land Person: He does have only one eye.

Fourth Summer Land Person: Let's welcome him back. Come join in our snake dance.

The singing and dancing begin again: "Wee gai wah neh," etc. Gluskabe is at the end of the line as the dancers circle the pot full of summer. When Gluskabe is close enough, he reaches in, grabs one of the summersticks, and breaks away, running back and forth.

Leader of The Summer Land People: He has taken one of our summersticks!

Second Summer Land Person: Someone stop him!

Third Summer Land Person: Crows, catch him!

Fourth Summer Land Person: Pull off his head!

The Crows swoop after Gluskabe. He reaches into his pouch and pulls out one of the balls. As each Crow comes up to him, he ducks his head down and holds up the ball. The Crow grabs the ball. Gluskabe keeps running, and pulls out another ball, repeating his actions until each of the Crows has grabbed a ball.

First Crow: *Gah-gah!* I have his head.

Second Crow: *Gah-gah!* No, I have his head!

Third Crow: *Gah-gah!* Look, I have his head!

Fourth Crow: *Gah-gah!* No, look—I have it too!

Leader of The Summer Land People: How many heads did that stranger have?

15 Key Ideas and Details
Ask: Why was Gluskabe able to join the Summer Land People?

Possible response: Gluskabe was clever and tricked the Summer Land People by saying he was one of them and by covering up his eye to look like them.

16 Key Ideas and Details
Ask: How does Gluskabe get away with grabbing a summerstick?

Possible response: He tricks the crows by holding up a ball so each crow takes a ball instead of his head.

17 Craft and Structure
Ask: What does the repetition of "I have" reveal about the four crows?

Possible response: Each of the crows thought it had Gluskabe's head. The crows were gullible and easily fooled by the balls.

DIFFERENTIATED INSTRUCTION

Enrichment for English Learners

Have students practice oral communication skills by having them present dramatic readings of the scenes from "Gluskabe and Old Man Winter." Divide students into four groups: four students for Scene 1, three students for Scene 2, five students for Scene 3 (have the four Summer Land people also be the four crows), and three students for the final scene. If you have a smaller class, divide students into two groups and have each group do two scenes. Assign the roles for each scene and have the groups practice acting out their assigned scenes. Encourage students to help one another with pronunciation and intonation. Suggest that students listen to the play in the *Student eText* or on the *Hear It!* CD-ROM before they practice. Finally, have students perform their scenes for the class.

18 Craft and Structure

Ask: What changes in setting does the author describe in the stage directions?

Possible response: The author describes how by bringing the summerstick to Old Man Winter's wigwam, Gluskabe changes the setting to be warm and allow the sun, flowers, and plants to come out.

19 Integration of Knowledge and Ideas

Ask: How do Gluskabe's actions reflect who he his? How might other people view him?

Possible response: Gluskabe was able to resolve the conflict with Old Man Winter and fulfill his challenge. This shows Gluskabe's cunningness. People may view him as a hero in defeating winter and bringing spring.

SECOND SUMMER LAND PERSON: He has tricked us. He got away.

Scene IV: *The Wigwam of Old Man Winter*

GLUSKABE *walks up to* **OLD MAN WINTER'S** *wigwam. He holds the summerstick in his hand and taps on the door.*

OLD MAN WINTER: Who is there!

GLUSKABE: It is Gluskabe.

OLD MAN WINTER: Ah, come inside and sit by my fire.

GLUSKABE *enters, sits, down, and places the summerstick in front of* **OLD MAN WINTER.**

GLUSKABE: You must go back to your home in the Winter Land.

OLD MAN WINTER: Oh, I must, eh? But tell me, do you like my fire?

GLUSKABE: Your fire is no longer cold. It is getting warmer. Your wigwam is melting away. You are getting weaker.

OLD MAN WINTER: No one can defeat me!

GLUSKABE: Old Man, you are defeated. Warm weather has returned. Go back to your home in the north.

18 *The blanket walls of* **OLD MAN WINTER'S** *wigwam collapse.* **OLD MAN WINTER** *stands up and walks away as swiftly as he can, crouching down as if getting smaller. People carrying the cutouts of the Sun, Flowers, and Plants come out and surround* **GLUSKABE** *as he sits there, smiling.*

19 **NARRATOR:** So Gluskabe defeated Old Man Winter. Because he brought only one small piece of summer, winter still returns each year. But, thanks to Gluskabe, spring always comes back again.

450 UNIT 4 • How do we decide who we are?

If you are using the Independent Practice as formative assessment, use the rubric below to evaluate students' performances.

Independent Practice Rubric	Rating Scale				
Close Reading: How well does the student use close reading strategies to answer the questions?	*not very* 1	2	3	4	*very* 5
Support/Elaboration: How well does the student support points with textual or other evidence?	1	2	3	4	5
Insight: How original, sophisticated, or compelling are the insights the student achieves?	1	2	3	4	5
Expression of Ideas: How well does the student use language, including word choice and conventions, in the expression of ideas?	1	2	3	4	5

Close Reading Activities

Comprehension: **Key Ideas and Details**

1. Interpret: In Scene I, what signs do you see that Gluskabe will successfully help the people?

2. (a) Find details in the stage directions that establish the seasons at various points in the play. **(b) Connect:** How are these details connected to the main conflict?

3. (a) Distinguish: How does the playwright characterize Old Man Winter? **(b) Infer:** What does this characterization suggest about the winter season?

4. Summarize: Write a brief objective summary of the drama. Cite story details in your writing.

Text Analysis: **Craft and Structure**

5. (a) What happens in each of the play's four scenes? **(b) Analyze:** Explain how the scenes form a plot with a conflict, rising action, climax, and resolution.

6. (a) Infer: Gluskabe speaks with Grandmother Woodchuck after Old Man Winter defeats him the first time. What

new information about Gluskabe do you learn from this conversation? **(b)** How does the dialogue move the story forward? Explain.

7. (a) What does the last stage direction describe? **(b) Analyze:** How is this stage direction essential to the play's plot?

Connections: **Integration of Knowledge and Ideas**

Discuss
Conduct a **small-group discussion** about the personification of winter and summer in the drama. Discuss why the Abenaki people might give human characteristics to these elements of nature.

Research
Briefly research several stories of the Abenaki culture. Consider these elements:

a. Gluskabe and other heroes

b. the use of stories as teaching tools

c. the role of nature

Take notes as you conduct your research. Then, write a brief **explanation** of the similarities one or more of the stories share with *Gluskabe and Old Man Winter*.

Write
Many traditional tales helped people make sense of the world. Write an essay in which you describe how *Gluskabe and Old Man Winter* explains an aspect of nature. Cite details from the play to support your analysis.

 How do we decide who we are?

(a) What are Gluskabe's strongest qualities? **(b)** How does he use his strengths to help his people? Cite specific details from the play in your answer.

Discuss
Students should recognize the contrasting human characteristics of winter (*harsh, cold*) and summer (*carefree, foolish*). Students might say the Abenaki find meaning in the characterization of the seasons.

Research
Students should use the identified elements of the Abenaki storytelling tradition to make clear, thoughtful connections with *Gluskabe and Old Man Winter*.

Write
Students should use details from the text to explain the nature and the changing of the seasons.

 How do we decide who we are?

(a) Gluskabe is determined, clever, and brave. **(b)** Gluskabe shows determination and bravery by continuing to fight Old Man Winter, despite being initially defeated by him. By being clever Gluskabe tricks the Summer Land People and finally brings spring and summer to help his people.

Possible responses appear below. Check to be sure students support their responses with evidence from the text.

1. Gluskabe is brave and confident. He says, "I will do what I can"; "Winter cannot beat me."

2. (a) Scene I: Winter (blankets). Scene II: Winter (Old Man Winter, a fire made of ice). Scene III: Summer. (a pot full of summer). Scene IV: Spring (sun, flowers, plants). **(b)** Gluskabe needs to get rid of Old Man Winter in order for spring and summer to come.

3. (a) Old Man Winter is fierce and aggressive. **(b)** The winter season can be harsh and cruel.

4. Old Man Winter is staying too long, so Gluskabe asks him to leave. After Old Man Winter defeats Gluskabe, Gluskabe travels to the Summer Land. By using a disguise, he is able to trick the Summer Land People and steal a summerstick. Gluskabe uses the summerstick to defeat Old Man Winter.

5. (a) Responses should summarize the action in each scene. **(b)** Conflict: Old Man Winter will not leave. Rising Action: Gluskabe decides to go to Summer Land. Climax: Gluskabe tricks the Summer Land People and steals a summerstick. Resolution: Old Man Winter is forced to leave.

6. (a) After learning about the traits of the Summer Land people, Gluskabe is able to come up with a cunning plan to bring summer back. **(b)** Their conversation sets in motion Gluskabe's defeat of Old Man Winter by bringing back summer.

7. (a) The last stage direction describes the collapse of Old Man Winter's wigwam, Old Man Winter's disappearance, and the appearance of the Sun, Flowers, and Plants. **(b)** This stage direction reveals the play's resolution: the end of winter and the arrival of spring.

❶ About the Quotation

Carl Sagan (1944–1996) was an American scientist and author.

Discussion Ask students to discuss the meaning of Sagan's quotation about imagination. Then ask them to decide whether they agree with the quotation. Have them explain and support their positions with sound reasoning and evidence.

❷ Critical Viewing

Pose the critical viewing question to the class. Then, guide the class in a discussion about the question. Encourage students to build upon each other's ideas as they share their responses. Remind students to support their responses with reasons and evidence.

❶ "**Imagination** will often carry us to **worlds that never were**, but without it we go nowhere."

—**Carl Sagan**

❓ DEVELOPING ESSENTIAL UNDERSTANDING

How do we decide who we are?

Explain to students that they will continue to consider the Big Question as they work through the selections in Part 2 of the unit.

- As students read each selection, they will look for details related to the Big Question and take notes.

- At the end of each selection, students will answer a Literary Analysis question that is related to the Big Question.

- Students will deepen their knowledge of the selections and their understanding of the Big Question through reading, speaking, listening, researching, and writing.

PART 2
TEXT ANALYSIS GUIDED EXPLORATION

ADVENTURE AND IMAGINATION

As you read the play in this section, you will explore a fantastic world filled with unusual characters, clever dialogue, and vivid settings. Take note of how the characters' behavior and feelings change as they navigate conflicts and challenges. The quotation on the opposite page will help you start thinking about how adventures—both imaginary and real—can expand your knowledge of yourself and the world around you.

2 ◄ **CRITICAL VIEWING** In what way is the girl in this picture using her imagination? What is the benefit of visiting "worlds that never were"?

3 **READINGS IN PART 2**

Drama
The Phantom Tollbooth, Act I
Susan Nanus
(p. 460)

Drama
The Phantom Tollbooth, Act II
Susan Nanus
(p. 490)

CLOSE READING TOOL

Use the Close Reading Tool to practice the strategies you learned in this unit.

3 **Readings in Part 2**
About the Texts
(For quantitative and qualitative measures of text complexity, see the rubrics on the opening pages of each selection.)

DRAMA: The Phantom Tollbooth, Act I

Summary In the drama, "The Phantom Tollbooth," Milo is a bored and restless boy who one day enters the Lands Beyond. In this fantasy world, Milo meets many fantastical, humorous characters who show him how to enjoy and value even the smallest things.

DRAMA: The Phantom Tollbooth, Act II

Summary Milo, Tock, and Humbug enter Digitopolis, a kingdom where characters are focused on numbers. After moving on through the Land of Ignorance into Castle-in-the-Air, Milo returns to his room, knowing more about how to spend time wisely.

CUSTOMIZING THE TEXT SET

Close Reading Tool
Use the Close Reading Tool to project the selections on a whiteboard and work through them as a whole-class activity. Students also have the opportunity to read these selections independently, with scaffolds available as needed.

Curriculum Builder
Customize this program by rearranging existing selections, adding selection titles of your choosing, and uploading your own resources—all online!

 **Audio**

Summary Audio is available in the *Student eText* and on the *Hear It!* CD-ROM.

Focus on Craft and Structure

❶ Elements of Drama

1. Introduce the elements of drama, using the instruction on the student page.

Have students compare and contrast drama to short stories and novels. **Ask:** Which elements of drama are similar to short stories and novels? Which elements are different?

Sample responses: *Similar—* Drama and other stories have plots, characters, settings, conflicts, resolutions, and themes. *Different—*Dramas have stage directions; dramas are meant to be performed; they are divided into acts; audiences learn about the plot and characters through dialogue (in a short story or novel, these can be conveyed through dialogue or narration); dramas are divided into acts and scenes, while novels are divided into chapters.

2. Referring to the chart on the student page, discuss the different elements of drama. Tell students to imagine that they are directing a play set in a forest at night. **Ask** what scenery and props they might use.

Sample response: Students might suggest a painted backdrop with trees and birds. Actors might use flashlights and backpacks as props.

❶ Elements of Drama

A drama is a story that is written to be performed by actors.

A **drama,** or play, is a story that is performed for an audience. You can read dramas, but they are really meant to be seen and heard. You can watch dramas on stage or on television, movie screens, or computer monitors.

In a drama, you meet **characters,** or fictional people. You watch their lives unfold in a particular **setting,** or time and place. Characters face a **conflict,** or problem, that moves them to act and react. The events that result form the **plot,** a series of actions that build to a **climax.** The climax is the plot's moment of greatest tension. After the climax, the action winds down. The conflict is settled—or left unsettled—in the **resolution,** or ending. Like most literary works, a drama expresses a **theme,** or insight about life.

The writer of a drama is called a **playwright** or **dramatist.** The written text of a drama is called a **script.** The script includes **dialogue,** or the words the actors speak. It may also include **stage directions** that describe the characters and setting.

Full-length dramas are divided into shorter sections, called **acts.** Each act may contain several **scenes.** A scene is like a little drama all by itself. It presents continuous action in a specific situation.

Elements of Drama	
Stage Directions	Stage directions are the playwright's instructions about how to perform the drama. They may include • details about the way the stage and characters should look; • instructions about where and how actors should move and speak; • details about other staging elements, such as scenery, lighting, sound, and costumes.
Dialogue	Conversation between characters is called dialogue. Through it, audiences learn about plot events and characters' feelings and actions.
Sets/Scenery	Sets and scenery are the constructions onstage that suggest the time and place of the action.
Props	Props are moveable items, such as books, coffee mugs, or newspapers. Actors use props to make their actions look realistic.
Acts and Scenes	Acts and scenes are units of action in dramas. Full-length dramas may have several acts, and each act may have several scenes.

454 UNIT 4 • How do we decide who we are?

② Forms of Drama: Past and Present

The oldest surviving dramas come from the ancient Greeks, who divided drama into two types:

- **Comedies** have happy endings. Their humor often comes out of the dialogue and situations. Like modern comedies, ancient comedies entertained but sometimes also expressed serious ideas about human nature.

- **Tragedies** show the downfall of a great person, known as the **tragic hero,** brought down by a fault, or **tragic flaw,** in his or her nature. The ancient tragedies were meant to teach and inspire with stories of legendary figures.

The experience of watching a play in ancient Greece was different from that of today. In ancient Greece, plays were performed in huge, open theaters. Thousands of spectators sat on stone benches that formed a semicircle around the performance space. The actors were all men, and some played more than one role. Each actor wore a mask to indicate his character's gender, age, and social position.

The next important era for drama took place in England in the late 1500s and early 1600s. Then, many audiences attended plays by William Shakespeare—perhaps the greatest playwright of all time. They sat in an open-air wooden playhouse, not as large as the Greek theater. All characters were still played by men, but they used makeup instead of masks.

Shakespeare and other playwrights of his time wrote tragedies that followed the Greek form, as well as comedies with romantic themes.

Today, modern dramas present serious subjects that mix both comedy and tragedy. We can watch a drama with live actors on a stage or watch a performance in a movie theater. We can even watch dramas alone at home in front of our televisions or computers.

Common Core State Standards

Reading Literature
3. Describe how a particular story's or drama's plot unfolds in a series of episodes as well as how the characters respond or change as the plot moves toward a resolution.
5. Analyze how a particular sentence, chapter, scene, or stanza fits into the overall structure of a text and contributes to the development of the theme, setting, or plot.

Live Theater	Film/Movies	Television Drama	Radio Play
• performed live for an audience • follows a written play **script** • uses scenery and lighting for effect	• recorded on film or digitally and shown in theaters • follows a script called a **screenplay** • uses camera angles for effect	• recorded or performed live • follows a script called a **teleplay** • like film, uses camera angles for effect	• recorded or performed live • follows a script called a **radio play** • uses dialogue and sound effects

PART 2 • Focus on Craft and Structure **455**

② Forms of Drama: Past and Present

1. Introduce the forms of drama, using the instruction on the student page.

2. Explain that both comedies and tragedies employ the elements of drama listed in the chart on the previous page.

3. Tell students that a major difference between a comedy and a tragedy is the way the drama ends. **Ask:** What type of ending would you expect each type of drama to have?

   Possible response: A comedy has a happy, upbeat ending. A tragedy has a sad or serious ending.

4. Review the forms of drama in the chart at the bottom of the student page.

5. **Ask:** Which dramatic form do you think would be the hardest to write? Why?

   Possible response: Students will probably say screenplays would be the hardest to write because they tend to be longer and more complex than shows on television or radio, and they include detailed information about camera angles.

⚙ DIFFERENTIATED INSTRUCTION

Support for Less Proficient Readers
Have students read the **Learning About Drama** pages for "Gluskabe and Old Man Winter" in the *Reader's Notebook: Adapted Version*. This version provides a basic-level introduction to drama.

ⓔ Support for English Learners
Have students read the **Learning About Drama** pages for "Gluskabe and Old Man Winter" in the *Reader's Notebook: English Learner's Version*. This version provides a basic-level introduction to drama.

❶ Analyzing Dramatic Elements

1. Introduce the dramatic elements, using the instruction on the student page.

2. Emphasize that unlike other forms of literature that are meant to be read, dramas make use of actions and dialogue to convey meaning. Review the three ways that playwrights use dialogue to reveal their characters.

3. Explain that sometimes, playwrights will make use of a special type of speech to give the audience information about the plot or characters. **Ask:** What is the difference between a monologue and a soliloquy?

   Answer: A monologue is a speech addressed to other characters who remain silent. A soliloquy is a speech a character delivers while alone.

   Ask: What is the difference between a soliloquy and an aside?

   Answer: An aside is always addressed to the audience. Sometimes a soliloquy is addressed to the audience, but other times, a character delivering a soliloquy is speaking to himself or herself.

4. **Ask:** Why are stage directions necessary in drama, but not in stories or novels?

   Possible response: Stories and novels develop plot by including descriptions and details. These elements are not usually part of a drama, so stage directions must describe the setting and tell how actors look, move, and speak.

❶ Analyzing Dramatic Elements

Most dramas focus on **characters** in **conflict** in order to express a **theme**.

The action in a drama is conveyed through the spoken dialogue and physical actions of its characters. A drama's plot may be full of twists and turns and ups and downs. When you read or watch a drama, you get to go along for the ride.

Keys to Character While some plays feature a narrator who gives the audience important information, most plays do not. Instead, audiences learn about characters from what they say. Playwrights use dialogue to reveal their characters in several ways:

- Characters may speak their inner thoughts, feelings, and conflicts out loud.
- Conversations among characters can reveal their feelings and personality traits.
- Characters may talk about each other. The reader or audience must decide whether to accept such comments as truth.

Most dramatic dialogue takes the form of conversations between or among characters. Sometimes, however, one character holds the spotlight with a special kind of speech.

- A **monologue** is a long, uninterrupted speech spoken by a character to other characters who remain silent. In a monologue, a character may reveal hidden feelings or may persuade another character to take action.
- A **soliloquy** is a speech a character delivers while alone. Sometimes the character speaks to the audience; sometimes only to himself or herself. Through a soliloquy, a character might explore an important question or make a decision.
- An **aside** is a comment made by a character to the audience. Other characters may be present, but an aside is not meant to be heard by anyone but the audience.

When you read a play, stage directions can provide important information about a character's feelings and personality. In the following example, the stage direction (printed in italics) reveals that the character is tired and perhaps frustrated.

> **Example:**
>
> Angela: *(pausing wearily before speaking)* What do you mean by that?

Great plays feature interesting characters whose stories hold the audience or reader's attention. The best dramas feature **complex characters** who have strengths and weaknesses and experience a variety of emotions. Complex characters are often pulled in different directions

because of the difficult situations that they face.

Conflict and Plot The problems, or conflicts, characters face are at the core of any drama. As characters respond to challenges and make decisions about how to solve conflicts, their feelings and behavior often change. These changes help move the plot from one event to another.

In drama, as in other types of literature, there are two main types of conflict. **External conflict** occurs between a character and an outside force, such as nature, society, or another character. **Internal conflict** occurs within the mind of a character. It arises when a character is torn between opposing feelings.

Type of Conflict	Examples
External Conflict *A character struggles against an outside force.*	• Against nature: A couple tries to climb a mountain. • Against society: A woman opposes a new city law. • Against another character: Two scientists claim the same discovery.
Internal Conflict *A character struggles against himself or herself.*	• An artist seeks fame but compromises her ideals. • A man has to choose between telling the truth and protecting his brother.

Scenes, or Episodes The events of a play are often presented in separate, connected episodes, or scenes. Every scene has a purpose. It may introduce or change the setting. For example, a scene at a train station may be followed by a scene on a train. A scene may also introduce a character, show a character making a decision, or begin an action that will lead to other actions.

Theme in Drama All the elements of a drama work together to create an illusion of reality, which is known as the *dramatic effect*. Dramatic elements also work to express a **theme,** or central idea about life. The conflict, characters' actions, and the resolution, or outcome of the story, all point to a play's theme. Viewers or readers may interpret that theme in different ways. A strong interpretation will take into account all the play's elements.

Dramatic Subject	Possible Theme
A young girl learns that she can have a full life in spite of her blindness.	With determination, we can overcome limitations.
War forces a family to flee their home and move to a new country.	Political conflicts disrupt innocent people's lives. Still, people survive.

The better a drama is, the more audiences connect with the characters, their situation, and the play's theme. When it is most powerful and effective, drama allows audiences to make discoveries about their own lives by identifying with the imagined lives of others.

5. Describe complex characters to students. Contrast complex characters with flat, one-dimensional characters and have students give examples of each type of character from dramas they have seen.

   Sample response: A character on my favorite TV show is complex because she is good at school, but she has a hard time making friends. She is happy by herself, but she gets nervous around others.

6. Remind students of the difference between external and internal conflict, and then review the conflict chart. Have students give examples of external and internal conflicts.

   Sample responses: External conflict: two cheerleaders are trying out for one position on a squad. Internal conflict: a boy is uncertain about whether to play football or focus more time on his studies.

7. Tell students that scenes are like chapters in novels—they separate the action into chunks. **Ask:** What is one way you can tell if you are watching a new scene?

   Possible response: The setting has changed.

8. Review the definition of a theme: the central insight expressed in a work of literature. **Ask:** What details help suggest the theme of a play?

   Sample response: what the conflict is, how it is resolved, how the characters relate to it, and how the story turns out

---

DIFFERENTIATED INSTRUCTION

Support for Special-Needs Students
Help students retain the information on dramatic elements by having them work in pairs to create graphic organizers in which to record important points. Have students make four-column charts with the headings *Character, Speeches, Conflict,* and *Theme* at the top of each column. Pairs should take turns reading and stop after each paragraph to note the most important details in their charts. Provide these examples of important details: Conflict: *problems characters face; two types: external (outer) and internal (inner).*

EL Support for English Learners
Support English Learners by previewing the page and giving them synonyms for new terms:
• *complex:* complicated
• *characters:* people
• *external:* outer
• *internal:* inner

   Encourage students to use a dictionary or thesaurus to find synonyms for other difficult words.

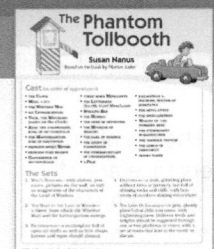

LESSON PACING GUIDE

The Phantom Tollbooth, Act I

DAY 1   Preteach/Teach

- Administer the Reading and Vocabulary Warm-ups, as necessary.
- Introduce the Key Ideas and Details skill: Summary.
- Introduce the Craft and Structure skill: Dialogue in Drama.
- Use the Close Reading Model to demonstrate the application of the skills.
- Review the selection vocabulary, as necessary, with students who need additional support.
- Prepare students to read the selection by reviewing with them the Multidraft Reading Strategies.

DAY 2   Teach

- Informally monitor comprehension while students read.
- Use the Comprehension questions to confirm understanding.
- Develop students' ability to summarize and analyze dialogue in drama using the sidenote questions.
- Reinforce vocabulary with the Vocabulary notes.
- Reinforce unit focus standards using the Spiral Review prompts.

DAY 3   Assess

- Assess students' comprehension and mastery of the skills by having them answer the Literary Analysis questions.
- Have students complete the Vocabulary activities.
- Develop students' understanding of roots and affixes by having them complete the Word Study activities.

DAY 4   Extend/Assess

- Build students' ability to master grammar concepts and conventions by having them complete the Conventions lesson.
- Have students complete the Writing to Sources activity and write a summary. (You may assign as homework.)
- Extend learning by having students complete the Research and Technology activity: a multimedia presentation.
- Administer the Selection Test or Open-Book Test.

Common Core State Standards

Reading Literature 2. Determine a theme or central idea of a text and how it is conveyed through particular details; provide a summary of the text distinct from personal opinions or judgments.

3. Describe how a particular story's or drama's plot unfolds in a series of episodes as well as how the characters respond or change as the plot moves toward a resolution.

5. Analyze how a particular sentence, chapter, scene, or stanza fits into the overall structure of a text and contributes to the development of the theme, setting, or plot.

6. Explain how an author develops the point of view of the narrator or speaker in a text.

Writing 4. Produce clear and coherent writing in which the development, organization, and style are appropriate to task, purpose, and audience.

6. Use technology, including the Internet.

8. Gather relevant information from multiple print and digital sources.

Speaking and Listening 5. Include multimedia components and visual displays in presentations to clarify information.

Language 1. Demonstrate command of the conventions of standard English grammar and usage when writing or speaking.

2.a. Use punctuation to set off nonrestrictive/parenthetical elements.

Daily Block Scheduling

Each day in this Lesson Pacing Guide represents a 40–50 minute period. Teachers using block scheduling may combine days to revise pacing. In addition, teachers may differentiate and support core instruction by integrating components for extended and intensive support as students require. See the Guide to Resources (facing page).

GUIDE TO RESOURCES

Section		L1	L2	L3	L4	EL	ALL	RESOURCES	PRINT	CD	ONLINE
Warm Up		✓	✓			✓		Vocabulary Warm-ups			✓
		✓	✓			✓		Reading Warm-ups			✓
							✓	Background Video			✓
							✓	Selection Audio		Hear It!	✓
Comprehension/ Selection Support							✓	Writing About the Big Question	Student Companion Workbook		✓
							✓	Literary Analysis	Student Companion Workbook		✓
							✓	Reading	Student Companion Workbook		✓
							✓	Vocabulary Builder	Student Companion Workbook		✓
					✓			Enrichment			✓
			✓	✓	✓			Conventions	Student Companion Workbook		✓
			✓	✓	✓			Writing to Sources	Student Companion Workbook		✓
			✓	✓	✓			Research and Technology	Student Companion Workbook		˙
Differentiated Instruction/ Additional Support							✓	Additional Standards Practice	Common Core Companion		✓
							✓	Close Reading Practice	Close Reading Notebook		✓
		✓	✓					Adapted Reader's Notebook			✓
						✓		English Reader's Notebook:			✓
						✓		Spanish Reader's Notebook			✓
						✓		Graphic Organizer A			✓
		✓	✓			✓		Graphic Organizer B			✓
		✓	✓			✓		"The Power to Move"	Reality Central Student Edition and Writing Journal		✓
		✓	✓			✓		Practice and Assess	Reading Kit		✓
Monitor Progress							✓	Selection Test		Exam View	✓
							✓	Open-Book Test		Exam View	✓
Digital Resources							✓	Close Reading Tool			✓
							✓	Online Writer's Notebook			✓

👥 One-on-one teaching ▦ Group work 👤 Whole class instruction 👤 Independent work Ⓐ Assessment 🖳 Digital Resource

LEARNER LEVELS

L1 Special-Needs Students **L3** On-Level Students (Tier 1) **EL** English Learners
L2 Below-Level Students (Tier 2) **L4** Advanced Students (Tier 1) **All** All Students

❶ How do we decide who we are?

Read • Discuss • Research • Write As students read, they will explore the Big Question through text analysis of the selection. Encourage students to take notes as they read and raise additional questions, using text evidence to support their thoughts. Students should refer to their notes to help them deepen their understanding of the selection through discussion, research, and writing.

❷ Close Reading Focus

1. Remind students that when they summarize, they have to record the main events, which requires leaving out most of the details.

2. Explain that when students analyze dialogue in drama as they read, they will have to imagine the speaker's facial expressions and body language. They can look for clues to tell them about the character: Why did he or she respond that way? What has already been said?

Meet the Author

Susan Nanus has written scripts for dramas, television miniseries, and movies. Like other screenwriters, she sometimes adapts, or reworks, novels to create screenplays for movies and scripts for stage plays. Her script for *The Phantom Tollbooth* was adapted from a novel by Norton Juster.

For a biography of Norton Juster, see page 488.

Common Core State Standards

Reading Literature
2. Determine a theme or central idea of a text and how it is conveyed through particular details; provide a summary of the text distinct from personal opinions or judgments.
3. Describe how a particular story's or drama's plot unfolds in a series of episodes as well as how the characters respond or change as the plot moves toward a resolution.
5. Analyze how a particular sentence, chapter, scene, or stanza fits into the overall structure of a text and contributes to the development of the theme, setting, or plot.
6. Explain how an author develops the point of view of the narrator or speaker in a text.

❶ How do we decide who we are?

Explore the Big Question as you read *The Phantom Tollbooth*. Take notes on ways in which the characters learn about themselves.

❷ CLOSE READING FOCUS

Key Ideas and Details: **Summary**

A **summary** of a literary work is a restatement of the work's main ideas and most important points. To summarize a drama, first reread to identify main events. In your summary, include only major events that move the story forward. Present the events in the order in which they happened.

Craft and Structure: **Dialogue in Drama**

A **drama** is a story that is written to be performed. Like short stories, dramas have characters, settings, and a plot that revolves around conflict. In dramas, however, these elements are developed mainly through **dialogue**, the words spoken by the characters. In the **script**, or written form of a drama, each character's name appears before his or her dialogue:

> **KATRINA.** I can't believe you said that!
> **WALLACE.** I was only kidding.

As you read this drama, notice how each character's point of view, or personality and beliefs, is developed through dialogue. Also, notice how the dialogue introduces conflict and moves the drama along.

Vocabulary

You will encounter the following words in *The Phantom Tollbooth*, Act I. Write the words, and then circle the two that share the same prefix. Write the meaning of the prefix, and explain how it changes the meaning of each base word.

ignorance	precautionary	unethical
ferocious	misapprehension	unabridged

ⓒ TEXT COMPLEXITY **RUBRIC**

The Phantom Tollbooth, Act I		Reader and Task Suggestions	
Qualitative Measures		**Preparing to Read the Text**	**Leveled Tasks**
Context/Knowledge Demands	Imaginary kingdoms; descriptive names; humor 1 2 ③ 4 5	• Point out the structure of a play in print. Discuss the differences on the page between stage directions, names of characters speaking, and the dialogue.	*Structure/Language* If students will have difficulty with the play format, have them note how the playwright uses brackets, italics, boldface, and capital letters to indicate setting and dialogue.
Structure/Language Conventionality and Clarity	Dialogue, sets and stage directions, word-play, long sentences 1 2 3 ④ 5		*Synthesizing* If students will not have difficulty with the play format, assign them to small groups to discuss one of the characters. Have them choose one of the settings in which the character appears and plan what items would be needed to create the set on stage.
Levels of Meaning/ Purpose/Concept Level	Accessible concept (valuing time and hard work) 1 2 ③ 4 5	• Guide students to use Multidraft Reading strategies (TE p. 460)	
Quantitative Measures			
Lexile	NP	**Text Length**	Word Count: 6,181

CLOSE READING MODEL

The passage below is from Susan Nanus's play *The Phantom Tollbooth*, Act I. The annotations to the right of the passage show how you can use close reading skills to summarize a drama and to analyze its dialogue.

from *The Phantom Tollbooth*, Act I

LETHARGARIAN 1. You're . . . in . . . the . . . Dol . . .drums . . . [*Milo looks around.*]

LETHARGARIAN 2. Yes . . . the . . . Dol . . . drums . . . [*A YAWN is heard.*]

MILO. [*Yelling.*] WHAT ARE THE DOLDRUMS?.

LETHARGARIAN 3. The Doldrums, my friend, are where nothing ever happens and nothing ever changes. [*Parts of the Scenery stand up or Six People come out of the scenery colored in the same colors of the trees or the road. They move very slowly and as soon as they move, they stop to rest again.*] [1] Allow me to introduce all of us. We are the Lethargarians at your service.

MILO. [*Uncertainly.*] Very pleased to meet you. I think I'm lost. Can you help me?

LETHARGARIAN 4. Don't say think. [*He yawns.*] It's against the law.

LETHARGARIAN 1. No one's allowed to think in the Doldrums. [*He falls asleep.*] [2]

LETHARGARIAN 2. Don't you have a rule book? It's local ordinance 175389-J. [*He falls asleep.*] [3]

Dialogue in Drama

1 This dialogue introduces aspects of character, setting, and plot. The Lethargarians are characters who appear tired, and speak very slowly. The setting is a place called the Doldrums. Milo's question tells you that he has no idea where he is.

Dialogue in Drama

2 This dialogue presents the surprising news that thinking is not allowed in the Doldrums. This information may hint at a possible conflict later in the plot.

Summary

3 To summarize this entire passage, you might write: "Milo finds himself in a strange land called the Doldrums, whose sleepy, slow-moving citizens, the Lethargarians, are forbidden to think."

For each class during which you will teach this selection, have students complete one of the five Vocabulary activities for Week 21 in *Daily Bellringer Activities*. You may wish to use additional activities that are applicable to this selection.

Vocabulary

If students require support with selection vocabulary, use this routine:

1. Write the following words and definitions on the board:

   ignorance *n.* lack of knowledge, education, or experience

   precautionary *adj.* done to prevent harm or danger

   unethical *adj.* not conforming to the moral standards of a group

   ferocious *adj.* wild and dangerous

   misapprehension *n.* misunderstanding

   unabridged *adj.* complete; not shortened

2. Have students say each word aloud.

3. Use the word in a sentence that defines the word.

DIFFERENTIATED INSTRUCTION

EL Extended Support— English Learners
Have students complete the **Reading and Vocabulary Warm-ups** for this selection in the *Student Companion All-in-One Workbook* before they read. Assign the prereading pages and the adapted selection in the *Reader's Notebook: English Learner's Version*. Then, have students listen to portions of the selection in the *Student eText* or on the *Hear It!* **CD-ROM.**

L1 L2 Extended Support— Struggling Readers
Have students complete the **Reading and Vocabulary Warm-ups** for this selection in the *Student Companion All-in-One Workbook* before they read. Assign the prereading pages and the adapted selection in the *Reader's Notebook: Adapted Version*. Then, have students listen to portions of the selection in the *Student eText* or on the *Hear It!* **CD-ROM** (adapted text).

Extended Support— Reluctant Readers
To build motivation and engagement before assigning the selection, have students read "The Power to Move" and "Taking Sides on Time," thematically related selections in *Reality Central*. Then, use the questions at the conclusions of the related selection to guide discussion.

MULTIDRAFT READING

To assist struggling readers and to deepen comprehension for all, assign the text in "chunks" and apply multidraft reading protocols. For each reading, have students set the purpose indicated:

- **First reading:** Students should read the selection independently and think about its basic meaning.
- **Second reading:** Students should analyze the text's key ideas and details and its craft and structure, and respond to the side-column prompts.
- **Third reading:** Students should integrate knowledge and ideas, connect the text to other texts and to the world, and answer the end-of-selection questions.

For more guidance, refer to the *Classroom Strategies and Teaching Routines* card on multidraft reading.

❶ Activating Prior Knowledge

Use the **Vocab-o-Gram** strategy (*Professional Development Guidebook,* p. 40) to introduce students to terminology and to make predictions about the play's characters, setting, and events. Write the following words on the board or overhead:

destination	fractions
words	Dictionopolis
Lethargarians	nap
slowly	square meal
Mathemagician	Royal Banquet
alarm	journey
light snack	Watchdog
Mountains of Ignorance	crags

Then give students the **Vocab-o-Gram** chart (*Professional Development Guidebook,* p. 40) and have them work with a partner or group to place the words in appropriate categories and make predictions about the play. Have students discuss or explain their word placements, their reasons, and their predictions. Students will re-examine their ideas after reading Act I.

❶ The Phantom Tollbooth

Susan Nanus
Based on the book by Norton Juster

Cast (in order of appearance)

- THE CLOCK
- MILO, A BOY
- THE WHETHER MAN
- SIX LETHARGARIANS
- TOCK, THE WATCHDOG (same as the clock)
- AZAZ THE UNABRIDGED, KING OF DICTIONOPOLIS
- THE MATHEMAGICIAN, KING OF DIGITOPOLIS
- PRINCESS SWEET RHYME
- PRINCESS PURE REASON
- GATEKEEPER OF DICTIONOPOLIS

- THREE WORD MERCHANTS
- THE LETTERMAN (fourth word Merchant)
- SPELLING BEE
- THE HUMBUG
- THE DUKE OF DEFINITION
- THE MINISTER OF MEANING
- THE EARL OF ESSENCE
- THE COUNT OF CONNOTATION
- THE UNDERSECRETARY OF UNDERSTANDING
- A PAGE

- KAKAFONOUS A. DISCHORD, DOCTOR OF DISSONANCE
- THE AWFUL DYNNE
- THE DODECAHEDRON
- MINERS OF THE NUMBERS MINE
- THE EVERPRESENT WORDSNATCHER
- THE TERRIBLE TRIVIUM
- THE DEMON OF INSINCERITY
- SENSES TAKER

The Sets

1. MILO'S BEDROOM—with shelves, pennants, pictures on the wall, as well as suggestions of the characters of the Land of Wisdom.

2. THE ROAD TO THE LAND OF WISDOM— a forest, from which the Whether Man and the Lethargarians emerge.

3. DICTIONOPOLIS—a marketplace full of open air stalls as well as little shops. Letters and signs should abound.

4. DIGITOPOLIS—a dark, glittering place without trees or greenery, but full of shining rocks and cliffs, with hundreds of numbers shining everywhere.

5. THE LAND OF IGNORANCE—a gray, gloomy place full of cliffs and caves, with frightening faces. Different levels and heights should be suggested through one or two platforms or risers, with a set of stairs that lead to the castle in the air.

🗨 VOCABULARY DEVELOPMENT

Thematic Vocabulary: The Big Question

As students are discussing *The Phantom Tollbooth,* Act I, encourage them to use the thematic vocabulary presented in Introducing the Big Question, pp. 440–441. You might encourage them with sentence starters like these:

1. At the beginning of the play, the *appearance* of a talking clock sets a mood of . . .

2. The Clock describes Milo's *personality* by saying . . .

3. When Milo receives a large package, his *expectations* are . . .

4. Each character Milo encounters has a *unique* way of . . .

5. When Milo tells Tock that he is "killing time," the Watchdog's *reaction* is . . .

Act I • Scene i

[The stage is completely dark and silent. Suddenly the sound of someone winding an alarm clock is heard, and after that, the sound of loud ticking is heard.]

[LIGHTS UP on the Clock, *a huge alarm clock. The* Clock *reads 4:00. The lighting should make it appear that the* Clock *is suspended in mid-air (if possible). The* Clock *ticks for 30 seconds.]*

Clock. See that! Half a minute gone by. Seems like a long time when you're waiting for something to happen, doesn't it? Funny thing is, time can pass very slowly or very fast, and sometimes even both at once. The time now? Oh, a little after four, but what that means should depend on you. Too often, we do something simply because time tells us to. Time for school, time for bed, whoops, 12:00, time to be hungry. It can get a little silly, don't you think? Time is important, but it's what you do with it that makes it so. So my advice to you is to use it. Keep your eyes open and your ears perked. Otherwise it will pass before you know it, and you'll certainly have missed something!
Things have a habit of doing that, you know. Being here one minute and gone the next.
In the twinkling of an eye.
In a jiffy.
In a flash!
I know a girl who yawned and missed a whole summer vacation. And what about that caveman who took a nap one afternoon, and woke up to find himself completely alone. You see, while he was sleeping, someone had invented the wheel and everyone had moved to the suburbs. And then of course, there is Milo. *[LIGHTS UP to reveal* Milo's *Bedroom. The* Clock *appears to be on a shelf in the room of a young boy—a room filled with books, toys, games, maps, papers, pencils, a bed, a desk. There is a dartboard with numbers and the face of the* Mathemagician, *a bedspread made from* King Azaz's *cloak, a kite looking like the Spelling Bee, a punching bag with the* Humbug's *face, as well as records, a television,*

◀ **Vocabulary**
ignorance (igʹ nə rəns)
n. lack of knowledge, education, or experience

Summary
How would you summarize the point Clock is making?

❸ Comprehension
How do you know what characters and sets are in this play?

---

❷ Summary

1. Remind students that a summary includes the main idea of a passage and only the most important points.

2. Have a volunteer read the bracketed dialogue. To reinforce that this is a drama, encourage the reader to use a voice that might sound like Clock's character.

3. **Ask** the Summary question. Tell students to state the main idea in their own words.

   Possible response: Make good use of your time before it's too late.

❸ Comprehension

Answer: The characters and the sets are listed on the first page of the play.

👥 DIFFERENTIATED INSTRUCTION

Support for Special-Needs Students
Students might benefit from noting the typographical clues within *The Phantom Tollbooth.* Call students' attention to how the playwright sets off information by using brackets, italics, boldfaced, and capital letters. Have students make a list of these treatments and note what each treatment signifies in the text.

EL Vocabulary for English Learners
To help students understand some of the characters and what they represent, review difficult vocabulary and discuss the meaning of characters' names and how they relate to their traits. Then help students apply what they have learned by asking them to describe the traits a character named Computer might have.

Video

Watch the Background Video online!

Audio

Selection audio is available in the **Student eText** and on the **Hear It!** CD-ROM.

4 Literature in Context

Culture Connection Private investors brought turnpikes to the United States in hopes of making money. Although turnpike companies improved American roads, they turned out to be poor investments. As a result, the United States government took over the job of road building and maintenance. Today, as in the past, the fee from a turnpike is used to cover the costs of building and maintaining the road.

Connect to the Literature
Before asking the question, have students imagine what they would do with a "genuine turnpike tollbooth" if they were given one as a gift.

Possible response: This gift might rescue Milo from his bored state of mind by causing him to use his own imagination.

---

4 LITERATURE IN CONTEXT

Culture Connection

Turnpike Tollbooth
A turnpike is a road that people pay a fee, or toll, to use. Long ago, long spears called "pikes" barred the road. The pikes were turned aside only after travelers paid the toll. A tollbooth is the booth or gate at which tolls are collected. The first record of tolls being collected dates from about 2000 B.C., when tolls were collected on a Persian military road between Babylon and Syria.

Connect to the Literature

How might the tollbooth—an unusual gift—affect Milo's bored state of mind?

Vocabulary ▶
precautionary (pri kô´ shə ner´ē) *adj.* done to prevent harm or danger

---

a toy car, and a large box that is wrapped and has an envelope taped to the top. The sound of FOOTSTEPS is heard, and then enter MILO *dejectedly. He throws down his books and coat, flops into a chair, and sighs loudly.*] Who never knows what to do with himself—not just sometimes, but always. When he's in school, he wants to be out, and when he's out he wants to be in. [*During the following speech,* MILO *examines the various toys, tools, and other possessions in the room, trying them out and rejecting them.*] Wherever he is, he wants to be somewhere else—and when he gets there, so what. Everything is too much trouble or a waste of time. Books—he's already read them. Games—boring. T.V.—dumb. So what's left? Another long, boring afternoon. Unless he bothers to notice a very large package that happened to arrive today.

MILO. [*Suddenly notices the package. He drags himself over to it, and disinterestedly reads the label.*] "For Milo, who has plenty of time." Well, that's true. [*Sighs and looks at it.*] No. [*Walks away.*] Well . . . [*Comes back. Rips open envelope and reads.*]

A VOICE. "One genuine turnpike tollbooth, easily assembled at home for use by those who have never traveled in lands beyond."

MILO. Beyond what? [*Continues reading.*]

A VOICE. "This package contains the following items:" [MILO *pulls the items out of the box and sets them up as they are mentioned.*] "One (1) genuine turnpike tollbooth to be erected according to directions. Three (3) precautionary signs to be used in a precautionary fashion. Assorted coins for paying tolls. One (1) map, strictly up to date, showing how to get from here to there. One (1) book of rules and traffic regulations which may not be bent or broken. Warning! Results are not guaranteed. If not perfectly satisfied, your wasted time will be refunded."

💬 VOCABULARY DEVELOPMENT

Word Analysis

Direct students' attention to the word *precautionary* and its definition on this page. Explain to students that the Latin *pre-*, meaning "before," is a clue that precautionary measures must be taken before something happens. Discuss with students other words that begin with *pre-*. Work together to define each one or allow students to find definitions based on the meaning of the prefix and root word. Words might include *prehistoric* (events that happened or objects that existed before written history), *preheat* (to heat to a specified temperature before using), *prepay* (to pay for something in advance), and *preview* (to see beforehand).

MILO. [*Skeptically.*] Come off it, who do you think you're kidding? [*Walks around and examines tollbooth.*] What am I supposed to do with this? [*The ticking of the* CLOCK *grows loud and impatient.*] Well . . . what else do I have to do. [MILO *gets into his toy car and drives up to the first sign.*]

VOICE. "HAVE YOUR DESTINATION IN MIND."

MILO. [*Pulls out the map.*] Now, let's see. That's funny. I never heard of any of these places. Well, it doesn't matter anyway. Dictionopolis. That's a weird name. I might as well go there. [*Begins to move, following map. Drives off.*]

CLOCK. See what I mean? You never know how things are going to get started. But when you're bored, what you need more than anything is a rude awakening.

[*The ALARM goes off very loudly as the stage darkens. The sound of the alarm is transformed into the honking of a car horn, and is then joined by the blasts, bleeps, roars and growls of heavy highway traffic. When the lights come up, Milo's bedroom is gone and we see a lonely road in the middle of nowhere.*]

Summary
Reread Scene i to identify and summarize the key events.

Scene ii • The Road to Dictionopolis

[*Enter* MILO *in his car.*]

MILO. This is weird! I don't recognize any of this scenery at all. [*A SIGN is held up before* MILO, *startling him.*] Huh? [*Reads.*] WELCOME TO EXPECTATIONS. INFORMATION, PREDICTIONS AND ADVICE CHEERFULLY OFFERED. PARK HERE AND BLOW HORN. [MILO *blows horn.*]

WHETHER MAN. [*A little man wearing a long coat and carrying an umbrella pops up from behind the sign that he was holding. He speaks very fast and excitedly.*] My, my, my, my, my, welcome, welcome, welcome, welcome to the Land of Expectations, Expectations, Expectations! We don't get many travelers these days; we certainly don't get many travelers. Now what can I do for you? I'm the Whether Man.

MILO. [*Referring to map.*] Uh . . . is this the right road to Dictionopolis?

Dialogue in Drama
What do you learn about the Whether Man from his first speech?

❼ Comprehension
What is in the package Milo opens?

❺ Summary

1. Have a volunteer point out where *Scene i* ends and explain how the reader knows that.

2. Read the Summary instructions. Allow time for students to reread the scene independently.

3. Then, ask volunteers to identify the key events in the scene. Have students record these events in their **Reading Skill Graphic Organizers** for this selection.

4. After students have identified key events, **ask** them to summarize *Scene i*, using the information on their graphic organizers.

   Possible response: Milo is bored. He receives a tollbooth as a gift. He decides to drive his toy car to a destination called Dictionopolis.

❻ Dialogue in Drama

1. Ask a volunteer to read the bracketed dialogue. Again, reinforce that this is a drama by encouraging readers to speak in a way that the character might speak.

2. **Ask** students to comment on something that is unusual about Whether Man's speech.

   Possible response: He speaks very quickly; he repeats words, as in "My, my, my, my, my, welcome, welcome, welcome, welcome."

3. **Ask** the Dialogue in Drama question.

   Possible Responses: Whether Man is very excitable. Whether Man is happy to see Milo and eager to help him.

❼ Comprehension

Answer: The package contains an unassembled tollbooth, signs, coins, a map, and a book of rules.

🏿 DIFFERENTIATED INSTRUCTION

⒠ Support for English Learners
Have students look up the words *whether* and *weather* in a dictionary. Then, have them work in small groups to make a list of how the word *whether* is depicted in the character traits of Whether Man. Discuss how the author might have depicted the character differently if the character's name had been Weather Man.

Enrichment for Gifted/Talented Students
Prearrange small groups of students and assign a setting from the play to each one. Have them discuss the description of their setting, then take on the roles of set designers. Tell them to decide on the props they need to make the set. Then have individuals sketch the set, incorporating items from the group's list of props. Provide time for students to share their sketches with the class.

❽ Dialogue in Drama

1. Using character voices, ask two students to read the bracketed dialogue.

2. Ask students where Milo is when he meets the Whether Man.

Answer: He is in the Land of Expectations.

3. Ask students where Milo is trying to go.

Answer: He is trying to go to Dictionopolis.

4. Ask the first Dialogue in Drama question.

Answer: Milo tries to see if he's on the right road to Dictionopolis. When he finds that Whether Man isn't that helpful, he decides to find his own way.

❾ Dialogue in Drama

1. Remind students that character, settings, and the plot in dramas are mainly developed through the words that characters say.

2. Have a volunteer read Milo's words.

3. Ask students to identify the main point that Milo is making.

Answer: Milo is in a hurry to move on.

4. Ask the second Dialogue in Drama question.

Possible response: His saying that he needs to get out of here fast causes the plot to jump forward to a new event.

Dialogue in Drama
What do you learn about the action from this dialogue between Milo and Whether Man?

Dialogue in Drama
How do Milo's words here move the plot along?

WHETHER MAN. Well now, well now, well now, I don't know of any wrong road to Dictionopolis, so if this road goes to Dictionopolis at all, it must be the right road, and if it doesn't, it must be the right road to somewhere else, because there are no wrong roads to anywhere. Do you think it will rain?

MILO. I thought you were the Weather Man.

WHETHER MAN. Oh, no, I'm the Whether Man, not the weather man. [*Pulls out a SIGN or opens a FLAP of his coat, which reads: "WHETHER."*] After all, it's more important to know whether there will be weather than what the weather will be.

MILO. What kind of place is Expectations?

WHETHER MAN. Good question, good question! Expectations is the place you must always go to before you get to where you are going. Of course, some people never go beyond Expectations, but my job is to hurry them along whether they like it or not. Now what else can I do for you? [*Opens his umbrella.*]

MILO. I think I can find my own way.

WHETHER MAN. Splendid, splendid, splendid! Whether or not you find your own way, you're bound to find some way. If you happen to find my way, please return it. I lost it years ago. I imagine by now it must be quite rusty. You did say it was going to rain, didn't you? [*Escorts MILO to the car under the open umbrella.*] I'm glad you made your own decision. I do so hate to make up my mind about anything, whether it's good or bad, up or down, rain or shine. Expect everything, I always say, and the unexpected never happens. Goodbye, goodbye, goodbye, good . . .

[*A loud CLAP of THUNDER is heard.*] Oh dear! [*He looks up at the sky, puts out his hand to feel for rain, and RUNS AWAY. MILO watches puzzledly and drives on.*]

MILO. I'd better get out of Expectations, but fast. Talking to a guy like that all day would get me nowhere for sure. [*He tries to speed up, but finds instead that he is moving slower and slower.*] Oh, oh, now what? [*He can barely move. Behind MILO, the LETHARGARIANS begin*

💬 VOCABULARY DEVELOPMENT

Descriptive Words

Remind students that the Whether Man said "Splendid, splendid, splendid" when Milo said he could find his own way. From left to right, write the words *acceptable, fine, good,* and *splendid.* Discuss how the degree of satisfaction expressed by the words increases from left to right. Using a thesaurus and a dictionary, work with students to list synonyms for *acceptable.* Then have teams of students list synonyms for the remaining words. Provide help where needed. Ask students to give their opinions about which would be the most interesting word to substitute for *splendid* in the dialogue.

to enter from all parts of the stage. They are dressed to blend in with the scenery and carry small pillows that look like rocks. Whenever they fall asleep, they rest on the pillows.] Now I really am getting nowhere. I hope I didn't take a wrong turn. [The car stops. He tries to start it. It won't move. He gets out and begins to tinker with it.] I wonder where I am.

LETHARGARIAN 1. You're . . . in . . . the . . . Dol . . . drums . . . [MILO looks around.]

LETHARGARIAN 2. Yes . . . the . . . Dol . . . drums . . . [A YAWN is heard.]

MILO. [Yelling.] WHAT ARE THE DOLDRUMS?

LETHARGARIAN 3. The Doldrums, my friend, are where nothing ever happens and nothing ever changes. [Parts of the Scenery stand up or Six People come out of the scenery colored in the same colors of the trees or the road. They move very slowly and as soon as they move, they stop to rest again.] Allow me to introduce all of us. We are the Lethargarians at your service.

MILO. [Uncertainly.] Very pleased to meet you. I think I'm lost. Can you help me?

LETHARGARIAN 4. Don't say think. [He yawns.] It's against the law.

LETHARGARIAN 1. No one's allowed to think in the Doldrums. [He falls asleep.]

LETHARGARIAN 2. Don't you have a rule book? It's local ordinance 175389-J. [He falls asleep.]

MILO. [Pulls out rule book and reads.] Ordinance 175389-J: "It shall be unlawful, illegal and unethical to think, think of thinking, surmise, presume, reason, meditate or speculate while in the Doldrums. Anyone breaking this law shall be severely punished." That's a ridiculous law! Everybody thinks.

ALL THE LETHARGARIANS. We don't!

▼ Critical Viewing
What details in this picture show what the Lethargarians are like?

◄ Vocabulary
unethical (un eth´ i kəl) adj. not conforming to the moral standards of a group

12 Comprehension
What are the Doldrums?

PART 2 • The Phantom Tollbooth, Act I **465**

10 Critical Viewing
Answer: The Lethargarians are shown sleeping on pillows that look like rocks. The details indicate that they are sluggish, sleepy creatures.

11 Connect
1. After students read the dialogue on this page, ask a volunteer to reread the bracketed text.
2. Have students return to p. 462. Read aloud the passage at the top, from "Who never knows what to do . . ." through "Another long, boring afternoon." (Do not include the stage direction in your reading.)
3. Remind students that, in this passage, the Clock is referring to Milo. **Ask:** What similarity is there between Milo's life at home and the Doldrums?

   Answer: "Another long, boring afternoon" for Milo is like the idea that "nothing ever happens, nothing ever changes" in the Doldrums.

12 Comprehension
Answer: The Doldrums is a place where nothing ever happens and nothing ever changes.

🔧 DIFFERENTIATED INSTRUCTION

Background for Less Proficient Readers
Teach students the words *lethargy* and *lethargic* so they can relate the Lethargarians to their characteristics. Then revisit the rules for living in the land of the Lethargarians. Have them reread the rules that Milo finds in the rulebook and restate the rules in their own words. Discuss why the rules are humorous and whether or not students think the rules are enforceable.

Enrichment for Advanced Readers
Students will likely be amused by the rules that start on this page. Call attention to the numbers of the ordinances, the language used in the rules, and the time limits on scheduled activities. Invite each student to make up his or her own preposterous rules for the classroom in the style of the Lethargarian rules. Post the rules for the class to enjoy.

PART 2 • The Phantom Tollbooth, Act I **465**

⓭ Dialogue in Drama

1. Have two volunteers read the bracketed dialogue between Lethargarian 5 and Milo.

2. **Ask** students what Milo was doing that was against the rules.

   Answer: He was laughing.

3. **Ask** the first Dialogue in Drama question.

   Possible response: It is a dull and humorless place that has too many rules about people's behavior. In the Doldrums, there is a lot of nothing to do.

⓮ Dialogue in Drama

1. Read aloud the instruction at the beginning of the Dialogue in Drama question: "Ellipsis points—three spaced periods—often indicate a pause or an unfinished thought."

2. Have volunteers read the bracketed dialogue. Encourage them to read the lines as sleepy, sluggish Lethargarians might. Remind them to pause when they come to each ellipsis.

3. **Ask** the second Dialogue in Drama question.

   Possible response: The punctuation shows me where to pause to suggest the sluggish, lethargic way the characters describe their schedule.

Dialogue in Drama
What does this dialogue reveal about the Doldrums?

Dialogue in Drama
Ellipsis points—three spaced periods—often indicate a pause or an unfinished thought. How does this punctuation help you understand the way the dialogue should be read?

LETHARGARIAN 2. And most of the time, you don't, that's why you're here. You weren't thinking and you weren't paying attention either. People who don't pay attention often get stuck in the Doldrums. Face it, most of the time, you're just like us. [*Falls, snoring, to the ground.* MILO *laughs.*]

LETHARGARIAN 5. Stop that at once. Laughing is against the law. Don't you have a rule book? It's local ordinance 574381-W.

MILO. [*Opens rule book and reads.*] "In the Doldrums, laughter is frowned upon and smiling is permitted only on alternate Thursdays." Well, if you can't laugh or think, what can you do?

LETHARGARIAN 6. Anything as long as it's nothing, and everything as long as it isn't anything. There's lots to do. We have a very busy schedule . . .

LETHARGARIAN 1. At 8:00 we get up and then we spend from 8 to 9 daydreaming.

LETHARGARIAN 2. From 9:00 to 9:30 we take our early mid-morning nap . . .

LETHARGARIAN 3. From 9:30 to 10:30 we dawdle and delay . . .

LETHARGARIAN 4. From 10:30 to 11:30 we take our late early morning nap . . .

LETHARGARIAN 5. From 11:30 to 12:00 we bide our time and then we eat our lunch.

LETHARGARIAN 6. From 1:00 to 2:00 we linger and loiter . . .

LETHARGARIAN 1. From 2:00 to 2:30 we take our early afternoon nap . . .

LETHARGARIAN 2. From 2:30 to 3:30 we put off for tomorrow what we could have done today . . .

LETHARGARIAN 3. From 3:30 to 4:00 we take our early late afternoon nap . . .

LETHARGARIAN 4. From 4:00 to 5:00 we loaf and lounge until dinner . . .

LETHARGARIAN 5. From 6:00 to 7:00 we dilly-dally . . .

466 UNIT 4 • How do we decide who we are?

💬 THINK ALOUD

Context Clues

Direct students' attention to the phrase *bide our time* on this page. Using a think-aloud process, model how to use context to infer the meaning of an unknown phrase. Say to students:

I'm going to think aloud to show you how I would figure out what *bide our time* means from its context.

One of the Lethargarians explains that they bide their time from 11:30 to 12:00.

When I look at the other activities on the Letharagarians' schedule I see activities such as dawdling, delaying, lingering, and loitering. This makes me think that *biding time* does not involve anything done quickly or actively. So I think that *biding time* means waiting, or slowly passing time.

Science Connection
Measuring Time
The Latin poet Ovid coined the phrase "Time flies." Through the ages, telling time has advanced from tracking shadows to measuring vibrations.

Egyptian shadow clocks, or sundials, tell time by measuring the length or angle of a shadow on the dial as the sun moves across the sky.

The quartz clock uses the vibrations of quartz crystal to generate an electric signal that drives the clock. Quartz powers digital watches.

3500 B.C.
Egyptian water clocks measured time by the flow of water through a small hole.

A.D. 100–1300
Chinese water clock towers, above, used water spilling from buckets to drive the wheels.

mid-1600s
This grandfather clock's weight-driven pendulum greatly improved timetelling accuracy.

1920s

1945
The atomic clock is the most accurate timepiece today. It tracks time by measuring movement between an atom's nucleus and surrounding electrons.

Connect to the Literature
Do you think Milo is interested in keeping track of time? Explain.

LETHARGARIAN 6. From 7:00 to 8:00 we take our early evening nap and then for an hour before we go to bed, we waste time.

LETHARGARIAN 1. [*Yawning.*] You see, it's really quite strenuous doing nothing all day long, and so once a week, we take a holiday and go nowhere.

LETHARGARIAN 5. Which is just where we were going when you came along. Would you care to join us?

MILO. [*Yawning.*] That's where I seem to be going, anyway. [*Stretching.*] Tell me, does everyone here do nothing?

LETHARGARIAN 3. Everyone but the terrible Watchdog. He's always sniffing around to see that nobody wastes time. A most unpleasant character.

MILO. The Watchdog?

⑯ **Comprehension**
Basically, what do the Lethargarians do all day?

GUIDED EXPLORATION

⑮ **Literature in Context**
Science Connection The International Bureau of Weights and Measures is keeper of the "official time" for the world. It uses Cesium Atomic Clocks in approximately 230 countries around the world as the basis for this time. These clocks are based on the vibration of the single electron of the Cesium 133 atom. There is a Cesium Atomic Clock in Boulder, Colorado. This clock is so accurate that it would not gain or lose a second in more than 60 million years.

Connect to the Literature
Before asking the question, have students think about whether or not Milo has paid any attention to the time so far.

Possible response: Milo is not interested in keeping track of time. He was very bored before this adventure began, so he probably doesn't think much about a schedule.

⑯ **Comprehension**
Answer: They spend all day doing nothing.

🗱 DIFFERENTIATED INSTRUCTION

Support for English Learners
The Lethargarians' dialogue presents an opportunity to teach synonyms. They describe their daily activities with words such as *dawdle, delay, linger, loiter, lounge, loaf,* and *dilly-dally.* Have each student think of other words that can be used to describe idle or time-wasting activities. After they compose their lists, pair students with proficient speakers to learn the connotations of the words they identified as well as the Lethargarians' words.

Support for Special-Needs Students
Students may benefit from a representation of the Lethargarians' schedule to help them visualize how they spend their time. On the left side of a piece of paper, have each student write time in half-hour increments, from 8:00 in the morning to 8:00 at night. Model filling in the blocks of time with the activities identified in the dialogue, pointing out that some activities take an hour and some take a half hour. When students have completed the schedule, discuss whether the Lethargarians do anything useful.

⑰ Summary

1. After students read the bracketed text, ask a volunteer to summarize what just happened.

Answer: Watchdog has just entered, and he scared off all of the Lethargarians.

2. **Ask** the Summary question.

Possible responses: Some students may include Watchdog's arrival because he or she appears to be an important character. Others may not include Watchdog because they are waiting to see if this is an important character.

▶ **Monitor Progress:** Ask students to share the most recent events they have recorded on their **Summary Graphic Organizers**.

Spiral Review

Character

1. Remind students that they studied the concept of character in the Unit 4 Focus on Craft and Structure (pp. 454–457).

2. **Ask** students the Spiral Review question.

Possible response: He is now more interested in thinking and paying attention to what he is doing.

⑱ Dialogue in Drama

1. **Ask** students to recall the rule regarding thinking in the Doldrums.

Answer: Thinking is against the rules.

2. **Ask** students what Milo is attempting to do.

Answer: He is trying to leave the Doldrums.

3. Have two volunteers read aloud the bracketed dialogue between Milo and Watchdog.

4. **Ask** the Dialogue in Drama question.

Possible response: Their conversation shows that the reason Milo can't drive on is that he has stopped thinking. Watchdog is encouraging Milo to use his brain and think again.

Summary
Would you include the arrival of the Watchdog in a summary of this scene? Why or why not?

Spiral Review
CHARACTER How has Milo changed as a result of visiting the Lethargarians?

Dialogue in Drama
How does the dialogue between Milo and the Watchdog help you understand the problem here?

LETHARGARIAN 6. THE WATCHDOG!

ALL THE LETHARGARIANS. [*Yelling at once.*] RUN! WAKE UP! RUN! HERE HE COMES! THE WATCHDOG! [*They all run off and ENTER a large dog with the head, feet, and tail of a dog, and the body of a clock, having the same face as the character* THE CLOCK.]

⑰ **WATCHDOG.** What are you doing here?

MILO. Nothing much. Just killing time. You see . . .

WATCHDOG. KILLING TIME! [*His ALARM RINGS in fury.*] It's bad enough wasting time without killing it. What are you doing in the Doldrums, anyway? Don't you have anywhere to go?

MILO. I think I was on my way to Dictionopolis when I got stuck here. Can you help me?

WATCHDOG. Help you! You've got to help yourself. I suppose you know why you got stuck.

MILO. I guess I just wasn't thinking.

WATCHDOG. Precisely. Now you're on your way.

⑱ **MILO.** I am?

WATCHDOG. Of course. Since you got here by not thinking, it seems reasonable that in order to get out, you must start thinking. Do you mind if I get in? I love automobile rides. [*He gets in. They wait.*] Well?

MILO. All right. I'll try. [*Screws up his face and thinks.*] Are we moving?

WATCHDOG. Not yet. Think harder.

MILO. I'm thinking as hard as I can.

WATCHDOG. Well, think just a little harder than that. Come on, you can do it.

⑳ **MILO.** All right, all right. . . . I'm thinking of all the planets in the solar system, and why water expands when it turns to ice, and all the words that begin with "q," and . . . [*The wheels begin to move.*] We're moving! We're moving!

WATCHDOG. Keep thinking.

468 UNIT 4 • How do we decide who we are?

💬 VOCABULARY DEVELOPMENT

Selection Vocabulary Reinforcement

Students will benefit from additional examples and practice with the selection vocabulary words. Reinforce their comprehension with "show-you-know" sentences. The first part of the sentence uses the word in an appropriate context. The second part of the sentence clarifies the first. Model the strategy with this example for *ignorance*:

Milo showed his *ignorance* of Doldrum rules; he laughed on a Tuesday.

1. The Clock cautioned against *ignorance*; ___.

Sample answer: it pointed out that a lack of knowledge of the importance of time leads people to carelessness.

2. Milo asked many questions as a *precautionary* measure: ___.
Sample answer: he wanted to make certain that he wouldn't get lost.

3. Laws in the Doldrums prohibited *unethical* behavior; ___.
Sample answer: bad actions would be punished.

MILO. [*Thinking.*] How a steam engine works and how to bake a pie and the difference between Fahrenheit and Centigrade . . .

WATCHDOG. Dictionopolis, here we come.

MILO. Hey, Watchdog, are you coming along?

TOCK. You can call me Tock, and keep your eyes on the road.

MILO. What kind of place is Dictionopolis, anyway?

TOCK. It's where all the words in the world come from. It used to be a marvelous place, but ever since Rhyme and Reason left, it hasn't been the same.

MILO. Rhyme and Reason?

TOCK. The two princesses. They used to settle all the arguments between their two brothers who rule over

19 ▲ **Critical Viewing**
Why is a clock part of this character's body?

21 **Comprehension**
What does Milo think about to get his car to move?

19 **Critical Viewing**
Answer: A clock is a part of the character's body because it is a "watch" dog.

20 **Connecting to the Big Question**

1. Point out that deciding who we are involves learning what we are capable of accomplishing.

2. Have students read the bracketed passage, beginning with Milo's speech on p. 468: "I'm thinking . . ." and ending with "What kind of place is Dictionopolis, anyway?" **Ask:** How does the definition of thinking as hard as he can change in this passage?

   Possible response: Milo surprises himself when he realizes that thinking does not have to be logical. He is amazed to learn that the force of his thoughts can power a car.

3. **Ask:** How does this knowledge change how Milo sees the world?

   Possible response: Instead of being only bored and tired, he is now curious and eager to get to his destination.

21 **Comprehension**
Answer: Milo thinks about planets in the solar systems, words with "q," steam engines, how to bake a pie, Fahrenheit and Centigrade.

DIFFERENTIATED INSTRUCTION

Culturally Responsive Instruction
The characters in this story express strong opinions and give Milo a lot of advice. Explain to students that sharing advice and offering the benefit of experience are a staple tradition of any culture. Respected authorities are people who have earned the right to give instruction or enforce rules. Encourage students to describe the authorities in their own experience, those people who preserve traditions of respect and good behavior. Then, have them consider examples of people who act with undeserved authority. Elicit that not all of the advice that is offered to Milo is good, and he must evaluate whether the advisor deserves to be trusted and whether the advice applies to his own circumstances.

㉒ Summary

1. After students have read the bracketed dialogue, **ask** them to review what they know about the characters having the conflict.

    Answer: Azaz is the king of Dictionopolis and the Mathemagician is the king of Digitopolis. They are the brothers of the princesses Rhyme and Reason.

2. **Ask** the Summary question.

    Answer: The argument is that Azaz believes that words are more important than numbers and the Mathemagician believes numbers are more important than words.

3. **Ask** students what clue suggests that this is a major event in the story.

    Answer: Tock describes the conflict as "an argument to end all arguments."

4. Remind students to add the event to their **Reading Skill Graphic Organizer.**

---

the Land of Wisdom. You see, Azaz is the king of Dictionopolis and the Mathemagician is the king of Digitopolis and they almost never see eye to eye on anything. It was the job of the Princesses Sweet Rhyme and Pure Reason to solve the differences between the two kings, and they always did so well that both sides usually went home feeling very satisfied. But then, one day, the kings had an argument to end all arguments. . . .

[*The LIGHTS DIM on* TOCK *and* MILO, *and come up on* KING AZAZ *of Dictionopolis on another part of the stage.* AZAZ *has a great stomach, a grey beard reaching to his waist, a small crown and a long robe with the letters of the alphabet written all over it.*]

AZAZ. Of course, I'll abide by the decision of Rhyme and Reason, though I have no doubt as to what it will be. They will choose words, of course. Everyone knows that words are more important than numbers any day of the week.

[*The* MATHEMAGICIAN *appears opposite* AZAZ. *The* MATHEMAGICIAN *wears a long flowing robe covered entirely with complex mathematical equations, and a tall pointed hat. He carries a long staff with a pencil point at one end and a large rubber eraser at the other.*]

MATHEMAGICIAN. That's what you think, Azaz. People wouldn't even know what day of the week it is without numbers. Haven't you ever looked at a calendar? Face it, Azaz. It's numbers that count.

Summary
Briefly explain the argument between Azaz and the Mathemagician.

AZAZ. Don't be ridiculous. [*To audience, as if leading a cheer.*] Let's hear it for WORDS!

MATHEMAGICIAN. [*To audience, in the same manner.*] Cast your vote for NUMBERS!

AZAZ. A, B, C's!

MATHEMAGICIAN. 1, 2, 3's! [*A FANFARE is heard.*]

AZAZ AND MATHEMAGICIAN. [*To each other.*] Quiet! Rhyme and Reason are about to announce their decision.

[RHYME *and* REASON *appear.*]

RHYME. Ladies and gentlemen, letters and numerals,

💬 VOCABULARY DEVELOPMENT

Dictionary Use

A discussion about the meaning of *reason* may help students better understand the concept of "rhyme and reason" and the traits of the princesses, Rhyme and Reason. Explain that it is generally believed that things should be done for their "rhyme"—or pleasing aspects—or their "reason"—their logic or practicality. To reinforce the meaning of *reason*, locate the word in a dictionary and read to students the definition that applies to the way *reason* is used in the drama: the power of understanding, inferring, or thinking, especially in orderly, sensible ways.

fractions and punctuation marks—may we have your attention, please. After careful consideration of the problem set before us by King Azaz of Dictionopolis [Azaz *bows.*] and the Mathemagician of Digitopolis [Mathemagician *raises his hands in a victory salute.*] we have come to the following conclusion:

Reason. Words and numbers are of equal value, for in the cloak of knowledge, one is the warp and the other is the woof.

Rhyme. It is no more important to count the sands than it is to name the stars.

Rhyme And Reason. Therefore, let both kingdoms, Dictionopolis and Digitopolis, live in peace.

[*The sound of CHEERING is heard.*]

Azaz. Boo! is what I say. Boo and Bah and Hiss!

23 Mathemagician. What good are these girls if they can't even settle an argument in anyone's favor? I think I have come to a decision of my own.

Azaz. So have I.

Azaz And Mathemagician. [*To the* PRINCESSES.] You are hereby banished from this land to the Castle-in-the-Air. [*To each other.*] *And as for you, KEEP OUT OF MY WAY!* [*They stalk off in opposite directions.*]

[*During this time, the set has been changed to the Market Square of Dictionopolis. LIGHTS come UP on the deserted square.*]

Tock. And ever since then, there has been neither Rhyme nor Reason in this kingdom. Words are misused and numbers are mismanaged. The argument between the two kings has divided everyone and the real value of both words and numbers has been forgotten. What a waste!

Milo. Why doesn't somebody rescue the Princesses and set everything straight again?

Tock. That is easier said than done. The Castle-in-the-Air is very far from here, and the one path which leads to

Summary
Reread this section to summarize the events leading to Rhyme and Reason's banishment.

24 Comprehension
What conclusion do Reason and Rhyme reach?

---

23 Summary

1. Select students to read the parts of the kings and princesses. Point out that the whole class will cheer as stated in the stage direction.

2. After rereading the bracketed text, **ask** the Summary question.

   Possible response: The kings agree to let Rhyme and Reason decide which is more important: words or numbers. The princesses' decision is that words and numbers have equal value. Neither king is happy with the decision, so they banish Rhyme and Reason.

3. Discuss which of these events is important enough to be included in a summary of the scene.

   Answer: The princesses' decision causes the kings to banish them.

24 Comprehension

Answer: They reach the conclusion that words and numbers have equal value.

:: DIFFERENTIATED INSTRUCTION

EL Support for English Learners
Examine some of the new names and words that students will read. Discuss that *Mathemagician* is a combination of *mathematics* and *magician*. Review the origins of the words *Dictionopolis* (*diction* [language] + *opolis* [city]) and *Digitopolis* (*digit* [number] + *opolis* [city]). Then ask students to explain why the king of words would rule Dictionopolis and the king of numbers would rule Digitopolis. Finally, ask students to think about the alphabet and explain why the name *Azaz* is humorous.

Enrichment for Advanced Readers
Call attention to Reason's metaphor on this page about the warp and the woof of knowledge. Have students use books or on-line reference sources to understand the metaphor. Direct them to the thesaurus, dictionary and materials describing methods and materials involved in wearing fabric. Then, ask each student to come up with metaphors about how words and numbers are both essential to our understanding of the world. Have students share their metaphors with the class.

25 Dialogue in Drama

1. Remind students that characters, setting, and plot are three elements that are developed through dialogue in a drama.

2. Have students read the bracketed dialogue.

3. **Ask** them what element or elements are developed through this specific part of the dialogue, and why.

   Possible responses: The plot is developed, because readers learn about how Milo enters Dictionopolis. The character of Gatekeeper is developed by showing how serious he is about his job.

4. **Ask** the Dialogue in Drama question.

   Possible responses: Dictionopolis is a place where you can buy or sell words. You must have a reason to enter Dictionopolis.

▶ **Monitor Progress:** To assess students' understanding of the Literary Analysis skill, **ask** them to describe what they know so far about the characters, setting, and plot of this drama. Encourage them to identify parts of the dialogue where they learned most about these elements.

▶ **Reteach:** If students have difficulty explaining how the dialogue helped them get to know the characters, setting, and plot, have them reread the explanation of the skill on the Building Knowledge page, p. 458. Then have students reread the dialogue between Milo and the Whether Man that begins on p. 463. Review with students what they learned about the characters, setting, and plot through this dialogue.

Vocabulary ▶
ferocious (fə rō´ shəs)
adj. wild and dangerous

Dialogue in Drama
What details does the Gatekeeper reveal about Dictionopolis?

it is guarded by ferocious demons. But hold on, here we are. [*A Man appears, carrying a Gate and a small Tollbooth.*]

GATEKEEPER. AHHHHREMMMM! This is Dictionopolis, a happy kingdom, advantageously located in the foothills of Confusion and caressed by gentle breezes from the Sea of Knowledge. Today, by royal proclamation, is Market Day. Have you come to buy or sell?

MILO. I beg your pardon?

GATEKEEPER. Buy or sell, buy or sell. Which is it? You must have come here for a reason.

MILO. Well, I . . .

GATEKEEPER. Come now, if you don't have a reason, you must at least have an explanation or certainly an excuse.

MILO. [*Meekly.*] Uh . . . no.

GATEKEEPER. [*Shaking his head.*] Very serious. You can't get in without a reason. [*Thoughtfully.*] Wait a minute. Maybe I have an old one you can use. [*Pulls out an old suitcase from the tollbooth and rummages through it.*] No . . . no . . . no . . . this won't do . . . hmmm . . .

MILO. [*To* TOCK.] What's he looking for? [TOCK *shrugs.*]

GATEKEEPER. Ah! This is fine. [*Pulls out a Medallion on a chain. Engraved in the Medallion is:* "WHY NOT?"] Why not. That's a good reason for almost anything . . . a bit used, perhaps, but still quite serviceable. There you are, sir. Now I can truly say: Welcome to Dictionopolis.

[*He opens the Gate and walks off.* CITIZENS *and* MERCHANTS *appear on all levels of the stage, and* MILO *and* TOCK *find themselves in the middle of a noisy marketplace. As some people buy and sell their wares, others hang a large banner which reads:* WELCOME TO THE WORD MARKET.]

MILO. Tock! Look!

MERCHANT 1. Hey-ya, hey-ya, hey-ya, step right up and take your pick. Juicy tempting words for sale. Get your fresh-picked "if 's," "and's" and "but's"! Just take a look at these nice ripe "where's" and "when's."

💬 VOCABULARY DEVELOPMENT

Word Forms

Expand students' vocabulary by helping them learn related forms of the selection vocabulary words. Three of the selection vocabulary words for "The Phantom Tollbooth, Act I" have related word forms. Give students a blank **Word Form Chart** (*Professional Development Guidebook*, p. 42) with *ignorance, precautionary,* and *misapprehension* in the correct columns. Work with the class, or have students work with a partner, to determine the related forms. Encourage students to integrate the related forms into their speaking and writing.

Noun	Verb	Adjective	Adverb
ignorance	ignore	ignorant	ignorantly
precaution		**precautionary**	
misapprehension	misapprehend		

MERCHANT 2. Step right up, step right up, fancy, best-quality words here for sale. Enrich your vocabulary and expand your speech with such elegant items as "quagmire," "flabbergast," or "upholstery."

MERCHANT 3. Words by the bag, buy them over here. Words by the bag for the more talkative customer. A pound of "happy's" at a very reasonable price . . . very useful for "Happy Birthday," "Happy New Year," "happy days," or "happy-go-lucky." Or how about a package of "good's," always handy for "good morning," "good afternoon," "good evening," and "goodbye."

MILO. I can't believe it. Did you ever see so many words?

TOCK. They're fine if you have something to say. [*They come to a Do-It-Yourself Bin.*]

MILO. [*To* MERCHANT 4 *at the bin.*] Excuse me, but what are these?

MERCHANT 4. These are for people who like to make up their own words. You can pick any assortment you like or buy a special box complete with all the letters and a book of instructions. Here, taste an "A." They're very good. [*He pops one into* MILO'S *mouth.*]

MILO. [*Tastes it hesitantly.*] It's sweet! [*He eats it.*]

MERCHANT 4. I knew you'd like it. "A" is one of our best-sellers. All of them aren't that good, you know. The "Z," for instance—very dry and sawdusty. And the "X"? Tastes like a trunkful of stale air. But most of the others aren't bad at all. Here, try the "I."

MILO. [*Tasting.*] Cool! It tastes icy.

MERCHANT 4. [*To* TOCK.] How about the "C" for you? It's as crunchy as a bone. Most people are just too lazy to make their own words, but take it from me, not only is it more fun, but it's also *de*-lightful, [*Holds up a "D."*] *e*-lating, [*Holds up an "E."*] and extremely *u*seful! [*Holds up a "U."*]

MILO. But isn't it difficult? I'm not very good at making words.

> Step right up, step right up, fancy, best-quality words here for sale.

26 **Comprehension**
What is sold in the Dictionopolis marketplace?

GUIDED EXPLORATION

26 **Connecting to the Big Question**

1. Point out that knowledge is built on experience, and things may not always be as they appear.

2. Direct students to read the bracketed passage, then **ask:** What does Milo learn at the Word Market?

   Possible response: He learns that words have not only meaning, but also taste.

3. **Ask:** What does Milo learn about himself here? Explain.

   Possible response: He is excited by the new possibilities offered by words, but he still feels that he is not very skilled at using them. He states that he is not very good at putting words together, judging by his past experience.

27 **Comprehension**

Answer: Words and letters are sold in the marketplace.

👥 DIFFERENTIATED INSTRUCTION

Strategy for Less Proficient Readers
As a group, help students use a **Venn diagram** (**Graphic Organizer** for this selection) to compare and contrast the Doldrums with Dictionopolis. Prompt their thinking by asking questions such as: "Do both places have the same level of activity? What happens in the Doldrums? What happens in Dictionopolis? What do the Lethargarians look like? Do the characters in Dictionopolis look the same? How are they different?"

Support for Less Proficient Readers
The dialogue in the Word Market scene is rich with details that may be overwhelming for some students. Break the scene into smaller segments by having students read the dialogue of the merchants, one at a time. After they read the words of each merchant, ask questions such as "What is Merchant 1 selling?" "Why does Merchant 3 say that *happy* is a very useful word?" "What does Merchant 4 say *Z* tastes like?"

28 Summary

1. Review what students have learned about summarizing. Specifically, ask them to explain how they decide which major events belong in a summary.

   Answer: Only the events that move the story forward should be included in the summary.

2. Have students reread the scene that takes place in the Word Market on pp. 472–475.

3. **Ask** the Summary question.

   Possible response: I would not include this scene. It is a funny scene that describes an event in Dictionopolis, but it does not move the story forward. Dictionopolis is a major destination of Milo's journey, not the Word Market.

---

28 Summary
Would you include the scene in the Word Market in a summary of Scene ii? Why or why not?

Vocabulary ▶
misapprehension
(mis´ ap rē hen´ shən)
n. misunderstanding

[*The* SPELLING BEE, *a large colorful bee, comes up from behind.*]

SPELLING BEE. Perhaps I can be of some assistance . . . a-s-s-i-s-t-a-n-c-e. [*The Three turn around and see him.*] Don't be alarmed . . . a-l-a-r-m-e-d. I am the Spelling Bee. I can spell anything. Anything. A-n-y-t-h-i-n-g. Try me. Try me.

MILO. [*Backing off,* TOCK *on his guard.*] Can you spell goodbye?

SPELLING BEE. Perhaps you are under the misapprehension . . . m-i-s-a-p-p-r-e-h-e-n-s-i-o-n that I am dangerous. Let me assure you that I am quite peaceful. Now, think of the most difficult word you can, and I'll spell it.

MILO. Uh . . . o.k. [*At this point,* MILO *may turn to the audience and ask them to help him choose a word or he may think of one on his own.*] How about . . . "Curiosity"?

SPELLING BEE. [*Winking.*] Let's see now . . . uh . . . how much time do I have?

MILO. Just ten seconds. Count them off, Tock.

SPELLING BEE. [*As* TOCK *counts.*] Oh dear, oh dear. [*Just at the last moment, quickly.*] C-u-r-i-o-s-i-t-y.

MERCHANT 4. Correct! [ALL *Cheer.*]

MILO. Can you spell anything?

SPELLING BEE. [*Proudly.*] Just about. You see, years ago, I was an ordinary bee minding my own business, smelling flowers all day, occasionally picking up part-time work in people's bonnets. Then one day, I realized that I'd never amount to anything without an education, so I decided that . . .

HUMBUG. [*Coming up in a booming voice.*] BALDERDASH! [*He wears a lavish coat, striped pants, checked vest, spats and a derby hat.*] Let me repeat . . . BALDERDASH! [*Swings his cane and clicks his heels in the air.*] Well, well, what have we here? Isn't someone going to introduce me to the little boy?

SPELLING BEE. [*Disdainfully.*] This is the Humbug. You can't trust a word he says.

HUMBUG. NONSENSE! Everyone can trust a Humbug. As I

🗨 THINK ALOUD

Making Inferences
Draw students' attention to Humbug's speech on this page. Use the following think aloud to model the process of making an inference. (The skill is introduced on p. 28):

   When I read the stage directions that introduce Humbug's entrance, I realize that an important clue about the character is given—he arrives and speaks his first line in a *booming* voice. This is confirmed by his exclamation *BALDERDASH!* The word is emphasized in the script by capital letters and an exclamation mark—further instruction to the actor in how to speak the line. I think about people I know who speak loudly and use many exclamations. I realize that they usually have strong opinions. I make an inference based on what I know of these people: I make the inference that this character has strong opinions, too! Then, when I read the detailed description of his costume, I see that he has strong opinions about fashion as well. These details confirm, or help prove, my first inference.

was saying to the king just the other day . . .

Spelling Bee. You've never met the king. [*To* Milo.] Don't believe a thing he tells you.

Humbug. Bosh, my boy, pure bosh. The Humbugs are an old and noble family, honorable to the core. Why, we fought in the Crusades with Richard the Lionhearted, crossed the Atlantic with Columbus, blazed trails with the pioneers. History is full of Humbugs.

Spelling Bee. A very pretty speech . . . s-p-e-e-c-h. Now, why don't you go away? I was just advising the lad of the importance of proper spelling.

Humbug. BAH! As soon as you learn to spell one word, they ask you to spell another. You can never catch up, so why bother? [*Puts his arm around* Milo.] Take my advice, boy, and forget about it. As my great-great-great-grandfather George Washington Humbug used to say . . .

Spelling Bee. You, sir, are an impostor i-m-p-o-s-t-o-r who can't even spell his own name!

Humbug. What? You dare to doubt my word? The word of a Humbug? The word of a Humbug who has direct access to the ear of a King? And the king shall hear of this, I promise you . . .

Voice 1. Did someone call for the King?

Voice 2. Did you mention the monarch?

Voice 3. Speak of the sovereign?

Voice 4. Entreat the Emperor?

29 ◀ **Critical Viewing**
How does this picture of Spelling Bee compare with his description in the play?

Dialogue in Drama
What does the dialogue between Humbug and Spelling Bee show about their relationship?

31 **Comprehension**
What advice does Spelling Bee give Milo?

PART 2 • The Phantom Tollbooth, Act I **475**

29 **Critical Viewing**
Answer: The picture of the bee shows qualities similar to those of Spelling Bee—both seem proud, triumphant, and quick.

30 **Dialogue in Drama**
1. Have two students read the bracketed conversation between Humbug and Spelling Bee. Remind them to read with expression and to follow the clues given by the use of punctuation.
2. Guide students to analyze the exchange between the characters. **Ask** them what is happening between Spelling Bee and Humbug, and why this is happening.

   Answer: They are arguing. They both want to impress Milo.
3. **Ask** the Dialogue in Drama question.

   Possible response: It shows that Spelling Bee and Humbug are very competitive and they do not think highly of one another.

31 **Comprehension**
Answer: He tells Milo not to trust a word that Humbug says.

DIFFERENTIATED INSTRUCTION

EL Support for English Learners
Students may not be familiar with the contest known as a *spelling bee*. Explain what a spelling bee is and how it is conducted. Then discuss Spelling Bee, the character. Ask students what they know about bees as insects. Help them use their own words to explain why the bee in the play is called Spelling Bee.

Enrichment for Gifted/Talented Students
Ask students to compare and contrast Spelling Bee and Humbug. Have students list the physical characteristics and personality of each character. Provide a **Venn diagram** (*Graphic Organizer*) for students to record their comparisons. Ask students to explain which character they think Milo should take advice from.

32 Analyze

1. Point out to students that sometimes characters act in a pattern to make a point. **Ask** students to glance down pp. 476–477 and note which characters speak in a pattern.

   Answer: The five ministers always speak one after the other in the same order and use words that mean the same thing.

2. **Ask** students what the pattern tells them about the ministers.

   Answer: They are similar characters.

3. Have students recall other characters in the drama who act in a pattern.

   Answer: The Lethargarians act in a pattern when they describe their schedule to Milo.

33 Dialogue in Drama

1. Call attention to the ministers' excessive use of words that mean the same thing.

2. **Ask** students to name the synonyms the ministers used for *country,* the synonyms they used for *of course,* and the ones they used for *nonsense.*

   Answer: *Country:* Nation, state, commonwealth, realm, empire, palatinate, principality; *Of course:* certainly, precisely, exactly, yes; *Nonsense:* ridiculous, fantastic, absurd, bosh.

3. **Ask** the Dialogue in Drama question.

   Answer: The use of many different words to say basically the same thing indicates that words are plentiful and important in Dictionopolis.

Voice 5. Hail his highness?

[*Five tall, thin gentlemen regally dressed in silks and satins, plumed hats and buckled shoes appear as they speak.*]

Milo. Who are they?

Spelling Bee. The King's advisors. Or in more formal terms, his cabinet.

Minister 1. Greetings!

Minister 2. Salutations!

Minister 3. Welcome!

Minister 4. Good Afternoon!

Minister 5. Hello!

Milo. Uh . . . Hi.

[*All the* Ministers, *from here on called by their numbers, unfold their scrolls and read in order.*]

Minister 1. By the order of Azaz the Unabridged . . .

Minister 2. King of Dictionopolis . . .

Minister 3. Monarch of letters . . .

32 Minister 4. Emperor of phrases, sentences, and miscellaneous figures of speech . . .

33 Minister 5. We offer you the hospitality of our kingdom . . .

Minister 1. Country

Minister 2. Nation

Minister 3. State

Minister 4. Commonwealth

Minister 5. Realm

Minister 1. Empire

Minister 2. Palatinate

Minister 3. Principality.

Milo. Do all those words mean the same thing?

Minister 1. Of course.

Minister 2. Certainly.

Vocabulary ▶
unabridged (un′ ə brijd′) *adj.* complete; not shortened

Dialogue in Drama
How does the dialogue of the five Ministers show the importance of words in Dictionopolis?

📖 VOCABULARY DEVELOPMENT

Dictionary Use

Point out that although synonyms are similar in meaning, they each have a slightly different definition. Focus students' attention on the word *palatinate.* Say to students:

I know from the context of the dialogue that *palatinate* has a similar meaning to *kingdom,* but what exactly does it mean? When I look up palatinate in the dictionary, I see it means "the territory of a palatine." What is a *palatine*? I need to find its definition. I see there's a relationship between the words *palatinate* and *palatine,* and there are several definitions of palatine. So I will decide which definition is related to a kingdom. One definition is "possessing royal privileges." That might be it, but let's see what else there is. Next is "a feudal lord having sovereign power." And the third is "of, relating to, or lying near the palate." Well, since a king could also be called a lord, I choose the second definition. Therefore, a *palatinate* is the territory of a king, in this case, Azaz.

Minister 3. Precisely.

Minister 4. Exactly.

Minister 5. Yes.

Milo. Then why don't you use just one? Wouldn't that make a lot more sense?

Minister 1. Nonsense!

Minister 2. Ridiculous!

Minister 3. Fantastic!

Minister 4. Absurd!

Minister 5. Bosh!

Minister 1. We're not interested in making sense. It's not our job.

Minister 2. Besides, one word is as good as another, so why not use them all?

Minister 3. Then you don't have to choose which one is right.

Minister 4. Besides, if one is right, then ten are ten times as right.

Minister 5. Obviously, you don't know who we are.

[*Each presents himself and* Milo *acknowledges the introduction.*]

Minister 1. The Duke of Definition.

Minister 2. The Minister of Meaning.

Minister 3. The Earl of Essence.

Minister 4. The Count of Connotation.

Minister 5. The Undersecretary of Understanding.

All Five. And we have come to invite you to the Royal Banquet.

Spelling Bee. The banquet! That's quite an honor, my boy. A real h-o-n-o-r.

Humbug. DON'T BE RIDICULOUS! Everybody goes to the Royal Banquet these days.

Summary
Briefly restate two ideas included in the Ministers' welcome.

35 Comprehension
What is the main responsibility of the Ministers?

34 Summary

1. Have students read the bracketed text.

2. **Read** the Summary instructions. Remind students to use their own words to tell the ideas.

Possible responses: Making sense is not part of their job description. Since many words have the same meaning, you don't have to choose just one.

3. **Ask** students to explain whether or not they would include the dialogue of the five ministers in a summary of the drama.

Possible response: No, their dialogue is funny, but it does not move the story forward. I would not consider this to be a major event.

35 Comprehension

Answer: Their main responsibility is to advise the king about the meaning of words.

DIFFERENTIATED INSTRUCTION

Pronunciation for English Learners
Refer students to the word *greetings* on the previous page. Write the word on the board, pronounce it distinctly, then have students repeat the word. Circle the base word *greet*. Next, write the word *gritting* on the board. Circle the base word *grit*. Model its pronunciation, and have students repeat it. Then, call a volunteer to the board. Say one or the other word, and have the volunteer point to the word you have said, and pantomime each word's meaning. Repeat with additional volunteers. For further practice with this sound, follow a similar routine with the following word pairs: *sleeping/sleep* and *slipping/slip*. Finally, extend the instruction by comparing *sleeping/slipping* and having students act out each word for the enjoyment of the class.

36 Dialogue in Drama

1. Direct students to the bracketed passage, paying special attention to the stage direction.

2. Ask the Dialogue in Drama question.

Answer: The stage directions reinforce that Azaz is an important character who demands respect. When he tells everyone to take their places, the stage directions indicate everyone rushing to follow his orders.

37 Connecting to the Big Question

1. Point out that a person's sense of self may be changed when other people pass judgment on him or her.

2. Have students read the bracketed passage. **Ask:** How does Milo feel at the banquet?

Possible response: He is very excited to be there, and graciously compliments the King on his beautiful palace.

3. Ask: Does Milo's mood change when the King calls him an ordinary boy?

Possible response: The King is only interested in a person with entertainment skills. He is not impressed by Milo's ability to count. Milo seems to feel less confident.

4. Finally, **ask** students whether they think Milo should allow his confidence to be shaken so easily by another person's perceptions.

Possible response: No, he should trust himself more.

5. Tell students to look as they read for more details showing how Milo decides who he is.

Dialogue in Drama
How do these stage directions reinforce Azaz's words?

SPELLING BEE. [*To the* HUMBUG.] True, everybody does go. But some people are invited and others simply push their way in where they aren't wanted.

HUMBUG. HOW DARE YOU? You buzzing little upstart, I'll show you who's not wanted . . . [*Raises his cane threateningly.*]

SPELLING BEE. You just watch it! I'm warning w-a-r-n-i-n-g you! [*At that moment, an ear-shattering blast of TRUMPETS, entirely off-key, is heard, and a* PAGE *appears.*]

PAGE. King Azaz the Unabridged is about to begin the Royal banquet. All guests who do not appear promptly at the table will automatically lose their place. [*A huge Table is carried out with* KING AZAZ *sitting in a large chair, carried out at the head of the table.*]

AZAZ. Places. Everyone take your places. [*All the characters, including the* HUMBUG *and the* SPELLING BEE, *who forget their quarrel, rush to take their places at the table.* MILO *and* TOCK *sit near the king.* AZAZ *looks at* MILO.] And just who is this?

MILO. Your Highness, my name is Milo and this is Tock. Thank you very much for inviting us to your banquet, and I think your palace is beautiful!

MINISTER 1. Exquisite.

MINISTER 2. Lovely.

MINISTER 3. Handsome.

MINISTER 4. Pretty.

MINISTER 5. Charming.

AZAZ. SILENCE! Now tell me, young man, what can you do to entertain us? Sing songs? Tell stories? Juggle plates? Do tumbling tricks? Which is it?

MILO. I can't do any of those things.

AZAZ. What an ordinary little boy. Can't you do anything at all?

MILO. Well . . . I can count to a thousand.

AZAZ. AARGH, numbers! Never mention numbers here. Only

🗣 THINK ALOUD

Context Clues
Direct students' attention to the word *substantial* on the next page. Using a think-aloud process, model how to use context to infer the meaning of an unknown word. Say to students:

> I'm going to think aloud to show you how I would figure out what *substantial* means from its context.

Humbug says that the meal of light rays is not very *substantial*. Then in the very next sentence, he suggests that Milo might ask for something a little more filling. This makes me think that a meal that is not substantial does not have a large quantity of food, whereas a *substantial* meal is one that does. So I think that *substantial* can refer to a large quantity of something.

use them when we absolutely have to. Now, why don't we change the subject and have some dinner? Since you are the guest of honor, you may pick the menu.

Milo. Me? Well, uh . . . I'm not very hungry. Can we just have a light snack?

Azaz. A light snack it shall be!

38 [Azaz *claps his hands. Waiters rush in with covered trays. When they are uncovered, Shafts of Light pour out. The light may be created through the use of battery-operated flashlights which are secured in the trays and covered with a false bottom. The Guests help themselves.*]

Humbug. Not a very substantial meal. Maybe you can suggest something a little more filling.

Milo. Well, in that case, I think we ought to have a square meal . . .

39 **Azaz.** [*Claps his hands.*] A square meal it is! [*Waiters serve trays of Colored Squares of all sizes. People serve themselves.*]

Spelling Bee. These are awful. [Humbug *coughs and all the Guests do not care for the food.*]

Azaz. [*Claps his hands and the trays are removed.*] Time for speeches. [*To* Milo.] You first.

Milo. [*Hesitantly.*] Your Majesty, ladies and gentlemen, I would like to take this opportunity to say that . . .

Azaz. That's quite enough. Mustn't talk all day.

Milo. But I just started to . . .

Azaz. NEXT!

Humbug. [*Quickly.*] Roast turkey, mashed potatoes, vanilla ice cream.

Spelling Bee. Hamburgers, corn on the cob, chocolate pudding p-u-d-d-i-n-g. [*Each Guest names two dishes and a dessert.*]

Azaz. [*The last.*] Pâté de foie gras, soupe à l'oignon, salade endives, fromage et fruits et demi-tasse. [*He claps his*

AARGH, numbers! Never mention numbers here.

Dialogue in Drama
How do the dialogue and stage directions show that "a light snack" has different meanings for Milo and Azaz?

40 **Comprehension**
What does Azaz forbid Milo to discuss?

PART 2 • The Phantom Tollbooth, Act I **479**

DIFFERENTIATED INSTRUCTION

Support for Less Proficient Readers
As the end of Act I is approaching, have students work in groups to review the play to this point. Have them talk about the major events noted on **Reading Skill Graphic Organizer A** for this selection and take turns drawing a picture that illustrates each event. Have them decide on captions for each picture. Encourage them to use the illustrations to check their summaries. Display the pictures and captions for the rest of the class to enjoy.

Enrichment for Advanced Learners
Challenge students to create wordplay in connection with some of their everyday school activities. They might enjoy literally rendering figurative or idiomatic expressions. Have students brainstorm ideas for their wordplay. If necessary, suggest these phrases as a springboard for thought: bag lunch, heavy schedule, cold facts, and hard test. Have them illustrate their choices as personification, like the characters in "The Phantom Tollbooth."

38 **Dialogue in Drama**

1. **Direct** students' attention to the bracketed dialogue and stage directions.

2. **Ask** students what Milo probably means when he suggests "a light snack." Then ask them to give examples of a light snack.

   Answer: He is talking about a small serving of food. An example might be a piece of fruit, some yogurt, or cheese and crackers.

3. **Ask** the Dialogue in Drama question.

   Answer: Milo meant a *light snack* to mean a small portion of food. The stage directions show a *light snack* as a serving of light rays on a tray.

39 **Connect**

1. Ask one volunteer to read aloud the characters' lines and another to read aloud the stage direction at the end of the bracketed passage.

2. Focus students' attention on Milo's statement, "I think we ought to have a square meal." Point out that, normally, the phrase "square meal" is an idiom.

3. **Ask** a volunteer to explain what an idiom is.

   Answer: An idiom is language that has a meaning that differs from its literal meaning.

4. Explain the phrase's idiomatic meaning: a square meal is one that is nourishing and substantial.

5. **Ask** students what the meaning of the phrase is in the context of the drama.

   Answer: It literally means that Milo is eating a meal of squares.

6. **Ask** students to identify other idiomatic phrases that have literal meaning in the banquet dialogue.

   Answer: light snack, eat my words

40 **Comprehension**

Answer: The king forbids Milo to talk about numbers.

PART 2 • The Phantom Tollbooth, Act I **479**

41 Dialogue in Drama

1. Explain to students that a pun is a humorous use of words, playing on different uses of the same word or on a similar sense or sound of different words.

2. Remind students about the character Whether Man. Point out that his name is a pun because Whether Man sounds like Weather Man.

3. Read the Dialogue in Drama instructions.

   Possible responses: *Somersault* sounds like "summer salt." *Rigamarole* sounds like a kind of bread roll. *Synonym bun* sounds like cinnamon bun.

42 Summary

1. Read aloud the Summary instruction.

2. Encourage students to reread the banquet scene on pp. 478–480. Tell them to make mental notes about the most important events at the banquet as they read.

3. Have students link the important events they noted to formulate a summary of the banquet scene.

   Possible response: Milo tries to speak at the banquet and the other characters cut him off. The other banquet guests list foods as menu items. Milo learns that the guests are expected to eat their words.

Dialogue in Drama
Identify one pun, or play on words, that adds humor to this dialogue. **41**

Summary **42**
Briefly summarize the events at the banquet.

---

hands. *Waiters serve each Guest his Words.*] Dig in. [*To* MILO.] Though I can't say I think much of your choice.

MILO. I didn't know I was going to have to eat my words.

AZAZ. Of course, of course, everybody here does. Your speech should have been in better taste.

MINISTER 1. Here, try some somersault. It improves the flavor.

MINISTER 2. Have a rigamarole. [*Offers breadbasket.*]

MINISTER 3. Or a ragamuffin.

MINISTER 4. Perhaps you'd care for a synonym bun.

MINISTER 5. Why not wait for your just desserts?

AZAZ. Ah yes, the dessert. We're having a special treat today . . . freshly made at the half-bakery.

MILO. The half-bakery?

AZAZ. Of course, the half-bakery! Where do you think half-baked ideas come from? Now, please don't interrupt. By royal command, the pastry chefs have . . .

MILO. What's a half-baked idea?

[AZAZ *gives up the idea of speaking as a cart is wheeled in and the Guests help themselves.*]

HUMBUG. They're very tasty, but they don't always agree with you. Here's a good one. [HUMBUG *hands one to* MILO.]

MILO. [*Reads.*] "The earth is flat."

SPELLING BEE. People swallowed that one for years. [*Picks up one and reads.*] "The moon is made of green cheese." Now, there's a half-baked idea.

[*Everyone chooses one and eats. They include:* "It Never Rains But Pours," "Night Air Is Bad Air," "Everything Happens for the Best," "Coffee Stunts Your Growth."]

AZAZ. And now for a few closing words. Attention! Let me have your attention! [*Everyone leaps up and Exits, except for* MILO, TOCK, *and the* HUMBUG.] Loyal subjects and friends, once again on this gala occasion, we have . . .

💬 VOCABULARY DEVELOPMENT

Multiple Meanings

Remind students that some words have more than one use. In the banquet scene, the idiomatic meaning of the word *swallowed* is "accepted something without question or protest." *Swallow* also refers to a kind of bird and the action of moving food from the mouth to the stomach. The word *subject* refers to "the topic of conversation" and "someone who is under the control of someone else." A school subject is a class or department of learning, such as mathematics. We think of the word *toe* as a part of our foot, but in the banquet dialogue *toe the line* means "follow the rules."

MILO. Excuse me, but everybody left.

AZAZ. [*Sadly.*] I was hoping no one would notice. It happens every time.

HUMBUG. They're gone to dinner, and as soon as I finish this last bite, I shall join them.

MILO. That's ridiculous. How can they eat dinner right after a banquet?

AZAZ. SCANDALOUS! We'll put a stop to it at once. From now on, by royal command, everyone must eat dinner before the banquet.

MILO. But that's just as bad.

HUMBUG. Or just as good. Things which are equally bad are also equally good. Try to look at the bright side of things.

MILO. I don't know which side of anything to look at. Everything is so confusing, and all your words only make things worse.

AZAZ. How true. There must be something we can do about it.

HUMBUG. Pass a law.

AZAZ. We have almost as many laws as words.

HUMBUG. Offer a reward. [AZAZ *shakes his head and looks madder at each suggestion.*] Send for help? Drive a bargain? Pull the switch? Lower the boom? Toe the line?

[*As* AZAZ *continues to scowl, the* HUMBUG *loses confidence and finally gives up.*]

MILO. Maybe you should let Rhyme and Reason return.

AZAZ. How nice that would be. Even if they were a bother at times, things always went so well when they were here. But I'm afraid it can't be done.

HUMBUG. Certainly not. Can't be done.

MILO. Why not?

HUMBUG. [*Now siding with* MILO.] Why not, indeed?

AZAZ. Much too difficult.

Things which are equally bad are also equally good.

44 Comprehension
Why has everyone left the banquet?

PART 2 • The Phantom Tollbooth, Act I **481**

43 **Connecting to the Big Question**

1. Point out that when people are exposed to many new situations, they may lose sight of their abilities and confidence.

2. Have students read the bracketed passage. **Ask:** How does Milo's question reflect his sense of self?

   Possible response: He sounds overwhelmed by the confusing words, messages, and expectations he has encountered.

3. **Ask:** How might Milo grow or change based on his experiences?

   Possible responses: He may find that he has a new interest in learning. He may be exhausted and want to return to his boring life.

44 Comprehension

Answer: They left the banquet to go to dinner.

≋ **FLUENCY**

Distribute copies of the previous page and this page. Have partners take turns reading the dialogue aloud. While one partner reads, the other should mark any words with which the one reading has difficulty. Collect students' marked-up copies of the story, and review difficult words and passages with the class. Look for these problem spots:

• If students have difficulty with the word *somersault,* have them cover up parts of the word with their thumb to sound out each syllable in turn. Point out that the words *fault* and *vault* rhyme with the final syllable. Then, explain that *somersault*

means "an acrobatic movement." Point out that this is one of many examples of wordplay in the script. Elicit that the final syllable of *somersault* sounds like the word *salt.* Guide students in understanding the humor created by the substitution. Repeat this process with the words *rigamarole* and *ragamuffin.*

• If students mispronounce the word *scandalous* on this page, guide them in identifying the letters and sounds in the word. Once students can pronounce the word, help them use context to infer its meaning.

45 Dialogue in Drama

1. **Ask** students to recall why Rhyme and Reason no longer live in the kingdom.

   Answer: They were banished because the kings did not like the way the princesses tried to settle the kings' argument about the importance of words and numbers.

2. Invite three students to read the bracketed lines for Milo, Azaz, and Humbug.

3. **Ask** the Dialogue in Drama question.

   Answer: They discuss the problem of how to get Rhyme and Reason back to the kingdom.

Dialogue in Drama
What major problem do Milo and Azaz discuss here?

HUMBUG. Of course, much too difficult.

MILO. You could, if you really wanted to.

HUMBUG. By all means, if you really wanted to, you could.

AZAZ. [*To* HUMBUG.] How?

MILO. [*Also to* HUMBUG.] Yeah, how?

HUMBUG. Why . . . uh, it's a simple task for a brave boy with a stout heart, a steadfast dog and a serviceable small automobile.

AZAZ. Go on.

HUMBUG. Well, all that he would have to do is cross the dangerous, unknown countryside between here and Digitopolis, where he would have to persuade the Mathemagician to release the Princesses, which we know to be impossible because the Mathemagician will never agree with Azaz about anything. Once achieving that, it's a simple matter of entering the Mountains of Ignorance from where no one has ever returned alive, an effortless climb up a two thousand foot stairway without railings in a high wind at night to the Castle-in-the-Air. After a pleasant chat with the Princesses, all that remains is a leisurely ride back through those chaotic crags where the frightening fiends have sworn to tear any intruder limb from limb and devour him down to his belt buckle. And finally after doing all that, a triumphal parade! If, of course, there is anything left to parade . . . followed by hot chocolate and cookies for everyone.

AZAZ. I never realized it would be so simple.

MILO. It sounds dangerous to me.

TOCK. And just who is supposed to make that journey?

AZAZ. A very good question. But there is one far more serious problem.

MILO. What's that?

AZAZ. I'm afraid I can't tell you that until you return.

MILO. But wait a minute, I didn't . . .

482 UNIT 4 • How do we decide who we are?

💬 VOCABULARY DEVELOPMENT

Vocab-o-Gram

Have students return to the **Vocab-o-Grams** they completed before reading the play. Have them refine their ideas about where the words belong in the chart and see if they can answer the questions they wrote. Have them review the vocabulary and clarify their meanings by returning to the selection or using reference sources. Ask them to write a definition for any unknown words they identified on the chart.

Azaz. Dictionopolis will always be grateful to you, my boy, and your dog. [Azaz *pats* Tock *and* Milo.]

Tock. Now, just one moment, sire . . .

Azaz. You will face many dangers on your journey, but fear not, for I can give you something for your protection. [Azaz *gives* Milo *a box.*] In this box are the letters of the alphabet. With them you can form all the words you will ever need to help you overcome the obstacles that may stand in your path. All you must do is use them well and in the right places.

Milo. [*Miserably.*] Thanks a lot.

Azaz. You will need a guide, of course, and since he knows the obstacles so well, the Humbug has cheerfully volunteered to accompany you.

Humbug. Now, see here . . . !

Azaz. You will find him dependable, brave, resourceful and loyal.

Humbug. [*Flattered.*] Oh, your Majesty.

Dialogue in Drama
Based on these lines, how does Azaz feel about the power of words?

48 Comprehension
What does Azaz give Milo for his journey?

PART 2 • The Phantom Tollbooth, Act I **483**

---

46 Dialogue in Drama

1. Have a student read the first bracketed text aloud.

2. **Ask** students to restate what Azaz directs Milo to do with the letters in the box.

   Answer: Azaz tells Milo to use the letters to form words that will help him on his difficult journey.

3. **Ask** the Dialogue in Drama question.

   Possible response: He feels that words are very powerful. If used correctly, they can offer protection.

47 Analyze

1. Tell students to read the bracketed dialogue independently.

2. Ask them to think about the tone of voice that Milo uses when he says, "I'm sure he'll be a great help."

3. **Ask** them to explain whether they think he is sincere in his response to Azaz or if he is being sarcastic.

   Possible response: I think Milo is being sarcastic. Up to this point, the character of Humbug has been pretty useless and not dependable in what he says. Milo probably doesn't think he will be a helpful companion on this dangerous journey.

48 Comprehension

Answer: The king gives Milo a box containing all the letters of the alphabet.

49 **Summary**

Read the Summary instructions and give students time to reread the entire scene. Remind students to use their graphic organizers.

Possible response: Milo meets Whether Man in Expectations and the Lethargarians in the Doldrums. Next, Tock the Watchdog arrives and tells Milo he must think hard to get out of the Doldrums. Tock tells Milo about the princesses Rhyme and Reason, and why they were banished by Azaz and the Mathemagician. In Dictionopolis, Milo and Tock meet Spelling Bee and Humbug, and they attend King Azaz's banquet. There, the King suggests that they rescue the princesses.

☑ **ASSESS**

Language Study
Vocabulary

1. ferocious; A dangerous, growling beast is ferocious.

2. misapprehension; A misapprehension, or misunderstanding, can lead to confusion or disagreement.

3. ignorance; Each means "lack of knowledge."

4. precautionary; Each word has to do with planning for future events.

5. unabridged; Each word means "not shortened."

Word Study
Part A

The Greek root -*eth*- means "character" or "custom." Ethics are a set of <u>customs</u> that describe proper moral conduct for a person of good <u>character</u>. *Ethnic* describes a group of people who share cultural traits and <u>customs</u>.

Part B
Sample answers:

1. No, it would be wrong, show bad <u>character</u>, and be *unethical* to take someone else's book.

2. Yes, an *ethicist* is someone who studies the <u>customs</u> of proper conduct and would be able to tell right from wrong.

 47

MILO. I'm sure he'll be a great help. [*They approach the car.*]

TOCK. I hope so. It looks like we're going to need it.

[*The lights darken and the* KING *fades from view.*]

AZAZ. Good luck! Drive carefully! [*The three get into the car and begin to move. Suddenly a thunderously loud NOISE is heard. They slow down the car.*]

MILO. What was that?

TOCK. It came from up ahead.

HUMBUG. It's something terrible, I just know it. Oh, no. Something dreadful is going to happen to us. I can feel it in my bones. [*The NOISE is repeated. They all look at each other fearfully as the lights fade.*]

49 **Summary**
Reread Scene ii and summarize the main events.

WORD STUDY

The **Greek root** -*eth*- means "character" or "custom." In this selection, Milo is told that to think in the land of the Doldrums is unethical, meaning that it shows poor character.

Language Study

Vocabulary The words listed below appear in *The Phantom Tollbooth*, Act I. Write a vocabulary word that fits with each of the numbered word groups. Explain your answers.

| ignorance | precautionary | ferocious |
| misapprehension | unabridged | |

1. growling, dangerous _____
2. confusion, disagreement _____
3. dullness, unawareness _____
4. carefully planned, safe _____
5. complete, entire _____

Word Study

Part A Explain how the **Greek root** -*eth*- contributes to the meanings of *ethics* and *ethnicity*. Consult a dictionary if necessary.

Part B Use context and what you know about the Greek root -*eth*- to explain your answer to each question.

1. Is it *ethical* to take a book that does not belong to you?
2. Can an *ethicist* tell right from wrong?

Literary Analysis

Possible responses appear below. Check to be sure students support their responses with evidence from the text.

1. **(a)** Through a tollbooth that Milo receives as a gift, he enters Lands Beyond. He meets Whether Man in the Land of Expectations. Then he enters the Doldrums, where he thinks hard to escape. On the way to Dictionopolis, Tock tells Milo about the princesses. Milo attends King Azaz's banquet, where he is asked to rescue the princesses. **(b)** These are the most important events because they move the story forward.

2. **(a)** Rhyme and Reason are the princesses who have been banished from the kingdom. **(b)** Their absence has made Dictionopolis unruly.

3. **(a)** Humbug makes the journey sound perilous. **(b)** It will be a dangerous journey. **(c)** Milo must enter mountains from which no one has ever returned alive, climb a dangerous staircase, and get past frightening fiends.

4. **(a)** The king gives Milo a box of alphabet letters. **(b)** They might help him make a sign to ask for help.

Literary Analysis

Key Ideas and Details

1. **Summary** **(a)** What events would you include in a summary of Act I? **(b)** Explain why they are the most important events.

2. **(a)** Who are Rhyme and Reason? **(b) Analyze Causes and Effects:** What effect does their absence have on Dictionopolis?

3. **(a)** How does Humbug describe the journey that Milo must make? **(b) Predict:** In Act II, Milo will start his journey. What do you think it will be like? **(c) Support:** Give three details from Act I to support your answer.

4. **(a)** What does King Azaz give Milo? **(b) Hypothesize:** Describe a situation in which the gift might help Milo.

Craft and Structure

5. **Dialogue in Drama** Complete a chart like the one on the right to explain what each passage of dialogue below reveals about a character, the setting, and an action. An example has been provided.
(a) MILO. Well, it doesn't matter anyway. Dictionopolis. That's a weird name. I might as well go there.
(b) GATEKEEPER. This is Dictionopolis, a happy kingdom, advantageously located in the foothills of Confusion and caressed by gentle breezes from the Sea of Knowledge.
(c) WATCHDOG. Do you mind if I get in? I love automobile rides.

Dialogue	What it Suggests
Passage (a)	Character: Milo is bored and uninterested.
Passage (b)	Setting:
Passage (c)	Action:

Integration of Knowledge and Ideas

6. **(a) Interpret:** So far, what theme, or insight about life, do you think the author is expressing? **(b) Hypothesize:** Who do you think is the main audience for this theme? **(c) Synthesize:** Why would that audience be interested in the theme?

7. **(a) Apply:** What advice would you give to Milo at the end of Act I? **(b) Support:** Why do you think it would be good advice? Explain your position, citing details from the play.

8. 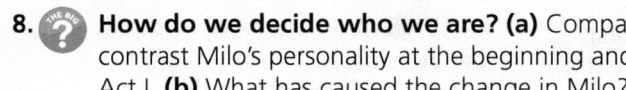 **How do we decide who we are? (a)** Compare and contrast Milo's personality at the beginning and end of Act I. **(b)** What has caused the change in Milo?

ACADEMIC VOCABULARY

As you write and speak about *The Phantom Tollbooth*, Act I, use the words related to identity that you explored on page 441 of this text.

8. **How do we decide who we are?**
(a) At the beginning of Act I, Milo is bored and uninterested in life. By the end of Act I, he is still easily discouraged and sarcastic, but much more engaged in his adventure. **(b)** Milo meets many characters who share their outlooks on life. He compares his beliefs to those he learns about, and his own views are sometimes strengthened and sometimes changed.

---

5. **(a)** Character: Milo is not interested in anything and is easily persuaded. **(b)** Setting: Dictionopolis is a pleasant place to live. **(c)** Action: Watchdog wants to come along on the journey.

6. **(a)** The theme is that people should live actively and seek out experiences eagerly, rather than being bored, in the doldrums, lazy, discouraged, or sarcastic. **(b)** The main audience for this theme is young people. **(c)** Young people would be interested in this

theme because they are just beginning to learn about life and about who they are, and they sometimes want advice.

7. **(a)** I would tell Milo to be brave and optimistic and that, if he is, he will succeed on his journey and find out some amazing things about himself and about life. **(b)** I think that would be good advice because I can tell that once Milo gets rid of his attitude of sarcasm and discouragement, he will be happier and more confident about his abilities.

 Online Writer's Notebook

Students can use the Online Writer's Notebook to record all responses.

Conventions

Introduce the skill, using the instruction on the student page.

Think Aloud: Model the Skill

Say to students:

When I say, "I will meet Roberto *in* the park," I am using a prepositional phrase, *in the park.* The phrase begins with the preposition *in* and includes the noun *park,* the object of the preposition. Prepositional phrases indicate where or when the action of the verb takes place.

An appositive phrase tells more about a noun or pronoun. When I say, "I will meet Roberto, my cousin, in the park," *my cousin* is an appositive phrase. It clarifies who Roberto is for those who may not know him.

Practice A

1. (on his bed)   4. (to the land) ;
2. (After school,)   (of Dictionopolis)
3. (In the play,)   5. (between Milo and the Humbug)

Reading Application

Sample answers: Milo traveled through the tollbooth. The Whether Man lives near the Land of Wisdom. The play begins in Milo's room.

Practice B

Sample answers:

1. Milo, (a young boy,)
2. Whether Man, (a little man) (wearing a coat,)
3. The novel (The Phantom Tollbooth)
4. A dog with a clock for a body, (Watchdog,)

Writing Application

Sample answers: Milo was bored by nearly everything. After opening the package, Milo becomes interested. On the road, Milo met many strange characters. Tock, a watchdog, described Dictionopolis. Milo, an inexperienced traveler, was now curious. Azaz, King of Words, sends Milo on an adventure.

Close Reading Activities Continued

Conventions: Prepositions and Appositives

A **preposition** relates a noun or pronoun to another word in the sentence. Common prepositions are *on, by,* and *from.*

A **prepositional phrase** begins with a preposition and includes a noun or pronoun called the **object of the preposition**.

An **appositive** is a noun or pronoun that identifies or explains another noun or pronoun in the sentence.

An **appositive phrase** includes an appositive and its modifiers. If an appositive is not essential to the meaning of the sentence, it is set off with commas or dashes. If an appositive is essential to the meaning of a sentence, it is not set off with commas.

Prepositions/Prepositional Phrases	Appositives/Appositive Phrases
Jenny stood _between_ the stage and the _audience._	Jenny, _a young girl_, stood between the stage and the audience. (not essential)
After the performance, the audience clapped and cheered.	My friend _Maria_ clapped and cheered. (essential)

Practice A

Rewrite each sentence, circling each preposition and underlining each object of the preposition.

1. Milo sat on his bed.
2. After school, Milo was bored.
3. In the play, the clock spoke.
4. Milo traveled to the land of Dictionopolis.
5. Tock rode between Milo and the Humbug.

Reading Application Reread the first act of *The Phantom Tollbooth* and identify at least three prepositional phrases.

Practice B

Rewrite each sentence, circling the appositive or appositive phrase. Underline the noun or pronoun it identifies or explains.

1. Milo, a young boy, stared into space.
2. The Whether Man, a little man wearing a coat, was not a weather man.
3. The novel *The Phantom Tollbooth* has been popular for decades.
4. A dog with a clock for a body, the Watchdog, hopped into the car.

Writing Application Write three sentences based on *The Phantom Tollbooth*, containing appositive or prepositional phrases.

▶ EXTEND THE LESSON

Sentence Modeling

Read aloud this sentence describing an incident from the selection students have read:

After he cleared his throat, the Gatekeeper, a proud man, welcomed the travelers to Dictionopolis.

Ask students what they notice about the sentence. Elicit from them that the sentence begins with a prepositional phrase. Ask them to identify the preposition *to* and the object of the preposition, *Dictionopolis.* Then, ask

what else they notice about the sentence. (The subject of the sentence, *Gatekeeper,* is a simple subject. It is followed by an appositive phrase that describes the subject: *a proud man.*)

Have students imitate the sentence in a sentence to describe a character of their own choosing from the play, matching each grammatical and stylistic feature discussed. Collect the sentences, and share them with the class.

Writing to Sources

Informative Text Write a brief **summary** of *The Phantom Tollbooth*, Act I.

- Review the play to decide which events, characters, and ideas are important.
- Present events in the order in which they occur, giving your summary a beginning, a middle, and an end.
- Provide enough information for readers to understand the main ideas and natural flow of the drama.
- Leave out unimportant details, and do not include opinions or evaluations.

Grammar Application Be sure that you have used prepositions and appositives correctly in your summary. If an appositive phrase is not essential, set it off with commas.

Research and Technology

Build and Present Knowledge Work with a small group to research and prepare a **multimedia presentation** on a topic related to drama. Because the audience for your presentation will be your class, choose your topic with your classmates' interests in mind. You might select from among these topics: actors, theaters, stage sets, playwrights, comedies, or serious dramas. Follow these steps to complete the assignment:

- Keep the backgrounds and interests of your audience in mind. Choose a topic your audience will find interesting.
- Conduct research on your topic, using reputable online or print resources. To ensure accuracy, confirm facts in at least two different sources.
- Include printouts, slides, photos, or drawings to illustrate the facts you present. Your illustrations should be lively to capture your audience's attention.
- Use other graphics, such as diagrams, timelines, and charts.
- Use audio aids, such as recordings and sound effects.

Practice your presentation, and then deliver it to the class.

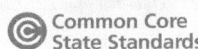

Common Core State Standards

Writing
4. Produce clear and coherent writing in which the development, organization, and style are appropriate to task, purpose, and audience.
6. Use technology, including the Internet.
8. Gather relevant information from multiple print and digital sources.

Speaking and Listening
5. Include multimedia components and visual displays in presentations to clarify information.

Language
1. Demonstrate command of the conventions of standard English grammar and usage when writing or speaking.
2.a. Use punctuation to set off nonrestrictive/parenthetical elements.

Writing

1. Review the assignment, using the instruction on the student page.
2. To give students guidance in writing their informative texts, give them **Support for Writing**, for this selection in the *Student Companion All-in-One Workbook*.
3. To evaluate the writing activity, use the summary rubrics, in *Professional Development Guidebook,* pp. 246–247. Evaluate for how well students summarize.

Grammar Application

Have students check their drafts for the correct use of prepositions and appositives.

Six Traits Focus

✓	Ideas	✓	Word Choice
✓	Organization	✓	Sentence Fluency
	Voice	✓	Conventions

Research and Technology

1. Review the assignment, using the instruction on the student page.
2. To support students' work on the assignment, have them complete the **Support for Extend Your Learning** page for this selection in the *Student Companion All-in-One Workbook*.

Time and Resource Manager

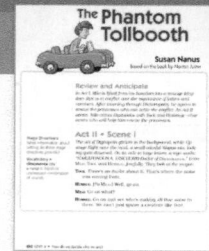

LESSON PACING GUIDE

The Phantom Tollbooth, Act II

DAY 1	Preteach/Teach

- Administer the Reading and Vocabulary Warm-ups, as necessary.
- Introduce the Key Ideas and Details skill: Compare and Contrast.
- Introduce the Craft and Structure skill: Stage Directions.
- Use the Close Reading Model to demonstrate the application of the skills.
- Review the selection vocabulary, as necessary, with students who need additional support.
- Prepare students to read the selection by reviewing with them the Multidraft Reading Strategies.

DAY 2	Teach

- Informally monitor comprehension while students read.
- Use the Comprehension questions to confirm understanding.
- Develop students' ability to compare and contrast and analyze stage directions using the sidenote questions.
- Reinforce vocabulary with the Vocabulary notes.
- Reinforce unit focus standards using the Spiral Review prompts.

DAY 3	Assess

- Assess students' comprehension and mastery of the skills by having them answer the Literary Analysis questions.
- Have students complete the Vocabulary activities.
- Develop students' understanding of roots and affixes by having them complete the Word Study activities.

DAY 4	Extend/Assess

- Build students' ability to master grammar concepts and conventions by having them complete the Conventions lesson.
- Have students complete the Writing to Sources activity and write a review. (You may assign as homework.)
- Extend learning by having students complete the Speaking and Listening activity: a group discussion.
- Administer the Selection Test or Open-Book Test.

Common Core State Standards

Reading Literature 5. Analyze how a particular sentence, chapter, scene, or stanza fits into the overall structure of a text and contributes to the development of the theme, setting, or plot.

7. Compare and contrast the experience of reading a story, drama, or poem to listening to or viewing an audio, video, or live version of the text, including contrasting what they "see" and "hear" when reading the text to what they perceive when they listen or watch.

Writing 1. Write arguments to support claims with clear reasons and relevant evidence.

1.a. Introduce claim(s) and organize the reasons and evidence clearly.

Speaking and Listening 1.c. Pose and respond to specific questions with elaboration and detail by making comments that contribute to the topic, text, or issue under discussion.

3. Delineate a speaker's argument and specific claims, distinguishing claims that are supported by reasons and evidence from claims that are not.

Language 1. Demonstrate command of the conventions of standard English grammar and usage when writing or speaking.

3. Use knowledge of language and its conventions when writing, speaking, reading, or listening.

3.a. Vary sentence patterns for meaning, reader/listener interest, and style.

6. Acquire and use accurately grade-appropriate general academic and domain-specific words and phrases; gather vocabulary knowledge when considering a word or phrase important to comprehension or expression.

Daily Block Scheduling

Each day in this Lesson Pacing Guide represents a 40–50 minute period. Teachers using block scheduling may combine days to revise pacing. In addition, teachers may differentiate and support core instruction by integrating components for extended and intensive support as students require. See the Guide to Resources (facing page).

GUIDE TO RESOURCES

		LEARNER LEVELS						RESOURCES	WHERE FOUND		
		L1	L2	L3	L4	EL	ALL		PRINT	CD	ONLINE
Warm Up		✔	✔			✔		Vocabulary Warm-ups			✔
		✔	✔			✔		Reading Warm-ups			✔
							✔	Background Video			✔
							✔	Selection Audio		Hear It!	✔
Comprehension/ Selection Support							✔	Writing About the Big Question	Student Companion Workbook		✔
							✔	Literary Analysis	Student Companion Workbook		✔
							✔	Reading	Student Companion Workbook		✔
							✔	Vocabulary Builder	Student Companion Workbook		✔
					✔			Enrichment			✔
				✔	✔	✔		Conventions	Student Companion Workbook		✔
				✔	✔	✔		Writing to Sources	Student Companion Workbook		✔
				✔	✔	✔		Speaking and Listening	Student Companion Workbook		
Differentiated Instruction/ Additional Support							✔	Additional Standards Practice	Common Core Companion		✔
							✔	Close Reading Practice	Close Reading Notebook		✔
		✔	✔					Adapted Reader's Notebook			✔
						✔		English Reader's Notebook:			✔
						✔		Spanish Reader's Notebook			✔
						✔		Graphic Organizer A			✔
		✔	✔			✔		Graphic Organizer B			✔
		✔	✔			✔		"Extreme Challenges"	Reality Central Student Edition and Writing Journal		✔
		✔	✔			✔		Practice and Assess	Reading Kit		✔
Monitor Progress							✔	Selection Test		Exam View	✔
							✔	Open-Book Test		Exam View	✔
Digital Resources							✔	Close Reading Tool			✔
							✔	Online Writer's Notebook			✔

👥 One-on-one teaching 👥 Group work 👥 Whole class instruction 👤 Independent work Ⓐ Assessment 💻 Digital Resource

LEARNER LEVELS

L1 Special-Needs Students   L3 On-Level Students (Tier 1)   EL English Learners
L2 Below-Level Students (Tier 2)   L4 Advanced Students (Tier 1)   All All Students

1 **How do we decide who we are?**

Read • Discuss • Research • Write As students read, they will explore the Big Question through text analysis of the selection. Encourage students to take notes as they read and raise additional questions, using text evidence to support their thoughts. Students should refer to their notes to help them deepen their understanding of the selection through discussion, research, and writing.

2 **Close Reading Focus**

1. Remind students that comparing and contrasting characters or events in a play can deepen their understanding of each character or event.

2. Explain to students that stage directions help bring a play to life. They tell to whom a character is speaking, give clues about his or her appearance, tell where the character is, and even explain the general mood of a scene.

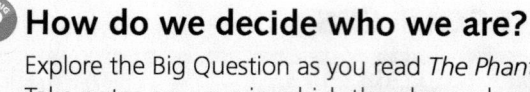

Building Knowledge

Meet the Author

Norton Juster (b. 1929) designed buildings and other structures during his career as an architect. He took up creative writing in his spare time "as a relaxation" from architecture. When he began writing *The Phantom Tollbooth,* the novel on which this drama is based, he thought it was just a short story for his own pleasure. Yet before long, Juster says, "it had created its own life, and I was hooked." The novel has been translated into several languages and adapted for an animated film.

 Common Core State Standards

Reading Literature
5. Analyze how a particular sentence, chapter, scene, or stanza fits into the overall structure of a text and contributes to the development of the theme, setting, or plot.

Language
6. Acquire and use accurately grade-appropriate general academic and domain-specific words and phrases; gather vocabulary knowledge when considering a word or phrase important to comprehension or expression.

1 **How do we decide who we are?**

Explore the Big Question as you read *The Phantom Tollbooth*, Act II. Take notes on ways in which the play explores how experiences can change a person.

2 **CLOSE READING FOCUS**

Key Ideas and Details: **Compare and Contrast**

When you **compare** two things, you tell how they are alike. When you **contrast** two things, you tell how they are different. As you read drama, picture the action to compare and contrast characters, situations, and events. Pay attention to the dialogue and the descriptions of how characters speak and act.

Craft and Structure: **Stage Directions**

A dramatic script contains two types of information. Lines of dialogue tell readers what the characters say. **Stage directions** are the words in a drama that the characters do not say. These directions tell performers how to move and speak. They also help readers picture the action, sounds, and scenery. Stage directions are usually printed in italics and set between brackets, as in this example.

> **CARLOS.** [*To* ISABEL.] Remember, don't make a sound! [*He tiptoes offstage.*]

Remember to read the stage directions when you read a play, or you may miss important information.

Vocabulary

You will encounter the following words in *The Phantom Tollbooth*, Act II. Decide whether you know each word well, know it a little bit, or do not know it at all. After you read the play, see how your knowledge of each word has increased.

dissonance	deficiency	admonishing
iridescent	malicious	transfixed

488 UNIT 4 • How do we decide who we are?

TEXT COMPLEXITY **RUBRIC**

The Phantom Tollbooth, Act II		Reader and Task Suggestions	
Qualitative Measures		**Preparing to Read the Text**	**Leveled Tasks**
Context/Knowledge Demands	Imaginary kingdoms; descriptive names; humor 1 2 ③ 4 5	• Use the Compare and Contrast note on TE p. 492 to discuss how the playwright uses language in the play.	*Structure/Language* If students will have difficulty with wordplay, discuss how the names *Dynne* (*din*) and *Dischord* are related to the word *dissonance*. Have students explain how their dialogue reflects the meaning of their names.
Structure/Language Conventionality and Clarity	Dialogue, long sentences, some challenging vocabulary, word play 1 2 3 ④ 5		
Levels of Meaning/Purpose/ Concept Level	Accessible concept (valuing time and hard work) 1 2 ③ 4 5	• Guide students to use Multidraft Reading strategies (TE p. 490)	*Analyzing* If students will not have difficulty with the wordplay, have them look at the illustration of Dodecahedron on p. 498 and identify the elements that make up his body. Discuss why the illustrator used these elements to create Dodecahedron.
Quantitative Measures			
Lexile	NP	Text Length	Word Count: 17,832	

CLOSE READING MODEL

The passage below is from Susan Nanus's play *The Phantom Tollbooth*, Act II. The annotations to the right of the passage show ways in which you can use close reading skills to compare and contrast characters, situations, and events, as well as analyze stage directions.

from *The Phantom Tollbooth*, Act II

MILO. [*Suspiciously.*] Just what kind of doctor are you? [1]

DISCHORD. Well, you might say, I'm a specialist. I specialize in noises, from the loudest to the softest, and from the slightly annoying to the terribly unpleasant. For instance, have you ever heard a square-wheeled steamroller ride over a street full of hardboiled eggs? [*Very loud CRUNCHING SOUNDS are heard.*] [2]

MILO. [*Holding his ears.*] But who would want all those terrible noises?

DISCHORD. [*Surprised at the question.*] Everybody does. Why, I'm so busy I can hardly fill all the orders for noise pills, racket lotion, clamor salve and hubbub tonic. That's all people seem to want these days. Years ago, everyone wanted pleasant sounds and business was terrible. But then the cities were built and there was a great need for honking horns, screeching trains, clanging bells and all the rest of those wonderfully unpleasant sounds we use so much today. [3] I've been working overtime ever since and my medicine here is in great demand. All you have to do is take one spoonful every day, and you'll never have to hear another beautiful sound again. Here, try some.

HUMBUG. [*Backing away.*] If it's all the same to you, I'd rather not. [4]

Stage Directions

1 The italic words in brackets signal a stage direction. This one tells you that Milo is suspicious of Dischord.

Stage Directions

2 These stage directions call for a sound effect. Someone backstage might create the effect by playing a recording or using objects that create a crunching sound.

Compare and Contrast

3 Dischord contrasts what his business was like years ago to what his business is like now that the cities are bustling.

Compare and Contrast

4 When you compare Dischord to a real-life doctor, his ideas about medicine may be the opposite of what you expect. Real-life doctors do not try to cure something positive such as the ability to hear beautiful sounds.

For each class during which you will teach this selection, have students complete one of the five Revision activities for Week 22 in *Daily Bellringer Activities*. You may wish to use additional activities that are applicable to this selection.

Vocabulary

If students require support with selection vocabulary, use this routine:

1. Write the following words and definitions on the board:

   dissonance *n.* harsh or unpleasant combination of sounds

   deficiency *n.* shortage or lack

   admonishing *adj.* disapproving

   iridescent *adj.* showing different colors when seen from different angles

   malicious *adj.* having or showing bad intentions

   transfixed *v.* made motionless by horror or fascination

2. Have students say each word aloud.

3. Use the word in a sentence that defines the word.

🏫 DIFFERENTIATED INSTRUCTION

🔵 Extended Support—English Learners
Have students complete the **Reading and Vocabulary Warm-ups** for this selection in the *Student Companion All-in-One Workbook* before they read. Assign the prereading pages and the adapted selection in the *Reader's Notebook: English Learner's Version.* Then, have students listen to portions of the selection in the *Student eText* or on the *Hear It!* CD-ROM.

🔲 🔲 Extended Support—Struggling Readers
Have students complete the **Reading and Vocabulary Warm-ups** for this selection in the *Student Companion All-in-One Workbook* before they read. Assign the prereading pages and the adapted selection in the *Reader's Notebook: Adapted Version.* Then, have students listen to portions of the selection in the *Student eText* or on the *Hear It!* CD-ROM (adapted text).

Extended Support—Reluctant Readers
To build motivation and engagement before assigning the selection, have students read have students read "Extreme Challenges," and "The Creative Connection," two thematically related selections in *Reality Central.* Then, use the questions at the conclusion of the related selection to guide discussion.

MULTIDRAFT READING

To assist struggling readers and to deepen comprehension for all, assign the text in "chunks" and apply multidraft reading protocols. For each reading, have students set the purpose indicated:

- **First reading:** Students should read the selection independently and think about its basic meaning.
- **Second reading:** Students should analyze the text's key ideas and details and its craft and structure, and respond to the side-column prompts.
- **Third reading:** Students should integrate knowledge and ideas, connect the text to other texts and to the world, and answer the end-of-selection questions.

For more guidance, refer to the *Classroom Strategies and Teaching Routines* card on multidraft reading.

❶ Activating Prior Knowledge

List the characters introduced in "The Phantom Tollbooth, Act I"—The Whether Man, the Lethargarians, Tock, Azaz, the Mathemagician, Princess Rhyme, Princess Reason, Spelling Bee, and Humbug. Have students describe each character.

Then list the characters in Act II— Kakafonous A. Dischord, The Awful Dynne, The Dodecahedron, The Everpresent Wordsnatcher, The Terrible Trivium, and Senses Taker. Ask students to predict the personality traits of these characters.

After they read Act II, have students return to the predictions about the names of characters and have them revise as necessary.

As necessary, have them revise their descriptions of the Act II characters to tell how they look and how their names are related to their character traits.

❷ Stage Directions

Ask the Stage Directions question.

Answer: They tell that Digitopolis is in the background and a colorful wagon is near the front of the stage.

The Phantom Tollbooth

Susan Nanus
Based on the book by Norton Juster

❶ Review and Anticipate

In Act I, Milo is lifted from his boredom into a strange kingdom that is in conflict over the importance of letters and numbers. After traveling through Dictionopolis, he agrees to rescue the princesses who can settle the conflict. As Act II opens, Milo enters Digitopolis with Tock and Humbug—characters who will help him rescue the princesses.

Stage Directions
What information about setting do these stage directions provide?

Vocabulary ▶
dissonance (dis´ə nəns) *n.* harsh or unpleasant combination of sounds

Act II • Scene i

The set of Digitopolis glitters in the background, while Upstage Right near the road, a small colorful Wagon sits, looking quite deserted. On its side in large letters, a sign reads: "KAKAFONOUS A. DISCHORD Doctor of Dissonance." Enter MILO, TOCK, *and* HUMBUG, *fearfully. They look at the wagon.*

TOCK. There's no doubt about it. That's where the noise was coming from.

HUMBUG. [*To* MILO.] Well, go on.

MILO. Go on what?

HUMBUG. Go on and see who's making all that noise in there. We can't just ignore a creature like that.

💬 VOCABULARY DEVELOPMENT

Thematic Vocabulary: The Big Question
As students are discussing *The Phantom Tollbooth,* Act II, encourage them to use the thematic vocabulary presented in Introducing the Big Question, pp. 440–441. You might encourage them with sentence starters like these:

1. Dischord's *appearance* leads Milo to believe that . . .
2. Dischord is interested in a *diverse* collection of . . .
3. The Dodecahedron thinks that the *custom* of giving more than one name to a person with one face is . . .
4. The Dodecahedron's many faces *reflect* . . .
5. Milo and his companions *respond* to danger by . . .

MILO. Creature? What kind of creature? Do you think he's dangerous?

HUMBUG. Go on, Milo. Knock on the door. We'll be right behind you.

MILO. O.K. Maybe he can tell us how much further it is to Digitopolis.

[MILO *tiptoes up to the wagon door and KNOCKS timidly. The moment he knocks, a terrible CRASH is heard inside the wagon, and* MILO *and the others jump back in fright. At the same time, the Door Flies Open, and from the dark interior, a Hoarse* VOICE *inquires.*]

VOICE. Have you ever heard a whole set of dishes dropped from the ceiling onto a hard stone floor? [*The Others are speechless with fright.* MILO *shakes his head.* VOICE *happily.*] Have you ever heard an ant wearing fur slippers walk across a thick wool carpet? [MILO *shakes his head again.*] Have you ever heard a blindfolded octopus unwrap a cellophane-covered bathtub? [MILO *shakes his head a third time.*] Ha! I knew it. [*He hops out, a little man, wearing a white coat, with a stethoscope around his neck, and a small mirror attached to his forehead, and with very huge ears, and a mortar and pestle in his hands. He stares at* MILO, TOCK *and* HUMBUG.] None of you looks well at all! Tsk, tsk, not at all. [*He opens the top or side of his Wagon, revealing a dusty interior resembling an old apothecary shop, with shelves lined with jars and boxes, a table, books, test tubes and bottles and measuring spoons.*]

MILO. [*Timidly.*] Are you a doctor?

DISCHORD. [VOICE.] I am KAKAFONOUS A. DISCHORD, DOCTOR OF DISSONANCE! [*Several small explosions and a grinding crash are heard.*]

HUMBUG. [*Stuttering with fear.*] What does the "A" stand for?

DISCHORD. AS LOUD AS POSSIBLE! [*Two screeches and a bump are heard.*] Now, step a little closer and stick out your tongues. [DISCHORD *examines them.*] Just as I expected. [*He opens a large dusty book and thumbs through the pages.*] You're all suffering from a severe lack of noise. [DISCHORD *begins running around, collecting bottles, reading the labels to himself as he goes along.*]

Stage Directions

What information about sound effects do you learn from these stage directions?

4 Comprehension

Why are Milo, Tock, and Humbug frightened?

---

3 Stage Directions

1. Call students' attention to the bracketed passage.

2. **Ask** them what visual clue the text provides to indicate sound effects.

   Answer: The sounds are written in capital letters.

3. **Ask** the Stage Directions question.

   Possible response: I learned that Milo knocks softly on the wagon door, and then he hears a huge crash coming from inside the wagon.

4. Remind students to use the **Literary Analysis Graphic Organizer** for this selection to help them picture the action and characters as they read the play.

4 Comprehension

Possible response: They are frightened because of the loud, disturbing noises they hear, and they don't know what is inside the wagon.

DIFFERENTIATED INSTRUCTION

Support for Less Proficient Readers
As students begin Act II, they are likely to be comfortable reading the play format. Allow time for sustained silent reading so they can develop fluency without interruption. Provide time for questions and clarification, but only after students have completed a significant portion of Act II.

EL Vocabulary for English Learners
Students may benefit from previewing the vocabulary terms and other difficult words throughout Act II. Have them check the definitions of unfamiliar words in a dictionary. Challenge them to use the new words in sentences.

 Video

Watch the Background Video online!

 **Audio**

Selection audio is available in the *Student eText* and on the *Hear It!* CD-ROM.

5 Critical Viewing

Possible Response: His large ears are a clue.

6 Compare and Contrast

Onomatopoeic words for loud or unpleasant noises often have a hard or harsh sound, just as onomatopoeic words for pleasant sounds often have many soft and pleasing sounds. Work with students to come up with lists of words for various types of sounds. Start with some of the words in the play that are used in puns and word play:

cacophonous

discord

crash

hoarse

screech

bump

clang

din

row

Work with students to come up with antonyms for these and other unpleasant sound words.

Possible responses:

melodious

harmony

float

smooth

murmur

brush

tinkle

hush

calm

Help students brainstorm about the effect that these words have when they hear them.

5 ▼ Critical Viewing
What aspect of Dischord's appearance might lead you to guess that he is interested in sounds?

Vocabulary ▶
deficiency (dē fish´ ən sē) *n.* shortage or lack

"Loud Cries." "Soft Cries." "Bangs, Bongs, Swishes. Swooshes." "Snaps and Crackles." "Whistles and Gongs." "Squeeks, Squawks, and Miscellaneous Uproar." [*As he reads them off, he pours a little of each into a large glass beaker and stirs the mixture with a wooden spoon. The concoction smokes and bubbles.*] Be ready in just a moment.

Milo. [*Suspiciously.*] Just what kind of doctor are you?

Dischord. Well, you might say, I'm a specialist. I specialize in noises, from the loudest to the softest, and from the slightly annoying to the terribly unpleasant. For instance, have you ever heard a square-wheeled steamroller ride over a street full of hard-boiled eggs? [*Very loud CRUNCHING SOUNDS are heard.*]

Milo. [*Holding his ears.*] But who would want all those terrible noises?

Dischord. [*Surprised at the question.*] Everybody does. Why, I'm so busy I can hardly fill all the orders for noise pills, racket lotion, clamor salve and hubbub tonic. That's all people seem to want these days. Years ago, everyone wanted pleasant sounds and business was terrible. But then the cities were built and there was a great need for honking horns, screeching trains, clanging bells and all the rest of those wonderfully unpleasant sounds we use so much today. I've been working overtime ever since and my medicine here is in great demand. All you have to do is take one spoonful every day, and you'll never have to hear another beautiful sound again. Here, try some.

Humbug. [*Backing away.*] If it's all the same to you, I'd rather not.

Milo. I don't want to be cured of beautiful sounds.

Tock. Besides, there's no such sickness as a lack of noise.

Dischord. How true. That's what makes it so difficult to cure. [*Takes a large glass bottle from the shelf.*] Very well, if you want to go all through life suffering from a noise deficiency, I'll just give this to Dynne for his lunch. [*Uncorks the bottle and pours the liquid into it. There is a rumbling and then a loud*

🧠 THINK ALOUD

Dictionary Use
On p. 493, direct students' attention to the name of Dynne's grandfather—the Dreadful Rauw. Then tell students that the grandfather's name is a wordplay involving the word *row*. Write the word on the board. Say to students:

I'm going to think aloud to show you how I would figure out which dictionary definition of *row* to choose based on the context of the drama. Ever since Milo and his companions have met Dischord, the

focus of the drama has been on noise. I see in the dictionary that there are many definitions for *row*. The first definition is "to propel a boat." That doesn't seem right; there are no boats in this scene. The next is "objects arranged in a straight line." Well, we're not talking about objects, so that's not right, either. The next definition is "a noisy disturbance or quarrel." Based on the context of the drama, this definition of *row* seems just right.

explosion accompanied by smoke, out of which DYNNE, *a smog-like creature with yellow eyes and a frowning mouth, appears.*]

DYNNE. [*Smacking his lips.*] Ahhh, that was good, Master. I thought you'd never let me out. It was really cramped in there.

DISCHORD. This is my assistant, the awful Dynne. You must forgive his appearance, for he really doesn't have any.

MILO. What is a Dynne?

DISCHORD. You mean you've never heard of the awful Dynne? When you're playing in your room and making a great amount of noise, what do they tell you to stop?

MILO. That awful din.

DISCHORD. When the neighbors are playing their radio too loud late at night, what do you wish they'd turn down?

TOCK. That awful din.

DISCHORD. And when the street on your block is being repaired and the drills are working all day, what does everyone complain of?

HUMBUG. [*Brightly.*] The dreadful row.

DYNNE. The Dreadful Rauw was my grandfather. He perished in the great silence epidemic of 1712. I certainly can't understand why you don't like noise. Why, I heard an explosion last week that was so lovely, I groaned with appreciation for two days. [*He gives a loud groan at the memory.*]

DISCHORD. He's right, you know! Noise is the most valuable thing in the world.

MILO. King Azaz says words are.

DISCHORD. NONSENSE! Why, when a baby wants food, how does he ask?

DYNNE. [*Happily.*] He screams!

DISCHORD. And when a racing car wants gas?

DYNNE. [*Jumping for joy.*] It chokes!

Stage Directions
How does this stage direction help you imagine what Dynne is like?

Compare and Contrast
How are Dischord's opinions different from most people's regarding sounds?

9 Comprehension
What caused people to want noise and hubbub rather than pleasant sounds?

DIFFERENTIATED INSTRUCTION

Support for Special-Needs Students
Help students understand the true meaning of the words *din* and *discord* and how the words are related to the characters' names. Define *discord* as "a harsh or unpleasant sound." Explain that this is an appropriate name for Doctor Dischord, because he specializes in noises, especially unpleasant ones. Define *din* as "a loud and continued noise." Tell students that Dynne is an appropriate name for this character, because he appreciates noise—especially loud explosions—and can't understand why anyone wouldn't like it.

Enrichment for Gifted/Talented Students
Challenge students to re-create one of the scenes in the play. Have them read the stage directions and other descriptions of the scenes. Then, encourage them to use paint, markers, clay, and other art media to make a drawing or diorama of a set. Suggest that they add scaled-down models of costumed characters to their sets.

7 Stage Directions

1. Have students close their eyes and listen as you read aloud the bracketed stage directions (beginning on the previous page). Tell them to picture the scene in their minds.

2. **Ask** the Stage Directions question.

   Possible response: Some students may visualize a small creature with a wispy, undefined shape because he materializes from smoke. Others may see Dynne as a larger, cloudlike form, particularly given the loud explosion.

3. **Ask** students to tell what information they learned about sound effects from the same stage directions.

   Answer: The action made a rumbling and a loud explosion.

4. Suggest that students add their visualization of Dynne to their **Literary Analysis Graphic Organizer** for this selection.

8 Compare and Contrast

1. Have a volunteer read the bracketed dialogue aloud.

2. **Ask** students to identify Dynne's reaction to the explosion he heard.

   Answer He thought it was a lovely sound and groaned in appreciation of it.

3. Point out that Dischord agrees that the explosion was lovely. **Ask** the Compare and Contrast question.

   Possible Response: Most people do not like to hear loud explosions and they complain about them. In contrast, Dischord says that noise is the most valuable thing in the world.

9 Comprehension

Answer: Once cities were built, there was a much greater need for warnings and alerts, such as honking horns, screeching trains, clanging bells, and all sorts of unpleasant sounds.

10 Compare and Contrast

1. Direct students' attention to the first bracketed text.

2. **Ask** students to paraphrase what Dynne does on his rounds.

Possible response: He wanders around the kingdom, searching for terrible sounds. He collects them and brings them in bags to the doctor.

3. **Ask** the Compare and Contrast question.

Possible response: On his or her rounds, a mail carrier travels on a specific route and delivers letters and packages. In his rounds, Dynne wanders throughout the kingdom and collects sounds for the doctor.

11 Stage Directions

1. Read aloud the bracketed stage directions.

2. **Ask** the Stage Directions question.

Answer: They tell us that he is looking for a specific package that he has misplaced.

3. If students were unfamiliar with the word *rummages,* **ask** them how they could use context clues to determine its meaning.

Answer: The words "Ah, here it is . . ." are a clue that Dischord was searching for something in particular.

Compare and Contrast
10 How are these rounds different from the daily rounds of people such as mail carriers?

Stage Directions
11 How do these stage directions help you understand what Dischord is doing?

DISCHORD. And what happens to the dawn when a new day begins?

DYNNE. [*Delighted.*] It breaks!

DISCHORD. You see how simple it is? [*To* DYNNE.] Isn't it time for us to go?

MILO. Where to? Maybe we're going the same way.

DYNNE. I doubt it. [*Picking up empty sacks from the table.*] We're going on our collection rounds. Once a day, I travel throughout the kingdom and collect all the wonderfully horrible and beautifully unpleasant sounds I can find and bring them back to the doctor to use in his medicine.

DISCHORD. Where are you going?

MILO. To Digitopolis.

DISCHORD. Oh, there are a number of ways to get to Digitopolis, if you know how to follow directions. Just take a look at the sign at the fork in the road. Though why you'd ever want to go there, I'll never know.

MILO. We want to talk to the Mathemagician.

HUMBUG. About the release of the Princesses Rhyme and Reason.

DISCHORD. Rhyme and Reason? I remember them. Very nice girls, but a little too quiet for my taste. In fact, I've been meaning to send them something that Dynne brought home by mistake and which I have absolutely no use for. [*He rummages through the wagon.*] Ah, here it is . . . or maybe you'd like it for yourself. [*Hands* MILO *a Package.*]

MILO. What is it?

DISCHORD. The sounds of laughter. They're so unpleasant to hear, it's almost unbearable. All those giggles and snickers and happy shouts of joy, I don't know what Dynne was thinking of when he collected them. Here, take them to the Princesses or keep them for yourselves, I don't care. Well, time to move on. Goodbye now and good luck! [*He has shut the wagon by now and gets in. LOUD NOISES begin to erupt as* DYNNE *pulls the wagon offstage.*]

494 UNIT 4 • How do we decide who we are?

💬 **VOCABULARY DEVELOPMENT**

Graphic Organizers
Point out that Dischord uses the terms *giggles, snickers,* and *happy shouts of joy* to describe various sounds of laughter. From left to right on a word continuum, write the words *snickers, giggles, laughter,* and *shrieks.* Discuss how the degree of sound expressed by the words increases from left to right on the graphic organizer. Using a thesaurus and a dictionary, work with students to list synonyms for *snickers.* Direct students to repeat the process for the remaining words. Then have students compare their lists.

Milo. [*Calling after them.*] But wait! The fork in the road . . . you didn't tell us where it is . . .

Tock. It's too late. He can't hear a thing.

Humbug. I could use a fork of my own, at the moment. And a knife and a spoon to go with it. All of a sudden, I feel very hungry.

Milo. So do I, but it's no use thinking about it. There won't be anything to eat until we reach Digitopolis. [*They get into the car.*]

Humbug. [*Rubbing his stomach.*] Well, the sooner the better is what I say. [*A SIGN suddenly appears.*]

> DIGITOPOLIS 5 Miles
> 1,600 Rods
> 8,800 Yards
> 26,400 Feet
> 316,800 Inches
> 633,600 Half Inches AND THEN SOME

⑫ ◄ Critical Viewing
How are the different measurements on this sign related?

Voice. [*A strange voice from nowhere.*] But which way will get you there sooner? That is the question.

Tock. Did you hear something?

Milo. Look! The fork in the road and a signpost to Digitopolis! [*They read the Sign.*]

Humbug. Let's travel by miles, it's shorter.

Milo. Let's travel by half inches. It's quicker.

Tock. But which road should we take? It must make a difference.

Milo. Do you think so?

Tock. Well, I'm not sure, but . . .

Humbug. He could be right. On the other hand, he could also be wrong. Does it make a difference or not?

⑬ Comprehension
What does Dischord give to Milo, and why?

Voice. Yes, indeed, indeed it does, certainly, my yes, it does make a difference.

⑫ Critical Viewing

Answer: Each is a measurement of length. The list begins with the longest measurement, miles, and ends with the shortest measurement, half inches.

⑬ Comprehension

Answer: He gives Milo a box containing the sounds of laughter. He wants to get rid of them because he thinks these sounds are unpleasant.

⚏ DIFFERENTIATED INSTRUCTION

🄴🄻 Support for English Learners
Clarify the two meanings of "fork," so that students can make a connection between Milo's and Humbug's dialogue. Explain that while most fork utensils split into three or four tines, the image of a fork utensil is often used to represent a place where a road splits into two different directions. On the board, draw an image of a fork in a road.

Enrichment for Advanced Readers
Interested students may enjoy working together to create a booklet of mathematical word problems based on "The Phantom Tollbooth." (Remind students to include answers.) You might suggest that they consult with a math teacher. After they have constructed their booklet, have students share problems with the rest of the class.

14 Stage Directions

1. Direct students' attention to the bracketed text and tell them to pay special attention to the stage directions as they read the section.

2. Tell them to picture what Dodecahedron looks like and how it moves.

3. **Ask** the Stage Directions question.

   Answer: The information would be important to the performers because it explains that each of Dodecahedron's faces has a different expression and describes how Dodecahedron moves.

4. Have students add the stage directions and what they show about Dodecahedron to their **Literary Analysis Graphic Organizer** for *The Phantom Tollbooth*, Act II.

Stage Directions
Why would the information presented here be important to a group performing the play?

Vocabulary ▶
admonishing (ad män´ ish in) *adj.* disapproving

[*The* DODECAHEDRON *appears, a 12-sided figure with a different face on each side, and with all the edges labeled with a small letter and all the angles labeled with a large letter. He wears a beret and peers at the others with a serious face. He doffs his cap and recites:*]

DODECAHEDRON. My angles are many.
　　　　My sides are not few.
　　　　I'm the Dodecahedron.
　　　　Who are you?

MILO. What's a Dodecahedron?

DODECAHEDRON. [*Turning around slowly.*] See for yourself. A Dodecahedron is a mathematical shape with 12 faces. [*All his faces appear as he turns, each face with a different expression. He points to them.*] I usually use one at a time. It saves wear and tear. What are you called?

MILO. Milo.

DODECAHEDRON. That's an odd name. [*Changing his smiling face to a frowning one.*] And you have only one face.

MILO. [*Making sure it is still there.*] Is that bad?

DODECAHEDRON. You'll soon wear it out using it for everything. Is everyone with one face called Milo?

MILO. Oh, no. Some are called Billy or Jeffery or Sally or Lisa or lots of other things.

DODECAHEDRON. How confusing. Here everything is called exactly what it is. The triangles are called triangles, the circles are called circles, and even the same numbers have the same name. Can you imagine what would happen if we named all the twos Billy or Jeffery or Sally or Lisa or lots of other things? You'd have to say Robert plus John equals four, and if the fours were named Albert, things would be hopeless.

MILO. I never thought of it that way.

DODECAHEDRON. [*With an* admonishing *face.*] Then I suggest you begin at once, for in Digitopolis, everything is quite precise.

MILO. Then perhaps you can help us decide which road we should take.

💬 VOCABULARY DEVELOPMENT

Selection Vocabulary Reinforcement
Students will benefit from additional examples and practice with the selection vocabulary words. Reinforce their comprehension with "show-you-know" sentences for the words they have already encountered in the text. The first part of the sentence uses the word in an appropriate context. The second part of the sentence clarifies the first. Model the strategy for *dissonance*: Most people consider traffic noises to be *dissonance*; however, Dischord loves all those unpleasant sounds.

　　Then give students these sentence prompts and coach them in creating the clarification part.

1. No matter how well the musician played, the old piano only created *dissonance*; _____ .
Sample answer: it was badly in need of tuning.

2. A *deficiency* of funds caused the town to close a library; _____ .
Sample answer: there was just not enough money in the budget to keep it open.

3. The father gave his children an *admonishing* look; _____ .
Sample answer: he disapproved of their behavior in the restaurant.

DODECAHEDRON. [*Happily.*] By all means. There's nothing to it. [*As he talks, the three others try to solve the problem on a Large Blackboard that is wheeled onstage for the occasion.*] Now, if a small car carrying three people at 30 miles an hour for 10 minutes along a road 5 miles long at 11:35 in the morning starts at the same time as 3 people who have been traveling in a little automobile at 20 miles an hour for 15 minutes on another road exactly twice as long as half the distance of the other, while a dog, a bug, and a boy travel an equal distance in the same time or the same distance in an equal time along a third road in mid-October, then which one arrives first and which is the best way to go?

HUMBUG. Seventeen!

MILO. [*Still figuring frantically.*] I'm not sure, but . . .

DODECAHEDRON. You'll have to do better than that.

MILO. I'm not very good at problems.

DODECAHEDRON. What a shame. They're so very useful. Why, did you know that if a beaver 2 feet long with a tail a foot and a half long can build a dam 12 feet high and 6 feet wide in 2 days, all you would need to build Boulder Dam is a beaver 68 feet long with a 51 foot tail?

HUMBUG. [*Grumbling as his pencil snaps.*] Where would you find a beaver that big?

DODECAHEDRON. I don't know, but if you did, you'd certainly know what to do with him.

MILO. That's crazy.

DODECAHEDRON. That may be true, but it's completely accurate, and as long as the answer is right, who cares if the question is wrong?

TOCK. [*Who has been patiently doing the first problem.*] All three roads arrive at the same place at the same time.

DODECAHEDRON. Correct! And I'll take you there myself. [*The blackboard rolls off, and all four get into the car and drive off.*] Now you see how important problems are. If you hadn't done this one properly, you might have gone the wrong way.

Compare and Contrast
Based on his words and actions, how is Dodecahedron different from Milo and Humbug?

...as long as the answer is right, who cares if the question is wrong?

16 Comprehension
Based on their responses to the problem Dodecahedron poses, who is best at mathematics: Milo, Tock, or Humbug?

15 Compare and Contrast

1. Invite three students to read the bracketed parts of Dodecahedron, Humbug, and Milo.

2. **Ask** students to picture Dodecahedron as he is describing the math problem. Then have them brainstorm for words and phrases that describe him.

   Possible responses: Students may say that Dodecahedron *is enthusiastic, loves math,* and *is brainy.*

3. **Ask** the Compare and Contrast question.

   Answer: He is very good at math and loves the subject. Humbug and Milo are not very good at solving math problems and they don't seem very interested in the subject.

16 Comprehension

Answer: Tock is the one with the correct answer.

DIFFERENTIATED INSTRUCTION

Support for Less Proficient Readers
Students may benefit from reviewing the characters in the play. Have each student select and make notes about a character. Student's observations should include a description of the character, notes about the character's first appearance in the play, and the major events the character has taken part in. Provide time for students to share their observations.

Support for Special-Needs Students
Students may be confused by the presence of the word problems in this part of the dialogue. The problems abruptly interrupt the play's forward motion and can lead some readers off on a tangent. Explain that they are included in the dialogue to give the reader clues about the character of Dodecahedron. Stress that they are not meant to solve the math problem, nor to actually understand it.

Critical Viewing

Possible response: Some students may say that the most interesting details are those that show the various math instruments that he is made from. Others may say that the expressions on the faces of the dodecahedron are the most interesting details.

18 **Connecting to the Big Question**

1. Point out to students that deciding who we are is a process involving change. As we experience new things and meet new people, we may grow in unpredictable ways.

2. Have students read the bracketed passage. **Ask:** Is Milo sure of himself when he states his feelings about numbers?

   Possible response: He states clearly that he never thought that they were very important.

3. **Ask:** How is Milo affected by the Dodecahedron's enthusiasm for numbers?

   Possible response: When he says, "All I meant was . . ." he is expressing some doubt about what he was more sure of earlier.

4. Tell students to look as they read for additional details showing Milo's questioning of his own beliefs.

17 ▼ **Critical Viewing**
Which qualities of Dodecahedron are the most interesting to you? Why?

MILO. But if all the roads arrive at the same place at the same time, then aren't they all the right road?

DODECAHEDRON. [*Glaring from his upset face.*] Certainly not! They're all the wrong way! Just because you have a choice, it doesn't mean that any of them has to be right. [*Pointing in another direction.*] That's the way to Digitopolis and we'll be there any moment. [*Suddenly the lighting grows dimmer.*] In fact, we're here. Welcome to the Land of Numbers.

HUMBUG. [*Looking around at the barren landscape.*] It doesn't look very inviting.

MILO. Is this the place where numbers are made?

DODECAHEDRON. They're not made. You have to dig for them. Don't you know anything at all about numbers?

MILO. Well, I never really thought they were very important.

DODECAHEDRON. NOT IMPORTANT! Could you have tea for two without the 2? Or three blind mice without the 3? And how would you sail the seven seas without the 7?

MILO. All I meant was . . .

DODECAHEDRON. [*Continues shouting angrily.*] If you had high hopes, how would you know how high they were? And did you know that narrow escapes come in different widths? Would you travel the whole world wide without ever knowing how wide it was? And how could you do anything at long last without knowing how long the last was? Why, numbers are the most beautiful and valuable things in the world. Just follow me and I'll show you. [*He motions to them and pantomimes walking through rocky terrain with the others in tow. A Doorway similar to the Tollbooth appears and the* DODECAHEDRON *opens it and motions the others to follow him through.*] Come along, come along. I can't wait for you all day. [*They enter the doorway and the lights are dimmed very low, as to simulate the interior of a cave. The SOUNDS of scrapings and tapping, scuffling and digging are heard all around them. He hands them Helmets with flashlights attached.*] Put these on.

18

💬 **VOCABULARY DEVELOPMENT**

Geometry Terms
Call students' attention to the illustration of Dodecahedron. Recall from the text that the figure has twelve faces. Tell students that the prefix *dodeca-* means twelve and *-hedron* means number of surfaces; a *dodecahedron* is a solid figure that has twelve surfaces. Next, point out that each of Dodecahedron's twelve faces has five sides and five angles; those flat faces, or plane figures, are called *pentagons*. Explain that the prefix *penta-* means five and *-gon* means angle. List related terms, such as *hexagon, heptagon, octagon, nonagon, decagon, hendecagon,* and *dodecagon*. Explain that they are plane figures with six, seven, eight, nine, ten, eleven, and twelve sides and angles.

MILO. [*Whispering.*] Where are we going?

DODECAHEDRON. We're here. This is the numbers mine. [*LIGHTS UP A LITTLE, revealing Little Men digging and chopping, shoveling and scraping.*] Right this way and watch your step. [*His voice echoes and reverberates. Iridescent and glittery numbers seem to sparkle from everywhere.*]

MILO. [*Awed.*] Whose mine is it?

VOICE OF MATHEMAGICIAN. By the four million eight hundred and twenty-seven thousand six hundred and fifty-nine hairs on my head, it's mine, of course! [*ENTER the MATHEMAGICIAN, carrying his long staff which looks like a giant pencil.*]

HUMBUG. [*Already intimidated.*] It's a lovely mine, really it is.

MATHEMAGICIAN. [*Proudly.*] The biggest number mine in the kingdom.

MILO. [*Excitedly.*] Are there any precious stones in it?

MATHEMAGICIAN. Precious stones! [*Then softly.*] By the eight million two hundred and forty-seven thousand three hundred and twelve threads in my robe, I'll say there are. Look here. [*Reaches in a cart, pulls out a small object, polishes it vigorously and holds it to the light, where it sparkles.*]

MILO. But that's a five.

MATHEMAGICIAN. Exactly. As valuable a jewel as you'll find anywhere. Look at some of the others. [*Scoops up others and pours them into MILO's arms. They include all numbers from 1 to 9 and an assortment of zeros.*]

DODECAHEDRON. We dig them and polish them right here, and then send them all over the world. Marvelous, aren't they?

TOCK. They are beautiful. [*He holds them up to compare them to the numbers on his clock body.*]

MILO. So that's where they come from. [*Looks at them and carefully hands them back, but drops a few which smash and break in half.*] Oh, I'm sorry!

◄ **Vocabulary**
iridescent (ir′ ə des′ ənt) *adj.* showing different colors when seen from different angles

Stage Directions
What information do these stage directions provide about the action?

20 Comprehension
What do Dodecahedron and Mathemagician find exciting and valuable?

19 Stage Directions

1. Remind students that one purpose of stage directions is to help the reader picture the action.
2. Read the bracketed stage direction. Tell students to listen for the verbs, or action words, in the stage directions.
3. **Ask** the Stage Directions question. Encourage students to pantomime the actions as they answer the question.

   Answer: They specifically identify the actions of Mathemagician. He reaches into the cart, pulls out an object, polishes it, and holds it up to the light.

20 Comprehension

Answer: They find numbers to be valuable and exciting.

✸ DIFFERENTIATED INSTRUCTION

Enrichment for Gifted/Talented Students
The text does not include any illustration of the numbers mine or the Little Men who toil there. Invite students to use colored pencils, markers, or pastels to illustrate how they envision a scene in the mine. Challenge them to find a way to make the numbers appear to be "iridescent and glittery" as described in the stage directions. Display their artwork for others to enjoy.

Enrichment for Advanced Readers
Have students closely examine the illustration of Dodecahedron. Challenge them to name all the parts used to make him (a dodecahedron for his head, triangles for his arms, rulers for his body, protractors for his legs, and triangles for his feet). Supply some of these mathematical tools and reference materials about them. Have students demonstrate the tools' use to the class.

㉑ Critical Viewing

Possible response: His robe and hat are covered with equations. He is holding his staff, with a pencil point at one end and an eraser at the other. He is surrounded by numbers that appear to be from the numbers mine.

㉑ ▲ Critical Viewing
Which details in the picture suggest that this is Mathemagician?

MATHEMAGICIAN. [*Scooping them up.*] Oh, don't worry about that. We use the broken ones for fractions. How about some lunch? [*Takes out a little whistle and blows it. Two miners rush in carrying an immense cauldron which is bubbling and steaming. The workers put down their tools and gather around to eat.*]

HUMBUG. That looks delicious! [*TOCK and MILO also look hungrily at the pot.*]

MATHEMAGICIAN. Perhaps you'd care for something to eat?

MILO. Oh, yes, sir!

TOCK. Thank you.

HUMBUG. [*Already eating.*] Ummm . . . delicious! [*All finish their bowls immediately.*]

MATHEMAGICIAN. Please have another portion. [*They eat and finish. MATHEMAGICIAN serves them again.*] Don't stop now. [*They finish.*] Come on, no need to be bashful. [*Serves them again.*]

MILO. [*To TOCK and HUMBUG as he finishes again.*] Do you want to hear something strange? Each one I eat makes me a little hungrier than before.

MATHEMAGICIAN. Do have some more. [*He serves them again. They eat frantically, until the MATHEMAGICIAN blows his whistle again and the pot is removed.*]

㉒ HUMBUG. [*Holding his stomach.*] Uggghhh! I think I'm starving.

MILO. Me, too, and I ate so much.

DODECAHEDRON. [*Wiping the gravy from several of his mouths.*] Yes, it was delicious, wasn't it? It's the specialty of the kingdom . . . subtraction stew.

500 UNIT 4 • How do we decide who we are?

💬 VOCABULARY DEVELOPMENT

Selection Vocabulary Reinforcement
To reinforce and assess students' comprehension of selection vocabulary words, give them sentences using the words in which the word may or may not be used correctly. Students must tell whether the use is correct and explain their answers. Use these sentences:

1. Most lullabies feature *dissonance* in their melodies.
Answer: No, *dissonance* is not used correctly. *Dissonance* is a harsh or unpleasant combination of sounds and would not encourage sleep.

2. The *deficiency* of rain in the past years has caused serious problems for local farmers.
Answer: Yes, *deficiency* is used correctly. A shortage of rain could be a problem for farmers because crops need water.

3. She chose the *iridescent* fabric for her costume because she didn't want it to change colors under the stage lights.
Answer: No, *iridescent* is not used correctly. An iridescent fabric would change colors when seen from different angles under the lights.

TOCK. [*Weak from hunger.*] I have more of an appetite than when I began.

MATHEMAGICIAN. Certainly, what did you expect? The more you eat, the hungrier you get, everyone knows that.

MILO. They do? Then how do you get enough?

MATHEMAGICIAN. Enough? Here in Digitopolis, we have our meals when we're full and eat until we're hungry. That way, when you don't have anything at all, you have more than enough. It's a very economical system. You must have been stuffed to have eaten so much.

DODECAHEDRON. It's completely logical. The more you want, the less you get, and the less you get, the more you have. Simple arithmetic, that's all. [TOCK, MILO *and* HUMBUG *look at him blankly.*] Now, look, suppose you had something and added nothing to it. What would you have?

MILO. The same.

DODECAHEDRON. Splendid! And suppose you had something and added less than nothing to it? What would you have then?

HUMBUG. Starvation! Oh, I'm so hungry.

DODECAHEDRON. Now, now, it's not as bad as all that. In a few hours, you'll be nice and full again . . . just in time for dinner.

MILO. But I only eat when I'm hungry.

MATHEMAGICIAN. [*Waving the eraser of his staff.*] What a curious idea. The next thing you'll have us believe is that you only sleep when you're tired.

[*The mine has disappeared as well as the Miners.*]

HUMBUG. Where did everyone go?

MATHEMAGICIAN. Oh, they're still in the mine. I often find that the best way to get from one place to another is to erase everything and start again. Please make yourself at home.

Compare and Contrast
How are the meals that characters eat in Digitopolis different from real-life meals?

23 Comprehension
What is the easiest way for Mathemagician to get from one place to another?

22 Compare and Contrast

1. Have volunteers read the bracketed script for Milo, Mathemagician, Dodecahedron, and Tock on the previous page and this page.
2. **Ask** students when people in Digitopolis eat meals.
   Answer: They eat meals when they are full.
3. **Ask** the Compare and Contrast question.
   Answer: The difference is that the meals in Digitopolis increase one's appetite; in real life, meals take away one's appetite.

23 Comprehension

Answer: He erases everything and starts again.

DIFFERENTIATED INSTRUCTION

Support for Special-Needs Students
To help students understand the play's events, have students listen to portions of the selection in the *Student eText* or on the *Hear It!* CD-ROM. Instruct students to take notes as they listen, pausing the CD when necessary so that they can write their notes and questions. In particular, tell them to note scene changes and the introduction of new characters.

Enrichment for Gifted/Talented Students
Invite students to work in groups to create menus for restaurants in Digitopolis. Have them come up with names of foods or meals that relate to mathematics, in the way that "Subtraction Stew" does. Suggest that they incorporate terms such as *addition, multiplication, division, fraction, sum,* and *total* into the names. Encourage them to find additional math terms in the play to include. Have them design and illustrate menus with descriptions of each menu item and prices.

㉔ Literature in Context

Cultural Connection

Plumb lines are used by people in many building trades. Bricklayers, carpenters, plumbers, and paper-hangers use plumb lines to ensure that their vertical lines are straight. The guiding principle behind the plumb line is gravity; a weight will fall in a straight line toward Earth. Similar lines, called sounding lines, are used to measure water depth.

Connect to the Literature

1. **Ask** the Connect to the Literature question.

2. Direct students' attention to the first stage direction following "No, indeed!". Tell them to use the information provided in the stage direction and Mathemagician's words to infer the answer to the question.

Answer: He uses the plumb line to determine the shortest distance between two points. No, this would not happen in real life, because a plumb line is used to measure the height of something or vertical straight lines; it is not used to measure the distance from one place to another.

㉔ LITERATURE IN CONTEXT

Cultural Connection

Plumb Line
A plumb line is a cord that has a weight, often called a *plumb or plumb bob,* at one end. The word *plumb* comes from the Old French word *plomb,* which means "lead." Not surprisingly, the weight on a plumb line is frequently made of lead. The weight keeps the line straight and makes it a useful tool for measuring heights and straight lines.

Connect to the Literature

For what purpose does Mathemagician use a plumb line? Would this work in real life? Why or why not?

[*They find themselves in a unique room, in which all the walls, tables, chairs, desks, cabinets and blackboards are labeled to show their heights, widths, depths and distances to and from each other. To one side is a gigantic notepad on an artist's easel, and from hooks and strings hang a collection of rulers, measures, weights and tapes, and all other measuring devices.*]

Milo. Do you always travel that way? [*He looks around in wonder.*]

Mathemagician. No, indeed! [*He pulls a plumb line from a hook and walks.*] Most of the time I take the shortest distance between any two points. And of course, when I have to be in several places at once . . . [*He writes $3 \times 1 = 3$ on the notepad with his staff.*] I simply multiply. [*Three Figures looking like the Mathemagician appear on a platform above.*]

Milo. How did you do that?

Mathemagician and The Three. There's nothing to it, if you have a magic staff. [*The Three Figures cancel themselves out and disappear.*]

Humbug. That's nothing but a big pencil.

Mathemagician. True enough, but once you learn to use it, there's no end to what you can do.

Milo. Can you make things disappear?

Mathemagician. Just step a little closer and watch this. [*Shows them that there is nothing up his sleeve or in his hat. He writes:*]
$4 + 9 - 2 \times 16 + 1 = 3 \times 6 - 67 + 8 \times 2 - 3 + 26 - 1 - 34 + 3 - 7 + 2 - 5 =$ [*He looks up expectantly.*]

Humbug. Seventeen?

Milo. It all comes to zero.

Mathemagician. Precisely. [*Makes a theatrical bow and rips off paper from notepad.*] Now, is there anything else you'd like to see? [*At this point, an appeal to the audience to see if anyone would like a problem solved.*]

💬 VOCABULARY DEVELOPMENT

Word Forms
Expand students' vocabulary by helping them learn related forms of the selection vocabulary words. All six of the Vocabulary Builder words for *The Phantom Tollbooth,* Act II have related word forms. Give students a blank **Word Forms Chart** (*Professional Development Guidebook,* p. 42) with *dissonance, deficiency,* *admonishing, transfixed, malicious,* and *iridescent* in the correct columns. Work with the class, or have students work with a partner, to determine the related forms. Encourage students to integrate the related forms into their speaking and writing.

MILO. Well . . . can you show me the biggest number there is?

MATHEMAGICIAN. Why, I'd be delighted. [*Opening a closet door.*] We keep it right here. It took four miners to dig it out. [*He shows them a huge "3" twice as high as the* **MATHEMAGICIAN.**]

MILO. No, that's not what I mean. Can you show me the longest number there is?

MATHEMAGICIAN. Sure. [*Opens another door.*] Here it is. It took three carts to carry it here. [*Door reveals an "8" that is as wide as the "3" was high.*]

MILO. No, no, that's not what I meant either. [*Looks helplessly at* **TOCK.**]

TOCK. I think what you would like to see is the number of the greatest possible magnitude.

MATHEMAGICIAN. Well, why didn't you say so? [*He busily measures them and all other things as he speaks, and marks it down.*] What's the greatest number you can think of? [*Here, an appeal can also be made to the audience or* **MILO** *may think of his own answers.*]

MILO. Uh . . . nine trillion, nine hundred and ninety-nine billion, nine hundred ninety-nine million, nine-hundred ninety-nine thousand, nine hundred and ninety-nine [*He puffs.*]

MATHEMAGICIAN. [*Writes that on the pad.*] Very good. Now add one to it. [**MILO** *or audience does.*] Now add one again. [**MILO** *or audience does so.*] Now add one again. Now add one again. Now add . . .

MILO. But when can I stop?

MATHEMAGICIAN. Never. Because the number you want is always at least one more than the number you have, and it's so large that if you started saying it yesterday, you wouldn't finish tomorrow.

HUMBUG. Where could you ever find a number so big?

MATHEMAGICIAN. In the same place they have the smallest number there is, and you know what that is?

Compare and Contrast
Based on Mathemagician's actions here, how does he see numbers differently from Milo?

26 Comprehension
What does Mathemagician teach Milo about numbers?

25 Compare and Contrast

1. Have a student read the bracketed text aloud.

2. **Ask** students what information the stage directions give about Mathemagician's actions.

    Answer: He is busily measuring numbers and writing down their measurements.

3. **Ask** the Compare and Contrast question.

    Possible response: He and Milo are using words that cause them to view the numbers differently. Mathemagician interprets "biggest" and "longest" to mean the numbers' physical size. Milo is talking about them in terms of their quantity.

26 Comprehension

Answer: He teaches Milo that he can always add one to any given number and divide any given number in half.

DIFFERENTIATED INSTRUCTION

EL Pronunciation for English Learners
Refer students to the word *pulls* in the first stage direction for Mathemagician on the previous page. Write the word on the board, pronounce it distinctly, then have students repeat the word. Next, write the word *pools* on the board. Model its pronunciation, and have students repeat it. Then, call a volunteer to the board. Say one or the other word, and have the volunteer point to the word you have said. Repeat with additional volunteers.

For further practice with this sound, follow a similar routine with the following word pair: *full/fool.* Extend the instruction by pointing out the sound similarities between the words *bull* and *wool.* Point out that these two words have similar spellings to the words in the pairings examined earlier, but *wool* is not pronounced like *pool* and *fool.* Point out that students must memorize irregular pronunciations.

27 Compare and Contrast

1. Read aloud the bracketed text.
2. **Ask** students to paraphrase Mathemagician's words.

   Possible response: It's so easy to be wrong that it's not even worth trying.

3. **Ask** the Compare and Contrast question.

   Possible response: Some students may agree with this statement. They may say that because it's so easy to be wrong, they'd rather put their effort into being right.

4. Invite students to identify real-life situations that support their point of view regarding this question.

Compare and Contrast 27
Do real-life situations support Mathemagician's statement about being wrong? Explain.

MILO. The smallest number . . . let's see . . . one one-millionth?

MATHEMAGICIAN. Almost. Now all you have to do is divide that in half and then divide that in half and then divide that in half and then divide that . . .

MILO. Doesn't that ever stop either?

MATHEMAGICIAN. How can it when you can always take half of what you have and divide it in half again? Look. [*Pointing offstage.*] You see that line?

MILO. You mean that long one out there?

MATHEMAGICIAN. That's it. Now, if you just follow that line forever, and when you reach the end, turn left, you will find the Land of Infinity. That's where the tallest, the shortest, the biggest, the smallest and the most and the least of everything are kept.

MILO. But how can you follow anything forever? You know, I get the feeling that everything in Digitopolis is very difficult.

MATHEMAGICIAN. But on the other hand, I think you'll find that the only thing you can do easily is be wrong, and that's hardly worth the effort.

MILO. But . . . what bothers me is . . . well, why is it that even when things are correct, they don't really seem to be right?

MATHEMAGICIAN. [*Grows sad and quiet.*] How true. It's been that way ever since Rhyme and Reason were banished. [*Sadness turns to fury.*] And all because of that stubborn wretch Azaz! It's all his fault.

MILO. Maybe if you discussed it with him . . .

MATHEMAGICIAN. He's just too unreasonable! Why just last month, I sent him a very friendly letter, which he never had the courtesy to answer. See for yourself. [*Puts the letter on the easel. The letter reads:*]

4738 1919,

667 394107 5841 62589 85371 14

39588 7190434 203 27689 57131 481206.

5864 98053,

62179875073

MILO. But maybe he doesn't understand numbers.

MATHEMAGICIAN. Nonsense! Everybody understands numbers. No matter what language you speak, they always mean the same thing. A seven is a seven everywhere in the world.

MILO. [*To* TOCK *and* HUMBUG.] Everyone is so sensitive about what he knows best.

TOCK. With your permission, sir, we'd like to rescue Rhyme and Reason.

MATHEMAGICIAN. Has Azaz agreed to it?

TOCK. Yes, sir.

MATHEMAGICIAN. THEN I DON'T! Ever since they've been banished, we've never agreed on anything, and we never will.

MILO. Never?

MATHEMAGICIAN. NEVER! And if you can prove otherwise, you have my permission to go.

MILO. Well then, with whatever Azaz agrees, you disagree.

MATHEMAGICIAN. Correct.

MILO. And with whatever Azaz disagrees, you agree.

28 MATHEMAGICIAN. [*Yawning, cleaning his nails.*] Also correct.

MILO. Then, each of you agrees that he will disagree with whatever each of you agrees with, and if you both disagree with the same thing, aren't you really in agreement?

MATHEMAGICIAN. I'VE BEEN TRICKED! [*Figures it over, but comes up with the same answer.*]

TOCK. And now may we go?

MATHEMAGICIAN. [*Nods weakly.*] It's a long and dangerous journey. Long before you find them, the demons will know you're there. Watch out for them, because if you

A seven is a seven anywhere in the world.

Stage Directions
What does this stage direction suggest about the Mathemagician's opinion of himself?

29 Comprehension
How does Milo outsmart Mathemagician?

🌠 DIFFERENTIATED INSTRUCTION

Support for Less Proficient Readers
As a group, help students use a Venn diagram to compare and contrast the kingdoms of Dictionopolis and Digitopolis. Prompt their thinking by asking questions such as: *Are they ruled by the same kings? What do inhabitants of Dictionopolis value most? What do inhabitants of Digitopolis value most? What do people eat in Dictionopolis? What do people eat in Digitopolis?*

Enrichment for Advanced Readers
Invite these students to conduct research about *cryptography* and discover codes that substitute numbers for letters. Working individually or in small groups, have students write messages from Mathemagician to Azaz in number codes and create the keys needed to decipher the code. Then have individuals or groups trade their messages for others to decipher. You might want to have students attempt to "crack" the codes, before viewing the keys.

---

28 Stage Directions

1. Direct students' attention to the bracketed stage direction.

2. Aside from being tired, **ask** students what it generally means when someone yawns during a conversation.

   Answer: It means that the person is bored.

3. **Ask** students to suggest why the author might have added the stage direction for Mathemagician to clean his nails.

   Possible response: This action can show that he is not really interested in what Milo has to say.

4. **Ask** the Stage Directions question.

   Possible response: It suggests that Mathemagician has a high opinion of himself and is confident in his beliefs.

▶ **Monitor Progress: Ask** students to share the most recent entries they have recorded on their **Literary Analysis Graphic Organizer** for this selection. Discuss what the stage directions showed about a character or an event.

▶ **Reteach:** If students have difficulty using stage directions to picture actions or to understand what characters are thinking and feeling, have them reread the explanation of the skill on the Building Knowledge page, p. 488. Scan pages of the play and discuss stage directions that help readers picture action (such as at the bottom of pp. 494 and 498) and ones that help readers understand what characters are thinking and feeling (such as near the bottom of p. 504).

29 Comprehension

Answer: Milo tricks him with a paradox. Getting the kings to agree to disagree with one another shows that they do agree about something.

30 Stage Directions

1. Have two students read the dialogue between Dodecahedron and Mathemagician that appears just before the BLACKOUT stage direction.

2. **Ask** students what question is waiting to be answered.

   Answer: The question is, "What is the serious obstacle that Mathemagician is referring to?"

3. Point out the BLACKOUT stage direction. **Ask** the Stage Directions question.

   Answer The blackout adds to the suspense by halting the forward motion of the play and prolonging the time until the question is answered.

31 Stage Directions

1. **Ask** the second Stage Directions question.

   Possible response: The stage direction signals the continuation of the play, which moves the action forward.

2. **Ask** students to explain what has happened on stage between the blackout and the time that the lights come back up.

   Answer: In this interval, the setting has been changed from the Mathemagician's office to the castle where the princesses are being held.

3. Point out that the change of scenery helps to move the action of the play forward.

Stage Directions
BLACKOUT means that all the lights focused on the stage are turned off. How does this add suspense here?

Stage Directions
What effect does the stage direction LIGHTS UP have on the action?

---

ever come face to face, it will be too late. But there is one other obstacle even more serious than that.

MILO. [*Terrified.*] What is it?

MATHEMAGICIAN. I'm afraid I can't tell you until you return. But maybe I can give you something to help you out. [*Claps hands. ENTER the* DODECAHEDRON, *carrying something on a pillow. The* MATHEMAGICIAN *takes it.*] Here is your own magic staff. Use it well and there is nothing it can't do for you. [*Puts a small, gleaming pencil in* MILO's *breast pocket.*]

HUMBUG. Are you sure you can't tell about that serious obstacle?

MATHEMAGICIAN. Only when you return. And now the Dodecahedron will escort you to the road that leads to the Castle-in-the-Air. Farewell, my friends, and good luck to you. [*They shake hands, say goodbye, and the* DODECAHEDRON *leads them off.*] Good luck to you! [*To himself.*] Because you're sure going to need it. [*He watches them through a telescope and marks down the calculations.*]

DODECAHEDRON. [*He re-enters.*] Well, they're on their way.

MATHEMAGICIAN. So I see. . . [DODECAHEDRON *stands waiting.*] Well, what is it?

DODECAHEDRON. I was just wondering myself, your Numbership. What actually is the serious obstacle you were talking about?

MATHEMAGICIAN. [*Looks at him in surprise.*] You mean you really don't know?

30 *BLACKOUT*

Scene ii • The Land of Ignorance

31 LIGHTS UP *on* RHYME *and* REASON, *in their castle, looking out two windows.*

RHYME. *I'm worried sick, I must confess*
I wonder if they'll have success
All the others tried in vain,
And were never seen or heard again.

REASON. Now, Rhyme, there's no need to be so pessimistic.

🗯 THINK ALOUD

Context Clues
Direct students' attention to the word *pessimistic* at the top of the next page. Using a think-aloud process, model how to use context to infer the meaning of an unknown word. Say to students:

> I'm going to think aloud to show you how I would figure out what *pessimistic* means from its context.

After Reason listens to Rhyme's speech, she tells her sister not to be so *pessimistic*. The point of Rhyme's speech is that she doubts Milo and his companions will be able to rescue them, because no one else has been able to do so. So, I think that *pessimistic* means doubtful that something will work well.

Milo, Tock, and Humbug have just as much chance of succeeding as they do of failing.

RHYME. *But the demons are so deadly smart*
They'll stuff your brain and fill your heart
With petty thoughts and selfish dreams
And trap you with their nasty schemes.

REASON. Now, Rhyme, be reasonable, won't you? And calm down, you always talk in couplets when you get nervous. Milo has learned a lot from his journey. I think he's a match for the demons and that he might soon be knocking at our door. Now come on, cheer up, won't you?

RHYME. I'll try.

[*LIGHTS FADE on the* PRINCESSES *and COME UP on the little Car, traveling slowly.*]

MILO. So this is the Land of Ignorance. It's so dark. I can hardly see a thing. Maybe we should wait until morning.

VOICE. They'll be mourning for you soon enough. [*They look up and see a large, soiled, ugly bird with a dangerous beak and a malicious expression.*]

MILO. I don't think you understand. We're looking for a place to spend the night.

BIRD. [*Shrieking.*] It's not yours to spend!

MILO. That doesn't make any sense, you see . . .

BIRD. Dollars or cents, it's still not yours to spend.

MILO. But I don't mean . . .

BIRD. Of course you're mean. Anybody who'd spend a night that doesn't belong to him is very mean.

TOCK. Must you interrupt like that?

BIRD. Naturally, it's my job. I take the words right out of your mouth. Haven't we met before? I'm the Everpresent Wordsnatcher.

MILO. Are you a demon?

BIRD. I'm afraid not. I've tried, but the best I can manage to be is a nuisance. [*Suddenly gets nervous as he looks beyond the three.*] And I don't have time to waste with you. [*Starts to leave.*]

◀ **Vocabulary**
malicious (mə lish´ əs) *adj.* having or showing bad intentions

Compare and Contrast
How is the bird like other characters Milo meets?

33 Comprehension
How does Reason reassure Rhyme?

32 Compare and Contrast

1. Have three volunteers reread aloud the dialogue between Milo, Tock, and the newly introduced character, Bird.
2. **Read** the Compare and Contrast question.
   Possible response: He is like Mathemagician, who also confuses words that are pronounced alike but have different meanings (homonyms) and uses the wrong meaning of multiple-meaning words.
3. **Ask** students to identify the words that he confuses.
   Answer: He confuses *sense/cents* and *weight/wait*. He also uses the wrong meaning of *spend*.

33 Comprehension
Answer: She points out that Milo has learned a lot from his journey and will be able to handle the demons.

DIFFERENTIATED INSTRUCTION

Enrichment for Advanced Readers
Suggest that students read the original novel *The Phantom Tollbooth* by Norton Juster. Have them write reports that compare the novel with the play version. Suggest criteria, such as setting, dialogue, and characters, for the comparisons. To extend the activity, have students present their reports to the class.

Enrichment for Gifted/Talented Students
The castle in which Rhyme and Reason are confined is not described in much detail. The description of the route to the castle, however, gives some clues about it. Invite students to draw sketches of the Castle-in-the-Air, using their imaginations to fill in the missing details.

34 Stage Directions

1. Direct students' attention to the bracketed text of Man's words and stage directions.

2. Ask students to identify the three tasks that Man would like help in accomplishing.

Answer: He needs to move a pile of sand with tweezers, empty a well with an eyedropper, and dig a hole in a cliff with a needle.

3. Ask the Stage Directions question.

Answer: The first set of stage directions shows that these tasks will take a very long time to accomplish. The final stage direction regarding the lights is meant to show that the time of day passes while Man stands around and stares into space.

4. Invite students to share what they wrote in their **Literary Analysis Graphic Organizers** for this selection.

Stage Directions
How do these stage directions move the action along?

Tock. What is it? What's the matter?

Milo. Hey, don't leave. I wanted to ask you some questions. . . . Wait!

Bird. Weight? Twenty-seven pounds. Bye-bye. [*Disappears.*]

Milo. Well, he was no help.

Man. Perhaps I can be of some assistance to you? [*There appears a beautifully dressed man, very polished and clean.*] Hello, little boy. [*Shakes* Milo's *hand.*] And how's the faithful dog? [*Pats* Tock.] And who is this handsome creature? [*Tips his hat to* Humbug.]

Humbug. [*To others.*] What a pleasant surprise to meet someone so nice in a place like this.

Man. But before I help you out, I wonder if first you could spare me a little of your time, and help me with a few small jobs?

Humbug. Why, certainly.

Tock. Gladly.

Milo. Sure, we'd be happy to.

Man. Splendid, for there are just three tasks. First, I would like to move this pile of sand from here to there. [*Indicates through pantomime a large pile of sand.*] But I'm afraid that all I have is this tiny tweezers. [*Hands it to* Milo, *who begins moving the sand one grain at a time.*] Second, I would like to empty this well and fill that other, but I have no bucket, so you'll have to use this eyedropper. [*Hands it to* Tock, *who begins to work.*] And finally, I must have a hole in this cliff, and here is a needle to dig it. [Humbug *eagerly begins. The man leans against a tree and stares vacantly off into space. The* LIGHTS *indicate the passage of time.*]

Milo. You know something? I've been working steadily for a long time, now, and I don't feel the least bit tired or hungry. I could go right on the same way forever.

Man. Maybe you will. [*He yawns.*]

Milo. [*Whispers to* Tock.] Well, I wish I knew how long it was going to take.

🗨 THINK ALOUD

Vocabulary: Context
Direct students' attention to the word *villainously* in the stage direction near the middle of the next page. Use the following think aloud to model the use of context clues to infer the meaning of an unknown word. Say to students:

I'm going to show you how I would figure out the meaning of the word *villainously*. In this stage direction, *villainously* tells me how Man laughs. I notice that the word resembles another word: *villain.* I know this word means "an evil character." I wonder whether *villainously* means "in an evil way." To check using context, I reread the sentences before the word. Rereading Man's first three lines on the next page gives me the idea that he is an unpleasant person. Next, I read ahead. In Man's next speech, I see that he is the Terrible Trivium, demon of petty tasks and worthless jobs. The words *ogre* and *monster* support the idea that he would have an evil laugh. Replacing *villainously* with *in an evil manner* makes sense, now that I know more about the character.

Tock. Why don't you use your magic staff and find out?

Milo. [*Takes out pencil and calculates. To* Man.] Pardon me, sir, but it's going to take 837 years to finish these jobs.

Man. Is that so? What a shame. Well then you'd better get on with them.

Milo. But . . . it hardly seems worthwhile.

Man. WORTHWHILE! Of course they're not worthwhile. I wouldn't ask you to do anything that was worthwhile.

Tock. Then why bother?

Man. Because, my friends, what could be more important than doing unimportant things? If you stop to do enough of them, you'll never get where you are going. [*Laughs villainously.*]

Milo. [*Gasps.*] Oh, no, you must be . . .

Man. Quite correct! I am the Terrible Trivium, demon of petty tasks and worthless jobs, ogre of wasted effort and monster of habit. [*They start to back away from him.*] Don't try to leave, there's so much to do, and you still have 837 years to go on the first job.

Milo. But why do unimportant things?

Man. Think of all the trouble it saves. If you spend all your time doing only the easy and useless jobs, you'll never have time to worry about the important ones which are so difficult. [*Walks toward them whispering.*] Now do come and stay with me. We'll have such fun together. There are things to fill and things to empty, things to take away and things to bring back, things to pick up and things to put down . . . [*They are* transfixed *by his soothing voice. He is about to embrace them when a* Voice *screams.*]

Voice. Run! Run! [*They all wake up and run with the Trivium behind. As the voice continues to call out directions, they follow until they lose the Trivium.*] RUN! RUN! This way! This way! Over here! Over here! Up here! Down there! Quick, hurry up!

Tock. [*Panting.*] I think we lost him.

PART 2 • The Phantom Tollbooth, Act II **509**

---

35 **Compare and Contrast**
In what ways are Man and the Everpresent Wordsnatcher different?

Compare and Contrast
How is Terrible Trivium similar to the Lethargarians, who appear in Act I?

◄ **Vocabulary**
transfixed (trans fikst′)
v. made motionless by horror or fascination

37 **Comprehension**
What does the Terrible Trivium ask Milo, Tock, and Humbug to do?

---

35 ● **Compare and Contrast**

1. **Ask** the first Compare and Contrast question.
2. Then, tell students to reread pp. 507 and 508 to locate information about each character.
3. Tell them to look for details about the characters' appearances as well as their personalities.

   Answer: The Everpresent Wordsnatcher, or Bird, is an ugly, dirty, mean-looking character who is impatient and annoying. In contrast, Man is a clean, beautifully dressed man with a lot of patience.

36 ● **Compare and Contrast**

1. Have students read the bracketed dialogue.
2. **Ask** them what name the character Man calls himself.

   Answer: He calls himself the Terrible Trivium.
3. **Ask** students if they can think of a word that is similar to *Trivium* that might explain what the name means.

   Possible response: *Trivium* sounds like *trivia*. It might mean that he does lots of small and unimportant things.
4. **Ask** the second Compare and Contrast question. **Answer:** Both he and the Lethargarians waste a lot of time doing only easy and useless things.

37 ● **Comprehension**

Answer: The Terrible Trivium asks Milo to move a pile of sand with tweezers, Tock to empty a well with an eye dropper, and Humbug to dig a hole with a needle.

✦ DIFFERENTIATED INSTRUCTION

EL Support for English Learners
Bring in a pair of tweezers, an eyedropper, and a needle to show to students. Seeing and handling these props will help students understand the hopelessness involved in the three tasks that Man needs help with. Then, ask students to explain why these tools are not good choices to accomplish the tasks.

Enrichment for Advanced Readers
Note for students that Man's speech beginning "Think of all the trouble it saves" on this page almost convinces the travelers to stay with the Trivium. Have students write a paragraph explaining why the Trivium's ideas are so attractive. Encourage students to explore whether the ideas are also destructive and why.

Connecting to the Big Question

1. Point out to students that not all advice is good advice. Advice delivered with a confident, forceful speaking tone may be mistaken for good advice.

2. Ask: What was the result of following Insincerity's advice?

Possible answer: Milo and his friends fell into a trap.

3. Ask: Why does Milo reject Insincerity's advice about climbing out of the trap?

Possible answer: Milo realizes that Insincerity is telling him only what he thought Milo wanted to hear.

4. Tell students to look for additional details that show that Milo is learning to think for himself.

39 Critical Viewing

Possible response: Alone, or even in pairs, they do not have the height needed to reach the top of the pit. They must all work together to overcome the difficulties they will face on their journey.

39 ▲ **Critical Viewing**
How does this image show that Milo, Tock, and Humbug need one another in order to succeed?

VOICE. Keep going straight! Keep going straight! Now step up! Now step up!

MILO. Look out! [*They all fall into a Trap.*] But he said "up!"

VOICE. Well, I hope you didn't expect to get anywhere by listening to me.

HUMBUG. We're in a deep pit! We'll never get out of here.

VOICE. That is quite an accurate evaluation of the situation.

MILO. [*Shouting angrily.*] Then why did you help us at all?

VOICE. Oh, I'd do as much for anybody. Bad advice is my specialty. [*A Little Furry Creature appears.*] I'm the demon of Insincerity. I don't mean what I say; I don't mean what I do; and I don't mean what I am.

MILO. Then why don't you go away and leave us alone!

INSINCERITY. (VOICE) Now, there's no need to get angry. You're a very clever boy and I have complete confidence in you. You can certainly climb out of that pit . . . come on, try. . .

MILO. I'm not listening to one word you say! You're just telling me what you think I'd like to hear, and not what is important.

INSINCERITY. Well, if that's the way you feel about it . . .

MILO. That's the way I feel about it. We will manage by ourselves without any unnecessary advice from you.

INSINCERITY. [*Stamping his foot.*] Well, all right for you! Most people listen to what I say, but if that's the way you feel, then I'll just go home. [*Exits in a huff.*]

510 UNIT 4 • How do we decide who we are?

📃 **VOCABULARY DEVELOPMENT**

Multiple Meanings
One at a time, point out the following words in the script: *pit* (p. 510), *hook* (p. 511), and *gross* (p. 511). Explain that, although each word means one thing in the context of the drama, it also has other uses. In the drama, a *pit* is a hole in the ground. *Pit* also refers to the stone of a piece of fruit and the space at the front of a theater in which the orchestra sits.

Hook is a verb that describes what Humbug does with his umbrella. When used as a noun, *hook* can mean the object you hang your coat on or the bent and barbed wire used to catch a fish. In the context of the play, *gross* means immediately obvious. However, *gross* can also mean crude and vulgar or represent a unit of measurement.

HUMBUG. [*Who has been quivering with fright.*] And don't you ever come back! Well, I guess we showed him, didn't we?

MILO. You know something? This place is a lot more dangerous than I ever imagined.

TOCK. [*Who's been surveying the situation.*] I think I figured a way to get out. Here, hop on my back. [MILO *does so.*] Now, you, Humbug, on top of Milo. [*He does so.*] Now hook your umbrella onto that tree and hold on. [*They climb over* HUMBUG, *then pull him up.*]

HUMBUG. [*As they climb.*] Watch it! Watch it, now. Ow, be careful of my back! My back! Easy, easy . . . oh, this is so difficult. Aren't you finished yet?

TOCK. [*As he pulls up* HUMBUG.] There. Now, I'll lead for a while. Follow me, and we'll stay out of trouble. [*They walk and climb higher and higher.*]

HUMBUG. Can't we slow down a little?

TOCK. Something tells me we better reach the Castle-in-the-Air as soon as possible, and not stop to rest for a single moment. [*They speed up.*]

MILO. What is it, Tock? Did you see something?

TOCK. Just keep walking and don't look back.

MILO. You *did* see something!

HUMBUG. What is it? Another demon?

TOCK. Not just one, I'm afraid. If you want to see what I'm talking about, then turn around. [*They turn around. The stage darkens and hundreds of Yellow Gleaming Eyes can be seen.*]

HUMBUG. Good grief! Do you see how many there are? Hundreds! The Overbearing Know-it-all, the Gross Exaggeration, the Horrible Hopping Hindsight, . . . and look over there! The Triple Demons of Compromise! Let's get out of here! [*Starts to scurry.*] Hurry up, you two! Must you be so slow about everything?

MILO. Look! There it is, up ahead! The Castle-in-the-Air! [*They all run.*]

HUMBUG. They're gaining!

Compare and Contrast
How is the way these new creatures make their entrance different from the way other characters appear on-stage?

42 Comprehension
Why are Milo and the others running?

PART 2 • The Phantom Tollbooth, Act II **511**

⚙ DIFFERENTIATED INSTRUCTION

Support for Special-Needs Students
Call students' attention to the illustration on p. 510. Have students identify the scene that is being illustrated and answer the following questions: Who is on the bottom? Who is in the middle? Who is on the top? What are they trying to do? Where are they trying to do it?

Support for Less Proficient Readers
Have students make a list of questions to ask Milo in an interview. Encourage students to use the basic questions (who, why, what, where, when, and how) as a starting point. Model the following questions to ask Milo: Who were you trying to rescue? Why did you want to rescue them? What troubles did you find along the way? Where did your journey take you? After they have completed their lists, have students take turns taking on the roles of Milo and interviewers to ask and answer the questions.

GUIDED EXPLORATION

40 Infer

1. Have a volunteer read aloud the bracketed passage. Then **ask:** What does Milo say about danger?

   Answer: He says The Land of Ignorance is more dangerous than he imagined.

2. **Ask** students to infer why Milo is beginning to realize how dangerous the land is.

   Answer: When Milo, Tock, and Humbug began the journey, Milo noted the darkness and wanted to wait until morning to travel. They are fooled by the Terrible Trivium. Then they are tricked by the demon of Insincerity and fall into a deep pit.

41 Compare and Contrast

1. Direct students' attention to the bracketed text containing Tock's words and stage directions.

2. **Ask** students to identify details that are given about the creatures.

   Answer: There are hundreds of them and they have yellow gleaming eyes.

3. **Ask** students to identify details that are *not* addressed in the description.

   Possible response: No details are given about their shape or size.

4. **Ask** the Compare and Contrast question.

   Possible response: All the other creatures have been illustrated or described in detail. Except for their eyes, these creatures are not described.

5. **Ask** students to suggest reasons why the author did not describe these particular creatures.

   Possible responses: They might symbolize the fear that's growing in Milo, Tock, and Humbug.

42 Comprehension

Answer: They are running because they have almost reached their destination and because the demons are close behind.

PART 2 • The Phantom Tollbooth, Act II **511**

43 Critical Viewing

Possible response: Students are likely to say that the illustration matches their own images of him. He wears spectacles, has ink stains all over his clothes, and is bent over his ledger.

44 ❓ Connecting to the Big Question

1. Point out that in an unfamiliar situation, a person can make inferences that will help him or her make decisions.

2. Have students read the bracketed passage. **Ask:** How does Milo reach the conclusion that he and his friends may be in danger?

   Possible response: He notices that the Senses Taker asks many questions and repeats himself, speaking slowly and deliberately. Milo infers that they will be delayed for a long time if they let the Senses Taker finish his work.

3. **Ask:** What does Milo do in response to this danger?

   Possible response: He calculates that the demons will arrive soon and speaks up.

4. Tell students to look for additional details showing that Milo is learning to think for himself, developing plans of action, and taking charge.

---

43 ▼ Critical Viewing
Does this picture of Senses Taker match the image you formed as you read his description in the stage directions? Explain.

MILO. But there it is!

HUMBUG. I see it! I see it!

[*They reach the first step and are stopped by a little man in a frock coat, sleeping on a worn ledger. He has a long quill pen and a bottle of ink at his side. He is covered with ink stains over his clothes and wears spectacles.*]

TOCK. Shh! Be very careful. [*They try to step over him, but he wakes up.*]

SENSES TAKER. [*From sleeping position.*] Names? [*He sits up.*]

HUMBUG. Well, I . . .

SENSES TAKER. *NAMES?* [*He opens book and begins to write, splattering himself with ink.*]

HUMBUG. Uh . . . Humbug, Tock and this is Milo.

SENSES TAKER. Splendid, splendid. I haven't had an "M" in ages.

MILO. What do you want our names for? We're sort of in a hurry.

SENSES TAKER. Oh, this won't take long. I'm the official Senses Taker and I must have some information before I can take your sense. Now if you'll just tell me: [*Handing them a form to fill. Speaking slowly and deliberately.*] When you were born, where you were born, why you were born, how old you are now, how old you were then, how old you'll be in a little while . . .

 MILO. I wish he'd hurry up. At this rate, the demons will be here before we know it!

SENSES TAKER. . . . Your mother's name, your father's name, where you live, how long you've lived there, the schools you've attended, the schools you haven't attended . . .

💬 VOCABULARY DEVELOPMENT

Selection Vocabulary Reinforcement
To reinforce and assess student's comprehension of selection vocabulary words, ask them the following questions:

1. What character is fond of *dissonance*? (Dischord)
2. What items in the play were *iridescent*? (Mathemagician's numbers)
3. What character was a nuisance and wore a *malicious* expression? (the Everpresent Wordsnatcher)
4. What character gave Milo an *admonishing* look? (Dodecahedron)

HUMBUG. I'm getting writer's cramp.

TOCK. I smell something very evil and it's getting stronger every second. [*To* SENSES TAKER.] May we go now?

SENSES TAKER. Just as soon as you tell me your height, your weight, the number of books you've read this year . . .

MILO. We have to go!

SENSES TAKER. All right, all right, I'll give you the short form. [*Pulls out a small piece of paper.*] Destination?

MILO. But we have to . . .

SENSES TAKER. *DESTINATION?*

MILO, TOCK AND **HUMBUG.** The Castle-in-the-Air! [*They throw down their papers and run past him up the first few stairs.*]

SENSES TAKER. Stop! I'm sure you'd rather see what I have to show you. [*Snaps his fingers; they freeze.*] A circus of your very own. [*CIRCUS MUSIC is heard.* MILO *seems to go into a trance.*] And wouldn't you enjoy this most wonderful smell? [*TOCK sniffs and goes into a trance.*] And here's something I know you'll enjoy hearing . . . [*To* HUMBUG. *The sound of CHEERS and APPLAUSE for* HUMBUG *is heard, and he goes into a trance.*] There we are. And now, I'll just sit back and let the demons catch up with you.

[MILO *accidentally drops his package of gifts. The Package of Laughter from* DR. DISCHORD *opens and the Sounds of Laughter are heard. After a moment,* MILO, TOCK *and* HUMBUG *join in laughing and the spells are broken.*]

MILO. There was no circus.

TOCK. There were no smells.

HUMBUG. The applause is gone.

SENSES TAKER. I warned you I was the Senses Taker. I'll steal your sense of Purpose, your sense of Duty, destroy your sense of Proportion—and but for one thing, you'd be helpless yet.

MILO. What's that?

Stage Directions
Without these stage directions, would you be able to picture the action here? Explain.

47 Comprehension
What happens to Senses Taker when Milo drops the Package of Laughter?

---

45 Analyze

1. Have two volunteers read the Senses Taker's lines and the stage directions within the bracketed passage.

2. Direct students to pay attention to how the Senses Taker stops the travelers.

3. Then, **ask** students what puts each of the individual travelers in a trance.

   Answer: Circus music puts Milo in a trance; smells put Tock in a trance; and cheers and applause put Humbug in a trance.

4. Lead students in a discussion about how the trap for each traveler is uniquely effective: Most children like circuses, so circus music is a good trap for Milo. Dogs have a strong sense of smell, so good smells are an effective trap for Tock. Humbug is very vain, so cheers and applause stop him effectively.

46 Stage Directions

1. Have a student read aloud the bracketed stage directions.

2. **Ask** what information the stage directions provide about action.

   Answer: They tell that Milo drops the package and it opens.

3. **Ask** what information the stage directions provide about sounds.

   Answer: They tell that the sound of laughter is heard.

4. **Ask** the Stage Directions question.

   Possible response: Students will likely say they would not be able to picture the action without these directions. The dialogue that follows the stage directions would not make sense if you didn't know that the Sounds of Laughter had escaped from the box.

47 Comprehension

Answer: He becomes powerless to steal the other characters' sense of humor now that they have the sound of laughter.

✿ DIFFERENTIATED INSTRUCTION

Support for Less Proficient Readers
As the end of Act II is approaching, have students work in groups to review the play up to this point. Have them talk about the major events in Act II and take turns drawing a picture that illustrates each event. Have them decide on captions for each picture. Then have them arrange the illustrations in order and use them to retell the story. They may add them to the drawings they made for Act I, if they wish, and share the whole story with the class.

Enrichment for Advanced Readers
Invite students to conduct research about the United States census. Have them write reports that include answers to the following questions: What information does the census provide? How is the information used? When was the first census taken in the United States? How often is a census taken? Have students share their findings with the class.

48 Compare and Contrast

1. Have students read the parts of Reason, Milo, Tock, the Princesses, and Humbug in the bracketed passage.

2. Then focus students' attention on Milo's lines and the stage directions in particular. **Ask** students to name words that describe Milo in this situation.

   Possible response: Students may suggest words such as *quick-thinking, smart, creative, problem-solver.*

3. **Ask** the Compare and Contrast question.

   Possible response: In the first scene, Milo was bored, thought everything was too much trouble to do, and didn't actively use his brain. Now Milo uses his brain to solve problems and acts quickly.

Senses Taker. As long as you have the sound of laughter, I cannot take your sense of Humor. Agh! That horrible sense of humor.

Humbug. HERE THEY COME! LET'S GET OUT OF HERE!

[*The demons appear in nasty slithering hordes, running through the audience and up onto the stage, trying to attack* Tock, Milo *and* Humbug. *The three heroes run past the* Senses Taker *up the stairs toward the Castle-in-the-Air with the demons snarling behind them.*]

Milo. Don't look back! Just keep going! [*They reach the castle. The two princesses appear in the windows.*]

Princesses. Hurry! Hurry! We've been expecting you.

Milo. You must be the Princesses. We've come to rescue you.

Humbug. And the demons are close behind!

Tock. We should leave right away.

Princesses. We're ready anytime you are.

Milo. Good, now if you'll just come out. But wait a minute—there's no door! How can we rescue you from the Castle-in-the-Air if there's no way to get in or out?

Humbug. Hurry, Milo! They're gaining on us.

Reason. Take your time, Milo, and think about it.

Milo. Ummm, all right . . . just give me a second or two. [*He thinks hard.*]

Humbug. I think I feel sick.

Milo. I've got it! Where's that package of presents? [*Opens the package of letters.*] Ah, here it is. [*Takes out the letters and sticks them on the door, spelling:*] E-N-T-R-A-N-C-E. Entrance. Now, let's see. [*Rummages through and spells in smaller letters:*] P-u-s-h. Push. [*He pushes and a*

Compare and Contrast
Based on Milo's actions here, how has he changed since leaving his bedroom?

💬 VOCABULARY DEVELOPMENT

Dictionary Use

Direct students' attention to the word *hordes* in the first stage direction on this page. Using a think-aloud process, model how to choose the correct definition of the word, using the actual definitions in your own dictionary. Say to students:

I'm going to think aloud to show you how to choose the definition of *horde,* as it is used here. When I find *horde* in the dictionary, I see that there are two entries.

The first definition is "a people or tribe of nomadic life." The second is "a teeming crowd or throng." When I substitute the word *hordes* in the stage direction with each definition, I find that the second definition makes sense: *The demons appear in a nasty, slithering, teeming crowd or throng.*

(48) *door opens. The* PRINCESSES *come out of the castle. Slowly, the demons ascend the stairway.*]

HUMBUG. Oh, it's too late. They're coming up and there's no other way down!

MILO. Unless . . . [*Looks at* TOCK.] Well . . . Time flies, doesn't it?

TOCK. Quite often. Hold on, everyone, and I'll take you down.

HUMBUG. Can you carry us all?

(49) TOCK. We'll soon find out. Ready or not, here we go! [*His alarm begins to ring. They jump off the platform and disappear. The demons, howling with rage, reach the top and find no one there. They see the* PRINCESSES *and the heroes running across the stage and bound down the stairs after them and into the audience. There is a mad chase scene until they reach the stage again.*]

HUMBUG. I'm exhausted! I can't run another step.

MILO. We can't stop now . . .

TOCK. Milo! Look out there! [*The armies of* AZAZ *and* MATHE-MAGICIAN *appear at the back of the theater, with the Kings at their heads.*]

AZAZ. [*As they march toward the stage.*] Don't worry, Milo, we'll take over now.

MATHEMAGICIAN. Those demons may not know it, but their days are numbered!

SPELLING BEE. Charge! C-H-A-R-G-E! Charge! [*They rush at the demons and battle until the demons run off howling. Everyone cheers. The* FIVE MINISTERS OF AZAZ *appear and shake* MILO'S *hand.*]

MINISTER 1. Well done.

MINISTER 2. Fine job.

MINISTER 3. Good work!

MINISTER 4. Congratulations!

MINISTER 5. CHEERS! [*Everyone cheers again. A fanfare interrupts. A* PAGE *steps forward and reads from a large scroll:*]

Stage Directions
How do these stage directions help you know what the characters are feeling?

(50) Comprehension
What does Milo do to get into the Castle-in-the-Air?

(49) Stage Directions

1. Tell students to read the text, paying attention to the words that describe actions.

2. **Ask** them to identify the actions that were named in the stage directions.

   Answer: The heroes and princesses *jump* and *disappear.* The demons *howl* and *bound.*

3. **Ask** the Stage Directions question. Tell students to think about the feelings associated with the action words they just listed.

   Possible response: When people run from something or someone, it is often an indication of fear. The demons howl "with rage," which demonstrates that they are angry.

(50) Comprehension

Answer: He uses his letters to make signs that say *Entrance* and *Push,* and then he pushes a door open.

DIFFERENTIATED INSTRUCTION

Support for Special-Needs Students
Students may have trouble following the quick action that takes place on pp. 514–515. Have them reread the text. Guide students through describing the action in their own words. You may want to prompt students with questions such as: *Why couldn't Milo get into the castle? What was in the package that Milo had? What words did he form with the letters? Where did he place the letters? Who arrived just as the princesses were freed? Then what happened? Who came to help Milo and his friends after the chase? Who won the battle?*

(EL) Support for English Learners
Point out to students that Milo, Tock, and Humbug can enter the Castle-in-the-Air because Milo made signs saying "Entrance" and "Push." Ask students to think of other words or phrases that could be used to gain access to the castle or, alternatively, stop the demons from coming up the stairs after the travelers. Possibilities include "Stop," "Travelers Only," "No Demons Allowed," and "Invited Guests Only." Then have students make signs for their phrases.

51  **Connecting to the Big Question**

1. Point out that knowing the risks involved in a challenge can guide a person to proceed with caution. At the same time, knowing the risks can also discourage a person from trying something that requires more strength or bravery than the person thinks he or she has.

2. **Ask:** Why didn't Azaz warn Milo before he left on his journey?

   Possible response: He didn't want to discourage Milo from starting out on the adventure.

3. **Ask:** Would Milo have gone on the quest if he had known before setting out that it was impossible?

   Possible response: He was bored and lazy before he left home, so he probably would have stayed there.

4. **Ask** students to evaluate whether Milo has been changed by his experiences.

   Possible response: He has changed from someone who was lazy and easily bored to someone who can face a challenge bravely. He has learned much and has performed an important deed.

52 **Compare and Contrast**

1. Have five volunteers reread aloud Milo, Reason, Azaz, Mathemagician, and Humbug's lines in the bracketed passage.

2. **Ask** them to use their own words to tell what lesson Milo has learned.

   Possible response: He learns that we can do more than we think we can and that we should not let the idea that something is impossible keep us from trying to do it.

3. **Ask** students the Compare and Contrast question.

   Possible response: Many students may believe that there are real-life situations in which his statement holds true. Ask them to support their opinions with examples.

PAGE. Henceforth, and forthwith,
Let it be known by one and all,
That Rhyme and Reason
Reign once more in Wisdom.

[*The* PRINCESSES *bow gratefully and kiss their brothers, the* Kings.]

And furthermore,
The boy named Milo,
The dog known as Tock,
And the insect hereinafter referred to as the Humbug
Are hereby declared to be Heroes of the Realm.

[*All bow and salute the heroes.*]

MILO. But we never could have done it without a lot of help.

REASON. That may be true, but you had the courage to try, and what you can do is often a matter of what you *will* do.

AZAZ. That's why there was one very important thing about your quest we couldn't discuss until you returned.

51

MILO. I remember. What was it?

AZAZ. Very simple. It was impossible!

MATHEMAGICIAN. *Completely* impossible!

52 **HUMBUG.** Do you mean . . . ? [*Feeling faint.*] Oh . . . I think I need to sit down.

AZAZ. Yes, indeed, but if we'd told you then, you might not have gone.

MATHEMAGICIAN. And, as you discovered, many things are possible just as long as you don't know they're impossible.

MILO. I think I understand.

RHYME. I'm afraid it's time to go now.

REASON. And you must say goodbye.

MILO. To everyone? [*Looks around at the crowd. To* TOCK *and* HUMBUG.] Can't you two come with me?

HUMBUG. I'm afraid not, old man. I'd like to, but I've arranged

Compare and Contrast
Do you think there are real-life situations in which Mathemagician's statement might hold true? Explain.

for a lecture tour which will keep me occupied for years.

Tock. And they do need a watchdog here.

Milo. Well, O.K., then. [Milo *hugs the* Humbug.]

Humbug. [*Sadly.*] Oh, bah.

Milo. [*He hugs* Tock, *and then faces everyone.*] Well, goodbye. We all spent so much time together, I know I'm going to miss you. [*To the* Princesses.] I guess we would have reached you a lot sooner if I hadn't made so many mistakes.

Reason. You must never feel badly about making mistakes, Milo, as long as you take the trouble to learn from them. Very often you learn more by being wrong for the right reasons than you do by being right for the wrong ones.

Milo. But there's so much to learn.

Rhyme. That's true, but it's not just learning that's important. It's learning what to do with what you learn and learning why you learn things that matters.

Milo. I think I know what you mean, Princess. At least, I hope I do. [*The car is rolled forward and* Milo *climbs in.*] Goodbye! Goodbye! I'll be back someday! I will! Anyway, I'll try. [*As* Milo *drives the set of the Land of Ignorance begins to move offstage.*]

Azaz. Goodbye! Always remember. Words! Words! Words!

Mathemagician. And numbers!

Azaz. Now, don't tell me you think numbers are as important as words?

Mathemagician. Is that so? Why I'll have you know . . . [*The set disappears, and* Milo's *Room is seen onstage.*]

Milo. [*As he drives on.*] Oh, oh, I hope they don't start all over again. Because I don't think I'll have much time in the near future to help them out. [*The sound of loud ticking is heard.* Milo *finds himself in his room. He gets out of the car and looks around.*]

The Clock. Did someone mention time?

Compare and Contrast
With which piece of advice—Reason's or Rhyme's—do you agree more? Explain.

Spiral Review
CHARACTER How do the words "I think I know what you mean" indicate that Milo has grown and learned from his experiences?

53 Compare and Contrast

1. Have students read the bracketed words of Rhyme and Reason.

2. **Ask** them to paraphrase each one's thoughts.

   Possible responses: Reason: Learning from mistakes can be an opportunity. Being wrong for the right reasons can teach you more than being right for the wrong reasons. Rhyme: Two important parts of the learning process are what you do with your knowledge and understanding why you learn things.

3. **Ask** the Compare and Contrast question.

   Possible response: Encourage students to support their responses with well thought out reasons. Students may be likely to find difficult the idea of not feeling badly about making mistakes and say that Rhyme's advice is more applicable.

Spiral Review
Character

1. Remind students that they studied the concept of character in the Unit 4 Focus on Craft and Structure (pp. 454–457).

2. **Ask** students the Spiral Review question.

   Possible response: He has a new appreciation for learning and for using common sense to solve problems. He has begun to see the value of education as well as experience. He has grown to be brave, and he learns from his mistakes.

 **54** Stage Directions

1. Read aloud the bracketed passage.

2. **Ask** students to explain why it is important that the stage directions specifically say that Milo looks at his belongings with great interest. **Possible response:** These are the very things that he was bored with at the beginning of the play.

3. **Ask** the Stage Directions question. **Possible response:** Milo feels that time moves slowly when he is bored and it moves quickly when he uses his imagination and keeps himself busy with worthwhile activities, such as reading and using his chemistry set.

☑ ASSESS

Language Study

Vocabulary

1. Sam wore an *iridescent* necktie, which changed colors as he moved.

2. Last night I was awakened by the unpleasant *dissonance* caused by two howling dogs.

3. Consuela showed cruel intentions when she spread *malicious* gossip.

4. The disapproving babysitter shot an *admonishing* glance in the rude child's direction.

5. A *deficiency* of vitamin C can cause bleeding gums and other problems, while taking enough of this important vitamin can heal those diseases.

Word Study

Part A

Sample answer:

Transform means to "change something completely <u>through</u>." A *transatlantic* ocean liner sails <u>across</u> the Atlantic Ocean.

Part B

Sample answers:

1. The prefix *trans-* means "across" or "through." A *transcontinental* trip would not be short because it continues <u>across</u> an entire continent.

2. Yes, a person can move money over or <u>across</u> from one bank to another through a bank *transfer*.

Stage Directions
Based on these stage directions, how do you think Milo now feels about time? **54**

WORD STUDY

The **prefix *trans-*** means "across" or "through." In *The Phantom Tollbooth*, Act II, Milo is *transfixed* by a soothing voice. He looks as if he has been fixed into place by something that has pierced through him.

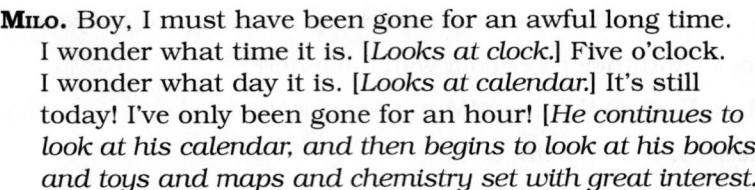

Milo. Boy, I must have been gone for an awful long time. I wonder what time it is. [*Looks at clock.*] Five o'clock. I wonder what day it is. [*Looks at calendar.*] It's still today! I've only been gone for an hour! [*He continues to look at his calendar, and then begins to look at his books and toys and maps and chemistry set with great interest.*]

Clock. An hour. Sixty minutes. How long it really lasts depends on what you do with it. For some people, an hour seems to last forever. For others, just a moment, and so full of things to do.

Milo. [*Looks at clock.*] Six o'clock already?

Clock. In an instant. In a trice. Before you have time to blink. [*The stage goes black in less than no time at all.*]

Language Study

Vocabulary The words listed below appear in *The Phantom Tollbooth*, Act II. For each numbered prompt below, write a sentence that includes a vocabulary word.

> **dissonance   deficiency   admonishing   iridescent   malicious**

1. a necktie that looks red or blue from different angles
2. the sounds that two yowling cats make
3. the act of spreading unkind gossip
4. a look that a baby sitter might give a rude child
5. a person's lack of enough Vitamin C

Word Study

Part A Explain how the **prefix *trans-*** contributes to the meanings of *transform* and *transatlantic*. Consult a dictionary if necessary.

Part B Use context and what you know about the prefix *trans-* to explain your answers to these questions.

1. Is a *transcontinental* trip a short one?
2. Can a person *transfer* money from one bank to another?

Literary Analysis

Possible responses appear below. Check to be sure students support their responses with evidence from the text.

Have students draw Venn diagrams or give them the **After You Read Graphic Organizer** for this selection.

1. Rhyme: sometimes speaks in rhymes, pessimistic, nervous; Reason: does not speak in rhymes, calm, hopeful; Both: is a princess, is trapped in Castle-in-the-Air, is wise

2. Humbug: insect, complains a lot; Tock: dog, problem-solver; Both: are faithful to Milo, courageous

3. **(a)** He wants them to do meaningless tasks that will waste their time. **(b)** They will not achieve their goal. **(c)** Milo learns the importance of using time wisely and not getting distracted by doing meaningless tasks.

4. **(a)** It is broken by the sound of laughter. **(b)** Milo learns that you can never take away a person's sense of humor.

Close Reading Activities

Literary Analysis

Key Ideas and Details

Compare and Contrast Create two Venn diagrams like the one shown on the right. Then, use details from Act II to compare and contrast these characters:

1. Rhyme and Reason

2. Humbug and Tock

3. (a) What does the Terrible Trivium want Milo, Tock, and Humbug to do? **(b) Deduce:** What will be the result if they follow his directions? **(c) Interpret:** What important lesson does Milo learn through his experience with the Terrible Trivium?

4. (a) How is the Senses Taker's spell broken? **(b) Draw Conclusions:** What does Milo learn about humor from his encounter with the Senses Taker?

Craft and Structure

5. Stage Directions (a) Describe one place in the play where stage directions are necessary for helping you understand what is happening. **(b)** Find one place in the play that has no stage directions. Write your own stage directions for that section of the play. Explain how your stage directions clarify the action.

Integration of Knowledge and Ideas

6. (a) Apply: Do you agree that the speed of time depends on what you are doing? **(b) Support:** Support your answer with examples from your own experience.

7. Evaluate: If you were Milo, would you want to return to the Lands Beyond? Why or why not? Support your position with details from the play.

8. **?** **How do we decide who we are?** With a small group, discuss the following question: In your opinion, which of Milo's experiences will lead him to the most important new interest or hobby? Explain your answer.

The Venn diagram shows two overlapping circles labeled "Character A" and "Character B" with the overlapping region labeled "How they are alike."

ACADEMIC VOCABULARY

As you write and speak about *The Phantom Tollbooth*, Act II, use the words related to identity that you explored on page 441 of this text.

and because I like the real world, which is my home.

8. **?** **How do we decide who we are?**
Milo's discovery that he has been gone for only one hour will lead him to appreciate how much he can experience in each moment—the opposite of being bored. Milo was a bored young man before he went on his adventure, and time crawled by. Now he has experienced the challenge, humor, conflict, and adventure that life can have.

5. (a) The stage directions on p. 513, which tell about Milo dropping the package of laughter, are necessary to understand how the Senses Taker's spells are broken. **(b)** Students may identify the dialogue on p. 497, in which Dodecahedron talks about the math problem involving the beaver and the dam. They might write stage directions in which he draws a beaver and a dam on the blackboard and labels the dimensions while demonstrating how to solve the problem. Stage directions could help reveal how Dodecahedron thinks and how serious he is in analyzing problems.

6. (a) Students may say that time passes more quickly when they are doing something they enjoy. **(b)** Examples may include time passing slowly on a very long car ride; however the time seems to go by more quickly when watching a movie or reading a good book.

7. Yes, I would want to return because it was an exciting adventure, I met many interesting characters, and I had experiences that made me more mature and wiser. No, I would not want to return because it was scary and I've already learned everything I could from it,

 Online Writer's Notebook

Students can use the Online Writer's Notebook to record all responses.

Conventions

1. Introduce the skill, using the instruction on the student page.
2. Discuss the definitions and the examples in the chart.

Think About: Model the Skill

Say to students:

When I say, "*The sleeping dog snored loudly,*" I am using an *-ing* verb form—*sleeping*—to describe the dog. I am using it as an adjective. When a verb form acts as an adjective, it is called a participle. A verb form ending in *-ing* can also act as a noun. When I say, "*Daydreaming is exercise for your mind,*" the word *daydreaming* is a noun.

Practice A

1. Milo finished <u>eating the numbers</u>.
2. In the Doldrums, <u>thinking</u> was strictly (prohibited.)
3. (Tired) from <u>traveling</u>, they rested.
4. Milo, (returning) to his room, was (amazed) at how much he had learned.

Reading Application
Sample answer:

The Lethargarians enjoy <u>napping</u> and <u>stretching their arms</u>. (Yawning,) they stretch their arms and do nothing. (Frustrated,) Milo tries to argue with them about their laws.

Practice B

1. asking questions—gerund phrase, noun
2. revealing—gerund, noun
3. Discouraged—past participle, adjective
4. Hugging—present participle, adjective

Writing Application

Learning more than he'd dared dream of, Milo returned home happy. *Learning* is fun.

Counting the hundreds of Yellow Gleaming Eyes, Humbug became quite frightened. *Counting* is important to the Mathemagician.

Seeing Milo, the Senses Taker began to ask him questions. Dischord is more interested in hearing than in *seeing*.

Conventions: Participles and Gerunds

A **participle** is a verb form that acts as an adjective.
A **present participle** is the *-ing* form of a verb: *Relaxing on the patio, I fell asleep.*

A **participial phrase** combines a present or past participle with other words to make a phrase. The entire phrase acts as an adjective.

A **gerund** is a verb form that ends in *-ing* and is used as a noun. A **gerund phrase** is a group of words containing a gerund and any modifiers or other words that relate to it: *Relaxing in your spare time is just as important as exercising.*

Both present participles and gerunds end in *-ing*. To identify each one, determine its function in a sentence. In the examples above, notice how *relaxing* was used as an adjective and as a noun.

Practice A
Rewrite each sentence, circling all the participles and participial phrases, and underlining all the gerunds and gerund phrases.

1. Milo finished eating the numbers.
2. In the Doldrums, thinking was strictly prohibited.
3. Tired from traveling, they rested.
4. Milo, returning to his room, was amazed at how much he had learned.

Reading Application Write a paragraph about *The Phantom Tollbooth* using at least one present participle, one past participle, one gerund, and one gerund phrase. Circle the participles and underline the gerund and gerund phrase.

Practice B
Complete each sentence with a gerund, a gerund phrase, a participle, or a participial phrase. Identify the part of speech for each one.

1. The Senses Taker was good at _____.
2. King Azaz delays _____ that the mission is impossible.
3. _____, Milo almost quit.
4. _____ Tock, Milo said goodbye to his friends.

Writing Application Write two sentences for each of the following words: *learning, counting, seeing*. In the first sentence, use the word as a participle. In the second sentence, use it as a gerund.

⇨ EXTEND THE LESSON

Sentence Modeling
Read aloud these sentences from the selection:

> But then the cities were built and there was a great need for honking horns, screeching trains, clanging bells and all the rest of those wonderfully unpleasant sounds we use so much today. You must never feel bad about making mistakes.

Ask students what they notice about the sentences.

Elicit from them that the first sentence contains participles, *honking, screeching, clanging*.

The second sentence contains a gerund, *making*. Point out that the gerund ends in *-ing* and is used as a noun. The participles also end in *-ing,* but they function as adjectives. Then, ask what else they notice about the sentences. (The first sentence is a compound sentence. The second sentence is a statement.)

Have students imitate the sentence in a sentence of their own construction that gives advice, matching each grammatical and stylistic feature discussed. Collect the sentences, and share them with the class.

Writing to Sources

Argumentative Text Imagine that you are a drama critic, and write a **review** of *The Phantom Tollbooth*. Follow these steps:

- Review Acts I and II. Take notes on the strengths and weaknesses of the plot and characters.

- Begin your review by stating your overall evaluation of the play. Then, logically organize the relevant examples from your notes to support your position and claims.

- Conclude by telling readers whether or not you recommend that they see this play.

Grammar Application Reread your review to be sure that you have used participles, participial phrases, gerunds, and gerund phrases correctly.

Speaking and Listening

Comprehension and Collaboration Now that you have read *The Phantom Tollbooth,* access the audio version of the play on your eText. Listen to the recording as a class. Then, hold a **group discussion** by forming small groups and talking about how the experience of reading the play was similar to and different from the experience of listening to it.

Use the following list of questions to guide your discussion. Choose a speaker to present your group's findings to the class.

- Did hearing the voices of different characters make the play easier to understand? Why or why not?

- What was the effect of hearing speakers emphasize certain words or phrases? Did the same words or phrases seem to require emphasis when you were reading the play? Why or why not?

- Did listening to the play help you imagine the action, or were you better able to imagine events and characters by reading about them? Explain your response.

Listen carefully to your classmates' arguments. Which of their claims were supported with strong evidence and reasons? Which claims were not?

 **Common Core State Standards**

Reading Literature
7. Compare and contrast the experience of reading a story, drama, or poem to listening to or viewing an audio, video, or live version of the text, including contrasting what they "see" and "hear" when reading the text to what they perceive when they listen or watch.

Writing
1. Write arguments to support claims with clear reasons and relevant evidence. **1.a.** Introduce claim(s) and organize the reasons and evidence clearly.

Speaking and Listening
1.c. Pose and respond to specific questions with elaboration and detail by making comments that contribute to the topic, text, or issue under discussion.
3. Delineate a speaker's argument and specific claims, distinguishing claims that are supported by reasons and evidence from claims that are not.

Language
1. Demonstrate command of the conventions of standard English grammar and usage when writing or speaking.
3. Use knowledge of language and its conventions when writing, speaking, reading, or listening. **3.a.** Vary sentence patterns for meaning, reader/listener interest, and style.

Writing to Sources

1. Review the assignment, using the instruction on the student page.

2. Help students understand that a review is not just a statement of whether or not you liked something. Each point you make, whether positive or negative, must be supported by details.

3. To give students guidance in writing their argumentative texts, give them **Support for Writing,** for this selection in the *Student Companion All-in-One Workbook.*

4. To evaluate the writing activity, use one of the Response to Literature rubrics in *Professional Development Guidebook,* pp. 224–225. Evaluate for how well students review the play.

Grammar Application

Have students check their drafts for the correct use of participles and gerunds.

Six Traits Focus

✓	Ideas	✓	Word Choice
	Organization	✓	Sentence Fluency
	Voice	✓	Conventions

Speaking and Listening

1. Review the assignment, using the instruction on the student page.

2. To support students' work on the assignment, have them complete the Support for Extend Your Learning page for this selection in the *Student Companion All-in-One Workbook.*

Daily Bellringer

For each class during which you will teach this selection, have students complete one of the five Research activities for Week 23 in the *Daily Bellringer Activities*. You may wish to use additional activities that are applicable to these selections.

 1 **How do we decide who we are?**

1. Review the assignment with the class.

2. Remind students that many qualities make up who they are, including personality, values, hopes, dreams, and experiences. Explain that the Big Question also relates to finding a purpose in life. Thinking about who we are helps us set and reach goals.

3. Remind students that when they read the texts, they should compare and contrast the purposes of the two authors and focus on how their writing supports those purposes.

MULTIDRAFT READING

To assist struggling readers and to deepen comprehension for all, assign the text in "chunks" and apply multidraft reading protocols. For each reading, have students set the purpose indicated:

• **First reading:** Students should read the selection independently and think about its basic meaning.

• **Second reading:** Students should analyze the text's key ideas and details and its craft and structure, and respond to the side-column prompts.

• **Third reading:** Students should integrate knowledge and ideas, connect the text to other texts and to the world, and answer the end-of-selection questions.

For more guidance, refer to the *Classroom Strategies and Teaching Routines* card on multidraft reading.

 ## How do we decide who we are?

1 Explore the Big Question as you read a scene from *You're a Good Man, Charlie Brown* and a drama review of a performance of that play.

READING TO COMPARE AUTHOR'S PURPOSE ACROSS GENRES

Playwright Clark Gesner and theater critic Matthew MacDermid write in two different genres, or forms of writing. Like all authors, however, each one writes with a purpose. When you finish reading, compare and contrast the ways that each author's writing supports his purpose.

from **You're a Good Man, Charlie Brown**

Clark Gesner (1938–2002)
Clark Gesner wrote *You're a Good Man, Charlie Brown* because he loved Charles Schulz's *Peanuts* comic strip. The production opened off-Broadway in 1967 and was immediately successful. Since then, it has become one of the most frequently produced musical comedies in the United States.

"Happiness is a Charming Charlie Brown at Orlando Rep"

Matthew MacDermid
Matthew MacDermid is a stage manager and theater critic. He has reviewed productions appearing in central Florida for *Talkin' Broadway*, an online theater resource. *Talkin' Broadway* provides current news about theater openings, revivals, and trends. It also provides a forum for interactive discussions on theatrical topics.

522 UNIT 4 • How do we decide who we are?

💬 ## VOCABULARY DEVELOPMENT

Vocabulary Knowledge Rating
Create a **Vocabulary Knowledge Rating Chart (Professional Development Guidebook**, p. 33) featuring the words glossed in the selections:

objectionable (p. 526)	*evoking* (p. 530)
tentatively (p. 526)	*embody* (p. 531)
civic (p. 527)	*abundantly* (p. 532)

Give students a copy of the chart, and read the words aloud. Have students mark their rating of each in the Before You Read column. To gauge how much instruction to provide, tally the students who think they know each word.

Explain that the words are defined in the margin at the point where they appear in the selection. Urge students to be alert to these words as they read the selections. They will rate their knowledge again when they finish.

❷ Comparing Author's Purpose Across Genres

An **author's purpose** is the author's main reason for writing a work. The purpose may be to inform, to entertain, to persuade, or to express emotions. Sometimes, an author may have more than one purpose for writing.

- When writing to **inform**, an author gives factual information on a subject to educate his or her audience.
- When writing to **persuade**, an author gives reasons, facts, and evidence to sway his or her readers to share the author's opinion.
- When writing to **entertain**, an author writes purely for the enjoyment of his or her audience.
- When writing to **express emotions**, an author uses words to convey the joy, sorrow, anger, or hope he or she feels.

An author chooses the genre, or specific form of writing, that will best enable him or her to achieve a specific purpose. For example, to fulfill the purpose of informing, an author might write an expository essay. To fulfill the purpose of entertaining, an author might write a short story, play, or humorous essay. Genre and purpose are usually closely related in functional texts, which convey information that is meant to be used in a specific way.

The scene by Clark Gesner is from a musical comedy, and the article by Matthew MacDermid is a review of a production of that show. The two selections are related, but the authors write in different genres and have different purposes for writing. As you read, use a chart like this one to note details from each selection that help you identify each author's unique purpose.

Selection	Details	Author's Purpose
from *You're a Good Man, Charlie Brown*		
"Happiness is a Charming Charlie Brown at Orlando Rep"		

Common Core State Standards

Reading Literature
9. Compare and contrast texts in different forms or genres in terms of their approaches to similar themes and topics.

Reading Informational Text
6. Determine an author's point of view or purpose in a text and explain how it is conveyed in the text.
9. Compare and contrast one author's presentation of events with that of another.

❷ Comparing Author's Purpose Across Genres

1. Introduce the skill.
2. Discuss the chart.
3. Give students a copy of **Comparing Author's Purpose Graphic Organizer B** for *You're a Good Man, Charlie Brown* and "Happiness is a Charming Charlie Brown at Orlando Rep." Tell them they will fill it in with details as they read.

Think Aloud: Model the Skill

Model a way to identify author's purpose. Say to students:

To understand author's purpose, I think about stories like "The Boy Who Cried Wolf" or "The Tortoise and the Hare." These fables end with a message, or moral, that explains what the story is about—they reveal the author's purpose at the end. In "Beauty and the Beast," the author also ends with a message; however, the author doesn't directly state what that message is. It is left to the reader to interpret the theme. Often, writers have more than one purpose in mind when they write.

🗐 TEACHING RESOURCES

	Print	Digital
All Common Core Companion, pp. 75–81, 137–143, 158–164	✓	✓
All Graphic Organizers A and B, for *You're a Good Man, Charlie Brown* and "Happiness is a Charming Charlie Brown at Orlando Rep"		✓
All Online Student Edition eText with audio and video		✓
All Online Teacher Edition		✓
L1 Professional Development Guidebook, p. 33		✓
All Student Companion All-in-One Workbook, *You're a Good Man, Charlie Brown* and "Happiness is a Charming Charlie Brown at Orlando Rep"	✓	✓

❶ Background

Peanuts on Stage The musical *You're a Good Man, Charlie Brown* is based on the characters in Charles Schultz's popular comic strip *Peanuts*. The show first opened in New York in 1967, and a production toured the country until 1971. In 1999, the show had a successful Broadway revival, winning two Tony Awards.

❷ Activating Prior Knowledge

Point out that people often find something they do not like about other people, even those they are very close to. Challenge students to write down some ways they would tell a best friend that they wish he or she would act differently in some way. Tell students they will return to these responses after reading the selection.

❸ About the Selection

Schroeder tells his friend Lucy that she is a crabby person. Upset, Lucy decides to seek the opinions of other friends. Charlie Brown says that she has only average crabbiness, but Patty and her brother Linus say she is very crabby. Lucy becomes depressed but is comforted when Linus tells her he loves her.

❹ Critical Viewing

Answer: Students might say that they know *Peanuts* is a cartoon, and that Charlie Brown, one of the leading characters, often encounters disappointments.

❶
❷
❸

from You're a Good Man, Charlie Brown

Clark Gesner

Based on the comic strip *Peanuts* by Charles M. Schulz

❹ ▲ **Critical Viewing** What do you already know about Charlie Brown and *Peanuts*?

❺

SCHROEDER. I'm sorry to have to say it right to your face, Lucy, but it's true. You're a very crabby person. I know your crabbiness has probably become so natural to you now that you're not even aware when you're being crabby, but it's true just the same. You're a very crabby person and you're crabby to just about everyone you meet. (LUCY *remains silent—just barely*) Now I hope you

524 UNIT 4 • How do we decide who we are?

ⓒ TEXT COMPLEXITY **RUBRIC**

from You're a Good Man, Charlie Brown		Reader and Task Suggestions	
Qualitative Measures		**Preparing to Read the Text**	**Leveled Tasks**
Context/Knowledge Demands	Contemporary U.S.; *Peanuts* comic strip 1　②　3　4　5	• Using the Background and About the Selection information on this page, discuss with students what they know about the character of Lucy.	*Levels of Meaning:* If students will have difficulty with meaning, use the Activating Prior Knowledge activity on this page to help students understand the situation in the play.
Structure/Language Conventionality	Simple sentences; on-level vocabulary 1　②　3　4　5	• Point out that even though there are some things we don't like about others, even our very best friends, we can still love and admire that person.	*Synthesizing:* If students will not have difficulty with meaning, ask students to think about some things they don't like about someone close to them. Then have volunteers explain how we can overlook a person's faults.
Levels of Meaning/Purpose/Concepts	Accessible concept (problems with friends) 1　2　③　4　5	• Guide students to use Multidraft Reading strategies (TE p. 522).	
Quantitative Measures			
Lexile	750L	**Text Length**	Word Count: 1,502

don't mind my saying this, Lucy, and I hope you'll take it in the spirit that it's meant. I think we should all be open to any opportunity to learn more about ourselves. I think Socrates was very right when he said that one of the first rules for anyone in life is "Know thyself." (LUCY *has begun whistling quietly to herself*) Well, I guess I've said about enough. I hope I haven't offended you or anything. (*He makes an awkward exit*)

LUCY. (*Sits in silence, then shouts offstage at* SCHROEDER) Well, what's Socrates got to do with it anyway, huh? Who was *he* anyway? Did he ever get to be king, huh! Answer me that, did he ever get to be king! (*Suddenly to herself, a real question*) *Did* he ever get to be king? (*She shouts offstage, now a question*) Who was Socrates, anyway? (*She gives up the rampage and plunks herself down*) "Know thyself," hmph. (*She thinks a moment, then makes a silent resolution to herself, exits and quickly returns with a clipboard and pencil.* CHARLIE BROWN *and* SNOOPY *have entered, still with baseball equipment*)

CHARLIE BROWN. Hey, Snoopy, you want to help me get my arm back in shape? Watch out for this one, it's a new fastball.

LUCY. Excuse me a moment, Charlie Brown, but I was wondering if you'd mind answering a few questions.

CHARLIE BROWN. Not at all, Lucy. What kind of questions are they?

LUCY. Well, I'm conducting a survey to enable me to know myself better, and first of all I'd like to ask: on a scale of zero to one hundred, using a standard of fifty as average, seventy-five as above average and ninety as exceptional, where would you rate me with regards to crabbiness?

CHARLIE BROWN. (*Stands in silence for a moment, hesitating*) Well, Lucy, I . . .

LUCY. Your ballots need not be signed and all answers will be held in strictest confidence.

CHARLIE BROWN. Well still, Lucy, that's a very hard question to answer.

Author's Purpose
What does your reaction to Lucy's behavior here tell you about the author's purpose?

You're a very crabby person and you're crabby to just about everyone you meet.

❺ Author's Purpose

1. Explain to students that Socrates was a philosopher from ancient Greece. In saying "Know thyself," Socrates was saying that the basis of wisdom was understanding one's own personality. Then, ask students to reread the bracketed passage.

2. **Ask** students to restate the main idea of what Schroeder said to Lucy.

   Answer: He said that she was crabby, though he hoped she was not hurt by hearing that.

3. **Ask** how Lucy responded, and what that shows about Schroeder's comment to her.

   Possible responses: She quickly became very angry, which shows that Schroeder was right and that what he said bothers her.

4. Finally, **ask** students the Author's Purpose question: What does your reaction to Lucy's behavior here tell you about the author's purpose? Have them explain their responses.

   Possible responses: His purpose is to entertain. Lucy's reaction is funny.

Connecting to the Big Question

6

1. Remind students of the Big Question by pointing out that emotions can get in the way of how people communicate, making it harder for us to know what other people really think about us.

2. Have students reread the bracketed passage, focusing on Charlie Brown's answers to Lucy's questions. Explain that *abstention* means "no response." **Ask** students how Charlie Brown responded to the questions about personality, friendliness, and appearance.

   Answer: He answered "forceful," he did not answer the friendliness question, and he said "you look just fine" to the appearance question.

3. **Ask** students if they think Charlie Brown is saying what he really thinks.

   Possible response: Charlie Brown clearly feels very uncomfortable answering Lucy's questions and is trying not to offend or anger Lucy.

4. Next, have students focus on Lucy's responses to Charlie Brown's answers. **Ask** if they think Lucy understands how Charlie Brown is feeling. Have them explain their answers.

   Possible response: Lucy records Charlie Brown's answers, though in the case of appearance, she turns "look just fine" into "stunning." She does not really see how uncomfortable Charlie Brown is or perceive that he is not quite telling her what he thinks.

5. Finally, **ask** students whether they think Lucy and Charlie Brown communicated clearly or unclearly. Have them explain their answers.

   Possible responses: The communication is unclear because Charlie Brown is hiding what he really thinks, and Lucy is not paying attention to what he really means. Tell students to look as they read for examples of clear and unclear communication.

Vocabulary ▶
objectionable (əb jek´ shən ə bəl) *adj.* disagreeable

LUCY. You may have a few moments to think it over if you want, or we can come back to that question later.

CHARLIE BROWN. I think I'd like to come back to it, if you don't mind.

LUCY. Certainly. This next question deals with certain character traits you may have observed. Regarding personality, would you say that mine is *A* forceful, *B* pleasing, or *C* objectionable? Would that be *A*, *B*, or *C*? What would your answer be to that, Charlie Brown, forceful, pleasing or objectionable, which one would you say, hmm? Charlie Brown, hmm?

CHARLIE BROWN. Well, I guess I'd have to say forceful, Lucy, but . . .

LUCY. "Forceful." Well, we'll make a check mark at the letter *A* then. Now, would you rate my ability to get along with other people as poor, fair, good or excellent?

6 CHARLIE BROWN. I think that depends a lot on what you mean by "get along with other people."

LUCY. You know, make friends, sparkle in a crowd, that sort of thing.

CHARLIE BROWN. Do you have a place for abstention?

LUCY. Certainly, I'll just put a check mark at "None of the above." The next question deals with physical appearance. In referring to my beauty, would you say that I was "stunning," "mysterious," or "intoxicating"?

CHARLIE BROWN. (*Squirming*) Well, gee, I don't know, Lucy. You look just fine to me.

LUCY. (*Making a check on the page*) "Stunning." All right, Charlie Brown, I think we should get back to that first question. On a scale of zero to one hundred, using a standard of fifty as average, seventy-five as . . .

CHARLIE BROWN. (*Loud interruption*) I . . . (*quieter*) . . . remember the question, Lucy.

Vocabulary ▶
tentatively (ten´ tə tiv lē) *adv.* in a hesitant way

LUCY. Well?

CHARLIE BROWN. (*Tentatively*) Fifty-one?

💬 VOCABULARY DEVELOPMENT

Thematic Vocabulary: The Big Question

As students are discussing *You're a Good Man, Charlie Brown,* ask them to use the thematic vocabulary presented in Introducing the Big Question, pp. 440–441. You might encourage them with sentence starters such as these:

1. Lucy's *reaction* to Schroeder's comment is . . .

2. Charlie Brown does not want to *respond* when . . .
3. When Lucy asks about her *appearance*, Charlie Brown says that . . .
4. Lucy does not seem to be *conscious* of . . .
5. Linus has a different *personality* from . . .

Lucy. (*Noting it down*) Fifty-one is your crabbiness rating for me. Very well then, that about does it. Thank you very much for helping with this survey, Charlie Brown. Your cooperation has been greatly appreciated. (*She shakes hands with* CHARLIE BROWN)

CHARLIE BROWN. (*Flustered*) It was a pleasure, Lucy, any time. Come on, Snoopy.

Lucy. Oh, just a minute, there is one more question. Would you answer "Yes" or "No" to the question: "Is Lucy Van Pelt the sort of person that you would like to have as president of your club or civic organization?"

CHARLIE BROWN. Oh, yes, by all means, Lucy.

Lucy. (*Making note*) Yes. Well, thank you very much. That about does it, I think. (CHARLIE BROWN exits, *but* SNOOPY *pauses, turns, and strikes a dramatic "thumbs down" pose to* LUCY) WELL, WHO ASKED YOU! (SNOOPY *makes a hasty exit.* LUCY *stands center stage, figuring to herself on the clipboard and mumbling*) Now let's see. That's a fifty-one, "None of the above," and . . . (*She looks up*) Schroeder was right. I can already feel myself being filled with the glow of self-awareness. (PATTY *enters. She is heading for the other side of the stage, when* LUCY *stops her*) Oh, Patty, I'm conducting a survey and I wonder if . . .

Patty. A hundred and ten, C, "Poor," "None of the above," "No," and what are you going to do about the dent you made in my bicycle! (PATTY *storms off.* LUCY *watches her go, then looks at the audience*)

Lucy. It's amazing how fast word of these surveys gets around. (LINUS *wanders in and plunks himself down in front of the TV.* LUCY *crosses to him, still figuring*)

Lucy. Oh, Linus, I'm glad you're here. I'm conducting a survey and there are a few questions I'd like to ask you.

Linus. Sure, go ahead.

Lucy. The first question is: on a scale of zero to one hundred, with a standard of fifty as average, seventy-five as above average and ninety as exceptional, where would you rate me with regards to crabbiness?

◀ **Vocabulary**
civic (siv´ ik) *adj.* representing a city or group of citizens

In referring to my beauty, would you say that I was "stunning," "mysterious," or "intoxicating"?

Spiral Review
Dialogue What does Patty's response show about her feelings for Lucy?

❼ Comprehension
What is the subject of Lucy's survey?

Spiral Review

Dialogue

1. Remind students that they studied the concept of dialogue in the Unit 4 Focus on Craft and Structure (pp. 454–457).

2. **Ask** students the Spiral Review question.

   Possible response: Patty doesn't like anything about Lucy, including her crabbiness, her personality, and her inability to get along well with others. She is angry with Lucy for denting her bicycle.

❼ Comprehension

Answer: The subject is how other people see Lucy in terms of crabbiness, personality, friendliness, appearance, and leadership.

⚏ DIFFERENTIATED INSTRUCTION

Strategy for Less Proficient Readers
Help students by preteaching vocabulary in this selection (taken from both dialogue and stage directions).

You may wish to start with a discussion, to see if some words and phrases are familiar: *crabby, awkward, rampage, conducting a survey, hesitating, held in strictest confidence, abstention, stunning, intoxicating, standard, exceptional,* and *candor.*

Assign a different word or phrase to each student. Have each student look up the assigned word in the dictionary and read aloud the definition. For phrases, help students put together the different words to create a meaning for the entire phrase. For individual words, help students form sentences using the word correctly.

Stop and review the meanings of these words and phrases as they are encountered in the text.

8 Author's Purpose

1. Remind students of their response to the Author's Purpose question on page 525.

2. Ask students to summarize what happens in the bracketed passage.

Answer: Lucy makes a big speech about how the survey has to be honest. In response, Linus honestly gives her a high rating in crabbiness, and she punches him. At first, Lucy is angry at Linus, but then she decides that she really is a crabby person.

3. Finally, **ask** students the Author's Purpose question: What further details does the author provide here to help you understand his purpose?

Possible responses: Lucy's speech about honesty in surveys, her punching of Linus, and her calling herself a "supercrab" are all exaggerated responses. These overblown reactions reinforce the comic effect of the scene, helping the author entertain us.

Linus. (*Slowly turns his head to look at her, then turns back to the TV*) You're my big sister.

Lucy. That's not the question.

Linus. No, but that's the answer.

Lucy. Come on, Linus, answer the question.

Linus. (*Getting up and facing* Lucy) Look, Lucy, I know very well that if I give any sort of honest answer to that question you're going to slug me.

Lucy. Linus. A survey that is not based on honest answers is like a house that is built on a foundation of sand. Would I be spending my time to conduct this survey if I didn't expect complete candor in all the responses? I promise not to slug you. Now what number would you give me as your crabbiness rating?

Linus. (*After a few moments of interior struggle*) Ninety-five. (Lucy *sends a straight jab to his jaw which lays him out flat*)

Lucy. No decent person could be expected to keep her word with a rating over ninety. (*She stalks off, busily figuring away on her clipboard*) Now, I add these two columns and that gives me my answer. (*She figures energetically, then finally sits up with satisfaction*) There, it's all done. Now, let's see what we've got. (*She begins to scan the page. A look of trouble skims over her face. She rechecks the figures. Her eternal look of self-confidence wavers, then crumbles*) It's true. I'm a crabby person. I'm a very crabby person and everybody knows it. I've been spreading crabbiness wherever I go. I'm a supercrab. It's a wonder anyone will still talk to me. It's a wonder I have any friends at all—(*She looks at the figures on the paper*) or even associates. I've done nothing but make life miserable for everyone. I've done nothing but breed unhappiness and resentment. Where did I go wrong? How could I be so selfish? How could . . . (Linus *has been listening. He comes and sits near her*)

Linus. What's wrong, Lucy?

Lucy. Don't talk to me, Linus. I don't deserve to be spoken to. I don't deserve to breathe the air I breathe. I'm no good, Linus. I'm no good.

Author's Purpose
What further details does the author provide here to help you understand his purpose?

8

🗨 THINK ALOUD

Identifying Traits and Motives of Characters

Model the way to use direct and indirect characterization to identify the traits and motives of characters (introduced on p. 28). Use this think aloud:

When I try to understand a character, I look at both what the character does and says (direct characterization) and how other characters react to him or her (indirect characterization). Look at the scene between Lucy and Linus. Lucy insists on getting an answer to her question. A person who is so persistent seems to be an aggressive person. When Linus says that he's afraid he'll be punched if he gives an honest answer, that confirms my idea that Lucy is aggressive. Both Lucy's own words and others' attitude toward her help reveal her character.

Encourage students to use the same method to analyze Linus's character.

Linus. That's not true, Lucy.

Lucy. Yes it is. I'm no good, and there's no reason at all why I should go on living on the face of this earth.

Linus. Yes there is.

Lucy. Name one. Just tell me one single reason why I should still deserve to go on living on this planet.

Linus. Well, for one thing, you have a little brother who loves you. (Lucy *looks at him. She is silent. Then she breaks into a great, sobbing "Wah!"*) Every now and then I say the right thing.

(Lucy *continues sobbing as she and* Linus *exit. A brief musical interlude, a change of light, and* Schroeder *and* Sally *come onstage*)

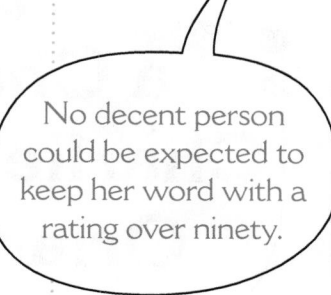

No decent person could be expected to keep her word with a rating over ninety.

Critical Thinking

1. **Key Ideas and Details (a)** What does Schroeder say that causes Lucy to develop the survey? **(b) Compare and Contrast:** How are Charlie Brown's answers different from Patty's responses? **(c) Interpret:** What do the different answers suggest about their contrasting feelings and personalities?

2. **Key Ideas and Details (a)** How does Snoopy react to Lucy? **(b) Infer:** What do Snoopy's gestures tell you about his feelings for Lucy?

3. **Key Ideas and Details (a)** Why is Linus afraid to tell Lucy the truth? **(b) Cause and Effect:** What happens when he tells the truth? **(c) Paraphrase:** Explain what Lucy means by the statement "No decent person could be expected to keep her word with a rating over ninety."

4. **Integration of Knowledge and Ideas (a)** What conclusion does Lucy draw about herself after the survey? **(b)** What does Linus say to try to change her mind? **(c)** What lesson might Lucy and the audience learn about "who we are"? Explain. *[Connect to the Big Question: How do we decide who we are?]*

 ASSESS

Critical Thinking

Possible responses appear below. Check to make sure students support their responses with evidence from the text.

1. **(a)** Schroeder says that Lucy is crabby. **(b)** Charlie Brown is much more hesitant to answer, and several of his answers are in the middle of ranges in the hopes he does not offend Lucy. Patty's answers are more honest and more harsh. **(c)** Charlie Brown's answers suggest that he is being careful. Patty is direct.

2. **(a)** He gives her a "thumbs-down" sign. **(b)** He does not approve of her.

3. **(a)** He is afraid that she will hit him. **(b)** She hits him. **(c)** Hearing such a harsh evaluation gives me the right to act on my hurt feelings.

4. **(a)** She decides she is "supercrabby." **(b)** Linus tells her he loves her. **(c)** We should learn that it is not just how people see us, but how they care about us that matters. We should realize that people still love one another even though nobody is perfect.

DIFFERENTIATED INSTRUCTION

Enrichment for Gifted/Talented Students
Have students perform a dramatic reading of this excerpt from *You're a Good Man, Charlie Brown.* You may wish to have students create or gather props based on both stage directions and the comic strips you shared. Encourage them to not simply read, but to add the emotions and even some of the actions to the dramatic reading. Allow time for students to gather props and rehearse, then have them give a presentation for the rest of the class.

Enrichment for Advanced Readers
Explain that an allusion is an indirect reference to something. Point out the allusions in this selection: Socrates (p. 525), famous for using questions to help people learn about themselves; a house built on a foundation of sand (p. 528), from the Bible, speaking of someone foolish enough to build on a foundation easily washed away; and Snoopy's thumbs down (p. 527), from the signal with which a Roman emperor could end a gladiator's life. Discuss how allusions enrich stories and how readers can understand them.

9 Background

Reviews Newspapers and magazines often publish reviews of plays, movies, books, concerts, and other events. The reviewer's task not only is to give background information about the author or performers but also to evaluate the work, explaining to readers what he or she did and didn't like and why.

10 Activating Prior Knowledge

Call on students to recall a time when they saw a movie or television show before a friend did. Invite volunteers to explain how they described the movie or show to the friend. Guide them with questions such as, How much of the plot did you tell? Did you focus on the acting or the story? Did you recommend that your friend see the movie or show or did you advise against it? Ask students to write a sentence or two explaining why two friends might have different opinions of a play, movie, or television show.

11 About the Selection

The theater critic for an Orlando (Fla.) newspaper writes a review of a production of *You're a Good Man, Charlie Brown*. The writer describes the performances of the principal actors, praising the three who play Linus, Lucy, and Snoopy in particular. The critic also comments on sets, costumes, music, and other aspects of the show as well as the work of the director.

Happiness is a Charming Charlie Brown at Orlando Rep

9
10
11

Matthew MacDermid

David Hsieh, courtesy of www.reacttheatre.org

Vocabulary ▶
evoking (ē vōk′ iŋ)
v. calling forth

At the conclusion of *You're A Good Man, Charlie Brown*—the classic musical based on Charles M. Schulz's "Peanuts" comic strip—the well-known characters of Charlie Brown, Sally Brown, Lucy, Linus, Schroeder and Snoopy sing of the simple joys in life that bring them happiness. The melody by Clark M. Gesner, along with the charming lyrics (such as "playing the drum in your own school band" and "being alone every now and then") make for a rather touching moment, allowing children and adults of all ages to ponder where they find happiness. At the Orlando Repertory Theatre, which is opening its fourth season with the revised version of this long-running Off-Broadway hit, happiness is alive and evident in a wonderful production evoking the original script's charm and the contemporary flair of new orchestrations by Michael Gibson, as well as additional dialogue and music by Michael Mayer and Andrew Lippa, respectively.

530 UNIT 4 • How do we decide who we are?

© TEXT COMPLEXITY **RUBRIC**

Happiness is a Charming Charlie Brown at Orlando Rep				Reader and Task Suggestions	
Qualitative Measures				**Preparing to Read the Text**	**Leveled Tasks**
Context/Knowledge Demands	Play review; theater critic 1 ② 3 4 5			• Using the Background and About the Selection information on this page, discuss the purpose of the review students will read.	*Structure/Language* If students will have difficulty with vocabulary, have them note words with which they will have difficulty. Use the Think Aloud note on TE p. 531 to help students define the words using context.
Structure/Language Conventionality	Accessible style, challenging vocabulary 1 2 ③ 4 5			• Point out that this review is written for a general adult audience and that there is some difficult vocabulary.	
Levels of Meaning/Purpose/Concepts	Accessible (positive review of a production) 1 ② 3 4 5			• Guide students to use Multidraft Reading strategies (TE p. 522).	*Synthesize* If students will not have difficulty with vocabulary, have students write short movie reviews. Then have students compare their reviews with a partner.
Quantitative Measures					
Lexile	1580L	**Text Length**	Word Count: 589		

You're A Good Man, Charlie Brown is really a series of comic strip vignettes taken directly from Schulz's funny pages. Delightful musical numbers are added to comment on the situations, allowing charismatic performers to bring cartoon characters to three-dimensional life. The Rep's cast is an outstanding blend of fresh, wide-eyed professional talent headed by the outstanding Michael Swickard as Charlie Brown. His round eyes and round head perfectly embody the lovable loser constantly battling his affection for the little red headed girl across the school yard and his inability to properly fly a kite. Karla Sue Schultz, as Charlie's sister Sally, establishes youth, naivete and a terrific sense of humor backed by a great voice in sketches about jumping rope and coathanger sculptures. She is especially effective in one of Lippa's new numbers, "My New Philosophy." Ronald E. Hornsby's Schroeder has less showy material, even with the new number "Beethoven's Birthday," but does his best with what he is given.

However, three performers take their characters to a higher level, stealing the spotlight with every opportunity and even chewing a bit of the scenery along the way. Shannon Bilo is a wonder as Lucy, with a clarion belt and expert comic timing that seems to go for days. Mark Catlett is outstanding as her kid brother Linus, sucking his thumb and doing the tango with his blanket, all the while exuding the mind-numbing intelligence of such a youngster. And Chris Layton stops the show with his rousing Snoopy, channeling the showbiz legends of yesteryear (including Carol Channing) in his celebratory "Suppertime."

Technically, this production remains on par with its performers, a perfect blend of design excellence from Alvin DeLeon's scenery, Simone Smith's costumes, Sam Hazell's props, David M. Upton's lighting and James E. Cleveland's sound. Justin S. Fischer's musical direction is also terrific, with his five-piece band perfectly executing Gibson's fresh orchestrations.

Myles Thoroughgood's musical staging is character driven and lovely, providing each performer with a

◀ **Vocabulary**
embody (em bäd´ ē) *v.* give bodily form to; represent

Author's Purpose
What do you think the author's purpose is for writing this article?

⑬ Comprehension
How does the critic feel about the overall production?

⑫ Author's Purpose

1. Have students reread the bracketed passage. **Ask** them to summarize the main points.

   Answer: The author discusses the play's original source and additions made for this production; he describes the performances of several actors, praising three in particular; and the author comments on the scenery, costumes, props, lighting, sound, and music.

2. **Ask** what details the author gives in describing the performances.

   Possible response: The author names the actors and talks about how the actors portray the characters and perform the different songs in the show.

3. Finally, **ask** students the Author's Purpose question: What do you think the author's purpose is for writing this article?

   Possible responses: The author's purpose is to inform. He wants to tell readers about the production and who took part in it. He also tries to communicate a sense of what the experience of seeing the show is like.

⑬ Comprehension

Answer: The critic is very favorable toward the production, rating the actors highly and saying that the scenery, costumes, and other elements are just as impressive.

🗨 **THINK ALOUD**

Vocabulary: Using Context
Call students' attention to the word *charming* in the title of the selection. Then use the following think aloud to show them how to use context to infer its meaning:

I'm going to think aloud to show you how I can figure out the meaning of *charming* from its context. I see in the title that *charming* is related to *happiness*, so I think that *charming* must be something pleasant. The first sentence of the review says that the play presents "simple joys." In that context, I think that

charming must mean something pleasant in a simple way. As I read the first paragraph, I see that the reviewer writes about the play's "charming lyrics." That sentence says that the lyrics help create a "touching moment," meaning that the writer and others in the audience felt a sweet emotional tug when they watched the scene. From these context clues, I can see that *charming* means something sweetly emotional, pleasant, and simple rather than complex.

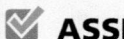 **ASSESS**

Critical Thinking

Possible responses appear below. Check to be sure students support their responses with evidence from the text.

1. **(a)** The play is based on stories in the comic strip, with music added. **(b)** The musical numbers bring the characters to life.

2. **(a)** The author praises all the performers. **(b)** The author singles out the actors who played Lucy, Linus, and Snoopy for special praise. **(c)** The actor who plays Snoopy seems to be his favorite, because he says that his performance stops the show.

3. **(a)** He says that the director's work was not up to the quality of the others' work. **(b)** He says the direction is inconsistent, that several scenes fall flat, and that some scenes "bring the show to a halt."

4. Students may say that each actor would have his or her own opinion of the quality of the performance and an actor would not be influenced by a review. Some might say that it would probably be gratifying to the actors to receive favorable reviews.

---

signature dance move that surfaces throughout. Jeffrey Revels' direction isn't quite up to the standard of everything else. While his work is mostly excellent, it is somewhat inconsistent, with several scene buttons falling flat and a couple that actually seem to bring the show to a halt. But what is good is great, and his decisions in casting have abundantly affected the success of his production.

Vocabulary ►
abundantly (ə bun′ dənt lē) *adv.* in an exceptional way

The Orlando Repertory Theatre has produced one of their best productions to date with this *Charlie Brown*. It runs in the 328-seat Edyth Busch Theatre, in the Rep complex at 1001 E. Princeton Street in Orlando, through October 1st.

Cast:
Charlie Brown—Michael Swickard
Lucy—Shannon Bilo
Snoopy—Chris Layton
Linus—Mark Catlett
Sally—Karla Sue Schultz
Schroeder—Ronald E. Hornsby

Critical Thinking

1. **Key Ideas and Details (a)** How does the play relate to the comic strip? **(b) Interpret:** According to the review, what make the play's subject suitable for theater?

2. **Key Ideas and Details (a)** How are the author's opinions of each actor's performance similar? **(b) Contrast:** How are his opinions different? **(c) Analyze:** Which actor seems to be his favorite? Explain.

3. **Key Ideas and Details (a)** Which member of the production does the author criticize? **(b) Summarize:** What weaknesses does the author cite as part of his criticism?

4. **Integration of Knowledge and Ideas** If you were an actor in this production, how much value would you give to this review? Why? *[Connect to the Big Question: How do we decide who we are?]*

📰 VOCABULARY DEVELOPMENT

Vocabulary Knowledge Rating

When students have completed reading and discussing *You're a Good Man, Charlie Brown* and "Happiness Is a Charming Charlie Brown at Orlando Rep," have them take out their **Vocabulary Knowledge Rating Chart.** Read the words aloud once more and have students rate their knowledge of the words again in the After Reading column. Clarify any words that are still problematic. Have students write their own definitions and examples in the appropriate column. Encourage students to use the words in further discussion and written work about these selections. Remind them that they will be accountable for these words on the **Selection Test.**

Writing to Sources

Comparing Author's Purpose

1. **(a)** What purpose did Clark Gesner have for writing his play *You're a Good Man, Charlie Brown?* **(b)** Explain what details helped you determine the author's purpose.

2. **(a)** What purpose did Matthew MacDermid have for writing his review? **(b)** Explain how details in the review helped you determine the author's purpose.

3. Complete a Venn diagram like the one below to show how the drama scene and the review are alike and different.

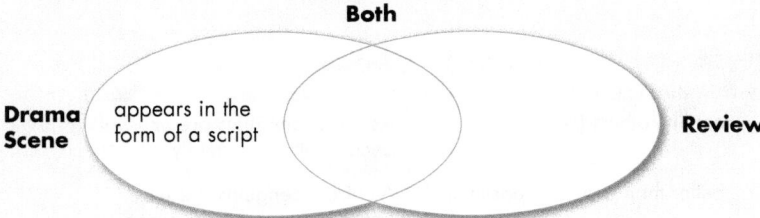

⏱ Timed Writing

Explanatory Text: Essay

In an essay, compare and contrast each author's purpose for writing and the way in which each genre—play and review—presents its topic. Provide textual evidence to support your understanding. **(30 minutes)**

5-Minute Planner

1. Read the prompt carefully and completely. Consider these questions to get started.

   • How does each selection convey ideas and information?

   • What type of information does each author provide?

   • What kind of audience is each genre—play and review—most likely to reach? Explain.

2. Use your notes on the selections and your answers to the questions above to formulate a response.

3. Reread the prompt, and then draft your essay.

USE ACADEMIC VOCABULARY

As you write, use academic language, including the following words or their related forms:

opinion

reflect

respond

specific

For more information about academic vocabulary, see pages xlvi–l.

ASSESSMENT RESOURCES

The following resources can be used to assess students' knowledge and skills.

L1 L2 EL Selection Test

L3 L4 Open-Book Test

✓ ASSESS

Comparing Author's Purpose

1. **(a)** Gesner's purpose is to entertain people. **(b)** Details such as Lucy's overreaction, Snoopy's thumbs-down, and the way Patty responds so brusquely to her are all funny, showing that the play is entertaining.

2. **(a)** MacDermid's purpose is to inform. **(b)** He gives many specific details about who took part in the production and how they did their jobs.

3. *Drama scene:* Appears in the form of a script; Tells a story; Uses dialogue and stage direction to relate a story; Is funny. *Both:* Involve the *Peanuts* characters. *Article:* Appears in the form of an essay; Describes one performance of the play; Evaluates the people who took part in the performance.

For other sample answers, see **After You Read Graphic Organizer A** for these selections and the **Additional Answers** section.

⏱ Timed Writing

1. Review the prompt with students.

2. Have students use the 5-Minute Planner to structure their time. Guide them in completing the bulleted instructions. For example, ask them where they are most likely to encounter a play or a play review.

3. Allow students 40 minutes to complete the assignment.

Six Traits Focus

✓	Ideas	Word Choice
✓	Organization	Sentence Fluency
	Voice	Conventions

 Online Writer's Notebook

Students can use the Online Writer's Notebook to record all responses.

Connotation and Denotation

1. Introduce the skill and review the examples in the chart.

2. Explain that the difference between denotation and connotation is similar to the way different pieces of furniture look and feel. A wooden chair and an upholstered chair can both be used as chairs, but the person sitting in them would notice a difference between the bare wood and the cushion. Similarly, two words with the same denotation, or definition, can have different connotations, or feelings that they evoke.

Think Aloud: Model the Skill

Say to students:

When I think of connotation, I think of different words to describe a pet dog. For instance, if I read about a "hairy dog," I think of an animal with lots of long hair. If the author describes the dog as "shaggy," I think the animal's hair hasn't been trimmed recently and might be sticking out in many different directions. If the author describes the dog as "fuzzy," I think of a cute puppy with soft fur.

Practice A
Answers:

1. *Dazzling* is more positive than *bright,* which is neutral.
2. *Discuss,* which is neutral, is more positive than the negative *argue.*
3. *Clever,* which is neutral, is more positive than *sly,* which is negative.
4. *Challenging,* which is neutral, is more positive than the negative *dangerous.*

 **Grammar Tutorials**

Grammar Tutorials in the *Student eText* provide additional support!

 Language Study

Connotation and Denotation

A word's **denotation** is its definition. You can find denotations in a dictionary. The associations or feelings that a word suggests are called its **connotation**. Connotations can be positive, negative, or neutral. For example, the words *inexpensive, cheap,* and *economical* are synonyms that mean "low-priced." However, *cheap* suggests something that is poorly constructed. It has a negative connotation. *Economical* suggests something that saves money. It has a positive connotation. *Inexpensive* does not carry either positive or negative feelings. It has a neutral connotation.

Word	Denotation	Connotation	Example Sentence
unusual	not common or ordinary	not like others (neutral)	As birds, penguins are *unusual* because they cannot fly.
exceptional		better than average (positive)	As birds, penguins are *exceptional* because they cannot fly.
strange		different in an unwelcome way (negative)	As birds, penguins are *strange* because they cannot fly.

 **Common Core State Standards**

Language
4.c. Consult reference materials, both print and digital, to find the pronunciation of a word or determine or clarify its precise meaning or its part of speech.
5. Demonstrate understanding of figurative language, word relationships, and nuances in word meanings.
5.c. Distinguish among the connotations (associations) of words with similar denotations (definitions).

TEACHING RESOURCES

	Print	Digital
All Language Study Worksheet, Connotation and Denotation		✓

Practice A

Each of the following words has a positive, neutral, or negative connotation. For each word pair, identify which word has a more positive connotation. Use a dictionary if you need help checking a word's denotation.

1. bright, dazzling
2. argue, discuss
3. clever, sly
4. challenging, dangerous

Practice B

Each of these verbs has a neutral connotation. Provide a synonym for each one using a dictionary or thesaurus if necessary. Then, label each of your synonyms *negative, positive,* or *neutral,* depending on its connotation. Finally, use five of your synonyms to write sentences that clearly show either a positive or a negative connotation.

1. ask
2. quiet
3. get
4. food
5. walk
6. car
7. laugh
8. curiosity
9. write
10. anticipate

Activity Each of the following words has a neutral connotation. Use a thesaurus to locate synonyms for each word. Find a synonym with a positive connotation and one with a negative connotation. Use a graphic organizer like this one to organize your synonyms. The first one has been completed as an example.

brave   warm   house   think   different

Synonyms with Negative Connotations		Synonyms with Positive Connotations
reckless	← brave →	heroic

> **Comprehension and Collaboration**
>
> Work with a partner to list as many synonyms as you can for the word *talk*. Then classify the synonyms, analyzing their shades of meaning. Divide the words into groups to show whether they have *negative, positive,* or *neutral* connotations.

Practice B

Sample answers:

1. Neutral: *question;* negative: *quiz, interrogate.* Sample sentence: The officers *interrogated* the suspect for ten hours.
2. Neutral: *calm, motionless;* positive: *tranquil, peaceful;* negative: *immobile.* Sample sentence: They paused by the *peaceful* lake.
3. Neutral: *obtain, acquire;* positive: *win, earn;* negative: *procure.* Sample sentence: He *acquired* the painting last year.
4. Neutral: *fare, diet;* positive: *nourishment, sustenance;* negative: *grub.* Sample sentence: The explorers didn't have enough *grub.*
5. Neutral: *step, tread;* positive: *stroll, stride, hike;* negative: *pace, march.* Sample sentence: The couple *strolled* along the lake.
6. Neutral: *auto;* positive: *limousine;* negative: *jalopy.* Sample sentence: The noise from the *jalopy* ruined the quiet night.
7. Neutral: *chuckle, giggle;* positive: *guffaw, roar;* negative: *snicker, sneer.* Sample sentence: The crowd *roared* at the joke.
8. Neutral: *interest;* positive: *inquisitiveness;* negative: *nosiness.* Sample sentence: Her *inquisitiveness* led her to learn new things.
9. Neutral: *pen, author;* positive: *compose, create;* negative: *scribble, scrawl.* Sample sentence: He sat down to *compose* a tribute to his father.
10. Neutral: *expect, envision;* positive: *foresee, hope;* negative: *dread, apprehend.* Sample sentence: She could *foresee* a better future.

Activity

Provide thesauruses and guide students in their use.

Students should list both negative and positive synonyms.

Comprehension and Collaboration

Provide thesauruses and guide students in their use. Divide the class into pairs to carry out the activity.

Students should group the words into those with negative, positive, and neutral connotations.

🏵 DIFFERENTIATED INSTRUCTION

EL Enrichment for English Learners
Place students in pairs. Instruct each student in the pair to write a story using five synonyms they found when completing the Activity. Instruct them to use only synonyms with negative or positive connotations. When they have completed their stories, have them exchange papers with partners. Then, have each student rewrite the partner's story, using only words with the opposite connotation.

Enrichment for Gifted/Talented Students
Direct students' attention to the lists of words in Practice B and the Activity. Have them draw pictures of three different concrete nouns, such as *car* or *house,* or three different action verbs, such as *walk* or *laugh.* The three pictures should reflect words with neutral, positive, or negative connotations. Challenge other students to match each picture to the correct synonym.

Learn the Skills

1. Introduce the workshop, including the activity on the next page.

2. Encourage students to consider both sides of the argument as they develop their speech. That way, they can better anticipate counterarguments.

3. Explain that the audience often remembers the last point best.

4. Remind students that a strong speech contains a clear position with solid evidence.

5. Have students read their entire speech to a partner. Remind them that they can keep their audience engaged by making eye contact and varying their tone of voice for emphasis.

6. Students should work with partners to identify the key points that form the strongest support.

7. Explain that a key difference between a persuasive composition and a persuasive speech is the repetition of key phrases or ideas.

8. Remind students that key points can be reinforced with visual aids.

 # Speaking and Listening

Delivering a Persuasive Speech

The purpose of a **persuasive speech** is to convince an audience to think or act in a certain way. The speaker presents a claim, or argument, and uses strategies to convince the audience that his or her claim is valid. The following strategies will help you deliver an effective persuasive speech.

Learn the Skills

Develop your argument. Select a topic that is important to you and that has at least two sides. Identify which side you support. Then, list the reasons you support that side. Include evidence such as facts, statistics, or quotations from experts to strengthen your claim.

Organize your ideas. Rank your reasons and evidence in order of importance. When you deliver your speech, save your most important reason for last.

Start strong. Begin with a startling comparison or an anecdote that will capture your audience's attention. Then, provide a clear statement of your position.

Convince your listeners. Your audience will hear your presentation only once, so make sure they hear each and every word. To convince your audience, use speaking strategies that will highlight your strongest support.

- Speak loudly and slowly enough to be heard and understood.

- Make eye contact with your audience.

- Vary the volume and tone of your voice to emphasize key points.

Repeat key points. After explaining your ideas, repeat your most important idea in a single sentence. Pause afterward to allow your listeners to process what you say.

Use visuals. A picture, graphic, or chart can provide a dramatic illustration of a point you are making. Use your visuals to provide relevant evidence.

Common Core State Standards

Speaking and Listening

3. Delineate a speaker's argument and specific claims, distinguishing claims that are supported by reasons and evidence from claims that are not.

4. Present claims and findings, sequencing ideas logically and using pertinent descriptions, facts, and details to accentuate main ideas or themes; use appropriate eye contact, adequate volume, and clear pronunciation.

5. Include multimedia components (e.g., graphics, images, music, sound) and visual displays in presentations to clarify information.

536 UNIT 4 • How do we decide who we are?

✔ STRATEGIES FOR DELIVERING A PERSUASIVE SPEECH

Give students these additional strategies for delivering a persuasive speech:

Explain the difference between logical and emotional appeals. Tell students that if they focus only on logical appeals, they risk losing the interest of their audience. If they focus only on emotional appeals, their argument will seem less credible. Then, review the different types of evidence that students can use to support their argument:

- Facts include information such as statistics, studies, and other research. Facts appeal to the audience's logic.

- Opinions include personal beliefs and judgments. They often appeal to the audience's emotions.

- Examples help support facts and opinions. They help the audience understand how ideas work in the world.

Practice the Skills

Presentation of Knowledge and Ideas Use what you have learned in this workshop to perform the following task.

ACTIVITY: Deliver a Persuasive Speech

Plan, write, and deliver your speech. Ask classmates to use the feedback form to give you advice on how you can improve your delivery. As you deliver your speech, remember these points:

- Provide strong evidence
- Engage listeners
- Repeat key points
- Use visuals

As your classmates deliver their persuasive speeches, consider whether or not they have been successful in convincing you to accept their views. Use the following form to evaluate their presentations.

Feedback Form for Persuasive Presentation

Rating System

Excellent	Average	Weak
+	✓	–

Content

___ Clearly stated claim
___ Logical organization
___ Strong reasons and evidence
___ Effective use of visuals

Respond honestly to these questions:

What impact did the presentation have on you?
What question does the presentation raise for you?
On what point would you challenge the speaker?
How can you affirm something the speaker has said?

Comprehension and Collaboration After you have delivered your speeches, get into small groups and discuss the responses to the feedback forms. Was your position clear? Was your evidence strong? Was the organization logical? Were visuals used effectively? As a group, discuss your classmates' most successful speeches and examine why they worked so well.

Practice the Skills

1. Review the assignment with students. Make sure that they understand the speech should make an argument about something. Students should choose a topic that has two sides, and consider both sides as they develop the speech.

2. Explain to students that they should use a copy of the Feedback Form to evaluate their own presentation and the presentations made by classmates.

3. Before students give their presentations to the class, remind listeners to ask questions if any points are unclear. To maintain order, encourage them to raise their hands and wait to be acknowledged by the presenter before stating their questions. Suggest that students making presentations scan the classroom from time to time so they will notice any students who have questions.

Evaluate the Activity

1. Evaluate students' presentations on the basis of the clarity of the argument, the quality of supporting details, and the speaker's skill with delivery.

2. When the class discusses the presentations that were most persuasive, encourage students to make note of the features of those presentations that made them effective and to incorporate those techniques in their future presentations.

:: DIFFERENTIATED INSTRUCTION

Strategy for Special-Needs Students

Students may benefit from working in groups of four to six to evaluate and revise their written speeches. Suggest that students identify strengths and weaknesses in both the written speeches and the deliveries. Then, students can work in pairs to help each other create visuals. They can even help each other by displaying the visuals during other students' speeches.

EL Strategy for English Learners

Students may be reluctant to deliver their own speeches to the class. Ask students to exchange speeches with a partner and to deliver the partner's speech instead. Students may not feel shy about delivering another student's speech, and they will probably work hard to make a good presentation on behalf of another student. The speakers may consult the writers as they prepare their deliveries.

Introducing the Writing Assignment

Review the assignment and the criteria.

Focus on Research

Remind students to keep the following tips in mind as they conduct research.

- Gather information from multiple authoritative print and digital sources.
- Assess the usefulness of each source in answering the research question.
- Integrate information into the text selectively.
- Synthesize information from multiple sources.
- Avoid plagiarism.
- Use a standard format for citations.

 Writing Process

Write an Argument

Problem-and-Solution Essay

Defining the Form In a **problem-and-solution essay,** the writer identifies and explains a problem and then proposes one or more possible solutions. The writer's goal is to persuade readers that the problem needs to be solved and that the proposed solution will solve the problem.

Assignment Think about a problem that affects your school, your community, or the world. Propose one or more solutions to the problem. Include these elements:

✓ a *thesis* stating the problem and your idea for a solution

✓ a *detailed explanation* of the problem

✓ a *step-by-step description* of your proposed solution

✓ *persuasive evidence* that supports your proposed solution

✓ *a consistent, logical organization*

✓ error-free writing, including *correct and varied use of sentences*

To preview the criteria on which your essay may be judged, see the rubric on page 545.

FOCUS ON RESEARCH

To write an effective problem-and-solution essay, you must explain the nature and seriousness of the problem. You must also present evidence to support the claim that your solution will solve the problem in a practical way. You can find information in these sources:

- government agencies that study various problems and issues
- print or online newspapers and magazines that cover public issues
- Web sites of national or local groups that focus on particular issues

Consider how objective, or fair-minded, each source is. Does the source reflect only one narrow point of view? If so, you might need to find other sources that look at the issue from a broader perspective.

538 UNIT 4 • How do we decide who we are?

Common Core State Standards

Writing
1. Write arguments to support claims with clear reasons and relevant evidence.
1.a. Introduce claim(s) and organize the reasons and evidence clearly.
1.b. Support claim(s) with clear reasons and relevant evidence, using credible sources and demonstrating an understanding of the topic or text.

EssayScorer

Students can use EssayScorer with automatic feedback and scoring to practice summarizing!

TEACHING RESOURCES

	Print	Digital
All Common Core Companion, pp. 184–195, 331–334, 335–338	✓	✓
All EssayScorer powered by WriteToLearn		✓
All Online Student Edition eText with audio and video		✓
All Online Teacher Edition		✓
L1 Professional Development Guidebook, Rubrics for Self-Assessment: Problem-and-Solution Essay, pp. 244–245		✓
All Student Companion All-in-One Workbook, Unit 4 Writing Process	✓	✓

Prewriting/Planning Strategy

Narrow your scope. Begin by choosing a topic you consider interesting and important. Be sure to narrow the scope of your problem to a manageable size. For example, pollution is a serious problem. Solutions to ending all air pollution are beyond the scope of this assignment. You could, however, discuss steps individuals can take to use less energy or recycle products instead of throwing them out. Use the examples in the chart for guidance on narrowing a topic.

Broad Topic	Narrower Topic	Narrow Topics
Problems in public schools	Improving student performance	• Strategies for building reading skills • Successful methods for teaching math • Effective tutoring programs • Ways to motivate students to learn

Determine your audience. Think about the audience you will address in your essay. Do you want to persuade public officials to adopt your solution? Do you hope to convince community leaders, such as school principals? Will you address your essay to your peers? Defining your audience will help you determine what kind of evidence to present, and which points to emphasize in your solution.

Gather information. Once you have identified a problem, you will need to gather information about it and about your proposed solution. Look for these types of evidence:

- facts or statistics about the extent of the problem
- quotations from experts about the scope or seriousness of the problem
- information that shows why your solution is a practical one
- examples of other people or groups who have succeeded in putting a solution like yours in place to solve a similar problem

If possible, interview experts who can comment on your solution.

Prewriting/Planning Strategy

1. Introduce the prewriting strategy and the graphic organizer on the student page.
2. Have students apply the strategy to gather details.

Six Traits Focus

✓	Ideas		Word Choice
	Organization		Sentence Fluency
	Voice		Conventions

✅ STRATEGIES **FOR CLARIFYING EXPECTED OUTCOMES**

Using Rubrics

- Before students begin work on this assignment, have them preview the Rubric for Self-Assessment (p. 545) to learn what qualities their problem-and-solution essay must have. A copy of this rubric appears in the *Graphic Organizer* for this workshop.
- Review the criteria in the rubric with the class. Before students use the rubric to assess their own writing, work with them to rate the Student Model (p. 544) using the rubric.

- If you wish to assess students' problem-and-solution essays with either a 5-point or a 6-point scoring rubric, see *Professional Development Guidebook*, pp. 244–245.

Drafting Strategies

1. Introduce the drafting strategies on the student page.
2. Have students apply the strategies as they draft their essays.

Teaching the Strategies

1. Tell students to begin their essay with an introductory paragraph that clearly states the problem and solution or solutions.
2. Suggest that students end with a concluding paragraph that spurs readers to support the solution or solutions they have suggested.

Think Aloud: Model Audience Consideration

Stress that readers are more likely to accept ideas that seem relevant to their lives. Say to students:

> For an audience of sixth graders, I might open an essay about the problem of rising fuel costs by showing how the rising costs affect them: *Have you been upset by rising prices at your favorite store? The price of everything rises when fuel gets more expensive because it costs more to deliver merchandise to stores.*

Six Traits Focus

✓	Ideas		Word Choice
✓	Organization		Sentence Fluency
	Voice		Conventions

Drafting Strategies

State your thesis. Begin your essay with a clear thesis—one sentence that states both the problem and your proposed solution.

Explain the problem. Before presenting your solution in detail, you need to define the problem fully. Explain the situation using the evidence you gathered in your research. Along with discussing the scope of the problem, you might briefly describe its causes and effects.

Detail your solution. After you explain the problem, develop your solution with examples and details. Provide relevant evidence that shows why your solution will work. In addition, address possible objections to your solution. See the chart for suggestions.

Possible Objection	Response
The solution is not practical.	Give a real-life example in which a similar solution solved the problem.
The solution is expensive.	Compare the cost of the solution to the cost of the problem.
People will not support the solution.	Interview people about the solution and quote responses in favor of it.

After addressing possible objections, discuss the effects of your proposed solution.

Develop your conclusion. In your conclusion, remind readers about the nature of the problem. Then restate your solution and summarize why you think it will work.

Consider your audience. To achieve your overall purpose of persuading others to accept your proposed solution, keep your audience—your readers—in mind as you draft. Choose details that will show how the problem and solution affects your audience. To make your argument more convincing, establish and maintain a formal style.

Common Core State Standards

Writing
1.c. Use words, phrases, and clauses to clarify the relationships among claim(s) and reasons.
1.d. Establish and maintain a formal style.
1.e. Provide a concluding statement or section that follows from the argument presented.

Support Your Ideas

Providing Support In drafting your problem-and-solution essay, your first step is to explain the causes and effects of the problem and to explain why the problem needs to be solved. Your next step is to convince readers that your ideas for a solution will work. To do this, support your ideas with facts, details, examples, and explanations. Ask yourself the following questions about your solution:

- Is my solution practical? Can it really be done? If so, how?
- Has my solution ever been tried? If so, what was the result?
- Have experts considered my solution in the past? What did they say?
- What are the disadvantages of my solution?

For each of your proposed solutions, use a chart like the one below to determine whether or not you have adequate support for your ideas. The following example examines an idea that solves this problem: *Many students do not get adequate nutrition from their diets.*

Idea 1

Serve healthy food in the lunchroom.

Detail	Explanation	Fact	Example
A peanut butter and banana sandwich on whole-wheat bread, a slice of watermelon, and a glass of milk provide protein, complex carbohydrates, calcium, and potassium.	Studies show that students who get better nutrition at even one meal a day do better in school and get sick less often.	When other school districts switched to healthier lunch menus, student grades improved and students were out sick less often.	Healthy food can be tasty. For example, a strawberry-yogurt fruit smoothie is loaded with nutrients and good taste.

Support Your Ideas

1. Introduce the prewriting skill, using the instructions on the student page.
2. Have students use the recommendations, bulleted questions, and chart to help them support their ideas.

Teaching the Strategies

1. Have students elaborate on the problem they have chosen to address by identifying the causes and effects of the problem.
2. Tell students to list the solution or solutions they plan to offer and then to examine the effectiveness of each solution by asking and answering the bulleted questions on the student page.
3. Have students list the sources they plan to use to obtain facts, expert opinions, and other examples to support the ideas in their essays. Remind students using online sources to choose reliable Web sites, such as those of government agencies and respected reference works. Point out that some topics can be researched in part by conducting a survey; for example, the subject of food in the school lunchroom, touched on in the graphic organizer, might require a survey of students to see what they would eat and what amount they would be prepared to pay.

Revising Strategy

1. Introduce the revising strategy and graphic organizer.
2. Have students apply the strategy.

Teaching the Strategies

1. Have students work in pairs to read each other's problem-and-solution essays and identify where stronger support is needed.
2. After students read through the draft and identify places where there is lack of support, have them discuss what type of information should be added. Students may need to reorder the steps, explain how the information relates to the problem or solution, or add more facts.
3. Tell students that there are common problems that can confuse readers as they read problem-and-solution essays.
   - Readers can become confused when they do not understand the connections between one idea and the next.
   - Readers can become confused when they do not understand how information relates to the problem or solution.
4. Have students revise their essays, adding support where needed.

Think Aloud: Model Using Transitions

Model the strategy of adding supporting details, using the following think aloud. Say to students:

> I know that especially in a problem-and-solution essay, I have to make sure there is enough support for my position. Suppose I have written these sentences: *Our school needs healthier lunch options. A better lunch menu would include more smoothies, which have a lot of nutrients.* I have a lack of logic in my text. Without evidence to explain why our current lunches are unhealthy, readers may not believe that there is a problem.

Six Traits Focus

Ideas		Word Choice
Organization	✓	Sentence Fluency
Voice		Conventions

Revising Strategy

Revise the introduction for effect. Your readers do not necessarily see the problem or the solution as you do. You need to convince them your ideas are valid. Revise your opening paragraph to highlight the problem. You might use startling statistics, a powerful quotation from an expert, or the details of a dramatic event linked to the problem. This type of strong beginning will capture your readers' attention and make them eager to hear your proposed solution to the problem.

Revise to add support. Make sure to offer strong support for your position. Take the point of view of someone who has to be convinced about your solution. Then re-read your explanation of the solution. Does every point make sense? Are the points connected logically? Is there evidence that supports each step in the solution? Revise to correct any problems in these areas. Use the chart below as a guide to your revisions.

Weakness	Possible Corrections
Poor explanation of a step	• Rewrite to clarify what the step entails • Revise to explain how the step addresses one part of the problem
Lack of logic in steps	• Reorder the steps if they are not in sequence • If necessary, add an intermediate step
Lack of evidence	• Add more statistics, examples, facts, or quotations from your research

Peer Review

Ask a partner to read your draft and identify places where you lack support for your definition of the problem or for your solution. Consider adding more details. Ask your partner to read your draft and mark instances where standard English is not used. Make any necessary corrections.

Common Core State Standards

Writing
1.c. Use words, phrases, and clauses to clarify the relationships among claim(s) and reasons.
1.d. Establish and maintain a formal style.
1.e. Provide a concluding statement or section that follows from the argument presented.

Language
3. Use knowledge of language and its conventions when writing, speaking, reading, or listening.
3.a. Vary sentence patterns for meaning, reader/listener interest, and style.

✔ STRATEGIES **FOR USING TECHNOLOGY IN WRITING**

Explain that many word-processing programs are capable of making grammar checks that can correct sentence fragments and incorrect end punctuation. To use this tool, students will need to make sure that they have checked the appropriate boxes in their computer options to indicate that the computer should be checking grammar and also that it should consider punctuation and fragments. Emphasize that students should never blindly accept a grammar correction made by a computer but should instead consider it to see if it makes sense.

Combining Sentences for Variety

To add variety to your sentences, include prepositional phrases, appositive phrases, participial phrases, and gerund phrases.

Type of Phrase	Use	Example
Prepositional phrase	• as an adjective • as an adverb	The boy **in the red jacket** is my brother. The book fell **off the table**.
Appositive phrase	• as a noun phrase	Jim, a **7-year-old boy**, agreed.
Participial phrase	• as an adjective	The **completed** painting was lifelike. **Arriving on Friday**, the package was late.
Gerund phrase	• as a noun	**Playing the guitar** is relaxing.

Combining Sentences for Variety

To add variety to your sentence patterns, include prepositional phrases, appositive phrases, participial phrases, or gerund phrases.

Combining Short Sentences The examples show how to use these four kinds of phrases to pack information into your sentences.

- **Using a Prepositional Phrase**
  Separate: The bus moved slowly. The road was wet.
  Combined: The bus moved slowly *along the wet road*.

- **Using an Appositive Phrase**
  Separate: Henry likes to ride a bike. He is a healthy 89-year-old.
  Combined: Henry, *a healthy 89-year-old,* likes to ride a bike.

- **Using a Participial Phrase**
  Separate: We ran out of water. We were thirsty.
  Combined: *Having run out of water,* we were thirsty.

- **Using a Gerund Phrase**
  Separate: Do not order beef. It would be a mistake.
  Combined: *Ordering beef* would be a mistake.

Fixing Choppy Sentences To fix choppy sentences, follow these steps:
1. **Look for the relationship among ideas.**
2. **Combine sentences to stress these connections among ideas.**

Grammar in Your Writing

Read your problem-and-solution essay, looking for pairs of short, related sentences. Using the examples as a guide, combine some for variety.

Combining Sentences for Variety

1. Introduce the grammar skill, using the instruction on the student page.

2. Discuss the rules and examples, as well as the strategies for fixing incorrect usage.

3. Have students follow the instruction under Grammar in Your Writing to correct errors in their drafts.

Teaching the Grammar Skill

Have students use the techniques described in the textbook to combine the following sentences.

Prepositional Phrase:

The house was dark. We couldn't find the stairs. (**Possible response:** We couldn't find the stairs inside the dark house.)

Appositive Phrase:

I went fishing with Sam. Sam is my neighbor's cousin. (**Possible response:** I went fishing with Sam, my neighbor's cousin.)

Participial Phrase:

It was a beautiful day. I went for a walk. (**Possible response:** It being a beautiful day, so I went for a walk.)

Gerund Phrase:

We couldn't get out of the parking lot. It was a nightmare. (**Possible response:** Getting out of the parking lot was a nightmare.)

Student Model

Review the Student Model with the class, using the annotations to analyze the writer's use of the elements of a problem-and-solution essay.

Teaching From the Student Model

1. Point out that Shamus opens his essay with a statement designed to spark reader interest by calling the panther interesting.

2. **Ask** students to identify the problem and two-step solution in the essay. (**Problem:** The Florida panther is nearing extinction; **Solutions:** Set aside enough land for panthers and make sure they can move through it safely.)

3. Elicit that the carefully researched statistics ("sixty panthers," "275 square miles," "42% of panther deaths," and so on) offer detailed support that makes the writer's ideas more convincing to readers.

4. **Ask** students to explain the cause-and-effect relationships in the third paragraph. (**Answer:** More houses cause more roads, which cause more panthers to die as road kill. Underpasses result in panthers being able to cross an area safely, which results in fewer panther deaths.)

5. Point out that Shamus concludes with a paragraph that sums up his ideas and helps convince readers to accept them. **Ask** what makes the last sentence convincing. (**Possible answer:** It suggests that readers are involved in "putting our heads together" and expresses confidence that the suggested solutions will work.)

Connecting to Real-Life Writing

Let students know that there are many careers and activities that call on short story writing skills. News reporters use literary elements to tell stories that are true. Magazines and newspapers often have story writing contests, and many high schools and colleges have literary magazines that print student work. In addition, the skills used to write stories can be transferred easily to writing for the stage, television, and movies.

STUDENT MODEL: **Shamus Cunningham, Dayton Beach, FL**  Common Core State Standards

Language
2.b. Spell correctly.

Panther Problems

The Florida panther is one of our state's most interesting animals, but sadly, it is also one of the rarest. There are currently only about sixty panthers in Florida. Panther numbers don't grow because of shrinking panther habitat and increasing traffic in areas populated by panthers. To save panthers from extinction, we must make sure there is enough land set aside for panthers to live on and that they have safe ways to move through the areas in which they live.

> Shamus states his thesis in the first paragraph and suggests a two-step solution to the problem.

A grown panther needs approximately 275 square miles to roam and hunt. If too many adult panthers occupy the same territory, they fight and injure or kill one another. In addition, panthers hunt other wild animals, such as deer, for food. To be a good habitat for a panther, an area must have prey animals for the panther to hunt. Because of development, the "wild" areas that panthers used to call home are now filled with houses and stores rather than food and hiding places. It is unlikely that development will suddenly stop or even slow down. Therefore, experts must plan ahead and set aside one or two large protected areas where panthers can live, rather than many smaller areas.

> The problem is explained in more detail so that readers will understand the value of the proposed solution.

> Transition words such as "because" and "therefore" show cause-and-effect relationships.

Loss of habitat isn't the only problem caused by development. More houses means more roads, and that means more problems for panthers. According to the Florida Game and Freshwater Fish Commission, 42% of panther deaths in a recent twenty-five-year period were road kills. Underpasses have been built to allow panthers and other animals to cross a territory without crossing a road. In an area known as Alligator Alley, one large underpass was built. Since then, there have been no reported killings of panthers by cars. The success of the underpass in this area shows that we can protect panthers without halting progress.

> Each part of the problem and its solution is addressed in a separate paragraph. Statistics provide evidence that a solution is needed and that the proposed solution is the right one.

The two solutions suggested here would meet the needs of humans and panthers. The solutions are costly, but they have been proven effective, and they are the least disruptive to the human community. Saving the Florida panther is a complex issue, but if we put our heads together, I'm confident we will make the right decisions.

✔ STRATEGIES **FOR TEST TAKING**

When taking a test that includes a problem-and-solution writing prompt, students should pay special attention to the clarity of their writing. Remind them to state clearly the problem and the solution or solutions they offer, supporting their ideas with ample evidence.

Students should carefully organize their essays with cause-and-effect terms such as *because, therefore,* and *for that reason* that help make the relationships between ideas clear. Before submitting their essays, students should review them for overall coherence and unity.

Editing and Proofreading

Proofread your draft to correct errors in spelling, grammar, and punctuation.

Focus on words with suffixes. **Suffixes** are word parts that are added to the ends of base words. To spell a word with a suffix, remember the following rules:

Suffixes that begin with a consonant *(-ful, -tion,-ly)*: Change final *y* to *i* in the base word, unless a vowel precedes the *y*.

Suffixes beginning with a vowel: Change final *y* to *i* in the base word, unless a vowel precedes the *y*. Usually, drop the final *e* in the base word.

Publishing and Presenting

Consider one of the following ways to share your writing:

Present a proposal. Use your problem-and-solution essay as the basis for a presentation.

Submit your paper for publication. Send a clean copy to your school paper or local newspaper. Include a cover letter.

Reflecting on Your Writing

Writer's Journal Jot down your answer to this question:
Who can implement the solutions proposed in your essay?

Rubric for Self-Assessment

Find evidence in your writing to address each category. Then, use the rating scale to grade your work.

Criteria	Rating Scale			
Purpose/Focus Presents a clear problem and proposed solution; supports the solution with clear reasons and relevant evidence, using credible sources; addresses possible objections to the solution	*not very* .... *very* 1	2	3	4
Organization Introduces the problem and solution; has a concluding section that follows logically from the argument presented	1	2	3	4
Development of Ideas/Elaboration Organizes reasons and evidence clearly and logically; establishes and maintains a formal style	1	2	3	4
Language Uses precise language to strengthen the argument; uses words, phrases, and clauses to clarify the relationships among ideas	1	2	3	4
Conventions Varies sentence patterns for meaning, interest, and style	1	2	3	4

Spiral Review
Earlier in the unit, you learned about **prepositions and appositives** (p. 486) and **participles and gerunds** (p. 520). Review your essay to be sure that you have used these elements correctly.

Editing and Proofreading

1. Introduce the editing and proofreading focus, using the instruction on the student page.
2. Have students edit and proofread their narratives, correcting grammar, spelling, punctuation, and word choice. Make sure they check for errors of the type noted in the lesson focus and the Spiral Review.

Teaching the Editing Focus

Clarify the spelling rules by providing examples:

When adding a suffix that begins with a consonant to a word that ends in a vowel + *y*, generally change the *y* to *i*: *day* + *-ly* = *daily*

When adding a suffix that begins with a vowel to a word that ends in a consonant + *y*, generally change the *y* to *i*: *family* + *-es* = *families*

Six Traits Focus

Ideas	Word Choice
Organization	Sentence Fluency
Voice	✓ Conventions

✅ ASSESS

Publishing and Presenting

1. Students' oral presentations should include charts or other visuals illustrating key points.
2. Tell students that the cover letter accompanying their newspaper submissions should identify the contents as a sixth-grade school essay being submitted as a guest editorial. Remind students to use proper business-letter form.

Reflecting on Your Writing

In responding to the question in their journals, tell students to consider individuals, private organizations, and government agencies that could implement their proposals.

 Interactive Whiteboard Activities

Use this tool to project and edit student writing!

🐾 DIFFERENTIATED INSTRUCTION

Strategy for Less Proficient Writers
Help students map out the causes and effects in their essays by using graphic organizers. Students should list each cause and then use an arrow to point to its effect, showing chain reactions of causes and effects where appropriate. When a cause has more than one effect, students should use multiple arrows.

EL Strategy for English Learners
Pair English learners with students whose native language is English to work on their essays. Student pairs should work together on the prewriting activities on pages 538–539 as they each draft their essays. They should also work together in the revising stage, offering suggestions for improvements.

Strategy for Gifted/Talented Students
Encourage students talented in art, drama, or music to use those talents in presenting their essays to classmates. For example, students might create computer graphics or sketches to illustrate oral presentations of their essays, or they might present their ideas in dramatic skits with musical accompaniment.

Assessment

In this assessment (pp. 546–551), students apply and reinforce their mastery of the Common Core State Standards and the skills taught in Unit 4. The assessment is divided into four sections, including a section of Constructed Response tasks.

1. Before assigning each section, review the relevant Common Core State Standards and Unit skills with students.

2. Set a time limit for the multiple choice items in each section, allowing a little over one minute per question. Allow twenty minutes for any Timed Writing questions.

3. Administer each of the first three sections of the assessment (pp. 546–549).

4. Use the Constructed Response tasks on pages 550–551 to assess the depth of students' mastery of standards taught in the unit. Follow the suggestions on teacher pages 550–551 for assigning tasks and for supporting and evaluating student performance.

Reteaching Skills

For each practice, use the Reteaching Plan on the same page as the answers to determine which skills require reteaching, given the items students answered incorrectly.

Question	Instructional Pages to Reteach
1	458
2	488
3	458
4	523
5	458
6	—
7	—
8	458, 488

Assessment: Skills

SELECTED RESPONSE

Common Core State Standards

RL.6.1, RL.6.2, RL.6.3, RL.6.4; W.6.3, W.6.4
[For the full wording of the standards, see the standards chart in the front of your textbook.]

I. Reading Literature

Directions: *Read the passage from the play* Pygmalion, *by George Bernard Shaw. Then, answer each question that follows.*

HENRY HIGGINS: The science of speech. That's my profession; also my hobby. Happy is the man who can make a living by his hobby! You can spot an Irishman or a Yorkshireman by his brogue. I can place any man within six miles. I can place him within two miles in London. Sometimes within two streets.

ELIZA: Ought to be ashamed of himself, unmanly coward!

COLONEL PICKERING: But is there a living in that?

HENRY HIGGINS: Oh yes. Quite a fat one. This is an age of upstarts. Men begin in Kentish Town with 80 pounds a year, and end in Park Lane with a hundred thousand. They want to drop Kentish Town; but they give themselves away every time they open their mouths. Now I can teach them—

ELIZA: Let him mind his own business and leave a poor girl—

HENRY HIGGINS: [Explosively.] Woman: cease this <u>detestable</u> boohooing instantly; or else seek the shelter of some other place of worship.

ELIZA: [With feeble defiance.] I've a right to be here if I like, same as you.

HENRY HIGGINS: A woman who utters such depressing and disgusting sounds has no right to be anywhere—no right to live. Remember that you are a human being with a soul and the divine gift of articulate speech: that your native language is the language of Shakespeare and Milton and The Bible; and don't sit there crooning like a bilious pigeon.

ELIZA: [Quite overwhelmed, and looking up at him in mingled wonder and deprecation without daring to raise her head.] Ah—ah—ah—ow—ow—oo!

HENRY HIGGINS: [Whipping out his book.] Heavens! what a sound! [He writes; then holds out the book and reads, reproducing her vowels exactly] Ah—ah—ah—ow—ow—oo!

ELIZA: [Tickled by the performance, and laughing in spite of herself.] Garn!

HENRY HIGGINS: You see this creature with her kerbstone English: the English that will keep her in the gutter to the end of her days. Well, sir, in three months I could pass that girl off as a duchess at an ambassador's garden party. I could even get her a place as lady's maid or shop assistant, which requires better English...

546 UNIT 4 • How do we decide who we are?

✓ STRATEGIES **FOR TEST TAKING**

Remind students to pace themselves when taking a test. Point out that writing questions take more time to answer than multiple-choice items, since they need time to analyze the prompt; develop their ideas; organize their response; write the assignment; and review their writing to fix any problems with spelling, grammar, or punctuation. Since these questions are more elaborate, students need to set aside more time for them.

1. **Part A** What main problem does the **dialogue** in this passage reveal?
   A. Henry Higgins cannot make a living.
   B. Henry Higgins does not like Eliza.
   C. Eliza does not like Henry Higgins.
   D. Eliza has poor English skills.

   Part B Which phrase from the passage's **dialogue** helped you determine the play's main problem?
   A. "Happy is the man who can make a living by his hobby!"
   B. "I've a right to be here if I like"
   C. "Remember that you are a human being"
   D. "the English that will keep her in the gutter to the end of her days"

2. Why do the **stage directions** in the play include descriptions such as *Explosively* and *With feeble defiance*?
   A. so actors will know where to stand
   B. so the audience will know where to look
   C. so actors will know how to react to one another
   D. so actors will know what to wear

3. **Part A** What does Henry Higgins's **dialogue** tell you about his character?
   A. He strongly believes that correct speech is of great value.
   B. He is easily excited.
   C. He has no desire to help anyone but himself.
   D. He thinks he is very smart, but he is not.

   Part B Which phrase from the passage best supports the answer to Part A?
   A. "Happy is the man who can make a living by his hobby!"

   B. "Remember that you are a human being with a soul and the divine gift of articulate speech"
   C. "Men begin in Kentish Town with 80 pounds a year"
   D. "I could pass that girl off as a duchess at an ambassador's garden party!"

4. Which of these is most likely the **author's purpose** for writing this play?
   A. to entertain   C. to inform
   B. to persuade   D. to explain

5. Which of these would most likely serve as a prop in this **drama**?
   A. a handkerchief   C. a pigeon
   B. a small notebook D. an umbrella

6. Why does Henry Higgins write down what Eliza says when she says "Ah—ah—ah—ow—ow—oo!"?
   A. He is mocking her poor speech.
   B. He is trying to tell if she is from Ireland.
   C. He is trying to make her go away.
   D. He wants to remember her words.

7. Which word is closest in meaning to the underlined word *detestable*?
   A. excited   C. amazing
   B. challenging D. hateful

 Timed Writing

8. In an essay, tell what the **stage directions** and **dialogue** in this passage reveal about Eliza. Support your analysis with details from the passage.

GO ON

 ASSESS

I. Reading Literature
1. **Part A:** D
   Part B: D
2. C
3. **Part A:** A
   Part B: B
4. A
5. B
6. A
7. D

Timed Writing
8. Student essays should tell what the stage directions and dialogue in this passage reveal about Eliza.

 **ASSESS**

II. Reading Informational Text

1. Part A: A
   Part B: C

II. Reading Informational Text

Directions: *Read the passage below. Then, answer each question that follows.*

 Common Core
State Standards

RI.6.1, RI.6.5; W.6.2.e;
L.6.1, L.6.2.a, L.6.3,
L.6.3.a, L.6.3.b
[For the full wording of the standards, see the standards chart in the front of your textbook.]

> It is important that our school begin a recycling program. Our trash cans are brimming with bottles and cans that students carelessly toss away. The school community wastes thousands of pieces of paper every day, all of which is discarded. Recycling can reduce this waste. My family has reduced our waste by 30% by recycling.
>
> Recycling has countless benefits for the school community and for the environment. Every ton of paper that is recycled will save 3.3 cubic yards of landfill space. Soda bottles can be turned into clothing or other useful items, instead of clogging landfills. Recycling will teach us all the value of working together to achieve a common goal. Some students have already voiced interest in this program.
>
> Currently, this school has no environmental initiative in place. Our town's Department of Public Works is willing to donate recycling bins in our cafeteria for bottles and cans, and bins for paper recycling in each classroom. Once a week, a recycling truck will pick up the recyclables, just as the garbage truck comes to pick up the trash. That leaves the school community to place their paper, bottles, and cans in the appropriate bins, instead of the trash cans. This program will prove to have many benefits.

1. Part A What is the main argument made by the author of the persuasive letter above?

   A. Students throw away too much trash.
   B. Recycling trucks help play a role in reducing the amount of trash in school.
   C. All schools should have some sort of environmental initiative in place.
   D. Recycling benefits the environment.

Part B What detail from the letter best supports the answer to Part A?

   A. "Every ton of paper that is recycled will save 3.3 cubic yards of landfill space."
   B. "Currently, this school has no environmental initiative in place."
   C. "Our trash cans are brimming with bottles and cans that students carelessly toss away."
   D. "Once a week, a recycling truck will pick up the recyclables, just as the garbage truck comes to pick up the trash."

III. Writing and Language Conventions

Directions: *Read the letter. Then, answer each question.*

> Mr. Allan Reeves
> 13 Riverside Circle
> New York, New York 10007
> Dear Mr. Reeves:
> (1) I just finished reading your book *Common Denominators.*
> (2) I can't believe how awesome it was! (3) I read the story of
> the people lost at sea. (4) I was struck by their courage after
> they suffered through several disasters. (5) After reading their
> story, I wondered if I could survive such a frightening situation.
> (6) I hope you continue to write stories of courage and survival
> against the odds. (7) I think these stories inspire others, especially
> young readers. (8) I know they inspire me.
> Sincerely yours,
> Savion Miller

1. Which sentence contains an **appositiive phrase**?

A. sentence 5
B. sentence 6
C. sentence 7
D. sentence 8

2. Which sentence contains a **prepositional phrase**?

A. sentence 5
B. sentence 6
C. sentence 7
D. sentence 8

3. Which word in sentence 1 is a **gerund**?

A. just
B. finished
C. reading
D. book

4. Which of the following revisions best combines sentences 3 and 4 using a **participial phrase?**

A. Reading the story of the people lost at sea, I was struck by their courage.
B. I read the story of the people lost at sea, struck by their courage.
C. Struck by their courage, I read the story of the people lost at sea.
D. I read the story of the people lost at sea, and I was struck by their courage.

✓ ASSESS

III. Writing and Language Conventions

1. C
2. B
3. C
4. A

Reteaching Plan

Question	Pages to Reteach
1	486, 543
2	486, 543
3	520, 543
4	520, 543

Constructed Response

Assigning Tasks/Reteaching Skills

Use the chart below to choose appropriate Constructed Response tasks by identifying which tasks assess lessons in the textbook that you have taught. Use the same lessons for reteaching when students' performance indicates a failure to fully master a standard. For additional instruction and practice, assign the *Common Core Companion* pages indicated for each task.

Task	Where Taught/ Pages to Reteach	Common Core Companion Pages
1	454–457	41–53, 184–195
2	454–457	54–60, 184–195
3	454–457	15–27, 184–195
4	454–457	28–40, 304–310, 335–338, 353–354
5	454–457, 523	61–67, 304–310
6	454–457	15–27, 246–252, 253–266

Assessment Pacing

In assigning the Writing tasks on this student page, allow a class period for the completion of a task. As an alternative, assign tasks as homework. In assigning the Speaking and Listening tasks on the facing page, consider having students do any required preparation as a homework assignment. Then, allow a class period for the presentations themselves.

Evaluating Constructed Response

Use the rubric at the bottom of this teacher edition page to evaluate students' mastery of the standards as demonstrated in their Constructed Responses. Review the rubric with students before they begin work so they know the criteria by which their work will be evaluated.

CONSTRUCTED RESPONSE

Directions: *Follow the instructions to complete the tasks below as required by your teacher.*

As you work on each task, incorporate both general academic vocabulary and literary terms you learned in Parts 1 and 2.

 Common Core State Standards

RL.6.2, RL.6.3, RL.6.4, RL.6.5; RI.6.6; W.6.2, W.6.2.b, W.6.2.c, W.6.7, W.6.8; SL.6.4; L.6.3, L.6.6

[For the full wording of the standards, see the standards chart in the front of your textbook.]

Writing

TASK 1 Literature [RL.6.4; W.6.2]

Analyze Connotation

Write an essay in which you analyze the connotative meanings of words and their impact on mood or tone in a drama.

- From one of the drama in Part 2 Consider the shades of meaning the words express.
- Analyze the impact that the connotative meanings of the words have on the mood or tone of the play. Explain the words' effect on the play's overall meaning.
- Write a short essay in which you tell how the mood or tone of the play would be affected if the author had chosen words with similar definitions but different connotations.
- Present your ideas in a logical order. Use details from the text to support your ideas.

TASK 2 Literature [RL.6.5; W.6.2.b, W.6.2.c; W.6.2]

Analyze Characters and Conflict

Write an essay in which you analyze how the dialogue used in two different dramas from Part 2 shows the conflicts felt by characters.

- Choose two dramas from Part 2. Look for stage directions and dialogue that show internal or external conflict among characters.

- Write a short essay in which you explain how the stage directions or dialogue present the conflict experienced by the characters.
- Develop your analysis with relevant details, information, or examples from the both dramas.
- Use appropriate transitions to show relationships between your ideas.

TASK 3 Literature [RL.6.2; W.6.2]

Summarize and Determine Theme

Write a summary of one of the dramatic selections in Part 2 and state the work's theme.

Part 1
- Choose a drama selection from Part 2.
- Identify the major events in the drama, and determine why each of these events is important. Make notes of your findings.

Part 2
- Write an essay in which you summarize the drama.
- State the theme of the drama. Your summary of important events and main points should lead to and support your statement of the theme.

CONSTRUCTED RESPONSE RUBRIC: STANDARDS MASTERY

	Rating Scale
Critical Thinking: How clearly and consistently does the student pursue the specific mode of reasoning or discourse required by the standard, as specified in the prompt (e.g., comparing and contrasting, analyzing, explaining)?	*not very* *very* 1 2 3 4 5
Focus: How well does the student understand and apply the focus concepts of the standard, as specified in the prompt (e.g., development of theme or of complex characters, effects of structure, and so on)?	*not very* *very* 1 2 3 4 5
Support/Elaboration: How well does the student support points with textual or other evidence? How relevant, sufficient, and varied is the evidence provided?	*not very* *very* 1 2 3 4 5
Insight: How original, sophisticated, or compelling are the insights the student achieves by applying the standard to the text(s)?	*not very* *very* 1 2 3 4 5
Expression of Ideas: How well does the student organize and support ideas? How well does the student use language, including word choice and conventions, in the expression of ideas?	*not very* *very* 1 2 3 4 5

Speaking and Listening

TASK 4 Literature [RL.6.3; SL.6.4; L.6.3, L.6.6]

Analyze Plot Structure

Give an oral presentation in which you analyze the plot of a drama from Part 2.

- Describe how the play's plot unfolds in episodes. Determine the conflicts—both internal and external—and the plot structure: points at which the conflicts are introduced (exposition), developed (rising action), reach their greatest tension (climax), begin to be settled (falling action), and the ending (resolution) of the play.
- Visually display the key episodes in a plot diagram. You might draw a poster or create a brief slide show.
- Accurately use academic vocabulary in your presentation.

TASK 5 Literature [RL.6.6; SL.6.4]

Analyze Author's Purpose

Give an oral presentation analyzing an author's purpose in a drama.

- Select a play from Part 2 and determine the author's purpose in writing it. For example, the author might be trying to persuade, inform, or entertain.
- Analyze the way in which the author's purpose is conveyed in the play. Use of evidence, reasoning, or persuasive language by a certain character may point to the author's purpose.
- Include a visual display such as a graphic organizer to help present your information clearly.
- As you present, speak loudly enough to be heard well, and pronounce your words clearly.

Research

TASK 6 Literature [RL.6.2; W.6.7, W.6.8]

 How do we decide who we are?

The plays in Part 2 explore the ways in which people learn about themselves and each other. Conduct a short research project on different situations that help people learn about themselves and others, such as learning new skills, visiting new places, getting to know people who are different from oneself, or facing a difficult challenge.

Use both the literature you have read and your research to reflect on this unit's Big Question. Review the following guidelines before you begin your research:

- Focus your research on one way people learn about themselves and others.
- Gather relevant information from at least two reliable sources. Your sources may be print or digital.
- Take notes as you research.
- Cite your sources.

When you have completed your research, write a response to the Big Question. Discuss how your initial ideas have been either changed or reinforced. Support your response with an example from literature and an example from your research.

✦ DIFFERENTIATED INSTRUCTION

Strategy for Less Proficient Readers

Assign a Constructed Response task, and then have students meet in groups to review the standard assessed in that task. Remind students of the selections or independent readings to which they have previously applied the standard. Have groups summarize what they learned in applying the standard and then present their summaries. Discuss, clarifying any points of confusion. After students have completed their tasks, have groups meet again to evaluate members' work. Encourage members to revise their work based on the feedback they receive.

ⓔ Strategy for English Learners

For each assigned Constructed Response task, review the instructions with students. Clarify the meaning of any unfamiliar vocabulary, emphasizing routine classroom words such as *evidence, excerpt,* and *explanation,* and academic vocabulary such as *describe.*

Next, have students note ideas for their responses. Pair students, and have them review each other's notes, asking questions to clarify meaning and suggesting improvements. Encourage students to ask for your assistance in supplying English words or expressions they may require.

Supporting Speaking and Listening

1. Consider having students work with partners or in groups to complete Constructed Response tasks involving listening and speaking. For tasks that you assign for individual work, you may still wish to have students rehearse with partners, who can provide constructive feedback.

2. As students rehearse, have them keep in mind these tips:
   - Present findings and evidence clearly and concisely.
   - Observe conventions of standard English grammar and usage.
   - Be relaxed and friendly but maintain a formal tone.
   - Make eye contact with the audience, pronounce words clearly, and vary your pace.
   - When working with a group, respond thoughtfully to others' positions, modifying your own in response to new evidence.

Linking Constructed Response to Independent Reading

If you wish to cover the standards with students' independent reading, adapt Constructed Response tasks of your choice to the works they have selected. (Independent reading suggestions appear on the next page.)

How do we decide who we are?

1. Remind students that the unit Big Question is "How do we decide who we are?"

2. Have students complete their responses to the prompt on the student page. Point out that they have read selections in this unit about different approaches to or views of self-knowledge and that they should draw on these selections in their responses. Remind them that they can also draw on their own experiences and what they have learned in other subject areas in formulating their answers.

❶ About the Quotation

H.L. Mencken (1880–1956) was an American journalist and social critic.

Discussion: Ask students to discuss the meaning of Mencken's quotation about Mark Twain. Then ask them to decide whether they agree with the quotation. Have them explain and support their positions with sound reasoning and evidence.

❷ Critical Viewing

Pose the critical viewing question to the class. Then, guide the class in a discussion about the question. Encourage students to build upon each other's ideas as they share their responses. Remind students to support their responses with reasons and evidence.

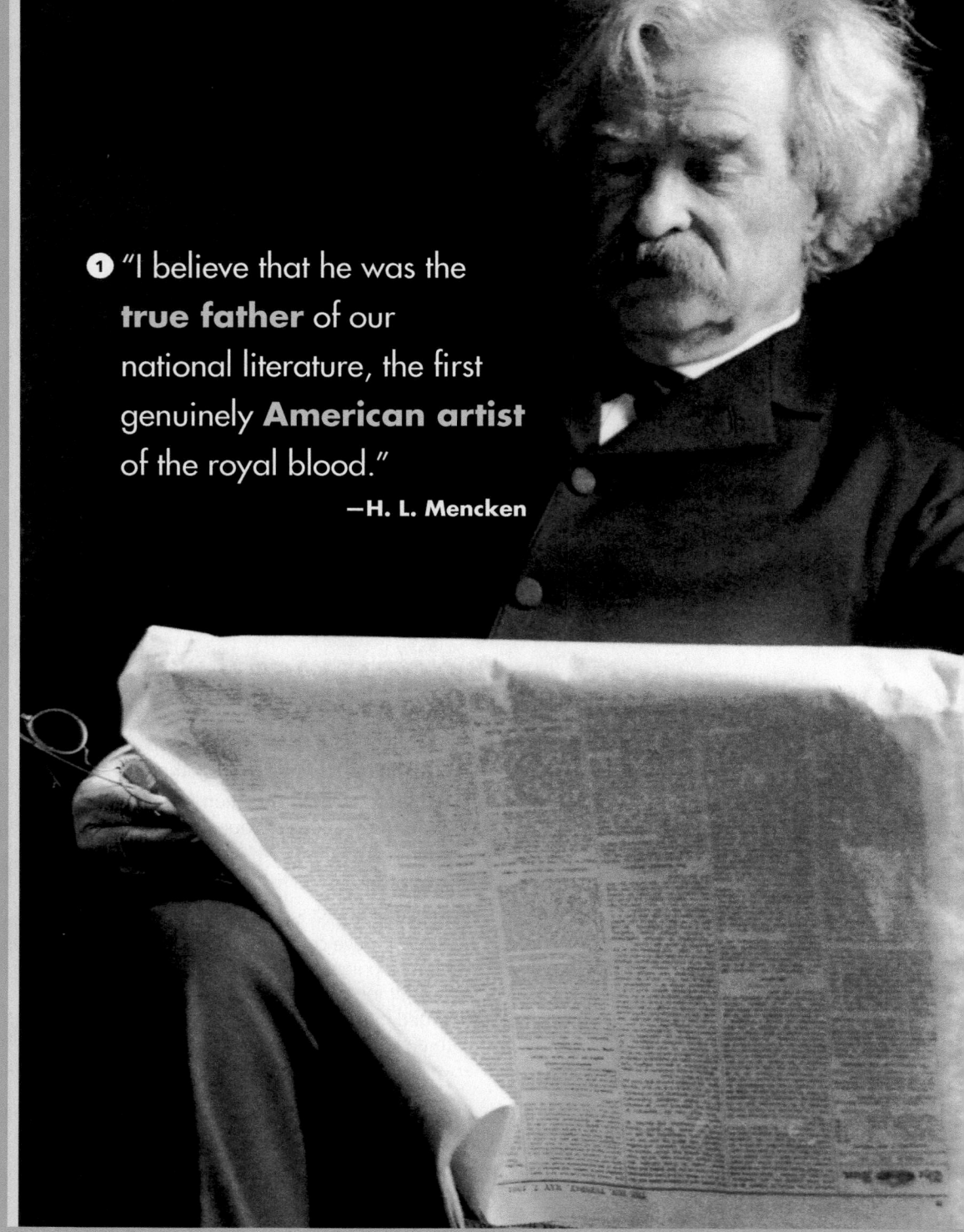

❶ "I believe that he was the **true father** of our national literature, the first genuinely **American artist** of the royal blood."

—H. L. Mencken

❓ DEVELOPING ESSENTIAL UNDERSTANDING

Mark Twain

Students will read several selections by and about Mark Twain. As a humorist, moralist, and novelist, Twain explored several aspects of human nature, including the effects of our actions and how we define our identities. Although many literary works offer views on identity, Twain's works often use humor to convey ideas and explore them in new ways. The selections in this multi-genre text set will help students develop essential understanding about Mark Twain by raising questions such as:

- How does Twain explore ideas about identity in his writing?
- How does Twain use his own experiences to define himself and create his characters?
- Why is it important to decide on and form your own identity?

PART 3
TEXT SETS DEVELOPING INSIGHT

MARK TWAIN

The selections in this unit all deal with the Big Question: **How do we decide who we are?** The texts that follow explore the distinctive identity and singular career of Mark Twain: as a novelist, a humorist, a public speaker, and even a father. As you read, consider the ways in which Mark Twain's personal reflections and experiences helped shape him into one of America's most remarkable literary voices.

2 ◀ CRITICAL VIEWING How does this image of Mark Twain compare and contrast with H. L. Menken's description?

🔍📧 **CLOSE READING TOOL**

Use the Close Reading Tool to practice the strategies you learned in this unit.

READINGS IN PART 3

ANCHOR TEXT
PLAY • NOVEL EXCERPT
The Prince and the Pauper • *from* The Prince and the Pauper
Mark Twain
(p. 554 • p. 572)

SPEECH
Stage Fright
Mark Twain (p. 580)

BIOGRAPHY
My Papa, Mark Twain
Susy Clemens (p. 584)

INTERVIEW
Mark Twain's First "Vacation"
The New York World
(p. 590)

QUOTATIONS
According to Mark Twain
Mark Twain (p. 594)

SHORT STORY
An Encounter With an Interviewer
Mark Twain (p. 596)

PART 3 • Mark Twain **553**

CUSTOMIZING THE TEXT SET

Close Reading Tool
Use the Close Reading Tool to project the anchor text on a whiteboard and work through it as a whole-class activity. Students also have the opportunity to read this selection independently, with scaffolds available as needed.

Curriculum Builder
Customize this program by rearranging existing selections, adding selection titles of your choosing, and uploading your own resources—all online!

3 Readings in Part 3
About the Texts

(For quantitative and qualitative measures of text complexity, see the rubrics on the opening pages of each selection.)

PLAY • NOVEL EXCERPT: The Prince and the Pauper • *from* The Prince and the Pauper

In the play a prince and a pauper exchange identities. The novel excerpt provides a description of each boy's birth and details about how the Prince and the pauper meet for the first time.

SPEECH: Stage Fright

Twain humorously explains his plan to make everything go perfectly during his first public lecture.

BIOGRAPHY: My Papa, Mark Twain

Twain's daughter shares humorous anecdotes about Twain.

INTERVIEW: Mark Twain's First "Vacation"

Twain describes his childhood adventure as a rain-soaked stowaway on a Mississippi steamboat.

QUOTATIONS: According to Mark Twain

This media text shows several of Twain's humorous advice quotations.

SHORT STORY: An Encounter With an Interviewer

This short story is a fictional interview of Twain, filled with humor and non-sensical dialogue.

Extended Reading Opportunity

INFORMATIONAL TEXT: Small Things Considered: Why There Is No Perfect Design

You may want to assign this extended reading to accompany the readings in Part 3. Further details about this text and other extended readings appear on the Independent Reading pages at the end of this unit.

 Audio

Summary Audio is available in the *Student eText* and on the *Hear It!* CD-ROM.

PART 3 • Mark Twain **553**

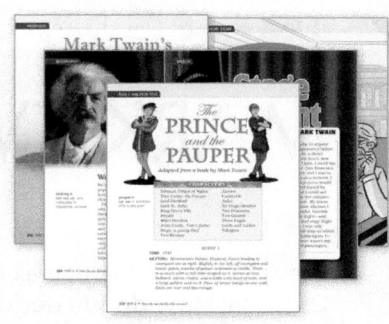

LESSON PACING GUIDE

ANCHOR TEXT (5 DAYS)

The Prince and the Pauper

DAY 1 Preteach/Teach

- Introduce the topic of the text set and its relationship to the Big Question.
- To motivate and engage students, discuss the quotation and the Critical Viewing question.
- Direct students to read the selection independently.

DAYS 2–4 Teach/Extend

- Use the Comprehension questions to confirm student understanding of the text.
- Develop vocabulary by assigning and monitoring the Language Study activities.
- Develop analytic ability by reviewing the Literary Analysis questions and instruction.
- Assign the Group Discussion and monitor responses to discussion questions.
- Assign the Writing to Sources activity, distributing copies of the Take Notes worksheet to help students organize their thoughts and information.

DAY 5 Extend/Assess

- Preview the Research activity, distributing copies of the Take Notes worksheet to help students plan their note-taking strategy. Assign the activity as homework.
- Administer the Selection Test or the Open-Book Test to monitor student progress.

RELATED TEXTS (2 DAYS EACH)

Stage Fright • My Papa, Mark Twain • Mark Twain's First "Vacation" • According to Mark Twain • An Encounter With an Interviewer

DAY 1 Preteach/Teach

- Review with students the topic of the text set and what they have learned from the previous readings.
- Build knowledge of the topic by directing students to read the text independently.
- Develop vocabulary by reviewing the Language Study activities.
- Build students' ability to think critically using the Literary Analysis questions.

DAY 2 Extend/Assess

- Extend exploration of the text through the Discuss, Research, and Write activities.
- Administer the Selection Test or the Open-Book Test to monitor student progress.

ASSESSMENT: SYNTHESIS (1–2 DAYS)

DAYS 1–2 Assess

- Review with the class the Criteria for Success for the Speaking and Listening activity. Assign the activity, and monitor student progress.
- Review with students the Criteria for Success for the Writing assignment, and assign the activity.
- Review with students the Self-Evaluation Rubric for the Writing to Sources activity. Direct students to complete the assignment.

**Common Core
State Standards**

Reading Literature 1, 2, 4, 5, 6
Reading Informational Text 1, 2, 3, 4, 5, 6
Writing 1, 1a, 2, 2a-f, 3, 4
Speaking and Listening 1, 1a-d, 2, 5
Language 4, 4a, 4d, 5, 6

Daily Block Scheduling

Each day in this Lesson Pacing Guide represents a 40–50 minute period. Teachers using block scheduling may combine days to revise pacing. In addition, teachers may differentiate and support core instruction by integrating components for extended and intensive support as students require. See the Guide to Resources (facing page).

GUIDE TO RESOURCES

RESOURCES	WHERE FOUND			ANCHOR TEXT The Prince and the Pauper	Stage Fright	My Papa, Mark Twain	Mark Twain's First "Vacation"	According to Mark Twain	An Encounter With an Interviewer
	PRINT	CD	ONLINE						
SELECTION SUPPORT 👤 👥 👨‍👩‍👦									
Close Reading Practice	CRN		✔	✔					
Academic Vocabulary	SCW		✔	✔	✔	✔	✔	✔	✔
Discussion: Take Notes worksheet	SCW		✔	✔	✔	✔	✔	✔	✔
Writing to Sources	SCW		✔	✔	✔	✔	✔	✔	✔
Research: Take Notes worksheet	SCW		✔	✔	✔	✔	✔	✔	✔
STANDARDS SUPPORT 👨‍👩‍👦									
Standards Instruction and Practice	CCC		✔	✔	✔	✔	✔	✔	✔
MONITOR PROGRESS Ⓐ									
Selection Test		EV	✔	✔	✔	✔	✔		✔
Open-Book Test		EV	✔	✔	✔	✔	✔		✔
ASSESSMENT: SYNTHESIS GRAPHIC ORGANIZERS AND RUBRICS 👤									
Speaking and Listening: Graphic Organizer			✔						
Writing: Graphic Organizer			✔						
Writing to Sources: Graphic Organizer			✔						
Self-Evaluation Rubric			✔						
DIGITAL RESOURCES 🖥️									
Close Reading Tool			✔	✔					
Online Writer's Notebook			✔	✔	✔	✔	✔	✔	✔

CRN Close Reading Notebook **SCW** Student Companion All-in-One Workbook **EV** ExamView **CCC** Common Core Companion

👥 Group work 👨‍👩‍👦 Whole class instruction 👤 Independent work Ⓐ Assessment 🖥️ Digital Resource

MULTIDRAFT READING

Essential Understanding

First, students should read the entire selection on their own. Then, to assist struggling readers and to deepen comprehension for all, you may wish to guide them through the selection by asking them the close reading questions provided in the margins. Have students apply the multidraft reading protocols as they examine specific "chunks" of text related to these questions. For each reading, have students set the purpose indicated:

- **First reading:** Students should read the selection independently and think about its basic meaning.

- **Second reading:** Students should analyze the text's key ideas and details and its craft and structure.

- **Third reading:** Students should integrate knowledge and ideas; connect to the Big Question, other texts, and the world; and use teacher-led Close Reading discussion questions to examine particularly rich and significant passages.

For more guidance, refer to the *Classroom Strategies and Teaching Routines* card on multidraft reading.

🔔 Daily Bellringer

For each class during which you teach these selections, have students complete one of the five Sentence Combining activities for Week 24 in *Daily Bellringer Activities*. You may wish to use additional activities that are applicable to these selections.

❶ Background

If you wish, point out that Twain adapted his book *The Prince and the Pauper* for the stage in 1890. Mention that although Twain took most of the material for the play from his book, he also added additional scenes to the drama. Include that *The Prince and the Pauper* has been made into several movies, including a 1915 silent version and a later version that used identical twin boys.

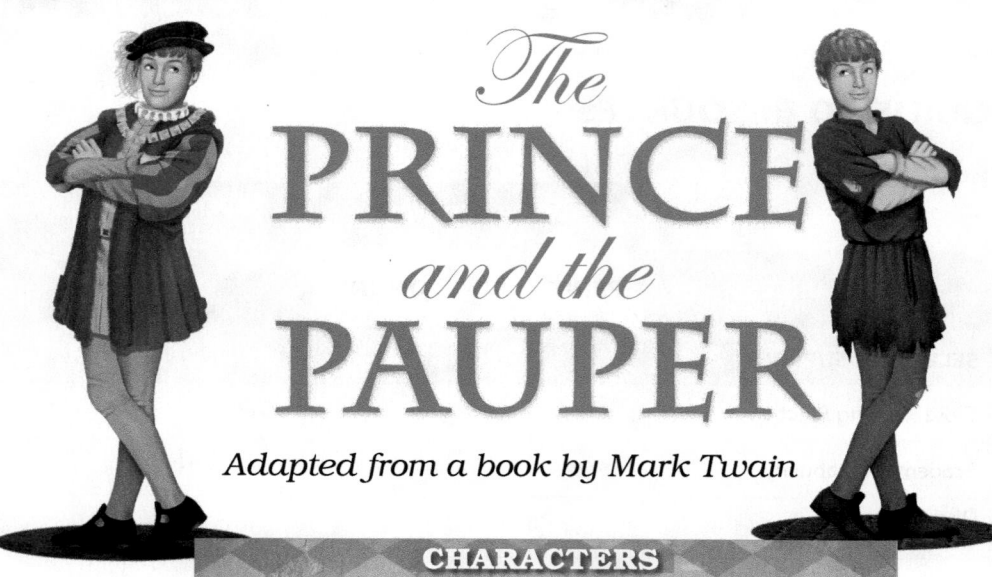

❶

The PRINCE and the PAUPER

Adapted from a book by Mark Twain

pauper ▶
(pô´ pər) *n.* someone who is very poor

CHARACTERS

Edward, Prince of Wales	Justice
Tom Canty, *the Pauper*	Constable
Lord Hertford	Jailer
Lord St. John	Sir Hugh Hendon
King Henry VIII	Two Prisoners
Herald	Two Guards
Miles Hendon	Three Pages
John Canty, *Tom's father*	Lords and Ladies
Hugo, *a young thief*	Villagers
Two Women	

SCENE 1

TIME. 1547.

SETTING. *Westminster Palace, England. Gates leading to courtyard are at right. Slightly to the left, off courtyard and inside gates, interior of palace anteroom is visible. There* ❷ *is a couch with a rich robe draped on it, screen at rear, bellcord, mirror, chairs, and a table with bowl of nuts, and a large golden seal on it. Piece of armor hangs on one wall. Exits are rear and downstage.*

554 UNIT 4 • How do we decide who we are?

©TEXT COMPLEXITY **RUBRIC**

The Prince and the Pauper (drama); The Prince and the Pauper (novel excerpt)

Qualitative Measures	Context/Knowledge Demands	England, mid 1500s, royal line of succession, poverty in Tudor England, references to royal court 1 2 3 ④ 5
	Structure/Language Conventionality and Clarity	Dialogue, British words and phrases, some difficult vocabulary and complex stage directions; references to London landmarks, difficult vocabulary, complex sentences 1 2 3 ④ 5
	Levels of Meaning/ Purpose/Concept Level	Accessible concepts (identity switch; class difference) 1 2 ③ 4 5
Quantitative Measures	Text Length	Word Counts: 5,212; 1,136
	Lexile	NP; 1240L

AT RISE, TWO GUARDS—*One at right, one at left—stand in front of gates, and several VILLAGERS hover nearby, straining to see into courtyard where PRINCE may be seen through fence, playing. TWO WOMEN enter right.*

1ST WOMAN. I have walked all morning just to have a glimpse of Westminster Palace.

2ND WOMAN. Maybe if we can get near enough to the gates, we can have a glimpse of the young prince. *(TOM CANTY, dirty and ragged, comes out of crowd and steps close to gates.)* I have always dreamed of seeing a real prince! *(Excited, he presses his nose against gates.)*

1ST GUARD. Mind your manners, you young beggar! *(Seizes TOM by collar and sends him sprawling into crowd. VILLAGERS laugh, as TOM slowly gets to his feet.)*

PRINCE. *(Rushing to gates)* How dare you treat a poor subject of the King in such a manner! Open the gates and let him in! *(As VILLAGERS see PRINCE, they take off their hats and bow low.)*

VILLAGERS. *(Shouting together)* Long live the Prince of Wales! *(GUARDS open gates and TOM slowly passes through, as if in a dream.)*

PRINCE. *(To TOM)* You look tired, and you have been treated cruelly. I am Edward, Prince of Wales. What is your name?

TOM. *(Looking around in awe)* Tom Canty, Your Highness.

PRINCE. Come into the palace with me, Tom. *(PRINCE leads TOM into anteroom. VILLAGERS pantomime conversation, and all but a few exit.)* Where do you live, Tom?

TOM. In the city, Your Highness, in Offal[1] Court.

PRINCE. Offal Court? That is an odd name. Do you have parents?

TOM. Yes, Your Highness.

PRINCE. How does your father treat you?

TOM. If it please you, Your Highness, when I am not able to beg a penny for our supper, he treats me to beatings.

---

1. **offal** (ô′ fəl) scraps left over when an animal is butchered.

PART 3 • The Prince and the Pauper **555**

❷ Close Reading

1. Key Ideas and Details
Ask: What key details help describe the setting? What inferences can be drawn from these details?

Possible response: The year, location, and anteroom indicate a historical play about English royalty. The villagers are fascinated by the young prince.

2. Craft and Structure
Ask: How does the author's description of the anteroom contribute to the setting?

Possible response: This description of objects like "a rich robe" and "a large gold seal" shows the Prince's wealth.

3. Integration of Knowledge and Ideas
Ask: How do descriptions of setting and action influence how you read the play? How would an audience know this information during a performance?

Possible response: The descriptions make it easy to imagine the action and dialogue. During a performance, the audience would gain this information from the sets, props, and lighting changes.

Vocabulary

1. Write the following words and definitions on the board:

pauper *n.* someone who is very poor

affliction *n.* pain, illness, suffering

masonry *n.* something built out of stone

2. Have students say each word aloud.

 **Video**

Watch the Background Video online!

🔊 **Audio**

Selection Audio is available in the *Student eText* and on the *Hear It!* CD-ROM.

©TEXT COMPLEXITY **READER AND TASK SUGGESTIONS**

The Prince and the Pauper (drama), The Prince and the Pauper (novel excerpt)

Preparing to Read the Text
• Discuss the difference between the structure of a novel and the written format of a play. Explain that a novel must describe all action and characters in detail, but a play provides a character list and stage directions to allow readers, actors, and directors to imagine and interpret the text.
• Guide students to use the Multidraft Reading strategies (TE p. 554).

Leveled Tasks
Clarity If students will have difficulty with structure, have them read Scene 1 in the play and the first three paragraphs of Chapter 3 in the novel excerpt. For the play, ask students to read the stage directions first, then reread the scene. Have them take notes on how each text describes action. Discuss students' notes and help clarify the effect of each format's structure.

Analyzing If students will not have difficulty with structure, have them read Scene 1 of the play and the first three paragraphs of the novel excerpt, taking notes on how each text emphasizes the differences between Tom and the Prince. As a class, discuss the benefits and drawbacks that writers should consider when using each format.

PART 3 • The Prince and the Pauper **555**

③ Close Reading

1. Key Ideas and Details Read aloud the passage to students. **Ask:** What happens in this passage?

Possible response: The boys wish that they could experience what it would be like to have a different life, so they exchange clothes.

2. Craft and Structure
Ask: Which words or phrases are repeated in this passage? How does this repetition contribute to the development of the plot?

Possible response: The author repeatedly uses the phrase "if I could wear" and makes numerous references to clothes. At this point in the story, clothes are the main physical difference between the two boys. By repeating the same words and phrases, the author emphasizes the importance of clothes in creating the characters' identities. The author also foreshadows that the boys will switch identities.

3. Integration of Knowledge and Ideas
Ask: What does this passage suggest about how people define identity?

Possible response: This passage emphasizes the importance of clothes as a way to pass for another person and as a symbol for a particular status. By trading clothes, the boys become different people. This action suggests that clothing and physical appearance are a large part of how people define themselves.

PRINCE. *(Shocked)* What! Beatings? My father is not a calm man, but he does not beat me. *(Looks at TOM thoughtfully)* You speak well and have an easy grace. Have you been schooled?

TOM. Very little, Your Highness. A good priest who shares our house in Offal Court has taught me from his books.

PRINCE. Do you have a pleasant life in Offal Court?

TOM. Pleasant enough, Your Highness, save when I am hungry. We have Punch and Judy shows,[2] and sometimes we lads have fights in the street.

PRINCE. *(Eagerly)* I should like that. Tell me more.

TOM. In summer, we run races and swim in the river, and we love to wallow in the mud.

PRINCE. *(Sighing, wistfully)* If I could wear your clothes and play in the mud just once, with no one to forbid me, I think I could give up the crown!

TOM. *(Shaking his head)* And if I could wear your fine clothes just once, Your Highness …

③ PRINCE. Would you like that? Come, then. We shall change places. You can take off your rags and put on my clothes—and I will put on yours. *(He leads TOM behind screen, and they return shortly, each wearing the other's clothes.)* Let's look at ourselves in this mirror. *(Leads TOM to mirror)*

TOM. Oh, Your Highness, it is not proper for me to wear such clothes.

PRINCE. *(Excitedly, as he looks in mirror)* Heavens, do you not see it? We look like brothers! We have the same features and bearing. If we went about together, dressed alike, there is no one who could say which is the Prince of Wales and which Tom Canty!

TOM. *(Drawing back and rubbing his hand)* Your Highness, I am frightened …

PRINCE. Do not worry. *(Seeing TOM rub his hand)* Is that a bruise on your hand?

TOM. Yes, but it is a slight thing, Your Highness.

---

2. Punch and Judy shows public puppet shows presented in Europe in the seventeenth century.

🗨 VOCABULARY DEVELOPMENT

Thematic Vocabulary: The Big Question
As students are discussing the play adaptation of and novel excerpt from *The Prince and the Pauper*, encourage them to use the thematic vocabulary presented in Introducing the Big Question, pp. 440–441. You might encourage them with sentence starters like these:

1. Both boys believe that if they change their *appearance* …

2. The Prince's dialogue shows that his *personality* is …
3. Other characters' *expectations* of Tom and the Prince are …
4. Tom's behavior suggests that he is *conscious* of …
5. The boys' decision to trade clothes goes against *custom* because …

PRINCE. *(Angrily)* It was shameful and cruel of that guard to strike you. Do not stir a step until I come back. I command you! *(He picks up golden Seal of England and carefully puts it into piece of armor. He then dashes out to gates.)* Open! Unbar the gates at once! *(2ND GUARD opens gates, and as PRINCE runs out, in rags, 1ST GUARD seizes him, boxes him on the ear, and knocks him to the ground.)*

1ST GUARD. Take that, you little beggar, for the trouble you have made for me with the Prince. *(VILLAGERS roar with laughter.)*

PRINCE. *(Picking himself up, turning on GUARD furiously)* I am Prince of Wales! You shall hang for laying your hand on me!

1ST GUARD. *(Presenting arms; mockingly)* I salute Your Gracious Highness! *(Then, angrily, 1ST GUARD shoves PRINCE roughly aside.)* Be off, you mad bag of rags! *(PRINCE is surrounded by VILLAGERS, who hustle him off.)*

VILLAGERS. *(Ad lib, as they exit, shouting)* Make way for His Royal Highness! Make way for the Prince of Wales! Hail to the Prince! *(Etc.)*

TOM. *(Admiring himself in mirror)* If only the boys in Offal Court could see me! They will not believe me when I tell them about this. *(Looks around anxiously)* But where is the Prince? *(Looks cautiously into courtyard. TWO GUARDS immediately snap to attention and salute. He quickly ducks back into anteroom as HERTFORD and ST. JOHN enter at rear.)*

HERTFORD. *(Going toward TOM, then stopping and bowing low)* My Lord, you look distressed. What is wrong?

TOM. *(Trembling)* Oh, I beg of you, be merciful. I am no Prince, but poor Tom Canty of Offal Court. Please let me see the Prince, and he will give my rags back to me and let me go unhurt. *(Kneeling)* Please, be merciful and spare me!

HERTFORD. *(Puzzled and disturbed)* Your Highness, on your knees? To me? *(Bows quickly, then, aside to ST. JOHN)* The Prince has gone mad! We must inform the King. *(To TOM)* A moment, Your Highness. *(HERTFORD and ST. JOHN exit rear.)*

TOM. Oh, there is no hope for me now. They will hang me for certain! *(HERTFORD and ST. JOHN re-enter, supporting*

---

❹ Close Reading

1. **Key Ideas and Details** Ask two students to read the passage aloud. Remind students to act out the information in the parentheses instead of reading the words. **Ask:** What is the conflict in this passage?

   Possible response: Based on what the Prince is wearing, the first guard assumes that the Prince is Tom. When the Prince insists that he is the Prince of Wales, the first guard and the villagers mock him.

2. **Craft and Structure**
   Ask: What types of sentences are being used? What do the type of sentences emphasize about the plot?

   Possible response: The passage uses exclamatory and imperative sentences. These sentences emphasize that the Prince furiously declares his identity. However, no one believes him.

3. **Integration of Knowledge and Ideas**
   Ask: How does this language reinforce the concept of identity?

   Possible response: The passage introduces the idea that a person's identity is more than what a person says or thinks. The first guard's assumption about the Prince in Tom's clothes suggests that others can make instant judgments about someone's identity based on items as seemingly innocent as clothes, despite what people proclaim, or say about themselves.

⁂ DIFFERENTIATED INSTRUCTION

Strategy for Special-Needs Students
To help students understand the action in this scene, have students look at the stage directions before reading the scene. Read aloud the stage directions and ask the students to read along with you. Remind students that stage directions tell what action should happen on stage and how the actors should read their lines. Then, have students make notes in the margins to tell when a new action takes place, such as *Prince leads Tom into palace* or *Tom and Prince trade clothes*. After students complete this task, have them read through the scene with a partner or in a group. Help students understand how dialogue and stage directions can help them imagine the scene by asking questions, such as, *How does the first guard treat Tom?* or *How does the Prince react to how the first guard treats Tom?*

KING. TOM *watches in awe as they help him to couch, where he sinks down wearily.)*

KING. *(Beckoning* TOM *close to him)* Now, my son, Edward, my prince. What is this? Do you mean to deceive me, the King, your father, who loves you and treats you so kindly?

TOM. *(Dropping to his knees)* You are the King? Then I have no hope!

KING. *(Stunned)* My child, you are not well. Do not break your father's old heart. Say you know me.

TOM. Yes, you are my lord the King, whom God preserve.

KING. True, that is right. Now, you will not deny that you are Prince of Wales, as they say you did just a while ago?

TOM. I beg you, Your Grace, believe me. I am the lowest of your subjects, being born a pauper, and it is by a great mistake that I am here. I am too young to die. Oh, please, spare me, sire!

KING. *(Amazed)* Die? Do not talk so, my child. You shall not die.

TOM. *(Gratefully)* God save you, my king! And now, may I go?

KING. Go? Where would you go?

TOM. Back to the alley where I was born and bred to misery.

KING. My poor child, rest your head here. *(He holds* TOM'S *head and pats his shoulder, then turns to* HERTFORD *and* ST. JOHN.*)* Alas, I am old and ill, and my son is mad. But this shall pass. Mad or sane, he is my heir and shall rule England. Tomorrow he shall be installed and confirmed in his princely dignity! Bring the Great Seal!

HERTFORD. *(Bowing low)* Please, Your Majesty, you took the Great Seal from the Chancellor two days ago to give to His Highness the Prince.

KING. So I did. *(To* TOM*)* My child, tell me, where is the Great Seal?

TOM. *(Trembling)* Indeed, my lord, I do not know.

affliction ▶
(ə flik´ shən) *n.* pain, illness, suffering

KING. Ah, your affliction hangs heavily upon you. 'Tis no matter. You will remember later. Listen, carefully! *(Gently, but firmly)* I command you to hide your affliction in all ways that be within your power. You shall deny to no one that you are the true prince, and if your memory should

💬 VOCABULARY DEVELOPMENT

Selection Vocabulary Reinforcement

To reinforce and assess students' comprehension of selection vocabulary words, give them sentences in which the word may or may not be used correctly. Students must tell whether the use is correct and explain their answer. Use these sentences:

1. The joyous birth of her first grandchild caused the new grandmother to be filled with *affliction*.
   Answer: No, *affliction* is not used correctly. It means the opposite of joyfulness or happiness.

2. The young man inherited millions of dollars from his uncle, which made him a *pauper*.
   Answer: No, *pauper* is not used correctly. It means "someone who is very poor," but someone who inherits millions of dollars is not very poor.

3. Its *masonry* made the castle one of the strongest stone structures in England.
   Answer: Yes, *masonry* is used correctly here. *Masonry* means "something built out of stone."

fail you upon any occasion of state, you shall be advised by your uncle, the Lord Hertford.

TOM. *(Resigned)* The King has spoken. The King shall be obeyed.

KING. And now, my child, I go to rest. *(He stands weakly, and* HERTFORD *leads him off, rear.)*

TOM. *(Wearily, to* ST. JOHN*)* May it please your lordship to let me rest now?

ST. JOHN. So it please Your Highness, it is for you to command and us to obey. But it is wise that you rest, for this evening you must attend the Lord Mayor's banquet in your honor. *(He pulls bellcord, and* THREE PAGES *enter and kneel before* TOM.*)*

TOM. Banquet? *(Terrified, he sits on couch and reaches for cup of water, but* 1ST PAGE *instantly seizes cup, drops on one knee, and serves it to him.* TOM *starts to take off his boots, but* 2ND PAGE *stops him and does it for him. He tries to remove his cape and gloves, and* 3RD PAGE *does it for him.)* I wonder that you do not try to breathe for me also! *(Lies down cautiously.* PAGES *cover him with robe, then back away and exit.)*

ST. JOHN. *(To* HERTFORD, *as he enters)* Plainly, what do you think?

HERTFORD. Plainly, this. The King is near death, my nephew the Prince of Wales is clearly mad and will mount the throne mad. God protect England, for she will need it!

ST. JOHN. Does it not seem strange that madness could so change his manner from what it used to be? It troubles me, his saying he is not the Prince.

HERTFORD. Peace, my lord! If he were an impostor and called himself Prince, that would be natural. But was there ever an impostor,

PART 3 • The Prince and the Pauper **559**

⑤ Close Reading

1. **Key Ideas and Details** Read aloud the passage to students. **Ask:** What do the court pages do in this passage?

   Possible response: Instead of letting Tom do anything himself, the court pages serve him a cup of water, take his boots, remove his cape and gloves, and cover him with a robe. Then they respectfully back away and leave the room.

2. **Craft and Structure** Ask students to focus on Tom's reactions and dialogue. **Ask:** What words, phrases, or lines illustrate Tom's feelings?

   Possible response: In the stage directions, words such as *terrified* and *cautiously* suggest that Tom is frightened and unsure about his situation. The line of dialogue "I wonder that you do not try to breathe for me also!" suggests that the pages' behavior baffles Tom. It also indicates that Tom thinks the pages' service is excessive and ridiculous.

3. **Integration of Knowledge and Ideas**
   Ask: How do the stage directions and Tom's lines show the difference in Tom's life now that people think he is the Prince?

   Possible response: The stage directions of the pages' extensive service illustrates that Tom's life has completely changed. Tom used to be severely mistreated and forced to beg for his supper, but he is constantly respected and served by others as soon as he is mistaken for the Prince.

⑥ Focus Passage

A Focus Passage is identified with brackets in the Student Edition of this page and the next for students' independent close reading and analysis. A question bank for the passage and possible responses appear at the end of the selection.

👥 DIFFERENTIATED INSTRUCTION

🔵 Vocabulary for English Learners
Although students may know that *mad* means "angry" or "upset," some students may not know that *mad* can also mean "insane" or "suffering from a mental disorder." Encourage students to look at how *mad* is used in this part of the play. Focus on examples such as "The Prince has gone mad" and "Mad or sane, he is my heir and shall rule England." Have students look at the words surrounding each example. Remind students that these context clues can help them determine which meaning of *mad* the author intended.

Enrichment for Advanced Readers
Discuss with students why the other characters in the play label the Prince and Tom as "mad." Have students look for examples from the text to support their ideas. After the discussion, encourage students to reflect on other texts that they have read. Have students make connections by asking themselves the following questions: *Why might a character be called mad? What similarities do you see between the different characters who are called mad or crazy? What conclusions can you draw based on the connections you found?*

7 Close Reading

1. Key Ideas and Details Read aloud the passage to students. **Ask:** How does Canty react to the Prince's demands?

Possible response: Canty repeatedly dismisses the Prince's demands and calls the Prince "mad" when he claims to be royalty. When the Prince insists that he is the Prince of Wales, Canty angrily proclaims that he will not tolerate this "madness."

2. Craft and Structure Ask students to carefully reread the passage, taking note of word choice. **Ask:** What words are repeated in this passage? Why is this repetition important?

Possible response: Canty repeatedly uses the word "mad" or "madness" to describe the Prince. The repetition shows that Canty will not change his mind about the Prince despite the Prince's claims. Canty only sees the clothes that the Prince wears and assumes he is a pauper.

3. Integration of Knowledge and Ideas **Ask:** How does this repetition relate to the overall dramatic irony in the play?

Possible response: Both boys insist on telling the truth and are repeatedly told that they are "mad." The reader or audience, however, knows that the boys are not mad, just honest. This knowledge makes the adults appear more irrational than the boys.

---

who being called Prince by the King and court, denied it? Never! This is the true Prince gone mad. And tonight all London shall honor him. *(HERTFORD and ST. JOHN exit. TOM sits up, looks around helplessly, then gets up.)*

6 **TOM.** I should have thought to order something to eat. *(Sees bowl of nuts on table)* Ah! Here are some nuts! *(Looks around, sees Great Seal in armor, takes it out, looks at it curiously.)* This will make a good nutcracker. *(He takes bowl of nuts, sits on couch and begins to crack nuts with Great Seal and eat them, as curtain falls.)*

SCENE 2

TIME. *Later that night.*

SETTING. *A street in London, near Offal Court. Played before the curtain.*

AT RISE. PRINCE *limps in, dirty and tousled. He looks around wearily. Several* VILLAGERS *pass by, pushing against him.*

PRINCE. I have never seen this poor section of London. I must be near Offal Court. If I can only find it before I drop! *(JOHN CANTY steps out of crowd, seizes PRINCE roughly.)*

CANTY. Out at this time of night, and I warrant you haven't brought a farthing home! If that is the case and I do not break all the bones in your miserable body, then I am not John Canty!

PRINCE. *(Eagerly)* Oh, are you his father?

CANTY. *His* father? I am *your* father, and—

PRINCE. Take me to the palace at once, and your son will be returned to you. The King, my father, will make you rich beyond your wildest dreams. Oh, save me, for I am indeed the Prince of Wales.

CANTY. *(Staring in amazement)* Gone stark mad! But mad or not, I'll soon find where the soft places lie in your bones. Come home! *(Starts to drag PRINCE off)*

7 **PRINCE.** *(Struggling)* Let me go! I am the Prince of Wales, and the King shall have your life for this!

CANTY. *(Angrily)* I'll take no more of your madness! *(Raises stick to strike, but PRINCE struggles free and runs off, and CANTY runs after him)*

SCENE 3

SETTING. *Same as Scene 1, with addition of dining table, set with dishes and goblets, on raised platform. Throne-like chair is at head of table.*

AT RISE. *A banquet is in progress.* TOM, *in royal robes, sits at head of table, with* HERTFORD *at his right and* ST. JOHN *at his left.* LORDS *and* LADIES *sit around table eating and talking softly.*

TOM. *(To* HERTFORD*)* What is this, my Lord? *(Holds up a plate)*

HERTFORD. Lettuce and turnips, Your Highness.

TOM. Lettuce and turnips? I have never seen them before. Am I to eat them?

HERTFORD. *(Discreetly)* Yes, Your Highness, if you so desire. *(*TOM *begins to eat food with his fingers. Fanfare of trumpets is heard, and* HERALD *enters, carrying scroll. All turn to look.)*

HERALD. *(Reading from scroll)* His Majesty, King Henry VIII, is dead! The King is dead! *(All rise and return to* TOM, *who sits, stunned.)*

ALL. *(Together)* The King is dead. Long live the King! Long live Edward, King of England! *(All bow to* TOM. HERALD *bows and exits.)*

HERTFORD. *(To* TOM*)* Your Majesty, we must call the council. Come, St. John. *(*HERTFORD *and* ST. JOHN *lead* TOM *off at rear.* LORDS *and* LADIES *follow, talking among themselves. At gates, down right,* VILLAGERS *enter and mill about.* PRINCE *enters right, pounds on gates and shouts.)*

PRINCE. Open the gates! I am the Prince of Wales! Open, I say! And though I am friendless with no one to help me, I will not be driven from my ground.

MILES HENDON. *(Entering through crowd)* Though you be Prince or not, you are indeed a gallant lad and not friendless. Here I stand to prove it, and you might have a worse friend than Miles Hendon.

1ST VILLAGER. 'Tis another prince in disguise. Take the lad and dunk him in the pond! *(He seizes* PRINCE, *but* MILES *strikes him with the flat of his sword. Crowd, now angry, presses forward threateningly, when fanfare of trumpets is heard offstage.* HERALD, *carrying scroll, enters up left at gates.)*

---

❽ Close Reading

1. Key Ideas and Details Ask a student to read aloud the passage. **Ask:** What does the Prince say in this passage?

Possible response: He demands that the gates be opened and repeats that he is the Prince of Wales. He also says that he will not leave the gates even though he has "no one to help" him.

2. Craft and Structure Ask students to reread the passage carefully. **Ask:** How is the word *I* used in this passage?

Possible response: The Prince's repetition of the word *I* suggests that he is trying desperately to prove who he is. The use of "I am" emphasizes the Prince's identity as the Prince of Wales and also his current situation as "friendless."

3. Integration of Knowledge and Ideas
Ask: What does the repetition show about how the Prince perceives himself?

Possible response: So far, the Prince has repeatedly declared his true identity. His use of the word "I" suggests that he is confident and determined not give up until someone finally believes his claims. The Prince does not conform to everyone else's thought of him.

👥 DIFFERENTIATED INSTRUCTION

Support for Less Proficient Readers

To help students understand the significance of the setting, point out the footnote at the bottom of p. 555. Then guide students to infer the meaning behind "Offal Court."

1. Have students reread the SETTING at the beginning of Scene 2 on p. 560. **Ask:** What does *offal* mean? (scraps left over when an animal is butchered) Explain to students that meat comes in different cuts. To make those cuts, butchers trim off extra pieces, which are usually discarded.
2. Help students connect this definition with the place by rereading what the Prince says about Offal Court. **Ask:** Why do you think the Prince has never seen Offal Court? (This section of London is poorer than the area surrounding Westminster Palace. A prince would not usually visit such a place.)
3. **Ask:** What is the significance of the name *Offal Court*? (Its name emphasizes that this place is the "leftover" part of London. It also suggests that residents of Offal Court, like Tom, are often forgotten or removed from the higher classes' experience of London.)

9 Close Reading

1. Key Ideas and Details Ask two students to read aloud the passage: one reading as the Prince and the other as Miles. **Ask:** What happens in this passage?

Possible response: The Prince thanks Miles and says that he will be rewarded. Although Miles does not believe the Prince's claims, he decides to humor him. The Prince is offended that Miles starts to sit, so Miles stands and serves the Prince.

2. Craft and Structure Have students reread the beginning of Scene 4 and concentrate on the stage directions. **Ask:** How does the structure of this passage show each character's point of view?

Possible response: The stage directions for the Prince show him continuing to act like royalty, such as when he reacts "(*Angrily*)" to Miles sitting in his presence. Miles's stage directions show that he hides his disbelief in the Prince's claims, for example he comments "(*To himself*) First he called himself Prince, and now he is King. Well, I will humor him."

3. Integration of Knowledge and Ideas

Ask: How do the stage directions of these two characters help create dramatic irony?

Possible response: The Prince thinks that Miles believes him and continues to behave like he would with any other subject or servant. Miles, however, does not believe the Prince and decides to play along with him. These differing points of view create dramatic irony because both characters are acting based on their contradicting ideas about the other character.

HERALD. Make way for the King's messenger! (*Reading from scroll*) His Majesty, King Henry VIII is dead! The King is dead! (*He exits right, repeating message, and* VILLAGERS *stand in stunned silence.*)

PRINCE. (*Stunned*) The King is dead!

1ST VILLAGER. (*Shouting*) Long live Edward, King of England!

VILLAGERS. (*Together*) Long live the King! (*Shouting, ad lib*) Long live King Edward! Heaven protect Edward, King of England! (*Etc.*)

MILES. (*Taking* PRINCE *by the arm*) Come, lad, before the crowd remembers us. I have a room at the inn, and you can stay there. (*He hurries off with stunned* PRINCE. TOM, *led by* HERTFORD, *enters courtyard up rear.* VILLAGERS *see them.*)

VILLAGERS. (*Together*) Long live the King! (*They fall to their knees as curtains close.*)

SCENE 4

SETTING. *Miles's room at the inn. At right is table set with dishes and bowls of food, a chair at each side. At left is bed, with table and chair next to it, and a window. Candle is on table.*

AT RISE. MILES *and* PRINCE *approach table.*

MILES. I have had a hot supper prepared. I'll bet you're hungry, lad.

PRINCE. Yes, I am. It's kind of you to let me stay with you, Miles. I am truly Edward, King of England, and you shall not go unrewarded. (*Sits at table*)

MILES. (*To himself*) First he called himself Prince, and now he is King. Well, I will humor him. (*Starts to sit*)

 Prince. (*Angrily*) Stop! Would you sit in the presence of the King?

Miles. (*Surprised, standing up quickly*) I beg your pardon, Your Majesty. I was not thinking. (*Stares uncertainly at* PRINCE, *who sits at table, expectantly.* MILES *starts to uncover dishes of food, serves* PRINCE *and fills glasses.*)

PRINCE. Miles, you have a gallant way about you. Are you nobly born?

🗨 THINK ALOUD

Vocabulary: Using Context

Direct students' attention to the word *gallant* on pages 561 and 562. Using a think-aloud process, model how to use context to determine the correct meaning of a word.

First, I look up the word *gallant* in the dictionary. Some meanings are "interesting or colorful clothing style," "grand or stately," "brave or courageous," and "polite or courteous." I am not sure which definition will work best, so I will reread the first sentence with the word *gallant*. "Though you be Prince or not, you are indeed a gallant lad and not friendless." Based on this sentence, I am still unsure of the correct meaning, so I will observe what the Prince is doing that might be considered "gallant." Before this sentence, the Prince demands to be let into the palace. I don't think this behavior is colorful or grand, and it is definitely not polite. So, "brave or courageous" seems to be the best definition.

Encourage students to try this process on their own with the second use of *gallant*. Remind students that the word's meaning could change depending on the context.

MILES. My father is a baronet,[3] Your Majesty.

PRINCE. Then you must also be a baronet.

MILES. *(Shaking his head)* My father banished me from home seven years ago, so I fought in the wars. I was taken prisoner, and I have spent the past seven years in prison. Now I am free, and I am returning home.

PRINCE. You have been shamefully wronged! But I will make things right for you. You have saved me from injury and possible death. Name your reward and if it be within the compass of my royal power, it is yours.

MILES. *(Pausing briefly, then dropping to his knee)* Since Your Majesty is pleased to hold my simple duty worthy of reward, I ask that I and my successors may hold the privilege of sitting in the presence of the King.

PRINCE. *(Taking MILES'S sword, tapping him lightly on each shoulder)* Rise and seat yourself. *(Returns sword to MILES, then rises and goes over to bed)*

MILES. *(Rising)* He should have been born a king. He plays the part to a marvel! If I had not thought of this favor, I might have had to stand for weeks. *(Sits down and begins to eat)*

PRINCE. Sir Miles, you will stand guard while I sleep. *(Lies down and instantly falls asleep)*

MILES. Yes, Your Majesty. *(With a rueful look at his uneaten supper, he stands up.)* Poor little chap. I suppose his mind has been disordered with ill usage. *(Covers PRINCE with his cape)* Well, I will be his friend and watch over him. *(Blows out candle, then yawns, sits on chair next to bed, and falls asleep. JOHN CANTY and HUGO appear at window, peer around room, then enter cautiously through window. They lift the sleeping PRINCE, staring nervously at MILES.)*

CANTY. *(In loud whisper)* I swore the day he was born he would be a thief and a beggar, and I won't lose him now. Lead the way to the camp, Hugo! *(CANTY and HUGO carry PRINCE off right, as MILES sleeps on and curtain falls.)*

---

3. **baronet** a member of the British upper class.

10 Close Reading

1. **Key Ideas and Details** Read aloud the passage to students. **Ask:** What happens in this passage? What details help you understand what is occurring?

   Possible response: The Prince asks Miles to guard him while he sleeps. Miles covers the sleeping Prince with his cape and then falls asleep himself. Afterwards, John Canty and Hugo enter through the window and take the Prince.

2. **Craft and Structure** Discuss foreshadowing with students. Explain that foreshadowing is when an author uses clues to hint at what might happen later in a story. This technique is often used to build suspense. **Ask:** What clues in this passage hint that something might happen to the Prince?

   Possible response: One clue is that the Prince asks Miles to guard him. Another clue is that Miles says he "will be [the Prince's] friend and watch over him" but seems to mean it figuratively since he immediately falls asleep after saying it.

3. **Integration of Knowledge and Ideas**
   Ask: How might Miles's promise to watch over the Prince foreshadow his future actions?

   Possible response: Even though Miles does not believe that the Prince is royalty, Miles's promise suggests that he still cares about the Prince. For this reason, Miles might appear later in the play and try to rescue the Prince or help him in some other way. As the play continues, the plot builds suspense as the audience waits for Miles to fulfill his promise to protect the Prince.

⑪ Close Reading

1. Key Ideas and Details Ask a student to read aloud the passage. **Ask:** What happens in this passage?

Possible response: The Prince refuses to beg or steal with Hugo. Hugo threatens the Prince and tells him to wait while he steals a woman's bundle. Then, Hugo places the bundle in the Prince's hands and tells the Prince to run after him. The Prince refuses and throws the bundle on the ground.

2. Craft and Structure
Ask: What do the repeated words and phrases emphasize?

Possible response: The Prince repeats the phrase "I will not," which shows his refusal to be part of the thieves and his continued resistance to how people treat him as a pauper. The Prince uses the word *suffer* to describe how he's been mistreated, and Hugo repeats it to describe how the Prince will be punished if he does not steal. Both uses of this word emphasize the changes in the Prince's life.

3. Integration of Knowledge and Ideas
Ask: How does the repetition deepen your understanding of how the Prince's life has changed?

Possible response: The Prince's life has changed dramatically from a life of luxury to a forced life of crime and suffering. Others no longer respect what he says.

SCENE 5

TIME. *Two weeks later.*

SETTING. *Country village street.*

BEFORE RISE. VILLAGERS *walk about.* CANTY, HUGO, *and* PRINCE *enter.*

CANTY. I will go in this direction. Hugo, keep my mad son with you, and see that he doesn't escape again! *(Exits)*

HUGO. *(Seizing* PRINCE *by the arm)* He won't escape! I'll see that he earns his bread today, or else!

PRINCE. *(Pulling away)* I will not beg with you, and I will not steal! I have suffered enough in this miserable company of thieves!

HUGO. You shall suffer more if you do not do as I tell you! *(Raises clenched fist at* PRINCE*)* Refuse if you dare! ⑪ *(*WOMAN *enters, carrying wrapped bundle in a basket on her arm.)* Wait here until I come back. *(*HUGO *sneaks along after* WOMAN, *then snatches her bundle, runs back to* PRINCE, *and thrusts it into his arms.)* Run after me and call, "Stop, thief!" But be sure you lead her astray! *(Runs off.* PRINCE *throws down bundle in disgust.)*

WOMAN. Help! Thief! Stop, thief! *(Rushes at* PRINCE *and seizes him, just as several* VILLAGERS *enter)* You little thief! What do you mean by robbing a poor woman? Somebody bring the constable! *(*MILES *enters and watches.)*

1ST VILLAGER. *(Grabbing* PRINCE*)* I'll teach him a lesson, the little villain!

PRINCE. *(Struggling)* Take your hands off me! I did not rob this woman!

MILES. *(Stepping out of crowd and pushing man back with the flat of his sword)* Let us proceed gently, my friends. This is a matter for the law.

PRINCE. *(Springing to* MILES'S *side)* You have come just in time, Sir Miles. Carve this rabble to rags!

MILES. Speak softly. Trust in me and all shall go well.

CONSTABLE. *(Entering and reaching for* PRINCE*)* Come along, young rascal!

MILES. Gently, good friend. He shall go peaceably to the Justice.

💬 VOCABULARY DEVELOPMENT

Vocabulary Reinforcement

Students will benefit from additional examples and practice with vocabulary words in the play. Reinforce their comprehension with "show-you-know" sentences. The first part of the sentence uses the vocabulary word in an appropriate context. The second part of the sentence—the "show-you-know" part—clarifies the first. Model the strategy with this example for *marvel:*

The circus offers *marvels* for all ages; its performers provided surprise and astonishment for the audience.

Then give students these sentence prompts, and coach them in creating the clarification part of the sentence:

1. The *marvel* of the evening was the amateur magician; _____.
   Possible response: his magic tricks gave the best surprises and most interesting sights that night.
2. The lost puppy wore a *rueful* expression; _____.
   Possible response: he seemed sad and lonely without his owners.
3. The *rabble* swarmed around the festival stage; _____.
   Possible response: each rowdy group of people seemed anxious for the show to start.

PRINCE. I will not go before a Justice! I did not do this thing!

MILES. *(Taking him aside)* Sire, will you reject the laws of the realm, yet demand that your subjects respect them?

PRINCE. *(Calmer)* You are right, Sir Miles. Whatever the King requires a subject to suffer under the law, he will suffer himself while he holds the station of a subject. *(CONSTABLE leads them off right. VILLAGERS follow. Curtain)*

* * * * *

SETTING. *Office of the JUSTICE. A high bench is at center.*

AT RISE. JUSTICE *sits behind bench.* CONSTABLE *enters with* MILES *and* PRINCE, *followed by* VILLAGERS. WOMAN *carries wrapped bundle.*

CONSTABLE. *(To JUSTICE)* A young thief, your worship, is accused of stealing a dressed pig from this poor woman.

JUSTICE. *(Looking down at PRINCE, then WOMAN)* My good woman, are you absolutely certain this lad stole your pig?

WOMAN. It was none other than he, your worship.

JUSTICE. Are there no witnesses to the contrary? *(All shake their heads.)* Then the lad stands convicted. *(To WOMAN)* What do you hold this property to be worth?

WOMAN. Three shillings and eight pence, your worship.

JUSTICE. *(Leaning down to WOMAN)* Good woman, do you know that when one steals a thing above the value of thirteen pence, the law says he shall hang for it?

WOMAN. *(Upset)* Oh, what have I done? I would not hang the poor boy for the whole world! Save me from this, your worship. What can I do?

JUSTICE. *(Gravely)* You may revise the value, since it is not yet written in the record.

WOMAN. Then call the pig eight pence, your worship.

JUSTICE. So be it. You may take your property and go. *(WOMAN starts off, and is followed by CONSTABLE. MILES follows them cautiously down right.)*

CONSTABLE. *(Stopping WOMAN)* Good woman, I will buy your pig from you. *(Takes coins from pocket)* Here is eight pence.

WOMAN. Eight pence! It cost me three shillings and eight pence!

---

⑫ Close Reading

1. **Key Ideas and Details** Read aloud the passage to students. **Ask:** What is Miles's argument? How does the Prince respond?

   Possible response: Miles argues that a king should respect the same laws that he expects his subjects to respect. The Prince agrees with this idea.

2. **Craft and Structure** Direct students to the repetition of the word *suffer*. **Ask:** How does the Prince use the word *suffer* in this passage?

   Possible response: The Prince uses *suffer* to mean "to obey or to live under." This use of the word *suffer* emphasizes that, although he does not want to do it, in this situation the Prince must obey the same laws as his subjects.

3. **Integration of Knowledge and Ideas**
   Ask: How has suffering influenced the Prince's life?

   Possible response: At the beginning of the story the Prince had never suffered. He has since experienced suffering. He now realizes that people should be treated fairly and that he should suffer the same consequences as everyone else.

👥 DIFFERENTIATED INSTRUCTION

Strategy for Less Proficient Readers
Because of the jump in time, the setting of Scene 5 may confuse some readers. Encourage students to use what they've read or learned so far—such as Tom's description of his father and the Prince's earlier escape from Canty—to help make inferences about what happened between Scene 4 and Scene 5. Use the following questions to help students make inferences: *What does Canty say after he and Hugo kidnap the Prince? What does this statement suggest about how the Prince will be treated?*

Strategy for Gifted/Talented Students
Have students write a scene at Offal Court that describes what may have occurred between the end of Scene 4 and the beginning of Scene 5. The one-page entry should include dialogue between the Prince, Canty, and Hugo. Based on their inferences, students should explain how the Prince reacted to his kidnapping and why he calls Canty and Hugo a "miserable company of thieves." Remind students to include stage directions in their scenes. When finished, students can read their scenes aloud in class.

CONSTABLE. Indeed! Then come back before his worship and answer for this. The lad must hang!

WOMAN. No! No! Say no more. Give me the eight pence and hold your peace. *(CONSTABLE hands her coins and takes pig. WOMAN exits, angrily. MILES returns to bench.)*

JUSTICE. The boy is sentenced to a fortnight in the common jail. Take him away, Constable! *(JUSTICE exits. PRINCE gives MILES a nervous glance.)*

MILES. *(Following CONSTABLE)* Good sir, turn your back a moment and let the poor lad escape. He is innocent.

CONSTABLE. *(Outraged)* What? You say this to me? Sir, I arrest you in—

MILES. Do not be so hasty! *(Slyly)* The pig you have purchased for eight pence may cost you your neck, man.

CONSTABLE. *(Laughing nervously)* Ah, but I was merely jesting with the woman, sir.

MILES. Would the Justice think it a jest?

CONSTABLE. Good sir! The Justice has no more sympathy with a jest than a dead corpse! *(Perplexed)* Very well, I will turn my back and see nothing! But go quickly! *(Exits)*

MILES. *(To PRINCE)* Come, my liege. We are free to go. And that band of thieves shall not set hands on you again, I swear it!

566 UNIT 4 • How do we decide who we are?

💬 VOCABULARY DEVELOPMENT

Words from Economics

Point out that different countries or allied nations often have their own currency, or systems of coins and bills. Currency can change over time depending on how governments choose to regulate it. Explain that during the 1500s the English used pounds, shillings, and pence. As the setting takes place in the past. Twain has his characters use this currency. Guide students to understand the value of the following currency words that are used in this selection:

pence: a coin with the smallest value in the English monetary system; worth one twelfth of a shilling

shilling: a coin worth twelve pence

value: the price or worth of something

PRINCE. *(Wearily)* Can you believe, Sir Miles, that in the last fortnight, I, the King of England, have escaped from thieves and begged for food on the road? I have slept in a barn with a calf! I have washed dishes in a peasant's kitchen, and narrowly escaped death. And not once in all of my wanderings did I see a courier searching for me! Is it no matter for commotion and distress that the head of state is gone?

MILES. *(Sadly, aside)* Still busy with his pathetic dream. *(To PRINCE)* It is strange indeed my liege. But come, I will take you to my father's home in Kent. We are not far away. There you may rest in a house with seventy rooms! Come, I am all impatience to be home again! *(They exit, MILES in cheerful spirits, PRINCE looking puzzled, as curtains close.)*

SCENE 6

SETTING. *Village jail. Bare stage, with barred window on one wall.*

AT RISE. TWO PRISONERS, *in chains, are onstage.* JAILER *shoves* MILES *and* PRINCE, *in chains, onstage. They struggle and protest.*

MILES. But I tell you I *am* Miles Hendon! My brother, Sir Hugh, has stolen my bride and my estate!

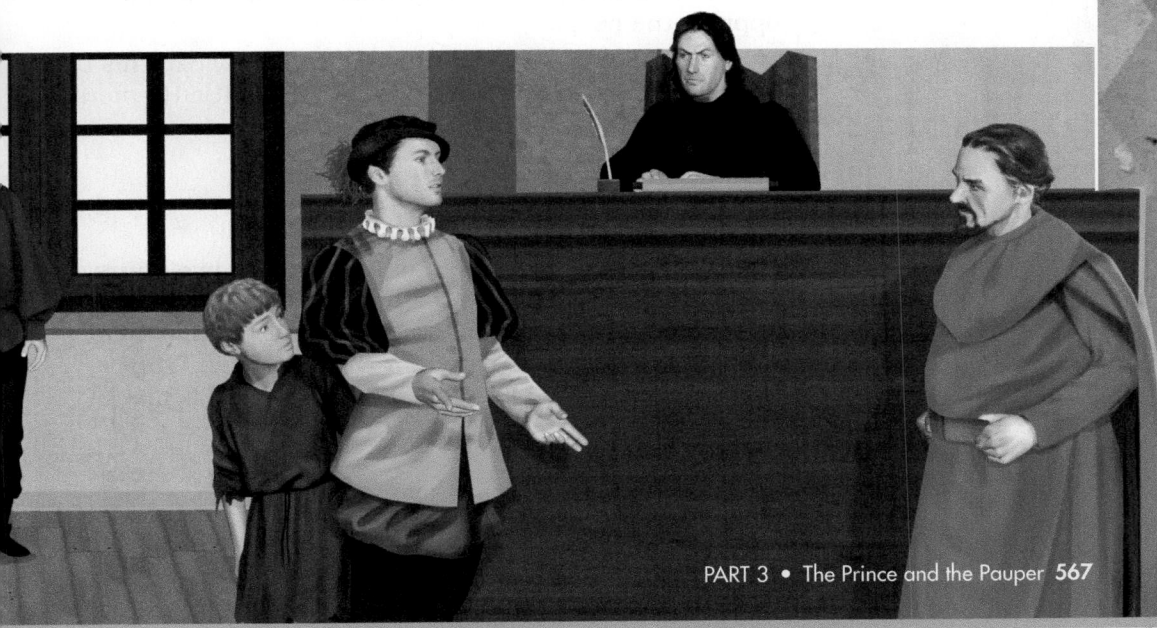

PART 3 • The Prince and the Pauper **567**

FLUENCY

Distribute copies of pages 566–567, and pair students. Have partners take turns reading the dialogue aloud. While one partner reads (all parts), the other should mark any words with which the reader has difficulty. Circulate to monitor the fluency of students' reading. Collect students' marked-up copies of the play excerpt, and review difficult words with the class. Look for the following challenge:

If students have difficulty with the words *perplexed* (p. 566) or *liege* (pp. 566 and 567), model how to pronounce each word.

⑬ Close Reading

1. Key Ideas and Details Ask a student to read aloud the passage. **Ask:** What does this passage reveal about the Prince's experience as a pauper?

Possible response: The Prince lists the experiences he has had since trading clothes with Tom: escaping from thieves, begging, sleeping in a barn, washing dishes, and escaping death. After these events, the Prince wonders hopelessly why no one is looking for him.

2. Craft and Structure Ask students to reread the passage and note how the Prince describes his experience. **Ask:** How does the Prince's use of the word *I* emphasize his feelings in this moment?

Possible response: "I, the King of England" emphasizes that the Prince continues to hold on to his identity as the king. The repetition of "I have" lists activities that are completely outside of the Prince's usual royal experience. Both uses of "I" suggest that the Prince does not understand his mistreatment or why no one notices that he is missing from the throne.

3. Integration of Knowledge and Ideas

Ask: How does this passage help you understand how much the Prince's life and identity has changed?

Possible response: Since trading clothes with Tom, the Prince experiences a life that is completely opposite to the one he was living as the Prince of Wales. The Prince originally thought it would be fun to live another life, but instead he has encountered many challenges. Although he knows that he should be the King, he is upset that no one else realizes this.

⑭ Close Reading

1. Key Ideas and Details Ask one student to read aloud the Jailer's lines and another student to read aloud Miles's lines. Remind students to act out the stage directions. **Ask:** What happened when Miles and the Prince went to Kent?

Possible response: When they arrived in Kent, Miles and the Prince found out that Sir Hugh forced Edith to marry him, stole Miles's estate, and claimed that the real Miles is dead. Sir Hugh also accused Miles of attacking him, so Miles and the Prince were arrested.

2. Craft and Structure Have students take note of how information about past events is revealed through dialogue. **Ask:** What does the repetition of "I" and "my" show?

Possible response: Miles repeats "I" and "my" to explain and reinforce who he is and what should have been his.

3. Integration of Knowledge and Ideas

Ask: How is the repetition of what Miles says similar to what the Prince has previously said? How has Miles's life become similar to the Prince's life?

Possible response: Both characters are mistaken for other people and no one believes their claims. Also, Miles is upset by the fact that his life has been taken from him and tries to convince others about his identity, which is similar to the Prince's situation.

JAILER. Be silent! Impostor! Sir Hugh will see that you pay well for claiming to be his dead brother and for assaulting him in his own house! *(Exits)*

MILES. *(Sitting, with head in hands)* Oh, my dear Edith … now wife to my brother Hugh, against her will, and my poor father … dead!

1ST PRISONER. At least you have your life, sir. I am sentenced to be hanged for killing a deer in the King's park.

2ND PRISONER. And I must hang for stealing a yard of cloth to dress my children.

PRINCE. *(Moved; to PRISONERS)* When I mount my throne, you shall all be free. And the laws that have dishonored you shall be swept from the books. *(Turning away)* Kings should go to school to learn their own laws and be merciful.

1ST PRISONER. What does the lad mean? I have heard that the King is mad, but merciful.

2ND PRISONER. He is to be crowned at Westminster[4] tomorrow.

PRINCE. *(Violently)* King? What King, good sir?

1ST PRISONER. Why, we have only one, his most sacred majesty, King Edward the Sixth.

2ND PRISONER. And whether he be mad or not, his praises are on all men's lips. He has saved many innocent lives, and now he means to destroy the cruelest laws that oppress the people.

PRINCE. *(Turning away, shaking his head)* How can this be? Surely it is not that little beggar boy! *(SIR HUGH enters with JAILER.)*

SIR HUGH. Seize the impostor!

MILES. *(As JAILER pulls him to his feet)* Hugh, this has gone far enough!

SIR HUGH. You will sit in the public stocks for two hours, and the boy would join you if he were not so young. See to it, jailer, and after two hours, you may release them. Meanwhile, I ride to London for the coronation! *(SIR HUGH exits and MILES is hustled out by JAILER.)*

---

4. **Westminster** Westminster Abbey, church in London that hosts coronations and other important ceremonies.

💭 THINK ALOUD

Character Development

Draw students' attention to the passage beginning with "1ST PRISONER. At least you have your life, sir." Use the following think aloud process to model identifying and analyzing character development.

When I read this passage, I notice that the Prince's reaction to his subjects seems different. To check my observation, I look back in the story. I know the Prince demands that the guard, Canty, and other commoners treat him as the Prince. I also remember that in Scene 5 the Prince refuses to go before the Justice when he is accused of stealing, which suggests that he thinks he is above the law. With that in mind, I look back at the passage on p. 564. At this point, the Prince has experienced unfair treatment in the streets, at the court, and at Kent. When the Prince says that kings should "learn their own laws and be merciful," he suggests that he wants to fix the laws to protect the people. I will keep reading to see if the Prince will act differently based on his realization. I will look for evidence in the text that shows how the Prince talks to and reacts to the prisoners.

PRINCE. Coronation! What does he mean? There can be no coronation without me! *(Curtain falls.)*

SCENE 7

TIME. *Coronation Day.*

SETTING. *Outside gates of Westminster Abbey, played before curtain. Painted screen or flat at rear represents Abbey. Throne is center. Bench is near it.*

AT RISE. LORDS *and* LADIES *crowd Abbey. Outside gates,* GUARDS *drive back cheering* VILLAGERS, *among them* MILES.

MILES. *(Distraught)* I've lost him! Poor little chap! He has been swallowed up in the crowd! *(Fanfare of trumpets is heard, then silence.* HERTFORD, ST. JOHN, LORDS *and* LADIES *enter slowly, in a procession followed by* PAGES, *one of whom carries crown on small cushion.* TOM *follows procession, looking about nervously. Suddenly,* PRINCE, *in rags, steps out from crowd, his hand raised.)*

PRINCE. I forbid you to set the crown of England upon that head. I am the King!

HERTFORD. Seize the little vagabond!

❶❺ TOM. I forbid it! He *is* the King! *(Kneels before* PRINCE*)* Oh, my lord the King, let poor Tom Canty be the first to say, "Put on your crown and enter into your own right again." *(*HERTFORD *and several* LORDS *look closely at both boys.)*

HERTFORD. This is strange indeed. *(To* TOM*)* By your favor, sir, I wish to ask certain questions of this lad.

PRINCE. I will answer truly whatever you may ask, my lord.

HERTFORD. But if you have been well trained, you may answer my questions as well as our lord the King. I need a definite proof. *(Thinks a moment)* Ah! Where lies the Great Seal of England? It has been missing for weeks, and only the true Prince of Wales can say where it lies.

TOM. Wait! Was the seal round and thick, with letters engraved on it? *(*HERTFORD *nods.)* I know where it is, but it was not I who put it there. The rightful King shall tell you. *(To* PRINCE*)* Think, my King, it was the very last thing you did that day before you rushed out of the palace wearing my rags.

---

❶❺ Close Reading

1. **Key Ideas and Details** Ask three volunteers to read aloud each part in the passage. **Ask:** What is happening in this passage?

   Possible response: The Prince stops the coronation and demands that he receive the crown. Tom stops Hertford and demands that everyone believe the Prince's claims.

2. **Craft and Structure** Ask students to reread the passage carefully, taking note of the interaction between the Prince and Tom. **Ask:** How does each character use the phrase "I forbid"?

   Possible response: The Prince uses "I forbid" as a decree aimed at stopping the coronation as well as an example of his royal authority. Tom knows that he can use "I forbid" because everyone assumes that he is the Prince. With this phrase, Tom uses the royal authority that has been forced on him to give the crown back to the real prince.

3. **Integration of Knowledge and Ideas**
   Ask: What do the words and actions tell you about both boys?

   Possible response: This passage shows that both boys want to correct the misunderstanding by telling the truth. The Prince uses the same approach that he has always used, claiming to be royalty, and Tom finally uses his false royal power to give the throne back to the Prince. Tom speaks up and also reinforces the truth by kneeling before the Prince.

⚙ DIFFERENTIATED INSTRUCTION

Support for Special-Needs Students

To help students understand the revelations in Scene 6, have students reread the scene several times. First, read aloud to students and ask them to read along with you. Then, ask questions to help students focus on the action in different parts of the scene, such as *What happens at the beginning of this scene? What does the Prince say to the prisoners? How does the Prince find out about the coronation?*

Remind students that action and dialogue can reveal new information about characters within and outside of the scene. Next, have students make notes in the margins to tell where action occurs, such as *Miles and the Prince are thrown in jail* or *Sir Hugh visits.* After students complete this task, have them reread the scene with a partner or in a group. Ask students to draw a square around the lines that reveal new information, such as "…he means to destroy the cruelest laws" which reveals that Tom has been reforming some of the king's laws. After they complete this activity, discuss what students have learned and correct any misunderstandings.

16 Close Reading

1. Key Ideas and Details

Ask: How is Tom trying to help the Prince in this passage?

Possible response: Tom gives the Prince hints to help him remember where he hid the Great Seal.

2. Craft and Structure

Ask: Which words emphasize the importance of the Prince remembering the Great Seal's hidden location?

Possible response: The similar words *recall, recollection,* and *remember* repeat to emphasize how important this memory is to help the Prince reclaim his identity.

3. Integration of Knowledge and Ideas

Ask: How does the action of remembering help prove the identity of the real King? What effect does this have on the plot?

Possible response: The Great Seal had been missing, so Hertford suggests that the true Prince of Wales will know where it is. This resolves the conflict that the Prince has of no one believing who he is.

17  **Big Question: Toward Essential Understanding**

1. Read aloud the passage, then draw students' attention to how characters react to the Prince and Tom.

2. Ask: How do the boys define themselves compared with how others see them?

Possible response: Both Tom and the Prince view themselves as the people they have always been: a pauper and a royal heir. Other characters have defined Tom and the Prince by their appearances.

3. Ask: How do the other characters react to the real identify of the boys.

Possible response: Hertford completely changes his mind about Tom and does not value him as a person anymore because of Tom's status. Miles wishes he would have known the truth because he probably would have treated the Prince differently.

PRINCE. *(Pausing)* I recall how we exchanged clothes, but have no recollection of hiding the Great Seal.

TOM. *(Eagerly)* Remember when you saw the bruise on my hand, you ran to the door, but first you hid this thing you call the Seal.

PRINCE. *(Suddenly)* Ah! I remember! *(To ST. JOHN)* Go, my good St. John, and you will find the Great Seal in the armor that hangs on the wall in my chamber. *(ST. JOHN hesitates, but at a nod from TOM, hurries off.)*

TOM. *(Pleased)* Right, my King! Now the scepter of England is yours again. *(ST. JOHN returns in a moment with Great Seal.)*

ALL. *(Shouting)* Long live Edward, King of England! *(TOM takes off his cape and throws it over PRINCE'S rags. Trumpet fanfare is heard. ST. JOHN takes crown and places it on PRINCE. All kneel.)*

HERTFORD. Let the small impostor be flung into the Tower![5]

PRINCE. *(Firmly)* I will not have it so. But for him, I would not have my crown. *(To TOM)* My poor boy, how was it that you could remember where I hid the Seal, when I could not?

TOM. *(Embarrassed)* I did not know what it was, my King, and I used it to ... to crack nuts. *(All laugh, and TOM steps back. MILES steps forward, staring in amazement.)*

MILES. Is he really the King? Is he indeed the sovereign of England, and not the poor and friendless Tom o' Bedlam[6] I thought he was? *(He sinks down on bench.)* I wish I had a bag to hide my head in!

1ST GUARD. *(Rushing up to him)* Stand up, you mannerless clown! How dare you sit in the presence of the King!

PRINCE. Do not touch him! He is my trusty servant, Miles Hendon, who saved me from shame and possible death. For his service, he owns the right to sit in my presence.

MILES. *(Bowing, then kneeling)* Your Majesty!

---

5. **Tower** the Tower of London, site of a prison and place of execution.
6. **Bedlam** British asylum for the mentally ill.

PRINCE. Rise, Sir Miles. I command that Sir Hugh Hendon, who sits within this hall, be seized and put under lock and key until I have need of him. *(Beckons to* TOM*)* From what I have heard, Tom Canty, you have governed the realm with royal gentleness and mercy in my absence. Henceforth, you shall hold the honorable title of King's Ward! *(*TOM *kneels and kisses* PRINCE'S *hand.)* And because I have suffered with the poorest of my subjects and felt the cruel force of unjust laws, I pledge myself to a reign of mercy for all! *(All bow low, then rise.)*

ALL. *(Shouting)* Long live the King! Long live Edward, King of England! *(Curtain)*

THE END

---

18 Close Reading

1. **Key Ideas and Details** Read aloud the passage to students. **Ask:** What does the Prince do in this passage?

   Possible response: He commands the arrest and imprisonment of Sir Hugh Hendon, appoints Tom as the King's Ward, and pledges to rule mercifully based on his experience as a poor subject.

2. **Craft and Structure** Ask students to reread the passage carefully. **Ask:** How does the language of this passage emphasize the play's time period?

   Possible response: The verbs that the Prince uses, such as *rise* and *seized* give him an authoritative and noble tone. Also, his use of *sir* and "honorable title" suggests that rank and status are very important. Based on this use of language, it is easy to imagine the Prince as a part of sixteenth-century society.

3. **Integration of Knowledge and Ideas**
   Ask: How does the time period affect how the characters in *The Prince and the Pauper* define themselves?

   Possible response: The period greatly affects how the characters define themselves. All of the characters value social rank, which determines how people should be treated and what privileges they enjoy. Throughout the play, the Prince defines himself by his social rank and tries to get other people to believe him. Tom, on the other hand, tries to tell others that he is a pauper but gives up because he does not want to be punished for pretending to be royalty.

❖ DIFFERENTIATED INSTRUCTION

EL Strategy for English Learners
Some students may have difficulty with language of the nobility and time period presented in *The Prince and the Pauper*. To help students understand what the noble characters are saying, guide them to rephrase confusing dialogue.

1. Read a confusing sentence aloud. For example, read Hertford's statement on p. 570, "Let the small impostor be flung into the Tower!"

2. Have students look around the sentence to identify context clues in surrounding sentences and other text features. Since the

Prince's identity has just been confirmed, Hertford must be talking about Tom. Hertford seems angry. Also, *Tower* has a footnote.

3. Use the context clues and features to determine the meaning of each part of the sentence. Tom is the *impostor,* or pretender, and the *Tower* is a prison. Also, Hertford probably wants Tom to be punished, so *flung* could mean "throw" or "lock away."

4. Rephrase the sentence so it is easier to understand: "Take the pretender to prison!"

⑲ Close Reading

1. Key Ideas and Details Read aloud the passage to students. **Ask:** What is being described in this passage? What inferences can you draw from this description?

Possible response: Twain is describing the different reactions to the birth of a pauper and the birth of a prince. Details like "who did not want him" suggest that Tom Canty was an unwelcome addition to his family. The sentence "All England wanted him too" suggest that Edward Tudor was considered a blessing for not only his family, but for all of England.

2. Craft and Structure Have students reread the text, taking notes on repeated words and phrases. **Ask:** How does Twain use repetition in this passage?

Possible response: He uses repetition to emphasize the differences between Tom and Edward. For example, Twain introduces Tom as "a boy was born to a poor family." He introduces Edward in an identical way as "another English child was born to a rich family." This repetition and other examples in the passage use language to directly contrast the boys, who will have opposite receptions from their families and opposite experiences in life.

3. Integration of Knowledge and Ideas

Ask: How does the repetition and contrast between Tom and Edward reflect class differences in this passage?

Possible response: Tom's birth was insignificant to everyone except the Canty family. Edward's birth, however, offered hope and inspired celebration to a country. This contrast suggests that a prince would be considered more valuable than an unwanted pauper.

---

from The Prince and the Pauper

Mark Twain

Chapter I. The birth of the Prince and the Pauper.

In the ancient city of London, on a certain autumn day in the second quarter of the sixteenth century, a boy was born to a poor family of the name of Canty, who did not want him. On the same day another English child was born to a rich family of the name of Tudor, who did want him. All England wanted him too. England had so longed for him, and hoped for him, and prayed God for him, that, now that he was really come, the people went nearly mad for joy. Mere acquaintances hugged and kissed each other and cried. Everybody took a holiday, and high and low, rich and poor, feasted and danced and sang, and got very mellow;[1] and they kept this up for days and nights together. By day, London was a sight to see, with gay banners waving from every balcony and housetop, and splendid pageants marching along. By night, it was again a sight to see, with its great bonfires at every corner, and its troops of revellers making merry around them. There was no talk in all England but of the new baby, Edward Tudor, Prince of Wales, who lay lapped[2] in silks and satins, unconscious of all this fuss, and not knowing that great lords and ladies were tending him and watching over him—and not caring, either. But there was no talk about the other baby, Tom Canty, lapped in his poor rags, except among the family of paupers whom he had just come to trouble with his presence.

---

1. **mellow** joyful or lighthearted.
2. **lapped** wrapped up or enfolded.

💬 VOCABULARY DEVELOPMENT

Academic Vocabulary

To reinforce and assess students' comprehension of academic vocabulary words, give them sentences using the words in which the word may or may not be used correctly. Students must tell whether the use is correct and explain their answer. Use these sentences:

1. The speaker looked around the room to judge his audience's *reaction* to his argument.
Answer: Yes, *reaction* is used correctly here. A reaction is a response to something done or said, like in a speech.

2. Every toy car was *unique,* so they all looked the same.
Answer: No, *unique* is not used correctly. It means "one of a kind," so something unique cannot look the same as something else.

3. The *diverse* student body included kids with exactly the same background.
Answer: No, *diverse* is not used correctly here. Diverse means the opposite of having exactly the same background.

Chapter III. Tom's meeting with the Prince.

Tom got up hungry, and sauntered hungry away, but with his thoughts busy with the shadowy splendours of his night's dreams. He wandered here and there in the city, hardly noticing where he was going, or what was happening around him. People jostled him, and some gave him rough speech; but it was all lost on the musing boy. By-and-by he found himself at Temple Bar,[3] the farthest from home he had ever travelled in that direction. He stopped and considered a moment, then fell into his imaginings again, and passed on outside the walls of London. The Strand[4] had ceased to be a country-road then, and regarded itself as a street, but by a strained construction; for, though there was a tolerably compact row of houses on one side of it, there were only some scattered great buildings on the other, these being palaces of rich nobles, with ample and beautiful grounds stretching to the river—grounds that are now closely packed with grim acres of brick and stone.

Tom discovered Charing Village presently, and rested himself at the beautiful cross built there by a bereaved king of earlier days; then idled down a quiet, lovely road, past the great cardinal's stately palace, toward a far more mighty and majestic palace beyond—Westminster. Tom stared in glad wonder at the vast pile of masonry, the wide-spreading wings, the frowning bastions and turrets,[5] the huge stone gateway, with its gilded bars and its magnificent array of colossal granite lions, and other the signs and symbols of English royalty. Was the desire of his soul to be satisfied at last? Here, indeed, was a king's palace. Might he not hope to see a prince now—a prince of flesh and blood, if Heaven were willing?

At each side of the gilded[6] gate stood a living statue—that is to say, an erect and stately and motionless man-at-arms, clad from head to heel in shining steel armour. At a respectful distance were many country folk, and people from the city,

◀ **sauntered**
(sôn´ tərd) *v.*
walked in a slow, relaxed manner

---

3. **Temple Bar** historic gate to the city of London.
4. **The Strand** street in London.
5. **bastions and turrets** projections and towers from the top or sides of a building.
6. **gilded** covered in gold.

PART 3 • *from* The Prince and the Pauper **573**

⓴ Close Reading

1. **Key Ideas and Details** Ask a student to read aloud the passage. **Ask:** What is being described in this passage? How does Tom react to this place?

   Possible response: This passage describes Westminster Palace. Tom is amazed and stares in awe at the masonry, the gate, and other magnificent features of the palace.

2. **Craft and Structure** Have students reread the passage, focusing on word choice. **Ask:** What examples of word choice emphasize the wealth of the royals?

   Possible response: Twain uses words like *gilded, magnificent,* and *splendid* to describe the palace. He also repeats these words several times within the passage, which suggests that the royal family has an abundance of wealth surrounding them.

3. **Integration of Knowledge and Ideas**
   Ask: Based on the word choice Twain uses, how is royalty defined?

   Possible response: This passage suggests that royalty is defined by how a palace looks and by how people react to the riches that surround it. Country folk and people from the city look on the Westminster Palace in wonder, which reflects how these people view royalty. This focus on appearance is similar to how appearance is defined in the play. In the play, other characters define Tom and the Prince based on their clothes and how they look.

👥 DIFFERENTIATED INSTRUCTION

Strategy for Special-Needs Students

To help students connect the play and the novel excerpt, help students review some of the key ideas from the play. Ask questions to prompt student responses, such as *How do Tom and the Prince meet?* or *How were Tom's and the Prince's backgrounds different?* Discuss these questions and their possible answers with students. Have students write the main ideas on sticky notes, making several copies of each idea. After the discussion, remind students that Twain explores the same ideas in the novel as he does in the play. Then, have students read along as you read the novel excerpt aloud. After the reading, have students work with a partner and reread the novel excerpt, placing the sticky notes where they see the key ideas appearing. Then discuss the passages students identified and correct any misunderstandings.

㉑ Close Reading

1. Key Ideas and Details Ask a student to read aloud the passage. **Ask:** What details lead Tom to decide that he is looking at the Prince?

Possible response: Details like "shining with jewels," "dainty buskins," and "a jaunty crimson cap...with a great sparkling gem" all suggest to Tom that he is looking at the Prince.

2. Craft and Structure Have students reread the passage, taking notes on word choice. **Ask:** How do the descriptive details in this passage show Tom's awe of the Prince?

Possible response: The descriptive details about the Prince, such as "lovely silks and satins" and "drooping plumes," appear in one complex sentence. This sentence structure, which jumps from one item to the next, suggests that the sight of the Prince overwhelms Tom. Also, the repetition of "prince" conveys Tom's excitement in finally seeing real royalty.

3. Integration of Knowledge and Ideas
Ask: How do these descriptions emphasize the idea that people are often defined by their appearance?

Possible response: This passage describes how the prince is dressed. Tom is defining the Prince's identity by the finery he sees. The phrase "without a shadow of a question" also suggests that people assume it is the Prince based on his clothes and that there is no need to question that assumption. This lack of questioning is also seen when the other characters do not believe Tom's and the Prince's claims of who they are based on their clothing.

⓴ waiting for any chance glimpse of royalty that might offer. Splendid carriages, with splendid people in them and splendid servants outside, were arriving and departing by several other noble gateways that pierced the royal enclosure.

⓴ Poor little Tom, in his rags, approached, and was moving slowly and timidly past the sentinels, with a beating heart and a rising hope, when all at once he caught sight through the golden bars of a spectacle that almost made him shout for joy. Within was a comely boy, tanned and brown with sturdy outdoor sports and exercises, whose clothing was all of lovely silks and satins, shining with jewels; at his hip a little jewelled sword and dagger; dainty buskins on his feet, with red heels; and on his head a jaunty crimson cap, with drooping plumes fastened with a great sparkling gem. Several gorgeous gentlemen stood near—his servants, without a doubt. Oh! he was a prince—a prince, a living prince, a real prince—without the shadow of a question; and the prayer of the pauper-boy's heart was answered at last.

Tom's breath came quick and short with excitement, and his eyes grew big with wonder and delight. Everything gave way in his mind instantly to one desire: that was to get close to the prince, and have a good, devouring look at him. Before he knew what he was about, he had his face against the gate-bars. The next instant one of the soldiers snatched him rudely away, and sent him spinning among the gaping crowd of country gawks and London idlers. The soldier said,—

"Mind thy manners, thou young beggar!"

The crowd jeered and laughed; but the young prince sprang to the gate with his face flushed, and his eyes flashing with indignation, and cried out,—

⓶⓶ "How dar'st thou use a poor lad like that? How dar'st thou use the King my father's meanest subject so? Open the gates, and let him in!"

You should have seen that fickle crowd snatch off their hats then. You should have heard them cheer, and shout, "Long live the Prince of Wales!"

🖻 VOCABULARY DEVELOPMENT

Graphic Organizers

To help students understand Twain's descriptive language, encourage students to create concept maps for the Prince of Poverty and the Prince of Limitless Plenty. Have students use the details on pages 574–575 that describe both Tom and the Prince. Encourage students to identify words that they do not know and look up each word. Remind students to use context clues to determine which dictionary definition fits each word best. After students define all of the unknown words, ask them to find synonyms for the words Twain uses to enlarge their concept maps. After students' have completed the activity, discuss students' concept maps and correct any misunderstandings.

The soldiers presented arms with their halberds,[7] opened the gates, and presented again as the little Prince of Poverty passed in, in his fluttering rags, to join hands with the Prince of Limitless Plenty.

Edward Tudor said—

"Thou lookest tired and hungry: thou'st been treated ill. Come with me."

Half a dozen attendants sprang forward to—I don't know what; interfere, no doubt. But they were waved aside with a right royal gesture, and they stopped stock still where they were, like so many statues. Edward took Tom to a rich apartment in the palace, which he called his cabinet. By his command a repast was brought such as Tom had never encountered before except in books. The prince, with princely delicacy and breeding, sent away the servants, so that his humble guest might not be embarrassed by their critical presence; then he sat near by, and asked questions while Tom ate.

"What is thy name, lad?"

"Tom Canty, an' it please thee, sir."

---

7. **halberds** (hal´ bərds) weapons used in the fifteenth and sixteenth centuries.

ABOUT THE AUTHOR

Mark Twain (1835–1910)

Mark Twain, who was born Samuel Langhorne Clemens, grew up along the Mississippi River in Hannibal, Missouri. He became a riverboat pilot at the age of twenty-three. Later, when he became an author, he adopted the pen name Mark Twain, a term used by riverboat pilots that means "two fathoms (twelve feet) deep." In addition to piloting riverboats and writing novels, Twain also worked as a journalist in the American West and travelled the world giving lectures. During his lifetime, he gained fame as both a writer and a very entertaining stage presence. Today, Twain's most popular novel is *Tom Sawyer*, but the book that most critics consider to be his masterpiece is *The Adventures of Huckleberry Finn*.

PART 3 • *from* The Prince and the Pauper **575**

22 Focus Passage

A Focus Passage is identified with brackets in the Student Edition for students' independent close reading and analysis. A question bank for the passage and possible responses appear at the end of the selection.

👥 DIFFERENTIATED INSTRUCTION

Culturally Responsive Instruction

Because Twain uses older language to establish the time period in the novel excerpt, some students may have difficulty understanding the dialogue on pages 574–575. Explain to students that the words *thou* and *thy* were used in the 1500s to mean *you* and *your*. Ask students to rewrite the dialogue using contemporary language. After they have finished writing, have students work in pairs to compare their dialogues with the passage. Monitor students' progress and correct any misunderstandings. Then, discuss students' comparisons as a class. Ask questions to encourage discussion, such as *Which dialogue is easier to understand and why?* or *Would the story have been more believable if Twain used more contemporary language? Why or why not?*

© **Close Reading Activities**

READ

Comprehension

1. Tom, the pauper, and the Prince change places.

2. The true prince becomes king, and the pauper is rewarded.

3. Tom presses his face against the gate to see the Prince. When the guards try to send him away, the Prince orders Tom to be let in.

4. He invites him in and feeds him.

Research: Clarify Details

Students should use their research to explain an unfamiliar detail in the story.

Summarize

Play summaries should include the switch, the Prince meeting Tom's father and Miles Hendon, the thievery incident and jail, and the events of Coronation Day. Novel excerpt summaries should include the two births, Tom's travels to Westminster, the incident with the guards, and meeting the Prince.

Language Study
Selection Vocabulary
Possible responses:

• *pauper:* someone who is very poor; The pauper wore shoes with holes; negative.

• *affliction:* pain, illness, suffering; His affliction kept him from playing sports; negative.

• *sauntered:* walked in a slow, relaxed manner; She sauntered to the park; neutral.

Diction and Style

1. (a) Tom's clothes are "fluttering rags." (b) His clothes may be flapping from holes and tears, from his excitement, or from both.

2. (a) The proper nouns are Prince of Poverty and Prince of Limitless Plenty. (b) **Possible responses:** The diction makes the boys represent poverty and plenty; the titles emphasize the contrast; the royal title emphasizes wealth.

READ

Comprehension
Reread to answer these questions.

1. In the play, who changes places?

2. What happens at the end of the play?

3. In the novel, how does Tom meet the prince?

4. In the novel, what does the prince do for Tom?

Language Study

Selection Vocabulary Define each boldfaced word and use it in a sentence. Then, identify each word's connotation—the feelings it suggests—as either negative, neutral, or positive.

• I am the lowest of your subjects, being born a **pauper**, and it is by a great mistake that I am here.

• Ah, your **affliction** hangs heavily upon you.

• Tom got up hungry, and **sauntered** hungry away, but with his thoughts busy with the shadowy splendours of his night's dreams.

Diction and Style Read this sentence from the novel excerpt and answer the questions that follow.

> The soldiers presented arms … as the little Prince of Poverty passed in, in his fluttering rags, to join hands with the Prince of Limitless Plenty.

1. (a) What words describe Tom's clothing? (b) What image do these words convey?

Conventions

(a) The appositive phrase "my father" identifies the noun *King*. (b) The Prince inserts this phrase to emphasize his true identity.

Academic Vocabulary

If students struggle with categorizing and defining the academic vocabulary words, use this routine:

Write the words and definitions on the board.

respond: answer or reply

technique: author's way of using words

similar: alike

Research: Clarify Details Research an unfamiliar detail in these works and explain how your research sheds light on the work.

Summarize Write an objective summary of "The Prince and the Pauper." Include only the main ideas and details. Do not include your opinions.

2. (a) What proper nouns describe the two boys? (b) What important idea about the boys do these words suggest?

Conventions Identify the appositive phrase in the lines from the play that appear below. (a) What noun does the phrase identify or explain? (b) Why does the prince include this information?

> **PRINCE.** Take me to the palace at once, and your son will be returned to you. The King, my father, will make you rich beyond your wildest dreams.

Academic Vocabulary

The following words appear in blue in the questions on the facing page.

respond   technique   similar

Copy the words in your notebook. Which word is a literary term? Which is an action? Which can be used to link words and describe nouns?

Have students say each word aloud. Then use the word in a sentence. Sample sentences should demonstrate the literary term (technique), the action word (respond), and the adjective (similar).

Literary Analysis

Reread the identified passages. The first is from the play; the second is from the novel excerpt. Then, respond to the questions that follow:

Focus Passage 1 *(pp. 559–560)*

ST. JOHN. Does it not seem strange … crack nuts with Great Seal and eat them, *as curtain falls*).

Focus Passage 2 *(p. 574)*

"Mind thy manners … "Long live the Prince of Wales!"

Key Ideas and Details

1. What troubles St. John?

2. Does Tom seem to feel at home in the palace? What details support your answer?

Craft and Structure

3. **(a)** What does Hertford say to reassure St. John? **(b) Interpret:** How do Hertford's remarks add humor to the play?

4. **(a)** At the end of the scene, what action of Tom's do the stage directions describe? **(b) Interpret:** What is funny about Tom's action?

Integration of Knowledge and Ideas

5. **(a) Draw Conclusions:** Which man has greater insight, Hertford or St. John? Support your answer.

6. **Synthesize:** What does this passage suggest about the life of a real prince?

Key Ideas and Details

1. **(a)** Who is the young beggar? **(b)** What does he want to do?

Craft and Structure

2. **(a) Compare and Contrast:** How does the crowd **respond** both before and after the prince speaks? **(b) Interpret:** What does this response tell you about the crowd?

3. **(a) Infer:** In this passage, who does the narrator address as "you"? **(b) Analyze:** What effect does Twain achieve by using this **technique**?

Integration of Knowledge and Ideas

4. **Draw Conclusions:** What does this passage suggest about human nature? **(b) Deduce:** Does Twain want his audience to laugh, to think, or both? Explain.

Theme

A **theme** is a central insight about life. As you reread the play, list details that reveal one or more themes.

1. **(a)** What does Miles do for the prince? **(b)** In the end, how is Miles rewarded?

2. **(a)** What does the constable do that he should not do? **(b)** What is the outcome for the constable and for the prince?

3. **(a)** How does Tom behave toward the prince throughout the play? **(b)** What is the outcome for Tom?

4. What theme do these **similar** events show?

Common Core State Standards

RL.6.1, RL.6.2, RL.6.4; L.6.4a, L.6.4d, L.6.6
[For full standards wording, see the chart in the front of this book.]

5. Hertford is logical but also does not care that the Prince is mad. St. John's troubled thoughts suggest he is closer to the truth because he finds the madness strange.

6. The passage suggests that a prince would still be honored and have royal duties despite being mad. The description of Tom saying that he should have ordered something to eat, shows that a prince can get whatever he wants.

Focus Passage 2

1. **(a)** The young beggar is Tom. **(b)** He wants to see what the Prince looks like.

2. **(a)** Before, people in the crowd jeer at Tom; after, they cheer and take off their hats. **(b)** The crowd responds to rank; the crowd reacts according to class or status; the crowd is fickle, or changes loyalties easily.

3. **(a)** The narrator is addressing the reader. **(b)** This technique allows the author to seem as if he is conspiring with the audience in making fun of the "fickle crowd" or of human nature.

4. **(a)** People will say and do what's best for them; people love celebrities. **(b)** Twain wants readers to laugh and think about human nature.

Theme

1. **(a)** Miles takes the Prince in and saves him from jail. **(b)** Miles will get back his estate and bride.

2. **(a)** He tries to get the pig cheaply. **(b)** The constable's corruption is exposed. He does not get what he wants, and the Prince goes free.

3. **(a)** Tom is always respectful and honest. **(b)** He becomes the King's Ward.

4. **Possible response:** Respect and kindness will be rewarded.

 Online Writer's Notebook

Students can use the Online Writer's Notebook to record all responses.

Literary Analysis

Possible responses appear below. Check to be sure students support their responses with evidence from the text.

Focus Passage 1

1. The Prince's change in manner, or behavior, bothers him.

2. At first Tom looks around helplessly and gets up, so he doesn't seem comfortable. But then he sits down to eat when he notices a bowl of nuts and seems more at home doing what he wants to do.

3. **(a)** He says it is unnatural for any person not to want to be called a prince. **(b)** His remarks add ironic humor because Tom is truthful when he denies being the Prince.

4. **(a)** They show him grabbing the Great Seal and using it to crack nuts. **(b)** The Great Seal is a symbol like the flag: it is both horrible and funny to think of it being used that way.

DISCUSS

From Text to Topic: Partner Discussion

Possible responses:

1. It does not matter if a king is real or not, or mad or not, as long as he does right by his people.

2. The Prince thinks there is only one real king, the heir by birth; only noble people can act like kings; he thinks that no beggar boy could be a good king.

WRITE

Writing to Sources: Informative Text

Introduce the assignment using the instruction on the student page.

Prewriting and Planning

1. Although most of the characters in *The Prince and the Pauper* confuse the two boys, some students may find it challenging to determine significant similarities and differences between the Prince and Tom. To guide their rereading and note-taking, provide struggling students with guiding questions, such as: *How does the author introduce each boy? Throughout the story, what key details about the characters stand out to you as being similar or different? Why does Tom stop trying to prove his identity when no one believes him? Why does the Prince continue to try to prove his identity, even when no one believes him?*

2. Provide students with copies of a Venn diagram to aid them in making comparisons.

3. Suggest that students use sticky notes to mark passages they may wish to cite.

Drafting

1. Review the two organizational structures for comparison-and-contrast writing: block method and point-by-point method.

2. Tell students to select the method that will help them organize their ideas in the clearest way.

DISCUSS

From Text to Topic **Partner Discussion**

Discuss the following passage with a partner. Contribute your own ideas, and support them with examples from the text. Take notes during your discussion.

> **PRINCE.** *(Violently)* King? What King, good sir?
> **1ST PRISONER.** Why, we only have one, his most sacred majesty, King Edward the Sixth.
> **2ND PRISONER.** And whether he be mad or not, his praises are on all men's lips. He has saved many innocent lives, and now he means to destroy the cruelest laws that oppress the people.
> **PRINCE.** *(Turning away, shaking his head)* How can this be? Surely it is not that little beggar boy! (p. 568)

WRITE

Writing to Sources **Informative Text**

> **Assignment**
> Write a **comparison-and-contrast essay** in which you analyze the two main characters in "The Prince and the Pauper."

Prewriting and Planning Reread both the play and the novel excerpt, looking for details that describe each boy's personality, behavior, and motivations. Record your notes in a Venn diagram.

Drafting Select a strategy for developing your ideas. Most comparison-and-contrast writing follows either a block or point-by-point organization (see p. 243 for information on these organizational patterns).

Cite specific examples from the texts to support your points.

Revising Reread your essay, making sure you clearly explain similarities and differences. Add or revise transitional words or phrases, such as those below, to connect your ideas.

in the same way	*also*	*similarly*	*likewise*
in contrast	*on the contrary*	*on the other hand*	*nevertheless*

Editing and Proofreading Make sure your transitional words and phrases show comparisons and contrasts.

QUESTIONS FOR DISCUSSION

1. What does this passage suggest about the real qualifications of a king?

2. What does the prince's surprise imply about differences between Tom and himself?

CONVENTIONS

When you use an adverb such as *similarly* to begin a sentence, place a comma after it.

Revising

1. Encourage students to review their drafts to ensure they have used transitional words and phrases to effectively convey comparisons and contrasts.

2. Remind students that their main points should be supported with specific examples from the text.

Editing and Proofreading

1. Encourage students to check that they have correctly used transitional words and phrases. For example, did they use *likewise* or *similarly* to convey points of comparison and *however* or *instead* to convey points of contrast?

2. Have students check that they have used a comma after an adverb, such as *similarly,* when it is used at the beginning of a sentence.

RESEARCH

Research **Investigate the Topic**

The Palace of Westminster In "The Prince and the Pauper, Mark Twain presents ideas about identity, partly by describing royalty and royal settings. One of the most famous royal settings in England is the Palace of Westminster.

> ### Assignment
>
> Conduct research to learn about the Palace of Westminster and its long history. Find out about the structure itself, as well as the associations this important site has had with British royalty and other key figures in British history. Consult credible print and Internet sources. Take clear notes so that you can easily access the information later. Share your findings in an **illustrated timeline**. In addition, write a paragraph in which you tell why you think Mark Twain chose the Palace of Westminster as a primary setting for his novel.

PREPARATION FOR ESSAY

You may use the knowledge you gain during this research assignment to support your claims in an essay at the end of this section.

Gather Sources Locate authoritative print and electronic sources. Look for expert authors and up-to-date facts. Follow links to new information, but remember to evaluate new sites for credibility.

Take Notes Take notes on each of your sources, either electronically or on note cards. Use an organized note-taking strategy.

- Clearly identify all the sources you consult. Note that many Web sites offer information on how to correctly cite them.
- Copy and paste only citation information, URLs, and exact words that you plan to quote.
- Paraphrase and summarize all other information on separate note cards or in separate files that clearly state each source.

Synthesize Multiple Sources Assemble data from your sources, including drawings, photographs, and diagrams. Use your notes and visuals to create your illustrated timeline. Create a Works Cited list as described in the Research Workshop in the Introductory Unit of this textbook.

Organize and Present Ideas Present your outline and paragraph to a small group of classmates. Be prepared to answer questions from your audience.

 Common Core
State Standards

W.6.2.a, W.6.2.b, W.6.2.c, W.6.2.d, W.6.2.f, W.6.4, SL.6.1.a-d
[For full standards wording, see the chart in the front of this book.]

RESEARCH

Investigate the Topic

Introduce the assignment, using the instruction on the student page.

Gather Sources

1. Arrange for students to visit your school's library or computer lab.
2. Remind students that some Internet sites provide unreliable information. Tell them that .gov, .edu, and .org Web sites are generally more reliable than .com Web sites.

Take Notes

1. Remind students that, in addition to directly quoting from a source, they can also summarize or paraphrase important information they learn from it, as long as they do so in their own words.
2. Emphasize that students must clearly state each source in their notes.

Synthesize Multiple Sources

1. Encourage students to draw conclusions and make connections between ideas from multiple sources.
2. Have students create an outline for their presentation. Point out that creating an outline will help them identify and organize the main points on which they want to focus.
3. Review the MLA style requirements for citing different kinds of print and online sources and provide examples. Have students create a Works Cited list that accurately identifies each source they reference.

Organize and Present Ideas

Remind students to practice so that they do not need to read directly from their presentation outlines and are prepared to answer any questions.

MULTIDRAFT READING

Essential Understanding

First, students should read the entire selection on their own. Then, to assist struggling readers and to deepen comprehension for all, you may wish to guide them through the selection by asking them the close reading questions provided in the margins. Have students apply the multidraft reading protocols as they examine specific "chunks" of text related to these questions. For each reading, have students set the purpose indicated:

- **First reading:** Students should read the selection independently and think about its basic meaning.
- **Second reading:** Students should analyze the text's key ideas and details and its craft and structure.
- **Third reading:** Students should integrate knowledge and ideas; connect to the Big Question, other texts, and the world; and use teacher-led Close Reading discussion questions to examine particularly rich and significant passages.

For more guidance, refer to the *Classroom Strategies and Teaching Routines* card on multidraft reading.

🔔 Daily Bellringer

For each class during which you teach these selections, have students complete one of the five Quick Write activities for Week 25 in *Daily Bellringer Activities*. You may wish to use additional activities that are applicable to these selections.

❶ Background

Explain that stage fright is a common fear for many people. It is a fight or flight response felt at the thought of appearing on stage.

Vocabulary

1. Write the following words and definitions on the board:

   compulsion *n.* driving force

   awed *adj.* filled with feelings of fear and wonder

   agonizing *adj.* making great efforts or struggling; being in great pain

2. Have students say each word aloud.

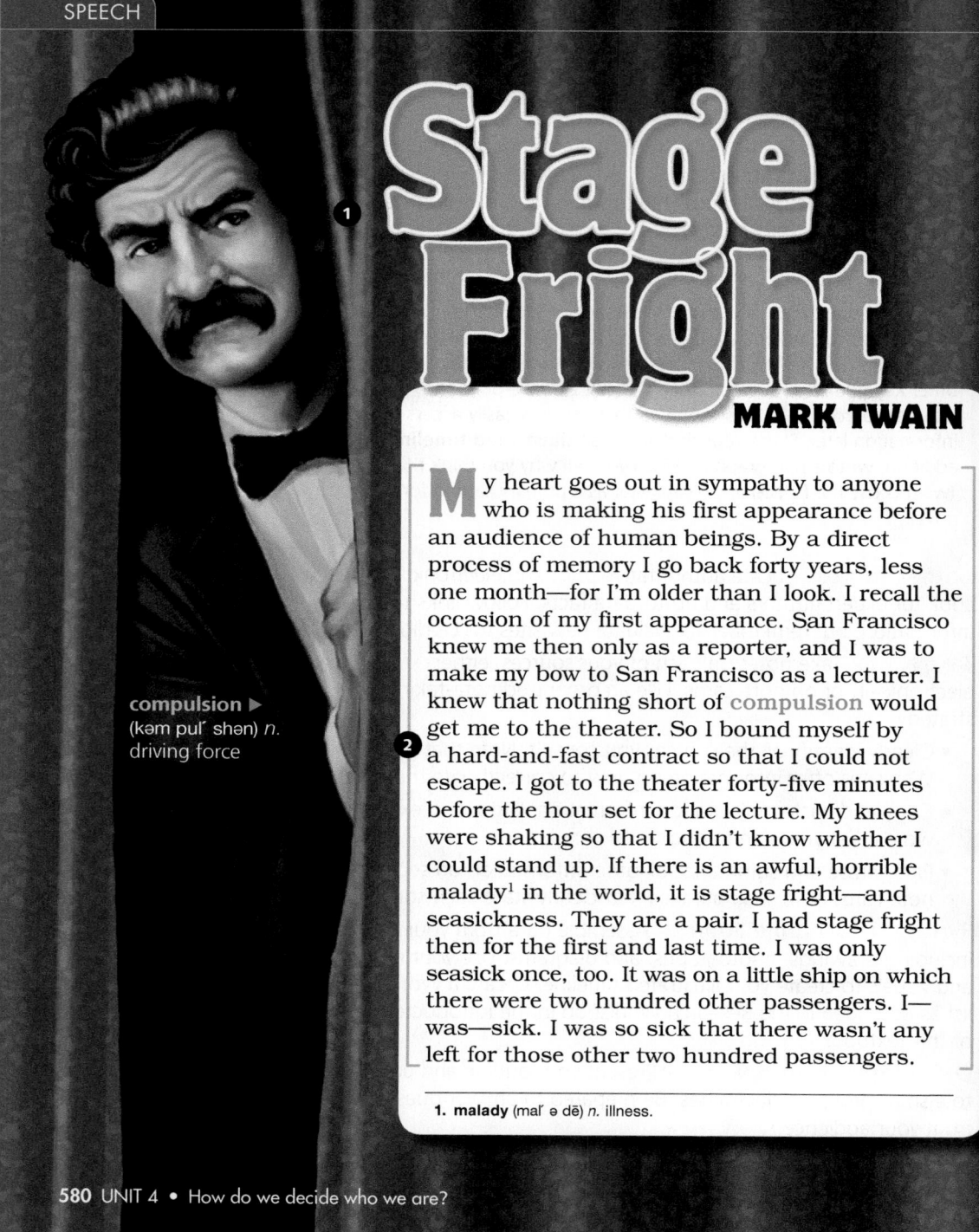

Stage Fright

MARK TWAIN

My heart goes out in sympathy to anyone who is making his first appearance before an audience of human beings. By a direct process of memory I go back forty years, less one month—for I'm older than I look. I recall the occasion of my first appearance. San Francisco knew me then only as a reporter, and I was to make my bow to San Francisco as a lecturer. I knew that nothing short of compulsion would get me to the theater. So I bound myself by a hard-and-fast contract so that I could not escape. I got to the theater forty-five minutes before the hour set for the lecture. My knees were shaking so that I didn't know whether I could stand up. If there is an awful, horrible malady[1] in the world, it is stage fright—and seasickness. They are a pair. I had stage fright then for the first and last time. I was only seasick once, too. It was on a little ship on which there were two hundred other passengers. I—was—sick. I was so sick that there wasn't any left for those other two hundred passengers.

compulsion ▶
(kəm pul′ shən) *n.* driving force

---

1. **malady** (mal′ ə dē) *n.* illness.

580 UNIT 4 • How do we decide who we are?

©TEXT COMPLEXITY **RUBRIC**

Stage Fright		
Qualitative Measures	Context/Knowledge Demands	Mid-1800s; humorous speech 1　2　③　4　5
	Structure/Language Conventionality and Clarity	Slightly dated; multiple meanings 1　2　3　④　5
	Levels of Meaning/ Purpose/Concept Level	Accessible concept (stage fright) 1　2　③　4　5
Quantitative Measures	Text Length	Word Count: 541
	Lexile	880L

It was dark and lonely behind the scenes in that theater, and I peeked through the little peek holes they have in theater curtains and looked into the big auditorium. That was dark and empty, too. By and by it lighted up, and the audience began to arrive.

I had got a number of friends of mine, stalwart[2] men, to sprinkle themselves through the audience armed with big clubs. Every time I said anything they could possibly guess I intended to be funny, they were to pound those clubs on the floor. Then there was a kind lady in a box up there, also a good friend of mine, the wife of the governor. She was to watch me intently, and whenever I glanced toward her she was going to deliver a gubernatorial laugh that would lead the whole audience into applause.

At last I began. I had the manuscript tucked under a United States flag in front of me where I could get at it in case of need. But I managed to get started without it. I walked up and down—I was young in those days and needed the exercise—and talked and talked.

Right in the middle of the speech I had placed a gem. I had put in a moving, pathetic part which was to get at the hearts and souls of my hearers. When I delivered it, they did just what I hoped and expected. They sat silent and awed. I had touched them. Then I happened to glance up at the box where the governor's wife was—you know what happened.

Well, after the first agonizing five minutes, my stage fright left me, never to return. I know if I was going to be hanged I could get up and make a good showing, and I intend to. But I shall never forget my feelings before the agony left me, and I got up here to thank you for her for helping my daughter, by your kindness, to live through her first appearance. And I want to thank you for your appreciation of her singing, which is, by the way, hereditary.

◀ **awed**
(ôd) *adj.* filled with feelings of fear and wonder

◀ **agonizing**
(ag′ ə nīz′ iŋ) *adj.* making great efforts or struggling; being in great pain

---

2. **stalwart** (stôul′ wərt) *adj.* strong; sturdy.

PART 3 • Stage Fright **581**

Ⓒ TEXT COMPLEXITY **READER AND TASK SUGGESTIONS**

Stage Fright	
Preparing to Read the Text • Discuss the language Twain uses. Review unfamiliar phrases, such as "direct process of memory," "make my bow to San Francisco." • Guide students to use Multidraft Reading strategies (TE p. 580).	**Leveled Tasks** *Language* If students will have difficulty with the language, have them suggest possible translations of difficult phrases. Encourage them to use the context to help them understand the phrases. *Synthesizing* If students will not have difficulty with the language, have them note humorous passages. Discuss Twain's use of humor in the last sentence on p. 580.

❷ Focus Passage

A Focus Passage is identified with brackets in the Student Edition for students' independent close reading and analysis. A question bank for the passage and possible responses appear at the end of the selection.

❸ Close Reading

1. **Key Ideas and Details** Read aloud the passage to students.
   Ask: What is Twain's plan for making his speech a success?

   Possible response: Twain's friends would pound clubs on the floor during funny parts and he asked a woman to laugh when he looks at her.

2. **Craft and Structure**
   Ask: How does Twain use word choice to create characterizations?

   Possible response: The "stalwart men" with "big clubs" might bully the audience into laughing. A "kind lady" with "a gubernatorial laugh" suggests a dignified woman.

3. **Integration of Knowledge and Ideas**
   Ask: How does Twain's characterization of his friends develop the tone of the essay?

   Possible response: It reinforces the humorous tone by emphasizing how Twain tried to deal with stage fright.

❹ ⑦ Big Question: Toward Essential Understanding

1. **Ask:** How has Twain's point of view about stage fright changed?

   Possible response: Having lived through his stage fright, Twain knows that he can succeed.

2. **Ask:** What influences the opinion we have about ourselves?

   Possible response: Twain suggests that our fears and experiences can influence the opinion we have about ourselves.

 Audio

Selection Audio is available in the *Student eText* and on the *Hear It!* CD-ROM.

PART 3 • Stage Fright **581**

Close Reading Activities

READ

Comprehension

1. He is on stage in a theater in San Francisco.

2. He arranges for people in the audience to act as if they are enjoying his performance.

3. His stage fright ends.

Research: Clarify Details

Students should use their research to clarify a detail that is unfamiliar.

Summarize

Students' summaries should mention Twain's nervousness, his plan for getting the audience response he desires, how the plan backfires, and the end of his stage fright.

Language Study

Possible responses:

- *compulsion:* driving force; compulsive, compulsory.
- *awed:* filled with feelings of fear and wonder; awe, awesome.
- *agonizing:* requiring great effort; painful; agony, agonize

Literary Analysis

Possible responses appear below. Check to be sure students support their responses with evidence from the text.

1. He sympathizes with anyone appearing before an audience for the first time.

2. (a) He compares it to seasickness. **(b)** He suggests a terrible or extreme physical response.

3. (a) Twain says that once he was was so sick no sickness was left for the other two hundred passengers. **(b)** It is funny; it shows how awful seasickness is.

4. Twains calls stage fright agonizing, describes it as among the worst things that can embarrass a person and cause physical discomfort. However, he also explains that he used strategies to help overcome his stage fright and had it only once.

READ

Comprehension

Reread to answer the following questions.

1. Where is Twain when he experiences stage fright?

2. What plan does Twain make before he speaks?

3. What happens after the first five minutes?

Language Study

Selection Vocabulary Define each boldfaced word, then list related words in different parts of speech. Use a dictionary if you need help.

- I knew that nothing short of **compulsion** would get me to the theater.

Literary Analysis

Reread the passage and answer the questions:

> **Focus Passage** *(p. 580)*
>
> My heart goes out in sympathy ... those other two hundred passengers.

Key Ideas and Details

1. For whom does Twain feel sympathy? Why?

Craft and Structure

2. (a) Connect: To what does Twain compare stage fright? **(b) Interpret:** What

Humor

Humor is writing that is intended to make readers laugh. Reread the speech, and take notes on how Twain uses humor.

1. (a) What does Twain say about his age? **(b)** Why is his remark funny?

Research: Clarify Details Research at least one unfamiliar detail in this speech and explain how your research sheds light on the work.

Summarize Write an objective summary of the speech. Remember that an objective summary does not include opinions or evaluations.

- They sat silent and **awed**.
- Well, after the first **agonizing** five minutes, my stage fright left me, never to return.

idea does he suggest by making this comparison?

3. (a) How does Twain use *hyperbole,* or exaggeration, to describe his experience on the "little ship"? **(b) Draw Conclusions:** What is the effect of this hyperbole?

Integration of Knowledge and Ideas

4. What is Twain's **opinion** of stage fright? Support your answer with details from the passage.

2. (a) What does the governor's wife do? **(b)** Why is her action funny?

3. (a) In the last line of the speech, what does Twain say about his daughter's talent? **(b)** Why is this funny?

Humor

1. (a) He says he is older than he looks. **(b)** He implies that he is young looking, which is not modest.

2. (a) She laughs on cue. **(b)** The cue is an accident, so she laughs at a serious moment.

3. (a) He says her talent of singing is hereditary. **(b)** He gives himself credit for her talent, which is not modest.

Stage Fright
MARK TWAIN

DISCUSS • RESEARCH • WRITE

From Text to Topic **Panel Discussion**

Discuss the following passage with a small group of classmates. Take notes during the discussion. Contribute your own ideas, and support them with examples from the text.

> At last I began. I had the manuscript tucked under a United States flag in front of me where I could get at it in case of need. But I managed to get started without it.

Research **Investigate the Topic**

Stage Fright In his speech, Twain says he feels sympathy for anyone going on stage for the first time.

Assignment

Conduct research to learn more about stage fright. Use a library database to find health studies about the human body's reaction to stage fright. Take clear notes and carefully identify your sources so that you can easily access the information later. Share your findings in a **brief research report**. Tell whether or not Twain describes a common reaction to stage fright in his speech.

Writing to Sources **Informational Text**

Mark Twain relates his own experience with stage fright. Develop a how-to essay to help people deal with stage fright.

Assignment

Write a **how-to essay** in which you include advice that Twain either follows himself or implies in his speech. Follow these steps:

- Introduce the topic, and organize your ideas by using bullets or numbers.
- Develop the topic with information from your research, from personal experience, and from Twain's speech.
- Use transitions to show the relationships among ideas.
- Establish and maintain a formal style.

QUESTIONS FOR DISCUSSION

1. What is Twain worried about?
2. For what purpose does he put the manuscript under a U.S. flag? Why is that funny?

PREPARATION FOR ESSAY

You may use the results of this research to support your ideas in the essay at the end of this section.

ACADEMIC VOCABULARY

Academic terms appear in blue on these pages. If these words are not familiar to you, use a dictionary to find their definitions. Then, use them as you speak and write about the text.

Common Core State Standards

RI.6.1, RI.6.2, RI.6.4, RI.6.5; SL.6.1; L.6.4, L.6.5, L.6.6; W.6.2

[For full standards wording, see the chart in the front of this book.]

Academic Vocabulary

If students struggle with defining the academic vocabulary words, use this routine:

Write the words and definitions on the board.

opinion: a personal belief

common: public, being used by everyone

purpose: the reason why something is done

Have students say each word aloud. Then have students use each word in a sentence.

DISCUSS • RESEARCH • WRITE

From Text to Topic: Panel Discussion

Possible responses:

1. He is worried that he may not remember what he wanted to say.
2. Twain thinks that the flag will protect him. It is funny because he feels he needs a special object to help him feel confident, but he does not really need it.

Research: Investigate the Topic

Introduce the assignment, using the instruction on the student page.

1. Arrange for students to visit your school's library or computer lab in order to use the library's database. Review strategies for using databases.
2. Remind students to take notes on the human body's reactions to stage fright as described in each source, either by directly quoting or summarizing in their own words. Remind students to identify sources in their notes so they can access the information later, if necessary.
3. Encourage students to draw conclusions and make connections between multiple health studies. Suggest that they prepare an outline for their presentation.
4. Suggest that students practice so that they do not need to read directly from their presentation outlines and are prepared to answer any questions.

Writing to Sources: Informational Text

Students' how-to essays should introduce the topic, format the advice using bullets or numbers, use transitions, use precise language, and maintain a formal style.

Online Writer's Notebook

Students can use the Online Writer's Notebook to record all responses.

PART 3 • Close Reading Activities 583

MULTIDRAFT READING

Essential Understanding

First, students should read the entire selection on their own. Then, to assist struggling readers and to deepen comprehension for all, you may wish to guide them through the selection by asking them the close reading questions provided in the margins. Have students apply the multidraft reading protocols as they examine specific "chunks" of text related to these questions. For each reading, have students set the purpose indicated:

- **First reading:** Students should read the selection independently and think about its basic meaning.

- **Second reading:** Students should analyze the text's key ideas and details and its craft and structure.

- **Third reading:** Students should integrate knowledge and ideas; connect to the Big Question, other texts, and the world; and use teacher-led Close Reading discussion questions to examine particularly rich and significant passages.

For more guidance, refer to the ***Classroom Strategies and Teaching Routines*** card on multidraft reading.

❶ Background

If you wish, describe to students how this biography offers a different perspective than most biographies. After reading Susy Clemens's biography of him, Twain said, "I have had no compliment, no praise, no tribute from any source that was so precious to me as this one was and still is." The author's account of Twain provides an adoring daughter's perspective of her father.

Vocabulary

If students require support with selection vocabulary, use this routine:

1. Write the following words and definitions on the board:

   striking *adj.* very noticeable or impressive; unusual

   incessantly *adv.* constantly; continually

   consequently *adv.* as a result

2. Have students say each word aloud.

3. Use the word in a sentence that defines the word.

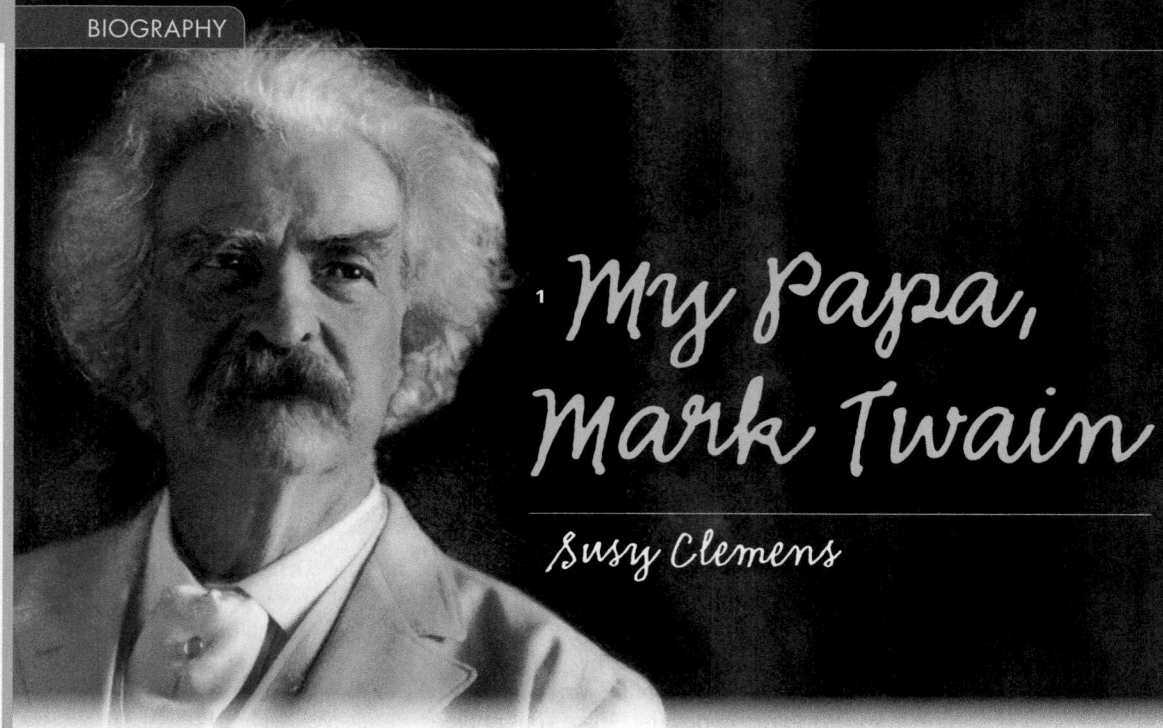

¹ My Papa, Mark Twain

Susy Clemens

We are a very happy family.

striking ▶
(strī′ kiŋ) *adj.* very noticeable or impressive; unusual

We consist of Papa, Mamma, Jean, Clara and me. It is papa I am writing about, and I shall have no trouble in not knowing what to say about him, as he is a *very* striking character.

❷ Papa's appearance has been described many times, but very incorrectly. He has beautiful gray hair, not any too thick or any too long, but just right; a Roman nose which greatly improves the beauty of his features; kind blue eyes and a small mustache. He has a wonderfully shaped head and profile. He has a very good figure—in short, he is an extrodinarily fine looking man. All his features are perfect except that he hasn't extrodinary teeth. His complexion is very fair, and he doesn't ware a beard. He is a very good man and a very funny one. He has got a temper, but we all of us have in this family. He is the loveliest man I ever saw or ever hope to see—and oh, so absent-minded.

584 UNIT 4 • How do we decide who we are?

Ⓒ TEXT COMPLEXITY **RUBRIC**

My Papa, Mark Twain		
Qualitative Measures	Context/Knowledge Demands	Late 1800s; teenager's biography of her father 1 ② 3 4 5
	Structure/Language Conventionality and Clarity	Intentional grammar and spelling errors; multiple meanings; period vocabulary 1 2 ③ 4 5
	Levels of Meaning/Purpose/Concept Level	Accessible concept (a daughter's admiration of her father) 1 ② 3 4 5
Quantitative Measures	Text Length	Word Count: 1,192
	Lexile	1360L

Papa's favorite game is billiards, and when he is tired and wishes to rest himself he stays up all night and plays billiards, it seems to rest his head. He smokes a great deal almost incessantly. He has the mind of an author exactly, some of the simplest things he can't understand. Our burglar alarm is often out of order, and papa had been obliged to take the mahogany room off from the alarm altogether for a time, because the burglar alarm had been in the habit of ringing even when the mahogany-room window was closed. At length he thought that perhaps the burglar alarm might be in order, and he decided to try and see; accordingly he put it on and then went down and opened the window; consequently the alarm bell rang, it would even if the alarm had been in order. Papa went despairingly upstairs and said to mamma, "Livy the mahogany room won't go on. I have just opened the window to see."

"Why, Youth," mamma replied. "If you've opened the window, why of course the alarm will ring!"

"That's what I've opened it for, why I just went down to see if it would ring!"

Mamma tried to explain to papa that when he wanted to go and see whether the alarm would ring while the window was closed he *mustn't* go and open the window—but in vain, papa couldn't understand, and got very impatient with mamma for trying to make him believe an impossible thing true.

Papa has a peculiar gait we like, it seems just to suit him, but most people do not; he always walks up and down the room while thinking and between each coarse at meals.

Papa is very fond of animals particularly of cats, we had a dear little gray kitten once that he named "Lazy" (papa always wears gray to match his hair and eyes) and he would carry him around on his shoulder, it was a mighty pretty sight! the gray cat sound asleep against papa's gray coat and hair. The names that he has give our different cats are really remarkably funny, they are named Stray Kit, Abner, Motley, Fraeulein, Lazy, Buffalo Bill, Soapy Sall, Cleveland, Sour Mash, and Pestilence and Famine.

Papa uses very strong language, but I have an idea not nearly so strong as when he first married mamma. A lady

◀ **incessantly**
(in ses´ ənt lē)
adv. constantly;
continually

◀ **consequently**
(kän´ si kwent´ lē)
adv. as a result

PART 3 • My Papa, Mark Twain **585**

❷ Close Reading

1. Key Ideas and Details
Ask: Who is being described? According to the author, what makes this description different?

Possible response: The passage describes Mark Twain. The author claims that others have described Twain "incorrectly."

2. Craft and Structure
Ask: How does Clemens's use of descriptive details create a more accurate description of Twain?

Possible response: Descriptive details capture each feature of Twain, from his "Roman nose" to his "kind blue eyes."

3. Integration of Knowledge and Ideas
Ask: How does this passage show that appearances influence people's opinions of someone?

Possible response: The way Clemens views her father reflects the traits she thinks are important.

❸ Close Reading

1. Key Ideas and Details
Ask: Which aspects of Twain's personality does Clemens describe?

Possible response: Clemens describes Twain's habit of pacing, his fondness for animals, and his habit of giving cats funny names.

2. Craft and Structure
Ask: Which words or phrases are repeated? How does this develop Clemens's description?

Possible response: Clemens repeats the word "gray," emphasizing the connection between Twain and his cats.

3. Integration of Knowledge and Ideas
Ask: How do the descriptions of Twain support Clemens's earlier claim that Twain is very funny?

Possible response: Twain's names for his cats show his humorous personality.

🔊 **Audio**

Selection Audio is available in the **Student eText** and on the **Hear It!** CD-ROM.

© **TEXT COMPLEXITY READER AND TASK SUGGESTIONS**

My Papa, Mark Twain	
Preparing to Read the Text • Discuss the overall effect of the misspellings and grammatical errors in the text. Point out examples of each of these errors. • Guide students to use Multidraft Reading strategies (TE p. 584).	**Leveled Tasks** *Language* If students will have difficulty with language, work with them to list the spelling and grammar errors. Help them correct the errors and reread the selection using the corrections. Discuss students' lists and help clarify language errors. *Evaluating* If students will not have difficulty with the language, have them discuss the author's vocabulary, picking out specific words that convey her love for her father. Encourage students to share their notes and conclusions.

4 Focus Passage

A Focus Passage is identified with brackets in the Student Edition for students' independent close reading and analysis. A question bank for the passage and possible responses appear at the end of the selection.

5 Close Reading

1. **Key Ideas and Details** Read aloud the passage to students. **Ask:** What is being compared in this passage?

   Possible response: Clemens compares how people view her father and how she views her father.

2. **Craft and Structure** Have students take notes in two-columns: Clemens's views and others' views. **Ask:** How does Clemens structure this passage?

   Possible response: First, Clemens offers her opinion of *The Prince and the Pauper*. Then, she includes a letter from one of Twain's readers and describes how it "enoyed" her. Next, she states that people do not know Twain and uses another writer's description of Twain as supporting evidence. She then returns to her point that *The Prince and the Pauper* reflects Twain's true nature.

3. **Integration of Knowledge and Ideas**

   Ask: How does this passage emphasize the contrast between how Clemens thinks of Twain versus the public?

   Possible response: Clemens sees Twain as her kind, graying father, but the public sees him as joking, red-headed writer.

He could listen to himself talk for hours ...

acquaintance of his is rather apt to interrupt what one is saying, and papa told mamma he thought he should say to the lady's husband "I am glad your wife wasn't present when the Deity said Let there be light."

4 Papa said the other day, "I am a mugwump[1] and a mugwump is pure from the marrow out." (Papa knows that I am writing this biography of him, and he said this for it.) He doesn't like to go to church at all, why I never understood, until just now, he told us the other day that he couldn't bear to hear anyone talk but himself, but that he could listen to himself talk for hours without getting tired, of course he said this in joke, but I've no dought it was founded on truth.

One of papa's latest books is "The Prince and the Pauper" and it is unquestionably the best book he has ever written, some people want him to keep to his old style, some gentleman wrote him, "I enjoyed Huckleberry Finn immensely and am glad to see that you have returned to your old style." That enoyed me, that enoyed me greatly, because it trobles me to have so few **5** people know papa, I mean realy know him, they think of Mark Twain as a humorist joking at everything; "And with a mop of reddish brown hair which sorely needs the barbar brush, a roman nose, short stubby mustache, a sad careworn face, with maney crows' feet" etc. That is the way people picture papa, I have wanted papa to write a book that would reveal something of his kind sympathetic nature, and "The Prince and the Pauper" partly does it. The book is full of lovely charming ideas, and oh the language! It is perfect. I think that one of the most touching scenes in it is where the pauper is riding on horseback with his nobles in the "recognition procession" and he sees his mother oh and then what followed! How she runs to his side, when she sees him throw up his hand palm outward, and is rudely pushed off by one of the King's officers, and then how the little pauper's conscience troubles him when he remembers the shameful words that were falling from his lips when she was turned from his side "I know you not woman" and how his

---

1. **mugwump** (mug´ wump´) *n*. Republican who refused to support the party candidates in the 1884 election.

grandeurs were stricken valueless and his pride consumed to ashes. It is a wonderfully beautiful and touching little scene, and papa has described it so wonderfully. I never saw a man with so much variety of feeling as papa has; now the "Prince and the Pauper" is full of touching places, but there is always a streak of humor in them somewhere. Papa very seldom writes a passage without some humor in it somewhere and I don't think he ever will.

Clara and I are sure that papa played the trick on Grandma about the whipping that is related in "The Adventures of Tom Sawyer": "Hand me that switch." The switch hovered in the air, the peril was desperate—"My, look behind you Aunt!" The old lady whirled around and snatched her skirts out of danger. The lad fled on the instant, scrambling up the high board fence and disappeared over it.

We know papa played "Hookey" all the time. And how readily would papa pretend to be dying so as not to have to go to school! Grandma wouldn't make papa go to school, so she let him go into a printing office to learn the trade. He did so, and gradually picked up enough education to enable him to do about as well as those who were more studious in early life.

ABOUT THE AUTHOR

Susy Clemens (1872–1896)

Olivia Susan Clemens, called Susy, was the oldest daughter of Mark Twain and his wife Olivia. Susy was born in Elmira, New York, and grew up in her family's luxurious home in Hartford, Connecticut. There, her parents entertained famous people of the time—and Susy had the opportunity to meet them. Her upbringing and education helped bring out her talents in dramatics, music, and writing. Her father was so pleased with portions of what Susy wrote about him that he used them in his own autobiography. It is said that Susy was her father's favorite daughter. After she died at age twenty-four, Twain's writing turned darker and more serious.

 Big Question: Toward Essential Understanding

1. Read aloud the passage.
2. **Ask:** What do these anecdotes illustrate about Twain?

   Possible response: They suggest that young Twain was similar to his characters.
3. **Ask:** How do our experiences affect who we are?

   Possible response: Some students will say that Twain's example suggests that experiences shape how we approach and think about the world around us. Others may say our experiences provide fun anecdotes to tell but do not necessarily shape who we are.

DIFFERENTIATED INSTRUCTION

Support for English Learners
To avoid possible confusion caused by the misspellings and grammatical errors included in the selection, have students listen to "My Papa, Mark Twain" on the *Student eText* or on the *Hear It!* CD-ROM. Tell students to note the pride, devotion, and support for Twain that the author's words convey through the reading. Suggest that students follow along in the text as they listen.

Enrichment for Gifted/Talented Students
Urge students to read excerpts from *The Prince and the Pauper* in order to better their understanding of Clemens's description in the text. Ask whether they agree with Clemens's estimation that it reveals her father's "kind sympathetic nature." Allow students the opportunity to explain their opinions.

READ

Comprehension

1. He is a very "fine looking man."
2. It is the best book he has ever written.
3. It was sufficient; he learned what he needed.

Research: Clarify Details

Students should use their research to clarify a detail that is unfamiliar.

Summarize

Students' summaries should mention the burglar alarm story and *The Prince and the Pauper;* they may also mention Twain's looks, his gait, his cats, his education, and other details.

Language Study

Possible responses:

- *striking:* The large, red hat completed the striking outfit.
- *incessantly:* Greg texted incessantly, day and night.
- *consequently:* Li skipped breakfast; consequently, she was starving by noon.

Literary Analysis

Possible responses appear below. Check to be sure students support their responses with evidence from the text.

1. Twain uses it, though not as much as when he was first married.
2. Clemens says he knows she is writing the biography and makes a political comment so that Clemens will include it in the biography.
3. **(a)** He told her about the lady acquaintance and what he wanted to say to her husband. **(b)** It is funny; it shows Twain wanting to misbehave.
4. **(a)** He likes listening to himself and could do so for hours. **(b)** The author calls it both a joke and founded on truth.
5. He is funny; he is egocentric; he has his own mind; he can go beyond some social boundaries; he is different.

READ

Comprehension

Reread to answer the following questions.

1. What conclusion does Clemens draw about her father's looks?
2. What is Clemens's opinion of *The Prince and the Pauper?*
3. What is her opinion of her father's education?

Language Study

Selection Vocabulary Use each boldfaced word in a sentence that shows it you know the word's meaning.

- … I shall have no trouble in not knowing what to say about him, as he is a very **striking** character.

- He smokes a great deal almost **incessantly**.
- Accordingly he put it on and then went down and opened the window; **consequently** the alarm bell rang.

Literary Analysis

Reread the passage and answer the questions:

> **Focus Passage** (pp. 585–586)
> Papa uses … it was founded on truth.

Key Ideas and Details

1. What does Clemens say about her father's use of strong language?
2. Does Twain support Clemens in her writing of his biography? Explain.

Point of View

Point of view is the perspective from which a story is told. Reread the biography, and take notes on the author's perspective.

1. Identify two details of Clemens's life that show her perspective.

Research: Clarify Details Choose at least one unfamiliar detail in the selection, and research it. Explain how your research sheds light on the biography.

Summarize Write an objective summary of the biography. Include only the most important ideas and details.

Craft and Structure

3. **(a)** What remark did Twain make to his wife? **(b)** Why does Clemens include this anecdote in her biography?
4. **(a)** What does Twain say about talking? **(b)** How are his words both hyperbole —or exaggeration— and fact?

Integration of Knowledge and Ideas

5. What key ideas about Mark Twain does this passage reveal?

2. How might the author's point of view be different if someone outside Twain's family had written this biography?
3. How credible is Susy Clemens as a biographer? Explain.

Point of View

1. Clemens is Twain's daughter and many of her anecdotes about Twain are memories from her own childhood.
2. A writer from outside the family might refer to different aspects of Twain's life and may praise or criticize Twain for different reasons based on his public persona and writings.
3. She is close to Twain, so she knows a lot. However, she is also biased because Twain is her father.

DISCUSS • RESEARCH • WRITE

From Text to Topic **Partner Discussion**

Discuss the following passage with a partner. Take notes during the discussion. Contribute your own ideas, and support them with examples from the text.

> I never saw a man with so much variety of feeling as papa has; now the "Prince and the Pauper" is full of touching places, but there is always a streak of humor in them somewhere. Papa very seldom writes a passage without some humor in it somewhere and I don't think he ever will.

Research **Investigate the Topic**

Twain According to Others Research to learn what other biographers have written about Mark Twain.

Assignment

Use library databases and other resources to find a reliable biography of Mark Twain. Read at least one chapter, and compare the biographer's portrayal of Twain with Susy Clemen's portrayal. Take clear notes and carefully identify your source so that you can easily access the information later. Share your findings in an **informal speech** for the class.

Writing to Sources **Argument**

In this selection, Mark Twain's biographer is his own daughter.

Assignment

Write an **argument** in which you make a claim stating whether or not a person's family member can make a good a biographer for that person. Follow these steps:

- Introduce your claim and organize your reasons clearly.
- Use evidence from "My Papa, Mark Twain" to support your claim.
- Consider and address opposing views.
- Establish and maintain a formal style.
- Provide an effective conclusion. For example, you might end with your most **convincing** point.

QUESTIONS FOR DISCUSSION

1. How is this passage typical of the entire biography?
2. How is Susy Clemens like a traditional biographer? How is she different?

PREPARATION FOR ESSAY

You may use the results of this research project to support your ideas in the essay at the end of this section.

ACADEMIC VOCABULARY

Academic terms appear in blue on these pages. If these words are not familiar to you, use a dictionary to find their definitions. Then, use them as you speak and write about the text.

 **Common Core State Standards**

RI.6.1, RI.6.2, RI.6.5, RI.6.6; L.6.4, L.6.6; SL.6.1; W.6.1
[For full standards wording, see the chart in the front of this book.]

Academic Vocabulary

If students struggle with defining the academic vocabulary words, use this routine:

Write the words and definitions on the board.

identify: to find or determine

credible: reasonable, believable

convincing: persuading by supporting an argument with evidence

Have students say each word aloud. Then have students use each word in a sentence.

DISCUSS • RESEARCH • WRITE

From Text to Topic: Partner Discussion

Possible responses:

1. She talks about Twain as a writer and humorist. Clemens inserts her opinions by including her reactions to *The Prince and the Pauper* and by stating that she does not think Twain will ever write something without humor in it.
2. She retells parts of a life. Unlike some biographers, she judges Twain, but she also sees everything in his life as positive.

Research: Investigate the Topic

Introduce the assignment, using the instruction on the student page.

1. Arrange for students to visit your school's library or computer lab. Review strategies for identifying reliable sources.
2. Remind students to take notes on how each biographer portrays Twain. Have them clearly identify their sources so that they can access information later.
3. Encourage students to make connections between other biographies and Clemens's portrayal of Twain. Suggest that they prepare an outline for their presentation.
4. Suggest that students practice so that they do not need to read directly from their presentation outlines and are prepared to answer any questions.

Writing to Sources: Argument

Students' arguments should make and support a clear claim, use formal style, and end effectively.

 Online Writer's Notebook

Students can use the Online Writer's Notebook to record all responses.

MULTIDRAFT READING

Essential Understanding

First, students should read the entire selection on their own. Then, to assist struggling readers and to deepen comprehension for all, you may wish to guide them through the selection by asking them the close reading questions provided in the margins. Have students apply the multidraft reading protocols as they examine specific "chunks" of text related to these questions. For each reading, have students set the purpose indicated:

- **First reading:** Students should read the selection independently and think about its basic meaning.

- **Second reading:** Students should analyze the text's key ideas and details and its craft and structure.

- **Third reading:** Students should integrate knowledge and ideas; connect to the Big Question, other texts, and the world; and use teacher-led Close Reading discussion questions to examine particularly rich and significant passages.

For more guidance, refer to the *Classroom Strategies and Teaching Routines* card on multidraft reading.

❶ Background

If you wish, explain to students that regular steamboat service on the lower Mississippi River began in 1812. Although trains eventually surpassed steamboats in efficiency, steamboats still had lasting effects on Twain, who wrote the memoir *Life on the Mississippi* to describe steamboat travel and his time as a steamboat captain.

❷ Big Question: Toward Essential Understanding

1. Read aloud the passage.

2. **Ask:** Based on this passage, what influences Twain's opinion of himself?

   Possible response: Some students will say that childhood dreams and adventures influence Twain's opinion of himself. Others may say that Twain's age influences how he views his behavior as a child.

---

❶ Mark Twain's First "Vacation"

from an interview in the *New York World*, 7 September 1902

"Do you know what it means to be a boy on the banks of the Mississippi, to see the steamboats go up and down the river, and never to have had a ride on one? Can you form any conception of what that really means? I think not.

❷ "Well, I was seven years old and my dream by night and my longing by day had never been realized. But I guess it came to pass. That was my first vacation." A pause.

"One day when the big packet[1] that used to stop at Hannibal rung up to the mooring at my native town, a small chunk of a lad might have been seen kiting[2] on to the deck and in a jiffy disappearing from view beneath a yawl[3] that was placed bottom up. I was the small chunk of a lad.

"They called it a life-boat," said Mr. Clemens, "but it was one of that kind of life-boats that wouldn't save anybody. Well, the packet started along all right, and it gave me great thrills of joy to be on a real sure-enough steamboat. But just then it commenced to rain. Now, when it rains in the ❸ Mississippi country it rains. After the packet had started I had crawled from beneath it and was enjoying the motion of the swift-moving craft. But the rain drove me to cover and that was beneath the yawl. No. It was not a life boat, for the manner in which that rain came pouring down upon me from the bottom of that yawl made me wonder if I was

---

1. **packet** boat that travels up and down a river or coast carrying people or goods.
2. **kiting** climbing up on.
3. **yawl** small boat, or dinghy.

ⓒ TEXT COMPLEXITY **RUBRIC**

Mark Twain's First "Vacation"		
Qualitative Measures	**Context/Knowledge Demands**	Mississippi, September 1902; steamboats, humor 1 2 ③ 4 5
	Structure/Language Conventionality and Clarity	Longer sentences; on-level vocabulary 1 2 ③ 4 5
	Levels of Meaning/ Purpose/Concept Level	Accessible concept (reflecting on a childhood adventure) 1 2 ③ 4 5
Quantitative Measures	**Text Length**	Word Count: 426
	Lexile	940L

ever to return home again. To add to the fun the red-hot cinders from the big stacks[4] came drifting down and stung my legs and feet with a remorseless vigor, and if it hadn't been a steamboat that I was on I would have wanted to be safe at home in time for supper. Well, it kept on raining and storming generally until toward evening, when, seventeen miles below Hannibal,[5] I was discovered by one of the crew." A very deliberate pause.

"They put me ashore at Louisiana." Another pause.

"I was sent home by some friends of my father's. My father met me on my return." A twinkle in the steel-blue eyes. "I remember that quite distinctly."

Then as an afterthought: "My mother had generally attended to that part of the duties of the household, but on that occasion my father assumed the entire responsibility." Reminiscently: "That was my first vacation and its ending"— he bit his cigar, "and I remember both."

◀ **vigor**
(vig´ ər) *n.* active force or strength

◀ **deliberate**
(di lib´ ər it) *adj.* intended or carefully planned

◀ **distinctly**
(di stiŋkt´ lē) *adv.* clearly or plainly

---

4. **stacks** smokestacks.
5. **Hannibal** town in Missouri on the Mississippi River, where Mark Twain grew up.

PART 3 • *Mark Twain's First "Vacation"* **591**

❸ Close Reading

1. Key Ideas and Details
Read aloud the passage to students. **Ask:** What happens on the life-boat?

Possible response: Twain hides in the life-boat, however it starts raining and the boats lets in water. He also gets burned from smockestacks.

2. Craft and Structure
Ask: Which descriptive details create humor in this passage?

Possible response: Details like "when it rains in Mississippi country it rains," "red-hot cinders," and "a remorseless vigor" emphasize and exaggerate Twain's experience to create humor.

3. Integration of Knowledge and Ideas
Ask: Based on this passage, how does the language reflect Twain's childhood?

Possible response: Twain defines his childhood as full of adventure. Twain's use of humor shows that he fondly reflects on these experiences.

❹ Focus Passage

A Focus Passage is identified with brackets in the Student Edition of this page for students' independent close reading and analysis. A question bank for the passage and possible responses appear at the end of the selection.

Vocabulary

1. Write the following words and definitions on the board:

vigor *n.* active force or strength

deliberate *adj.* intended or carefully planned

distinctly *adv.* clearly or plainly

2. Have students say each word aloud.

3. Use the word in a sentence that defines the word.

 **Audio**

Selection Audio is available in the *Student eText* and on the *Hear It!* CD-ROM.

ⓒ TEXT COMPLEXITY **READER AND TASK SUGGESTIONS**

Mark Twain's First "Vacation"

Preparing to Read the Text
• Using the Background and other material on TE p. 590, discuss Twain's memories of the Mississippi River and steamboats.
• Discuss with students how an author can create humor within a narrative.
• Guide students to use Multidraft Reading strategies (TE p. 590).

Leveled Tasks
Knowledge Demands If students have difficulty with knowledge demands, have them first read to identify the order of events. Then, have them reread, taking notes on the word choice and tone Twain uses to describe each event. Discuss students' notes, offering clarification about which passages are humorous.

Synthesizing If students will not have difficulty with knowledge demands, have them note as they read ways in which Twain creates humor. Tell them to consider how this text is similar to other Twain texts they have read. As a class, discuss students' notes and ideas.

Close Reading Activities

READ

Comprehension

1. He snuck aboard a riverboat and took a seventeen-mile journey.
2. He spent the time under a yawl.
3. He was discovered, sent home, and met by his father.

Research: Clarify Details

Students should use their research to clarify a detail that is unfamiliar.

Summarize

Students' summaries should begin with Twain's desire at age seven to experience a riverboat, his sneaking aboard and crawling under the yawl, his being discovered and sent home, and his punishment.

Language Study

Possible responses:

- *vigor:* synonym—*pep, energy;* Juana attacked the sandwich with vigor.
- *deliberate:* synonym—*purposeful;* Her silence was deliberate and meant to hurt him.
- *distinctly:* synonym—*clearly;* A ship was distinctly visible on the horizon.

Literary Analysis

Possible responses appear below. Check to be sure students support their responses with evidence from the text.

1. His father met him.
2. He remembers the vacation and its ending.
3. **(a)** Twain's mother performed them. **(b)** *Duties* consist of punishments. **(c)** It leaves the punishment to the reader's imagination, which makes it funny.
4. The things that Twain does not say and lets the reader imagine make the passage funny.

Plot

1. **(a)** The conflict is the strong desire to get on the boat. **(b)** He tells about sneaking aboard and riding for seventeen miles in the rain.

READ

Comprehension

Reread to answer the following questions.

1. What did Twain do when he was seven?
2. Where did he spend his time on the packet?
3. How did his adventure end?

Language Study

Selection Vocabulary Write a synonym for each boldfaced word. Then write a sentence using each boldfaced word.

- To add to the fun the red-hot cinders from the big stacks came drifting down and

Literary Analysis

Reread the passage and answer the questions:

> **Focus Passage** *(p. 591)*
> "I was sent home by some friends of my father's … and I remember both."

Key Ideas and Details

1. Who met Twain when he got home?
2. What two things does Twain remember clearly about his adventure?

Plot

Plot is the sequence of events in a narrative. Reread the interview, and take notes on how Twain develops a plot.

1. **(a)** What is the **conflict** in Twain's story? **(b)** How does Twain develop the conflict?

Research: Clarify Details Choose at least one unfamiliar detail in the selection, and briefly research it. Explain how your research sheds light on the interview.

Summarize Write an objective summary of the interview. Remember to leave out your opinions and evaluations.

stung my legs and feet with a remorseless **vigor** …

- A very **deliberate** pause.
- I remember that quite **distinctly**.

Craft and Structure

3. **(a)** Who usually performed the "duties" when Twain had done something wrong? **(b) Infer:** What does Twain mean by "duties"? **(c) Speculate:** Why does Twain use this *euphemism,* or vague and mild word, instead of directly stating what the "duties" were?

Integration of Knowledge and Ideas

4. **Analyze:** What makes this passage funny?

2. **(a)** What is the climax of Twain's story? **(b)** Why is it exciting?

3. What makes Twain a good storyteller? Cite details from the interview to support your answer.

---

2. **(a)** The climax is getting discovered. **(b)** The reader knows that trouble will follow.

3. The conflict is engaging, there is a lot of action, readers know it will not go well for Twain, and the ending of the story is funny.

DISCUSS • RESEARCH • WRITE

From Text to Topic **Group Discussion**

Discuss the following passage with a group of classmates. Take notes during the discussion. Contribute your own ideas, and support them with examples from the text.

> Well, it kept on raining and storming generally until toward evening, when, seventeen miles below Hannibal, I was discovered by one of the crew." A very deliberate pause.
>
> "They put me ashore at Louisiana." Another pause.
>
> "I was sent home by some friends of my father's. My father met me on my return." A twinkle in the steel-blue eyes. "I remember that quite distinctly."

Research **Investigate the Topic**

Twain's First Riverboat Journey Make a poster based on "Mark Twain's First 'Vacation'."

Assignment

Conduct research to find out about riverboats on the Mississippi River before the Civil War. Use maps to speculate on Twain's journey. Take clear notes and carefully identify your sources so that you can easily access the information later. Share your findings in a **visual presentation** for the class.

Writing to Sources **Narrative**

Mark Twain tells his story by looking back on an event that occurred when he was seven years old.

Assignment

Write a **narrative** that **retells** Mark Twain's "Vacation" from the point of view of Twain's father. Follow these steps:

- Reread the interview to find details to use in your narrative.
- Develop a narrative with a clear sequence of events.
- Write from Twain's father's point of view, imagining how he might feel and react to the events.
- Use dialogue, and appropriate pacing in your narrative.
- Provide a satisfying conclusion.

QUESTIONS FOR DISCUSSION

1. What details does the interviewer add to the text? What effect do these details achieve?

2. How is the format of this interview different from other interviews you have read?

PREPARATION FOR ESSAY

You may use the results of this research project to support your ideas in the essay at the end of this section.

ACADEMIC VOCABULARY

Academic terms appear in blue on these pages. If these words are not familiar to you, use a dictionary to find their definitions. Then, use them as you speak and write about the text.

 **Common Core State Standards**

RI.6.1, RI.6.2, RI.6.3, RI.6.4, RI.6.5; L.6.4, L.6.6; SL.6.1, SL.6.2, SL.6.5; W.6.3
[For full standards wording, see the chart in the front of this book.]

DISCUSS • RESEARCH • WRITE

From Text to Topic: Group Discussion

1. He inserts pauses and describes a twinkle in the eye. The inserts slow down the story, affecting the pacing. They help show Twain's humor.

2. The interviewer lets Twain tell the whole story and only adds a few observations for effect about the way Twain tells it.

Research: Investigate the Topic

Introduce the assignment, using the instruction on the student page.

- Arrange for students to visit your school's library or computer lab. Review strategies for identifying reliable sources.

- Have students find images of riverboats and use maps of the Mississippi River from before the Civil War.

- Encourage students to take clear notes about each source and connect ideas between multiple sources. Suggest that they create a Works Cited list that identifies each of their sources.

- Suggest that students choose the best images for their visual presentations. Encourage students to practice their presentation.

Academic Vocabulary

If students struggle with defining the academic vocabulary words, use this routine:

Write the words and definitions on the board.

conflict: a problem

achieve: accomplish, complete

retells: tells again, relates

Have students say each word aloud. Then have students use each word in a sentence.

Writing to Sources: Narrative

Students' narratives should retell the events of the interview from the point of view of Twain's father. The narrative should have a clear sequence of events, use dialogue and effective pacing, use transitions, and end in a satisfying way.

📝 Online Writer's Notebook

Students can use the Online Writer's Notebook to record all responses.

Big Question: Toward Essential Understanding

1. Read aloud the quotations. **Ask:** What do these quotations have in common?

   Possible response: These quotations usually start off as practical advice and end humorously.

2. **Ask:** How do these quotations connect to the Big Question: *How do we decide who we are?*

   Possible response: Some students may say that the quotations suggest that we decide who we are through our actions and whether we decide to tell the truth. Others may say that these quotations suggest that we decide who we are by comparing our words and actions with the words and actions of others.

Close Reading

1. **Key Ideas and Details**

   Ask: What is the purpose of these quotations?

   Possible response: To provide Twain's opinion and advice to others.

2. **Craft and Structure**

   Ask: What is the sentence structure of most of the quotations? How does the structure influence the purpose of the quotations?

   Possible response: Many of the quotations are compound or complex sentences and explain two thoughts. Twain uses compound and complex questions to humorously compare and contrast or explain human nature.

3. **Integration of Knowledge and Ideas**

   Ask: What do these quotations tell you about Twain's view of people?

   Possible response: Students may respond that Twain believes people should act honestly.

According to Mark Twain

It is better to remain silent and be thought a fool than to open one's mouth and remove all doubt.

A person who won't read has no advantage over one who can't read.

If you tell the truth, you don't have to remember anything.

Action speaks louder than words but not nearly as often.

Always do right. This will gratify some people and astonish the rest.

Never put off till tomorrow what you can do the day after tomorrow.

A lie can travel halfway around the world while the truth is putting on its shoes.

To believe yourself brave is to be brave; it is the one only essential thing.

Everybody's private motto: It's better to be popular than right.

💬 VOCABULARY DEVELOPMENT

Academic Vocabulary

If students require support with academic vocabulary, write the following words and definitions on the board:

- **modify:** change the form or quality of
- **quotation:** the words of a source
- **establish:** bring into being; show to be true

Have students say each word aloud. Then use the word in a sentence that defines it. Point out that academic vocabulary words can be used across disciplines. For example, a historian can *establish* what causes led to war, while an author class can *establish* a scene.

READ • RESEARCH • WRITE

Comprehension

Reread all or part of the text to help you answer the following questions.

1. In your own words, what does Twain say about keeping silent?

2. In your own words, what does Twain say about truth and lies?

3. According to Twain, how do people respond when someone does the right thing?

Critical Analysis

Key Ideas and Details

1. Analyze: On what topics does Twain give advice?

Craft and Structure

2. (a) Distinguish: Identify one quotation that uses hyperbole, or exaggeration. **(b) Draw Conclusions:** How does hyperbole make the advice more memorable or entertaining?

3. (a) Analyze: In which quotation does Twain seem to make fun of, or satirize, traditional advice? **(b) Deduce:** How does Twain use humor to modify the advice?

Integration of Knowledge and Ideas

4. Compare and Contrast: How is Twain's advice similar to and different from other common sayings you have heard?

Research **Investigate the Topic**

Conduct research to find additional quotations from Twain. Classify the quotations according to the literary devices Twain uses, such as word choice and hyperbole. Make a generalization about how Twain creates humor in his advice.

Writing to Sources **Argument**

Write a brief **argument** supporting one side of this claim: Mark Twain's advice about believing yourself brave is completely serious/ is completely humorous. Support your claim with an analysis of the exact words of the quotation. As you write, establish and maintain a formal style.

Common Core State Standards

RI.6.1, RI.6.4; W.6.1.a
[For full standards wording, see the chart in the front of this book.]

ACADEMIC VOCABULARY

Academic terms appear in blue on these pages. If these words are not familiar to you, use a dictionary to find their definitions. Then, use them as you speak and write about the text.

READ • RESEARCH • WRITE

Comprehension

1. He says it is better than talking foolishly.

2. He says the truth is simpler and easier, and lies spread fast.

3. They are surprised or shocked.

Critical Analysis

Possible responses appear below. Check to be sure students support their responses with evidence from the text.

1. He gives advice on silence, reading, truth, right actions, procrastination, bravery, and identity.

2. (a) "A person who won't read ..." or "A lie can travel ..." **(b)** Exaggeration makes his sayings seem direct and funny.

3. (a) He starts out with traditional advice in the saying "Action speaks louder...." **(b)** He adds additional information to explain that the opposite of the advice usually happens.

4. Twain's advice, like other advice in common sayings that show wisdom about human nature, is short and precise. His sayings differ because they are funny.

Research: Investigate the Topic

Students should identify additional quotations, classify them by literary devices, and make a generalization about how Twain creates humor.

Writing to Sources: Argument

Students' arguments should make and support a clear claim about whether the proverb is serious or humorous and should use a formal style.

 Online Writer's Notebook

Students can use the Online Writer's Notebook to record all responses.

MULTIDRAFT READING

Essential Understanding

First, students should read the entire selection on their own. Then, to assist struggling readers and to deepen comprehension for all, you may wish to guide them through the selection by asking them the close reading questions provided in the margins. Have students apply the multidraft reading protocols as they examine specific "chunks" of text related to these questions. For each reading, have students set the purpose indicated:

- **First reading:** Students should read the selection independently and think about its basic meaning.

- **Second reading:** Students should analyze the text's key ideas and details and its craft and structure.

- **Third reading:** Students should integrate knowledge and ideas; connect to the Big Question, other texts, and the world; and use teacher-led Close Reading discussion questions to examine particularly rich and significant passages.

For more guidance, refer to the *Classroom Strategies and Teaching Routines* card on multidraft reading.

❶ Background

If you wish, explain to students that over his lifetime, Mark Twain published more than 30 books plus hundreds of articles, and he wrote hundreds of manuscript pages that he did not publish. Point out to students that the selection, a satire, was written by Twain as a way of poking fun at the many people that interviewed him after he became famous.

Vocabulary

If students require support with selection vocabulary, use this routine:

1. Write the following words and definitions on the board:

   astonishing *adj.* amazing or surprising

   rapture *n.* expression of joy

   notorious *adj.* famous for negative behavior or qualities

2. Have students say each word aloud.

3. Use the word in a sentence that defines the word.

An Encounter With An ❶ Interviewer

Mark Twain

596 UNIT 4 • How do we decide who we are?

© TEXT COMPLEXITY **RUBRIC**

An Encounter With An Interviewer		
Qualitative Measures	**Context/Knowledge Demands**	Fictional interview; humor, irony 1 2 3 ④ 5
	Structure/Language Conventionality and Clarity	Conversational dialogue; Q and A interview format; some difficult vocabulary; occasional difficulty in identifying speaker 1 2 3 ④ 5
	Levels of Meaning/ Purpose/Concept Level	Challenging concept (interview) 1 2 3 ④ 5
Quantitative Measures	**Text Length**	Word Count: 1,373
	Lexile	520L

The nervous, dapper, "peart"[1] young man took the chair I offered him, and said he was connected with the Daily Thunderstorm, and added:

"Hoping it's no harm, I've come to interview you."

"Come to what?"

"Interview you."

"Ah! I see. Yes—yes. Um! Yes—yes."

I was not feeling bright that morning. Indeed, my powers seemed a bit under a cloud. However, I went to the bookcase, and when I had been looking six or seven minutes I found I was obliged to refer to the young man. I said:

"How do you spell it?"

"Spell what?"

"Interview."

"Oh, my goodness! what do you want to spell it for?"

"I don't want to spell it; I want to see what it means."

"Well, this is astonishing, I must say. I can tell you what it means, if you—if you—"

"Oh, all right! That will answer, and much obliged to you, too."

"In, in, ter, ter, inter—"

"Then you spell it with an h."

"Why certainly!"

"Oh, that is what took me so long."

"Why, my dear sir, what did you propose to spell it with?"

"Well, I—I—hardly know. I had the Unabridged, and I was ciphering around in the back end, hoping I might tree her among the pictures.[2] But it's a very old edition."

"Why, my friend, they wouldn't have a picture of it in even the latest e— My dear sir, I beg your pardon, I mean no harm in the world, but you do not look as—as—intelligent as I had expected you would. No harm—I mean no harm at all."

"Oh, don't mention it! It has often been said, and by

◀ **astonishing**
(ə stän′ ish in)
adj. amazing or surprising

---

1. **peart** (pērt) pert; lively.
2. **Unabridged . . . among the pictures** Twain says he was hoping to find the word in the back of a dictionary, where it might be illustrated with a picture.

❷ Close Reading

1. **Key Ideas and Details** Ask three students to read aloud the passage: one as the narrator, one as the narrator speaking, and one as the interviewer. **Ask:** How do the details in this passage describe the two characters?

   Possible response: The words *nervous, dapper, "peart"* describe the young man. The narrator describes himself as "a bit under a cloud," which suggests that he is not in the mood to be interviewed.

2. **Craft and Structure**
   Ask: How do you know who is speaking in the interview dialogue?

   Possible response: The author places clues to identify each speaker. The first speaker is the interviewer because the narrator notes that the interviewer explains his connection with a newspaper and then "added" or spoke. Since only two people are in the scene, the next statement must be from the narrator.

3. **Integration of Knowledge and Ideas**
   Ask: Why might the narrator act like he does not understand what an interview is?

   Possible response: The narrator's confusion might be his way of stalling the interview or his attempt to humor or frustrate the interviewer.

❸ 🅱 Big Question: Toward Essential Understanding

1. Read aloud the passage, and then draw students' attention to the narrator's response.

2. **Ask:** Do the opinions of others influence how the narrator defines himself? Explain.

   Possible response: No, his casual response suggests that he is amused and unaffected by people's opinions of his intelligence.

 **Audio**

Selection Audio is available in the *Student eText* and on the *Hear It!* CD-ROM.

© TEXT COMPLEXITY **READER AND TASK SUGGESTIONS**

An Encounter With An Interviewer

Preparing to Read the Text
• Use the Background note on TE p. 596 to discuss Mark Twain.
• Discuss with students types of narration and perspective in fiction. Ask students to think about how authors manipulate these elements of fiction in order to present their stories and convey ideas in a certain way.
• Guide students to use Multidraft Reading strategies (TE p. 596).

Leveled Tasks
Levels of Meaning If students will have difficulty with levels of meaning, have them first read the story and make notes about the interviewer's questions and Twain's answers. Discuss students' notes and help clarify meanings.

Analyzing If students will not have difficulty with levels of meaning, ask them to read and note details that reveal how Twain feels about being interviewed. Tell them to look for implicit as well as explicit clues. Encourage students to share their notes and conclusions.

④ Focus Passage

A Focus Passage is identified with brackets in the Student Edition of this page for students' independent close reading and analysis. A question bank for the passage and possible responses appear at the end of the selection.

⑤ Close Reading

1. **Key Ideas and Details** Read aloud the passage to students.
   Ask: What type of questions does the interviewer ask the narrator?

   Possible response: The interviewer asks the narrator simple, factual questions about his life.

2. **Craft and Structure** Have students reread the passage.
   Ask: How do the narrator's responses establish the tone of the interview?

   Possible response: The narrator gives nonsensical responses to the interviewer's questions. These responses build on the humor from earlier in the selection and help establish a playful tone.

3. **Integration of Knowledge and Ideas**
   Ask: Why do you think the narrator responds to the interviewer in this way?

   Possible response: Some students may say that the narrator's responses suggest that he does not take the interview seriously. Others may say that the narrator responds in this way because he thinks the interviewer is unintelligent.

rapture ▶
(rap′chər) *n.*
expression of joy

notorious ▶
(nō tôr′ ē əs) *adj.*
famous for negative behavior or qualities

③ people who would not flatter and who could have no inducement to flatter, that I am quite remarkable in that way. Yes—yes; they always speak of it with rapture."

"I can easily imagine it. But about this interview. You know it is the custom, now, to interview any man who has become notorious."

"Indeed, I had not heard of it before. It must be very interesting. What do you do it with?"

"Ah, well—well—well—this is disheartening. It ought to be done with a club in some cases; but customarily it consists ④ in the interviewer asking questions and the interviewed answering them. It is all the rage now. Will you let me ask you certain questions calculated to bring out the salient points of your public and private history?"

"Oh, with pleasure—with pleasure. I have a very bad memory, but I hope you will not mind that. That is to say, it is an irregular memory—singularly irregular. Sometimes it goes in a gallop, and then again it will be as much as a fortnight[3] passing a given point. This is a great grief to me."

"Oh, it is no matter, so you will try to do the best you can."

"I will. I will put my whole mind on it."

"Thanks. Are you ready to begin?"

"Ready."

Q. How old are you?
A. Nineteen, in June.
Q. Indeed. I would have taken you to be thirty-five or six. Where were you born?
⑤ A. In Missouri.
Q. When did you begin to write?
A. In 1836.
Q. Why, how could that be, if you are only nineteen now?
A. I don't know. It does seem curious, somehow.
Q. It does, indeed. Whom do you consider the most remarkable man you ever met?
A. Aaron Burr.[4]
⑥ Q. But you never could have met Aaron Burr, if you are only nineteen years!

---

3. **fortnight** two weeks.
4. **Aaron Burr** vice president of the United States from 1801–1805.

 VOCABULARY DEVELOPMENT

Selection Vocabulary Reinforcement

To reinforce and assess students' comprehension of selection vocabulary words, give them sentences in which the word may or may not be used correctly. Students must tell whether the use is correct and explain their answer. Use these sentences:

1. It was *astonishing* to see the dolphin jump out of the water to play with us.
   Answer: Yes, *astonishing* is used correctly. It would be amazing to be able to play with a dolphin.

2. I had a feeling of *rapture* when I accidentally cut myself.
   Answer: No, *rapture* is not used correctly. One would not feel joy upon hurting oneself.

3. Bill was *notorious* for volunteering at the soup kitchen on Thanksgiving.
   Answer: No, *notorious* is not used correctly. Volunteering at a soup kitchen is a positive quality.

A. Now, if you know more about me than I do, what do you ask me for?

Q. Well, it was only a suggestion; nothing more. How did you happen to meet Burr?

A. Well, I happened to be at his funeral one day, and he asked me to make less noise, and—

Q. But, good heavens! if you were at his funeral, he must have been dead, and if he was dead how could he care whether you made a noise or not?

A. I don't know. He was always a particular kind of a man that way.

Q. Still, I don't understand it at all, You say he spoke to you, and that he was dead.

A. I didn't say he was dead.

Q. But wasn't he dead?

A. Well, some said he was, some said he wasn't.

Q. What did you think?

A. Oh, it was none of my business! It wasn't any of my funeral.

Q. Did you—However, we can never get this matter straight. Let me ask about something else. What was the date of your birth?

A. Monday, October 31, 1693.

Q. What! Impossible! That would make you a hundred and eighty years old. How do you account for that?

A. I don't account for it at all.

Q. But you said at first you were only nineteen, and now you make yourself out to be one hundred and eighty. It is an awful discrepancy.

A. Why, have you noticed that? (Shaking hands.) Many a time it has seemed to me like a discrepancy, but somehow I couldn't make up my mind. How quick you notice a thing!

Q. Thank you for the compliment, as far as it goes. Had you, or have you, any brothers or sisters?

A. Eh! I—I—I think so—yes—but I don't remember.

Q. Well, that is the most extraordinary statement I ever heard!

A. Why, what makes you think that?

Q. How could I think otherwise? Why, look here! Who is this a picture of on the wall? Isn't that a brother of yours?

Well, some said he was, some said he wasn't.

❻ Close Reading

1. Key Ideas and Details Read aloud the passage to students. **Ask:** What causes the interviewer to change how he talks to the narrator?

Possible response: The interviewer does not believe the narrator's answer to a previous question. Instead of moving to another question, the interviewer challenges the narrator.

2. Craft and Structure Have students reread the passage, focusing on the format of the passage. **Ask:** How does Twain use the interview format to create humor in this passage?

Possible response: Twain's use of the interview format creates humor by going against what readers expect from an interview. For example, when the interviewer questions the logic of the narrator's answers, the narrator asks "what do you ask me for?" This interaction reverses the traditional interviewer/interviewee roles so that the narrator is in the role of interviewer.

3. Integration of Knowledge and Ideas **Ask:** What role does an interview play in showing who people are? How is this interview different from most interviews?

Possible response: An interview usually is meant to find out what a person is like. In this section the interviewer points out that the narrator is giving nonsensical answers. Readers need to determine why the narrator is not giving truthful answers to understand the narrator's personality. It could be because the narrator intends to confuse or make fun of the interviewer, or perhaps he wants to evade describing himself.

🔅 DIFFERENTIATED INSTRUCTION

Strategy for Less Proficient Readers
Some students may have difficulty with the above-level vocabulary in this selection. Help them by preteaching difficult words.

- *unabridged*: full-length edition of a reference work, such as a dictionary
- *ciphering*: solving a math problem
- *inducement*: incentive, encouragement
- *disheartening*: saddening, discouraging
- *discrepancy*: a difference between things that should be the same

- *defunct*: no longer existing or working
- *solemn*: serious; sad
- *gloom*: a dark or sad feeling
- *procession*: a march

Write the words and their definitions on the board. Review the words and their definitions with students, and have them copy them down. Assist students in using the words in a sentence.

7 Close Reading

1. Key Ideas and Details Read aloud the passage to students. **Ask:** What happens in this passage? What details help you understand what is occurring?

Possible response: The narrator describes the death of his twin brother at the age of two weeks and the burial at the funeral that followed. The twin boys "got mixed in the bathtub" and one boy "was drowned."

2. Craft and Structure Have students reread the passage, taking note of the word choice. **Ask:** What repeated words or phrases show the confusion surrounding the death and burial of the narrator's brother?

Possible response: The word *mystery* and the phrase "some think it was" are used several times to show the confusing results. The similar phrases "that was me," "that child," and "the one that was drowned" also create confusion by suggesting that the narrator was the one who drowned, even though he is obviously still alive.

3. Integration of Knowledge and Ideas

Ask: What is the narrator suggesting happened with his identity?

Possible response: The narrator suggests that he questions his own identity. He wonders if he was the one who had drowned and if he is actually his brother. However, it seems unlikely that the narrator, at two weeks old, would know that he had switched identities with his dead brother.

A. Oh, yes, yes, yes! Now you remind me of it; that was a brother of mine. That's William—Bill we called him. Poor old Bill!

Q. Why? Is he dead, then?

A. Ah! well, I suppose so. We never could tell. There was a great mystery about it.

Q. That is sad, very sad. He disappeared, then?

A. Well, yes, in a sort of general way. We buried him.

Q. Buried him! Buried him, without knowing whether he was dead or not?

A. Oh, no! Not that. He was dead enough.

Q. Well, I confess that I can't understand this. If you buried him, and you knew he was dead.

A. No! no! We only thought he was.

Q. Oh, I see! He came to life again?

A. I bet he didn't.

Q. Well, I never heard anything like this. Somebody was dead. Somebody was buried. Now, where was the mystery?

A. Ah! that's just it! That's it exactly. You see, we were twins—defunct—and I—and we got mixed in the bathtub when we were only two weeks old, and one of us was drowned. But we didn't know which. Some think it was Bill. Some think it was me.

Q. Well, that is remarkable. What do you think?

A. Goodness knows! I would give whole worlds to know. This solemn, this awful mystery has cast a gloom over

💬 THINK ALOUD

Tone

Draw students' attention to the passage beginning with "Well, I never heard anything like this." Remind students that context is important when considering the tone of a passage. Use the following think aloud process to model analyzing tone.

> Sentences like "this awful mystery has cast a gloom over my whole life" suggest that the narrator is disturbed by his uncertain identity. If I only read this, I might think that this interview is very serious. As I keep reading, however, I notice that the narrator

is not as disturbed as I originally thought. The narrator says "don't mention it where the family can hear it" and uses the phrase "Heaven knows," both of which suggest that the narrator is dismissing his "gloom." This illogical conclusion is surprising and that makes it funny. Based on this evidence, Twain is actually using a humorous and playful tone.

Encourage students to try this process on their own with earlier parts of the selection.

my whole life. But I will tell you a secret now, which I never have revealed to any creature before. One of us had a peculiar mark—a large mole on the back of his left hand; that was me. That child was the one that was drowned!

Q. Very well, then, I don't see that there is any mystery about it, after all.

A. You don't? Well, I do. Anyway, I don't see how they could ever have been such a blundering lot as to go and bury the wrong child. But, 'sh!—don't mention it where the family can hear of it. Heaven knows they have heartbreaking troubles enough without adding this.

Q. Well, I believe I have got material enough for the present, and I am very much obliged to you for the pains you have taken. But I was a good deal interested in that account of Aaron Burr's funeral. Would you mind telling me what particular circumstance it was that made you think Burr was such a remarkable man?

A. Oh! it was a mere trifle![5] Not one man in fifty would have noticed it at all. When the sermon was over, and the procession all ready to start for the cemetery, and the body all arranged nice in the hearse, he said he wanted to take a last look at the scenery, and so he got up and rode with the driver.

Then the young man reverently withdrew. He was very pleasant company, and I was sorry to see him go.

---

5. **trifle** something of little importance.

DIFFERENTIATED INSTRUCTION

Strategy for Less Proficient Readers
Long and compound sentences like the one beginning "When the sermon was over…" on p. 601 may prove a barrier to some students' enjoyment of the story. Have students break down long sentences like these by first identifying the independent clauses and then reading them separately.

Strategy for Gifted/Talented Students
Have small groups of students work together to research interviews of Mark Twain. Suggest that they research Rudyard Kipling's interview with Twain. Then have students write questions they would want to ask Twain. Have students use their questions to stage a mock interview. Encourage students to act out their interview in class.

Close Reading Activities

READ

Comprehension

1. Readers are meant to believe Mark Twain himself is narrating the story.

2. The interviewer is surprised by Twain's seeming lack of intelligence.

3. The interviewer listens to the Twain's answers without questioning the logic behind the statements.

Research: Clarify Details

Students should use their research to explain the significance of a particular detail from the interview.

Summarize

Students' summaries should include the arrival of the interviewer, the question about spelling *interview*, and exchanges about Aaron Burr and Bill.

Language Study

Possible responses:

- *astonishing*: The boy gave an astonishing piano performance; *-ing* means consisting of, and it forms an adjective.

- *rapture*: She greeted the gift with rapture; *-ure* means the act of, result, and it forms a noun.

- *notorious*: Yan became notorious for his bad jokes; *-ious* means full of, and it forms an adjective.

Literary Analysis

Possible responses appear below. Check to be sure students support their responses with evidence from the text.

1. **(a)** The interviewer speaks in the first and third paragraph, and Twain speaks in the second and fourth paragraphs. **(b)** The interviewer talks about how he is going to conduct the interview, and Twain mentions the interview "is such a grief to me."

2. **(a)** He says interviews should be done with a club in some cases. **(b)** It shows interviews as a way of "beating answers" out of people.

3. **(a)** The narrator says his memory is "singularly irregular": it can

READ

Comprehension

Reread and answer the questions.

1. Who are readers meant to believe is narrating this story?

2. What is the interviewer's attitude toward the narrator at the beginning of the story?

3. What is the interviewer's attitude toward the narrator at the end of the story?

Language Study

Selection Vocabulary Use each boldfaced word in a sentence of your own. For the words with suffixes, explain what each suffix means.

- Well, this is **astonishing**, I must say.

Literary Analysis

Reread the identified passage:

> **Focus Passage** *(p. 598)*
> "I can easily imagine it ... This is a great grief to me."

Key Ideas and Details

1. **(a)** Who is the speaker in each paragraph? **(b) Analyze:** How can you tell?

Craft and Structure

2. **(a)** What does the interviewer say about the way that interviews ought to be

Tone

Tone is the writer's attitude toward his or her audience and subject. Reread "An Encounter With An Interviewer," and take notes on the elements that develop tone.

Research: Clarify Details Research an unfamiliar detail from the story and explain how what you learned sheds light on an aspect of the story.

Summarize Write an objective summary of the story. Leave out your opinions and evaluations.

- Yes, yes; they always speak of it with **rapture**.

- You know, it is the custom, now, to interview any man who has become **notorious**.

done? **(b) Interpret:** What does this remark suggest about interviews in general?

3. **(a)** What does the narrator say about his memory? **(b) Interpret:** What do these remarks suggest about the quality of his interview answers?

Integration of Knowledge and Ideas

4. Based on this passage, what is Mark Twain's opinion of interviews? Cite details in the text that support your response.

1. **(a)** Whom does the narrator say is the most remarkable man he has ever met? **(b)** Why is this a ridiculous answer?

2. How does the narrator's tone show his attitude toward interviews?

gallop or go very slow. **(b)** They are going to be unreliable or exaggerated.

4. Interviews are a bother; Twain makes the interview difficult for the interviewer and warns that he has a bad memory.

Tone

1. **(a)** Aaron Burr **(b)** Burr was dead before Twain was born.

2. The narrator's tone shows that Twain thinks interviews are ridiculous. He mocks both the interviewer and his questions.

DISCUSS • RESEARCH • WRITE

From Text to Topic **Small Group Discussion**

Discuss the following passage with a small group of classmates. Take notes during the discussion. Contribute your own ideas, and support them with examples from the text.

> Q. Well, I believe I have got material enough for the present ... I was sorry to see him go. (pp. 600–601)

Research **Investigate the Topic**

Real Twain Interviews After he became famous, Mark Twain was interviewed many times. Find out how Twain, as an interview subject, was similar to or different from the narrator of this story.

Assignment

Conduct research to locate one or more **interviews** that Twain gave during his lifetime. Consult Mark Twain Web sites and library resources. Take clear notes and carefully identify your sources so that you can easily access the information later. Share your findings in an **oral presentation** to the class. Compare and contrast the real Twain with the narrator of the story.

Writing to Sources **Argument**

In "An Encounter with an Interviewer," the narrator gently makes fun of interviews and interviewers.

Assignment

Write an **argument** in which you use evidence from Twain's story to argue that interviews are a bothersome, inaccurate, or otherwise poor means of gathering information. Follow these steps:

- State your claim and organize the reasons that support it in order of importance.
- **Refer** to evidence from "An Encounter with an Interviewer" as you support your claims.
- Use precise words to clearly convey the main points of your argument.
- Provide a concluding section or statement.

QUESTIONS FOR DISCUSSION

1. Is the narrator really sorry to see the interviewer go? How can you tell?

2. Why does the narrator **pose** as an unreliable interview subject?

PREPARATION FOR ESSAY

You may use the results of this research project to support your ideas in the essay at the end of this section.

ACADEMIC VOCABULARY

Academic terms appear in blue on these pages. If these words are not familiar to you, use a dictionary to find their definitions. Then, use them as you speak and write about the text.

 **Common Core State Standards**

RL.6.1, RL.6.2, RL.6.5, RL.6.6; L.6.4, L.6.6; SL.6.1; W.6.1
[For full standards wording, see the chart in the front of this book.]

Academic Vocabulary

If students struggle with defining the academic vocabulary words, use this routine:

Write the words and definitions on the board.

pose: to act, pretend

interviews: conversations conducted by reporters to ask questions

refer: to make reference

Have students say each word aloud. Then have students use each word in a sentence.

DISCUSS • RESEARCH • WRITE

From Text to Topic: Small Group Discussion

Possible responses:

1. The narrator may have been having fun making up answers and watching the interviewer struggle to do his job.

2. He wants to show that most interviews are unreliable. He implies that an interviewee can say anything, and a foolish reporter will believe it.

Research: Investigate the Topic

Introduce the assignment, using the instruction on the student page.

1. Arrange for students to visit your school's library or computer lab. Review strategies for identifying reliable sources with students.

2. Remind students to take notes. Tell them to take note of elements of Twain's actual interviews that evoke the interview in "An Encounter With An Interviewer."

3. Have students note the sources they used and to create a list of Works Cited.

4. Have that students prepare an outline for their speech or presentation. Suggest that students practice before giving their speech or presentation so that they do not read directly from their outline as they present to the class.

Writing to Sources: Argument

Students' arguments should make a clear claim about the inaccuracy of interviews as a source of information, organize reasons for the claim in order of importance, use evidence from the text, use transitions, and provide a concluding section.

 Online Writer's Notebook

Students can use the Online Writer's Notebook to record all responses.

Assessment: Synthesis

Speaking and Listening: Group Discussion

Introduce the assignment using the instruction on the student page.

1. **Conduct discussions.** Help students recall and apply their knowledge of the selections in this section to answer the discussion questions. For example, **ask:**

   - How did Mark Twain use his own experiences in his writing? Do you think writing was an opportunity for him to reveal his true identity?

   - How do the characters of the prince and the pauper change?

   - What effect does humor have on Twain's writing?

2. **Summarize and present your ideas.** Remind students that when they summarize their findings, they should strive to represent a range of ideas that emerged from their group's discussion.

Criteria for Success

Circulate around the room and observe group discussions. Support groups in their efforts to conduct organized, focused, balanced, and respectful discussions. Ask guiding questions if the conversation stagnates, and encourage students to make connections between ideas and experiences from different sources and to explore contrasts in the texts' portrayals or points of view. Emphasize that students should support all points with specific text evidence.

Use New Vocabulary

Assist students in using new vocabulary during group discussion. For example, **ask:**

- Can people *deliberately* determine their own identity, or is it shaped by their upbringing, environment, education, and so on?

- For some, finding oneself can be an *agonizing* ordeal. Do you think that deciding who you are is worth the effort?

Speaking and Listening: **Group Discussion**

Mark Twain and Identity The texts in this section all comment in some way, either seriously or humorously, on choices that affect who we are. Even when Mark Twain pokes fun at these choices, his work addresses the Big Question for this unit: **How do we decide who we are?**

Assignment

Conduct discussions. With a small group of classmates, conduct a discussion about Mark Twain and what his work seems to say about identity. Refer to the texts in this section, other texts you have read, and your personal experience and knowledge to support your ideas. Begin your discussion by addressing the following questions:

- How does Twain use humor to present serious ideas? What does this reveal about Twain as a person?

- Does Twain seem to believe that people can change for the better?

- In what ways do Twain's characters represent people in general?

- Twain is considered one of the greatest American writers and humorists of all time. Why do you think that is so?

Summarize and present your ideas. After you have fully explored the topic, summarize your discussion for the class.

Criteria for Success

✓ **Organizes the group effectively**
Appoint a group leader and a timekeeper. The group leader should present the discussion questions. The timekeeper should make sure the discussion takes no longer than 20 minutes.

✓ **Maintains focus of discussion**
As a group, stay on topic and avoid straying into other subject areas.

✓ **Involves all participants equally and fully**
No one person should monopolize the conversation. Rather, everyone should take turns speaking and contributing ideas.

✓ **Follows the rules for collegial discussion**
As each group member speaks, others should listen carefully. Express disagreement respectfully.

604 UNIT 4 • How do we decide who we are?

© Common Core
State Standards

SL.6.1.a-d
[For full standards wording, see the chart in the front of this book.]

USE NEW VOCABULARY

As you speak and share ideas, work to use the vocabulary words you have learned in this unit. The more you use new words, the more you will "own" them.

Writing: Fictional Narrative

Mark Twain and Identity In Mark Twain's *The Prince and the Pauper*, two boys exchange identities. Their deception leads to problems, but in the end, each boy learns important lessons.

> **Assignment**
>
> Write a **fictional narrative**, or short story, in which a case of mistaken identity creates a conflict that eventually lead the main character to learn an important lesson. Refer to the research you conducted on Twain and his work to help you develop the conflict and resolution in your story.

Criteria for Success

Purpose/Focus

✓ **Connects specific incidents with larger ideas**
Make meaningful connections between the character's choices or experiences and the texts you have read in this section.

✓ **Clearly conveys the significance of the story**
Provide a conclusion in which the character learns an important lesson.

Organization

✓ **Sequences events logically**
Structure your narrative so that individual events build on one another to create a coherent whole.

Development of Ideas/Elaboration

✓ **Supports insights**
Include details based on the texts you have read in this section.

✓ **Uses narrative techniques effectively**
Use pacing to build suspense in your story.

Language

✓ **Uses description effectively**
Use descriptive details that help readers picture settings and characters.

Conventions

✓ **Does not have errors**
Correct errors in grammar, spelling, and punctuation.

 **Common Core State Standards**

W.6.3.a-e
[For full standards wording, see the chart in the front of this book.]

WRITE TO EXPLORE

Writing is a way to clarify what you feel and think. This means that you may change your mind or get new ideas as you work. Allowing for this will improve your final draft.

Writing: Fictional Narrative

Introduce the assignment using the instruction on the student page.

Criteria for Success

1. **Purpose/Focus** Encourage students to identify meaningful connections or contrasts between their experiences, their research, and ideas explored in the texts. For example, **ask:**

   How might your character respond if he or she was thrown into a new identity? Would your character make the best of it? Would your character let it negatively affect his or her life? Would the character learn from the situation and try to behave differently in the future?

2. **Organization** Encourage students to structure their narratives in a logical way. Chronological order may be the most practical structure for most students.

3. **Development of Ideas/ Elaboration** Encourage students to vividly convey real people and events through the use of detail and dialogue. Point out effective models in the texts, such as the exchange between Tom Canty and the Prince in the play *The Prince and the Pauper*.

4. **Language** Instruct students to use sensory language to create images that appeal to the five senses.

5. **Conventions** In addition to a self-review, students should have someone else read their narratives to check for errors.

Write to Explore

Point out that students' thoughts and feelings about what they experienced might deepen or change as they write and reflect. As they conclude their narratives, encourage them to carefully consider what they have learned over the course of the writing experience in order to identify important observations they have made, insights they have gained, or conclusions they have drawn.

Writing to Sources: Informative/ Explanatory Essay

Introduce the assignment using the instruction on the student page.

Prewriting and Planning

1. Choose texts. Explain that in order to understand Mark Twain's ideas on human nature, students will need to analyze in depth the characters and ideas in two or more of the texts that they explored.

2. Gather details and identify key ideas.

- Remind students that key ideas from the texts will support their analysis of Twain's philosophies.

- Instruct students to go back into the texts they have selected and review passages that are connected to the concept of human nature.

- Encourage them to use a chart like the one shown to record each significant passage and identify what ideas it suggests about the concepts.

- Students may also wish to raise questions that the passage may help answer, such as *How is identity formed? Does one's identity change over time? Is it human nature to be satisfied with who one is and what one has?*

- They can then use these ideas to identify and explain Mark Twain's views on human nature.

Incorporate Research

Remind students to consider how they might use their prior research—about Mark Twain's use of hyperbole and word choice in some of his famous quotes—to support their claim in this essay.

Writing to Sources: Informative/Explanatory Essay

Mark Twain and Identity The related readings in this section show that in his writing, Mark Twain used humor to express important ideas about human nature. The selections raise questions, such as the following, about the reasons why people behave as they do:

- Why do people make poor choices? Do all poor choices lead to disaster? Does a positive outcome ever result from a poor choice?

- Is the use of humor an effective way to make a serious point or teach an important lesson?

- What are some reasons why people poke fun at others? Why do they poke fun at themselves?

Focus on the question or questions that intrigue you the most, and then complete the following assignment.

> ### Assignment
> Write an essay in which you explore and analyze some of Mark Twain's ideas about human nature. Clearly present, develop, and support your ideas with examples and details from the texts.

Prewriting and Planning

Choose texts. Review the texts in the section to determine which ones you will cite in your essay. Select at least two texts that will provide strong material to support your ideas.

Gather details and identify key ideas. Use a chart like the one shown to develop your key ideas.

Focus Question: Why do people make poor choices?

Text	Passage	Notes
The Prince and the Pauper	**TOM.** ...and sometimes we lads have fights in the streets. **PRINCE.** *(Eagerly)* I should like that ...	It is human nature to want something different from what you have, but when the Prince chooses Tom's life, he is sorry.
"According to Mark Twain"	Never put off till tomorrow what you can do the day after tomorrow.	People decide to put off things they should be doing. Twain humorously suggests delaying even further.

Example Claim: Twain suggests that people sometimes make poor choices before they consider the possible consequences.

Common Core State Standards

W.6.2.a-e
[For full standards wording, see the chart in the front of this book.]

INCORPORATE RESEARCH

Make sure to introduce each supporting fact and example in a way that shows a clear connection between the researched material and the point it supports in your essay.

Drafting

Define and develop your focus. Review your prewriting notes to find a main idea or focus for your essay. Then write one strong sentence that states your focus. Include this sentence in your introduction, and elaborate on it in the body of your essay.

Use examples to provide support. Use examples from the selections in this section and from your research to help you support your main argument or claims. For example, refer to a specific scene, character, or image that illustrates one of your key points. Be sure to use quotation marks if you include the exact words of a text or source.

Revising and Editing

Revise to organize around your strongest idea. Review your draft and circle your strongest point—the key argument or quotation that pulls your essay together. Consider moving this point to the end, just before your concluding statement. Then, revise your last paragraph to add a transition sentence that clearly explains the connection between this point and your other ideas.

 **Common Core State Standards**

W.6.2.a-e
[For full standards wording, see the chart in the front of this book.]

CITE RESEARCH CORRECTLY

Review your draft to make sure your citations are formatted properly. Refer to the Research Workshop in the Introductory Unit for information on how to cite sources.

Self-Evaluation Rubric

Use the following criteria to evaluate the effectiveness of your essay.

Criteria	Rating Scale
Purpose/Focus Introduces a specific topic; provides a concluding section that follows from and supports the information or explanation presented	*not very .... very* 1 2 3 4
Organization Organizes complex ideas, concepts, and information to make important connections and distinctions; uses appropriate and varied transitions to link the major sections, create cohesion, and clarify relationships among ideas	1 2 3 4
Development of Ideas/Elaboration Develops the topic with well-chosen, relevant and sufficient facts, extended definitions, concrete details, quotations or other information and examples appropriate to the audience's knowledge of the topic	1 2 3 4
Language Uses precise language and domain-specific vocabulary to manage the complexity of the topic; establishes and maintains a formal style and objective tone	1 2 3 4
Conventions Uses correct conventions of grammar, spelling, and punctuation	1 2 3 4

Drafting

1. **Define and develop your focus.**
   - Encourage students to create informal outlines to organize the main ideas in their essays.
   - Remind students to clearly and carefully introduce their topic and main ideas, using a strategy such as comparison/contrast.

2. **Use examples to provide support.**
   - Have students refer to their prewriting and planning notes to develop the topic with relevant details and facts.
   - Remind students to include quotations where they are appropriate or add interest to the essay.

Revising and Editing

1. **Revise to organize around your strongest idea.** Suggest that students share a draft of their essay with a classmate or family member. Students should ask the reviewer the following questions.
   - What is my topic?
   - What are the strongest details that support my topic? What are the weakest?
   - Is it clear when I transition from one supporting detail to another?
   - What other details might I include to make my analysis more complete or interesting?
   - Is my conclusion clear and does it effectively sum up my essay?

Remind students to confirm that the relationships among their topic, details, and ideas are clear. Encourage them to include words, phrases, and clauses to reinforce these links.

Self-Evaluation Rubric

Encourage students to rate their own essays objectively and to use the results to guide their revision process.

Cite Research Correctly

Review with students the correct format for citing different sources, such as books and printed or online news articles. Provide examples of proper citations. Then have students create a Works Cited list that correctly lists each source they refer to in their essays.

Independent Reading

Titles featured on the Independent Reading pages at the end of each unit represent a range of reading, including stories, dramas, and poetry, as well as literary nonfiction and other types of informational text. Throughout, labels indicate the works that are CCSS Exemplar Texts. Choosing from among these featured titles will help students read works at increasing levels of text complexity in the grades 6–8 text complexity band.

Online Text Set

The selections that are a part of the Online Text Set are located in the *Student eText*.

Using Literature Circles

A literature circle is a temporary group in which students independently discuss a book.

Use the guidance in the *Professional Development Guidebook,* pp. 47–49, as well as the teaching notes on the facing page, for additional suggestions for literature circles.

Ⓒ Meeting Unit 4 Common Core State Standards

Students can use books listed on this page to apply and to reinforce their mastery of the Common Core State Standards covered in this unit.

Introducing Featured Titles

Have students choose a book or books for independent reading. Assist them by previewing the titles, noting their subject matter and level of difficulty. **Note:** Before recommending a work to students, preview it, taking into account the values of your community as well as the maturity of your students.

Independent Reading

Titles for Extended Reading

In this unit, you have read texts in a variety of genres. Continue to read on your own. Select works that you enjoy, but challenge yourself to explore new authors and works of increasing depth and complexity. The titles suggested below will help you get started.

INFORMATIONAL TEXT

Welcome to the Globe!
The Story of Shakespeare's Theatre
by Linda Martin

The Globe Theatre in London is where Shakespeare's plays were performed. This illustrated **nonfiction book** teaches the history of this famous theatre.

Small Things Considered:
Why There Is No Perfect Design
by Henry Petroski   EXEMPLAR TEXT Ⓒ

This **nonfiction book** explores the fascinating world of design. It includes the article "The Evolution of the Grocery Bag" and other essays that describe the thinking behind the design of everyday items such as telephone keypads and toothbrushes.

Tiger Tales
by Deborah Chancellor

This **nonfiction** book uncovers the truth about how the number of wild tigers and other animal populations are decreasing because of hunting.

LITERATURE

You're a Good Man, Charlie Brown
by Clark Gesner
Random House, Inc., 1967

This **musical comedy** is based on the hugely popular cartoon series *Peanuts* by Charles Schulz and features Snoopy, Lucy, Linus, and the gang.

608 UNIT 4 • How do we decide who we are?

James and the Giant Peach: A Play
by Roald Dahl

James goes on an adventure inside a giant peach in this **play** based on Roald Dahl's beloved children's story. Complete with ideas for props and costumes, this play is one you could stage with your friends.

Seven Plays of Mystery and Suspense

This collection of **plays** will delight lovers of mystery and suspense stories. Expect to be on the edge of your seat as you read.

The Collected Poems of
Langston Hughes
by Langston Hughes
Vintage, 1995   EXEMPLAR TEXT Ⓒ

This complete collection of Hughes's **poems** contains his life's work. Hughes celebrates African American life and shares the beauty of his language and the wisdom of his insights.

ONLINE TEXT SET

SPEECH
My Heart is in the Highlands Jane Yolen

NOVEL EXCERPT
from **Roll of Thunder, Hear My Cry** Mildred D. Taylor

POEM
Alphabet Naomi Shihab Nye

Ⓒ TEXT COMPLEXITY **ALIGNING TEXTS WITH READERS AND TASKS**

Texts	Readers And Tasks
• *Welcome to the Globe!* (Lexile: 710L) • *James and the Giant Peach: A Play*	**Below-Level Readers** Allow students to focus on reading for content, and challenge them to interpret multiple perspectives.
• *You're a Good Man, Charlie Brown* • *Seven Plays of Mystery and Suspense* • *The Collected Poems of Langston Hughes*	**Below-Level Readers** Challenge students as they read for content. **On-Level Readers** Allow students to focus on reading for content, and challenge them to interpret multiple perspectives. **Advanced Readers** Allow students to focus on interpreting multiple perspectives.
• *Small Things Considered: Why There Is No Perfect Design* • *Tiger Tales* (Lexile 820L)	**On-Level Readers** Challenge students as they read for content. **Advanced Readers** Allow students to focus on reading for content, and challenge them to interpret multiple perspectives.

Preparing to Read Complex Texts

Attentive Reading As you read on your own, ask yourself questions like these to enrich your reading experience.

When reading drama, ask yourself…

Comprehension: **Key Ideas and Details**

- Who is the main character? What struggles does this character face?
- What other characters are important? How do these characters relate to the main character?
- Where and when does the play take place? Do the time and place of the setting affect the characters? If so, how?
- Do the characters, settings, and events seem real? Why or why not?
- How does the play end? How does the ending make me feel?

Text Analysis: **Craft and Structure**

- Does the playwright include background information? If so, how does this help me understand what I am reading?
- How many acts are in this play? What happens in each act?
- Does the dialogue sound like real speech? Are there passages that seem especially real? Are there any that seem false?
- What do the stage directions tell me about the ways characters move, speak, and feel? In what other ways do I learn about the characters?
- At what point in the play do I feel the most suspense? Why?
- What speech or passage in the play do I like the most? Why?
- Does the playwright seem to have a positive or a negative point of view? How do I think the playwright's point of view affects the story?

Connections: **Integration of Knowledge and Ideas**

- How does this play compare with others I have read or seen?
- What new ideas have I gained from reading this play?
- If I were to be in this play, what role would I want?
- Would I recommend this play to others? Why or why not?

Common Core State Standards

Reading Literature/ Informational Text
10. By the end of the year, read and comprehend literature, including stories, dramas, and poems, and literary nonfiction in the grades 6–8 text complexity band proficiently, with scaffolding as needed at the high end of the range.

PART 4 • Independent Reading **609**

© TEXT COMPLEXITY **READER AND TASK SUPPORT SUGGESTIONS**

Independent Reading

Increased Support Suggest that students choose a book that they feel comfortable reading and one that is a bit more challenging. Pair a more proficient reader with a less proficient reader and have them work together on the more challenging text. Partners can prepare to read the book by reviewing questions on this student page. They can also read difficult passages together, sharing questions and insights. They can use the questions on the student page to guide after-reading discussion.

Increased Challenge Encourage students to integrate knowledge and ideas by combining the Big Question and the Unit Focus concepts in their approach to two or more featured titles.

For example, students might consider the approaches to self-knowledge in *You're a Good Man, Charlie Brown* and *James and the Giant Peach: A Play*. In addition, students can focus on the ways in which characters' points of view, personalities, and beliefs are developed through dialogue.

Preparing to Read Complex Texts

1. Tell students they can be attentive readers by bringing their experience and imagination to the texts they read and by actively questioning those texts. Explain that the questions they see on the student page are examples of types of questions to ask about works of drama.

2. Point out that, like writing, reading is a "multidraft" process, involving several readings of complete works or passages, revising and refining one's understanding each time.

Key Ideas and Details

3. As an example, review and amplify the third bulleted item. **Ask:** How would you determine where and when the play takes place?

   Possible response: You might point out that the setting is stated indirectly in characters' dialogue or stated directly in the stage directions.

Craft and Structure

4. **Ask:** What details of craft and structure would you examine to learn about how the characters move, speak, and feel?

   Possible response: You might point to the characters' dialogue as evidence of how they speak or to their actions as evidence of how they feel.

Integration of Knowledge and Ideas

5. **Ask:** How would you determine whether or not the play reminds you of others you have read?

   Possible response: You might compare and contrast features of the plays, such as characters, plot, and theme.

6. Finally, explain to students that they should cite key ideas and details, examples of craft and structure, or instances of the integration of knowledge and ideas as evidence to support their points during a book discussion. After hearing the evidence, the group might reach a consensus or might agree to disagree.

PART 4 • Independent Reading **609**

© **UNIT 5**

THE BIG ? How much do our communities shape us?

UNIT PATHWAY

PART 1	PART 2	PART 3	PART 4
SETTING EXPECTATIONS	**TEXT ANALYSIS** GUIDED EXPLORATION	**TEXT SET** DEVELOPING INSIGHT	**DEMONSTRATING INDEPENDENCE**
• INTRODUCING THE BIG QUESTION • CLOSE READING WORKSHOP	SHARED LESSONS 	PEOPLE AND ANIMALS 	• INDEPENDENT READING • ONLINE TEXT SET 

CLOSE READING TOOL

Use this tool to practice the close reading strategies you learn.

STUDENT eTEXT

Bring learning to life with audio, video, and interactive tools.

WRITER'S NOTEBOOK

Easily capture notes and complete assignments online.

611

1 **How much do our communities shape us?**

1. Read aloud the first paragraph.
   Ask: How do communities shape their members?
   Possible response: They have laws or rules that the members must follow.

2. **Ask** students the Big Question, "How much do our communities shape us?"
   Possible response: It depends on the community—our neighborhood and our country can affect us differently.

3. Point out that folk tales are the literature of a given community, often handed down orally. Remind students to keep the Big Question in mind as they read the folk tales in this unit.

2 **Exploring the Big Question**

Collaboration: One-on-One Discussion

1. Introduce the activity, using the instruction on the student page.

2. Have students work individually to list examples. As they complete their lists, remind them to include some examples of their own experiences.

3. Review the Big Question vocabulary on the next page, following the teaching suggestions. Have students use the vocabulary as they complete the activity on this page.

Connecting to the Literature

Explain the Big Question strand in the unit, referring to the text at the bottom of this page.

How much do our communities shape us?

The word community usually refers to a group of people who have common needs and interests. In fact, this word comes from a Latin word that means "common." People in a community may live near each other, or they may live far apart. One type of community is a neighborhood. Another can be an organization whose members live in different areas. People in communities often share languages and values. They may exchange information, support one another, and work together to solve problems. While individual members contribute to the shape of a community, the opposite is also true: a community can shape its members.

2 Exploring the Big Question

Collaboration: One-on-One Discussion Start thinking about the Big Question by examining different types of communities. Briefly describe how the following groups are influenced by their communities:

- students in a classroom
- workers in a factory
- members of a sports team
- citizens of a town
- members of a choir or theater group

Share your lists and descriptions with a partner. Talk about your own experiences as a member of a community. Use the Big Question Vocabulary in your discussion.

Connecting to the Literature Each reading in this unit will give you additional insight into the Big Question. As you read, pause to consider the ways in which characters benefit from the support of their communities.

❓ DEVELOPING ESSENTIAL UNDERSTANDING

How much do our communities shape us?
Explain to students that they will continue to consider the Big Question as they work through Unit 5.

- As students read each selection, they will look for details related to the Big Question and take notes.
- At the end of each selection, students will answer a Literary Analysis question that is related to the Big Question.
- Throughout the unit, students will deepen their knowledge of the selections and their understanding of the Big Question through

reading, speaking, listening, researching, and writing. By the end of the unit, students should understand how each selection relates to the Big Question individually and how the selections connect to one another through the Big Question.

- Tell students that their goal will be to gain a deeper understanding of literature and to develop a more sophisticated way of discussing the Big Question. Ultimately, students should use the Big Question as a springboard for their own questions that relate to their interests and concerns.

❸ Vocabulary

Acquire and Use Academic Vocabulary Academic vocabulary is the language you encounter in textbooks and on standardized tests. Review the definitions of these academic vocabulary words.

> **common** (käm´ən) *adj.* ordinary; shared
>
> **influence** (in´floo əns) *v.* sway or persuade
>
> **involve** (in välv´) *v.* include
>
> **isolate** (ī´sə lāt´) *v.* set apart
>
> **participation** (pär tis´ə pā´ shən) *n.* taking part in an event or activity
>
> **support** (sə pôrt´) *v.* stand behind; back up

Gather Vocabulary Knowledge Additional vocabulary words are listed below. Categorize the words by deciding whether you know each one well, know it a little bit, or do not know it at all.

> | | | |
> |---|---|---|
> | belief | culture | group |
> | community | family | history |
> | connection | generation | values |

Then, do the following:

1. Write the definitions of the words you know.
2. Consult a dictionary to confirm the meanings of the words whose definitions you wrote down. Revise your definitions if necessary.
3. Using a print or an online dictionary, look up the meanings of the words you do not know. Then, write the meanings.
4. Write true or false statements about each word. For example, *A persuasive advertisement may <u>influence</u> what you buy. (true) If I <u>support</u> Mayor Green, I will not vote for him. (false)*
5. Exchange your sentences with a partner to test each other on your knowledge of the words. Label each statement true or false and offer a brief explanation for each answer.

Ⓒ Common Core State Standards

Speaking and Listening
1. Engage effectively in a range of collaborative discussions with diverse partners on grade 6 topics, texts, and issues, building on others' ideas and expressing their own clearly.

Language
6. Acquire and use accurately grade-appropriate general academic and domain-specific words and phrases; gather vocabulary knowledge when considering a word or phrase important to comprehension or expression.

PART 1 • Introducing the Big Question **613**

---

❸ Vocabulary

Acquire and Use Academic Vocabulary

1. Introduce the academic vocabulary words in the first word bank on the student page. Have students preview the words.
2. For each word, have students say the word aloud. Then, use the word in a sentence that defines the word.

Gather Vocabulary Knowledge

1. With the class, review the steps in the activity on the student page. Have students complete the activity independently, with partners, or in small groups.
2. Before students complete the last step, review the words and their meanings as a class. (Definitions appear at the bottom of this page.) Then, have students complete their sentences.

💬 GATHER VOCABULARY KNOWLEDGE

belief (bə lēf´) *n.* accepted idea

community (kə myoo´nə tē) *n.* group living in a particular area

connection (kə nek´shən) *n.* tie; link

culture (kul´chər) *n.* customs of a group or community

family (fam´ə lē) *n.* people related by blood

generation (jen´ər ā´shən) *n.* people living at the same time and about the same age

group (groop) *n.* collection or set

history (his´tə rē) *n.* record of past events

values (val´yooz) *n.* beliefs about what is important

▶ Video

Watch the Background Video online!

❶ Close Reading: Folk Literature

In the Close Reading Workshop, students will practice using close reading strategies within the context of a particular genre. They will use the features of this genre to help them access the text. All of the close reading strategies align with the Common Core State Standards reading domains:

- **Comprehension:** Key Ideas and Details focuses on what the text says.
- **Text Analysis:** Craft and Structure focuses on how the author conveys the text.
- **Connections:** Integration of Knowledge and Ideas focuses on what the text means and how it changes the reader's view of the world.

MULTIDRAFT READING

Essential Understanding
Explain to students that close reading works best when they read a text multiple times, focusing on different aspects of the text each time.

- **First reading:** Students should read independently to unlock the basic meaning of the text.
- **Second reading:** Students should focus on analyzing key ideas and details and the craft and the structure of the text.
- **Third reading:** Students should focus on integrating knowledge and ideas by connecting the text to the Big Question. The essential understanding students gain from making this connection will help them connect the text to other texts and to the world.

© Close Reading Workshop

In this workshop you will learn an approach to reading that will deepen your understanding of literature and will help you better appreciate the author's craft. The workshop includes models for close reading, discussion, research, and writing activities. After you have reviewed the strategies and models, practice your skills with the Independent Practice selection.

© Common Core State Standards
RL.6.1, RL.6.2; W.6.2.b, W.6.7, W.6.9.a; SL.6.1
[For full standards wording, see the standards chart in the front of this book.]

❶ CLOSE READING: FOLK LITERATURE

Use these strategies as you read the works of folk literature in this unit.

Comprehension: **Key Ideas and Details**

- Read first to unlock basic meaning.
- Use context clues to help you determine the meanings of unfamiliar words.
- Identify unfamiliar details that you might need to clarify through research.

Ask yourself questions such as these:
- Who are the main characters? What are their distinctive traits?
- Where and when is the story set? What is interesting or unusual about the setting?
- What is the conflict in the story?

Text Analysis: **Craft and Structure**

- Identify elements of folk literature, including the use of fantasy, exaggeration, and repeated narrative patterns.
- Examine how the literary work presents a culturally perspective or a universal theme.

Ask yourself questions such as these:
- What details in the story reflect the background, customs, and beliefs of the culture from which the story comes?
- What insight or lesson does the story present?

Connections: **Integration of Knowledge and Ideas**

- Recognize common characters, settings, and conflicts among various works of folk literature.
- Compare and contrast this work with other works you have read that express the same or similar themes.

Ask yourself questions such as these:
- How has this work increased my knowledge of folk literature?
- Why have people retold this story as part of a cultural tradition?

614 UNIT 5 • How much do our communities shape us?

© ACTIVE READING FOR COMMON CORE

Read • Discuss • Research • Write
In this workshop, students will learn how to access text through reading, discussing, researching, and writing. In the first half of the workshop, these activities are modeled for students. In the second half, students have the opportunity to partake in these activities independently.

Read: Students will read and comprehend the Reading Model selection. Annotations call out key points that students should focus on. These annotations model the types of things students should notice when they read the Independent Practice selection later.

Discuss: Students will deepen their understanding of the text through collaborative discussion.

Research: Students will clarify and expand their understanding of the text by conducting research.

Write: Students will synthesize their thoughts and research and will write a response to the text, supporting their ideas with evidence.

❷ Read

As you read this piece of folk literature, take note of the annotations that model ways to closely read the text.

from *Black Ships Before Troy: The Story of the Iliad* by Rosemary Sutcliff

In the high and far-off days when men were heroes and walked with the gods, Peleus, king of the Myrmidons, took for his wife a sea nymph called Thetis, Thetis of the Silver Feet. Many guests came to their wedding feast, and among the mortal guests came all the gods of high Olympus. **1**

But as they sat feasting, one who had not been invited was suddenly in their midst: Eris, the goddess of discord, had been left out because wherever she went she took trouble with her; yet here she was, all the same, and in her blackest mood, to avenge the insult. **2**

All she did—it seemed a small thing—was to toss down on the table a golden apple. Then she breathed upon the guests once, and vanished.

The apple lay gleaming among the piled fruits and the brimming wine cups; and bending close to look at it, everyone could see the words "To the fairest" traced on its side. **3**

❸ Then the three greatest of the goddesses each claimed that it was hers. Hera claimed it as wife to Zeus, the All-father, and queen of all the gods. Athene claimed that she had the better right, for the beauty of wisdom such as hers surpassed all else. Aphrodite only smiled, and asked who had a better claim to beauty's prize than the goddess of beauty herself.

They fell to arguing among themselves; the argument became a quarrel, and the quarrel grew more and more bitter, and each called upon the assembled guests to judge between them. But the other guests refused, for they knew well enough that, whichever goddess they chose to receive the golden apple, they would make enemies of the other two. **4**

In the end, the three took the quarrel home with them to Olympus. The other gods took sides, some with one and some with another, and the ill will between them dragged on for a long while. More than long enough in the world of men for a

Key Ideas and Details

1 The opening lines describe a time "when men were heroes and walked with the gods." These fantastic details help identify the story as a myth.

Craft and Structure

2 The goddess Eris is an outcast, a familiar character type in folk literature. Though uninvited, she comes to the feast seeking revenge. This event sets the plot in motion.

Integration of Knowledge and Ideas

3 You may connect the apple and the words "the fairest" to the fairy tale "Snow White," in which an evil queen tricks Snow White into eating a poisoned apple. This may lead you to predict that a conflict has been set in motion.

Craft and Structure

4 The idea that it is dangerous to anger the gods is a familiar theme in classical mythology.

PART 1 • Close Reading Workshop **615**

❷ Read

Before students begin reading the model, explain to them that the annotations call out important points in the story related to Key Ideas and Details, Craft and Structure, and Integration of Knowledge and Ideas. Tell students that their understanding and interpretation of the text should not be limited by the existing annotations. Encourage students to use the annotations as a starting point to help them analyze the story further.

❸ Integration of Knowledge and Ideas

To move students toward essential understanding, draw their attention to bracketed annotation 3 in the Teacher Edition. **Ask:** How are the goddesses affected by the goddess Eris? Explain.

Possible response: The goddesses Hera, Athene, and Aphrodite began to fight amongst themselves and others in their community because Eris wanted them to choose which one was the fairest.

👥 DIFFERENTIATED INSTRUCTION

Strategy for Less Proficient Readers

If students struggle with some of the literary terminology referenced on the previous page, provide them with the following definitions:

- **character traits:** qualities, attitudes, and values that a character has or displays.
- **setting:** the time and place of the action. In most literary works, the setting serves as a backdrop—a context in which the characters interact.

- **plot:** the sequence of events in which each event results from a previous one and causes the next.
- **conflict:** struggle between opposing forces. An internal conflict takes place in the mind of a character struggling to take an action or overcome a feeling. An external conflict is one in which a character struggles against some outside force.

 Audio

Selection Audio is available in the *Student eText* and on the *Hear It!* CD-ROM.

4 Integration of Knowledge and Ideas

To move students toward essential understanding, draw their attention to bracketed annotation 4 in the Teacher Edition. **Ask:** How is Paris's life shaped by the king's decision to have him abandoned in the wilderness?

Possible response: Paris is raised in the country by a herdsman and grows up to become a herdsman himself. His life is dramatically affected by the king's decision to abandon him.

child born when the quarrel first began, to grow to manhood and become a warrior or a herdsman. But the immortal gods do not know time as mortals know it. **5**

Now on the northeast coast of the Aegean Sea, there was a city of men. Troy was its name, a great city surrounded by strong walls, and standing on a hill hard by the shore. It had grown rich on the tolls that its kings demanded from merchant ships passing up the nearby straits to the Black Sea cornlands and down again. Priam, who was now king, was lord of wide realms and long-maned horses, and he had many sons about his hearth. And when the quarrel about the golden apple was still raw and new, a last son was born to him and his wife Queen Hecuba, and they called him Paris.

There should have been great rejoicing, but while Hecuba still carried the babe within her, the soothsayers had foretold that she would give birth to a firebrand that should burn down Troy. And so, when he was born and named, the king bade a servant carry him out into the wilderness and leave him to die. The servant did as he was bid; but a herdsman searching for a missing calf found the babe and brought him up as his own. **6**

The boy grew tall and strong and beautiful, the swiftest runner and the best archer in all the country around. **7** So his boyhood passed among the oak woods and the high hill-pastures that rose toward Mount Ida. And there he met and fell in love with a wood nymph called Oenone, who loved him in return. She had the gift of being able to heal the wounds of mortal men, no matter how sorely they were hurt.

Among the oak woods they lived together and were happy—until one day the three jealous goddesses, still quarreling about the golden apple, chanced to look down from Olympus, and saw the beautiful young man herding his cattle on the slopes of Mount Ida.

They knew, for the gods know all things, that he was the son of Priam, king of Troy, though he himself did not know it yet; but the thought came to them that he would not know who they were, and therefore he would not be afraid to judge between them. They were growing somewhat weary of the argument by then.

So they tossed the apple down to him, and Paris put up his hands and caught it. After it the three came down, landing before him so lightly that their feet did not bend the mountain grasses, and bade him choose between them, which was the fairest and had best right to the prize he held in his hand. **8**

Key Ideas and Details

5 A baby boy grows to manhood as the goddesses continue to quarrel. This distorted passage of time could only occur in an exaggerated world of fantasy.

Craft and Structure

6 This paragraph presents common elements of folk literature. Details such as a soothsayers' warning and a character's lack of knowledge about his true identity appear in many other folk stories.

Key Ideas and Details

7 Many characters in folk literature have exaggerated traits. In addition to being "tall strong and beautiful," Paris is "the swiftest runner" and "the best archer" in the land.

Craft and Structure

8 The goddesses are "weary of the argument." They decide to use Paris—without his knowledge—to settle the issue. The gods' manipulation of human "destiny" is a common idea in mythology.

🗨 THINK ALOUD

Vocabulary: Using Context

To model the process of using context clues to guess the meaning of an unfamiliar word, point students to the third paragraph on this page and read aloud the first sentence. Then, say:

> I see the word *soothsayers*. I'm not sure what this word means, so I'll see if there are any clues in the paragraph that will help me guess its meaning. The sentence says that

everyone should have been celebrating, but that while Queen Hecuba was pregnant, soothsayers foretold that she would give birth to someone who would burn down Troy. I know that *foretold* means "predicted, often by using magical powers." Therefore, soothsayers are people, such as fortune-tellers, who can predict the future.

First Athene, in her gleaming armor, fixed him with sword-gray eyes and promised him supreme wisdom if he would name her.

Then Hera, in her royal robes as queen of heaven, promised him vast wealth and power and honor if he awarded her the prize.

Lastly, Aphrodite drew near, her eyes as blue as deep-sea water, her hair like spun gold wreathed around her head, and, smiling honey-sweet, whispered that she would give him a wife as fair as herself if he tossed the apple to her.

And Paris forgot the other two with their offers of wisdom and power, forgot also, for that moment, dark-haired Oenone in the shadowed oak woods; and he gave the golden apple to Aphrodite. [9]

Integration of Knowledge and Ideas

9 The repetition of the word *forgot* emphasizes a common theme in folk literature: when faced with temptation, a person can forget everything he or she once valued.

? DEVELOPING ESSENTIAL UNDERSTANDING

How much do our communities shape us?

After students have finished reading the model, ask them the following questions to help them deepen their understanding of how the story relates to the Big Question:

- How are characters affected by the actions, decisions, and values of the community around them?

- To what extent are characters free to determine their own destiny, independently of their community?

- What are the drawbacks of living in a community? What are the benefits?

    Remind students that as they read the rest of the selections in this unit, they should ask themselves similar questions to help them connect the texts with the Big Question.

❺ Discuss

Throughout the unit, students will be engaging in discussions about the selections they read. As students discuss, remind them of the following points:

- Come to discussions prepared.
- Support ideas with text evidence.
- Pose and respond to questions that connect the selection to broader themes and ideas.
- Respond thoughtfully to diverse perspectives.

❻ Research

As students conduct research, remind them of the following tips:

- Focus your research question so that it's not too broad or too complex.
- Try to be as precise as possible when doing a key word search online. Otherwise, you'll have too many results to evaluate. You might also try using more than one search engine.
- Make sure the Web sites you use are reputable ones. Sites that end in .gov, .edu, or .org are generally reliable.

❺ Discuss

Sharing your own ideas and listening to the ideas of others can deepen your understanding of a text and help you look at a topic in a whole new way. As you participate in collaborative discussions, work to have a genuine exchange in which classmates build upon one another's ideas. Support your points with evidence and ask meaningful questions.

Student 1: I wonder why the three goddesses keep trying to decide which of them is "the fairest." Do they think that being "the fairest" is better than being queen of the gods, the goddess of wisdom, or the goddess of beauty?

Student 2: I think they don't have anything better to do. They're immortal. All that time stretches out in front of them, so they make their arguments last as long as they can. Also, in a lot of myths the gods act like human beings. Sometimes they're stubborn.

Student 3: That's true. Another point, though, is that what the gods do in myths usually has major consequences for human beings. I think their contest will cause some kind of problem for Paris, his family in Troy, or both.

❻ Research

Targeted research can clarify unfamiliar details and shed light on various aspects of a text. Consider questions that arise in your mind as you read, and use those questions as the basis for research.

Research Model

Questions: *How do the consequences of Paris's choice affect his future or the future of his family?*

Key Words for Internet Search: Paris AND Troy

Result: history of the Trojan War

What I Learned: When Aphrodite asks Paris to choose her as "the fairest," she promises to give him the most beautiful woman in the world, Helen of Sparta. Helen is already married to the king of Sparta in Greece, but Paris kidnaps her. The Greeks go to Troy to avenge her kidnapping, which sets off the Trojan War.

❼ Write

Writing about a text will deepen your understanding of it and will also allow you to share your ideas more formally with others. The following model essay identifies a theme in the work and cites evidence to support the main ideas.

Writing Model

Don't Blame Paris

In this excerpt from Rosemary Sutcliff's *Black Ships Before Troy*, three goddesses take advantage of Paris, a human who does not have the knowledge to understand what is going on. Although Paris makes a choice that ultimately leads to a terrible war, he cannot be blamed because the goddesses tricked him into making that choice.

The author first introduces a mythological setting in which gods and humans live together. The conflict begins when "the three greatest of the goddesses"—Hera, Athene, and Aphrodite—quarrel about who should win the prize of a golden apple, and be declared "the fairest." Their argument continues for a long time because "the immortal gods do not know time as mortals know it." During the argument, a boy named Paris grows up without knowing that he is the son of King Priam of Troy, and that it was foretold he would someday destroy his father's city.

The author describes the goddesses' argument as their reason for interfering in Paris's life. Their quarrel brings out petty human emotions in the goddesses, and their pride, bitterness, and jealousy prevent them from resolving the conflict. Because they "know all things," the goddesses realize that Paris does not know their identities so they can use him to decide the winner of their contest. If Paris had been raised by his true parents, they might have taught him to recognize the goddesses and to beware of their possible trickery.

Paris, however, is does not suspect the goddesses. When asked to choose "the fairest," he picks Aphrodite because she offers him a beautiful wife. This is Helen of Sparta, who is already married to a Greek king. Paris's choice sets in motion a chain of events that lead to war: Paris captures Helen for his wife, which causes the Greeks to seek revenge. However, these events are not Paris's fault. The goddesses use deception to influence Paris's actions. The myth presents an important theme of classical mythology: the gods often use humans for their own personal gain. Therefore, the gods, and not Paris, are the cause of the deadly war.

In the introductory paragraph, the writer states a claim and explains the essay's title.

Important background information helps readers understand the topic.

The writer interprets story details to draw a conclusion that supports the main idea.

The writer incorporates information from research in this statement of cause and effect.

The concluding statement restates the writer's claim.

---

❼ Write

Review the writing model with the class, using the annotations to analyze how the writer uses evidence to support his or her ideas.

Genre Requirements

Remind students that when they write responses to literature, they should do the following:

- Introduce the topic at the beginning of the essay.
- Organize ideas and information in order to make important connections.
- Support claims with specific details from the literary work.
- Provide a conclusion that supports the information presented.

Teaching from the Writing Model

1. Point out to students that the last sentence of the introduction is the writer's thesis.
2. Point out that each body paragraph uses text evidence or facts to support the thesis.
3. The conclusion presents further evidence and restates the thesis.

CLOSE READING TOOL

Students may close read and mark the text using the **Close Reading Tool**, which is available online. Scaffolds are provided for students who need help. Students who do not have online access may use the **Close Reading Notebook** to mark the text with their close reading responses.

8 Independent Practice

The Independent Practice is an optional assignment. You may wish to administer it at this point and use it as formative assessment, or you may wish to administer it at the end of Part 1 as summative assessment. If you wish to administer the Independent Practice but feel your students will struggle with it, you can use the questions in the side margins of this Teacher Edition to help guide them.

9 Key Ideas and Details

Ask: What types of descriptions does the author use to convey the setting? What is the effect of these descriptions?

Possible response: The author uses figurative language to vividly and imaginatively describe the land and sky. The descriptions give the setting a magical quality.

10 Craft and Structure

Ask: What does this description reveal about Bob? What technique does the author use to emphasize Bob's abilities?

Possible response: Bob was an enslaved person who never learned to read, so he learns from studying animals. The author uses exaggeration. He says Bob *is* a horse because he is good at making the horses believe he is one of them.

🔊 Audio

Selection Audio is available in the **Student eText** and on the **Hear It!** CD-ROM.

---

8 As you read the following story, apply the close reading strategies you have learned. You may need to read the story multiple times.

Black Cowboy, Wild Horses: A True Story

by Julius Lester

First Light. Bob Lemmons rode his horse slowly up the rise. When he reached the top, he stopped at the edge of the bluff. He looked down at the corral where the other cowboys were beginning the morning chores, then turned away and stared at **9** the land stretching as wide as love in every direction. The sky was curved as if it were a lap on which the earth lay napping like a curled cat. High above, a hawk was suspended on cold threads of unseen winds. Far, far away, at what looked to be the edge of the world, land and sky kissed.

He guided Warrior, his black stallion, slowly down the bluff. When they reached the bottom, the horse reared, eager to run across the vastness of the plains until he reached forever. Bob smiled and patted him gently on the neck. "Easy. Easy," he whispered. "We'll have time for that. But not yet."

He let the horse trot for a while, then slowed him and began peering intently at the ground as if looking for the answer to a question he scarcely understood.

It was late afternoon when he saw them—the hoofprints of mustangs, the wild horses that lived on the plains. He stopped, dismounted, and walked around carefully until he had seen all the prints. Then he got down on his hands and knees to examine them more closely.

Some people learned from books. Bob had been a slave and never learned to read words. But he could look at the ground and read what animals had walked on it, their size **10** and weight, when they had passed by, and where they were going. No one he knew could bring in mustangs by themselves, but Bob could make horses think he was one of them—because he was.

He stood, reached into his saddlebag, took out an apple, and gave it to Warrior, who chewed with noisy enthusiasm. It was a herd of eight mares, a colt, and a stallion. They had passed

Meet the Author

Julius Lester (b. 1939), a native of St. Louis, Missouri, has been a folk singer, a civil rights photographer, a writer, and a professor of African American Studies and Judaic Studies. His works include novels, stories, poetry, nonfiction, and a memoir.

CLOSE READING TOOL

Read and respond to this selection online using the **Close Reading Tool**.

© ACTIVE READING FOR COMMON CORE

Read • Discuss • Research • Write

In the Independent Practice section of the Close Reading Workshop, students will practice the reading, discussing, researching, and writing strategies they learned in the modeling section. They will also deepen their essential understanding of the Big Question.

Read: Students will read and comprehend the selection. They should note significant points in the text that relate to Key Ideas and Details, Craft and Structure, and Integration of Knowledge and Ideas. They should use the annotations in the Reading Model that they read earlier as a guide. After students have

finished reading the story, they will answer Literary Analysis questions.

Discuss: Students will deepen their understanding of the text through collaborative discussion.

Research: Students will clarify and expand their understanding of the text by conducting research.

Write: Students will synthesize their thoughts and research by writing a response to the text, supporting their ideas with evidence.

there two days ago. He would see them soon. But he needed to smell of sun, moon, stars, and wind before the mustangs would accept him.

The sun went down and the chilly night air came quickly. Bob took the saddle, saddlebag, and blanket off Warrior. He was cold, but could not make a fire. The mustangs would smell the smoke in his clothes from miles away. He draped a thick blanket around himself, then took the cotton sack of dried fruit, beef jerky, and nuts from his saddlebag and ate. When he was done, he lay his head on his saddle and was quickly asleep. Warrior grazed in the tall, sweet grasses.

As soon as the sun's round shoulders came over the horizon, Bob awoke. He ate, filled his canteen, and saddling Warrior, rode away. All day he followed the tracks without hurrying.

Near dusk, clouds appeared, piled atop each other like mountains made of fear. Lightning flickered from within them like candle flames shivering in a breeze. Bob heard the faint but distinct rumbling of thunder. Suddenly lightning vaulted from cloud to cloud across the curved heavens.

Warrior reared, his front hooves pawing as if trying to knock the white streaks of fire from the night sky. Bob raced Warrior to a nearby ravine as the sky exploded sheets of light. And there, in the distance, beneath the ghostly light, Bob saw the herd of mustangs. As if sensing their presence, Warrior rose into the air once again, this time not challenging the heavens but almost in greeting. Bob thought he saw the mustang stallion rise in response as the earth shuddered from the sound of thunder.

Then the rain came as hard and stinging as remorse. Quickly Bob put on his poncho, and turning Warrior away from the wind and the rain, waited. The storm would pass soon. Or it wouldn't. There was nothing to do but wait.

Finally the rain slowed and then stopped. The clouds thinned, and there, high in the sky, the moon appeared as white as grief. Bob slept in the saddle while Warrior grazed on the wet grasses.

The sun rose into a clear sky and Bob was awake immediately. The storm would have washed away the tracks, but they had been going toward the big river. He would go there and wait.

By mid-afternoon he could see the ribbon of river shining in the distance. He stopped, needing only to be close enough to see the horses when they came to drink. Toward evening he saw a trail of rolling, dusty clouds.

◀ **Vocabulary**
ravine (rə vēn´) *n.* long, deep hollow in the earth's surface

◀ **Vocabulary**
remorse (ri môrs´) *n.* guilt over a wrong one has done

⓫ Key Ideas and Details
Ask: What is Bob's quest?

Possible response: Bob's quest is to have the mustangs accept him as one of their own.

⓬ Craft and Structure
Ask: How might the weather affect the development of the story?

Possible response: The weather might make the horses afraid. It might force Bob to return to the corral alone.

⓭ Integration of Knowledge and Ideas
Ask: What does Bob's reaction to the weather tell you about his attitude toward nature?

Possible response: Bob's reaction indicates he knows he cannot change nature; he is respectful of its power.

14 Craft and Structure

Ask: Why is the stallion's reaction important to the outcome of Bob's quest?

Possible response: If the stallion accepts Bob, then he can become part of the herd. If not, he will have failed in his quest.

15 Key Ideas and Details

Ask: What unique abilities enable Bob to track the horses successfully?

Possible response: Bob can be very still, moving only when the herd moves. He can act and smell like a horse.

16 Integration of Knowledge and Ideas

Ask: What central idea about nature does Bob's reaction to the snake help develop?

Possible response: It develops the central idea that humans should not interfere with nature.

In front was the mustang herd. As it reached the water, the stallion slowed and stopped. He looked around, his head raised, nostrils flared, smelling the air. He turned in Bob's direction and sniffed the air again.

14 Bob tensed. Had he come too close too soon? If the stallion smelled anything new, he and the herd would be gone and Bob would never find them again. The stallion seemed to be looking directly at him. Bob was too far away to be seen, but he did not even blink his eyes, afraid the stallion would hear the sound. Finally the stallion began drinking and the other horses followed. Bob let his breath out slowly. He had been accepted.

The next morning he crossed the river and picked up the herd's trail. He moved Warrior slowly, without sound, without dust. Soon he saw them grazing. He stopped. The horses did not notice him. After a while he moved forward, slowly, quietly. The stallion raised his head. Bob stopped.

15 When the stallion went back to grazing, Bob moved forward again. All day Bob watched the herd, moving only when it moved but always coming closer. The mustangs sensed his presence. They thought he was a horse. So did he.

The following morning Bob and Warrior walked into the herd. The stallion eyed them for a moment. Then, as if to test this newcomer, he led the herd off in a gallop. Bob lay flat across Warrior's back and moved with the herd. If anyone had been watching, they would not have noticed a man among the horses.

When the herd set out early the next day, it was moving slowly. If the horses had been going faster, it would not have happened.

The colt fell to the ground as if she had stepped into a hole and broken her leg. Bob and the horses heard the chilling sound of the rattles. Rattlesnakes didn't always give a warning before they struck. Sometimes, when someone or something came too close, they bit with the fury of fear.

16 The horses whinnied and pranced nervously, smelling the snake and death among them. Bob saw the rattler, as beautiful as a necklace, sliding silently through the tall grasses. He made no move to kill it. Everything in nature had the right to protect itself, especially when it was afraid.

The stallion galloped to the colt. He pushed at her. The colt struggled to get up, but fell to her side, shivering and kicking feebly with her thin legs. Quickly she was dead.

Already vultures circled high in the sky. The mustangs milled aimlessly. The colt's mother whinnied, refusing to leave the side of her colt. The stallion wanted to move the herd from there, and pushed the mare with his head. She refused to budge, and he nipped her on the rump. She skittered away. Before she could return to the colt, the stallion bit her again, this time harder. She ran toward the herd. He bit her a third time, and the herd was off. As they galloped away, Bob looked back. The vultures were descending from the sky as gracefully as dusk.

It was time to take over the herd. The stallion would not have the heart to fight fiercely so soon after the death of the colt. Bob galloped Warrior to the front and wheeled around, forcing the stallion to stop quickly. The herd, confused, slowed and stopped also.

Bob raised Warrior to stand high on his back legs, fetlocks pawing and kicking the air. The stallion's eyes widened. He snorted and pawed the ground, surprised and uncertain. Bob charged at the stallion.

Both horses rose on hind legs, teeth bared as they kicked at each other. When they came down, Bob charged Warrior at the stallion again, pushing him backward. Bob rushed yet again.

The stallion neighed loudly, and nipped Warrior on the neck. Warrior snorted angrily, reared, and kicked out with his forelegs, striking the stallion on the nose. Still maintaining his balance, Warrior struck again and again. The mustang stallion cried out in pain. Warrior pushed hard against the stallion. The stallion lost his footing and fell to the earth. Warrior rose, neighing triumphantly, his front legs pawing as if seeking for the rungs on which he could climb a ladder into the sky.

The mustang scrambled to his feet, beaten. He snorted weakly. When Warrior made as if to attack again, the stallion turned, whinnied weakly, and trotted away.

Bob was now the herd's leader, but would they follow him? He rode slowly at first, then faster and faster. The mustangs followed as if being led on ropes.

Throughout that day and the next he rode with the horses. For Bob there was only the bulging of the horses' dark eyes, the quivering of their flesh, the rippling of muscles and bending of bones in their bodies. He was now sky and plains and grass and river and horse.

17 Craft and Structure

Ask: What pattern does the author use in this passage to move the action of the story along?

Possible response: The author uses the pattern of threes—the stallion bites the mother three times before she runs toward the herd.

18 Integration of Knowledge and Ideas

Ask: The clash between animals and humans is a common theme in the oral tradition. How is the conflict between Bob and the stallion important to the development of the story? Why are such conflicts common in folk literature?

Possible response: The conflict is important because Bob must win the fight in order to become the herd leader and complete his quest of directing the horses to the corral. Such conflicts may be common in folk literature because humans have often struggled to impose their will on other animals in order to survive.

19 **Integration of Knowledge and Ideas**

Ask: What problem has Bob solved? How does the ending compare to that of other stories about folk heroes you have read or heard?

Possible response: Bob has solved the problem of how to get the horses into the corral. It is similar to other endings because the hero (Bob) successfully and cleverly completes his quest.

When his food was almost gone, Bob led the horses on one last ride, a dark surge of flesh flashing across the plains like black lightning. Toward evening he led the herd up the steep hillside, onto the bluff, and down the slope toward the big corral. The cowboys heard him coming and opened the corral gate. Bob led the herd, but at the last moment he swerved Warrior aside, and the mustangs flowed into the fenced enclosure. The cowboys leaped and shouted as they quickly closed the gate.

Bob rode away from them and back up to the bluff. He stopped and stared out onto the plains. Warrior reared and whinnied loudly.

"I know," Bob whispered. "I know. Maybe someday."

Maybe someday they would ride with the mustangs, ride to that forever place where land and sky kissed, and then ride on. Maybe someday.

If you are using the Independent Practice as formative assessment, use the rubric below to evaluate students' performances.

Independent Practice Rubric	Rating Scale				
Close Reading: How well does the student use close reading strategies to answer the questions?	*not very* 1	2	3	4	*very* 5
Support/Elaboration: How well does the student support points with textual or other evidence?	1	2	3	4	5
Insight: How original, sophisticated, or compelling are the insights the student achieves?	1	2	3	4	5
Expression of Ideas: How well does the student use language, including word choice and conventions, in the expression of ideas?	1	2	3	4	5

Comprehension: **Key Ideas and Details**

1. (a) Identify examples of Bob Lemmons's legendary ability. **(b) Infer:** What danger does Bob face in approaching the mustangs too soon?

2. (a) How does Bob depend on Warrior? **(b) Connect:** Why does it seem that Warrior's goals match Bob's goals?

3. (a) What does Bob do after he leads the mustangs to the corral? **(b) Interpret:** What do his actions suggest about the life of a legendary hero?

4. Summarize: Write a brief, objective summary of the story. Cite story details in your writing.

Text Analysis: **Craft and Structure**

5. (a) Describe the setting, including the weather. **(b) Interpret:** How does the setting affect the story's development?

6. Evaluate: The author states that Bob "could make horses think he was one of them—because he was." Why is this exaggeration meaningful?

7. (a) Why does Bob decide not to kill the rattler? **(b) Generalize:** What central idea about Bob does his decision convey?

Connections: **Integration of Knowledge and Ideas**

Discuss
Conduct a **small-group discussion** about the character of Bob. Identify qualities that make him seem like a real person, as well as exaggerated abilities that make him seem like a legend. Then compare the character of Bob to other legendary characters you know.

Research
Bob Lemmons was a real-life "mustanger" who worked to gain the trust of wild horses. Research Lemmons's life and the methods he used to gather horses. Consider the following:

a. Lemmons's personal history and motivations

b. the job of capturing wild horses in the old West

c. horse training tactics that are practiced today

Take notes as you perform your research. Then, write a brief **explanation** of why Bob Lemmons makes a good legendary character.

Write
Warrior plays an important role in the story. Write an **essay** in which you analyze Warrior as a character from folk literature. Consider, for example, the stallion's heroic traits and unusual abilities. Support your analysis with story details.

 How much do our communities shape us?

(a) What is Bob Lemmons's "community"? **(b)** How does this community influence Bob's life and personality? Explain.

---

1. (a) He can use the ground to gather information about animals and can capture mustangs. **(b)** He might scare off the mustangs and not find them again.

2. (a) Warrior helps him become part of the herd. **(b)** Warrior does exactly what Bob needs him to do.

3. (a) He rides away and stares out onto the plains with Warrior, hoping to someday ride with the mustangs again. **(b)** The hero's life is solitary.

4. Summaries should describe how Bob uses his abilities to convince a herd of wild mustangs that he is one of them. He tames their leader and then leads them to the corral.

5. (a) The story takes place on a vast plain that also has a hill above a corral. The weather can be stormy. **(b)** The story starts and ends at the corral. Most action takes place on the plains, where a storm forces Bob and Warrior to stop.

6. The exaggeration is meaningful because it helps to convey Bob's uncanny ability to understand horses.

7. (a) He believes that "everything in nature had the right to protect itself." **(b)** Bob respects nature, which helps him become one with the horses.

Discuss
Responses should mention Bob's strategy for bringing in the horses and his ability to blend into the herd so the mustangs do not detect him. Legendary characters like Bob can often communicate with animals.

Research
Students should explain why Bob Lemmons is an appropriate character for a legendary story, supporting their analysis with evidence gathered from research.

Write
Student essays should mention Warrior's ability to carry out Bob's wishes and the horse's desire to run out of this world, to "that forever place," an image that appears at the beginning and the end of the story.

 How much do our communities shape us?

(a) His community is the animal world. **(b)** Because of his affinity for animals, Bob earns his living by working with animals, spending most of his time communing with them.

❶ About the Quotation

Helen Keller (1880–1968) became a noted writer and lecturer despite having been stricken blind and deaf by childhood illness. The story of how Keller broke into the world of language is told in the play and film *The Miracle Worker*.

Discussion Ask students to discuss the meaning of Keller's quotation about life's lessons. Ask them how their knowledge of Keller's life influences their understanding of the quotation. Then ask them if they agree with the quotation. Have them explain and support their position with sound reasoning and evidence.

❷ Critical Viewing

Pose the critical viewing question to the class. Then, guide the class in a discussion about the question. Encourage students to build upon each other's ideas as they share their responses. Remind students to support their responses with reasons and evidence.

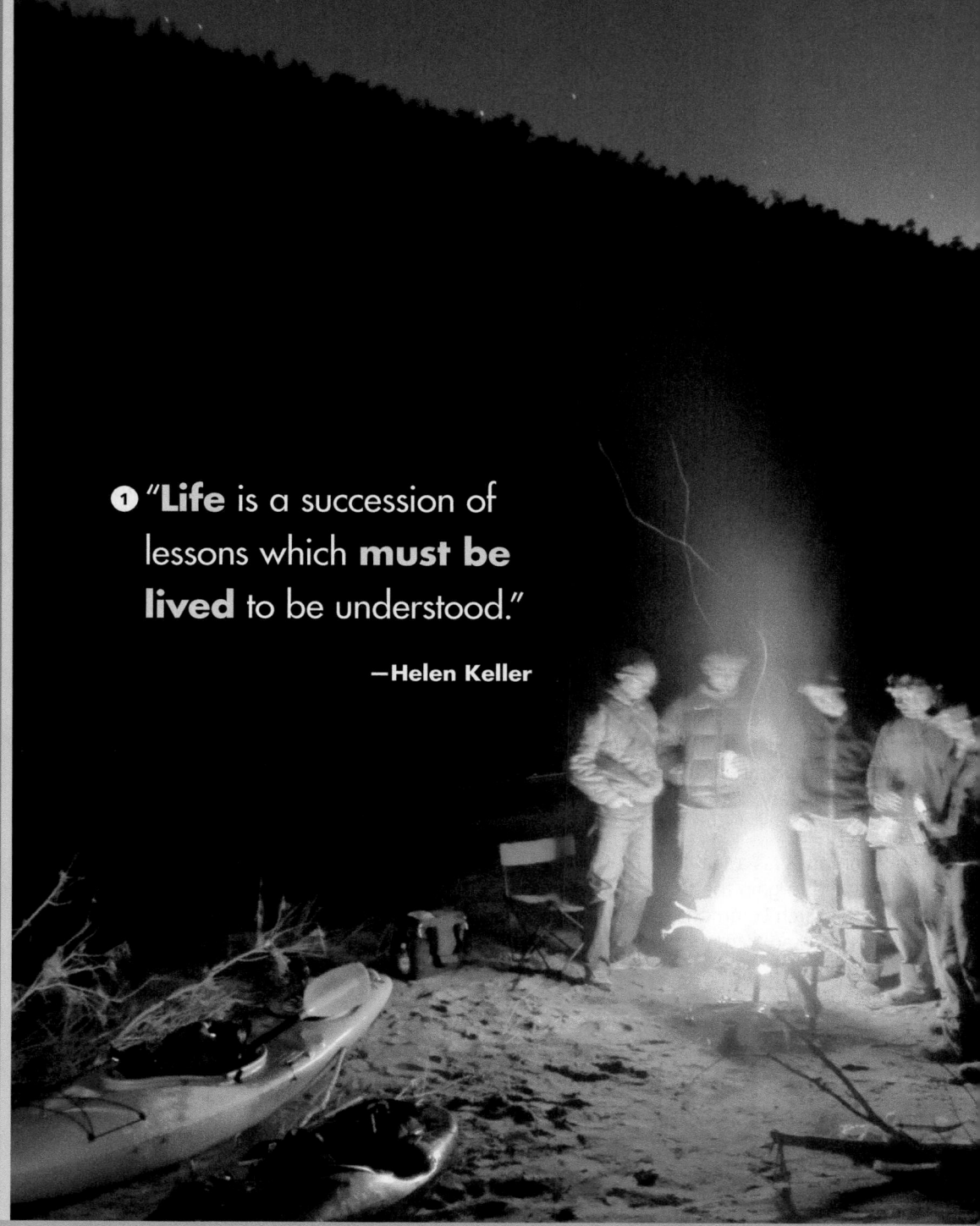

❶ "**Life** is a succession of lessons which **must be lived** to be understood."

—Helen Keller

❓ DEVELOPING ESSENTIAL UNDERSTANDING

How much do our communities shape us?
Explain to students that they will continue to consider the Big Question as they work through the selections in Part 2 of the unit.

• As students read each selection, they will look for details related to the Big Question and take notes.

• At the end of each selection, students will answer a Literary Analysis question that is related to the Big Question.

• Students will deepen their knowledge of the selections and their understanding of the Big Question through reading, speaking, listening, researching, and writing.

PART 2

TEXT ANALYSIS GUIDED EXPLORATION

SHARED LESSONS

As you read the folk literature in this section, explore the ways in which tales from the oral tradition can reveal the values, beliefs, and customs of the cultures from which they originated. The quotation on the opposite page will help you start thinking about ways in which learning from past mistakes or experiences can help you understand common themes about life.

2 ◀ **CRITICAL VIEWING** How can a person benefit from sharing his or her experiences with others in a situation such as the one shown in the photo?

3 READINGS IN PART 2

FABLE • RUSSIAN FOLK TALE
The Tiger Who Would Be King • The Ant and the Dove
James Thurber • Leo Tolstoy
(p. 634) • (p. 636)

GREEK MYTH
Arachne
Olivia Coolidge
(p. 642)

FOLK TALE
The Stone
Lloyd Alexander
(p. 652)

FOLK TALE
Why the Tortoise's Shell Is Not Smooth
Chinua Achebe
(p. 668)

CLOSE READING TOOL

Use the Close Reading Tool to practice the strategies you learned in this unit.

PART 2 • Shared Lessons **627**

CUSTOMIZING THE TEXT SET

Close Reading Tool
Use the Close Reading Tool to project the selections on a whiteboard and work through them as a whole-class activity. Students also have the opportunity to read those selections independently, with scaffolds available as needed.

Curriculum Builder
Use the Curriculum Builder to customize this program by rearranging existing selections, adding selection titles of your choosing, and uploading your own resources—all online!

3 Readings in Part 2
About the Texts
(For quantitative and qualitative measures of text complexity, see the rubrics on the opening pages of each selection.)

FABLE • RUSSIAN FOLK TALE: The Tiger Who Would Be King • The Ant and the Dove

Summary In "The Tiger Who Would Be King," all of the jungle creatures fight until death—except the tiger, who is mortally wounded.

In "The Ant and the Dove," a dove does a kind deed for an ant. Later, the ant saves the dove, proving that one can never predict when a kindness may be repaid.

GREEK MYTH: Arachne

Summary Arachne is famous for her weaving skills. Arachne insists she has developed her skill through hard work and not even Athene can create finer cloth. Athene challenges Arachne to a contest. Angered by scenes that Arachne weaves into her cloth, Athene turns Arachne into a spider.

FOLK TALE: The Stone

Summary Maibon passes an old man on the road and starts thinking about the problems of old age. Later, he frees a dwarf who is trapped under a log and asks the dwarf to reward him with a stone that will stop him from growing old. The stone keeps Maibon and everything around him from changing, often with negative results.

FOLK TALE: Why the Tortoise's Shell Is Not Smooth

Summary Tortoise convinces the birds to lend him some feathers so that he can fly with them. Tortoise uses his cunning to trick the birds, and the birds get their revenge. This tale provides an explanation for the markings on a tortoise's shell.

 **Audio**

Summary Audio is available in the *Student eText* and on the *Hear It!* CD-ROM.

PART 2 • Shared Lessons **627**

➊ Elements of Folk Literature

1. Introduce the elements of folk literature, using the instruction on the student page.

   Ask students how folk literature originated.

   Possible response: Folk literature began as stories passed along by word of mouth.

2. Read aloud the instruction on theme and universal themes. **Ask** students to describe the difference between a theme and a universal theme.

   Possible response: A theme is a message or insight about life. A universal theme is a message or insight that is broad enough to be understood by many different people.

3. Referring to the graphic organizer on the student page, discuss the different elements. **Ask** students to name examples of folk literature they have read or seen.

   Possible response: Answers will vary, but students might mention the tales of King Arthur or stories about Paul Bunyan or Brer Rabbit.

Focus on Craft and Structure

➊ Elements of Folk Literature

Folk literature is a genre of writing that has its origins in the **oral tradition.**

The Oral Tradition Long before writing or books were invented, people told stories. These stories were passed along by word of mouth from one generation to the next. You may have experienced a similar sharing of stories among your family or friends. The passing along of stories is known as the **oral tradition.** Folk literature—including folk tales, fairy tales, fables, wise sayings, folk songs, legends, and myths—originated in the stories of the oral tradition.

Theme is the central message or insight in a literary work. The themes in folk literature have survived the test of time and place. This is because many themes in folk literature are universal.

Universal themes express ideas, values, and insights into human nature that people from different cultures and eras have found meaningful and important. For example, universal themes might warn of the dangers of greed or the value of kindness. Sometimes, the theme of a folk story is **culturally specific.** Such themes reflect the background, customs, and beliefs of a particular culture.

Purposes of Folk Literature The **purpose** of a literary work is the reason it is created. In folk literature, that purpose may be to teach a lesson, to explain something in nature, or simply to entertain. In folk literature, the purpose may be tied closely to the theme.

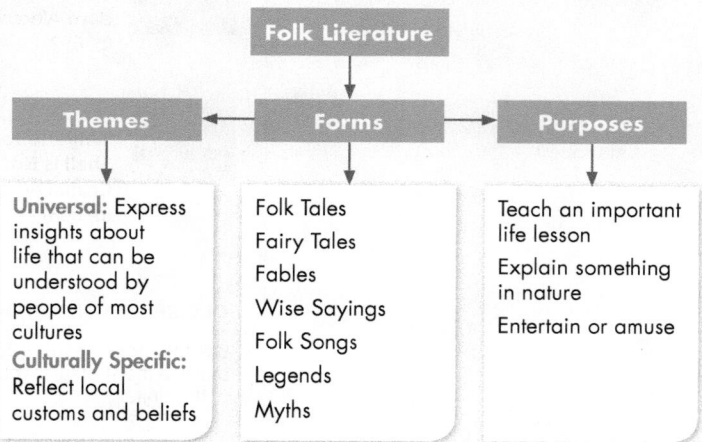

❷ The Oral Tradition in Print

Once writing and books were invented, stories from the oral tradition were collected and put into print. Today, collections of folk literature are generally classified by type.

Folk Tales are stories that often deal with heroes, adventure, magic, or romance. They were told not only to entertain but also to communicate the shared ideas of a culture.

Fables are brief stories or poems that teach lessons, or morals. These morals are usually stated directly at the ends of the fables. The main characters are often animals with human characteristics.

Folk songs present the ideas, values, feelings, and beliefs of a culture in musical form. With simple melodies and repeated lines, they tell stories of war, adventure, and romance.

Myths are fictional tales that explore the actions of gods and heroes or explain why things are a certain way in the natural world. Every ancient culture has its own **mythology.** The mythology of ancient Greece and Rome is known as **classical mythology.**

Legends are traditional, familiar stories about the past. Legends usually have some basis in fact. However, over time and through many retellings, the factual details have often been changed, making the legends more fiction than fact.

Characteristics of Folk Literature The different types of folk literature have many common characteristics.

Characteristic	Definition
Fantasy	writing that is highly imaginative and contains elements not found in real life
Personification	type of figurative language in which a nonhuman subject is given human characteristics
Hyperbole	exaggeration or overstatement that is often used to create a comic effect
Irony	involves surprises, unexpected events, and interesting or amusing contradictions
Dialect	form of language spoken by people of a particular region or group

Common Core State Standards

Reading Literature
2. Determine a theme or central idea of a text and how it is conveyed through particular details; provide a summary of the text distinct from personal opinions or judgments.

PART 2 • Focus on Craft and Structure **629**

---

❷ The Oral Tradition in Print

1. Introduce the types of folk literature, using the instruction on the student page.
2. Have students identify the type of folk literature of each of these examples:
   - a story about a cat and a mouse that teaches a moral
     Answer: fable
   - a tale about a Greek god
     Answer: myth
   - a fictional story about a real historical king and queen
     Answer: legend
   - a story that explains why the sun is so hot
     Answer: myth
   - a story about an African American hero that tells about her culture
     Answer: folk tale
   - a story of war told in musical form
     Answer: folk song
3. Have students review the information in the chart. **Ask:** Which types of folk literature often feature personification?

   Possible responses: fables; myths

❖ DIFFERENTIATED INSTRUCTION

Support for Less Proficient Readers
Have students read the **Learning About Folk Literature** pages for "Black Cowboy, Wild Horses" in the *Reader's Notebook: Adapted Version.* This version provides a basic-level introduction to folk literature.

EL Support for English Learners
Have students read the **Learning About Folk Literature** pages for "Black Cowboy, Wild Horses" in the *Reader's Notebook: English Learner's Version.* This version provides a basic-level introduction to folk literature.

❶ Analyzing Structure and Theme in Folk Literature

1. Introduce the concepts of structure and themes in folk literature, using the instruction on the student page.

2. Have students describe in their own words the difference between a stated and implied theme.

Possible response: A stated theme is expressed directly in the story. An implied theme is suggested. To find it you must pay attention to the characters and events and notice any symbols in the story.

3. Review the use of symbols in themes and common themes in folk literature with students. Encourage students to think of folk tales or fairy tales they know.

Ask: Which folk tales or fairy tales do you know that express these themes? Explain.

Possible responses: "The Frog Prince"—an unappealing outward appearance may disguise a noble soul: the frog turns out to be a prince. "Cinderella"—the virtues of kindness, generosity, and modesty are stronger than their opposites—cruelty, greed, and pride: the prince falls in love with Cinderella, not her evil stepsisters.

❶ Analyzing Structure and Theme in Folk Literature

Works of folk literature express **themes**—central messages that provide insights into life and human nature.

For modern readers, folk literature is a source of entertainment and insights. Elements of adventure, romance, and drama provide the entertainment. However, it is the themes—the deeper meanings of these stories—that provide insights into human nature.

Stated and Implied Theme

Themes in folk literature are expressed in many different ways. In a fable, the theme is often stated at the end of the story as a moral, or lesson. Look at the following example.

Example: The Boy Who Cried Wolf

While watching his father's sheep, a boy decided to trick the local villagers. "Wolf! Wolf!" he cried, loud enough for all to hear. When the villagers ran to help him, they discovered that there was no wolf. The boy continued playing this trick for several days. Then one day, a wolf actually appeared. The boy cried, "Wolf! Wolf!" but the villagers thought the boy was playing his trick again. They ignored his pleas for help. As a result, the wolf ate the sheep.

Moral: If you always tell lies, no one will believe you when you tell the truth.

Not all themes in folk literature are so clearly stated, however. Sometimes, a theme is implied, or suggested.

In these cases, readers must analyze the characters, setting, and events in the story to determine what the theme is.

Symbols and Theme A symbol is a person, place, or object that represents something beyond its literal meaning. For example, a mirror might symbolize vanity in a fairy tale or folk tale. As you read, pay attention to objects that seem to represent important ideas. Understanding the deeper meaning of a symbol can help you determine a story's theme.

Common Themes in Folk Literature Here are some common themes in folk literature:

- Often, those who seem foolish are actually wise.
- Too much pride can lead to a fall.
- Wisdom comes through suffering.
- The virtues of kindness, generosity, and modesty are stronger than their opposites—cruelty, greed, and pride.
- An unappealing outward appearance may disguise a noble soul.

🗨 THINK ALOUD

Finding the Theme

To model the skill of finding an implied theme, use this think aloud. Say:

If the theme of "The Boy Who Cried Wolf" were not directly stated, I could still find it. First, I could look at the characters and their actions. The characters are a boy who takes care of sheep and some villagers. The boy likes to trick villagers by lying. He cries "Wolf!" when there is no wolf, and villagers come to help him each time. The villagers must get pretty frustrated with the boy because when a wolf actually comes, they think he is lying and do not come. Because of his lies, the sheep are killed. The moral, or theme, of the story is if you tell lies all the time, people will not know when you're telling the truth.

Folk literature has several unique characteristics and structural devices that contribute to the development of theme. Keep these in mind as you read.

Simple Diction Diction is an author's choice of words, phrases, and sentence structure. The simple diction in much of folk literature is characterized by plain, common words, everyday language, and simple sentence construction. The use of simple diction helps convey theme in a way that people of all backgrounds can easily recognize and understand.

Repetition The repetition of events, lines of dialogue, descriptions, and sound patterns is a familiar element in folk literature. A **refrain,** often found in folk songs and poems, is the repetition of a phrase, line, or verse at regular intervals in the text. Repetition adds a pleasing rhythm to a story. In addition, it probably helped listeners and storytellers of the past remember the details of a story or song.

Patterns In folk literature, the story structure often follows a familiar and regular pattern. For example, many folk stories begin with simple phrases such as *Once upon a time...* or *Long ago, in a far-off land....* Another pattern often found in folk literature is the introduction of "threes"— for example, three characters or three events. The fairy tale "Rumpelstilskin" is a good example of the use of "threes."

Example: Rumpelstiltskin
• A young girl must spin <u>three</u> rooms of straw into gold.
• She has <u>three</u> days to complete her task.
• She gets <u>three</u> tries to guess the name of the odd little man who helps her.

Archetypes An **archetype** is an element that recurs regularly in literature and has similar meanings to people of different cultures and eras. Oral storytellers used archetypes to explore universal themes such as the dangers of greed and the importance of courage. Here are some common archetypes found in folk literature:

Common Archetypes in Folk Literature	
Plot	• dangerous journey • quest to prove one's honor • search for a valuable item
Characters	• enchanted princess • superhuman heroes and villains • trickster, or wise fool • talking animals
Ideas	• good vs. evil • magic in the normal world • hero or heroine aided by supernatural forces • evil disguised as good

4. Point out that because folk literature originated in the oral tradition, these stories use the simple language that oral storytellers used. In addition to being easy to understand, simple language was easy for oral storytellers to remember and pass on to others.

5. Tell students that openings such as "once upon a time" and "long ago, in a far-off land" cue the listener or reader that he or she is about to enter into a distant setting that could be anywhere—no particular time or place is given. **Ask:** What else comes to mind when you hear "once upon a time" or "long ago, in a far-off land"?

   Possible responses: I am going to hear a story that is made up. I am going to hear a fairy tale. I am going to hear about a magical time and place.

6. Explain that the pattern of threes is common in folk tales. Have students think of other examples.

   Possible response: "Goldilocks and the Three Bears," "The Three Little Pigs"

7. Have a volunteer read the instruction on archetypes. Then, review the chart as a class. Lead a discussion in which students discuss archetypal plots, characters, and ideas that appear in currently popular movies, television shows, and books.

Time and Resource Manager

LESSON PACING GUIDE

The Tiger Who Would Be King/The Ant and the Dove

DAY 1	Preteach/Teach

- Administer the Reading and Vocabulary Warm-ups, as necessary.
- Introduce the Key Ideas and Details skill: Cause and Effect.
- Introduce the Craft and Structure skill: Fables and Folk Tales.
- Use the Close Reading Model to demonstrate the application of the skills.
- Review the selection vocabulary, as necessary, with students who need additional support.
- Prepare students to read the selection by reviewing with them the Multidraft Reading Strategies.

DAY 2	Teach

- Informally monitor comprehension while students read.
- Use the Comprehension questions to confirm understanding.
- Develop students' ability to identify cause and effect and analyze fables and folk tales using the sidenote questions.
- Reinforce vocabulary with the Vocabulary notes.
- Reinforce unit focus standards using the Spiral Review prompts.

DAY 3	Assess

- Assess students' comprehension and mastery of the skills by having them answer the Literary Analysis questions.
- Have students complete the Vocabulary activities.
- Develop students' understanding of roots and affixes by having them complete the Word Study activities.

DAY 4	Extend/Assess

- Build students' ability to master grammar concepts and conventions by having them complete the Conventions lesson.
- Have students complete the Writing to Sources activity and write a fable. (You may assign as homework.)
- Extend learning by having students complete the Speaking and Listening activity: an oral report.
- Administer the Selection Test or Open-Book Test.

Common Core State Standards

Reading Literature 2. Determine a theme or central idea of a text and how it is conveyed through particular details.

Writing 3.b. Use narrative techniques, such as dialogue, pacing, and description, to develop experiences, events, and/or characters.

3.c. Use a variety of transition words, phrases, and clauses to convey sequence and signal shifts from one time frame or setting to another.

3.e. Provide a conclusion that follows from the narrated experience or events.

6. Use technology, including the Internet, to produce and publish writing.

7. Conduct short research projects to answer a question, drawing on several sources and focusing the inquiry when appropriate.

Speaking and Listening 5. Include multimedia components and visual displays in presentations to clarify information.

Language 1. Demonstrate command of the conventions of standard English grammar and usage when writing or speaking.

4.b. Use common, grade-appropriate Greek or Latin affixes and roots as clues to the meaning of a word.

Daily Block Scheduling

Each day in this Lesson Pacing Guide represents a 40–50 minute period. Teachers using block scheduling may combine days to revise pacing. In addition, teachers may differentiate and support core instruction by integrating components for extended and intensive support as students require. See the Guide to Resources (facing page).

GUIDE TO RESOURCES

| | LEARNER LEVELS | | | | | | RESOURCES | WHERE FOUND | | |
	L1	L2	L3	L4	EL	ALL		PRINT	CD	ONLINE
Warm Up	✔	✔			✔		Vocabulary Warm-ups			✔
	✔	✔			✔		Reading Warm-ups			✔
						✔	Background Video			✔
						✔	Selection Audio		Hear It!	✔
Comprehension/ Selection Support						✔	Writing About the Big Question	Student Companion Workbook		✔
						✔	Literary Analysis	Student Companion Workbook		✔
						✔	Reading	Student Companion Workbook		✔
						✔	Vocabulary Builder	Student Companion Workbook		✔
			✔				Enrichment			✔
		✔	✔	✔			Conventions	Student Companion Workbook		✔
		✔	✔	✔			Writing to Sources	Student Companion Workbook		✔
		✔	✔	✔			Speaking and Listening	Student Companion Workbook		✔
Differentiated Instruction/ Additional Support						✔	Additional Standards Practice	Common Core Companion		✔
						✔	Close Reading Practice	Close Reading Notebook		✔
	✔	✔					Adapted Reader's Notebook			✔
					✔		English Reader's Notebook:			✔
					✔		Spanish Reader's Notebook			✔
					✔		Graphic Organizer A			✔
	✔	✔			✔		Graphic Organizer B			✔
	✔	✔			✔		"Help You, Help Me"	Reality Central Student Edition and Writing Journal		✔
	✔	✔			✔		Practice and Assess	Reading Kit		✔
Monitor Progress						✔	Selection Test		Exam View	✔
						✔	Open-Book Test		Exam View	✔
Digital Resources						✔	Close Reading Tool			✔
						✔	Online Writer's Notebook			✔

👥 One-on-one teaching 👥 Group work 👥 Whole class instruction 👤 Independent work Ⓐ Assessment 🖥 Digital Resource

LEARNER LEVELS

L1 Special-Needs Students
L2 Below-Level Students (Tier 2)
L3 On-Level Students (Tier 1)
L4 Advanced Students (Tier 1)
EL English Learners
All All Students

❶ How much do our communities shape us?

Read • Discuss • Research • Write As students read, they will explore the Big Question through text analysis of the selection. Encourage students to take notes as they read and raise additional questions, using text evidence to support their thoughts. Students should refer to their notes to help them deepen their understanding of the selection through discussion, research, and writing.

❷ Close Reading Focus

1. Remind students that when they identify causes and effects, they are able to understand the reasons why something happened. Sometimes there can be multiple events, actions, or feelings that are the causes of an effect. Encourage students to use a two-column chart to note the causes in the first column and the effects in the second column.

2. Provide familiar examples of fables and folk tales to help students recognize the elements of each. Explain that "The Tortoise and the Hare" is a fable because it is fairly short, has animals as main characters, and teaches a clear lesson—slow and steady wins the race. "Beauty and the Beast" is a folk tale for the following reasons: the main character is human, the story has adventure and romance, and it hints at a lesson (that real beauty is inside). Tell students that they can look for these elements to find out whether a story is a fable or folk tale.

Meet the Author

James Thurber (1894–1961) wrote for his high school and college newspapers in Ohio. After military service in World War I, Thurber began writing and cartooning. Much of his early work appeared in *The New Yorker* magazine. Although failing eyesight forced him to give up drawing, Thurber kept making people laugh through his writing.

Leo Tolstoy (1828–1910) was born into a wealthy family in Russia and inherited the family estate. By the time he was fifty, he had written some of the world's most famous novels, including *War and Peace*. In midlife, Tolstoy began to reject his life of luxury. He surrendered the rights to many of his works and gave his property to his family. This world-famous writer died alone in a remote train station in Russia.

Ⓒ **Common Core State Standards**

Reading Literature
2. Determine a theme or central idea of a text and how it is conveyed through particular details.
Language
4.b. Use common, grade-appropriate Greek or Latin affixes and roots as clues to the meaning of a word.

❶ How much do our communities shape us?

Explore the Big Question as you read "The Tiger Who Would Be King" and "The Ant and the Dove."

❷ CLOSE READING FOCUS

Key Ideas and Details: **Cause and Effect**

A **cause** is an event, an action, or a feeling that produces a result. The result is called an **effect**. Sometimes an effect is the result of several causes. Other times, one cause can produce several different effects. To help you identify the relationship between an event and its causes, reread important passages in a literary work, looking for connections.

Craft and Structure: **Fables and Folk Tales**

Fables and **folk tales** are part of the oral tradition, in which stories and poems were passed from generation to generation by word of mouth.

- **Fables** are brief stories that often have animal characters. A fable teaches a lesson, or moral, that is usually stated at the end of the story.
- **Folk tales** often have clever characters who outsmart their superiors. These stories may contain elements of magic and adventure.

Some fables and folk tales have *ironic*, or surprising, endings because they do not turn out as you expect. The twist ending helps you see the story's theme, or message. As you read a fable or folk tale, notice how the setting, characters, and events introduce and develop the story's theme.

Vocabulary

You will encounter the following words in these tales. Write the words in your notebook, underlining the verbs.

prowled	inquired	repulse
monarch	startled	repaid

Ⓒ TEXT COMPLEXITY **RUBRIC**

The Tiger Who Would Be King; The Ant and the Dove		Reader and Task Suggestions	
Qualitative Measures		**Preparing to Read the Text**	**Leveled Tasks**
Context/Knowledge Demands	Animal Kingdom 1 2 ③ 4 5	• Tell students that fables use animal characters who demonstrate human virtues or vices. • Guide students to use Multidraft Reading strategies (TE p. 634)	*Knowledge Demands* If students will have difficulty with knowledge demands, use the Activating Prior Knowledge note on TE p. 634 to discuss the animal characters in fables and why these stories are so popular. *Synthesizing* If students will not have difficulty with knowledge demands, discuss why storytellers used allusions in fables, folk tales, and myths.
Structure/Language Conventionality and Clarity	Conversational; on-level vocabulary; short selections 1 ② 3 4 5		
Levels of Meaning/Purpose/ Concept Level	Accessible concept (power struggle; a favor returned) 1 2 ③ 4 5		
Quantitative Measures			
Lexile	860L, 750L	**Text Length** Word Count: 381, 116	

CLOSE READING MODEL

The passages below are from the fables "The Tiger Who Would Be King" and "The Ant and the Dove." The annotations to the right of the passages show ways in which you can use close reading skills to analyze cause and effect and to interpret fables and folk tales.

from **"The Tiger Who Would Be King"**

One morning the tiger woke up in the jungle and told his mate that he was king of beasts.

"Leo, the lion, is king of beasts," she said. [1]

"We need a change," said the tiger. "The creatures are crying for a change."

The tigress listened but she could hear no crying, except that of her cubs.

"I'll be the king of beasts by the time the moon rises," said the tiger. [2]

Fables and Folk Tales

1 A tiger announces that he is king of beasts, and his mate responds. The fact that these animals think and speak like humans can help you identify the story as a fable or folk tale.

Cause and Effect

2 Although the tigress does not hear the animals "crying for a change," the tiger insists he will replace the lion as king. You might predict that the tiger's plan to become king will become the cause of a conflict.

from **"The Ant and the Dove"**

A few days later a hunter was about to catch the dove in his net. When the ant saw what was happening, it walked right up to the man and bit him on the foot. Startled, the man dropped the net. [3] And the dove, thinking that you never can tell how or when a kindness may be repaid, flew away. [4]

Cause and Effect

3 The man's attempt to catch the dove causes the ant to bite the man. The effect of the bite is that the man drops the net.

Fables and Folk Tales

4 To discover the moral or theme of a folk tale, look for direct statements that reflect a general truth or an important idea about life.

Daily Bellringer

For each class during which you will teach this selection, have students complete one of the five Sentence Modeling activities for Week 26 in *Daily Bellringer Activities.* You may wish to use additional activities that are applicable to this selection.

Vocabulary

If students require support with selection vocabulary, use this routine:

1. Write the following words and definitions on the board:

   prowled *v.* moved around quietly and secretly

   inquired *v.* asked

   repulse *v.* drive back; repel an attack

   monarch *n.* single or sole ruler

   startled *adj.* surprised

   repaid *v.* did or gave in return

2. Have students say each word aloud.

3. Use the word in a sentence that defines the word.

:: DIFFERENTIATED INSTRUCTION

EL Extended Support— English Learners
Have students complete the **Reading and Vocabulary Warm-Ups** for this selection in the *Student Companion All-in-One Workbook* before they read. Assign the prereading pages and the adapted selection in the *Reader's Notebook: English Learner's Version.* Then, have students listen to portions of the selection in the *Student eText* or on the *Hear It!* CD-ROM.

L1 L2 Extended Support— Struggling Readers
Have students complete the **Reading and Vocabulary Warm-Ups** for this selection in the *Student Companion All-in-One Workbook* before they read. Assign the prereading pages and the adapted selection in the *Reader's Notebook: Adapted Version.* Then, have students listen to portions of the selection in the *Student eText* or on the *Hear It!* CD-ROM (adapted text).

Extended Support— Reluctant Readers
To build motivation and engagement before assigning the selection, have students read "Help You, Help Me," a thematically related selection in *Reality Central.* Then, use the questions at the conclusion of the related selection to guide discussion.

MULTIDRAFT READING

To assist struggling readers and to deepen comprehension for all, assign the text in "chunks" and apply multidraft reading protocols. For each reading, have students set the purpose indicated:

- **First reading:** Students should read the selection independently and think about its basic meaning.

- **Second reading:** Students should analyze the text's key ideas and details and its craft and structure, and respond to the side-column prompts.

- **Third reading:** Students should integrate knowledge and ideas, connect the text to other texts and to the world, and answer the end-of-selection questions.

For more guidance, refer to the *Classroom Strategies and Teaching Routines* card on multidraft reading.

❶ Activating Prior Knowledge

Ask students to recall stories about animals that they read or heard when they were young. As each volunteer mentions a story, ask what point, if any, the tale tries to make about human behavior. Tell students that many cultures around the world use animal tales to teach lessons about human behavior. Have students speculate about why such tales are so popular. Tell students they will revisit their thoughts about which selection will teach a more valuable lesson at the end of the selections.

THE TIGER WHO WOULD BE KING ❶

JAMES THURBER

Vocabulary ▶
prowled (prould)
v. moved around quietly and secretly

inquired (in kwīrd´)
v. asked

One morning the tiger woke up in the jungle and told his mate that he was king of beasts.

"Leo, the lion, is king of beasts," she said.

"We need a change," said the tiger. "The creatures are crying for a change."

The tigress listened but she could hear no crying, except that of her cubs.

"I'll be king of beasts by the time the moon rises," said the tiger. "It will be a yellow moon with black stripes, in my honor."

"Oh, sure," said the tigress as she went to look after her young, one of whom, a male, very like his father, had got an imaginary thorn in his paw.

The tiger prowled through the jungle till he came to the lion's den. "Come out," he roared, "and greet the king of beasts! The king is dead, long live the king!"

Inside the den, the lioness woke her mate. "The king is here to see you," she said.

"What king?" he inquired, sleepily.

"The king of beasts," she said.

"I am the king of beasts," roared Leo, and he charged out of the den to defend his crown against the pretender.

It was a terrible fight, and it lasted until the setting of the sun. All the animals of the jungle joined in, some taking the side of the tiger and others the side of the lion. Every creature from the aardvark to the zebra took part in the struggle to overthrow the lion or to repulse the tiger, and some did not know which they were fighting for, and some fought for both, and some fought whoever was nearest, and some fought for the sake of fighting.

"What are we fighting for?" someone asked the aardvark.

"The old order," said the aardvark.

"What are we dying for?" someone asked the zebra.

"The new order," said the zebra.

When the moon rose, fevered and gibbous,[1] it shone upon a jungle in which nothing stirred except a macaw[2] and a cockatoo,[3] screaming in horror. All the beasts were dead except the tiger, and his days were numbered and his time was ticking away. He was monarch of all he surveyed, but it didn't seem to mean anything.

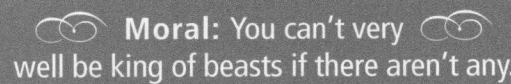

Moral: You can't very well be king of beasts if there aren't any.

---

1. **gibbous** (gib´ əs) *adj.* more than half but less than completely illuminated.
2. **macaw** (mə kô´) *n.* bright-colored, harsh-voiced parrot of Central or South America.
3. **cockatoo** (kok´ ə tü´) *n.* crested parrot with white feathers tinged with yellow or pink.

---

❷ LITERATURE IN CONTEXT

Language Connection

Allusions

James Thurber uses an allusion in his description of the tigress who attends to her male cub with an imaginary thorn in his paw. An *allusion* is a reference to a person, place, or thing in another artistic work. Thurber makes an allusion to the fable of a shepherd who boldly relieves a lion from the pain caused by a thorn in his paw. Later, when the shepherd is in danger, the lion remembers the shepherd's kindness and saves him.

Connect to Literature

Why does Thurber allude to the fable about the lion and the shepherd?

◀ **Vocabulary**

repulse (ri puls´) *v.* drive back; repel an attack

monarch (män´ ərk) *n.* single or sole ruler

❸ **Fables and Folk Tales**
What conflict or problem does this fable address?

❷ Literature in Context

Language Connection

The word *allusion* comes from a Latin word that means "playing." Allusions are common in folk tales and fables, as well as myths and legends. Storytellers, especially in times when literature was often shared orally, could assume that their readers or listeners knew certain other stories. The storytellers could then add meaning to their stories by alluding to—or referring to—stories from ancient times, knowing that these stories were familiar to most people.

Connect to Literature Have students read the Literature in Context feature, and present the additional background information above. Then, **ask** the Connect to Literature question: Why does Thurber allude to the fable about the lion and the shepherd?

Answer: He wants to add meaning to his story. The allusion stresses that real kindness is rewarded but that imaginary complaints probably won't be. Since the tiger's complaint about the lion, like that of his son, is imaginary, it will lead to a bad end.

❸ Fables and Folk Tales

Ask the Fables and Folk Tales question.

Possible Response: Some conflicts have no winner and the losses are great.

 Video

Watch the Background Video online!

 **Audio**

Selection audio is available in the *Student eText* and on the *Hear It!* CD-ROM.

PART 2 • The Tiger Who Would Be King **635**

Spiral Review

Character

1. Remind students that they studied the concept of character in the Unit 5 Focus on Craft and Structure (pp. 628–631).

2. **Ask** students the Spiral Review question.

   Possible response: The characters in this story are typical of fables in that the animals have human characteristics.

☑ ASSESS

Language Study

Vocabulary

Sample answers:

1. A wolf might have <u>prowled</u> near a river hoping to catch some prey.

2. People are <u>repulsed</u> by garbage because it smells bad and may contain bugs.

3. <u>Startled</u> people might gasp, shout, or run away.

4. You might have <u>inquired</u> about a friend's health to show your concern.

5. The United States does not have a <u>monarch</u> because it has an elected President instead.

Word Study

Part A

Sample answers:

The suffix *-ment* means "act," or "art" or "process of." An *argument* is the <u>act of</u> arguing. A *payment* is the <u>process</u> of paying.

Part B

Sample answers:

1. The suffix *-ment* means "act of." You give your friends *encouragement,* or the <u>act of</u> encouraging, when they are feeling unsure.

2. The suffix *-ment* means "process of." You get a *measurement* from the <u>process of</u> measuring.

Literary Analysis

Possible responses appear below. Check to be sure students support their responses with evidence from the text.

1. **(a)** Causes include that the tiger claims that he is king of the jungle, and that the lion needs to

---

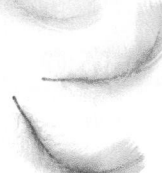

The Ant and the Dove
Russian Folk Tale • Leo Tolstoy

Spiral Review
CHARACTERS How are the characters in this story typical of fables?

Vocabulary ▶
startled (stärt′ əld) *adj.* surprised

repaid (ri pād′) *v.* did or gave in return

A thirsty ant went to the stream to drink. Suddenly it got caught in a whirlpool and was almost carried away.

At that moment a dove was passing by with a twig in its beak. The dove dropped the twig for the tiny insect to grab hold of. So it was that the ant was saved.

A few days later a hunter was about to catch the dove in his net. When the ant saw what was happening, it walked right up to the man and bit him on the foot. Startled, the man dropped the net. And the dove, thinking that you never can tell how or when a kindness may be repaid, flew away.

Language Study

Vocabulary Respond to each item below based on your knowledge of the italicized vocabulary words.

| prowled | inquired | repulse | monarch | startled |

1. Explain why a wolf might have *prowled* near a river.
2. Provide two reasons why garbage might *repulse* people.
3. Identify three things that a *startled* person might do.
4. Explain why you might have *inquired* about a friend's health.
5. Explain why the United States does not have a *monarch*.

Word Study

WORD STUDY

The **suffix** *-ment* means the "act," "art," or "process of." A word ending in *-ment* is usually a noun. "The Ant and the Dove" is a story about the **repayment** of a favor, or the act of paying back a favor.

Part A Explain how the **suffix** *-ment* contributes to the meanings of *argument* and *payment.* Consult a dictionary if necessary.

Part B Use context and what you know about the suffix *-ment* to explain your answer to each question.

1. When do you give your friends *encouragement*?
2. How do you get a *measurement*?

---

defend his position as king. **(b)** The effect is that all the animals kill one another until only the wounded tiger is left.

2. **(a)** The dove drops a twig so the ant does not drown. **(b)** By climbing onto the twig, the ant stays above water and does not drown.

3. The end effect is that the ant later saves the dove.

4. Title—"The Tiger Who Would Be King"; "The Ant and the Dove"; Characters—tiger, Leo the lion, tigress, lioness, zebra, aardvark; ant, dove, man; Moral or Theme—Impulsive, aggressive behavior often results in conflicts in which

nobody wins. People should be kind and help others because someday that kindness may be repaid.

5. **(a)** It is ironic that all the beasts are dead, so the tiger has no one to rule. **(b)** The costs of conflict can be greater for both sides than any benefits it may produce.

6. **(a)** The lion and the tiger fight to rule. **(b)** Some of them react without thinking about the outcome of their actions. **(c)** The animal characters show greed, impulsiveness, and aggression.

Literary Analysis

Key Ideas and Details

1. Cause and Effect (a) In "The Tiger Who Would Be King," identify two causes of the fight in the jungle. **(b)** What is the effect of the fight?

2. (a) What does the dove in "The Ant and the Dove" do for the ant? **(b) Make Inferences:** How does this action save the ant?

3. Cause and Effect What is the end effect of the dove's action in "The Ant and the Dove?"

Craft and Structure

4. Fables and Folk Tales Make a chart like the one on the right to identify the elements of fables and folk tales in the two stories.

5. Fables and Folk Tales (a) What is **ironic**, or surprising, about the ending of "The Tiger Who Would Be King"? **(b)** What theme does the ending suggest?

Title	
Characters	Moral or Theme

Integration of Knowledge and Ideas

6. (a) Which two animals fight to rule in "The Tiger Who Would Be King"? **(b) Make Inferences:** Some of the animals join the fight for the sake of fighting. What does this suggest about them? **(c) Apply:** What human qualities does Thurber show in these animals?

7. Relate: Does "The Ant and the Dove" remind you of any other stories you have read? Explain.

8. ❓ **How much do our communities shape us?** With a small group, discuss the following questions: **(a)** In "The Tiger Who Would Be King," what action in the community could have saved the animals? Support your answer with details. **(b) Draw Conclusions:** Explain why the animals did not take that action.

ACADEMIC VOCABULARY

As you write and speak about "The Tiger Who Would Be King" and "The Ant and the Dove," use the words related to cooperation that you explored on page 613 of this text.

7. Students might name Aesop's tales "The Lion and the Mouse" or "The Serpent and the Eagle"; William Steig's *Amos and Boris*; the Brothers Grimm's "The Frog Prince." They should support their responses with explanations.

8. ❓ **How much do our communities shape us?**
(a) If the community had convinced the tiger not to fight the lion, this could have saved the community. **(b)** Some of the animals wanted to defeat the lion, some liked to fight, and some were just bored. They could not agree on an action to take together.

 Online Writer's Notebook

Students can use the Online Writer's Notebook to record all responses.

Conventions

1. Introduce the skill.
2. Discuss the examples.

Think Aloud: Model the Skill

Say to students:

Linking verbs join subjects to descriptions. They do not have objects. When I say "Jeremiah is a talented violinist," the predicate noun *violinist* identifies the subject, *Jeremiah.* The linking verb *is* joins the subject to the word that identifies it. When I say, "His violin is very valuable," the linking verb *is* joins the subject *violin* to the predicate adjective *valuable.* By contrast, action verbs do take objects. In the sentence *Jeremiah plays a valuable violin,* I am using a direct object, *violin,* to tell *what* Jeremiah plays.

Practice A

1. king, predicate noun
2. angry, predicate adjective
3. busy, predicate adjective
4. war, predicate noun
5. fierce, predicate adjective
6. king, predicate noun

Reading Application
Sample answers:

Predicate noun: "Leo, the lion is *king* of beasts."; "It will be a yellow *moon*"; "I am the *king* of beasts"; "It was a terrible *fight*"; "He was *monarch* of all he surveyed."

Predicate adjective: "The king is *dead*"; "The king is *here* to see you"; "All the beasts were *dead* except the tiger."

Practice B
Sample answers:

1. helpful, predicate adjective; The ant is brave.
2. hunter, predicate noun; The man became a teacher.
3. kind, predicate adjective; The ant's action was surprising.
4. thankful, predicate adjective; The dove seems safe now.

Writing Application
Sample answer:

A fable is really a (lesson.) "The Tiger Who Wanted to Be King" is my favorite (fable.) The story is (exciting) and the characters are (funny.)

Conventions: **Subject Complements**

A **subject complement** is a noun, a pronoun, or an adjective that appears with a linking verb and tells something about the subject of the sentence.

A **predicate noun** renames or identifies the subject. A **predicate adjective** describes the subject.

Predicate Noun	Predicate Adjective
Lucy is an excellent *doctor.*	This toast tastes *burnt.*
That fruit appears to be a *quince.*	Frank seemed *relieved* to hear the news.
The caterpillar became a *butterfly.*	You've grown *tall* this summer!
Her piggy bank was a small *cat.*	If the cheese smells *moldy,* don't eat it.

Practice A
Identify the predicate noun or predicate adjective in each sentence.

1. The lion is king of the beasts.
2. The tiger grows angry.
3. The tigress was busy with her cubs.
4. The argument became a war.
5. His roar sounds fierce.
6. The tiger became the king.

Reading Application In "The Tiger Who Would Be King," find at least two predicate nouns and two predicate adjectives. Copy the sentences with subject complements and label each complement *predicate noun* or *predicate adjective.*

Practice B
Identify the predicate noun or predicate adjective in each sentence. Then, rewrite each sentence, replacing the predicate noun or predicate adjective to change the meaning of the sentence.

1. The ant is helpful to the dove.
2. The man became a hunter.
3. The ant's action was kind.
4. The dove seems thankful now.

Writing Application Write a description of one of the fables. Use at least two predicate adjectives and two predicate nouns in your description. Circle the predicate adjectives and the predicate nouns you use.

▶ EXTEND THE LESSON

Sentence Modeling
Write these sentences from "The Tiger Who Would Be King" on the board.

"I am the king of beasts," roared Leo, and he charged out of the den to defend his crown against the pretender.

The king is dead, long live the king!

Ask students what they notice about the sentences. Elicit from them that the first sentence uses a predicate noun and the second sentence uses a predicate adjective. Then, ask what else they notice. (In the first sentence a conjunction connects two clauses joining two different actions. In the second sentence only a comma joins two ideas.)

Have students imitate one of the sentences in a sentence on a topic of their own choosing, matching each grammatical and stylistic feature discussed. Collect the sentences, and share them with the class.

Writing to Sources

Narrative Text Write a **fable** that teaches the same lesson as one of the selections you read.

- First, reread the selection to determine what lesson it teaches. Then, brainstorm for situations in which characters could learn that lesson.
- Decide who your characters will be, then use dialogue and description to develop the characters.
- Use effective pacing in your fable. To slow the pace as you introduce scenes, use longer sentences and more details. To move faster and create tension, use short sentences.
- Use transitions to clearly show how story events lead to the lesson learned.
- Provide a moral at the end that logically follows from the events.

Grammar Application Review your fable to identify and correct errors in grammar and punctuation.

Speaking and Listening

Presentation of Ideas Prepare an **oral report** on either James Thurber or Leo Tolstoy.

- Research the author's life using the Internet or print sources. Answer questions you have about the author's background and key published works. Add questions or change your focus, if necessary, as your research develops.
- Take notes on the key points you want to share in your report. Then, use your notes to compose an interesting oral presentation. Include information that tells how some of the author's other works are similar to and different from the one you read in your textbook.
- Prepare visual aids, such as pictures, timelines, and graphs to grab your audience's attention and to support your ideas.
- Practice delivering your presentation. Speak expressively, emphasizing key points. When you are ready, share your report with the class.

 **Common Core State Standards**

Writing
3.b. Use narrative techniques, such as dialogue, pacing, and description, to develop experiences, events, and/or characters. **3.c.** Use a variety of transition words, phrases, and clauses to convey sequence and signal shifts from one time frame or setting to another. **3.e.** Provide a conclusion that follows from the narrated experience or events.
6. Use technology, including the Internet, to produce and publish writing.
7. Conduct short research projects to answer a question, drawing on several sources and focusing the inquiry when appropriate.

Speaking and Listening
5. Include multimedia components and visual displays in presentations to clarify information.

Language
1. Demonstrate command of the conventions of standard English grammar and usage when writing or speaking.

Writing to Sources

1. Review the assignment, using the instruction on the student page.
2. To give students guidance in writing narrative texts, give them the **Support for Writing,** for this selection in the *Student Companion All-in-One Workbook.*
3. To evaluate the writing activity, use one of the **Short Story** rubrics, pp. 226–227 in *Professional Development Guidebook.* In addition, you might evaluate for how well students show cause-and-effect relationships and how well the action of the fable supports the lesson.

Grammar Application

Have students check their drafts for the correct use of subject complements.

Six Traits Focus

✓	Ideas	Word Choice
✓	Organization	Sentence Fluency
	Voice	Conventions

Speaking and Listening

1. Review the assignment, using the instruction on the student page.
2. To support students' work on the assignment, have them complete the **Support for Extend Your Learning** for this selection in the *Student Companion All-in-One Workbook.*

LESSON PACING GUIDE

Arachne

DAY 1	**Preteach/Teach**

- Administer the Reading and Vocabulary Warm-ups, as necessary.
- Introduce the Key Ideas and Details skill: Cause and Effect.
- Introduce the Craft and Structure skill: Myths.
- Use the Close Reading Model to demonstrate the application of the skills.
- Review the selection vocabulary, as necessary, with students who need additional support.
- Prepare students to read the selection by reviewing with them the Multidraft Reading Strategies.

DAY 2	**Teach**

- Informally monitor comprehension while students read.
- Use the Comprehension questions to confirm understanding.
- Develop students' ability to identify cause and effect and analyze myths using the sidenote questions.
- Reinforce vocabulary with the Vocabulary notes.
- Reinforce unit focus standards using the Spiral Review prompts.

DAY 3	**Assess**

- Assess students' comprehension and mastery of the skills by having them answer the Literary Analysis questions.
- Have students complete the Vocabulary activities.
- Develop students' understanding of roots and affixes by having them complete the Word Study activities.

DAY 4	**Extend/Assess**

- Build students' ability to master grammar concepts and conventions by having them complete the Conventions lesson.
- Have students complete the Writing to Sources activity and write a brief compare-and-contrast essay. (You may assign as homework.)
- Extend learning by having students complete the Research and Technology activity: an annotated bibliography entry.
- Administer the Selection Test or Open-Book Test.

 **Common Core State Standards**

Reading Literature 2. Determine a theme or central idea of a text and how it is conveyed through particular details.

5. Analyze how a particular sentence, chapter, scene, or stanza fits into the overall structure of a text and contributes to the development of the theme, setting, or plot.

Writing 2. Write informative/explanatory texts to examine a topic and convey ideas, concepts, and information through the selection, organization, and analysis of relevant content.

2.a. Introduce a topic; organize ideas, concepts, and information, using strategies such as definition, classification, comparison/contrast, and cause/effect.

2.d. Use precise language and domain-specific vocabulary to inform about or explain the topic.

2.e. Establish and maintain a formal style.

8. Gather relevant information from multiple print and digital sources, assess the credibility of each source, and quote or paraphrase the data and conclusions of others while avoiding plagiarism and providing basic bibliographic information for sources.

Language 3. Use knowledge of language and its conventions when writing, speaking, reading, or listening.

4.b. Use common, grade-appropriate Greek or Latin affixes and roots as clues to the meaning of a word.

Daily Block Scheduling

Each day in this Lesson Pacing Guide represents a 40–50 minute period. Teachers using block scheduling may combine days to revise pacing. In addition, teachers may differentiate and support core instruction by integrating components for extended and intensive support as students require. See the Guide to Resources (facing page).

GUIDE TO RESOURCES

		LEARNER LEVELS						RESOURCES	WHERE FOUND		
		L1	L2	L3	L4	EL	ALL		PRINT	CD	ONLINE
Warm Up		✔	✔			✔		Vocabulary Warm-ups			✔
		✔	✔			✔		Reading Warm-ups			✔
							✔	Background Video			✔
							✔	Selection Audio		Hear It!	✔
Comprehension/ Selection Support							✔	Writing About the Big Question	Student Companion Workbook		✔
							✔	Literary Analysis	Student Companion Workbook		✔
							✔	Reading	Student Companion Workbook		✔
							✔	Vocabulary Builder	Student Companion Workbook		✔
				✔				Enrichment			✔
			✔	✔	✔			Conventions	Student Companion Workbook		✔
			✔	✔	✔			Writing to Sources	Student Companion Workbook		✔
			✔	✔	✔			Research and Technology	Student Companion Workbook		✔
Differentiated Instruction/ Additional Support							✔	Additional Standards Practice	Common Core Companion		✔
							✔	Close Reading Practice	Close Reading Notebook		✔
		✔	✔					Adapted Reader's Notebook			✔
						✔		English Reader's Notebook:			✔
						✔		Spanish Reader's Notebook			✔
						✔		Graphic Organizer A			✔
		✔	✔			✔		Graphic Organizer B			✔
		✔	✔			✔		"Mentors Make a Difference"	Reality Central Student Edition and Writing Journal		✔
		✔	✔			✔		Practice and Assess	Reading Kit		✔
Monitor Progress							✔	Selection Test		Exam View	✔
							✔	Open-Book Test		Exam View	✔
Digital Resources							✔	Close Reading Tool			✔
							✔	Online Writer's Notebook			✔

One-on-one teaching　　Group work　　Whole class instruction　　Independent work　　A Assessment　　Digital Resource

LEARNER LEVELS

L1 Special-Needs Students
L2 Below-Level Students (Tier 2)
L3 On-Level Students (Tier 1)
L4 Advanced Students (Tier 1)
EL English Learners
All All Students

❶ How much do our communities shape us?

Read • Discuss • Research • Write As students read, they will explore the Big Question through text analysis of the selection. Encourage students to take notes as they read and raise additional questions, using text evidence to support their thoughts. Students should refer to their notes to help them deepen their understanding of the selection through discussion, research, and writing.

❷ Close Reading Focus

1. Remind students that to help them identify causes and effects, they can look for clue words. Students can also ask themselves questions to understand why something happened. The reasons why something happened can be the causes.

2. Tell students that they can remember the elements of a myth by thinking of a hero's journey through a dark forest. A journey has a beginning, just as myths often tell how a culture or universe *began*. The journey takes place in nature, and myths often explain *nature,* such as why the trees are so tall. Explain that a hero needs certain qualities to succeed on his journey and that he may learn from his experience. Similarly, myths often stress a value, such as the courage needed to travel safely through a dark forest. They may also express a theme, or message about life, such as the belief that we must keep going even if we can't see the path clearly.

Building Knowledge

Meet the Author

Olivia E. Coolidge **(1908–2006)** lived in both Europe and the United States. She taught English, Latin, and Greek, but was best known as a writer. In addition to writing about subjects from classical mythology, such as the Trojan War, she wrote about colonial times in American history. Coolidge was known for the accuracy of her historical fiction and for her attention to detail. She said that she enjoyed writing about legends and myths because they express ancient values that are still important in the modern world.

© Common Core State Standards

Reading Literature
2. Determine a theme or central idea of a text and how it is conveyed through particular details.
5. Analyze how a particular sentence, chapter, scene, or stanza fits into the overall structure of a text and contributes to the development of the theme, setting, or plot.

Language
4.b. Use common, grade-appropriate Greek or Latin affixes and roots as clues to the meaning of a word.

---

❶ How much do our communities shape us?

Explore the Big Question as you read "Arachne." Take notes on ways in which the myth expresses the values of ancient Greek society.

❷ CLOSE READING FOCUS

Key Ideas and Details: **Cause and Effect**

A **cause** is an event, action, or emotion that makes something happen. An **effect** is what happens. When an effect occurs, it can then become the cause of another event. In most stories, the plot unfolds as a series of linked events—causes and effects—that are organized into sentences, paragraphs, and scenes.

As you read, look for clue words such as *because, so,* and *as a result* that signal cause-and-effect relationships. Then, ask questions such as "What happened?" and "Why did this happen?" to help you follow the structure of cause-and-effect.

Craft and Structure: **Myths**

Myths are fictional tales that describe the actions of gods or heroes. Every culture has its own myths. A myth can do one or more of the following:

- Tell how the universe or a culture began
- Explain something in nature, such as thunder
- Express a theme, or insight—often one that emphasizes the importance of a value, such as honesty or bravery

The characters, plot, and imagery in a myth often provide a glimpse into the culture from which the myth came.

Vocabulary

You will encounter the following words in "Arachne." Which word is an adverb? How can you tell?

obscure	humble	mortal
indignantly	obstinacy	strive

© TEXT COMPLEXITY RUBRIC

Arachne			Reader and Task Suggestions	
Qualitative Measures			**Preparing to Read the Text**	**Leveled Tasks**
Context/Knowledge Demands	Ancient Greece; ancient Greek gods and myths 1 2 ③ 4 5		• Tell students that myths usually explain some aspect of the world or emphasize a cultural value.	*Knowledge Demands* If students will have difficulty with myths, review the Close Reading Focus. Discuss myths students have read.
Structure/Language Conventionality and Clarity	Conversational; on-level vocabulary 1 2 ③ 4 5			*Synthesizing* If students will not have difficulty with myths, discuss the Literature in Context note on TE p. 645. Ask students to list other Greek gods and goddesses that they know something about.
Levels of Meaning/Purpose/ Concept Level	Accessible concept (struggle between gods and mortals) 1 ② 3 4 5		• Guide students to use Multidraft Reading strategies (TE p. 642).	
Quantitative Measures				
Lexile	1270L	**Text Length**	Word Count: 982	

CLOSE READING MODEL

The passage below is from Olivia Coolidge's retelling of the myth "Arachne." The annotations to the right of the passage show ways in which you can use close reading skills to analyze cause and effect and interpret myths.

from "Arachne"

"Stupid old woman," said Arachne indignantly, "who gave you a right to speak in this way to me? It is easy to see that you were never good for anything in your day, or you would not come here in poverty and rags to gaze at my skill. If Athene resents my words, let her answer them herself. I have challenged her to a contest, but she, of course, will not come. It is easy for the gods to avoid matching their skill with that of men." ¹

At these words the old woman threw down her staff and stood erect. The wondering onlookers saw her grow tall and fair and stand clad in long robes of dazzling white. They were terribly afraid as they realized that they stood in the presence of Athene. Arachne herself flushed red for a moment, for she had never really believed that the goddess would hear her. ² Before the group that was gathered there she would not give in; so pressing her pale lips together in obstinacy and pride, she led the goddess to one of the great looms and set herself before the other. ³

Myths

1 Arachne says she has challenged Athene, and complains that the gods avoid competition with humans. These details help you infer that Athene is a goddess and that this tale is a myth. Arachne's boastful attitude suggests that the myth might convey an important idea about pride.

Cause and Effect

2 Blushing red is an effect, caused by Arachne's realization that she has insulted Athene. Here, the word *for* means "because" and signals a cause-and-effect relationship.

Cause and Effect

3 Arachne is too proud to give in. This feeling of pride causes her to compete against Athene.

🔔 **Daily Bellringer**

For each class during which you will teach this selection, have students complete one of the five Vocabulary activities for Week 27 in *Daily Bellringer Activities*. You may wish to use additional activities that are applicable to this selection.

Vocabulary

If students require support with selection vocabulary, use this routine:

1. Write the following words and definitions on the board:

   obscure *adj.* not well known

   humble *adj.* modest; not proud

   mortal *adj.* referring to humans, who eventually die

   indignantly *adv.* in a way that expresses anger

   obstinacy *n.* stubbornness

   strive *v.* struggle; compete

2. Have students say each word aloud.

3. Use the word in a sentence that defines the word.

🔧 DIFFERENTIATED INSTRUCTION

EL Extended Support— English Learners
Have students complete the **Reading and Vocabulary Warm-Ups** for this selection in the *Student Companion All-in-One Workbook* before they read. Assign the prereading pages and the adapted selection in the *Reader's Notebook: English Learner's Version*. Then, have students listen to portions of the selection in the *Student eText* or on the *Hear It!* CD-ROM.

L1 L2 Extended Support— Struggling Readers
Have students complete the **Reading and Vocabulary Warm-Ups** for this selection in the *Student Companion All-in-One Workbook* before they read. Assign the prereading pages and the adapted selection in the *Reader's Notebook: Adapted Version*. Then, have students listen to portions of the selection in the *Student eText* or on the *Hear It!* CD-ROM (adapted text).

Extended Support— Reluctant Readers
To build motivation and engagement before assigning the selection, have students read "Mentors Make a Difference," a thematically related selection in *Reality Central*. Then, use the questions at the conclusion of the related selection to guide discussion.

MULTIDRAFT READING

This icon ● marks natural pauses in the selection. To assist struggling readers and to deepen comprehension for all, assign the text in "chunks," separated by the icons, and apply multidraft reading protocols. For each reading, have students set the purpose indicated:

- **First reading:** Students should read the selection independently and think about its basic meaning.
- **Second reading:** Students should analyze the text's key ideas and details and its craft and structure, and respond to the side-column prompts.
- **Third reading:** Students should integrate knowledge and ideas, connect the text to other texts and to the world, and answer the end-of-selection questions.

For more guidance, refer to the *Classroom Strategies and Teaching Routines* card on multidraft reading.

❶ Activating Prior Knowledge

1. Use the **Vocab-o-Gram** strategy (*Professional Development Guidebook,* p. 39) to introduce students to terminology and to make predictions about the myth's characters, setting, and events. Post the following words:

Arachne	weave	pale
noose	proud	spider
goddess	gray old	skills
ask pardon	graceful	matching
insult	looms	

2. Then, distribute the **Vocab-o-Gram Chart** and have partners or groups place the words in appropriate categories and make predictions about the myth. Have students discuss their word placements.

3. For further guidance, see the *Classroom Strategies and Teaching Routines* card for **Using a Graphic Organizer.** Students will re-examine their ideas after reading "Arachne."

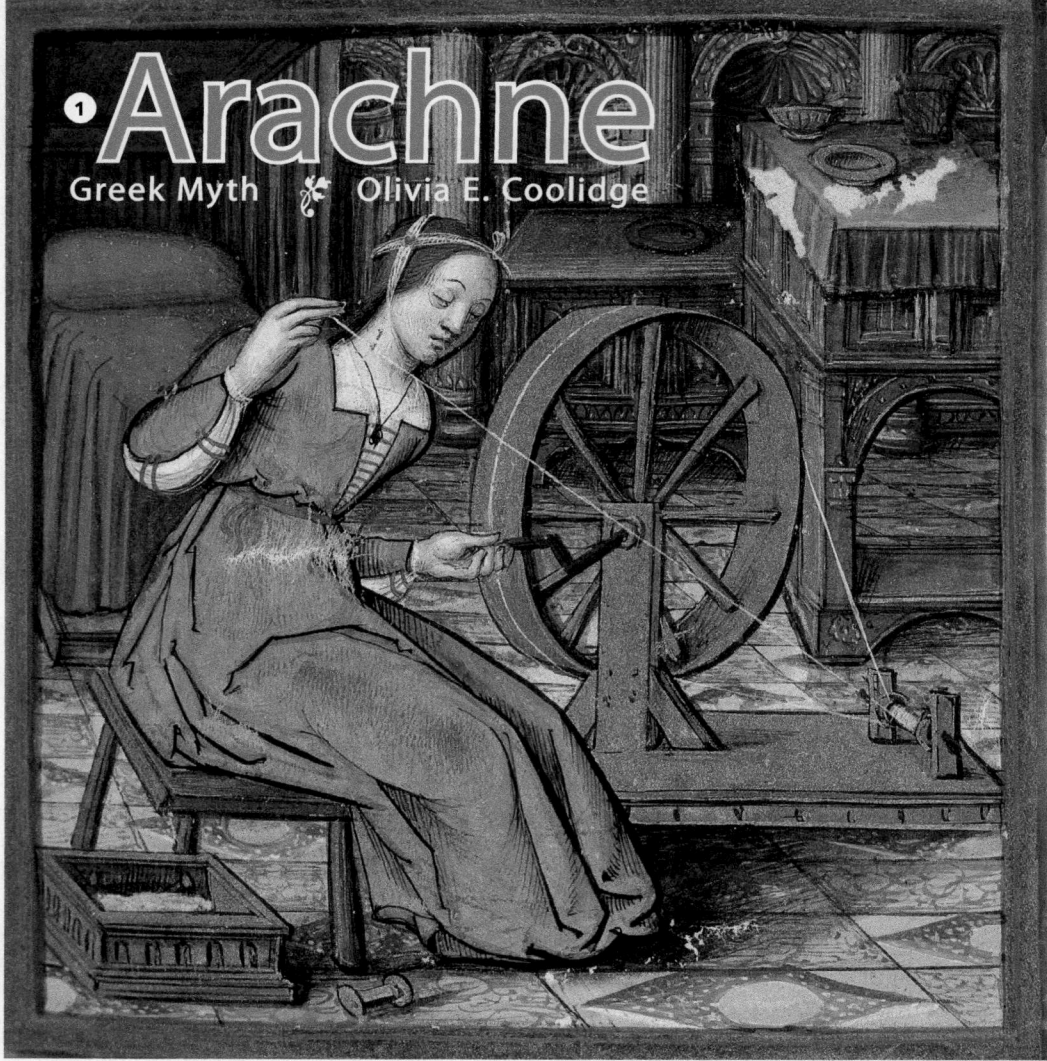

❶ Arachne
Greek Myth ❦ Olivia E. Coolidge

Vocabulary ▶
obscure (əb skyoor´) *adj.* not well known

humble (hum´bəl) *adj.* modest; not proud

Arachne [ə rak´ nē] was a maiden who became famous throughout Greece, though she was neither wellborn nor beautiful and came from no great city. She lived in an obscure little village, and her father was a humble dyer of wool.

642 UNIT 5 • How much do our communities shape us?

💬 VOCABULARY DEVELOPMENT

Thematic Vocabulary: The Big Question
As students are discussing "Arachne," encourage them to use the thematic vocabulary presented in Introducing the Big Question, pp. 612–613. You might encourage them with sentence starters like these:

1. Arachne was foolish enough to question the *influence* of . . .
2. No one could change her *belief* that . . .
3. Arachne didn't think anyone in the *community* could . . .
4. She made the *common* human mistake of having too much . . .
5. Arachne learned the hard way of important *values* such as . . .

In this he was very skillful, producing many varied shades, while above all he was famous for the clear, bright scarlet which is made from shellfish, and which was the most glorious of all the colors used in ancient Greece. Even more skillful than her father was Arachne. It was her task to spin the fleecy wool into a fine, soft thread and to weave it into cloth on the high, standing loom within the cottage. Arachne was small and pale from much working. Her eyes were light and her hair was a dusty brown, yet she was quick and graceful, and her fingers, roughened as they were, went so fast that it was hard to follow their flickering movements. So soft and even was her thread, so fine her cloth, so gorgeous her embroidery, that soon her products were known all over Greece. No one had ever seen the like of them before.

At last Arachne's fame became so great that people used to come from far and wide to watch her working. Even the graceful nymphs[1] would steal in from stream or forest and peep shyly through the dark doorway, watching in wonder the white arms of Arachne as she stood at the loom and threw the shuttle from hand to hand between the hanging threads, or drew out the long wool, fine as a hair, from the distaff[2] as she sat spinning. "Surely Athene[3] herself must have taught her," people would murmur to one another. "Who else could know the secret of such marvelous skill?"

Arachne was used to being wondered at, and she was immensely proud of the skill that had brought so many to look on her. Praise was all she lived for, and it displeased her greatly that people should think anyone, even a goddess, could teach her anything. Therefore when she heard them murmur, she would stop her work and turn round indignantly to say, "With my own ten fingers I gained this skill, and by hard practice from early morning till night. I never had time to stand looking as you people do while another maiden worked. Nor if I had, would I give Athene credit because the girl was more skillful than I. As

---

1. **nymphs** (nimfz) *n.* minor nature goddesses, represented as beautiful maidens living in rivers, trees, and mountains.
2. **distaff** (dis´ taf) *n.* stick on which flax or wool is wound for spinning.
3. **Athene** (ə thē´ ne) *n.* Greek goddess of wisdom, skills, and warfare.

Cause and Effect
What causes Arachne's work to be known all over Greece?

Spiral Review
SETTING In this paragraph, what do you learn about the world of this story?

PART 2 • Arachne **643**

GUIDED EXPLORATION

❷ Analyze

1. Have a volunteer read the first bracketed description of Arachne aloud.

2. Have students make a comparison. How is Arachne similar to a spider?

   Answer: Both are dusty brown, small, and pale. Both are quick and graceful with flickering, fast "fingers."

❸ Cause and Effect

1. Have students reread the second bracketed text independently. **Ask** them to identify the adjectives used to describe the thread, the cloth, and the embroidery.

   Answer: The adjectives are *soft* and *even*, *fine*, and *gorgeous*.

2. **Ask** the Cause and Effect question. Tell students to respond with a sentence that includes the word *because*.

   Answer: Her work is known all over Greece because her thread is soft and even, her cloth is fine, and her embroidery is gorgeous.

Spiral Review
Setting

1. Remind students that they studied the concept of setting in the Unit 1 Focus on Craft and Structure (pp. 14–17).

2. Have students reread the paragraph. Then, **ask** the Spiral Review question.

   Possible response: From this paragraph, you learn that the people in the world of this story believe in gods and goddesses who seem to have a direct effect on people's behavior.

⚙ DIFFERENTIATED INSTRUCTION

Support for Less Proficient Readers
Preview the selection with students. Help them decode the long sentences. Then, have students read the myth aloud, stopping to discuss the sentences that are confusing. Guide them to break long sentences into meaningful chunks as they read, identifying the most important nouns and verbs.

Enrichment for Gifted/Talented Students
Invite students to create an illustration of the cloth patterns described in the myth—Athene's, which include pictures of the awful fate of those who competed with the gods, and Arachne's, which show the gods' misbehavior. Have students investigate Greek mythology for further myths and legends to illustrate. Encourage students to use a variety of materials such as chalk, crayons, acrylics, colored pencils, and watercolors to create their art.

 Video

Watch the Background Video online!

 **Audio**

Selection audio is available in the *Student eText* and on the *Hear It!* CD-ROM.

④ Cause and Effect

1. Have a student read aloud the first bracketed passage, which begins on the previous page.

2. **Ask** students to tell whether the passage seems to be a cause or an effect and ask them to explain their responses.

   Possible response: The passage seems to be a cause because that kind of bragging has the effect of making people angry.

3. **Ask** the Cause and Effect question.

   Possible response: Some students might predict that Arachne will suffer a downfall as a result of her bragging. Others might specifically predict that Athene will reveal herself as a goddess and challenge her to a weaving contest.

⑤ Connecting to the Big Question

1. Recall a time when a friend warned you against certain behavior, such as eating food that often upsets your stomach. Ask students how such warnings hint at events to come.

2. Have students read the second bracketed passage on this page. **Ask:** What warning does the old woman give to Arachne? What lesson do you think Arachne will learn in this story?

   Possible response: The old woman warns Arachne not to claim equality with the gods. Arachne will probably learn the lesson of why she shouldn't claim such equality.

3. Tell students to try to connect Arachne's behavior with the Big Question: How do our communities shape us? Urge them to consider how the old woman represents the community, how she tries to shape Arachne's behavior, and whether she succeeds.

   Possible response: The old woman represents the community's values, or beliefs. She tries to shape Arachne by sharing those beliefs. She does not succeed.

Cause and Effect
What do you think will be the effect of Arachne's bragging? ④

Vocabulary ▶
mortal (môr´ təl) *adj.* referring to humans, who eventually die

indignantly (in dig´ nənt lē) *adv.* in a way that expresses anger

obstinacy (äb´ stə nə sē) *n.* stubbornness

strive (strīv) *v.* struggle; compete

for Athene's weaving, how could there be finer cloth or more beautiful embroidery than mine? If Athene herself were to come down and compete with me, she could do no better than I."

One day when Arachne turned round with such words, an old woman answered her, a gray old woman, bent and very poor, who stood leaning on a staff and peering at Arachne amid the crowd of onlookers. "Reckless girl," she said, "how dare you claim to be equal to the immortal gods themselves? I am an old woman and have seen much. Take my advice and ask pardon of Athene for your words. Rest content with your fame of being the best spinner and weaver that mortal eyes have ever beheld."

"Stupid old woman," said Arachne indignantly, "who gave you a right to speak in this way to me? It is easy to see that you were never good for anything in your day, or you would not come here in poverty and rags to gaze at my skill. If Athene resents my words, let her answer them herself. I have challenged her to a contest, but she, of course, will not come. It is easy for the gods to avoid matching their skill with that of men."

At these words the old woman threw down her staff and stood erect. The wondering onlookers saw her grow tall and fair and stand clad in long robes of dazzling white. They were terribly afraid as they realized that they stood in the presence of Athene. Arachne herself flushed red for a moment, for she had never really believed that the goddess would hear her. Before the group that was gathered there she would not give in; so pressing her pale lips together in obstinacy and pride, she led the goddess to one of the great looms and set herself before the other. Without a word both began to thread the long woolen strands that hang from the rollers, and between which the shuttle[4] moves back and forth. Many skeins lay heaped beside

---

4. **shuttle** (shut´ əl) *n.* instrument used in weaving to carry thread back and forth.

💬 VOCABULARY DEVELOPMENT

Vocab-o-Gram
Have students return to their **Vocab-o-Grams** and refine their ideas. They may work on their own or in their original groups. Have students check their predictions and modify them based on their knowledge of the story. Review the vocabulary with the group and clarify words by returning to the selection or other reference sources.

them to use, bleached white, and gold, and scarlet, and other shades, varied as the rainbow. Arachne had never thought of giving credit for her success to her father's skill in dyeing, though in actual truth the colors were as remarkable as the cloth itself.

Soon there was no sound in the room but the breathing of the onlookers, the whirring of the shuttles, and the creaking of the wooden frames as each pressed the thread up into place or tightened the pegs by which the whole was held straight. The excited crowd in the doorway began to see that the skill of both in truth was very nearly equal, but that, however the cloth might turn out, the goddess was the quicker of the two. A pattern of many pictures was growing on her loom. There was a border of twined branches of the olive, Athene's favorite tree, while in the middle, figures began to appear. As they looked at the glowing colors, the spectators realized that Athene was weaving into her pattern a last warning to Arachne. The central figure was the goddess herself competing with Poseidon for possession of the city of Athens; but in the four corners were mortals who had tried to strive with gods and pictures of the awful fate that had overtaken them. The goddess ended a little before Arachne and stood back from her marvelous work to see what the maiden was doing.

Never before had Arachne been matched against anyone whose skill was equal, or even nearly equal to her own. As she stole glances from time to time at Athene and saw the goddess working swiftly, calmly, and always a little faster than herself, she became angry instead of frightened, and an evil thought came into her head. Thus as Athene stepped back a pace to watch Arachne finishing her work, she saw that the maiden had taken for her design a pattern of scenes which showed evil or unworthy actions of the gods, how they had deceived fair maidens, resorted to trickery, and appeared on earth from time to time in the form of poor and humble people. When the goddess saw this insult glowing in bright colors on Arachne's loom, she did not wait while the cloth was

Culture Connection

Athene

As goddess of wisdom and warfare, Athene was a key figure in Greek mythology. Athene protected her favorites, such as Odysseus and Heracles (or Hercules), and punished those who displeased her, including Arachne and Ajax, a famous Greek warrior. According to one story, the people of a major Greek city wanted to name their city after either Poseidon, the sea god, or Athene, depending on who gave them the more useful gift. Poseidon created horses, and Athene created olive trees. The gods judged Athene's gift more useful, so Athens was named for her. To honor Athene, the city built a great temple, called the Parthenon.

Connect to the Literature

Which of Athene's character traits does this myth illustrate?

7 **Comprehension**
Why is Arachne upset when people say Athene must have taught her to spin?

---

6 Literature in Context

Cultural Connection Athene, the daughter of Zeus, had many roles and titles. Like her father, she controlled the sky and could send storms, lightning, and thunder bolts to scare off enemies. She was an inventor, credited with inventing the plough, the rake, the flute, the trumpet, the spindle and the olive tree. Athene was also a teacher who taught mortals to tame horses and instructed gods to build ships.

Connect to the Literature

1. **Ask** students to reread the information about Athene, trying to identify character traits that are either stated or inferred. Ask students to name the traits they identify.

   Possible response: Athene is wise, harsh, quick to impose punishments, quarrelsome, and protective.

2. **Ask** the Connect to the Literature question.

   Possible response: The myth illustrates that she is harsh and quick to punish.

7 Comprehension

Possible response: She has practiced very hard to achieve her skill, without help from anyone.

⓼ Myths

1. Have a student read aloud the first bracketed passage, which begins on the previous page.
2. **Ask** the first Myths question.
   Answer: It insults the gods by showing their evil and unworthy actions.

⓽ Myths

1. Read aloud the second bracketed passage on this page.
2. Then, read aloud the description of Arachne at the top of p. 643. **Ask** the second Myths question.
   Answer: It explains why spiders are little dusty brown creatures with quick "fingers" and excellent weaving skills.

☑ ASSESS

Language Study
Vocabulary
Sample answers:

1. No one in the class had heard of the <u>obscure</u> novel.
2. Her <u>obstinacy</u> makes her difficult to get along with.
3. Mr. Vallone was a poor and <u>humble</u> tailor.
4. "No, thank you," she said <u>indignantly</u>.
5. The two brothers never <u>strive</u> to help each other.

Word Study
Part A
Sample answers:

The Latin root -*mort*- means "death." Sample answers: Something that is *immortal* cannot <u>die</u>. A *mortician* prepares bodies after <u>death</u>.

Part B
Sample answers:

1. No; the root -*mort*- means "death." A *mortal* wound causes death.
2. The root -*mort*- means "death." A person who is *mortified* is so embarrassed that he or she wishes to die.

Myths
Why is Arachne's design disrespectful to the gods?

Myths
What traits of spiders does this myth explain?

⓼ judged, but stepped forward, her gray eyes blazing with anger, and tore Arachne's work across. Then she struck Arachne across the face. Arachne stood there a moment, struggling with anger, fear, and pride. "I will not live under this insult," she cried, and seizing a rope from the wall, she made a noose and would have hanged herself.

The goddess touched the rope and touched the maiden. "Live on, wicked girl," she said. "Live on and spin, both you and your descendants. When men look at you they may remember that it is not wise to strive with Athene." At that ⓽ the body of Arachne shriveled up, and her legs grew tiny, spindly, and distorted. There before the eyes of the spectators hung a little dusty brown spider on a slender thread.

All spiders descend from Arachne, and as the Greeks watched them spinning their thread wonderfully fine, they remembered the contest with Athene and thought that it was not right for even the best of men to claim equality with the gods.

Language Study

Vocabulary The words in blue appear in "Arachne." Rewrite each sentence below, using a vocabulary word so that the new sentence has the opposite meaning of the original.

obscure	humble	indignantly	obstinacy	strive

1. Everyone in the class had heard of the famous novel.
2. Her agreeable nature makes her easy to get along with.
3. Mr. Vallone was a rich and famous tailor.
4. "No, thank you," she said in a cheerful way.
5. The two brothers always try to help each other.

WORD STUDY

The **Latin root -*mort*-** means "death." Unlike a god or goddess, who cannot die, Arachne is a mortal—a human being, who will not live forever.

Word Study

Part A Explain how the **Latin root -*mort*-** contributes to the meanings of *immortal* and *mortician*. Consult a dictionary if necessary.

Part B Use context and what you know about the Latin root -*mort*- to explain your answer to each question.

1. If an ancient Greek warrior received a *mortal* wound, would he recover?
2. How strongly embarrassed is someone who is *mortified*?

Literary Analysis

Possible responses appear below. Check to be sure students support their responses with evidence from the text.

1. Her skill draws much praise and admiration from all over Greece.
2. Arachne has claimed to be more skillful than Athene at weaving.
3. **(row 1)** Athene reveals her identity and accepts Arachne's challenge. **(row 2)** Arachne sees that Athene has worked faster and has created a warning design. **(row 3)** Arachne is changed into a spider.
4. **(a)** She values praise. **(b)** She is conceited about her weaving talent. **(c)** She shows conceit and disrespect when she dares Athene to compete with her at the loom.
5. **(a)** the goddess herself, competing with Poseiden for possession of the city **(b)** She wanted to give Arachne a warning. **(c)** Arachne insulted the gods.
6. It explains why spiders are little dusty brown creatures with quick "fingers" and excellent weaving skills.
7. The values of humility, modesty, and respect for the gods are taught through the theme of this myth.

Close Reading Activities

Literary Analysis

Key Ideas and Details

1. **Cause and Effect** What is the effect of Arachne's skill as a weaver?

2. **Cause and Effect** What causes Athene to visit Arachne?

3. **Cause and Effect** Complete the chart on the right to show other causes and effects in "Arachne."

4. **(a)** What does Arachne value more than anything else?
(b) Interpret: Why does Arachne refuse to accept the advice of the old woman? **(c) Analyze:** What character traits does Arachne reveal through her behavior?

5. **(a)** What design does Athene weave? **(b) Make Inferences:** What is Athene's original intention toward Arachne?
(c) Deduce: What makes Athene angry?

Causes	Effects
Arachne challenges Athene.	
	Arachne's design shows unworthy actions of the gods.
Athene touches the rope and touches Arachne.	

Craft and Structure

6. **Myths** What does this myth explain about spiders?

7. **Myths** What beliefs and values about behavior are taught through the theme of this myth?

Integration of Knowledge and Ideas

8. **(a) Make a Judgment:** Do you think it was fair of Athene to turn Arachne into a spider? **(b) Defend:** Share and defend your judgment with a partner. Then decide together on a single answer to share with the class.

9. **Compare and Contrast:** Think of another myth you have read. Then, explain the ways in which "Arachne" is similar to and different from that myth.

10. 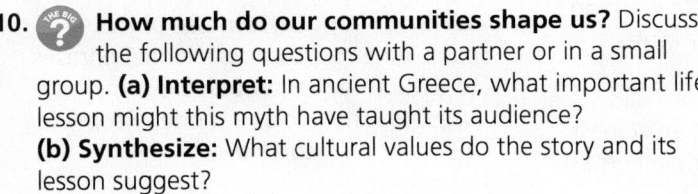 **How much do our communities shape us?** Discuss the following questions with a partner or in a small group. **(a) Interpret:** In ancient Greece, what important life lesson might this myth have taught its audience?
(b) Synthesize: What cultural values do the story and its lesson suggest?

ACADEMIC VOCABULARY

As you write and speak about "Arachne," use the words related to values that you explored on page 613 of this text.

---

8. **(a)** Some students may say that it was fair because Arachne was too conceited. Others may say the punishment was too harsh.
(b) Have partners share their decisions and reasons. Partners may agree that Arachne's behavior was so contemptuous that the punishment was deserved.

9. Students may choose another Greek myth or a myth from another culture. The myth of the golden apple is similar to "Arachne" because a goddess becomes angry. It is different from "Arachne" because the problem involves many gods and goddesses, instead of one person.

10. 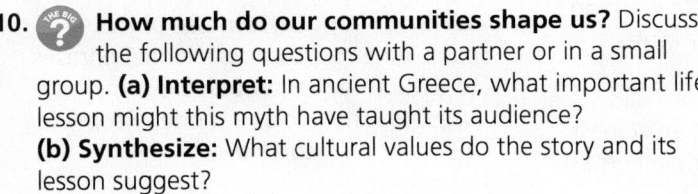 **How much do our communities shape us?**
(a) It might have taught that too much pride can lead to one's downfall. **(b)** The story and its lesson suggest that humility is a cultural value.

 Online Writer's Notebook

Students can use the Online Writer's Notebook to record all responses.

Conventions

1. Introduce the skill, using the instruction on the student page.
2. Discuss the definitions and the examples in the chart.

Think Aloud: Model the Skill

Say to students:

I remember that a direct object receives the action of the verb and answers the question *Who?* or *What?* In the sentence, "Jose told a joke," *joke* is the direct object. In the sentence, "Jose told Maria a joke." *Maria* is the indirect object. She is the person Jose told the joke *to*. The indirect object answers the question "To or for whom or what?"

Practice A

1. direct object: *art*; indirect object: *her*. **Sample answer:** Arachne's father taught her the *rules* of a game.
2. direct object: *warning*; indirect object: *Arachne*. **Sample answer:** The goddess gave Arachne a *punishment*.
3. direct object: *anger*; prepositional phrase: *to the crowd*. **Sample answer:** Arachne showed her *weaving* to the crowd.

Reading Application

Sample answer: At these words the old woman threw down her staff and stood erect. The goddess touched the rope and touched the maiden. Then she struck Arachne across the face.

Practice B Sample answers:

1. direct object and indirect object: *The girl gave me a gift.* direct object and prepositional phrase: *The girl gave a gift to her teacher.*
2. direct object and indirect object: *The boy bought me lunch.* direct object and prepositional phrase: *The boy bought lunch for me.*
3. direct object and indirect object: *We made ourselves a promise.* direct object and prepositional phrase: *We made a promise to ourselves.*

Writing Application

Check students' sentences for correct use of object complements and prepositional phrases.

 Close Reading Activities Continued

Conventions: Object Complements

There are two kinds of **object complements**: direct objects and indirect objects. A **direct object** is a noun or pronoun that receives the action of the verb and answers the question *Who* or *What?* An **indirect object** names the person or thing to whom or for whom an action is done, and answers the question *To or for whom?* or *To or for what?*

Sentence	Question	Answer	Direct/Indirect Object
Elsa baked bread.	Baked *what?*	*bread*	*bread* (direct object)
Mimi brought us a surprise.	Brought *what?* Brought *to whom?*	*surprise* *us*	*surprise* (direct object) *us* (indirect object)

An indirect object appears between the verb and the direct object.

If a noun or pronoun is followed by a preposition such as *to* or *for*, the noun or pronoun after the preposition becomes the object of the preposition. It is not an indirect object because it always follows the preposition.

Example: I threw the ball <u>to *Jack*</u>.

Practice A

Find the direct object and either the indirect object or the prepositional phrase in the following sentences. Then, rewrite each sentence with a different direct object.

1. Arachne's father taught her the art of weaving.
2. The goddess gave Arachne a warning.
3. Arachne showed her anger to the crowd.

Reading Application Identify at least three examples of object complements in "Arachne."

Practice B

Use the following verbs to write sentences that contain direct objects, indirect objects, and prepositional phrases. Label each direct object, indirect object, and prepositional phrase.

1. give   2. bought   3. made

Writing Application Use object complements and propositional phrases to write three sentences about myths. Use this sentence as a model: *People tell myths to their children.*

⏩ EXTEND THE LESSON

Sentence Modeling

Model the skill using this sentence from "Arachne":

Nor if I had, would I give Athene credit because the girl was more skillful than I.

Ask students what they notice about the sentence. (A direct object receives the action of the verb and answers *What?*) Point out the indirect object that names the person for whom the action is done. Then, ask students what else they notice. (The sentence is complex.)

Have students imitate the sentence in a sentence on a topic of their own choosing, matching each grammatical and stylistic feature discussed. Collect the sentences, and share them with the class.

Writing to Sources

Explanatory Text Write a brief **compare-and-contrast essay** in which you analyze ways in which the characters of Arachne and Athene are alike and different.

- Reread the myth to find details that describe the personality, appearance, motivations, and actions of each character. Record your notes in a two-column chart or Venn diagram.

- Choose an organizational structure—such as the block or point-by-point method (see p. 243)—that will help you present your ideas clearly.

- Use language that expresses your meaning precisely and is appropriately formal for academic work.

- Support your ideas with details from the myth.

Grammar Application Use object complements in your essay to add information to your sentences.

Research and Technology

Build and Present Knowledge Imagine that you are writing an essay that explains how "Arachne" reflects the cultural values of ancient Greece. Find two reliable research sources that provide information on that topic. Then write an **annotated bibliography entry** for each source.

- Use a library catalog or do a keyword search on the Internet to find reliable sources of information.

- Sources should be well-known for accuracy and recently published. Consult Web sites that have *.edu, .gov,* or *.org* at the ends of their addresses.

- Write down publication information from two sources.

- Read each source. Paraphrase, or restate, key ideas in your own words in order to avoid plagiarism.

- Write an annotated bibliography entry for each source. Include the publication information, your paraphrases, and an explanation of why the source is reliable and valuable.

 **Common Core State Standards**

Writing
2. Write informative/explanatory texts to examine a topic and convey ideas, concepts, and information through the selection, organization, and analysis of relevant content. **2.a.** Introduce a topic; organize ideas, concepts, and information, using strategies such as definition, classification, comparison/contrast, and cause/effect. **2.d.** Use precise language and domain-specific vocabulary to inform about or explain the topic. **2.e.** Establish and maintain a formal style.
8. Gather relevant information from multiple print and digital sources, assess the credibility of each source, and quote or paraphrase the data and conclusions of others while avoiding plagiarism and providing basic bibliographic information for sources.

Language
3. Use knowledge of language and its conventions when writing, speaking, reading, or listening.

Writing to Sources

1. Review the assignment, using the instruction on the student page.

2. Help students find details that are specific to both of the characters.

3. To give students guidance in writing their explanatory texts, give them the **Support for Writing,** page for this selection in the *Student Companion All-in-One Workbook.*

4. To evaluate students' essays, use one of the rubrics for a **Compare-and-Contrast** essay in *Professional Development Guidebook,* pp. 234–235.

Grammar Application

Have students check their drafts to make sure that they have used direct and indirect objects.

Six Traits Focus

✓	Ideas		Word Choice
✓	Organization		Sentence Fluency
	Voice		Conventions

Research and Technology

1. Review the assignment, using the instruction on the student page.

2. To support students' work on the assignment, have them complete the **Support for Extend Your Learning** page for this selection in the *Student Companion All-in-One Workbook.*

The Stone
·Lloyd Alexander·

LESSON PACING GUIDE

The Stone

| **DAY 1** | **Preteach/Teach** |

- Administer the Reading and Vocabulary Warm-ups, as necessary.
- Introduce the Key Ideas and Details skill: Setting a Purpose.
- Introduce the Craft and Structure skill: Universal Theme.
- Use the Close Reading Model to demonstrate the application of the skills.
- Review the selection vocabulary, as necessary, with students who need additional support.
- Prepare students to read the selection by reviewing with them the Multidraft Reading Strategies.

| **DAY 2** | **Teach** |

- Informally monitor comprehension while students read.
- Use the Comprehension questions to confirm understanding.
- Develop students' ability to set a purpose for reading and analyze universal themes using the sidenote questions.
- Reinforce vocabulary with the Vocabulary notes.
- Reinforce unit focus standards using the Spiral Review prompts.

| **DAY 3** | **Assess** |

- Assess students' comprehension and mastery of the skills by having them answer the Literary Analysis questions.
- Have students complete the Vocabulary activities.
- Develop students' understanding of roots and affixes by having them complete the Word Study activities.

| **DAY 4** | **Extend/Assess** |

- Build students' ability to master grammar concepts and conventions by having them complete the Conventions lesson.
- Have students complete the Writing to Sources activity and write a plot proposal. (You may assign as homework.)
- Extend learning by having students complete the Research and Technology activity: a written and visual report.
- Administer the Selection Test or Open-Book Test.

 **Common Core State Standards**

Reading Literature 2. Determine a theme or central idea of a text and how it is conveyed through particular details; provide a summary of the text distinct from personal opinions or judgments.

Writing 4. Produce clear and coherent writing in which the development, organization, and style are appropriate to task, purpose, and audience.

6. Use technology, including the Internet, to produce and publish writing.

8. Gather relevant information from multiple print and digital sources.

Speaking and Listening 1. Engage effectively in a range of collaborative discussions with diverse partners on grade 6 topics, texts, and issues, building on others' ideas and expressing their own clearly.

Language 1. Demonstrate command of the conventions of standard English grammar and usage when writing or speaking.

2.a. Use punctuation (commas, parentheses, dashes) to set off nonrestrictive/parenthetical elements.

6. Acquire and use accurately grade-appropriate general academic and domain-specific words and phrases; gather vocabulary knowledge when considering a word or phrase important to comprehension or expression.

Daily Block Scheduling

Each day in this Lesson Pacing Guide represents a 40–50 minute period. Teachers using block scheduling may combine days to revise pacing. In addition, teachers may differentiate and support core instruction by integrating components for extended and intensive support as students require. See the Guide to Resources (facing page).

GUIDE TO RESOURCES

	L1	L2	L3	L4	EL	ALL	RESOURCES	PRINT	CD	ONLINE
Warm Up	✓	✓			✓		Vocabulary Warm-ups			✓
	✓	✓			✓		Reading Warm-ups			✓
						✓	Background Video			✓
						✓	Selection Audio		Hear It!	✓
Comprehension/ Selection Support						✓	Writing About the Big Question	Student Companion Workbook		✓
						✓	Literary Analysis	Student Companion Workbook		✓
						✓	Reading	Student Companion Workbook		✓
						✓	Vocabulary Builder	Student Companion Workbook		✓
				✓			Enrichment			✓
		✓	✓	✓			Conventions	Student Companion Workbook		✓
		✓	✓	✓			Writing to Sources	Student Companion Workbook		✓
		✓	✓	✓			Research and Technology	Student Companion Workbook		
Differentiated Instruction/ Additional Support						✓	Additional Standards Practice	Common Core Companion		✓
	✓	✓					Adapted Reader's Notebook			✓
					✓		English Reader's Notebook:			✓
					✓		Spanish Reader's Notebook			✓
					✓		Graphic Organizer A			✓
	✓	✓			✓		Graphic Organizer B			✓
	✓	✓			✓		"Age and Beauty"	Reality Central Student Edition and Writing Journal		✓
	✓	✓			✓		Practice and Assess	Reading Kit		✓
Monitor Progress						✓	Selection Test		Exam View	✓
						✓	Open-Book Test		Exam View	✓
Digital Resources						✓	Close Reading Tool			✓
						✓	Online Writer's Notebook			✓

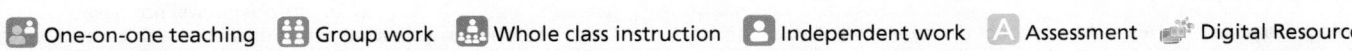

One-on-one teaching Group work Whole class instruction Independent work Assessment Digital Resource

LEARNER LEVELS

L1 Special-Needs Students
L2 Below-Level Students (Tier 2)
L3 On-Level Students (Tier 1)
L4 Advanced Students (Tier 1)
EL English Learners
All All Students

❶ **How much do our communities shape us?**

Read • Discuss • Research • Write As students read, they will explore the Big Question through text analysis of the selection. Encourage students to take notes as they read and raise additional questions, using text evidence to support their thoughts. Students should refer to their notes to help them deepen their understanding of the selection through discussion, research, and writing.

❷ Close Reading Focus

1. Explain to students that they should set a purpose for their reading. Their reading rate can be influenced by their reading purpose. If part of a selection is complicated, students can slow down and read more carefully to make sure they understand the concepts and theme.

2. Provide an example of a familiar experience to help students understand universal theme. Tell students to think about a girl who has asthma. Explain that she goes to school even when she doesn't feel her best and has to remember to take medicine. But she knows that she must make the right choices to care for herself. Explain that these details point to a theme—facing challenges leads to maturity and independence—and that details in literature also point to theme.

Building Knowledge

❶ **How much do our communities shape us?**

Explore the Big Question as you read "The Stone." Take notes on ways in which the story explores how one individual's actions can impact his family and community.

❷ CLOSE READING FOCUS

Key Ideas and Details: **Setting a Purpose**

Setting a purpose, or reason, for reading gives you a focus as you read. Once you have set your purpose, adjust your reading rate to help you accomplish that purpose.

- When you are reading to learn facts, read slowly and carefully. Pause periodically to think about what you have read. Your reading rate should also be slow when you read descriptive passages that are heavy with details.
- When you are reading for enjoyment, you can read faster. For example, you might read dialogue quickly to imitate the flow of conversation.

Craft and Structure: **Universal Theme**

The theme of a literary work is its central idea or message about life and human nature. A **universal theme** is a message that is expressed regularly in many cultures and time periods. Examples of universal themes include the importance of courage, the power of love, and the danger of greed. You can find a story's universal theme by examining its conflict and the actions of the main character. Notice the changes he or she undergoes and the effects of those changes.

Vocabulary

You will encounter the following words in this story. Write synonyms for the words you know.

feeble	vanished	plight
jubilation	rue	sown

Meet the Author

Lloyd Alexander (1924–2007) shocked his parents by telling them he wanted to become a writer. "My family pleaded with me to forget literature and do something sensible, such as find some sort of useful work," he recalled. He eventually became a successful author, after working in a bank, serving in World War II, and writing for a magazine. He wrote more than forty books for children and young adults.

© Common Core State Standards

Reading Literature
2. Determine a theme or central idea of a text and how it is conveyed through particular details; provide a summary of the text distinct from personal opinions or judgments.

Language
6. Acquire and use accurately grade-appropriate general academic and domain-specific words and phrases; gather vocabulary knowledge when considering a word or phrase important to comprehension or expression.

© TEXT COMPLEXITY **RUBRIC**

The Stone		Reader and Task Suggestions	
Qualitative Measures		**Preparing to Read the Text**	**Leveled Tasks**
Context/Knowledge Demands	Folk tale; farm setting; dwarf with magical power 1 2 3 ④ 5	• Discuss the fact that many tales about wishes involve poor peasants.	*Knowledge Demands* If students will have difficulty with knowledge demands, review elements of farm life and the consequences if the normal order of farm life is thrown out of whack.
Structure/Language Conventionality and Clarity	Dialogue; challenging vocabulary 1 2 ③ 4 5	• Guide students to use Multidraft Reading strategies (TE p. 652)	*Evaluating* If students will not have difficulty with knowledge demands, discuss the results of the farmer's selfishness on his family. What point is the author making with this story?
Levels of Meaning/Purpose/Concept Level	Accessible concept (be careful what you wish for) 1 2 ③ 4 5		
Quantitative Measures			
Lexile	740L	**Text Length**	Word Count: 2,852

CLOSE READING MODEL

The passage below is from Lloyd Alexander's folk tale "The Stone." The annotations to the right of the passage show ways in which you can use close reading skills to set a purpose for reading and to analyze universal themes.

from "The Stone"

There was a cottager named Maibon, and one day he was driving down the road in his horse and cart when he saw an old man hobbling along, so frail and feeble he doubted the poor soul could go many more steps. Though Maibon offered to take him in the cart, the old man refused; and Maibon went his way home, shaking his head over such a pitiful sight, [1] and said to his wife, Modrona:

"Ah, ah, what a sorry thing it is to have your bones creaking and cracking, and dim eyes, and dull wits. [2] When I think this might come to me, too! A fine, strong-armed, sturdy-legged fellow like me? One day to go tottering, and have his teeth rattling in his head, and live on porridge, like a baby? There's no fate worse in all the world."

"There is," answered Modrona, "and that would be to have neither teeth nor porridge. [3] "Get on with you, Maibon, and stop borrowing trouble. Hoe your field or you'll have no crop to harvest, and no food for you, nor me, nor the little ones." [4]

Setting a Purpose

1 At this point, your purpose for reading might be to find out if Maibon will see the old man again.

Universal Themes

2 Maibon thinks the old man's signs of age are "a sorry thing," and he dreads growing old himself. The fear of getting older and closer to death appears in many stories. You may recognize it as a universal theme.

Setting a Purpose

3 When you come to the conversation between Maibon and Modrona, you may decide to read more quickly, so that their dialogue sounds like a real-life conversation.

Universal Themes

4 Madrona tells Maibon that it is better to have little than to have nothing. You may recognize this idea as a universal theme.

Daily Bellringer

For each class during which you will teach this selection, have students complete one of the five Revision activities for Week 28 in *Daily Bellringer Activities*. You may wish to use additional activities that are applicable to this selection.

Vocabulary

If students require support with selection vocabulary, use this routine:

1. Write the following words and definitions on the board:

    feeble *adj.* weak

    vanished *v.* disappeared

    plight *n.* awkward, sad, or dangerous situation

    jubilation *n.* great joy; triumph

    rue *v.* feel sorrow or regret for something

    sown *v.* planted; scattered with seeds

2. Have students say each word aloud.

3. Use the word in a sentence that defines the word.

✦ DIFFERENTIATED INSTRUCTION

EL Extended Support— English Learners
Have students complete the **Reading and Vocabulary Warm-Ups** for this selection in the *Student Companion All-in-One Workbook* before they read. Assign the prereading pages and the adapted selection in the *Reader's Notebook: English Learner's Version*. Then, have students listen to portions of the selection in the *Student eText* or on the *Hear It!* CD-ROM.

L1 L2 Extended Support— Struggling Readers
Have students complete the **Reading and Vocabulary Warm-Ups** for this selection in the *Student Companion All-in-One Workbook* before they read. Assign the prereading pages and the adapted selection in the *Reader's Notebook: Adapted Version*. Then, have students listen to portions of the selection in the *Student eText* or on the *Hear It!* CD-ROM (adapted text).

Extended Support— Reluctant Readers
To build motivation and engagement before assigning the selection, have students read "Age and Beauty," a thematically related selection in *Reality Central*. Then, use the questions at the conclusion of the related selection to guide discussion.

MULTIDRAFT READING

This icon ● marks natural pauses in the selection. To assist struggling readers and to deepen comprehension for all, assign the text in "chunks," separated by the icons, and apply multidraft reading protocols. For each reading, have students set the purpose indicated:

- **First reading:** Students should read the selection independently and think about its basic meaning.
- **Second reading:** Students should analyze the text's key ideas and details and its craft and structure, and respond to the side-column prompts.
- **Third reading:** Students should integrate knowledge and ideas, connect the text to other texts and to the world, and answer the end-of-selection questions.

For more guidance, refer to the *Classroom Strategies and Teaching Routines* card on multidraft reading.

❶ Activating Prior Knowledge

1. Ask students what they think the perfect age is. Suppose that by some magical means they had an opportunity to remain that age all their lives. Would they choose to do so?

2. Encourage students to examine the pros and cons of this hypothetical situation. **Ask:** What would be gained? What would be lost? Have students list their answers in a two-column chart labeled *Pros* and *Cons*. After completing their reading, students should re-examine the chart they created in which they listed the pros and cons of what they thought was the perfect age. Have them discuss if the events of the story influenced their thinking.

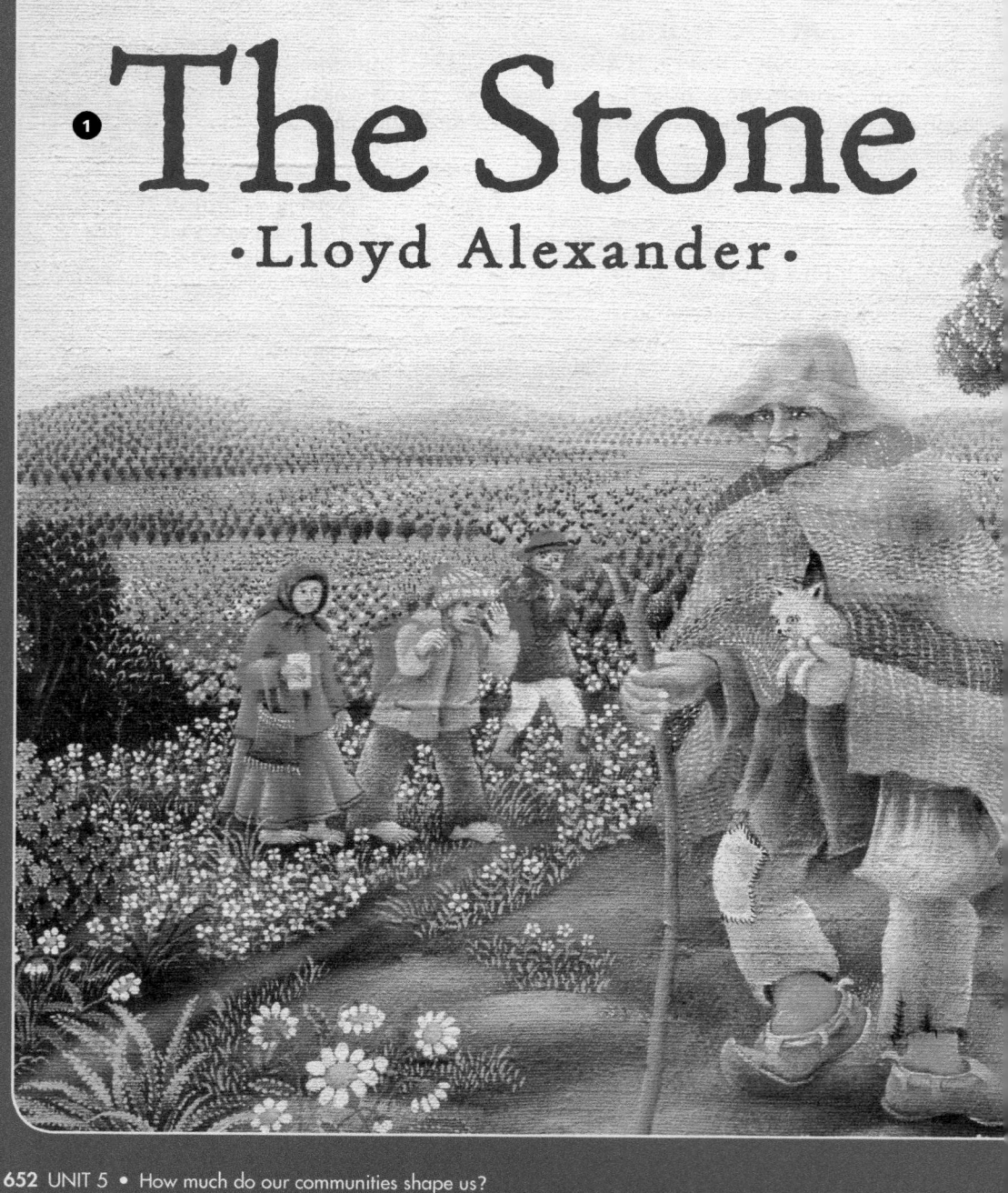

❶ # The Stone
•Lloyd Alexander•

652 UNIT 5 • How much do our communities shape us?

💬 VOCABULARY DEVELOPMENT

Thematic Vocabulary: The Big Question
As students are discussing "The Stone," encourage them to use the thematic vocabulary presented in Introducing the Big Question, pp. 612–613. You might encourage them with sentence starters like these:

1. As soon as Maibon gets *involved* with the dwarf . . .
2. Maibon's *belief* in his own importance . . .
3. He uses his *influence* over the dwarf only to . . .
4. Because of Maibon's *choices*, his *family* . . .
5. Surprisingly, the stone *isolates* Maibon from his *community* because . . .

2 Critical Viewing

Possible response: The picture gives the impression that old age is an unhappy time because the old man is frowning, has patched clothes, and needs a tree branch to serve as a cane. Even his pet has a very serious expression.

3 Comprehension

Answer: Maibon is upset at the prospect of growing older because he sees only the negative aspects of old age, such as creaking bones, poor eyesight, and a decrease in alertness.

There was a cottager named Maibon, and one day he was driving down the road in his horse and cart when he saw an old man hobbling along, so frail and feeble he doubted the poor soul could go many more steps. Though Maibon offered to take him in the cart, the old man refused; and Maibon went his way home, shaking his head over such a pitiful sight, and said to his wife, Modrona:

"Ah, ah, what a sorry thing it is to have your bones creaking and cracking, and dim eyes, and dull wits. When I think this might come to me, too! A fine, strong-armed, sturdy-legged fellow like me? One day to go tottering, and have his teeth rattling in his head, and live on porridge, like a baby? There's no fate worse in all the world."

"There is," answered Modrona, "and that would be to have neither teeth nor porridge. Get on with you, Maibon, and stop borrowing trouble. Hoe your field or you'll have no crop to harvest, and no food for you, nor me, nor the little ones."

◀ **Vocabulary**
feeble (fē′ bəl)
adj. weak

3 Comprehension
Why is Maibon upset?

2 ◀ Critical Viewing
What impression of old age is conveyed by this picture?

DIFFERENTIATED INSTRUCTION

Strategy for Less Proficient Readers
Use the art on pp. 652–653 and 654 to help students understand the setting of the story. Have students preview the art, and then ask them to infer answers to questions such as the following: Where does Maibon live? What does he do for a living? Discuss clues that the art provides, and remind students that an inference is a logical guess based on clues and personal knowledge or experience. Have students check their answers as the story progresses.

EL Support for English Learners
Maibon uses two hyphenated words, "strong-armed" and "sturdy-legged" (both on p. 653) to describe himself. Explain to students that hyphens connect two words that are used together as one adjective. Encourage students to list other hyphenated adjectives as they continue reading. (Examples include "close-fitting," "ham-handed," and "heavy-footed," all on p. 655.)

 Video

Watch the Background Video online!

 **Audio**

Selection audio is available in the *Student eText* and on the *Hear It!* CD-ROM.

❹ Setting a Purpose

1. Read aloud the bracketed passage. **Ask:** What are Maibon's complaints?

Possible response: His tools are worn. They do not work as well as they did when they were new. He also finds fault with the sun that doesn't warm him and the moon that looks wilted. He feels that he is in bad shape and will grow worse as he ages.

2. **Ask** students the Setting a Purpose question.

Possible response: Students may say that they would read the descriptive passage slowly because it contains details that are important to understanding the story.

Setting a Purpose
At what rate would you read this descriptive passage? Why?

Sighing and grumbling, Maibon did as his wife bade him. Although the day was fair and cloudless, he took no pleasure in it. His ax-blade was notched, the wooden handle splintery; his saw had lost its edge; and his hoe, once shining new, had begun to rust. None of his tools, it seemed to him, cut or chopped or delved[1] as well as they once had done.

"They're as worn out as that old codger I saw on the road," Maibon said to himself. He squinted up at the sky. "Even the sun isn't as bright as it used to be, and doesn't warm me half as well. It's gone threadbare as my cloak. And no wonder, for it's been there longer than I can remember. Come to think of it, the moon's been looking a little wilted around the edges, too.

"As for me," went on Maibon, in dismay, "I'm in even a worse state. My appetite's faded, especially after meals. Mornings, when I wake, I can hardly keep myself from yawning. And at night, when I go to bed, my eyes are so heavy I can't hold them open. If that's the way things are now, the older I grow, the worse it will be!"

In the midst of his complaining, Maibon glimpsed something bouncing and tossing back and forth beside a fallen tree in a corner of the field. Wondering if one of his piglets had squeezed out of the sty and gone rooting for

---

1. **delved** (delvd) *v.* dug.

💬 VOCABULARY DEVELOPMENT

Word Analysis

Explain to students that a suffix is a syllable or group of syllables added to a word or word base to form a new word. Some suffixes change function.

Call attention to the word *cloudless* in the bracketed passage on this page. The suffix *-less* means "without" or "lacking." A *cloudless* sky has no clouds. Ask students to watch for these words and define them by analyzing their structure: *speechless* (p. 655), *toothless* (p. 660), *calfless* (p. 660), and *fruitless* (p. 660).

The suffix *-ly* often turns adjectives into adverbs that tell *when, how,* or *in what way* an action happens. The adjective *rapid* is turned into an adverb when *ly* is added: *rapidly* (p. 655), which means "in a fast way." Give students these words to watch for and to analyze: *reluctantly* (p. 658), *regretfully* (p. 659), *unwillingly* (p. 659), and *desperately* (p. 660).

acorns, Maibon hurried across the turf. Then he dropped his ax and gaped in astonishment.

There, struggling to free his leg which had been caught under the log, lay a short, thickset figure: a dwarf with red hair bristling in all directions beneath his round, close-fitting leather cap. At the sight of Maibon, the dwarf **⑤** squeezed shut his bright red eyes and began holding his breath. After a moment, the dwarf's face went redder than his hair; his cheeks puffed out and soon turned purple. Then he opened one eye and blinked rapidly at Maibon, who was staring at him, speechless.

"What," snapped the dwarf, "you can still see me?"

"That I can," replied Maibon, more than ever puzzled, "and I can see very well you've got yourself tight as a wedge under that log, and all your kicking only makes it worse."

At this, the dwarf blew out his breath and shook his fists. "I can't do it!" he shouted. "No matter how I try! I can't make myself invisible! Everyone in my family can disappear—Poof! Gone! Vanished! But not me! Not Doli! Believe me, if I could have done, you never would have found me in such a plight. Worse luck! Well, come on. Don't stand there goggling like an idiot. Help me get loose!"

At this sharp command, Maibon began tugging and heaving at the log. Then he stopped, wrinkled his brow, and scratched his head, saying:

"Well, now, just a moment, friend. The way you look, and all your talk about turning yourself invisible—I'm thinking you might be one of the Fair Folk."

"Oh, clever!" Doli retorted. "Oh, brilliant! Great clodhopper! Giant beanpole! Of course I am! What else! Enough gabbling. Get a move on. My leg's going to sleep."

⑥ "If a man does the Fair Folk a good turn," cried Maibon, his excitement growing, "it's told they must do one for him."

"I knew sooner or later you'd come round to that," grumbled the dwarf. "That's the way of it with you ham-handed, heavy-footed oafs. Time was, you humans got along well with us. But nowadays, you no sooner see a Fair Folk than it's grab, grab, grab! Gobble, gobble, gobble! Grant my wish! Give me this, give me that! As if we had nothing better to do!

"Yes, I'll give you a favor," Doli went on. "That's the rule,

◄ **Vocabulary**
vanished (va´ nisht) v. disappeared

plight (plīt) n. awkward, sad, or dangerous situation

Universal Theme
What problem does Maibon face?

⑦ Comprehension
What is unusual about Doli?

PART 2 • The Stone **655**

---

⑤ Analyze

1. Remind students that folklore is filled with creatures who have magical powers. Fairies and elves, usually depicted as tiny and graceful, are represented in human form. In Irish folklore, a leprechaun is a fairy in the form of a little old man. If you catch a leprechaun, the story goes, he will reveal a hiding place of treasure.

2. **Ask** students to brainstorm for a list of reasons why these creatures help writers explore universal themes.

   Possible responses: Creatures with magical powers allow the storyteller to go beyond the boundaries of day-to-day events. These creatures let the reader imagine what he or she might do if presented with certain choices that raise important issues. Some examples are: What life would I choose if I could choose anything at all? What is happiness?

⑥ Universal Theme

1. Students can consult their copies of the **Literary Analysis Graphic Organizer B** for "The Stone" and add details that focus on the theme of the story.

2. Read aloud the bracketed text. **Ask** students the Universal Theme question.

   Answer: Maibon must decide whether or not to help Doli.

⑦ Comprehension

Answer: Doli is a dwarf with red hair and red eyes, who is grumpy and short-tempered. Unlike the rest of his family, he is unable to make himself invisible. Maibon calls him one of the Fair Folk, who have magic powers.

👥 DIFFERENTIATED INSTRUCTION

Strategy for Special-Needs Students
Help students visualize segments of the story. Have them read aloud or listen to the paragraphs on this page and the previous page in which Maibon discovers the dwarf trying to free his leg from under the log (the audio version can be found on the **Hear It!** CD-ROM). Discuss the reactions of Maibon and the dwarf to each other. Have students brainstorm a list of ways to produce images based on the text, such as creating a mural or a comic strip. Divide students into small groups and have each group create a visual representation of the paragraphs.

Enrichment for Advanced Readers
After students have read this story, recommend that they find and read other stories about magicians, such as "Aladdin and the Wonderful Lamp" from *The Arabian Nights* and the stories in T. H. White's *The Once and Future King*. Each student should select his or her favorite story to summarize in a written report. The report should include the main character(s), the plot, the theme, the setting, and the main events.

8 Universal Theme

1. Assign students to read the parts of Maibon, Doli, and the narrator. Have the students read the bracketed passage.

2. Ask students to respond to the Universal Theme question.

Possible response: Doli thinks human beings are not sensible. The usual reward they want is gold or jewels or fine clothes rather than something practical.

3. Ask students to relate Doli's complaints to the theme of the story.

Possible response: Doli is advising Maibon that the stones are "greatly overrated" and that it is better to wish for something useful rather than something that will change his life in unforeseen ways. In other words, human beings should accept change and aging as inevitable and not try to interfere with the natural order of things.

Universal Theme
Why is Doli frustrated by Maibon and other humans?

8

I'm obliged to. Now, get on with it."

Hearing this, Maibon pulled and pried and chopped away at the log as fast as he could, and soon freed the dwarf.

Doli heaved a sigh of relief, rubbed his shin, and cocked a red eye at Maibon, saying:

"All right. You've done your work, you'll have your reward. What do you want? Gold, I suppose. That's the usual. Jewels? Fine clothes? Take my advice, go for something practical. A hazelwood twig to help you find water if your well ever goes dry? An ax that never needs sharpening? A cook pot always brimming with food?"

"None of those!" cried Maibon. He bent down to the dwarf and whispered eagerly, "But I've heard tell that you Fair Folk have magic stones that can keep a man young forever. That's what I want. I claim one for my reward."

Doli snorted. "I might have known you'd pick something like that. As to be expected, you humans have it all muddled. There's nothing can make a man young again. That's even beyond the best of our skills. Those stones you're babbling about? Well, yes, there are such things. But greatly overrated. All they'll do is keep you from growing any older."

"Just as good!" Maibon exclaimed. "I want no more than that!"

Doli hesitated and frowned. "Ah—between the two of us, take the cook pot. Better all around. Those stones—we'd sooner not give them away. There's a difficulty—"

"Because you'd rather keep them for yourselves," Maibon broke in. "No, no, you shan't cheat me of my due. Don't put me off with excuses. I told you what I want, and that's what I'll have. Come, hand it over and not another word."

💬 VOCABULARY DEVELOPMENT

Selection Vocabulary Reinforcement

To reinforce and assess students' comprehension of the selection vocabulary words, give them sentences in which the word may or may not be used correctly. Students must tell whether the use is correct and explain their answers. Use these sentences:

1. The newspaper articles described the *plight* of residents whose homes were destroyed by the earthquake.

Answer: Yes, *plight* is used correctly. A *plight* is a predicament or sad situation.

People who have lost their homes in a natural catastrophe would suffer.

2. There was great *jubilation* when we learned that our after-school programs were cut as a result of budgetary shortfalls.

Answer: No, *jubilation* refers to great rejoicing and happiness. Cutting extracurricular activities from a school would cause people to feel disappointed rather than elated.

Doli shrugged and opened a leather pouch that hung from his belt. He spilled a number of brightly colored pebbles into his palm, picked out one of the larger stones, and handed it to Maibon. The dwarf then jumped up, took to his heels, raced across the field, and disappeared into a thicket. ●

Laughing and crowing over his good fortune and his cleverness, Maibon hurried back to the cottage. There, he told his wife what had happened, and showed her the stone he had claimed from the Fair Folk.

"As I am now, so I'll always be!" Maibon declared, flexing his arms and thumping his chest. "A fine figure of a man! Oho, no gray beard and wrinkled brow for me!"

Instead of sharing her husband's jubilation, Modrona flung up her hands and burst out:

"Maibon, you're a greater fool than ever I supposed! And selfish into the bargain! You've turned down treasures! You didn't even ask that dwarf for so much as new jackets for the children! Nor a new apron for me! You could have had the roof mended. Or the walls plastered. No, a stone is what you ask for! A bit of rock no better than you'll dig up in the cow pasture!"

Crestfallen[2] and sheepish, Maibon began thinking his wife was right, and the dwarf had indeed given him no more than a common field stone.

"Eh, well, it's true," he stammered, "I feel no different than I did this morning, no better nor worse, but every way the same. That redheaded little wretch! He'll rue the day if I ever find him again!"

So saying, Maibon threw the stone into the fireplace. That night he grumbled his way to bed, dreaming revenge on the dishonest dwarf.

Next morning, after a restless night, he yawned, rubbed his eyes, and scratched his chin. Then he sat bolt upright in bed, patting his cheeks in amazement.

"My beard!" he cried, tumbling out and hurrying to tell his wife. "It hasn't grown! Not by a hair! Can it be the dwarf didn't cheat me after all?"

"Don't talk to me about beards," declared his wife as

---

2. **crestfallen** (krest′ fôl′ ən) *adj.* made sad or humble; disheartened.

◄ **Vocabulary**
jubilation
(jōō′ bə lā′ shən) *n.* great joy; triumph

rue (rōō) *v.* Feel sorrow or regret for something

Setting a Purpose
How does your reading rate change when you read dialogue? Explain.

❿ **Comprehension**
Why does Maibon's wife say he's a fool?

❾ **Setting a Purpose**

1. **Ask** students if they are comfortable with their reading rate so far. To answer, have them summarize what has happened to Maibon since he received the stone from Doli.

   Possible response: At first, he is jubilant. He is pleased with himself for being so clever, and he is delighted at the thought that he will not grow any older. After his wife scolds him for being a selfish fool, he becomes disheartened and starts to distrust the dwarf, believing he has been cheated.

2. Have students work in groups to read the bracketed passage aloud. Urge them to read the entire passage several times until everyone is comfortable with the reading rate. **Ask** groups to describe that rate.

   Possible response: The reading rate is slower for the descriptions and faster for the dialogue.

3. **Ask** students to respond to the Setting a Purpose question.

   Possible response: Reading rate speeds up when reading dialogue because we want the dialogue to "sound" like real people speaking.

❿ **Comprehension**

Answer: Modrona thinks Maibon is a fool for using his wish on his own vanity instead of to improve life for his family.

DIFFERENTIATED INSTRUCTION

EL Pronunciation for English Learners
To help students pronounce initial *f*, post these words: *fine/pine, find/bind,* and *feel/peel.* Pronounce each word, stressing the initial consonant sound. Have students echo. Call out words at random as students write them. Have students compare and discuss results with a fluent partner, discussing incorrect choices as the fluent partner models correct pronunciation.

Enrichment for Gifted/Talented Students
Fantasy stories provide excellent material for visual representation. Have gifted/talented students work in pairs or small groups to select a scene from "The Stone" and create a small three-dimensional stage set for their selection. Students can use construction paper to cover grocery cartons for their models. Have students design appropriate costumes for the characters, create an original backdrop, and furnish their sets with appropriate props.

11 ❓ **Connecting to the Big Question**

1. Ask students what happens to a family when one member is away from the home. Discuss ways that each family member's contribution is important to the group.

2. Have students read the bracketed passage. **Ask:** How do Maibon's actions impact his family here?

   Possible response: The chickens aren't hatching, the cow hasn't borne her calf, the seeds have not sprouted, and the apple tree has not made apples. Remind students that family is a type of community.

3. **Ask:** Is Maibon thinking about his family? Does he see that his actions shape that community? Explain.

   Possible response: No, Maibon is thinking only of himself and his desire to avoid old age. He doesn't realize that his actions are freezing the family in time as well.

12 **Critical Viewing**

Answer: The painting depicts a life similar to that of Maibon and his wife because the subject of the painting seems to be a group of family members harvesting crops on their farm. Details include the horse and cart, the fields where crops are grown, and trees.

Maibon went to the fireplace, picked out the stone, and clutched it safely in both hands. "There's trouble enough in the chicken roost. Those eggs should have hatched by now, but the hen is still brooding on her nest."

"Let the chickens worry about that," answered Maibon. "Wife, don't you see what a grand thing's happened to me? I'm not a minute older than I was yesterday. Bless that generous-hearted dwarf!"

"Let me lay hands on him and I'll bless him," retorted Modrona. "That's all well and good for you. But what of me? You'll stay as you are, but I'll turn old and gray, and worn and wrinkled, and go doddering into my grave! And what of our little ones? They'll grow up and have children of their own. And grandchildren, and great-grandchildren. And you, younger than any of them. What a foolish sight you'll be!"

But Maibon, gleeful over his good luck, paid his wife no heed, and only tucked the stone deeper into his pocket. Next day, however, the eggs had still not hatched.

11 "And the cow!" Modrona cried. "She's long past due to calve, and no sign of a young one ready to be born!"

"Don't bother me with cows and chickens," replied Maibon. "They'll all come right, in time. As for time, I've got all the time in the world!"

Having no appetite for breakfast, Maibon went out into the field. Of all the seeds he had sown there, however, he was surprised to see not one had sprouted. The field, which by now should have been covered with green shoots, lay bare and empty. ●

"Eh, things do seem a little late these days," Maibon said to himself. "Well, no hurry. It's that much less for me to do. The wheat isn't growing, but neither are the weeds."

Some days went by and still the eggs had not hatched, the cow had not calved, the wheat had not sprouted. And now Maibon saw that his apple tree showed no sign of even the smallest, greenest fruit.

"Maibon, it's the fault of that stone!" wailed his wife. "Get rid of the thing!"

"Nonsense," replied Maibon. "The season's slow, that's all."

Nevertheless, his wife kept at him and kept at him so much that Maibon at last, and very reluctantly, threw the stone out the cottage window. Not too far, though, for he

Vocabulary ▶
sown (sōn) *v.* planted; scattered with seeds

12 ▶ **Critical Viewing** Find three details that suggest that the people in this picture lead a life similar to that of Maibon and his wife.

🗨 **THINK ALOUD**

Vocabulary: Context Clues
Direct students' attention to the word *doddering* in the second full paragraph on this page. Using a think-aloud process, model how to use context to infer the meaning of an unknown word. Say to students:

I'm going to think aloud to show you how I would figure out the meaning of *doddering* from its context.

In this sentence, doddering is used to describe how Modrona imagines herself approaching death. We know from the words "old and gray" and "worn and wrinkled" that she pictures herself as very old. The word doddering refers to the way a very old person would move, so I think it means "walking unsteadily" or "tottering." I then use a dictionary to confirm my inference.

had it in the back of his mind to go later and find it again.

Next morning he had no need to go looking for it, for there was the stone sitting on the window ledge.

"You see?" said Maibon to his wife. "Here it is back again. So, it's a gift meant for me to keep."

"Maibon!" cried his wife. "Will you get rid of it! We've had nothing but trouble since you brought it into the house. Now the baby's fretting and fuming. Teething, poor little thing. But not a tooth to be seen! Maibon, that stone's bad luck and I want no part of it!"

Protesting it was none of his doing that the stone had come back, Maibon carried it into the vegetable patch. He dug a hole, not a very deep one, and put the stone into it.

Next day, there was the stone above ground, winking and glittering.

"Maibon!" cried his wife. "Once and for all, if you care for your family, get rid of that cursed thing!"

13 Seeing no other way to keep peace in the household, Maibon regretfully and unwillingly took the stone and threw it down the well, where it splashed into the water and sank from sight.

But that night, while he was trying vainly to sleep, there came such a rattling and clattering that Maibon clapped his hands over his ears, jumped out of bed, and went stumbling into the yard. At the well, the bucket was jiggling back and forth and up and down at the end of the rope;

14 Comprehension
What is the stone doing to everything on Maibon's farm?

PART 2 • The Stone **659**

---

13 Draw Conclusions

1. **Ask** students to summarize the basic conversations that Maibon and Modrona have had since Maibon was given the stone.

   Answer: He has been delighted in his good luck. She has identified problems that the stone has created for the family. She has asked him to get rid of the stone. He has resisted and half-heartedly tried to discard it.

2. Have students read the bracketed passage. **Ask:** What does Modrona want Maibon to do? How does Maibon feel about the request?

   Possible response: She wants him to get rid of the stone. He feels regretful and unwilling to do so, but he tries to discard it.

3. **Ask** students to draw a conclusion about what Maibon hoped the stone would do for him and what these hopes suggest about his character.

   Possible response: Maibon hopes that the stone will bring him eternal youth. He remains interested in keeping the stone, despite repeated requests from his wife and much evidence that the stone is harming his family. He appears to be a selfish man.

14 Comprehension

Answer: As a result of the stone's influence, nothing on Maibon's farm is experiencing change. The hens' eggs have not hatched, the calf has not been born, the seeds Maibon planted have not sprouted, the apple tree has not produced fruit, and the baby is teething, but no tooth has appeared.

:: DIFFERENTIATED INSTRUCTION

EL Strategy for English Learners
Point out the following sentence from this page: "Maibon, that stone's bad luck and I want no part of it!" Identify it as a compound sentence. Tell students that a compound sentence is made up of two or more independent clauses and may be joined by a coordinating conjunction. Point out that the coordinating conjunction in this sentence is *and*. Model how to read each independent clause as a separate sentence. Then, combine the two meanings for an overall meaning.

Culturally Responsive Instruction
Point out that this tale focuses on interaction between a human and a dwarf. Acknowledge that fairies and dwarves have prominent places in folk tales from many cultures. Encourage students to share stories from their home culture that feature dwarves or fairies. As a class, compare and contrast the roles that the dwarves and fairies play in the folklore of several cultures.

⑮ Literature in Context

Literature Connection Invite students to tell stories in which stones play a role. Here are some examples you may cite:

- Perhaps the most famous stone in literature is the stone that holds a sword in the Arthurian legend. When Arthur withdraws the sword, he is acknowledged to be king of Britain.

- In the fairy tale of Hansel and Gretel, Hansel stuffs his pockets with pebbles and throws them on the road into the forest. By moonlight the children are then able to find their way back to their house.

- In "Stone Soup," another tale from folklore, a clever man finds a way to feed a village during a famine. In some accounts he is a peddler who drops a stone into a cauldron of boiling water. He gets everyone to contribute one ingredient until the soup becomes a delicious meal for all.

Connect to the Literature

Have students read the Literature in Context feature, and present the additional information above. Then, **ask** the Connect to the Literature question.

Possible response: Perhaps the best way to apply the power of the stone is to keep great art, books, buildings, and other landmarks of civilization from being destroyed by the ravages of time.

⑯ Setting a Purpose

1. Invite two students to read aloud the bracketed conversation, which continues onto the next page. **Ask** students to describe the mood of the conversation.

   Answer: The mood is tense and angry.

2. **Ask:** How do people speak when they are angry and tense?

   Possible response: They often speak quickly because their emotions are driving their speech.

3. **Ask** the Setting a Purpose question.

   Possible response: Students may say they would read it quickly because the tension in the scene causes the characters to speak quickly.

---

⑮ LITERATURE IN CONTEXT

Literature Connection

Rocks and Roles
Stones play a role in many stories. For example, in Aesop's fable "The Crow and the Pitcher," a thirsty crow tries to drink from a pitcher, but the water is too far down for his beak to reach. After much thought, the crow solves his problem by dropping pebbles into the pitcher until the water rises enough that he can drink it. The moral: Necessity is the mother of invention.

In "The Stone," a rock causes problems rather than solving them when Maibon makes foolish choices.

Connect to the Literature

How might Maibon have used his stone wisely?

Setting a Purpose
At what rate would you read dialogue such as this? Why?

---

and in the bottom of the bucket was the stone.

Now Maibon began to be truly distressed, not only for the toothless baby, the calfless cow, the fruitless tree, and the hen sitting desperately on her eggs, but for himself as well.

"Nothing's moving along as it should," he groaned. "I can't tell one day from another. Nothing changes, there's nothing to look forward to, nothing to show for my work. Why sow if the seeds don't sprout? Why plant if there's never a harvest? Why eat if I don't get hungry? Why go to bed at night, or get up in the morning, or do anything at all? And the way it looks, so it will stay for ever and ever! I'll shrivel from boredom if nothing else!"

"Maibon," pleaded his wife, "for all our sakes, destroy the dreadful thing!"

Maibon tried now to pound the stone to dust with his heaviest mallet; but he could not so much as knock a chip from it. He put it against his grindstone without so much as scratching it. He set it on his anvil and belabored it with hammer and tongs, all to no avail.

At last he decided to bury the stone again, this time deeper than before. Picking up his shovel, he hurried to the field. But he suddenly halted and the shovel dropped from his hands. There, sitting cross-legged on a stump, was the dwarf. ●

"You!" shouted Maibon, shaking his fist. "Cheat! Villain! Trickster! I did you a good turn, and see how you've repaid it!"

The dwarf blinked at the furious Maibon. "You mortals are an ungrateful crew. I gave you what you wanted."

"You should have warned me!" burst out Maibon. ⑯

"I did," Doli snapped back. "You wouldn't listen. No, you yapped and yammered, bound to have your way. I told you we didn't like to give away those stones. When you mortals get hold of one, you stay just as you are—but so does everything around you. Before you know it, you're mired in time like a rock in the mud. You take my advice.

16 Get rid of that stone as fast as you can."

"What do you think I've been trying to do?" blurted Maibon. "I've buried it, thrown it down the well, pounded it with a hammer—it keeps coming back to me!"

17 "That's because you really didn't want to give it up," Doli said. "In the back of your mind and the bottom of your heart, you didn't want to change along with the rest of the world. So long as you feel that way, the stone is yours."

"No, no!" cried Maibon. "I want no more of it. Whatever may happen, let it happen. That's better than nothing happening at all. I've had my share of being young, I'll take my share of being old. And when I come to the end of my days, at least I can say I've lived each one of them."

"If you mean that," answered Doli, "toss the stone onto the ground, right there at the stump. Then get home and be about your business."

Spiral Review
REPETITION What feeling is created by Maibon's repeated attempts to get rid of the stone?

Universal Theme What message about change does Doli try to share with Maibon?

PART 2 • The Stone **661**

Spiral Review
Repetition

1. Remind students that they studied the concept of repetition in the Unit 5 Focus on Craft and Structure (pp. 628–631).

2. **Ask** students the Spiral Review question.

   Possible response: The repeated attempts create a feeling of anxiety and distress.

17 Universal Theme

1. Have students read aloud the second bracketed passage. **Ask:** What insight does Doli have into Maibon's nature?

   Possible response: He knows that although Maibon has made attempts to get rid of the stone, he doesn't really want to give it up.

2. **Ask** students the Univeral Theme question.

   Possible response: Doli suggests that without change, there is no growth or development. Maibon has learned that change is essential because without it, nothing happens and life is dull and meaningless.

▶ **Monitor Progress:** Review students' graphic organizers to ensure that they are including salient details about the main character's change, the meaning of the change, and the universal theme expressed in the events of the story.

▶ **Reteach:** Using their **Literacy Analysis Graphic Organizers**, have students compare and contrast the two scenes in which Maibon and Doli meet (pp. 655–656 and pp. 660–661). Students should describe how Maibon changes after he sees the stone's effect and what the change in his attitude means. Students should then relate this change in the character to the theme of the story—the importance of accepting aging as a natural and inevitable process.

☑ ASSESS

Language Study

Vocabulary

Sample answers:

1. You can solve a hungry person's <u>plight</u> by providing food, which would help alleviate the problem.

2. No, <u>jubilation</u> is great joy. I would feel unhappy if I lost a contest.

3. No, my <u>feeble</u> uncle would not be strong enough to carry my suitcase.

4. No, I celebrate the day rather than <u>rue</u> it.

5. No, seeds need soil to grow, so they cannot be <u>sown</u> in the desert, where there is only sand.

Word Study

Part A

Sample answers:

The Latin root *-van-* means "empty." If you struggle *vainly* to accomplish something, your results are <u>empty</u>, or without success. *Evanescence* is the quality of disappearing, or becoming <u>empty</u>, very quickly.

Part B

Sample answers:

1. The root *-van-* means "empty." If you have too much *vanity*, you have <u>empty</u> pride in yourself.

2. The root *-van-* means "empty." It would be an insult to be called *vain* and considered <u>empty</u> of true substance or character.

Literary Analysis

Possible responses appear below. Check to be sure students support their responses with evidence from the text.

1. descriptive passage on p. 654— slowly; dialogue between Maibon and Modrona on p. 657—quickly

2. It makes sense to read the first passage slowly in order to appreciate the details of what Maibon sees and how he reacts to it. It makes sense to read the second passage quickly to capture the tension of the conversation between Maibon and Modrona.

3. **(a)** Maibon gets the stone by freeing a red-headed dwarf named Doli. **(b)** He chooses the

---

Maibon flung down the stone, spun around, and set off as fast as he could. When he dared at last to glance back over his shoulder, fearful the stone might be bouncing along at his heels, he saw no sign of it, nor of the redheaded dwarf.

Maibon gave a joyful cry, for at that same instant the fallow field was covered with green blades of wheat, the branches of the apple tree bent to the ground, so laden they were with fruit. He ran to the cottage, threw his arms around his wife and children, and told them the good news. The hen hatched her chicks, the cow bore her calf. And Maibon laughed with glee when he saw the first tooth in the baby's mouth.

Never again did Maibon meet any of the Fair Folk, and he was just as glad of it. He and his wife and children and grandchildren lived many years, and Maibon was proud of his white hair and long beard as he had been of his sturdy arms and legs.

"Stones are all right, in their way," said Maibon. "But the trouble with them is, they don't grow."

Language Study

Vocabulary The words listed below appear in "The Stone." Explain your answers to the numbered questions.

feeble	plight	jubilation	rue	sown

1. How could you solve a hungry person's *plight*?
2. Would you react with *jubilation* if you lost a contest?
3. Would you ask your *feeble* uncle to carry your suitcase?
4. Do you *rue* the day you met your best friend?
5. Can seeds be *sown* in the desert?

Word Study

WORD STUDY

The **Latin root -van-** means "empty." In this story, the stone **vanished**, or disappeared, leaving an empty space.

Part A Explain how the **Latin root -van-** contributes to the meanings of *vainly* and *evanescence*. Consult a dictionary if necessary.

Part B Use context to explain your answers to these questions:

1. What are the dangers of having too much *vanity*?
2. Would you feel insulted if someone described you as *vain*?

---

stone because he does not want to grow older. **(c)** He cannot get rid of it because he does not really want to.

4. Doli wants Maibon to understand that the magic stone will not make him happy.

5. Change is a necessary part of life.

6. Maibon shows the theme when he finally discards the stone with conviction, then cries out with joy to discover that it is gone and that change has returned to the world.

7. **(a)** Maibon's new belief is that getting old is better than always staying the same.

(b) Maibon is "proud" of his white hair and long beard. **(c)** The author wants to show that Maibon has accepted that he is willing to change and grow old.

8. Some students may reason that it is good to remain young in mind and aspirations so that life is filled with purpose and interest. Other students may argue that people need to accept the realities of aging and not think of aging in a negative light.

Close Reading Activities

Literary Analysis

Key Ideas and Details

1. **Setting a Purpose** Choose two passages from the folk tale. In a chart like the one on the right, tell your **reading rate** for each passage.

2. **Setting a Purpose** Use the information in your chart to explain when and why you changed your reading rate as you read.

3. **(a)** How does Maibon get the stone? **(b) Make Inferences:** Why does he choose the stone over other gifts? **(c) Interpret:** Why is Maibon unable to get rid of the stone?

Passage
Reading Rate

Craft and Structure

4. **Universal Theme** What lesson is Doli trying to teach Maibon when he says that the stones are greatly overrated?

5. **Universal Theme** What universal theme is revealed in the folk tale, just after Doli explains why the stone would not go away?

6. **Universal Theme** Which of Maibon's actions best supports the theme? Why?

Integration of Knowledge and Ideas

7. **(a) Analyze:** What new belief finally allows Maibon to rid himself of the stone? **(b) Connect:** What emotion does Maibon show at the end of the story? **(c) Support:** Why do you think the author uses this detail?

8. **Apply:** Many messages in advertisements and on consumer products promote youthfulness. Do you think this is a good message? Why or why not?

---

9. **How much do our communities shape us?** With a small group, discuss the following questions:
(a) Hypothesize: How might the stone have affected Maibon's neighbors if he had kept it? **(b) Synthesize:** Based on this story, what obligations do you think each individual has to his or her neighbors or community? Explain.

ACADEMIC VOCABULARY

As you write and speak about "The Stone," use the words related to family and community that you explored on page 613 of this text.

9. **How much do our communities shape us?**
(a) The stone might have frozen Maibon's neighbors in time along with him and his family. **(b)** Individuals have an obligation not to harm neighbors or the community through their own actions.

Online Writer's Notebook

Students can use the Online Writer's Notebook to record all responses.

Conventions

1. Introduce the skill.
2. Discuss the definitions and the examples in the chart.

Think Aloud: Model the Skill

Say to students:

We use independent and subordinate clauses when we write and speak. Suppose I say, "Before I go home, I will lock the door." I express the main idea—I will lock the door—with a complete thought. Words such as *before, after, when,* and *because* help me recognize and create subordinate clauses that depend on the rest of the sentence for meaning.

Practice A Sample answers:

1. *Maibon rescues a dwarf named Doli,* whose leg is caught under a log.
2. *Doli suggests a useful reward* that is brimming with food.
3. When Maibon makes his wish, *he isn't thinking clearly.*
4. *Modrono calls her husband a fool* because she is angry.
5. *Maibon will be happy* if Doli helps him.

Reading Application
Sample answers:

independent clauses: "You'll stay as you are"; "I'll turn old and gray"; subordinate clause: "When he dared at last to glance back over his shoulder"; relative clause: "who was staring at him, speechless"

Practice B Sample answers:

1. Modrona scolds him *when he brings home the stone.* (subordinate)
2. Maibon searches for Doli, *who can get rid of the stone.* (relative)
3. Maibon was proud of his hair, *which had grown long and white.* (relative)
4. Wishes can cause trouble *because you may not know the effects.* (subordinate)

Writing Application
Sample answers:

Maibon, who is not the smartest person on earth, makes a foolish choice.

Maibon regrets his choice of a reward after he sees the effects.

Conventions: Independent and Dependent Clauses

The Stone
·Lloyd Alexander·

A **clause** is a group of words with its own subject and verb.

An **independent clause** has a subject and a verb and can stand by itself as a complete sentence. A **dependent clause** has a subject and a verb, but it cannot stand alone as a complete sentence.

There are two kinds of dependent clauses: A **subordinate clause** begins with a subordinating conjunction, such as *if, when, because, or since.* A **relative clause** begins with a relative pronoun, such as *who, whom, whose, which,* or *that.*

I can hear you	because you are speaking loudly.
independent clause	subordinate clause
There is the brave person	who saved my dog's life.
independent clause	relative clause

If a relative clause is not necessary in order to understand the main idea of the sentence, it is called a **nonrestrictive clause**. A nonrestrictive clause is set off by commas, dashes, or parentheses.

Example: Dan, *who grew up in Nevada,* moved to Vermont last year.

Practice A
Add an independent clause to each dependent clause to make a complete sentence.

1. whose leg is caught under a log
2. that is brimming with food
3. When Maibon makes his wish
4. because she is angry
5. if Doli helps him

Reading Application Scan "The Stone" to find two independent clauses, one subordinate clause, and one relative clause.

Practice B
Add a dependent clause to each of the following independent clauses to make a new sentence. State whether the dependent clause is *subordinate* or *relative.*

1. Modrona scolds him
2. Maibon searches for Doli
3. Maibon was proud of his hair
4. Wishes can cause trouble

Writing Application Write a sentence about "The Stone" that contains an independent clause and a dependent clause.

▶ EXTEND THE LESSON

Sentence Modeling

Present these sentences from "The Stone."

Although the day was fair and cloudless, he took no pleasure in it.

I told you we didn't like to give away those stones.

Remind students of the lesson on independent and subordinate clauses. Ask students what they notice about the sentences. (They contain an independent and a subordinate clause.) Then ask what else students notice.

(In the first sentence the subordinate clause comes first, setting the scene but also delaying the main idea. In the second sentence the main clause comes first, with the subordinate clause giving more detail about the main clause.)

Have students imitate one of the sentences in a sentence on a topic of their own choosing, matching each grammatical and stylistic feature discussed. Collect the sentences, and share them with the class.

Writing to Sources

Narrative Text Write a **plot proposal**—a plan of story events—that illustrates the universal theme of "The Stone."

- Review "The Stone" to identify the universal theme your new story will convey.
- Brainstorm for a situation that illustrates the theme. Use your imagination and your own experience to develop your idea. Decide how the setting, characters, and plot will work together to reveal the theme.
- Write a brief description of the plot.
- When you finish writing, check to be sure that your proposal clearly illustrates the universal theme.
- Proofread your proposal to check for correct capitalization, spelling, and punctuation.

Grammar Application Use independent and dependent clauses correctly in your plot proposal. Set off nonrestrictive clauses with commas, dashes, or parentheses.

Research and Technology

Build and Present Knowledge With a small group, prepare a **written and visual report** on human aging. Follow these steps to complete the assignment:

- Decide how to divide the responsibilities of the assignment among your group members.
- Type keywords, such as "human aging process," into an Internet Web browser to find information from multiple sources.
- Get together as a group to discuss what you have learned. Then, create an outline to organize your information.
- Decide how to pair pictures and other graphics with facts.
- Practice your presentation in your group before presenting to the rest of the class. In your presentation, connect the information you learned through your research to descriptions of aging that appear in "The Stone."

 **Common Core State Standards**

Writing
4. Produce clear and coherent writing in which the development, organization, and style are appropriate to task, purpose, and audience.
6. Use technology, including the Internet, to produce and publish writing.
8. Gather relevant information from multiple print and digital sources.

Speaking and Listening
1. Engage effectively in a range of collaborative discussions with diverse partners on grade 6 topics, texts, and issues, building on others' ideas and expressing their own clearly.

Language
1. Demonstrate command of the conventions of standard English grammar and usage when writing or speaking.
2.a. Use punctuation (commas, parentheses, dashes) to set off nonrestrictive/parenthetical elements.

Writing to Sources

1. Review the assignment, using the instruction on the student page.
2. Then, review the elements that make up a plot: *exposition, conflict, rising action, climax, falling action,* and *resolution.* To help students come up with ideas for their stories, ask them to identify the conflict of the story they read.
3. To give students guidance writing a plot proposal, give them the **Support for Writing** for this selection in the *Student Companion All-in-One Workbook.*

Grammar Application

Have students check their drafts for the correct use of independent and dependent clauses.

Six Traits Focus

✓ Ideas	Word Choice
Organization	Sentence Fluency
Voice	Conventions

Research and Technology

1. Review the assignment, using the instruction on the student page.
2. To support students' work on the assignment, have them complete the **Support for Extend Your Learning** page for this selection in the *Student Companion All-in-One Workbook.*

Time and Resource Manager

LESSON PACING GUIDE

Why the Tortoise's Shell Is Not Smooth

DAY 1	**Preteach/Teach**

- Administer the Reading and Vocabulary Warm-ups, as necessary.
- Introduce the Key Ideas and Details skill: Purpose for Reading.
- Introduce the Craft and Structure skill: Personification.
- Use the Close Reading Model to demonstrate the application of the skills.
- Review the selection vocabulary, as necessary, with students who need additional support.
- Prepare students to read the selection by reviewing with them the Multidraft Reading Strategies.

DAY 2	**Teach**

- Informally monitor comprehension while students read.
- Use the Comprehension questions to confirm understanding.
- Develop students' ability to set a purpose for reading and analyze personification using the sidenote questions.
- Reinforce vocabulary with the Vocabulary notes.
- Reinforce unit focus standards using the Spiral Review prompts.

DAY 3	**Assess**

- Assess students' comprehension and mastery of the skills by having them answer the Literary Analysis questions.
- Have students complete the Vocabulary activities.
- Develop students' understanding of roots and affixes by having them complete the Word Study activities.

DAY 4	**Extend/Assess**

- Build students' ability to master grammar concepts and conventions by having them complete the Conventions lesson.
- Have students complete the Writing to Sources activity and write an invitation. (You may assign as homework.)
- Extend learning by having students complete the Speaking and Listening activity: a dramatic reading.
- Administer the Selection Test or Open-Book Test.

 **Common Core State Standards**

Reading Literature 4. Determine the meaning of words and phrases as they are used in a text, including figurative and connotative meanings; analyze the impact of a specific word choice on meaning and tone.

Writing 4. Produce clear and coherent writing in which the development, organization, and style are appropriate to task, purpose, and audience.

Speaking and Listening 6. Adapt speech to a variety of contexts and tasks, demonstrating command of formal English when indicated or appropriate.

Language 1. Demonstrate command of the conventions of standard English grammar and usage when writing or speaking.

3.a. Vary sentence patterns for meaning, reader/listener interest, and style.

5.a. Interpret figures of speech in context.

5.b. Use the relationship between particular words to better understand each of the words.

Daily Block Scheduling

Each day in this Lesson Pacing Guide represents a 40–50 minute period. Teachers using block scheduling may combine days to revise pacing. In addition, teachers may differentiate and support core instruction by integrating components for extended and intensive support as students require. See the Guide to Resources (facing page).

GUIDE TO RESOURCES

		L1	L2	L3	L4	EL	ALL	RESOURCES	PRINT	CD	ONLINE
Warm Up		✔	✔			✔		Vocabulary Warm-ups			✔
		✔	✔			✔		Reading Warm-ups			✔
							✔	Background Video			✔
							✔	Selection Audio		Hear It!	✔
Comprehension/ Selection Support							✔	Writing About the Big Question	Student Companion Workbook		✔
							✔	Literary Analysis	Student Companion Workbook		✔
							✔	Reading	Student Companion Workbook		✔
							✔	Vocabulary Builder	Student Companion Workbook		✔
					✔			Enrichment			✔
				✔	✔	✔		Conventions	Student Companion Workbook		✔
				✔	✔	✔		Writing to Sources	Student Companion Workbook		✔
				✔	✔	✔		Speaking and Listening	Student Companion Workbook		
Differentiated Instruction/ Additional Support							✔	Additional Standards Practice	Common Core Companion		✔
		✔	✔					Adapted Reader's Notebook			✔
						✔		English Reader's Notebook:			✔
						✔		Spanish Reader's Notebook			✔
						✔		Graphic Organizer A			✔
		✔	✔			✔		Graphic Organizer B			✔
		✔	✔			✔		"Seeking Student Success"	Reality Central Student Edition and Writing Journal		✔
		✔	✔			✔		Practice and Assess	Reading Kit		✔
Monitor Progress							✔	Selection Test		Exam View	✔
							✔	Open-Book Test		Exam View	✔
Digital Resources							✔	Close Reading Tool			✔
							✔	Online Writer's Notebook			✔

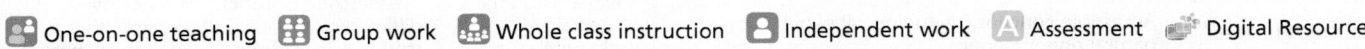

👥 One-on-one teaching   ⬛ Group work   👥 Whole class instruction   👤 Independent work   Ⓐ Assessment   💻 Digital Resource

LEARNER LEVELS

L1 Special-Needs Students   **L3** On-Level Students (Tier 1)   **EL** English Learners
L2 Below-Level Students (Tier 2)   **L4** Advanced Students (Tier 1)   **All** All Students

❶ How much do our communities shape us?

Read • Discuss • Research • Write As students read, they will explore the Big Question through text analysis of the selection. Encourage students to take notes as they read and raise additional questions, using text evidence to support their thoughts. Students should refer to their notes to help them deepen their understanding of the selection through discussion, research, and writing.

❷ Close Reading Focus

1. Explain to students that before they start reading, they should set a purpose. Students can ask themselves, "Why am I reading this text?" Reading with a purpose helps people focus on the text and what they want to gain from reading. Encourage students to preview the text and text features to understand the topic of the text and help develop reasons why they will read it.

2. To help students understand personification, point out the base word *person*, and explain that *personification* means "described like a person." As an example, read the sentence, "The cat shouted, 'There is no way I'm going into that bathtub!'" and ask students what they think of when they hear it. Explain that, while we know a cat can't really talk, this description shows us that the cat really did not want a bath. Tell students that personification can also be funny and can help them understand and enjoy folk literature.

Building Knowledge

Meet the Author

Chinua Achebe (1930–2013) liked to retell stories from his native country of Nigeria. Achebe attended the local mission school where his father taught, and then went to universities in Nigeria and England. He won acclaim with his novel, *Things Fall Apart* (1958), about changing times in Africa. He moved to the United States when the political climate in Nigeria made it too dangerous for him to stay. He once wrote, "Any good story, any good novel, should have a message."

 Common Core State Standards

Reading Literature
4. Determine the meaning of words and phrases as they are used in a text, including figurative and connotative meanings; analyze the impact of a specific word choice on meaning and tone.

Language
5.a. Interpret figures of speech in context. **5.b.** Use the relationship between particular words to better understand each of the words.

❶ How much do our communities shape us?

Explore the Big Question as you read "Why the Tortoise's Shell Is Not Smooth." Take notes on ways in which the story explores what happens when a community's rules are broken.

❷ CLOSE READING FOCUS

Key Ideas and Details: **Purpose for Reading**

Your **purpose for reading** is the reason you read a text. Sometimes you choose a text based on a purpose you already have. Other times, you set a purpose based on the kind of text you are about to read. Setting a purpose helps you focus your reading. For example, you might read to learn about a subject, to gain understanding, or simply to be entertained. Preview the text by looking at the title, the pictures, and the beginnings of paragraphs before you read. This will help you set a purpose or decide whether the text will fit a purpose you already have.

Craft and Structure: **Personification**

Figurative language is language that is used imaginatively rather than literally. **Personification** is figurative language in which a nonhuman subject is described as if it had human qualities. In the example, *rain kisses her cheek*, the rain behaves like a person.

Writers use personification to make text lively or to emphasize an important point. In folk tales, personification is often used to give human qualities to animal characters. The animals' behavior illustrates human traits and problems in a humorous way.

Vocabulary

You will encounter the following words in this story. Decide whether you know each word well, know it a little bit, or do not know it at all. After you read, see how your knowledge of each word has increased.

cunning	famine	orator
custom	eloquent	compound

©TEXT COMPLEXITY **RUBRIC**

Why the Tortoise's Shell Is Not Smooth		Reader and Task Suggestions	
Qualitative Measures		**Preparing to Read the Text**	**Leveled Tasks**
Context/Knowledge Demands	Folk tale involving animals; oral tradition 1 2 ③ 4 5	• Tell students that this story contains both a moral lesson and an explanation for a natural phenomenon. • Guide students to use Multidraft Reading strategies (TE p. 668)	*Levels of Meaning* If students will have difficulty with meaning, discuss the story's plot with them. Discuss the animals' character traits and the lessons the tortoise and birds learn. *Synthesizing* If students will not have difficulty with meaning, discuss other stories students may know that are part of the oral tradition.
Structure/Language Conventionality and Clarity	On-level vocabulary; simple sentences; dialogue 1 ② 3 4 5		
Levels of Meaning/Purpose/ Concept Level	Accessible concept (mythological explanation of natural phenomenon) 1 2 ③ 4 5		
Quantitative Measures			
Lexile	770L	Text Length	Word Count: 1,103

CLOSE READING MODEL

The passage below is from Chinua Achebe's folk tale "Why the Tortoise's Shell Is Not Smooth." The annotations to the right of the passage show ways in which you can use close reading skills to set a purpose and analyze personification.

from "Why the Tortoise's Shell Is Not Smooth" [1]

Low voices, broken now and then by singing, reached Okonkwo from his wives' huts as each woman and her children told folk stories. Ekwefi and her daughter, Ezinma, sat on a mat on the floor. It was Ekwefi's turn to tell a story.

"Once upon a time," she began, "all the birds were invited to a feast in the sky. [2] They were very happy and began to prepare themselves for the great day. They painted their bodies with red cam wood and drew beautiful patterns on them with dye. [3]

"Tortoise saw all these preparations and soon discovered what it all meant. Nothing that happened in the world of the animals ever escaped his notice; he was full of cunning. As soon as he heard of the great feast in the sky his throat began to itch at the very thought. [4] There was a famine in those days and Tortoise had not eaten a good meal for two moons. His body rattled like a piece of dry stick in an empty shell. So he began to plan how he would go into the sky." [4]

Purpose for Reading

1 Previewing the title tells you that this folk tale explains something in nature. You might set a purpose to learn why, according to the tale, the tortoise's shell is not smooth.

Purpose for Reading

2 You may recognize the words, "Once upon a time" as a traditional beginning for many fairy tales and folk tales. At this point, you might decide that your purpose is to read for enjoyment.

Personification

3 The birds are "very happy" and paint their bodies the way humans in an African village might decorate themselves for a special occasion. The personification of animals is a common feature of folk tales.

Personification

4 Tortoise plots to join the feast in a way a human might. Imagining Tortoise with human characteristics helps you understand his cunning.

For each class during which you will teach this selection, have students complete one of the five Research activities for Week 29 in *Daily Bellringer Activities*. You may wish to use additional activities that are applicable to this selection.

Vocabulary

If students require support with selection vocabulary, use this routine:

1. Write the following words and definitions on the board:

   cunning *n.* slyness; deception

   famine *n.* shortage of food

   orator *n.* person who speaks well in public

   custom *n.* usual way of doing things

   eloquent *adj.* persuasive and expressive

   compound *n.* grounds surrounded by buildings

2. Have students say each word aloud.

3. Use the word in a sentence that defines the word.

DIFFERENTIATED INSTRUCTION

EL Extended Support—English Learners
Have students complete the **Reading and Vocabulary Warm-Ups** for this selection in the *Student Companion All-in-One Workbook* before they read. Assign the prereading pages and the adapted selection in the *Reader's Notebook: English Learner's Version*. Then, have students listen to portions of the selection in the *Student eText* or on the *Hear It!* CD-ROM.

L1 L2 Extended Support—Struggling Readers
Have students complete the **Reading and Vocabulary Warm-Ups** for this selection in the *Student Companion All-in-One Workbook* before they read. Assign the prereading pages and the adapted selection in the *Reader's Notebook: Adapted Version*. Then, have students listen to portions of the selection in the *Student eText* or on the *Hear It!* CD-ROM (adapted text).

Extended Support—Reluctant Readers
To build motivation and engagement before assigning the selection, have students read "Seeking Student Success," a thematically related selection in *Reality Central*. Then, use the questions at the conclusion of the related selection to guide discussion.

MULTIDRAFT READING

This icon ● marks natural pauses in the selection. To assist struggling readers and to deepen comprehension for all, assign the text in "chunks," separated by the icons, and apply multidraft reading protocols. For each reading, have students set the purpose indicated:

- **First reading:** Students should read the selection independently and think about its basic meaning.

- **Second reading:** Students should analyze the text's key ideas and details and its craft and structure, and respond to the side-column prompts.

- **Third reading:** Students should integrate knowledge and ideas, connect the text to other texts and to the world, and answer the end-of-selection questions.

For more guidance, refer to the *Classroom Strategies and Teaching Routines* card on multidraft reading.

Why the TORTOISE'S SHELL Is Not SMOOTH
— Chinua Achebe

💬 VOCABULARY DEVELOPMENT

Thematic Vocabulary: The Big Question
As students are discussing "Why the Tortoise's Shell Is Not Smooth," encourage them to use the thematic vocabulary presented in Introducing the Big Question, pp. 612–613. You might encourage them with sentence starters like these:

1. Tortoise uses fine words to *influence* the birds to . . .
2. He wants to join their *community* because . . .
3. It takes the efforts of the whole *group* to make Tortoise . . .
4. The people of the sky think that the birds' *culture* includes . . .
5. The birds are angry at Tortoise because he *values* . . .

Low voices, broken now and again by singing, reached Okonkwo (ō kōn´ kwō) from his wives' huts as each woman and her children told folk stories. Ekwefi (e kwe´ fē) and her daughter, Ezinma (e zēn´ mä), sat on a mat on the floor. It was Ekwefi's turn to tell a story.

"Once upon a time," she began, "all the birds were invited to a feast in the sky. They were very happy and began to prepare themselves for the great day. They painted their bodies with red cam wood[1] and drew beautiful patterns on them with dye.

"Tortoise saw all these preparations and soon discovered what it all meant. Nothing that happened in the world of the animals ever escaped his notice; he was full of cunning. As soon as he heard of the great feast in the sky his throat began to itch at the very thought. There was a famine in those days and Tortoise had not eaten a good meal for two moons. His body rattled like a piece of dry stick in his empty shell. So he began to plan how he would go to the sky."

"But he had no wings," said Ezinma.

"Be patient," replied her mother. "That is the story. Tortoise had no wings, but he went to the birds and asked to be allowed to go with them.

"'We know you too well,' said the birds when they had heard him. 'You are full of cunning and you are ungrateful. If we allow you to come with us you will soon begin your mischief.'

" 'You do not know me,' said Tortoise. 'I am a changed man. I have learned that a man who makes trouble for others is also making it for himself.'

---

1. **red cam** (cam) **wood** hard West African wood that makes red dye.

> **❶ Purpose for Reading**
> What purpose for reading does this story's title present?

> **◄ Vocabulary**
> **cunning** (kun´ iŋ) *n.*
> slyness; deception
>
> **famine** (fam´ in) *n.*
> shortage of food

> **❷ Comprehension**
> Why is the tortoise hungry?

❶ Purpose for Reading

1. Have a volunteer read the story title aloud. Point out the word *why* and **ask** students what clue it offers to the story's purpose.

   Answer: The word *why* suggests that the story will answer a question.

2. **Ask** the Purpose for Reading question.

   Possible response: Students may say the purpose for reading suggested by the title is to get information.

3. **Ask** students how the story's purpose might direct their reading purpose.

   Answer: It gives readers an idea of the kind of information the text will contain.

4. Give students a copy of **Reading Skill Graphic Organizer A** for "Why the Tortoise Shell Is Not Smooth" and have them fill it in as they preview the text.

❷ Comprehension

Answer: There has been a famine.

🔅 DIFFERENTIATED INSTRUCTION

Strategy for Less-Proficient Readers
Prepare an Anticipation Guide (*Professional Development Guidebook*, p. 38) with the following statements:

- Most tales in the oral tradition have a stated or implied moral.
- The animal characters in folk tales are recognizable as animals.
- Folk tales reflect the customs and values of the culture they come from.

Give students a copy of the prepared **Guide** and have them mark their responses in the Me column. Have students discuss the statements in pairs and mark their responses in the Group column. After they're done reading the selection, have students fill in the After Reading column.

Video

Watch the Background Video online!

Audio

Selection audio is available in the *Student eText* and on the *Hear It!* CD-ROM.

Spiral Review

Plot

1. Remind students that they learned about the concept of plot in the Unit 5 Focus on Craft and Structure (pp. 628–631).

2. Ask the Spiral Review question.

Possible response: Student responses will vary but might include the evidence that Tortoise has a reputation for causing mischief and having a "sweet tongue."

❸ Analyze

1. As they read the bracketed text, have students note how precisely the feast is described. **Ask:** Why might a storyteller include names of specific foods in a tale?

Possible response: The foods would be familiar to the audience that the storyteller is addressing. The specific foods also let the reader know which culture the story comes from.

2. Ask: What special preparations are made for this feast?

Possible response: The birds decorate their bodies with dye. The hosts bring out several courses freshly cooked, and one of the hosts tastes the food in each pot to make sure that it is good enough for the guests.

Spiral Review
PLOT What evidence suggests that the story might involve trickery?

Vocabulary ▶

orator (ôr´ ət ər) *n.* person who speaks well in public

custom (kus´ təm) *n.* usual way of doing something; habit

eloquent (el´ ə kwənt) *adj.* persuasive and expressive

"Tortoise had a sweet tongue, and within a short time all the birds agreed that he was a changed man, and they each gave him a feather, with which he made two wings.

"At last the great day came and Tortoise was the first to arrive at the meeting place. When all the birds had gathered together, they set off in a body. Tortoise was very happy as he flew among the birds, and he was soon chosen as the man to speak for the party because he was a great orator.

"'There is one important thing which we must not forget,' he said as they flew on their way. 'When people are invited to a great feast like this, they take new names for the occasion. Our hosts in the sky will expect us to honor this age-old custom.'

"None of the birds had heard of this custom but they knew that Tortoise, in spite of his failings in other directions, was a widely traveled man who knew the customs of different peoples. And so they each took a new name. When they had all taken, Tortoise also took one. He was to be called *All of you.* •

"At last the party arrived in the sky and their hosts were very happy to see them. Tortoise stood up in his many-colored plumage and thanked them for their invitation. His speech was so eloquent that all the birds were glad they had brought him, and nodded their heads in approval of all he said. Their hosts took him as the king of the birds, especially as he looked somewhat different from the others.

"After kola nuts had been presented and eaten, the people of the sky set before their guests the most delectable dishes Tortoise had ever seen or dreamed of. The soup was brought out hot from the fire and in the very pot in which it had been cooked. It was full of meat and fish. Tortoise began to sniff aloud. There was pounded yam and also yam pottage[2] cooked with palm oil and fresh fish. There were also pots of palm wine. When everything had been set before the guests, one of the people of the sky came forward and tasted a little from each pot. He then invited the birds to eat. But Tortoise jumped to his feet and asked: 'For whom have you prepared this feast?'

---

2. **yam** (yam) **pottage** (pät´ ij) *n.* thick stew made of sweet potatoes.

"'For all of you,' replied the man.

"Tortoise turned to the birds and said: 'You remember that my name is *All of you.* The custom here is to serve the spokesman first and the others later. They will serve you when I have eaten.'

"He began to eat and the birds grumbled angrily. The people of the sky thought it must be their custom to leave all the food for their king. And so Tortoise ate the best part of the food and then drank two pots of palm wine, so that he was full of food and drink and his body grew fat enough to fill out his shell.

"The birds gathered round to eat what was left and to peck at the bones he had thrown all about the floor. Some of them were too angry to eat. They chose to fly home on an empty stomach. But before they left, each took back the feather he had lent to Tortoise. And there he stood in his hard shell full of food and wine but without any wings to fly home. He asked the birds to take a message for his wife, but they all refused. In the end Parrot, who had felt more angry than the others, suddenly changed his mind and agreed to take the message.

"'Tell my wife,' said Tortoise, 'to bring out all the soft things in my house and cover the compound with them so that I can jump down from the sky without very great danger.'

"Parrot promised to deliver the message, and then flew away. But when he reached Tortoise's house he told his wife to bring out all the hard things in the house.

Personification
What human qualities does Tortoise have?

◀ **Vocabulary**
compound (käm´ pound) *n.* grounds surrounded by buildings

"When people are invited to a great feast like this, they take new names for the occasion."

PART 2 • Why the Tortoise's Shell Is Not Smooth **671**

❹ Personification

1. Remind students that when animal characters are personified, they are shown to have human traits and behaviors.

2. Have students read the bracketed passage, which begins on the previous page. Instruct them to look for statements that describe Tortoise directly and then to look for characteristics revealed by his words and actions. **Ask** the Personification question.

Possible response: Tortoise is "full of cunning," and the birds say he is ungrateful. He is known for making mischief. He is a gifted speaker and persuades the birds to trust him. He is treacherous and betrays the birds' trust by trickery. He is also a glutton.

❺ Connecting to the Big Question

1. Tell students to imagine a friend has tricked them. Discuss what students might do. Will they confront the friend and ask him or her to change behavior? Will they end the friendship in anger? Are there other choices?

2. Have students read the second bracketed passage on this page. **Ask:** How would you react if you saw Tortoise act this way? Explain.

Possible response: Students may say that they would try to stop Tortoise, either verbally or physically. Others may say that they too would fly home in anger, even if it meant going hungry.

3. Ask: How does the community respond to Tortoise's actions? How is the community shaping Tortoise, and is he shaping the community?

Possible response: The community gets angry at Tortoise but does nothing to stop his bad behavior. The community shapes Tortoise by its lack of reaction. He shapes the community by not caring about its feelings.

🌊 **FLUENCY**

Distribute copies of this page, and pair students. Have listeners mark text with which readers struggle. Circulate to monitor students' fluency, then collect the marked-up pages. Review difficult words and passages, such as these:

• If students stumble over the use of two types of quotation marks (" '), clarify that there is a story within a story. Remind students that on the first page of the story the people are speaking and after this, the animals are

speaking. The regular quotation marks show that Ekwefi is telling the story. The single quotation marks show that she is quoting the words of an animal character.

• If students stumble over the italicized phrase *All of you* on the previous page, clarify that this is the name the Tortoise wants to use. Model how to flow the individual words into a phrase, using names such as Betty Sue or James Lee as examples.

6 Purpose for Reading

1. Have students review the purpose they set before reading the tale, then have them read the final story paragraph.

2. **Ask** students to write a few sentences to answer the Purpose for Reading question. Use the following sentence starters as a guide.

   1. My purpose was to find out what explanation would be given for the appearance of the tortoise's shell. What I learned was . . .

      Possible response: that his own cunning got the best of him.

   2. My purpose was to read an entertaining story. I liked this folk tale because . . . OR I didn't enjoy the folk tale because . . .

      Possible response: I find animal stories amusing OR I do not like animal stories.

☑ ASSESS

Language Study

Vocabulary

1. orator
2. eloquent
3. famine
4. cunning
5. compound

Word Study

Part A

Sample answers:

The suffix -*ary* means "related to" or "connected with." A *primary* event or reason is <u>related to</u> being first in order or importance. A *legendary* character is one <u>connected</u> with a legend.

Part B

Sample answers:

1. Yes, the suffix -*ary* means "related to" and *cautionary* means "related to caution."

2. Yes, the suffix -*ary* means "connected with" and science fiction authors have grand visions of the future or imaginary places. Their stories are <u>connected</u> to these visions.

And so she brought out her husband's hoes, machetes, spears, guns, and even his cannon. Tortoise looked down from the sky and saw his wife bringing things out, but it was too far to see what they were. When all seemed ready he let himself go. He fell and fell and fell until he began to fear that he would never stop falling. And then like the sound of his cannon he crashed on the compound."

"Did he die?" asked Ezinma.

"No," replied Ekwefi. "His shell broke into pieces. But there was a great medicine man in the neighborhood. Tortoise's wife sent for him and he gathered all the bits of shell and stuck them together. That is why Tortoise's shell is not smooth."

Purpose for Reading
Did you achieve your purpose for reading this folk tale? Why or why not?

Language Study

Vocabulary The words listed below appear in the folk tale. Use one of the words to complete each *analogy* item below. In an analogy, pairs of words share a relationship.

cunning   famine   orator   eloquent   compound

1. *speech* is to *speaker* as *oration* is to _____
2. *tiresome* is to *boring* as *persuasive* is to _____
3. *eating* is to *feast* as *starving* is to _____
4. *attractiveness* is to *beauty* as *craftiness* is to _____
5. *tree* is to *forest* as *building* is to _____

WORD STUDY
The **suffix -*ary*** means "related to" or "connected with." In this folk tale, the birds think it is **customary**, or related to the usual practice, for the king to eat all the food at a feast.

Word Study

Part A Explain how the **suffix -*ary*** contributes to the meaning of *primary* and *legendary*. Consult a dictionary if necessary.

Part B Explain your answer to each question.

1. Does a *cautionary* tale instruct you to be careful?
2. Are science fiction authors likely to be *visionary* writers?

Literary Analysis

Possible responses appear below. Check to be sure students support their responses with evidence from the text.

1. **(a)** Some students may say their purpose was to read an entertaining story. Others may say that they wanted to learn the explanation the folk tale gives for the appearance of a tortoise's shell. **(b)** One's purpose would be to learn the scientific facts about the scaled plates of the tortoise shell.

2. The title indicates that the tale will offer an explanation for the appearance of a tortoise's shell. The photos of tortoise shells emphasize the focus of the folk tale.

3. **(a)** Tortoise wants to go to the feast because he has not eaten in two months. **(b)** The birds do not trust Tortoise.

4. **(a)** The birds decide to help Tortoise because he convinces them, by using his "sweet tongue," that he is a "changed man." **(b)** The birds choose Tortoise because he is an eloquent speaker. **(c)** Tortoise takes advantage of his privilege by eating the best part of the food.

Literary Analysis

Key Ideas and Details

1. **Purpose for Reading (a)** What was your purpose for reading this folk tale? **(b)** How might your purpose be different if you were reading a nonfiction article about tortoises?

2. **Purpose for Reading** How well did previewing the title and pictures give you a sense of what the folk tale would be about? Explain.

3. **(a) Analyze Causes and Effects:** Why does Tortoise want to go to the great feast? **(b) Make Inferences:** Why do the birds not want to take him at first?

4. **(a) Analyze Causes and Effects:** Why do the birds eventually decide to help Tortoise go to the feast? **(b) Deduce:** Why do they choose him to speak for the group? **(c) Assess:** How does Tortoise make use of this privilege?

5. **(a) Interpret:** Explain how Tortoise's new name allows him to eat before the birds eat. **(b) Draw Conclusions:** What lesson do the birds learn about Tortoise?

Craft and Structure

6. **Personification** Complete a chart like the one on the right to analyze one of the animal characters. Use details from the text to support your entries.

7. **Personification (a)** In the text, find three examples of personification in the description of Tortoise's character. **(b)** What effect does the use of personification have on the story?

Integration of Knowledge and Ideas

8. At the end of the folk tale, the birds learn that Tortoise has not changed. **(a) Interpret:** Based on the ending, what lesson do you think this folk tale teaches? **(b) Hypothesize:** Why do you think the author has written about this lesson? Cite details from the text to support your answer.

9. **How much do our communities shape us?**
   (a) Synthesize: What unwritten community rules does Tortoise break? Explain. **(b) Speculate:** How do you think the birds will treat Tortoise after this incident? Explain.

Character's Name:
Animal Qualities:
Human Qualities:

ACADEMIC VOCABULARY

As you write and speak about "Why the Tortoise's Shell Is Not Smooth," use the words related to communities that you explored on page 613 of this text.

9. **How much do our communities shape us?**
   (a) Tortoise breaks the rules against greed and selfishness. **(b)** The birds will treat Tortoise with anger and suspicion because he has tricked them for his own gain.

---

5. **(a)** His new name, "All of you," is the answer to the question, "For whom have you prepared this feast?" **(b)** The birds learn that they should never have trusted Tortoise as he is cunning and greedy.

6. Tortoise: Animal Qualities—suffers from famine; body rattles in his empty shell; has no wings; grows fat and fills out his shell; Human Qualities—cunning and ungrateful; known for mischief; great orator; deceives birds

7. **(a)** Examples of personification include: "he was full of cunning" (p. 669) "Tortoise had a sweet tongue" (p. 670) "he was a great orator" (p. 670) **(b)** Personification makes the story easier to connect to, by making the animal characters familiar.

8. **(a)** This folk tale teaches a lesson about not believing everything you hear. **(b)** The author writes about this lesson to show how important it is not to be greedy and selfish within a community. Example: Tortoise plays a mean and selfish trick on the birds, who then make Tortoise suffer.

Online Writer's Notebook

Students can use the Online Writer's Notebook to record all responses.

Conventions

1. Introduce the skill.
2. Discuss the definitions.

Think Aloud: Model the Skill

Say to students:

> I use a variety of sentences when I write. I choose simple sentences when I want my meaning to be as clear as possible. I choose complex sentences when I want to stress one main idea but also show its connection to related details.

Practice A

1. Independent clause: *Tortoise longed to join the feast* Dependent clause: *who was very hungry.* Complex sentence
2. Independent clause: *Tortoise tried to trick the birds.* Simple sentence
3. Independent clause: *Tortoise crashed.* Independent clause: *his shell broke.* Compound sentence

Reading Application
Sample answers:

Simple: Tortoise began to sniff aloud. Compound: At last the party arrived in the sky and their hosts were very happy to see them. Complex: Tortoise was very happy as he flew among the birds, and he was soon chosen as the man to speak for the party because he was a great orator.

Practice B Sample answers:

1. The people of the sky invited the birds to a feast.
2. The birds went to the feast, and Tortoise joined them.
3. Tortoise, who thought of a sneaky plan, changed his name to "All of you."

Writing Application
Sample answers:

Tortoise is starving. (simple) He joins the birds for their feast, but he tricks them and gets all the food. (compound) By tricking Tortoise into falling from the sky, the birds take revenge. (complex) A medicine man repairs Tortoise's shell, which is no longer smooth. (complex)

Conventions: Simple, Compound, and Complex Sentences

Sentences can be classified according to the number and kinds of their clauses—groups of words with their own subjects and verbs.

An **independent clause** can stand alone as a sentence because it expresses a complete thought. A **dependent clause** cannot stand alone because it does not express a complete thought. A dependent clause may begin with a relative pronoun, such as *who, which,* or *that.* Relative pronouns indicate that the clause may not be able to stand alone. This chart shows how clauses are used to create the three types of sentence structures.

Simple Sentences	Compound Sentences	Complex Sentences
A single independent clause	Two or more independent clauses	One independent clause and one or more dependent clauses
The dog barked. He and I walked home. The girl in the front row is the class president.	Brad cooked the meal, Kai set the table, and I washed dishes. I like baseball, but he prefers soccer.	The other travelers, (who were very tired), climbed onto the bus. (Because the storm came), our game was postponed.

Practice A
Copy each sentence, underlining independent clauses and circling dependent clauses. Then tell what kind of sentence each is.

1. Tortoise, who was very hungry, longed to join the feast.
2. Tortoise tried to trick the birds.
3. Tortoise crashed, and his shell broke.

Reading Application In the folk tale, find and record a simple, a compound, and a complex sentence.

Practice B
Add to each group of words to make the kind of sentence indicated.

1. The people of the sky (simple)
2. The birds went to the feast (compound)
3. who thought of a sneaky plan (complex)

Writing Application Write a brief summary of "Why the Tortoise's Shell Is Not Smooth." Include simple, compound, and complex sentences.

674 UNIT 5 • How much do our communities shape us?

➤ EXTEND THE LESSON

Sentence Modeling
Use this sentence from "Why the Tortoise's Shell Is Not Smooth."

> *If we allow you to come with us you will soon begin your mischief.*

Remind students of the lesson on sentence types. Ask students what they notice about the sentence. Elicit from them that the sentence is a complex sentence. Then, ask what else students notice. (A subordinate clause comes before the independent clause, explaining why the birds do not want the tortoise to come with them.)

Have students imitate the sentence in a sentence on a topic of their own choosing, matching each grammatical and stylistic feature discussed. Collect the sentences, and share them with the class.

Writing to Sources

Informative Text Write an **invitation** to the feast in the sky in "Why Tortoise's Shell Is Not Smooth." Choose the best format for your invitation. For example, you may write a letter, create a card, or develop a poster. Follow these steps to include important information:

- Review the folk tale to find details to include in your invitation.
- Identify the event and explain its purpose.
- Include the date, time, and location of the event.
- Provide directions for getting to the location.
- Ask your guests to let you know if they will attend.
- Include a phone number or an e-mail address for replies.

Grammar Application Proofread your invitation, and correct any grammatical errors you find.

Speaking and Listening

Comprehension and Collaboration With a group, present a **dramatic reading** of "Why the Tortoise's Shell Is Not Smooth." Act out the scene in which Tortoise asks the birds if he can go with them to the feast.

Follow these steps to complete the assignment:

- Assign a role to each member of your group.
- Act out the parts of the characters using exact words from the folk tale.
- Practice reading fluently and with appropriate pacing, intonation, and expression.
- Vary the tone and volume of your voice to show different levels of feeling. Use gestures to bring the words to life.
- Have classmates watch your dramatic reading and provide feedback. Then, practice and deliver the reading again.

Common Core State Standards

Writing
4. Produce clear and coherent writing in which the development, organization, and style are appropriate to task, purpose, and audience.

Speaking and Listening
6. Adapt speech to a variety of contexts and tasks, demonstrating command of formal English when indicated or appropriate.

Language
1. Demonstrate command of the conventions of standard English grammar and usage when writing or speaking.
3.a. Vary sentence patterns for meaning, reader/listener interest, and style.

Writing to Sources

1. Review the assignment, using the instruction on the student page.
2. To provide students with guidance in writing this informative text, give them the **Support for Writing** page for this selection in the *Student Companion All-in-One Workbook*.
3. Review the essential information that should appear on the invitation. Evaluate how well students describe the purpose of the meeting and if they include the details of date, time, and place.

Grammar Application

Have students check their drafts for the correct use of simple, compound, and complex sentences.

Six Traits Focus

✓	Ideas	✓	Word Choice
	Organization		Sentence Fluency
	Voice	✓	Conventions

Speaking and Listening

1. Review the assignment, using the instruction on the student page.
2. To support students' work on the assignment, have them complete the **Support for Extend Your Learning** page for this selection in the *Student Companion All-in-One Workbook*.

Daily Bellringer

For each class during which you will teach this selection, have students complete one of the five Sentence Combining activities for Week 30 in the *Daily Bellringer Activities*. You may wish to use additional activities that are applicable to this selection.

1 **How much do our communities shape us?**

1. Review the assignment with the class.

2. Remind students that there are many different types of communities—from families to neighborhoods and towns. Explain that the Big Question also relates to how individuals shape their communities and how communities shape individuals. Thinking about our own communities can help us understand this concept.

3. Remind students that when they read the texts, they should compare and contrast the similarities and differences between the two works.

MULTIDRAFT READING

To assist struggling readers and to deepen comprehension for all, apply multidraft reading protocols. For each reading, have students set the purpose indicated:

- **First reading:** Students should read the selection independently and think about its basic meaning.

- **Second reading:** Students should analyze the text's key ideas and details and its craft and structure, and respond to the side-column prompts.

- **Third reading:** Students should integrate knowledge and ideas, connect the text to other texts and to the world, and answer the end-of-selection questions.

For more guidance, refer to the *Classroom Strategies and Teaching Routines* card on multidraft reading.

 Comparing Texts

 How much do our communities shape us?

1 Explore the Big Question as you read these selections. Take notes on the ways that each main character reacts to being in an unusual community.

READING TO COMPARE FANTASY

Authors Rudyard Kipling and Roald Dahl use elements of fantasy in the stories that follow. You may be familiar with fantasy from movies about superheroes or space travel. Sometimes the fantastic elements or special effects dominate these movies. Other times, the fantastic elements serve as a background for stories about very believable human characters. When you finish reading these selections, compare how the two authors make use of fantasy.

SHORT STORY

Mowgli's Brothers
Rudyard Kipling

"Mowgli's Brothers"

Rudyard Kipling (1865–1936)
Rudyard Kipling was born in India to British parents. When he was very young, his Indian nurses told him folk tales that featured talking animals. These stories inspired the characters in many of Kipling's works, such as *The Jungle Book*, in which "Mowgli's Brothers" appears. As a boy, Kipling was sent to school in England. At age sixteen, he returned to India as a journalist. His work as a reporter, writer, and poet earned him the 1907 Nobel Prize.

FICTION

from *James and the Giant Peach*

Roald Dahl (1916–1990)
As a boy growing up in Wales, Roald Dahl loved books and stories. When he was eight years old, he began keeping a diary, and hid it in a box tied to a high tree branch. Years later, Dahl began his writing career by describing his experiences in the Royal Air Force during World War II. Dahl became interested in writing stories for children while making up bedtime stories for his daughters. "I have a passion for teaching kids to become readers," he once said.

676 UNIT 5 • How much do our communities shape us?

VOCABULARY DEVELOPMENT

Vocabulary Knowledge Rating
Create a **Vocabulary Knowledge Rating Chart** (*Professional Development Guidebook*, p. 33) featuring the words glossed in the selections:

quarry (p. 682)	dispute (p. 685)
fostering (p. 683)	intently (p. 690)
monotonous (p. 685)	colossal (p. 694)

Give students a copy of the chart, and read the words aloud. Have students mark their rating of each in the Before You Read column. To gauge how much instruction to provide, tally the students who think they know each word.

Explain that the words are defined in the margin at the point where they appear in the selection. Urge students to be alert to these words as they read the selections. They will rate their knowledge again when they finish.

② Comparing Elements of Fantasy

Fantasy is imaginative writing that contains elements not found in real life. Many fantastic stories balance imagination with realistic elements—characters, events, or situations that are true to life. These realistic details help readers relate to an inventive or unusual story. This blend of the impossible and the possible makes fantasy an enjoyable genre. Use these questions to identify the fantastic and realistic elements in the stories that follow:

- Which elements of the story's setting could not exist in real life? Which elements could exist?
- Which elements of a character's behavior could not occur in real life? Which elements could occur?
- Which elements of the situation could not happen in real life? Which elements could happen?

Create a chart like the one below. Then, record the fantastic and realistic elements in each story.

Title:		
Element	Fantastic or Realistic	Why?

Fantasy and Theme

Although works of fantasy are not realistic, they can convey serious **themes**. In "Mowgli's Brothers," for example, readers learn about the importance of belonging. In the excerpt from *James and the Giant Peach*, readers learn that communities can be imperfect but still valuable. The lessons are true even though the stories are not.

Fantasy elements can actually make a message stronger or highlight a story's lesson. Through the appeal of fantasy, the lessons reach readers effectively. As you read, think about each story's message and how the fantasy genre helps make the message understandable.

© **Common Core State Standards**

Reading Literature
2. Determine a theme or central idea of a text and how it is conveyed through particular details.

Writing
2.a. Introduce a topic; organize ideas, concepts, and information, using strategies such as definition, classification, comparison/contrast, and cause/effect.

② Comparing Elements of Fantasy

1. Introduce the skill.
2. Discuss the bulleted list.
3. Give students a copy of **Comparing Elements of Fantasy Graphic Organizer B** for "Mowgli's Brothers" and *James and the Giant Peach*. Tell them they will fill it in with details as they read.

Think Aloud: Model the Skill

Model a way to distinguish elements of fantasy from realistic elements. Say:

When I think about fantasy, I think about science fiction movies. When the movie has spaceships that travel from star to star, I know that the filmmakers are using fantasy elements. The technology does not yet exist. The aliens that space travelers meet are fantasy, too. Still, human characters in the movie have the same emotions as people today—concern for each other, curiosity, fear, and so on. Those are realistic elements.

Fantasy and Theme

1. Introduce the skill, using the instruction on the student page.
2. Point out that works of fantasy convey important themes about values, beliefs, and life lessons found in the culture from which the stories originate. Characters in works of fantasy may be talking animals or imaginary creatures, and they all play a part in teaching the lessons.
3. Explain that when characters place a special emphasis on aspects of behavior, they are reflecting the culture's beliefs about values and standards of acceptable behavior. Have students look for details that reflect the theme as they read each story.

📑 TEACHING RESOURCES

	Print	Digital
All Common Core Companion, pp. 15–27, 184–195	✓	✓
All Graphic Organizers A and B, "Mowgli's Brothers," *from* "James and the Giant Peach"		✓
All Online Student Edition eText with audio and video		✓
All Online Teacher Edition		✓
L1 Professional Development Guidebook, p. 33		✓
All Student Companion All-in-One Workbook, "Mowgli's Brothers," *from* "James and the Giant Peach"	✓	✓

① Background

Wolf Children There have been several verified stories of wolves raising human babies. The best documented case is of two children named Kamala and Amala, who were raised by wolves in India. Their story came to light in 1920, years after Kipling wrote of Mowgli, but this case suggests that Kipling knew of such incidents. Unlike in this fantasy story, children raised by wild animals are not healthy and wise, and they do not adjust well to being around humans. Some never learn to speak more than a few words. It is because we admire many traits of animals that we like to believe humans could live with animals and still be fully human, but this is not the case in real life.

② Activating Prior Knowledge

Have students discuss characteristics of wild animals that make them both interesting and scary. Discuss how students think these characteristics would be conveyed in dialogue, if animals could speak. Students will return to this discussion after they have read the story.

③ About the Selection

One evening, Father Wolf discovers a human child near his cave. Father Wolf brings the child inside and places him with the pups. Mother Wolf names the child Mowgli, but she knows that she cannot keep Mowgli unless the pack approves. With the help of Baloo the Bear and Bagheera the Black Panther, the child is accepted into the pack and begins a new life among the animals.

① ② ③ Mowgli's Brothers
— Rudyard Kipling

Now Chil the Kite[1] brings home the night
    That Mang the Bat sets free—
The herds are shut in byre[2] and hut
    For loosed till dawn are we.
This is the hour of pride and power,
    Talon and tush[3] and claw.
Oh hear the call!—Good hunting all
    That keep the Jungle Law!
        —Night-Song in the Jungle

---

1. **Kite** (kit) *n.* bird of the hawk family.
2. **byre** (bir) *n.* cow barn.
3. **tush** (tush) *n.* tusk.

678 UNIT 5 • How much do our communities shape us?

© TEXT COMPLEXITY **RUBRIC**

Mowgli's Brothers		
Qualitative Measures	**Context/Knowledge Demands**	Indian jungle, late 1800s 1 2 ③ 4 5
	Structure/Language Conventionality and Clarity	Long sentences, unusual syntax; challenging vocabulary 1 2 3 ④ 5
	Levels of Meaning/ Purpose/Concept Level	Challenging concept (wolves adopt human baby, form a government) 1 2 3 ④ 5
Quantitative Measures	**Text Length**	Word Count: 3,223
	Lexile	970L

It was seven o'clock of a very warm evening in the Seeonee hills[4] when Father Wolf woke up from his day's rest, scratched himself, yawned, and spread out his paws one after the other to get rid of the sleepy feeling in their tips. Mother Wolf lay with her big gray nose dropped across her four tumbling, squealing cubs, and the moon shone into the mouth of the cave where they all lived. "Augrh!" said Father Wolf, "it is time to hunt again"; and he was going to spring downhill when a little shadow with a bushy tail crossed the threshold and whined: "Good luck go with you, O Chief of the Wolves; and good luck and strong white teeth go with the noble children, that they may never forget the hungry in this world."

It was the jackal—Tabaqui the Dishlicker—and the wolves of India despise Tabaqui because he runs about making mischief, and telling tales, and eating rags and pieces of leather from the village rubbish-heaps. But they are afraid of him too, because Tabaqui, more than anyone else in the jungle, is apt to go mad, and then he forgets that he was ever afraid of anyone, and runs through the forest biting everything in his way. Even the tiger runs and hides when little Tabaqui goes mad, for madness is the most disgraceful thing that can overtake a wild creature. We call it hydrophobia, but they call it *dewanee*—the madness—and run.

"Enter, then, and look," said Father Wolf, stiffly; "but there is no food here."

"For a wolf, no," said Tabaqui; "but for so mean a person as myself a dry bone is a good feast. Who are we, the Gidur log [the jackal-people], to pick and choose?" He scuttled to the back of the cave, where he found the bone of a buck with some meat on it, and sat cracking the end merrily.

"All thanks for this good meal," he said, licking his lips. "How beautiful are the noble children! How large are their eyes! And so young too! Indeed, indeed, I might have remembered that the children of Kings are men from the beginning."

Now, Tabaqui knew as well as anyone else that there is nothing so unlucky as to compliment children to their faces; and it pleases him to see Mother and Father Wolf look uncomfortable.

4. **Seeonee** (sē ō′ nē) **hills** hills in central India.

Elements of Fantasy
What element of fantasy is introduced in this paragraph? Explain.

Elements of Fantasy
What is fantastic about Tabaqui's behavior? What is realistic about it?

6 Comprehension
Why do the wolves despise Tabaqui?

© TEXT COMPLEXITY **READER AND TASK SUGGESTIONS**

Mowgli's Brothers

Preparing to Read the Text
- Use the Background information on the previous page to explain that this story is a fantasy.
- Use the About the Selection note on the previous page to explain how this fantasy creates an animal society of families, government, and laws.
- Guide students to use Multidraft Reading strategies (TE p. 676).

Leveled Tasks
Levels of Meaning If students will have difficulty with concepts, review the Comparing Elements of Fantasy feature and the Think Aloud note on TE p. 677 to discuss how the animals in this story mirror human behavior. *Synthesizing* If students will not have difficulty with the concepts in this story, discuss how all cultures have laws that people need to follow for a community to function properly. Discuss how the students' community's laws or rules compare to those in the story.

---

4 Elements of Fantasy

1. **Ask** what elements of fantasy might be found in an animal story.

   Possible response: Animals talking, acting, and thinking like humans.

2. **Ask** students the first Elements of Fantasy question.

   Answer: The wolves talk. In real life, animals do not talk.

5 Elements of Fantasy

1. Explain that jackals are wolf-like animals (although they are smaller than wolves) that usually follow larger hunting animals, such as tigers, and scavenge whatever leftovers the larger animals leave behind. They have a reputation as being cowards, though this reputation has been exaggerated. They smell bad, and it is said that their cry is distressing to humans. Tell students to be alert to details about Tabaqui that reflect this perception of the jackal.

2. **Ask** students the second Elements of Fantasy question.

   Possible response: The fantastical elements are that he talks, that he believes in luck (or bad luck), and that he enjoys making the wolves uncomfortable by trying to bring bad luck to them. The realistic response element is that, like a real jackal, he is getting leftovers from a larger hunter.

3. Explain that hydrophobia—"the madness" described here—is the disease rabies. The disease is transmitted through the bite of an infected animal, which is why the animals fear the bite of a jackal when it goes mad.

6 Comprehension

Possible answer: He makes mischief, he tells tales, and he eats rags and pieces of leather from the village rubbish-heaps.

Spiral Review

Folk Tale

1. Remind students that they studied the concept of folk tales in the Unit 5 Focus on Craft and Structure (pp. 628–631).

2. **Ask** the Spiral Review question.

   Possible responses: One element that this story shares with other folk tales is the setting: challenging landscapes, rugged mountains, darkness and light, and so on. Another element might be the characters; there are talking animals, good and evil characters, as well as characters with heroic traits.

❼ Elements of Fantasy

1. Point out how Tabaqui threatens Father Wolf, in offering to tell Shere Khan of the wolf's "gratitude." Relate that writers often use fictional and even fantastic elements to reveal things that are real. Here, we see a realistic depiction of a nasty tattletale, even though it is through the fantasy element of a talking animal. Encourage students to think about how fantasy elements can reflect real life.

2. **Ask** students the Elements of Fantasy question.

   Answer: While having animals talk is fantastic, the other behaviors are realistic, the description of the noise the tiger makes while hunting seems realistic, and it is realistic that hearing a tiger would make people run.

3. Explain that, until recently, the term *man* was used to mean "human." The reference to "Man" in this passage means all human beings, male and female, young and old.

4. **Ask** students what clues are given on this page that Shere Khan is the "bad guy" of the story.

   Answer: Shere Khan is hunting Man, which is breaking the Law of the Jungle.

Spiral Review
Folk Tale Although this story does not come from the oral tradition, what elements does it share with folk tales? Explain.

Elements of Fantasy
Do you think the behavior described in this paragraph is fantastic or realistic? Explain.

❼

Tabaqui sat still, rejoicing in the mischief that he had made: then he said spitefully:

"Shere Khan, the Big One, has shifted his hunting-grounds. He will hunt among these hills for the next moon, so he has told me."

Shere Khan was the tiger who lived near the Waingunga River, twenty miles away.

"He has no right!" Father Wolf began angrily—"By the Law of the Jungle he has no right to change his quarters without due warning. He will frighten every head of game within ten miles, and I—I have to kill for two, these days."

"His mother did not call him Lungri [the Lame One] for nothing," said Mother Wolf, quietly. "He has been lame in one foot from his birth. That is why he has only killed cattle. Now the villagers of the Waingunga are angry with him, and he has come here to make our villagers angry. They will scour the Jungle for him when he is far away, and we and our children must run when the grass is set alight. Indeed, we are very grateful to Shere Khan!"

"Shall I tell him of your gratitude?" said Tabaqui.

"Out!" snapped Father Wolf. "Out and hunt with thy master. Thou hast done harm enough for one night."

"I go," said Tabaqui, quietly. "Ye can hear Shere Khan below in the thickets. I might have saved myself the message."

Father Wolf listened, and below in the valley that ran down to a little river, he heard the dry, angry, snarly, singsong whine of a tiger who has caught nothing and does not care if all the Jungle knows it.

"The fool!" said Father Wolf. "To begin a night's work with that noise! Does he think that our buck are like his fat Waingunga bullocks?"[5]

"H'sh! It is neither bullock nor buck he hunts tonight," said Mother Wolf. "It is Man." The whine had changed to a sort of humming purr that seemed to come from every quarter of the compass. It was the noise that bewilders woodcutters and gypsies sleeping in the open, and makes them run sometimes into the very mouth of the tiger.

"Man!" said Father Wolf, showing all his white teeth. "Faugh! Are there not enough beetles and frogs in the tanks

---

5. **bullocks** (bool′ əks) *n.* steers.

🗨 THINK ALOUD

Indirect Characterization

Model the way to interpret indirect characterization (introduced on page 28) with this think aloud. Say to students:

I'm going to show you how I use indirect characterization to gain clues about a character. When Tabaqui tells Father and Mother Wolf that Shere Khan has come to hunt in their hills, Father Wolf becomes angry. He complains that Shere Khan scares all the game away. In doing so, he shows

he has no regard for the law of the jungle. From these comments, I conclude that Shere Khan is only interested in his own desires. This idea is confirmed a few paragraphs later, when Father Wolf reveals that Shere Khan even eats humans, another violation of the jungle law. Clearly, Shere Khan is a selfish character with no regard for the other animals or the law.

that he must eat Man and on our ground too!"

The Law of the Jungle, which never orders anything without a reason, forbids every beast to eat Man except when he is killing to show his children how to kill, and then he must hunt outside the hunting-grounds of his pack or tribe. The real reason for this is that man-killing means, sooner or later, the arrival of white men on elephants, with guns, and hundreds of brown men with gongs and rockets and torches. Then everybody in the jungle suffers. The reason the beasts give among themselves is that Man is the weakest and most defenseless of all living things, and it is unsportsmanlike to touch him. They say too—and it is true—that man-eaters become mangy,[6] and lose their teeth.

The purr grew louder, and ended in the full-throated "Aaarh!" of the tiger's charge.

Then there was a howl—an untigerish howl—from Shere Khan. "He has missed," said Mother Wolf. "What is it?"

Father Wolf ran out a few paces and heard Shere Khan muttering and mumbling savagely, as he tumbled about in the scrub.

"The fool has had no more sense than to jump at a woodcutter's campfire, and has burned his feet," said Father Wolf, with a grunt. "Tabaqui is with him."

"Something is coming up hill," said Mother Wolf, twitching one ear. "Get ready."

The bushes rustled a little in the thicket, and Father Wolf dropped with his haunches under him, ready for his leap. Then, if you had been watching, you would have seen the most wonderful thing in the world—the wolf checked in mid-spring. He made his bound before he saw what it was he was jumping at, and then he tried to stop himself. The result was that he shot up straight into the air for four or five feet, landing almost where he left ground.

"Man!" he snapped. "A man's cub. Look!"

Directly in front of him, holding on by a low branch, stood a naked brown baby who could just walk—as soft and as dimpled a little atom[7] as ever came to a wolf's cave at night. He looked up into Father Wolf's face, and laughed.

Elements of Fantasy
Do you think Father Wolf's behavior here could occur in real life? Why or why not?

❾ Comprehension
Why does the Law of the Jungle generally forbid man-killing?

6. **mangy** (mān′ jē) *adj.* having mange, a skin disease of mammals that causes sores and loss of hair.
7. **atom** (at′ əm) *n.* tiny piece of matter.

❽ Elements of Fantasy

1. Point out that before the "man cub" appears, Shere Khan has leapt into a woodcutter's campfire. **Ask** students what this suggests about the man cub.

   Answer: Adults must have made the fire, perhaps the child's parents. The adults must have run away, leaving behind the child.

2. **Ask** students the Elements of Fantasy question: Do you think Father Wolf's behavior here could occur in real life? Why or why not?

   Possible responses: Yes, a wolf would want to spring on anything that is attacking. It might be possible that real wolves, like the wolf here, would not want to kill humans. (Some students may even have seen pets leap in the air and then change their minds. It is not that uncommon a behavior.)

❾ Comprehension

Answer: If animals kill man, then white men will come with guns, and brown men will come with gongs and rockets and torches. Also, it makes the man-eater mangy.

⚏ DIFFERENTIATED INSTRUCTION

Strategies for Special-Needs Students
To help students picture the animal characters, show them illustrations of the animals in the story: wolf, jackal, tiger, brown bear, and black panther. After displaying each picture and identifying the type of animal it shows, call on the students to connect the picture to the correct character. Have a volunteer write the correct name (or names, in the case of wolves) under the picture. Display the pictures for students to use as references.

EL Support for English Learners
Students may need help with the formal language and inverted sentence structure of some of the dialogue. Explain that English once had different forms of "you." *Ye* is the plural form of *you*, spoken to two or more. *Thou* is *you* spoken to an individual. *Thy* means *your*.

10 **Connecting to the Big Question**

1. Remind students of the Big Question by pointing out that wolves are social animals, meaning that they live in groups and depend on each other, whereas tigers are solitary hunters.

2. Have students re-read the bracketed passage. **Ask** them to summarize what takes place.

   Answer: Shere Khan comes to the wolves' den to demand the man-cub. Father Wolf refuses to yield him, claiming that he only obeys the commands of the Head of the Pack. Shere Khan angrily repeats his claim to the boy.

3. **Ask** students what Shere Khan's speech reveals about his attitude toward the wolves.

   Possible response: His words show that he thinks he is superior to the wolves.

4. **Ask** students on what Shere Khan and Father Wolf base their claims to the boy. Have them explain how these reasons reflect the nature of tigers and wolves.

   Possible responses: Shere Khan seems to think that he has a right to the boy because he is superior. Since tigers are solitary hunters, it is logical that they would be concerned only about themselves. Father Wolf bases his claim on the law of the jungle. As social animals, wolves learn to follow rules.

Tell students to look as they read for more clues about the role of the Pack in the wolves' lives.

Vocabulary ▶
quarry (kwôr´ ē) *n.* prey; anything being hunted or pursued

10

"Is that a man's cub?" said Mother Wolf. "I have never seen one. Bring it here."

A wolf accustomed to moving his own cubs can, if necessary, mouth an egg without breaking it, and though Father Wolf's jaws closed right on the child's back not a tooth even scratched the skin, as he laid it down among the cubs.

"How little! How naked, and—how bold!" said Mother Wolf, softly. The baby was pushing his way between the cubs to get close to the warm hide. "Ahai! He is taking his meal with the others. And so this is a man's cub. Now, was there ever a wolf that could boast of a man's cub among her children?"

"I have heard now and again of such a thing, but never in our Pack or in my time," said Father Wolf. "He is altogether without hair, and I could kill him with a touch of my foot. But see, he looks up and is not afraid."

The moonlight was blocked out of the mouth of the cave, for Shere Khan's great square head and shoulders were thrust into the entrance. Tabaqui, behind him, was squeaking: "My lord, my lord, it went in here!"

"Shere Khan does us great honor," said Father Wolf, but his eyes were very angry. "What does Shere Khan need?"

"My quarry. A man's cub went this way," said Shere Khan. "Its parents have run off. Give it to me."

Shere Khan had jumped at a woodcutter's campfire, as Father Wolf had said, and was furious from the pain of his burned feet. But Father Wolf knew that the mouth of the cave was too narrow for a tiger to come in by. Even where he was, Shere Khan's shoulders and forepaws were cramped for want of room, as a man's would be if he tried to fight in a barrel.

"The Wolves are a free people," said Father Wolf. "They take orders from the Head of the Pack, and not from any striped cattle-killer. The man's cub is ours—to kill if we choose."

"Ye choose and ye do not choose! What talk is this of choosing? By the bull that I killed, am I to stand nosing into your dog's den for my fair dues? It is I, Shere Khan, who speak!"

The tiger's roar filled the cave with thunder. Mother Wolf shook herself clear of the cubs and sprang forward, her eyes, like two green moons in the darkness, facing the blazing eyes of Shere Khan.

"And it is I, Raksha [The Demon], who answer. The man's cub is mine, Lungri—mine to me! He shall not be killed. He shall live to run with the Pack and to hunt with the Pack; and in the end, look you, hunter of little naked cubs— frog-eater—fish-killer— he shall hunt thee! Now get hence, or by the Sambhur that I killed (I eat no starved cattle), back thou goest to thy mother, burned beast of the Jungle, lamer than ever thou camest into the world! Go!" •

Father Wolf looked on amazed. He had almost forgotten the days when he won Mother Wolf in fair fight from five other wolves, when she ran in the Pack and was not called The Demon for compliment's sake. Shere Khan might have faced Father Wolf, but he could not stand up against Mother Wolf, for he knew that where he was she had all the advantage of the ground, and would fight to the death. So he backed out of the cave-mouth growling, and when he was clear he shouted:

"Each dog barks in his own yard! We will see what the Pack will say to this fostering of man-cubs. The cub is mine, and to my teeth he will come in the end, O bush-tailed thieves!"

Mother Wolf threw herself down panting among the cubs, and Father Wolf said to her gravely:

"Shere Khan speaks this much truth. The cub must be shown to the Pack. Wilt thou still keep him, Mother?"

"Keep him!" she gasped. "He came naked, by night, alone and very hungry; yet he was not afraid! Look, he has pushed one of my babies to one side already. And that lame butcher would have killed him and would have run off to the Waingunga while the villagers here hunted through all our

11 ▲ Critical Viewing
Do you think this tiger is friendly to humans? Why or why not?

◄ Vocabulary
fostering (fôs′ tər iŋ) *n.* taking care of

12 Comprehension
How does Mother Wolf respond to Shere Kahn's demands?

PART 2 • Mowgli's Brothers **683**

11 Critical Viewing
Possible answer: No, it is not friendly to humans. The tiger looks as if it is from the wild, and wild tigers are not friendly.

12 Comprehension
Answer: Mother Wolf becomes enraged by Shere Khan's demands. She springs forward and insults and threatens the tiger.

⁙ DIFFERENTIATED INSTRUCTION

Strategy for Less Proficient Readers
The inverted sentence structure that Mother Wolf uses in her speech at the top of the page might give students some difficulty. Assist them by pointing to an earlier example; on page 679, Tabaqui says "How beautiful are the noble children!" Explain that this can be "translated" into a more normal sentence pattern by saying "The noble children are beautiful!" Then, direct them to Mother Wolf's statement on this page that reads "back thou goest to thy mother." First, explain that *goest* is an old-fashioned form of "go." Then, call on volunteers to "translate" this sentence into normal word order. Guide them to see that the sentence means the same as "Go back to your mother." Have students look for and interpret other examples of inverted sentences in the story.

PART 2 • Mowgli's Brothers **683**

⓲ Elements of Fantasy

1. Remind students that in a fantasy, completely unrealistic details, such as talking animals, can seem quite normal.

2. Point out that when wolves howl, they really are communicating, although they are not using words. Discuss ways humans communicate without words or sounds. Examples are waving, raising hands in class, winking, nodding "yes," shaking their heads "no," saying "mmmm," and other body language and non-verbal messages. Discuss how not using words limits what can be communicated. **Ask** students what limitations would occur if the animals did not have the ability to use words.

Answer: Without words, they could not really debate the law or what might happen to Mowgli.

3. Ask students the Elements of Fantasy question: What details about this meeting at Council Rock are realistic? What details are fantastic?

Possible responses: All the wolves gathering around the leader of the pack is realistic, as is the staying together of parents and cubs. However, the idea of animals gathering together to discuss the law is fantastic. What people call "the law of the jungle" is a combination of instinct, learned behavior, and a desire to survive, not the result of discussions and reasoning. (It is also unlikely, in nature, for wolves, a bear, a panther, and a tiger to stay near each other.)

Elements of Fantasy
What details about this meeting at Council Rock are realistic? What details are fantastic?

---

lairs in revenge! Keep him? Assuredly I will keep him. Lie still, little frog. O thou Mowgli—for Mowgli the Frog I will call thee—the time will come when thou wilt hunt Shere Khan as he has hunted thee."

"But what will our Pack say?" said Father Wolf. The Law of the Jungle lays down very clearly that any wolf may, when he marries, withdraw from the Pack he belongs to; but as soon as his cubs are old enough to stand on their feet he must bring them to the Pack Council, which is generally held once a month at full moon, in order that the other wolves may identify them. After that inspection the cubs are free to run where they please, and until they have killed their first buck no excuse is accepted if a grown wolf of the Pack kills one of them. The punishment is death where the murderer can be found; and if you think for a minute you will see that this must be so.

⓲ Father Wolf waited till his cubs could run a little, and then on the night of the Pack Meeting took them and Mowgli and Mother Wolf to the Council Rock—a hilltop covered with stones and boulders where a hundred wolves could hide. Akela, the great gray Lone Wolf, who led all the Pack by strength and cunning, lay out at full length on his rock, and below him sat forty or more wolves of every size and color, from badger-colored veterans who could handle a buck alone, to young black three-year-olds who thought they could. The Lone Wolf had led them for a year now. He had fallen twice into a wolf-trap in his youth, and once he had been beaten and left for dead; so he knew the manners and customs of men. There was very little talking at the Rock. The cubs tumbled over each other in the center of the circle where their mothers and fathers sat, and now and again a senior wolf would go quietly up to a cub, look at him carefully, and return to his place on noiseless feet. Sometimes a mother would push her cub far out into the moonlight, to be sure that he had not been overlooked. Akela from his rock would cry: "Ye know the Law—ye know the Law. Look well, O Wolves!" and the anxious mothers would take up the call: "Look—look well, O Wolves!"

At last—and Mother Wolf's neck-bristles lifted as the time came—Father Wolf pushed "Mowgli the Frog," as they called him, into the center, where he sat laughing and playing

---

💬 VOCABULARY DEVELOPMENT

Word Forms

Expand students' vocabulary by helping them learn related forms of the selection vocabulary words. Three of the selection vocabulary words for "Mowgli's Brothers" have related forms. Give students a blank **Word Form Chart** (***Professional Development Guidebook***, p. 42), with *fostering, monotonous,* and *dispute* in the correct columns. Work with the class, or have students work with a partner, to determine the related forms. The final chart should look like the one shown.

Hold students accountable for integrating the related forms of the words into their speaking and writing.

Noun	Verb	Adjective	Adverb
fostering	foster	foster	
monotone		**monotonous**	monotonously
dispute	dispute	disputable	disputably

with some pebbles that glistened in the moonlight.

Akela never raised his head from his paws, but went on with the monotonous cry: "Look well!" A muffled roar came up from behind the rocks—the voice of Shere Khan crying: "The cub is mine. Give him to me. What have the Free People to do with a man's cub?" Akela never even twitched his ears: all he said was: "Look well, O Wolves! What have the Free People to do with the orders of any save the Free People? Look well!"

There was a chorus of deep growls, and a young wolf in his fourth year flung back Shere Khan's question to Akela: "What have the Free People to do with the man's cub?" Now the Law of the Jungle lays down that if there is any dispute as to the right of a cub to be accepted by the Pack, he must be spoken for by at least two members of the Pack who are not his father and mother.

"Who speaks for this cub?" said Akela. "Among the Free People who speaks?" There was no answer, and Mother Wolf got ready for what she knew would be her last fight, if things came to fighting.

Then the only other creature who is allowed at the Pack Council—Baloo, the sleepy brown bear who teaches the wolf cubs the Law of the Jungle: old Baloo, who can come and go where he pleases because he eats only nuts and roots and honey—rose up on his hind quarters and grunted.

"The man's cub—the man's cub?" he said. "I speak for the man's cub. There is no harm in a man's cub. I have no gift of words, but I speak the truth. Let him run with the Pack, and be entered with the others. I myself will teach him."

"We need yet another," said Akela. "Baloo has spoken, and he is our teacher for the young cubs. Who speaks besides Baloo?"

A black shadow dropped down into the circle. It was Bagheera the Black Panther, inky black all over, but with the panther marking showing up in certain lights like the pattern of watered silk. Everybody knew Bagheera, and nobody cared to cross his path; for he was as cunning as Tabaqui, as bold as the wild buffalo, and as reckless as the wounded elephant. But he had a voice as soft as wild honey dripping from a tree, and a skin softer than down.

"O Akela, and ye the Free People," he purred, "I have no

◄ **Vocabulary**
monotonous
(mə nät′ n əs) *adj.*
unchanging

dispute (di spyoot′) *n.*
argument; debate; quarrel

Elements of Fantasy
Does Baloo's speech in favor of keeping the child seem true to life or fantastic? Explain.

⑮ Comprehension
According to the Law of the Jungle, how must the Pack settle a dispute over accepting a cub?

PART 2 • *Mowgli's Brothers* **685**

⑭ Elements of Fantasy

1. **Ask** students why they think Kipling includes the idea of a bear teaching the cubs—with what other element of fantasy is this connected?

   Answer: The other element of fantasy is the Law of the Jungle as a set of rules that all the animals know and understand. If all the animals know the same laws, then one kind of animal could teach the laws to another kind.

2. **Ask** students the Elements of Fantasy question: Does Baloo's speech in favor of keeping the child seem true to life or fantastic? Explain.

   Possible answers: The fact that he is speaking, of course, is fantastic, but the speech seems realistic for the character and the situation. And he tells the truth—a baby is harmless.

3. The entire discussion among the animals about points of law is clearly fantasy, but **ask** students if they think the discussion reflects how humans really debate in important meetings.

   Answer: It realistically portrays a group of humans arguing over issues and points of law. There are a few major players and many who jump in with comments or go along with the last one to speak.

⑮ Comprehension

Answer: The cub must be spoken for by at least two members of the Pack who are not his father and mother. Another way to settle the dispute is for the life of the cub to be bought at a price.

⁂ DIFFERENTIATED INSTRUCTION

Enrichment for Gifted/Talented Students
Have students make animal masks representing the characters in the story. Suggest that they use paints, fake fur, fabric, and other items to embellish the masks. Then, have students wear the masks as they perform dramatic readings of segments of the story. Encourage students to use expressive voices and gestures to enhance the drama of their presentations.

Enrichment for Advanced Readers
Encourage students to continue reading *The Jungle Book*, to find out what happens to Mowgli and to learn if the prediction made by Bagheera about Mowgli and Shere Khan will come true. Direct them to summarize the rest of the story for the class.

16 Critical Viewing

Possible response: They might show respect toward the panther, or perhaps fear.

17 Elements of Fantasy

1. Ask students to think of the combination of realistic and fantastic elements in the story so far.

2. **Ask** students the Elements of Fantasy question on the next page: Which behavior described here is not likely to occur in real life?

   Possible response: It is unlikely that a child would not notice a lot of wild animals coming to look at him.

3. **Ask** students what element of the real laws of the jungle—the ones in actuality, not the rules in the story—is reflected in Akela's thoughts.

   Answer: That, in time, he will be killed by the pack when he becomes too feeble to lead.

right in your assembly; but the Law of the Jungle says that if there is a doubt which is not a killing matter in regard to a new cub, the life of that cub may be bought at a price. And the Law does not say who may or may not pay that price. Am I right?"

"Good! good!" said the young wolves, who are always hungry. "Listen to Bagheera. The cub can be bought for a price. It is the Law."

"Knowing that I have no right to speak here, I ask your leave."

"Speak then," cried twenty voices.

"To kill a naked cub is shame. Besides, he may make better sport for you when he is grown. Baloo has spoken in his behalf. Now to Baloo's word I will add one bull, and a fat one, newly killed, not half a mile from here, if ye will accept the man's cub according to the Law. Is it difficult?"

There was a clamor of scores of voices, saying: "What matter? He will die in the winter rains. He will scorch in the sun. What harm can a naked frog do us? Let him run with the Pack. Where is the bull, Bagheera? Let him be accepted." And then came Akela's deep bay, crying: "Look well—look well, O Wolves!"

Mowgli was still deeply interested in the pebbles, and he did not notice when the wolves came and looked at him one by one. At last they all went down the hill for the dead bull, and only Akela, Bagheera, Baloo, and Mowgli's own wolves were left. Shere Khan roared still in the night, for he was

16 ▲ Critical Viewing
How do you think the other animals might behave toward a panther like the one shown? Explain.

686 UNIT 5 • How much do our communities shape us?

VOCABULARY DEVELOPMENT

Selection Vocabulary Reinforcement
To reinforce and assess students' comprehension of selection vocabulary words, give them sentences using the words in which the word may or may not be used correctly. Students must tell whether the use is correct and explain their answers. You can use these sentences or create your own.

1. She completely ignored the baby bird she was *fostering*.
   Answer: No, *fostering* means taking care of something, not ignoring it.

2. The *monotonous* drip, drip, drip of the old faucet drove her crazy.
   Answer: Yes, an unchanging drip, drip, drip would be tiresome.

3. During the *dispute*, everyone smiled and nodded in agreement.
   Answer: No, *dispute* is an argument or quarrel, so people would not agree.

4. When I drag a toy mouse across the floor, my cat acts as if it is her *quarry*.
   Answer: Yes, the cat would be hunting the toy mouse.

17 very angry that Mowgli had not been handed over to him.

"Ay, roar well," said Bagheera, under his whiskers; "for the time comes when this naked thing will make thee roar to another tune, or I know nothing of man."

"It was well done," said Akela. "Men and their cubs are very wise. He may be a help in time."

"Truly, a help in time of need; for none can hope to lead the Pack forever," said Bagheera.

Akela said nothing. He was thinking of the time that comes to every leader of every pack when his strength goes from him and he gets feebler and feebler till at last he is killed by the wolves and a new leader comes up—to be killed in his turn.

"Take him away," he said to Father Wolf, "and train him as befits one of the Free People."

And that is how Mowgli was entered into the Seeonee wolf-pack at the price of a bull and on Baloo's good word.

Elements of Fantasy
Which behavior described here is not likely to occur in real life?

Spiral Review
Theme How do Akela's thoughts suggest a possible theme?

Critical Thinking

1. **Key Ideas and Details (a)** How is Mowgli similar to the wolf cubs? How is he different? **(b) Analyze:** What qualities in Mowgli does Mother Wolf find appealing?

2. **Key Ideas and Details (a)** Who pays for Mowgli's life? **(b) Evaluate:** Are this character's reasons based on his own self-interest or on what is good for the pack? **(c) Support:** What examples from the story support your answer?

3. **Key Ideas and Details (a)** Describe how the wolves in the pack make decisions. **(b) Take a Position:** Do you think the process is effective? Explain.

4. **Integration of Knowledge and Ideas** "Mowgli's Brothers" takes place in a community that has many rules. **(a)** What is the purpose of the rules? **(b)** In what ways do the rules shape the actions of the characters? *[Connect to the Big Question: How much do our communities shape us?]*

PART 2 • Mowgli's Brothers **687**

Spiral Review
Theme

1. Remind students that they studied the concept of theme in the Unit 5 Focus on Craft and Structure (pp. 628–631).

2. **Ask** students the Spiral Review question.

   Possible response: He is thinking of the cycle of life and the survival of the fittest.

✓ ASSESS

Critical Thinking

Possible responses appear below. Check to be sure students support their responses with evidence from the text.

1. **(a)** Like the cubs, Mowgli is bold and unafraid. He is different because he is human. **(b)** She likes his boldness and is intrigued by his humanity.

2. **(a)** Bagheera pays for Mowgli's life. **(b)** His reason is based on both self-interest and the good of the pack. **(c)** He says that he believes Mowgli will one day hunt Shere Khan, and this would benefit all the animals, including him and the pack.

3. **(a)** They discuss the situation and the law. Everyone has a say in the decision. **(b)** It is time consuming, but it is effective. The law is kept in the forefront of the discussion, and the law is followed.

4. **(a)** The purpose of the rules is to keep the society—all the animals living in the jungle—ordered. **(b)** The wolves carefully follow the rules. Shere Khan ignores them when he can, but when confronted by all the other animals, he has to give in to their decisions.

18 Background

Meet James James Henry Trotter is nine years old. An orphan, he lives with his dreadful aunts, Sponge and Spiker. James misses his parents and dreams of escaping. A mysterious old man gives James a bag of magic, green, crystal-like "crocodile tongues," which he says can make dreams come true. James spills them on the ground near a peach tree, and a giant peach soon appears. When James takes a bite, a large hole opens that leads to the center of the peach. Inside, he finds that other things have grown because of the spilled "crocodile tongues."

19 Activating Prior Knowledge

Have students discuss what they know about insects, spiders, and worms. What is it that makes some of them creepy and some interesting? What role do insects play in nature? Discuss what students think insects would be like if they were as large as humans and could speak. Students will return to this discussion after they have read the story.

20 About the Selection

James enters the hole that has opened in the side of the peach and crawls to the giant pit. There, he finds a door that admits him into a company of insects, worms, and a spider that are as overgrown as the peach. James panics at first, but begins to discover that the creatures mean him no harm, and in fact say that they have been waiting for him. He begins to learn about the person-alities of his new friends, but by the time he has helped the Centipede remove all of his boots, it is time to bed down in the hammock the spider has spun for him.

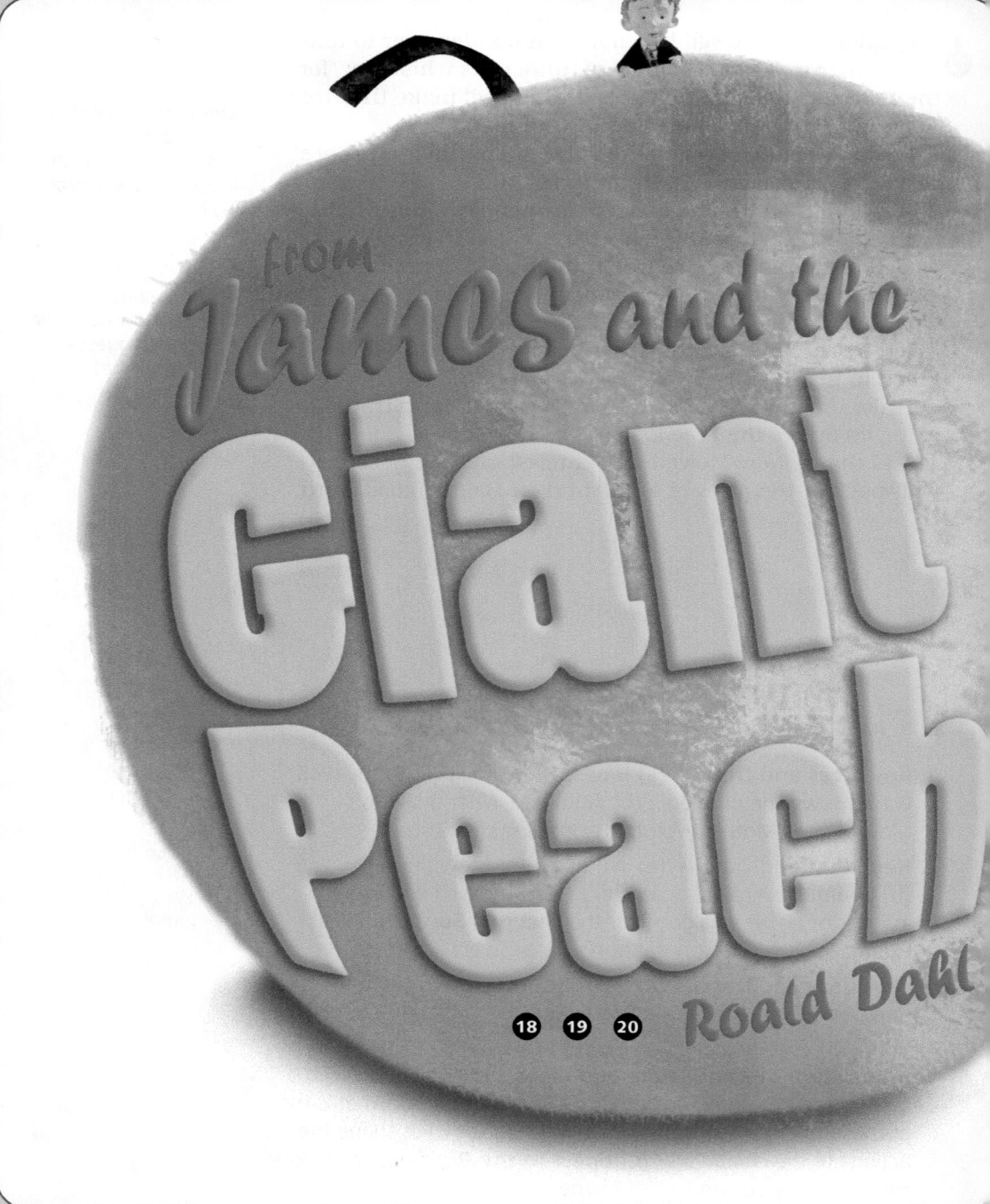

from James and the Giant Peach

18 19 20 Roald Dahl

688 UNIT 5 • How much do our communities shape us?

© TEXT COMPLEXITY **RUBRIC**

from James and the Giant Peach		
Qualitative Measures	Context/Knowledge Demands	Understanding of the elements of fantasy 1 2 ③ 4 5
	Structure/Language Conventionality and Clarity	Accessible syntax; on-level vocabulary 1 ② 3 4 5
	Levels of Meaning/ Purpose/Concept Level	Accessible concept (boy finding safe world with fun friends) 1 ② 3 4 5
Quantitative Measures	Text Length	Word Count: 1,908
	Lexile	790L

It was quite a large hole, the sort of thing an animal about the size of a fox might have made.

James knelt down in front of it and poked his head and shoulders inside.

He crawled in.

He kept on crawling.

This isn't just a hole, he thought excitedly. It's a tunnel!

The tunnel was damp and murky, and all around him there was the curious bittersweet smell of fresh peach. The floor was soggy under his knees, the walls were wet and sticky, and peach juice was dripping from the ceiling. James opened his mouth and caught some of it on his tongue. It tasted delicious.

He was crawling uphill now, as though the tunnel were leading straight toward the very center of the gigantic fruit. Every few seconds he paused and took a bite out of the wall. The peach flesh was sweet and juicy, and marvelously refreshing.

He crawled on for several more yards, and then suddenly—bang—the top of his head bumped into something extremely hard blocking his way. He glanced up. In front of him there was a solid wall that seemed at first as though it were made of wood. He touched it with his fingers. It certainly felt like wood, except that it was very jagged and full of deep grooves.

"Good heavens!" he said.

"I know what this is! I've come to the stone in the middle of the peach!"

Then he noticed that there was a small door cut into the face of the peach stone. He gave a push. It swung open. He crawled through it, and before he had time to glance up and see where he was, he heard a voice saying, "Look who's here!" And another one said, "We've been waiting for you!"

James stopped and stared at the speakers, his face white with horror.

He started to stand up, but his knees were shaking so much he had to sit down again on the floor. He glanced behind him, thinking he could bolt back into the tunnel the way he had come, but the doorway had disappeared. There was now only a solid brown wall behind him.

21 ◄ Critical Viewing
Which details of this picture are fantastic? Which are realistic?

Elements of Fantasy
Identify one fantastic element and one realistic element in this paragraph.

23 Comprehension
What clues help James guess what the solid wall really is?

21 Critical Viewing

Answer: A tiny boy climbing on a huge peach is fantastic. Other than its size, the peach itself is realistic.

22 Elements of Fantasy

1. Explain that, because the plot and setting for this story are so much more fantastic than those for "Mowgli's Brothers," students may need to look more closely at the story to find the realistic elements.

2. **Ask** students if they think it is realistic for a nine-year-old boy to climb into a hole in a giant peach.

   Possible responses: Yes, nine-year-old boys like to explore. No, it would just be too weird being inside a sticky, dripping tunnel.

3. **Ask** students the Elements of Fantasy question: Identify one fantastic element and one realistic element in this paragraph.

   Possible responses: It is fantastic that there is a door in a giant pit at the center of a giant peach. It is realistic that a nine-year-old boy who has already crawled through a tunnel would open the door.

23 Comprehension

Answer: It is hard, jagged, and full of deep grooves, plus he knew he was inside a peach and had been crawling toward the center.

© TEXT COMPLEXITY **READER AND TASK SUGGESTIONS**

from James and the Giant Peach

Preparing to Read the Text
- Use the Background information on the previous page to introduce students to James and to explain how James finds himself in the fantastic world of this story.
- Use the About the Selection note on the previous page to introduce some of the fantastic elements and creatures in the story.
- Guide students to use Multidraft Reading strategies (TE p. 676).

Leveled Tasks
Knowledge Demands If students will have difficulty with the knowledge demands, review the difference between fantastic and realistic story elements. Have students give examples of each element from the story (for example, the peach is gigantic, which is an element of fantasy, but it smells and tastes sweet and delicious, which is realistic).
Analyzing If students will not have difficulty with the knowledge demands, have them identify human emotions and characteristics the creatures display. Discuss what these creatures might represent.

24 Make Predictions

1. Direct students to reread the bracketed passage.

2. Ask them how they think James feels now that he has encountered these giant creatures.

Possible responses: He feels frightened and puzzled. Their large size and the strange light worry him.

3. Ask them how they think he will respond to these three speeches by Spider, the Old-Green-Grasshopper, and Ladybug.

Possible response: The news that they are hungry is likely to scare him even more.

James's large frightened eyes traveled slowly around the room.

The creatures, some sitting on chairs, others reclining on a sofa, were all watching him intently.

Creatures?

Or were they insects?

An insect is usually something rather small, is it not? A grasshopper, for example, is an insect.

Vocabulary ▶
intently (in tent′ lē) *adv.* with great attention or determination

So what would you call it if you saw a grasshopper as large as a dog? As large as a large dog. You could hardly call that an insect, could you?

There was an Old-Green-Grasshopper as large as a large dog sitting on a stool directly across the room from James now.

And next to the Old-Green-Grasshopper, there was an enormous Spider.

And next to the Spider, there was a giant Ladybug with nine black spots on her scarlet shell.

Each of these three was squatting upon a magnificent chair.

On a sofa nearby, reclining comfortably in curled-up positions, there was a Centipede and an Earthworm.

On the floor over in the far corner, there was something thick and white that looked as though it might be a Silkworm. But it was sleeping soundly and nobody was paying any attention to it.

Every one of these "creatures" was at least as big as James himself, and in the strange greenish light that shone down from somewhere in the ceiling, they were absolutely terrifying to behold.

"I'm hungry!" the Spider announced suddenly, staring hard at James.

"I'm famished!" the Old-Green-Grasshopper said.

"So am I!" the Ladybug cried.

The Centipede sat up a little straighter on the sofa.

24

🗨 **THINK ALOUD**

Vocabulary: Using Context
Direct students' attention to the word *famished* at the bottom of this page. Model how to use context to infer the meaning of an unknown word with this think aloud. Say to students:

> I'm going to think aloud to show how I would figure out the meaning of *famished* from its context.
>
> In the sentence just before this word is first used, the spider announces that she

is hungry. In the sentence right after the Centipede says he is famished, he exclaims, "We need food!" From the discussion of hunger and the exclamation that the characters need food, I can guess that *famished* has something to do with being hungry. The fact that exclamation points are used each time suggests that they are very hungry.

"Everyone's famished!" he said. "We need food!"

Four pairs of round black glassy eyes were all fixed upon James.

The Centipede made a wriggling movement with his body as though he were about to glide off the sofa—but he didn't.

There was a long pause—and a long silence.

The Spider (who happened to be a female spider) opened her mouth and ran a long black tongue delicately over her lips. "Aren't you hungry?" she asked suddenly, leaning forward and addressing herself to James.

Poor James was backed up against the far wall, shivering with fright and much too terrified to answer.

"What's the matter with you?" the Old-Green-Grasshopper asked. "You look positively ill!"

"He looks as though he's going to faint any second," the Centipede said.

"Oh, my goodness, the poor thing!" the Ladybug cried. "I do believe he thinks it's him that we are wanting to eat!"

There was a roar of laughter from all sides.

"Oh dear, oh dear!" they said. "What an awful thought!"

"You mustn't be frightened," the Ladybug said kindly. "We wouldn't dream of hurting you. You are one of us now, didn't you know that? You are one of the crew. We're all in the same boat."

Elements of Fantasy
Identify one fantastic detail in this paragraph.

Spiral Review
Folk Tale How are the characters in this modern story similar to those in many folk tales? Explain.

26 **Comprehension**
Why do the creatures laugh at James's fright?

27 ◄ **Critical Viewing**
What part of the story do you think this picture shows?

PART 2 • *from James and the Giant Peach* **691**

👥 DIFFERENTIATED INSTRUCTION

Support for Special-Needs Students
Spend extra time explaining the difference between elements that are fantastic and those that are realistic, giving examples from the story. For example, the peach is gigantic, which is an element of fantasy, but it still smells and tastes sweet and delicious, which is realistic.

Prepare students for the fantastic elements of the story by discussing the images of the characters shown in the text. Have students make a list of all the characters in the story (James, Old-Green-Grasshopper, Miss Spider, Centipede, Earthworm, Ladybug, Silkworm), and then have them write down as they read what the characters are like or what they say. Encourage them to add notes based on the artwork, too. Tell students to look at what they have already written for a character when they encounter the character again, so they can continue to build on what they know. This will help them keep all the characters straight and will help them build complete pictures of each character.

25 **Elements of Fantasy**

1. Remind students that a fantasy is often a mix of both fantastic and realistic details.

2. **Ask** students why they think James is so frightened.

   Answer: He is surrounded by giant insects, worms, and the Spider. Even worse, all of them are hungry, and they are all looking at him.

3. **Ask** students what they know about spiders in particular that might make James's fear a realistic element.

   Answer: Spiders catch and eat insects—they are not vegetarians.

4. Point out that the fact that because none of the insects are afraid of the spider, James is convinced he is safe.

5. **Ask** students the Elements of Fantasy question: Identify one fantastic detail in this paragraph.

   Possible response: A spider does not have a tongue or lips.

Spiral Review
Folk Tale

1. Remind students that they studied the concept of folk tales in the Unit 5 Focus on Craft and Structure (pp. 628–631).

2. **Ask** the Spiral Review question.

   Possible responses: Some of the common character elements this story shares with other folk tales are characters with heroic traits, good and evil characters, and characters with magical qualities.

26 **Comprehension**

Answer: They laugh because eating James is so unthinkable to them.

27 **Critical Viewing**

Possible responses: From the frightened look on James's face, this probably shows the part of the story where the creatures say they are hungry and he fears they are going to eat him.

28 Elements of Fantasy

1. Invite a volunteer to read aloud the bracketed passage. **Ask** students what is fantastic about the Centipede aside from its size.

Answer: He is wearing boots; he is conceited; he lies about how many legs he has.

2. The Centipede and Earthworm are proud of very different things. **Ask** students what they take pride in.

Answer: The Earthworm is proud of being useful and much loved. The Centipede is proud of being a pest.

3. Ask students how realistic these kinds of feelings are.

Answer: People do take pride in different things. While it is better to take pride in being useful, some people take pride in being pests.

4. Ask students the Elements of Fantasy question: Could a conversation such as this one occur in real life? Explain.

Possible response: While the arguing and name-calling may occur in real life, the actual discussion could not take place in real life, because people don't slither and things that slither don't talk.

Elements of Fantasy
Could a conversation such as this one occur in real life? Explain.

"We've been waiting for you all day long," the Old-Green-Grasshopper said. "We thought you were never going to turn up. I'm glad you made it."

"So cheer up, my boy, cheer up!" the Centipede said. "And meanwhile I wish you'd come over here and give me a hand with these boots. It takes me hours to get them all off by myself."

James decided that this was most certainly not a time to be disagreeable, so he crossed the room to where the Centipede was sitting and knelt down beside him.

"Thank you so much," the Centipede said. "You are very kind."

"You have a lot of boots," James murmured.

"I have a lot of legs," the Centipede answered proudly. "And a lot of feet. One hundred, to be exact."

"There he goes again!" the Earthworm cried, speaking for the first time. "He simply cannot stop telling lies about his legs! He doesn't have anything like a hundred of them! He's only got forty-two! The trouble is that most people don't bother to count them. They just take his word. And anyway, there is nothing marvelous, you know, Centipede, about having a lot of legs."

"Poor fellow," the Centipede said, whispering in James's ear. "He's blind. He can't see how splendid I look."

"In my opinion," the Earthworm said, "the really marvelous thing is to have no legs at all and to be able to walk just the same."

"You call that walking!" cried the Centipede. "You're a slitherer, that's all you are! You just slither along!"

"I glide," said the Earthworm primly.

"You are a slimy beast," answered the Centipede.

"I am not a slimy beast," the Earthworm said. "I am a useful and much loved creature. Ask any gardener you like. And as for you . . ."

"I am a pest!" the Centipede announced, grinning broadly and looking round the room for approval.

692 UNIT 5 • How much do our communities shape us?

🗯 THINK ALOUD

Vocabulary: Using Context
Model the way to decode the meaning of words by using context with this think aloud. Say to students:

I'm going to show you how I come to understand the meaning of an unfamiliar word by using context. Centipede tells James that he feels sorry for Earthworm because without eyes, he cannot see how

splendid Centipede looks. I know that Centipede is very proud of his feet. He clearly thinks very highly of himself. He sees himself as someone special. From these clues, I conclude that *splendid* means "marvelous" or "wonderful." Centipede thinks that he looks great.

"He is so proud of that," the Ladybug said, smiling at James. "Though for the life of me I cannot understand why."

"I am the only pest in this room!" cried the Centipede, still grinning away. "Unless you count Old-Green-Grasshopper over there. But he is long past it now. He is too old to be a pest any more."

The Old-Green-Grasshopper turned his huge black eyes upon the Centipede and gave him a withering look. "Young fellow," he said, speaking in a deep, slow, scornful voice, "I have never been a pest in my life. I am a musician."

"Hear, hear!" said the Ladybug.

"James," the Centipede said. "Your names is James, isn't it?"

29 ▲ Critical Viewing
Which characters are represented in this picture?

30 Comprehension
How do the Centipede and the Earthworm get along?

29 Critical Viewing
Answer: The picture shows (*from left*) Old-Green-Grasshopper, James, Ladybug, Centipede, and Earthworm.

30 Comprehension
Possible responses: They do not get along very well, since they seem to argue a great deal. Each seems not to like the other.

31 Elements of Fantasy

1. Point out the way the creatures respond, interrupt, and change the subject. If the speakers and topics were different, the flow and tone of the conversation could easily be among real people.

2. Remind students that careful reading can help them understand characters. For example, when the narrator says that James likes the Centipede, the "but" in the sentence shows us that he does so not because the Centipede is a rascal, but in spite of it. James is simply drawn to the laughter. **Ask** students if they think this is realistic.

   Possible response: Yes, people are often drawn to someone who is fun, even when they know the person is a troublemaker.

3. **Ask** students the Elements of Fantasy question: Which aspects of this good-natured teasing are realistic and which are fantastic?

   Answer: People tease each other all the time about physical differences, such as hair color, height, or wearing glasses, and people often use the expression "pulling his leg" to speak of teasing that involves telling tall tales, so these are realistic. So is the laughter over the obvious inappropriateness of speaking of an earthworm's legs. It is the characters who are doing the teasing and the elements of that teasing (too many feet, no legs) that are fantastic.

Vocabulary ▶
colossal (kə läs´ əl) *adj.* very large; huge

Elements of Fantasy
Which aspects of this good-natured teasing are realistic and which are fantastic?

"Yes."

"Well, James, have you ever in your life seen such a marvelous colossal Centipede as me?"

"I certainly haven't," James answered. "How on earth did you get to be like that?"

"Very peculiar," the Centipede said. "Very, very peculiar indeed. Let me tell you what happened. I was messing about in the garden under the old peach tree and suddenly a funny little green thing came wriggling past my nose. Bright green it was, and extraordinarily beautiful, and it looked like some kind of a tiny stone or crystal . . ."

"Oh, but I know what that was!" cried James.

"It happened to me, too!" said the Ladybug.

"And me!" Miss Spider said. "Suddenly there were little green things everywhere! The soil was full of them!"

"I actually swallowed one!" the Earthworm declared proudly.

"So did I!" the Ladybug said.

"I swallowed three!" the Centipede cried. "But who's telling this story anyway? Don't interrupt!"

"It's too late to tell stories now," the Old-Green-Grasshopper announced. "It's time to go to sleep."

"I refuse to sleep in my boots!" the Centipede cried. "How many more are there to come off, James?"

"I think I've done about twenty so far," James told him.

"Then that leaves eighty to go," the Centipede said.

"Twenty-two, not eighty!" shrieked the Earthworm. "He's lying again."

The Centipede roared with laughter.

"Stop pulling the Earthworm's leg," the Ladybug said.

This sent the Centipede into hysterics. "Pulling his leg!" he cried, wriggling with glee and pointing at the Earthworm. "Which leg am I pulling? You tell me that?"

James decided that he rather liked the Centipede. He was obviously a rascal, but what a change it was to hear somebody laughing once in a while. He had never heard Aunt Sponge or Aunt Spiker laughing aloud in all the time he had been with them.

"We really must get some sleep," the Old-Green-Grasshopper said. "We've got a tough day ahead of us tomorrow. So would you be kind enough, Miss Spider, to make the beds?" •

💬 VOCABULARY DEVELOPMENT

Word Analysis

Knowing the meanings of word roots can help students remember the words and decode other words with the same roots.

In this story, James encounters a centipede. Explain that the Latin root *-cent-* means "hundred," and *-ped-* means "foot." Tell students that centipedes do not really have a hundred feet, but they have so many feet that this seemed like an appropriate name. (Point out that the centipede in the story believes it is a hundred, so even *he* has not counted his own feet!)

List on the board *century, centimeter, cent, pedal, pedestal,* and *quadruped.* Ask students which words they already know. Have them give the definitions of these words and what *-cent-* and *-ped-* contribute to the meaning of the word. For words that are unknown, have a volunteer look up the word and read the definition. Discuss how knowing *-cent-* or *-ped-* can help students remember the words and how it might help them figure out the meaning of a new word with one of these roots.

A few minutes later, Miss Spider had made the first bed. It was hanging from the ceiling, suspended by a rope of threads at either end so that actually it looked more like a hammock than a bed. But it was a magnificent affair, and the stuff that it was made of shimmered like silk in the pale light.

"I do hope you'll find it comfortable," Miss Spider said to the Old-Green-Grasshopper. "I made it as soft and silky as I possibly could. I spun it with gossamer. That's a much better quality thread than the one I use for my own web."

"Thank you so much, my dear lady," the Old-Green-Grasshopper said, climbing into the hammock. "Ah, this is just what I needed. Good night, everybody. Good night."

Then Miss Spider spun the next hammock, and the Ladybug got in.

After that, she spun a long one for the Centipede, and an even longer one for the Earthworm.

"And how do you like your bed?" she said to James when it came to his turn. "Hard or soft?"

"I like it soft, thank you very much," James answered.

Elements of Fantasy
Would you call Miss Spider's bed-making behavior fantastic or realistic? Why?

33 Comprehension
How did the creatures get to be big?

32 Elements of Fantasy

1. Remind students that fantasy stories often mix some realistic details with some fantastical ones. **Ask** students to identify realistic details about the different creatures that have appeared in the story so far.

   Possible responses: Centipede has many legs, like real centipedes do. Earthworm has no legs and cannot see, which is like real earthworms. Ladybug has spots on her shell. All the creatures, of course, can talk and have personalities similar to humans, which are fantastic details.

2. Then, invite volunteers to read aloud the bracketed passage. **Ask** the Elements of Fantasy question: Would you call Miss Spider's bed-making behavior fantastic or realistic? Why?

   Possible responses: It is realistic that spiders spin webs, but it is fantastic that Miss Spider would spin beds for the other creatures to sleep. Spiders spin webs for them to live in and to trap food.

33 Comprehension

Answer: They ate "funny little green things." (If students remember the Background note from the beginning of the tale, they may identify these green things as the "crocodile tongues" that James dropped at the base of the tree.)

🕮 DIFFERENTIATED INSTRUCTION

Enrichment for Gifted/Talented Students
Have students work in a group to create a diorama of the scene in the peach pit. Have different students work on the furniture and each of the different creatures. Have students collect materials such as felt, pipe cleaners, modeling clay, construction paper, crayons, markers, and any other art supplies they might need for this project. Encourage students to use their imaginations to figure out how to construct the characters and arrange them so that all the characters could see each other and James. (A box turned on its side might make a good room/peach pit for them.) Suggest that James be about five or six inches tall and everything else be scaled in relation to that size.

ASSESS

Critical Thinking

Possible responses appear below.
Check to be sure students support their
responses with evidence from the text.

1. **(a)** He is afraid. **(b)** He thinks they are going to eat him.

2. **(a)** He asks James to help take off his boots. **(b)** He is conceited and a rascal, but he is funny and likes laughing. **(c)** Though there are disagreements and teasing, they seem to get along well, because they all agree on important things, such as bedtime and not eating James. Most of them seem very polite, saying "thank you" and calling the spider "dear lady."

3. **(a)** Yes, he is beginning to like them, because the spider has spun him a web and the Centipede laughs. No, he doesn't like them yet; he is still nervous, and the Centipede makes him work, but James is beginning to relax. **(b)** James and the creatures will probably embark on an adventure to leave the peach and go home or start a new life somewhere else, since they were all unexpectedly brought to the peach by strange circumstances.

4. **THE BIG ?** Some students will say that he will get used to them, and they will get used to him, and they will all become friends. Others may say that he will still think it strange to be associating with a group of giant bugs.

"For goodness' sake stop staring round the room and get on with my boots!" the Centipede said. "You and I are never going to get any sleep at this rate! And kindly line them up neatly in pairs as you take them off. Don't just throw them over your shoulder."

James worked away frantically on the Centipede's boots. Each one had laces that had to be untied and loosened before it could be pulled off, and to make matters worse, all the laces were tied up in the most complicated knots that had to be unpicked with fingernails. It was just awful. It took about two hours. And by the time James had pulled off the last boot of all and had lined them up in a row on the floor—twenty-one pairs altogether—the Centipede was fast asleep.

Critical Thinking

1. **Key Ideas and Details (a)** What is James's first reaction when he encounters the creatures in the peach? **(b) Infer:** How does he interpret their actions and words at first?

2. **Key Ideas and Details (a)** What does the Centipede ask James to do? **(b) Infer:** What words would you use to describe the Centipede's personality? **(c) Analyze:** As a group, how do the creatures seem to get along? Give examples from the text to support your answer.

3. **Key Ideas and Details (a)** By bedtime, do you think James is beginning to like the creatures? Why or why not? **(b) Speculate:** What do you think will happen to James and his new friends? Why?

4. **Integration of Knowledge and Ideas** If James stays with the creatures for a year, how do you think his reaction to them might change? Explain. *[Connect to the Big Question: How much do our communities shape us?]*

💬 VOCABULARY DEVELOPMENT

Vocabulary Knowledge Rating
When students have completed reading and discussing "Mowgli's Brothers" and the selection from *James and the Giant Peach*, have them take out their **Vocabulary Knowledge Rating Chart**. Read the words aloud once more and have students rate their knowledge of the words again in the After Reading column. Clarify any words that are still problematic.

Have students write their own definitions and examples or sentences in the appropriate column. Encourage students to use the words in further discussion and written work about these selections. Remind them that they will be accountable for these words on the **Selection Test**.

Writing to Sources

Comparing Elements of Fantasy

1. **Integration of Knowledge and Ideas** For each selection, complete a chart like the one shown to list the fantastic and realistic elements in each category.

Category	Fantastic Element	Realistic Element
Animals		
Human		
Setting		
Situation		

⏱ Timed Writing

Explanatory Text: Essay

In an essay, compare and contrast the use of fantastic and realistic elements in "Mowgli's Brothers" and the excerpt from *James and the Giant Peach*. Use the information in your charts and the questions below to get started. **(30 minutes)**

5-Minute Planner

1. Read the prompt carefully and completely.

2. Organize your ideas by answering these questions:

   • In which story do the animals seem more realistic? Why?

   • Is the boy in either story fantastic in some way? If so, how?

   • Which story's setting seems more realistic?

   • Could either situation happen in real life? Explain.

   • What might be the author's reason for including fantastic elements?

   • Do the fantastic elements help readers understand the message of the story? Explain.

3. Reread the prompt, and then draft your essay.

USE ACADEMIC VOCABULARY

As you write, use academic language, including the following words or their related forms:

conflict

convince

encounter

unique

For more information about academic vocabulary, see pages xlvi–l.

Comparing Elements of Fantasy

"Mowgli's Brothers" [col. 2]: [row 1] animals talk [row 2] child unafraid [row 3] animals that would not be together in nature gather [row 4] animals discuss child's future

[col. 3]: [row 1] animals look real, behave realistically [row 2] child is curious [row 3] jungle and cave realistic [row 4] child being lost

James and the Giant Peach [col. 2]: [row 1] giant insects, worm, spider wear clothes, talk, sit on chairs [row 2] boy climbs inside giant peach [row 3] room inside giant peach [row 4] boy inside peach with giant insects

[col 3]: [row 1] teasing, vanity, laughter, kindness [row 2] children like exploring. [row 3] people often sit around and talk. [row 4] children in new situations with new people

For other sample answers, see **Comparing Elements of Fantasy Graphic Organizer A** for these selections.

⏱ Timed Writing

1. Review the prompt with students.

2. Have students use the 5-Minute Planner to structure their time. Guide them in completing the bulleted instructions by helping them identify the realistic and fantastic elements in each story and the basic message of each story.

3. Allow students 30 minutes to complete the assignment.

Six Traits Focus

✓	Ideas		Word Choice
✓	Organization		Sentence Fluency
	Voice		Conventions

ASSESSMENT RESOURCES

The following resources can be used to assess students' knowledge and skills.

L1 L2 **EL** Selection Test

L3 L4 Open-Book Test

 Online Writer's Notebook

Students can use the Online Writer's Notebook to record all responses.

Idioms

1. Introduce the skill, using the instruction on the student page.

2. Review the examples in the chart.

3. Help students see how the literal meaning of the original words can sometimes be related to the meaning of the idiom. For instance, a carpenter would want to hit a nail squarely rather than on the side to drive it correctly into wood. Then, write this sentence on the board: "That remark of yours hit the nail right on the head." Guide students to see that, as used in sentences, the idioms make no sense if taken literally. The figurative meaning, though, does make sense.

4. Give students some examples of sentences with common idioms that they might be familiar with, such as "The boss told the workers to put the brakes on the new project" or "He made a pig of himself." Call on volunteers to explain what the idioms mean.

Think Aloud: Model the Skill

Model the skill of recognizing idioms to decode word meanings. Say to students:

I know I've found an idiom when an expression can't possibly make any sense literally. Suppose I read a story where one woman ends a phone conversation with her sister by saying, "Keep in touch." I know that she's not saying they should literally be touching. After all, they weren't even touching when they were talking on the phone. I see that she is just using an expression to say that she wants to stay in communication with her sister.

Language Study

Idioms

An **idiom** is an expression that has a different meaning from the literal meanings of the words it contains. For example, if a baseball game was postponed because it was "raining cats and dogs," it was postponed because it was raining very hard.

Some idioms are very common and easily understood. Others, however, can be confusing. Look for context clues in sentences that contain an idiom. For example, the sentence above contains the context clue that the game was "postponed." When you add your own background knowledge you can determine that a baseball game would be *postponed* if it was raining too hard to play.

Idioms usually develop in some specialized field where they originally make sense. Look at these common idioms and their sources:

Idiom	Source	Meaning
to watch like a hawk	wildlife	to look at something very closely
to hit the nail on the head	carpentry	to do or say something in exactly the right way
to be on an even keel	sailing	to be balanced, steady, and heading in the right direction

Common Core State Standards

Language
5.a. Interpret figures of speech in context.

TEACHING RESOURCES

	Print	Digital
All Language Study Worksheet, Idioms		✓

G Grammar Tutorials

Grammar Tutorials in the *Student eText* provide additional support!

Practice A

Identify the idiom in each sentence.

1. We all worked like ants to finish the class art project.
2. Tom dropped the ball when he forgot to buy a birthday gift for Ana.
3. The members of the soccer team cut down on their snacks.
4. I think I might be coming down with a cold.
5. She let the cat out of the bag when she revealed the secret.

Practice B

Identify the idiom in each sentence. Then, use context clues to figure out the meaning of the idiom. Restate the idiom in your own words.

1. I didn't want to apologize to my sister, but I had to face the music.
2. Kyle wanted to play a role he could sink his teeth into.
3. Leila was putting out fires all day at work until she came home and relaxed.
4. Mrs. Fine's grandchild was the apple of her eye.
5. When Gerald lost the chess match, he was fit to be tied.

Activity Think of three idioms you know. Then, using note cards like the one shown, describe the source of each idiom. For example, your example may be an idiom that relates to an animal, nature, or a kind of food. Next, explain the meaning of each idiom. Finally, write a sentence using each idiom.

Idiom:
Source:
Meaning:
Example sentence:

Comprehension and Collaboration

With a partner, conduct online research to find idioms from another language, such as Spanish or Japanese. Try to find at least five examples. Share your findings with others in the class.

Practice A
Answers

1. "Worked like ants" is the idiom.
2. "Dropped the ball" is the idiom.
3. "Cut down" is the idiom.
4. "Coming down with" is the idiom.
5. "Let the cat out of the bag" is the idiom.

Practice B
Answers

1. The idiom is "face the music." It means that the speaker had to do a difficult thing—apologize to her sister—despite not wanting to do so.
2. The idiom is "sink his teeth into." It means that Kyle wanted a part in the play that was substantial.
3. The idiom is "putting out fires." It means that Leila was constantly solving problems.
4. The idiom is "apple of her eye," which means that her grandchild was very special to her.
5. The idiom is "fit to be tied," which means that Gerald was very upset.

Activity

Provide dictionaries for students and guide them in their use so they can carry out the activity.

In their responses, students should list three idioms, explain their origins and meanings, and use them correctly in a sentence.

Comprehension and Collaboration

Divide the class into pairs to carry out the activity, and give them time to carry out the required online research.

Sample answer: The English idiom, "You're pulling my leg!" means "You're joking with me!" In Spanish, you would express the same idea by saying "¡Me estás tomando el pelo!" (literally, "You're taking my hair").

DIFFERENTIATED INSTRUCTION

Strategy for Less Proficient Readers
Explain that students can test to see if a phrase is an idiom by replacing the words in the phrase with substitutes. If those substitutions make no sense, the expression is probably an idiom. Have students substitute "take a bite out of" for the idiom in Practice B, sentence 2. They should see that the sentence that results is nonsense. Encourage students to try this strategy of substitution with the idioms that appear in Practice A or B.

EL Strategy for English Learners
Point out that many idioms are defined in a dictionary. If students recognize that an expression is an idiom but they cannot make out its meaning because the context is unclear, they can consult a dictionary. Explain that they would look the expression up under the key word. As examples, have them find the meanings of "beat around the bush" (look under *bush*); "foot in the door" (*foot*); and "between a rock and a hard place" (*rock*).

Learn the Skills

1. Introduce the workshop, including the activity on the next page.

2. Guide students as they develop their interpretations.

- Help them clarify their ideas. Point out that a few well-developed ideas will be easier to understand than many ideas that lack support.

- Remind students their response centers on a literary work. Opinions are most easily supported using evidence from the text, including examples and quotations.

3. Ask volunteers to model speaking with different tones, volume levels, and pacing to show the impact of these changes on listeners' interest in the presentation. Challenge them to maintain eye contact with the audience, using notes only for main ideas and direct quotations.

© Speaking and Listening

Oral Response to Literature

After you have read a literary work, you may be asked to deliver an oral response to literature. An oral response includes many of the characteristics of a written response.

Learn the Skills

The first step toward preparing a successful oral response is to read the literary work carefully and thoughtfully to develop an interpretation.

Developing your response

- **Organize around clear ideas.** Organize your response around a number of clear ideas, premises, or images. Your introduction should include a thesis statement that expresses your interpretation of the work. The body of the speech should present clearly related and logically organized ideas. Conclude your response by restating your interpretation and sharing your opinion.

- **Create clear transitions among ideas.** Make sure your listeners can follow the flow of your ideas. To do so, use transitional words and phrases. Introduce examples and details with words and phrases such as *for example, for instance, namely,* and *particularly.* Indicate emphasis with words like *above all* and *chiefly.*

- **Use examples and quotations from the text.** To develop your interpretation, use examples from the literature, including direct quotations, to support your opinion.

Delivering your response

- **Use nonverbal elements.** Use nonverbal cues such as eye contact and hand gestures to help the audience follow your main ideas and to emphasize *salient*, or important, points.

- **Use effective rate, volume, and tone.** Use a strong, clear voice that can be heard in the back of the room. Speak slowly and enunciate every word. Do not be afraid to pause before reading a quotation or introducing a new thought.

© Common Core State Standards

Speaking and Listening

1.c. Pose and respond to specific questions with elaboration and detail by making comments that contribute to the topic, text, or issue under discussion.

1.d. Review the key ideas expressed and demonstrate understanding of multiple perspectives through reflection and paraphrasing.

4. Present claims and findings, sequencing ideas logically and using pertinent descriptions, facts, and details to accentuate main ideas or themes; use appropriate eye contact, adequate volume, and clear pronunciation.

☑ STRATEGIES FOR DELIVERING AN ORAL PRESENTATION

Explain to students that once they have organized their thoughts and prepared their note cards, they must rehearse their presentations. Doing so will give them confidence and allow them to experiment with different tones of voice and nonverbal gestures. Share the following tips:

- Rehearse with a partner. Watch and listen carefully. Share constructive ideas about how to improve the presentation.

- Videotape a rehearsal. If possible, urge partners to record their presentations and then discuss what worked and what might be changed.

- Prepare a marked-up copy of the notes. Based on partner feedback, urge students to mark up their presentation notes, setting up cues for effective pauses and shifts in volume.

Practice the Skills

Presentation of Knowledge and Ideas Use what you have learned in this workshop to perform the following task.

> ### ACTIVITY: **Oral Response to Literature**
>
> Present an oral response to literature to your class. Follow the steps below.
> - Choose a work of literature on which to base your response.
> - Organize your interpretation using the strategies in this workshop.
> - Present your response to the class.
> - Use a Speaking Guide like the one below.

Use a Speaking Guide like the one below to prepare and organize your presentation.

> ### Speaking Guide
>
> **Preparing the response:**
>
> Novel, short story, or collection title: _____
>
> Author: _____
>
> Main points: _____
>
> Supporting details: _____
>
> Interpretation: _____
>
> **Delivering the response:**
>
> Before you present, practice these tips:
>
> ❑ Hold up the book in which the literary work appears.
>
> ❑ When reading a passage or a quotation, read directly from the work. Use sticky notes to mark pages before the presentation.
>
> ❑ Use props. Hold up an object mentioned in your presentation.
>
> **Speaking techniques:**
>
> ❑ Employ eye contact and use natural gestures.
>
> ❑ Use an appropriate speaking rate and volume.
>
> ❑ Use a clear voice and enunciate your words.
>
> ❑ Use correct conventions of language.

Comprehension and Collaboration Evaluate and discuss a classmate's presentation. Listen to and interpret the verbal and nonverbal cues in the presentation. After paraphrasing the major ideas and supporting evidence, ask the speaker questions to clarify his or her purpose, perspective, or any other confusing points.

Practice the Skills

1. Review the assignment with students. Review listening skills, urging students to pay attention to both verbal and nonverbal messages, and to ask questions to clarify the speaker's purpose and perspective.

2. Explain to students that they should use a copy of the Speaking Guide to evaluate their own presentation and the presentations made by classmates.

3. Before students give their presentations to the class, remind listeners to ask questions if any points are unclear. To maintain order, encourage them to raise their hands and wait to be acknowledged by the presenter before stating their questions. Suggest that students making presentations scan the classroom from time to time so they will notice any students who have questions.

Evaluate the Activity

1. Evaluate students' presentations on the basis of the clarity of their interpretation, their use of supporting details as evidence, and their delivery technique.

2. When the class discusses the presentations that were most effective, encourage students to make note of the features of those presentations that made them effective and to incorporate those techniques in their future presentations.

✿ DIFFERENTIATED INSTRUCTION

🅔 Strategies for English Learners

Teach students how to add variety to their oral responses by introducing different grammatical structures, such as simple and compound sentences. Give an example for each sentence type.

Ask students to review their oral responses and to combine simple sentences into compound sentences. Provide students with a list of connecting words to choose from, such as *and, or, if,* and *because.*

Guide students in combining sentences with related meanings into compound sentences. Then, have pairs work together to join simple sentences into compound sentences. Finally, have students edit their own work to reflect different sentence types.

Introducing the Writing Assignment

Review the assignment and the criteria, using the instruction on the student page.

Focus on Research

Remind students to keep the following tips in mind as they conduct research.

- Gather information from multiple authoritative print and digital sources.
- Assess the usefulness of each source in answering the research question.
- Integrate information into the text selectively.
- Synthesize information from multiple sources.
- Avoid plagiarism.
- Use a standard format for citations.

Writing Process

Write an Explanatory Text

Cause-and-Effect Essay

Defining the Form A **cause-and-effect essay** is a piece of expository writing that explains the reasons or the results for something that happens. You might use elements of this form in social studies reports, scientific lab reports, or news reports.

Assignment Write a cause-and-effect essay to explain the reasons leading to an event or situation and the results of that event or situation. Your essay should feature the following elements:

✓ a *thesis* that states the causes and effects of a situation

✓ *relevant facts and details* that support the thesis statement

✓ a *coherent* organizational pattern that emphasizes cause-and-effect relationships and has a *clear introduction* and *logical conclusion*

✓ a *formal style* and effective *word choice*

✓ *transitions* that make connections between ideas

✓ error-free writing, including correct use of *commas, parentheses, and dashes*

To preview the criteria on which your cause-and-effect essay may be judged, see the rubric on page 709.

FOCUS ON RESEARCH

When you write a cause-and-effect essay, you might conduct research to:

- learn background information about the event or situation.
- locate facts, statistics, or other details that describe the scope and nature of the causes and effects.
- find quotations from experts about the significance of the causes and effects.

Cite your source when you use a direct quotation. The Research Workshop in the Introductory Unit explains how to cite sources properly.

702 UNIT 5 • How much do our communities shape us?

Common Core State Standards

Writing
2. Write informative/explanatory texts to examine a topic and convey ideas, concepts, and information through the selection, organization, and analysis of relevant content.

READING-WRITING CONNECTION

To get the feel for cause-and-effect writing, read the essay "Birds Struggle to Recover from Egg Thefts of 1800s" by Edie Lau on page 148.

🗐 TEACHING RESOURCES

	Print	Digital
All Common Core Companion, pp. 184–195; 214–226; 331–334; 335–338	✓	✓
All EssayScorer powered by WriteToLearn		✓
All Online Student Edition eText with audio and video		✓
All Online Teacher Edition		✓
L1 Professional Development Guidebook, Rubrics for Self-Assessment: Cause-and-Effect Essay pp. 238–239		✓
All Student Companion All-in-One Workbook, Unit 5 Writing Process	✓	✓

📝 EssayScorer

Students can use EssayScorer with automatic feedback and scoring to practice summarizing!

Prewriting/Planning Strategies

Brainstorm. In a group, discuss possible topics. You may wish to begin with a general idea such as "historical events" or a fill-in-the-blank exercise such as "What causes_____?" Review the results and choose an idea from the list as your topic.

Browse media sources. Look through the newspaper or a favorite magazine for topics that interest you. Circle key words or ideas and consider their causes or effects. Choose a topic based on your findings.

Use a topic web. Create a topic web like the one shown to help you evaluate and narrow your topic. First, write your topic inside a circle. Then, write connected ideas, or subtopics, inside circles surrounding your topic. Label each idea "cause" or "effect." When you have finished, review your completed web. To narrow your topic, focus on a single one of your subtopics.

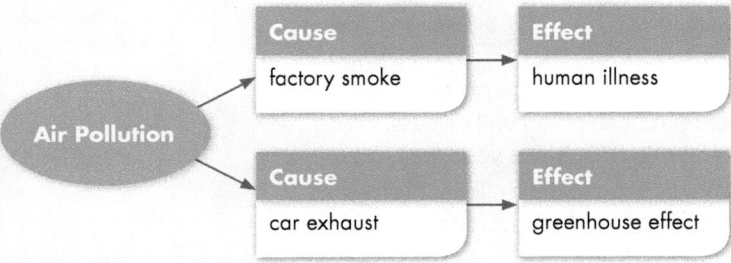

Use a T-chart in research. To find facts and examples that explain cause-and-effect relationships, you may need to conduct research. Use a T-chart to organize your ideas.

Fact	Example

✔ STRATEGIES **FOR CLARIFYING EXPECTED OUTCOMES**

Using Rubrics
- Before students begin work on this assignment, have them preview the Rubric for Self-Assessment (p. 709) to know what qualities their essays must have. A copy of this rubric appears in the *Graphic Organizers* for this workshop.
- Review the criteria in the rubric with the class. Before students use the rubric to assess their own writing, work with them to rate the Student Model (p. 708) using the rubric.

- If you wish to assess students' cause-and-effect essays with either a 4-point or a 6-point scoring rubric, see *Professional Development Guidebook*, pp. 238–239.

Prewriting/Planning Strategies

1. Introduce the prewriting and planning strategies.
2. Have students apply the strategies to choose a topic.

Teaching the Strategies
1. Divide the class into separate groups for browsing and brainstorming. Browsing works well with groups of three to six.
2. Other general ideas for brainstorming could include current events and natural phenomena.
3. As students create their topic webs, note that topics that generate more than fifteen causes and effects are probably too broad.
4. Give students an opportunity to conduct research.

Think Aloud: Model Narrowing a Topic
Say to students:

Let's say I have brainstormed for a good topic and have chosen "pollution." Once I start listing causes and effects involved in pollution, I realize the topic is huge! Pollution is caused by many things, including cars, factories, litterbugs, and so on. It has many effects, including effects on the atmosphere, on people's health, and on animals. I could write a whole book on pollution. For an essay, I need to choose just one of the subtopics I have identified. For example, I might choose pollution caused by cars and its effects.

Six Traits Focus

✓	Ideas	Word Choice
✓	Organization	Sentence Fluency
	Voice	Conventions

Drafting Strategies

1. Introduce the drafting strategies, using the instruction on the student page.
2. Have students apply the strategies as they draft.

Teaching the Strategies

1. Before students review the information they have gathered for their cause-and-effect essays, warn them to stop and think if they identify a simple cause and effect. If this is the case, do they have enough to write about? Will their paper be too simple and obvious? Will it include interesting and relevant details?
2. Emphasize the importance of crafting a focused thesis statement. Remind students that all information in their essays should support or elaborate on their thesis statement.

Think Aloud: Model Using Transitions

Model the use of transitions, using the following "think aloud." Say to students:

When I write a cause-and-effect essay, it's important to show how causes and effects relate to one another. So, I place causes *before* effects and use transitional words and phrases to show a relationship between events. Suppose I have written: *The company failed to monitor the bacteria level in their soup. Many people became sick.* If I add a transitional phrase, the relationship between the cause and effect becomes much clearer to the reader: *The company failed to monitor the bacteria level in their soup. As a result, many people became sick.*

Six Traits Focus

✓	Ideas		Word Choice
✓	Organization		Sentence Fluency
	Voice		Conventions

Drafting Strategies

Organize details. You may have identified a single cause and a single effect, or multiple causes for a single effect. This chart shows an example of a single cause with several effects. Select an organization for your essay from the following two common patterns.

- **Many Causes/Single Effect** If a number of unrelated events leads to a single result, focus one paragraph on each cause.
- **Single Cause/Many Effects** If one cause produces several effects, focus one paragraph on each effect.

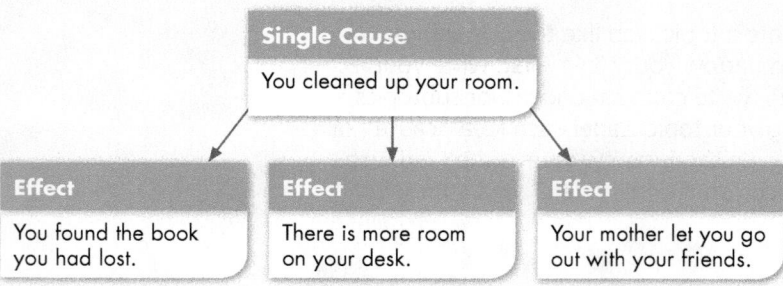

Single Cause
You cleaned up your room.

Effect
You found the book you had lost.

Effect
There is more room on your desk.

Effect
Your mother let you go out with your friends.

Focus your writing with a strong thesis statement. Consider the cause-and-effect relationship you will discuss. Using your notes, craft one thesis sentence that states your main idea.

Example: If the city builds a new sports stadium, local businesses will get the benefit of increased sales.

Include enough information to build a link. Make sure that your sentences show readers exactly how the events or situations are linked in cause-and-effect relationships. Provide supporting details that are precise rather than vague.

Vague: If your skin is damaged, you are at risk for illness.

Clear: If you are fair-skinned and spend a lot of time in the sun without wearing sunscreen, you are more likely to get skin cancer.

Connect with transitions. Choose transitional words and phrases that show clear cause-and-effect relationships.

To show a cause: *Because* of the flood, many homes were damaged.

To show an effect: *As a result*, people have to rebuild.

 Common Core State Standards

Writing
2.a. Introduce a topic; organize ideas, concepts, and information, using strategies such as definition, classification, comparison/contrast, and cause/effect; include formatting, graphics, and multimedia when useful to aiding comprehension.
2.b. Develop the topic with relevant facts, definitions, concrete details, quotations, or other information and examples.
2.c. Use appropriate transitions to clarify the relationships among ideas and concepts.

Language
2.a. Use punctuation (commas, parentheses, dashes) to set off nonrestrictive/parenthetical elements.

Using Commas, Parentheses, and Dashes

A **comma** signals readers to pause. It is used to separate words or groups of words in a series.

Examples: School supplies include pencils, erasers, and notebooks.
I went home, studied for my test, and went to bed.

Commas are also used to set off phrases, clauses, or nonessential elements in a sentence.

Set off Appositive Phrase	Set off Introductory Phrase	Set off Nonessential Element
The fire truck, *bright red*, shone in the sunlight.	*In the moonlight*, the tree glowed a ghostly white.	The store, which I love, is in the Riverside mall.

Parentheses separate words, phrases, or clauses from the rest of the sentence. However, parentheses enclose information that can be omitted from the rest of the sentence without changing the sentence's basic meaning.

Example: On Saturday (Jeff's birthday) we are leaving the city and going home.

Like commas and parentheses, **dashes** also separate words, phrases, or clauses from the rest of the sentence, but they indicate a more sudden and stronger interruption in thought.

Example: Take the sauce off the burner—be careful, it's hot—and pour it into a bowl.

Fixing Errors in Usage

1. For words in a series, make sure to place a comma after each word or group of words, including the last word or group of words before the word *and*.

2. Reread any sentence that includes parentheses to be sure the information in parentheses is not essential to the sentence's meaning.

Grammar In Your Writing

Choose two paragraphs in your cause-and-effect essay. Underline every sentence that contains commas, parentheses, or dashes. Correct any usage errors you find.

Using Commas, Parentheses, and Dashes

1. Introduce the skill, using the instruction on the student page.

2. Discuss the definitions and the examples in the chart.

Teaching the Grammar Skill

1. Remind students that commas are used to signal pauses in reading. They are also used to separate items in a list. Dashes are also used to signal pauses; however, their purpose is to inflect a longer pause. Parentheses separate information from the rest of the passage and are almost read as asides. They are thoughts that could be omitted without changing the meaning of the sentence.

2. Encourage students to read their drafts out loud and look for natural pauses in their speaking. Have them pencil in these pauses. When finished, they should go back and decide if a comma, dash or, perhaps a parenthesis, belongs at each pause.

3. A final read of the draft should always include a check for usage of commas, dashes, and parentheses. Make sure students check any lists or serial thoughts to ensure they are separated by commas. Also, remind them to look for any unnecessary punctuation and edit as needed.

Think Aloud: Model the Skill

Model the skill of using commas. Say to students:

Commas help me communicate clearly. For example, if I want you to bring materials for a project, I can say "Bring three cups, a red pen, and a piece of fabric." Notice that I pause after each item. This helps you know that each item is separate. In writing, I use a comma to stand for that pause.

Revising Strategies

1. Introduce the revising strategy, using the instruction on the student page.

2. Have students apply the strategy as they revise.

Teaching the Strategies

Have students identify the following transitional words and phrases as cause-and-effect or chronological.

After lunch, we will leave for the lake. (**Answer:** chronological)

As a result of an accounting error, the checks will not be mailed this week. (**Answer:** cause and effect)

After years of consuming contaminated feed, the fish population began to die off. (**Answer:** cause and effect)

I will go to bed when my TV show is over. (**Answer:** chronological)

When sodium is added to the mixture, it bursts into flames. (**Answer:** cause and effect)

Think Aloud: Model Revising for Support

Model the strategy of revising for support, using the following "think aloud." Say to students:

I can revise to make sure that my topic sentences are supported by every other sentence in the paragraph. If my topic sentence is *Research has shown that a nutritious breakfast is important to helping students work well in school,* I might include a sentence such as, *Oatmeal or eggs provide the calories needed for a good start to the day.* However, I would delete a sentence that does not support the topic sentence, such as *Most students surveyed prefer hot cereal to cold.*

Six Traits Focus

✓	Ideas	✓	Word Choice
✓	Organization		Sentence Fluency
	Voice		Conventions

Revising Strategies

Test for logical organization. Examine the connections between your paragraphs. Follow these steps to be sure the topic sentences in each paragraph support the thesis of your essay.

1. Highlight the topic sentence of each paragraph.

2. Label each connection to the topic as *cause* or *effect*.

3. Read the topic sentences in the order in which they appear.

4. If necessary, reorder sentences or paragraphs for clarity.

5. Write a concluding statement that follows from the topic sentences of your essay.

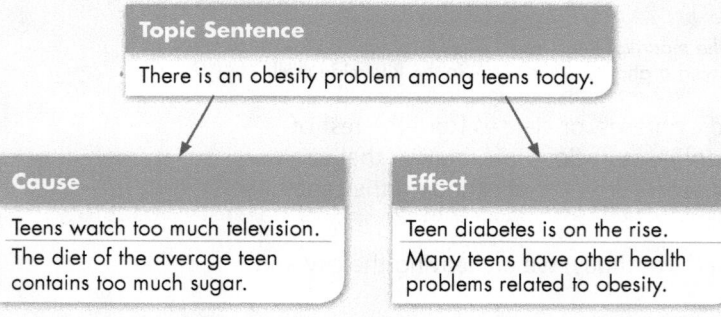

Topic Sentence
There is an obesity problem among teens today.

Cause
Teens watch too much television.
The diet of the average teen contains too much sugar.

Effect
Teen diabetes is on the rise.
Many teens have other health problems related to obesity.

Confirm the link. Make sure your essay describes events that are truly connected by cause and effect, not related only because one event happened after another.

Chronology:	We finished the dishes, then started our homework.
Cause and Effect:	I studied so hard for the test that I was able to do well.

Confirm accuracy. Compare your notes against your draft to ensure that your writing correctly reflects the facts.

Add graphics. Some cause-and-effect relationships are complicated for readers to grasp through words alone. Visual aids, such as diagrams or flowcharts, make complex processes easier to understand. Look for places to add graphics in your essay.

Peer Review

Share your essay with a partner. Ask your reader to tell you whether all of your cause-and-effect relationships are reliable, logical, and clearly explained.

706 UNIT 5 • How much do our communities shape us?

Common Core State Standards

Writing
2.a. Introduce a topic; organize ideas, concepts, and information, using strategies such as definition, classification, comparison/contrast, and cause/effect; include formatting, graphics, and multimedia when useful to aiding comprehension.

2.f. Provide a concluding statement or section that follows from the information or explanation presented.

5. With some guidance and support from peers and adults, develop and strengthen writing as needed by planning, revising, editing, rewriting, or trying a new approach.

Language
2. Demonstrate command of the conventions of standard English capitalization, punctuation, and spelling when writing.

2.a. Use punctuation (commas, parentheses, dashes) to set off nonrestrictive/parenthetical elements.

3. Use knowledge of language and its conventions when writing, speaking, reading, or listening.

⚙ DIFFERENTIATED INSTRUCTION

EL Strategies for English Learners
Suggest that students focus on a topic that is already familiar to them. Tell students to make a list of words that are associated with their topics. Then, have them work with partners proficient in English to make sure they are using the correct words with the appropriate connotations.

Revising Choppy Sentences

Direct objects and indirect objects are called *complements* because they are used to complete the meaning of a sentence. You can combine choppy sentences in your writing by using compound complements. (For more on complements, see pages 638 and 648.)

Sentence Combining Using Complements This chart shows how combining complements can eliminate choppy sentences.

Complement	Choppy Sentences	Compound Complements
predicate adjective	Tennis is **fast-paced**. It is **fun**.	Tennis is **fast-paced** and **fun**.
predicate noun	One great sport is **tennis**. Another is **badminton**.	Two great sports are **tennis** and **badminton**.
direct object	Playing tennis well requires **equipment**. It requires **practice**.	Playing tennis well requires **equipment** and **practice**.
indirect object	Tennis gives **me** great exercise. It gives **Ed** exercise.	Tennis gives **Ed** and **me** great exercise.

Punctuation Tip You may want to include interesting details that are not essential. Set off nonessential elements with **commas**, **dashes**, or **parentheses**.

Example: Tennis, which requires practice, is a fun sport.

Example: Tennis is fun, as is the related sport of badminton.

Example: Tennis is fun—both to watch and to play.

Example: Tennis requires equipment (rackets, balls, and shoes), as well as practice.

Fixing Choppy Sentences In a pair of sentences, look at the complements that follow each verb. Then, combine the sentences with compound complements when it makes sense to do so.

Grammar in Your Writing

Reread the draft of your cause-and-effect essay aloud. Listen for pairs of choppy sentences that can be combined with complements.

Revising Choppy Sentences

1. Introduce the grammar skill, using the instruction on the student page.
2. Discuss the rules and examples, as well as the strategies for fixing choppy writing.
3. Have students follow the instruction under Grammar in Your Writing to improve their sentence variety.

Teaching the Grammar Skill

1. Review complements by having students identify the underlined part of speech in each of the following sentences.

   Give <u>her</u> the book.
   Answer: indirect object

   Elizabeth I was a powerful English <u>queen</u>. **Answer:** predicate noun

   The weather is <u>frigid</u>.
   Answer: predicate adjective

   Mother made <u>meatloaf</u> for dinner.
   Answer: direct object

2. Have students combine the following pairs of sentences using compound complements.

   Snakes make good pets. Iguanas make good pets. **Possible response:** Both snakes and iguanas make good pets.

   Vincent is smart. Vincent is athletic. **Possible response:** Vincent is smart and athletic.

   The author has written two novels. He also has written numerous short stories. **Possible response:** The author has written two novels and numerous short stories.

   Lorenzo told me what happened. He told my sister, too. **Possible response:** Lorenzo told my sister and me what happened.

Student Model

Review the Student Model with the class, using the annotations to analyze the writer's use of the elements of a cause-and-effect essay.

Teaching from the Student Model

1. Explain that the Student Model is a sample and that essays can be longer.

2. Have students identify the effects of sun on the skin. (**Answer:** skin damage and an increased risk of skin cancer) Note how the first paragraph presents facts and observations to support the writer's thesis.

3. Have a volunteer read the second paragraph of the Student Model aloud, and draw students' attention to the sentence that is bracketed by the third annotation. Point out that the writer has summarized information from his research in this sentence. Explain to students that they will have to paraphrase and summarize the research they find for their essays.

4. Ask students to point out transitional words or phrases that the writer uses to show cause and effect. (**Possible responses:** *because, if, once, as a result*)

5. Read aloud the final two paragraphs of the Student Model. Point out that the writer clearly explains the cause-and-effect relationship between sun exposure and skin damage and that this adds weight to the writer's message.

Connecting to Real-Life Writing

Explain that information about causes and effects can be found almost everywhere. Discuss with the class how information in news articles often explains causes and effects of problems in a community. Have students find at least three examples of cause-and-effect text structures that affect a community and bring them to class.

STUDENT MODEL: **Bryson McCollum, Cumming, GA**

Common Core State Standards

Language
2.b. Spell correctly.

Don't Get Burned

Sunscreen should always be worn when you are out in the sun because the sun can be very dangerous to your skin. If your skin is exposed to the sun's ultraviolet rays without sunscreen, it will turn red, burn, and hurt. Many people believe that burning their skin is one step closer to their desire of getting a tan. They do not realize that both burning and tanning your skin can damage it. Once you burn or tan and the redness or color begins to fade, the damaged skin may begin to peel, leaving a new, unhealthy, thin, and sensitive layer of skin.

What you do to your skin as a child and as a young adult will affect your skin for your full life. Sunscreen can help. Doctors recommend that children apply sunscreen often and at least 30 minutes before going out in the sun. Adults, children, and young adults will benefit from using sunscreens with sun protection factor (SPF) numbers of 15 or more. The SPF numbers give some idea of how long you can stay out in the sun without burning. For example, an SPF of 15 should protect you for approximately 150 minutes—nearly two and a half hours—in the sun. While some sunscreens say they are waterproof, they do not give you total protection from water and sweat. As a result, it is also recommended that sunscreen be applied often.

Nobody's skin is immune to skin cancer. If your skin is damaged a lot by the sun during your childhood and adult years, your chances of getting skin cancer are greater than they are for people who have taken better steps toward protection. Some signs of skin cancer are leathery scab-like patches of skin that may be discolored, bleed, or burn. If you have been burned several times in a short period of time, you should be checked by a doctor because some forms of skin cancer cannot be detected.

So, think twice the next time you are at the beach or the pool without sunscreen, hoping to absorb the sun. Be careful and apply sunscreen to protect yourself from skin damage. Remember that even though a tan may look nice for a few days, it may cause you health problems and unhealthy-looking skin in the future.

Bryson begins by stating his thesis, the cause-and-effect relationship he will show.

Details about the sun's ability to damage the skin help support the writer's purpose.

The writer uses examples to make doctors' recommendations clear.

Each paragraph focuses on a cause or an effect related to Bryson's thesis.

Editing and Proofreading

Correct errors in grammar, spelling, and punctuation.

Focus on spelling. In words with multiple syllables, use a dictionary to help you spell the unstressed vowel sound. The sound, known as a *schwa*, is an open neutral sound like you hear in the words *ago*, *agent*, and *sanity*. The *schwa* sound can be spelled with almost any vowel. In a dictionary, the *schwa* is represented with the symbol ə.

Publishing and Presenting

Consider one of the following ways to share your writing:

Make a movie proposal. Treat your cause-and-effect essay like a script for a short film. Create a storyboard that shows what different scenes might look like.

Make an oral presentation. Read your essay aloud to classmates or family members. Then, invite questions and discussion.

Reflecting on Your Writing

Writer's Journal Jot down your answers to this question:
How do you view your topic differently now that you have analyzed its related causes and effects?

Rubric for Self-Assessment

Find evidence in your writing to address each category. Then, use the rating scale to grade your work.

Criteria	Rating Scale
Purpose/Focus Develops an informative and explanatory text that analyzes clear cause-and-effect relationships	*not very* .... *very* 1 2 3 4
Organization Introduces the topic clearly; organizes information to show cause and effect; provides a concluding statement that follows from the information presented	1 2 3 4
Development of Ideas/Elaboration Presents a clear thesis statement; develops the topic with relevant facts, definitions, concrete details, quotations, and examples	1 2 3 4
Language Uses appropriate transitions to clarify relationships among ideas and concepts	1 2 3 4
Conventions Uses proper capitalization, spelling, and punctuation, including correct use of commas, parentheses, and dashes	1 2 3 4

PART 2 • Writing Process **709**

Spiral Review
Earlier in the unit, you learned about **subject complements** (p. 638) and about **object complements** (p. 648). Review your essay to be sure that you have used complements correctly.

Editing and Proofreading

1. Introduce the editing and proofreading focus, using the instruction on the student page.

2. Have students edit and proofread their essays, correcting grammar, spelling, punctuation, and word choice. Make sure they look for errors of the type noted in the lesson focus and the Spiral Review.

Teaching the Editing Focus

1. Explain to students that in words with several syllables, it is sometimes hard to determine how to spell the syllable that contains a *schwa*, or "uh" sound, for its vowel. Suggest that they become more familiar with these words by looking them up in a dictionary.

2. As a class, correct the spelling of the misspelled word in each of the following sentences:

   We are studying French *litereture*.
   Answer: *literature*
   I am *optamistic* about my grades this quarter.
   Answer: *optimistic*

Six Traits Focus

	Ideas		Word Choice
	Organization		Sentence Fluency
	Voice	✓	Conventions

✅ ASSESS

Publishing and Presenting

1. Suggest students make rough sketches for their storyboards or use pictures from magazines.

2. Have students practice reading their papers aloud to a partner before presenting to a larger audience.

Reflecting on Your Writing

Suggest students compare the various drafts of their essay to identify any new insights they had during the writing process.

 Interactive Whiteboard Activities

Use this tool to project and edit student writing!

PART 2 • Writing Process **709**

✅ STRATEGIES **FOR TEST TAKING**

When responding to a prompt for a cause-and-effect essay, suggest that students proceed as follows:

- **Review the passage,** if one is given, writing down the main causes it mentions.

- **Create a cluster diagram** by circling each cause you noted and then adding more circles with items related to the main causes. Then, connect each of these additional items with lines to the related main cause, and number them sequentially.

- **Organize the details** by making an outline of the main causes with the related events underneath. Use the numbers in the cluster diagram to put the events in order. List only as many main causes as the question specifies.

- **Elaborate** by referring to your outline for details. Explain how each main cause resulted in the situation under discussion, describing events in sequence.

Assessment

In this assessment (pp. 710–715), students apply and reinforce their mastery of the Common Core State Standards and the skills taught in Unit 5. The assessment is divided into four sections, including a section of Constructed Response tasks.

1. Before assigning each section, review the relevant Common Core State Standards and unit skills with students.

2. Set a time limit for the multiple choice items in each section, allowing a little over one minute per question. Allow twenty minutes for any Timed Writing questions.

3. Administer each of the first three sections of the assessment (pp. 710–713).

4. Use the Constructed Response tasks on pages 714–715 to assess the depth of students' mastery of standards taught in the unit. Follow the suggestions on teacher pages 714–715 for assigning tasks and for supporting and evaluating student performance.

Reteaching Skills

For each practice, use the Reteaching Plan on the same page as the answers to determine which skills require reteaching, given the items students answered incorrectly.

Question	Instructional Pages to Reteach
1	632
2	650
3	629
4	629
5	632, 640
6	650, 677
7	—
8	650, 666

Assessment: Skills

SELECTED RESPONSE

I. Reading Literature

Common Core State Standards

RL.6.1, RL.6.2, RL.6.4; W.6.3, W.6.3.d, W.6.4
[For the full wording of the standards, see the standards chart in the front of your textbook.]

Directions: *Read the passage from "A Crippled Boy," by My-Van Tran. Then, answer each question that follows.*

Long, long ago there was a boy called Theo. He was crippled in both legs and could hardly walk. Since he could not work, he had no choice but to live on rice and vegetables which kind people gave him…

…To amuse himself Theo practiced throwing pebbles at targets. Hour after hour he would spend practicing his aim…

One day Theo was under his favorite banyan tree. To his surprise, he heard a drumbeat… It happened that the King was out for a country walk with some of his officials and was passing by Theo's tree…

Theo was very frightened and tried to get away; but he could not crawl very far. The King asked Theo what he had been doing. Theo told the King his story.

Then the King asked Theo to <u>demonstrate</u> his skill at pebble throwing… The King was impressed and asked Theo to return with him to the palace where the King said, "I have a little job for you to do."

The following day, before the King had a meeting with his mandarins, he ordered Theo to sit quietly behind a curtain. The King had ordered a few holes to be made in the curtain so that Theo could see what was going on.

"Most of my mandarins talk too much," the King explained. "They never bother to listen to me or let me finish my sentence. So if anybody opens his mouth to speak while I am talking, just throw a pebble into his mouth. This will teach him to shut up."

Sure enough, just as the meeting was about to start one mandarin opened his big mouth, ready to speak.

Oops! Something got into his mouth and he quickly closed it.

Another mandarin opened his mouth to speak but strangely enough he, too, shut his mouth without saying a word.

A miracle had happened. Throughout the whole meeting all the mandarins kept their silence.

For once the King could speak as much as he wanted without being interrupted. The King was extremely pleased with his success and the help that Theo had given him.

After that he always treasured Theo's presence and service…

710 UNIT 5 • How much do our communities shape us?

✔ STRATEGIES **FOR TEST TAKING**

Remind students to get sufficient sleep the night before taking standardized tests. With rest, their minds will be sharper and they will be better able to focus. Emphasize that cramming the night before an exam is a poor strategy to use, because details are often forgotten.

1. **Part A** Many **folk tales** feature characters who represent moral values or good behavior. Whose good behavior is highlighted in this story?

   A. Theo's
   B. the King's
   C. the King's officials'
   D. the mandarins'

   Part B Which phrase from the passage best supports the answer to Part A?

   A. "Hour after hour he would spend practicing his aim"
   B. "I have a little job for you to do."
   C. "just as the meeting was about to start one mandarin opened his big mouth"
   D. "Most of my mandarins talk too much."

2. What is the **universal theme** of this folk tale?

   A. It is good to work for the King.
   B. Some people talk too much.
   C. Skill and practice will be rewarded.
   D. Some people are luckier than others.

3. **Part A** In folk literature, **irony** involves surprises, unexpected events, and interesting contradictions. What ironic situation occurs in the story?

   A. Theo relied on others to support him.
   B. The King thought that Theo's pebble-throwing skill could be useful.
   C. The King passed by Theo's tree.
   D. Theo could see from his hiding place.

   Part B Which phrase from the passage best supports the answer to Part A?

   A. "he had no choice but to live on rice and vegetables which kind people gave him"
   B. "The King had ordered a few holes to be made in the curtain"

   C. "The King was out for a country walk"
   D. "The King was impressed and asked Theo to return with him to the palace"

4. What other **ironic** situation arises in the story?

   A. Theo was at first frightened of the King.
   B. Although Theo could not work in his village, he does valued work for the King.
   C. The King was impressed with Theo.
   D. The King felt that his mandarins talked too much and never listened to him.

5. What effect did the King hope that Theo's pebble-throwing skill would have?

   A. Theo would not be scared of the King.
   B. The mandarins would be scolded.
   C. Theo will no longer have to live alone.
   D. People will learn to stop talking while the King is speaking.

6. What **theme** does the ending of the story help to express?

   A. It is always better to talk too little rather than too much.
   B. Physical weakness does not equal a lack of skill.
   C. Do not rely on a King for help.
   D. People who know how to throw pebbles can learn other skills.

7. Which phrase is closest in meaning to the underlined word *demonstrate*?

   A. show clearly
   B. protest
   C. officials
   D. a disability

🕐 Timed Writing

8. Write an original story that has a **universal theme**. Include figurative language such as **personification**.

➡ **GO ON**

☑ **ASSESS**

I. Reading Literature

1. **Part A:** A
   Part B: A

2. C

3. **Part A:** D
   Part B: C

4. B

5. D

6. B

7. A

🕐 **Timed Writing**

8. Students should write an original story that exemplifies a universal theme and that uses figurative language.

 **ASSESS**

II. Reading Informational Text

1. **Part A:** A
   Part B: C

II. Reading Informational Text

Directions: *Read the excerpt from an online article. Then, answer each question that follows.*

 **Common Core State Standards**

RI.6.2, RI.6.5; W.6.5; L.6.1, L.6.3.a
[For the full wording of the standards, see the standards chart in the front of your textbook.]

To plan for a trip to Washington, D.C., Lucinda has prepared an outline of sites she wants to visits at the National Mall. She expects to learn and see many new things on this enriching trip.

I. Memorials and Monuments
   A. Lincoln Memorial
      1. built in 1922 and pictured on pennies
      2. 36 columns representing the states of the Union when Lincoln died
   B. Vietnam Veterans Memorial
      1. called "the wall"
      2. inscribed with the names of about 58,000 American armed troops killed during the Vietnam War
   C. Washington Monument
      1. 555.5-foot obelisk near east end of reflecting pool
      2. designed by architect Robert Mills

II. Museums
   A. United States Holocaust Memorial Museum
      1. most visited site in the mall
      2. remembers victims of the Holocaust
   B. Freer Gallery
      1. museum of American and Asian Art
   C. Hirshorn Museum and Sculpture Garden
      1. one of the best collections of modern art in the world
      2. includes art by Edward Hopper and Georgia O'Keeffe
      3. outside is a sculpture garden

1. **Part A** According to Lucinda's outline, what is she most interested in visiting?
   A. museums, memorials, and monuments
   B. Lincoln Memorial
   C. Hirshorn Museum and Sculpture Garden
   D. sites dedicated to sad events

Part B What part of the outline best supports the answer to Part A?
   A. The Lincoln Memorial appears at the top of the first list, so it must be most important to her.
   B. The Hirshorn Museum and Sculpture Garden has three supporting details, more than any other subtopic listed.
   C. "Memorials and Monuments" and "Museums" are the main ideas of this outline.
   D. Both the Vietnam Veterans Memorial and the United States Holocaust Memorial Museum are dedicated to sad events.

III. Writing and Language Conventions

Directions: *Read the following excerpt from a multimedia report. Then, answer each question that follows.*

> **Script for Multimedia Report: Maui**
>
> (1) **Visual:** photo of beach in Maui (2) Maui has 120 miles of coastline. (3) Maui has over 30 miles of beaches. (4) Maui is a large island. (5) **Visual:** photo of Maui taken from the air. (6) The most interesting thing to do in Maui is hike up the Haleakala Crater. (7) Haleakala is the largest dormant volcano on earth. (8) At the top, the fog is very thick and it is surprisingly cold. (9) **Visual:** photo of crater (10) Because of Maui's diverse landscape, there are enough activities to keep anyone busy.

1. Which revision to sentences 2 and 3 properly combines **complements** to eliminate choppy sentences?
   A. Maui has 120 miles of coastline and it also has over 30 miles of beaches.
   B. Maui has 120 miles of coastline, but only 30 miles of beaches.
   C. Maui's coastlines and beaches are over 120 miles and 30 miles.
   D. Maui has 120 miles of coastline and over 30 miles of beaches.

2. Which portion of sentence 10 is a **subordinate clause**?
   A. Because of Maui's diverse landscape
   B. there are enough
   C. activities to keep
   D. anyone busy

3. What kind of **sentence** is sentence 7?
   A. complex sentence
   B. compound sentence
   C. simple sentence
   D. subordinate setnence

4. Identify the **predicate noun** in sentence 4.
   A. Maui
   B. is
   C. large
   D. island

 **ASSESS**

III. Writing and Language Conventions

1. D
2. A
3. C
4. D

Reteaching Plan

Question	Pages to Reteach
1	638, 648
2	664
3	674
4	638

Constructed Response

Assigning Tasks/Reteaching Skills

Use the chart below to choose appropriate Constructed Response tasks by identifying which tasks assess lessons in the textbook that you have taught. Use the same lessons for reteaching when students' performance indicates a failure to fully master a standard. For additional instruction and practice, assign the *Common Core Companion* pages indicated for each task.

Task	Where Taught/ Pages to Reteach	Common Core Companion Pages
1	628–631, 632, 650	54–60, 184–195, 267–274
2	628–631, 632	28–40, 321–330
3	628–631, 632	15–27, 267–274
4	628–631, 666	41–53, 286–292
5	628–631, 650	15–27, 304–310, 311–312
6	610	15–27, 246–252, 253–266

Assessment Pacing

In assigning the Writing tasks on this student page, allow a class period for the completion of a task. As an alternative, assign tasks as homework. In assigning the Speaking and Listening and Research tasks on the facing page, consider having students do any required preparation as a homework assignment. Then, allow a class period for the presentations themselves.

Evaluating Constructed Response

Use the rubric at the bottom of this teacher edition page to evaluate students' mastery of the standards as demonstrated in their Constructed Responses. Review the rubric with students before they begin work so they know the criteria by which their work will be evaluated.

CONSTRUCTED RESPONSE

Directions: *Follow the instructions to complete the tasks below as required by your teacher.*

As you work on each task, incorporate both general academic vocabulary and literary terms you learned in Parts 1 and 2.

Common Core State Standards
RL.6.2, RL.6.3, RL.6.4, RL.6.5; W.6.2, W.6.7, W.6.8, W.6.9.a; SL.6.1, SL.6.4, SL.6.5; L.6.1
[For the full wording of the standards, see the standards chart in the front of your textbook.]

Writing

TASK 1 Literature [RL.6.5; W.6.2; W.6.9.a]

Analyze a Key Scene

Write an essay in which you analyze how a key scene in a literary work from Part 2 helps to communicate the work's universal theme.

- Identify and describe an important scene from a selection in Part 2.
- Determine the universal theme of the work.
- Explain how the scene you chose contributes to the development of the universal theme. Include details from the scene that help readers understand the message of the work.
- Provide a conclusion that sums up your analysis.

TASK 2 Literature [RL.6.3; L.6.1]

Analyze Structure and Theme

Write an essay in which you analyze how two pieces of folk literature use various structures to develop theme.

- Identify a work of folk literature from Part 2 that features a structural device such as repetition, patterns, or archetypes.
- Write an essay in which you discuss how the structural device helps develop the work's theme. Explain whether or not the device makes the work more effective, and why.

- Identify a second work of folk literature that features a different structural device. Analyze the device's role in the development of theme, and evaluate the effectiveness of the device.
- Compare and contrast the effectiveness of the structural devices in the two stories you chose.
- Make sure your sentences are not fragments and that they contain complete ideas.

TASK 3 Literature [RL.6.2; W.6.9.a]

Evaluate Theme

Write an essay in which you evaluate the theme of a work that contains fantasy.

Part 1

- Identify a story in Part 2 in which the theme is affected by the use of fantasy. As you are reviewing the story, take notes on the the theme.

Part 2

- Write an essay in which you analyze the ways in which fantastic elements strengthen the theme in the work.
- Use a formal writing style and tone.
- Sum up your analysis in a strong conclusion.

714 UNIT 5 • How much do our communities shape us?

CONSTRUCTED RESPONSE RUBRIC: STANDARDS MASTERY

	Rating Scale
Critical Thinking: How clearly and consistently does the student pursue the specific mode of reasoning or discourse required by the standard, as specified in the prompt (e.g., comparing and contrasting, analyzing, explaining)?	not very very 1 2 3 4 5
Focus: How well does the student understand and apply the focus concepts of the standard, as specified in the prompt (e.g., development of theme or of complex characters, effects of structure, and so on)?	not very very 1 2 3 4 5
Support/Elaboration: How well does the student support points with textual or other evidence? How relevant, sufficient, and varied is the evidence provided?	not very very 1 2 3 4 5
Insight: How original, sophisticated, or compelling are the insights the student achieves by applying the standard to the text(s)?	not very very 1 2 3 4 5
Expression of Ideas: How well does the student organize and support ideas? How well does the student use language, including word choice and conventions, in the expression of ideas?	not very very 1 2 3 4 5

Speaking and Listening

TASK 4 Literature [RL.6.4; SL.6.1]

Compare Uses of Personification

Lead a discussion in which you analyze and compare the portrayals of animal characters in one or more literary works from Part 2.

- Come to the discussion prepared with general ideas about the reasons folk tales and fables often include animals with human qualities. In addition, prepare specific questions about at least two animal characters from Part 2 and their similarities and differences.
- Pose your questions and respond to ideas contributed by group members.
- Review the key ideas expressed by the group and state any new ideas you arrive at during the discussion.

Research

TASK 6 Literature [RL.6.2; W.6.7, W.6.8]

 How much do our communities shape us?

In this unit, you have read literature that examines the ways that people and groups are shaped by their communities. Now you will conduct a short research project about how people shape the communities they live in. Use both literature you have read and your research to reflect on this unit's Big Question. Review the following guidelines before you begin your research:

- Focus your research on people or groups who have worked hard to make changes that improved their communities.

TASK 5 Literature [RL.6.2; SL.6.4, SL.6.5]

Analyze Theme

Prepare and present an oral presentation in which you evaluate the theme of a work of literature from Part 2.

- State the theme of the work you selected.
- Explain how the theme is conveyed through particular details in the work. Consider character, plot, setting, elements of fantasy, and cultural details.
- Organize your presentation by sequencing your ideas in a way that helps your audience follow your reasoning.
- If you have the technology available, prepare a slideshow to accompany your oral presentation. Alternatively, create a poster or other visual display.

- Gather relevant information from at least two reliable sources. Your sources may be print or digital.
- Take notes as you research the improvements people and groups make to communities.
- Cite your sources.

When you have completed your research, write a response to the Big Question. Discuss how your initial ideas have changed or been reinforced. Support your response with an example from literature and an example from your research.

PART 2 • Assessment: Skills **715**

---

1. Consider having students work with partners or in groups to complete Constructed Response tasks involving listening and speaking. For tasks that you assign for individual work, you may still wish to have students rehearse with partners, who can provide constructive feedback.

2. As students rehearse, have them keep in mind these tips:

   - Present findings and evidence clearly and concisely.
   - Observe conventions of standard English grammar and usage.
   - Be relaxed and friendly but maintain a formal tone.
   - Make eye contact with the audience, pronounce words clearly, and vary your pace.
   - When working with a group, respond thoughtfully to others' positions, modifying your own in response to new evidence.

Linking Constructed Response to Independent Reading

If you wish to cover the standards with students' independent reading, adapt Constructed Response tasks of your choice to the works they have selected. (Independent reading suggestions appear on the next page.)

How much do our communities shape us?

1. Remind students that the unit Big Question is "How much do our communities shape us?"

2. Have students complete their responses to the prompt on the student page. Point out that they have read selections in this unit about different approaches to or views of community and that they should draw on these selections in their responses.

:: DIFFERENTIATED INSTRUCTION

Strategy for Less Proficient Readers
Assign a Constructed Response task and then have students meet in groups to review the standard assessed in that task. Remind students of the selections or independent readings to which they have previously applied the standard. Have groups summarize what they learned in applying the standard and then present their summaries. Discuss, clarifying any points of confusion. After students have completed their tasks, have groups meet again to evaluate members' work. Encourage members to revise their work based on the feedback they receive.

EL Strategy for English Learners
For each assigned Constructed Response task, review the instructions with students. Clarify the meaning of any unfamiliar vocabulary, emphasizing routine classroom words such as *scene, message,* and *traits,* and academic vocabulary such as *evaluate.*

Next, have students note ideas for their responses. Pair students, and have them review each other's notes, asking questions to clarify meaning and suggesting improvements. Encourage students to ask for your assistance in supplying English words or expressions they may require.

PART 2 • Assessment: Skills **715**

❶ About the Quotation

Paul McCartney (b. 1942) is an English singer, songwriter, and composer.

Discussion: Ask students to discuss the meaning of McCartney's quotation about people and animals. Then, ask them to decide whether they agree with the quotation. Have them explain and support their positions with sound reasoning and evidence.

❷ Critical Viewing

Possible response: Pose the critical viewing question to the class. Then, guide the class in a discussion about the question. Encourage students to build upon each other's ideas as they share their responses. Remind students to support their responses with reasons and evidence.

"You can judge a man's ❶ **true character** by the way he **treats** his fellow animals."

—Paul McCartney

❷ DEVELOPING ESSENTIAL UNDERSTANDING

People and Animals

People and animals interact on a daily basis in most communities. Communities are continuously reminded about the importance of animals in the lives of people in a community and vice versa, whether it is a guide dog helping a visually impaired person or a pet rescue facility saving the lives of stray dogs and cats. The selections in this text set will help students develop essential understanding about the relationship between people and animals by raising questions such as:

• Why do people help animals in need?

• In what ways do animals help people?

• How do animals and humans benefit from helping each other?

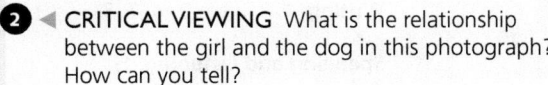

PART 3
TEXT SETS DEVELOPING INSIGHT

PEOPLE AND ANIMALS

The selections in this unit all deal with the Big Question: **How much do our communities shape us?** Members of a community often benefit from working together. In the texts that follow, humans and animals cooperate in a variety of ways to help one another. As you read, think about the ways that mutual support can be beneficial to all the creatures that share a community.

2 ◄ **CRITICAL VIEWING** What is the relationship between the girl and the dog in this photograph? How can you tell?

CLOSE READING TOOL

Use the Close Reading Tool to practice the strategies you learned in this unit.

 READINGS IN PART 3

 ANCHOR TEXT **MYTH**
Prologue from The Whale Rider
Witi Ihimaera (p. 718)

 **MAGAZINE ARTICLE**
The Case of the Monkeys That Fell From the Trees
Susan E. Quinlan (p. 726)

 **WEB ARTICLE**
Rescuers to Carry Oxygen Masks for Pets
Associated Press (p. 734)

 **INFOGRAPHIC**
2012 Pet Ownership Statistics
American Pet Products Association (p. 738)

 **SHORT STORY**
The Old Woman Who Lived With the Wolves
Chief Luther Standing Bear (p. 740)

 **NEWS RELEASE**
Satellites and Sea Lions
NASA (p. 746)

 **NARRATIVE ESSAY**
Turkeys
Bailey White (p. 750)

PART 3 • People and Animals **717**

CUSTOMIZING THE TEXT SET

Close Reading Tool
Use the Close Reading Tool to project the anchor text on a whiteboard and work through it as a whole-class activity. Students also have the opportunity to read this selection independently, with scaffolds available as needed.

Curriculum Builder
Customize this program by rearranging existing selections, adding selection titles of your choosing, and uploading your own resources—all online!

---

3 **Readings in Part 3**
About the Texts
(For quantitative and qualitative measures of text complexity, see the rubrics on the opening pages of each selection.)

MYTH: *Prologue from* The Whale Rider

Summary A myth explains the coming of the Maori people to New Zealand and their respect for nature.

MAGAZINE ARTICLE: The Case of the Monkeys That Fell From the Trees

Summary Scientists research the eating habits of howler monkeys.

WEB ARTICLE: Rescuers to Carry Oxygen Masks for Pets

Summary One Wisconsin community decides to supply fire trucks with oxygen masks for small pets.

INFOGRAPHIC: 2012 Pet Ownership Statistics

SHORT STORY: The Old Woman Who Lived With the Wolves

Summary When a young Sioux woman takes shelter from a storm, wolves befriend and protect her.

NEWS RELEASE: Satellites and Sea Lions

Summary Oceanographers tag animals to learn about the ocean.

NARRATIVE ESSAY: Turkeys

Summary The author recalls how her childhood illness led to the renewal of a wild turkey population.

Extended Reading Opportunity
LITERATURE: Myths and Stories from the Americas

You may want to assign this extended reading to accompany the readings in Part 3. Further details about this text and other extended readings appear on the Independent Reading pages at the end of this unit.

 **Audio**

Summary Audio is available in the *Student eText* and on the *Hear It!* CD-ROM.

LESSON PACING GUIDE

ANCHOR TEXT (5 DAYS)

Prologue from **The Whale Rider**

DAY 1 Preteach/Teach

- Introduce the topic of the text set and its relationship to the Big Question.
- To motivate and engage students, discuss the quotation and the Critical Viewing question.
- Direct students to read the selection independently.

DAYS 2–4 Teach/Extend

- Use the Comprehension questions to confirm student understanding of the text.
- Develop vocabulary by assigning and monitoring the Language Study activities.
- Develop analytic ability by reviewing the Literary Analysis questions and instruction.
- Assign the Group Discussion and monitor responses to discussion questions.
- Assign the Writing to Sources activity, distributing copies of the Take Notes worksheet to help students organize their thoughts and information.

DAY 5 Extend/Assess

- Preview the Research activity, distributing copies of the Take Notes worksheet to help students plan their note-taking strategy. Assign the activity as homework.
- Administer the Selection Test or the Open-Book Test to monitor student progress.

RELATED TEXTS (2 DAYS EACH)

The Case of the Monkeys That Fell From the Trees • Rescuers to Carry Oxygen Masks for Pets • 2012 Pet Owner Statistics • The Old Woman Who Lived With the Wolves • Satellites and Sea Lions • Turkeys

DAY 1 Preteach/Teach

- Review with students the topic of the text set and what they have learned from the previous readings.
- Build knowledge of the topic by directing students to read the text independently.
- Develop vocabulary by reviewing the Language Study activities.
- Build students' ability to think critically using the Literary Analysis questions.

DAY 2 Extend/Assess

- Extend exploration of the text through the Discuss, Research, and Write activities.
- Administer the Selection Test or the Open-Book Test to monitor student progress.

ASSESSMENT: SYNTHESIS (1–2 DAYS)

DAYS 1–2 Assess

- Review with the class the Criteria for Success for the Speaking and Listening activity. Assign the activity, and monitor student progress.
- Review with students the Criteria for Success for the Writing assignment, and assign the activity.
- Review with students the Self-Evaluation Rubric for the Writing to Sources activity. Direct students to complete the assignment.

Common Core State Standards

Reading Literature 1, 2, 3, 4
Reading Informational Text 1, 2, 5, 6
Writing 1, 2, 2.a-c, 3, 4, 7, 8, 9.a
Speaking and Listening 1, 2, 4
Language 1, 2, 3, 4, 4.b, 5, 6

Daily Block Scheduling

Each day in this Lesson Pacing Guide represents a 40–50 minute period. Teachers using block scheduling may combine days to revise pacing. In addition, teachers may differentiate and support core instruction by integrating components for extended and intensive support as students require. See the Guide to Resources (facing page).

GUIDE TO RESOURCES

RESOURCES	PRINT	CD	ONLINE	ANCHOR TEXT Prologue from The Whale Rider	The Case of the Monkeys That Fell From the Trees	Rescuers to Carry Oxygen Masks for Pets	2012 Pet Ownership Statistics	The Old Woman Who Lived With the Wolves	Satellites and Sea Lions	Turkeys
SELECTION SUPPORT										
Close Reading Practice	CRN		✔	✔						
Academic Vocabulary	SCW		✔	✔	✔	✔	✔	✔	✔	✔
Discussion: Take Notes worksheet	SCW		✔	✔	✔	✔	✔		✔	✔	✔
Writing to Sources	SCW		✔	✔	✔	✔	✔	✔	✔	✔	✔
Research: Take Notes worksheet	SCW		✔	✔	✔	✔	✔		✔	✔	✔
STANDARDS SUPPORT										
Standards Instruction and Practice	CCC		✔	✔	✔	✔	✔	✔	✔	✔	✔
MONITOR PROGRESS										
Selection Test		EV	✔	✔	✔	✔	✔		✔	✔	✔
Open-Book Test		EV	✔	✔	✔	✔	✔		✔	✔	✔
ASSESSMENT: SYNTHESIS GRAPHIC ORGANIZERS AND RUBRICS										
Speaking and Listening: Graphic Organizer			✔							
Writing: Graphic Organizer			✔							
Writing to Sources: Graphic Organizer			✔							
Self-Evaluation Rubric			✔							
DIGITAL RESOURCES										
Close Reading Tool			✔	✔						
Online Writer's Notebook			✔	✔	✔	✔	✔	✔	✔	✔

CRN Close Reading Notebook   **SCW** Student Companion All-in-One Workbook   **EV** ExamView   **CCC** Common Core Companion

Group work   Whole class instruction   Independent work   Assessment   Digital Resource

MULTIDRAFT READING

Essential Understanding

First, students should read the entire selection on their own. Then, to assist struggling readers and to deepen comprehension for all, you may wish to guide them through the selection by asking them the close reading questions provided in the margins. Have students apply the multidraft reading protocols as they examine specific "chunks" of text related to these questions. For each reading, have students set the purpose indicated:

- **First reading:** Students should read the selection independently and think about its basic meaning.

- **Second reading:** Students should analyze the text's key ideas and details and its craft and structure.

- **Third reading:** Students should integrate knowledge and ideas; connect to the Big Question, other texts, and the world; and use teacher-led Close Reading discussion questions to examine particularly rich and significant passages.

For more guidance, refer to the *Classroom Strategies and Teaching Routines* card on multidraft reading.

🔔 Daily Bellringer

For each class during which you teach this selection, have students complete one of the five Quick Write activities for Week 31 in *Daily Bellringer Activities*. You may wish to use additional activities that are applicable to this selection.

❶ Background

In the Maori legend of Paikea, Kahutia Te Rangi is carried by the whale Paikea to New Zealand's North Island. He then assumes the name of the whale and makes his home on the island.

Vocabulary

1. Write the following words and definitions on the board:

   yearning *n.* feeling of wanting something very much

   teemed *v.* was full of

   apex *n.* highest point

2. Have students say each word aloud.

---

❶ *Prologue from* The

Whale Rider

Witi Ihimaera

yearning ▶
(yʉr′ niŋ) *n.* feeling of wanting something very much

❷ In the old days, in the years that have gone before us, the land and sea felt a great emptiness, a yearning. The mountains were like a stairway to heaven, and the lush green rainforest was a rippling cloak of many colors. The sky was iridescent, swirling with the patterns of wind and clouds; sometimes it reflected the prisms of rainbow or southern aurora.[1] The sea was ever-changing, shimmering and seamless to the sky. This was the well at the bottom of the world, and when you looked into it you felt you could see to the end of forever.

---

1. **southern aurora** (ô rôr′ ə) *n.* streamers or arches of light appearing above Earth in the Southern Hemisphere.

718 UNIT 5 • How much do our communities shape us?

© TEXT COMPLEXITY RUBRIC

Prologue from **The Whale Rider**		
Qualitative Measures	Context/Knowledge Demands	Coast of New Zealand; Maori culture 1 2 ③ 4 5
	Structure/Language Conventionality and Clarity	Challenging vocabulary and diction; complex sentence structure; foreign words 1 2 3 4 ⑤
	Levels of Meaning/ Purpose/Concept Level	Challenging concept (arrival of humankind) 1 2 3 ④ 5
Quantitative Measures	Text Length	Word Count: 1,309
	Lexile	970L

This is not to say that the land and sea were without life, without vivacity. The tuatara, the ancient lizard with its third eye, was sentinel here, unblinking in the hot sun, watching and waiting to the east. The moa browsed in giant wingless herds across the southern island. Within the warm stomach of the rainforests, kiwi,[2] weka,[3] and the other birds foraged for *huhu* and similar succulent insects. The forests were loud with the clatter of tree bark, chatter of cicada, and murmur of fish-laden streams. Sometimes the forest grew suddenly quiet, and in wet bush could be heard the filigree of fairy laughter like a sparkling glissando.[4]

The sea, too, teemed with fish, but they also seemed to be waiting. They swam in brilliant shoals, like rains of glittering dust, throughout the greenstone depths—*hapuku, manga, kahawai, tamure, moki,* and *warehou*—herded by shark or *mango ururoa*. Sometimes from far off a white shape would be seen flying through the sea, but it would only be the serene flight of the *tarawhai*, the stingray with the spike on its tail.

Waiting. Waiting for the seeding. Waiting for the gifting. Waiting for the blessing to come.

◄ **teemed**
(tēmd) *v.* was full of

---

2. **kiwi** (kē′ wē) *n.* small, flightless New Zealand bird.
3. **weka** (wā′ kä) *n.* flightless New Zealand wading bird.
4. **glissando** (gli sän′ dō) *n.* quick sliding up or down the musical scale.

PART 3 • *Prologue from The Whale Rider* 719

DEVELOPING INSIGHT

❷ Close Reading

1. **Key Ideas and Details** Read aloud the passage to students. **Ask:** What details describe the setting? What can you infer from those details?

   Possible response: Details about the land, sea, mountains, and sky help describe the setting. They suggest that nature was vibrant.

2. **Craft and Structure**
   Ask: What are examples of similes and metaphors in the passage? What does this figurative language emphasize?

   Possible response: The simile "The mountains were like a stairway to heaven" and metaphor "the lush green rainforest was a rippling cloak of many colors" emphasize how special the world looked in the past.

3. **Integration of Knowledge and Ideas**
   Ask: How does the author use literary devices to set a certain mood?

   Possible response: The author uses metaphors, similes, and personification to set a mood of anticipation. For example, personification in the first sentence suggests that the land and sea are waiting for something.

© TEXT COMPLEXITY **READER AND TASK SUGGESTIONS**

Prologue from The Whale Rider

Preparing to Read the Text
- Using the Background note on TE p. 718, discuss the Maori people and their legends.
- Tell students to use vocabulary notes and footnotes to help them with the difficult vocabulary in the story.
- Guide students to use Multidraft Reading strategies (TE p. 718).

Leveled Tasks
Structure/Language If students will have difficulty with language, discuss ways to understand complex sentences. Model how to construct meaning from the main clause and then using details from the other clauses.

Evaluating If students will not have difficulty with language, point out how the author's style evokes a sense of a dreamy mythological past. As a class, discuss how the images affect the reader.

 Video

Watch the Background Video online!

 Audio

Selection Audio is available in the *Student eText* and on the *Hear It!* CD-ROM.

❸ Focus Passage

A Focus Passage is identified with brackets in the Student Edition of this page for students' independent close reading and analysis. A question bank for the passage and possible responses appear at the end of the selection.

❹ Close Reading

1. **Key Ideas and Details** Read aloud the passage to students. **Ask:** What happens in this passage? What key idea does the song at the end convey?

   Possible response: A large creature from the depths of the ocean has been sighted. The song suggests that the land and sea will finally get what they have been anticipating.

2. **Craft and Structure** Ask volunteers to locate the descriptive word choices. Invite students to write the words on the board. **Ask:** What feelings do the words evoke?

   Possible response: The author's descriptive word choices include *dark shape rising, awesome, leviathan, breaching, and hurling itself skyward.* These phrases create feelings of awe at what is being witnessed.

3. **Integration of Knowledge and Ideas**
   Ask: What mood does the descriptive words help the author create? What does the author leave unstated?

   Possible response: These descriptive phrases create a mood of suspense because the author does not directly describe what the creature from the ocean is.

apex ▶
(ā′ peks′) *n.*
highest point

❸ Suddenly, looking up at the surface, the fish began to see the dark bellies of the canoes from the east. The first of the Ancients were coming, journeying from their island kingdom beyond the horizon. Then, after a period, canoes were seen to be returning to the east, making long cracks on the surface sheen. The land and the sea sighed with gladness:
We have been found.
The news is being taken back to the place of the Ancients.
Our blessing will come soon.

In that waiting time, earth and sea began to feel the sharp pangs of need, for an end to the yearning. The forests sent sweet perfumes upon the eastern winds and garlands of *pohutukawa* upon the eastern tides.

The sea flashed continuously with flying fish, leaping high to look beyond the horizon and to be the first to announce the coming; in the shallows, the chameleon sea horses pranced at attention. The only reluctant ones were the fairy people, who retreated with their silver laughter to caves in glistening waterfalls.

❹ The sun rose and set, rose and set. Then one day, at its noon apex, the first sighting was made. A spume on the horizon. A dark shape rising from the greenstone depths of the ocean, awesome, leviathan, breaching through the surface and hurling itself skyward before falling seaward again. Underwater the muted thunder boomed like a great door opening far away, and both sea and land trembled from the impact of that downward plunging.

Suddenly the sea was filled with awesome singing, a song with eternity in it, a song to the land:
You have called and I have come,
bearing the gift of the Gods.

The dark shape rising, rising again. A whale, gigantic. A sea monster. Just as it burst through the sea, a flying fish leaping high in its ecstasy saw water and air streaming like thunderous foam from that noble beast and knew, ah yes, that the time had come. For the sacred sign was on the monster, a swirling tattoo imprinted on the forehead.

Then the flying fish saw that astride the head, as it broke skyward, was a man. He was wondrous to look upon, the whale rider. The water streamed away from him and he opened his mouth to gasp in the cold air. His eyes were shining with

💬 VOCABULARY DEVELOPMENT

Thematic Vocabulary: The Big Question
As students are discussing the prologue from *The Whale Rider*, encourage them to use the thematic vocabulary presented in Introducing the Big Question, pp. 612–613. You might encourage them with sentence starters like these:

1. This myth explains the Maori *beliefs* about …

2. The entire *community* of nature is waiting for …
3. The animals of the land and sea feel a *connection* to …
4. The whale rider story *influences* Maori *culture* by …

splendor. His body dazzled with diamond spray. Upon that beast he looked like a small tattooed figurine, dark brown, glistening, and erect. He seemed, with all his strength, to be pulling the whale into the sky.

Rising, rising. And the man felt the power of the whale as it propelled itself from the sea. He saw far off the land long sought and now found, and he began to fling small spears seaward and landward on his magnificent journey toward the land.

Some of the spears in midflight turned into pigeons, which flew into the forests. Others, on landing in the sea, changed into eels. And the song in the sea drenched the air with ageless music, and land and sea opened themselves to him, the gift long waited for: *tangata*, man. With great gladness and thanksgiving, the man cried out to the land,

> *Karanga mai, karanga mai, karanga mai.*

Call me. But there was one spear, so it is told, the last, that, when the whale rider tried to throw it, refused to leave his hand. Try as he might, the spear would not fly.

So the whale rider uttered a prayer over the wooden spear, saying, "Let this spear be planted in the years to come, for there are sufficient spear already implanted. Let this be the one to flower when the people are troubled and it is most needed."

And the spear then leaped from his hands with gladness and soared through the sky. It flew across a thousand years. When it hit the earth, it did not change but waited for another hundred and fifty years to pass until it was needed.

The flukes of the whale stroked majestically at the sky.

Hui e, haumi e, taiki e.

Let it be done.

Try as he might, the spear would not fly.

ABOUT THE AUTHOR

Witi Ihimaera (b. 1944)

Witi Ihimaera was raised in the Maori culture of New Zealand. He became interested in writing at an early age and recalls scribbling stories across a wall of his room at his family farm. Ihimaera is the first Maori to publish both a novel and a collection of short stories. He says that he sees writing as a way to express his experience of being a Maori. *The Whale Rider*, a book that he wrote in just three weeks in 1978, inspired the successful 2002 movie *The Whale Rider*.

PART 3 • *Prologue from* The Whale Rider **721**

---

❺ Focus Passage

A Focus Passage is identified with brackets in the Student Edition of this page for students' independent close reading and analysis. A question bank for the passage and possible responses appear at the end of the selection.

❻ Big Question: Toward Essential Understanding

1. Read aloud the passage to students. **Ask:** Why does the human ask for the spear to be planted in the future?

   Possible response: He realizes that the last spear is not needed right now. By saving extra resources, the whale rider is preparing for the future communities that might need it.

2. **Ask:** What do the whale rider's actions suggest about the building of communities?

   Possible response: Communities grow and change, so present needs will probably be different in the future. His actions suggest that part of building a community is making sure that it will thrive in the present and in the future.

🔹 DIFFERENTIATED INSTRUCTION

🔵 Vocabulary for English Learners

Some students may have difficulty with descriptive language. To help students understand unfamiliar words, guide them to use context clues to find a word's meaning. For example, have students look at *astride* on p. 720. Explain that the sentence before this word describes a whale with a tattoo on its forehead. The sentence after *astride* calls someone a "whale rider," which suggests that this person is riding on the whale. Ask students to substitute *riding on* for *astride* to see if the sentence still makes sense. Encourage students to try this method with other unfamiliar words.

Strategy for Gifted/Talented Students

Have students write about an event from history in the style used in the prologue from *The Whale Rider*. Their writing should use similes and metaphors as well as descriptive language to describe the event. Have volunteers share their writing with the class.

© **Close Reading Activities**

READ

Comprehension

1. They had a feeling of "a great emptiness, a yearning."
2. A whale rose from the water with a rider on its head.
3. The spear "refused to leave his hand."

Research: Clarify Details

Students should use their research to explain the significance of a particular detail in the myth.

Summarize

Summaries should include the yearning of the land and sea, the visit of the Ancients, the rising of the whale and whale rider from the sea, the throwing of the spears, and the last spear meant to help people in the future.

Language Study

Selection Vocabulary
Possible responses:

- *yearning*: Dad has a yearning to see his hometown.
- *teemed*: Bees teemed around the hive.
- *apex*: The climbers reached the apex of the mountain yesterday.

Diction and Style

1. **(a)** hearing **(b)** *loud, clatter, chatter, murmur*
2. The forests were alive with the sounds of living things.

Conventions

Students should identify the following: "It flew across a thousand years," independent clause; "When it hit the earth," dependent clause; "it did not change but ... to pass," independent clause; "until it was needed," dependent clause. The sentence variety comes from the author's use of a simple sentence followed by a complex sentence.

READ

Comprehension

Reread to answer the following questions.

1. What feeling did the land and sea have in the old days?
2. What amazing sight rose from the sea?
3. What happened when the whale rider tried to throw the last spear?

Language Study

Selection Vocabulary Use each boldfaced word from the myth in an original sentence that shows its meaning.

- ... the land and sea felt a great emptiness, a **yearning**.
- The sea, too, **teemed** with fish, but they also seemed to be waiting.
- Then one day, at its noon **apex**, the first sighting was made.

Diction and Style Reread the sentence and answer the questions that follow.

> The forests were loud with the clatter of tree bark, chatter of cicada, and murmur of fish-laden streams.

1. **(a)** To which of the five senses does this passage appeal? **(b)** What specific words relate to this sense?
2. Based on its **sensory** language, what is the main idea of the passage?

Research: Clarify Details Research one unfamiliar detail from the myth. Then, explain how your research sheds light on an aspect of the myth.

Summarize Write an objective summary of the myth. Do not include your opinions or evaluations.

Conventions Identify the independent and dependent clauses in this passage. Then, explain how the clauses add sentence variety.

> It flew across a thousand years. When it hit the earth, it did not change but waited for another hundred and fifty years to pass until it was needed.

Academic Vocabulary

The following words appear in blue in the instructions and questions on the facing page.

sensory   observe   reveal

Copy the words into your notebook. For each word, find at least one related word that is built on the same root (for example, appreciate/appreciation).

Academic Vocabulary

If students struggle with defining the academic vocabulary words, use this routine:

Write the words and definitions on the board.

sensory: related to the sense of sight, hearing, smell, taste, and touch

observe: notice or see

reveal: show or uncover

Have students say each word aloud and then use the word in a sentence. Sample sentences should demonstrate that the words can be used across disciplines.

Literary Analysis

Reread the identified passages. Then, respond to the questions that follow.

> **Focus Passage 1** *(p. 720)*
>
> Suddenly, looking up at the surface, the fish began … *Our blessing will come soon.*

> **Focus Passage 2** *(p. 721)*
>
> Rising, rising. And the man felt … the spear would not fly.

Key Ideas and Details

1. (a) What do the fish observe about the directions in which the canoes move? **(b) Infer:** Why are the land and sea excited about the arrival of the Ancients?

2. Interpret: Why are the land and the sea happy to see the Ancients leave?

Craft and Structure

3. (a) In the passage, find an example of personification—figurative language in which a nonhuman subject is given human characteristics. **(b) Assess:** What is the effect of this personification?

Integration of Knowledge and Ideas

4. Speculate: How might the events described in the passage bring a blessing to the land and sea?

Myth

A **myth** is a fictional tale that often explains how elements of nature originated. Myths are part of the oral tradition. Reread the myth, and take notes on ways the author explains elements of nature.

1. People and Animal (a) What does this myth explain? **(b)** Do you think the whale rider is a mortal or a god?

Key Ideas and Details

1. Interpret: Why does the man cry out to the land?

2. Analyze: How is the last spear different from the other spears?

Craft and Structure

3. Generalize: The narrator says the man is on a "magnificent journey." What meaning does the word *magnificent* give to the passage?

4. Analyze: How do the phrases "song in the sea" and "ageless music" contribute to the atmosphere of the passage?

Integration of Knowledge and Ideas

5. Infer: What information does this passage reveal about the culture that first told the story of the whale rider?

Use details from the myth to support your answer.

2. What values does this myth teach?

Common Core State Standards

RL.6.1, RL.6.2, RL.6.4; L.6.4, L.6.5, L.6.6
[For full standards wording, see the chart in the front of this book.]

Focus Passage 2

1. The land was "long sought," and now he has found it. He is full of joy.

2. The last spear will not leave his hand, whereas the first spears left his hand and became pigeons and eels. The last spear will help people in the future instead of immediately adding animals to the land and sea.

3. It suggests the journey is noble, awesome, and grand. It gives the journey significance.

4. They add feelings of joy, gladness, and permanence.

5. The community values all living things and can plan for the future.

Myth

1. (a) The myth explains how the land was populated with creatures and people. **(b)** The whale rider may be a god because he has the ability and endurance to ride a whale underwater and the strength to throw spears great distances. The whale rider may be a man because he is the ancestor of the people who tell this tale.

2. The myth teaches the beauty of things in nature, the gifts people can bring to the land, and the cooperation of animals and humans.

Literary Analysis

Possible responses appear below. Check to be sure students support their responses with evidence from the text.

Focus Passage 1

1. (a) They first observe the canoes arriving from the east, and later see them returning to the east. **(b)** They believe they have been discovered.

2. They believe the Ancients will take word of their discovery to "their island kingdom beyond the horizon" and their "blessing will come soon."

3. (a) An example of personification is "The land and the sea sighed with gladness." **(b)** It brings the animals and scenery alive as characters.

4. Arrival of people will end the period of waiting and yearning and fill the "great emptiness."

DISCUSS

From Text to Topic: Partner Discussion

Possible responses:

1. Whales are large and powerful creatures. They live in the ocean but come up to the surface for air where people can see and possibly interact with them.

2. If an equally large and awesome creature appeared in the sea, the passage might have the same impact. If the creature were a smaller creature, the impact could be different.

WRITE

Writing to Sources: Informative Text

Introduce the assignment using the instruction on the student page.

Prewriting and Planning

1. Because this story is a myth, students may find it difficult to identify cause-and-effect relationships. To guide their rereading and note taking, provide struggling students with guiding questions, such as: *What causes the land and sea to sigh with gladness? Why do the flying fish leap high continuously after the Ancients return to the east? What is an effect of the whale's jumping and plunging back into the sea?*

2. Have students create a cause-and-effect chart to help them clarify the cause-and-effect relationships in the selection.

3. Suggest that students use sticky notes for passages they may wish to cite.

Drafting

1. Remind students that their drafts should include all the points from their prewriting, adding details to fill out points as they write.

2. Explain that the points they include should clearly show how events are linked. For each cause, there should be an effect.

DISCUSS

From Text to Topic **Partner Discussion**

Discuss the following passage with a partner. Take notes during the discussion. Contribute your own ideas, and support them with examples from the text.

> The sun rose and set, rose and set.... trembled from the impact of that downward plunging. (p. 720)

WRITE

Writing to Sources **Informative Text**

> **Assignment**
>
> Write a **cause-and-effect essay** in which you analyze events in the Prologue from *The Whale Rider*. In particular, consider the actions of both the Ancients and the whale rider. Explore how these actions affect the land, the sea, and the people.

Prewriting and Planning Reread the myth, looking for details that describe the land and sea at different points in the story: before the canoes arrive, after the canoes return to the east, and after the whale and whale rider change them. Record your notes in a web or chart.

Drafting In your draft, cite specific examples from the myth to support your points. Make sure the information you provide clearly shows how events are linked in cause-and-effect relationships. If your supporting details seem vague or unclear, review the myth to find additional information to include in your essay.

Revising Reread your essay, making sure you have used transitional words and phrases that clarify cause-and-effect relationships. Choose from among the examples below.

because	*as a result*	*so*
due to	*for this reason*	*consequently*

Editing and Proofreading Check to see that you have used a variety of sentence structures, including simple and complex sentences. Revise to correct any errors in grammar, spelling, or punctuation.

QUESTIONS FOR DISCUSSION

1. What characteristics of whales might inspire people to develop myths about them?

2. Would this passage have the same impact if a different type of creature had appeared in the sea? Why or why not?

CONVENTIONS
Use a comma after a dependent clause at the beginning of a sentence.

Revising

1. Encourage students to review their drafts to ensure that they have used transitional words and phrases successfully to clarify cause-and-effect relationships.

2. Remind students that their main points should be supported with specific examples from the text.

Editing and Proofreading

1. Encourage students to check that they have used a variety of sentence structures including simple and complex sentences.

2. Have students check that they have used correct grammar, spelling, and punctuation.

RESEARCH

Research **Investigate the Topic**

The Role of Myths The whale and the whale rider in this myth represent certain beliefs and values of the Maori culture.

Assignment

Conduct research to find out about the role of myths in society, and to learn what myths from different cultures have in common. Focus your research on myths that have both human and animal characters. Take clear notes and carefully identify your sources. Share your findings in an **oral presentation** for the class.

PREPARATION FOR ESSAY

You may use the knowledge you gain during this research assignment to support your claims in an essay at the end of this section.

Gather Sources Locate authoritative sources. Search print sources, such as anthologies and reference books. Conduct key word searches, using terms such as *creation myths*, to locate appropriate Web sites. Look for sources with expert authors.

Take Notes Take notes on each of your sources, either electronically or on note cards. Use an organized note-taking strategy.

- Use two columns, with key words in the first column and details in the second, or use an outline with general headings followed by specific details.
- Record source information to use in citations.
- Write legibly so that you can read your notes later.

Synthesize Multiple Sources Assemble data from your sources and organize it into a cohesive presentation. Use your notes to construct an outline for your presentation. Follow accepted conventions to cite all of the sources you used in developing your presentation. See the Citing Sources pages in the Introductory Unit of this textbook for additional guidance.

Organize and Present Ideas Review your outline and practice delivering your presentation. Be prepared to answer questions from your audience.

 **Common Core State Standards**

SL.6.1, SL.6.4; W.6.2.a–c, W.6.7, W.6.8, W.6.9.a; L.6.2, L.6.3
[For full standards wording, see the chart in the front of this book.]

RESEARCH

Investigate the Topic

Introduce the assignment, using the instruction on the student page.

Gather Sources

1. Arrange for students to visit your school's library or computer lab.
2. Remind students that some Internet sites provide unreliable or undocumented information. Tell them that .gov, .edu, and .org Web sites are generally more reliable than .com Web sites.

Take Notes

1. Point out to students that taking notes in an organized way will help them when they draft their essays.
2. Remind students that all sources, whether they are from a print or online reference, should be given proper credit in a list of Works Cited.

Synthesize Multiple Sources

1. Encourage students to make connections between ideas from multiple sources.
2. Have students use their notes to create an outline for their speech or presentation. Point out that creating an outline will help them identify and organize the main points of their presentation.
3. Use examples to review the MLA style requirements for citing different kinds of print and online sources. Have students create a Works Cited list that identifies each source they reference.

Organize and Present Ideas

Remind students to practice so that they do not need to read directly from their presentation outlines and are prepared to answer any questions.

MULTIDRAFT READING

Essential Understanding

First, students should read the entire selection on their own. Then, to assist struggling readers and to deepen comprehension for all, you may wish to guide them through the selection by asking them the close reading questions provided in the margins. Have students apply the multidraft reading protocols as they examine specific "chunks" of text related to these questions. For each reading, have students set the purpose indicated:

• **First reading:** Students should read the selection independently and think about its basic meaning.

• **Second reading:** Students should analyze the text's key ideas and details and its craft and structure.

• **Third reading:** Students should integrate knowledge and ideas; connect to the Big Question, other texts, and the world; and use teacher-led Close Reading discussion questions to examine particularly rich and significant passages.

For more guidance, refer to the *Classroom Strategies and Teaching Routines* card on multidraft reading.

🏫 Daily Bellringer

For each class during which you teach this selection, have students complete one of the five Sentence Modeling activities for Week 32 in *Daily Bellringer Activities*. You may wish to use additional activities that are applicable to this selection.

❶ Background

If you wish, point out that howler monkeys, also called howling monkeys, reside in the rain forests of Central and South America. Troops of monkeys live and feed in territories ranging from 3 to 25 acres. The monkeys spend much of their time sleeping or resting in the treetops. Howler monkeys use their loud, booming sounds to protect their territories. It is said that the monkeys howl loudly in the morning and again at night to keep others away from the food source in their territory. Since their diet consists mainly of leaves, the monkeys have a great stake in protecting whatever young and nutritious leaves they find.

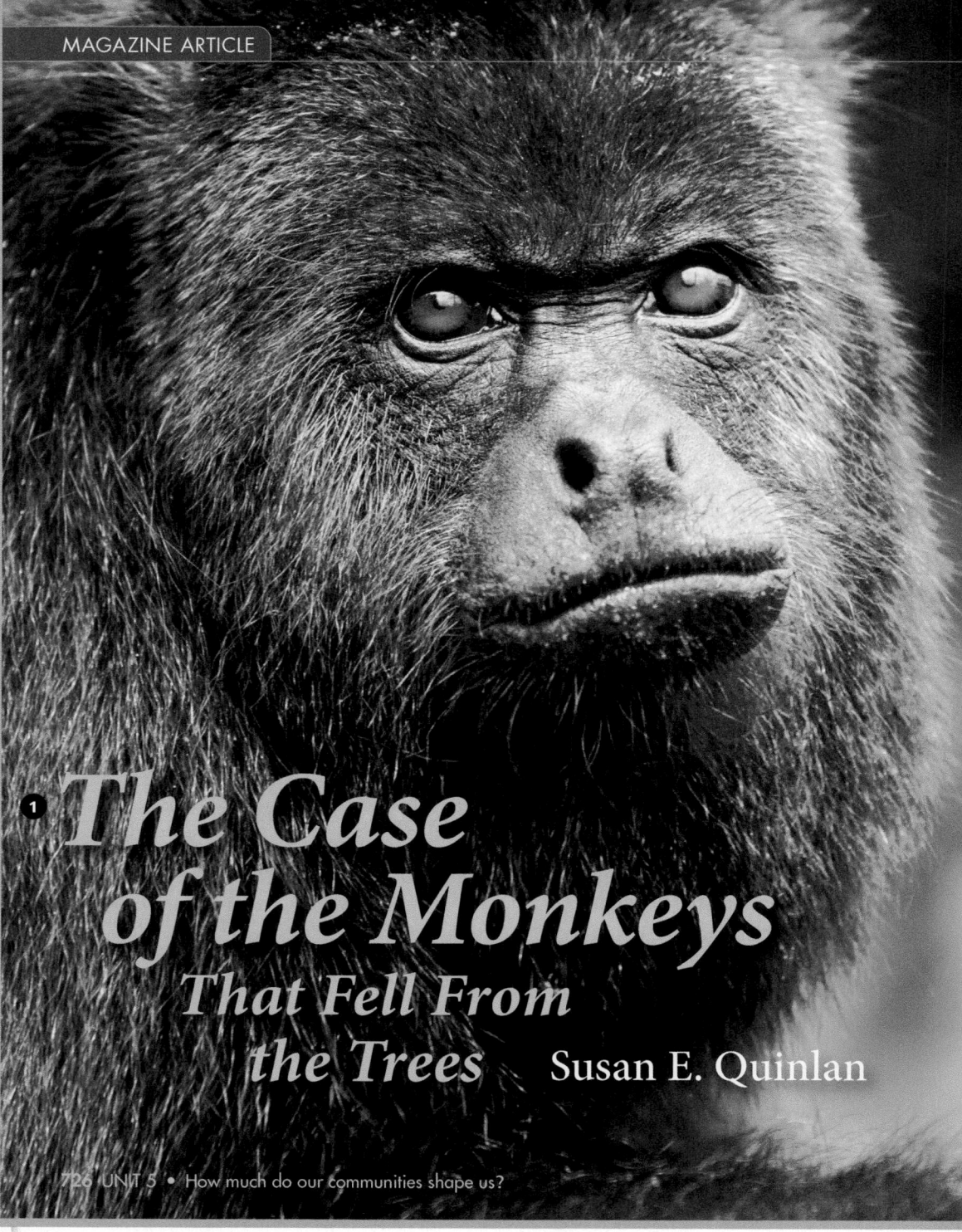

❶ *The Case of the Monkeys That Fell From the Trees* — Susan E. Quinlan

726 UNIT 5 • How much do our communities shape us?

©TEXT COMPLEXITY **RUBRIC**

The Case of the Monkeys That Fell From the Trees		
Qualitative Measures	Context/Knowledge Demands	Nonfiction; twentieth-century Costa Rica; rain forest 1 2 ③ 4 5
	Structure/Language Conventionality and Clarity	Some long sentences; technical, challenging vocabulary 1 2 3 ④ 5
	Levels of Meaning/ Purpose/Concept Level	Challenging concept (detailed descriptions of animal research) 1 2 3 ④ 5
Quantitative Measures	Text Length	Word Count: 1,711
	Lexile	1110L

W hen the incidents began in August 1972, biologist Ken Glander and his wife, Molly, had been studying the eating habits of a troop of howling monkeys in northwestern Costa Rica for nearly three months. Then, over a two-week period, seven monkeys from various troops in the area fell out of trees and died. Another fell but climbed back up.

One morning the Glanders watched a female howling monkey with a ten-day-old baby turn in tight circles on a tree branch. Abruptly, she fell off the branch. For a moment she hung upside down, suspended by her long tail. Then her grip failed and she plunged thirty-five feet to the forest floor. Dazed but still alive, she climbed back up, carrying her clinging infant. She stopped on a thick branch and sat there without eating for the next twenty-four hours.

Normally, howling monkeys are skilled, nimble climbers. They often leap ten feet or more between tree limbs, and they almost never fall. Why were monkeys suddenly falling from trees?

Glander wondered if a disease or parasite[1] might be involved. He asked scientists in the microbiology department at the University of Costa Rica to examine some of the dead monkeys and look for clues. The scientists found no signs of disease or parasites. Nor had the monkeys starved. All had died in apparently healthy condition. Glander began to think they had been poisoned. But who or what would poison wild monkeys? Glander had several green, leafy suspects in mind, all of them tropical forest trees.

Many tropical trees have similar-looking leaves and trunks, so it is difficult to determine their species.[2] But tropical plant expert Paul Opler had identified all the trees in the Glanders' study area. Several poisonous species were present. Suspiciously, some of the monkeys that fell had been feeding in trees known to have poisonous leaves. Yet Glander knew this proved nothing.

◄ **incidents**
(in ´sə dənts´)
n. events;
occurrences

◄ **abruptly**
(ə brupt´ lē)
adv. suddenly

---

1. **parasite** (par´ə sīt) plant, animal, or insect that lives on or in another living thing, called "the host." The parasite gets its food from the blood or tissue of the host.
2. **species** (spē´ sēz) group of plants or animals, scientifically classified because of similar traits.

PART 3 • The Case of the Monkeys That Fell From the Trees **727**

❷ Close Reading

1. **Key Ideas and Details** Read aloud the passage to students. **Ask:** How does Quinlan begin this article? Use the introduction to find the main idea of the article.

   Possible response: Quinlan begins by mentioning "the incidents" and then describing how howler monkeys were falling out of trees. Based on the introduction, the main idea of the article is finding the mystery of why the howler monkeys are falling from the trees.

2. **Craft and Structure** Have students reread the passage. **Ask:** How does the introduction grab the reader's attention?

   Possible response: Quinlan opens midaction, which creates immediate interest about the researchers and monkeys.

3. **Integration of Knowledge and Ideas**
   Ask: What does the introduction of this informational text have in common with the introduction of a mystery?

   Possible response: This introduction describes incidents that are unusual and do not have explanations. In the rest of the text Quinlan will explain the mystery and what the researchers discovered about the group of monkeys.

Vocabulary

If students require support with selection vocabulary, use this routine:

1. Write the following words and definitions on the board:

   incidents *n.* events; occurrences

   abruptly *adv.* suddenly

   distress *n.* serious pain or sadness

2. Have students say each word aloud.

3. Use the word in a sentence that defines the word.

 **Audio**

Selection Audio is available in the **Student eText** and on the **Hear It!** CD-ROM.

Ⓒ TEXT COMPLEXITY **READER AND TASK SUGGESTIONS**

The Case of the Monkeys That Fell From the Trees

Preparing to Read the Text	Leveled Tasks
• Use the Background note on TE p. 726 to discuss facts about howler monkeys. • Discuss the vocabulary that scientists and scientific articles use. • Guide students to use Multidraft Reading strategies (TE p. 726).	*Language/Clarity* If students will have difficulty with vocabulary, encourage them to write down technical words as they read the selection for the first time. Then, have them share and discuss their word lists with one another. Discuss students' lists and help clarify meanings. *Analyzing* If students will not have difficulty with vocabulary, have them write sentences with other uses of these vocabulary words. Encourage students to share and discuss their sentences as a class.

❸ Close Reading

1. Key Ideas and Details Have a volunteer read aloud the passage. **Ask:** What main idea does Quinlan develop in this paragraph?

Possible response: Glander is suspicious about certain trees, but he needs to collect some evidence.

2. Craft and Structure Have students reread the passage, taking note of word choice. **Ask:** How does this word choice mimic a criminal investigation?

Possible response: The words and phrases *suspected, killers, evidence, point fingers,* and *make a case* mimic terms used in criminal investigations. These words show that scientific research is also an investigation that must be approached just as methodically as a criminal investigation.

3. Integration of Knowledge and Ideas

Ask: How does the word choice contribute to the overall tone?

Possible response: The words that mimic a criminal investigation suggest a seriousness about the deaths and the researchers' determination to figure out the cause.

distress ▶
(di stres´) *n.* serious pain or sadness

All plants produce chemicals called secondary compounds, many of which are poisonous. Plants make these chemicals for a variety of purposes. Some ward off plant-eating animals, especially insects. But howling monkeys eat nothing except plants, so they could not survive unless they were able to digest or tolerate plant poisons. Other scientists had observed howlers eating leaves from many kinds of trees, including poisonous species, without any signs of distress. As a result, most scientists assumed that howling monkeys had an unlimited food supply in their lush tropical forest homes. Glander wasn't so sure.

The monkeys that fell from the trees strengthened his belief that howling monkeys could not eat leaves from just any tree. He suspected that certain trees were monkey killers, but he needed evidence before he could point fingers. He and Molly began collecting the data they needed to make a case.

Their days started around 4 or 5 a.m. That's when the monkeys awoke, often greeting the day with roars and growls. The monkeys soon set off, alternating bouts of feeding with periods of crawling, leaping, and climbing through the treetops. Wherever the monkeys went, the Glanders followed on foot.

That's when the monkeys awoke, often greeting the day with roars and growls.

At midday, the monkeys settled down. Draping themselves over large branches, their arms and legs dangling, the howlers slept with their tails wrapped around branches to anchor them in place. Late in the day, when the air cooled a few degrees, the monkeys stirred. They climbed and fed until settling down for the night at sunset.

For twelve months, the Glanders endured long days, mosquitoes, heavy rains, and temperatures that sometimes soared over 100°F. They did this in order to make their observations of the monkey troop as continuous as possible. Throughout each day, they recorded how many minutes the monkeys spent sleeping, eating, and moving. They recorded which of 1,699 individually numbered trees the monkeys slept in and ate from, and exactly which parts the monkeys ate—leaves, fruits, flowers, or stems.

Each day, the scientists collected samples of leaves from every tree the monkeys fed in that day, and leaves from nearby trees of the same species. The monkeys had visited these trees but did not feed in them. The Glanders tagged the leaves with wire labels, noting the tree, the date, and the time that the sample was collected.

728 UNIT 5 • How much do our communities shape us?

💬 VOCABULARY DEVELOPMENT

Multiple Meanings: Words From Science and Social Studies

Write the following definitions for *troop* on the board.

1. a unit of students with an adult leader
2. a unit of soldiers
3. a large group of people, animals, or things that are alike
4. to move or gather together as a large group
5. to march

Point out the word *troop* in the sentence "They did this in order to make their observations of the monkey troop as continuous as possible." Explain that *troop* has different meanings and that it can be different parts of speech. Discuss the definitions, and ask volunteers to suggest the correct definition for *troop* as it is used in the sentence. Emphasize that the Glanders observed groups of howler monkeys as the monkeys ate, slept, and played.

Next, they dried the leaves in an oven, then packed them in zippered plastic bags for later study.

The Glanders soon noticed that the howlers ate new leaves whenever they could, only occasionally eating fruits, flowers, or mature leaves. In certain trees, the monkeys plucked off the leaves, then stripped and tossed away the leaf blades. They ate only the remaining leaf stems. Other scientists thought this messy feeding behavior meant that howling monkeys could afford to be wasteful in a forest where food was so abundant. Glander wasn't convinced.

After thousands of hours of field work, including nearly two thousand hours of observing monkeys, Glander reviewed all the records he and Molly had gathered. Their careful data showed that howlers had not eaten leaves from just any trees in the forest. Indeed, the monkeys had rarely eaten leaves from the most common tree species. Instead, they spent most of their feeding time in a few uncommon kinds of trees. All told, the monkeys had eaten from only 331 of the 1,699 trees in the area. More surprisingly, they had spent three-quarters of their feeding time in just 88 trees. The data showed that the monkeys selected only certain tree species for feeding.

Glander discovered something even more surprising. The monkeys had not eaten leaves from all the trees of favored species. Instead, they ate leaves from just a few individual trees of most species. For example, the monkeys traveled through most of the 149 madera negra trees in the area, but they ate mature leaves from only three of these. This pattern fascinated Glander, because the madera negra is one of the most toxic[3] trees in the forest. Its leaves are used to make rat poison.

To learn more, Glander chemically analyzed all the leaves he and Molly had collected from the madera negra trees in the study area during their field studies. The results were startling. The three individual trees from which the monkeys had eaten mature leaves showed no traces of poison alkaloids.[4] But leaves collected from the other madera negras were packed with these poisons. Somehow, the monkeys had picked out those very few trees whose leaves were not poisonous.

---

3. **toxic** (tăk′ sik) poisonous.
4. **alkaloids** (al′ kə loidz) group of chemical substances, some poisonous, found in plants.

❹ Focus Passage

A Focus Passage is identified with brackets in the Student Edition of this page for students' independent close reading and analysis. A question bank for the passage and possible responses appear at the end of the selection.

🐾 DIFFERENTIATED INSTRUCTION

Vocabulary for Less Proficient Readers
This selection, which features above-level vocabulary and technical language, might challenge students. Help them by preteaching difficult words in the selection.

- **nimble** (p. 727): able to move quickly and lightly
- **data** (p. 728): bits of information
- **alternating** (p. 728): changing between one thing and another

- **consistently** (p. 730): regularly
- **edible** (p. 730): able to be eaten
- **technique** (p. 730): method
- **toxicity** (p. 730): state of being poisonous

Write the words and their definitions on the board. Review the words and their definitions with students, and then have students copy them down.

Big Question: Toward Essential Understanding

1. Read aloud the passage to students. **Ask:** What is the main idea of this passage? What details support the main idea?

Possible response: The main idea is that monkeys have a system for finding the poisonous trees. Details that support this main idea include Glander's observation about the purpose of "sampling" and his suspicion that monkeys must sample trees often.

2. Ask: How do the monkeys that sample the leaves benefit their community?

Possible response: The monkeys benefit their community by risking sickness or death so that others in their community do not become sick or die. They risk their lives for the benefit of the community.

Chemical analyses of mature leaves from other kinds of trees revealed a similar pattern. The howling monkeys had consistently selected the most nutritious, most digestible, and least poisonous leaves available in their patch of forest. Glander noted that howlers ate only the leaf stems in some trees because the stems contained fewer poisons than the leaves. His data showed that instead of being sloppy eaters awash in a sea of food, howling monkeys are cautious, picky eaters in a forest filled with poisons.

But the mystery of the monkeys that fell from the trees was not solved. If howling monkeys can identify and avoid the most toxic leaves, why would they ever become poisoned and fall? Glander uncovered more clues by studying plants and their poisons.

The concentration of poison is not uniform among those plants that produce poisonous secondary compounds. The kinds and amounts of poison present vary widely among plant species, among individual plants of a single species, and even within the parts of a single plant. In fact, individual plants make varying amounts of poisons at different times of year and under different growing conditions. Some plants produce more poisons after their leaves or twigs are eaten by plant-eating animals. These same plants make fewer poisons if they are not damaged by plant-eaters. Due to these constant changes, Glander realized that monkeys could not simply learn which trees had poisonous leaves and which had edible ones. Their task was far more complicated. How did the monkeys do it?

Again, Glander found an answer in his field records. Howlers had fed in 331 of the trees in the study area, but they made only one stop in 104 of these trees. In each case, a solitary adult monkey visited the tree briefly, ate just a little bit, and then moved on. Glander thinks these monkeys were "sampling" the leaves for poisons. If the plant parts were toxic, they probably tasted bad or made the monkey who sampled them feel slightly ill. He suspects that each monkey troop finds out which trees currently have the least poisonous leaves by regularly and carefully sampling from trees throughout the area. By using this technique, the monkeys would avoid eating too many of the most toxic plant poisons.

Considering the ever-changing toxicity of the leaves in a forest, however, Glander reasoned that individual monkeys may sometimes make mistakes. They may eat too many of the wrong leaves. More importantly, when edible leaves are scarce due to unusual

---

📃 VOCABULARY DEVELOPMENT

Word Analysis

Write the words *nutritious, poisonous,* and *cautious* on the board. Underline the suffix *-ous* in each word. Tell students that the suffix *-ous* means "full of." Have students identify the base word in *nutritious* (*nutrition*), *poisonous* (*poison*), and *cautious* (*caution*). Point out that each of the base words is a noun. The addition of the suffix *-ous* changes each of these nouns into an adjective.

Challenge students to find these adjectives on p. 730 and identify the words each of the adjectives describes. (*Nutritious* and *poisonous* describe the leaves, and *cautious* describes the monkeys.)

conditions, monkeys may be forced to eat leaves they wouldn't otherwise choose. Glander first saw monkeys falling from trees during a severe drought[5] year, when the howlers' food choices were quite limited. Because some poisons produced by tropical plants affect animal muscles and nerves, eating the wrong leaves could certainly cause illness, dizziness, and deadly falls.

Today, after more than thirty years of studying monkeys, Ken Glander is convinced that the falling monkeys he and Molly observed were poisoned by eating leaves from the wrong trees at the wrong time. His work shows that a tropical forest is like a pantry filled with a mixture of foods and poisons. Only the most selective eaters can avoid the poisons and find enough edible food to survive.

However, the monkeys' poison-filled pantry has a silver lining. Poison chemicals used in small amounts often have medicinal value. Many human medicines contain plant poisons, including aspirin, quinine, atropine, morphine, digitoxin (a heart medicine), and cancer-fighting vincristine and paclitaxel. In fact, an estimated one-fourth of all medicines prescribed in the United States today come from plants.

Glander and other researchers have gathered some evidence that howlers and other monkeys sometimes select poisonous leaves for medicinal purposes, such as ridding themselves of parasites. Glander thinks scientists searching for new medicines for people might get some useful tips from howlers. The monkeys' behavior might help scientists select those plants most worth sampling.

6

---

5. **drought** (drout) period of little or no rain.

ABOUT THE AUTHOR

Susan E. Quinlan (b. 1954)
Susan E. Quinlan and her husband, Bud Lehnhausen, have worked together for more than twenty-five years conducting wildlife research and teaching natural history courses.

A biologist, writer, and educator, Quinlan is inspired by her love of wildlife. "I write about nature and the work of scientists because I want to share my fascination in these topics with young readers," she says.

6 Close Reading

1. **Key Ideas and Details** Read aloud the passage to students. **Ask:** What part of the article is this? How do you know?

   Possible response: This is the conclusion because the first sentence summarizes the body paragraphs of the article. The next two sentences conclude the article.

2. **Craft and Structure** Have students reread the paragraph, focusing on how the author structures the conclusion. **Ask:** Is this paragraph an effective conclusion? Why or why not?

   Possible response: Yes, this paragraph is an effective conclusion because the author expands on her main ideas. After describing in previous paragraphs how Glander solved the howler monkeys mystery, she extends the main idea by suggesting that people might benefit from researching the medical properties of the leaves that monkeys select.

3. **Integration of Knowledge and Ideas**
   Ask: What does this concluding passage illustrate about the relationship between people and animals?

   Possible response: The passage shows that people can learn from animals' instinctive behavior. By carefully observing and researching nature, people can understand how to use and benefit from natural resources in more effective ways.

DIFFERENTIATED INSTRUCTION

EL Support for English Learners
Students may have difficulty grasping the meaning of longer complex sentences, such as "The concentration of poison is not uniform among those plants that produce poisonous secondary compounds." Slowly read aloud sentences such as these. Write them on the board, and use a vertical line to break the sentence into chunks. As you review each chunk with students, clarify difficult vocabulary terms. Then, have students read the complete sentence out loud. Encourage students to summarize the sentence in their own words.

Enrichment for Advanced Readers
Have pairs of students work together on posters that illustrate the Glanders' discoveries. Suggest that each pair outline the scientists' hypotheses, observations, and findings and then use their outlines as the basis for their poster. Encourage students to use captions, labels, arrows, and color to highlight the information in the poster. Provide space for students to display their posters. The posters may help less proficient readers understand the concepts in the selection.

Close Reading Activities

READ

Comprehension

1. Why do howling monkeys that almost never fall suddenly start falling from trees?

2. They observe and record information about the monkeys' habits and the trees in which they sleep and eat. They collect leaf samples, label them, and package them for study.

3. One monkey from the troop samples the leaves.

4. The monkeys that died ate leaves from the wrong trees at the wrong time.

Research: Clarify Details

Students should explain how their research findings helped them understand the text.

Summarize

Summaries should explain the problem of the falling monkeys, how the Glanders collected data, the conclusion the Glanders drew, and the implications for medicine.

Language Study

Possible responses:

- *incidents*: events; Three similar incidents had occurred.

- *abruptly*: suddenly; She abruptly quit her job.

- *distress*: suffering; We heard a cry of distress from next door.

Literary Analysis

Possible responses appear below. Check to be sure students support their responses with evidence from the text.

1. The monkeys feed in a small percentage of the available trees, and only from some species.

2. **(a)** The author describes the data about the exact number of trees in the area and the trees that the monkeys select for feeding. **(b)** The details about the data show that the Glanders' research was thorough and precise.

3. The long hours produce detailed notes that support Ken Glander's hypothesis about what monkeys eat.

READ

Comprehension

Reread as needed to answer the questions.

1. What mystery do Ken and Molly Glanders want to solve?

2. How do the Glanders gather information?

3. How do the monkeys know which leaves to eat?

4. What do the Glanders conclude?

Language Study

Selection Vocabulary Define each boldfaced word and use it in a sentence of your own.

- When the **incidents** began in August 1972 …

Literary Analysis

Reread the identified passage. Then, respond to the questions that follow.

> **Focus Passage** *(p. 729)*
> After thousands of hours of field work, … species for feeding.

Key Ideas and Details

1. What does the Glanders' **study** reveal about the monkeys' eating habits?

Expository Writing

Expository texts explain concepts or provide information on real people, places, or events.

1. **(a)** Who are the real people in the article? **(b)** What facts lead them to **investigate** a problem?

Research: Clarify Details Conduct research to learn about one unfamiliar detail from the article. Explain how your research sheds light on the article.

Summarize Write an objective summary of the article. Remember to leave out your opinions and evaluations.

- **Abruptly**, she fell off the branch.
- Other scientists have observed howlers eating leaves from many kinds of trees, including poisonous species, without any signs of **distress**.

Craft and Structure

2. **(a) Classify:** What specific types of details does the author provide in this passage? **(b) Evaluate:** What do these details suggest about the Glanders' research?

Integration of Knowledge and Ideas

3. **Speculate:** What makes the Glanders' long hours of **observation** and recording worthwhile in the end?

2. After collecting leaves, what do the researchers do?

3. **People and Animals** What does the Glanders' work show about the relationship between scientists and animals?

Expository Writing

1. **(a)** The real people are Ken Glander, his wife Molly, and other researchers. **(b)** Monkeys begin falling from trees; the Glanders also see one monkey fall and get back up.

2. The researchers dry the leaves in an oven and pack them in plastic bags. Then they chemically analyze the leaves for the presence of poisons.

3. **Possible response:** Scientists can learn a lot about animals by quietly and carefully watching them for extended periods of time.

DISCUSS • RESEARCH • WRITE

From Text to Topic **Panel Discussion**

Conduct a panel discussion with four or five classmates. Take notes during the discussion. Contribute your own ideas, and support them with examples from the text.

> Glander and other researchers have gathered some evidence that howlers and other monkeys sometimes select poisonous leaves for medicinal purposes, such as ridding themselves of parasites. Glander thinks scientists searching for new medicines for people might get some useful tips from howlers.

Research **Investigate the Topic**

The Scientific Method Scientists follow particular steps in order to ask and answer scientific questions. The steps can vary, but they usually follow a process known as the scientific method.

> **Assignment**
>
> Conduct research to find out more about the scientific method and how and when it was developed. Consult online encyclopedias or print sources. Take notes and carefully identify your sources. Share your findings in **an annotated chart**. Include a paragraph in which you explain how scientists can use the scientific method in their research about animals.

Writing to Sources **Informational Text**

This article describes how the Glanders investigated an incident they observed. They spent a year studying howler monkeys and kept extensive field records before arriving at their conclusion.

> **Assignment**
>
> Write an **explanation** of the Glanders' method of investigating why the howling monkeys fell from trees in Costa Rica. Follow these steps:
>
> • Introduce the Glanders' question and explain their method clearly.
>
> • Use relevant facts and concrete details from the article.
>
> • Clarify relationships. For example, use words that show order—such as *first* and *next*—to present the steps the Glanders followed.
>
> • Provide a conclusion that explains how the steps led to answers about the falling monkeys.

QUESTIONS FOR DISCUSSION

1. How might information learned through scientific research lead Glander and others to new research questions?

2. What does the passage reveal about a way in which howlers are like people?

PREPARATION FOR ESSAY

You may use the results of this research project to support your ideas in the essay at the end of this section.

ACADEMIC VOCABULARY

Academic terms appear in blue on these pages. If these words are not familiar to you, use a dictionary to find their definitions. Then, use them as you speak and write about the text.

 Common Core State Standards

RI.6.1, RI.6.2, RI.6.6; W.6.2, W.6.7; SL.6.1, SL.6.4; L.6.4.b, L.6.6
[For full standards wording, see the chart in the front of this book.]

DISCUSS • RESEARCH • WRITE

From Text to Topic: Panel Discussion

Possible responses:

1. In investigating why the howling monkeys were falling from trees, Glander gathered data showing that howling monkeys sometimes choose poisonous leaves on purpose to cure themselves. He suggests looking at the monkeys' behavior to get clues for research into new medicines for people.

2. Howlers and other monkeys eat plants for "medicinal purposes," much as people do.

Research: Investigate the Topic

Introduce the assignment using the instruction on the student page.

1. Arrange for students to visit your school's library or computer lab. Review strategies for identifying reliable sources.

2. Remind students to take notes on main ideas encountered in each source, either by directly quoting or summarizing in their own words.

3. Encourage students to draw conclusions and make connections between ideas in multiple sources. Suggest that they prepare an outline for their presentation and create a Works Cited list that identifies each source they reference.

4. Suggest that students practice so that they do not need to read directly from their notes and are prepared to answer any questions.

Writing to Sources: Informational Text

Students should clearly explain the Glanders' methods. Remind students to support their topic with facts and details.

> **Online Writer's Notebook**
>
> Students can use the Online Writer's Notebook to record all responses.

Academic Vocabulary

If students struggle with defining the academic vocabulary words, use this routine:

Write the words and definitions on the board.

study: research of a subject

observation: an act of noticing

investigate: to search and examine to learn the facts about something

Have students say each word aloud. Then, have students use each word in a sentence.

MULTIDRAFT READING

Essential Understanding

First, students should read the entire selection on their own. Then, to assist struggling readers and to deepen comprehension for all, you may wish to guide them through the selection by asking them the close reading questions provided in the margins. Have students apply the multidraft reading protocols as they examine specific "chunks" of text related to these questions. For each reading, have students set the purpose indicated:

- **First reading:** Students should read the selection independently and think about its basic meaning.
- **Second reading:** Students should analyze the text's key ideas and details and its craft and structure.
- **Third reading:** Students should integrate knowledge and ideas; connect to the Big Question, other texts, and the world; and use teacher-led Close Reading discussion questions to examine particularly rich and significant passages.

For more guidance, refer to the *Classroom Strategies and Teaching Routines* card on multidraft reading.

❶ Background

If you wish, point out to students that although there are no official fire department statistics, some sources estimate that anywhere between 40,000 and 150,000 pets die yearly in fires, mostly from smoke inhalation.

Vocabulary

If students require support with selection vocabulary, use this routine:

1. Write the following words and definitions on the board:

   resuscitation *n.* act of bringing back to life or consciousness; act of reviving

   unsolicited *adj.* not requested

   inhalation *n.* breathing in

2. Have students say each word aloud.

3. Use the word in a sentence that defines the word.

❶ Rescuers to Carry
Oxygen Masks for Pets

734 UNIT 5 • How much do our communities shape us?

Ⓒ TEXT COMPLEXITY **RUBRIC**

Rescuers to Carry Oxygen Masks for Pets		
Qualitative Measures	Context/Knowledge Demands	Nonfiction; 21st century; Appleton, Wisconsin 1 2 ③ 4 5
	Structure/Language Conventionality and Clarity	Some long sentences; clear language 1 ② 3 4 5
	Levels of Meaning/Purpose/Concept Level	Straightforward concept (oxygen masks for pets) 1 ② 3 4 5
Quantitative Measures	Text Length	Word Count: 297
	Lexile	1150L

By Associated Press
Updated: 9/3/2006

APPLETON, Wis. Pets here will be breathing a little easier now that local rescuers will be carrying oxygen masks designed for animals.

Six Appleton fire trucks and 13 ambulances will be equipped with masks intended for use on dogs, cats and other small animals.

Alderman Richard Thompson initiated the program after he saw a newspaper photograph of a firefighter in Superior giving mouth-to-mouth **resuscitation** to a cat rescued from a house fire.

"A pet is family to most people," he said. "I know I wouldn't want to lose Maggie, my collie, or Lucy, my Tabby cat, to a fire, carbon monoxide poisoning or who knows what else."

The money to pay for each $49 mask came from donations by local animal lovers.

"It was something to see," Thompson said. "There was no organized solicitation effort. People and community groups just read or heard about the program and stepped up to the plate."

The masks, which come in three sizes, will be distributed to each of six fire stations and to the Appleton Police Department K-9 unit, he said.

The Madison Fire Department carries similar masks on its seven ambulances, said Lori Wirth, the department's community education officer.

The Madison department also bought its masks with money raised from **unsolicited** donations, she said. In fact, the department raised so much money it was able to buy mask kits for several neighboring communities.

Wirth said the department's firefighters haven't had to use the masks yet but they're trained and willing.

"What we've done so far is use the masks as a way to remind people to get out of their residence in the event of a fire and don't go searching for pets," she said. "Firefighters will care for any pets we find in the event they suffer from smoke **inhalation**."

◀ **resuscitation**
(ri sus′ə tā′ shən)
n. act of bringing back to life or consciousness; act of reviving

◀ **unsolicited**
(un′sə lis′it′ ed) *adj.*
not requested

◀ **inhalation**
(in′hə lā′shən) *n.*
breathing in

PART 3 • Rescuers to Carry Oxygen Masks for Pets **735**

❷ Close Reading

1. Key Ideas and Details Read aloud the passage to students. **Ask:** What detail is the most striking in this passage? What does that detail suggest?

Possible response: The image of a firefighter resuscitating a cat suggests that pets need emergency care.

2. Craft and Structure
Ask: Why does the author choose to describe this scene?

Possible response: This image is shocking and immediately draws in the reader.

3. Integration of Knowledge and Ideas
Ask: What does this passage say about the relationship between people and animals?

Possible response: It suggests that animals require emergency care just like people. It also suggests that humans are responsible for saving pets.

❸ Focus Passage

A Focus Passage is identified with brackets in the Student Edition of this page for students' independent close reading and analysis. A question bank for the passage and possible responses appear at the end of the selection.

❹ Big Question: Toward Essential Understanding

1. Ask: How does this passage show the community's attitude toward animals?

Possible response: Details such as the unsolicited donations show that the community loves animals.

2. Ask: How does a community shape the people in it?

Possible response: It encourages people to support a common goal, such as getting masks for animals, and to help other communities.

 **Audio**

Selection Audio is available in the *Student eText* and on the *Hear It!* CD-ROM.

ⓒ TEXT COMPLEXITY **READER AND TASK SUGGESTIONS**

Rescuers to Carry Oxygen Masks for Pets

Preparing to Read the Text	Leveled Tasks
• Discuss the purpose of news articles and the type of language used in articles. • Guide students to use Multidraft Reading strategies (TE p. 734).	*Structure/Language* If students will have difficulty with vocabulary, have them write down words that are unfamiliar to them as they read the selection. Then, have students share and discuss their word lists with one another. Discuss students' notes and help clarify meanings. *Analyzing* If students will not have difficulty with the vocabulary in the selection, have them write sentences giving examples of other uses of these vocabulary words. Encourage students to share and discuss their sentences as a class.

READ

Comprehension

1. Thompson saw a photo of a fire-fighter resuscitating a cat.

2. They raise money through donations. People heard about the program and started to donate money.

Research: Clarify Details

Students should explain how their research findings helped them understand an unfamiliar detail.

Summarize

Students' summaries should describe the oxygen mask program, why it began, and how the program works in Madison.

Language Study

Possible responses:

Resuscitation and *inhalation* have the suffix *-tion*, which changes the verbs *resuscitate* (meaning "revive") and *inhale* (meaning "breathe in") into nouns.

- *resuscitation*: The suffix *-tion* changes the word *resuscitate* from a verb to a noun. She was saved by resuscitation after being rescued.

- *unsolicited*: The donations were unsolicited.

- *inhalation*: The suffix *-tion* changes the word *inhale* from a noun to a verb. Inhalation of smoke is dangerous to animals.

Literary Analysis

Possible responses appear below. Check to be sure students support their responses with evidence from the text.

1. (a) Anyone who owns a pet in Appleton, Wisconsin, would want to know. **(b)** Thompson owns pets.

2. Volunteers donated money to pay for the masks.

3. (a) People are ready to help or do a certain task. **(b)** It makes Thompson sound friendly and the article seem casual.

4. The quotation shows how a community leader feels about pets and adds personal interest to the article.

 Close Reading Activities

READ

Comprehension

Answer these questions.

1. Why did Richard Thompson start the program described in this article?

2. How do the cities of Appleton and Madison, Wisconsin, raise money for the oxygen masks?

Language Study

Selection Vocabulary Identify the suffix two of the boldfaced words share. Explain how this suffix changes the part of speech of the root word. Then use each word in a sentence.

- … a firefighter in Superior giving mouth-to-mouth **resuscitation** to a cat …

Literary Analysis

Reread the identified passage.

> **Focus Passage** *(p. 735)*
> "A pet is family to most people," he said. … stepped up to the plate."

Key Ideas and Details

1. (a) Infer: According to Thompson, who would be interested in this program? **(b) Analyze:** How is Thompson like those people?

Text Features

Text features give structure to a text and help readers find information. Text features include headlines, bylines, headings, and captions. Reread the article and take notes on the text features.

Research: Clarify Details Choose at least one unfamiliar detail from the Web article and briefly research it. Then, explain how your research sheds light on the article.

Summarize Write an objective summary of the article.

- The Madison department also bought its masks with money raised from **unsolicited** donations, she said.

- Firefighters will care for any pets we find in the event they suffer from smoke **inhalation**.

---

2. How did individuals **support** the program?

Craft and Structure

3. (a) What does "stepped up to the plate" mean? **(b) Analyze:** How does the use of this expression affect the tone of article?

Integration of Knowledge and Ideas

4. Draw Conclusions: What does the first **quotation** add to the article as a whole?

---

1. Identify three text features in the article and explain what information each feature provides.

2. People and Animals What do the text features show about animals in Appleton?

Text Features

1. Three text features are the headline, dateline, and photograph. The headline summarizes the article's content, the dateline tells where and when the story takes place, and the photograph gives information in a visual way.

2. Possible response: The text features show that people in Appleton, Wisconsin, including firefighters, care about pets.

DISCUSS • RESEARCH • WRITE

From Text to Topic **Partner Discussion**

Discuss the following passage with a partner. Take notes during the discussion. Contribute your own ideas, and support them with examples from the text.

> "What we've done so far is use the masks as a way to remind people to get out of their residence in the event of a fire and don't go searching for pets," she said. "Firefighters will care for any pets we find in the event they suffer from smoke inhalation."

Research **Investigate the Topic**

Oxygen Masks Why do animals need oxygen after a fire?

Assignment

Conduct research to find out why people and animals may need oxygen after being exposed to a fire, and why pets need specialized oxygen masks. Consult online sources and look for authorities you can trust. Take clear notes and carefully identify your sources. Share your findings in a **short research paper**.

Writing to Sources **Nonfiction Narrative**

Alderman Thompson says, "A pet is family to most people." Many families in the U.S. have pets.

Assignment

Write a **nonfiction narrative** in which you describe the actions someone took to make sure a pet was safe. You may base the narrative on your own experience or on a situation you witnessed or read about. Follow these steps:

- Introduce your narrative with evidence from the article that explains why people care for pets.
- Use vivid words to precisely describe both the pet and the situation.
- Explain the specific steps that ensured the pet's safety.
- Write a strong conclusion, in which you reflect on what the people involved learned from the experience.

QUESTIONS FOR DISCUSSION

1. What did the Madison Fire Department hope would happen after it provided pet oxygen masks to firefighters?
2. How might use of the masks help accomplish this goal?

PREPARATION FOR ESSAY

You may use the results of this research project to support your ideas in the essay at the end of this section.

ACADEMIC VOCABULARY

Academic terms appear in blue on these pages. If these words are not familiar to you, use a dictionary to find their definitions. Then, use them as you speak and write about the text.

 **Common Core State Standards**

RI.6.1, RI.6.2, RI.6.5; SL.6.1; W.6.3, W.6.7; L.6.4, L.6.6
[For full standards wording, see the chart in the front of this book.]

DISCUSS • RESEARCH • WRITE

From Text to Topic: Partner Discussion

1. The department hoped knowing about the masks would encourage people to get out of burning homes without taking time to search for pets.
2. **Possible response:** Knowing that the firefighters can care for pets may reassure people that their pets will be safe.

Research: Investigate the Topic

Introduce the assignment using the instruction on the student page.

1. Arrange for students to visit your school's library or computer lab. Review strategies for identifying reliable online sources.
2. If possible, have students visit a local fire department and/or veterinarian to learn more about why people and animals may need oxygen after being exposed to a fire and why pets need specialized oxygen masks.
3. Remind students to take notes as they review each source and as they interview people.
4. Encourage students to draw conclusions and make connections between ideas in their notes.
5. Remind students to use their notes as they write their short paper. They should organize their paper in a progression that will help explain their findings in a clear and precise way. Remind students to include a Works Cited list that identifies each source they reference.

Academic Vocabulary

If students struggle with defining the academic vocabulary words, use this routine:

Write the words and definitions on the board.

support: help, assist

quotation: words that are used from another passage

authorities: people having legal power to enforce the law

Have students say each word aloud. Then, have students use each word in a sentence.

Writing to Sources: Nonfiction Narrative

Students' nonfiction narratives should incorporate evidence from the article, describe a pet and an incident with precise words, and use appropriate transitions.

 Online Writer's Notebook

Students can use the Online Writer's Notebook to record all responses.

1 Big Question: Toward Essential Understanding

1. Have students carefully review the data in each graph.

   Ask: What do the graphs have in common?

   Possible response: All the graphs describe an aspect of pet ownership.

2. Review the data in the charts and graphs on the page with students.

   Ask: How do these data connect to the Big Question: *How much do our communities shape us?*

   Possible response: The data show that many people in the United States have pets and spend money caring for them. These graphs suggests that owning and taking care of pets is an important part of a community.

Critical Viewing

Tell students that there are several types of statistics on the page. Each analyzes a different aspect of pet ownership in the United States. Review with students the different types of charts on the page. Remind students that pie charts and circle graphs compare information in relation to the whole. Point out that there are different types of bar graphs as well. Bar graphs can be used to show percentage, dollar amount, or number of several items and how they relate to one another.

Also discuss the use of shading to represent different data sets in each chart. For example, point out the key for the bar graph at the bottom left of the page and the key for the pie chart. On the pie chart, for example, light blue represents food, dark blue represents vet care, and so on.

2012 PET OWNERSHIP STATISTICS

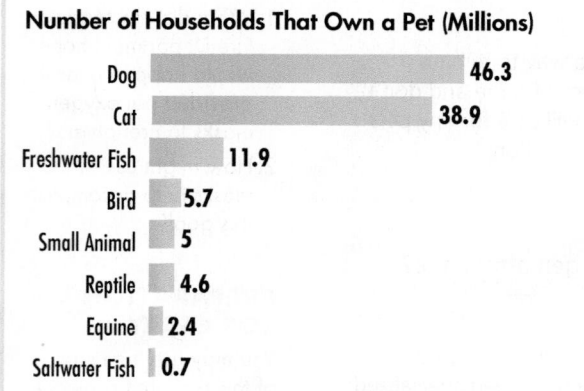

Number of Households That Own a Pet (Millions)

Dog	46.3
Cat	38.9
Freshwater Fish	11.9
Bird	5.7
Small Animal	5
Reptile	4.6
Equine	2.4
Saltwater Fish	0.7

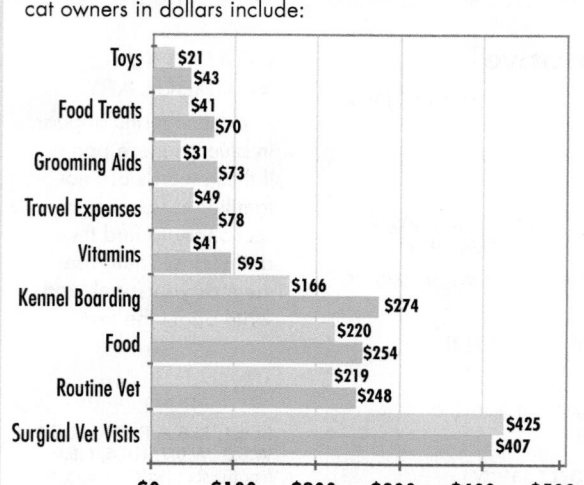

According to the **2011–2012 APPA National Pet Owners Survey**, basic annual expenses for dog and cat owners in dollars include:

	CATS	DOGS
Toys	$21	$43
Food Treats	$41	$70
Grooming Aids	$31	$73
Travel Expenses	$49	$78
Vitamins	$41	$95
Kennel Boarding	$166	$274
Food	$220	$254
Routine Vet	$219	$248
Surgical Vet Visits	$425	$407

$0 $100 $200 $300 $400 $500

■ **CATS**   ■ **DOGS**

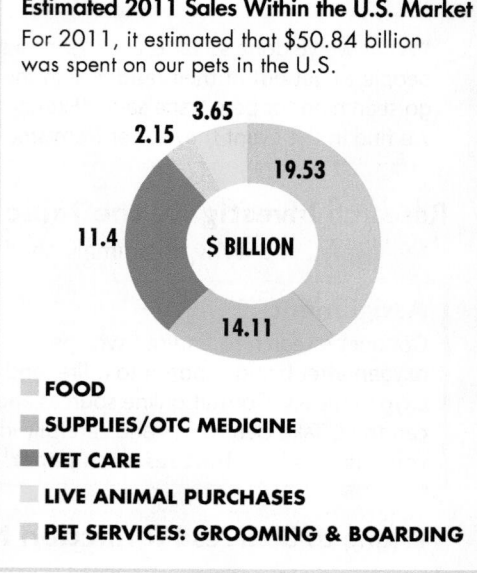

Estimated 2011 Sales Within the U.S. Market

For 2011, it estimated that $50.84 billion was spent on our pets in the U.S.

3.65
2.15
19.53
11.4
$ BILLION
14.11

■ **FOOD**
■ **SUPPLIES/OTC MEDICINE**
■ **VET CARE**
■ **LIVE ANIMAL PURCHASES**
■ **PET SERVICES: GROOMING & BOARDING**

738 UNIT 5 • How much do our communities shape us?

■ VOCABULARY DEVELOPMENT

Academic Vocabulary

If students require support with academic vocabulary, write the following words and definitions on the board:

- **subject:** topic
- **generalization:** broad statement
- **explain:** to give the reason for or cause of

   Have students say each word aloud. Then, use the word in a sentence that defines it.

Point out that academic vocabulary words can be used across disciplines. For example, in science, a *subject* can be a person who is part of a study. In literature, a *subject* can be the topic of a story. A *generalization* can be supported by data in a graph. Typically, some discussion is needed to *explain* the data in a graph. In literature, a reader can make a *generalization* about a character and *explain* a character's motives.

READ • DISCUSS • WRITE

Comprehension

Study the infographic to answer these questions.

1. (a) According to the first graph, what is the most commonly owned pet? **(b)** What is the least commonly owned pet?

2. What is similar about the **subject** of the graph on the bottom left and the subject of the graph on the right?

Critical Analysis

Key Ideas and Details

1. (a) In general, who spends more money each year—a cat owner or a dog owner? **(b) Analyze:** What is the exception to your **generalization** about which pet is more expensive?

Craft and Structure

2. Interpret: What is the purpose of the color key that accompanies the graph on the right?

Integration of Knowledge and Ideas

3. (a) Speculate: Which animals might be included under the heading "Small Animals" in the first graph? **(b) Infer:** Why are all the "small animals" grouped together under one heading?

From Text to Topic Class Discussion

Discuss the infographic with classmates. Explore questions such as the following in your conversation.

1. Why might kennel boarding be more of an expense for dog owners than for cat owners?

2. How can you **explain** the large difference between the number of people who own freshwater fish and saltwater fish?

Writing to Sources Argument

Write a brief **argument** in which you claim either that the benefits of owning a pet outweigh the costs, or that the costs of owning a pet outweigh the benefits. Include some information from the graphs. You may also refer to your own experiences or to other selections you have read in this section.

Common Core State Standards

RI.6.1; W.6.1; SL.6.1, SL.6.2
[For full standards wording, see the chart in the front of this book.]

ACADEMIC VOCABULARY

Academic terms appear in blue on these pages. If these words are not familiar to you, use a dictionary to find their definitions. Then, use them as you speak and write about the text.

READ • DISCUSS • WRITE

Comprehension

1. (a) dogs **(b)** saltwater fish

2. Both charts show the amount of money spent on pets.

Critical Analysis

Possible responses appear below. Check to be sure students support their responses with evidence from the text.

1. (a) A dog owner spends more each year. **(b)** Cat owners spend more for surgical vet visits.

2. The color key shows the categories of products sold to pet owners.

3. (a) Small animals might include hamsters, gerbils, and guinea pigs. **(b)** The number of households for each type of small pet might be too small to list; there may be too many different types of pets to list them all.

From Text to Topic: Class Discussion

1. Cats can stay alone in a home longer than dogs can, so there is less need to board them.

2. Possible responses: Freshwater fish may be less expensive to buy and maintain. Freshwater fish may be easier to find in pet stores.

Writing to Sources: Argument

Students should argue for or against owning a pet and connect the benefits and costs of pet ownership to the information in the various graphs.

 Online Writer's Notebook

Students can use the Online Writer's Notebook to record all responses.

MULTIDRAFT READING

Essential Understanding

First, students should read the entire selection on their own. Then, to assist struggling readers and to deepen comprehension for all, you may wish to guide them through the selection by asking them the close reading questions provided in the margins. Have students apply the multidraft reading protocols as they examine specific "chunks" of text related to these questions. For each reading, have students set the purpose indicated:

- **First reading:** Students should read the selection independently and think about its basic meaning.
- **Second reading:** Students should analyze the text's key ideas and details and its craft and structure.
- **Third reading:** Students should integrate knowledge and ideas; connect to the Big Question, other texts, and the world; and use teacher-led Close Reading discussion questions to examine particularly rich and significant passages.

For more guidance, refer to the *Classroom Strategies and Teaching Routines* card on multidraft reading.

❶ Background

If you wish, explain to students that the Sioux view animals as wise and powerful and as messengers between themselves and supernatural powers. The Sioux also appreciate nature. A Sioux quote describes a view of nature—"Even sticks and stones have a spiritual essence, a manifestation of the mysterious power that fills the Universe."

Vocabulary

If students require support with selection vocabulary, use this routine:

1. Write the following words and definitions on the board:

   coaxed *v.* persuaded by gentle urging

   traversed *v.* went across

   mystified *v.* made someone feel confused or unable to understand something

2. Have students say each word aloud.

3. Use the word in a sentence that defines the word.

SHORT STORY

THE OLD WOMAN WHO LIVED WITH THE WOLVES

Chief Luther Standing Bear

The Sioux were a people who traveled about from place to place a great deal within the borders of their own country. They did not trespass upon the territory of their neighbor Indians, but liked to make their home first here and then there upon their own ground, just as they pleased. It was not like moving from one strange town to another, but wherever they settled it was home. Taking down and putting up the tipis was not hard for them to do.

The reasons for their moving were many. Perhaps the grass for their ponies ran short, or the water in the creek became low. Maybe the game had gone elsewhere, and maybe the people just moved the camp to a fresh green spot, for the Sioux loved pure water, pure air, and a clean place on which to put their tipis.

❷ One day, long ago, a Sioux village was on the march. There were many people in the party, and many children. A great number of horses carried the tipis, and herds of racing and war horses were being taken care of by the young men. In this crowd was a young woman who carried with her a pet dog. The dog was young and playful, just past the puppy

740 UNIT 5 • How much do our communities shape us?

ⓒ TEXT COMPLEXITY **RUBRIC**

The Old Woman Who Lived With the Wolves		
Qualitative Measures	Context/Knowledge Demands	Sioux Indian territory 1 2 ③ 4 5
	Structure/Language Conventionality and Clarity	Sophisticated diction; culturally specific vocabulary 1 2 3 ④ 5
	Levels of Meaning/ Purpose/Concept Level	Challenging concept (survival tale of a Sioux girl who learns to communicate with wolves) 1 2 3 ④ 5
Quantitative Measures	Text Length	Word Count: 1,090
	Lexile	1310L

age. The young woman was very fond of her pet, as she had cared for it since it was a wee little thing with eyes still closed. She romped along with the pup, and the way seemed short because she played with it and with the young folks when not busy helping her mother with the packing and unpacking.

One evening Marpiyawin missed her dog. She looked and she called, but he was not to be found. Perhaps someone liked her playful pet and was keeping him concealed, but after a search she became satisfied that no one in camp was hiding him. Then she thought that perhaps he had lain down to sleep somewhere along the way and had been left behind. Then, lastly, she thought that the wolves had enticed him to join their pack. For oftentimes the Sioux dogs were coaxed away and ran with the wolf-pack, always returning, however, in a few days or weeks to the village.

So Marpiyawin, thinking the matter over, decided that she would go back over the way her people had journeyed and that somewhere she would find her dog. She would then bring him back to camp with her. Without a word to anyone, she turned back, for she had no fear of becoming lost. Nothing could befall her, so why should she fear? As she walked back, she came to the foothills at the base of the mountains where her village people had spent the summer. As she slept that night, the first snowfall of the autumn came so silently that it did not awaken her. In the morning everything was white with snow, but it was not far to the place where the village had been in camp and so determined was she to find her dog that she decided to keep going. Marpiyawin now felt that her pet had gone back to the old camping-ground, as dogs often do, and was now there howling and crying to be found.

That afternoon the snow fell thicker and faster and Marpiyawin was forced to seek shelter in a cave, which
3 was rather dark, but warm and comfortable. She was not hungry, for in her little rawhide[1] bag was still some wasna.[2] She was tired, however, so it was not long till she fell asleep,

◄ **coaxed**
(kōkst) *v.* persuaded by gentle urging

---

1. **rawhide** (rô´ hīd) *n.* rough leather.
2. **wasna** (wäs´ nuh) *n.* meat and berries pounded and pressed together in flat strips to make a nutritious food that is easy to carry.

PART 3 • The Old Woman Who Lived With the Wolves **741**

❷ Close Reading

1. **Key Ideas and Details** Read aloud the sentence to students. **Ask:** What happens in this sentence?

   Possible response: There is a Sioux village that is on the march, or moving.

2. **Craft and Structure**
   Ask: How does the word choice in this sentence create a timeless quality? How do the words help draw the reader in?

   Possible response: "One day, long ago" could refer to a day in the lifetimes of Sioux ancestors. The words make the narrator sound like an experienced storyteller. Also, their intimate tone makes it seem as if the narrator is speaking directly to the reader.

3. **Integration of Knowledge and Ideas**
   Ask: What does this one sentence tell you about the type of story this is?

   Possible response: The phrase "One day, long ago" is typical of legends, so that means this story is probably a myth or legend.

❸ Focus Passage

A Focus Passage is identified with brackets in the Student Edition for students' independent close reading and analysis. A question bank for the passage and possible responses appear at the end of the selection.

ⓒTEXT COMPLEXITY READER AND TASK SUGGESTIONS

The Old Woman Who Lived With the Wolves	
Preparing to Read the Text • Using the Background note on TE p. 740, discuss the Sioux relationship with nature. • Discuss why it is important to have respect for animals and nature. • Guide students to use Multidraft Reading strategies (TE p. 740).	**Leveled Tasks** *Levels of Meaning* If students will have difficulty with meaning, have them read the first two pages of the selection, taking notes on Marpiyawin's relationship with her dog. Next, ask students to review their notes and use them to write a description of how Marpiyawin's actions reflect a love for all living things. Discuss students' descriptions and clarify any misunderstandings. *Analyzing* If students will not have difficulty with meaning, have them read the entire selection and take notes on how Marpiyawin reacts to dangerous situations. Have students use their notes to discuss Marpiyawin as a character. Encourage students to make connections between her reactions and the relationship between people and animals.

Audio

Selection Audio is available in the *Student eText* and on the *Hear It!* CD-ROM.

➍ Close Reading

1. Key Ideas and Details Read aloud the passage to students. **Ask:** What is this passage describing? What does this description suggest about how Marpiyawin is feeling?

Possible response: It describes Marpiyawin's journey back to her people. She is feeling sad for leaving the wolves but is also grateful for their help.

2. Craft and Structure Ask students to reread the passage and focus on the description of Marpiyawin's communication with the wolves. **Ask:** In this passage, how does the author's word choice show that this story is a myth?

Possible response: In this passage, the author describes a conversation between the wolves and Marpiyawin. The wolves "offered" to lead Marpiyawin back to her people. Marpiyawin "thanked all the wolves" for the kindness. This word choice suggests that the story is a myth because it implies that Marpiyawin and the wolves are able to speak to each other. In reality, animals cannot communicate with people in this way.

3. Integration of Knowledge and Ideas

Ask: What does the author's choice of language say about the relationship between the Sioux and the animals found in nature? Why was this myth told?

Possible response: The Sioux respect nature and the animals within nature. They also believe that all things in nature serve a purpose. The Sioux used myths to help people understand their views about nature and animals.

---

traversed ▶
(trə vurst´) v.
went across

mystified ▶
(mist´ tə fid´) v.
made someone feel confused or unable to understand something

➌ and while she slept she had a most wonderful vision. In her dream the wolves talked to her and she understood them, and when she talked to them they understood her too. They told her that she had lost her way, but that she should trust them and they would not see her suffer from cold or hunger. She replied that she would not worry, and when she awoke it was without fear, even though in the cave with her were the wolves sitting about in a friendly manner.

The blizzard raged outside for many days, still she was contented, for she was neither cold nor hungry. For meat the wolves supplied her with tender rabbits and at night they kept her body warm with their shaggy coats of fur. As the days wore on, she and the wolves became fast friends.

But clear days finally came and the wolves offered to lead her back to her people, so they set out. They traversed many little valleys and crossed many creeks and streams; they walked up hills and down hills, and at last came to ➍ one from which she could look down upon the camp of her people. Here she must say "Good-bye" to her friends and companions—the wolves. This made her feel very sad, though she wanted to see her people again. Marpiyawin thanked all the wolves for their kindness to her and asked what she might do for them. All they asked was that, when the long winter months came and food was scarce, she bring to the top of the hill some nice fat meat for them to eat. This she gladly promised to do and went down the hill toward the camp of her people.

As Marpiyawin neared the village, she smelled a very unpleasant odor. At first it mystified her, then she realized it was the smell of human beings. At once the knowledge came to her that the smell of humans was very different from the smell of animals. This was why she now knew that animals so readily track human beings and why the odor of man is oftentimes so offensive to them. She had been with the wolves so long that she had lost the odor of her people and now was able to see that, while man often considers the animal offensive, so do animals find man offensive.

Marpiyawin came to the camp of her people and they were happy to see her, for they had considered her lost and thought she had been taken by an enemy tribe. But she pointed to the top of the hill in the distance, and there

---

💬 VOCABULARY DEVELOPMENT

Selection Vocabulary Reinforcement

To reinforce and assess students' comprehension of selection vocabulary words, give them sentences using the words in which the word may or may not be used correctly. Students must tell whether the use is correct and explain their answer. Use these sentences:

1. Jane *coaxed* the kitten out from under the car and took it home.
   Answer: Yes, *coaxed* is used correctly. Jane would have to gently urge the cat to come out from under the car.

2. The first English settlers *traversed* the ocean without knowing what they would find.
   Answer: Yes, *traversed* is used correctly. Early settlers crossed the ocean to come to North America.

3. The professor was confidently *mystified* while teaching the class.
   Answer: No, *mystified* is not used correctly. It means that someone feels "confused," and a professor teaching a class cannot be both confident and confused.

sat her friends, their forms black against the sky. In great surprise her people looked, not knowing what to say. They thought she must have just escaped a great danger. So she explained to them that she had been lost and would have perished had not the wolves saved her life. She asked them to give her some of their fat meat that she might carry it to the top of the hill. Her people were so grateful and happy that a young man was sent about the camp telling of the safe return of Marpiyawin and collecting meat from each tipi. Marpiyawin took the meat, placed the bundle on her back, and went up the hill, while the village people looked on in wonder. When she reached the hilltop she spread the meat on the ground and the wolves ate it.

THEY THOUGHT SHE MUST HAVE ESCAPED A GREAT DANGER.

Ever after that, when the long winter months came and food was scarce, and hard to find, Marpiyawin took meat to her friends the wolves. She never forgot their language and oftentimes in the winter their voices calling to her would be heard throughout the village. Then the people would ask the old woman what the wolves were saying. Their calls would be warnings that a blizzard was coming, or that the enemy was passing close, and to send out a scout or to let the old woman know that they were watching her with care.

And so Marpiyawin came to be known to the tribe as "The Old Woman Who Lived with the Wolves," or, in the Sioux language as, "Win yan wan si k'ma nitu ompi ti."

ABOUT THE AUTHOR

CHIEF LUTHER STANDING BEAR (1868–1939)

A member of the Oglala Sioux, Chief Standing Bear was originally named *Ota K'Te* (Plenty Kill). He later called himself Standing Bear because it was his father's name. He graduated from the Carlisle Indian School in Pennsylvania and became a writer who fought for Native American rights. In his work, Chief Standing Bear describes the customs and beliefs of the Sioux, including their special relationship with nature. In *Land of the Spotted Eagle,* he wrote, "Earth was bountiful and we were surrounded with the blessings of the great mystery."

5 **?** **Big Question: Toward Essential Understanding**

1. Read aloud the passage to students. **Ask:** How have the wolves affected Marpiyawin's community?

   Possible response: The wolves helped Marpiyawin survive during a blizzard. Through their kindness, Marpiyawin returned to her community, which made the community very happy.

2. **Ask:** How is Marpiyawin shaped by the two communities: the Sioux and the wolves?

   Possible response: The Sioux community shaped Marpiyawin's respect for nature and the creatures that live within it. The wolves give Marpiyawin a new insight into how animals see the world and humans.

👥 DIFFERENTIATED INSTRUCTION

Strategy for Less Proficient Readers
Some students may have difficulty reading long and compound sentences. Draw students' attention to the sentence beginning with "They traversed many little valleys and crossed many creeks and streams" (p. 742). Guide students to break the sentence into independent clauses, and the read these separately. Ask students what each part means, and then have students put the meanings together to determine what the whole sentence is saying. (Marpiyawin and the wolves traveled throughout the land until they finally found Marpiyawin's camp.) Repeat this activity with other long sentences in the selection.

Enrichment for Advanced Readers
Using books and online resources, have students research the Sioux. Tell them to investigate where the Sioux lived, aspects about their nomadic way of life, their conflict with the United States government, and famous Sioux leaders. Encourage them to present their findings to the class in posters, photo essays, or oral reports.

READ

Comprehension

1. They may need new resources, such as food and water, or they may just want a new area to live.

2. Marpiyawin cannot find her dog and retraces the way she had traveled with her people to find him.

3. She finds shelter in a cave where wolves bring her food and keep her warm with their fur.

Research: Clarify Details

Students should explain how their research helped them understand an unfamiliar detail.

Summarize

Students' summaries should include details about the Sioux way of life, Marpiyawin's separation from her people, the wolves' help, the conflict Marpiyawin feels about returning to her people, and how she becomes known as "The Old Woman Who Lived With the Wolves."

Language Study

Possible responses:

- *coaxed*: urged; Josie coaxed me to volunteer as a student guide.

- *traversed*: traveled across; Pioneers traversed the mountains on foot and horseback.

- *mystified*: puzzled; The disappearance of the pens mystified Katie until she caught her kitten taking one.

Literary Analysis

Possible responses appear below. Check to be sure students support their responses with evidence from the text.

1. **(a)** Marpiyawin takes shelter in a cave during a storm, and when she wakes up, wolves are in the cave with her. **(b)** The wolves in her dream told her if she trusted them she would survive, so she trusts the wolves in the cave instead of being afraid.

2. **(a)** The author describes the setting and Marpiyawin's dream with sensory details such as "thicker," "dark," "warm," "comfortable," and "cold" to

---

© Close Reading Activities

READ

Comprehension

Answer the following questions.

1. Why do the Sioux move from place to place?

2. How does Marpiyawin get separated from the rest of her tribe?

3. How does Marpiyawin survive harsh conditions?

Language Study

Selection Vocabulary Define each boldfaced word from the story. Then use the word in a sentence of your own.

- … Sioux dogs were **coaxed** away and ran with the wolf-pack …

Literary Analysis

Reread the identified passage. Then, respond to the questions that follow.

> **Focus Passage** *(pp. 741–742)*
> That afternoon the snow fell thicker … sitting about in a friendly manner.

Key Ideas and Details

1. **(a)** How does Marpiyawin come to spend time with the wolves? **(b) Interpret:** Why is she not afraid of the wolves?

Conflict and Resolution

In an **external conflict**, a character struggles against an outside force. An **internal conflict** takes place inside a character. The **resolution** is the outcome of a conflict. Reread the short story, and take notes on the conflict and resolution.

Research: Clarify Details Research an unfamiliar detail from the story, and explain how the information you learn sheds light on the story.

Summarize Write an objective summary of the story. Remember to leave out your opinions and evaluations.

- They **traversed** many little valleys and crossed many creeks …

- At first it **mystified** her, then she realized it was the smell of human beings.

Craft and Structure

2. **(a)** What **sensory** images does the author provide in the passage? **(b) Interpret:** How do these images help you understand Marpiyawin's situation?

Integration of Knowledge and Ideas

3. **Draw Conclusions:** What does Marpiyawin's experience with the wolves **indicate** about the relationship of the Sioux people to nature?

---

1. Which type of conflict develops when Marpiyawin becomes lost?

2. **People and Animals** How does Marpiyawin's trust in animals help her **resolve** the conflict?

---

create a visual image of the setting with the wolves. **(b)** The images help readers understand Marpiyawin's need to find shelter and why she is not fearful of being with the wolves.

3. The experience shows that the Sioux have a deep respect for nature.

Conflict and Resolution

1. An external conflict develops because Marpiyawin has to struggle against harsh weather.

2. In a dream, the wolves tell Marpiyawin they will help if she trusts them. She does, and she survives.

DISCUSS • RESEARCH • WRITE

From Text to Topic **Group Discussion**

Discuss the following passage with a group of classmates. Take notes during the discussion. Contribute your own ideas, and support them with examples from the text.

> The blizzard ranged outside … toward the camp of her people. (p. 742)

Research **Investigate the Topic**

Humans and Animals For thousands of years, humans have raised, kept, and farmed with animals. Animals have helped humans survive in difficult times, just as the wolves helped Marpiyawin in this story.

Assignment

Conduct research to find out when and how people domesticated, or tamed, dogs, sheep, cows, and horses. How did both humans and animals benefit? Consult online databases and reference sources. Take clear notes and carefully identify your sources so that you can easily access the information later. Share your findings in an **informal speech** to the class.

Writing to Sources **Informative Essay**

"The Old Woman Who Lived With Wolves" is about one community of people living close to nature.

Assignment

Write an **informative essay** in which you make a claim about how the Sioux in the story benefit from Marpiyawin's experiences with the wolves. Follow these steps:

- Introduce your claim about the benefits of Marpiwan's experiences upon her people. Organize the reasons that support your claim.
- Develop your essay with details and examples from the story.
- Use transition words and phrases such as *for this reason* and *because* to clarify the relationships between your claim and supporting details.

QUESTIONS FOR DISCUSSION

1. What does Marpiyawin learn from living with the wolves?
2. How are the communities of the wolves and the Sioux alike?

PREPARATION FOR ESSAY

You may use the results of this research project to support your ideas in the essay at the end of this section.

ACADEMIC VOCABULARY

Academic terms appear in blue on these pages. If these words are not familiar to you, use a dictionary to find their definitions. Then, use them as you speak and write about the text.

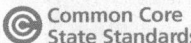 **Common Core State Standards**

RL.6.1, RL.6.2, RL.6.3, RL.6.4; SL.6.1, SL.6.4; W.6.1, W.6.7, W.6.8; L.6.1, L.6.4
[For full standards wording, see the chart in the front of this book.]

From Text to Topic: Group Discussion

Possible responses:

1. Marpiyawin learns to experience the world from the wolves' point of view.
2. Both groups protect their members and respect the members of the other community.

Research: Investigate the Topic

Introduce the assignment using the instruction on the student page.

1. Arrange for students to visit your school's library or computer lab. Review strategies for identifying reliable online sources.
2. Tell students to take notes on main ideas and details that support the main idea of each source. Remind students that they can choose to quote directly or summarize in their own words as they take notes.
3. Remind students that they should try to make connections between the ideas and facts in the different sources. Encourage students to draw their own conclusions from the information.
4. Suggest that students practice giving their speech or presentation so that they do not need to read directly from their notes.

Academic Vocabulary

If students struggle with defining the academic vocabulary words, use this routine:

Write the words and definitions on the board.

sensory: relating the to sense of touch, smell, hearing, tasting, or sight

indicate: to point out

resolve: to find an answer

Have students say each word aloud. Then, have students use each word in a sentence.

Writing to Sources: Informative Essay

Students' informative essays should make a claim about one or more benefits of Marpiyawin's experiences to the Sioux community and use facts and examples from the story to support the claim. Students should use transition words and phrases to show relationships between their claims and their reasons.

 Online Writer's Notebook

Students can use the Online Writer's Notebook to record all responses.

MULTIDRAFT READING

Essential Understanding

First, students should read the entire selection on their own. Then, to assist struggling readers and to deepen comprehension for all, you may wish to guide them through the selection by asking them the close reading questions provided in the margins. Have students apply the multidraft reading protocols as they examine specific "chunks" of text related to these questions. For each reading, have students set the purpose indicated:

- **First reading:** Students should read the selection independently and think about its basic meaning.
- **Second reading:** Students should analyze the text's key ideas and details and its craft and structure.
- **Third reading:** Students should integrate knowledge and ideas; connect to the Big Question, other texts, and the world; and use teacher-led Close Reading discussion questions to examine particularly rich and significant passages.

For more guidance, refer to the *Classroom Strategies and Teaching Routines* card on multidraft reading.

❶ Background

If you wish, explain to students that oceanographers are scientists who study the world's oceans and seas. Oceanographers study varying aspects of the ocean, including the properties of its saltwater, its movement, changes in its basins or other features, and the life cycles of its animal and plant life. This type of research allows scientists to make predictions about how weather and climate changes affect the ocean. It also helps them study humans' positive and negative impact on the ocean.

Vocabulary

1. Write the following words and definitions on the board:

   navigate *v.* find the way

   marine *adj.* relating to the ocean or ocean life

   meteorologists *n.* scientists who study the atmosphere and weather

2. Have students say each word aloud.

---

❶ SATELLITES AND SEA LIONS:
Working Together to Improve Ocean Models

NASA News Release
Updated 2/6/07

navigate ▶
(nav´ə gāt´) *v.*
find the way

marine ▶
(mə rēn´) *adj.*
relating to the
ocean or ocean life

❷

The best oceanographers in the world never studied at a university. Yet they know how to **navigate** expertly along oceanic fronts, the invisible boundaries between waters of different temperatures and densities. These ocean experts can find rich fishing in places and at depths that others would assume are barren. They regularly visit the most interesting and dynamic parts of the sea.

Sea lions, seals, sharks, tuna, and other top ocean predators share some of their experiences with human researchers, thanks to electronic tags. Besides tracking the animals, these sensors also collect oceanographic data, such as temperature and salinity. Scientists are beginning to incorporate this rich store of information into ocean models providing new insights into the inner workings of the ocean and the lives of its creatures.

"Our goal is to produce a three-dimensional model of the ocean," says oceanographer Dr. Yi Chao. Chao uses data from satellites, ships, buoys and floats to map the currents, heat content and different water densities beneath the ocean surface. When Chao heard Dr. Dan Costa, a professor of **marine** biology at the University of California, Santa Cruz, present some of his animal tagging data at a scientific meeting a few years ago, he saw an opportunity to improve his ocean models. Costa recognized a chance to get a clearer picture of the place where his research subjects live. .

The research collaboration now includes Dr. Barbara Block, a professor of marine sciences at Stanford University, Palo Alto, Calif., and the scientists have added tagging data collected from tuna and sharks to their studies. Together with a group called TOPP, for Tagging of Pacific Pelagics, they are now working to expand the use of environmental and biological data collected by ocean inhabitants.

ⓒ TEXT COMPLEXITY **RUBRIC**

Satellites and Sea Lions: Working Together to Improve Ocean Models		
Qualitative Measures	Context/Knowledge Demands	Use of data from different sources to map the ocean 1 2 ③ 4 5
	Structure/Language Conventionality and Clarity	Some long sentences; technical, challenging vocabulary 1 2 3 ④ 5
	Levels of Meaning/ Purpose/Concept Level	Challenging concept (descriptions of data collected and how best to interpret) 1 2 3 ④ 5
Quantitative Measures	Text Length	Word Count: 664
	Lexile	1360L

"We are at the forefront of knowing how animals use the ocean," says Costa. "But we want to understand the environment better. We still see the ocean primarily as deep or shallow or near-shore or offshore. But just as there are different habitats on land, the ocean has fine-scale features that are very important to animals," he explains. "We want to be able to look at the ocean and say the equivalent of 'this is a grassland' or 'this is a forest.'"

In late January, Costa and his research group headed up the California coast to begin tagging elephant seals and collecting tags that were deployed last spring. The work is strictly regulated to ensure that the animals are protected from harm, and it requires a permit from the National Marine Fisheries Service. . . .

"Marine scientists have been tracking marine animals for years," says Chao. "It's an interesting challenge, though, to use the data. There are all sorts—from tuna, sharks, seals—you name it. Some of these data sets have small errors, others much larger errors. Figuring out how to put these in our system is a challenge," he says. "But five years from now, we should be able to see the ocean the way a turtle sees it."

"As we are getting more data from the sea and improving our computer models," says Chao, "we should be able to make routine ocean forecasts, similar to what **meteorologists** have been doing in the past few decades. People who open the newspaper or turn on the TV in the morning will see the updated ocean forecast and make appropriate decisions as they plan their activities on the sea."

What is most important about using marine animals as ocean sensors is that the work benefits the animals, Costa explains. "Collaborations between biologists like Barbara Block and me and physical oceanographers like Yi are critical for understanding why the animals go where they go," he says, "as we need to know and understand the ocean physics and its relationship to climate processes. Further, the ability to understand how climate change is affecting the world oceans is not only of benefit to humans, but is vital for trying to figure out what is going to happen to habitats of marine animals."

◄ **meteorologists**
(mē′tē ə räl′ə jist) *n.* scientists who study the atmosphere and weather

❷ Close Reading

1. **Key Ideas and Details**
   Ask: Based on the first passage, what will this selection be about?

   Possible response: The selection is about oceans, their inhabitants, and researchers.

2. **Craft and Structure**
   Ask: How does the author use structure to surprise the reader? How is the first paragraph different from the second one?

   Possible response: First the author leads the reader to believe that the best oceanographers are humans. Then the reader discovers that the author is referring to ocean animals.

3. **Integration of Knowledge and Ideas**
   Ask: Why does the author describe these ocean animals in terms of oceanographers?

   Possible response: The author recognizes the ocean animals' intelligence and their vast knowledge of the oceans.

❸ Focus Passage

A Focus Passage is identified with brackets in the Student Edition of this page for students' independent close reading and analysis. A question bank for the passage and possible responses appear at the end of the selection.

❹ **Big Question: Toward Essential Understanding**

1. **Ask:** How are marine animal communities shaping the research?

   Possible response: Marine animal communities are helping scientists collect data.

2. **Ask:** How is the research shaping the marine communities?

   Possible response: The research helps scientists understand how climate change can affect marine animal habitats. Researchers may then be able to propose solutions to keep the marine habitat healthy.

 **Audio**

Selection Audio is available in the **Student eText** and on the **Hear It!** CD-ROM.

ⓒ TEXT COMPLEXITY **READER AND TASK SUGGESTIONS**

Satellites and Sea Lions: Working Together to Improve Ocean Models

Preparing to Read the Text	Leveled Tasks
• Use the Background note on TE p. 746 to discuss the purpose of oceanography. • Discuss technical, scientific vocabulary and how that vocabulary differs from language used in other professions. • Guide students to use Multidraft Reading strategies (TE p. 746).	*Language/Clarity* If students will have difficulty with selection vocabulary, have them read the first three paragraphs and identify examples of scientific language. Then, have students use context clues to determine the meaning of each scientific word. Discuss students' definitions and help clarify meanings. *Analyzing* If students will not have difficulty with selection language, tell them to consider the difficulties oceanographers would encounter recording the same information without the help of ocean predators. Encourage students to use scientific language to help explain their ideas. Then, ask students to discuss their notes and conclusions as a class.

READ

Comprehension

1. Oceanographers can now use tagged sea animals to gather information about the ocean and the behavior of sea creatures.

2. This information will help scientists understand how climate change is affecting oceans and marine life. Scientists want to predict how climate change will affect marine habitats in the future.

Research: Clarify Details

Students' research should explain how their findings helped them understand a concept in the news release.

Summarize

Students' summaries should describe information from the news release about cooperation among the scientists to use data from tagged animals and satellites, ships, buoys, and floats to improve models of the ocean and its inhabitants.

Language Study
Possible responses:

- *navigate*: find the way; The captain knows how to navigate in rough seas.

- *marine*: relating to the ocean or ocean life; Sea lions are marine animals.

- *meteorologists*: scientists who study the atmosphere and weather; Meteorologists predicted a major snowstorm in the Midwest.

Literary Analysis

Possible responses appear below. Check to be sure students support their responses with evidence from the text.

1. **(a)** They are studying tuna, sharks, seals, and other animals. **(b)** They are collecting tracking data from tagged marine animals to add to computer models of the ocean.

2. No, it will be difficult. The data may contain errors, and Chao calls it a "challenge."

READ

Comprehension

Reread as needed to answer these questions.

1. What is the main idea of the news release?

2. How can the research described in the news release benefit animals in the future?

Language Study

Selection Vocabulary Define each boldfaced word below. Then, use the word in a sentence of your own.

- Yet they know how to **navigate** expertly along oceanic fronts …

Literary Analysis

Reread the passage and answer the questions.

> **Focus Passage** *(p. 747)*
> "Marine scientists have been tracking … as they plan their activities on the sea."

Key Ideas and Details

1. **(a)** What kinds of animals are the scientists studying? **(b) Interpret:** What data are the scientists collecting, and why?

Expository Writing

Expository writing explains or informs. Reread the selection, noting reasons why the news release is an example of expository writing.

1. What topic does the news release explain?

Research: Clarify Details Research at least one unfamiliar detail from the news release and explain how the information you learn sheds light on the text.

Summarize Write an objective summary of the news release. Remember to leave out your opinions and judgments.

- … Dr. Barbara Block, a professor of **marine** sciences at Stanford University …

- … similar to what **meteorologists** have been doing in the past few decades.

2. **Infer:** Will it be easy for scientists to use the data to make ocean forecasts? Cite textual evidence to support your answer.

Craft and Structure

3. **Deduce:** What do the quotations from Chao add to the passage?

Integration of Knowledge and Ideas

4. **(a)** What effect will the computer models have on people's everyday lives? **(b) Infer:** Why is this kind of modeling useful?

2. **People and Animals** How does the news release present information that shows how the scientists' work will benefit people and animals?

---

3. They add authenticity to the report. The author allows the scientist to explain things for himself.

4. **(a)** They will allow scientists to create ocean forecasts to help people plan their activities on the water. **(b)** People will be able to stay safe when they work or play in the ocean, such as fishing or sailing.

Expository Writing

1. It explains how scientists track marine animals with electronic tags and collect information about the ocean.

2. **Possible response:** The news release introduces information, includes quotes from scientists, and then makes the claim that the research will help scientists understand how oceans can be affected by climate change. Understanding how oceans can change will help both humans and animals in the future.

DISCUSS • RESEARCH • WRITE

From Text to Topic **Class Discussion**

Discuss the following passage with your class. Take notes during the discussion. Contribute your own ideas, and support them with examples from the text.

> What is most important about using marine animals … what is going to happen to habitats of marine animals." (p. 747)

Research **Investigate the Topic**

Oceanographers All oceanographers study the ocean. However, there are different fields of study within oceanography. For example, chemical oceanographers study the chemical composition of oceans and the **interaction** that take place between the oceans and the atmosphere.

Assignment

Conduct research to find out about different types of scientists who study the ocean and its creatures. Consult **credible** online and print sources about oceanographers. Take clear notes and carefully identify your sources so that you can easily locate the information later. Share your findings in a **visual report**.

Writing to Sources **Argument**

The news release focuses on ways that scientists have learned about animals and oceans by working **collaboratively**.

Assignment

Write a **persuasive letter** to NASA in which you argue for increased spending on marine study. Promote collaboration among scientists on new research about ocean animals. Follow these steps:

- Present your claim about supporting new research.
- Acknowledge and refute the opposing position.
- Support your claim with reasons and evidence from the text.
- Use transitional words and phrases to clarify the relationships among the reasons and evidence that support your claim.
- Conclude with a statement that summarizes your argument.

QUESTIONS FOR DISCUSSION

1. How does sharing information lead people to a better understanding of animals?
2. What information about climate can the researchers learn from animals?

PREPARATION FOR ESSAY

You may use the results of this research project to support your ideas in the essay at the end of this section.

ACADEMIC VOCABULARY

Academic terms appear in blue on these pages. If these words are not familiar to you, use a dictionary to find their definitions. Then, use them as you speak and write about the text.

 **Common Core State Standards**

RI.6.1, RI.6.2, RI.6.5; W.6.1, W.6.7, W.6.8; SL.6.1; L.6.4, L.6.6
[For full standards wording, see the chart in the front of this book.]

DISCUSS • RESEARCH • WRITE

From Text to Topic: Class Discussion

Possible responses:

1. Scientists who study the ocean water can share information with scientists who study plant and animal life in the ocean to learn how animals use the ocean.
2. Researchers can learn how climate change is affecting the oceans by monitoring where animals go.

Research: Investigate the Topic

Introduce the assignment using the instruction on the student page.

1. Arrange for students to visit your school's library or computer lab. Review strategies for identifying reliable sources with students.
2. Remind students to take notes on main ideas and supporting details of each source. Remind students that they can choose to quote directly or summarize in their own words as they take notes.
3. Have students note the sources they used. Encourage them to make a list of Works Cited.
4. Encourage students to draw conclusions and make connections between ideas in multiple sources.
5. Have students prepare an outline for their presentation. Suggest that students practice before giving their speech or presentation so that they do not need to read directly from their outline as they present to the class.

Academic Vocabulary

If students struggle with defining the academic vocabulary words, use this routine:

Write the words and definitions on the board.

interaction: the influence of people or things on one another

credible: believable, reliable

collaboratively: together

Have students say each word aloud. Then, have students use each word in a sentence.

Writing to Sources: Argument

Students' persuasive letters should be addressed to NASA and promote scientific collaboration. Letters should include a clear claim, recognition of the opposing position, reasons and text evidence to support the claim, appropriate transitions, and a conclusion that sums up the argument.

 Online Writer's Notebook

Students can use the Online Writer's Notebook to record all responses.

MULTIDRAFT READING

Essential Understanding

First, students should read the entire selection on their own. Then, to assist struggling readers and to deepen comprehension for all, you may wish to guide them through the selection by asking them the close reading questions provided in the margins. Have students apply the multidraft reading protocols as they examine specific "chunks" of text related to these questions. For each reading, have students set the purpose indicated:

- **First reading:** Students should read the selection independently and think about its basic meaning.

- **Second reading:** Students should analyze the text's key ideas and details and its craft and structure.

- **Third reading:** Students should integrate knowledge and ideas; connect to the Big Question, other texts, and the world; and use teacher-led Close Reading discussion questions to examine particularly rich and significant passages.

For more guidance, refer to the *Classroom Strategies and Teaching Routines* card on multidraft reading.

❶ Background

If you wish, explain to students that conservation became a political issue in the United States in the early 1900s when President Theodore Roosevelt established the first wildlife refuge at Pelican Island, Florida. For many years, hunters had been killing birds on Pelican Island for their colorful plumage. Many people feared that the island's entire bird population would be wiped out. After many unsuccessful attempts to stop the hunting there, a group of people brought their concerns and frustrations to President Roosevelt's attention. He asked, "Is there any law preventing me from declaring Pelican Island a Federal Bird Reservation?" When he was informed there was not—as the land was owned by the government—he responded, "Very well, then I so declare it." His conservation efforts for birds did not stop there. He later set aside more than 140 million acres nationwide as forest reserves.

NARRATIVE ESSAY

Turkeys
Bailey White

❶

Something about my mother attracts ornithologists.[1] It all started years ago when a couple of them discovered she had a rare species of woodpecker coming to her bird feeder. They came in the house and sat around the window, exclaiming and taking pictures with big fancy cameras. But long after the red cockaded woodpeckers had gone to roost, the ornithologists were still there. There always seemed to be three or four of them wandering around our place and staying for supper.

In those days, during the 1950's, the big concern of ornithologists in our area was the wild turkey. They were rare, and the pure-strain wild turkeys had begun to

---

1. **ornithologists** (ôr′ nə thäl′ ə jists) *n.* people who study birds.

ⓒ TEXT COMPLEXITY **RUBRIC**

Turkeys		
Qualitative Measures	Context/Knowledge Demands	Rural Georgia in the 1950s; ornithology 1 ②　3　4　5
	Structure/Language Conventionality and Clarity	Simple sentence structure; scientific vocabulary 1　2　③　4　5
	Levels of Meaning/Purpose/Concept Level	Accessible concept (amusing narrative about a serious childhood experience) 1　2　③　4　5
Quantitative Measures	Text Length	Word Count: 862
	Lexile	890L

interbreed with farmers' domestic stock. The species was being degraded. It was extinction by dilution, and to the ornithologists it was just as tragic as the more dramatic demise of the passenger pigeon or the Carolina parakeet.

One ornithologist had devised a formula to compute the ratio of domestic to pure-strain wild turkey in an individual bird by comparing the angle of flight at takeoff and the rate of acceleration. And in those sad days, the turkeys were flying low and slow.

It was during that time, the spring when I was six years old, that I caught the measles. I had a high fever, and my mother was worried about me. She kept the house quiet and dark and crept around silently, trying different methods of cooling me down.

◀ **dilution**
(di lōō´ shən)
n. process of weakening by mixing with something else

◀ **demise**
(di mīz´) *n.* end of existence; death

PART 3 • Turkeys **751**

② Close Reading

1. **Key Ideas and Details** Read aloud the passage to students. **Ask:** What does this passage describe?

   Possible response: The author describes a formula ornithologists used to figure out whether a turkey is a pure-strain wild turkey.

2. **Craft and Structure** Ask students to reread the passage. **Ask:** What type of language does the author use to describe what is happening in this passage? What words help you determine the type of language? What effect do the author's word choices create?

   Possible response: The passage uses scientific language, such as *compute the ratio of domestic* and informal language, such as *flying low and slow.* The word choices give the reader a sense of the work ornithologists do.

3. **Integration of Knowledge and Ideas**
   Ask: What does the contrast in language suggest about how scientists—compared with other people—observe wild turkeys?

   Possible response: The scientists used a complicated formula to identify basic information about the flight of the turkey. However, anyone could see that the turkeys were flying low and slow.

Vocabulary

If students require support with selection vocabulary, use this routine:

1. Write the following words and definitions on the board:

   dilution *n.* process of weakening by mixing with something else

   demise *n.* end of existence; death

   vigilance *n.* watchfulness

2. Have students say each word aloud.

3. Use the word in a sentence that defines the word.

 **Audio**

Selection Audio is available in the **Student eText** and on the **Hear It!** CD-ROM.

ⓒ TEXT COMPLEXITY **READER AND TASK SUGGESTIONS**

Turkeys

Preparing to Read the Text
- Using the Background note on the previous page, discuss the birds on Pelican Island.
- Discuss the purpose of using scientific language in a narrative essay. Ask students to describe other instances in which scientific language would be used.
- Guide students to use Multidraft Reading strategies (TE p. 750).

Leveled Tasks
Structure/Language If students will have difficulty with vocabulary, encourage them to write down technical words as they read the selection for the first time. Then, have them share and discuss their word lists with one another. Discuss students' lists and help clarify meanings.

Analyzing If students will not have difficulty with vocabulary, have them write sentences giving examples of other uses of these terms. Encourage students to share and discuss their sentences as a class.

③ Close Reading

1. Key Ideas and Details Have a volunteer read aloud the passage. **Ask:** What is White thinking when she sees the "worried faces" of the ornithologists? Is she right?

Possible response: White thinks that the ornithologists are worried about her well-being. They are concerned about her, but they are more concerned with trying to ensure that the wild turkey eggs hatch.

2. Craft and Structure Reread the passage to students. Ask them to listen for similes in the passage. **Ask:** How does the author's use of simile act as foreshadowing?

Possible response: The author uses a simile to compare the faces of the ornithologists to those of glowing eggs. This image foreshadows the real purpose of the visit by the ornithologists.

3. Integration of Knowledge and Ideas

Ask: What does the language in this passage reveal about the narrator?

Possible response: The passage shows how she is in a dreamlike state because of her illness. She does not fully understand what is happening.

④ Focus Passage

A Focus Passage is identified with brackets in the Student Edition of this page for students' independent close reading and analysis. A question bank for the passage and possible responses appear at the end of the selection.

Even the ornithologists stayed away—but not out of fear of the measles or respect for a household with sickness. The fact was, they had discovered a wild turkey nest. According to the formula, the hen was pure-strain wild—not a taint of the sluggish domestic bird in her blood—and the ornithologists were camping in the woods, protecting her nest from predators and taking pictures.

One night our phone rang. It was one of the ornithologists. "Does your little girl still have measles?" he asked.

"Yes," said my mother. "She's very sick. Her temperature is 102."

"I'll be right over," said the ornithologist.

In five minutes a whole carload of them arrived. They marched solemnly into the house, carrying a cardboard box. "A hundred and two, did you say? Where is she?" they asked my mother.

They crept into my room and set the box down on the bed. I was barely conscious, and when I opened my eyes, their **③** worried faces hovering over me seemed to float out of the darkness like giant, glowing eggs. They snatched the covers off me and felt me all over. They consulted in whispers.

"Feels just right, I'd say."

"A hundred two—can't miss if we tuck them up close and she lies still."

I closed my eyes then, and after a while the ornithologists drifted away, their pale faces bobbing up and down on the black wave of fever.

④ The next morning I was better. For the first time in days I could think. The memory of the ornithologists with their whispered voices was like a dream from another life. But when I pulled down the covers, there staring up at me with googly eyes and wide mouths were sixteen fuzzy baby turkeys, and the cracked chips and caps of sixteen brown speckled eggs.

I was a sensible child. I gently stretched myself out. The eggshells crackled, and the turkey babies fluttered and cheeped and snuggled against me. I laid my aching head back on the pillow and closed my eyes. "The ornithologists," I whispered. "The ornithologists have been here."

It seems the turkey hen had been so disturbed by the elaborate protective measures that had been undertaken

💬 VOCABULARY DEVELOPMENT

Selection Vocabulary Reinforcement

As students are discussing "Turkeys," reinforce their comprehension of selection vocabulary with "show-you-know" sentences. The first part of the sentence uses the vocabulary word in an appropriate context. The second part of the sentence—the "show-you-know" part—clarifies the first. You might encourage them with sentence starters like these:

1. I made a *dilution* of the soup by _____.
   Possible response: adding more broth.

2. Scientists are concerned about the *demise* of pure-strain wild turkeys because _____.
   Possible response: their population was rapidly decreasing.

3. The *vigilance* of the ornithologists was evident when they _____.
   Possible response: went to great lengths to make sure that all of the eggs hatched.

on her behalf that she had abandoned her nest on the night the eggs were due to hatch. It was a cold night. The ornithologists, not having an incubator on hand, used their heads and came up with the next best thing.

The baby turkeys and I gained our strength together. When I was finally able to get out of bed and feebly creep around the house, the turkeys peeped and cheeped around my ankles, scrambling to keep up with me and tripping over their own big spraddle-toed feet. When I went outside for the first time, the turkeys tumbled after me down the steps and scratched around in the yard while I sat in the sun.

Finally, in late summer, the day came when they were ready to fly for the first time as adult birds. The ornithologists gathered. I ran down the hill, and the turkeys ran too. Then, one by one, they took off. They flew high and fast. The ornithologists made Vs with their thumbs and forefingers, measuring angles. They consulted their stopwatches and paced off distances. They scribbled in their tiny notebooks. Finally they looked at each other. They sighed. They smiled. They jumped up and down and hugged each other. "One hundred percent pure wild turkey!" they said.

Nearly forty years have passed since then. Now there's a vaccine for measles. And the woods where I live are full of pure wild turkeys. I like to think they are all descendants of those sixteen birds I saved from the vigilance of the ornithologists.

◀ **vigilance**
(vij ́ ə ləns)
n. watchfulness

ABOUT THE AUTHOR

Bailey White (b. 1950)
Baily White's father, Robb, wrote children's stories and television and movie scripts. Inspired by her father's love of words, White began writing in her teen years. Her mother, Rosalie, was a farmer. Through her mother, White gained an admiration for nature. As a teacher in Thomasville, Georgia, White did not expect to become famous. However, she became an essayist on National Public Radio, where she shared her observations with listeners across the country. White's collection of essays, *Mama Makes Up Her Mind and Other Dangers of Southern Living,* was on the bestseller list for 55 weeks.

❺ Close Reading

1. **Key Ideas and Details** Read aloud the passage to students. **Ask:** What happens here?

   Possible response: The baby turkeys began to follow White around as she gained her strength.

2. **Craft and Structure**
   Ask: What vivid verbs does the author use? How do these verbs characterize the author and the turkeys?

   Possible response: The author uses the verbs *creep, peep, cheep, scramble, trip, tumble,* and *scratch* in her description. These verbs characterize the baby turkeys as being eager but uncoordinated as they follow the narrator.

3. **Integration of Knowledge and Ideas**
   Ask: What does this passage say about relationships between people and animals?

   Possible response: This passage suggests that people and animals can have relationships similar to animals with other animals or people with other people. For example, the turkeys continuously follow the narrator, who recognizes their need for a mother and acts as a surrogate.

❻ Big Question: Toward Essential Understanding

1. **Ask:** What happens in this passage? Compare the experience of people and animals in the past and present.

   Possible response: In the past, there was no vaccine for measles and there were few wild turkeys in the woods where the author lives. Today there are both.

2. **Ask:** Which community may have shaped the narrator more, that of people or that of turkeys and nature?

   Possible response: Both communities shaped the author. As a child, the narrator was surrounded by people and animals. The incident with the turkeys left an impression because she wrote about it almost forty years later.

🔅 DIFFERENTIATED INSTRUCTION

Support for Special-Needs Students
Some students may have difficulty understanding why this narrative essay describes the ornithologists and White's illness. To help students understand the purpose of these seemingly separate topics, have students reread pp. 752–753. First, read aloud to students and ask them to read along with you. Then, ask questions to help students think about connections, such as: *How do the ornithologists react to White's illness at first? How do they treat her illness later in the story? How does White's illness affect the wild turkeys?*
Discuss students' answers and clarify any misunderstandings.

🔵 Pronunciation for English Learners
Refer students to the word *ornithologists* in the first sentence on p. 750. Write the word on the board, pronounce it distinctly, and then have students repeat the word. Next, write the word *solemnly* on the board. Model its pronunciation, and have students repeat it. Repeat with other difficult vocabulary from the selection.

READ

Comprehension

1. Wild turkeys are in danger of extinction by dilution, or inter-breeding with domestic turkeys.

2. They are studying and protecting a wild turkey hen's nest.

3. Their plan works because the eggs hatch and the turkeys survive.

Research: Clarify Details

Students should explain how their research helped them understand a detail in the text.

Summarize

Students' summaries should explain why the ornithologists were near White's home, the problem they faced, what happened to the turkey hen's eggs, and how the problem was solved.

Language Study

Possible responses:

- *dilution*: process of weakening by mixing with something else; This dilution of the juice is too watery.

- *demise*: end of existence, death; Wildlife groups work to prevent the demise of endangered animals.

- *vigilance*: watchfulness; The detective's vigilance solved the mystery.

Literary Analysis

Possible responses appear below. Check to be sure students support their responses with evidence from the text.

1. White's 102-degree temperature is crucial.

2. They run the risk that White is not warm enough to incubate the eggs or that she might roll over in her sleep and accidentally crush them.

3. **(a)** White uses the phrase "a dream from another life" to describe her memories from when she had a fever. **(b)** Yes, the reader knows that White is unaware of what is happening around her. We get this sense by her surprise the next morning to find 16 baby turkeys in the bed with her.

READ

Comprehension

Reread as needed to answer the questions.

1. In the essay, what problem threatens the wild turkeys?

2. What are the ornithologists doing in the woods?

3. What is the final result of the ornithologists' plan to save the eggs?

Language Study

Selection Vocabulary Define each boldfaced word and use it in a sentence of your own.

- It was extinction by **dilution** …

- … the more dramatic **demise** of the passenger pigeon or the Carolina parakeet.

- … those sixteen birds I saved from the **vigilance** of the ornithologists.

Literary Analysis

Reread the identified passage. Then, respond to the questions that follow.

> **Focus Passage** *(p. 752)*
> "Feels just right … brown speckled eggs.

Key Ideas and Details

1. **Analyze:** What key detail is **crucial** to the success of the ornithologists' plan?

2. **Interpret:** What risks do the ornithologists take by following their plan?

Author's Influences

An **author's influences** are factors that affect his or her writing. These factors include the author's cultural background and the time in which he or she lives. Reread the narrative essay, and take notes on the factors that influenced the author.

Research: Clarify Details Research at least one unfamiliar detail and explain how the information you learn sheds light on an aspect of the narrative essay.

Summarize Write an objective summary of the essay. Do not include your opinions or evaluations.

Craft and Structure

3. **(a)** What words and phrases does White use to describe the feeling of having a fever? **(b) Evaluate:** Does White convey the feeling effectively? Why or why not?

Integration of Knowledge and Ideas

4. **Draw Conclusions:** What does the ornithologists' plan show about the ways in which scientists use problem-solving skills?

---

1. **(a)** Where and when did the events take place? **(b)** What details of White's situation made these events possible?

2. **People and Animals** How does the author feel about the event nearly forty years later?

---

4. It shows that ornithologists think outside the box when they need to find a solution for which there is no readily available scientific protocol.

Author's Influences

1. **(a)** The events take place at the author's home in the 1950s, when she was a child. **(b)** White became very ill, her mother befriended some ornithologists, and some wild turkey eggs were about to hatch.

2. White likes to think that she helped save the wild turkeys from extinction.

DISCUSS • RESEARCH • WRITE

From Text to Topic **Class Discussion**

Discuss the following passage with a group of classmates. Take notes during the discussion. Contribute your own ideas, and support them with examples from the text.

> Finally, in late summer, the day came … with their thumbs and forefingers, measuring angles. (p. 753)

Research **Investigate the Topic**

Wild Turkeys When the events that White describes took place, wild turkeys were threatened with extinction. Today, these turkeys have made a comeback. There are five different types of wild turkey in North America.

Assignment

Conduct research to find out about wild turkeys and how people helped them make a comeback. Consult print and online resources. Carefully identify your sources so that you can easily access the information later. Share your findings in an **informal presentation** for the class.

Writing to Sources **Argument**

Bailey White and the ornithologists are responsible for helping to save sixteen wild turkeys. Some scientists and activists, called *conservationists*, work to keep animals from becoming extinct.

Assignment

Write a **persuasive essay** from the point of view of a conservationist who wants to save the wild turkey. Argue for the value of saving the species using information from the narrative essay to support your claims. Follow these steps:

- Introduce your claim.
- Support your claim with logical reasoning and information from the text.
- Use transition words, phrases, and clauses to connect your claim and reasons.
- Provide a strong concluding statement.

QUESTIONS FOR DISCUSSION

1. What does it mean that the turkeys took off flying high and fast?

2. Why do the ornithologists make Vs with their thumbs and fingers? What do they hope to discover?

PREPARATION FOR ESSAY

You may use the results of this research project to support your ideas in the essay at the end of this section.

ACADEMIC VOCABULARY

Academic terms appear in blue on these pages. If these words are not familiar to you, use a dictionary to find their definitions. Then, use them as you speak and write about the text.

Common Core State Standards

RL.6.1, RL.6.2, RL.6.3; SL.6.1; W.6.1, W.6.4; L.6.4, L.6.6
[For full standards wording, see the chart in the front of this book.]

DISCUSS • RESEARCH • WRITE

From Text to Topic: Class Discussion

1. Since flying low and slow meant birds had some domestic turkey in them, flying high and fast suggests they are pure-strain wild turkeys.

2. The ornithologists are measuring the angle of the turkeys' flight because it shows whether they are pure-strain wild turkeys.

Research: Investigate the Topic

Introduce the assignment using the instruction on the student page.

1. Arrange for students to visit your school's library or computer lab. Review strategies for identifying reliable sources with students.

2. Remind students to take notes on main ideas and supporting details of each source.

3. Have students note the sources they used and create a list of Works Cited.

4. Have students prepare an outline for their presentation. Suggest that students practice before giving their speech or presentation so that they do not need to read directly from their outline as they present to the class.

Academic Vocabulary

If students struggle with defining the academic vocabulary word, use this routine:

Write the word and definition on the board.

crucial: important

Have students read the word aloud. Then, have students use the word in a sentence.

Writing to Sources: Argument

Students' persuasive essays should introduce a claim about saving the wild turkeys and use details and facts from the text to support the claim. Students should connect the claim and reasons with transition words, phrases, and clauses and provide a concluding statement.

 Online Writer's Notebook

Students can use the Online Writer's Notebook to record all responses.

Speaking and Listening: Small Group Discussion

Introduce the assignment using the instruction on the student page.

1. Conduct discussions. Help students recall and apply their knowledge of the selections in this section to answer the discussion questions. For example, **ask:**

- What types of people or organizations help abandoned or injured animals?

- How did White benefit from caring for the wild turkeys? How did the wild turkeys benefit from White's involvement?

- What do the statistics about pet ownership in the United States say about the importance of animals in our communities?

2. Summarize and present your ideas. Remind students that when they summarize their findings, they should strive to represent a range of ideas that emerged from their group's discussion.

Criteria for Success

Circulate around the room and observe group discussions. Support groups in their efforts to conduct organized, focused, balanced, and respectful discussions. Ask guiding questions if the conversation stagnates, and encourage students to make connections between ideas and experiences from different sources and to explore contrasts in the texts' portrayals or points of view. Emphasize that students should support all points with specific text evidence.

Use New Vocabulary

Assist students in using new vocabulary during group discussion. For example, **ask:**

- What were the sea and animals *yearning* for in the Maori myth?

- What *incidents* from your personal life show how animals are important in your community?

 Assessment: Synthesis

Speaking and Listening: **Small Group Discussion**

People, Animals, and Communities The texts in this section vary in genre, length, style, and perspective. However, all of the texts comment in some way on the idea that animals can make valuable contributions to human communities. The issues surrounding the many ways animals and people can help one another are fundamentally related to the Big Question addressed in this unit: **How much do our communities shape us?**

Assignment

Conduct discussions. With a small group of classmates, conduct a discussion about issues surrounding people, animals, and communities. Refer to the texts in this section, other texts you have read, and your personal experience and knowledge to support your ideas. Begin your discussion by addressing the following questions:

- How do people help abandoned or injured animals?
- How can people benefit from caring for animals? How can animals benefit from being cared for by people?
- How can animals help people and their communities?

Summarize and present your ideas. After you have fully explored the topic, summarize your discussion and present your findings to the class as a whole.

Criteria for Success

✓ Organizes the group effectively
Appoint a group leader and a timekeeper. The group leader should present the discussion questions. The timekeeper should make sure the discussion takes no longer than 20 minutes.

✓ Maintains focus of discussion
As a group, stay on topic and avoid straying into other subject areas.

✓ Involves all participants equally and fully
No one person should monopolize the conversation. Rather, everyone should take turns speaking and contributing ideas.

✓ Follows the rules for collegial discussion
As each group member speaks, others should listen carefully. Build on one another's ideas and support viewpoints and opinions with sound reasoning and evidence. Express disagreement respectfully.

756 UNIT 5 • How much do our communities shape us?

Common Core State Standards

SL.6.1, SL.6.4, SL.6.6
[For full standards wording, see the chart in the front of this book.]

USE NEW VOCABULARY

As you speak and share ideas, work to use the vocabulary words you have learned in this unit. The more you use new words, the more you will "own" them.

Writing: **Narrative**

People, Animals, and Communities Many kinds of communities help animals, and many groups of animals help people. For example, people may help animals by forming groups to support wildlife preservation or working together at animal shelters. Animals may help people by working to herd other animals, providing transportation, or aiding people with disabilities.

Assignment

Write a nonfiction **narrative** that describes a situation in which people and animals help each other. Your narrative may be based on a personal experience, or on a situation with which you are familiar. Use sensory language and dialogue to bring your narrative to life. Include relevant facts and examples from the texts in this section.

Criteria for Success

Purpose/Focus
✓ **Connects specific incidents with larger ideas**
Make meaningful connections between the situations you describe and the texts you have read in this section.

Organization
✓ **Organize ideas and information logically**
Structure your narrative so that your facts, details, or examples relate to the topic to create a coherent whole.

Development of Ideas/Elaboration
✓ **Supports insights**
Include both personal examples and details from the texts you have read in this section.

✓ **Uses narrative techniques effectively**
Consider using dialogue to help readers "hear" how characters sound.

Language
✓ **Uses description effectively**
Effectively uses descriptive details.

Conventions
✓ **Does not have errors**
Eliminate errors in grammar, spelling, and punctuation.

 **Common Core State Standards**

W.6.3; L.6.2, L.6.3
[For full standards wording, see the chart in the front of this book.]

WRITE TO EXPLORE

Writing is a way to clarify what you feel and think. This means that you may change your mind or get new ideas as you work. Allowing for this will improve your final draft.

Writing: **Narrative**
Introduce the assignment using the instruction on the student page.

Criteria for Success

1. **Purpose/Focus** Encourage students to identify meaningful connections or contrasts between their experiences, their research, and ideas explored in the texts. For example, **ask:** In what ways have animals helped you or the people in your community? In what ways have people in your community helped animals?

2. **Organization** Encourage students to structure their narratives in a logical way.

3. **Development of Ideas/ Elaboration** Encourage students to include personal examples and details from the texts. Point out that using dialogue will help readers better relate to characters in their narrative.

4. **Language** Instruct students to use descriptive words and details. Explain that this will give readers a more vivid mental image of the setting and characters.

5. **Conventions** In addition to a self-review, students should have someone else read their narratives to check for errors.

Write to Explore

Point out that students' thoughts and feelings about what they experienced might deepen or change as they write and reflect. As they conclude their narratives, encourage them to carefully consider what they have learned over the course of the writing experience in order to identify important observations they have made, insights they have gained, or conclusions they have drawn.

Writing to Sources: Expository Essay

Introduce the assignment using the instruction on the student page.

Prewriting and Planning

1. **Choose texts.** Explain that in order to identify and develop their own thoughts and feelings about how people and animals help one another and shape communities, students will need to analyze in depth the communities of people and animals in two or more of the texts that they explored.

2. **Gather details and craft a working thesis, or topic.**

   - Instruct students to go back into the texts they have selected and review passages that are connected to the concept of people and animals in a community and how each is shaped by the other.

   - Encourage them to use a chart like the one shown to record each significant passage and identify what ideas it suggests about the concepts.

   - Students may also wish to raise questions that the passage may help answer, such as: *Why might people need animals in their lives? Why do animals sometimes need humans?*

   - They can then use these ideas to identify and develop an overall thesis about people and animals in a community.

Incorporate Research

Remind students to consider how they might use their prior research—about how people and animals help each other in some way—to support their claim in this essay.

Writing to Sources: Expository Essay

People, Animals, and Communities The related readings in this section present a range of ideas about the ways that people and animals help one another in communities. The selections raise questions, such as the following, about community values and beliefs:

- What part can animals play in a culture's values and beliefs?
- How can observation and scientific research help both people and animals?
- What role do pets play in family life?
- How can people and animals aid in one another's survival?

Focus on the question that intrigues you the most, and then complete the following assignment.

> **Assignment**
>
> Write an essay in which you explain how people and animals help one another and shape communities. Build evidence by analyzing the communities of people and animals in two or more texts from this section. Clearly present, develop, and support your ideas with examples and details from the texts.

Prewriting and Planning

Choose texts. Review the texts in the section to determine which ones you will cite in your essay. Select at least two texts that will provide strong material to support your exposition.

Gather details and craft a working thesis, or topic. Use a chart like the one shown to develop your informative essay.

Focus Question: How can people and animals help each other survive?

Text	Passage	Notes
Prologue from The Whale Rider	The news is being taken back to the place of the Ancients. Our blessing will come soon.	The land and sea are glad because they have waited for people to come.
"The Old Woman Who Lived With the Wolves"	As the days wore on, she and the wolves became fast friends. But clear days finally came and the wolves offered to lead her back to her people.	The girl belongs to a community of people and becomes part of a community of wolves.

Example Thesis: Communities of people and animals both benefit when one group shares resources with the other.

 **Common Core State Standards**

W.6.2.a-b, W.6.9.a-b
[For full standards wording, see the chart in the front of this book.]

INCORPORATE RESEARCH

In your essay, use information you gathered as you completed the brief research assignments related to the selections in this section.

Drafting

Write a strong introduction. Your introduction is the first thing your audience will read. Include a sentence or two that clearly presents your topic, and then identify the main points you will make in your essay.

Develop your ideas. Decide which facts from your reading and research are relevant to your topic. If appropriate, write an extended definition. Review your notes to find the strongest details, quotations, examples that support your ideas.

Use the SEE technique. For each main idea you identify, use the SEE technique to add depth to your essay. In a paragraph, first write a **S**tatement. Next, write a sentence that **E**xtends the idea. Finally, write a sentence that **E**laborates on the extension.

Revising and Editing

Use the appropriate verb tense. Make sure that your topic or thesis is clearly stated and that you have supported it with convincing evidence from the texts. Underline main ideas in your paper and confirm that each one is supported. Add additional details or examples, if necessary.

Review style. Check that you have found the clearest, simplest way to communicate your ideas. Omit unnecessary words.

 **Common Core State Standards**

W.6.2, W.6.4, W.6.5, W.6.9, W.6.10; L.6.2, L.6.3
[For full standards wording, see the chart in the front of this book.]

CITE RESEARCH CORRECTLY

Avoid plagiarism by properly crediting the ideas of others. See the Citing Sources pages in the Introductory Unit of this textbook for guidance.

Self-Evaluation Rubric

Use the following criteria to evaluate the effectiveness of your essay.

Criteria	Rating Scale			
Purpose/Focus Introduces a specific topic; provides a concluding section that follows from and supports the information or explanation presented	*not very .... very* 1	2	3	4
Organization Organizes complex ideas, concepts, and information to make important connections and distinctions; uses appropriate and varied transitions to link the major sections, create cohesion, and clarify relationships among ideas	1	2	3	4
Development of Ideas/Elaboration Develops the topic with well-chosen, relevant and sufficient facts, extended definitions, concrete details, quotations or other information and examples appropriate to the audience's knowledge of the topic	1	2	3	4
Language Uses precise language and domain-specific vocabulary to manage the complexity of the topic; establishes and maintains a formal style and objective tone	1	2	3	4
Conventions Uses correct conventions of grammar, spelling, and punctuation	1	2	3	4

PART 3 • Assessment: Synthesis **759**

Self-Evaluation Rubric

Encourage students to rate their own essays objectively and to use the results to guide their revision process.

Cite Research Correctly

Review with students the correct format for citing different sources, such as books and printed or online news articles. Provide examples of proper citations. Then, have students create a Works Cited list that correctly lists each source they refer to in their essays.

Drafting

1. Write a strong introduction.

- Remind students to include a sentence or two at the beginning of the essay that clearly presents the topic and identifies the main points the essay will make.

- Remind students that each of their points should be supported by details.

2. Develop your ideas.

- Have students refer to their prewriting and planning notes on developing ideas.

- Remind students to support all of their points with details.

3. Use the SEE technique.

- Remind students that the introduction of their essay should grab the reader's attention and give them a general statement of the topics that will be discussed in the main body of the essay.

- The body of their essay should extend their main ideas. Students should use specific details from the texts to support their ideas.

- The conclusion should restate the main idea and elaborate on the main topic of the essay.

Revising and Editing

1. Use the appropriate verb tense. Suggest that students share a draft of their argument with a classmate or family member. Students should ask the reviewer the following questions:

- Is my topic clearly stated?

- Have I supported my topic with convincing evidence from the texts?

- Is each of my main ideas supported?

- Do I use sufficient details and examples?

Remind students to confirm that they have used the correct verb tense in their essay. Encourage them to include vivid and colorful verbs to add interest for readers.

2. Review style. If students are using a computer to type their papers, remind them to utilize the grammar and spell-check features.

PART 3 • Assessment: Synthesis **759**

Independent Reading

Titles featured on the Independent Reading pages at the end of each unit represent a range of reading, including stories, dramas, and poetry, as well as literary nonfiction and other types of informational text. Throughout, labels indicate the works that are CCSS Exemplar Texts. Choosing from among these featured titles will help students read works at increasing levels of text complexity in the grades 6–8 text complexity band.

Online Text Set

The selections that are a part of the Online Text Set are located in the *Student eText.*

Using Literature Circles

A literature circle is a temporary group in which students independently discuss a book.

Use the guidance in the *Professional Development Guidebook,* pp. 47–49, as well as the teaching notes on the facing page, for additional suggestions for literature circles.

Ⓒ Meeting Unit 5 Common Core State Standards

Students can use books listed on this page to apply and to reinforce their mastery of the Common Core State Focus Standards covered in this unit.

Introducing Featured Titles

Have students choose a book or books for independent reading. Assist them by previewing the titles, noting their subject matter and level of difficulty. **Note:** Before recommending a work to students, preview it, taking into account the values of your community as well as the maturity of your students.

Ⓒ Independent Reading

Titles for Extended Reading

In this unit, you have read texts in a variety of genres that originated in the oral tradition. Continue to read on your own. Select works that you enjoy, but challenge yourself to explore new writers and works of increasing depth and complexity. The titles suggested below will help you get started.

INFORMATIONAL TEXT

Discoveries: Finding Connections

This collection of **essays** explores the importance of communities in "The Maori Culture of New Zealand," "Natural Disasters," "The Delta Blues," and "Numbers: The Universal Language."

Understanding the Holy Land
by Mitch Frank

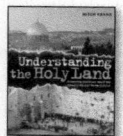

The Israeli-Palestinian conflict may be familiar to you, but how much do you really know? This **nonfiction book** explains why this conflict is important and how it affects the rest of the world.

The Circuit
by Francisco Jiménez

In this **autobiography**, Jiménez tells of his difficult early years as part of a family of migrant farm workers. To him, life consisted of constant moving around and work, with school wedged in around harvesting jobs.

LITERATURE

Black Ships Before Troy: The Story of the Iliad
by Rosemary Sutcliff
Laurel Leaf, 2005   EXEMPLAR TEXT Ⓒ

Sutcliff retells the grand **epic** of the Greeks' ten-year-long battle against the city of Troy in exciting and vivid detail. She breathes life into classical and mythical characters and also re-creates some of the brutal realities of battle.

Sleeping Ugly
by Jane Yolen

This funny **fairy tale** turns the original version upside down. Princess Miserella is beautiful but mean. Plain Jane is homely but sweet. To this pair of opposites, Jane Yolen adds a magical mix-up and an unsuspecting prince.

Myths and Stories from the Americas

This collection of **myths** and **folk tales** includes stories of creation, tricksters, love, and adventure from North America, Hawaii, the Caribbean, Central America, and South America.

This Big Sky
by Pat Mora

This book of fourteen **poems** combines Mora's vivid imagery with cut-paper collages to bring the awe-inspiring American Southwest to life for the reader.

ONLINE TEXT SET

AUTOBIOGRAPHY
The Market Square Dog James Herriot

SHORT STORY
Aaron's Gift Myron Levoy

REFLECTIVE ESSAY
Childhood and Poetry Pablo Neruda

760 UNIT 5 • How much do our communities shape us?

Ⓒ TEXT COMPLEXITY **ALIGNING TEXTS WITH READERS AND TASKS**

Texts	Readers And Tasks
• *Sleeping Ugly* (Lexile: 590L) • *The Circuit* (Lexile: 880L)	**Below-Level Readers** Allow students to focus on reading for content, and challenge them to interpret multiple perspectives.
• *Myths and Stories from the Americas* • *This Big Sky* • *Discoveries: Finding Connections*	**Below-Level Readers** Challenge students as they read for content. **On-Level Readers** Allow students to focus on reading for content, and challenge them to interpret multiple perspectives. **Advanced Readers** Allow students to focus on interpreting multiple perspectives.
• *Understanding the Holy Land* (Lexile: 1130L) • *Black Ships Before Troy: The Story of the Iliad* (Lexile: 1300L)	**On-Level Readers** Challenge students as they read for content. **Advanced Readers** Allow students to focus on reading for content, and challenge them to interpret multiple perspectives.

Preparing to Read Complex Texts

Attentive Reading As you read on your own, ask yourself questions like these to enrich your reading experience.

© **Common Core State Standards**

Reading Literature/ Informational Text
10. By the end of the year, read and comprehend literature, including stories, dramas, and poems, and literary nonfiction in the grades 6–8 text complexity band proficiently, with scaffolding as needed at the high end of the range.

When reading texts from the oral tradition, ask yourself ...

Comprehension: **Key Ideas and Details**

- From what culture does this text come? What do I know about that culture?
- What type of text am I reading? For example, is it a myth, a legend, or a tall tale? What characters and events do I expect to find in this type of text?
- What elements of the culture do I see in the text? For example, do I notice beliefs, foods, or settings that have meaning for the people of this culture?

Text Analysis: **Craft and Structure**

- Who is retelling or presenting this text? Do I think the author has changed the text from the original? If so, how?
- Does the text include characters and tell a story? If so, are the characters and plot interesting?
- What do I notice about the language used in the text? Which aspects seem similar to or different from the language used in modern texts?
- Does the text include symbols? If so, do they have a special meaning in the original culture of the text? Do they also have meaning in modern life?

Connections: **Integration of Knowledge and Ideas**

- What does this text teach me about the culture from which it comes?
- What, if anything, does this text teach me about people in general?
- How does this text compare with others I have read?
- Do I know of any modern versions of this text? How are they similar to or different from this one?
- If I were researching this culture for a report, would I include passages from this text? If so, what would those passages show?

© **TEXT COMPLEXITY READER AND TASK SUPPORT SUGGESTIONS**

Independent Reading

Increased Support Suggest that students choose a book that they feel comfortable reading and one that is a bit more challenging. Pair a more proficient reader with a less proficient reader and have them work together on the more challenging text. Partners can prepare to read the book by reviewing questions on this student page. They can also read difficult passages together, sharing questions and insights. They can use the questions on the student page to guide after-reading discussion.

Increased Challenge Encourage students to integrate knowledge and ideas by combining the Big Question and the Unit Focus concepts in their approach to two or more featured titles.
  For example, students might consider the characters' relationships with community in *Black Ships Before Troy: The Story of the Iliad*. In addition, students can focus on identifying characteristics of folk literature such as personification, hyperbole, and dialect.

Preparing to Read Complex Texts

1. Tell students they can be attentive readers by bringing their experience and imagination to the texts they read and by actively questioning those texts. Explain that the questions they see on the student page are examples of types of questions to ask about texts from the oral tradition.

2. Point out that, like writing, reading is a "multidraft" process, involving several readings of complete works or passages, revising and refining one's understanding each time.

Key Ideas and Details

3. As an example, review and amplify the second bulleted item. **Ask:** What key ideas and details could you cite as evidence that the text met your expectations?

   Possible response: You might cite evidence that a text contained certain features that met your expectations. For example, you might point out that a myth featured a hero or that a tall tale included exaggerated elements.

Craft and Structure

4. **Ask:** What details of craft and structure would you use to determine whether or not a text differed from the original?

   Possible response: You might point to modern details the author uses to update the story or to plot points from the text that differ from the original.

Integration of Knowledge and Ideas

5. **Ask:** How would you determine what a text teaches you about the culture from which it comes?

   Possible response: You would consider what the text teaches you about the beliefs, traditions, and values of the culture it describes.

6. Finally, explain to students that they should cite key ideas and details, examples of craft and structure, or instances of the integration of knowledge and ideas as evidence to support their points during a book discussion. After hearing the evidence, the group might reach a consensus or might agree to disagree.

Resources

Literary Handbook **R1**

    Literary Terms R1

    Tips for Literature Circles.. R9

    Tips for Improving Reading Fluency R10

Writing Handbook **R12**

    Types of Writing R12

    Writing Friendly Letters R14

    Writing Business Letters R15

    Guide to Rubrics R16

Grammar, Usage, and Mechanics Handbook **R20**

Vocabulary Handbook **R24**

    Glossary R24

    Spanish Glossary R30

Indexes..**R36**

    Index of Skills R36

    Index of Authors and Titles.. R41

Acknowledgments **R44**

Credits **R48**

Literary Terms

ALLITERATION *Alliteration* is the repetition of initial consonant sounds. Writers use alliteration to draw attention to certain words or ideas, to imitate sounds, and to create musical effects.

ALLUSION An *allusion* is a reference to a well-known person, event, place, literary work, or work of art. Understanding what a literary work is saying often depends on recognizing its allusions and the meanings they suggest.

ANALOGY An *analogy* makes a comparison between two or more things that are similar in some ways but otherwise unalike.

ANECDOTE An *anecdote* is a brief story about an interesting, amusing, or strange event. Writers tell anecdotes to entertain or to make a point.

ANTAGONIST An *antagonist* is a character or a force in conflict with a main character, or protagonist.

See *Conflict* and *Protagonist.*

ARGUMENT See *Persuasion.*

ATMOSPHERE *Atmosphere,* or *mood,* is the feeling created in the reader by a literary work or passage.

AUTHOR'S INFLUENCES An *author's influences* are things that affect his or her writing. These factors include the author's time and place of birth and cultural background, as well as world events that took place during the author's lifetime.

AUTHOR'S STYLE *Style* is an author's typical way of writing. Many factors determine an author's style, including diction; tone; use of characteristic elements such as figurative language, dialect, rhyme, meter, or rhythmic devices; typical grammatical structures and patterns; typical sentence length; and typical methods of organization.

AUTOBIOGRAPHY An *autobiography* is the story of the writer's own life, told by the writer. Autobiographical writing may tell about the person's whole life or only a part of it.

Because autobiographies are about real people and events, they are a form of nonfiction. Most autobiographies are written in the first person.

See *Biography, Nonfiction,* and *Point of View.*

BIOGRAPHY A *biography* is a form of nonfiction in which a writer tells the life story of another person. Most biographies are written about famous or admirable people. Although biographies are nonfiction, the most effective ones share the qualities of good narrative writing.

See *Autobiography* and *Nonfiction.*

CHARACTER A *character* is a person or an animal that takes part in the action of a literary work. The main, or *major,* character is the most important character in a story, poem, or play. A *minor* character is one who takes part in the action but is not the focus of attention.

Characters are sometimes classified as flat or round. A *flat character* is one-sided and often stereotypical. A *round character,* on the other hand, is fully developed and exhibits many traits—often both faults and virtues. Characters can also be classified as dynamic or static. A *dynamic character* is one who changes or grows during the course of the work. A *static character* is one who does not change.

See *Characterization, Hero/Heroine,* and *Motive.*

CHARACTERIZATION *Characterization* is the act of creating and developing a character. Authors use two major methods of characterization—*direct* and *indirect.* When using *direct* characterization, a writer states the *character's traits,* or characteristics.

When describing a character *indirectly,* a writer depends on the reader to draw conclusions about the character's traits. Sometimes the writer tells what other participants in the story say and think about the character.

See *Character* and *Motive.*

CHARACTER TRAITS *Character traits* are the qualities, attitudes, and values that a character has or displays—for example, dependability, intelligence, selfishness, or stubbornness.

CLIMAX The *climax,* also called the turning point, is the high point in the action of the plot. It is the moment of greatest tension, when the outcome of the plot hangs in the balance.

See *Plot.*

COMEDY A *comedy* is a literary work, especially a play, that is light, is often humorous or satirical, and ends happily. Comedies frequently depict ordinary characters faced with temporary difficulties and conflicts. Types of comedy include *romantic comedy,* which involves problems between lovers, and the *comedy of manners,* which satirically challenges social customs of a society.

CONCRETE POEM A *concrete poem* is one with a shape that suggests its subject. The poet arranges the letters, punctuation, and lines to create an image, or picture, on the page.

CONFLICT A *conflict* is a struggle between opposing forces. Conflict is one of the most important elements of stories, novels, and plays because it causes the action. There are two kinds of conflict: external and internal. An *external conflict* is one in which a character struggles against some outside force, such as another person. Another kind of external conflict may occur between a character and some force in nature.

An *internal conflict* takes place within the mind of a character. The character struggles to make a decision, take an action, or overcome a feeling.

See *Plot.*

CONNOTATIONS The *connotation* of a word is the set of ideas associated with it in addition to its explicit meaning. The connotation of a word can be personal, based on individual experiences. More often, cultural connotations—those recognizable by most people in a group—determine a writer's word choices.

See also *Denotation.*

DENOTATION The *denotation* of a word is its dictionary meaning, independent of other associations that the word may have. The denotation of the word *lake,* for example, is "an inland body of water." "Vacation spot" and "place where the fishing is good" are connotations of the word *lake.*

See also *Connotation.*

DESCRIPTION A *description* is a portrait, in words, of a person, place, or object. Descriptive writing uses images that appeal to the five senses—sight, hearing, touch, taste, and smell.

See *Image.*

DEVELOPMENT See *Plot.*

DIALECT *Dialect* is the form of a language spoken by people in a particular region or group. Dialects differ in pronunciation, grammar, and word choice. The English language is divided into many dialects. British English differs from American English.

DIALOGUE A *dialogue* is a conversation between characters. In poems, novels, and short stories, dialogue is usually set off by quotation marks to indicate a speaker's exact words.

In a play, dialogue follows the names of the characters, and no quotation marks are used.

DRAMA A *drama* is a story written to be performed by actors. Although a drama is meant to be performed, one can also read the script, or written version, and imagine the action. The *script* of a drama is made up of dialogue and stage directions. The *dialogue* is the words spoken by the actors. The *stage directions,* usually printed in italics, tell how the actors should look, move, and speak. They also describe the setting, sound effects, and lighting.

Dramas are often divided into parts called *acts.*

The acts are often divided into smaller parts called *scenes.*

DYNAMIC CHARACTER See *Character.*

ESSAY An *essay* is a short nonfiction work about a particular subject. Most essays have a single major focus and a clear introduction, body, and conclusion.

There are many types of essays. An *informal essay* uses casual, conversational language. A *historical essay* gives facts, explanations, and insights about historical events. An *expository essay* explains an idea by breaking it down. A *narrative essay* tells a story about a real-life experience. An *informational essay* explains a process. A *persuasive essay* offers an opinion and supports it.

See *Exposition, Narration,* and *Persuasion.*

EXPOSITION In the plot of a story or a drama, the *exposition,* or introduction, is the part of the work that introduces the characters, setting, and basic situation.

See *Plot.*

R2 Literary Terms

EXPOSITORY WRITING *Expository writing* is writing that explains or informs.

EXTENDED METAPHOR In an *extended metaphor,* as in a regular metaphor, a subject is spoken or written of as though it were something else. However, extended metaphor differs from regular metaphor in that several connected comparisons are made.

See *Metaphor.*

EXTERNAL CONFLICT See *Conflict.*

FABLE A *fable* is a brief story or poem, usually with animal characters, that teaches a lesson, or moral. The moral is usually stated at the end of the fable.

See *Irony* and *Moral.*

FANTASY A *fantasy* is highly imaginative writing that contains elements not found in real life. Examples of fantasy include stories that involve supernatural elements, stories that resemble fairy tales, stories that deal with imaginary places and creatures, and science-fiction stories.

See *Science Fiction.*

FICTION *Fiction* is prose writing that tells about imaginary characters and events. Short stories and novels are works of fiction. Some writers base their fiction on actual events and people, adding invented characters, dialogue, settings, and plots. Other writers rely on imagination alone.

See *Narration, Nonfiction,* and *Prose.*

FIGURATIVE LANGUAGE *Figurative language* is writing or speech that is not meant to be taken literally. The many types of figurative language are known as *figures of speech.* Common figures of speech include metaphor, personification, and simile. Writers use figurative language to state ideas in vivid and imaginative ways.

See *Metaphor, Personification, Simile,* and *Symbol.*

FIGURE OF SPEECH See *Figurative Language.*

FLASHBACK A *flashback* is a scene within a story that interrupts the sequence of events to relate events that occurred in the past.

FLAT CHARACTER See *Character.*

FOLK TALE A *folk tale* is a story composed orally and then passed from person to person by word of mouth. Folk tales originated among people who could neither read nor write. These people entertained one another by telling stories aloud—often dealing with heroes, adventure, magic, or romance. Eventually, modern scholars collected these stories and wrote them down.

Folk tales reflect the cultural beliefs and environments from which they come.

See *Fable, Legend, Myth,* and *Oral Tradition.*

FOOT See *Meter.*

FORESHADOWING *Foreshadowing* is the author's use of clues to hint at what might happen later in the story. Writers use foreshadowing to build their readers' expectations and to create suspense.

FREE VERSE *Free verse* is poetry not written in a regular, rhythmical pattern, or meter. The poet is free to write lines of any length or with any number of stresses, or beats. Free verse is therefore less constraining than *metrical verse,* in which every line must have a certain length and a certain number of stresses.

See *Meter.*

GENRE A *genre* is a division or type of literature. Literature is commonly divided into three major genres: poetry, prose, and drama. Each major genre is, in turn, divided into lesser genres, as follows:

1. *Poetry:* lyric poetry, concrete poetry, dramatic poetry, narrative poetry, epic poetry

2. *Prose:* fiction (novels and short stories) and nonfiction (biography, autobiography, letters, essays, and reports)

3. *Drama:* serious drama and tragedy, comic drama, melodrama, and farce

See *Drama, Poetry,* and *Prose.*

HAIKU The *haiku* is a three-line Japanese verse form. The first and third lines of a haiku each have five syllables. The second line has seven syllables. A writer of haiku uses images to create a single, vivid picture, generally of a scene from nature.

HERO/HEROINE A *hero* or *heroine* is a character whose actions are inspiring, or noble. Often heroes and heroines struggle to overcome the obstacles and problems that stand in their way. Note that the term *hero* was originally used only for male characters, while heroic female characters were always called *heroines.* However, it is now acceptable to use *hero* to refer to females as well as to males.

HISTORICAL FICTION In *historical fiction,* real events, places, or people are incorporated into a fictional or made-up story.

IMAGERY See *Images.*

IMAGES *Images* are words or phrases that appeal to one or more of the five senses. Writers use images to describe how their subjects look, sound, feel, taste, and smell. Poets often paint images, or word pictures, that appeal to your senses. These pictures help you experience the poem fully.

INTERNAL CONFLICT See *Conflict.*

IRONY *Irony* is a contradiction between what happens and what is expected. The three main types of irony are *situational irony, verbal irony,* and *dramatic irony.*

JOURNAL A *journal* is a daily, or periodic, account of events and the writer's thoughts and feelings about those events. Personal journals are not normally written for publication, but sometimes they do get published later with permission from the author or the author's family.

LEGEND A *legend* is a widely told story about the past—one that may or may not have a foundation in fact. Every culture has its own legends—its familiar, traditional stories.
See *Folk Tale, Myth,* and *Oral Tradition.*

LETTERS A *letter* is a written communication from one person to another. In personal letters, the writer shares information and his or her thoughts and feelings with one other person or group. Although letters are not normally written for publication, they sometimes do get published later with the permission of the author or the author's family.

LIMERICK A *limerick* is a humorous, rhyming, five-line poem with a specific meter and rhyme scheme. Most limericks have three strong stresses in lines 1, 2, and 5 and two strong stresses in lines 3 and 4. Most follow the rhyme scheme *aabba.*

LYRIC POEM A *lyric poem* is a highly musical verse that expresses the observations and feelings of a single speaker. It creates a single, unified impression.

MAIN CHARACTER See *Character.*

MEDIA ACCOUNTS *Media accounts* are reports, explanations, opinions, or descriptions written for television, radio, newspapers, and magazines. While some media accounts report only facts, others include the writer's thoughts and reflections.

METAPHOR A *metaphor* is a figure of speech in which something is described as though it were something else. A metaphor, like a simile, works by pointing out a similarity between two unlike things.
See *Extended Metaphor* and *Simile.*

METER The *meter* of a poem is its rhythmical pattern. This pattern is determined by the number of *stresses,* or beats, in each line. To describe the meter of a poem, read it while emphasizing the beats in each line. Then, mark the stressed and unstressed syllables, as follows:

Mў fáth | ĕr wás | thĕ firśt | tŏ héar |

As you can see, each strong stress is marked with a slanted line (´) and each unstressed syllable with a horseshoe symbol (˘). The weak and strong stresses are then divided by vertical lines (|) into groups called *feet.*

MINOR CHARACTER See *Character.*

MOOD See *Atmosphere.*

MORAL A *moral* is a lesson taught by a literary work. A fable usually ends with a moral that is directly stated. A poem, novel, short story, or essay often suggests a moral that is not directly stated. The moral must be drawn by the reader, based on other elements in the work.
See *Fable.*

MOTIVATION See *Motive.*

MOTIVE A *motive* is a reason that explains or partially explains a character's thoughts, feelings, actions, or speech. Writers try to make their characters' motives, or motivations, as clear as possible. If the motives of a main character are not clear, then the character will not be believable.

Characters are often motivated by needs, such as food and shelter. They are also motivated by feelings, such as fear, love, and pride. Motives may be obvious or hidden.

MYTH A *myth* is a fictional tale that explains the actions of gods or heroes or the origins of elements of nature. Myths are part of the oral tradition. They are composed orally and then passed from generation to generation by word of mouth. Every ancient culture has its own mythology, or collection of myths. Greek and Roman myths are known collectively as *classical mythology.*

See *Oral Tradition.*

NARRATION *Narration* is writing that tells a story. The act of telling a story is also called narration. Each piece is a *narrative.* A story told in fiction, nonfiction, poetry, or even in drama is called a narrative.

See *Narrative, Narrative Poem,* and *Narrator.*

NARRATIVE A *narrative* is a story. A narrative can be either fiction or nonfiction. Novels and short stories are types of fictional narratives. Biographies and autobiographies are nonfiction narratives. Poems that tell stories are also narratives.

See *Narration* and *Narrative Poem.*

NARRATIVE POEM A *narrative poem* is a story told in verse. Narrative poems often have all the elements of short stories, including characters, conflict, and plot.

NARRATOR A *narrator* is a speaker or a character who tells a story. The narrator's perspective is the way he or she sees things. A *third-person narrator* is one who stands outside the action and speaks about it. A *first-person narrator* is one who tells a story and participates in its action.

See *Point of View.*

NONFICTION *Nonfiction* is prose writing that presents and explains ideas or that tells about real people, places, objects, or events. Autobiographies, biographies, essays, reports, letters, memos, and newspaper articles are all types of nonfiction.

See *Fiction.*

NOVEL A *novel* is a long work of fiction. Novels contain such elements as characters, plot, conflict, and setting. The writer of novels, or novelist, develops these elements. In addition to its main plot, a novel may contain one or more subplots, or independent, related stories. A novel may also have several themes.

See *Fiction* and *Short Story.*

NOVELLA A fiction work that is longer than a short story but shorter than a novel.

ONOMATOPOEIA *Onomatopoeia* is the use of words that imitate sounds. *Crash, buzz, screech, hiss, neigh, jingle,* and *cluck* are examples of onomatopoeia. *Chickadee, towhee,* and *whippoorwill* are onomatopoeic names of birds.

Onomatopoeia can help put the reader in the activity of a poem.

ORAL TRADITION *Oral tradition* is the passing of songs, stories, and poems from generation to generation by word of mouth. Folk songs, folk tales, legends, and myths all come from the oral tradition. No one knows who first created these stories and poems.

See *Folk Tale, Legend,* and *Myth.*

OXYMORON An *oxymoron* (pl. *oxymora*) is a figure of speech that links two opposite or contradictory words, to point out an idea or situation that seems contradictory or inconsistent but on closer inspection turns out to be somehow true.

PERSONIFICATION *Personification* is a type of figurative language in which a nonhuman subject is given human characteristics.

PERSPECTIVE See *Narrator* and *Point of View.*

PERSUASION *Persuasion* is used in writing or speech that attempts to convince the reader or listener to adopt a particular opinion or course of action. Newspaper editorials and letters to the editor use persuasion. So do advertisements and campaign speeches given by political candidates. An *argument* is a logical way of presenting a belief, conclusion, or stance. A good argument is supported with reasoning and evidence.

See *Essay.*

PLAYWRIGHT A *playwright* is a person who writes plays. William Shakespeare is regarded as the greatest playwright in English literature.

PLOT *Plot* is the sequence of events in which each event results from a previous one and causes the next. In most novels, dramas, short stories, and narrative poems, the plot involves both characters and a central conflict. The plot usually begins with an exposition that introduces the setting, the characters, and the basic situation. This is followed by the *inciting incident,* which introduces the central conflict. The conflict then increases during the *development* until it reaches a high point of interest or suspense, the *climax.* The climax is followed by the *falling action,* or end, of the central conflict. Any events that occur during the *falling action* make up the *resolution,* or *denouement.*

Some plots do not have all of these parts. Some stories begin with the inciting incident and end with the resolution.

See *Conflict.*

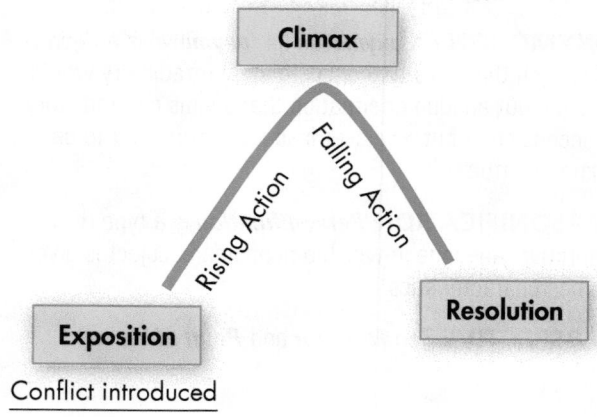

POETRY *Poetry* is one of the three major types of literature, the others being prose and drama. Most poems make use of highly concise, musical, and emotionally charged language. Many also make use of imagery, figurative lan-guage, and special devices of sound such as rhyme. Major types of poetry include lyric poetry, narrative poetry, and concrete poetry.

See *Concrete Poem, Genre, Lyric Poem,* and *Narrative Poem.*

POINT OF VIEW *Point of view* is the perspective, or vantage point, from which a story is told. The storyteller is either a narrator outside the story or a character in the story. *First-person point of view* describes a story told by a character who uses the first-person pronoun "I."

The two kinds of *third-person point of view,* limited and omniscient, are called "third person" because the narrator uses third-person pronouns such as "he" and "she" to refer to the characters. There is no "I" telling the story.

In stories told from the *omniscient third-person point of view,* the narrator knows and tells about what each character feels and thinks.

In stories told from the *limited third-person point of view,* the narrator relates the inner thoughts and feelings of only one character, and everything is viewed from this character's perspective.

See *Narrator.*

PROBLEM See *Conflict.*

PROSE *Prose* is the ordinary form of written language. Most writing that is not poetry, drama, or song is consid-ered prose. Prose is one of the major genres of literature and occurs in two forms—fiction and nonfiction.

See *Fiction, Genre,* and *Nonfiction.*

PROTAGONIST The *protagonist* is the main character in a literary work. Often, the protagonist is a person, but sometimes it can be an animal.

See *Antagonist* and *Character.*

REFRAIN A *refrain* is a regularly repeated line or group of lines in a poem or a song.

REPETITION *Repetition* is the use, more than once, of any element of language—a sound, word, phrase, clause, or sentence. Repetition is used in both prose and poetry.

See *Alliteration, Meter, Plot, Rhyme,* and *Rhyme Scheme.*

RESOLUTION The *resolution* is the outcome of the conflict in a plot.

See *Plot.*

RHYME *Rhyme* is the repetition of sounds at the ends of words. Poets use rhyme to lend a songlike quality to their verses and to emphasize certain words and ideas. Many traditional poems contain *end rhymes,* or rhyming words at the ends of lines.

Another common device is the use of *internal rhymes,* or rhyming words within lines. Internal rhyme also emphasizes the flowing nature of a poem.

See *Rhyme Scheme.*

RHYME SCHEME A *rhyme scheme* is a regular pattern of rhyming words in a poem. To indicate the rhyme scheme of a poem, one uses lowercase letters. Each rhyme is assigned a different letter, as follows in the first stanza of "Dust of Snow" by Robert Frost:

The way a crow	*a*
Shook down on me	*b*
The dust of snow	*a*
From a hemlock tree	*b*

Thus, the stanza has the rhyme scheme *abab.*

RHYTHM *Rhythm* is the pattern of stressed and unstressed syllables in spoken or written language.

See *Meter.*

ROUND CHARACTER See *Character.*

SCENE A *scene* is a section of uninterrupted action in the act of a drama.

See *Drama.*

SCIENCE FICTION *Science fiction* combines elements of fiction and fantasy with scientific fact. Many science-fiction stories are set in the future.

SENSORY LANGUAGE *Sensory language* is writing or speech that appeals to one or more of the five senses.

See *Images.*

SETTING The *setting* of a literary work is the time and place of the action. The setting includes all the details of a place and time—the year, the time of day, even the weather. The place may be a specific country, state, region, community, neighborhood, building, institution, or home. Details such as dialects, clothing, customs, and modes of transportation are often used to establish setting. In most stories, the setting serves as a backdrop—a context in which the characters interact. Setting can also help create a feeling, or atmosphere.

See *Atmosphere.*

SHORT STORY A *short story* is a brief work of fiction. Like a novel, a short story presents a sequence of events, or plot. The plot usually deals with a central conflict faced by a main character, or protagonist. The events in a short story usually communicate a message about life or human nature. This message, or central idea, is the story's theme.

See *Conflict, Plot,* and *Theme.*

SIMILE A *simile* is a figure of speech that uses *like* or *as* to make a direct comparison between two unlike ideas. Everyday speech often contains similes, such as "pale as a ghost," "good as gold," "spread like wildfire," and "clever as a fox."

SPEAKER The *speaker* is the imaginary voice a poet uses when writing a poem. The speaker is the character who tells the poem. This character, or voice, often is not identified by name. There can be important differences between the poet and the poem's speaker.

See *Narrator.*

STAGE DIRECTIONS *Stage directions* are notes included in a drama to describe how the work is to be performed or staged. Stage directions are usually printed in italics and enclosed within parentheses or brackets. Some stage directions describe the movements, costumes, emotional states, and ways of speaking of the characters.

STAGING *Staging* includes the setting, lighting, costumes, special effects, music, dance, and so on that go into putting on a stage performance of a drama.

See *Drama.*

STANZA A *stanza* is a group of lines of poetry that are usually similar in length and pattern and are separated by spaces. A stanza is like a paragraph of poetry—it states and develops a single main idea.

STATIC CHARACTER See *Character.*

SURPRISE ENDING A *surprise ending* is a conclusion that is unexpected. The reader has certain expectations about the ending based on details in the story. Often, a surprise ending is *foreshadowed,* or subtly hinted at, in the course of the work.

See *Foreshadowing* and *Plot.*

SUSPENSE *Suspense* is a feeling of anxious uncertainty about the outcome of events in a literary work. Writers create suspense by raising questions in the minds of their readers.

SYMBOL A *symbol* is anything that stands for or represents something else. Symbols are common in everyday life. A dove with an olive branch in its beak is a symbol of peace. A blindfolded woman holding a balanced scale is a symbol of justice. A crown is a symbol of a king's status and authority.

SYMBOLISM *Symbolism* is the use of symbols. Symbolism plays an important role in many different types of literature. It can highlight certain elements the author wishes to emphasize and also add levels of meaning.

THEME The *theme* is a central message, concern, or purpose in a literary work. A theme can usually be expressed as a generalization, or a general statement, about human beings or about life. The theme of a work is not a summary of its plot. The theme is the writer's central idea.

Although a theme may be stated directly in the text, it is more often presented indirectly. When the theme is stated indirectly, or implied, the reader must figure out what the theme is by looking carefully at what the work reveals about people or about life.

TONE The *tone* of a literary work is the writer's attitude toward his or her audience and subject. The tone can often be described by a single adjective, such as *formal* or *informal, serious* or *playful, bitter,* or *ironic.* Factors that contribute to the tone are word choice, sentence structure, line length, rhyme, rhythm, and repetition.

TRAGEDY A *tragedy* is a work of literature, especially a play, that results in a catastrophe for the main character. In ancient Greek drama, the main character is always a significant person—a king or a hero—and the cause of the tragedy is a tragic flaw, or weakness, in his or her character. In modern drama, the main character can be an ordinary person, and the cause of the tragedy can be some evil in society itself. The purpose of tragedy is not only to arouse fear and pity in the audience but also, in some cases, to convey a sense of the grandeur and nobility of the human spirit.

TURNING POINT See *Climax.*

UNIVERSAL THEME A *universal theme* is a message about life that is expressed regularly in many different cultures and time periods. Folk tales, epics, and romances often address universal themes like the importance of courage, the power of love, or the danger of greed.

Tips for Literature Circles

As you read and study literature, discussions with other readers can help you understand and enjoy what you have read. Use the following tips.

- ## Understand the purpose of your discussion

  Your purpose when you discuss literature is to broaden your understanding of a work by testing your own ideas and hearing the ideas of others. Keep your comments focused on the literature you are discussing. Starting with one focus question will help to keep your discussion on track.

- ## Communicate effectively

  Effective communication requires thinking before speaking. Plan the points that you want to make and decide how you will express them. Organize these points in logical order and use details from the work to support your ideas. Jot down informal notes to help keep your ideas focused.

  Remember to speak clearly, pronouncing words slowly and carefully. Also, listen attentively when others are speaking, and avoid interrupting.

- ## Consider other ideas and interpretations

  A work of literature can generate a wide variety of responses in different readers. Be open to the idea that many interpretations can be valid. To support your own ideas, point to the events, descriptions, characters, or other literary elements in the work that led to your interpretation. To consider someone else's ideas, decide whether details in the work support the interpretation he or she presents. Be sure to convey your criticism of the ideas of others in a respectful and supportive manner.

- ## Ask questions

  Ask questions to clarify your understanding of another reader's ideas. You can also use questions to call attention to possible areas of confusion, to points that are open to debate, or to errors in the speaker's points. To move a discussion forward, summarize and evaluate conclusions reached by the group members.

  When you meet with a group to discuss literature, use a chart like the one shown to analyze the discussion.

Work Being Discussed:	
Focus Question:	
Your Response:	Another Student's Response:
Supporting Evidence:	Supporting Evidence:

Tips for Improving Reading Fluency

When you were younger, you learned to read. Then, you read to expand your experiences or for pure enjoyment. Now, you are expected to read to learn. As you progress in school, you are given more and more material to read. The tips on these pages will help you improve your reading fluency, or your ability to read easily, smoothly, and expressively.

Keeping Your Concentration

One common problem that readers face is the loss of concentration. When you are reading an assignment, you might find yourself rereading the same sentence several times without really understanding it. The first step in changing this behavior is to notice that you do it. Becoming an active, aware reader will help you get the most from your assignments. Practice using these strategies:

- Cover what you have already read with a note card as you go along. Then, you will not be able to reread without noticing that you are doing it.

- Set a purpose for reading beyond just completing the assignment. Then, read actively by pausing to ask yourself questions about the material as you read.

- Use the Reading Strategy instruction and notes that appear with each selection in this textbook.

- Stop reading after a specified period of time (for example, 5 minutes) and summarize what you have read. To help you with this strategy, use the Reading Check questions that appear with each selection in this textbook. Reread to find any answers you do not know.

Reading Phrases

Fluent readers read phrases rather than individual words. Reading this way will speed up your reading and improve your comprehension. Here are some useful ideas:

- Experts recommend rereading as a strategy to increase fluency. Choose a passage of text that is neither too hard nor too easy. Read the same passage aloud several times until you can read it smoothly. When you can read the passage fluently, pick another passage and keep practicing.

- Read aloud into a tape recorder. Then, listen to the recording, noting your accuracy, pacing, and expression. You can also read aloud and share feedback with a partner.

- Use *Hear It!* Prentice Hall Literature Audio program CDs to hear the selections read aloud. Read along silently in your textbook, noticing how the reader uses his or her voice and emphasizes certain words and phrases.

Understanding Key Vocabulary

If you do not understand some of the words in an assignment, you may miss out on important concepts. Therefore, it is helpful to keep a dictionary nearby when you are reading. Follow these steps:

- Before you begin reading, scan the text for unfamiliar words or terms. Find out what those words mean before you begin reading.

- Use context—the surrounding words, phrases, and sentences—to help you determine the meanings of unfamiliar words.

- If you are unable to understand the meaning through context, refer to the dictionary.

Paying Attention to Punctuation

When you read, pay attention to punctuation. Commas, periods, exclamation points, semicolons, and colons tell you when to pause or stop. They also indicate relationships between groups of words. When you recognize these relationships you will read with greater understanding and expression. Look at the chart below

Punctuation Mark	Meaning
comma	brief pause
period	pause at the end of a thought
exclamation point	pause that indicates emphasis
semicolon	pause between related but distinct thoughts
colon	pause before giving explanation or examples

Using the Reading Fluency Checklist

Use the checklist below each time you read a selection in this textbook. In your Language Arts journal or notebook, note which skills you need to work on and chart your progress each week.

Reading Fluency Checklist
☐ Preview the text to check for difficult or unfamiliar words.
☐ Practice reading aloud.
☐ Read according to punctuation.
☐ Break down long sentences into the subject and its meaning.
☐ Read groups of words for meaning rather than reading single words.
☐ Read with expression (change your tone of voice to add meaning to the word).

Reading is a skill that can be improved with practice. The key to improving your fluency is to read. The more you read, the better your reading will become.

Types of Writing

Good writing can be a powerful tool used for many purposes. Writing can allow you to defend something you believe in or show how much you know about a subject. Writing can also help you share what you have experienced, imagined, thought, and felt. The three main types of writing are argument, informative/explanatory, and narrative.

Argument

When you think of the word *argument*, you might think of a disagreement between two people, but an argument is more than that. An argument is a logical way of presenting a belief, conclusion, or stance. A good argument is supported with reasoning and evidence.

Argument writing can be used for many purposes, such as to change a reader's point of view or opinion or to bring about an action or a response from a reader.

There are three main purposes for writing a formal argument:

- to change the reader's mind

- to convince the reader to accept what is written

- to motivate the reader to take action, based on what is written

The following are some types of argument writing:

Advertisements An advertisement is a planned message meant to be seen, heard, or read. It attempts to persuade an audience to buy a product or service, accept an idea, or support a cause. Advertisements may appear in print, online, or in broadcast form.

Several common types of advertisements are public service announcements, billboards, merchandise ads, service ads, and political campaign literature.

Persuasive Essay A persuasive essay presents a position on an issue, urges readers to accept that position, and may encourage a specific action. An effective persuasive essay

- Explores an issue of importance to the writer

- Addresses an issue that is arguable

- Uses facts, examples, statistics, or personal experiences to support a position

- Tries to influence the audience through appeals to the readers' knowledge, experiences, or emotions

- Uses clear organization to present a logical argument

Forms of persuasion include editorials, position papers, persuasive speeches, grant proposals, advertisements, and debates.

Informative/Explanatory

Informative/explanatory writing should rely on facts to inform or explain. Informative/explanatory writing serves some closely related purposes: to increase readers' knowledge of a subject, to help readers better understand a procedure or process, or to provide readers with an enhanced comprehension of a concept. It should also feature a clear introduction, body, and conclusion. The following are some examples of informative/explanatory writing:

Cause-and-Effect Essay A cause-and-effect essay examines the relationship between events, explaining how one event or situation causes another. A successful cause-and-effect essay includes

- A discussion of a cause, event, or condition that produces a specific result

- An explanation of an effect, outcome, or result

- Evidence and examples to support the relationship between cause and effect

- A logical organization that makes the explanation clear

Comparison-and-Contrast Essay A comparison-and-contrast essay analyzes the similarities and differences between or among two or more things. An effective comparison-and-contrast essay

- Identifies a purpose for comparison and contrast

- Identifies similarities and differences between or among two or more things, people, places, or ideas

- Gives factual details about the subjects

- Uses an organizational plan suited to the topic and purpose

Descriptive Writing Descriptive writing creates a vivid picture of a person, place, thing, or event. Most descriptive writing includes

- Sensory details—sights, sounds, smells, tastes, and physical sensations

- Vivid, precise language

- Figurative language or comparisons

R12 Types of Writing

- Adjectives and adverbs that paint a word picture

- An organization suited to the subject

Types of descriptive writing include descriptions of ideas, observations, travel brochures, physical descriptions, functional descriptions, remembrances, and character sketches.

Problem-and-Solution Essay A problem-and-solution essay describes a problem and offers one or more solutions to it. It describes a clear set of steps to achieve a result. An effective problem-and-solution essay includes

- A clear statement of the problem, with its causes and effects summarized for the reader

- The most important aspects of the problem

- A proposal of at least one realistic solution

- Facts, statistics, data, or expert testimony to support the solution

- A clear organization that makes the relationship between problem and solution obvious

Research Writing Research writing is based on information gathered from outside sources. A research paper—a focused study of a topic—helps writers explore and connect ideas, make discoveries, and share their findings with an audience. An effective research paper

- Focuses on a specific, narrow topic, which is usually summarized in a thesis statement

- Presents relevant information from a wide variety of sources

- Uses a clear organization that includes an introduction, body, and conclusion

- Includes a bibliography or works-cited list that identifies the sources from which the information was drawn

Other types of writing that depend on accurate and insightful research include multimedia presentations, statistical reports, annotated bibliographies, and experiment journals.

Workplace Writing Workplace writing is probably the format you will use most after you finish school. In general, workplace writing is fact-based and meant to communicate specific information in a structured format. Effective workplace writing

- Communicates information concisely

- Includes details that provide necessary information and anticipate potential questions

- Is error-free and neatly presented

Common types of workplace writing include business letters, memorandums, résumés, forms, and applications.

Narrative

Narrative writing conveys experience, either real or imaginary, and uses time to provide structure. It can be used to inform, instruct, persuade, or entertain. Whenever writers tell a of story, they are using narrative writing. Most types of narrative writing share certain elements, such as characters, a setting, a sequence of events, and, often, a theme. The following are some types of narration:

Autobiographical Writing Autobiographical writing tells a true story about an important period, experience, or relationship in the writer's life. Effective autobiographical writing includes

- A series of events that involve the writer as the main character

- Details, thoughts, feelings, and insights from the writer's perspective

- A conflict or an event that affects the writer

- A logical organization that tells the story clearly

- Insights that the writer gained from the experience

Types of autobiographical writing include autobiographical sketches, personal narratives, reflective essays, eyewitness accounts, and memoirs.

Short Story A short story is a brief, creative narrative. Most short stories include

- Details that establish the setting in time and place

- A main character who undergoes a change or learns something during the course of the story

- A conflict or a problem to be introduced, developed, and resolved

- A plot, the series of events that make up the action of the story

- A theme or message about life

Types of short stories include realistic stories, fantasies, historical narratives, mysteries, thrillers, science-fiction stories, and adventure stories.

Writing Friendly Letters

Writing Friendly Letters

A friendly letter is much less formal than a business letter. It is a letter to a friend, a family member, or anyone with whom the writer wants to communicate in a personal, friendly way. Most friendly letters are made up of five parts:

- ✔ the heading
- ✔ the salutation, or greeting
- ✔ the body
- ✔ the closing
- ✔ the signature

The purpose of a friendly letter is often one of the following:

- ✔ to share personal news and feelings
- ✔ to send or to answer an invitation
- ✔ to express thanks

Model Friendly Letter

In this friendly letter, Betsy thanks her grandparents for a birthday present and gives them some news about her life.

11 Old Farm Road
Topsham, Maine 04011

April 14, 20—

Dear Grandma and Grandpa,

Thank you for the sweater you sent me for my birthday. It fits perfectly, and I love the color. I wore my new sweater to the carnival at school last weekend and got lots of compliments.

The weather here has been cool but sunny. Mom thinks that "real" spring will never come. I can't wait until it's warm enough to go swimming.

School is going fairly well. I really like my Social Studies class. We are learning about the U.S. Constitution, and I think it's very interesting. Maybe I will be a lawyer when I grow up.

When are you coming out to visit us? We haven't seen you since Thanksgiving. You can stay in my room when you come. I'll be happy to sleep on the couch. (The TV is in that room!!)

Well, thanks again and hope all is well with you.

Love,

Betsy

> The **heading** includes the writer's address and the date on which he or she wrote the letter.

> The **body** is the main part of the letter and contains the basic message.

> Some common **closings** for personal letters include "Best wishes," "Love," "Sincerely," and "Yours truly."

Writing Business Letters

Formatting Business Letters

Business letters follow one of several acceptable formats. In **block format,** each part of the letter begins at the left margin. A double space is used between paragraphs. In **modified block format,** some parts of the letter are indented to the center of the page. No matter which format is used, all letters in business format have a heading, an inside address, a salutation or greeting, a body, a closing, and a signature. These parts are shown and annotated on the model business letter below, formatted in modified block style.

Model Business Letter

In this letter, Yolanda Dodson uses modified block format to request information.

Students for a Cleaner Planet
c/o Memorial High School
333 Veteran's Drive
Denver, CO 80211

January 25, 20—

Steven Wilson, Director
Resource Recovery Really Works
300 Oak Street
Denver, CO 80216

Dear Mr. Wilson:

Memorial High School would like to start a branch of your successful recycling program. We share your commitment to reclaiming as much reusable material as we can. Because your program has been successful in other neighborhoods, we're sure that it can work in our community. Our school includes grades 9–12 and has about 800 students.

Would you send us some information about your community recycling program? For example, we need to know what materials can be recycled and how we can implement the program.

At least fifty students have already expressed an interest in getting involved, so I know we'll have the people power to make the program work. Please help us get started.

Thank you in advance for your time and consideration.

Sincerely,

Yolanda Dodson

Yolanda Dodson

The **heading** shows the writer's address and organization (if any) and the date.

The **inside address** indicates where the letter will be sent.

A **salutation** is punctuated by a colon. When the specific addressee is not known, use a general greeting such as "To whom it may concern:"

The **body** of the letter states the writer's purpose. In this case, the writer requests information.

The **closing** "Sincerely" is common, but "Yours truly" or "Respectfully yours" are also acceptable. To end the letter, the writer types her name and provides a **signature.**

Guide to Rubrics

What is a rubric?

A rubric is a tool, often in the form of a chart or a grid, that helps you assess your work. Rubrics are particularly helpful for writing and speaking assignments.

To help you or others assess, or evaluate, your work, a rubric offers several specific criteria to be applied to your work. Then the rubric helps you or an evaluator indicate your range of success or failure according to those specific criteria. Rubrics are often used to evaluate writing for standardized tests.

Using a rubric will save you time, focus your learning, and improve the work you do. When you know what the rubric will be before you begin writing a persuasive essay, for example, as you write you will be aware of specific criteria that are important in that kind of an essay. As you evaluate the essay before giving it to your teacher, you will focus on the specific areas that your teacher wants you to master—or on areas that you know present challenges for you. Instead of searching through your work randomly for any way to improve it or correct its errors, you will have a clear and helpful focus on specific criteria.

How are rubrics constructed?

Rubrics can be constructed in several different ways.

- Your teacher may assign a rubric for a specific assignment.

- Your teacher may direct you to a rubric in your text-book.

- Your teacher and your class may construct a rubric for a particular assignment together.

- You and your classmates may construct a rubric together.

- You may create your own rubric with criteria you want to evaluate in your work.

How will a rubric help me?

A rubric will help you assess your work on a scale. Scales vary from rubric to rubric but usually range from 6 to 1, 5 to 1, or 4 to 1, with 6, 5, or 4 being the highest score and 1 being the lowest. If someone else is using the rubric to assess your work, the rubric will give your evaluator a clear range within which to place your work. If you are using the rubric yourself, it will help you make improvements to your work.

What are the types of rubrics?

- A **holistic rubric** has general criteria that can apply to a variety of assignments. See p. R29 for an example of a holistic rubric.

- An **analytic rubric** is specific to a particular assignment. The criteria for evaluation address the specific issues important in that assignment. See p. R28 for examples of analytic rubrics.

Sample Analytic Rubrics

Rubric With a 4-point Scale

The following analytic rubric is an example of a rubric to assess a persuasive essay. It will help you evaluate focus, organization, support/elaboration, and style/convention.

	Focus	Organization	Support/Elaboration	Style/Convention
4	Demonstrates highly effective word choice; clearly focused on task.	Uses clear, consistent organizational strategy.	Provides convincing, well-elaborated reasons to support the position.	Incorporates transitions; includes very few mechanical errors.
3	Demonstrates good word choice; stays focused on persuasive task.	Uses clear organizational strategy with occasional inconsistencies.	Provides two or more moderately elaborated reasons to support the position.	Incorporates some transitions; includes few mechanical errors.
2	Shows some good word choices; minimally stays focused on persuasive task.	Uses inconsistent organizational strategy; presentation is not logical.	Provides several reasons, but few are elaborated; only one elaborated reason.	Incorporates few transitions; includes many mechanical errors.
1	Shows lack of attention to persuasive task.	Demonstrates lack of organizational strategy.	Provides no specific reasons or does not elaborate.	Does not connect ideas; includes many mechanical errors.

Rubric With a 6-point Scale

The following analytic rubric is an example of a rubric to assess a persuasive essay. It will help you evaluate presentation, position, evidence, and arguments.

	Presentation	Position	Evidence	Arguments
6	Essay clearly and effectively addresses an issue with more than one side.	Essay clearly states a supportable position on the issue.	All evidence is logically organized, well presented, and supports the position.	All reader concerns and counterarguments are effectively addressed.
5	Most of essay addresses an issue that has more than one side.	Essay clearly states a position on the issue.	Most evidence is logically organized, well presented, and supports the position.	Most reader concerns and counterarguments are effectively addressed.
4	Essay adequately addresses issue that has more than one side.	Essay adequately states a position on the issue.	Many parts of evidence support the position; some evidence is out of order.	Many reader concerns and counterarguments are adequately addressed.
3	Essay addresses issue with two sides but does not present second side clearly.	Essay states a position on the issue, but the position is difficult to support.	Some evidence supports the position, but some evidence is out of order.	Some reader concerns and counterarguments are addressed.
2	Essay addresses issue with two sides but does not present second side.	Essay states a position on the issue, but the position is not supportable.	Not much evidence supports the position, and what is included is out of order.	A few reader concerns and counterarguments are addressed.
1	Essay does not address issue with more than one side.	Essay does not state a position on the issue.	No evidence supports the position.	No reader concerns or counterarguments are addressed.

Sample Holistic Rubric

Holistic rubrics such as this one are sometimes used to assess writing assignments on standardized tests. Notice that the criteria for evaluation are focus, organization, support, and use of conventions.

Points	Criteria
6 Points	• The writing is strongly focused and shows fresh insight into the writing task. • The writing is marked by a sense of completeness and coherence and is organized with a logical progression of ideas. • A main idea is fully developed, and support is specific and substantial. • A mature command of the language is evident, and the writing may employ characteristic creative writing strategies. • Sentence structure is varied, and writing is free of all but purposefully used fragments. • Virtually no errors in writing conventions appear.
5 Points	• The writing is clearly focused on the task. • The writing is well organized and has a logical progression of ideas, though there may be occasional lapses. • A main idea is well developed and supported with relevant detail. • Sentence structure is varied, and the writing is free of fragments, except when used purposefully. • Writing conventions are followed correctly.
4 Points	• The writing is clearly focused on the task, but extraneous material may intrude at times. • Clear organizational pattern is present, though lapses may occur. • A main idea is adequately supported, but development may be uneven. • Sentence structure is generally fragment free but shows little variation. • Writing conventions are generally followed correctly.
3 Points	• Writing is generally focused on the task, but extraneous material may intrude at times. • An organizational pattern is evident, but writing may lack a logical progression of ideas. • Support for the main idea is generally present but is sometimes illogical. • Sentence structure is generally free of fragments, but there is almost no variation. • The work generally demonstrates a knowledge of writing conventions, with occasional misspellings.
2 Points	• The writing is related to the task but generally lacks focus. • There is little evidence of organizational pattern, and there is little sense of cohesion. • Support for the main idea is generally inadequate, illogical, or absent. • Sentence structure is unvaried, and serious errors may occur. • Errors in writing conventions and spellings are frequent.
1 Point	• The writing may have little connection to the task and is generally unfocused. • There has been little attempt at organization or development. • The paper seems fragmented, with no clear main idea. • Sentence structure is unvaried, and serious errors appear. • Poor word choice and poor command of the language obscure meaning. • Errors in writing conventions and spelling are frequent.
Unscorable	The paper is considered unscorable if: • The response is unrelated to the task or is simply a rewording of the prompt. • The response has been copied from a published work. • The student did not write a response. • The response is illegible. • The words in the response are arranged with no meaning. • There is an insufficient amount of writing to score.

R18 Guide to Rubrics

Student Model

Persuasive Writing

This persuasive essay, which would receive a top score according to a persuasive rubric, is a response to the following writing prompt, or assignment:

Most young people today spend more than 5 hours a day watching television. Many adults worry about the effects on youth of seeing too much television violence. Write a persuasive piece in which you argue against or defend the effects of television watching on young people. Be sure to include examples to support your views.

Until the television was invented, families spent their time doing different activities. Now most families stay home and watch TV. Watching TV risks the family's health, reduces the children's study time, and is a bad influence on young minds. Watching television can be harmful.

> The writer clearly states a position in the first paragraph.

The most important reason why watching TV is bad is that the viewers get less exercise. For example, instead of watching their favorite show, people could get exercise for 30 minutes. If people spent less time watching TV and more time exercising, then they could have healthier bodies. My mother told me a story about a man who died of a heart attack because he was out of shape from watching television all the time. Obviously, watching TV put a person's health in danger.

> Each paragraph provides details that support the writer's main point.

Furthermore, watching television reduces childern's study time. For example, children would spend more time studying if they didn't watch television. If students spent more time studying at home, then they would make better grades at school. Last week I had a major test in science, but I didn't study because I started watching a movie. I was not prepared for the test and my grade reflected my lack of studying. Indeed, watching television is bad because it can hurt a student's grades.

Finally, watching TV can be a bad influence on children. For example, some TV shows have inappropriate language and too much violence. If children watch programs that use bad language and show violence, then they may start repeating these actions because they think the behavior is "cool." In fact, it has been proven that children copy what they see on TV. Clearly, watching TV is bad for children and its affects children's behavior.

In conclusion, watching television is a bad influence for these reasons: It reduces people's exercise time and students' study time and it shows children inappropriate behavior. Therefore, people should take control of their lives and stop allowing television to harm them.

> The conclusion restates the writer's position.

Grammar, Usage, and Mechanics Handbook

Parts of Speech

Nouns A **noun** is the name of a person, place, or thing. A **common noun** names any one of a class of people, places, or things. A **proper noun** names a specific person, place, or thing.

Pronouns A **pronoun** is a word that stands for a noun or for a word that takes the place of a noun. A **personal pronoun** refers to (1) the person speaking, (2) the person spoken to, or (3) the person, place, or thing spoken about.

	Singular	*Plural*
First Person	I, me, my, mine	we, us, our, ours
Second Person	you, your, yours	you, your, yours
Third Person	he, him, his, she, her, hers, it, its	they, them, their, theirs

A **reflexive pronoun** is a word that ends in self or selves and names the person or thing receiving the action when that person or thing is the same as the one performing the action.

A **demonstrative pronoun** directs attention to a specific person, place, or thing.

These are the juiciest pears I have ever tasted.

An **interrogative pronoun** is used to begin a question.

Who is the author of "Jeremiah's Song"?

An **indefinite pronoun** refers to a person, place, or thing, often without specifying which one.

Everyone bought something.

Verbs A **verb** is a word that expresses time while showing an action, a condition, or the fact that something exists. An **action verb** indicates the action of someone or something. A **linking verb** connects the subject of a sentence with a noun or a pronoun that renames or describes the subject. A **helping verb** can be added to another verb to make a single verb phrase.

Adjectives An **adjective** describes a noun or a pronoun or gives a noun or a pronoun a more specific meaning. Adjectives answer the questions *what kind, which one, how many,* or *how much.*

The articles the, a, and an are adjectives. An is used before a word beginning with a vowel sound.

A noun may sometimes be used as an adjective.

family home   *science* fiction

A **proper adjective** is (1) a proper noun used as an adjective or (2) an adjective formed from a proper noun. When this, that, these, or those appears immediately before a noun, that word is functioning as a **demonstrative adjective.**

Adverbs An **adverb** modifies a verb, an adjective, or another adverb. Adverbs answer the questions *where, when, in what way,* or *to what extent.*

Prepositions A **preposition** relates a noun or a pronoun following it to another word in the sentence.

Conjunctions A **conjunction** connects other words or groups of words. A **coordinating conjunction** connects similar kinds or groups of words. **Correlative conjunctions** are used in pairs to connect similar words or groups of words.

both Granpa *and* Grandma   *neither* they *nor I*

A **Subordinating conjunctions** is a word used to join two complete ideas by making one of the ideas dependent on the other.

Interjections An interjection is a word that expresses feeling or emotion and functions independently of a sentence.

Phrases, Clauses, and Sentences

Sentences A **sentence** is a group of words with two main parts: a complete subject and a complete predicate. Together, these parts express a complete thought.

A **fragment** is a group of words that does not express a complete thought.

Subject The **subject** of a sentence is the word or group of words that tells whom or what the sentence is about. The **simple subject** is the essential noun, pronoun, or group of words acting as a noun that cannot be left out of the complete subject. A **complete subject** is the simple subject plus any modifiers.

A **compound subject** is two or more subjects that have the same verb and are joined by a conjunction.

Neither the horse nor the driver looked tired.

Predicate The **predicate** of a sentence is the verb or verb phrase that tells what the complete subject of the sentence does or is. The **simple predicate** is the essential verb or verb phrase that cannot be left out of the complete predicate. A **complete predicate** is the simple predicate plus any modifiers or complements.

Pony express riders carried packages more than 2,000 miles.

A **compound predicate** is two or more verbs that have the same subject and are joined by a conjunction.

She *sneezed and coughed* throughout the trip.

Complement A **complement** is a word or group of words that completes the meaning of the predicate of a sentence. Five different kinds of complements can be found in English sentences: *direct objects, indirect objects, objective complements, predicate nominatives,* and *predicate adjectives.*

A **direct object** is a noun, pronoun, or group of words acting as a noun that receives the action of a transitive verb.

We watched the *liftoff.*

An **indirect object** is a noun, pronoun, or group of words that appears with a direct object and names the person or thing that something is given to or done for.

He sold the *family* a mirror.

An **objective complement** is an adjective or noun that appears with a direct object and describes or renames it.

I called Meg my *friend.*

A **subject complement** is a noun, pronoun, or adjective that appears with a linking verb and tells something about the subject. A subject complement may be a *predicate nominative* or a *predicate adjective.*

A **predicate nominative** is a noun or pronoun that appears with a linking verb and renames, identifies, or explains the subject.

Kiglo was the *leader.*

A **predicate adjective** is an adjective that appears with a linking verb and describes the subject of a sentence.

Roko became *tired.*

Sentence Types A **simple sentence** consists of a single independent clause. A **compound sentence** consists of two or more independent clauses joined by a comma and a coordinating conjunction or by a semicolon. A **complex sentence** consists of one independent clause and one or more subordinate clauses. A **compound-complex sentence** consists of two or more independent clauses and one or more subordinate clauses. A **declarative sentence** states an idea and ends with a period. **Interrogative Sentence** An interrogative sentence asks a question and ends with a question mark. An **imperative sentence** gives an order or a direction and ends with either a period or an exclamation mark. An **exclamatory sentence** conveys a strong emotion and ends with an exclamation mark.

Phrases A **phrase** is a group of words, without a subject and a verb, that functions in a sentence as one part of speech. A **prepositional phrase** is a group of words that includes a preposition and a noun or a pronoun that is the object of the preposition. An **adjective phrase** is a prepositional phrase that modifies a noun or a pronoun by telling what kind or which one. An **adverb phrase** is a prepositional phrase that modifies a verb, an adjective, or an adverb by pointing out *where, when, in what manner,* or *to what extent.* An **appositive phrase** is a noun or a pronoun with modifiers, placed next to a noun or a pronoun to add information and details. A **participial phrase** is a participle modified by an adjective or an adverb phrase or accompanied by a complement. The entire phrase acts as an adjective.

Running at top speed, he soon caught up with them.

An **infinitive phrase** is an infinitive with modifiers, complements, or a subject, all acting together as a single part of speech.

At first I was too busy enjoying my food *to notice how the guests were doing.*

Gerunds A **gerund** is a noun formed from the present participle of a verb ending in *—ing.* Like other nouns, gerunds can be used as subjects, direct objects, predicate nouns, and objects of prepositions.

Gerund Phrases A **gerund phrase** is a gerund with modifiers or a complement, all acting together as a noun.

Clauses A **clause** is a group of words with its own subject and verb. An **independent clause** can stand by itself as a complete sentence.

A **subordinate clause** has a subject and a verb but cannot stand by itself as a complete sentence; it can only be part of a sentence.

"Although it was late"

Using Verbs, Pronouns, and Modifiers

Principal Parts A **verb** has **four principal parts:** the *present,* the *present participle,* the *past,* and the *past participle.* Regular verbs form the past and past participle by adding -ed to the present form.

Irregular verbs form the past and past participle by changing form rather than by adding *-ed.*

Verb Tense A **verb tense** tells whether the time of an action or condition is in the past, the present, or the future. Every verb has six tenses: *present, past, future, present perfect, past perfect,* and *future perfect.* The **present tense** shows actions that happen in the present. The **past tense** shows actions that have already happened. The **future tense** shows actions that will happen. The **present perfect tense** shows actions that begin in the past and continue to the present. The **past perfect tense** shows a past action or condition that ended before another past action. The **future perfect tense** shows a future action or condition that will have ended before another begins.

Pronoun Case The **case** of a pronoun is the form it takes to show its use in a sentence. There are three pronoun cases: *nominative, objective,* and *possessive.* The **nominative case** is used to name or rename the subject of the sentence. The nominative case pronouns are *I, you, he, she, it, we, you, they.* The **objective case** is used as the direct object, indirect object, or object of a preposition. The objective case pronouns are *me, you, him, her, it, us, you, them.* The **possessive case** is used to show ownership. The possessive pronouns are *my, your, his, her, its, our, their, mine, yours, his, hers, its, ours, theirs.*

Subject-Verb Agreement To make a subject and a verb agree, make sure that both are singular or both are plural. Two or more singular subjects joined by *or* or *nor* must have a singular verb. When singular and plural subjects are joined by *or* or *nor*, the verb must agree with the closest subject.

Pronoun-Antecedent Agreement Pronouns must agree with their antecedents in number and gender. Use singular pronouns with singular antecedents and plural pronouns with plural antecedents. Many errors in pronoun-antecedent agreement occur when a plural pronoun is used to refer to a singular antecedent for which the gender is not specified.

Incorrect: Everyone did their best.

Correct: Everyone did his or her best.

The following indefinite pronouns are singular: *anybody, anyone, each, either, everybody, everyone, neither, nobody, no one, one, somebody, someone.*

The following indefinite pronouns are plural: *both, few, many, several.*

The following indefinite pronouns may be either singular or plural: *all, any, most, none, some.*

Modifiers The **comparative** and **superlative** degrees of most adjectives and adverbs of one or two syllables can be formed in either of two ways: Use *–er* or *more* to form a comparative degree and *–est* or *most* to form the superlative degree of most one- and two-syllable modifiers.

More and *most* can also be used to form the comparative and superlative degrees of most one- and two- syllable modifiers. These words should not be used when the result sounds awkward, as in "A greyhound *is more* fast than a beagle."

Glossary of Common Usage

accept, except: *Accept* is a verb that means "to receive" or "to agree to." *Except* is a preposition that means "other than" or "leaving out." Do not confuse these two words.

affect, effect: *Affect* is normally a verb meaning "to influence" or "to bring about a change in." *Effect* is usually a noun, meaning "result."

among, between: *Among* is usually used with three or more items. *Between* is generally used with only two items.

bad, badly: Use the predicate adjective *bad* after linking verbs such as *feel, look,* and *seem.* Use *badly* whenever an adverb is required.

beside, besides: *Beside* means "at the side of" or "close to." *Besides* means "in addition to."

can, may: The verb *can* generally refers to the ability to do something. The verb *may* generally refers to permission to do something.

different from, different than: *Different from* is generally preferred over *different than.*

farther, further: Use *farther* when you refer to distance. Use *further* when you mean "to a greater degree or extent" or "additional."

fewer, less: Use *fewer* for things that can be counted. Use *less* for amounts or quantities that cannot be counted.

good, well: Use the predicate adjective *good* after linking verbs such as *feel, look, smell, taste,* and *seem.* Use well whenever you need an adverb.

its, it's: The word *its* with no apostrophe is a possessive pronoun. The word *it's* is a contraction for *it is.* Do not confuse the possessive pronoun *its* with the contraction *it's,* standing for "it is" or "it has."

lay, lie: Do not confuse these verbs. *Lay* is a transitive verb meaning "to set or put something down." Its principal parts are *lay, laying, laid, laid. Lie* is an intransitive verb meaning "to recline." Its principal parts are *lie, lying, lay, lain.*

like, as: *Like* is a preposition that usually means "similar to" or "in the same way as." *Like* should always be followed by an object. Do not use *like* before a subject and a verb. Use *as* or *that* instead.

of, have: Do not use *of* in place of have after auxiliary verbs like *would, could, should, may, might,* or *must.*

raise, rise: *Raise* is a transitive verb that usually takes a direct object. *Rise* is intransitive and never takes a direct object.

set, sit: *Set* is a transitive verb meaning "to put (something) in a certain place." Its principal parts are *set, setting, set, set. Sit* is an intransitive verb meaning "to be seated." Its principal parts are *sit, sitting, sat, sat.*

than, then: The conjunction *than* is used to connect the two parts of a comparison. Do not confuse *than* with the adverb *then,* which usually refers to time.

that, which, who: Use the relative pronoun *that* to refer to things or people. Use *which* only for things and *who* only for people.

when, where, why: Do not use *when, where,* or *why* directly after a linking verb such as *is.* Reword the sentence.

Faulty: Suspense is when an author increases the reader's tension.

Revised: An author uses suspense to increase the reader's tension.

who, whom: In formal writing, remember to use *who* only as a subject in clauses and sentences and *whom* only as an object.

Capitalization and Punctuation

Capitalization

1. Capitalize the first word of a sentence.
2. Capitalize all proper nouns and adjectives.
3. Capitalize a person's title when it is followed by the person's name or when it is used in direct address.
4. Capitalize titles showing family relationships when they refer to a specific person, unless they are preceded by a possessive noun or pronoun.
5. Capitalize the first word and all other key words in the titles of books, periodicals, poems, stories, plays, paintings, and other works of art.
6. Capitalize the first word and all nouns in letter salutations and the first word in letter closings.

Punctuation

End Marks

1. Use a **period** to end a declarative sentence, an imperative sentence, and most abbreviations.
2. Use a **question mark** to end a direct question or an incomplete question in which the rest of the question is understood.
3. Use an **exclamation mark** after a statement showing strong emotion, an urgent imperative sentence, or an interjection expressing strong emotion.

Commas

1. Use a comma before the conjunction to separate two independent clauses in a compound sentence.
2. Use commas to separate three or more words, phrases, or clauses in a series.
3. Use commas to separate adjectives of equal rank. Do not use commas to separate adjectives that must stay in a specific order.
4. Use a comma after an introductory word, phrase, or clause.
5. Use commas to set off parenthetical and nonessential expressions.
6. Use commas with places and dates made up of two or more parts.
7. Use commas after items in addresses, after the salutation in a personal letter, after the closing in all letters, and in numbers of more than three digits.

Semicolons

1. Use a semicolon to join independent clauses that are not already joined by a conjunction.
2. Use a semicolon to join independent clauses or items in a series that already contain commas.

Colons

1. Use a colon before a list of items following an independent clause.
2. Use a colon in numbers giving the time, in salutations in business letters, and in labels used to signal important ideas.

Quotation Marks

1. A **direct quotation** represents a person's exact speech or thoughts and is enclosed in quotation marks.
2. An **indirect quotation** reports only the general meaning of what a person said or thought and does not require quotation marks.
3. Always place a comma or a period inside the final quotation mark of a direct quotation.
4. Place a question mark or an exclamation mark inside the final quotation mark if the end mark is part of the quotation; if it is not part of the quotation, place it outside the final quotation mark.

Titles

1. Underline or italicize the titles of long written works, movies, television and radio shows, lengthy works of music, paintings, and sculptures.
2. Use quotation marks around the titles of short written works, episodes in a series, songs, and titles of works mentioned as parts of collections.

Hyphens

1. Use a **hyphen** with certain numbers, after certain prefixes, with two or more words used as one word, and with a compound modifier that comes before a noun.

Apostrophes

1. Add an **apostrophe** and s to show the possessive case of most singular nouns.
2. Add an apostrophe to show the possessive case of plural nouns ending in *s* and *es.*
3. Add an apostrophe and s to show the possessive case of plural nouns that do not end in *s* or *es.*
4. Use an apostrophe in a contraction to indicate the position of the missing letter or letters.

Glossary

Big Question vocabulary appears in **blue type**. High-utility Academic vocabulary is <u>underlined</u>.

A

abruptly (uh BRUHPT lee) *adv.* suddenly; unexpectedly

absent-minded (ab suhnt MYND uhd) *adj.* forgetful

accompanied (uh KUHM puh need) *v.* went along with; joined

accusers (uh KYOO zuhrz) *n.* those who find fault or blame

acquainted (uh KWAYNT uhd) *v.* know or become familiar with

admonishing (ad MON ihsh ihng) *adj.* disapproving

agonizing (AG uh nyz ihng) *v.* making great efforts or struggling; being in great pain

amid (uh MIHD) *prep.* in the middle of; surrounded by

anecdotes (AN ihk dohtz) *n.* short, entertaining tales

anxious (ANGK shuhs) *adj.* eager

anxiously (ANGK shuhs lee) *adv.* in a worried or uneasy way

apex (AY pehks) *n.* the highest point

<u>appearance</u> (uh PIHR uhns) *n.* how a person or thing looks

applications (AP luh KAY shuhnz) *n.* forms filled out to make a request

<u>argue</u> (AHR gyoo) *v.* fight using words; debate

asphalt (AS fawlt) *n.* a brown or black mixture of substances used to pave roads

astray (uh STRAY) *adv.* away from the correct path

awed (awd) *adj.* filled with feelings of fear and wonder

B

barriers (BAR ee uhrz) *n.* something that makes progress difficult; obstacles

battle (BAT uhl) *n.* fight or major dispute

belief (bih LEEF) *n.* accepted idea

beseech (bih SEECH) *v.* beg

bewildered (bih WIHL duhrd) *v.* confused as by something complicated

billowing (BIHL oh ihng) *v.* a large swelling mass

bound (bownd) *v.* tied

C

catastrophe (kuh TAS truh fee) *n.* a disaster or misfortune

cavernous (KAV uhr nuhs) *adj.* huge and hollow; like a cavern

<u>challenge</u> (CHAL uhnj) *n.* a dare; a calling into question

chaotic (kay OT ihk) *adj.* completely confused

charitable (CHAR uh tuh buhl) *adj.* kind and generous in giving help to others in need

choral (KAWR uhl) *adj.* relating to a singing group or choir

chorus (KAWR uhs) *n.* the sound produced by many voices singing or speaking at the same time

classified (KLAS uh fyd) *adj.* secret; available only to certain persons

clatter (KLAT uhr) *n.* rattling sound

coaxed (kohkst) *v.* persuaded by gentle urging or pleading

<u>common</u> (KOM uhn) *adj.* ordinary or expected

communicate (kuh MYOO nuh kayt) *v.* share thoughts or feelings, usually in words

community (kuh MYOO nuh tee) *n.* group of people living in a particular area

compete (kuhm PEET) *v.* contend; take part in a sport, game, or contest

composed (kuhm POHZD) *v.* made up of

compound (KOM pownd) *n.* an enclosed space with a building or a group of buildings

compulsion (kuhm PUHL shuhn) *n.* driving force

<u>concept</u> (KON sehpt) *n.* general idea or notion

<u>conclude</u> (kuhn KLOOD) *v.* to bring to a close; to end

condemnation (kon dehm NAY shuhn) *n.* an expression of strong disapproval

<u>confirm</u> (kuhn FURM) *v.* support; show to be correct

confiscated (KON fihs kayt uhd) *v.* seized often by a governmental authority

connection (kuh NEHK shuhn) *n.* link or tie

conscious (KON shuhs) *adj.* awake or aware

consequently (KON suh kwehnt lee) *adv.* as a result

consoled (kuhn SOHLD) *v.* comforted

consumption (kuhn SUHMP shuhn) *n.* eating; drinking; using up

<u>convince</u> (kuhn VIHNS) *v.* to persuade

cordial (KAWR juhl) *adj.* warm and friendly

correspond (kawr uh SPOND) *v.* agree with or be similar to

covetousness (KUHV uh tuhs ness) *n.* enviousness; wanting what another person has

craned (kraynd) *v.* stretched out for a better look

crippled (KRIHP uhld) *adj.* having a disability that prevents normal motion in a person's limbs or body

crude (krood) *adj.* lacking polish; not carefully made

cuddly (KUHD lee) *adj.* having a quality which invites hugging or holding in one's arms

culture (KUHL chuhr) *n.* collected customs of a group or community

cunning (KUHN ihng) *adj.* sly; crafty; deceptive

custody (KUHS tuh dee) *n.* protection or supervision

custom (KUHS tuhm) *n.* accepted practice

custom (KUHS tuhm) *n.* usual way of doing something; habit

D

decision (dih SIHZH uhn) *n.* choice; result of judging

declined (dih KLYND) *v.* refused

deem (deem) *v.* hold as an opinion; judge

defend (dih FEHND) *v.* guard from attack; protect

deficiency (dih FIHSH uhn see) *n.* shortage or lack

demented (dih MEHN tihd) *adj.* insane; mad

demise (dih MYZ) *n.* end of existence; death

demonstrate (DEHM uhn strayt) *v.* show clearly; prove

descendants (dih SEHN duhnts) *n.* a person's children, grandchildren, great grandchildren and so on

determine (dih TUR muhn) *v.* settle; reach a conclusion

devoured (dih VOWRD) *v.* ate hungrily or greedily

dialogue (DY uh lawg) *n.* conversation or exchange of words

dignity (DIHG nuh tee) *n.* being worthy of esteem or honor; proper pride and self respect

dilution (duh LOO shuhn) *n.* process of weakening by mixing with something else

dimensions (duh MEHN shuhnz) *n.* scope or importance

dismal (DIHZ muhl) *adj.* causing gloom or misery

dispersed (dihs PURST) *v.* distributed in many directions

dissonance (DIHS uh nuhns) *n.* harsh or unpleasant combination of sounds

distinguish (dihs TIHNG gwihsh) *v.* mark as different; set apart

distorted (dihs TAWRT uhd) *v.* twisted out of normal shape

distracted (dihs TRAKT uhd) *adj.* unable to concentrate

diverse (duh VURS) *adj.* many and different; from different backgrounds

diverse (duh VURS) *adj.* various; with differing characteristics

drone (drohn) *n.* continuous humming sound

E

eloquent (EHL uh kwuhnt) *adj.* vivid, persuasive and expressive

embedded (ehm BEHD ihd) *adj.* firmly fixed in surrounding material

embraced (ehm BRAYSD) *v.* hugged; clasped in the arms to show affection

emigrated (EHM uh grayt uhd) *v.* left one country to settle in another

endured (ehn DURD) *v.* suffered through

engulfing (ehn GUHLF ihng) *adj.* swallowing up; overwhelming

enroll (ehn ROHL) *v.* to place oneself on a register or list

enviously (EHN vee uhs lee) *adv.* with jealousy

equipped (ih KWIHPT) *v.* having what is needed

escorting (EHS kawrt ihng) *v.* going with as a companion

etiquette (EHT uh keht) *n.* acceptable social manners

evidence (EHV uh duhns) *n.* proof in support of a claim or statement

evident (EHV uh duhnt) *adj.* easy to see; very clear

evolved (ih VOLVD) *v.* grew gradually; developed

exact (ehg ZAKT) *v.* demand with force or authority

examine (ehg ZAM uhn) *v.* study in depth; look at closely

exhaust (ehg ZAWST) *v.* use up

exhausted (ehg ZAWST uhd) *adj.* very tired

expectations (EHKS pehk TAY shuhnz) *n.* feelings that something is about to happen

expression (ehk SPREHSH uhn) *n.* figure of speech

exuded (ehg ZOOD uhd) *v.* gave off; oozed

F

fact (fakt) *n.* idea or thought that is real or true

family (FAM uh lee) *n.* people related by blood or having a common ancestor

famine (FAM uhn) *n.* shortage of food

fantasy (FAN tuh see) *n.* idea or thought that is imagined or unreal

fascinated (FAS uh nayt uhd) *adj.* strongly attracted to something interesting or delightful

Glossary **R25**

feeble (FEE buhl) *adj.* weak

fellow (FEHL oh) *n.* a man or boy

ferocious (fuh ROH shuhs) *adj.* wild and dangerous

fiction (FIHK shuhn) *n.* imagined or made-up thought or claim

flaw (flaw) *n.* crack; defect

flee (flee) *v.* to run away as from danger

flickering (FLIHK uhr ihng) *v.* burning unsteadily

fragments (FRAG muhntz) *n.* small, broken off parts

fragrant (FRAY gruhnt) *adj.* having a pleasant odor

frenzied (FREHN zeed) *adj.* acting in a wild, uncontrolled way

fulfilling (ful FIHL ihng) *v.* carrying out a promise; satisfying an obligation

G

game (gaym) *n.* contest; type of play in which there is usually one winner

generation (jehn uh RAY shuhn) *n.* people living at the same time and/or of about the same age

gesture (JEHS chuhr) *n.* motion of the hand or body to show or point

gilded (GIHLD uhd) *adj.* covered with gold or golden color

gnawing (NAW ihng) *v.* biting and cutting with teeth

greed (greed) *n.* a selfish desire for more than one's share of something

group (groop) *n.* collection or set, as of people

grudgingly (GRUHJ ihng lee) *adv.* in an unwilling or resentful way

guess (gehs) *n.* estimate based on little or no information

H

hence (hehns) *adv.* from this place or time

hereditary (huh REHD uh tehr ee) *adj.* a characteristic passed down from generation to generation

hesitated (HEHZ uh tayt uhd) *v.* stopped because of indecision

history (HIHS tuhr ee) *n.* record of past events

hollowed (HOL ohd) *v.* created a cavity or a space within

homey (HOHM ee) *adj.* comfortable; having a feeling of home

horrid (HAWR ihd) *adj.* shockingly dreadful; extremely unpleasant

howl (howl) *v.* make a loud, sorrowful sound

humble (HUHM buhl) *adj.* modest; not proud

I

ideals (y DEE uhlz) *n.* models or standards of excellence or perfection

idle (Y duhl) *adj.* not working or active; doing nothing

ignorance (IHG nuhr uhns) *n.* lack of knowledge, education, or experience

ignore (ihg NAWR) *v.* pay no attention to

imitate (IHM uh tayt) *v.* copy; mimic

immense (ih MEHNS) *adj.* huge

impatient (ihm PAY shuhnt) *adj.* feeling or showing annoyance because of delay

incessantly (ihn SEHS uhnt lee) *adv.* constantly; continuously

indignantly (ihn DIHG nuhnt lee) *adv.* expressing anger or scorn

individuality (ihn duh vihj u AL uh tee) *n.* way in which a person or thing stands apart or is different

inedible (ihn EHD uh buhl) *adj.* not fit to be eaten

inevitably (ihn EHV uh tuh blee) *adv.* unavoidably

infamous (IHN fuh muhs) *adj.* having a bad reputation

influence (IHN floo uhns) *v.* to sway or affect in some other way

inhabited (ihn HAB iht uhd) *adj.* lived in; occupied

inquired (ihn KWYRD) *v.* asked

inscribed (ihn SKRYBD) *v.* written on

instinctively (ihn STIHNGK tihv lee) *adv.* done automatically without thinking

integrate (IHN tuh grayt) *v.* remove all barriers and allow free association; bring together as a whole

intently (ihn TEHNT lee) *adv.* purposefully; earnestly

investigate (ihn VEHS tuh gayt) *v.* examine thoroughly, as an idea

involve (ihn VOLV) *v.* include

iridescent (ihr uh DEHS uhnt) *adj.* showing different colors when seen from different angles

irrational (ih RASH uh nuhl) *adj.* unreasonable

isolate (Y suh layt) *v.* set apart

issue (IHSH oo) *n.* problem or point on which there is disagreement

J

jubilation (joo buh LAY shuhn) *n.* great joy; triumph

judge (juhj) *v.* form an opinion of or pass judgment on

K

knowledge (NOL ihj) *n.* result of learning; awareness

L

lair (ler) *n.* den or resting place of a wild animal

language (LANG gwihj) *n.* form of communication between people

leisurely (LEE zhuhr lee) *adj.* in an unhurried way

liable (LY uh buhl) *adj.* likely to do something or to happen

limit (LIHM iht) *n.* as far as something can go; farthest extreme

lose (looz) *v.* to fail in a game or dispute

lure (lur) *v.* tempt or attract

M

malicious (muh LIHSH uhs) *adj.* having or showing evil intentions

mauled (mawld) *v.* badly injured by being attacked

measure (MEHZH uhr) *v.* place a value on

message (MEHS ihj) *n.* written or spoken communication

methods (MEHTH uhdz) *n.* ways of doing something

migrated (MY grayt uhd) *v.* moved from one place to another

miniscule (MIHN uh skyool) *adj.* very small; tiny

misapprehension (mihs ap rih HEHN shuhn) *n.* misunderstanding

mistook (mihs TUK) *v.* identified incorrectly; to misunderstand

mode (mohd) *n.* a way of acting, doing, or being

monarch (MON uhrk) *n.* the single or sole ruler of a state

mortal (MAWR tuhl) *adj.* referring to humans who eventually die

murmured (MUR muhrd) *v.* made a low, continuous sound

mystified (MIHS tuh fyd) *v.* perplexed; bewildered

N

narrow (NAR oh) *adj.* limited in extent, not wide

negotiate (nih GOH shee ayt) *v.* to settle or come to an agreement

nigh (ny) *adv.* near

nonverbal (nohn VUR buhl) *adj.* not involving or using words or speech

O

obscure (uhb SKYUR) *adj.* not well known

observant (uhb ZUR vuhnt) *adj.* quick to notice; alert; watchful

observe (uhb ZURV) *v.* notice or see

obstinacy (OB stuh nuh see) *n.* stubbornness

offense (uh FEHNS) *n.* harmful act; a violation of law

offensive (uh FEHN sihv) *adj.* unpleasant

official (uh FIHSH uhl) *adj.* formal; prescribed by an authority

olden (OHL duhn) *adj.* ancient; old

opinion (uh PIHN yuhn) *n.* personal view or belief

orator (AWR uh tuhr) *n.* a person who can speak well in public

P

participation (pahr tihs uh PAY shuhn) *n.* the act of taking part in an event or activity

peaceable (PEE suh buhl) *adj.* harmonious; tranquil

peculiar (pih KYOOL yuhr) *adj.* out of the ordinary; odd

persisted (puhr SIHST uhd) *v.* refused to give up

personality (pur suh NAL uh tee) *n.* the sum of behaviors and feelings that define an individual

perspective (puhr SPEHK tihv) *n.* point of view

petition (puh TIHSH uhn) *n.* document that people sign to express demands

pitiless (PIHT uh lihs) *adj.* without mercy

plagued (playgd) *v.* troubled or annoyed

pleaded (PLEED uhd) *v.* begged

pleasant (PLEHZ uhnt) *adj.* agreeable; delightful

plight (plyt) *n.* awkward, sad or dangerous situation

plunging (PLUHN jihng) *v.* moving suddenly forward or downward

precautionary (prih KAW shuh nehr ee) *adj.* done to prevent harm or danger

precious (PREHSH uhs) *adj.* dear; beloved

prejudiced (PREHJ uh dihst) *adj.* having unreasonable hostile feelings toward a racial, religious or other group

prelude (PREHL yood) *n.* introduction to a main event

prove (proov) *v.* establish the truth of, as in a claim or statement

provided (pruh VYD uhd) *v.* supplied; furnished

prowled (prowld) *v.* moved around quietly and secretly

pulsating (PUHL sayt ihng) *adj.* beating or throbbing rhythmically

purpose (PUR puhs) *n.* what something is used for

pursue (puhr SOO) *v.* be involved in; follow

pursuers (puhr SOO uhrz) *n.* those who follow in an effort to capture

Q

question (KWEHS chuhn) *v.* challenge the accuracy of; place in doubt

quote (kwoht) *v.* refer to the words of a source

R

rage (rayj) *n.* very strong anger

rancor (RANG kuhr) *n.* bitter hate or ill will

ravaged (RAV ihjd) *v.* violently destroyed; ruined

ravenous (RAV uh nuhs) *adj.* greedily hungry

reaction (ree AK shuhn) *n.* response or course of action taken in response to something said or done

realistic (ree uh LIHS tihk) *adj.* true to life; having to do with reality

recognize (REHK uhg nyz) *v.* know and remember

refer (rih FUR) *v.* point back to, as an authority or expert

reflect (rih FLEHKT) *v.* think about or consider

reflecting (rih FLEHKT ihng) *v.* thinking seriously

reluctant (rih LUHK tuhnt) *adj.* showing doubt or unwillingness

reluctantly (rih LUHK tuhnt lee) *adv.* unwillingly; unenthusiastically

repaid (rih PAYD) *v.* did or gave in return

repentance (rih PEHN tuhns) *n.* deep sorrow and regret; feeling of sorrow for wrongdoing

repulse (rih PUHLS) *v.* drive back; repel an attack

resident (REHZ uh duhnt) *adj.* living in a particular place

resist (rih ZIHST) *v.* to oppose actively; to refuse to give in

resolve (rih ZOLV) *v.* to settle or bring to an end

respond (rih SPOND) *v.* to reply or answer

retaliated (rih TAL ee ayt uhd) *v.* punished in return for an injury or wrong done

reunion (ree YOON yuhn) *n.* gathering of people who have been separated

reveal (rih VEEL) *v.* to show or uncover

revolution (rehv uh LOO shuhn) *n.* a complete or radical change of any kind

routine (roo TEEN) *n.* a customary or regular procedure

rue (roo) *v.* to be sorrowful or regretful

S

savoring (SAY vuhr ihng) *v.* enjoying; tasting with delight

scarce (skairs) *adj.* not enough to satisfy need

scarcely (SKAIRS lee) *adv.* hardly

scrawny (SKRAW nee) *adj.* very thin, skinny, and boney

sculpted (SKUHLPT uhd) *v.* shaped or molded

sensible (SEHN suh buhl) *adj.* logical; practical; intelligent

sentiment (SEHN tuh muhnt) *n.* a tender feeling or emotion

share (shair) *v.* to communicate with, such as an idea or experience

similar (SIHM uh luhr) *adj.* alike

skimming (SKIHM ihng) *v.* gliding; moving swiftly and lightly over a surface

slanderous (SLAN duhr uhs) *adj.* untrue and damaging statements

smugly (SMUHG lee) *adv.* in a way that shows satisfaction with oneself

soprano (suh PRAN oh) *n.* a singer who can sing two octaves or more above middle C

sour (sowr) *adj.* having the sharp acid taste of lemon or vinegar

source (sawrs) *n.* person or book that provides information

sown (sohn) *v.* scattered or planted seeds for growing

spasm (SPAZ uhm) *n.* sudden short burst of energy or activity

splendor (SPLEHN duhr) *n.* gorgeous appearance; magnificence

splendor (SPLEHN duhr) *n.* great brightness

startled (STAHR tuhld) *adj.* surprised

starvation (stahr VAY shuhn) *n.* a state of extreme hunger

striking (STRY kihng) *adj.* very noticeable or impressive; unusual

strive (stryv) *v.* struggle; compete

stubby (STUHB ee) *adj.* short and thick; bristly

study (STUHD ee) *n.* research or investigation into a claim

study (STUHD ee) *v.* to look into deeply

sublime (suh BLYM) *adj.* majestic; impressive because of great beauty

summit (SUHM iht) *n.* highest part

superb (su PURB) *adj.* extremely fine; excellent

support (suh PAWRT) *v.* to stand behind or back up

surmise (suhr MYZ) *v.* to infer without evidence; to guess

surplus (SUR pluhs) *adj.* an amount greater than what is needed

survival (suhr VY vuhl) *n.* the act of lasting or continuing to live

symbolize (SIHM buh lyz) *v.* to stand for

sympathize (SIHM puh thyz) *v.* to share in a feeling; to feel compassion

sympathy (SIHM puh thee) *n.* understanding and sharing another person's feelings

systematic (SIHS tuh MAT ihk) *adj.* orderly

T

teemed (teemd) *v.* was full of

temporarily (tehm puh REHR uh lee) *adv.* not permanently

test (tehst) *n.* method or process for proving or disproving a claim

thicket (THIHK iht) *n.* dense growth of shrubs or small trees

thorny (THAWR nee) *adj.* prickly; full of thorns

thrashing (THRASH ihng) *v.* wild moving

thrives (thryvz) *v.* grows well

timidly (TIHM ihd lee) *adv.* in a way that shows fear or shyness

trace (trays) *n.* mark left behind by something

transfixed (trans FIHKSD) *v.* made motionless

transport (trans PAWRT) *v.* carry from one place to another

traversed (TRAV uhrsd) *v.* went across

treacheries (TREHCH uhr eez) *n.* acts of betrayal

trend (trehnd) *n.* tendency or general direction

trespass (TREHS pahs) *v.* to go on another's land without permission

trotted (TROT uhd) *v.* a run by a four-legged animal in which the front foot and the opposite hind foot lift at the same time

trudged (truhjd) *v.* walked as if tired or with effort

true (troo) *adj.* real; genuine

tyrant (TY ruhnt) *n.* a harsh cruel ruler

U

unbelievable (UHN bih LEE vuh buhl) *adj.* not likely; hard to accept as true

undulating (UHN juh layt ihng) *adj.* moving in waves, like a snake

unethical (uhn EHTH uh kuhl) *adj.* not conforming to moral standards or to the standards of a group

unique (yoo NEEK) *adj.* one of a kind

V

values (VAL yooz) *n.* beliefs of a person or group

vanish (VAN ihsh) *v.* disappear

verbal (VUR buhl) *adj.* involving or using words or speech

vigilance (VIHJ uh luhns) *n.* watchfulness

vigorously (VIHG uhr uhs lee) *adv.* forcefully or energetically

visual (VIHZH u uhl) *adj.* able to be seen or understood with the eyes

vow (vow) *n.* promise or pledge

W

whirs (hwurz) *v.* flies or moves quickly with a buzzing sound

win (wihn) *v.* to gain a victory or come out ahead

winced (wihnsd) *v.* drew back slightly as if in pain

wintry (WIHN tree) *adj.* being very cold, like winter weather

Y

yearning (YURN ihng) *n.* deep or anxious longing

Spanish Glossary

El vacabulario de Gran Pregunta aparece en **azul**. El vocabulario academico de alta utilidad está <u>subrayado</u>.

A

abruptly / súbitamente *adv.* repentinamente; inesperadamente

absent-minded / distraído *adj.* olvidadizo

accompanied / acompañó *v.* fue en compañía de otro; se unió; se juntó

accusers / acusadores *s.* personas que culpan

acquainted / conocer *v.* saber algo o familiarizarse con algo

admonishing / amonestado *adj.* desaprobado

agonizing / agonizando *v.* haciendo un gran esfuerzo o luchando; con mucho dolor

amid / entre *prep.* en el medio de; rodeado de

anecdotes / anécdotas *s.* relatos cortos y entretenidos

anxious / ansioso *adj.* deseoso

anxiously / ansiosamente *adv.* con preocupación o intranquilidad

apex / cumbre *s.* punto más alto

appearance / apariencia *s.* aspecto de una persona o cosa

applications / solicitudes *s.* formularios que se completan para hacer una petición

<u>**argue / discutir**</u> *v.* debate; desacuerdo verbal

asphalt / asfalto *s.* mezcla marrón o negra de sustancias que se usa para pavimentar carreteras

astray / descarriar *v.* alejar del camino correcto

awed / sobrecogido *adj.* con sentimientos de temor y asombro

B

barriers / barreras *s.* algo que dificulta el progreso; obstáculo

battle / lucha *s.* pelea; gran disputa

belief / creencia *s.* idea conforme

beseech / suplicar *v.* rogar

bewildered / desconcertado *adj.* confundido por algo complejo

billowing / hinchado *adj.* inflamado o inflado

bound / sujetó *v.* amarró

C

catastrophe / catástrofe *s.* desastre o desgracia

cavernous / cavernoso *adj.* enorme y hueco; como una caverna

<u>**challenge / desafío**</u> *s.* un reto; el acto de cuestionar

chaotic / caótico *adj.* completamente confuso

charitable / caritativo *adj.* que presta ayuda a los necesitados de una manera amable y generosa

choral / coral *adj.* relacionado con un grupo de cantantes o un coro

chorus / coro *s.* sonido que producen muchas voces al cantar o hablar al mismo tiempo

classified / clasificado *adj.* secreto; disponible solo para ciertas personas

clatter / traqueteo *s.* vibración

coaxed / convenció *v.* persuadió de manera sutil

<u>**common / común**</u> *adj.* ordinario; frecuente y esperado

<u>**communicate / comunicar**</u> *v.* compartir pensamientos o sentimientos, usualmente con palabras

community / comunidad *s.* grupo de personas que tienen un interés en común o que viven cerca el uno del otro

compete / competir *v.* contender; participar en un deporte, juego o concurso

composed / compuesto *adj.* formado por

compound / complejo residencial *s.* área que tiene una o varias edificaciones

compulsion / compulsión *s.* impulso irresistible

<u>**concept / concepto**</u> *s.* idea general o noción

<u>**conclude / concluir**</u> *v.* finalizar; terminar

condemnation / condena *s.* fuerte expresión de desaprobación

<u>**confirm / confirmar**</u> *v.* apoyar o corroborar

confiscated / confiscó *v.* embargó; acción que generalmente ejecuta el gobierno

connection / conección *s.* enlace o vínculo

conscious / conciente *adj.* que está despierto o tiene presente

consequently / consecuentemente *adv.* como resultado de

consoled / consoló *v.* alivió la pena

consumption / consumo *s.* uso alimentos o bebidas; utilización

<u>**convince / convencer**</u> *v.* persuadir; incitar a aceptar cierto punto de vista

cordial / cordial *adj.* afectuoso y amable

correspond / corresponder *v.* acordar en algo o asemejarse

covetousness / codicia *s.* envidia; deseo de tener lo que otra persona posee

craned / estiró *v.* se extendió para ver mejor

crippled / lisiado *adj.* persona que tiene una incapacidad física que previene el movimiento normal de los brazos y las piernas; el uso del equivalente en inglés de esta palabra para referirse a una persona es ofensivo

crude / crudo *adj.* sin pulir; hecho sin cuidado

cuddly / mimoso *adj.* que le encantan las caricias y los abrazos; muy afectuoso

culture / cultura *s.* conjunto de modos de vida y costumbres de un grupo o una comunidad

cunning / astuto *adj.* hábil; taimado; engañoso

custody / custodia *s.* protección o supervisión

custom / costumbre *s.* lo que se hace comúnmente

custom / costumbre *s.* manera común de hacer algo; hábito

D

decision / decisión *s.* elección; resultado de un juicio

declined / declinar *v.* rechazar

deem / considerar *v.* juzgar

defend / defender *v.* resguardar de un ataque; proteger

deficiency / deficiencia *s.* escasez o carencia

demented / demente *adj.* loco

demise / fallecimiento *s.* fin de la existencia; muerte

demonstrate / demostrar *v.* enseñar claramente; probar

descendants / descendientes *s.* hijos, nietos, bisnietos de una persona; generaciones que siguen a una persona

determine / determinar *v.* decidir; llegar a una conclusión

devoured / devoró *v.* comió con ansia o apresuradamente

dialogue / dialogar *s.* conversación; intercambio de palabras

dignity / dignidad *s.* cualidad de una persona que merece aprecio o trato con honor; comportamiento con orgullo y dándose a respetar

dilution / dilución *s.* proceso mediante el cual se diluyen los componentes mezclándolos

dimensions / dimensiones *s.* alcance o importancia

dismal / sombrío *adj.* que causa tristeza o melancolía

dispersed / dispersó *v.* distribuyó en varias direcciones

dissonance / disonancia *s.* conjunto desagradable de sonidos

distinguish / distinguir *v.* diferenciar; considerar por separado

distorted / distorsionó *adj.* torció de tal manera que cambia la forma original

distracted / distraído *adj.* que no se puede concentrar

diverse / diverso *adj.* en cantidad y variado; de orígenes diferentes

diverse / diverso *adj.* variado; con diferentes características

drone / zumbido *s.* sonido continuado y bronco

E

eloquent / elocuente *adj.* vívido, persuasivo y expresivo

embedded / incrustado *adj.* fijado fuertemente en otro material

embraced / abrazó *v.* rodeó con los brazos como muestra de afecto

emigrated / emigró *v.* se marchó de un país para establecerse en otro

endured / aguantó *v.* soportó una situación difícil

engulfing / arrollador *adj.* destructor; derribador; que puede sepultar

enroll / matricular *v.* inscribirse o registrarse

enviously / con envidia *adv.* con celos

equipped / equipado *adj.* con lo necesario

escorting / acompañar *v.* ir con otra persona

etiquette / etiqueta *s.* buenos modales que se debe tener en actos sociales

evidence / evidencia *s.* prueba que apoya una aseveración o argumento

evident / evidente *adj.* aparente; muy claro

evolved / evolucionó *v.* creció gradualmente; se desarrolló

exact / exigir *v.* pedir con fuerza y autoridad

examine / examinar *v.* estudiar a fondo; observar detenidamente

exhaust / agotar *v.* usar todo; terminar

exhausted / agotado *adj.* muy cansado

expectations / expectativas *s.* sensación de que algo está por ocurrir

expression / expresión *s.* figura retórica

exuded / exudar *v.* emitir; rezumar

F

fact / hecho *s.* idea o pensamiento real o verdadero

family / familia *s.* personas de relación consanguínea o que tienen un ancestro en común

famine / hambruna *s.* escasez de alimentos

fantasy / fantasía *s.* producto de la imaginación; ficción

fascinated / fascinado *adj.* atraído fuertemente a algo interesante o encantador

feeble / débil *adj.* flojo

fellow / tipo *s.* hombre o joven

ferocious / feroz *adj.* salvaje y peligroso

fiction / ficción *s.* lo inventado o imaginado

flaw / imperfección *s.* grieta; defecto

flee / huir *v.* alejarse apresuradamente del peligro, escaparse

flickering / parpadear *v.* titilar

fragments / fragmentos *s.* pequeños pedazos de algo

fragrant / fragante *adj.* que tiene un aroma agradable

frenzied / frenético *adj.* que actúa de manera alocada y desenfrenada

fulfilling / satisfacer *v.* cumplir con una promesa o con una obligación

G

game / juego *s.* concurso, tipo de diversión en el que usualmente hay un ganador

generation / generación *s.* personas que viven en en mismo período de tiempo y/o son de la misma edad

gesture / gesto *s.* movimiento de la mano o del cuerpo para demostrar o señalar

gilded / dorado *adj.* cubierto de oro o de color áureo

gnawing / morder *v.* apretar y cortar con los dientes

greed / codicia *s.* deseo egoísta de tener más de la porción establecida

group / grupo *s.* conjunto o agrupación, como de personas

grudgingly / a regañadientes *adv.* de mala gana o con resentimiento

guess / conjetura *s.* estimado basado en poca o ninguna información

H

hence / por lo tanto *adv.* desde ahora

hereditary / hereditario *adj.* característica que se pasa de generación a generación

hesitated / dudar *v.* detenerse por estar indeciso

history / historia *s.* récord de sucesos del pasado

hollowed / ahuecó *v.* abrió una cavidad o un espacio dentro de algo

homey / hogareño *adj.* cómodo; que genra el sentimiento de estar en el hogar

horrid / horrible *adj.* espantoso; muy desagradable

howl / aullar *v.* hacer un ruido alto y triste

humble / humilde *adj.* modesto; sin vanidad

I

ideals / ideales *s.* modelos o estándares de excelencia o perfección

idle / holgazán *adj.* ocioso, desocupado; que no trabaja; inactivo

ignorance / ignorancia *s.* falta de conocimiento, educación o experiencia

ignore / ignorar *v.* no prestar atención

imitate / imitar *v.* copiar; emular

immense / inmenso *adj.* enorme

impatient / impaciente *adj.* que siente o demuestra molestia por algún retraso

incessantly / sin cesar *adv.* constante; continuo

indignantly / con indignación *adv.* expresando ira o desprecio

individuality / individualidad *s.* forma en la que alguien o algo se diferencia de otros

inedible / incomible *adj.* que no se puede comer

inevitably / inevitablemente *adv.* que no se puede eludir

infamous / infame *adj.* que tiene mala reputación

influence / influencia *v.* poder o efecto sobre algo

inhabited / habitó *adj.* sitio donde se ha vivido, que ha sido ocupado

inquired / informado *v.* preguntado

inscribed / inscribir *v.* escribir o grabar en algún material

instinctively / instintivamente *adv.* automáticamente, sin pensar

integrate / integrar *v.* eliminar las barreras y permitir la libre asociación; unificar

intently / intencionadamente *adv.* seriamente, con atención

investigate / investigar *v.* examinar detenidamente, como una idea

involve / involucrar *v.* incluir

iridescent / iridiscente *adj.* que muestra colores distintos cuando se observa desde diferentes ángulos

irrational / irracional *adj.* que carece de razón

isolate / aislar *v.* considerar por separado

issue / asunto *s.* problema o punto en el que hay un desacuerdo

J

jubilation / júbilo *s.* gran alegría; triunfo

judge / juzgar *v.* formar una opinión o pronunciar juicio

K

knowledge / conocimiento *s.* el resultado del aprendizaje; tener presente

L

lair / guarida *s.* cueva o lugar donde guarecen los animales salvajes

language / lenguaje *s.* sistema de comunicación entre personas

leisurely / tranquilamente *adj.* sin apresuramiento

liable / responsable *adj.* que es probable que haga algo

R32 Spanish Glossary

limit / límite *s.* punto en el que no se puede seguir; extremo máximo

lose / perder *v.* fallar o fracasar en un juego o disputa

lure / atraer *v.* tentar o interesar

M

malicious / malicioso *adj.* que tiene o demuestra malas intenciones

mauled / magullar *v.* herir gravemente al atacar

measure / evaluar *v.* reconocer su valor

message / mensaje *s.* comunicación escrita o verbal

methods / métodos *s.* maneras de hacer las cosas

migrated / migró *v.* se fue de un lugar a otro

miniscule / minúsculo *adj.* muy pequeño; pequeñito

misapprehension / malentendido *s.* mala interpretación

mistook / equivocarse *v.* identificar incorrectamente; malentender

mode / modo *s.* manera de actuar o ser

monarch / monarca *s.* soberano de un estado

mortal / mortal *adj.* se refiere a seres que pueden morir

murmured / murmuró *v.* hizo un sonido bajo y continuo

mystified / desconcertó *v.* dejó perplejo; aturdió

N

narrow / estrecho *adj.* de extensión limitada; que no es ancho

negotiate / negociar *v.* decidir; llegar a un acuerdo

nigh / contiguo *adv.* cercano

nonverbal / no verbal *adj.* que no involucra o usa palabras o el habla

O

obscure / críptico *adj.* no muy conocido, oscuro, enigmático

observant / observador *adj.* que se da cuenta rápidamente; alerta; vigilante

observe / observar *v.* notar o ver

obstinacy / obstinación *s.* terquedad

offense / ofensa *s.* acto perjudicial; violación de la ley

offensive / ofensivo *adj.* desagradable

official / oficial *adj.* formal; dictado por una figura de la autoridad

olden / pasado *adj.* antiguo; viejo

opinion / opinión *s.* punto de vista personal o creencia

orator / orador *s.* persona que habla bien en público

P

participation / participación *s.* el acto de tomar parte en un evento o actividad

peaceable / grato *adj.* armonioso; tranquilo

peculiar / peculiar *adj.* fuera de lo normal; extraño

persisted / persistirse *v.* rehusarse a darse por vencido

personality / personalidad *s.* el conjunto de comportamientos y sentimientos que definen a un individuo

perspective / perspectiva *s.* punto de vista

petition / petición *s.* documento firmado para solicitar algo

pitiless / despiadado *adj.* sin piedad, cruel

plagued / asediar *v.* molestar o importunar a alguien sin descanso

pleaded / suplicó *v.* rogó

pleasant / placentero *adj.* agradable, apacible

plight / situación grave *s.* suceso muy extraño, triste o que puede causar peligro

plunging / desplomar *v.* caer repentinamente

precautionary / preventivo *adj.* algo que se hace para evitar daño o peligro

precious / precioso *adj.* muy querido; de mucho valor

prejudiced / prejuiciado *adj.* que tiene sentimientos hostiles e irracionales contra un grupo racial, religioso, etc.

prelude / preludio *s.* introducción a un evento

prove / probar *v.* establecer la veracidad de algo, como de una aseveración o argumento

provided / proveer *v.* suministrar; facilitar

prowled / rondar *v.* moverse por un lugar silenciosamente y en secreto

pulsating / pulsando *v.* latiendo o palpitando a cierto ritmo

purpose / propósito *s.* intención por la cual se usa algo

pursue / perseguir *v.* seguir; tratar de alcanzar algo

pursuers / perseguidores *s.* personas que buscan con el propósito de capturar

Q

question / cuestionar *v.* la precisión de algo; poner en duda

quote / citar *v.* relatar las palabras de una fuente de información

R

rage / rabia *s.* ira

rancor / rencor *s.* odio o mala voluntad

ravaged / devastó *v.* destruyó violentamente; arruinó

ravenous / hambriento *adj.* que tiene mucha hambre

reaction / reacción s. respuesta o acción que responde a algo dicho o hecho

realistic / realista adj. sensato; relacionado a la realidad

recognize / reconocer v. saber y recordar

refer / referir v. aludir a, como a una autoridad o a un experto

reflect / reflejar v. pensar en algo o considerar

reflecting / reflexionando v. pensando detenidamente

reluctant / reacio adj. que demuestra duda o poca voluntad para hacer algo

reluctantly / de mala gana adv. sin voluntad; sin entusiasmo

repaid / retribuyó v. hizo o dio a cambio de algo

repentance / remordimiento s. gran sentimiento de pena y arrepentimiento; sentimiento de pena por haber actuado incorrectamente

repulse / repeler v. rechazar un ataque obligando; alejar algo con fuerza

resident / residente adj. que vive en un lugar en particular

resist / resistir v. oponerse activamente; negarse a ceder

resolve / resolver v. decidir; finalizar

respond / responder v. replicar; contestar

retaliated / tomar represalias v. castigar por haber herido o por haber hecho una maldad

reunion / reunión s. congregación de personas que han estado separadas

reveal / revelar v. mostrar; descubrir

revolution / revolución s. cambio total o radical

routine / rutina s. proceso habitual o regular

rue / lamentar v. sufrir una pena o arrepentirse

S

savoring / saboreando v. degustando o apreciando con placer

scarce / escaso adj. insuficiente

scarcely / escasamente adv. difícilmente

scrawny / esquelético adj. muy delgado, flaco y huesudo

sculpted / esculpió v. dio forma o moldeó

sensible / sensato adj. lógico; práctico; inteligente

sentiment / sensación s. ternura o emoción

share / compartir v. comunicar una idea o experiencia

similar / similar adj. semejante

skimming / rasar v. deslizarse; moverse rápida y ligeramente por una superficie

slanderous / calumnioso adj. que contiene argumentos falsos y perjudiciales

smugly / presuntuoso adv. se refiere a las personas que muestran extrema satisfacción consigo mismas

soprano / soprano s. persona que puede cantar dos octavos o más por encima del do central

sour / ácido adj. con el sabor fuerte y ácido de limón o vinagre

source / fuente s. persona o texto que provee información

sown / sembró v. regó o plantó semillas

spasm / arranque s. ímpetu de energía o inicio repentino de una actividad

splendor / esplendor s. belleza impresionante; magnificencia

splendor / resplandor s. brillo intenso

startled / sobresaltado adj. sorprendido

starvation / inanición s. falta extrema de alimento

striking / destacado adj. muy notable o impresionante; inusual

strive / esforzarse v. luchar; competir

stubby / regordete adj. bajo y grueso

study / estudiar v. examinar; observar a fondo

study / estudio s. búsqueda o investigación de un tema

sublime / sublime adj. mejestuoso; impresionante por su belleza

summit / cumbre s. la parte más alta

superb / espléndido adj. extremadamente fino; excelente

support / apoyar v. basar; fundar

surmise / presumir v. inferir sin evidencia; figurarse

surplus / excedente adj. cantidad mayor a la que se necesita

survival / supervivencia s. lo que perdura o continua viviendo

symbolize / simbolizar v. atribuir; representar

sympathize / compadecer v. compartir un sentimiento; sentir compasión

sympathy / compasión s. comprensión de los sentimientos de otra persona

systematic / sistemático adj. ordenado

T

teemed / repleto v. lleno de

temporarily / temporalmente adv. por algún tiempo, pero no de manera permanente

test / prueba s. método o proceso de probar o desmentir una aseveración

thicket / matorral s. terreno denso de arbustos y pequeños árboles

thorny / espinoso adj. lleno de espinas

thrashing / golpear v. mover de manera repentina y violenta un cuerpo contra otro

thrives / prosperar v. crecer muy bien

timidly / tímidamente adv. con temor o modestia

trace / rastro *s.* huella que deja algo o alguien a su paso

transfixed / paralizar *v.* detener el movimiento

transport / transportar *v.* llevar de un lugar a otro

traversed / atravesó *v.* cruzó

treacheries / traiciones *s.* actos desleales

trend / tendencia *s.* inclinacion o dirección en general

trespass / entrar sin autorización *v.* pasar a territorio ajeno sin permiso

trotted / trotar *v.* manera de correr de un animal cuadrúpedo en la cual la pata delantera y la pata trasera opuesta se usan al mismo tiempo

trudged / marchar fatigosamente *v.* caminar de manera cansada o con mucho esfuerzo

true / cierto *adj.* real; auténtico

tyrant / tirano *s.* gobernador cruel y severo

U

unbelievable / increíble *adj.* que no es probable; difícil de aceptar como cierto

undulating / ondulado *adj.* que se mueve en oleadas, como una serpiente

unethical / poco ético *adj.* que no respeta los estándares morales o los de un grupo

unique / único *adj.* sin otro de su especie

V

values / valores *s.* creencias de una persona o grupo

vanish / desvanecer *v.* desaparecer

verbal / verbal *adj.* que involucra o usa palabras o el habla

vigilance / vigilancia *s.* supervisión

vigorously / vigorosamente *adv.* con fuerza o energía

visual / visual *adj.* que se puede ver o entender por medio de la vista

vow / juramento *s.* promesa o compromiso

W

whirs / runrunear *v.* que vuela o se mueve rápidamente emitiendo un zumbido

win / ganar *v.* vencer; terminar por delante

winced / retorcer *v.* moverse por causa de dolor

wintry / invernal *adj.* muy frío, como el clima de invierno

Y

yearning / anhelo *s.* deseo profundo o ansioso

Index of Skills

Literary Analysis

Acts (drama), 454
Alliteration, 134, 311, 352, R1
Allusion, 236, 635, R1
Analogy, 672, R1
Anecdote, 183, 195, 205, R1
Antagonist, R1
Archetype, 631
Argument, 240, 273, 429, 521, 538, 589, 595, 603, R1
Author's influences, 206, 754, R1
Author's perspective, 184, 261, 588
Author's point of view, 182, 261
Author's purpose, 146, 182, 428, 523, 533
Author's style, R1
Autobiographical narrative, 184, 185, 193, 195, 269, 295, 403
Autobiographical writing, 181
Autobiography, 181, R1
Bandwagon/anti-bandwagon approach, 238
Biography, R1
Cause, 632, 640
Central idea, 183, 216, 422 See also Main idea
Character, 14, 17, 454, 456, R1
Character motives, 14, 17, 456
Character traits, 14, 456, R1
Characterization, 14, 16, 278, R1
    direct/indirect, 17, 28
Chronological organization, 100
Claim (assertion), lxiv, lxv, 273
Climax, 15, 18, 454, R1
Comedy, 455, R2
Conclusions, 58, 137
Concrete poem, R2
Conflict, 14, 15, 16, 17, 18, 44, 454, 457, 744, R2
Connotation, 182, 312, 534, R2
Context clues, 90, 316, 332
Cultural context, 628
Denotation, 312, 534, R2
Details
    key, 28, 206
Development. See Plot, R2

Dialect, 629, R2
Dialogue, 442, 454, 458, 485, R2
    drama, 454, 458, 485
Diaries and journals, 181, 409
Diction, 631
Direct characterization, 28
Drama, 442, 454, 455, 458, 485, R2
    See also Dialogue; Stage directions
Editorial, 181
Effect, 632, 640
Emotional appeal, 238
Essay, 181, 229, 374, 377, R2
    cause-and-effect, 702, 724
    comparison-and-contrast, 262, 374, 377, 423, 488, 578, 697
    expository, 181, 296, 396, 745, 758, R2
    how-to, 583
    narrative, 181, R2
    persuasive, 181, 240, 429, 434, R2
    problem-and-solution, 229, 538, 544
    reflective, 181, 419
Explanatory writing, 229, 331, 369, 451, 533
Exposition, 15, 18, R2
Expository essay, 181, 296, 396, 697, 758
Expository writing, 235, 732, 748, R3
Extended metaphor, R3
Fable, 629, 632, R3
Facts, 183, 194
Falling action, 15, 18
Fantasy, 676, 677, 697, R3
Fiction, R3
    theme, 14
Figurative language, 183, 312, 332, 333, R3
Figures of speech, R3 See Figurative language
Flashback, 73, 97, 268, R3
Flat character, R3
Folk literature, 614, 628
    characteristics, 628, 629
    structure, 614, 628, 630
    theme, 628, 630
Folk song, 629
Folk tale, 629, 632, R3
Foot, R3 See Meter
Foreshadowing, 73, 97, 408, R3
Functional texts, 181

Free verse, R3
Grounds (evidence), lxiv, lxv
Haiku, 342, 345, R3
Hyperbole, 312, 629
Idioms, 698
Imagery, 152, 364, 365, 367, R4
Images, 365, 367, R4
Indirect characterization, 28
Informative text, 262, 396, 487
Interpreting themes, 520
Ironic endings, 632, 637
Irony, 629, R4
Key idea, 183, 206, 216 See also Central idea
Legend, 629, R4
Letters, 181, 279, 331, R4
    to an author, 331
    business, 749
Limerick, 342, 348, R4
Lines (poetry), 310
Literary nonfiction, 180
Lyric poem, R4
Main character, R4
Main idea, 183, 206, 216, 422
Memoir, 181
Metaphor, 312, 332, R4
Meter, R4
Minor character, R4
Monologue, 205
Mood, 14, 216, 369, R4
Moral, R4
Motivation, R5 See also Character motives
Motive, R5 See also Character motives
Myth, 629, 640, 723, R5
Mythology, 629
Narration, R5
Narrative, 593, R5
    Narrative essay, 181, 593, 605, 757
Narrative nonfiction, 180, 184, 195, 757
Narrative poem, 313, R5
Narrator, 184, 310, R5 See also Author's perspective; Point of view
Nonfiction, 180, R5
    central ideas in, 180, 422
    elements, 180, 182
    forms of, 181

literary, 180
  narrative, 180, 184, 194
  structure, 180
  types of, 181
Novel, R5
Novella, R5
Objective Summary, 458
Onomatopoeia, 311, 352, R5
Opinions, 194, 748
Oral tradition, 628, 629, R5
Organization, 377
  chronological, 706
  flashback, 73, 97
Paraphrasing, 25, 342, 343, 352
Patterns, 631
Personification, 303, 312, 332, 629, 666, R5
Perspective, R5 See Author's perspective; Narrator; Point of view
Persuasive essay, 181, 429, 434, 749, 755
Persuasive speeches, 273, 536
Plot, 14, 18, 25, 73, R6
  drama, 454, 457, 458
  elements, 15, 18, 73, 457
  folk literature, 614, 628, 631
  short story, 14, 15, 18, 592
  structure, 14, 18, 73, 97
  techniques, 97
Poetry, 302, 310, 313, R6 See also Meter; Rhyme; Rhythm
  concrete poem, 313, 342
  elements, 310
  forms, 313, 342
  free verse, 313
  haiku, 313, 342, 345
  limerick, 313, 342, 348
  lyric poem, 313
  narrative poem, 313 See Narrative poem
  song lyrics, 132
Point of view, 184, 261, 588, R6 See also Author's perspective;
  first/third person, 104, 184
  nonfiction, 182
Prediction, 18, 184
Props, 454
Prose, R6
Protagonist, R6
Quotations, 402
Reflective essay, 181, 419
Refrain, 631, R6
Repetition, 311, 352, R6
Resolution, R6 See also Plot, 15, 18, 44, 454, 744

Response to literature
  letter,
    review, 521, 532
Rhetorical devices, lxvi, lxvii
Rhyme, 302, 310, 311, 316, 317, R7
Rhyme scheme, R7
Rhythm, 302, 310, 311, 316, 317, R7
Rising action, 15, 18
Round character, R7
Rubrics, 109, 247, 381, 545
Scenes (drama), 454, 457, R7
Science fiction, R7
Screenplay, 455
Script, 442, 454, 455, 458
Sensory language, R7
  poetry,
Set, 454
Setting, 14, 16, 129, 454, R7
Short story, 4, 14, R7
  analyzing, 4
  characterization, 14
  elements, 4
  structure of, 4
Simile, 312, 332, 388, 395, R7
Soliloquy, 456
Song lyrics, 132
Sound devices, 311, 352
  poetry, 302, 311, 352
Speaker, 310, R7 See also Narrator
Speeches, 270, 580
Stage directions, 442, 454, 458, 488, 499, R7
Staging, R7
Stanza, 303, 310, R7
Static character, R7
Step-by-step organization, 538
Structure
  folk literature, 614, 628
  poetry, 302, 310, 313
  short story, 15, 16
Supporting details, 244
Surprise ending, R7
Suspense, R8
Symbol, 418, 630, R8
Symbolism, R8
Teleplay, 455
Testimony, 238
Theme, 14, 58, 312, 313, 457, 577, 630, 640, 650, R8 See also Universal theme

Tone/emotion, 180, 182, 194, 203, 312, 353, 602, R8
Topic sentence, 706
Tragedy, 455, R8
  tragic flaw, 455
  tragic hero, 455
Turning point, R8 See Climax
Universal theme, 628, 650, 651, 656, 661, R8
Word choice, 182, 290

Comprehension Skills

Asking questions, 100, 103, 105, 302, R9
Author's conclusions, evaluating, 213
Author's purpose, recognizing, 180, 182, 185, 206, 261, 428, 523, 533
Authors' styles, comparing, 180, 182, 522
Autobiography, comparing, 193
Cause and effect, identifying, 632, 633, 640, 702, 704
Characters' motives, comparing, 14, 17, 456
Close reading, 4, 11, 614, 632
  drama, 488
  fiction, 4, 27, 45, 59
  folk literature, 614, 628, 632, 633, 641, 667
  nonfiction, 207, 217
  poetry, 302, 312, 333
  short story, 4, 11, 15, 27, 29, 45, 59
Compare and contrast, 235, 261, 296, 374, 423, 442, 488, 523, 533, 578, 676
  analyzing, 519
Conclusions, drawing, 55, 58, 59, 69, 96, 191, 213, 519
Connections, to identify, 64
Context clues, using, 235, 302, 316, 317, 332, 333
Details, important/unimportant, identifying, 193, 216, 376, 442
Details, recognizing/using, 28, 76, 193, 302, 523, 704
Elements of fantasy, comparing, 676, 677, 697
Evidence, evaluating, 194
Fact/opinion, recognizing, 194, 195, 196, 238
Fiction, comparing, 72
Flashback, comparing, 72, 73, 97
Foreshadowing, 75, 76, 408, R3
  comparing, 72, 73, 97

Generalizations, making, 55, 368

Imagery, comparing, 364, 369

Inferences, making, 28, 29, 31, 41, 44, 55, 87, 302, 663

Key details, identifying, 4, 11, 76, 183, 191, 193, 206, 442
main idea map,

Main events, rereading to identify, 485, 639

Main idea, identifying, 206, 207, 213, 217, 485

Main ideas, connecting and clarifying, 375

Multiple-step instructions, following, 100

Nonfiction, comparing, 181
chart, 180, 181, 183

Organizational features, analyzing, 180, 376, 377

Paraphrasing, 25, 100, 342

Poetry reading guide, using, 365 181

Predictions, making, 18, 19, 25, 184

Prior knowledge, using, 44

Propaganda techniques, recognizing, 238

Purpose for reading, setting, 650, 651, 657, 666

Questions, asking, 100, 103, 105

Reading ahead, to verify predictions, 666

Reading fluency, 302, 675
reading aloud for, Reading rate, adjusting, 663

Sensory language, comparing, 302

Setting, 14, 16 comparing,

Structural features, identifying, 15, 16, 18, 73, 184, 194, 216, 312, 631, 736

Summarizing, 451, 458, 459, 487

Theme, 58, 69
comparing, 630, 677

Vocabulary

Big Question/Academic Vocabulary, 3, 163, 184, 299, 441

Building speaking vocabulary, 163

Domain-specific academic vocabulary, 3

General academic vocabulary, 163, 299, 441, 613

Increasing word knowledge, 163, 613

Language Study
Connotations and Denotations, 312, 534
Idioms,
Using a Dictionary and Thesaurus, 98
Word Origins, 24, 40, 54, 68, 190, 212,

226, 236, 328, 338, 360, 484
Etymology, 98
Words with Multiple-Meaning, 370

Grammar, Usage, and Mechanics

Action verbs, 204, R20

Adjective phrase, R21

Adjectives, 330, 340, R20

Adverb phrase, R21

Adverbs, 330, 340, R20

Antecedent, 107

Apostrophes, R23

Appositive phrase, 486, 543, 576, R21

Capitalization, R23

Clauses, 664, 674, R21

Colons, R23

Commas, 379, 705, R23

Common nouns, 26, R20

Comparative adjectives, 342

Comparative modifiers, 342, R22

Complements, 638, 648, R20

Complete predicate, 362, R20

Complete subject, R20

Complex sentences, 674, R21

Compound-complex sentences, 674, R21

Compound predicate, R20

Compound sentences, 674, R21

Compound subject, 362, R20

Conjunctions, 350, 379, R20

Connotation, 312

Coordinating conjunctions, 379, R20

Correlative conjunctions, R20

Declarative sentences, 362, R21

Demonstrative adjectives, R20

Demonstrative pronouns, R20

Denotation, 312

Dependent clause, 664, 674

Dictionary, using, 98

Direct object, 648, 707, R21

Exclamation mark, R23

Exclamatory sentences, 362, R21

Future perfect tense, 228, R21

Future tense, 214, R21

Gerund/gerund phrase, 520, 543, R21

Glossary of common usage, R22

Helping verbs, R20

Homophones, 109

Hyphens, R23

Idioms, 698

Imperative sentences, 362, R21

Indefinite pronouns, 56, R20

Independent clause, 664, 674, R21

Indirect object, 648, 707, R21

Infinitive phrase, R21

Intensive pronouns, 56

Interjections, 350, R20

Interrogative pronouns, 56, R20

Interrogative sentences, 362, R21

Irregular verbs, 192, 245

Linking verbs, 204, 638, R20

Modifiers, 330, 340, R22

Nouns, 26, R20

Objective complement, R21

Objects, 648, 707

Parentheses, 707

Participial phrase, 520, 543, R21

Participles, 520

Past participle, 245

Past perfect tense, 228, 262, R21

Past tense, 214, 262, R21

Perfect tenses, 228

Periods, R21

Personal pronouns, 42, R20

Phrase, R21

Possessive nouns, 26

Possessive pronouns, 42

Predicate, R20

Predicate adjectives, 638, 707, R21

Predicate nominative, R21

Predicate nouns, 638, 707

Preposition, R20 prepositional phrase, 486, 543, R21

Present participle, 245

Present perfect tense, 228, R21

Present tense, 214, R21

Pronoun-antecedent agreement, 107, R22

Pronoun case, 70, R21
Nominative, 70, R21
Objective, 70, R21
Possessive, 70, R21

Pronouns, 42, 56, 107, R20

Proper adjectives, R20

Proper nouns, 26, R20

Punctuation, 27, R23

Question marks, R23

Quotation marks, R23

Reflexive pronouns, 56, R20
Regular verbs, 192
Semicolons, R23
Sentence fragments, 362
Sentence types, 362, R21
Sentences, 362, R20
Simple predicate, 362, R20
Simple sentences, 674, R21
Simple subject, 362, R20
Simple tenses, 214
Subject, R20
Subject complement, 638, R21
Subject-verb agreement, 378, R22
Subordinate clause, 664, R21
Subordinating conjunctions, R20
Superlative adjectives, 340
Superlative modifiers, 340, R22
Synonyms, 260
Thesaurus, using, 98
Troublesome verbs, 245
Verb tenses, 192, 214, 228, 262, R21
Verbs, 192, 204, 245, 262, R20 See also
   Verb tenses, R21
Words with multiple meanings, 370, 371

Writing Applications

Anecdote, personal, 195, 205
Argument, 57, 235, 240, 273, 538, 589,
   595, 603, 739, 749
Autobiographical narrative, 185, 269, 737
   Writing Process, 538
Business letter, model, R15
Cause-and-effect essay, 702, 724
   Student Model, 708
   Writing Process, 702
Compare-and-contrast essay, 296, 374,
   377, 380, 423, 488, 519, 578, 649, 697
   Student Model, 380
   Venn diagram, 376, 423, 519, 533
   Writing Process, 374
Description of a character, 71
Descriptive essay
   Student Model, 246
   Writing Workshop,
Essay comparing imagery, 369
Essay evaluating evidence, 240, Timed
   Writing,
Explanation, Timed Writing, 97, 369, 533,
   697, 733, 745
Fable, 639

Fictional narrative, 102, 433, 605 Timed
   Writing, 135
Invitation, 675
Journal entry, 215, 293, 545
Letter, 279, 331, R14
Narrative, 757
   Conventions, 757
   Development of ideas, 757
   Language, 757
   Organization, 757
   Purpose, focus, 757
Personal letter, model, R14
Persuasive essay, 156, 429, 434,
   749, 755
Rubric for self-assessment, 435
   Writing Process, 240
Persuasive speech, 57, 273
Poem, 303, 306, 341, 351
Problem-and-solution essay, 538
   Student Model, 544
   Writing Workshop,
Prose description, 363
Response to Big Questions
   Do we need words to communicate
      well? 298, 309, 332, 352
   How do we decide who we are?
      458, 522
   How much do our communities shape
      us? 632, 640, 676, 756
   Is conflict always bad? 18, 58, 72
   What is important to know?
      184, 194
Response to drama/review, 521
Response to literature/letter, 331
   Student Model,
   Writing Workshop,
Response to literature/review, 305
   Student Model,
   Writing Workshop,
Sentence starters
   Do we need words to communicate
      well? 316, 332, 352, 364
   How do we decide who we are?
      458, 522
   How much do our communities shape
      us? 632, 640, 650, 666, 676
   Is conflict always bad?, 11
Short story
   Student Model, 108
   Timed writing,
   Writing Process, 102
Statement of positions, Timed Writing,
   235
Summary of literature, 487

Writing Strategies

Prewriting:
Argument, build, 241, 273, 589
Art and photos, review, 103
Audience, define, 539
Brainstorm, 703
Characters, create, 103
Chart, use, 43, 242, 541, 697
Conflicts, discuss/list, 103
Counter-arguments, anticipate, 241
Decide which elements are important,
   538
Details, add, 539
Details, chart, 103, 376
Details, gather, 102, 376, 539
Details, organize, 376, 539
Evidence, collect, 241, 538
Freewriting, 103
Graphic organizer, use, 237, 241,
   369, 535
Graphics/illustrations, match to
   text, 706
Ideas, support, 244, 541
Media sources, review, 241, 703
Note cards, use, 725
Notes, jot/take, 725
Notes, organize, 725
Outline, use, 725
Position, present/support, 235, 244
Primary sources, locate, 374, 538
Round table, organize, 241
Solution strategy, consider, 229, 540
Solutions, explain, 540
Solutions, justify, 540, 541
State problem, 540, 541
Step-by-step solutions, provide, 538,
   540, 541
T-chart, use, 703
Thesis statement, develop, 240, 375
Title, choose, 103
Tone, use appropriate, 105
Topic, choose, 375, 539
Topic, narrow, 193, 241, 375, 539
Topic list, create, 375
Topic web, create/use, 703
Two-sided topic, select, 241
Venn diagram, use, 376, 533
Word choice, use appropriate,
   243, 290
Drafting:
Audience, consider, 539, 540
Audience, target, 242, 539
Block method of organization, follow,
   377, 578
Cause and effect, organize to
   show, 704
Cause and effect, show, 704
Causes/effects, identify, 704

Causes/effects, show links, 706
Conclusion, write, 396, 540
Counter-arguments, address, 156, 157, 242, 435
Details, include, 376, 540
Details, organize, 376, 540, 704
Facts, summarize, 539, 540
Ideas, clarify/support, 157, 541, 759
Information, organize, 143
Information, present adequate, 704
Introduction, plan, 376, 759
Introduction, write, 376, 396, 759
Main ideas, support with facts, 242, 540
Organization pattern, follow, 377
Organizational structure, choose, 242, 377
Plagiarism, avoid, 435, 759
Plot, develop, 104, 665
Plot diagram, use, 104
Point-by-point method of organization, follow, 377, 578
Point of view, write from, 104
Points, support, 242, 244
Sensory details, include, 104
Thesis, state, 242, 244, 540, 704
Thesis statement, prepare, 242, 704
Tone, use appropriate, 242
Transitional words, use, 244, 376, 704
Transitions, use, 376, 704
Word choice, review, 243, 290

Revising:
Accuracy, confirm, 157, 706
Balance, check, 378
Bead chart, use, 106
Cause/effect, confirm link, 706
Chart, use, 542
Choppy sentences, combine, 543, 707
Connections, identify and strengthen, 106
Coordinating conjunctions, using, 379
Dialogue, use, 106
Identify sentences to combine, 543
Improve support, 244, 542
Irregular verbs, identifying/correcting errors, 245
Logical connections, create, 706
Narrative voice, 105
Opening, strengthen, 542
Organization, check, 378, 706
Peer review, use, 244, 542, 706
Peer review, use/consider, 378, 542
Point of view, evaluate, 106
Pronoun/antecedent agreement, identifying/fixing errors, 107
Punctuation, identify/correct errors, 379, 705

Related details, color-code,
Sentence functions, identify/correct errors, 379
Sentence length, vary, 543
Sentence structure, evaluate, 543
Sentences, combine for variety, 379, 543, 707
Sentences, combine with participial phrases, 543
Sentences, show relationships, 244
Sentences, vary, 543
Short sentences, combine, 543
Subject-verb agreement, check, 378
Topic sentence, write, 706
Transitions, check, 106
Troublesome verbs, identifying/correcting errors, 245
Verb errors, identifying/correcting, 245
Word choices, vary, 106, 243, 290
Word traps, avoid, 243

Writer's Toolbox:
Conventions, 107, 245, 378, 379, 543, 705, 707
Ideas, 541
Organization, 378, 541, 705
Sentence fluency, 244, 379, 543, 707
Word choice, 105, 243, 245, 290
Voice, 105, 107

Editing/Proofreading:
Double comparisons, avoid, 381
Grammar errors, correct, 245, 759
Sources, credit, 157, 297, 435, 607, 759
Spelling, focus on, 109
Spelling errors, correct, 247
Suffixes, focus on, 545

Publishing/Presenting:
Audio recording, 381
Bulletin board posting, 247
Group discussion, 279, 756
Oral presentation, 545
Picture essay, 381
Publication, submitting for, 109
Reading, 109
Speech, 247
Submission to publisher, 545

Rubric for Self-Assessment:
4-point scale rubric, 109, 247, 381, 545, 759, R17
6-point scale rubric, R17
Argumentative essay, 157, 383, 435, R19
Cause-and-effect essay, 709
Compare-and-contrast essay, 297, 381
Holistic rubric, R16
Problem-and-solution essay, 545
Short story, 109

Speaking and Listening
Activities:
Advertisement, evaluate, 238, 239
Conversation, written, 193
Debate, 423
Discussing literature, 589
Discussion, informal, 6, 11, 71, 154, 162, 229, 238, 269, 403, 578, 604, 739
Dramatic reading, 675
Dramatic poetry reading, 341
Emotion, identify, 700
Group discussion, 11, 135, 262, 279, 285, 291, 294, 409, 429, 432, 444, 521, 603, 625, 724, 734, 745, 749, 755
Instructional presentation, 745
Literature circles, R9
Monologue, 205, 456
Mood, identify,
Multi-step oral directions, carry out, 100, 701
Oral presentation, 725
Oral report, 639
Oral response to literature, 700, 701
Panel discussion, 273, 583, 733
Persuasive message, evaluate, 238
Persuasive speech, 536, 537
Problem-solution proposal, 372, 373
Tone, identify, 700

Research
Research and Technology:
Annotated bibliography entries, 649
Brochure, 27
Chart, compare-and-contrast, 43, 57
Illustrated booklet, 331
Multimedia presentation, 487
Presentation, 57, 215, 263, 273, 285, 351, 419, 423, 429, 579, 603, 733, 755
Research project, 304, 403
Resume for a poet, 363
Written and visual report, 291, 397, 431, 665, 737, 749

Research the Topic:
The Gold Rush, 131, 135, 143, 147, 153
Baseball, 263, 269, 273, 279, 285, 291, 293
Determination 397, 403, 409, 419, 423, 429, 431
Mark Twain, 579, 583, 589, 593, 595, 603
People and Animals, 725, 733, 737, 739, 745, 749, 755

Index of Authors and Titles

The following authors and titles appear in the print and online versions of Pearson Literature.

2012 Pet Ownership Statistics, 738

A

Abuelito Who, 337
Achebe, Chinua, 668
Adams, John, 420
According to Mark Twain, 594
Adventures of Isabel, 322
Aiken, Joan, 74
Alexander, Lloyd, 652
Alvarez, Julia, 196
Angelou, Maya, 324
Angela Duckworth and the Research on "Grit," 398
Anonymous, 350
Ant and the Dove, The, 636
April Rain Song, 338
Arachne, 642
Art, Architecture, and Learning in Egypt, 233

B

Ballou, Mary B., 138
Bashò, Matsuo, 347
Birds Struggle to ecover from Egg Thefts of 1800s, 148
Black Cowboy, Wild Horses: A True Story, 620
Black Ships Before Troy: The Story of the Iliad, 615
Bradbury, Ray, 410
Brighton Beach Memoirs, from, 443
Brooks, Gwendolyn, 362
Bruchac, Joseph, 446
Burns, Ken, 256

C

Carroll, Lewis, 326
Case of the Monkeys That Fell From the Trees, The, 726
Charles, Dorthi, 349
Chinese and African Americans in the Gold Rush, 144
Circuit, The, 60
Cisneros, Sandra, 337
Clemens, Olivia Susan (Susy), 96

Clemens, Samuel Langhorn. *See* Twain, Mark
Concrete Cat, 349
Coolidge, Olivia E., 642
Cummings, E. E., 368
Cynthia in the Snow, 362

D

Dahl, Roald, 688
Determination, 430
Dickinson, Emily, 340
Dream Within a Dream, A, 321
Drive-In Movies, The, 186
Dunham, H. J., 132
Durbin, Richard, 270
Dust of Snow, 370

E

Encounter With An Interviewer, An, 596

F

Fairies' Lullaby, The, from A Midsummer Night's Dream, 360
Fame Is a Bee, 340
Fenway Park Celebrates 100 Years as America's Oldest Working Major League Park, 280
Filipović, Zlata, 168
Frost, Robert, 370

G

George, Jean Craighead, 8
Gesner, Clark, 524
Giovanni, Nikki, 339
Gluskabe and Old Man Winter, 446
Gold Rush: The Journey by Land, 136
Greenfield, Eloise, 208

H

Haiku, 347
Hanford, Emily, 398
Hansen, Joyce, 30
Happiness is a Charming Charlie Brown at Orlando Rep, 530
Hughes, Langston, 338

I

Ihimaera, Witi, 718

J

Jackie Robinson: Justice at Last, 256
James and the Giant Peach, from, 688
Jeremiah's Song, 88
Jiménez, Francisco, 60
Juster, Norton, 460, 490

K

Keller, Helen, 424
King of Mazy May, The, 118
Kipling, Rudyard, 678

L

Langston Terrace, 208
Lau, Edie, 148
Lester, Julius, 620
"Letter on Thomas Jefferson," from, 420
Life Doesn't Frighten Me, 324
Limerick, 350
Line, Molly, 280
Lob's Girl, 74
London, Jack, 118

M

MacDermid, Matthew, 530
Mark Twain's First "Vacation," 590
Memories of an All-American Girl, 264
Merriam, Eve, 392
Midsummer Night's Dream, from *A,* 648
Morrison, Lillian, 348
Mowgli's Brothers from The Jungle Book, 678
My Papa, Mark Twain, 584
Myers, Walter Dean, 88

N

Names/Nombres, 196
Nanus, Susan, 460, 490
Nash, Ogden, 322
Navajo, 305
Newman, Mark, 286
No Thank You, 358

O

Ode to Family Photographs, 310
"Old Grandfather and His Little Grandson, The," 5
Old Woman Who Lived With the Wolves, The, 740
Oranges, 308

P

Partridge, Elizabeth, 165
Pauls, Carmen, 264
Paz, Octavio, 357
Phantom Tollbooth, The, 460, 490
Pigman & Me, The, from, 218
Poe, Edgar Allan, 321
Preserving a Great American Symbol, 280
Prince and the Pauper, The, 554
Prince and the Pauper, The, from, 572

Q

Quinlan, Susan E., 726

R

Race to the End of the Earth, 404
Rescuers to Carry Oxygen Masks for Pets, 734
Rylant, Cynthia, 20

S

Satellites and Sea Lions, 746
Scheller, William G., 404

Seven Wonders of the World, The, 231
Shakespeare, William, 360
Sidewalk Racer or On the Skateboard, The, 348
Silverstein, Shel, 358
Simile: Willow and Ginkgo, 392
Simon, Neil, 443
Singer, Isaac Bashevis, 46
Soto, Gary, 186, 308, 310
Sound of Summer Running, The, 410
Southpaw, The, 274
Stage Fright, 104
Standing Bear, Chief Luther, 740
Stone, The, 652
Stray, 20
Sutcliff, Rosemary, 615

T

Tail, The, 30
Ted Williams Baseball Card, 292
This Land Was Made for You and Me, 165
Thurber, James, 634
Tiger Who Would Be King, The, 634
To Klondyke We've Paid Our Fare, 132
Tolstoy, Leo, 5, 636
Turkeys, 750
Twain, Mark, 554, 572, 580, 590, 594, 596
Twelfth Song of Thunder, 305

V

Viorst, Judith, 274

W

Walrus and the Carpenter, The, 326
Ward, Geoffrey C., 256
Water, 424
Whale Rider, Prologue from The, 718
White, Bailey, 750
who knows if the moon's, 368
Why the Tortoise's Shell Is Not Smooth, 668
Why We Love Baseball, 286
Wind and water and stone, 357
Woman's View of the Gold Rush, A, 138
World is Not a Pleasant Place to Be, The, 339
Wounded Wolf, The, 8

Y

You're a Good Man, Charlie Brown, from, 524

Z

Zindel, Paul, 218
Zlata's Diary, from, 168
Zlateh the Goat, 46

Additional Selections: Author and Title Index

The following authors and titles appear in the Online Literature Library.

A

Aaron's Gift
Aesop
Alegría, Ricardo E.
All-American Slurp, The
Alphabet
Ankylosaurus
Anonymous
Asimov, Isaac

B

Backwoods Boy, A, from *Lincoln: A Photobiography*
Baker, Russell
Becky and the Wheels-and-Brake Boys
Benét, Rosemary
Benét, Stephen Vincent
Berry, James

C

California Sea Lions
Chang, Diana
Childhood and Poetry
Child on Top of a Greenhouse
Clarke, Arthur C.
Crippled Boy, A

D

Dogan, Reginald T.
Dragon, Dragon

E

Eleven

F

Feathered Friend
Field, Rachel
Fitzgerald, F. Scott
Freedman, Russell

Freedom Writer's Diary, from Foreword to *The*
Fulghum, Robert
Fun They Had, The

G

Gardner, John
Greyling

H

Haiku
Hamilton, Virginia
Hard as Nails
He Lion, Bruh Bear, and Bruh Rabbit
Herriot, James
Homecoming, The

J

Jake Wood Baseball League Is the Start of Something Special

K

Katz, Rachel

L

Lady and the Spider, The
La Leña Buena
Letter from a Concentration Camp
Letter to Scottie, A
Levoy, Myron
Library Card Application
Library Card Information
Lion and the Bulls, The
Limerick

M

Market Square Dog, The
McKissack, Fredrick, Jr.
McKissack, Patricia C.
Metric Metric: It's so nice, we'll say it twice!

Musò Soseki
My Heart Is in the Highlands

N

Namioka, Lensey
NASA Finally Goes Metric
Neruda, Pablo
Nye, Naomi Shihab

P

Parade
Prelutsky, Jack

R

Roethke, Theodore
Roll of Thunder, Hear My Cry, from

S

Santos, John Phillip
Saying Yes
Shutout, The
Something to Declare, from
Soseki, Musò

T

Taylor, Mildred D.
Tran, My-Van
Three Wishes, The

W

Why Monkeys Live in Trees: African Folk Tale
Wilbur Wright and Orville Wright
World of Escher Tessellation Contest

U

Uchida, Yoshiko

Y

Yep, Laurence
Yolen, Jane

Acknowledgments

Grateful acknowledgment is made to the following for copyrighted material:

English—Language Arts Content Standards for California Public Schools reproduced by permission, California Department of Education, CD Press, 1430 N Street, Suite 3207, Sacramento, CA 95814.

Airmont Publishing Company, Inc. "Water" by Helen Keller from *The Story of My Life*. Copyright © 1965 by Airmont Publishing Company, Inc. Used by permission of Airmont Publishing Company, Inc.

Ricardo E. Alegría "The Three Wishes" selected and adapted by Ricardo E. Alegría from *The Three Wishes: A Collection of Puerto Rican Folktales*. Copyright © 1969 by Ricardo E. Alegría. Used by permission of Ricardo E. Alegría.

American Red Cross National Headquarters "Red Cross Helps Florida Residents Recover From Tornadoes" by Arindam Mukherjee, December 29, 2006 posted on *www.redcross.org*. Used by permission courtesy of the American National Red Cross. All rights reserved in all countries.

The Associated Press "Rescuers to Carry Oxygen Masks for Pets" from *www.postcrescent.com*. Copyright © 2007 The Associated Press. Used with permission. All rights reserved.

Atheneum Books for Young Readers, an imprint of Simon & Schuster "Stray" by Cynthia Rylant from *Every Living Thing*. Copyright © 1985 by Cynthia Rylant. Used by permission of Atheneum Books for Young Readers, an imprint of Simon & Schuster Children's Publishing Division.

The Bancroft Library, Administrative Offices "Letter from a Concentration Camp" by Yoshiko Uchida from *The Big Book For Peace*. Text copyright © 1990 by Yoshiko Uchida. Courtesy of the Bancroft Library University of California, Berkeley. Used with permission.

Bantam Doubleday Dell Publishing "Black Ships Before Troy: The Story of The Iliad" by Rosemary Sutcliff from *Delacorte Press*. Copyright © 1993 by Frances Lincoln Limited.

Susan Bergholz Literary Services "Abuelito Who" by Sandra Cisneros from *My Wicked Wicked Ways*. Copyright © 1987 by Sandra Cisneros. Published by Third Woman Press and in hardcover by Alfred A. Knopf. Used by permission of Third Woman Press and Susan Bergholz Literary Services, New York. "Names/Nombres" by Julia Alvarez from *Nuestro, March, 1985*. Copyright © 1985 by Julia Alvarez. First published in *Nuestro. March, 1985*. "Something to Declare" (Introduction) by Julia Alvarez. Copyright © 1998 by Julia Alvarez. From *Something To Declare,* published by Plume, an imprint of Penguin Group (USA), in 1999 and originally in hardcover by Algonquin Books of Chapel Hill. "Eleven" from *Woman Hollering Creek* by Sandra Cisneros. Copyright © 1991 by Sandra Cisneros. Published by Vintage Books, a division of Random House, Inc., New York and originally in hardcover by Random House, Inc. Used by permission of Susan Bergholz Literary Services, New York, NY and Lamy, NM. All rights reserved.

Robert Bly "Friends All of Us" from *Childhood and Poetry* by Pablo Neruda. Reprinted from *Neruda and Vallejo: Selected Poems,* by Robert Bly, Beacon Press, Boston, 1993. Used by permission.

BOA Editions, Ltd. c/o The Permissions Company "Alphabet" by Naomi Shihab Nye from *Fuel*. Copyright © 1998 by Naomi Shihab Nye. All rights reserved. Used by permission of BOA Editions Ltd., www.boaeditions.org.

Georges Borchardt, Inc. "Dragon, Dragon" from *Dragon, Dragon And Other Tales* by John Gardner. Copyright © 1975 by Boskydell Artists, Ltd. Used by permission of Georges Borchardt, Inc., for the Estate of John Gardner.

Brandt & Hochman Literary Agents, Inc. "Wilbur Wright and Orville Wright" by Stephen Vincent Benét, from *A Book of Americans* by Rosemary and Stephen Vincent Benét. Copyright © 1933 by Rosemary and Stephen Vincent Benét. Copyright © renewed 1961 by Rosemary Carr Benét. "Lob's Girl" from *A Whisper in the Night* by Joan Aiken. Delacorte Press. Copyright © 1984 by Joan Aiken Enterprises, Ltd. Used by permission of Brandt & Hochman Literary Agents, Inc.

John Brewton, George M. Blackburn & Lorraine A. Blackburn "Limerick (Accidents--More or Less Fatal)" from *Laughable Limericks*. Copyright © 1965 by Sara and John E. Brewton. Used by permission of Brewton, Blackburn and Blackburn.

Brooks Permissions "Cynthia In the Snow" from *Bronzeville Boys and Girls* by Gwendolyn Brooks. Copyright © 1956 by Gwendolyn Brooks. Used by consent of Brooks Permissions.

Curtis Brown Ltd. From *The Pigman & Me (Learning the Rules)* by Paul Zindel. Copyright © 1992 by Paul Zindel. First published by HarperCollins. "Adventures of Isabel" by Ogden Nash from *Parents Keep Out*. Originally published by *Nash's Pall Mall Magazine*. Copyright © 1936 by Ogden Nash. All rights reserved. "Greyling" by Jane Yolen from *Greyling: A Picture Story from the Islands*. Copyright © 1968, 1996 by Jane Yolen. First published by Penguin Putnam. Used by permission of Curtis Brown, Ltd.

Diana Chang (Diana C. Herrmann) "Saying Yes" by Diana Chang. Copyright by Diana Chang. Used by permission of the author.

Chronicle Books "Oranges" from *New and Selected Poems* by Gary Soto. Copyright © 1995 by Gary Soto. Visit www.chroniclebooks.com. Used with permission of Chronicle Books LLC, San Francisco.

Clarion Books, a division of Houghton Mifflin "A Backwoods Boy" from *Lincoln: A Photobiography*. Copyright © 1987 by Russell Freedman. Used by permission of Clarion Books/Houghton Mifflin Company. All rights reserved.

Ruth Cohen Literary Agency, Inc. "The All-American Slurp" by Lensey Namioka, copyright © 1987, from *Visions*, ed. by Donald R. Gallo. Used by permission of Lensey Namioka. All rights reserved by the Author.

Don Congdon Associates, Inc. "The Sound of Summer Running" by Ray Bradbury from *The Saturday Evening Post, 2/18/56*. Copyright © 1956 by the Curtis Publishing Company, copyright © renewed 1984 by Ray Bradbury. "Hard As Nails" from *The Good Times* by Russell Baker. Copyright © 1989 by Russell Baker. Used by permission of Don Congdon Associates, Inc.

Gary N. DaSilva Excerpt from *Brighton Beach Memoirs* by Neil Simon from *McGraw Hill Glencoe*, copyright © 1984 by Neil Simon.

Dell Publishing, a division of Random House, Inc. "Jeremiah's Song" by Walter Dean Myers, from *Visions* by Donald R. Gallo, Editor, copyright © 1987 by Donald R. Gallo. "The Tail" Copyright © 1992 by Joyce Hansen from *Funny You Should Ask* by David Gale, Editor. Used by permission of Dell Publishing, a division of Random House, Inc.

Dial Books for Young Readers, a division of Penguin Young Readers Group *Black Cowboy, Wild Horses* written by Julius Lester and illustrated by Jerry Pinkney. Text copyright © 1998 by Julius Lester. Illustrations copyright © 1998 by Jerry Pinkney. "Gluskabe and Old Man Winter: Abenaki" by Joseph Bruchac from *Pushing Up the Sky*. Copyright © 2000 by Joseph Bruchac, text. Used by permission of Dial Books for Young Readers, A Division of Penguin Young Readers Group, A Member of Penguin Group (USA).

Doubleday, a division of Random House, Inc. "Child on Top of a Greenhouse" by Theodore Roethke from *The Collected Poems of Theodore Roethke*, copyright © 1946 by Editorial Publications, Inc. "The Fun They Had" from *Isaac Asimov: The Complete Stories of Vol. I*, by Isaac Asimov, copyright © 1957 by Isaac Asimov. Used by permission of Doubleday, a division of Random House, Inc.

Dover Publications, Inc. "Rendezvous with Despair" by Thomas E. Dewey from *The World's Great Speeches*, copyright © 1958, 1973 by Dover Publications, Inc.

Paul S. Eriksson "My Papa, Mark Twain" by Susy Clemens from *Small Voices* by Josef and Dorothy Berger. Copyright © 1966 by Josef and Dorothy Berger in arrangement with Paul S. Eriksson, Publisher. Used by permission.

Jean Grasso Fitzpatrick "The Ant and the Dove" by Leo Tolstoy from *Fables and Folktales Adapted from Tolstoy*. Translated by Jean Grasso Fitzpatrick. Used with permission.

Florida Fish and Wildlife Conservation Commission Manatee Decal Art Contest from *http://myfwc.com/manatee/decals/contest2007.htm*. Copyright © 2007 Florida Fish and Wildlife Conservation Commission. Used by permission.

Samuel French, Inc. "The Phantom Tollbooth" from *The Phantom Tollbooth: A Children's Play in Two Acts* by Susan Nanus and Norton Juster. Copyright © 1977 by Susan Nanus and Norton Juster. Used by permission of Samuel French, Inc. All rights reserved. CAUTION: Professionals and amateurs are hereby warned that "The Phantom Tollbooth," being fully protected under the copyright laws of the United States of America, the British Commonwealth countries, including Canada, and the other countries of the Copyright Union, is subject to royalty. All rights, including professional, amateur, motion picture, recitation, lecturing, public reading, radio, television and cable broadcasting, and the rights of translation into foreign languages, are strictly reserved. Any inquiry regarding the availability of performance rights, or the purchase of individual copies of the authorized acting edition, must be directed to Samuel French, Inc., 45 West 25th Street, NY, NY 10010 with other locations in Hollywood and Toronto, Canada.

Greenwillow Books, a division of HarperCollins "Ankylosaurus" by Jack Prelutsky from *Tyrannosaurus Was a Beast*. Text copyright © 1988 by Jack Prelutsky. Used by permission of HarperCollins Publishers.

Harcourt, Inc. "Ode to Family Photographs" from *Neighborhood Odes*, copyright © 1992 by Gary Soto. Used by permission of Harcourt, Inc.

Harcourt Education Limited "Why the Tortoise's Shell Is Not Smooth" by Chinua Achebe from *Things Fall Apart*. Copyright © 1959 by Chinua Achebe. Used with permission of Harcourt Education.

HarperCollins Publishers, Inc. "No Thank You" by Shel Silverstein from *Falling Up*. Copyright © 1996 by Shel Silverstein. All rights reserved. "Zlateh the Goat" by Isaac Bashevis Singer from *Zlateh the Goat and Other Stories*. Text copyright © 1966 by Isaac Bashevis Singer, copyright © renewed 1994 by Alma Singer. Art copyright © 1966 by Maurice Sendak, copyright © renewed 1994 by Maurice Sendak. "The Homecoming" by Laurence Yep from *The Rainbow People*. Copyright © 1989 by Laurence Yep. From *The Wounded Wolf* by Jean Craighead George. Text copyright © 1978 by Jean Craighead George. Used by permission of HarperCollins Publishers. "Langston Terrace" by Eloise Greenfield, from *Childtimes: A Three-Generation Memoir*, copyright © 1979 by Eloise Greenfield and Lessie Jones Little. "Aaron's Gift" from *The Witch of Fourth Street and Other Stories* by Myron Levoy. Text copyright © 1972 by Myron Levoy.

Harper's Magazine "Preserving a Great American Symbol," (originally titled "Desecrating America") by Richard Durbin from *Harper's Magazine, October 1989, p.32*. Copyright © 1989 by *Harper's Magazine*. All rights reserved. Reproduced from the October issue by special permission.

Harvard University Press "Fame Is a Bee" (#1763) by Emily Dickinson is used by permission of the publishers and the Trustees of Amherst College from *The Poems of Emily Dickinson*, Thomas H. Johnson, editor, Cambridge, Mass.: The Belknap Press of Harvard University Press, Copyright © 1951, 1955, 1979, 1983 by the President and Fellows of Harvard College.

Sara Hightower Regional Library System Sara Hightower Regional Library Systems Card Policies and Application from *http://www.romelibrary.org/card.htm*. Copyright © 2007 Sara Hightower Regional Library System. Used by permission.

The Barbara Hogenson Agency, Inc. "The Tiger Who Would Be King" by James Thurber, from *Further Fables for Our Time*. Copyright © 1956 James Thurber. Copyright © renewed 1984 by Rosemary A. Thurber. Used by arrangement with Rosemary A. Thurber and The Barbara Hogenson Agency, Inc.

Henry Holt and Company, Inc. "Dust of Snow" by Robert Frost from *The Poetry of Robert Frost* edited by Edward Connery Lathem. Copyright © 1923, 1969 by Henry Holt & Company. Copyright © 1951 by Robert Frost. "The Stone" from *The Foundling And Other Tales Of Prydain* by Lloyd Alexander. Copyright © 1973, 2002 by Lloyd Alexander. Used by permission of Henry Holt and Company, LLC.

Houghton Mifflin Company, Inc. "Arachne" from *Greek Myths*. Copyright © 1949 by Olivia E. Coolidge; copyright © renewed 1977 by Olivia E. Coolidge. Used by permission of Houghton Mifflin Company. All rights reserved.

Imaginova c/o Space.com "NASA Finally Goes Metric" from *www.space.com/news/070108_moon_metric.html*. Copyright © 2007 Space.com. Used by permission.

Information Please "The Seven Wonders of the World" *www. infoplease.com./ipa/A0001327.html*, Info Please Database © 2007 Pearson Education, Inc. Used by permission of Pearson Education, Inc. publishing as Info Please. All rights reserved.

Dr. Francisco Jiménez "The Circuit" by Francisco Jiménez from *America Street: A Mulicultural Anthology Of Stories.* Copyright © 1993 by Anne Mazer. Used with permission of the author Francisco Jiménez.

Alfred A. Knopf Children's Books "Jackie Robinson: Justice at Last" from *25 Great Moments* by Geoffrey C. Ward and Ken Burns with S.A. Kramer, copyright © 1994 by Baseball Licensing International, Inc., "He Lion, Bruh Bear, and Bruh Rabbit" from *The People Could Fly: American Black Folktales* by Virginia Hamilton illustrated by Leo and Diane Dillon, copyright © 1985 by Virginia Hamilton. Illustrations copyright © 1985 by Leo and Diane Dillon. "April Rain Song" from *The Collected Poems of Langston Hughes* by Langston Hughes, edited by Arnold Rampersad with David Roessel, Associate Editor, copyright © 1994 by The Estate of Langston Hughes. From *James and the Giant Peach* by Roald Dahl. Text copyright © 1961 by Roald Dahl. Text copyright renewed 1989 by Roald Dahl. Illustrations copyright © 1996 by Lane Smith. Used by permission of Alfred A. Knopf, an imprint of Random House Children's Books, a division of Random House, Inc.

The Lazear Literary Agency "Turkeys" by Bailey White from *Mama Makes Up Her Mind.* Copyright © 1993 by Bailey White. Used by permission.

Lescher & Lescher, Ltd. "The Southpaw" by Judith Viorst. Copyright © 1974 by Judith Viorst. From *Free To Be...You And Me.* This usage granted by permission of Lescher & Lescher, Ltd. All rights reserved.

Nelson Mandela Foundation "Nelson Mandela's Address to Rally in Cape Town on His Release from Prison" by Nelson Mandela from *db.nelsonmandela.org.* Used by permission.

The Marine Mammal Center "California Sea Lion" from *www.tmmc.org.* Copyright © 2007 The Marine Mammal Center. www.marinemammalcenter.org. All rights reserved. Used by permission.

Eve Merriam c/o Marian Reiner "Simile: Willow and Ginkgo" by Eve Merriam from *A Sky Full of Poems.* Copyright © 1964, 1970, 1973, 1986 by Eve Merriam. All rights reserved. Used by permission of Marian Reiner, Literary Agent, for the author.

Minnesota Public Radio Angela Duckworth and the Research on 'Grit' by Emily Hanford. Copyright (c) 2013. Minnesota Public Radio.

MLB Advanced Media, L.P. Why we love baseball - Players, management and fans chime in on Valentine's Day by Mark Newman. Copyright (c) 2007. MLB Advanced Media, L.P.

Lillian Morrison c/o Marian Reiner "The Sidewalk Racer or On the Skateboard" by Lillian Morrison from *The Sidewalk Racer and Other Poems of Sports and Motion.* Copyright © 1965, 1967, 1968, 1977 by Lillian Morrison. Used by permission of Marian Reiner, for the author.

William Morrow & Company, Inc., a division of HarperCollins "The World is Not a Pleasant Place To Be" from *My House* by Nikki Giovanni. Copyright © 1972 by Nikki Giovanni. Used by permission

of William Morrow & Company, Inc., a division of HarperCollins Publishers, Inc.

NASA Jet Propulsion Laboratory "Satellites and Sea Lions: Working Together to Improve Ocean Models" by Rosemary Sullivant from *http://www.nasa.gov/vision/earth/lookingatearth/sealion-20070206.html.* Used by permission of NASA/JPL-Caltech.

National Geographic World From *Race to the End of the Earth* by William G. Scheller from *National Geographic World, Number 294, February 2000.* Copyright © 2000 by National Geographic Society. Reproduction of the whole or any part of the contents of National Geographic World without permission is prohibited. Used by permission. All rights reserved.

New Directions Publishing Corporation "Wind and Water and Stone" by Octavio Paz, translated by Eliot Weinberger, from *Collected Poems 1957-1987.* Copyright © 1984 by Octavio Paz and Eliot Weinberger. Used by permission of New Directions Publishing Corp.

Orchard Books, an imprint of Scholastic Inc. "Becky and the Wheels-and-Brake Boys" from *A Thief In The Village And Other Stories* by James Berry. Published by Orchard Books, an imprint of Scholastic, Inc. Copyright © 1987 by James Berry. Used by permission.

PARS International Corporation Birds struggle to recover from egg thefts of 1800s by Edie Lau. Copyright © 1998. PARS International Corporation.

Carmen Pauls Memories of an All-American Girl by Carmen Pauls Orthner. © 2005–2012.

Pearson Education "Gilgamesh" from *Scott Foresman Social Studies: The World.* Pg. 44 Copyright © 2003. Pearson Education, Inc., or its affiliates. Used by permission. All rights reserved. *The Prince and the Pauper* Adapted from a book by Mark Twain, in Short Dramas and Teleplays. Copyright © 2000. Pearson Education, Inc., or it's affiliates. Used by permission. All rights reserved.

Pearson Prentice Hall Egyptian Pyramids from *California Social Studies Ancient Civilizations (Grade 6/Section 5 - Pp. 118-121).* Copyright © 2006 by Pearson Education, Inc. or its affiliates. Used by permission.

Penguin Group (USA) Inc. "Roll of Thunder, Hear My Cry" by Mildred D. Taylor from *Puffin Books.* Copyright © Mildred D. Taylor, 1976. "This Land Was Made for You and Me: Life & Songs of Woodie Guthrie" by Elizabeth Partridge from *Viking.* Copyright © Elizabeth Partridge, 2002. All rights reserved.

Pensacola News Journal "Jake Wood Baseball League is the Start of Something Special" by Reginald T. Dogan from *www.pensacolanewsjournal.com.* Copyright © 2007 Pensacola News Journal. Used by permission. All rights reserved.

Random House, Inc. From *You're a Good Man, Charlie Brown* by Clark Gesner. Copyright © 1967 by Clark Gesner. Coypright © 1965, 1966, 1967 by Jeremy Music, Inc. "Life Doesn't Frighten Me" copyright © 1978 by Maya Angelou, from *And Still I Rise* by Maya Angelou. Used by permission of Random House, Inc.

Reed Publishing (NZ) Ltd. "Prologue from The Whale Rider" by Witi Ihimaera from *The Whale Rider.* Copyright © 1987 Witi Ihimaera. All rights reserved. Used by permission of Reed Publishing (NZ) Ltd.

Marian Reiner, Literary Agent "Haiku ("An old silent pond…")" by Matsuo Basho translated by Harry Behn from *Cricket Songs: Japanese Haiku*. Copyright © 1964 by Harry Behn; Copyright © renewed 1992 Prescott Behn, Pamela Behn Adam and Peter Behn. "Haiku ("Over the wintry")" by Muso Soseki translated by Harry Behn from *Cricket Songs: Japanese Haiku*. Copyright © 1964 Harry Behn. Copyright renewed © 1992 by Prescott Behn, Pamela Behn Adam, and Peter Behn. Used by permission of Marian Reiner.

The Sacramento Bee "The Journey by Land" from *The Great American Gold Rush* by Rhoda Blumberg, *The Gold Rush* by Liza Ketchum, *The California Gold Rush*, published by American Heritage, *The California Gold Rush* by Elizabeth Van Steenwyk, *Hunting for Gold* by William Downie, *Sea Routes to the Gold Fields* by Oscar Lewis, *If You Traveled West in a Covered Wagon* by Ellen Levine, *The East Indiamen* by Russell Miller, Steve and Eric Chrissman of the National Nautical Heritage Society.

San Francisco Chronicle "O'Neil Belongs Inside this Hall" by Scott Ostler from *http://sfgate.com/*. Copyright © 2006 by San Francisco Chronicle. Used by permission of San Francisco Chronicle via Copyright Clearance Center.

San Francisco Public Library San Francisco Public Library Card Policies and Application from *http://sfpl.lib.ca.us/services/librarycard. htm*. Copyright © 2002-2006 by San Francisco Public Library. Used by permission.

Sarasota County Library Sarasota County Library Card Services, Policies, and Application from *http://suncat.co.sarasota.fl.us/services/librarycard.aspx*. Copyright © 2007 Sarasota County Library. Used by permission.

Scholastic Inc. "The Shutout" from *Black Diamond: The Story Of The Negro Baseball Leagues* by Patricia C. McKissack and Fredrick McKissack, Jr. Copyright © 1994 by Patricia C. McKissack and Fredrick McKissack, Jr. "Why Monkeys Live in Trees" from *How Many Spots Does A Leopard Have? And Other Tales* by Julius Lester. Copyright © 1989 by Julius Lester. Reproduced by permission of Scholastic Inc.

Scovil Chichak Galen Literary Agency, Inc. "Feathered Friend" from *The Other Side Of the Sky* by Arthur C. Clarke. Copyright © 1958 by Arthur C. Clarke. Used by permission of the author and the author's agents, Scovil Chichak Galen Literary Agency, Inc.

Scribner, a division of Simon & Schuster "Letter to Scottie" by F. Scott Fitzgerald, from *F. Scott Fitzgerald: A Life in Letters*, edited by Matthey J. Bruccoli. Used by permission of Scribner, an imprint of Simon & Schuster Adult Publishing Group. Copyright © 1994 by The Trustees under Agreement dated July 3, 1975. Created by Frances Scott Fitzgerald Smith.

Simon & Schuster Books for Young Readers "Parade" used by the permission of Simon & Schuster Books for Young Readers, an imprint of Simon & Schuster Children's Publishing Division from *Branches Green* by Rachel Field. Copyright © 1934 Macmillan Publishing Company; copyright © renewed 1962 by Arthur S. Pederson.

The Center for Social Organization of Schools Chinese and African Americans in the Gold Rush. © Johns Hopkins University. Reprinted with the permission of the Center for Social Organization of Schools, Johns Hopkins University School of Education

St. Martin's Press "The Market Square Dog" from *James Herriot's Treasury for Children* by James Herriot. Copyright © 1989 James Herriot. Used by permission of St. Martin's Press, LLC.

William Strauss, Director, The Cappies "You're a Good Man, Charlie Brown at Robert E. Lee (High School)" by Brianna Sonnefeld from *www.cappies.com/nca/news/reviews/06-07/le.htm*. Copyright © 2005 The Cappies, Inc., All Rights Reserved. Used by permission.

Talkin' Broadway "Happiness is a Charming Charlie Brown at Orlando Rep "by Matthew MacDermid from *www.talkinbroadway.com*. Copyright © TalkinBroadway.com, a project of www.TalkinBroadway.org, Inc. Used by permission.

Thorgate, LLC "Metric Metric: It's so nice, we say it twice!™" from *www.metricmetric.com*. Copyright © 2007 Metric Metric. Used by permission.

Dr. My-Van Tran "A Crippled Boy" from *Folk Tales from Indochina* by Dr. My-Van Tran. First published in 1987. Copyright © Vietnamese Language and Culture Publications and Tran My-Van. Used by permission.

University of Nebraska Press "The Old Woman Who Lived With the Wolves" reprinted from *Stories Of The Sioux* by Luther Standing Bear. Used by permission of the University of Nebraska Press. Copyright © 1934 by Luther Standing Bear. Copyright © renewed 1961 by May M. Jones.

University Press of New England "The Drive-In Movies" from *A Summer Life* copyright © 1990 by University Press of New England, Hanover, NH. Used by permission.

Viking Penguin, Inc. "La lena buena," (retitled) pages 113-144 from *Places Left Unfinished At The Time Of Creation* by John Phillip Santos, copyright © 1999 by John Phillip Santos. From *Zlata's Diary* by Zlata Filipovic from *Zlata's Life: A Child's Life in Sarajevo*. Translated by Christina Pribichevich-zoric. Copyright © 1994 Editions Robert Laffont/Fixot. Used by permission of Viking Penguin, a division of Penguin Group (USA) Inc.

Villard Books, a division of Random House, Inc. "The Lady and the Spider" from *All I Really Need to Know I Learned In Kindergarten* by Robert L. Fulghum. Copyright © 1986, 1988 by Robert L. Fulghum. Used by permission of Villard Books, a division of Random House, Inc.

World Book, Inc. From "Tornado" by Howard B. Bluestein from *World Book Reference Center*. Copyright © 2007. World Book, Inc. Used by permission of publisher. *www.worldbookonline.com*.

World of Escher "World of Escher Tessallation Contest" from *www.worldofescher.com/contest*. Copyright © 1995-2007 WorldofEscher.com. All rights reserved. Used by permission.

Jane Yolen "My Heart is in the Highlands" by Jane Yolen from *My Heart Is In The Highlands*. Copyright © Jane Yolen.

Credits

F cover Andrey Bayda/Shutterstock

© Kyle George / Aurora /AGE Fotostock; © David Tipling/Alamy; © Horizon International Images Limited / Alamy; © Blend Images / Alamy; ©RAMON ESPINOSA/AP Photos; ©Associated Press; ©Louie Chin/ Art Reps NYC; Réunion des Musées Nationaux/Art Resource, NY; HIP/ Art Resource, NY; Art Resource, NY; The Jacob and Gwendolyn Lawrence Foundation/ Art Resource, NY; The Art Archive / Musée Thomas Dobrée Nantes / Dagli Ort/ Art Resource; Miriam Berkley; © Cheron Bayna; © Ocean/Corbis; © Bettmann/CORBIS; © Chuck Savage/Corbis; © David J. & Janice L. Frent Collection/CORBIS; © Lawrence Manning/ CORBIS; © JUSTIN LANE/epa/Corbis; © Blue Lantern Studio/Corbis; © Jeff Albertson/CORBIS; © Corbis; © Ikon Images/Corbis; © C.E. Bolles/ Corbis; © Philip Gould/CORBIS; © Bettmann/Corbis; © Lomen Brothers/ Corbis Images; © Terry Cryer/CORBIS; © Lomen Brothers/ Corbis; © Randy Faris/ Corbis; © Car Culture/ Corbis Images; © Little Blue Wolf Productions/ Corbis; © Bettmann/CORBIS; © Robert Maass/ Corbis; © Randy Faris/CORBIS; © Seth Resnick/CORBIS; © Lew Robertson/ CORBIS; © Terry Cryer/CORBIS; Image Source/Corbis Images; © Frank Krahmer/Zefa/Corbis Images; © Blue Lantern Studio/Corbis Images; © Sea World of California/Corbis Images; © Mimmo Jodice/ Corbis; © Frank Krahmer/zefa/ Corbis; © Julian Calder/CORBIS; ©Images.com/ Corbis; ©Nancy Crampton; Didi Cutler/ Isabel Cutler Photography; DK Images; Richard Bonson/ DK Images; Mike Dunning/ Dorling Kindersley; John Woodcock/ Dorling Kindersley; Photo: Mike Eddowes; © Argus/ Fotolia; © Larry Ye/Fotolia; ©Goinyk Volodymyr/ Fotolia; © Kalabukhava Iryna/Fotolia; © Chris Hill/Fotolia; © vivalapenler/Fotolia; © rafo/Fotolia; © 1xpert/Fotolia; © yanlev/Fotolia; © Tetiana Shamenko/Fotolia; © kak-tus2536/Fotolia; © Matthew Cole/Fotolia; © Goinyk Volodymyr/Fotolia; © Eky Chan/Fotolia; © SIRIPONG JITCHUM/Fotolia; © Farinoza/Fotolia; © Eric Isselée/Fotolia; © EcoView/Fotolia.com; © leksele/Fotolia; Richard Megna/ Fundamental Photographs, NY; © Clarissa Leahy/Stone+/Getty Images; © Lori Epstein/National Geographic/Getty Images; © Jasper James/Stone/Getty Images; © picturegarden/Getty Images; © Getty Images; © Herb Scharfman/Sports Imagery/Getty Images; © Gilbert Mayers/Getty Images; © Image Source/Getty Images; © Ryan McVay/ Getty Images; Boston Globe via Getty Images; © American School/ Getty Images; © David Alquezar/Getty Images; © Blend Images/PBNJ Productions/Getty Images; © Zoran Milich/Allsport/Getty Images; © Frank Driggs Collection/ Getty Images; © Orlando/Hulton Archive/Getty Images, Inc; © Time & Life Pictures/Getty Images; © Space Frontiers/ Hulton Archive/ Getty Images; © Judy Dole/The Image Bank/ Getty Images; © Alan Sirulnikoff/ Getty Images; © C Squared Studios/ Getty Images; © Matt Henry Gunther/Getty Images, Inc.; © Neil Robinson/ Getty Images; © Frank Driggs Collection/ Getty Images; © Museum of the City of New York/Getty Images; © Ciaran Griffin/ Getty Images; © Cosmo Condina/ Getty Images; © Photodisc/ Getty Images; © John Foxx/Getty Images; © James Warwick/ Getty Images; © Hola Images/ Getty Images, Inc.; © Michael Grimm / Getty Images, Inc.; Photo by Monica Greenfield; Charles Gupton; Emily Hanford; Photograph by Austin V. Hansen, Jr.; from "Zlateh the Goat and Other Stories" by Isaac Bashevis Singer, illustrations by Maurice Sendak © 1966, HarperCollins Publishers, Inc.; illustrations copyright © 1995 by Jerry Pinkney. Ued by permission of Harper Collins Publishers; HarperCollins Publishers; Houghton Mifflin Company; Designpics/ Inmagine.com; TAPshooter / iStockphoto.com; Marcela Brasse/ iStockphoto; Valerie Loiseleux/ istockphoto.com; GeoPappas / iStock International, Inc.; PN_Photo / iStockphoto; Charles Taylor/istockphoto; dononeg/ iStockphoto; tedestudio / iStockphoto; narvikk / iStockphoto; Stan Rohrer/ iStockphoto Marcela Brasse / istockphoto; Valerie Loiseleux/ istockphoto; iStockphoto; Frank Boellmann / iStockphoto; Vladislav

Lebedinski iStockphoto; iStock International, Inc.; GeoPappas / iStock International; © Jan Cobb Photo LTD; Library of Congress, Prints & Photographs Division, FSA/OWI Collection, [8b31654a]; The Mark Twain House and Museum/ Mark Twain Memorial; Mary Evans Picture Library; Picture History/Newscom; KIKE CALVO/Newscom; akgim-ages/Newscom; Daily Mirror Mirrorpix/Newscom; Chuck Myers/MCT/ Newscom; Don Hammond/Design Pics/Newscom; Phoebe Beasley/ Omni-Photo/UIG; © Bryan Orthner; © Rogerio Soud/Painted Words; © Pearson Education; Photo Researchers, Inc.; David Macias/Photo Researchers, Inc.; Felicia Martinez/ Photo Edit; Bill Aron/ PhotoEdit; Walt Disney Pictures/Photofest; Cynthia Rylant; Charles Barry, Santa Clara University; Courtesy of the Saskatchewan Sports Hall of Fame; © Paul Cotney/Shutterstock; © David Thyberg/Shutterstock; © Semisatch/ Shutterstock; © greenland/Shutterstock; © rodho/Shutterstock; © Fernando Jose V. Soares/Shutterstock; © L F File/Shutterstock; © Flashon Studio/Shutterstock; © Elenamiv/Shutterstock; © 3drender-ings/Shutterstock; © Eric Isselee/Shutterstock; © Jackie Stukey/ Shutterstock; © mexrix/Shutterstock; © Olgysha/Shutterstock; © PusitGuru/Shutterstock; © Joanne Weston/Shutterstock; Courtesy of Sony Music Entertainment; Used by permission of Gary Soto; L. N. Tolstoi, I. E. Repin, Sovfoto/Eastfoto; John Newcomb/SuperStock; Helen Vaugh/ SuperStock; Gilbert Mayers/ SuperStock; Jessie Coates/ SuperStock; SuperStock; Bridgeman Art Library International; Private Collection, © Look and Learn / The Bridgeman Art Library International; Fairy Art Museum, Tokyo, Japan/ The Bridgeman Art Library; The Granger Collection, New York City; David Hsieh; © Courtesy of Topps; Reuters America LLC; Ralph Orlowski/Reuters; U.S. Department of Commerce; © Ralph Voltz/Deborah Wolfe Limited; © Ted Hammond/ Deborah Wolfe

Staff Credits

Dori Amtmann, Tricia Battipede, Rachel Beckman, Nancy Bolsover, Laura Brancky, Odette Calderon, Pam Carey, Kelly Casanova, Geoff Cassar, Jessica Cohn, Kyle Cooper, Sarah Cunningham, Anthony DeSacia, Kim Doster, Irene Ehrmann, Andy Ekedahl, Sandy Engleman, Samantha Fahy, Janet Fauser, Amy Fleming, Pam Gallo, Mark Gangi, Nicole Gee, Susan Graef, Leslie Griffin, Elaine Goldman, Brian Hawkes, Steve Hernacki, Martha Heller, Amanda House, Rick Hickox, Patricia Isaza, Etta Jacobs, Blair Jones, Jim Kelly, Nathan Kinney, Sarah Kraus, Gregory Lynch, Nancy Mace, Jim McPherson, Charles Morris, Pa Moua, Elizabeth Nielsen, Kim Ortell, Kathleen Pagliaro, Jennie Rakos, Sheila Ramsay, Karen Randazzo, Julianne Regnier, Christopher Richardson, Melissa Schreiner, Hillary Schwei, Jeff Shagawat, Susan Sheehan, Charlene Smith, DeAnn Smith, Sheila Smith, Cynthia Summers, Morgan Taylor, Brian Thomas, Lucia Tirondola, Karen Tully, Merle Uuesoo, Kristen Varina, Jackie Westbrook, Jessica White